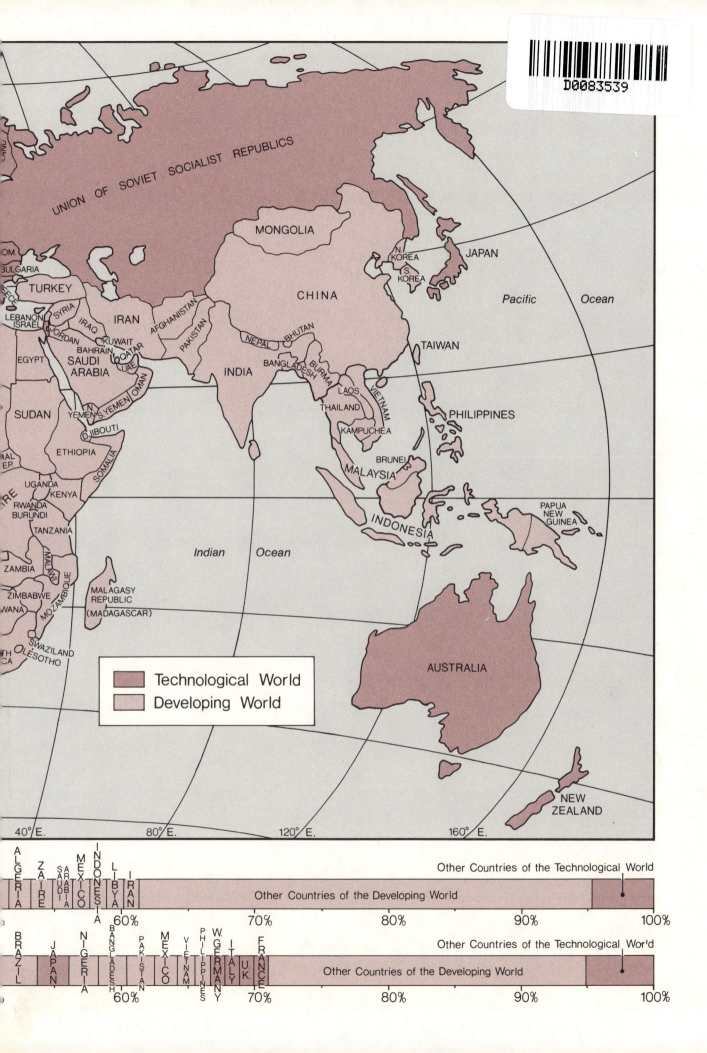

D0083539

UNION OF SOVIET SOCIALIST REPUBLICS

MONGOLIA

N. KOREA
S. KOREA
JAPAN

CHINA

Pacific   Ocean

TURKEY

BULGARIA

LEBANON
ISRAEL
SYRIA
IRAQ
JORDAN
KUWAIT
BAHRAIN
QATAR
UAE

IRAN

AFGHANISTAN

PAKISTAN

NEPAL
BHUTAN

TAIWAN

EGYPT

SAUDI
ARABIA

OMAN

INDIA

BANGLADESH
BURMA

LAOS
VIETNAM

PHILIPPINES

SUDAN

N.
YEMEN
S. YEMEN

DJIBOUTI

THAILAND

KAMPUCHEA

ETHIOPIA

SOMALIA

BRUNEI

MALAYSIA

UGANDA
KENYA

RWANDA
BURUNDI

TANZANIA

INDONESIA

PAPUA
NEW
GUINEA

Indian   Ocean

ZAMBIA

MALAWI

ZIMBABWE

MOZAMBIQUE

WANA

MALAGASY
REPUBLIC
(MADAGASCAR)

SWAZILAND
LESOTHO

CA

AUSTRALIA

Technological World
Developing World

40° E.   80° E.   120° E.   160° E.

NEW
ZEALAND

WORLD REGIONAL GEOGRAPHY

A Question of Place

THIRD EDITION

WORLD REGIONAL GEOGRAPHY

A Question of Place

PAUL WARD ENGLISH

Professor of Geography
University of Texas at Austin

JAMES A. MILLER

Associate Professor of Geography
Clemson University

JOHN V. COTTER

Cartography

WILEY

JOHN WILEY & SONS

NEW YORK   **CHICHESTER**   **BRISBANE**   **TORONTO**   **SINGAPORE**

Text Design—Karin Gerdes Kincheloe
Cover Design—Madelyn Lesure
Cover photos:
   Machu Picchu, Kal Muller, Woodfin Camp & Assoc.
   Manhattan Skyline, Gerd Ludwig, Woodfin Camp & Assoc.
Photo Researcher—Chris Migdol

Library of Congress Cataloging-in-Publication Data:

English, Paul Ward.
   World regional geography.

   Bibliography: p. B1
   1. Geogrpahy. I. Miller, James Andrew.
II. Cotter, John V. III. Title.

G128.E53 1989   910   88-27903
ISBN 0-471-61648-6

Printed in the United States of America

10 9 8 7 6 5 4 3

For you
In reminiscence, *The Song of Solomon*, 2:10–12.

PREFACE

About four million years ago, our ancestors embarked on a journey—an odyssey of the spirit—at a place called Olduvai Gorge in Africa. In the time since, human beings spread across the globe and reshaped the earth. They transformed landscapes and continually devised new ways of living. Modern geography is the study of the interactions between people and their environments—past and present. It tells the ongoing story of the world as we know it—the latest stage in the journey that began long ago in the East African highlands.

THE HUMAN WORLD REMADE

Until the last few thousand years of our four million year history, people lived in a very different world from ours today. Only 20,000 years ago, the human race amounted to five million men and women living in small groups spread across the globe. They secured food as **hunters and gatherers** by collecting plants and killing animals within their reach. Their knowledge, energy, and technology were limited. So was their use of the resources of the earth. Then, two periods of explosive change altered their way of life and transformed the geography of the planet.

The Environmental Transformation

During the first period of change, the **Environmental Transformation,** people invented agriculture and tamed animals. The break-through came first in the Middle East about 10,000 years ago. Soon after, agri-culture appeared in India, China, Southeast Asia, Europe, and much later in Mexico and Peru. Exactly why human beings became farmers and herders at this particular time still eludes us. But when they did, they opened the way to a more humanized world.

These farmers and herders soon clustered together in new and larger settlements, cities. Here, people first became "civilized" in our sense of the word. These cities became the centers of organized agricultural civilizations.

By the beginning of the sixteenth century (A.D. 1500), the Environmental Transformation—food production and urbanism—had created a new global geography. Farming and herding gave people a more reliable supply of food. As a result, 500 million human beings inhabited the planet. Sophisticated urban civilizations existed in Western Europe, the Mediterranean, the Middle East, India, China, and in the Aztec and Incan realms of Mexico and Peru. In each of these regions farmers grew the food to nourish elite city dwellers who lived in urban capitals, trading towns, and religious centers. Farmers also provided much of the wealth and labor that built the temples, shrines, and palaces that fascinate tourists today.

The world in 1500 was divided into a number of **culture regions.** Each culture region had a distinctive religion, language, society, and economy. No single civilization was capable of imposing its will on the others, although attempts to do so were frequent. The distances between regions were too long, and communications were too slow. Manpower, energy, and technology were too limited for one civilization to dominate another for very long.

Then, with the beginning of the second major period of change, the Scientific Transformation, Europe became the first society with global capacity. Beginning in the age of Columbus and continuing into the twentieth century, Europeans sailed around the world and subdued civilizations in Asia, Africa, and the New World. These events and their after-effects created the interlocking economic and political realities that we live with today.

The Scientific Transformation

The **Scientific Transformation** started in the 1500s when Europeans began to explore new worlds—geographically and intellectually—to create one of the most exciting eras in human history. In the 1500s, European explorers opened up new routes of communication and trade throughout the world. At the same time, advances in science and technology led to new inventions. It was in this climate of terrestrial and scientific exploration that the **Industrial Revolution** occurred in England in 1750.

The productive powers of machine technology unleashed a torrent of change. Coal, and later oil-powered machines, transformed raw materials into finished goods. New industries emerged, and production of goods soared. New patterns of trade and commerce linked distant parts of the globe. The higher productivity of a new ecomomic system—**capitalism**—combined with advances in science to spur rapid population growth.

By 1800, there were one billion people in the world. Many of these people sought jobs in rapidly growing cities. The city became the home of more and more people; the factory became their work environment. A new and different human geography emerged. These changes brought many improvements in life, but also caused many of today's basic social and economic problems.

The spread of the Scientific Transformation took place in the 1800s and 1900s. Before this, colonies of Europeans were settled along the coasts of North and South America and in South Africa. Elsewhere, a handful of Europeans worked in trading stations on the oceanic rims of Asia and Africa. But generally, Europeans were few and far between outside of Europe.

Beginning in the 1800s, however, millions of emigrants swept out of Europe. They settled in North America, southern South America, South Africa, and Australia—all regions with environments similar to Europe. In each of these areas, the ties of European language and culture remained strong long after new countries like the United States declared their political independence from Europe. In time, these regions settled by European immigrants integrated the capital, resources, and social institutions needed to become industrial nations, members of the Technological World. In North America, the Soviet Union, and Japan the Scientific Transformation took root and blossomed beyond the frontiers of Europe.

In most of Latin America, Africa, and Asia, the impact of the Scientific Transformation was quite different. These areas produced agricultural and mineral products highly valued in the marketplaces of Europe, but their environments were largely unattractive to Europeans. As a result, Europeans came to form a tiny but well-armed minority in the tropics. They established plantations and founded mines as they lived among but apart from native peoples as **colonial** rulers. Europeans provided the capital and technological know-how; native Latin Americans, Africans, and Asians provided the muscle. **Dependency economies** emerged in these areas, reliant on the production and sale of raw materials to industrial countries. When these colonial societies finally achieved political independence, they did so in a world designed by and for Europeans. The former colonies have not yet fully integrated the Scientific Transformation. Today, they remain less developed and poorer members of the global family, and are often termed the Developing World.

The Scientific Transformation, then, did not spread evenly across the globe. In the Technological World, where science and technology form the basis of society, people live longer, eat better, are healthier, consume more energy, and steadily increase their standards of living. In the Developing World, where science and technology long remained in the hands of European colonialists, life spans and standards of living increased, but at much slower rates than in industrial nations. As a result, vast inequalities separate the haves and have-nots of the world today. One quarter of the five billion people on the planet are relatively well-fed, healthy, and long-lived, and three quarters are not.

GEOGRAPHY AND DEVELOPMENT: A TALE OF TWO WORLDS

These human differences form the core of much study by modern geographers. Interactions between environment, population, culture, and location lie at the heart of geography. Geographic issues involve the distribution of people, food, energy, and resources, and affect each of us, whether we are in the Developing or the Technological World.

Books, newspapers, and television constantly remind us of the global nature of everyday life. American grain shipments to the Soviet Union and hunger in Africa are issues that have affected Americans directly. Global energy crises have changed driving habits, household economies, food production, and industry. Even a country as vast in size and as rich in resources as the United States must import over 120 vital commodities to maintain its standard of living. And, for the first time, it is within the reach of human beings to put an end to the future tense.

Needless to say, people in the Technological World and the Developing World view this situation very differently and have different hopes for the future. In the Technological World, people work to preserve the current world economic system because it produces their wealth. They support political stability so that their positions and the status quo can be maintained. Achieving higher standards of living is of importance to most people.

In the Developing World, by contrast, dissatisfaction with the world economic system is wide-spread. Here, world political stability is less important to people than a greater share in the global balance of wealth and power. Their goal is to overtake the richer nations by developing their own resource bases and by acquiring the technology and skills needed to raise standards of living. But during the last 50 years, the distribution of wealth and poverty has remained pretty much the same.

In the Technological World, countries have extensive trade contacts, well-developed transportation networks, high rates of energy production and consumption, and high **gross national products.** As a whole, their people are well supplied with medical facilities, have low rates of population growth, and are highly urbanized. Nearly everyone is literate, and most people are able to earn relatively high incomes. The higher living standards in these countries are the result of diversified commercial and industrial economies.

The poorer countries of the Developing World, by contrast, are weighed down by marginal environments, inadequate natural resource development, poorly connected transportation systems, and low gross national products. Their people are mainly engaged in **subsistence** activities, have high rates of population growth, and low standards of living.

The sources of poverty vary. In South Asia, rapid population growth consumes economic gains that could improve standards of living. In most of the Middle East, dry environments retard national development. In Africa, the legacy of colonialism weighs heavy. In South America, population growth is high and control of the physical environment is inadequate. Although the causes vary from region to region, poverty is now a persistent and pervasive fact of life in the less developed countries.

Several outcomes are possible. The wealthy may continue to provide assistance to less developed countries through organizations like the **World Bank.** The poor may remain poor, except in those countries where determined leaders or the discovery of new resources spur rapid development. Or countries in the Technological World may decide to curtail their standards of living in order to raise living standards in the Developing World. But none of these futures seems likely to resolve world tensions or to be accomplished without great turmoil.

On a day-to-day basis, these long-term issues do not appear to be immediate or compelling. Nearly two thirds of the world's population still lead the simple, lethal, and vulnerable lives of their ancestors. They dwell in the same cities, practice crafts, till fields, and herd flocks much like 300 generations of their ancestors before them. But in a very basic way everything has changed in this generation—and you can sense it.

In Ethiopia, a plowman still uses the broken branch of a tree to cultivate the land, but he knows that with cash he could buy a metal plow. In the Middle East, villagers live in homes similar to those built at the time of Christ, but they know that their children must leave the village if they are to lead better lives. In South Asia, the back-breaking toil of cultivating rice kills women so rapidly that there is a shortage of wives, and the women know it. In Latin America, men leave their families to find work in the city, because the good land is owned by wealthy landlords.

In a sense, all of these people—your contemporaries—are enduring much as their ancestors endured, but now they have been afflicted by hope. The knowledge of wealth has made them feel poorer; the availability of life has made them resentful of dying. Rising expectations are an important force that will shape the geographical issues of the coming generation.

And so the journey begun at Olduvai Gorge continues. Although the world has changed dramatically through the force of human endeavor, geographical questions of current importance must have occupied our ancestors during those long ages so mysteriously remote from us now. Like us, they were caught up in the business of living. Decisions had to be made about how to assess environmental potential, how to maximize available opportunities, whether to migrate, which course of action to follow, and what the future held. These questions are at the core of modern geography. They engage the concern of most thinking people today.

WORLD REGIONAL GEOGRAPHY: A QUESTION OF PLACE

This book provides a coherent, organized human geography of the world as we now know it—where we are, where we seem to be heading. Regional discussions of interactions among environments, populations, ways of life, and locations—subjects much studied by modern geographers—from the body of the text.

Organization of the Book

World Regional Geography: A Question of Place is divided into three major parts. The first part, The Human World Remade, provides the logic for presenting the geography of the modern world in two groupings of countries. These groupings form the second and third parts of the book, The Technological World and The Developing World.

Part 1, The Human World Remade, briefly outlines events during the two periods of cataclysmic change that gave human beings greater control over the earth. The Environmental Transformation created those agriculture-based civilizations that still encompass the life experience of most people on the planet. The Scientific Transformation created the industrial and commercial societies that have governed world affairs for the last two centuries. Forces originating during these two periods of change have divided the globe into two sets of countries: the Technological World and the Developing World.

Part 2, The Technological World, presents a discussion of five world regions—Western Europe, North America; the Soviet Union and Eastern Europe; Japan and Korea; and Australia, New Zealand, and the Pacific World—where the full elaboration of the modern experience has produced unprecedented levels of material well-being and mastery of the environment. Despite differences in tradition, culture, economy, and environment, each of these world regions is highly urbanized and has a diversified economy, a high level of economic productivity, and a well-developed resource base. The chapters of each region of The Technological World use the same system of organization. First, the progress of modernization is traced; second, the contempory human geography of the region is described; and third, salient problems of current concern are discussed. This consistency of approach is intended to enable students to appreciate the differences in land and life in each world region, while recognizing the similar processes and problems that exist throughout the Technological World.

Part 3, The Developing World, introduces those six world regions—Latin America, China, South Asia, Southeast Asia, the Middle East and North Africa, and Africa—where advances in living standards generated by the Scientific Transformation have yet to be fully experienced. Each of these world regions has a high rate of population growth, an agriculture-based economy, urbanization without industrialization, a low level of economic productivity, and a poorly developed resource base. Again, each regional chapter in The Developing World follows a consistent format. First, the traditional culture and society of the region is described; second, the contemporary human geography is discussed; and third, the impact of modernization and major problems confronting each society are delineated. As in Part II, this similarity of treatment is intended to enable students to understand the diversity that exists among these regions, while comprehending the commonalities of life in the Developing World.

Special Features

To support these discussions of every major country in the world, three special features are embodied in the regional chapters. These are Mapscan, Geolab, and Geostatistics.

Mapscan is an important innovation in this book. Essentially, Mapscan is a short course in map interpretation intended to provide students with the basic skills needed to read and use maps with a higher level of understanding. In each regional chapter, Mapscan introduces a basic element of cartographic knowledge using data from the region under study, including the following topics.

- The Beginnings of Cartography
- Map Projections
- Map Scale
- Map Symbols
- Isolines
- Topographic Maps
- Cartograms
- Mapping Population
- Urban Mapping
- Mapping Water Need
- Remote Sensing of the Environment

Maps are a fundamental tool in geographical research and writing; better understanding of their construction, purpose, and best use is essential for all students of world regional geography.

Geolab is a second special feature in this book. In each regional chapter, Geolab introduces a fundamental idea or area of research developed by geographers to analyze the world around them. Each Geolab is based on data from the region under study, including the following subjects.

- Formal Regions
- Spatial Diffusion
- Environmental Perception
- Natural Hazards
- Elevation and Environment
- Climographs of Human Comfort
- The Monsoon
- Rural Settlement Patterns
- Megalopolis
- Location Theory
- Central Place Theory
- Culture Regions

These ideas are important subjects of debate among professional geographers, fertile areas of research still under study. They provide students with an introduction to ongoing study in the discipline as well as preparing them for further exploration in more advanced courses.

Geostatistics, a third special feature provided in each regional chapter, is a statistical profile of each country in the world. Frequently used solely for reference, these tables illuminate patterns of life and livelihood within and among world regions and merit the attention of serious students.

ACKNOWLEDGMENTS

Completing any long work provides authors with a moment of reflection, a quiet time to express appreciation and recognition. The ideas and materials embodied in this book derive from an array of literature in the discipline. The publications of many of these professionals are acknowledged in figure references and bibliographies in the text. Still more derive from discussions with colleagues, friends, and fellow students.

First, among my colleagues at the University of Texas at Austin and elsewhere, I thank J. A. Allan (School of Oriental and African Studies, University of London), James A. Bill, Paul W. Blank (Middleburg College), Barbara Brower, Michael E. Bonine (University of Arizona), Karl W. Butzer, George Carter (Texas A&M University), Christopher Shane Davies, William E. Doolittle, Robin W. Doughty, Hafez F. Farmayan, Kenneth E. Foote, Thomas E. Glick (Boston University), Ann Helgeson, Michael C. Hillmann, Robert K. Holz, David L. Huff, Mohammad Ali Jazayery, J. Richard Jones, Terry G. Jordan, Gregory W. Knapp, Keith McLachlan (School of Oriental and African Studies, University of London), Jan R. Manners, Robert C. Mayfield, Donald W. Meinig (Syracuse University), James J. Nasuti, Gundars Rudzitis (University of Idaho), Joseph E. Schwartzberg (University of Minnesota), Frederick J. Simoons (University of California at Davis), Robert Spayne (University of Massachuetts), and Philip L. Wagner (University of British Columbia) for their reflections and critism. Reviewers of preliminary drafts of the manuscript include Alan Best (Boston University), Clyde Browning (University of North Carolina-Chapel Hill), Michael D. Cummins (Normandale Community College, Minnesota), Sam B. Hilliard (Louisiana State University), Shannon McCune, Professor Emeritus (University of Florida), and Thomas Poulsen (Portland State University, Oregon). The special contribution of John V. Cotter in designing the cartographic program merits special recognition.

Second, staff and assistants at the University of Texas at Austin who contributed to this book include Cherie Crass, Robert D. Edwards, Jeffery S. Schwartz, and Carol Vernon. Among them, the constant charm, competence, and intelligence of Beverly Beaty-Benadom stands apart. The staff at John Wiley ably led by editor Stephanie Happer contributed their professional expertise: Suzanne Hendrickson in production, Maddy Lesure in book design, Stella Kupferberg in photo research, and Martin Bentz in map design.

Finally, we dedicate this book to those whom we love.

PWE
JAM

CONTENTS

THE
HUMAN
WORLD
REMADE

1

THE HUMAN WORLD REMADE

3

*H*uman understanding and control over personal survival and the environment grew during two periods of explosive change (Fig. 1.1). During the first period, the Environmental Transformation, people's relationships with nature changed. Beginning about 10,000 years ago, humans invented agriculture, domesticated animals, and then built cities in the **culture hearths** of the Old World. The first civilizations were supported by food supplies produced by agriculture. **Hunters and gatherers** were pushed into less attractive **environments.** Farmers and urbanites forged new patterns of living that every populous society—from the earliest civilizations in Mesopotamia to the medieval monarchies of China, India, Europe, and Russia— came to share.

During a second broad period of change known as the Scientific Transformation, a new scale of technological understanding emerged in Europe in the 1700s. People harnessed **inanimate energy** sources. Human control expanded to global dimensions. Scientific understanding of nature increased beyond the imagination of those who had lived just a few generations earlier.

The agricultural basis of life in medieval Europe expanded to support emerging cities, industries, and elites. Commerce became a world venture; resource utilization, a global affair. The tentacles of an international economy penetrated remote areas. As this system evolved and **diffusion** took place, the world split into two: (1) the Technological World, whose component states became primary producers of industrial technology and the principal consumers of energy and resources; and (2) the Developing World, whose societies now seek parity in an unequal world.

The human world was remade by these two transformations (Fig. 1.1). Each led to a substantial increase in population, to control over new forms of energy, and to changes in food production. Where one lived and worked, levels of wealth and well-being, and patterns of birth and death changed as each transformation created its own human geography. Today's global patterns reflect fundamental changes wrought by the Environmental and Scientific Transformations.

THE ENVIRONMENTAL TRANSFORMATION

The Environmental Transformation took place in two phases. First, *The Discovery of Food Production* led to new levels of human control over the environment. The Agricultural Revolution that took place in the ancient Middle East was succeeded by *The Rise of Cities* after several thousand years. Urban-based civilizations controlling sizable **hinterlands** existed in the river valleys of the Middle East in the fourth millennium B.C., in the Aegean by the third millennium B.C., in West Africa and East Asia in the second millennium B.C., and in the New World 2000 years later.

The dynamics of the Environmental Transformation must have differed substantially from one region to another, and *The Diffusion of the Environmental Transformation* is not fully understood. It is generally accepted, however, that the first farmers and the first urbanites lived in the Middle East.

The Discovery of Food Production

In the first phase of the Environmental Transformation, people learned how to tend plants and tame animals. These changes began some 10,000 years ago and are often termed the "Agricultural Revolution." Grain cultivation, sheep and goat herding, planting tree crops, and the use of the plow established the basis of village life.

Before this time, the human population was both low and sparse. Perhaps five million people formed the entire population of the earth. They were concentrated in environments favorable to **hunting and gathering** techniques. Their lives were dependent on the natural distribution of wild foodstuffs. Domesticated plants and animals were unknown. Landscapes evolved by the laws of nature, barely touched by the efforts of hunters and gatherers to wrest a living from their environments.

Between 8000 and 2500 B.C., agricultural societies appeared in a wide variety of places. Each of these places is often considered a distinct **culture hearth** of agricultural origins. The best archaeological evidence places the first farmers in the ancient Middle East, although a growing body of evidence leads us to consider other early culture hearths as well. In the lowlands of the Huang He in North China, for example, intensive hoe cultivation was the dominant economy by 3000 B.C. In Southeast Asia, early farmers planted root crops and domesticated

THE HUMAN WORLD REMADE

The human geography of the modern world was forged by two periods of rapid change—the Environmental Transformation and the Scientific Transformation. This graph shows the impact of these periods on population, economy, income, food production, material progress, transportation, and communication.

Adapted from: Daniel Noin, Géographie de la population. Paris: Masson, 1979, fig. 87, pp. 318–319.

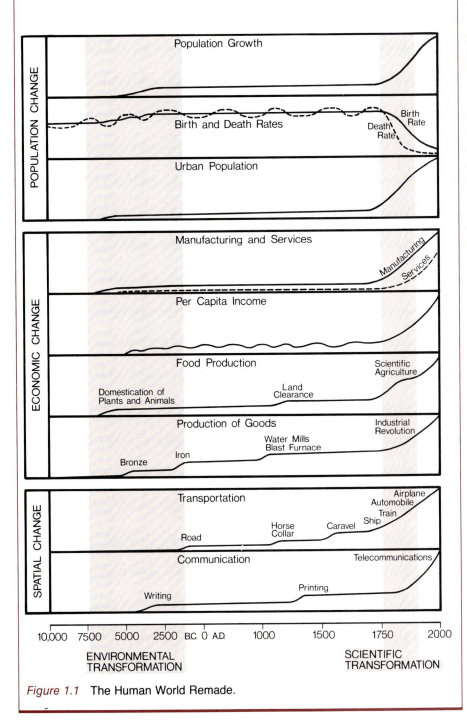

Figure 1.1 The Human World Remade.

pigs and chickens. In Mexico and Peru, native Americans focused their efforts on domesticating squash, beans, and corn. And in the Old World, farmers may have tended fields in the Danube River Valley near the Black Sea in Europe and in the Indus River Valley in what is modern Pakistan nearly as early as farmers did in the Middle East.

Some observers suggest that the process of diffusion—the spread and exchange of ideas and environmental knowledge—connected some or all of these culture hearths over time. Future archaeology will undoubtedly reveal much about linkages among these early agricultural societies. It appears clear today, however, that these societies developed food production and village life later than in the Middle East.

In the Middle East and in other culture hearths, early agricultural societies exhibited a set of common cultural characteristics. Cultivation of plants and animal keeping led to more reliable food supplies. Populations increased slowly and clustered in permanent villages. As life became more reliant upon human-controlled plants and animals, hunting and gathering receded into peripheral areas.

And the environment itself was transformed. Agricultural societies took center stage and altered the landscapes of favored cradle areas. New land was brought into cultivation as farming populations extended their sway over much of the earth. Forests were leveled, hillsides **terraced**, and dry lands **irrigated**. In transforming nature, these people transformed themselves. They created the economic base for the stable, settled village communities that still dominate much of the human world.

The Fertile Crescent

The earliest experiment in food production probably took place in the **piedmont** of the Fertile Crescent in

Domesticated plants and animals, supplemented by wild game and fish, formed the food base of Egyptian civilization. The discovery of food production is illustrated here by the making of wine from domestic grapes (above) and the preparation of domestic fowl (below).

the Middle East (Fig. 1.2). The Fertile Crescent, so called for its relatively abundant precipitation, sweeps northward from the coastal highlands of the eastern Mediterranean, encircles the Tigris-Euphrates Valley along the Taurus Mountains of Turkey and then arches southward along the western slopes of the Zagros Mountains of Iran. In these foothills, a variety of vegetation zones are found at different elevations. In general, grassy lowlands give way to oak and pistachio forests at middle altitudes, with wooded mountain valleys and **alpine meadows** high above. The area generally receives enough precipitation to support cultivation without irrigation.

The richest resource zone in the Fertile Crescent was located in the oak and pistachio forests at elevations of 1000 to 3000 feet. Here the diversity of plants and animals was high. The area was rich enough in resources to enable hunters and gath-erers to live there during the long period of experimentation that preceded the achievement of full food production. Many of our domesticated plants and animals are native to this piedmont core area.

Toward the end of the last Ice Age, around 20,000 years ago, preagricultural peoples were widely distributed throughout the Fertile Crescent. Larger and more **sedentary** populations were located in environments with the most resources. Smaller migratory bands occupied less favored areas. Once established in local environments, patterns of living changed very slowly. Population densities stayed well below levels that would lead to resource exhaustion.

These people began to establish new dietary patterns. They broadened their diets to include a greater variety of food sources, in which everything from water turtles to land snails was eaten. Many of these ad-ditional food resources were small in size and could be stored.

Later, toward 10,000 B.C., pots and baskets appeared. This "container revolution," as the urban historian Lewis Mumford calls it, was only one of a series of changes in human behavior that accompanied broad-spectrum gathering. These two advances—a greater variety of food sources and food storage—made larger and more concentrated populations possible.

The new broad-spectrum pattern of gathering probably involved women and children in the food economy to a much greater degree. The division of labor between the sexes became common. Men, the organizers of the social unit, appear as hunters in the archeological record; women and children were gatherers of wild grains, nuts, and small invertebrates. Women's contributions to the total diet became more substantial. Their knowledge of edible plants, animals, and insects gained importance.

The resource potential of local environments in the Middle East began to play a greater role in the distribution of population. People became more and more concentrated in the piedmont oak and pistachio forests, which was the best environment for food collection for several reasons. First, the uplands had the widest assortment of nuts, fruits, wild grasses, and small game. Second, the soils of the oak and pistachio forests could be worked with a **digging stick,** a simple implement used to pry stones, prod plants, and uncover roots. Third, many of the large mammals of this area—sheep, goats, gazelles, and wild asses—have a tendency toward herd behavior, a feature understandably attractive to hunters. For these reasons, hunters and gatherers peopled this rich environment in relatively large numbers by 10,000 B.C.

It is likely, however, that the beginnings of agriculture did not occur in the resource-rich forests of oak and pistachio but instead in less favored environments on their margins. Lit-

THE FERTILE CRESCENT OF THE MIDDLE EAST

The Fertile Crescent is an arc of productive, well-watered land extending from the highlands of the eastern Mediterranean through the foothills of the Taurus Mountains of southern Turkey and the Zagros Mountains of western Iran. This was the culture hearth in which agriculture and herding were discovered in the Middle East nearly 10,000 years ago.

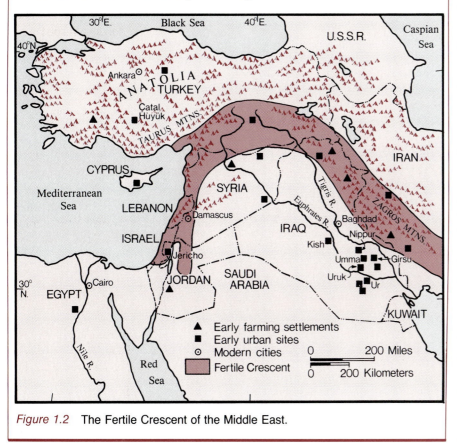

Figure 1.2 The Fertile Crescent of the Middle East.

tle stimulus for planting held sway in the foothills because pure stands of wild grains are found throughout the region. A recent experiment suggests that an experienced family of food gatherers could reap a ton of grain, more than a year's supply, in a three-week harvesting season—and without working very hard. Given these conditions, planting would clearly be unnecessary in the richer zones.

These favored **environmental niches** may have acted as regional centers of population growth that spawned colonies in less favored areas nearby. In marginal regions on the fringes of the Fertile Crescent, agriculture may have begun as a logical extension of food gathering practices. Migrants from the oak and pistachio forests recreated the dense stands of grasses that occurred naturally in their homelands. It may be that agriculture, in its earliest phases, was a simple alternative to hunting and gathering and that only after long periods of experimentation did it become the dominant economy in the foothills of the Fertile Crescent.

If this is true—and the evidence is far from complete—the origins of agriculture and herding are not rooted in a dramatic environmental change or in the foresight of an unknown prehistoric genius. Instead, these discoveries occurred as a simple extension of the food-gathering practices of preagricultural people spurred by a rather limited population explosion. People may have accidentally, unintentionally developed the capacity to control plants and animals.

The Domestication of Plants

By 7000 B.C., domesticated wheat and barley were being cultivated in villages throughout the foothills of the Fertile Crescent—on the western flanks of the Zagros Mountains, in southern Anatolia, and in northern Palestine (Fig. 1.2). At approximately this same time, the bones of domesticated sheep and goats begin to appear in the remains of ancient village farming sites. In most places, cultivated plants and animals are found together. But at some sites, domesticated animals preceded cultivated plants by almost 2000 years.

All available evidence, however, points to the importance of the foothills of the Middle East as a primary culture hearth of both plant and animal domestication. The important questions are: How did domestication occur? Why did people cultivate plants and herd animals to create the economic base for a new human environment?

Wild cereal grains and cultivated varieties differ greatly. The difference lies in their method of seed dispersal. Wild wheat and barley have fragile, seed-holding spikes that open at maturity. Any movement of the plant caused by passing animals, by wind, or by food gatherers shakes these seeds onto the ground. This ensures a new crop in the following year. The seeds of cultivated wheat and barley, by contrast, cling tenaciously to the stalk. Thus, in a natural setting, cultivated wheat and barley had a low survival capacity.

For this reason, most plants in wild wheat and barley fields had fragile, brittle heads. Only small patches of wild cereal grains held ripened grain firmly on the stalk. When preagricultural gatherers entered these fields, however, plant populations began to change. Gradually, hard-holding wheat and barley plants became more prevalent because gatherers slapped their seeds off the stalk and collected, carried, and dropped these seeds throughout the humanized area.

People unconsciously ensured the spread of hard-holding varieties of wheat and barley. When they migrated to new environments, they brought these plants with them. These practices created the very kind of grain needed for farming—grain picked from the plant rather than from the ground.

The Domestication of Animals

The domestication of animals in the Fertile Crescent may also have been an unplanned process pursued as a natural extension of the activities of hunters and gatherers. The first animal domesticated in the Middle East was the sheep, which in those days looked more like a modern deer. Shortly thereafter, goats and probably pigs were domesticated in this region. Several thousand years later, cattle were domesticated.

The earliest physical evidence of animal domestication occurs between 9000 and 8000 B.C. when sheep bones begin to outnumber those of goats by sixteen to one in some archeological sites. This suggests the development of sheepherding and the beginnings of animal domestication. Between 8000 and 7000 B.C., similar changes in goat populations begin to appear in other archeological sites and goat horns shrink in size and change in shape. Soon, these domesticated sheep and goats are found throughout the foothills of the Fertile Crescent.

Animal domestication must have posed problems to hunters and gatherers and to early agriculturalists. First, herds of domesticated sheep and goats had to be protected from larger, wild predators. This task was probably more easily accomplished by sedentary folk than by **nomads.** Second, herds had to be fed throughout the year and particularly during the summer when natural pastures in the lowlands dry up. Agriculturalists probably fed animals chaff and grain from their fields; nomads in the Zagros Mountains could take herds to alpine meadows during the dry season. But people involved in animal domestication, whether agriculturalists or gatherers, had to have a sufficiently reliable year-round food supply, so that they were not tempted to consume their herds.

These people must have had a motive to expend the considerable energy necessary for animal domestication. Wild sheep and goats did not produce milk or wool. Meat and hides already were acquired by hunters, so, it is necessary to look beyond food and clothing needs to identify possible motives.

Young animals that formed the nucleus of a herd may have been originally kept for religious purposes, for sacrifice at festivals, or for the value of their horns. Large horned animals played important symbolic and religious roles in the lives of these people. Young animals brought into a village by a hunter may also have survived as pets or as hunting decoys. By any or all of these means, once the nucleus of a herd of young sheep or goats was established, villagers would probably reject the most aggressive, unmanageable animals. As in the domestication of plants, an accidental, unplanned selection of animals began that ultimately led to specialized stock breeding.

Village Farming in the Middle East

By 6000 B.C., after 3000 years of experimentation, the basic elements of the Middle Eastern food-producing complex—wheat and barley cultivation, domesticated sheep and goats, and permanent village settlement— had spread throughout the uplands of the Middle East. Village farming combined with hunting and gathering had emerged as an attractive and reliable way of life. Under this new economic system, population densities probably increased ten to twenty times. People appear to have concentrated at those sites most suitable for farming. This resulted in fewer but larger human settlements in the uplands of the Middle East.

The discovery of agriculture and herding provided people with a more reliable food base, but it would be a mistake to view the process as simply economic. Life in these new agricultural villages must have differed substantially from that of hunters and gatherers. Day-to-day living was increasingly tied to the seasonal activities of farming. Sowing in the fall, harvesting in early summer, lambing in spring, and moving herds to upland pastures in the summer were repetitive events marked by festivals in early religions. These events formed a regular pattern of village activity far more disciplined than that of hunters and gatherers.

The village farming system both expanded and limited human horizons. Geographically, individual patterns of movement became more restricted: the village, then as now, was a rooted community. Yet patterns of trade and commerce over long distances indicate that these communities were not isolated. A flow of goods and ideas existed in the Fertile Crescent from the Mediterranean Sea to the Arabian/Persian Gulf (Fig. 1.2). Although personal knowledge of distant places must have been more limited in settled villages, intense, local environmental experience contributed to the control and augmentation of plant and animal resources.

The Rise of Cities

The rise of cities, the second phase of the Environmental Transformation, followed food production in each of the major hearths of agriculture.

Small settled villages, cultivated grainfields, and domesticated sheep and goats were primary elements in the Middle Eastern food-producing complex. The pigeon towers in the background housed doves kept for food and fertilizer.

In the Tigris-Euphrates Valley, Egypt, the Indus Valley, North China, central Mexico, and the northern Andes, 4000 years separate the beginnings of agriculture from the emergence of large and complex urban settlements. Compared to the long span of human time before the origins of agriculture, cities appear quickly in the archaeological record.

Before cities could develop, however, two conditions had to exist. First, a reliable **food surplus** had to be available to feed city dwellers. Unless surrounding environments produced agricultural surpluses for nonfood producers—urban leaders, craft specialists, merchants, priests— no city, then or now, could long survive. Second, a social organization was needed to manage the collection, storage, and redistribution of food

surpluses. Whether for religious, political, or economic reasons, rural farmers, fisherfolk, and herders had to be persuaded to exchange their food surpluses in return for urban goods and services. In these early cities, the first large-scale attempt to organize human energy occurred. This energy was channeled into the building of walls, temples, and pyramids.

The Rise of Cities in Mesopotamia

After 4000 B.C., agriculturalists living in small villages in the foothills of the Fertile Crescent began to move downslope into the Tigris-Euphrates Valley in modern Iraq, the ancient Mesopotamian hearth of civilization. These farmers brought with them cultivated wheat and barley; domesticated sheep, goats, and cattle; and

a tradition of settled village life. Their movement was probably the result of modest increases in population. The farmers very gradually ate and sowed their way down into the valley.

The Tigris-Euphrates Valley environment presented new problems and opportunities. First, low rainfall in these lowlands made **irrigation** essential for cultivation. Wheat and barley fields, interspersed with date palm groves, were planted on the marshy banks of stream channels. These crops were watered by simple diversion channels. Second, the summer heat and drought scorched vegetation off the plains, making it difficult to feed the cattle and donkeys needed for plowing during this season of the year. Third, building stones were not available on the **alluvial plains,** so that most structures were built of reeds or sun-dried brick. These houses were periodically threatened by torrential floods fed by the spring melting of snow on surrounding mountains. Adapting to this new environment must have been difficult. Early Mesopotamian religious texts describe a society living in fear of environmental dangers.

Despite these problems, the plains of Mesopotamia were fertile and produced food surpluses far greater than previously known. Irrigated agriculture, generally five to six times more productive than **dry farming,** became the technological basis of everyday life. Higher yields on irrigated land enabled society to feed a growing population. A large, stable farming population evolved in the lowlands of Mesopotamia.

What sparked the emergence of cities was a social structure capable of organizing society's food surplus and channeling human energy into directed activities. This direction was apparently provided by a specialized class of priests. Religious authorities acted as both economic administrators and spiritual leaders in early Sumer, the first of a succession of civilizations located in the Mesopotamian Plains.

Religion was intimately associated with environmental conditions in the valley. Early on, priests became involved in feeding domesticated animals during the summer drought when local grazing lands were parched. Agricultural land was set aside to grow animal fodder; priests organized the winter storage and summer distribution of fodder to herdsmen. Not incidentally, this gave the priests partial control over wool, a major item of trade. Gradually, religion became central to the organization of the Mesopotamian agricultural economy.

The Sumerian City-State

These processes of environmental adaptation and social organization culminated in the emergence of the first Mesopotamian urban-based civilization, Sumer. The basis of this civilization was the **city-state,** organized and run by priests and kings. Its citizens included merchants, artisans, and slaves. Each city-state in Sumer had monumental structures, exerted territorial control over surrounding agricultural areas, and participated in international trade.

By 2500 B.C., ten to twelve major Sumerian urban centers existed in Mesopotamia. These cities served a rural population of upwards of 1 million people living on the alluvial plains between the Tigris and Euphrates rivers (Fig. 1.2). The largest cities—places like Kish, Nippur, and Ur—enclosed as much as 250 acres of land within their fortifications.

The largest Sumerian city, Uruk, had a population of roughly 50,000 people and covered an area of 1100 acres. It was encircled by a double city wall, approximately 6 miles long, reinforced by nearly 1000 semicircular towers. Temple complexes covered many acres of land inside the city. These structures included a warren of storerooms, warehouses, and shrines occupied by priests, scribes, craftspeople, and laborers. The main temple was often a massive step pyramid or **ziggurat.** One such religious complex at Uruk was so large that an estimated 1500 slaves working ten-hour days for five years were required to complete it.

By 2500 B.C., every large city in Sumer was a walled fortress. Battlements protected Sumerians from nomadic raids and from invasions by rulers of neighboring city-states. Fear of starvation was replaced by fear of war. The people of Sumer no longer prayed for subsistence but for safety. Kingship was the political response to incessant warfare, and royal palaces grew to rival temples in size, wealth, and complexity.

At the heart of the Sumerian city, massive temples, palaces, and other public buildings occupied vast amounts of space. Wide, straight, unpaved streets connected this urban core with the outer gates in city walls. Wealthy residents lived in large houses that featured spacious courtyards and sewage removal. These were normally located on major avenues near the center of the city. Off the major streets, the densely packed houses of the poorer classes were often less secure than those of the rich. Commercial activity was concen-

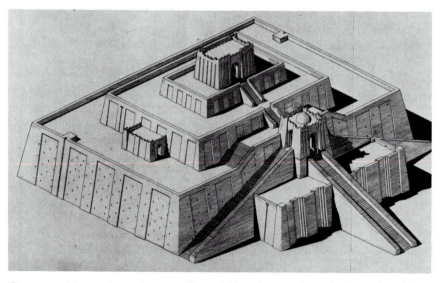

Step pyramids, or ziggurats, were the main temple complexes in Sumerian cities. The structures, which were economic as well as religious centers, show that early civilizations were able to organize people to work on large-scale projects. This ziggurat at Uruk took at least five years to complete.

THE DECLINE OF SUMER: AN EARLY ECOLOGICAL CRISIS

After 1000 years of growth, the center of civilization in the Tigris-Euphrates Valley moved northward from Sumer to Akkad near modern Baghdad. Historians have offered several reasons for this northward shift: heavy military burdens, invasion by mountain peoples to the north and east, and even a change in climate that led to the drying up of southern Mesopotamia. Recent evidence, however, suggests that increases in soil salinity caused by human abuse of the land contributed to the decline of Sumer.

Salinization, the accumulation and concentration of salts in the soil, is a problem wherever irrigation is practiced carelessly. If salts carried by irrigation water accumulate in fields, plants are less able to absorb water, soil texture is damaged, land fertility and crop yields decline, and the land must be abandoned. To reduce salt accumulation, one can use water with a low salt content or alternatively flush salt from the root zone down into the **groundwater** by large-scale applications of water.

In Sumer, salt accumulation was initially controlled by limiting irrigation and by cultivating land in alternate years. But warfare and population pressure led to overirrigation and continuous cultivation. These practices increased salini-

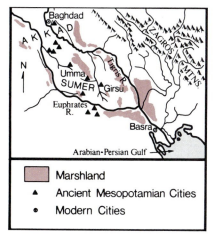

Figure 1.3 Salinization in Sumer.

zation in Sumer between 2400 and 1700 B.C. and were factors in its decline.

For 150 years during this period, two neighboring cities, Girsu and Umma, located on tributaries of the Tigris and Euphrates rivers, were in conflict over fertile land near their mutual frontier (Fig. 1.3). When Girsu began to prevail, the people of Umma, who were located upstream, blocked the canals that fed water to the disputed territory. In response, the king of Girsu had a canal constructed directly from the Tigris River to the disputed zone. This canal became an important source of irrigation water, but when combined with water from the Euphrates, it caused the **water table** with its accumulated salts to rise.

Similar decisions spurred by conflict must have been common in Sumer. At Girsu, patches of saline ground appeared almost immediately after the construction of the Tigris Canal. Land surveys over the next 300 years prove that land previously described as salt free had become saline. Throughout Sumer, shifts from wheat cultivation to more salt-tolerant barley suggest that salinization was a chronic problem. By 1700 B.C., wheat was no longer cultivated in southern Mesopotamia, and crop yields were one-third those recorded for earlier periods. The implications of this destruction of the food base of cities with large populations, temple complexes, palaces, and professional armies must have been staggering. The alluvial plains of Mesopotamia, once sufficiently fertile to provide a reliable food surplus, were severely damaged by salinization, and population declined and shifted northward.

Adapted from: Thorkild Jacobsen and Robert M. Adams, "Salt and Silt in Ancient Mesopotamian Agriculture," *Science,* Vol. 128 (1958), pp. 1251–1258.

trated along the waterfront, on river banks, and at the city gates. Large open areas in the city were still used for cultivation.

This diversification of urban land use reflected a growing social stratification in Sumerian life. At the top of Sumerian society were the king, palace administrators, priests, and temple officials. These leaders administered huge estates to supply food to the army, the palace, and the temple. They became wealthy, as they do in modern societies, in the performance of their duties.

Despite the great control exercised by the palace and the temple over human and agricultural resources in Sumer, it appears that small agricultural producers cultivating their own land formed two thirds of the population. Most people in Sumer were, after all, still primary producers—herders, fisherfolk, and farmers—and it is unlikely that more than a fifth of the total society was ever freed from growing food at any one time. The hallmarks of **preindustrial** society appear early in Sumer.

The civilization that arose in Sumer was similar to those that later arose in Egypt, the Mediterranean Basin, China, the Indus Valley of Pakistan, Europe, and the New World. The best and the worst of human achievements were represented here. Fashion, music, art, a literary tradition, organized religion, huge public structures, and large-scale irrigation networks stood in contrast with militarism, exploitation of the weak, slavery, bureaucratic regulation, and environmental destruction (Fig. 1.3).

The Diffusion of the Environmental Transformation

The agriculture, domesticated animals, sedentary villages, and town life of the Environmental Transformation diffused outward from the culture hearths of the Old and New Worlds into new environments. The spread was slow and uneven. Centuries were needed for people, plants, and animals to adapt to different climates and for social organization to develop in different regions. This new way of life diffused persistently, however. By A.D. 1500, the world supported a population of 500 million. Sophisticated urban-based civilizations existed in the Middle East, throughout the Mediterranean and elsewhere in Europe, in China, India, Southeast Asia, Mexico, and Peru. The routes of diffusion and interaction among these centers are subjects of lively debate in geography. All agree, however, that the Environmental Transformation changed the face of the planet.

The Diffusion of Agriculture

About 6000 years ago, village farming began to spread from the Fertile Crescent of the Middle East down to

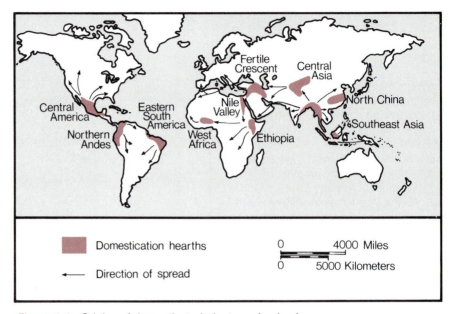

Figure 1.4 Origins of domesticated plants and animals.

the alluvial lowlands of the Tigris and Euphrates rivers of Mesopotamia. Agriculture diffused somewhat later into the Nile River Valley. By 4000 B.C., the food-producing revolution was widespread in the Middle East.

The essential elements of the food-producing complex then spread westward across the Anatolian Plateau in Turkey into Europe moving slowly along the coast of the Mediterranean (Fig. 1.4). It took thousands of years for agriculture to spread from Eastern Europe to the far corners of Scandinavia. On average, agriculture probably spread at a rate of one-half mile a year, but the exact routes and rates of dispersal are not fully known. When cultivation and animal husbandry spread away from the Mediterranean world, adjustments to different climates, soils, and vegetation were necessary.

The first non-Mediterranean area settled by farmers was the Danube River Valley adjacent to the Black Sea. In the fifth millenium B.C., people practiced a form of **shifting cultivation,** growing wheat, barley, and other plants on the Danube lowlands. They also kept domesticated cattle and pigs, but sheep and goats were of minor importance. Similar settlements existed in other lowland river basins of Europe, apparently the most attractive regions to early agriculturalists. Cultivation extended much later into the more difficult forest environments of Europe.

This expansion of cultivators into the forest environments of Europe did not occur until after 3000 B.C.,

The Nile River enabled farmers to establish themselves in a desert landscape. Floodwaters were trapped in basins to irrigate crops, an adaptation that increased agricultural production.

ORIGINS OF DOMESTICATED PLANTS AND ANIMALS

Hearth	Plants	Animals
Old World		
Southeast Asia	Bamboo, banana, black pepper, citrus, eggplant, mango, sugarcane, taro, tea, yam	Cat,* cattle,* chicken, dog, duck, goose, pig,* water buffalo
North China	Apricot, cabbage, millet, mulberry, peach, persimmon, plum, radish, rice, sorghum, soybean, tea	Chicken,* dog, horse, pig,* silkworm
Central Asia	Almond, apple, carrot, cherry, flax, hemp, lentil, melon, onion, pea, pear, turnip, walnut	Bactrian camel, bee, cattle, chicken, dog, horse,* reindeer, sheep, yak
Fertile Crescent	Almond, barley, cabbage, date, fig, grape, oats, olive, onion, pea, rutabaga, rye, turnip, wheat	Bee, cattle,* dog, dromedary camel, goat, pig,* pigeon, sheep
Ethiopia	Coffee	
Nile Valley	Cotton, cucumber, lentil, melon, millet, pea, sesame, sorghum	Cat, dog, donkey
West Africa	Cowpea, kola, rice, watermelon, yam	
New World		
Central America	Amaranth, avocado, bean, chili pepper, cocoa, corn, cotton, manioc, papaya, pineapple,* potato, pumpkin, squash, sunflower, tobacco, tomato	Dog, guinea pig, turkey
Northern Andes	Beans, potato, pumpkin, squash, strawberry	Alpaca, guinea pig, llama
Eastern South America	Bean, cocoa, manioc, peanut, pineapple,* squash, sunflower, sweet potato	Dog, duck

Note: *Indicates possible origin.

Table adapted from: Marvin W. Mikesell, *Patterns and Imprints of Mankind.* Chicago: Rand McNally, 1968, p. xxx; *Encyclopaedia Britannica,* s.v. "Domestication, Plant and Animal." Map adapted from: Peter Haggett, *Geography: A Modern Synthesis,* 3rd ed., New York: Harper & Row, 1983, fig. 12-4, p. 278.

when agriculturalists began to use fire to clear the land, to plant cereals in the ashes, and to herd animals in meadows created in these clearings. Over wide areas of Europe, oak and elm forests were destroyed by farmers using **slash and burn** techniques. As farmers moved northward into cooler climates, wheat and barley were gradually replaced by oats and rye, hardier cereal grains.

At this same time, agriculture and herding also diffused westward along the North African **littoral** and up the Nile Valley as far as the modern city of Khartoum. The environment in this region was similar to that of the Fertile Crescent, so that little adjustment in subsistence strategy was needed.

The dry climates of the Sahara, however, did require **ecological** adaptation. Some cereal agriculture was practiced in a limited way in mountain oases in this desert, but the dominant economy of the Sahara in the fourth millennium B.C. was cattle herding. It is generally assumed that traders from the Nile Valley transmitted their knowledge of agriculture into sub-Saharan Africa. Some writers, however, suggest that an independent culture hearth of plant domestication existed in West Africa at the headwaters of the Niger River (Fig. 1.4).

The diffusion of Middle Eastern food production eastward into Asia was every bit as slow as its westward spread into Europe. By 5000 B.C., wheat and barley were cultivated as far east as Afghanistan and Pakistan. But beyond the Indus Valley, food production apparently came much later. By 2000 B.C., farmers in central India cultivated grain and vegetables and herded domesticated animals. In North China, cultivators combined Southeast Asia's agricultural techniques with the grain cultivation of the Middle East. Southeast Asia, in turn, had a different pattern of farming based on vegetative reproduction of plants through cuttings (Fig. 1.4). Tuber plants played an important role, as did the pig and the chicken. The geographic relationships between agriculture in eastern Asia and the Middle East remain unclear.

In the New World, an independent but parallel shift from hunting and gathering to food production took place in Central America and the northern Andes (Fig. 1.4). In the Middle East, people domesticated many animals and few plants, but in the New World the reverse was true. White and sweet potatoes were domesticated as well as sunflowers, beans, pumpkins, chilies, squash, and most important, corn. New World animal domesticates included the llama and the alpaca of the Peruvian highlands, and the turkey and hairless dog in Central America.

The Spread of Cities

Urban centers sprang up in the river valleys of Egypt, India, North China, and Southeast Asia after the emergence of the Sumerian cities. In each case, cities follow the introduction of agriculture. By the third millennium B.C., cities existed in Mesopotamia, the Nile Valley, the Indus Valley, and shortly thereafter throughout the Mediterranean Basin. Most of these cities were control centers for relatively dense populations living in agricultural hinterlands. Very quickly, however, they became exchange centers in expanding networks of interregional trade. By the second millennium B.C., city life existed in North China, in the river valleys of Southeast Asia, and along the Niger River in West Africa. Some 2000 years later, New World civilizations in Central America and the Andes were urban based.

By the time of Christ, world population had grown to around 300 million people. Fully 80 percent of these people were concentrated in three highly organized urban systems: an estimated 40 percent on the Indian subcontinent, another 25 percent in North China, and the remainder in the Middle Eastern-Mediterranean core area. Beyond these fertile culture hearths, vast regions of the globe remained thinly populated and still largely the realm of hunters and gatherers.

In Europe, nearly 1000 years passed before cities spread from the Mediterranean to the western reaches of the continent (Fig. 1.5). Under the Romans, urbanism spread north and west into Spain, France, and finally Britain. Population subsequently increased, particularly in newly settled areas. Although many of these cities collapsed with the decline of the Roman Empire, some European cities remained important centers of civilization throughout the Dark Ages, during the medieval period, and on into the present. Similarly in India, China, and the New World, cities extended their reach to encompass broader hinterlands and larger populations.

By A.D. 1500, the eve of the Scientific Transformation, the overlapping diffusion of agriculture and ur-

THE SPREAD OF CITIES IN EUROPE

Urban centers appear in southeastern Europe as early as 2000 B.C., but the major spread of city building across Europe coincided with the expansion of the Roman Empire. This slow spread of **urbanism** took centuries, so that 1100 years elapsed between the construction of cities on the coast of the Aegean Sea and the beginnings of urban life in the northern reaches of the British Isles.

Adapted from: Norman J. G. Pounds, "The Urbanization of the Classical World," *Annals of the Association of American Geographers,* Vol. 59 (1969), pp. 135–157; fig. 6, p. 148.

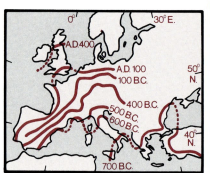

Figure 1.5 The spread of cities in Europe.

WORLD PATTERNS OF LAND USE IN A.D. 1500

By 1500, the Environmental Transformation had spread widely throughout the Old and the New World. Agriculture formed the basis of urban civilizations in East and South Asia, the Middle East, West Africa, Europe, and the New World. These patterns changed radically when the Scientific Transformation gave Europeans the technology to dominate the world.

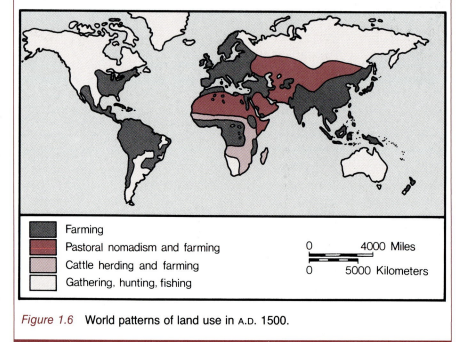

Farming
Pastoral nomadism and farming
Cattle herding and farming
Gathering, hunting, fishing

0　　4000 Miles
0　　5000 Kilometers

Figure 1.6 World patterns of land use in A.D. 1500.

banism had altered the economy of vast areas of the Old World (Fig. 1.6). Throughout Europe, the Middle East and North Africa, Central Asia, China,

and India, grain cultivation was the mainstay of human life. In Southeast Asia and Africa, tuber cultivation was the basis of agriculture. Specialized nomadic herding economies prevailed in the **deserts** and **steppes** of the Middle East and North Africa as well as in the northern reaches of Scandinavia and Siberia. Agriculture had not yet spread to Australia, and scattered groups still practiced hunting and gathering in parts of southern and central Africa and along the Arctic fringe. By and large, however, agriculture had effectively replaced earlier economies as the predominant basis of human existence.

Similarly, in the New World, cultivation of maize, beans, and squash was practiced throughout Central America and in eastern North America as far north as the Great Lakes and the St. Lawrence River (Fig. 1.6). In South America, only the dry and cool south, the uplands of northeastern Brazil, and the Amazon Basin did not have an agricultural economy. Complex urban civilizations existed in Mexico, parts of Central America, and the Andes highlands. Comparable in architectural sophistication, political organization, and economy to the ancient civilizations of the Old World, these societies quickly collapsed before the onslaught of the military technology of an expanding Europe.

THE SCIENTIFIC TRANSFORMATION

The Environmental Transformation created a world in which regional civilizations controlled different spheres of the globe. No single society possessed the long-term power to impose its will on the others. With the beginning of the Scientific Transformation, however, Europe became the first society with the capacity for global influence. *The Medieval Agricultural Revolution* expanded settlement and population in northern and western Europe between A.D. 1000 and 1500. New areas were brought into cultivation. The forests of Europe were felled. Larger agricultural

surpluses supported larger and more intense human concentrations.

In the phase that followed, *The Industrial Revolution,* scientific knowledge was applied to technology, and inanimate sources of energy were brought under control. England became the world's first industrial and urban country in the eighteenth and nineteenth centuries. Largely as a result of this intellectual and technological growth, Europeans began to dominate other world cultures.

New patterns of human relations were created by *The Diffusion of the Scientific Transformation.* An inner sphere of technologically advanced societies, the Technological World, began to control an outer sphere of technologically less advanced societies, the Developing World. For the first time in history, divisions between peoples across the face of the earth were based on the possession of scientific knowledge and technology.

The Medieval Agricultural Revolution

In the Medieval, or Middle, Ages, changes in the organization of agriculture in northern and western Europe caused a major expansion of population beginning about A.D. 1000. In the next 500 years, forests were cut, towns were established, and population nearly tripled.

This initial phase of the Scientific Transformation established the agricultural basis for a later flowering of European society. The changes of this early period are often ignored because medieval patterns of growth were obscured by plagues and warfare in the fourteenth and fifteenth centuries. Nonetheless, the distinctive features of modern Europe are lodged in the rural prosperity of medieval times.

Rural Life in Medieval Europe

In the early Middle Ages, rural life was universal in Western Europe. The first millenium A.D. had seen dramatic shifts in population. European

population decreased from 36 million in A.D. 200 to 26 million in A.D. 600, the low point of the Dark Ages. At A.D. 1000, the early medieval period, population had again risen to 36 million. Yet England and Germany had virtually no urban centers. Elsewhere, towns were few and far between. Agricultural productivity was so low that even in cities, most people were still directly engaged in agriculture.

Much as in the early Environmental Transformation, villages were the basic unit of settlement. Human existence centered on these fixed places, which were widely separated one from another by empty spaces. Village boundaries were marked by hedges to form enclosures containing huts, animal pens, stores of food, and vegetable gardens, or tofts.

Village location was fixed in law and for environmental reasons. The soil inside village enclosures was fertilized by household wastes and animal manure. Here, peasants cultivated their tofts year-round, growing herbs, root crops, vines, and other vegetables. Outside the enclosures, fields of wheat, rye, and oats ringed with hedges were planted in the least exposed, most accessible places.

Villages owned by lords, monasteries, or religious orders were large and employed many local peasants and servants (Fig. 1.7). The Church played a particularly important role in the economic life of medieval Europe. Monasteries were widely distributed across the landscape and controlled large holdings of agricultural land. They were active in opening up new lands to cultivation in frontier regions, like the English marshes. They were engaged in sheep raising in the uplands. In this way, lords and priests controlled the activities of peasants by controlling the land. Some estates were as large as 25,000 to 50,000 acres. Their principal economic function was to support a few people in wealth and comfort.

Generally, the cultivated area was small. Over much of Europe the landscape was covered by natural pasture and forest. The forests served as grazing areas for pigs; the meadows, for sheep, goats, and cattle. A good part of the peasants' food supply still came from hunting, fishing, and trapping. The vast majority of people lived through a combination of cultivation, animal husbandry, and gathering.

Most villages were located on light, easily worked, and well-drained soils. In England, this meant cultivation of the uplands and avoidance of lowland regions with their heavy clay soils and dense vegetation. In the Low Countries, villagers also avoided areas of heavy soils, creating a spotty pattern of settlement. Agricultural expansion was difficult because the fragile wooden tools of the peasantry were not equal to the task of clearing wooded areas or turning heavy soils.

As a result, although total population was small, favored ecological zones in Western Europe tended to be overpopulated, and this population pressure could not easily be relieved by colonization. According to most surveys of the time, the villages of France, the Netherlands, western Germany, Switzerland, and northern Italy were overpopulated during the 200 years before the year A.D. 1000. The main preoccupations of European peasants were to survive the perils of cultivating cereals with inferior tools in unfavorable climates, to meet the demands of landlords and priests, and to avoid periodic attacks by invaders. Life was a hazardous, hand-to-mouth affair.

Changes in Medieval Agriculture

A series of changes in medieval technology, energy, and economy altered the fabric of country life in Western Europe to reduce the precariousness of peasant existence, reshape the landscape of northern Europe, and create a vastly more productive agricultural system. The three most important elements contributing to these changes in agricultural life were (1)

LAND USE IN A MEDIEVAL VILLAGE

Medieval land was divided into the enclosed fields of the local lord (bottom of illustration) and the open lands of the village (top of illustration). Planting strategies were determined by the village commune, a corporate body directed by the lord or his steward. Villagers grazed a certain number of cattle on common land; some lords allowed timber and firewood to be taken from the woodlot.

The enclosed fields of the lord's manor were not open to the villagers. Open fields were held in common or owned by the church, the lord, or an individual villager. The meadow in some cases belonged to the lord and in others was open to general use. A portion of the open fields was set aside for support of the church in addition to "God's acre," the parson's field.

Figure 1.7 Land use in a medieval village.

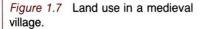

the heavy plow, which opened wet clay soils to cultivation; (2) the use of horses for plowing and transport; and (3) the development of a three-field system of **crop rotation,** which increased agricultural production.

The heavy, or iron, plow came into use in northern Europe between the eighth and tenth centuries. This plow had distinct advantages over the old wooden plow. The heavy plow turned wet, thick soils so effectively that **cross plowing** was no longer needed. This cut the labor of plowing in half, enabling peasants to cultivate more land in the same amount of time. The heavy plow also enabled peasants to cultivate heavy lowland soils that were inherently more fertile than those of surrounding uplands. The combination of savings in labor, improvements in field drainage, and the opening of new lands to cultivation raised production and revolutionized agriculture in northern Europe.

The heavy plow also stimulated so-

cial and economic changes in village life. This plow needed eight oxen instead of the customary two to turn the soil effectively. Because few peasants owned eight oxen, a pooling of resources was required. This involved new patterns of social cooperation and a reorganization of village lands into more efficiently sized, large open fields plowed in long strips. These strips were assigned to the group of peasants who owned the plow and oxen. The land was worked communally. Disputes and management decisions were placed in the hands of a village council. By the end of the Middle Ages, the typical village economy in northern Europe involved the use of the heavy plow, **strip farming** of open fields, and communal husbandry.

A second major change in medieval agriculture was the growing use of horses for plowing and planting in northwestern Europe. The major advantages of horses over oxen lay in their greater speed and endurance. Although both animals had equal pulling power, horses plowed twice as rapidly and could work for one to two hours more each day than oxen. By 1200, horses were widely used for plowing on the plains of northern Europe. A century later, they were common in England. Horses never penetrated Mediterranean Europe, probably because oats, their primary food, did not grow well there.

The shift from oxen to horses had important effects on communication and transport in medieval Europe. In the early Middle Ages, every castle, monastery, or town was likely to be visited occasionally by wandering monks and peddlers, but regular connections between settlements were few. Obstacles to communication were formidable: roads were poor and unsafe; bridges were not maintained. A normal day's travel for a caravan of merchants amounted to only 20 miles.

The widespread adoption of the horse altered this pattern. Hamlets in the vicinity of larger settlements were abandoned as peasants moved to larger centers and commuted to their fields on horseback. Substantial villages of 100 or more families with facilities such as a church, tavern, and school appeared on the European landscape, laying the foundation for the later shift from rural to urban life.

The three-field rotation system, the last element of agricultural change, was adopted in northern Europe during the 1200s. Under the traditional two-field system, half the agricultural land was planted in grain and half left unplanted each year to maintain soil fertility. With the cultivation of new soil-enriching **legumes,** such as peas and beans, village land could be divided into thirds. On each third, grain was planted the first year; legumes, barley, and oats the second year; and the land was left fallow the third year.

Like the plow and the horse, the three-field system sharply increased productivity. In the two-field system, half the land was unproductive. With the three-field system, only a third lay fallow, so that more food could be grown in the same area. Moreover, spring planting of barley and oats was important for feeding horses, so that a change from a two-field rotation system often coincided with the shift from oxen to horses.

The heavy plow, the horse, and the three-field rotation system had a significant impact on rural life in medieval Europe. Obstacles that had limited cultivation in the past were removed. New villages sprang up and old ones grew larger. Towns began to dot the countryside. Greater agricultural productivity and a better diet provided the energy for new and demanding ventures. The great forests of the region were cut down. As the empty spaces disappeared, closer patterns of human association were established.

In this scene from the Flemish *Hours of the Virgin,* a heavy plow pulled by a team of horses prepares a field for sowing. The area is fenced to keep domesticated pigs rooting for acorns (upper left) out of the grainfields.

Population Growth and Agricultural Expansion

In the twelfth and thirteenth centuries, the population of Western Europe grew sharply to 83 million people (Fig. 1.8). Although **birth rates** were no higher, larger numbers of people survived. Population grew at different rates in different places because growth was based on improvements in agricultural techniques, which diffused unevenly. In England, the overall population rose from 1.1 million in 1086 to 3.7 million in 1346, but Devon in the south remained a wilderness. In France, by far the largest country in Europe, the population shot from 6.5 million in A.D. 1000 to 16 million in 1300. The region near Paris, already densely settled, experienced a substantial population increase, whereas other regions in France remained virtually uninhabited.

Despite these variations, the larger number of people in Europe was generally accommodated by an enlargement of **arable** land at the expense of forest, swamps, and pasture. In the Netherlands, this meant the draining of swamps, the building of dikes, and the construction of **polder.** In France and Germany, forests were cleared and new villages founded. In the Alps, villages reached high elevations, subsequently abandoned in modern times.

The assault on the European wilderness was started in the eleventh century by peasant pioneers who, spurred by population pressure and possessing better tools and equipment, began to enlarge the cultivated lands in the vicinity of their village (Fig. 1.9). Fields were brought into cultivation on the fringes of older settlements or on sites previously cleared for shifting cultivation. Cultivated fields enclosed by hedges also took over common pastures.

Deeper in the forests, peasants, hermits, charcoal burners, shepherds, and iron makers cut clearings in the woodland (Fig. 1.9). These pioneer efforts were often sizable mi-

THE POPULATION OF MEDIEVAL EUROPE

The population curve of medieval Europe shows the overall increase spurred by advances in agriculture between A.D. 1000 and 1350, the devastating effects of bubonic plague in the fourteenth century, and the later recovery that preceded the Industrial Revolution.

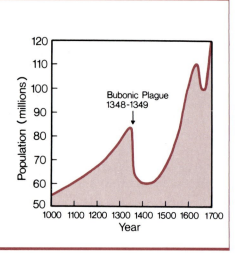

Figure 1.8 The population of medieval Europe.

grations. Monks were not, as has often been said, the chief agents of landscape change. The great abbeys of the Benedictines and Cistercians were usually established on previously cleared land. Many new religious orders, however, did settle the wilderness to rediscover the dignity of manual labor.

The second phase in the clearing of the European wilderness was characterized by the foundation of new villages by groups of settlers led by prominent social leaders. The forests of Europe generally belonged to the nobility and the Church, and churchmen and nobles both saw advantages in supporting the development of unused lands. In some cases, new villages were located on roads to ensure collection of tolls. Others were founded to produce additional sources of rent. The inhabitants of these new villages were usually poorer peasants and younger sons with no rights to inheritance. Old, crowded villages

THE ASSAULT ON THE EUROPEAN WILDERNESS

This local area southeast of Munich, West Germany, depicts the various stages of forest clearing during the medieval period. In the first stage, settlements (lower left) were located in isolated clearings surrounded by forest. Somewhat later, clearings were enlarged (center), until finally so much forest had been cleared that only patches of trees remained (upper right). The impenetrable forests of medieval Europe were gradually replaced by farms, villages, and towns.

Figure 1.9 The assault on the European wilderness.

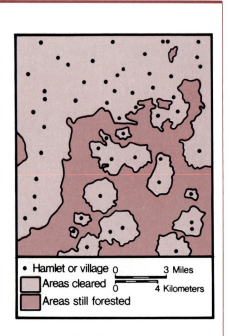

served as launching pads for pioneers attracted by promises of new land, equipment, and houses.

The final phase of settlement of the European wilderness was marked by an ebbing of the tide of new villages and a filling of the intervening spaces by individual settlers living in dispersed single farmsteads. The end of the thirteenth century witnessed the closing of the European frontier. This once impenetrable wilderness had been settled, and a landscape similar to that of modern Europe emerged.

The Changing Tempo of Medieval Life

Medieval growth in population and agricultural activity dramatically altered European systems of economic organization, commerce, and communication. The most immediate effect was to intensify human concentrations. Improvements in transportation aided urban growth. Bridges were thrown across rivers. Old roads were rebuilt and new ones constructed. The heavy bricks of the Roman roads were replaced by light

This medievel Dutch market town with its church, guild hall (right), and cluster of houses reflects the growth in population and urbanization that accompanied the clearing and settlement of the European wilderness.

gravel surfaces that were easily repaired. In England, new roads cut wide swaths through the countryside. To protect merchants from lurking highwaymen, trees were forbidden within 200 feet of the highway. Growth of land and water transport contributed directly to increased commerce on which expanding urban populations relied.

Cities had sprung up in every region of northern Europe. Most of these towns were small, less than a half mile in radius. Some had been in existence since Roman times; others became important as new religious centers. Still others grew up at fortified strategic points protected by the strength of a lord's castle. Some 2500 new cities were established in Germany alone during the late medieval period, and they attracted a flood of peasants from the countryside. The largest cities of the period were Paris and Venice, with populations of 40,000—hardly large by modern standards. Yet an urban mentality and social structure incubated in these cities.

A new urban middle class was developing, one less tied to the rhythm of the seasons and increasingly indispensable to the changing economy of the region. This medieval middle class owed virtually everything to trade. In the Mediterranean,

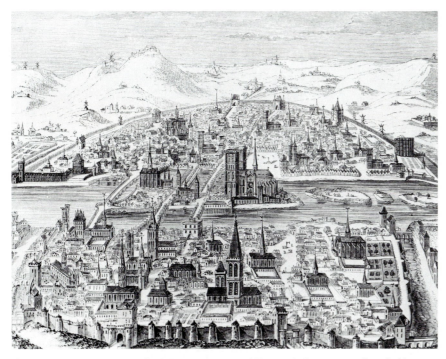

Paris, with a population of 40,000, was one of Europe's largest medieval cities. This print of Paris in 1607 shows the Seine River, Notre Dame Cathedral on Île de la Cité, and the walls and moats that surrounded the city.

merchants of Venice and Genoa vied for control of coastal hinterlands. In northern Europe, the Hanseatic League, an association of merchant groups, controlled commerce. Cloth dominated the medieval economy as completely as steel does now. From France to Italy, city weavers produced cloth for local and foreign markets. This revival of commerce was stimulated by the flow of coinage and precious metals into Western Europe. Previously trade had served only a wealthy elite.

What happened was a general loosening of economic conditions. The peasantry was deeply affected by urban markets and by a growing awareness of broader horizons. Peasants now bought iron and cloth in neighboring towns. They sold grain and livestock to urbanites and became sophisticated in exchange. This flowering of culture and civilization in medieval Europe, despite the destruction that soon followed, formed the background of the Industrial Revolution of the eighteenth and nineteenth centuries. In a real sense, it was the womb in which the Technological World was conceived.

The Industrial Revolution

While the medieval period was marked by slow but steady changes in Western Europe, the momentum of these changes gave rise to one of the most exciting and dynamic eras in human history—the Industrial Revolution—the second phase of the Scientific Transformation.

After centuries of looking backward toward the wisdom of Greece and Rome for inspiration, Europeans once more became adventurous—intellectually and geographically. By the mid-1400s, European expeditions had charted the shores of West Africa and brought gold and slaves back to Europe. Other explorers quickly followed, and a flood of new wealth was injected into the European economy. These voyages cul-

minated in the circumnavigation of the globe by the Magellan expedition (1519–1522). The Age of Exploration unveiled a new and larger world to the Europeans, ushering in a period when, for the first time in history, every part of the planet was accessible.

Simultaneously, another new world—scientific and technological—was being explored by European mathematicians and physicists, like Copernicus, Kepler, Galileo, and Descartes. From their work, a world view emerged that old concepts of space, time, motion, and matter could not explain. This new world was discovered by careful observation and experimentation, what we now call the scientific method. The earth moved, and it moved regularly. It formed a minor part of a broader universe and was not even located at the center. Mechanical clocks controlled time, telescopes and compasses comprehended space. A thirst for new knowledge and a torrent of discovery engulfed Europe. By 1750, this thirst

began to transform every aspect of land and life.

In the Industrial Revolution that followed, four processes are of particular geographic importance: (1) a rapid growth in population generated by continued high birth rates and a decline in **death rates;** (2) a heightened pace of technological change, which harnessed inanimate energy and fostered rises in production to support the larger population; (3) a spatial reordering of society brought about by new patterns of resource utilization, communication, and growing urbanization; and (4) the emergence of the industrial town as a new human environment.

Population Increase

England and Wales embarked on the Industrial Revolution with a population of only 6.5 million people. Eighty years later, in 1800, the total population of England and Wales had soared to 14 million. This spectacular doubling of population in less than a century, virtually unknown in prein-

The Great Paris Sewer (shown above) was one of a number of improvements in urban sanitation, medicine, and health care that made it possible for more people to live longer.

dustrial societies, was caused by the interplay of two forces—traditionally high birth rates and declining death rates.

In fact, birth rates actually rose slightly in Britain. This was principally caused by people marrying earlier and having more children. Young men, long tied to craft apprenticeships, married earlier when they took jobs in factories, and this led to higher birth rates and larger families. Childbearing was also encouraged by the demand for child labor in these new factories. Children were preferred in the cotton mills because they were more responsive to regimentation, had quicker hands, and could be paid less. In the mines, women and children were employed to drag coal from small narrow tunnels to the main passages. Because the average worker earned only 8 shillings a week and needed 14 for basic necessities, the stimulus to have children who could earn money was substantial. After 1795, government subsidy of family incomes based on the number of children made them worth more than ever.

While birth rates increased slowly, death rates dropped rapidly because more children were surviving. In large part, this was due to improvements in medical techniques and the availability of hospitals in urban areas. In the eighteenth century, some 100 hospitals and dispensaries were built in London, and in one of them, **infant mortality** declined sixfold between 1750 and 1800. The decline in infant mortality was part of a broader trend that lowered the death rate in England by half during this same period.

A variety of factors was involved. Broad-scale famines were eliminated by increased agricultural productivity at home, greater food imports from abroad, and the availability of meat year round. Improvements in medicine, particularly vaccination against smallpox (1796), played a role. Availability of cheap cotton cloth for underclothes and of cheap soap that

The hand-powered spinning jenny invented by James Hargreaves in the 1760s spun cotton into thread. It accomplished eight times the work of one person, thereby contributing to the growth of England's textile industry. It was one of a number of technological inventions that powered the Industrial Revolution.

killed typhus-carrying lice were also important factors. Later, the paving and draining of streets, slate roofs instead of straw, piped water supplies, and even government regulation of gin tended to lower the death rate.

As a result of these forces, the population of England was increasing steadily at a rate of about 2 percent each year by the beginning of the nineteenth century. More people were surviving because of significantly better living conditions. The population was getting younger. If industrial employment had not been available for these young men and women in the cities of England at this time, Thomas Malthus's 1798 prediction of a disastrous famine would have become a reality. Industrial employment was available because of the rapid pace of technological change in eighteenth-century England.

Technological Change

The English were fascinated with the application of science to technological problems in the late seventeenth and eighteenth centuries. This fas-

cination became business as social and economic forces encouraged the growth of industrial manufacturing.

Many factors were involved. Capital acquired from two centuries of commerce, slave trading, and piracy had injected new vigor into the English economy. Merchants, who had once retired as country squires, now invested money in new ventures at low rates of interest. Simultaneously, the geographic shift of European economic activity from the Mediterranean to the North Atlantic opened up new opportunities for British merchants. Most important, a broad stream of British scientific thought, based on the genius of Francis Bacon (1561–1626), Robert Boyle (1627–1691), and Sir Isaac Newton (1642–1727) had spawned a generation keenly concerned with invention and technological application (Fig. 1.10).

England had money and a sustained interest in science. Soon the critical inventions of Sir Richard Arkwright (the spinning frame), James Watt (the steam engine), and Henry

TECHNOLOGICAL CHANGE AND ECONOMIC GROWTH

The relative invention rate, based on patent statistics, shows the key role technological change played in the Industrial Revolution (Fig. 1.10). Major inventions below contributed substantially to economic growth in Europe and the United States. This table shows major British, European, and American inventions of the eighteenth and nineteenth centuries.

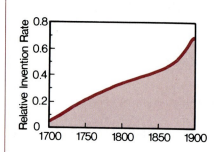

Figure 1.10 Technological change and economic growth.

Graph adapted from: S. Lilley, *Men, Machines and History.* London: Cobbett Press, 1948, p. 193.

Table adapted from: Marvin W. Mikesell, *Patterns and Imprints of Mankind.* Chicago: Rand McNally, 1969, p. xl.

Year	Invention	Country
1764	Spinning jenny	England
1765	Steam engine	England
1769	Self-propelled steam vehicle	France
1783	Puddling iron furnace	England
1785	Power loom	England
1786	Threshing machine	Scotland
1793	Cotton gin	United States
1802	Steamboat	United States
1811	Cylinder printing press	Germany
1824	Portland cement	England
1825	Steam locomotive	England
1831	Electric generator	England
1834	Grain reaper	United States
1839	Photography (daguerreotype)	France
1839	Vulcanization of rubber	United States
1844	Telegraph	United States
1845	Rotary printing press	United States
1850	Corn picker	United States
1851	Refrigerating machine	United States
1855	Bessemer process of steelmaking	England
1859	Gas engine	France
1859	Oil-well drilling	United States
1861	Passenger elevator	United States
1866	Open-hearth steel furnace	United States
1867	Reinforced concrete	France
1869	Railway air brake	United States
1876	Four-cycle gas engine	Germany
1876	Telephone	United States
1879	Incandescent light	United States
1882	Steam turbine	France
1884	Artificial silk (rayon)	France
1884	Linotype	United States
1884	Photographic roll film	United States
1888	Pneumatic tire	Ireland
1892	Diesel engine	Germany
1892	Electric motor (alternating current)	United States
1892	Gasoline automobile	United States
1893	Motion pictures	United States
1895	Wireless telegraphy	Italy
1900	Caterpillar tractor	United States

Cort (iron processing) along with a host of lesser innovations harnessed new forms of energy and generated a surge in industrial production.

The effect of these technological changes struck first in the cotton textile industry. One of the major problems in textiles was the inability of thread spinners to keep pace with the looms of the more technically advanced weavers. In the 1760s, James Hargreaves developed a hand-pow-

ered machine, the spinning jenny, that could spin as many as eight threads simultaneously. These machines were cheap, easy to construct, and small enough to fit in a spinner's cottage. In thirty years, more than 2000 spinning jennies were distributed across the English landscape.

Unfortunately, the thread from the spinning jenny was too soft to be used for the warp cords of the cloth, so that a good deal of thread still had to

be spun by hand. In 1768, however, Richard Arkwright developed the water-powered spinning frame, which produced a strong, coarse cotton thread suitable for either warp or woof. This device could not be turned by hand and was too large to fit in a cottage. Thus the factory was born. To have waterpower, mills using spinning frames were located on streams. After 1790, when James Watt's steam engine came into use, however, spinning factories could be located anywhere coal supplies were available. By the turn of the century, Manchester, destined to become one of the world's first industrial cities, had fifty-two textile mills. The factory town had been born.

Production soared. Cotton imports went from 5 million to 60 million pounds in twenty years. England became the world's leading producer of cotton cloth, even though no cotton grew in England and the English had always worn wool. Cotton textiles made up a phenomenal 40 percent of Britain's exports by 1806. A **colonial** frontier to control cotton production was established overseas—in the American South, in the West Indies, and later in Egypt and India.

The impact of technological change on the critical coal and iron mining industries was much slower and less dramatic. The extraction of both coal and iron ore remained in the hands of small gangs of miners well into the eighteenth century. The scale of iron making was so small that in 1750 a typical swordmaker probably used only 3 to 5 tons of iron a year. Even in the largest mines, the most advanced technical discovery in the first

half of the eighteenth century was the introduction of ponies for hauling. This practice freed men to do the mining and led to the hiring of women and children to control the horses.

Step by step, however, discoveries in metallurgy, machine tooling, and engineering led to the gradual replacement of wood by metal and to substantial increases in iron production. Abraham Darby discovered a method of smelting iron with refined coal, **coke,** instead of with charcoal made from wood. By 1750, iron smelters moved from the forests to the coalfields. Later Henry Cort discovered a new technique for refining crude pig iron into a purer form, and iron forges joined the smelters in the coalfields.

Production rose accordingly. Coal production had quadrupled between 1750 and 1800 to reach 11 million tons. The yearly production of iron ore, half of which had to be imported in 1750, grew to 227,000 tons by 1800. The significance of these early increases was that the growing availability of cheap iron made it possible to mechanize other industries.

The rapid pace of technological change was based on new knowl-

edge, new forms of power, and new machinery. These changes led to a reorganization of society and economy in England. People migrated to urban factories, and farmers began to desert the English landscape. Industries moved to take advantage of energy and mineral resources. New patterns of commerce favored the expansion of some cities and the decline of others. The growth of manufacturing concentrations created the first industrial landscapes. England was the first nation to exhibit these new patterns of living. Other nations of the Technological World, particularly those of northern Europe, soon followed.

Changing Spatial Patterns
The industrialization of England prompted a spatial restructuring of society and economy. Four spatial processes were set in motion: (1) the **urbanization** of the English population, (2) new patterns of resource utilization and industrial location, (3) an expansion of transportation networks, and (4) the emergence of **urban hierarchies** and regional manufacturing specializations.

As England industrialized, it also urbanized. Villagers gradually aban-

Coal powered the factories, heated the homes, and dominated the landscape and atmosphere of England's new industrial cities. This is a view of the city of Leeds from nearby Richmond Hill.

doned the countryside and migrated to factories in new industrial towns. In 1700, less than a quarter of England's population lived in cities. Over 60 percent lived in southern England, which was better suited for farming than elsewhere.

But starting in 1750, the geographic center of gravity began to shift toward manufacturing centers located on coalfields in the north. The attraction, of course, was jobs in the textile mills of Manchester and Liverpool and in the coalfields of the Pennine Mountains. Between 1800 and 1900, the number of people living in cities increased from 27 to 64 percent, and nearly half of England's population lived in the industrial north. This tide from the countryside converted England from a country of farmers into a nation of city dwellers.

To accommodate this urban flow, new cities were built. Between 1750 and 1850, the number of cities in England tripled, from 159 to 460. Most of these were small towns that expanded because of migration from the countryside, the rising birth rate, and the growth of small-scale manufacturing. Their median size was quite small, between 3000 and 5000 residents. Only 24 of the 460 cities were larger than 50,000, and only 4—London, Liverpool, Manchester, and Birmingham—could count more than 200,000 people. As time passed, seaports and cities favored by location and energy resources came to dominate.

The most important new pattern of resource utilization was the substitution of coal for other energy sources. The technological innovations of Darby and Cort enabled iron producers to substitute coke for charcoal. Because coke crumbled when being transported and then was useless for purifying iron, iron furnaces and forges were forced to move to the coalfields.

This concentration of iron processing led to the emergence of large, integrated industries that controlled the industrial refinement of iron from the mine to the finished product. Iron production converged on four major coalfields in Britain: the Midlands, the Northeast, Wales, and Scotland. Here the landscape was laid waste with pits and slag heaps, so thick in the "black country" around Birmingham that travelers were warned that roads might be undermined by mine shafts.

In the cotton textile industry, cheap waterpower was originally the primary location factor. But with the shift from water to coal-fired steam power, locational patterns changed. Near Manchester, the commercial heart of Lancashire, the original location of cotton mills was governed by the distribution of waterfalls outside the city. But when the steam engine replaced the waterwheel, location on coalfields became not only desirable, but also virtually mandatory to reduce transportation costs. The textile industry shifted to the city of Manchester as a result of this new locational principle.

Availability of resources, then, was critical to the growth of industrial complexes in England. Because availability was defined in terms of transport costs, town leaders throughout England attempted to enhance the relative location of their cities by building roads and canals. These canals were fundamental links in the growth of regional transportation networks. The first long-distance canal, linking the cotton industry of Manchester with the growing port of Liverpool in 1767, cut the cost of coal in Manchester by half. Merchants, industrialists, and entrepreneurs in other cities soon set up transportation trusts to build canal and highway networks. By 1775, every English city with a population of more than 20,000 was located on or near a navigable waterway. In 1805, the Grand Junction Canal linked the metropolis of London to the industrial north.

In the middle of the nineteenth century, this transportation network was reinforced by the construction of a network of railroads. Stephenson's steam locomotive, the Rocket, established the potential of rail transport on the Manchester-Liverpool line in 1829. The journey between these cities was cut from a day and a half by barge to two hours by rail. The cost of transport was halved, and in the first three months of operation 130,000 passengers made the intercity trip. In only twenty years, every major city in England was served by rail. These railroads strengthened the emerging patterns of urban interdependence and industrial expansion. They contributed to regional specializations and the growth of urban hierarchies.

By the middle of the nineteenth century, the full impact of the Industrial Revolution on patterns of human settlement had been felt. Urbanization had taken hold as in no earlier society. Some 42 percent of England's population lived in an urban arc extending from London to Lancashire. Three urban hierarchies had grown up alongside the coalfields in the Midlands, northeastern England, and the Scottish Lowlands, to complement London. Reductions in transportation costs favored large already established industrial complexes. This reinforced the early dominance of cotton milling in Lancashire, woolen textiles in Yorkshire, and iron and steel manufacturing in the Midlands. Villagers migrating from the countryside in search of work and a more comfortable life were more attracted to large urban centers than to smaller cities. These centers, in turn, extended their tentacles ever deeper into regional hinterlands to ensure regular and dependable food supplies for laborers in their mills. In the hinterlands, towns developed specialized functions related to local resources and traditions. The emergence of these urban hierarchies of the early Industrial Revolution foreshadowed the later growth of **meg-**

LONDON: THE EMERGENCE OF A METROPOLIS

The explosive growth of London during the Industrial Revolution is dramatically portrayed in Figure 1.11. In 1840, the entire city was contained within a 4-mile radius. Forty years later, the built-up area expanded to include places 6 miles from the city center. By World War I, London extended over 10 miles out from the city center.

Adapted from: S. E. Rasmussen, *London: The Unique City*. Cambridge: MIT Press, 1967, pp. 134–139.

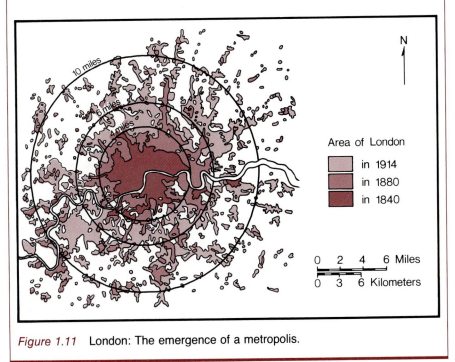

Area of London

	in 1914
	in 1880
	in 1840

0 2 4 6 Miles
0 3 6 Kilometers

Figure 1.11   London: The emergence of a metropolis.

---

alopolises, first in England and later in other nations of the Technological World (Fig. 1.11).

Manchester—The First Industrial City

Manchester was the first industrial city to spring from the economic and social revolution that swept England in the eighteenth and nineteenth centuries. In medieval times, Manchester was a small town, boasting a weekly market and an annual fair. By the late 1700s, Manchester was a thriving commercial town. In the nineteenth century it became an important industrial center and England's second largest city.

With the development of the steam engine, Manchester became the cotton manufacturing center of the country. Its population quadrupled in the first quarter of the nineteenth century and doubled every twenty years thereafter. Waves of migrants from rural England, Wales, and Ireland labored in the weaving sheds, cotton mills, and foundries of the city.

Manchester, in short, experienced explosive urban growth. In the process, **slums** spread over large areas, and slum landlords fed off the poor. The wealthy fled to the first modern suburbs. In the central city, pollution, sanitation, and housing became major problems. Middle-class apathy diluted efforts toward reform. What is now called the "urban crisis"—with poverty-stricken residents permanently in the central city and rich residents in distant suburbs—began in the city of Manchester. Manchester's nineteenth-century urban **ecology** carries a discouraging ring of familiarity.

Rural migrants came to the factories of Manchester in search of work and moved into the densely crowded slums of the central city. By 1820, the density of population in central Manchester was 70 people per acre (44,800 per square mile) as compared with less than 10 per acre in the suburbs. The greatest crowding was next to the textile mills, located on rivers. In these districts, land speculators constructed dense masses of cottages, which they rented at exorbitant rates. Streets were unpaved and unlit. Whole families lived in single rooms, and sanitation was poor. Major avenues in Manchester were scavenged to remove waste, but the poorer districts were cleaned only once a month. The urban poor relied on rain, polluted wells, and rivers. It was they who died in wave after wave of typhoid and cholera epidemics.

The worst of these slums was the Irish ghetto, Little Ireland. Here, Catholic immigrants lived adjacent to marshlands so low that chimneys of three-story buildings barely reached road level. Little Ireland adjoined densely concentrated mills and was by any reckoning, the most unhealthy part of the city. In this new industrial world, the ghetto Irish lived a marginal existence.

Air pollution had already become a major problem in Manchester. As early as the 1600s, the cities of industrial England were darkened by the smoke of innumerable hearth fires. Occasionally, the courts of Manchester fined factory owners for causing undue smoke, but few such cases were tried in Manchester and the fines were small. Dense clouds of smoke covered the industrial sec-

Railroads conquered distance and altered patterns of human settlement in England and later in continental Europe. This is an illustration of a new express locomotive introduced on the London and Northwestern Railroad in 1852.

tions of the city and the "nuisance committee" established to limit industrial smoke did little.

Conditions in the factories of Manchester were abysmal. Mill workers labored twelve to sixteen hours a day, six days a week, with breaks of a half hour for breakfast and an hour for lunch. Many of the workers were women and children who labored for a pittance to secure family survival. Some of the poor were taken off the street, sent to poorhouses, and forced to work in factories "to teach them industry." Even the simplest safety measures were not taken, which produced legions of nine-fingered people. Objections to bad working conditions took the form of petitions, strikes, riots in the streets, and the destruction of machines. From the viewpoint of the factory owners, however, increases in wages contributed to laziness, so that demonstrations were brutally put down. Industrial stability took precedence over social justice.

In spite of these grim conditions, the standard of living of the factory worker improved throughout the course of the Industrial Revolution. Per capita income and consumption of material goods rose steadily. Bad as the industrial slums were, they were better than poverty in the countryside. The poor walked off the land and into factories as fast as possible, and they continue to do so. In Manchester, a new way of life and a new human environment arose as the city became the locus of technological society and the factory the social habitat.

The Diffusion of the Scientific Transformation

The diffusion of the Scientific Transformation from England and the European culture hearth did not begin in earnest until the nineteenth century. Between 1500 and 1800, the growth of Europe was essentially internal. New towns and villages were founded, woodlands were cleared, and human settlements and communications intensified. There were few Europeans abroad. Small colonies of Europeans had settled the coasts of North America, South America, and South Africa. Elsewhere, a handful of Europeans sought fortunes: Spanish conquistadors in Mexico and Peru, Dutch merchants in the East Indies,

English and French traders in West and East Africa, and the British East India Company in South Asia.

Except in Spanish America, European colonization was confined to the coasts of the new continents, peripheral outposts on the flanks of sophisticated urban civilizations. Trading stations clung tenaciously to the oceanic rim of Asia and Africa. Fortunes were made by acquiring and transporting luxury goods to the urban markets of Europe. Gold and silver were found in Peru and Mexico; silk, spices, and tea in South and East Asia; sugar in the Caribbean and Brazil; and gold, ivory, slaves, and spices in West and East Africa. For the most part, these traders survived by the grace of traditional native monarchs. They were confined by the Manchu emperors of China to the port city of Canton; to Bombay, Madras, and Calcutta by the Moguls of India; and to the trading stations of West and East Africa by African kings who were jealous of their control of the trading routes into the interior. But in the nineteenth and twentieth centuries, this modest coastal presence expanded. A wave of some 52 million European migrants penetrated the continents, colonizing and settling the **midlatitude** environments in North America, southern South America, South Africa, and Australia and establishing **plantations** in the **tropical** regions of Latin America, Africa, and Asia.

Settler Colonization

European expansion by settler-colonizers was for the most part confined to **temperate** latitudes. Here, the agricultural experiences and preferences of European immigrants were more or less directly transferred to expanding frontiers in the New World, Africa, and Australia.

In North America, settlement along the eastern seaboard was initiated by a variety of northern Europeans seeking religious freedom and economic opportunity. In Canada, French and English fur traders and fisherfolk established themselves on the coast and penetrated the St. Lawrence Valley. In New England and the Middle Colonies, dissident religious groups sought self-expression. In the South, gentlemen-adventurers searched for gold and spices but eventually settled for less.

By 1800, two centuries after the founding of Jamestown, the European population of the United States was less than 5 million. Gradually, however, a tide of European immigrants from the industrial centers and densely settled countryside of nineteenth-century Europe sought fortunes and land in the New World. Between 1840 and 1930, some 34 million immigrants, 80 percent of them from Europe, arrived in the United States. Agricultural settlement expanded into the interior, dislodging and destroying native peoples. Europeans effectively occupied the continent.

In Australia, South Africa, and South America, European settler colonization took somewhat different forms. In Australia and New Zealand, settlement was not begun until the late eighteenth and early nineteenth centuries, and the colonial population of these regions grew slowly. In South Africa, dense native African populations prevented the establishment of a predominately European population. Conflict between Dutch and British immigrants and native Africans became dominant issues. In Argentina and Uruguay, the only South American countries with European majorities, Spanish, German, and Italian migrations established a significant European presence.

In time, each of these areas, populated by an emigrating European population of more than 50 million, aspired to independence although ties of language and culture remained strong. The technological experience and skills immigrants brought to these regions gave the United States, Canada, Australia, New Zealand, the white minority of South Africa, and to a lesser extent leaders in Argentina and Uruguay direct access to the Scientific Transformation. The diffusion of the Scientific Transformation was culture bound. European populations in midlatitude colonies provided the capital, technology, social institutions, and labor needed to make their nations members of the inner sphere of the Technological World.

Mercantile Colonialism

In the tropical regions of Latin America, Africa, and South and East Asia, the impact of the Scientific Transformation was quite different. Unattractive to European agricultural settlers, these tropical areas produced raw materials highly valued in European markets. Collection of agricultural products and minerals became the dominant economy.

European overseers established plantations and mines. Local or imported laborers produced goods for export to Europe. In the Caribbean, tropical islands were planted to sugar. Other parts of Latin America became known for the cultivation of coffee and rubber. In West Africa, peanuts, cacao, rubber, and spices came to dominate the export-oriented colonial economy, as did diamonds, gold and copper in southern Africa. In India, tea and opium plantations were founded; in Southeast Asia, it was rubber plantations. The lure of territorial expansion and furs led the Russians eastward to Central Asia, Siberia, and Alaska. Later, Middle Eastern oil became the object of serious European commercial effort.

Everywhere Europeans formed a tiny minority that provided capital and management skills. Native peoples were used as cheap labor to increase profits. When labor demands in the New World outstripped local native populations, 10 million slaves from Africa were transported to Brazil, the Caribbean, and the American South. A similar migration of 20 million contract laborers from India and China was drawn to tropical plantations throughout the world. By the late nineteenth century, Europeans controlled every significant non-Western society except China and Japan.

In all these regions, access to technology, capital, and science was retained by the European minority, who lived within but apart from native cultures. The effect was to create economies subordinate to Europe and other technological societies. Entire nations became dependent on the production of a single crop. After World War II, most of these colonial societies achieved political independence, but they did so in a world economically designed by Europeans. Today they share a legacy of **colonialism**, expanding populations, and dependence on exports to technological societies. With rare exceptions, they became members of today's Developing World.

Beyond the Technological World and the Developing World, the Scientific Transformation failed to penetrate vast stretches of the globe. In the heart of the tropics, the deserts of North Africa and the Middle East, the high mountains of South America and Asia, and the **polar latitudes** of North America and Eurasia, technological penetration remains minimal. Although individual mines, radar bases, oases, and plantations provide evidence of the tenacity of human purpose, these regions remain stubborn reminders of the environmental limits of modern humanity.

2

THE GEOGRAPHY OF DEVELOPMENT

*T*he scientific transformation spread unevenly across the globe. It created two different human domains—the rich and the poor, the haves and the have-nots, the North and the South, the lesser developed and the developed, or as they are called here, the Developing World and the Technological World (Fig. 2.1).

The differences between these two domains permeate every aspect of life on our planet. Standards of living, levels of education and health, length and quality of life, rates of agricultural and industrial production, and command of political power are high in those countries that have fully integrated technology, control of energy, and scientific knowledge into their ways of living. But the majority of the world's people live in countries that are struggling to achieve modernization, development, and industrialization.

In the Developing World, societies are burdened by limited technologies, rapidly growing populations, poorly developed resource bases, inadequate capital, and **neocolonial** economies. With few exceptions, their leaders desire to modernize. Thus far, only Japan has fully succeeded. Except for the oil-rich states of the Middle East and North Africa and some small countries on the rim of East Asia, few societies appear to have the human and physical resources needed to accom-

plish the task. In the Technological World, by contrast, countries—most of which were originally populated by Europeans—continue to expand their consumption of energy and resources, to increase their standards of living, and to maintain a balance of power in world affairs. In North America, Western Europe, Australia, New Zealand, the Soviet Union, parts of Eastern Europe, and Japan, urban industrial societies have achieved unprecedented levels of wealth.

Although the data used to measure global differences between countries in the Technological World and Developing World are incomplete and in many cases unreliable, and although the methods of measuring levels of development are not fully understood, the overall impact of the scientific transformation on the world is abundantly clear. One quarter of humanity is relatively well fed, healthy, and long-lived. Three quarters are not, and the most deprived 1 billion people on earth live in near total degradation and deprivation. The same proportions hold for literacy rates, energy consumption, income levels, and various other measures of the quality of human existence. These differences occur not as isolated variables, but as a set of interlocking conditions that provide a framework for discussion.

THE GEOGRAPHY OF WEALTH AND POVERTY

Today poor people form a majority of the world's population. This has always been the case. The rich get richer—the poor have children. In the twentieth century, however, a number of countries are truly wealthy for the first time in history: most of their people—not just an elite—live well. The global disparity between rich and poor is rapidly becoming the central issue of our time.

The rich countries—those of the Technological World—are interested in maintaining political stability, the present world economic sys-

tem, technological superiority, and high standards of living. For them, international conferences, foreign aid, trade, and political or military intervention in minor global disturbances are primarily methods of maintaining the status quo. In each country, policies are forged to sustain supplies of food, fuel, and income to provide citizens with levels of physical well-being that were attained only by royalty in the past.

In the poorer countries—those of the Developing World—leaders strive to carve out a new place in the world economic system and to acquire the technology and skills needed to raise standards of living. Changing, not maintaining, the status quo is their

central interest. In such countries, progress is measured in increases in calorie consumption, lower infant mortality rates, miles of roadway constructed, and gains in **gross national product (GNP)**. Local policies of birth control, **land reform,** agrarian change, and education engage virtually everyone on a personal and private level. The scientific transformation has left only the most remote and isolated communities unaffected.

In every country in the world, policies and programs are designed to fit local culture and environment, national values and ideology. The Chinese, the Indians, the states of Africa, the Middle East, and Latin

THE TECHNOLOGICAL WORLD AND THE DEVELOPING WORLD

The 23 countries of the Technological World have less than one quarter of the world's population, midlatitude locations and environments, and—with the exception of Japan—are culturally related to Western Europe. The Developing World includes 143 countries with three quarters of the world's population. They are primarily located in the tropics and are separated by language and tradition from Western Europe.

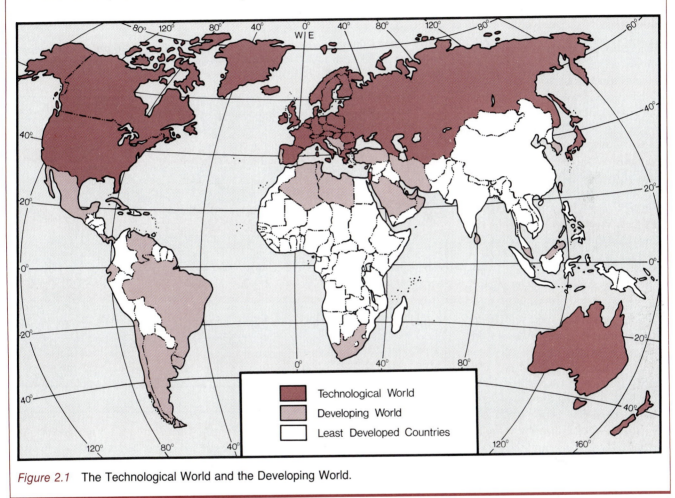

Figure 2.1 The Technological World and the Developing World.

America—all face development and modernization within the context of their own histories, economies, and societies. Similarly, Western Europe, Japan, the USSR, and the United States—all integrate science and technology differently within their own national systems. At a more general level, however, the countries of the Developing World possess one set of characteristics; those of the Technological World yet another.

The gap between these two worlds is awesome. Pressures to distribute global wealth in a more equitable way have grown, especially with the independence of former colonial societies in the 1950s and 1960s. The issues are poverty, hunger, transfer of technology, and redistribution of wealth. Currently, the United States consumes 60 percent of the world's resources and is by far the richest country on earth. Overall, the Tech-

nological World controls 90 percent of the world's industrial capacity. By contrast, Africa, Asia, and Latin America contain three quarters of the world's people but produce only 20 percent of its wealth. On these continents, raw materials represent 85 percent of all exports. Given these figures, Robert McNamara, former president of the **World Bank,** states that despite a quarter century of change and progress in the Developing World, some 800 million individuals continue to be trapped in absolute poverty, "a condition of life so characterized by malnutrition, illiteracy, disease, squalid surroundings, high infant mortality and low life expectancy as to be beneath any reasonable definition of human decency."

Measures of Development

During the last thirty years, a number of methods have been used by geographers to portray the global distribution of wealth and poverty. The geographer William Warntz attempted to map "the socio-economic terrain" of world population and world income in 1960. The two maps shown here illustrate a clear concentration of (1) people in the Developing World (Fig. 2.2) and (2) wealth in the Technological World (Fig. 2.3). They also show that the highest densities and the greatest mass of people lived in South and East Asia, whereas wealth was concentrated in the Eastern United States and Western Europe. Fifteen years later, in the mid-1970s, two population geographers—using fourteen demographic, economic, and social variables for eighty-nine countries—attempted to plot the global distribution of wealth and poverty. The conclusions of that study confirmed the dichotomy between the Technological World and the Developing World suggested in the earlier study by Warntz. Finally, the world map of GNP in the 1980s demonstrates that the distribution of wealth and poverty has not changed significantly in the last quarter century (Fig. 2.4). This persistent disparity between rich and poor is the salient geographical fact of our time, and the basis for the organization of this book.

Rich countries are endowed with extensive trade relations, well-developed internal communications systems, dense transportation networks, high rates of energy production and consumption, and high GNP. Their people are well supplied with schools, universities and medical fa-

WORLD POPULATION POTENTIAL AND WORLD INCOME POTENTIAL IN 1960

The two maps shown here illustrate the global distribution of population and wealth in 1960. Figure 2.2 is of world population potential (expressed in terms of thousands of people per square mile) and depicts the huge concentration of people in South and East Asia, nearly half of the world total. Figure 2.3 is of world income potential (expressed in millions of dollars per square mile) and illustrates that when population is weighted by income, the countries of North America and Europe are the wealthiest in the world. The gap between the global distribution of people and the global distribution of income is apparent when these two maps are compared.

Adapted from: W. Warntz, *Macrogeography and Income Fronts.* Philadelphia: Regional Science Research Institute, 1965, figs. 19, 24; pp. 92, 111.

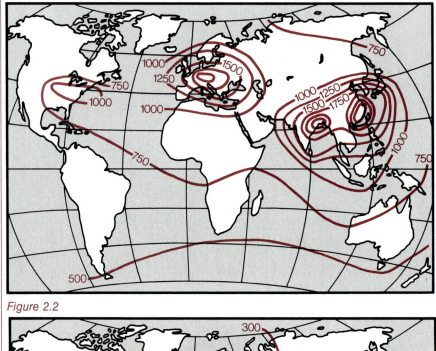

Figure 2.2

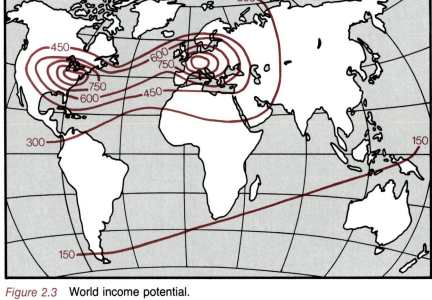

Figure 2.3 World income potential.

PER CAPITA GNP, 1988

The GNP is the total value of all goods and services produced by an economy during a one-year period. Although the reliability of these figures varies from country to country, the global distribution of wealth and poverty appears to have changed little in the last quarter century, except where high levels of income have been generated in a few oil-based countries, like Libya and Saudi Arabia. Countries in the Technological World have per capita GNP of $5000 or more; states in the Developing World have considerably less.

Source: World Population Data Sheet, 1988.

Figure 2.4 World per capita GNP.

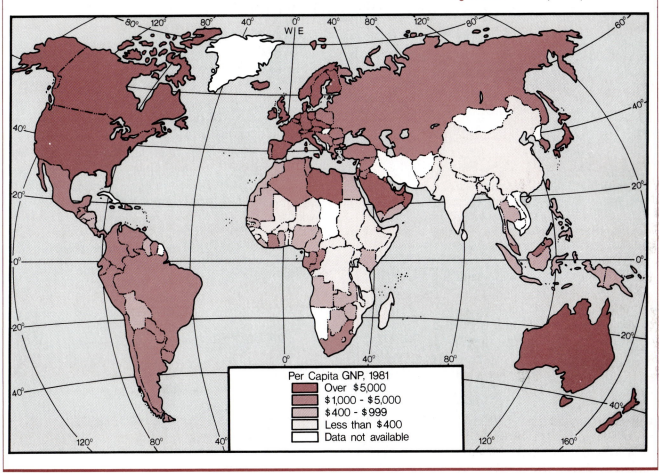

Per Capita GNP, 1981
- Over $5,000
- $1,000 - $5,000
- $400 - $999
- Less than $400
- Data not available

cilities, have low rates of population growth, and are highly urbanized. The higher living standards in the countries of the Technological World, virtually all of which have midlatitude locations and environments of relative abundance, are the result of diversified commercial economies.

The poorer countries of the Developing World, by contrast, often have marginal environments, subsistence economies, high rates of population growth, and low standards of living. Transport and trade networks are less developed; levels of energy production and consumption are relatively low. In three crucial areas—population, economy, and spatial organization—these "Two Worlds" show great global differences.

POPULATION AND DEVELOPMENT

The most important effect of the scientific transformation on the world today has been the postponement of death—the extension of life. Tens of thousands of years were required before the human population reached 1 billion around 1800; only 125 years were required to attain 2 billion, 33 years to reach 3 billion in the late 1950s, and 17 years to reach 4 billion in 1965. Five billion was reached in 1987. In 1990, world population will be an estimated 5.25 billion, and will grow by 84 million in that single year. Six billion will be attained by the year 2000. Techniques of environmental and medical technology combined with more productive economic systems enable more people to survive.

The countries of the Technological World want to maintain the status quo—politically, economically, and socially—throughout the world. Military intervention in minor regional conflicts is one means of maintaining control over world affairs. Here, a member of the UN "Peace-keeping" force in Lebanon scans the horizon.

Some one billion people in the Developing World live in conditions "beneath any reasonable definition of human decency." This family in Ethiopia in northeast Africa suffers from the effects of two decades of war, drought, and neglect.

As births outstrip deaths, population grows. The quality of life people lead is now a fundamental question.

The Demographic Transition

A four-stage **model** of population called the **demographic transition** that is based on the historic experience of Western Europe has accompanied industrialization, and consequent modernization, in many parts of the world (Figs. 2.5, 2.6).

In the first, or **high stationary,** stage, which lasted in Western Europe until about 1750, high birth rates were canceled out by high death rates. Population growth was relatively limited. Fluctuations in total population were largely a function of minor changes in the death rate. Periodic famines and wars increased the number of deaths; times of peace and plenty caused modest gains in total population. This pattern of deaths balancing births governed world population growth prior to the scientific transformation. A number of extremely poor, isolated countries, like North Yemen, Ethiopia, and Nepal have recently departed the high-stationary phase of the demographic transition. Until the 1940s, many of today's developing countries were still in this first phase of the demographic transition, and their populations had remained relatively stable for very long periods of time.

In the second stage of the demographic transition, the early expanding phase, which extended from 1750 to 1875 in Western Europe, birth rates remained high but death rates fell. Improvements in health care, medical knowledge, sanitation, and standards of living began to take hold. Life expectancy increased and total population quadrupled in Europe. In the third or late expanding stage, between 1875 and 1925 in Europe, death rates remained low and birth rates in the now urbanized, industrialized societies of Western Europe began to fall. The rate of **natural increase**

THE DEMOGRAPHIC TRANSITION

These two graphs portray the four-stage demographic transition. The change from low-survivor to high-survivor societies is depicted in idealized form in Figure 2.5, and is shown as it actually occurred in England and Wales in Figure 2.6. The first stage of the idealized model suggests limited control over the environment and high vulnerability to natural calamities. It is characteristic of premodern societies in general and of the poorest societies of the Developing World until recent times. Total population rises most dramatically in the second, or early-expanding stage, but continues to grow during the third stage, called the late expanding, because of the momentum of a large, young population base. Growth of population is much like money in the bank, gaining interest on the principal.

The effects of industrialization and ur-

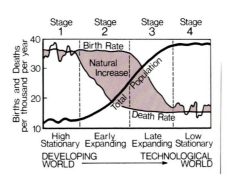

Figure 2.5 The demographic transition.

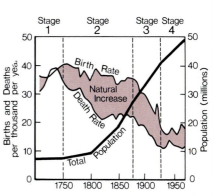

Figure 2.6 The demographic transition in England and Wales.

banization on population in England and Wales from 1750 to 1950 is shown in Figure 2.6. As the death rates fell in Stage 2, birth rates remained high, resulting in rapid population growth. This represents a population "explosion." In Stage 3, birth rates plummeted and death rates continued to decrease. Finally, relative population stability occurs in Stage 4 when both death rates and birth rates are low. These conditions have obtained in England and Wales since the 1920s and characterize the Technological World's societies today in general.

slowed down but total population continued to grow. Likewise, the populations of most countries in the Developing World now have more births than deaths and are experiencing rapid population growth.

In the final or low stationary stage, both birth and death rates are low in Western Europe. Population growth is limited. Unlike the high stationary phase that preceded the scientific transformation, however, fluctuations in population in the low stationary phase are caused by variations in the birth rate, not, as before, by changes in the death rate.

The Demographic Transition Today

When this four-phase model of population change is applied worldwide, a marked difference between populations in the Technological World and the Developing World is apparent. So, too, is their history of de-

mographic growth and change. Western Europe, North America, the USSR, Australia–New Zealand, and Japan are in the final or low-stationary stage. Rates of population growth are 1 percent a year or less, and these rates continue to decline. In some industrialized countries, such as West Germany and Denmark, **zero population growth** or even negative rates of population growth have been achieved. In parts of remote and underdeveloped countries, like Afghanistan, North Yemen, Indonesia, and Mauritania, the first or high-stationary stage is still detectable. More advanced developing countries, like Cuba, Thailand, Taiwan, the Philippines, and Turkey, are in the late expanding stage.

But substantial portions of Latin America, Africa, and Asia fall into the early expanding stage in which high birth rates and lowering death rates create rapid population growth. In these regions, the rate of natural in-

crease is between 2 and 3 percent a year. Although these percentage differences seem relatively minor, a country whose population is growing at a rate of 1 percent doubles it population every 87 years, at 2 percent every 35 years, and at 3 percent every 25 years.

Because a majority of countries in the Developing World are in the early or late expanding stages of the demographic transition, world population is increasing at a rate of 90 million per year; in the decade between 1970 and 1980, more than 80 percent of the estimated 1 billion people added to the population were born in those countries least able to provide basic services to any increased number of people.

In Western Europe, medical knowledge accumulated slowly over two centuries, allowing time to absorb larger populations. But in the Developing World, the rapid spread of accumulated knowledge can create chaos. In Sri Lanka (Ceylon), for example, the death rate fell 30 percent—from 20 to 14 per 1000 population—in a single year, 1947, when the introduction of DDT wiped out malarial mosquitos. The same thing happened in Mauritius, an island in the Indian Ocean, in the early 1950s. In Madagascar, penicillin cured a venereal disease that previously had sterilized one third of all women; use of this antibiotic caused a dramatic rise in the birth rate. The differences are graphically illustrated in the age distributions of populations in the areas of population growth versus the areas with stable or slow-growing populations (Fig. 2.7).

As a result, changes in population that took a century or more to accomplish in the nineteenth century in Western Europe and the United States occur in less than a decade in some developing states. This kind of change is identified as **death control**—the relatively easy, and often well-meaning, ability of technologically capable authorities to introduce health care into local-level societies and change things overnight. This creates incredible levels of social stress. What they change is the death rate, not the birth rate or levels of technological intervention of the environment—resources, food, shelter, habitat—for the babies that survive. New jobs, more food, and more houses are required for growing populations. The bulk of this growth, however, occurs as a result of lower infant mortality rates. Children under fifteen—who cannot contribute to economic development—now make up half the population in many nations in the Developing World (Fig. 2.7). This places enormous stress on educational, medical, and social services in the very countries that are least able to afford the cost.

THE ECONOMICS OF DEVELOPMENT

The different levels of living in the Technological World and the Developing World are produced by two quite different economic systems.

The scientific transformation enabled Europe to master new sources of energy in the form of coal, petroleum, and natural gas, which increased human productivity and

WORLD POPULATION UNDER 15 YEARS OF AGE

Figure 2.7 shows the percentage of children under the age of 15 and illustrates the high concentration of young people in the countries of Latin America, Africa, and Asia. The larger the proportion of children who are too young to work in any society, the greater the burden on the working population to pay for their needs. Countries with a high percentage of children are undergoing rapid population growth.

Source: World Population Data Sheet, 1988.

High rates of infant mortality—death during the highly vulnerable first year of life—are characteristic of many countries in the Developing World.

spurred a reorganization of society and economy. In England, this knowledge became available at a time when wood was in short supply, large deposits of coal were available, and a group of maritime entrepreneurs had become wealthy through a century of global commerce. This combination of ideas, resources, and capital led to an extraordinary increase in the amount of energy available to the society. Between 1860 and 1960, world production of inanimate energy increased nearly four times as fast as population growth. But production of energy took place in one part of the world, population growth took place in another.

Currently, the states of the Technological World, with approximately

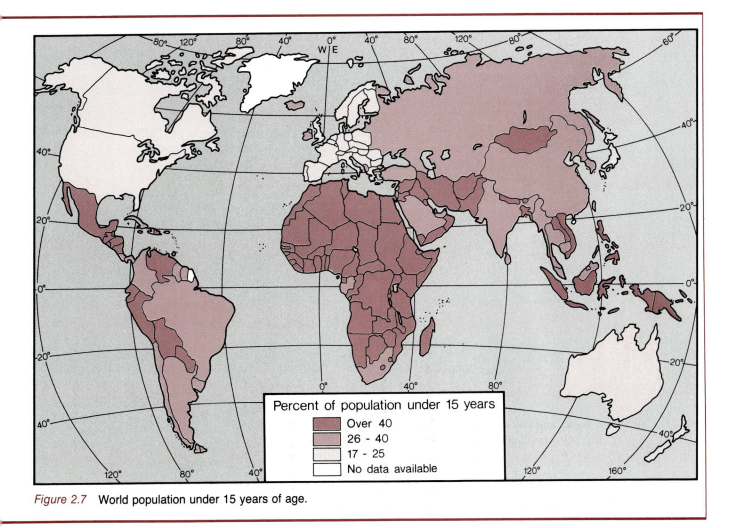

Figure 2.7 World population under 15 years of age.

a quarter of the world's population, consume 85 percent of all inanimate energy. Six countries—the United States, the USSR, China (because of sheer demographic size), Great Britain, West Germany, and Japan—account for two thirds of the world's energy consumption. Any one of these countries consumes more energy than the eighty least developed nations combined.

Agriculture, Industry, and Urbanization

In the Technological World, new energy budgets based on coal, petroleum, and natural gas had important effects on the nature of production and employment.

New materials, such as iron and steel, form the basis of construction. Steam and electricity concentrate energy in both space and time. Newly discovered resources cause shifts in population to the sources of production and lead to the construction of transport networks with higher levels of connectivity and interdependence. Large factories of higher productivity and efficiency replace smaller, low-energy family businesses. Per capita income rises with per capita energy consumption because of the higher productivity of large-scale enterprises. Employment shifts from agriculture to manufacturing and **service occupations.**

Industrialization defines a society as urban. Three of every four Amer-

icans and more than half of all Western Europeans are urbanites (Fig. 2.8). Less than one quarter of the population in most technological societies is required for the production of food because advances in agricultural technology have increased farm productivity. With mass production comes mass consumption and that dramatic increase in quality of life that is found in the wealthier countries of the world.

In the Developing World, the shift to inanimate forms of energy is under way, but people and animals are still the principal labor machines. As a result, productivity is low, per capita income is low, and the economic surplus is limited. People are distributed in villages, and 50 to 70 percent of the population is engaged in food production (Fig. 2.9). Growth in population increases pressure on agricultural land and encourages migration to industrializing urban centers. Yet the money needed to create new factories and jobs for these people is not available. Because many countries experienced modernization under colonial rule, **dual econ-** **omies** with a small modern, European-oriented, extractive sector and a large traditional agricultural sector lead to economic growth without social development. In Africa and Latin America, many countries rely heavily on the export of one or two raw materials to the industrial world. For most states, this means extreme vulnerability to fluctuations in inter-

The skeleton of this new building under construction in the Technological World reflects the accumulated knowledge of scientists, engineers, and skilled workers as well as a high level of control over natural resources. These are characteristics of technologically advanced, industrial societies.

WORLD LEVELS OF URBANIZATION

High levels of urbanization are characteristic in the industrialized countries of the Technological World. Lower levels generally are found in the less industrialized economies of the Developing World.

Source: World Population Data Sheet, 1988.

national markets. Although energy production rises every year, so do population and consumer demands.

The Need for Investment

For most countries in the Developing World, the last thirty years have involved a successful political struggle to gain independence and an unsuccessful economic battle to transform the nature of their societies from an agricultural to an industrial base. Their goal is to achieve higher levels of productivity and wealth by shifting from **animate** to inanimate energy. Their problem is to accumulate the surplus capital needed to modernize agriculture, construct roads and railroads, and

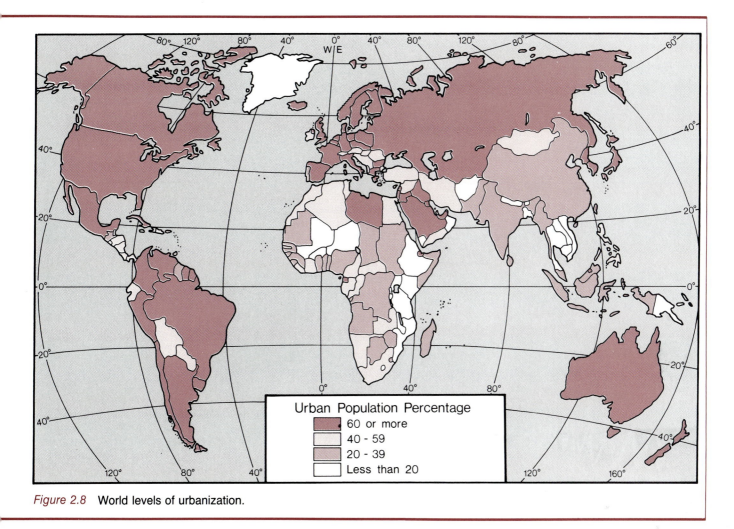

Figure 2.8 World levels of urbanization.

build factories and industry. Generally, high capital costs have frustrated development efforts, leaving many countries of the Developing World trapped in cycles of poverty. Low levels of productivity, income, and savings ensure an economy of stagnation.

Poverty breeds poverty. Most developing countries can afford to invest only 4 to 5 percent of their national income in industrial development each year. To transform their societies, development specialists estimate that 12 to 15 percent is needed. But when the average incomes of people amount to less than $300 per year, little money can be saved for investment because most is spent for food. In these circumstances, capital investment in higher

agricultural yields, irrigation projects, new businesses, or large-scale industry is difficult, if not impossible. A paralyzing poverty pervades virtually every facet of an underdeveloped economy. The landscape has too few factories, paved roads, power lines, and machines. The population has little to invest in health, education, and welfare.

THE SPATIAL ORGANIZATION OF DEVELOPMENT

The landscapes of developing and technological countries reflect differences in the social organization of

space. In the Technological World, networks of market centers, **central places,** have evolved to facilitate the regular exchange of goods and services between producers and consumers. This systematic organization of space permits economic specialization, facilitates the growth of economic regions, and enhances optimal utilization of resources.

The spatial basis of England's remarkable eighteenth-century economic growth can be found in the existence of a tightly woven network of market towns—preindustrial central places. The emergence of trading towns in Belgium played a similar role in transforming its agricultural landscape. In Meiji Japan, castle towns became marketplaces acting as links between small villages and large

WORLD POPULATION ENGAGED IN AGRICULTURE

In the Technological World, less than a quarter of the population is directly engaged in agriculture. In the Developing World, as much as four fifths of the total population earn their living by farming. The central problem these countries face is that modernization requires money. But if money is withdrawn from agriculture to build up industry, lower food production may result in malnutrition or even starvation. Which sector should be developed first or whether both need to be developed simultaneously is under debate in many countries.

Source: World Population Data Sheet, 1988.

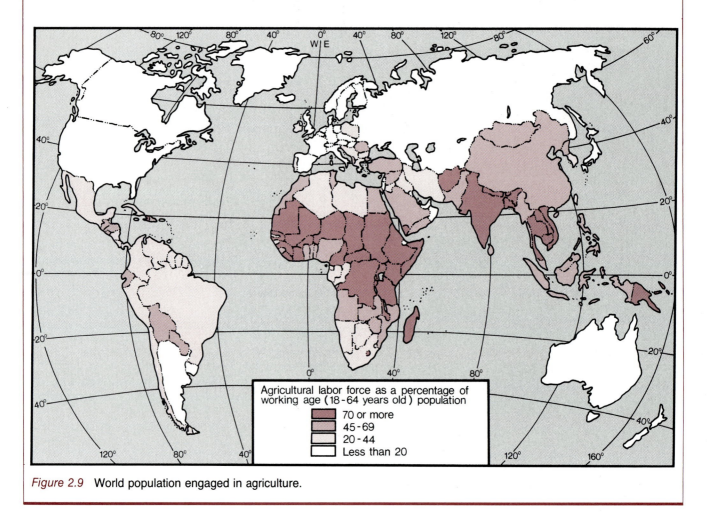

Agricultural labor force as a percentage of working age (18-64 years old) population

- 70 or more
- 45-69
- 20-44
- Less than 20

Figure 2.9 World population engaged in agriculture.

cities. Once railroads overcame mountain barriers, this **hierarchy** of settlements formed the spatial basis of Japan's economic growth. The same economic organization of space occurred in the American Midwest despite the geometric patterns imposed on the landscape by the rectangular land survey and the railroads.

In the Developing World, by contrast, landlords, religious leaders, and military elites imposed their will on landscapes. Spatial organization was designed to facilitate tax collection, the administration of justice, military control, and religious practice. Economic forces played a smaller role in locational decisions. Today, market centers are scattered, the organization of production and distribution is inadequate, and connections between villages, regional markets, and urban centers are poorly developed.

Many of India's half-million villages, for example, have only minimal contact with higher level marketing centers, hindering the implementation of government programs of modernization. In many former colonial countries in Latin America and Africa, railroads and air routes have only recently opened up **landlocked** areas to economic development. In China, by contrast, an imperial network of administrative centers formed a market hierarchy

Human muscles are the primary source of energy in many countries in the Developing World. Thousands of hours will be required to build this road between Jaipur and New Delhi in India.

that has facilitated economic development. But in most developing countries, efforts to forge more efficient transport and settlement systems based on market forces are just beginning.

Spatial Systems in the Developing World

The entire process of economic growth in the Developing World is closely related to the articulation of communication networks. Based on research in Ghana, Nigeria, Brazil, East Africa, and Malaysia, geographers have developed a four-stage model that identifies certain regularities in the growth of transportation systems (Fig. 2.10).

In the first stage, which in Africa lasted well into the nineteenth century, small ports and trading posts are scattered along the coast, inland connections are limited to immediate hinterlands, and coastal linkages are weak. In the second stage, usually associated with colonialism, a few major lines of penetration connect selected coastal ports with areas in the interior where minerals or agricultural products are found. As these

This firewood collector in Afghanistan reflects the low levels of transport and spatial organization found throughout many parts of the Developing World.

THE EVOLUTION OF TRANSPORT NETWORKS IN THE DEVELOPING WORLD

The model in Figure 2.10 is based on empirical research and suggests a four-stage sequence in which transport facilities are extended inland. These stages are (1) scattered ports and trading posts, (2) penetration lines and port concentration, (3) early interconnections, and (4) emergence of high-priority linkages. It is not certain how widely this model can be applied beyond colonial seaboard areas or, indeed, whether all four stages have occurred in every developing country.

Adapted from: E. J. Taaffe, R. L. Morrill, and P. R. Gould, "Transport Expansion in Underdeveloped Countries: A Comparative Analysis," *Geographical Review,* Vol. 53 (1963), p. 504.

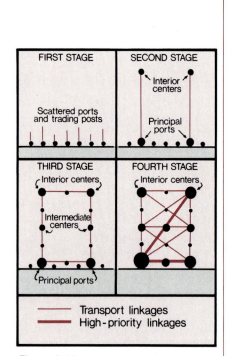

Figure 2.10   A model of transportation networks in the Developing World.

A CENTURY OF SPATIAL DEVELOPMENT IN BRAZIL

The evolution of spatial organization in southeastern Brazil over the last century is presented in Figure 2.11 as an example of the historical development of transportation linkages in a developing country.

As in Figure 2.10, Brazil's development was achieved in stages that reached outward into the interior from early established principal ports of trade and development.

Adapted from: Peter Haggett, *Locational Analysis in Human Geography.* London: Edward Arnold, 1965, p. 81.

Figure 2.11   Spatial development in Brazil, 1869–1955.

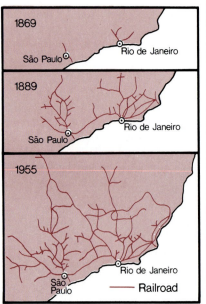

ports grow, local hinterlands expand and new routes focus on these emerging centers (Fig. 2.10). In the third stage, typical of many modern developing countries, seaport terminals and the interior centers continue to grow, and intermediate centers spring up along the routes of penetration. In the final stage, high-priority linkages between the most important centers are formed. The best paved roads, the most heavily used rail lines, and the most intense traffic occur along these main routes.

The extension of railroad lines and emergence of major port centers in Brazil over the last century illustrate the typical evolution of spatial networks in less developed areas (Fig. 2.11). In southeastern Brazil, the cities of São Paulo and Rio de Janeiro began as separate gateways to the interior, seen in the limited nature of their railroad development in 1869; both cities had developed connections and interior extensions by 1889; São Paulo and Rio had fully integrated city-based railroad networks by 1955 (Fig. 2.11).

For most countries in the Developing World, the enormous costs of connecting resources by road or rail with distribution points have prevented the full extension of effective transportation networks. Except for a few well-connected regions, usually source areas of mineral or agricultural wealth, spatial interaction in most developing countries still is based on premodern methods of transport.

Spatial Systems in the Technological World

In the Technological World, complex systems of roads, railroads, and sea and air transport compete to carry passengers and freight. The central problem is not the construction of new transport networks. Connections among resource areas, production centers, industrial districts, and markets have long since been estab-

THE ADJUSTMENT OF TRANSPORT NETWORKS IN THE TECHNOLOGICAL WORLD

The model in Figure 2.12 depicts the evolution of spatial organization in advanced areas by route substitution. The settlements, which are assumed to be equally spaced and of equal size in the first stage, have differentiated in the second and third stages, with a few places emerging as major economic centers.

Transport networks evolve, bypassing smaller places and linking larger centers with long-distance optimum routes.

Adapted from: August Lösch, *The Economics of Location* (trans. W. H. Woglorn and W. F. Stolper). New Haven, Conn.: Yale University Press, 1954, p. 127.

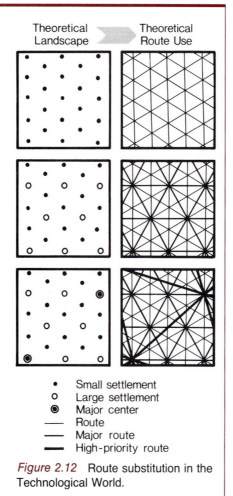

Theoretical Landscape → Theoretical Route Use

- • Small settlement
- ○ Large settlement
- ◎ Major center
- — Route
- — Major route
- **—** High-priority route

Figure 2.12 Route substitution in the Technological World.

Global Accessibility

From a global viewpoint, these different patterns of spatial organization and communication in the Developing World and the Technological World stand out clearly (Fig. 2.13). Adequate transportation is associated with higher levels of urbanization and industrialization. The most elaborate transportation networks, therefore, are found in the United States, southern Canada, Western Europe, Japan, and the densely populated western part of the Soviet Union. Here, road and rail connections are nearly continuous. Virtually no region is inaccessible.

Similar but less dense transportation networks are located in Argentina and eastern Brazil, in eastern Australia, in India (a colonial inheritance), and in parts of the Mediterranean Middle East.

But vast reaches of the Developing World remain unconnected: the arid cores of the Middle Eastern deserts, the tropical heartlands of South America and Africa, the interior of China, and the uninhabited eastern stretches of the Soviet Union, northern Canada, and western Australia. In general, the distribution of surface transportation networks provides an index of the intensity of human occupance in various world regions.

THE RICH AND THE POOR

During the last thirty years, poverty and wealth have retained roughly the same world distribution. In spite of intensive national programs of economic and social development and substantial levels of international aid, the rich nations have grown progressively richer, the poor relatively poorer. The income gap between the two worlds continues to widen.

The sources of poverty vary. In India, Sri Lanka, and Bangladesh, pop-

lished. Instead, the problem is to adjust existing spatial systems to changes in industrial location, urban expansion, changing travel patterns, and rising standards of living.

In the technological societies, functioning spatial networks adjust to new conditions by route substitution (Fig. 2.12). Some centers attain greater importance than others, and old routes are modified to bypass smaller centers. Alternatively, new routes are created to accommodate increased demand and to reduce overuse, traffic congestion, and deterioration of transport facilities.

The economist August Lösch proposed a three-stage model of this process (Fig. 2.12). In the initial stage, settlements are presumed to be equally spaced and a network of intersecting routes links each settlement with its neighbors. In the second stage, higher levels of economic development stimulate specialization and concentration of economic activity. A smaller number of higher level centers emerges. Smaller places located on high-priority routes that connect the higher level centers are bypassed. In the third stage, this process of route substitution and concentration of economic activity intensifies. A new and smaller set of major centers is connected by a new set of optimum routes, and a larger number of smaller centers are bypassed.

WORLD DISTRIBUTION OF SURFACE TRANSPORTATION

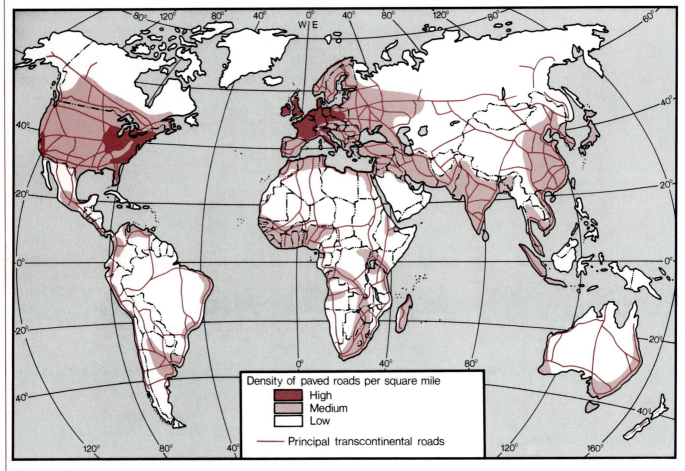

Figure 2.13 World distribution of surface transportation.

ulation growth appears to be the critical variable. In North Africa and parts of the Middle East, aridity retards the development of resources. In central Africa, the legacy of colonialism weighs heavy. In South America, control of the physical environment is inadequate. In many countries, political leadership is corrupt and repressive. Whatever the specific cause, poverty is now a persistent and pervasive feature of human life in the Developing World.

Few experts think this condition will change soon.

Cumulative Causation

One social scientist, Gunnar Myrdal, explains the stubborn resistance of depressed nations to developmental change in terms of a theory of **cumulative causation.** In this view, the "play of market forces" tends to increase rather than decrease inequalities between countries. Highly de-

veloped regions attract higher levels of development; less developed regions, proportionately less. The same effects can be detected at different geographic scales—world regions, countries themselves, or local regions.

Two forces are at work: spread effects and backwash effects. Spread effects emanate from high-growth regions to less developed areas because of growing demand for raw materials and agricultural products. Backwash

Figure 2.13 shows that surface transportation is highly integrated in technological societies, but less so in developing countries. The most striking global contrast, however, lies between the densely settled and thinly populated regions of the world.

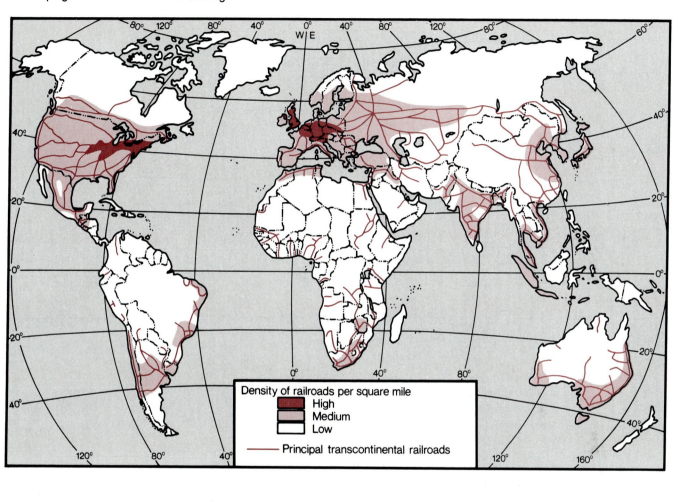

Density of railroads per square mile
High
Medium
Low
——— Principal transcontinental railroads

effects refer to the magnetic attraction of high-growth regions for skilled and intellectually trained persons, new investment, and advanced technology.

These differences in the levels of life between regions and countries intensify over time. The two forces, according to Myrdal, are not in equilibrium. Backwash effects tend to dominate. Thus, once a country gains an initial advantage, a cumulative process is set in motion that increases this advantage by draining human and physical resources from backward regions.

This **core-periphery** view of the world accords well with the demographic, economic, and spatial differences that now exist between the rich countries and the poor. If this theory is valid, the futures of many countries in the Developing World will be much like their pasts. They will remain peripheral—outsiders—to the world economy, contributing raw materials to more sophisticated and specialized states, sharing only one fifth of world trade, and experimenting with one new plan after another to accomplish the elusive goal of modernization.

Stages of Economic Growth

By contrast, the economic historian Walt W. Rostow has advanced a five-stage analysis of the process of development based on historical data (Fig. 2.14). In the initial stage (probably nonexistent today), *Preindustrial Agricultural Society* with traditional modes of production and consumption and traditional sources of knowledge prevails. In stage two, the *Preconditions for Take-off* are initiated by changes in attitudes in the population, a desire for higher standards of living, and modest increases in production. Then, the "revolution of rising expectations" begins, a condition that today has penetrated virtually every corner of the globe.

The third stage, **Take-off** is the crucial phase in the shift from traditional to modern economic organization. New modes of production are adopted, and savings are invested in roads, buildings, and the infra-

STAGES OF ECONOMIC GROWTH

In Figure 2.14, twenty countries are classified by Walt W. Rostow according to their stage of economic growth. Note that the countries of the Technological World all achieved mass consumption within this century, whereas those in the Developing World are involved in earlier stages of economic development.

Adapted from: Walt W. Rostow, *The World Economy: History and Prospect.* New York: Macmillan, 1978.

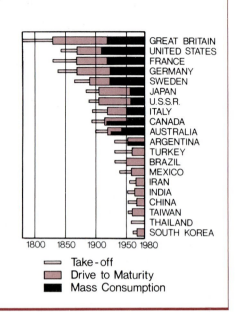

Figure 2.14 The stages of economic growth in twenty countries.

Wellington, which began as a small port in nineteenth-century New Zealand, has grown into a major export center of meat, wool, and milk products.

Highly developed spatial networks are characteristic of countries in the Technological World. Route substitution, often by the construction of freeways and interstate highways, causes some places to grow in importance while others are bypassed.

structure of the economy more generally. Political power shifts from a landed aristocracy to an urban-based elite, and industrialization occurs. The fourth stage, the *Drive to Maturity*, extends and intensifies this process, and long-term investments in health, education, and welfare are made. Most countries in the Developing World today fall in one of these latter two stages. The fifth and final stage of economic growth is the emergence

of the *Mass Consumption Society*, the full articulation of the scientific transformation in countries of the Technological World.

The Meaning of Development

Development and modernization are terms that defy clear definition because they describe a set of processes

that simultaneously permeate the lives of individuals, govern the policies of countries, and shape the affairs of the world. Usually, these terms are used to mean change that is considered desirable by the person who uses them. More broadly, however, they distinguish levels of living. Underdeveloped, less developed, or developing means poverty in all of its manifestations. Advanced, industrialized, or technological means wealthy. This distinction splits the modern world, underlies growing world tensions, and sets the global agenda for the future.

Most observers believe global differences in level of development will increase. The highest rates of population growth are in Africa and Latin America. The greatest number of people are located in the developing countries of Asia. Nearly a quarter of the world's population lives not in poverty, but in destitution. Scarcities of food and fuel are more intense today than at any time in this century. World food reserves are less than they were fifteen years ago. Food is scarce because of population growth in the Developing World and rising consumption in the Technological World. The costs of energy are similarly rising. The rich and the poor compete for oil. Global debt is higher than ever before.

Several outcomes are possible. The wealthy may assist less developed countries, although economic progress cannot keep up with rising expectations. The poor may quietly grow poorer except in countries where determined leadership, the discovery of new resources, or the successful integration of technology enables individual countries to move from one world to the other. Barring massive scientific breakthroughs in food and energy production, the countries of the Technological World may be forced to curtail their standards of living to accommodate a rise in world standards. It is at this point that experts on disaster—the prophets of war, famine, and environmental collapse—begin to speak.

These young people in Accra, Ghana, live in poverty, but they know that it is possible to live more comfortably. Their desire to achieve a higher standard of living is a powerful—if unmeasured—force for change and/or upheaval.

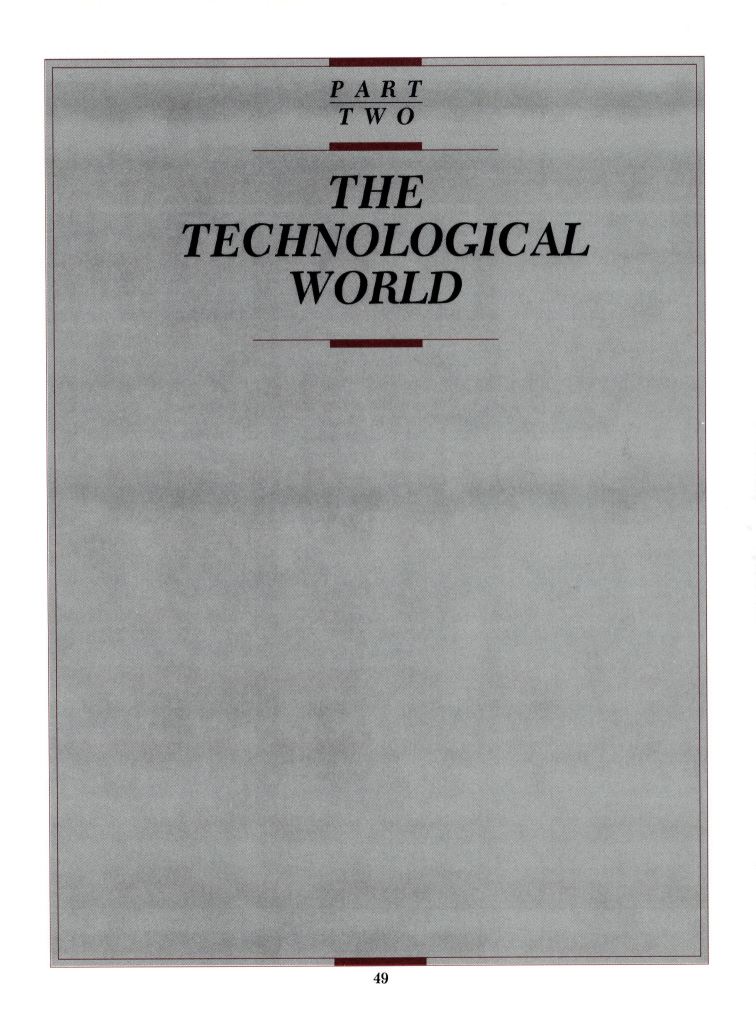

PART
TWO

THE TECHNOLOGICAL WORLD

50

3

WESTERN EUROPE

PROLOGUE

Western Europe began the twentieth century as the cockpit of the world. It was the core area in a new global economy and society. Today, Europe is no longer the headquarters of the world, and disputes over its national boundaries, which precipitated two world wars earlier in this century, seem minor in a world governed by larger, more powerful societies.

For Europeans today, the central question is not how to strengthen their respective frontiers, but how to diminish the limitations that national borders place on material progress.

To meet this challenge, movements toward European political and economic integration have worked to develop a united Europe comparable in size and resources to the United States and the Soviet Union. Under concerted economic leadership, they argue, the eighteen countries of Western Europe can regain the European prominence in world affairs lost almost overnight when European empires suddenly dissolved and 500 million colonial people became citizens of independent states in the 1950s and 1960s.

Decolonization signified the demographic and economic dwarfing of Western Europe. This enforced withdrawal from world governance had a profound psychological effect on Europeans and was a principal force behind the establishment of the European Community. While still maintaining strong relationships with former colonies, Europeans have turned inward in search of new geographical solutions to their diminished economic and political position.

The European Community, or EC 12, is Western Europe's most compelling example of cooperation, but it remains, despite the visions of its founding fathers, an elaborate customs union forged for mutual economic benefit. Yet the Community is successful, and Western Europe ranks among the foremost economic powers on the globe. Taken as a unit, Western Europe's eighteen countries produce twice the wealth of Japan, a bit more than that of the Soviet Bloc, and two-thirds that of the United States and Canada (Fig. 3.1).

Economic growth and prosperity have increased substantially in Western Europe. The automobile has transformed the distribution of production and population just as railroads did a century earlier. To be sure, there are still many problems. The contrast between the dynamic industrial core and the less developed periphery of Western Europe has become ever greater. Dependence on exterior resources has increased. Concentration and immigration has brought problems of urban slums, pollution, and racism. But thus far government planning has provided basic social services and economic growth while preserving the central ideals of liberal democracy. Through cooperation rather than competition, Western Europeans enjoy standards of living second only to those of North America.

In this sense, Western Europe provides a model for economic progress for the divided states of Latin America, Africa, Southeast Asia, and the Middle East, which have found it difficult to compete in the world economy. Whether the next logical step, political union, will become a reality in Western Europe depends on the relative strength of cultural and national allegiances versus economic pressures for international merger. If a united Europe should arise, and countries such as Germany and Italy—themselves born of such ideals in the nineteenth century—should fully merge, Western Europe would provide a model for integration in geographically jumbled areas of the Developing World such as Central America, South America, and Africa, whose national resource bases are too limited to fulfill the aspirations of their people.

Perhaps the most interesting foreign part of the world for North Americans, Europe holds great attraction for students of world regional geography because of its long history, understandable ways of life, and strong geographic pull on the culture and mind of the world. How Western Europe managed to exert itself over the life of the world is presented here.

GEOSTATISTICS

	Capital	Area (square miles)	Population (millions)	Rate of Natural Increase (%)	Number of Years to Double Population	Population Projected for A.D. 2000	Infant Mortality Rate	Life Expectancy at Birth	Urban Population (%)	Per Capita GNP ($)	Energy Consumption per capita (kg of oil equivalent)
Austria	Vienna	32,375	7.6	0.0	—	7.3	10	75	55	10,000	3,217
Belgium	Brussels	11,749	9.9	0.1	1,034	9.7	10	75	95	9,230	4,666
Denmark	Copenhagen	16,629	5.1	−0.1	—	5.1	8	75	84	12,640	4,001
Finland	Helsinki	130,127	4.9	0.3	247	5.0	6	74	62	12,180	4,589
France	Paris	211,208	55.9	0.4	166	57.9	8	75	73	10,740	3,673
Greece	Athens	50,942	10.1	0.2	330	10.3	12	74	58	3,680	1,841
Iceland	Reykjavik	39,768	0.2	0.9	79	0.3	5	77	90	13,370	—
Ireland (Eire)	Dublin	27,135	3.5	0.8	88	4.1	9	73	56	5,080	2,627
Italy	Rome	116,305	57.3	0.0	3,465	57.2	10	75	72	8,570	2,600
Luxembourg	Luxembourg	992	0.4	0.1	770	0.4	8	74	78	15,920	—
Netherlands	Amsterdam	14,405	14.7	0.4	169	15.2	8	76	89	10,050	5,138
Norway	Oslo	125,181	4.2	0.2	330	4.3	9	76	71	15,480	8,920
Portugal	Lisbon	35,552	10.3	0.3	231	10.5	16	73	30	2,230	1,312
Spain	Madrid	194,896	39.0	0.4	154	40.7	9	76	91	4,840	1,932
Sweden	Stockholm	173,730	8.4	0.1	673	8.3	6	77	83	13,170	6,482
Switzerland	Bern	15,942	6.6	0.3	277	6.6	7	77	61	17,840	3,952
West Germany	Bonn	95,977	61.2	−0.1	—	59.6	9	75	94	12,080	4,451
United Kingdom	London	94,525	57.1	0.2	408	57.3	10	75	91	8,920	3,603

Sources: World Population Data Sheet, 1988; World Development Report, 1987.

THE ASCENT OF EUROPE

The economies of Europe developed productive capacities of unprecedented strength and wealth in the nineteenth century. New technologies were harnessed in agriculture and industry, population grew, society became urbanized, and a new and complex way of life emerged.

This process started with *The Beginnings of Industrialization in Britain* and then *The Spread of Industrialization to the Continent.* By the latter half of the century, Europe held a virtual monopoly on machine technology and its new military strength dominated the globe. The technological conquest of distance brought natural resources for industry under European control. Gradually this small continent came to govern *The International Economy.* The wealth generated by these new capacities led to fundamental changes in patterns of population growth, urbanization, and to the rise of new classes—to a *European Society in Change: The Proud Tower.* But in 1914, nationalism led to World War I and ultimately to *The Decline of Europe.* The international economy of the West was badly damaged by World War I. Europe, drifting through the depression of the 1930s toward yet another war, lost its position as the central force in the world economy.

The Beginnings of Industrialization in Britain

While revolutions in America (1776) and France (1789) were creating sweeping changes in political and social life, a development of even greater significance was occurring in Britain in the eighteenth century. For the first time in history, agricultural and industrial production was outstripping population growth. New energy sources and new technologies were creating the outlines of a new human geography. Manufacturing was becoming oriented to national rather than local markets.

Early Industrialization

A constellation of industrial towns, linked by a network of canals and later by railroads, emerged on the British landscape. Coal production tripled in a century. Iron, previously an expensive metal, became commonly available and cheap. In 1829, the first steam locomotive proved the practicality of steam power by hauling a 13-ton load at the unheard-of speed of 29 miles per hour. The costs of transport plummeted as new and more powerful engines were designed. Coal and other bulk commodities could be moved cheaply to factories located in urban settings. In 1850, the rate of economic growth in Britain was unparalleled in the world.

The growth of economic productivity in Britain between 1750 and 1850 enlarged the privileged economic class. Many more people than ever before became wealthy. But the very rapidity of change in Britain obscured the slow but steady gains average people made in income, health, education, and diet.

Figure 3.1 Political map of Western Europe

1 NETHERLANDS
2 BELGIUM
3 LUXEMBOURG
4 SWITZERLAND

The flight from the land, the shift to mechanized factory employment, the new experience of city living, periodic financial recessions, and desperately inadequate environmental facilities in the smog-bound industrial towns—in short, industrialization and urbanization in rapid sequence—were traumatic changes for all economic groups. For the poor, these changes were frequently catastrophic. Not only were old trades, ancient skills, and small communities jeopardized but also traditional values and regional ways of life disappeared. Tension and class strife, strikes, and social inequity tore at the fabric of British society.

Britain's Industrial Advantages

Despite these difficulties, Britain became the primary supplier of textile goods, machinery, and railroad materials to continental Europe. England was recognized as the industrial workshop of the world, although why the **Industrial Revolution** occurred first in Britain rather than elsewhere in Europe, is still a matter of conjecture.

Several factors played important roles. First, Britain had a large internal market capable of purchasing the growing production of manufactured goods. The population of England and Wales doubled between 1750 and 1832, thereby doubling the size of the domestic market. Second, Britain was a free-trade area, so that within its boundaries trade barriers did not hinder economic exchange. Third, Britain played a key role in international trade, which filled British coffers with money that was used to finance industrial expansion at home. Finally, technological progress was a powerful stimulus to the growth of manufacturing in Britain. These four factors thrust Britain into the lead, a pioneer on the frontiers of the Technological World.

By contrast, continental Europe remained a realm of country estates, peasant holdings, and domestic workshops much longer. As late as the middle of the nineteenth century, Britain, with a population only half that of France, was producing two-thirds the coal and more than half the iron and cotton cloth in the world. Early efforts to emulate the British example generally failed. A series of obstacles to industrialization slowed the spread of the Industrial Revolution on the Continent.

The first of these obstacles was the scale and complexity of the European landmass. The sheer size of Europe, broken by physiographic barriers, like the Alps and the Pyrenees, made transportation difficult and expensive. A second reason for the advance of Britain over the Continent was that the resource base of continental Europe was less favorable to industrialization. The textile industry in France, Germany, and the Low Countries was forced to import cotton from places like the American South, Egypt, and India where British agents held monopolies. Most of their wool also came from foreign sources. In addition, although coal and iron deposits on the Continent were accessible, they were widely separated from one another. Furthermore, the widespread availability of timber in Europe prolonged traditional wood-fired methods of iron production. Finally, the poor people of continental Europe were even poorer than those of Britain, and this limited the market for inexpensive manufactured goods.

For all these reasons, economic activity remained a social enterprise on the Continent, and craft guilds retained control over the scale and techniques of industrial production. To be sure, there were some early centers of specialized economic activity, particularly in the Low Countries, northeastern France, and Germany. But well into the nineteenth century, by and large, the markets and manufacturing centers of continental Europe remained small, preindustrial, self-sufficient regions served by local artisans.

The Spread of Industrialization to the Continent

The governments of continental Europe could not ignore the British economic challenge. Economic growth was accurately identified as the key to increased wealth. A favorable balance of trade was seen as the basis of economic and political power. Government leaders also recognized that full employment was important in preserving domestic peace. But the geographic and social limitations on industrialization in Europe remained strong long after technological inventions spread to the Continent. A knowledge of mechanics and machines was one thing; the implementation of an industrial revolution was quite another.

Gradual Change: 1800–1850

During the first half of the nineteenth century, the diffusion of technology from Britain to the Continent was sporadic. Unlike Britain, where specific industries clustered in favored locations to take advantage of available labor or local natural resources, a large number of small, less efficient industrial centers persisted in Europe. The growth of large-scale industrial complexes comparable to those of Yorkshire or the Midlands was slow. Poor transportation networks, limited markets, and cultural resistance to industrial life were barriers to change.

The textile industry is a case in point. In France, the most important continental producer of cotton cloth, the textile industry was scattered across the country. Cotton textiles were manufactured in virtually every province of France with vast differences in efficiency, quality of product, and technology. Textile factories still remained small, family-run concerns, and the industry remained widely dispersed. The new machine technology developed in Britain was seen as destroying the old system of production with no assurance that it would create a new one.

The changeover to new techniques and new fuels was equally slow in heavy industry. In 1850, three quarters of the iron of France was still produced in small charcoal-burning forges located near sources of iron, timber, and water. Similarly, in the German states, iron smelters continued to be widely dispersed and to use craft techniques. In Italy, iron and coal resources were poor in quality, transport duties were high, and heavy industry remained limited. South of the Pyrenees and in Scandinavia, there was virtually no heavy industry at all.

Only Belgium, of all the states on the Continent, kept pace with Britain. Its modern landscapes of factories, mines, and row housing—a continental analogy to the British Midlands—still reflects this early industrialization. The seeming abundance of the Belgian coal and iron fields near the Sambre and Meuse rivers and the scarcity of charcoal made conversion to modern methods more attractive in Belgium than elsewhere. By mid-century, Belgium was the largest coal producer on the Continent and was exporting significant quantities of iron to Germany. In 1835, Belgium inaugurated the first national railroad network in continental Europe. The length of its rails, hard-surfaced roads, and navigable waterways per unit area soon exceeded those of Britain.

In 1850, then, the countries of the Continent lagged a generation behind Britain in industrialization. The concentration of industrial workers in urban factories had barely begun, and nothing like the slums of Manchester could be found. Contemporary writers in France and Germany congratulated themselves on avoiding the penalties of unbridled growth. But the persistence of the old social order on the Continent also meant a persistence of rural poverty, less visible in dispersed villages than in great cities, but nonetheless real. With populations growing throughout Europe and few industries to provide jobs, a reckoning was bound to come. In the 1840s, depression and famine produced misery and death across the face of Europe. Strikes, riots, and popular uprisings alerted political leaders: the price of slow industrial-

John Constable's *The White Horse*, captures the slow pace of rural life in nineteenth-century Europe before the Industrial Revolution.

RAILROADS, IRON, AND COAL IN NINETEENTH-CENTURY EUROPE

These three graphs illustrate the close relationship between the construction of railroads and the expansion of heavy industry in the United Kingdom, Germany, and France in the second half of the nineteenth century. Railroads broke down the barriers of distance. Transport of heavy industrial goods became feasible.

Source: William L. Langer (ed.), *Western Civilization,* Vol. 2. New York: Harper & Row, 1968, pp. 433, 441.

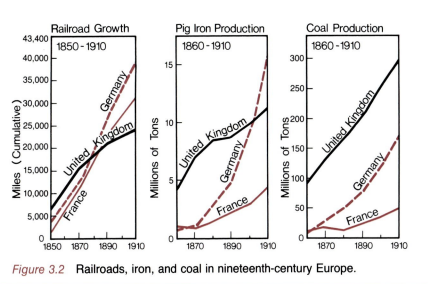

Figure 3.2 Railroads, iron, and coal in nineteenth-century Europe.

Railroads and Industrial Growth: 1850–1900

In the second half of the century, the pace of economic life on the Continent quickened, and the gap between Britain and the rest of Europe closed rapidly. Perhaps the single most important factor in this transformation was the construction of railroads. A web of steel came to stretch across Western Europe and include even the slowly developing countries of southern Europe.

Between 1850 and 1870, the rail network of Europe tripled in length (Fig. 3.2). Some 50,000 miles of track were laid, and strategic trunk lines connected state capitals, industrial centers, and ports. In the German states, railroads were built more quickly than elsewhere. The coal of the Ruhr Valley shuttled across Germany. In France, railroad lines radiated out from Paris like the spokes of a wheel. In the south, engineers pierced the Alps with the Mont Cenis and Saint Gotthard tunnels to bring Italy within hours of Central Europe. A line traversed the Pyrenees to connect France and Spain.

Everywhere these railroads broke down barriers to trade on the Continent. Many inefficient industries previously protected from competition by distance and **topography** were forced to shut down. Heavy raw materials moved from one end of Europe to the other on strands of steel. People experienced a new mobility.

This conquest of distance stimulated an extraordinary increase in industrial activity (Fig. 3.3). The appetite of European economies for raw materials grew apace. An industrial economy was recognized as a political necessity—a matter of national prestige—and the basis of a modern military force.

Nowhere did industrialization proceed more rapidly than in Germany where, by 1870, iron and coal production exceeded that of France. The Ruhr emerged as the greatest center of industry in Western Europe. By the 1890s, German steel production surpassed that of Great Britain and was second only to the United States (Fig. 3.2).

In France and Holland, by contrast, the pace of industrial growth was slow, almost stately. Some observers claim to this day that the French have never experienced an industrial revolution. In northeastern France, a zone of heavy industry did develop based on the Lorraine iron ores and coal from the Saar. But the conservative, measured French approach to industrial growth caused France to fall farther behind Britain, Belgium, and Germany in industrial output.

Elsewhere, industrial centers developed in the Po Valley of northern Italy, in northeastern Spain around Barcelona, and in the Sudetenland in modern Czechoslovakia. In Sweden, new railroad lines stimulated the export of iron ore and timber. In Denmark, the technological revolution found its place in agriculture; the nation's dairy and poultry industries were reorganized and mechanized. In short, by the turn of the century, Europe held primacy in the world economic order and the economic map of Europe took the form it has maintained to the present.

Technological Change: 1850–1900

A large part of Europe's industrial preeminence sprang from scientific

THE IMPACT OF RAILROADS ON TIME AND DISTANCE

Railroads reduced travel time between London and other British cities between 1750 and 1850. Transport costs were reduced, travel became possible year round, and the isolation of rural life diminished. This telescoping of time and distance foreshadowed the age of mass transit.

Source: E. J. Hobsbawn, *Industry and Empire.* London: Penguin, 1969, fig. 16.

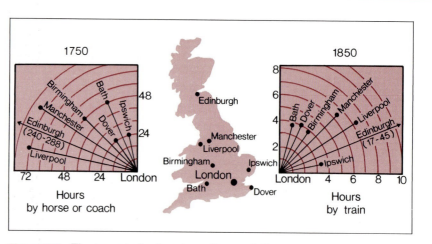

Figure 3.3 The impact of railroads on time and distance.

and technological advances made in the second half of the nineteenth century. The age of coal and iron was replaced by a new age of steel and electricity, which spurred a second generation of industrial growth.

The Bessemer converter made it possible for forges to remove the exact amount of carbon from iron necessary to convert iron ore into steel, a material of surpassing strength, hardness, and flexibility. The Bessemer process and open hearth methods of steel production cut the cost of steel by a factor of ten. Shortly thereafter, the petroleum industry blossomed and internal combustion engines were developed for automobiles. In the cities, coal was harnessed for electrical power, illumination, and telecommunications. Machines for both commerce and the home—sewing machines, scissors, manufactured shoes, watches, and typewriters—became commonplace.

Equally profound changes were occurring in the countryside. Scientific advances in organic chemistry produced chemical fertilizers that rejuvenated the ancient agricultural soils of Europe, doubling and sometimes tripling local harvests. Synthetic dyes, chemical drugs, inexpensive soap,

synthetic cloth (rayon), and dynamite were additional products of this new science.

Many entrepreneurs, followers of the economist Adam Smith, engaged in competition for raw materials and markets in the four industrialized nations of Western Europe—Great Britain, Germany, France, and Belgium. But as leadership shifted from Britain to Germany, free trade began to give way to protective tariffs, isolation, and patterns of international competition. German, French, Belgian, and American manufactures began to dislodge British products both at home and overseas.

As Britain's industrial monopoly

The Bessemer process of steel production lowered the cost of steel by 90 percent. This photo of the Bessemer Works at Sheffield, England, in 1896 reflects the gradual shift from animal to machine power that took place over the course of a century.

EUROPEAN EMIGRATION: 1846–1915

In the second half of the nineteenth century, a mass exodus of Europeans changed the complexion of the populations of North America, South America, and Australia. Great Britain, with its limited resource base, was the principal source of emigrants. German **migration** was greatest in the 1890s; Italians and Austro-Hungarians peaked a decade later. French migration was low throughout the period.

Source: William L. Langer (ed.), *Western Civilization,* Vol. 2. New York: Harper & Row, 1968, p. 446.

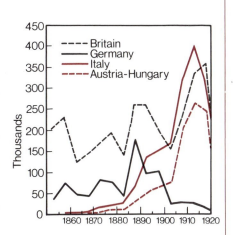

Figure 3.4 European emigration: 1846–1915.

gave way to continental competition, the contradictions between the interdependence of the world economy and the politics of **nationalism** in Europe became apparent.

The International Economy

What the railroads did to economic organization within Europe, the steamship did to communication among continents. Economic interdependence among technological countries and between them and the rest of the world increased sharply. The value of international trade expanded ten times between 1850 and 1913 as reductions in international shipping rates had important effects both in Europe and abroad.

The cost of American wheat shipped to Western Europe fell drastically, making it impossible for many European farmers to compete with cheap grain from the New World. Argentine beef and Australian mutton found new markets in Europe, as did European manufactures abroad. Less developed regions began to specialize in particular products—Egyptian cotton, Indian tea, Malayan rubber, Cuban sugar, Chilean nitrates, Bra-

zilian coffee, Bolivian tin, and the minerals of the Congo Basin.

European capital financed these commercial developments. By 1914, Britain was the banker of the world and had one quarter of its national wealth invested abroad. For the most part, Europeans controlled both ends of these trade lines. Although less developed countries experienced sudden prosperity as new markets for their raw materials opened up in Europe, they also became vulnerable and highly sensitive to commodity prices in the world economy.

The Dispersal of the Europeans

In the new international economy of 1850–1914, Europeans began to move about the world as freely as goods and capital—from one corner of Europe to another, from the countryside to the city, and from one continent to another. Passports and visas were not required. Steamship companies offered cheap fares to migrants. They served as human ballast, and, enabled the British Cunard Line, among others, to show a profit.

This mass movement of Europeans began in the 1840s when potato blight destroyed the agricultural economy of Ireland. From then on, each political or economic crisis in Europe propelled fresh waves of **migrants**

Migration of Europeans to the United States was one adjustment to the tensions caused by population growth, urbanization, and industrialization in Europe. Here, newly arrived immigrants, having checked in at Ellis Island, wait for a ferry to New York City in 1900.

abroad (Fig. 3.4). Between 1850 and 1900, an average of 400,000 people a year left European ports for overseas destinations. After 1900, this figure rose to over 1 million a year. All told, between 1870 and 1914, 34 million Europeans left the Continent; 27 million came to the United States, and the rest went to Canada, Argentina, Brazil, Australia, and South Africa. The Irish formed an important part of the exodus from the British Isles. Germany was a principal source of migrants until 1890. After 1890, the less industrial periphery of Europe—Eastern Europe and the Mediterranean states—formed the principal platform for emigration.

This vast migration of Europeans was caused by the interplay of two forces—population growth and industrialization. The characteristics of the demographic transition spread southward from northwestern Europe to the Mediterranean during the nineteenth century. As first occurred in Britain and then later in Germany, Italy, and other southern European countries, death rates fell, and birth rates remained high. Population pressures intensified. A new generation could not find jobs, compelling waves of migrants from less developed regions to seek employment overseas. After industrialization took hold in Britain and then spread across the rest of Western Europe, emigration rates fell. Growing factory towns began to absorb the bulk of the population increase.

It was not, however, simply a movement of poor peasants from overcrowded Europe. Artisans and craftsmen migrated as well. Early in the twentieth century, the movement of unemployed agriculturalists as well as urban Italian, Polish, Ukrainian, Croatian, and Serbian families to the factories of Pittsburgh and Chicago was substantial. The sheer scale of this movement testified to the human dislocation unleashed by the new social and economic forces at work in Europe.

European Society in Change: The Proud Tower

The inhabitants of the "Proud Tower," as the contemporary historian Barbara Tuchman calls Europe before World War I, had absorbed and turned to their advantage the most accelerated rate of change in history. For most Europeans, the superiority of their values and their civilization were facts—articles of faith—that demonstrated a unique European capacity to adapt to technology, to seize new opportunities, and to create a society of prosperity and peace. In retrospect, they were merely the first to cross the watershed between traditional society and modern society. Their capacities in transportation and communication, production and consumption, energy and commerce had expanded enormously.

If large-scale emigration from Europe was a symptom of social and economic tensions, it was also an example of European ingenuity and confidence. If there were new pressures of wealth and need, of crowded cities and class antagonisms, of national pride and international tensions, the inhabitants of Europe, the Proud Tower, would withstand them and accommodate. Underlying these pressures to expand, which along with industrialization propelled Europeans to world domination, were three forces: population growth, urbanization, and the rise of new classes.

Population Growth

Between 1800 and 1900, the European population doubled, rising from 150 to 312 million. The birth rate remained steady or rose in most countries, whereas the death rate was cut in half by advances in medicine and more reliable food supplies. This created an unprecedented rate of population increase, which affected even relatively underdeveloped countries like Spain, Portugal, Italy, and Greece. Although emigration

drained off a significant portion of this surplus, population densities across Europe were rising, thickening the human texture and generating competition for land and for personal advancement.

Increased agricultural and industrial production, stemming from technological progress, supported this larger population. Britain (pop. 42 million) and Germany (pop. 50 million) were the most populous European countries in 1900, with their growth rates holding steady at better than 1 percent per year. They had become predominantly urban as their populations passed into the late expanding phase of the demographic transition. England relied on cheap grain from abroad to feed its increasingly urban, industrial population. As the saying went, an Englishman could "produce more food making shoes than growing wheat." Germany remained self-sufficient in foodstuffs by using tariffs to limit imports of foreign grain.

With the application of new technologies to agriculture, many European farmers achieved higher grain yields. Along with the Dutch and Swiss, whose populations doubled in the nineteenth century, and the Danes, who tripled in number, German farmers became the richest and most productive in Europe. In Spain and Italy, population growth was not matched by comparable levels of industrial or agricultural progress. Land remained in the hands of the state, absentee landlords, and the Church. Overpopulation led to rural poverty, **fragmentation** of land, and declining rural standards of living.

France did not experience the surging population growth prevalent everywhere else in Europe. In 1800, France was the richest and most populous country in Europe. But in the nineteenth century, the French population grew slowly, from an estimated 27 million in 1800 to 41 million in 1900. By contrast, Germany grew by 32 million people in the nineteenth century; Austria-Hungary, by 23 million; Britain, by 26 million; and Italy, by 16 million.

The French birth rate fell almost as rapidly as the death rate, a departure from the expected patterns of the demographic transition. Some have suggested that inheritance laws, which required a division of property among all children in the family, caused French peasants to limit their number of children. Others have pointed out that abortion and birth control were more prevalent in France than elsewhere in Europe, despite its Roman Catholic faith. Finally, some modern geographers believe that France had a low birth rate precisely because it was a more advanced country than others in Europe; that high levels of education and aspiration, growing cities, and an expanding middle class tended to limit population growth. By the turn of the century more than half the districts of France had achieved zero population growth and abandoned villages were becoming a common feature of the landscape.

Urbanization

Most of Europe's immense increase in population was absorbed in medieval cities that spilled beyond their walls into the surrounding countryside. Industrial resources, such as iron ore, coal, and waterpower, were still location bound. It was cheaper to move people than raw materials. So, new urban centers sprang up alongside the mines and mills.

By 1914, 80 percent of the British population, 60 percent of all Germans, 45 percent of the French, and a third of the populations of less industrialized countries, such as Denmark, were urban. In the Ruhr Valley, the English Midlands, and the French northeast, networks of factory towns devoured the intervening countryside and formed smoke-palled **conurbations.**

Traditional administrative and political centers, such as London, Paris,

Brussels, Vienna, and Madrid, also expanded. London in 1900 was a sprawling city of 6.6 million people—a full 15 percent of the population of the country. Paris had a population of 3.7 million; Berlin, 2.7 million; and Vienna, 1.7 million. The industrial centers of Manchester, Liverpool, Birmingham, Hamburg, and Barcelona grew to more than 500,000 people, as did the political capitals, industrial centers, and port cities of Glasgow, Marseilles, Brussels, Amsterdam, Copenhagen, Budapest, Rome, and Milan. In a continent that had barely twenty cities with populations of 100,000 in 1800,

a massive shift in the human center of gravity had occurred. This shift created a new social environment to herald the twentieth century.

The rapid growth of cities in the nineteenth century completely transformed the nature and setting of life in Europe. In 1800, except in England and to a certain extent in the Netherlands, European cities were centers of royalty and religion, populated by the nobility, bureaucrats, politicians, soldiers, priests, and artisans. Madrid was such a city, as were Paris, Vienna, and Rome. All reflected long-standing patterns of cultural and social homogeneity but-

This slum in Newcastle, England, in 1880 was home to members of the working class who labored in the mines, mills, and factories of the country. Unemployment, illness, and early death deprived these people of any sense of security.

tressed by time and tradition. The influx of millhands and factory workers from the countryside into the cities disrupted traditional urban cultures and societies as surely as sprawling acres of tenements and workers' cottages altered city size and physical appearance.

The tensions and budding antagonisms that accompanied this human invasion were played out in squalid urban districts ill equipped to deal with large population increases. In Manchester, Lille, and Essen, slums grew up around the factories, railroads, and mills, spreading outward from the medieval urban core.

Living conditions were ghastly, although probably no worse than in the preindustrial villages of the European past. Miserable quarters were hastily constructed to house an expanding work force, and these areas rapidly declined into slums. Water supplies were inadequate, and facilities for sewage and garbage disposal were virtually nonexistent. Crowding was intense. Minority groups suffered the worst degradation—as with the Poles in the coal mines of the Ruhr and northeastern France, or the Irish in Liverpool and Manchester.

As Benjamin Disraeli, the British prime minister, put it, Europe was fast splitting into two nations—the rich and the poor—and both were thrown together in the city.

The Rise of Two New Classes

In Europe's growing cities, two new social orders—the middle and the working classes—put their stamp on the nineteenth century. The upper middle class, composed of industrial entrepreneurs, bankers, business leaders, and professionals, set the tone of urban life. They replaced an older order—the aristocracy, the Church, and the **gentry**—who gradually receded from the realities of the industrial age.

The ethics, manners, and tastes of these people were remarkably uniform from one nation to another.

The manners, morals, tastes, and dress of the British middle class are evident in this 1909 photograph of Oxford Street in London. Note the double-decker horse-drawn buses, the cobbled street, and gas-lighting.

Neatness, thrift, preservation of order, and avoidance of sensual pleasure were primary virtues. Wealth was viewed as heaven's reward and poverty as the product of laziness and irresponsibility. The middle class was quick to condemn the behavior of other social groups as immoral and to impose its code of morality on European society as a whole.

The upper middle class also pressed for social reforms. They were responsible for abolishing serfdom in Europe, for removing discriminatory religious and ethnic laws, and for sponsoring public education, the emancipation of women, and the organization of labor unions. These reforms probably spared Europe—given the antagonisms of the time—from widespread and bloody revolution. Artistically eclectic and obsessed by morality, the upper middle class molded public aspirations and social ideas. Beneath it, a lower middle class of shopkeepers, bureaucrats, and domestics copied its manners, eager to climb the social ladder.

For that other new class, the working class, high aspirations were unrealistic. Having abandoned the rhythm of the farm in search of a better life in the city, these factory workers, miners, and mechanics were plagued by the most basic forms of social insecurity—unemployment, illness, and early death. Harnessed to machines and engaged in dangerous, monotonous work, they bitterly resented the luxury and security afforded the upper and middle classes.

Industrial death rates were high. Fatal accidents in the coal mines were commonplace. Each trade was known for its own health risk: for potters, it was lead poisoning; for miners, tuberculosis and black lung disease; for spinners, bronchial illnesses; and for match makers, phosphorus poisoning. Mass production did make more creature comforts available to more people. But these amenities filtered down to the working class in the form of municipal improvements, such as paved streets, sewers, lighting, water supply systems, plumbing, hospitals, police and fire protection—services that made urban life less dangerous for all.

The only other significant rise in the standard of living of the working poor came near the end of the nineteenth century when cheap food from overseas led to better diets. The festering tensions that resulted from the economic gap between working-class poverty and middle-class ease fostered labor movements that forced European governments to improve the conditions of factory employment and job security and to provide the workers with a life of reasonable comfort.

The Decline of Europe

For most Europeans, the dawn of the twentieth century boded well, and many considered it a golden age, the "Belle Epoque." The French Riveria had become the playground of world socialites, of American millionaires, European aristocrats, and captains of industry. Few Europeans seriously thought that rising nationalism, imperial competition, and social unrest would spawn a conflict of unprecedented destructiveness, World War I.

World War I

When war came, it was sparked by a trivial incident. In June of 1914, Serbian terrorists assassinated the Austrian Archduke Francis Ferdinand in the obscure town of Sarajevo in modern Yugoslavia. Assassination itself was not an unusual occurrence; anarchists had killed prominent statesmen with frightful regularity. But in the case of Francis Ferdinand, Austria gave Serbia an ultimatum and demanded and received support from Germany. Serbia asked for help from Russia, which, in turn, invoked its treaty of alliance with France. Britain, worried about possible German dominance on the Continent, joined in. Through action and reaction, an intricate series of European treaties forged a chain of reciprocal responsibility that ensnared virtually everyone in a continentwide conflict.

The Proud Tower, free from large-scale war since Napoleonic times, entered the fray happily. In one year, illusions were shattered. This was the first war in which modern technology was applied to the art of killing, and the loss of human lives and property was enormous. Machine guns, artillery, and poison gas—basic equipment for trench warfare—created a four-year stalemate on the battlefield.

A generation of European men was destroyed. In the Somme offensive, the British, after losing 60 percent of their officers and 40 percent of their ranks on the first day, penetrated German lines a distance of 7 miles at a cost to both sides of 1 million men— one body for each 4 yards of contested ground. The psychological consequences of this mechanical slaughter were devastating. Overall, 10 million people died and the cost ran to hundreds of billions of dollars. When it was over, France had lost 1.5 million men, half the prewar male population of military age. Germany, ringed by the British naval blockade, faced starvation. The British themselves were deeply in debt. Europe was shattered.

World War I accelerated a shift in the world balance of economic and social power. It created a new set of international conditions. Industrial leadership shifted to the United States. After the Bolshevik Revolution of 1917, Communist Russia withdrew from the international economy. Nationalism spread from Europe to European colonies, and new competitors, such as Japan, vied for markets and produced merchandise previously monopolized by Europeans. The free-trade system that had brought prosperity to Europe began to weaken and, during the Depression of the 1930s, collapsed. This, in turn, led to the rise of economic nationalism and ultimately, a second world war.

The Breakdown of the International Economy

Europe, therefore, emerged from World War I a debtor continent. Britain and France paid war debts to the United States. Private American lenders extended credit to Germany, which, in turn, paid reparations to the European victors. In the process, America replaced Europe as the banker of the world.

European trade declined substantially. Although a temporary wartime loss of markets had been expected, it soon became clear that the nature of overseas markets had changed per-

During the "Belle Epoque," few suspected that World War I would destroy Europe's position of world dominance, certainly not these ladies, gentlemen, and soldiers attending the Sunday dog races at Harlingham, England, in 1908.

manently. The United States was now a prominent industrial exporter, and Japan had taken over markets in the Pacific. India, Argentina, Australia, and a number of other countries created home industries. New centers of production had emerged outside the European sphere.

In Great Britain, the three leading industries—coal mining, iron and steel production, and textile manufacture—all experienced great difficulties. German reparations in the form of coal from the Ruhr deprived Britain of European markets for its coal. British steel mills were, compared with the newer plants in Germany and the United States, obsolete. Britain's cotton textile industry also declined, while Japan and India emerged as major textile exporters. It was still necessary for Britain to import large quantities of raw materials to sustain its industrial economy.

Carved up by the Treaty of Versailles, Germany had lost one third of its coal resources, three quarters of its iron mines, and one tenth of its population. France took Alsace-Lorraine, Denmark received northern Schleswig, and Belgium annexed three small communes. The Saar region and its coalfields were placed under French control for fifteen years. In the east, the Posen (now Poznań) region was granted to the new state of Poland, as were the industrial centers of Upper Silesia. West Prussia became a Polish corridor to the sea separating German East Prussia from Germany proper. Combined with high reparations payments, these territorial losses saddled the German economy with unmanageable inflation. France, by contrast, was relatively better off, having gained important resources in Alsace-Lorraine and maintained its balanced, less industrialized economy.

Economic Nationalism, Social Change

In these circumstances of divided states, cycles of debt and changing global markets, the countries of Europe struggled to build their separate economies while bound in one way or another to the powerful financial structure of the United States. When the New York stock market crashed on Black Thursday in 1929, the impact on Europe was direct and immediate. In a single year, prices and production fell precipitously all over the world; in Europe, unemployment increased by half. In Austria and Germany, banks closed. A general economic depression settled over Europe.

Thrown back on its own resources, each country in Europe withdrew to the extent possible from the international economy. A collection of closed-off, largely antagonistic national economies resulted. Every nation erected barriers to imports while seeking agreements with other nations that would maximize exports. Production everywhere became oriented to domestic markets, and for Europe as a whole, this meant a drastic reduction in jobs and wealth. In the world labor force, 30 million people—a fifth of the total—were jobless.

The breakdown of free trade was soon followed by the decline of two other basic European institutions—liberal democracy and the power of the middle class. Faith in liberal democracy, badly damaged by the devastation of World War I, was strained by new social tensions. Breadlines and bankruptcies became common. Extremists gained credibility as the old bases of European economic strength crumbled. In Italy, fascism took root under Mussolini. Germany, humiliated by treaty and economically deprived, was taken over by Hitler's National Socialist Party.

Europe plunged into World War II, when Nazi Germany strove to create an empire independent of the world economy. This second struggle among Europe's fragmented states completed the destruction of the Continent as the global center of political and economic power. After this war, no illusions remained. In a world dominated by the Soviet Union and the United States, Europeans were forced to seek a new role and a new human geography.

THE HUMAN GEOGRAPHY OF WESTERN EUROPE

Western Europe's landscapes of industrial countries are set in mid- to north-latitude environments. In Europe, the broad **latitudinal** bands of climate and vegetation so prominent in the Soviet Union and North America are altered and compartmentalized by two factors: the **maritime** influences of the Atlantic Ocean and the Mediterranean Sea and the intrusion of mountain terrain.

The maritime influences of the Atlantic and Mediterranean moderate the temperatures of Western Europe (Fig. 3.5). In southern Ireland, at the same latitude as Calgary, Alberta, temperatures below 20 degrees Fahrenheit have never been recorded. At the same latitude as Quebec, palm trees can be grown on the British coast. Rome and Athens, located in Europe's southern perimeter, are at the same latitudes as Philadelphia and Washington, D.C., but cannot be considered "southern" except as compared with the northerly position of the rest of Western Europe. Indeed, European centers of population are clustered further north than in any other world region. Maritime influences have contributed substantially to making it an attractive human environment.

From the time Benjamin Franklin observed the northeastward drift of Atlantic waters, it was believed that northwestern Europe basked in warm water from the Gulf of Mexico, shunted north and eastward across the North Atlantic. However, physical geographers have now determined that the current of warm Atlantic water influencing Europe, the

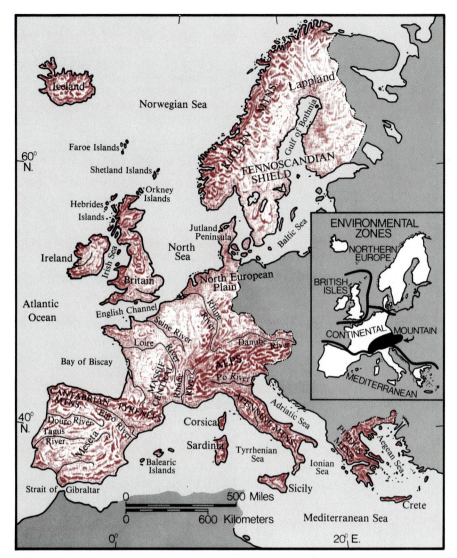

Figure 3.5 Physical features of Western Europe.

zone distinct from maritime Britain, Northern Europe, the mountains, and the Mediterranean south.

On these environmental bases, Western Europe can be divided into five broad subregions—*The British Isles, Northern Europe, Continental Europe, Mountain Europe*, and *Mediterranean Europe*—which provide a framework for viewing large-scale similarities. But the 357 million people of Western Europe live in small, intensively exploited realms. Each nation of Western Europe has its own language, culture, and ideals; each is in global terms a self-contained and powerfully communicative culture. As a result, Europeans speak to their landscapes in intimate terms as a succession of distinctive countrysides, each representing a culture and a region in its own right. The French word **pays** conveys a sense of distinct cultural identity set down over time in a specific countryside. This sense of place reflects a long history of human occupance, now in fundamental change.

The British Isles

The British Isles are separated from the European mainland by the North Sea and the English Channel. A population of 60.6 million people, roughly one sixth of that of Western Europe, lives on two main islands: Ireland in the west and Great Britain in the east. England, Scotland, and Wales are geographically located on the island of Great Britain, but each has its own language, culture, and outlook. The United Kingdom is a political entity that includes these three **culture regions** as well as Northern Ireland. The Irish Republic (Eire), independent of the United Kingdom since 1922, shares a common history with its neighbors in Northern Ireland on the island of Ireland. Eire has experienced a separate evolution from the rest of the British Isles, but periods of isolation from, and proximity to, the English have played a major role.

North Atlantic Drift, surges out of the central Atlantic and is deflected northeastward toward Europe. The warming action of the Mediterranean, a closed continental sea, plays a similar role in southern Europe. More than 3000-feet deep, the Mediterranean acts as a heat reservoir; its waters warm rapidly in spring and early summer, and cool slowly during the autumn.

The limits of Atlantic and Mediterranean influence in Europe are drawn by chains of mountains that have historically acted as boundaries of human activity (Fig. 3.5). The highest of these—the Pyrenees between Spain and France and the Alps

of France, Italy, Switzerland, Germany, Austria, and northern Yugoslavia—form a barrier between the Atlantic north and the Mediterranean south. Both ranges were scoured by **glaciation** (Fig. 3.6). Wide mountain valleys, distinguished by U-shaped contours and often dotted with lakes, tend to make the Alps relatively accessible despite their height and extent. In contrast, the narrow, V-shaped valleys of the Pyrenees make it one of the most effective obstacles to human contact in Western Europe. Between the mountains and the Atlantic, the broad expanse of France, West Germany, and the Benelux countries forms a transition

THE GLACIATION OF EUROPE

Some 20,000 years ago much of the northern part of Europe was covered by an ice mass thousands of feet deep. This ice mass scoured the land while advancing. It left behind a glaciated surface with distinctive landforms, soils, and drainage patterns when the ice cap retreated. All of Northern Europe, most of the British Isles, part of the North European Plain as well as the higher reaches of the Alps and the Pyrenees were covered by ice (Fig. 3.6).

As a result, these regions have irregular drainage patterns that are marked by braided and disrupted stream patterns carved out by glacial meltwater as well as **kettle lakes** that were formed where masses of ice pitted the land sur-

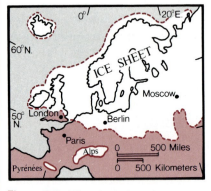

Figure 3.6 The glaciation of Europe.

face (Fig. 3.7). The soils of these regions are composed of **glacial drift**—the debris of rock, gravel, and sand left behind when the ice melted. Landforms, such as terminal and recessional **mo-**

raines, formed at the edge of the ice; **eskers** mark the position of ice tunnels; **outwash plains** made up of stratified drift were laid down by streams flowing from the glacier; and small rounded, oval

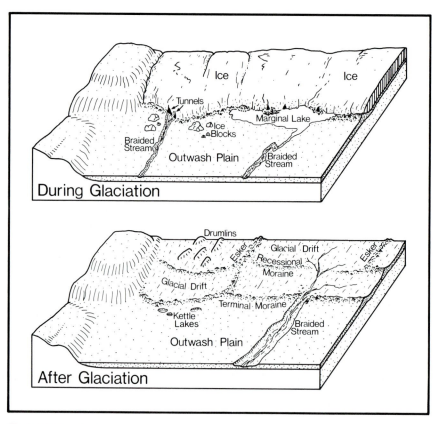

Figure 3.7 Effects of continental glaciation on landforms and drainage patterns.

Much of the physical geography of the British Isles is similar to that of Northern Europe (Fig. 3.5). The landscapes of the area are **glaciated;** its climate is continually moist and cool. Winter harshness increases poleward, but the British Isles generally have mild winters and cool summers.

Seen from the air, the agricultural landscapes of Britain and Ireland resemble those of Belgium, Germany, and northern France—a mosaic of neat farmsteads, well-kept pastures, meadows, and crop fields outlined by

hedgerows. Although British farms are highly productive, less than a tenth of the nation's area is devoted to the production of food, and only 3 percent of its people are farmers. Britain, therefore, must trade its manufactured goods and raw materials to feed its population. Ireland, by contrast, has a substantial agricultural population.

A fuller measure of life in Britain, and for that matter in much of northwestern Europe, is visible from the night sky. Chains of urban lights illuminate the industrial basis of mod-

ern European life. Fully 91 percent of the British and 56 percent of the Irish are townspeople. With the exception of London, most large British cities are located on or near coalfields, but topography has also shaped patterns of occupance. Highland Britain, generally a treeless land deforested by grazing sheep and goats, shares a common geologic history with Scandinavia.

The United Kingdom

Throughout the United Kingdom, the distinction between settlement in

hills of uncertain origin, called **drum-lins,** dot the modern landscape. The impact of this ancient ice mass on the distribution of economic activity in glaciated areas of Europe today is apparent. Soils are generally stony, acidic, and of low fertility except on outwash plains; **bogs** and swamps dot a land scoured by ice. Human settlements tend to follow patterns first set by nature.

Adapted from: Arthur N. Strahler and Alan H. Strahler, *Environmental Geoscience.* Santa Barbara, Calif.: Hamilton, 1973, pp. 439, 444.

Rock and gravel debris deposited when the glacier melted dominates the landscape of much of northern Europe.

highlands and lowlands is manifest. The United Kingdom, the political state, includes Scotland, England, Wales, and Northern Ireland (Fig. 3.5). Nowhere is the highland–lowland difference clearer than in Scotland, where northern and southern highlands are divided by the Scottish Lowlands. The Lowlands extend coast to Scottish coast from the Firth of Clyde on the west to the Firth of Forth on the east. Four fifths of Scotland's 5.1 million people are clustered in the Lowlands. Glasgow, the industrial capital of Scotland and its largest city with 1.8 million in the metropolitan area, lies at the western end of the lowland corridor. Edinburgh (pop. 460,000), the political and cultural capital, lies to the east.

Outside this lowland belt, Scotland is thinly populated because of its rugged terrain and harsh weather. Much of the Scottish north resembles the Norwegian coast with a small, self-contained fishing and farming communities located on deepwater **fjords.** Aberdeen, in particular, has grown in response to the development of North Sea oil since the 1970s.

But the North is still far removed in spirit from the Lowlands' industrial complex based on specialized trades such as whisky, heavy metals, shipbuilding, and petrochemicals. To the south of the Scottish Lowlands, a block of highlands breaks this lowland ribbon of urbanization. Southern Scotland is much lower in elevation than the North, but this area served as an effective barrier between the Scots and the English for centuries.

Crossing this border, the Pennine Mountains course southward from Scotland into England, which, with its population of 47.7 million, dominates the British Isles. The Pennines are broken by an important series of east-west gaps connecting the farmlands and pastures of Yorkshire in the east with the urban complex of Merseyside in the west. On the flanks of the Pennines, a belt of cities sprang up during the Industrial Revolution on the basis of local coal and iron deposits, available waterpower, and agricultural resources. In northeast England, Newcastle on the River Tyne was born on the rich coalfields of Northumberland and became a transshipment point for coal. In the east, in Yorkshire, wool gave rise to the textile industry. Westward across the Pennines, in Liverpool (pop. 1.5 million) and Manchester (pop. 2.7 million), commerce was based on cotton and other colonial products shipped to these ports on the Mersey River and its canals.

As the narrow ridge of the Pennines flattens out, the Midlands form an industrial band in central England. Birmingham (pop. 2.7 million), on the western fringe, is the heart of the West Midlands, the "black country" of England—an area densely industrialized for two centuries. The East Midlands is less heavily industrialized, although the coal fields of Nottingham produce about half the total British output, making this the most important mining district in Britain. In all, the intensity of human activity and industrial development in the English Midlands is matched in all of Western Europe only by the German Ruhr.

Southwest of the Midlands, the rugged mountains of Wales (pop. 2.8 million) have isolated that country and, to some degree, preserved the Celtic identity of its people. But Wales, conquered by the English in the thirteenth century, has hardly escaped industrialization and urbanization. South Wales is a major coalfield forming the basis for an important industrial region. Its major port, Cardiff, developed much like Newcastle in the English northeast.

With the exception of Cornwall and Devon in the far southwest, most of southern England is lowland country dominated by London, only recently replaced by New York, then Tokyo, and now Mexico City, as the largest city in the world. Much of the southeastern plain of England is productive agricultural land devoted to the cultivation of grains, cattle, and intensively worked vegetable farms and orchards. The share of the British labor force in agriculture (2.3%), however, is the lowest in Western Europe.

London's influence in this part of the British Isles overshadows all else. Some 40 miles from the mouth of the Thames River, 13 million Londoners, one fourth of the British population, live in a city open to world trade. Greater London is the primary focus of British society. The city spreads out over a considerable portion of the southeast countryside (see Fig. 1.11). Its size, remarkable among British cities even before the Industrial Revolution, has been attributed to its proximity to the Continent and its populous and productive hinterland. The area covered by urban London has grown many times in the past 100 years, devouring farmland in a country whose finite land resources make unrestricted urban growth unrealistic. Government policies now protect a **greenbelt** around the city from being entirely engulfed by urbanization. **New towns,** entirely planned before construction, have been built beyond this greenbelt. As elsewhere in Britain, new towns represent an experiment in urban geography marked by varying degrees of success.

The United Kingdom also includes the territory of Northern Ireland on the Irish isle across the Irish Sea. These 5452 square miles of rolling hills are a political remnant of English domination of Ireland. Northern Ireland's population of 1.5 million is divided on religious grounds that have their origins in the English control of all of Ireland from the time of Cromwell (1642) to the establishment of the Irish Republic (Eire) in 1922. Protestants are a majority in Northern Ireland. Serious civil strife, focused on the provincial capital of Belfast, has persisted for the last twenty-five years between these people and the indigenous Catholic Irish, who form a relatively depressed minority.

Republic of Ireland (Eire)

Ireland shares the same heritage of Celtic language and civilization that once flourished in Scotland, Wales, Cornwall, and in the French province of Brittany. In each of these regions, Celtic culture has diminished greatly, although Ireland still clings to its separate language, tradition, and literature.

Most of Ireland is a level plain under 500-feet elevation. The interior of Ireland is a basin studded by glacial moraines and barren rock outcrops; its coast is cut by deeply etched valleys whose lower extremities are drowned in the Atlantic (Fig. 3.7). Except in the east, the coast is rimmed by low mountains that shelter centers of population in coastal coves. Dublin (pop. 670,000) is the primary seaport and manufacturing center of the republic. Farm workers form the largest job category in Ireland, but farmers who constituted more than 50 percent of the work force in the 1950s, are less than 15% of the Irish labor pool today. The island today has just three fifths the population of 8.2 million recorded before the great potato famine struck the land in 1841. Even with this small population, however, Ireland remains poor with few industrial raw materials, little capital, and limited markets.

Northern Europe

Geologically akin to the British Isles, Northern Europe is composed of the **continental** states of Norway, Sweden, Denmark, and Finland and the outlying island of Iceland. Here, 6 percent of Western Europe's popu-

Geiranger fjord, located between Bergen and Trondheim on the west coast of Norway, exhibits the U-shaped valley, protected harbor, and limited level land characteristic of these ocean-flooded glacial troughs.

lation (22.8 million) lives on one third of the total area of Western Europe.

Northern Europe's thin population is a consequence of the harsh climate, glacial landscapes, and acidic soils that generally prevail in this region (Fig. 3.7). Fishing, forestry, and agriculture play important roles in the economies of these countries. Despite small populations and limited natural resource bases, Northern Europe has high standards of wealth and pioneering programs of social service that provide living environments as unique as its landscapes.

Norway, Sweden, Denmark, and Iceland all share related Scandinavian languages and closely interwoven histories. Finland, by contrast, is an outlier of Central Asian languages, but sheer geographic commonalities place it within this European region.

The Scandinavian Peninsula: Norway and Sweden

Norway, which occupies the western half of the 1200-mile-long Scandinavian **peninsula,** is dominated by the rugged landscapes of the Fennoscandian shield, an outcropping of the ancient crystalline crust of the European continent. Far to the north, Norway has severe Arctic climates and **tundra** vegetation. Called the Finnmark, this region is occupied by 30,000 Lapps. These native pastoral reindeer herders range freely across northern Norway, Sweden, and Finland. Were it not for the moderating maritime influence of the North Atlantic, this area would be a Siberian wasteland.

Fjords, Norway's most distinctive landscape feature punctuate the Atlantic coast. Fjords are U-shaped valleys partially filled by the sea that reach outward from the Kjölen

Mountains, the highland spine of the Scandinavian peninsula. Scooped out by glaciation, Norwegian fjords are quite deep and well protected from Atlantic storms, although they provide limited level land for human settlement. A succession of fjords that stretch from northernmost Norway to the milder southwest serve as maritime bases for the Norwegian fishing industry. The only Atlantic-facing cities with substantial populations and relatively large hinterlands—Bergen, Trondheim, and Stavanger—are located in the most protected fjords in the south. These cities are growing as the shore facilities needed to exploit North Sea oil expand.

In the past, the heartland of Norwegian culture oscillated between Trondheim and Bergen. Today the center of Norwegian population and economy lies at Oslo (pop. 455,000) in the southeast. In contrast to the rugged Atlantic coast, eastern Norway is a land of wide, wooded valleys with lower rainfall and warmer summers. Dotted with small urban centers with diverse industrial bases, eastern Norway now accounts for more than half the national population of 4.2 million and is growing rapidly. But in European terms, Norway is an empty land. The harshness of the environment and limited economic opportunities have prompted more than half the Norwegian population to emigrate overseas in the last century.

Sweden, the largest country in Northern Europe with a population of 8.4 million, is located on the east side of the Scandinavian peninsula. The country has a low-lying glacial landscape shielded from the direct effects of the North Atlantic and Arctic oceans by the Kjölen Mountains. Fast-flowing rivers course down these mountains in northern Sweden. In the central part of Sweden and the southern half of Finland is a patchwork of lakes and streams separated by numerous eskers and morainic deposits of assorted rocks and soil left behind by retreating glaciers (Fig. 3.7).

In southern Sweden, the country projects far south to end in the Skåne peninsula. Here, the climate is warmer because the maritime influences of the North Sea penetrate farther inland than elsewhere in Scandinavia. This region has level arable land and is the most densely populated area of Sweden, Norway, or Finland. Small farms, few larger than 50 acres, are intensively cultivated. Dairy cattle and poultry are raised; wheat, sugar beets, and fodder crops are cultivated. Malmö is the principal port and center of population in the south. Its economy is based on the processing and export of agricultural products.

Central Sweden is the heartland of Swedish population and commerce today. Dominated by the Stockholm metropolitan area (pop. 1.5 million), it is a region of large-scale agriculture and diversified urban centers. Three great lakes—the Mälaren, Vättern, and Vänern—are like landlocked inland seas, linked together by rivers and canals. Göteborg on the west and Stockholm on the east frame this region, which is noted for abundant mineral resources in the east and timber and grain in the west. Although industrial pursuits dominate the area today, the traditional communal agricultural organization of central Sweden, the **bergslag**, provides the foundation for the social solidarity and democratic institutions for which the country is famous.

Like the Norwegian north, northern Sweden has low population densities. This region is an immense forest of pine, spruce, and birch. Settlement has progressed inland since the 1600s from ports on the Gulf of Bothnia in search of timber. Today, the streams of northern Sweden provide cheap hydroelectric power for developing industries. In the far north, rugged sub-Arctic tundra forms the summer pastures of the Lapps. Here, rich deposits of high-grade iron ore have been developed in the pioneering regions of Kiruna and Gällivare.

Finland

Finland stands apart from Norway and Sweden. Its population is of different origin; its easterly location is farther removed from moderating influences of the North Atlantic Drift. The 4.9 million Finns are a Central Asiatic people who settled in the lake-dotted lowlands of this region in the eighth century. Finland's climate is more continental than elsewhere in Scandinavia. Winters are colder and drier; summers are briefer and hotter. Helsinki (pop. 892,000), the capital, occasionally experiences frosts in June and September. Harbors on the Gulf of Finland are jammed with ice for a good part of the winter.

Finnish settlement patterns mirror those of its Scandinavian neighbors. The topography of the country imposes special problems. The southern and western low-lying plains are much more intensely settled than the interior lake country. The southern coast has a population density of over 300 per square mile, including the city of Helsinki, whereas the lake provinces in the interior have densities of just 40 people per square mile.

The bustling economy of the country is based on timber, paper, forest products, machinery, furs and hides, and some new industries, such as chemicals and electronics. Although typically Scandinavian, the development of Finland has been hampered by a terrain shredded by glaciation and a history of political subservience. Finland was Swedish territory until 1809 and then belonged to Russia until 1917. After siding against the Soviet Union (but not with Nazi Germany) in World War II, Finland lost 18,000 square miles to Russia in 1944. Since that time, the country has involved itself in Western European efforts at economic cooperation, but has maintained a position of strict political neutrality.

Denmark and Iceland

Denmark, with a population of 5.1 million, is far less rugged and more evenly settled than any of its neighbors in Northern Europe. No point in the country exceeds 550 feet in elevation. With the exception of isolated undrained marshes, the Danish landscape forms an unbroken carpet of rich agricultural land laced by a network of villages and market towns. Agriculture is a highly specialized, export-oriented enterprise in Denmark. More than three quarters of the territory of the country is cultivated, and average poultry and dairy yields are among the highest in the world.

Despite its image as an agricultural nation, Danish society is strongly focused on a small number of important cities. Some 84 percent of the Danes live in cities. Copenhagen, the capital, is a metropolis of 1.4 million people. It is the premier port on the Baltic Sea and the site of almost all Danish industry.

Iceland, an island nation proud of its separate heritage as an outpost of Norse exploration in the Atlantic, was colonized during what may have been a warmer climatic period in the tenth century A.D. Norwegians fled political disturbances at home and settled the island. The Danes took over in 1381 and used it as an outfitting center for further exploration and fishing—a satellite state within reach of Greenland and Newfoundland. Since 1918, Iceland has been an independent nation and a center of fisheries and communications in an otherwise inhospitable sea.

The terrain of Iceland is distinguished by Arctic mountains, **glaciers, crevasses, caverns, geysers,** and **volcanoes.** Settlement is most dense in the southwestern part of the island. Here, proximity to the North Atlantic Drift has enabled a population of 84,000 to survive in Reykjavik, the capital. Most of the remainder of the 231,000 Icelanders live near the capital, the site of major British and American naval and air bases.

Continental Europe

The core of Western Europe is composed of France, Western Germany, Belgium, the Netherlands, and Luxembourg. With a combined total of 142.1 million people, 40 percent of the population of Western Europe, Continental Europe is located in a transitional environment surrounded by maritime Britain, the Arctic landscapes of Northern Europe, the mountains of Central Europe, and the Mediterranean south. Each flank of this region reflects different influences; its 335,000 square miles of territory accommodate great cultural diversity.

The population core of this region is concentrated in a band of industry that arcs inland from northern France and the Benelux countries southward along the Rhine River. On the glacial plains north of this industrial zone and in the French Mediterranean to the south, agriculture predominates. Between them lies the economic core of Western Europe and the European Community.

France

Compared with other Western European countries, France has a favored environment and location (Fig. 3.10). For the most part unglaciated, France borders the Atlantic Ocean and the North and Mediterranean seas. It has a varied topography. The Alps (15,771 feet at Mont Blanc) are a barrier to the east, and the Pyrenees, an 11,000-foot mountain wall, separate France from Spain.

Marked regional differences characterize France, which is the largest West European country. Like Italy, Sweden, and West Germany, France has strong latitudinal differences. The natural and human environments of the south (the Midi) are profoundly different form those of the north. But the origins of the local human regions of France—the distinctive **pays**—belong to the past, not the present. These differences notwithstanding, France today, with a population of 55.9 million people, is a highly centralized state. Every region in France depends on the resources and services of Paris for the functioning of its culture, economy, and administration. Only recently have provincial administrators been locally elected rather than centrally appointed.

Paris, a **metropolitan** area of 8.5 million people, stands at the confluence of several important river systems in the Paris Basin (Figs. 3.8, 3.9). This basin commands the geographical **heartland** of France. To the northeast, the Paris Basin extends to the marshlands settled by the Dutch and Flemings. To the east lies Germany, rimmed by the upland topography of the forested Ardennes and the Vosges Mountains. The Lorraine lowland lies between them and serves as an open eastern gate to conquest. Brittany to the west is a vestigial Celtic culture hearth long incorporated into France. The rich French countryside that extends south from Paris through pays such as the Loire, Champagne, and Burgundy has been the undisputed homeland of the French nation since the Middle Ages.

In northern France, a tapestry of cities weaves outward from Paris. Orléans, Rouen, Amiens, Reims, and Troyes form a first ring some 70 to 80 miles away. A second web of cities farther outward includes the industrial districts of Lille, Metz, Nancy, and Strasbourg in the north and east. To the west and southwest of Paris, the intensity of urbanization is much less. This part of France remains predominantly agricultural. Its cities process the specialized products of their surroundings pays. To the south of Paris, Lyon (pop. 1.2 million) guards the gateway to the enclosed Rhône River Valley, which stretches south-

The Cité, an island in the Seine River, is occupied by government buildings and Notre Dame Cathedral. It is the heart of old Paris. Skyscrapers in the background signal changes now taking place in this metropolitan capital of Western Europe's largest nation.

ward and broadens out to embrace the cities and countryside of the Mediterranean lowlands of the Midi (Fig. 3.9).

The Mediterranean coast of France—ancient Provence—is a densely settled region identifiable by its **Mediterranean climate** and agriculture. The whole of Mediterranean France has a history of distinctive languages and political affiliations. A ribbon of coastal cities at the foot of the Alps stretches east toward Italy. To the southwest, the lowland plain toward Spain is also highly urbanized. The primary urban center of Mediterranean France is Mar-

seilles, a major seaport and manufacturing center of over 1 million population.

Unlike its industrial neighbors to the north and across the English Channel, France remains an important agricultural nation and the largest food producer in Western Europe. Some 46 million acres of diversified cropland employ 7 percent of the French labor force. In addition, some 3.5 million migrant workers, largely from North Africa and other Mediterranean lands, work in French agriculture and industry. France has large expanses of good farmland and important industrial re-

sources, giving France a privileged status among Western European countries.

West Germany

Neither as large nor as favorably endowed as France, the West German population of 61.2 million lives in two distinct physical environments: the northern plains and the mountainous south. The North European Plain, broadening to the east, is rolling countryside mostly below 300 feet in elevation. As in Denmark and coastal Sweden and Finland, the Plain has been glaciated; moraines, bogs, and

MAPSCAN

MAP SCALE

A map is a graphic representation of a portion of the earth's surface, and every map is smaller than the portion of the earth represented on the map. In other words, **cartographers** reduce the size of reality—bring it down to scale—to depict the world on maps. Distances measured on the earth's surface in miles (or kilometers) appear on maps in inches (or centimeters). To convert distance on the earth to distance on a map, a reduction factor called **scale** is used to preserve consistency and accuracy. The scale of a map tells you how many miles on the earth each inch on the map represents.

Scale is usually expressed as a **representative fraction** or as a **linear** (or **bar**) **scale.** A representative fraction states the ratio of map distance to earth distance. For example, if a map has a scale of 1:63,360, it means that every inch on the map equals 63,360

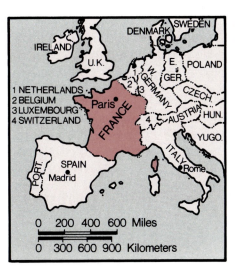

Figure 3.9 Medium-scale map of Paris in France.

inches or 1 mile on the earth. Linear scale, used throughout this book, is simply a small ruler (bar scale) printed on each map. This scale measures out units of distance on the map, usually in terms of real-world distance in whole numbers of miles or kilometers.

The three maps shown here focus on the city of Paris. They illustrate the effect of scale on level of generalization. Figure 3.8 is a detailed or **large-scale** map of the city and its surroundings presented at a scale of 1:1,000,000—1 inch equals about 16 miles. This map is not detailed enough to guide one through the city, nor general enough to show the location of Paris within France. It does, however, illustrate the extent of the built-up area of Paris and distances between the city center and suburbs like Versailles, Vincennes, and Orly. Figure 3.9, a less detailed or medium

scale map, shows Paris in its national context at a scale of 1:16,000,000—1 inch equals about 250 miles. On this map, the suburbs of Paris disappear, but distances between the capital and other French cities like Bordeaux, Lyon, and Marseilles can be calculated. Figure 3.10 at a **small scale** shows Paris and France in the context of Western Europe at a scale of 1:45,000,000 or 1 inch equals about 700 miles. On this map, distances between major European capitals can be measured and the relative location of each country is apparent.

The level of generalization—the scale of the map—must be appropriate in each case to the data presented and the questions asked. The cartographer must decide whether the focus of attention is on the Paris Basin, France, or Western Europe and proceed accordingly.

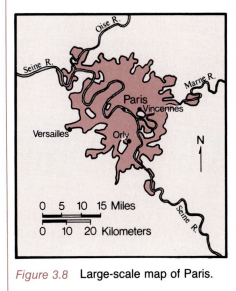

Figure 3.8 Large-scale map of Paris.

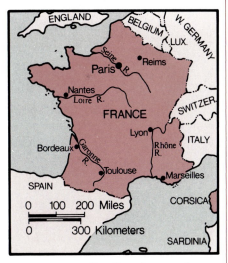

Figure 3.10 Small-scale map of France in Western Europe.

lakes are scattered across the landscape (Fig. 3.7). The Plain covers the northern third of West Germany and widens east of the Elbe River to include much of East Germany, Poland, and the Soviet Union beyond.

Near the North and the Baltic seas, glacial depressions have warped the land into low-lying fields, **peat bogs,** and marshes with heavy, damp soils. The physical landscape resembles that of Holland, and some of the land still

lies unreclaimed, providing a rare European haven for wildlife.

Isolated in East Germany, the divided metropolis of Berlin (pop. 2 million) was the urban focus of the eastern districts of the North European plain. Yet West Germany's north does have an expanding economy. The port cities of Hamburg (pop. 1.7 million), Bremen, Kiel, and Lübeck are growing. They have been the main resettlement zones for 10 million refugees from East Germany.

South of the North European Plain, a series of low mountain ranges rise and ultimately culminate in the Alps at the Swiss and Austrian borders. Densely settled lowlands nestle in the Central Uplands throughout southern Germany. The uplands hold important reserves of timber today endangered by **acid rain;** the lowlands are a checkerboard of prosperous small farms that vie for space with urban centers, like Munich (pop. 1.3 million), Stuttgart, and Nürnberg. Many West German cities have lost at least part of their hinterlands to the closed, Soviet-oriented economy of East Germany.

The cities of the middle Rhine River, paralleling the French border, form a dense ribbon of industrial towns whose contemporary importance is rooted in their early industrialization. Along the upper reaches of the Rhine from Karlsruhe to Frankfurt they contain over 2 million people, not counting the inhabitants of secondary towns and associated rural areas. To the west, tucked away in territory historically disputed between Germany and France, is the Saar, a center of heavy industry set in an agricultural area known for the excellence of its wines and fruit.

Farther downstream, the Rhine broadens to accommodate oceangoing vessels at Cologne and is a main artery of European maritime traffic.

The postwar West German capital, Bonn, is located on the Rhine just upstream. Few landscapes in the world can rival that of the lower Rhine for intensity of urbanization and industrialization. The Rhineland is an immense alluvial fan of cities. The area, usually called the Ruhr, is the largest megalopolis in continental Europe. Over sixty cities of note lie in this industrial belt. Within a perimeter of 100 miles, 9 million people are engaged in the treatment of ores, the production of metals, and the manufacture of a wide variety of finished products.

West Germany, then, has a highly industrialized economy and a strongly urbanized society. Some 94 percent of the people of West Germany are city dwellers; only 5 percent are in agriculture. The country has Europe's largest and richest economy. Yet on the plains of the north and in the mountains of the south, the landscape retains some of its wilderness past. Its open lands contrast strongly with the intensely humanized landscapes of its neighbors toward the sea—the Benelux countries of Belgium, the Netherlands, and Luxembourg.

The Benelux Countries

In the Benelux countries, the level North European Plain sweeps south along the North Sea. The Netherlands is totally included within this arc; only the Ardennes uplands of the Belgian interior and the independent Duchy of Luxembourg are not part of the North European Plain. With a total population of 25 million people and only a tiny fraction of the West European landmass, this area is more intensively utilized than any other in Europe.

The Netherlands sits astride two great rivers: the Maas, which originates in French Lorraine, and the Rhine, which enters the country as one river but quickly subdivides into numerous **distributaries.** In this **delta** land of swamps and marshes, the

Coal piles and factories cover the Ruhr, the industrial core of West Germany, where 9 million people are engaged in the production of metals, the treatment of ores, and the manufacture of finished goods.

POLDER: LAND RECLAIMED FROM THE SEA

Over half of the land area of the Netherlands and substantial parts of Belgium lie below sea level. This land has been reclaimed from the sea over the centuries by the construction of dikes, dams, and levees. This reclaimed land, called polder, has been vastly extended in this century by two massive hydraulic engineering projects, the Zuider Zee and the Rhine Delta. These projects are the largest of a considerable number of reclamation efforts in the **Low Countries** designed to create usable land out of sea bottom, to provide freshwater lakes, and to prevent coastal flood damage. In all, the Dutch have reclaimed 2600 square miles from the North Sea over the last 700 years.

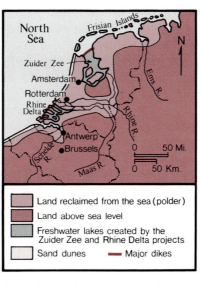

	Land reclaimed from the sea (polder)
	Land above sea level
	Freshwater lakes created by the Zuider Zee and Rhine Delta projects
	Sand dunes — Major dikes

Figure 3.11   Land reclaimed from the sea.

Dutch have created a human landscape out of drained **estuaries** and shallow sea bottom.

Polder, land protected from the sea by seawalls, dikes, and dams, covers a significant portion of the modern Dutch landscape (Fig. 3.11). Reclamation began in the early Renaissance period and has continued to the present, expanding in size with increasing technological capacity.

Modern reclaimed areas, carefully organized into productive farmland, give the Netherlands a scientifically designed landscape, one developed for maximum utilization. Although dairy foods, poultry, and flower bulbs are produced for export, the Netherlands must import most of its food.

Overall, however, the Netherlands, with a population of 14.7 million, is an urban nation. Only 4.6 percent of its people are employed in agriculture, and the country relies on its trading location at the mouth of the Rhine and on skilled labor for industrial products. Amsterdam, a city of 1 million people, is the premier metropolis of the country, with an urban zone whose influence extends over the entire nation.

In the south, on the Maas, Rotterdam, another city of 1 million people, is the busiest port in Europe. Much of Rotterdam's postwar growth has been rooted in the oil industry, and its new deep harbor—Europoort—handles much of the Middle Eastern oil flowing into the European continent. The Dutch landscape is dotted with other urban centers, linked together by the nation's 4000 miles of canals.

South of the Netherlands, Belgium forms a human transition zone between German and Dutch culture to the north and French to the south. Belgium unites two diverse populations: the Flemings, who speak Flemish (a variety of Dutch) and the Walloons, who speak French with a distinctive accent. Flemings are more numerous—55 percent of Belgium's 9.9 million people—but the Walloons, with 33 percent of the population, until recently dominated the cultural and political life of the country.

The landscapes of Belgium, however, reflect the more general patterns of terrain found along the North Sea—coastal lowlands, an interior plain, succeeded by highlands. Most of the Belgian population was, until modern times, concentrated at the transitional zones between these three distinct landscapes. Brussels and Antwerp dominate Belgium today. Brussels, the national capital, is the headquarters of both the European Community and the North Atlantic Treaty Organization (NATO). It is connected by canal to the Schelde River, granting its population of 1.1 million access to oceangoing vessels and prompting growth in the industrial sector. Antwerp, the port rival of Rotterdam, is the second city of Belgium, with a metropolitan population of 673,000. One of the first countries in Europe to industrialize, only 3 percent of Belgium's workforce is in farming today—the lowest percentage on the Continent.

The smallest of the Benelux countries, Luxembourg, with a population of 356,000, is remarkable to have survived as an independent nation. It is only 50 miles long and nowhere more than 30 miles across. Located in the hilly Ardennes and surrounded by Belgium, West Germany, and France, Luxembourg is a significant world producer of steel made from iron ore deposits in the area adjoining French Lorraine. The Luxembourgeois retain a separate language related to both French and German. A remnant of a much larger medieval state, Luxembourg has been politically independent since 1867.

Mountain Europe

Switzerland and Austria are landlocked countries framed by the Alps, which serve to separate Continental from Mediterranean Europe (Fig. 3.5). They share somewhat similar environments, but are quite different in their historical experiences. Austria is a vestige of the Austro-Hungarian Empire, a vast realm composed of southern Germans, Balkan peoples, Magyars, and many other ethnic groups. Switzerland has been independent and has pursued a policy of neutrality, since 1815. Comparing the two, Switzerland is half as large, has a smaller population (6.6 million compared with Austria's 7.6 million), and is the geographical center of Western Europe, straddling three streams of cultural influence—Italian, French, and German. Together, these two alpine states constitute 4 percent of the land area and population of Western Europe. Both have capitalized on their mountain environments, and are winter resorts for Europe and the world.

Switzerland

Switzerland is a remarkable multiethnic confederation whose national cohesion has been formed in a geographical zone where different linguistic and cultural groups meet. Unlike most other West Europeans, the Swiss do not speak a common language. The Swiss speak either German (64 percent), French (18 percent) or Italian (12 percent). A tiny minority speaks Romansh, an ancient dialect of Latin. All four languages hold equal status in national affairs. Nor is there uniformity of religion in Switzerland: religious allegiance is equally divided between Catholicism and Protestantism. The country is an exception to the West European pattern of cultural uniformity derived from competitive nationalism. The origins of confederation in Switzerland were based on cultural cooperation, a rare long-term quality.

Switzerland is confined on the west by the heights of the Jura, shared with France, and on the south and east by the Italian and Austrian Alps, which cover over half the area of Switzerland. Stretched between these mountain ranges lie the Swiss lowlands or "Mittelland," a series of highland valleys where nearly three quarters of the Swiss live on one third of the national space. Population density in the lowlands is very high—approaching the Dutch average. Agricultural production of dairy products, poultry, and grains is intense.

In the southwest, the city of Geneva is the center of French language in Switzerland and a world diplomatic capital. International organizations hold 30,000 conferences a year in Geneva. Zurich in the northeast is the largest Swiss city (pop. 707,000). Its financial markets and banks make it as important in international commerce as New York, London, or Paris. Basel to the northwest is an important manufacturing center. Bern, centrally located, is the Swiss capital as well as headquarters of the International Postal Union.

Dependent on the rest of the world for most of its fuel and raw materials, Switzerland has been able to base its industry on a highly skilled urban labor force; 92 percent of the Swiss population is employed in nonagricultural pursuits. Over half a million foreign workers have been attracted to work in Switzerland. Exporting precision mechanical and electronic products, the Swiss have developed far beyond the limits of their natural resource base. Well over half the work force is employed in the service, or tertiary, sector—in banking, finance, and insurance.

Austria

Framed by the Danube Valley in the north and by the eastern projection of the Alps in the south, modern Austria is a fraction of its former size. After World War I, when new independent states were created in Eastern Europe out of the former Austro-Hungarian Empire, Austria became a small country seeking equilibrium within a much reduced geographic space. Vienna, the imperial capital, had grown to a graceful world city of 2 million people by World War I. After the War, Vienna began to lose population as the city was shorn of its broad eastern hinterland which was carved up into independent Hungary, Yugoslavia, Bulgaria, and Romania. The population of the country was reduced from 50 million to 7 million by the diplomats' and cartographers' pens. Austria was annexed by Nazi Germany before World

The Alps frame the landlocked nations of Switzerland and Austria. Historically these mountains have been a barrier between northern and southern Europe.

War II; until 1955, Vienna was administered much like Berlin by the Allied Powers. Vienna has gradually regrown to a population of 1.7 million today from a demographic low point reached in 1951.

Austria has two distinct physical environments. The Alps dominate the south; the Austrian Plain of the Danube River Valley frames the north.

The Alps arc horizontally east-west across southern Austria, reaching elevations of over 12,000 feet along the Italian border. Sheep and cattle are important in the upland zones, where patches of fertile lowlands are worked much like gardens, and **transhumance** remains important. Forest covers over 40 percent of Austria, and so lumber and wood products are important. Fast-flowing alpine rivers sweep down to the Danube and provide hydroelectric power for industry, particularly iron and steel, paper, textiles, and electrical equipment. In addition to its central role in the world of winter sports, highland Austria is a notable producer of geothermal electricity—power generated directly from geysers.

Lowland Austria, holding 60 percent of the population, is composed of the Austrian Valley of the Danube River. The capital, Vienna, long controlled the traffic of the entire length of the Danube, which flows southeast through Budapest and Belgrade and eventually empties into the Black Sea. Hydroelectric plants along the river produce a quarter of Austria's energy needs today. Regaining its independence in 1955, Austria, like Switzerland, declared its neutrality and does not participate in European military or political alliances. The country, almost entirely German-speaking, is predominantly Roman Catholic in religion. About half Austria's employment is today in the service sector of the economy. Emblematic of the shift toward **postindustrial** prosperity is Austria's demographic profile, in which the death rate has exceeded the birth rate since 1975 and population has decreased.

Mediterranean Europe

The four countries of Mediterranean Europe—Portugal, Spain, Italy, and Greece—have a combined population of 116.7 million, nearly a third that of Western Europe, and a comparable share of its land area (Fig. 3.5). Yet population pressures in these countries are intense in part because long abuse of the environment has resulted in widespread **deforestation** and soil **erosion.** Relatively underdeveloped modern economies exacerbate these conditions. Mediterranean climate, with its dry summers and wet winters, creates environments highly sensitive to human pressure. Successive layers of civilization—Phoenician, Minoan, Greek, Roman, Byzantine, Arab, and modern—have severely stripped the resources of the region. Many areas in Mediterranean Europe are still strongly dependent on agriculture. With growing populations, they are a source of emigrant laborers to industrial centers farther north.

Iberia: Spain and Portugal

Spain and Portugal, composing the Iberian Peninsula, form a separate European reality. Cut off from France by the Pyrenees and from Atlantic Europe by distance, **Iberia** is nearly surrounded by the Mediterranean and the Atlantic. Like Greece, Iberia has been strongly affected by non-Eu-

Tile-roofed stucco buildings, cultivated fields, and small towns dot the Mediterranean coast of Spain.

GEOLAB

LOCATION THEORY: THE VON THÜNEN MODEL

Johann Heinrich von Thünen (1783–1850) was a German scholar-farmer. At the age of 27, he acquired an estate near Rostock in the province of Mecklenburg along the Baltic coast in what is now East Germany. A lively intellect, von Thünen was deeply interested in how the cost of transporting agricultural goods affected the location of agricultural activities. In 1826, he published a volume, *Der Isolierte Staat (The Isolated State)*, proposing a general model of agricultural land use. This classic work is regarded as one of the first attempts to formulate a general location theory to explain the underlying forces that govern the spatial distribution of human activity.

Von Thünen's relatively simple model attempted to show the hypothetical distribution of agricultural activities in an "isolated (or ideal) state" where: (1) only one market center was available to rural farmers, all of whom grew crops for sale rather than subsistence; (2) the physical environment of the countryside was uniform in quality and all points had equal access to the market center; and (3) all farmers tried to maximize their profits. In essence, von Thünen held other variables constant, so that distance expressed in terms of the cost of transporting goods became the principal factor influencing the distribution of agricultural activity.

On this basis, von Thünen concluded that the spatial arrangement of agricultural activities around his single market center would form five concentric zones, or circles (Fig. 3.12). Closest to the market center, high-value perishable crops, like market vegetables and dairy products, would be grown. The second zone would be allocated to forest land, reflecting the high cost of transporting wood in nineteenth century Germany. Still farther from the market center lay zones devoted to extensive grain cropping and animal grazing. Farthest away lay

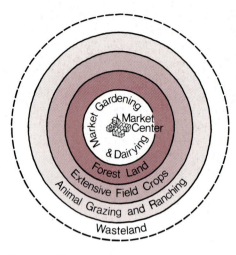

Figure 3.12 Land use in von Thünen's "Isolated State."

wasteland. Underlying this concentric arrangement of economic activity lay the basic concept of land use competition.

As a farmer, von Thünen was well aware that variations in access to transportation routes, competing market centers, and differences in soil fertility would alter zones of land use. He produced modified diagrams to show the impact these types of variations might produce (Fig. 3.13). The river provides low-cost transport and extends the reach of each zone; competing market centers provide alternative points of sale for farmers and each center has its own zones; and changes in soil fertility affect which

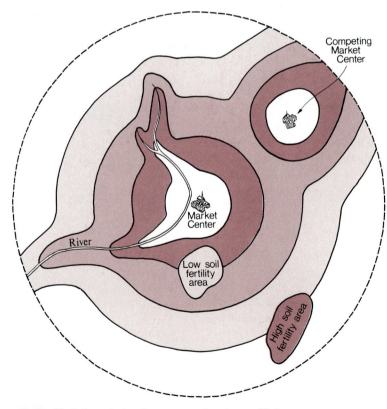

Figure 3.13 Variations in land use according to von Thünen.

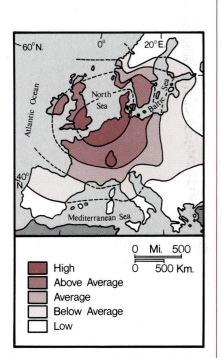

Figure 3.14 Agricultural intensity in Western Europe.

High
Above Average
Average
Below Average
Low

0   Mi.   500
0   500 Km.

changes in soil fertility affect which land use scheme can be practiced. Despite the distortions of the original concentric zones, the principle of location retains its explanatory value.

In the last century, changes in means of transport, agricultural technology, market scale, and a host of other variables have led to modifications of von Thünen's original proposition. But many researchers have used his exploration of location theory as a basis for understanding patterns of human activities. The map of agricultural intensity in modern Europe (Fig. 3.14) is simply one example where the power of von Thünen's original hypothesis still exerts sway; other examples of research conducted throughout the world justify his reputation as a pioneer in geographical thought.

Adapted from: Samuel Van Valkenburg and Colbert C. Held, *Europe.* New York: Wiley, 1952, p. 102.

ropean cultures. It was an integral part of Muslim civilization for over three centuries.

Spain, the second largest European nation in area, has a population of only 39 million and a population density that is among the lowest in Europe—some twenty-five people per square mile. The central plateau, the Meseta, dominates the country in size, aridity, and rural poverty. The Mediterranean coastline is rimmed by high mountains. The industrialized northern coast has an Atlantic climate and is separated from other centers of economic activity by the Cantabrian Mountains. Stretching from France to Africa, Spain is a nation of contrasting landscapes and sharply defined human habitats.

The north is a relatively fertile land rimmed by a succession of mountain ranges that intensify maritime influences on the coast and distinguish this area from the drier and colder interior. Galicia, Spain's most humid region with an annual rainfall of over 65 inches, lies in the northwest. This highland region resembles western France. Farmlands are planted to northern crops, such as apples, rye, wheat, and potatoes. The coastline is deeply etched by bays that extend far inland and provide shelter for important urban centers. Farther east along the Atlantic coast, high-grade iron ore deposits near Bilbao and the country's primary coal field at Oviedo have given rise to a zone of heavy industry at the foot of the Cantabrian Mountains, which grade eastward into the Pyrenees.

Central Spain, the bulk of the Iberian peninsula, is occupied by the Meseta, a series of elevated plains bordered on the north by the Cantabrian Mountains and the Ebro River and on the south by the Guadalquivir River and the high Sierra Nevada. The Meseta is a harsh landscape: almost uniformly above 1500 feet in elevation, it is dry, lacks adequate underground sources of water, and is largely deforested. Madrid (pop. 4

million), the capital and a cultural focus for the entire Spanish-speaking world, is located in the heart of the Meseta.

The Mediterranean coast of Spain is bordered by fertile lowlands where intensive cultivation of citrus fruits, olives, nuts, and other fruit trees is interspersed with vegetable crops grown for world markets. Traditional garden cultivation in small, fertile coastal valleys is today conducted under high-technology conditions. Miles of tomatoes and lettuce, grown under plastic, line the Spanish coast and are destined for export to the United Kingdom, Germany, and Canada.

Dense populations and numerous cities dot the coast. In the northeast, along the Costa Brava, Barcelona (pop. 1.7 million) is the primary port and industrial complex as well as the capital of Catalonia, one of the ancient provinces of Spain. Site of the 1992 Summer Olympics, this is the most business-oriented part of Spain. Hydroelectric power has been harnessed to provide energy for cotton mills and chemical factories; the Ebro River and its **tributaries** have been tapped for irrigation.

Farther south along the Mediterranean coast, a number of cities are important centers of farming, industry, and tourism. The rural core of Andalusia in the south, is the rich valley of the Guadalquivir River. This valley is the largest expanse of agricultural land in Spain—a fertile Mediterranean environment that stretches some 160 miles to the Atlantic.

Although Portugal, with a population of 10.3 million, is the most Atlantic-oriented of the continental nations of Western Europe, its climate and vegetation are largely Mediterranean. It is a continuation of Spain in climate and topography, yet its cultural geography is clearly different. It is an intensely manicured landscape of Mediterranean agriculture.

There are three subregions in Portugal. Rainfall decreases and temperatures increase southward, and vegetation is more lush and relief more pronounced to the north. Northern Portugal is centered on the Douro River Valley, a region of winter snows and oak and pine forests. The Douro and its hinterland are famous for cork; Porto is the urban core of this intensely inhabited region, which has one of the highest densities of population in Europe.

Southward, the Tagus River Valley extends over 100 miles inland, carving out the largest expanse of farmland in the country. Rice, fruit orchards, and forests of cork oak trees alternate with extensive irrigated fields. Metropolitan Lisbon, the capital, has a population of 2 million and functions as the center of virtually every facet of Portuguese life. South of the city, the country is considerably drier. Agriculture is dependent on irrigation, and sheep grazing is important. The low Algarve Mountains frame the southern coast and enclose a region undergoing extensive development as a center of tourism.

North-south differences in environment and development are strong in Portugal, with much of the south still reflecting a Europe of long ago. Twenty-three percent of the Portuguese work force is employed in **primary sector** pursuits. Some 70 percent of the population lives in rural areas. Industrialization, however, has begun to change the face of Portugal. Textile mills and chemical plants have been developed to capitalize on the nation's waterpower resources and low labor costs. West German, British, French, and Italian firms have set up local assembly plants for electronic equipment and automobiles. As with Spain, Portugal's entry into the EC in 1986 bodes rapid and fundamental geographic change.

Italy

Italy, in 1870, was one of the last countries in Europe to unite under one government. Today, its population of 57.3 million is one in race, language, religion, and political structure. In economic structure and levels of prosperity, however, the Italians are divided, north and south.

The long (500 miles) Italian **peninsula** is built upon the backbone of the Apennine Mountains, which rise to 9500 feet. More than any other point in Italy, Rome the capital, tends to mark the transition between the Italian North and the Italian South.

The North, highly industrialized and focused on the rich agricultural plains of the Po River Valley, stands in strong contrast to the South. The central Po Valley is reclaimed marshland whose **watershed** is characterized by early fall flooding. Intensive, highly mechanized agriculture of rice, corn, hemp, olives, and fruit takes place on farms each averaging less than 12 acres in size. Italy ranks second only to France as a West European food producer and exporter of grain, wine, and olives.

The Po lowland is ringed by important centers of commerce along the foothills of both the Alps and Apennines. In the western Po Valley, Turin (pop. 1.2 million) is the capital of the Piedmont, a province with strong historical attachments to France. Milan, more central in position, rules the plain and is the headquarters of many Italian companies. The second largest city in Italy after Rome, its metropolitan population approaches 2 million. The urban outlet of the Po plain is Venice, 30 miles north of the delta at the head of the Adriatic Sea. Long a center of east-west trade and of fine arts, Venice is a city beset by environmental difficulties today.

Venice's regional population of some 400,000 is spread across a unique urban setting of land and water. The historic urban core is located on 118 tiny islands grouped together in a shallow **lagoon**. Some 120,000 people live in this floating Renaissance creation. The other two thirds of the population live in "industrial Venice," a city that has grown up on the neighboring mainland. Industrial Venice has had a disastrous effect on the Renaissance city, polluting both air and water.

Today, the old city is sinking below sea level, and floodwaters rushing into the lagoon swamped the city in 1966 and again in 1980. International efforts to save its Renaissance buildings have to some degree succeeded. In many ways, Venice mirrors the problems that have beset post World War II Italy and much of Mediterranean Europe as well. Population pressures in the countryside have forced the Italians to sponsor industrial expansion at all cost. Jobs are scarce and emigration to northern centers of economic activity in Continental Europe is substantial.

South of the Po Valley, the Apennine Mountains trend southeastward across the peninsula. Cut by short streams on the coast of the Adriatic Sea and by longer, more mature rivers on the west, the Apennines are the source of most of Italy's major rivers, each associated with a separate economy and major city. In the north, Florence, on the Arno River, is distinguished by its artistic past and present. Rome, the center of empire in classical times, is on the Tiber River at the geographical center of Italy. A congested national capital with a metropolitan population of 3 million, Rome remains an international center of fashion and art.

Naples is the regional capital of southern Italy, the backward Mezzogiorno. It is a sprawling industrial port city of 1.3 million and an island of industrialization and job opportunities. The problems of the Mezzogiorno—feudal landowning practices; an environment of rugged, broken mountains and low rainfall; a large **peasant** population subsisting on a finite resource base—are all reflected in the complex urban texture of Naples. Misery intensifies south of Naples down to the toe of the Italian "boot." The island of Sicily across the Strait of Messina is only partially in modern Europe. It is the largest island in the Mediterranean Sea. Of almost primeval beauty, Sicily produces Mediterranean agricultural products that meet stiff competition in world markets: citrus, olives, and wine. Italy's other large island, Sardinia, lies 170 miles west of Rome and 250 miles northwest of the Sicilian capital of Palermo. It is less densely populated than most of Italy. Still isolated from the mainstreams of modernization, iron ore, lead mines and tourism have begun to change the face of Sardinia.

Greece

Greece, with a population of 10.1 million, has figured large in its contributions to Western civilization. It is a mountainous country consisting of a large peninsula, the Peloponnesus, connected to the mainland by the **Isthmus** of Corinth and separated from it by the Corinth canal; the large Mediterranean island of Crete to the southeast; and 165 smaller inhabited isles along the coast of the Ionian Sea and in the Aegean Sea that together compose a fifth of the Greek land area.

Northern Greece is a broken landscape dominated by the Pindus Mountains. Its three important coastal lowland plains contain substantial populations and are the most productive farmlands in Greece. In the northern regions of Macedonia and Thrace, emigration has traditionally been important, although northern Greece is now undergoing delayed and rapid industrialization. The northern urban focus, Thessaloníki, is an important Greek manufacturing center and a free port open to Yugoslavian exports.

Some 140 miles to the south, the Greek landscape is quite different. Dry, hot summers and a limestone topography characterize this eastern Mediterranean environment. Athens (pop. 2.5 million), the **primate city** of Greece, is located here. The administrative, industrial, educational, and political life of the nation is concentrated in Athens to a degree unequaled elsewhere in Europe. More

than a fourth of the modern Greek population is located within 30 miles of the ancient Acropolis, yet Greece is the most agriculturally based of all EC members; 27 percent of the Greek population is engaged in farming, fishing, or forestry—primary economic activities.

The Peloponnesus, Greece's southern peninsula, is a rugged rural landscape with mountains that rise to elevations above 6000 feet. In lowland valleys and on terraced hillsides, the countryside forms a mosaic of olive orchards, vineyards, and pastures. The Greek islands beyond the Peloponnesus stretch out over an area many times larger than their land surface, rendering communications difficult with all but the largest towns on the Greek isles. As one might expect of a country with a long seafaring tradition, Greece has a large merchant fleet spread throughout the world's seas. Tourism adds significantly to Greece's gross national product (GNP), but on the whole, Greece remains one of Europe's poorest countries. Greek incomes are only one-fifth the amount of those in Switzerland, which has Europe's highest per capita income.

The problems of Greece—isolation from the main currents of industrial Europe until very recent times; an environment prone to drought, heat, erosion, deforestation, and earthquake; rural overpopulation and a history of emigration—are masked by the beauty of the **landscape,** worked through time by successive layers of civilization.

MODERN WESTERN EUROPE: ECONOMIC INTEGRATION AND SOCIAL CHANGE

In 1945, the people of Western Europe—the initiators of the Industrial Revolution—found themselves bracketed between two superpow-

ers, the United States and the Soviet Union, whose military and industrial potential completely overshadowed their own. Most of their leaders recognized that Western Europe had fallen sharply behind in technology, power, and productivity. If this recognition was galling to most West Europeans, it was also an impetus for change.

Western Europe was weary of war. Its people demanded social and economic reform, and a just measure of stability and prosperity. Keenly aware of the economic, political, and social limitations of their small size, a number of countries embarked on *The Search for a New Europe*. By integrating their national economies into a larger geographical unit called the European Community, Western Europe launched a period of sustained economic growth and prosperity. This period brought its literate and talented population one of the highest standards of living in the world.

The key to this growth was *Industrial Resurgence* based on the adoption of new technologies, modernization of the industrial base, and diversification of sources of energy and raw materials. The band of industry in the "European growth corridor," which stretches from England to Italy, rapidly became one of the most intense and productive manufacturing and mining complexes in the world. Increased urbanization and industrialization, however, have created *Changes in Agriculture* as Europeans abandoned rural, isolated, and upland areas and sought better futures in the economic growth regions of their countries.

These forces are now leading to new patterns of *Population and Environment*. Western Europe is moving from an industrial to a postindustrial society. A fundamental shift in land and life is occurring, marked by changes in population patterns, the breakdown of traditional ways of living, and new problems of environmental deterioration.

The Search for a New Europe

At the end of World War II, the war-torn landscapes, exhausted peoples, and impoverished economies of Western Europe were physical evidence that the region faced a bleak future. The heart of the problem was Europe's political disunity. National traditions, linguistic and ethnic differences, varying levels of development, and economic competition divided the eighteen states of Western Europe. Indeed, these differences were at the root of two twentieth-century wars that had all but destroyed the heartland of Western civilization.

Overall, the region had a substantial and well-trained population and an adequate resource base. But Europe's industrial and agricultural economies were geared to eighteen small, protective national markets. Even today, ten West European countries have fewer than 10 million citizens each, and only four—West Germany, the United Kingdom, Italy, and France—have populations larger than 50 million. Productivity inside these national compartments has mostly been geared to the size of the national population. The large investments and huge enterprises common in the economies of the United States and the Soviet Union were largely beyond the reach of any single European nation. Trapped between the Communist Soviet Union to the east and the United States to the west, divided Europe seemed destined to fall steadily behind both superpowers as the twentieth century progressed.

Economic Integration

Europe found a geographical solution to these problems through economic integration, the merger of individual national economies into larger geographic units. Larger markets make possible larger inputs of capital, economies of scale, greater specialization among industries and re-

Through economic integration in the European Community, or EC 12, Western Europe is regaining its position as a dynamic center of world trade. This is a photograph of the first meeting of the European Commission at Brussels, Belgium, after the entry of Spain and Portugal enlarged the European Community to twelve member states in 1986.

gions, and more economical locations for human activity. European leaders recognized that badly needed modernization, technological improvement, and economic competitiveness required a larger geographical context.

In 1958, six nations—West Germany, France, Italy, the Netherlands, Belgium, and Luxembourg—formed the European Community, the EC (or Common Market) to accomplish these goals. The much looser European Free Trade Association (EFTA), composed of the "outer seven"—the United Kingdom, Ireland, Norway, Sweden, Iceland, Switzerland, and Austria—stood on the perimeter. In 1973, the United Kingdom and Ireland left EFTA, and along with Denmark, joined the European Community. In 1981, Greece joined to make 10, and Spain and Portugal acquired membership in 1986, making 12 members today. Through this organization, Europe is again a dynamic global economic center, accounting for 40 percent of world trade, of which two thirds takes place within Europe itself.

Western Europe's postwar economic problems were substantial. For nearly a century, this region had depended on international trade. Europe sold industrial products worldwide in return for foreign imports of raw materials and food. Many foreign investments had been lost or liquidated during the war. Traditional trade relationships between Western Europe and the more agricultural countries of Eastern Europe were blocked by the Iron Curtain. Growing populations in the Developing World were consuming food previously exported to Europe. Industrialization had progressed in a number of countries that had previously relied on European manufactures.

In this crisis, the United States under the Marshall Plan channeled $13 billion into Western Europe between 1947 and 1952 to rebuild the war-torn economic **infrastructure** and get the economies of Europe moving again. European transportation systems and industries were rebuilt. Although housing was in short supply and agriculture recovered more slowly than industry, by 1952 most European countries had regained prewar (1939) levels of production. Today, the American investment in Europe has been repaid many times over. EC 12–U.S. trade amounts to nearly $133 billion per year, and taken as a whole, the EC 12 is the United States' biggest export market.

From National to International Planning

During World War II, the governments of Europe centralized production, employment, and resource allocation to meet military demands. Postwar demands for full employment and welfare programs reinforced the tendency toward central planning, and many European countries developed economies characterized by government funded corporations. In the United Kingdom, for example, coal mines, communications, electric utilities, insurance, and the Bank of England were nationalized. Heavy taxation reduced income differences. A national health program was initiated. In France, similar government economic planning was also accepted. Planning was more cautious in West Germany, however, because government control raised the specter of the Third Reich. In Scandinavia, extensive programs of social welfare were implemented. In Eastern Europe, **command economies** using central planning of the Soviet type were imposed on the satellite countries. The new economic order based in national planning, expanded to the international level within Western Europe. By the 1950s, nothing less than the integration of the entire Western European economy was being encouraged by farsighted European leaders.

A step in this direction occurred in 1951, when France, West Germany, Belgium, the Netherlands, Luxembourg, and Italy agreed to place their coal and steel industries under a single authority, the European Coal and Steel Community (ECSC). Important motives for this union were cooperative control over the resources of the Ruhr and an end to the historical rivalry between France and Germany. Although the ECSC was not an economic success, it established patterns of cooperation among the member states that led to the formation of the European Community.

Under the provisions of the Treaty of Rome in 1958, the six members of ECSC reorganized into the European Community, which envisioned social and political integration as well as economic cooperation. Internal barriers to trade were progressively abolished over a period of ten years, creating a customs union of "The Six." Goods flowed freely from country to country. When the process was complete in 1968, internal trade had tripled in volume. Next, a common tariff on external trade was imposed on goods flowing into the European Community from those European nations that had failed to join as well as non-European economic competitors, like the United States and Japan.

Despite these trade barriers, the increasing prosperity of the countries in the European Community attracted a great volume of imports. Trade with nonmember nations doubled in the first decade of its existence. In 1968, free international movement of labor was allowed in the European Community, providing manpower from depressed agricultural regions in southern Europe for the industrial core areas of northwestern Europe. In 1973, 1981, and 1986, the EC enlarged to include six additional national economies, encompass larger markets, and broaden its productive capacities. Joined together in the pursuit of economic growth, the 12 member states have not relinquished political sovereignty. The hopes of the founders of the European Community for a political union in the form of a United States of Europe, a "second America" as French planner Jean Monnet called it, have not yet been realized.

A United States of Europe?

The EC has, however, endeavored to develop political and social structures that reach beyond the "Common Market" approach to unity. With an annual budget reaching $40 billion in the late 1980s, the European Community has established institutions with some of the legislative, executive, and judicial powers traditionally exercised at the national level. The EC Commission in Brussels proposes and implements Community policy and enforces EC treaties. The Council of Ministers, composed of cabinet-rank Ministers from each of the member states, serves as the final decision-making body for the Commission's proposals. In the middle stands the European Parliament, a directly elected standing congress of 518 members, which scrutinizes actions of both the Commission and the Council. The Parliament meets in Strasbourg, but has not yet been given the legislative powers of national parliaments. An important step toward greater European unity is the creation of the European Currency Unit (ECU), which serves as the EC's accounting unit and has become increasingly popular as a global unit of currency used by both businesses and individuals. Passports of European Community members are now issued as EC passports first and, say, Dutch or French passports second. Moreover, according to the 1986 treaty known as the "Single Act," new dimensions to "Europeaness" will arrive in 1992, when common EC legal, environmental, research, and technological policies are scheduled to come into effect.

Progress toward a truly united Europe has been slow, with EC member states quick to put national interests ahead of Community interest. Indeed, recent polling has found that 25 percent of Europeans—ranging from 66 percent in Denmark to 12 percent in Belgium, Germany, and Ireland—reject the idea of a "United States of Europe." However, an important fact in the geography of modern Europe remains: 12 European countries, many of whom were adversaries on the battlefield not so long ago, have ceded some of their sovereignty, welded vital sectors of their economies, and developed common policies in many areas. Peace and prosperity have become a Western European condition.

Industrial Resurgence

The postwar industrial resurgence of Western Europe is principally the result of the adoption of new technologies, better systems of industrial organization, and more efficient utilization of resources. The larger market created by economic integration in the European Community encouraged the emergence of large-scale industries geared to world markets and expanded the role of multinational corporations.

New patterns of resource use—primarily the shift from coal to petroleum for industrial energy and increased reliance on imported raw materials—are dispersing the historic concentration of manufacturing and heavy industry away from the "European growth corridor." European industry is shifting toward high technology; for this reason, availability of skilled labor, capital, centers of research and development, and environmental amenities are becoming powerful locational determinants. In short, Western Europe, like other regions of the Technological World, is moving rapidly from an industrial to a postindustrial economy and society.

Industrial Growth and Modernization

The growth and modernization of European industry is leading to a movement of large-scale industry away from the European growth corridor. This region—which stretches southward from the English Midlands and the London conurbation, through the Heavy Industrial Triangle of the Low Countries, the French northeast, the German Ruhr, and the Mittelland of Switzerland to the Po Valley of northern Italy—was largely created during the Industrial Revolution when availability of coal, iron, and waterpower were of crucial importance. This economic heartland still contains over half the population and produces three quarters of the manufactured goods of Western Europe. More industry in Europe is still located near coalfields than in any other major world region. Today, however, more flexible locational factors are coming into play. Technological modernization, advances in transport, and changing world markets are altering the historic clustering of Europe's three major industries—steel, automobiles, and chemicals. New centers of economic growth are being created and aging industrial cores left behind.

The European Community produces between 100 and 150 million tons of steel each year, depending on market demand. The Community is a formidable world supplier and consumer of finished steel, comparable

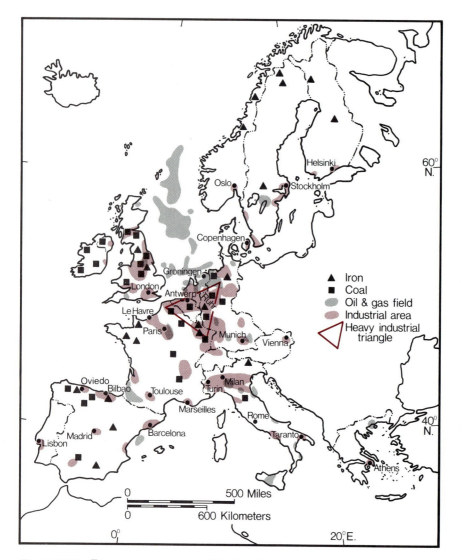

Figure 3.15 Economic resources of Western Europe.

in scale to the United States and the Soviet Union. More than half of this steel-producing capacity is located in the Heavy Industrial Triangle in the French northeast, the Low Countries, and the German Ruhr—the most centrally located and densest concentration of heavy industry in the European Community (Fig. 3.15).

The preeminence of this industrial **region** was spurred by local supplies of high-grade coal and iron, cheap transportation provided by the Rhine waterway and its network of canals, and easy access to world markets through the coastal ports of Amsterdam, Rotterdam, and Antwerp. Dominant since the nineteenth century, the older industrial concentrations of the Heavy Industrial Triangle have been enlarged. New industrial zones engaged in heavy engineering and chemicals have grown up around its major urban centers. Through technological progress, this pivot of the European growth corridor remains the largest steel-producing region in Western Europe, a continental complement to the British nexus of heavy industry in the Midlands.

Fundamental changes are occurring in the scale, location, and structure of heavy industry in Western Europe. Steel plants increased dramatically in size and decreased accordingly in number. By the late 1980s, 9 large companies controlled 60 percent of Western Europe's steel production, compared with more than 100 companies in 1960. This economy of scale is directly related to the larger market and expanded intracommunity trade fostered by economic cooperation within the EC 12.

Government and European Community loans have been invested in modernizing and automating steel plants to increase efficiency of production. Perhaps the most vivid example is Italy. Lacking local raw materials, Italy has built completely modern steel complexes—the largest of which is Taranto on the southeast coast—based on imported ores

and energy. The shift to large-scale integrated coastal steelworks, which now produce a third of the steel in the European Community, reflects the growing reliance of Western Europe on imported raw materials. Deepwater ports handling giant ore carriers and supertankers operate at several locations on the shores of the North Sea, at Europoort in the Netherlands, Port Talbot in South Wales, and Fos near Marseilles in southern France.

These technological changes, alternative sources of raw materials, and new locational imperatives are converting the old coal-based industrial complexes of the British Midlands, South Wales, and the Low Countries—but not the Ruhr—into depressed industrial areas characterized by high levels of unemployment, aging plant facilities, and blighted environments. Western Europe's coal industry has steadily declined in production and employment for the last three decades. Old, coal-based industrial centers have emerged as the primary victims of industrial modernization.

Many coal mines have closed, mining employment is dropping, and some of Western Europe's largest industrial regions are facing difficult times. In the Ruhr, with a tenth of the West German population and nearly three quarters of its coal, iron, and steel production, employment in the coal industry is dropping, even though productivity is increasing. Local iron mines have closed as reliance on high-quality ores imported from Sweden, Spain, and North Africa has risen. Similarly, in South Wales, the number of coal miners has dropped so drastically that it has left the mining villages of this region bereft of a future.

Unemployment in these areas has been alleviated by the introduction of new industries, retraining of younger miners, and a variety of welfare programs, but these efforts have met with limited success. In landscapes dotted with obsolete factories, old-

fashioned mines, pillaged land, poor housing, and plagued by widespread air and water pollution, initiative is blocked by inertia and attractions are few. The workers in these old industrial cores are social casualties of modernity.

The chemical and automobile industries, by contrast, have benefited from changing patterns of European consumption and the enlarged market created by economic integration. The chemical industry has developed at twice the rate of other large-scale industries in Western Europe, accounting for a third of the world's output. Production of plastics and synthetic fibers doubled in West Germany, France, the United Kingdom, and Italy. American investment by such companies as DuPont, Union Carbide, and Monsanto was attracted to the expanding European market. Technological and managerial innovations from across the Atlantic were imported intact. In the late 1980s, in turn, European technology and capital have geographically flowed back across the Atlantic to rejuvenate the American textile and chemical industries.

In the automotive industry, the European Community is producing nearly 11 million automobiles each year, and the European auto market has reached that of the United States in size. Upward of 110 million cars stream across Western Europe, one for every three people. The largest European manufacturers—Fiat, Volkswagen, Renault/Peugeot, and British Leyland—have expanded to fill domestic demand and play an important role in world markets. In France, the car industry now absorbs a quarter of national steel production. The Fiat plant at Turin is the social and economic backbone of the industrial complex in the Italian north. Heavily infiltrated by American investment, Ford, GM, and Chrysler control substantial portions of British, West German, and French production. The automobile industry is critical to the European economy.

The Resource Base

Dramatic increases in industrial output and rising standards of living have increased Western Europe's dependence on foreign imports of energy and other basic raw materials. Petroleum, the fuel of the age, is imported to meet this demand. The rising cost of imported oil in the 1970s triggered an intense search for alternative sources of energy in Europe. With less than 8 percent of the world's population, the eighteen nations of Western Europe consume 20 percent of the global energy output and refine 30 percent of the world's oil. For every four units of energy produced in the European Community, six units must be imported. Whereas only a tenth of the energy consumed in Western Europe's cities was imported in 1950 by the late 1980s half originated from foreign sources. Although energy consumption has declined from 1975 to 1985 because of sluggish economic con-

ditions and stringent conservation measures, long-term, reliable sources of energy and other raw materials are fundamental to the maintenance of the European economy.

As in other regions of the Technological World, petroleum has replaced coal as the primary source of Western Europe's industrial energy. This transition has also occurred since the early 1950s. With coal mines getting deeper and labor costs rising, the coal industry stagnated as petroleum products competed for the energy market. By the 1970s, coal provided less than a quarter of this region's overall energy. But the oil crises of 1973 and 1979 halted this decline. The United Kingdom, West Germany, and, to a far lesser degree, France are still important world producers. Although Western Europe imports 20 percent of its coal, Europe's coalfields form a bulwark against excessive dependence on foreign energy (Fig. 3.15).

Today, Western Europe imports more than half its energy needs. These imports are primarily in the form of petroleum. Oil refineries are becoming the new coalfields of Europe; port cities, such as Rotterdam, Amsterdam, Hamburg, Le Havre, and Marseilles, are being rejuvenated as refining centers, nodes in a pipeline network that carries energy to the region's primary urban and industrial centers from sources in North Africa and the Soviet Arctic (Fig. 3.16).

In the 1970s, faced with large trade deficits from the costs of imported Middle Eastern oil and natural gas, northwestern Europe invested in the development of major new oil and natural gas fields beneath the shallow bottom of the North Sea (Fig. 3.15). Five countries bordering the North Sea—the United Kingdom, the Netherlands, West Germany, Denmark, and Norway—mapped out concession areas. Oil exploration as far north as the Shetland Islands dis-

The oil terminal at Rotterdam in the Netherlands, the world's busiest port, is the largest in Europe. Overall, Western Europe must import half its energy needs, principally in the form of petroleum.

SOVIET NATURAL GAS FOR WESTERN EUROPE

Energy needs in Western Europe have led to a joint energy project linking the natural gas fields of the Soviet Union with energy markets in Western Europe. Construction of a 3400-mile-long pipeline from the huge natural gas fields of the northeast Arctic, which contain a quarter of the world's supply, to the heart of the European Community has begun.

The Soviets aim to sell a total of 40 billion cubic meters of natural gas each year for twenty-five years, primarily to West Germany, France, and Italy. Contracts were signed in 1983 for 20 billion cubic meters per year. The pipeline will enter Western Europe at Waidhausen on the Czech-West German border and connect with the existing European grid. The cost of the project is estimated at $5 billion. It requires 2500 miles of specially welded, 56-inch-diameter pipe, fifty new railroad depots to transport the pipe, and forty-one compressor stations. Planners have worked out the logistics of laying down 2.7 million tons of steel pipe in two years.

This expansion of trade between the

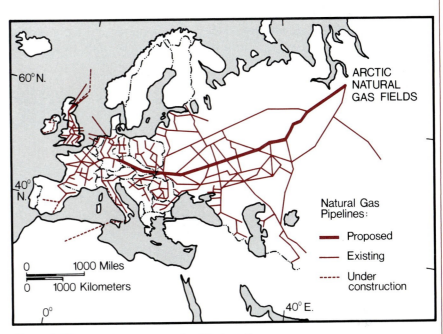

Figure 3.16 Soviet natural gas for Western Europe.

Soviet Union and Western Europe raised fears in the United States because the proposed natural gas network involves complex political and strategic risks. Europeans see diversification of sources, including reliance on Soviet gas, as less dangerous than continued dependence on Middle Eastern oil. The Soviet Union, second largest producer of natural gas in the world, has vast excess capacity and lies within reach of Western Europe; Western Europe has few sources and strong demand. The geogrpahic match is obvious.

closed large reserves of oil and natural gas. These fields produce enough energy to make the United Kingdom more than self-sufficient; Norway, too, has ample reserves and supplies to sell to the world. The energy discoveries in the North Sea combined with the development of large gas fields at Groningen in the Netherlands have drastically altered Europe's energy future. The Netherlands now ranks third in production of natural gas in the world.

Western Europe continues to diversify its energy base to reduce vulnerability to fluctuations in the world economy. Many countries have natural gas deposits, and efforts to increase local supplies are intensifying.

Hydroelectric power is a major source of energy in Switzerland, France, Austria, Italy, and the Scandinavian countries. The best sites for hydroelectric dams are already in use. More important, Western Europe has turned to nuclear energy as an alternative to both coal and petroleum. With the exceptions of Austria, Luxembourg, Ireland, Portugal, and Iceland, all Western European nations either have or are planning to generate nuclear power. By the late 1980's some 137 nuclear power plants were in operation and 34 others were under construction. About 75 percent of these are in France, West Germany, and the United Kingdom. France, the most nuclear oriented of

all countries, has built or planned 62 nuclear plants and intends to generate 90 percent of its power from nuclear sources by the year 2000. Growing political opposition to nuclear power, particularly in West Germany, coupled with general concern over the long-range effects of Chernobyl, could have significant consequences on the future of nuclear generation throughout Europe.

Perhaps the most controversial European effort to secure diversified sources of energy is the 3400-mile-long pipeline that carries Soviet natural gas from the Soviet Arctic to Western Europe (Fig. 3.16). Although several pipelines already carry Soviet natural gas into Europe, the

This week-long antinuclear march from Malville in southern France to Paris reflects growing opposition to Western Europe's high investment in nuclear energy. The "no thanks" symbol on the banner is found in almost every country.

Arctic pipeline substantially increases West European reliance on Soviet gas to as much as 30 percent of natural gas consumption in countries like France, West Germany, Italy, and Austria. It amounts to 6 percent of the total European Community energy budget.

The pipeline, under construction in the mid-1980s, attracted European governments because sizable orders for heavy machinery and steel pipe created thousands of jobs in stagnating industries in the United Kingdom, France, and West Germany. West Germany, France, Italy, Switzerland, and Austria signed agreements to buy Soviet gas for twenty-five years. These agreements emphasized the need of the European Community to ensure long-term energy supplies to maintain their industrial base. Their future needs extend beyond projected production from within Western Europe.

European controversy over alternate foreign sources of energy emphasizes the overall raw material dependence that characterizes the industrial economy of Western Europe. Heavy demand, intense ex-

ploitation of local resources, and high production relative to proved reserves require large imports of minerals and metals. Iron ore, an essential reserve behind any modern industrialized economy, is in such short supply that two thirds of all iron ore must come from outside sources, primarily Canada and the Soviet Union. Western Europe is also an important importer of sensitive raw materials such as copper, tungsten, chrome, zinc, lead, and phosphates. On the whole, imports of these raw materials require vast foreign expenditures. In the future, Western Europe is likely to become even more import-oriented, requiring the production of large quantities of finished goods to pay for needed energy, metals, and minerals.

The Shift to High Technology

The decline of traditional industries such as steel, shipbuilding, and textiles, which rely on imports and compete on world markets only with the assistance of large government subsidies, has turned the attention of Western European corporations and governments to expanding fields in

high technology. New jobs and wealth for their educated population are the goals. In these highly competitive fields, however, Europe faces a number of difficulties.

Deep concern emerged in the 1970s when a technological gap between Europe and the United States was revealed. The United States, it was discovered, was spending six times as much on industrial research and development as the European Community and three times as much as Western Europe as a whole. In advanced technological fields, such as automation, computers, aerospace, nuclear energy, and space satellites, Europe was not competitive with either the Soviet Union or the United States. Discoveries in data processing, telecommunications, meteorology, and oceanography—all regarded as fields of the future—were being rapidly developed with limited European participation.

Part of the problem was that large West European industrial companies outgrew their small domestic markets, but genuinely European corporations comparable in scale to the industrial giants of Japan and the United States did not emerge. Strong national affiliations and loyalties slowed such mergers. Further, as many as 50,000 to 60,000 scientists and engineers were migrating across the Atlantic each year to seek their fortunes in more dynamic industries, universities, and laboratories in North America. For Western Europe, no longer a primary producer of industrial staples and reliant on technological advancement for high standards of living, these losses of human resources were of crucial importance.

To cope with this situation, the United Kingdom, France, and West Germany have dramatically increased investment in advanced fields of research and technology. Training of scientists and engineers is being given high priority, and the Community has developed its own space capability based on European advances in high-energy physics. France, in particular, is pouring funds into high technology research. A ten-year development program is converting the French southwest, one of its poorest rural areas, into a center of electronics and aerospace industry focused on the city of Toulouse. A comparable program to convert the fishing villages and farms of traditional Brittany to a New England type economy based on tourism and advanced technology cottage industry has also received government support. In the United Kingdom, the government has channeled funds into research on biotechnology and robotics. In West Germany, by contrast, the development of microchips, computers, and electronic processing is generally left to private corporations.

Today, Europe is teeming with hundreds of small, high technology firms producing computers, industrial robots, and telecommunications equipment. Individual countries, like Britain and France, continue to safeguard domestic advances in high technology. As they have elsewhere in the world, American and Japanese firms have penetrated and even dominated certain sectors of the European economy. At the same time, however, Europeans have played an increasingly important role in global trade and investment. The British, Dutch, West Germans, and Swiss, for example, held $124 billion in direct investments in the United States in 1986, versus $46 billion in similar investments in 1980. European industrial design, fashion, and consumer technology industries have retained their positions of global prominence.

Changes in Agriculture

The agricultural landscapes of Western Europe were also drastically affected by postwar economic resurgence. Rapid population growth in the nineteenth century was accompanied by agricultural expansion.

Cultivated land expanded in most regions, and mechanization came to European farms as larger populations consuming more and better quality food encouraged modernization. Agricultural self-sufficiency was a primary goal in most countries, so, governments subsidized farmers. Even Sweden and Switzerland designed agricultural policies to produce as much food as possible from their own resources despite their difficult environments. Only the United Kingdom, confident of its control of world trade, revoked domestic agricultural subsidies in favor of less expensive imported food from former colonies such as Canada, Australia, and New Zealand.

The principal effect of the tendency toward national self-sufficiency on European agriculture was to encourage farmers to remain on the land. Significant areas of Western Europe, poorly endowed by nature, were left farmed by small holders producing food at prices well above world market levels during the first half of the twentieth century. Even the industrious farmers of Denmark and Holland were hard pressed to

compete in world markets because the small national populations they served did not encourage efficient, large-scale production. The United Kingdom was the exception in Western Europe because government policies had already driven small farmers off the land and into the cities.

Agriculture was a major problem when the European Community formed in 1958. With too many farmers, and particularly too many small farmers, the income gap between industrial workers and agriculturalists was widening significantly. Rural poverty was becoming a dangerous political issue in France, West Germany, and Italy. When farmers began to use chemical fertilizers, improved seeds, and new techniques of production in an effort to better their incomes, the resulting overproduction of food at prices above world market levels became a critical issue. To make things worse, the least efficient farmers in isolated parts of the Continent faced new competition from lower priced products trucked in on improved roads from the better endowed farming areas of Europe.

On this electronic farm at Lignieres in central France, computers monitor all phases of cattle breeding and farm operation. Video screens are used to film cows about to calve and to keep the manager in constant touch with activities in different farm buildings.

The sheer scale of the farm problem made agriculture a sensitive political issue, perhaps the most difficult the European Community has faced in implementing economic integration. A third of all workers in France, Italy, Austria, Ireland, and Norway and a fifth in West Germany, Denmark, Switzerland, and Sweden were farmers in 1958. Around the Mediterranean, farmers formed half the work force in Spain, Portugal, and Greece as well as two fifths of the workers in Italy. As late as 1970, there were still 12 million agriculturalists in the original six European Community countries.

The Common Agricultural Policy (CAP)

To deal with this problem, the European Community forged a Common Agricultural Policy (CAP). Originally this policy was intended to modernize European agriculture, eliminate agricultural surpluses, and encourage industrialization. Price supports for farm products were to be maintained at modest levels, so that efficient farmers would stay on the land and inefficient farmers would move to urban industrial centers. But member states with large agricultural surpluses, Belgium, France, Italy, and the Netherlands, kept agricultural price supports high to offset anticipated influxes of high-priced industrial products from West Germany. Agricultural price supports also guaranteed social stability in the countryside and rural political support for the enabling political parties.

The CAP of the European Community immediately led to overproduction because farmers were guaranteed high prices, protection from external competition, and subsidies to enable them to sell surplus products on the world market. Massive surpluses of wheat, butter, sugar, and wine piled up in Western Europe. By 1988, an enormous 1.2 million tons of surplus butter, a veritable "butterberg," had accumulated. With subsidized prices, farmers produce

more, and urbanites pay relatively high prices for butter and other commodities, while surpluses have been sold in foreign countries at great losses only to result in trade wars with the United States. Large surpluses of other agricultural products, from beef to barley to olive oil, have resulted in similar market situations. Drastic structural reforms are clearly needed.

Today, the European Community is one of the world's largest exporters of dairy products and a major exporter of grain, meat, sugar, and wine. Most of the Community's annual budget is spent buying up surplus butter, meat, wine, and other foodstuffs, and farm spending is increasing. Quixotically, the EC 12 is also the world's largest importer of food, mainly because industrial nations, particularly the United Kingdom and West Germany, buy large amounts of food on world markets in addition to Community products.

Pressure for reform of the CAP is intense and delayed the entrance of Spain and Portugal—both major agricultural producers—into the European Community. But the obstacles to reform are formidable. Agricultural nations, like France, Italy, and Ireland, want their farmers to stay on the land because high unemployment and slow industrial growth in cities would worsen if these people left the countryside. Furthermore, agricultural exports help pay for oil imports. Industrial nations, on the other hand, could lower their budgets substantially by purchasing low-priced food on world markets. This is the major factor that induced the United Kingdom to attempt to renegotiate its relationship with the European Community.

Flight from the Land

The European farmers that the CAP was designed to retire, retrain, and move off the land have already been strongly influenced by the transportation revolution that occurred as Europe truly entered the automobile age in the 1950s. The distribution of

market centers in Western Europe was forged in the age of foot and water traffic. The railroad grid, superimposed on existing settlements in the nineteenth century, did not substantially alter this pattern. Great as the effects of railroads were on European agriculture, they did not reach down to the village level to reorganize the structure of farming in large stretches of rural Western Europe.

But as better roads penetrated these regions, upland farmers, who account for much of the cultural variety and economic poverty in Europe, were exposed to new competitive forces. Thus populations of hill towns in central Italy, southern France, the Alps, and other remote areas are dwindling in size. Settlements whose villagers have farmed the land and tended herds for generations are being abandoned.

Both food processing and commodity marketing have been centralized as European road systems have reworked farm–market relations. New facilities and marketing procedures have brought greater efficiency and lower food costs to the Continent. For example, the famous central food market of Paris, Les Halles, has moved to suburban Rungis to take advantage of highway connections. Supermarket shopping by car is the norm in many European lives today. As these changes transpire, the highly diversified European landscapes geographers have described so eloquently are gradually disappearing. Zones of rural underdevelopment and poverty today stand in juxtaposition to modern and prosperous, but crowded, industrial cores.

As peasant landscapes of small villages and small farms began to disappear from the European countryside over the 1960s, 1970s, and 1980s, the structural characteristics of European agriculture changed too. The total number of people working on farms has dropped. About 17.5 million people were employed on farms in the original six-country Community in the mid-1950s. Only 5.8 million worked on farms in these countries in the mid-1980s. Farms smaller than 12 acres accounted for 85 percent of all Italian holdings, 55 percent of German farms, and 35 percent of French farms back in the 1950s. Farm size has grown, so that the average farm in the European Community had 31 acres of arable land by the mid-1980s, although there are wide variations in this figure. British farms are the largest in Europe, with an average arable size of 160 acres; Greek farms have, on the average, just 9 acres of arable land. Furthermore, the origins of the work force on the farms of Western Europe have changed dramatically. No longer do villages have excess labor. Villagers work in the city or have moved there altogether, leaving the village populated by part-time farmers, old people, commuters, and weekend households. In the prosperous fields of France, French farmers rely on Moroccan workers from North Africa. Turks herd sheep in the German hills; Portuguese, Sicilians, and Greeks work as hired hands on fields throughout the Community.

The disintegration of traditional rural communities in parts of Western Europe underlines the serious problem of regional underdevelopment that exists in the European periphery—in central France, the Alps, southern Italy, Scotland, Ireland, northern Scandinavia, and large parts of central Spain, rural Portugal, and Greece. Part of the problem is environmental. The northern regions have **climates** that are suited only to raising animals. Overproduction of dairy products is driving marginal farmers off the land. In France, the rocky and elevated landscapes of the Massif Central, the Pyrenees, and the Alps are not suitable for modern agriculture. In the Mediterranean, soils cultivated since antiquity are exhausted.

Regional planners have attempted to stem the tide by encouraging decentralization of industry and the

Department stores, like this one in Paris, are common sights in Western European cities. The continent is rapidly adopting the trappings of an American-style consumer society.

growth of tourism. Factories have been constructed in Brittany and in central and southwestern France in an effort to create nuclei that will spur local economic revivals. Italy envisions a ten-year allocation of public investment into the poorest, most backward parts of the country—the Mezzogiorno, Sicily, and Sardinia. In the United Kingdom, incentives are provided to new industrial ventures that locate outside the London conurbation. The goal is to create a

more balanced pattern of regional growth. But the costs of combating rural poverty are complicated by unemployment in industrial areas, budget deficits, mounting urban social demands, high energy costs, and the maintenance of agricultural price supports.

Population and Environment

Technological renewal and economic integration were the keys that unlocked a new era of prosperity in the European Community. National incomes rose substantially in most countries. Although many people did not fully participate in this economic miracle, European life and livelihood changed dramatically.

A consumer society emerged as families purchased automobiles, television sets, refrigerators, and other household appliances, as Americans had done earlier. Industries supplying consumer goods expanded rapidly compared with declining iron and coal industries. Pockets of poverty and social tension arose in areas that had supported these old industries. Skyscrapers changed the look of cities; supermarkets began to replace grocery stores; corner shops became less important in everyday life. Regional differences between the wealth of the industrial cores and metropolitan centers and the poverty of rural areas intensified (Fig. 3.17). These forces have led to major changes in population and environment in Western Europe.

Population Change

Despite advances in transportation systems and mass communication, general cultural and linguistic patterns remain intact throughout Western Europe. In Southern Europe, the peoples of Spain, Portugal, Italy, and France speak Romance languages derived from Latin and are generally Roman Catholic in faith. In Northern Europe, Germanic languages, like English, modern German, the Scandinavian tongues, and Dutch, are spoken and Protestantism outweighs Catholicism. Overall, national frontiers still act as containers for language groups, with the exception of the multilingual countries of Belgium and Switzerland; the French-German border regions; the Basque country of Spain and France; and in the Celtic-speaking areas of Brittany, Scotland, Wales, and Ireland.

The formation of the European Community and the affluence it has generated set in motion new popu-

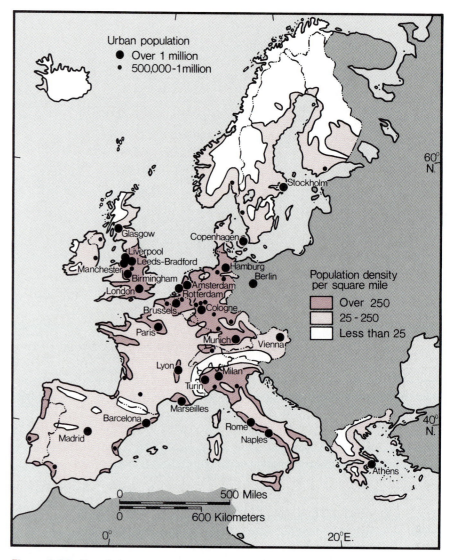

Figure 3.17 Population map of Western Europe.

lation forces. First, the rate of population growth is slowing dramatically. Second, free movement of labor in the European Community, external immigration, and migrant laborers from abroad are leading to greater racial and ethnic complexity in Europe's large cities. Third, greater mobility is creating greater concentrations of people in the urban-industrial cores (Fig. 3.17). Finally, regional consciousness based on language and faith is experiencing a resurgence as a cultural reaction to the growing homogenization of European life.

In the last two decades, the population of Western Europe has virtually stopped growing. Falling birth rates have concerned politicians, planners, and population geographers (Fig. 3.18). In Scandinavia, West Germany, Belgium, the Netherlands, Switzerland, Austria, and Luxembourg, populations have reached a plateau. France's population continues to grow principally because of large-scale immigration from North Africa. Except for France, only the poorer nations of the European periphery—Spain, Portugal, Greece, and Ireland have birth rates above replacement level and these rates, too, have been dropping rapidly over the last ten years. Even they are very low in global terms. All this means that in the next fifty years, the pro-

EUROPE'S DECLINING POPULATION GROWTH RATE

Compared to most other world regions, Europe's population growth rate has been declining rapidly over the last three decades, largely because of a rapid fall in birth rates. Population geographers predict that Europe will reach a point of zero growth by the year 2000 and that this will have profound effects on society and economy in this region. As Figure 3.18 shows, North America has followed a similar pattern.

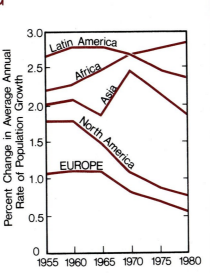

Figure 3.18 Population growth rates by continent.

portion of children will decrease and the percentage of older people in Western Europe—already high—will become higher. In Northern European countries, for example, already more than 5 percent of the population is over the age of sixty-five. On the other hand, the productive population will remain the same or get smaller. This demographic change, identified as the **graying** of society suggests that Western Europe may face a future in which social and economic initiative will shift to younger, more dynamic societies elsewhere. Or, it may continue to encourage immigration to Europe from the global periphery of Europe—the Middle East, North Africa, tropical Africa, the Caribbean, and the Indian subcontinent.

The causes of this drastic decline in birth rates, which started in most Western European countries in the middle 1960s, are not fully understood. The major factor, however, may be the social changes wrought by the transformation of Europe's agrarian society into a modern consumer society of abundance. Sophisticated welfare programs support the aged, the ill, and the unemployed. Reliance on children for support in their declining years no longer influences

most parents. Changes in the status of women, their large-scale movement into the work force, and the easy availability of contraceptive measures are still other factors. Further, the migration from the land to the great cities of the region has probably reduced the incentive to have large families. Children, a boon to farming families, may be viewed as financial burdens in the context of Europe's prosperous urban society. As in other postindustrial societies, a vacation home and a second car begin to weigh against the costs of child rearing.

The graying of Western Europe means that, within the next fifteen years, most of the region will probably achieve zero population growth. Fewer workers will support a larger retired population and future economic growth may be problematic. Some observers fear that an aging European population will be less open to creativity and innovation, which most view as a vital necessity in a postindustrial society.

Migration, Mobility, and Cultural Change

Faced with labor shortages during economic boom times in the 1960s and 1970s, Western Europe opened

its borders to some 13 to 14 million permanent immigrants and guest workers from overseas. In West Germany, 2 million foreign workers with an additional 2 million dependents—the vast majority from Yugoslavia, southern Italy, and Turkey—live and labor in the country's industrial districts and urban centers and comprise 8 percent of the work force. In France, 3.5 million foreigners from southern Europe and North Africa labor at jobs native Frenchmen find unattractive. In the United Kingdom, 2.4 million nonwhites of Pakistani, Indian, Caribbean, and African origin comprise 4 percent of the total population. In the 1980s, economic recession and unemployment has fostered competition for jobs, housing, and social services as well as high levels of social tension. Increasing numbers of racial incidents, broad-scale discrimination in housing, and stiffer barriers to entry are becoming common. These problems of a multiracial society are relatively new to Western Europe. They are exacerbated by the ghettolike concentration of nonwhites in the region's largest urban and industrial centers. A recent (1986) study by the city of Dusseldorf, however, pinpoints the importance of Europe's migrant workers to the economic base of Western Europe. The study showed that the industries and public services of Dusseldorf would grind to a halt if the "gastarbeiten," or immigrant workers, withdrew their labor. It would appear that international labor substitution for Europe's "birth dearth" is a permanent—and growing—fact of life if Europe is to sustain its levels of prosperity and economic growth.

The movement of Europeans away from isolated, rural, and upland regions of the Continent to the region's great metropolitan centers and medium-sized cities has rendered Western Europe the most highly urbanized region in the world (Fig. 3.17). European planners must deal with complex core-periphery problems.

The population axis of Western Europe has shifted to the city, leaving less favored agricultural areas behind. Europe's great cities—London, Paris, Rome, Madrid, Hamburg, Berlin, and Vienna—are destination points for rural migrants, foreign immigrants, and new industries. Medium-sized cities in the industrial cores of the English Midlands, the Heavy Industrial Triangle, and the Po Valley of Italy are experiencing sustained population growth, reflecting the mobility of Europeans as they seek jobs, urban amenities, and social services over a broader social space.

Paradoxically, many of Europe's less developed regions have become centers of tourist activity. Tides of tourists and their wealth flood the hotels, restaurants, railroad stations, airports, and highways of Western Europe year round. Over half the European population take their long (four weeks by law in France) holidays away from home each year. Tourists from abroad bring the total to a staggering 189 million vacationers moving freely across the European landscape each year.

Mobility, migration, mass communications, and effective transportation networks are changing the social fabric of Western Europe and reducing the diversity of its cultural landscapes. These forces of modernization are intruding most dramatically on the regional consciousness of more isolated regions where local cultural identity has remained strong. They are also threatening the survival of some of Western Europe's most distinctive cultural groups.

In Wales, the Welsh-speaking region is progressively diminishing as the English language penetrates along the geographic pathways of modernization—coastal and valley towns—and leaves Welsh speakers confined to areas of hilly terrain (Fig. 3.19). Only 20 percent of the Welsh population still speak their native tongue. Welsh nationalists, believing that their language is a surer barrier to cultural

RETREAT OF THE WELSH LANGUAGE

Welsh ("Cymru" in Welsh) is a Celtic language spoken in Wales, a region dominated by the English since the thirteenth century. During the last fifty years, the territorial extent of Welsh language has steadily contracted. Between 1931 and 1971, the number of Welsh speakers declined from 900,000 to less than half a million, less than 20 percent of the 2.8 million people in Wales. Accusing the English of "linguistic imperialism," a Welsh Language Society has been established and the Welsh language has been made coequal under the law. A Welsh nationalist party has played an interesting role in modern British politics. Many believe that Welsh culture and language is doomed in urban Wales—a casualty of a civilization of consumption—and can only survive in isolated villages in the mountains. A similar decline in Celtic languages has occurred in Scotland, Ireland, and French Brittany.

Adapted from: Terry G. Jordan and Lester Rowntree, *The Human Mosaic,* 3rd ed. New York: Harper & Row, 1982, p. 159.

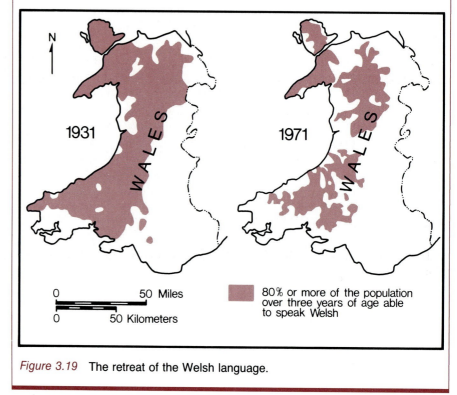

80% or more of the population over three years of age able to speak Welsh

Figure 3.19   The retreat of the Welsh language.

invasion than any fortress or river, have burned down English holiday cottages, established a Welsh language television station, and had Welsh accepted as part of the curriculum in many schools. In Ireland, similar efforts to maintain Celtic culture and language have punctuated the recent cultural history of the country. Cultural identity is a major wellspring of the vicious conflict between Catholics and Protestants in Northern Ireland. In Spain, Basque nationalists have used terror to achieve self-determination. Regional identity in the province of Catalonia is another strong force for separation in Spain.

These dramatic examples of cultural resistance to modern forces expose a subtle, general uneasiness among Western Europeans that they are losing undefined but valuable qualities of land and life—summarized by the French conceptualization of their landscapes as a series of pays—to a consumer society expanding and taking root on European soil. European writers speak of a cultural invasion, of the erosion of centuries-old ways of life, and the destruction of time-tested human values and environmental qualities. Crowded metropolitan centers, polluted industrial districts, despoiled beaches, and abandoned rural ways of life are frequently cited as products of these modern forces. Although Europeans move freely from the land to the city, from one job to another, and from traditional to modern patterns of living, a sense of geographic loss invades recent advances in technology and standards of living.

Environmental Change

The continued growth of the urban core at the expense of the rural periphery in Western Europe has led to dense concentrations of people and industry. Over the last century, the amount of land available per person has been halved, so that today 357 million Europeans live in an area one-third the size of the United States. Twenty-six European metropolitan areas have populations of 1 million or more (Fig. 3.17). Urbanites form better than 70 percent of the populations of the United Kingdom, West Germany, Spain, Italy, Greece, France, the Benelux, and Scandinavia. In Ireland, Austria, Switzerland, and Portugal many still live on the land, but their number dwindles yearly. With nearly 270 million people living in cities and an industrial economy, the environment of Western Europe has serious problems of pollution.

With local exceptions, automobile exhaust has affected the atmosphere of every city in Europe, and use of high-sulfur petroleum from the Middle East for industry and domestic heating has raised air pollution lev-

els. European governments and the EC have enacted a variety of clean air acts.

After a **smog** over London in December 1952 was declared medically responsible for some 3500 to 4000 deaths, public demands for the improvement of air quality began. During the next two decades, a series of clean air acts was put into effect in the United Kingdom to control smoke and levels of particulate emissions. By the 1980s smoke levels had fallen

by more than half and sulfur dioxide concentrations by a third. Winter sunshine levels showed remarkable improvement; the yellow pall of smoke has disappeared from many British industrial centers. West Germany has also enacted an ambitious antipollution bill to accomplish this same purpose, adopting the Japanese formula of forcing polluters to pay for pollution. In addition, France, Belgium, the Netherlands, and Italy have passed various pollution-control

Acid rain is rapidly destroying the forests of northern and central Europe. These striking photos near Göttingen in the Harz Mountains east of the Ruhr were taken ten years apart. Air pollution has inexorably changed this forest into a wasteland.

AIR POLLUTION: AN INTERNATIONAL PROBLEM

To determine how air pollutants disperse across Western Europe, specific units of air from the Ruhr industrial complex in West Germany were tracked every third day for one year. In Figure 3.20, dots show the average distribution of the Ruhr's pollutant "units" after 24 hours and after 60 hours. The large circles enclose one half of all units studied.

The prevailing westerly flow of winds at this latitude carried most Ruhr pollutants eastward in the first 24 hours, directly affecting Eastern Europe; but the air dispersed much more widely after 60 hours. By measuring pollutant flows for the entire year, the broad and complex pattern of dispersal illustrates the difficulties involved in identifying specific source areas of air pollution for such areas as Scandinavia, the Alps, and the Mediterranean.

Adapted from: Simon Harper (trans.), *Acidification Today and Tomorrow.* Stockholm: Ministry of Agriculture, 1982, p. 44.

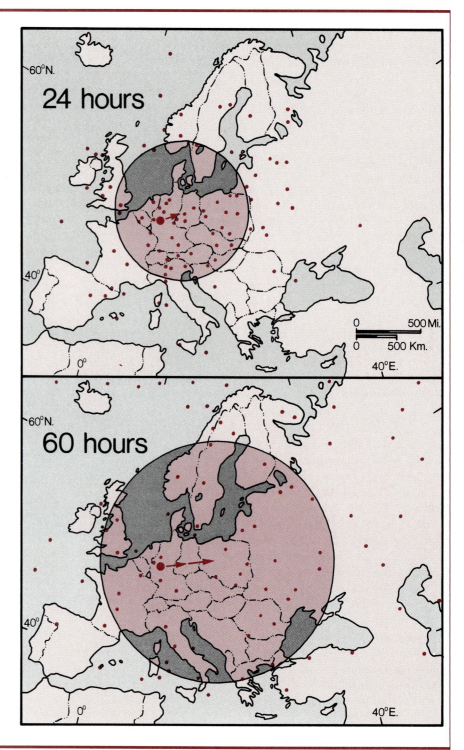

Figure 3.20 Air pollutants carried by wind after 24 hours and after 60 hours.

measures, from limitations on emissions from gas and diesel engines to control of industrial wastes.

The international dimensions of pollution problems in Europe are clearly demonstrated in Scandinavia.

Industrial air pollution from northwestern Europe, particularly the United Kingdom, has increased the level of acid rain that falls in Norway and Sweden (Fig. 3.20). Swedish geographers have been able to trace

the source of high sulfate and acid levels in Scandinavian precipitation to the heavily industrialized areas south and west of the North Sea.

When **temperature inversions** and stagnant air over the Midlands or the

WATER POLLUTION: THE NORTH SEA AND THE

The North Sea and the Mediterranean Sea have become heavily polluted as population and industry have grown along their coasts. Along the shores of the North Sea—near the United Kingdom, Belgium, the Netherlands, West Germany, and southern Norway—domestic sewage, industrial waste and offshore marine traffic have contributed to the environmental decline of this important water body (Fig. 3.22). Britain pours ash waste directly into the North Sea and permits toxic wastes to be burned offshore in "incinerator ships"

In the Mediterranean, the situation is even more critical (Fig. 3.21). Fifteen countries with a combined population of over 370.0 million people line its shores. Over 90 percent of the sewage from these countries flows into the Mediterranean untreated, and industrial pollution and tanker traffic have further damaged water quality. Moreover, unlike the North Sea, the Mediterranean is not flushed by tidal action, evaporation rates are high, and pollutants are driven by the westerly water currents deeper into the basin. Swimming in the "Med" can be serious sport, indeed.

Adapted from: Gunter Weichart, "The North Sea," *Environment,* Vol. 16 (1974), p. 32; OECD, *The State of the Environment in OECD Member Countries.* Paris: OECD, 1979, p. 59.

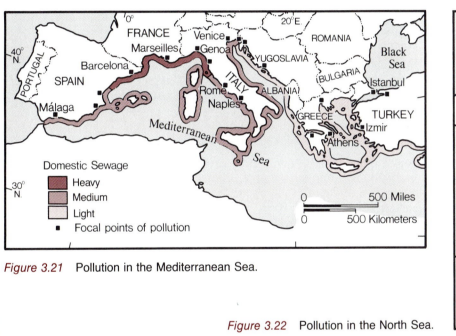

Figure 3.21   Pollution in the Mediterranean Sea.

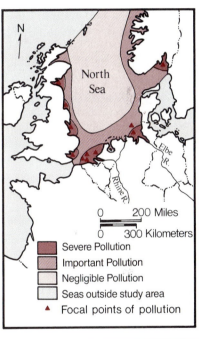

Figure 3.22   Pollution in the North Sea.

Ruhr create masses of pollutant-saturated air, the general westerly circulation of the atmosphere carries this air north and east (Fig. 3.20). Rain with high levels of sulfuric acid falls on the Scandinavian Peninsula, increasing the already high acidity of the soils of Scandinavia. Similarly, an estimated 3.5 million tons of sulfur dioxide fall on West Germany each year, threatening vast areas of forest land. Denuded and dying forests in Eastern Europe are now also being attributed to acid rain. The European Community is attempting to forge a common environmental pol-

icy, but implementation requires unprecedented degrees of cooperation among the small, crowded nations of Western Europe.

Water pollution is even more intense, or at least more apparent, in Western Europe than air pollution (Figs. 3.21, 3.22). Most large cities are located on rivers that provide water for domestic and industrial purposes. As the European population has grown and become more concentrated, urban and industrial pollution has severely damaged the rivers.

In France, the distribution of pol-

luted rivers coincides almost directly with population density. The waters of the Seine, Rhône, Loire, and Garonne as well as the canals of the industrial north are chronically polluted. In the Netherlands, river water can be neither drunk nor used on gardens without filtration. In the United Kingdom, clean water acts have revived the Thames, but many miles of polluted inland waterways remain. Even the picturesque alpine lakes of Switzerland, West Germany, Italy, and France are contaminated by airborne pollutants and by domestic sewage. The fish populations of Lake Geneva and Lake Constance are diminishing rapidly. Measurements at Lake Maggiore in the Italian Alps indicate high levels of nitrates and phosphates. At Lake Lugano, hydrogen sulfide in the water has led to frequent bans on swimming. To the south, the beaches of the Riviera must be regularly sprayed to limit the spread of communicable diseases, such as cholera, and to dissolve the tar dropped by tankers carrying Middle Eastern oil into the tideless Mediterranean Sea (Fig. 3.21).

Some forty international conferences have been held in Europe over the last 100 years to discuss water pollution, many of them concerned with the Rhine River. Despite this attention, pollution in the Rhine has risen with population density and industrial growth, and it now has reached toxic levels. As the Rhine flows northward, it passes through five different countries and a near-continuous band of dense urbanization and heavy industry. Waste water and sewage from the city of Basel in Switzerland and residues from large chemical factories begin the process. At the French border, potash mines around Mulhouse dump tons of salt each year into the Rhine, a primary reason water must be desalinized before agricultural use in the Netherlands. By the time the river reaches Strasbourg, swimming is forbidden. In West Germany, chemical in-

dustries at Ludwigshafen contribute poisonous wastes to the Rhine, and the Neckar River, which joins the Rhine after serving as a sewage disposal system for the cities of Stuttgart and Tübingen, adds more pollutants. At Koblenz, the seat of the international pollution commission, nuclear plants on the banks of the river raise water temperatures and encourage bacterial action, thereby reducing the water's oxygen level. Farther north, industrial wastes from the Lorraine iron mines, the Saar coalfields, and more potash mines pour into the river. Thereafter, the Rhine enters the industrial Ruhr. When it crosses the Dutch border of Emmerich, it is carrying a staggering total of 24 million tons of solid waste a year, 65,753 tons a day.

The Rhine and other rivers from nine European nations ultimately dump their waste materials into the North Sea, one of the most heavily polluted water bodies in the world (Fig. 3.22). Salt from potash mines, phosphates in urban sewage, heavy metal wastes from steel mills, and agricultural pesticides flow into the North Sea in unmodified form. Some 15,000 tons of phosphorus and 60,000 tons of fixed nitrogen reach the North Sea from the east coast of Britain each year. An additional 40,000 tons of phosphorus and 500,000 tons of fixed nitrogen come from the Rhine, Elbe, Weser, and Ems rivers. The Rhine alone contributes 80,000 tons of iron,

20,000 tons of zinc, 6000 tons of manganese, and more than 1000 tons of chromium, nickel, copper, lead, and arsenic. Additional pollutants are introduced by shipping and direct dumping of urban wastes, organic chemicals, and radioactive substances.

Interestingly, the large-scale development of off-shore oil in the North Sea has increased awareness of the potential damage of pollution to marine and coastal **ecosystems.** Because the North Sea is cleansed by currents from the Atlantic circulating around Scotland, pollution is concentrated in the southern portion of the North Sea, the area most heavily used and most densely ringed by population (Fig. 3.22).

Pollution is symptomatic of a deterioration in the quality of the European environment that has paralleled this region's remarkable surge to affluence in the postwar period. Human pressure on picturesque landscapes is severe. Urban congestion, traffic, inadequate housing, and excessive noise are now characteristic of most European metropolises. Yet expanding urban economies continue to attract increasing numbers of people at the expense of rural regions. The changes now occurring in European land and life are rapidly reformulating the nature of the world's initial industrial societies.

NORTH AMERICA

With 5.3 percent of the world's population, North America occupies a fortunate position among the world's peoples. Despite their **agrarian** history, the United States and Canada took on the characteristics of industrial society rapidly. The population of the United States was more urban than rural by 1920; the Canadian population reached the same level by 1931. Agricultural workers as a percentage of the work force have steadily declined in both countries.

In contrast to Europe, however, the North American birth rate has remained relatively higher longer, sustaining levels of natural population growth greater than in other technological countries. With a combined population of 272.2 million, the United States and Canada have, like the Soviet Union, large, sparsely populated areas and small concentrations of densely populated land (Fig. 4.1).

Like other countries in the Technological World, North Americans have high levels of personal income and literacy, very high levels of energy consumption, low death rates, and long life expectancies. The conditions that stimulated industrial growth in North America are similar to those in highly developed regions elsewhere, but they are distinctive in terms of scale and abundance.

The achievement of material abundance has solved most basic problems of human existence in North America. For this reason, North Americans have been able to accommodate many different social questions.

The scale and variety of their resource base and the enormous size of their environment have provided room for dissidents, new lands for the landless, and dynamic opportunities for personal development. Yet North Americans are faced today with highly complex social and economic issues that must be solved within North America as well as in the rest of the world.

The global view now affects many national questions, and many national actions echo throughout the world. Over a quarter of the American economy is now entwined in the international economic system. North American policies on international trade, world energy markets, food, and monetary affairs affect other countries directly. Less directly, national debates on personal freedom, racial harmony, social equality, economic growth, foreign policy, environmental management, and quality of life carry weight in the attitudes and aspirations of many individuals and groups throughout the world. New directions taken in North American society will have impact on both the Technological World and the Developing World.

Although widely criticized as conservative societies, North Americans have traditionally attempted to preserve radical principles—personal freedom, political liberty, and justice. Viewed in a global framework, North American society is at peace, rich, free, well fed, well housed, and healthy. Despite current economic and social difficulties, despite promises unfulfilled, the vitality of North America is intact.

THE WORLD'S FIRST NEW NATIONS

Over the course of 250 years, the societies of the United States and Canada evolved differently from societies in their original homelands in Europe. In the words of the French traveler Alexis de Tocqueville, North Americans were "born free instead of becoming so," and they inhabited "one vast forest in the middle of which they carved some clearings." Struck by America's dynamic mobility, enormous resources, individualism, and faith in progress, de Tocqueville, in 1835, underestimated the difficulties and hazards that faced the pioneers who gave these two democracies form.

During *The Beginnings of European Colonization,* four culture hearths were precariously implanted on the east coast of North America. They were established by people of varied backgrounds and different ambitions, linked only by their willingness to explore the unknown. Over the course of two centuries, the *Population and Economy of Colonial America* expanded significantly as Americans won their independence from Britain and Canadians achieved Dominion status in 1867. Crossing the Appalachians, *Westward Expansion* by pioneers opened up the resources of an extraordinarily rich swath of midlatitude land. The growth of transportation networks led to economic specialization and *The Conquest of a Continent.* After a century of independence, the *Centennial* celebration of freedom in the United States mirrored the emergence of two vibrant, expansive democratic soci-

GEOSTATISTICS

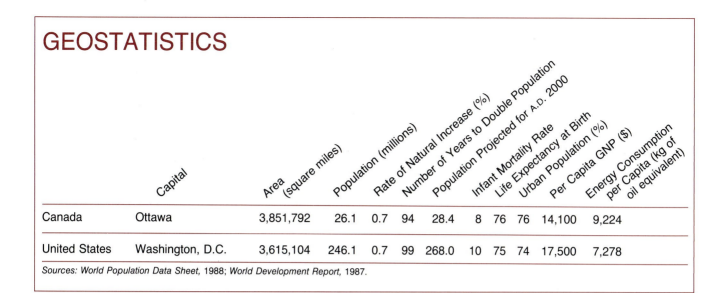

	Capital	Area (square miles)	Population (millions)	Rate of Natural Increase (%)	Number of Years to Double Population	Population Projected for A.D. 2000	Infant Mortality Rate	Life Expectancy at Birth	Urban Population (%)	Per Capita GNP ($)	Energy Consumption per Capita (kg of oil equivalent)
Canada	Ottawa	3,851,792	26.1	0.7	94	28.4	8	76	76	14,100	9,224
United States	Washington, D.C.	3,615,104	246.1	0.7	99	268.0	10	75	74	17,500	7,278

Sources: World Population Data Sheet, 1988; World Development Report, 1987.

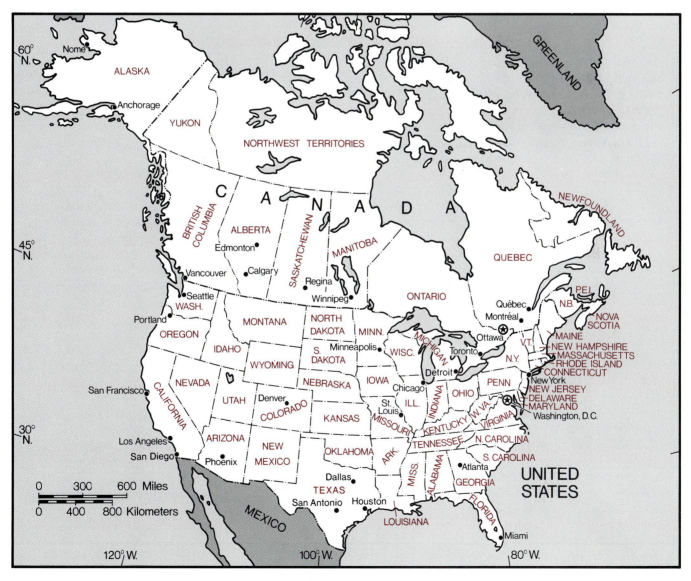

Figure 4.1   Political regions of North America.

eties—the world's first new nations, the United States and Canada.

The Beginnings of European Colonization

The French and the British began to colonize the New World a century after the Spanish and Portuguese had established colonial empires in Latin America. European explorers had groped along the Atlantic coast of North America and were familiar with its outlines. By 1600, explorers had searched in vain for a northwest passage to China, a highway of trade that might bring northern Europe closer to the wealth of the East Indies. Failing that, finding no gold but a continent instead, the explorers who established temporary bases on the Atlantic coast were unable to generate sufficient interest at home to sustain colonial adventures. The geography of North America was too forbidding, and the monarchs of Britain and France were preoccupied with affairs in Europe.

Motives for Colonization

At the beginning of the seventeenth century, new European energies were released to colonize North America. The first spur to colonial development was the hope that American colonies would provide wealth in the form of gold, spices, and raw materials for shipbuilding—tar, pitch, turpentine, and rope—commodities that were in short supply at home. Second, France and Britain wanted to challenge Spanish dominance in the New World. North American colonies, it was argued, could become bases for pirates and privateers to plunder Spanish ships carrying gold and silver from Mexico and Peru back to Europe. A third spur to colonization was high unemployment in England, which had created a new class of urban drifters that posed a threat to law and order. Better for England to let them migrate. Finally, dissident religious minorities seeking liberty to practice their be-

COLONIAL CULTURE HEARTHS

Each of the four North American culture hearths—French Canada, New England, the Middle Colonies, and the South—differed in social origin, economic growth, and environmental setting. For 150 years, except in French Canada, European immigrants were restricted to the Atlantic coast by the densely forested ridges of the Appalachians and were separated from Europe by 3000 miles of ocean.

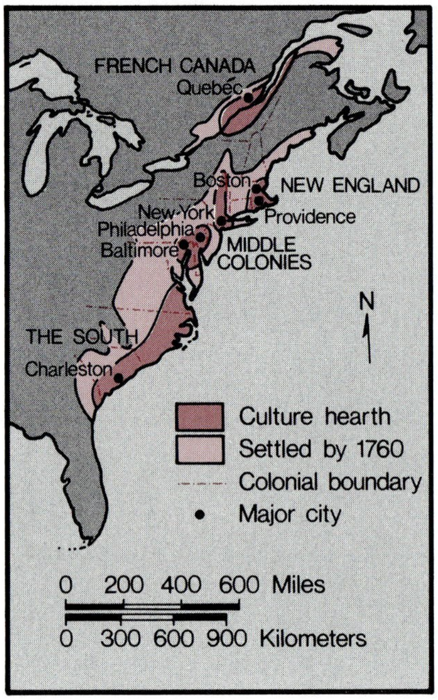

Figure 4.2 The beginnings of European colonization in the seventeenth century.

liefs, adventurous nobles looking for conquests, and families in search of land were disruptive to the established social order in Western Europe. Getting rid of them seemed a good idea.

In the 1600s, therefore, emigrants from Western Europe arrived on the Atlantic coast of North America. Tens of thousands came from England, a trickle from France, a thousand or two from Spain, and a small number from Holland and Portugal. Different motives, different methods of colonization, and different adaptations to the environments of North America produced a variety of ways of life. A new human geography was created by Europeans seeking gold, religious freedom, new prospects, land, and empire. By 1650, four colonial culture hearths appeared on the Atlantic coast in French Canada, New England, the South, and the Middle Colonies (Fig. 4.2).

The Fur Traders of French Canada

The first permanent French settlements in New France (now Canada)

were established at Annapolis Royal (1604) in Nova Scotia and at Québec (1608) by the French explorer, Samuel de Champlain (1567?–1635). Champlain and his successors scouted inland along the St. Lawrence River and the shores of the Great Lakes. The French staked out an elongated New World empire along the glacial waterways that drain the southern rim of the Canadian **Shield.**

It was the discovery of beaver that precipitated a rush of trappers and fur traders into the St. Lawrence Valley. Sixteenth-century French fashion favored beaver pelt, particularly for men's hats. A royal fur company was established that exported as many as 25,000 beaver pelts a year from Canada to France. Montréal, Trois-Rivières, and Québec became **market centers** where fleets of Indian canoes carrying beaver skins converged each spring to trade pelts for pots and pans, guns, blankets, and liquor. As local supplies of beaver were exhausted, French trappers and traders, the **voyageurs,** moved deep in the forests and dealt directly with Indians on their own ground. Thinly scattered across a forest frontier penetrating 2000 miles into the North American interior, the fur traders of New France probably numbered no more than 2000 in 1650.

With the number of English settlers in New England and Virginia increasing rapidly and with British plans for expeditions into Hudson Bay in progress, the French recognized that they had to establish a more substantial presence in North America or face losing their colony. In 1663, Canada became a province of France governed directly by the crown. Enormous grants of land in the more temperate St. Lawrence lowlands were given to feudal lords, seigneurs. It was their responsibility to clear the forests and serve the French crown in time of war. These feudal estates were subdivided and rented out to **tenant** farmers, while the **seigneurs** retained timber rights and the right to draft labor for road building and other public works. People, livestock, and seed were sent out from France to tame the Canadian wilderness.

The **seigneurial** system of landholding created a distinctive cultural landscape in French Canada. To avoid road building, colonists used rivers for transportation. Because taxes were levied on the basis of river frontage, landowners arranged their farms so that as little land as possible bordered the St. Lawrence. Long strips of farm land running back from the river, called **long lots** or seigneuries, came to line the St. Lawrence River and its tributaries.

Despite efforts by France to encourage colonization in Canada, population remained low. Settlement was difficult in this harsh climate, and population grew slowly. By 1750, the 80,000 French who had settled along the St. Lawrence River, the shores of the Great Lakes, and the Mississippi River were flanked by more than 1 million British colonists tightly clustered on the Atlantic **coastal plain.**

Although the French penetration of North America started generally earlier than the English and despite French control of the two major gateways to the American interior, the St. Lawrence and Mississippi rivers, the French population was too thinly scattered over too large an area to hold this vast territory. Britain defeated France and emerged as the primary political power in North America in 1763. English perceptions, political and social institutions, settlement forms, and systems of thought came to dominate the human geography of North America. French Canada was left an island of French culture in an English-speaking continent.

Religious Dissenters in New England

In December 1620, a small group of English religious dissenters, Pilgrims, bound for Virginia, drifted north of their original destination and landed at Plymouth, in what is now Massachusetts. Rather than risk a winter sea voyage south to Virginia, they decided to disembark and established the Plymouth Colony. These Pilgrims had earlier fled from England to Holland to escape religious persecution. Their goal was to create a new settlement where they could live as "a distinct body by themselves." Half the members of the expedition died of starvation and disease in the unexpected cold of that first New England winter. But the Plymouth Colony survived. Additional Protestant religious sects, most notably the Puritans, fled to New England. In twenty years, 25,000 emigrants journeyed from Britain to the new Commonwealth of Massachusetts in search of religious freedom.

This freedom, however, rarely extended beyond members of each individual religious group. Splinter groups left Massachusetts and established new colonies in Rhode Island, Connecticut, New Hampshire, and Maine. Each religious dispute produced a new settlement inhabited by a small, compact cluster of believers. In this fashion, New Englanders created a landscape of tightly organized religious **townships** and superimposed a topography of the mind on the wilderness of New England. Having fled Europe for religious freedom, they never looked back. And this distinguished the earliest settlers of New England from the three other culture hearths on the Atlantic coast of North America.

The typical unit of settlement in New England was a small town—the only Old World village in the United States—inhabited by a single religious congregation. Most of these townships were located in one of the many narrow, protected valleys that trend southward between folds in the Appalachian Mountains. Houses were built close together; public buildings usually consisted of a church, a public meetinghouse, a courthouse, and an inn. Along with the cemetery adjoining the church, the heart of the village was dominated by the greensward of the commons, a common pasture in the center of the town.

In town meetings, citizens debated local issues. A strong tradition of political freedom and majority rule was firmly established. Higher education began with the establishment of Harvard College in 1636, only sixteen years after the landing of the Pilgrims at Plymouth. Rigorous codes of conduct were laid down. Offenders were subjected to public scorn and ridicule in the pillory or the stocks.

Common action arrived at by common consent was an important force that enabled New Englanders to cope with their difficult environment. The coastal plain was narrow, the soils of the interior stony and sandy—a **glacial landscape** of forest and bare rock poorly suited to agriculture. With mammoth labor and unwavering belief, fields were cleared of trees and stones. Clearings originally cultivated by Indians—open fields—were settled. An estimated 85 percent of these early New Englanders became subsistence farmers. They cultivated

Indian crops, such as corn, beans, and squash, as well as European wheat, barley, and rye. Poultry and livestock were imported from Europe. Cod fishing proved a profitable supplement to agriculture, as did fur trading and the export of timber.

A relatively self-sufficient society of free farmers, traders, fisherfolk, and artisans reshaped the landscapes of New England and, on the anvil of this new land, hammered out the values of hard work, thrift, piety, and equality—an **ethos** that played a conspicuous role in the growth of American culture.

The Plantation South

In 1607, a group of about 100 settlers sponsored by the London Company arrived in southeastern Virginia to found Jamestown, the first English settlement in North America. Their goal was to colonize Virginia for commercial purposes, hoping to find mines of gold and silver like those already known in Spanish Peru and Mexico.

Their members were, in the words of one British historian, "ne'er-do-wells and misfits." The contract they signed, requiring seven years of compulsory labor before taking up private land, failed to attract serious farmers and artisans. Furthermore, the company insisted that colonists devote themselves to exotic pursuits, like hunting for gold, silkworm raising, and exploring for a passage to China. Poorly led, the Jamestown settlers established themselves in a malarial lowland and failed to get a first-year crop in the ground. Colonists died from disease, starvation, and Indian raids. By 1622, only one of every three settlers sent over by the London Company was still alive.

What saved the Jamestown colony was tobacco, a New World crop in great demand in Europe. Tobacco provided southern settlers with funds to pay for imported manufactures from Europe, and a rich export trade between Virginia and England ensued. As tobacco colonies prospered, new

grants of land in the South were secured by English aristocrats and merchant companies.

Tobacco flourished in the warm, wet summers and rich soils of both the **tideland** and the inland piedmont. But the labor requirements of tobacco cultivation were high. In England, companies ran advertisements to attract settlers to colonies in Virginia, the Carolinas, and Georgia. When supplies of English indentured servants and laborers fell short, black slaves were imported from Africa. They worked in the tobacco fields, on rich plantations bordering the tidal rivers and freshwater swamps of the southern coast, and in the upland piedmont where **indigo** was grown to provide a blue dye needed by British woolen manufacturers.

The commercial production of tobacco, rice, and indigo had important effects on the development of the southern colonies. Prices of these commodities fluctuated widely, driving small planters into bankruptcy. Moreover, tobacco can quickly exhaust soil fertility. Shifting cultivation was a common practice. Small farmers, lacking sufficient land to rotate cultivation from one field to another, were frequently unable to compete with wealthy planters who had large holdings worked by slaves. As market instability grew and competition became stiffer, the social gulf between landed planters on the **tidewater** and small farmers on the Appalachian piedmont widened. Because planters traded directly with British merchants from their own docks and warehouses on coastal **inlets,** no **mercantile** middle class emerged in Virginia.

Slavery further distorted society in the southern colonies. Government was by the rich, the well born, the propertied, and the able. Schooling for most people was rudimentary and haphazard, but the children of the wealthy were educated by European tutors. More a reflection of the Europe of that time than any other colonial culture hearth, the American

South developed rigid class lines, dependence on agricultural exports, a **dual economy,** and a **dual society.** On the Appalachian frontier, however, society was more egalitarian, and subsistence farmers soon turned their backs on the colonial South and moved west.

Immigrant Farmers in the Middle Colonies

The Middle Colonies—Pennsylvania, New Jersey, New York, Delaware, and Maryland—formed a geographic and social transition zone between the compact religious settlements of New England located in environments of rocky soils and severe winters and the tidewater plantations and piedmont farms of the warm, humid American South. Commercial crops, such as sugar, tobacco, rice, and indigo, were not as easily grown here as in Virginia and the Carolinas, but food grains, like wheat and corn, grew far better on the mid-Atlantic coastal plain than in glaciated New England.

European immigrants of diverse ancestries and faiths came to this temperate environment in the Middle Colonies. Dutch colonists came to New Netherland, or New York, as it became known when the English took control of the colony in 1664. Swedes came to Delaware. Quakers, Mennonites, and Moravians settled in William Penn's community in Pennsylvania. Huguenots and Jews were attracted by the religious tolerance of Lord Baltimore's colony in Maryland. And waves of English, German, Scotch, and Irish settlers were drawn to the rich, open lands of the mid-Atlantic region.

Both northern and southern types of economies developed. Dutch landlords established large estates along the Hudson River, and tobacco plantations were successful in eastern Maryland. But most settlers in the Middle Colonies became self-supporting farmers living on single-family farms dispersed across the countryside—a departure from the

European pattern of clustered village settlement. Education in log-cabin public schoolhouses provided basic reading, writing, and arithmetic to all. Port cities like New York, Philadelphia, and Baltimore became **central places** serving rich agricultural hinterlands.

Differences in faith and background bred tolerance. More balanced and diverse in economy and society than New France, New England, or the South, the Middle Colonies produced self-educated frontiersmen who pioneered the wilderness, earned their livings in agriculture, commerce, and trade, and practiced religious liberty and democracy as we have come to know them.

Population and Economy of Colonial America

In the 1600s, the colonial economy and other aspects of American life lay yet underdeveloped. Boston, New York, and Philadelphia, were active small seaports. Population was sparse and labor continually in short supply. Most colonists were farmers engaged in clearing forests and fields, combating hostile Indians, and bringing the land into productivity. In the 1700s, these tasks were largely accomplished east of the Appalachian Mountains, and populations in the culture hearths of New England, the Middle Colonies, and the South began to increase rapidly.

Population Distribution in 1750

By 1750, an American population of 1.6 million spanned the shores of the Atlantic from Massachusetts to Georgia. Most of these new Americans still lived on the coast, although settlement was beginning to push west-

Port cities on the Atlantic played an important role in the growth of the American economy. Of these, New York City, at the mouth of the Hudson River, was the largest and most important.

ward beyond the Appalachian Mountains. Because increase in population in the colonies resulted largely from high American birth rates, the coastal areas of New England, the Middle Colonies, and the South remained predominantly English in population and culture. But other nationalities, drawn by the attractions of the New World and driven by hardship in Europe, began to migrate, settle, and transform the ethnic map of North America.

Of all coastal regions, the tightly woven social fabric of New England was the most hostile to outsiders. Incoming German, Scottish, and Irish immigrants were deflected southward to other colonies. Maine, Vermont, and New Hampshire were still mostly wilderness.

In the Middle Colonies of New York and New Jersey, the cultural imprint of Europeans from the Germanic states and the Low Countries was strong. Incoming German immigrants bypassed Dutch landholdings in the Hudson River Valley and occupied the northern frontiers of settlement. The most distinctive regional concentration of German immigrants, however, was in Pennsylvania, where a third of the colony's rural population were popularly called the Pennsylvania Dutch (from "deutsch," meaning German). Moving inland, German settlers also occupied the rich farmlands of the interior valleys, a 600-mile-long band of German settlement in the shadow of the Appalachians.

As more German colonists settled in the South, English settlers began to fear that they would be culturally engulfed. Highland Scots settled central Georgia, but most immigrants from Britain in the mid-1700s were Irish and Scotch-Irish (from Northern Ireland) settlers. Flinty and aggressive, solitary types, these new arrivals populated the back country of the Appalachian frontier and gained fame as hunters, trappers, and Indian fighters. The backbone of plantation agriculture in the South, however, was formed by 300,000 black slaves.

On the eve of the American Revolution, only 60 percent of the colonial population was English; 14 percent was Scottish or Scotch-Irish, and 9 percent was German. As the American patriot Thomas Paine observed in his pamphlet *Common Sense*, "Europe, and not England, is the parent country of America." He forgot Africa. In 1776, 2.7 million people inhabited coastal America—a fifth of them African, a smaller number native Indian, and the remainder whites. They were people with diverse languages and backgrounds, thinly scattered over 200,000 square miles of organized territory.

The Growth of Transatlantic Trade

With a growing population and an expanding agricultural economy, colonial America emerged as an active center of transatlantic commerce in the 1700s. Of the twenty largest cities in North America, nineteen were ports. Each of these ports specialized in products reflecting the economy of their hinterlands and the environmental diversity of the Atlantic seaboard.

In New England, about a quarter of the population depended on nonagricultural pursuits such as fishing, lumbering, and trade. Farms in this difficult environment produced little to export, so the region imported a considerable part of its grain from the Middle Colonies. But the sea proved a profitable alternative for New Englanders. The fish catch from the waters off the coast of Newfoundland and the Grand Banks was larger than that of the North Sea. In the 1700s, New England ports were exporting tons of fish to southern Europe and the West Indies.

Related New England industries were based on forest products principally used in shipbuilding. Shipyards dotted the coast from Maine to Philadelphia, and by the outbreak of the Revolutionary War, over a third of Britain's ships were made in America. Tapping the interior forests along the entire coast, the colonies exported timber for masts, lumber, and barrel staves to Europe, which was rapidly becoming **deforested.** Naval stores, like turpentine, tar, and rosin were additional exports, as was iron produced from a growing number of forges distributed from Pennsylvania to Massachusetts. According to one estimate, North America in the 1770s produced one seventh of the world's iron.

The Middle Colonies produced a large exportable surplus of food. Wheat, bread flour, flaxseed, corn, beef, and pork were shipped to Europe in 1770. Farther south, in Maryland and Virginia, tobacco was the principal export product. In the Carolinas and Georgia, rice and indigo sustained plantation society (Fig. 4.3).

Transatlantic trade tripled between 1750 and 1775, although the value of colonial exports never kept up with the price of imported manufactures from Europe. American exports, however, began to play a key role in some European economies. By the beginning of the American Revolution, it was apparent that North America had a rich and diverse resource base.

Commercial relationships between England and America were clearly defined under the policy of **mercantilism.** The colonies produced raw materials in return for manufactures from Europe. Manufacturing in America was actively discouraged by the British. Taxes were levied on imports, and all European goods sold to the colonies had to be sent through Britain. These restrictions would certainly have hampered a more complex American economy, but the American economy was still relatively simple—it was agrarian from New England to Georgia. Mutual needs kept conflict to a minimum.

COLONIAL TRADING PATTERNS

Colonial America increasingly based its prosperity on transatlantic trade. Overall, this trade amounted to an exchange of New World raw materials and foodstuffs for manufactures from Europe.

The most famous trading pattern was the **triangular trade,** which involved the shipment of distilled rum and iron from New England and the Middle Colonies to West Africa, where these goods were exchanged for African slaves, who, in turn, were brought to the Caribbean and the American South for sale. In the New World, slaves were exchanged for the molasses and sugar, which were distilled into rum in New England. The cycle was profitable in three locations with three commodities.

Adapted from: Max Savelle, *A History of Colonial America,* 3rd ed. New York: Dryden Press, 1973, p. 526.

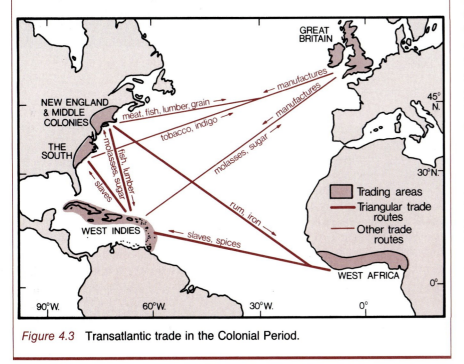

Figure 4.3 Transatlantic trade in the Colonial Period.

Besides, English administrators were notoriously incompetent, so that merchants and business people could generally do as they pleased.

Independence

The situation changed, however, after the successful defeat of the French by British and colonial troops in the French and Indian War (1758–1763). Britain had gained half a continent, but the cost of the war doubled Britain's national debt. From the British point of view, it seemed only right that the colonies should pay part of this financial burden. In 1763, the year the war ended, the British enacted a series of tax measures toward this purpose. The Americans, however, viewed the war against the French as a means of enlarging British territory. Why, then, should Americans pay Britain's debt?

Tensions between crown and colony intensified. In Virginia, Patrick Henry asserted that Britain had no right to tax the colonies at all. Thomas Paine challenged loyalists to the crown to "show a single advantage that this continent can reap by being connected with Great Britain." In Massachusetts, tons of tea were dumped in Boston Harbor, and battle was joined at Lexington and Concord in 1776.

In England, George III opted for conflict rather than conciliation. The war lost, loyalists fled north to Canada and gave root to the proud independence Canadians maintain with respect to the United States today. Britain had underestimated the competitive, individualistic living that characterized its New World descendants and never understood the degree to which an ocean separated the two cultures. As the British geographer James Watson notes: "Few places or times offered more freedom than North America, and few peoples carried freedom so far."

Westward Expansion

After independence, Americans turned to the West as an outlet for growth and development. No longer hemmed in by the Appalachian Mountains and no longer pinned to the sea as a coastal extension of European colonization, settlers swept into the interior plains of North America. As a society, Americans had a bent toward migration and movement, always attracted by greener pastures, better soils, and greater opportunities.

The pace of westward expansion was rapid, and in three generations, the conquest of the West was over. Individuals, families, and small groups—largely on their own initiative—built homes in the wilderness, harnessed the resources of a continent, forged the territorial outlines of modern America, and created the ethos of freedom, individualism, and self-sufficiency that remains deeply rooted in modern American culture.

Pioneering became a common experience. Pioneers moved out onto the vast interior plains of the conti-

Americans enveloped a continent as wagon trains of pioneers swept westward across the Central Plains.

nent. They crossed the Rocky Mountains, which some advocated as an ideal western border for the United States because it stood like "a Chinese Wall"—an impregnable barrier. Everywhere the frontier outpaced the law. In the resulting chaos of rapid geographic expansion, vast herds of buffalo were exterminated, American Indians were decimated or relegated to reservations, and forests were leveled.

Open land, considered an American birthright, was added in great chunks—the Louisiana Territory, Texas, California, and New Mexico—any one of them as large as a substantial European country. The new nation, although yet barely formed, doubled and tripled in size until it stretched from ocean to ocean.

The Moving Frontier

At the close of the Revolution, few Americans knew what lay beyond the Allegheny Mountains, but soon Scotch-Irish and German settlers began to penetrate the region. They carved landscapes of small farms out of towering forests and established small towns spaced along primitive roads and trails.

A new human geography began to take shape. Immigrants, escaping the feudal regime of the plantation South and the religious rigidity of New England, spread westward into Ohio, Kentucky, and Tennessee to carve out farmsteads. Diffusion across the new West was sporadic and irregular. Settlers generally followed rivers in search of fertile land, bypassing more rugged terrain that was occupied later. Indian resistance was fierce, but settlers continued to come, pouring through gaps in the Appalachian Mountains to plant corn patches in the forest and live in iso-

lated log-cabin **homesteads** in the wilderness.

In the frontier environment, settlers developed a new sense of social and economic independence. The frontier experience bred conflict between the settled areas of the East and the rapidly unfolding West. In the Carolinas, differences between the backcountry settlers of the piedmont and the gentry of the coast nearly led to civil war. In Pennsylvania, government taxation of corn whiskey led to the unsuccessful Whiskey Rebellion of 1794—an uprising that re-

Westward expansion enveloped a continent, but it did so a mile at a time. Here, the first railroad train (accompanied by wagons) heads north from Orlando to Perry near Stillwater, Oklahoma, on September 16, 1893.

THE SPATIAL ORGANIZATION OF WESTERN LAND

The organization of western lands into civil divisions began in 1785 with the survey of the Old Northwest—the territory lying north and west of the Ohio River. In Figure 4.4, (A) shows Michigan and Wisconsin organized by two surveyor's reference lines: (1) an east-west base line, or as it was known, the "geographer's line," corresponding to one degree of latitude; and (2) lines of **longitude** or **meridians** running north-south. Next, (B) enlarges the perspective to show the organization of the land into townships and ranges. The north-south location of each area is identified as a township, counted off in sets of four, north and south of the base line. The east-west location is specified by range, counted in sets of six, east and west of the meridian. Each **civil division,** in this case the township, therefore, is identified by its north-south and east-west location in relation to a base line and a meridian. Here in (B), township *A* is labeled T 1 N, R 1 E—in the first row north of the base line (Township 1 North) and in the first tier east of the meridian (Range 1 East). In (C), township *A*, 6-miles square, is further divided into thirty-six sections. In (D), one section of township

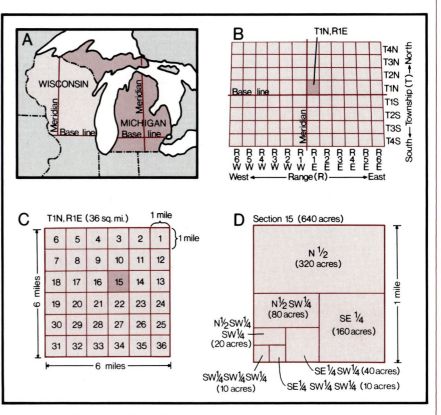

Figure 4.4 The township and range system.

A, section 15, is 1-mile square as are all 36 sections in the township. It is shown subdivided into many units like those settled by individual families and worked as new farms in the western landscape.

Adapted from: Arthur N. Strahler, *Introduction to Physical Geography,* 3rd ed. New York: John Wiley, 1973, p. 447.

quired a larger army than George Washington had ever commanded during the Revolutionary War. Similar friction existed between coastal and upstate New York, Boston and western Massachusetts, the plantation South and the small farms of the Appalachian piedmont. However much historians would later admire frontier men and women, many leaders of American society in Boston, New York, Philadelphia, and Charleston considered them unruly, uneducated people, prone to violence, and were delighted to see them leave.

The western lands soon proved to be too valuable to be left to random pioneer settlement. In 1802, the area between the Appalachian Mountains and the Mississippi River was declared public land. A federal plan, the United States rectangular survey or **township and range** system, was initiated to regularize the geography of settlement (Fig. 4.4). However, the warrant system, based on landmarks and property lines or **metes and bounds,** was already in use in many areas of the Appalachian frontier and the South (Fig. 4.5). Under this system, pioneers received rights to new land and traveled into the interior settling wherever they wished. The North, however, followed the more organized rectangular system

of land development, with tier after tier of townships planned to regulate the western advance into the trans-Appalachian interior.

Ultimately, the patterns of the North prevailed. All public lands were divided by the United States rectangular survey into townships 6-miles square, which, in turn, were subdivided into thirty-six **sections** of 640 acres each. Every second township was sold as a unit to groups of settlers, reflecting the community tradition of New England. The others were auctioned off by single sections, a compromise to the southern tradition of individual pioneers. In this way, a geometrical grid was imposed

THE IMPACT OF SURVEY SYSTEMS ON THE CULTURAL LANDSCAPE

A century and a half after the original surveyors completed their work, two environmentally similar areas demonstrate the persistent impact of the township and range and the metes and bounds systems of land division on field patterns and property lines. The distinctive human geometry of these systems is a permanent and prominent feature of the **cultural landscape.**

Source: Norman J. W. Thrower, *Original Survey and Land Subdivision: A Comparative Study of the Form and Effect of Contrasting Cadastral Surveys.* Chicago: Rand McNally, 1966, pp. 40, 63, 84, (AAG Monograph No. 4).

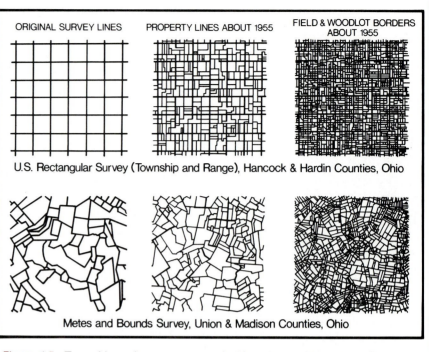

ORIGINAL SURVEY LINES — PROPERTY LINES ABOUT 1955 — FIELD & WOODLOT BORDERS ABOUT 1955

U.S. Rectangular Survey (Township and Range), Hancock & Hardin Counties, Ohio

Metes and Bounds Survey, Union & Madison Counties, Ohio

Figure 4.5 Township and range compared with metes and bounds in Ohio.

---

on the new lands east of the Mississippi. After the Louisiana Purchase in 1803, public lands were extended to the Rocky Mountains. With the acquisition of Oregon and California, the geometry of the township and range system was impressed on the American landscape from the Appalachians to the Pacific coast.

Between 1790 and 1820, the population of the United States tripled to 9.6 million and the area of the country doubled to nearly 1.8 million square miles. In this period, almost all population growth in the United States was due to **natural increase.** By 1840, the population of the United States reached 17.1 million, and hordes of settlers continued to roll westward.

An Irish journalist, John L. O'Sullivan, captured the mood of the new nation when he referred to America's "manifest destiny to overspread the continent." It was an idea of powerful geographic logic that subdued those who believed that the Great Plains west of the Mississippi consisted of the "Great American

Desert" and that the Far West was too remote to be governed effectively.

Stage by stage, westward expansion enveloped the continent. Statehood was accorded to Texas in 1845, Iowa in 1846, and California in 1850. In 1853, the Gadsden Purchase of the Gila River country of southern Arizona and New Mexico rounded out the frontiers of the continental United States. In Canada, the union of the provinces of New Brunswick and Nova Scotia with Québec and Ontario in 1867 marked the beginnings of nationhood and provided a method for **assimilating** the western provinces. While the Spanish dominions in the New World became fragmented into many small new countries, the United States and Canada governed regions continental in scope, a geographic key to the markedly different evolutions of North America and South America.

Spatial Integration

The enormous land acquisitions and westward expansion of the United

States and Canada posed difficult problems of communications and transport. The demand for food and cotton in urban America and Europe encouraged westward expansion to open up new lands for agriculture. But in 1800, only farmers located near seaport cities or on navigable streams and rivers could transport their grain, cotton, tobacco, or timber to market. Overland transport was so expensive that the cost of moving goods 30 miles over inland roads was roughly equal to prices paid for shipping goods 3000 miles across the Atlantic. Small wonder that pioneers became **subsistence farmers** and that Americans remained pinned to the Atlantic coast for nearly two centuries. Even along the eastern seaboard, roads were inadequate. Indeed, news of the signing of the Declaration of Independence in Philadelphia in 1776 took twenty-nine days to reach Charleston, South Carolina.

In the first half of the nineteenth century, efforts began to improve transportation systems (Fig. 4.6). Private companies as well as state and

THE CONQUEST OF DISTANCE

The North American interior became accessible in the first half of the nineteenth century as turnpikes, canals, and railroads provided the technology to conquer distance. These contour maps of overland travel times in 1800, 1830, and 1857 illustrate how quickly the barriers to communication were reduced in a brief fifty-year period.

Adapted from: Charles O. Paullin and John K. Wright, *Atlas of the Historical Geography of the United States*. Washington, D.C. and New York: Carnegie Institution and New York Geographical Society, 1932.

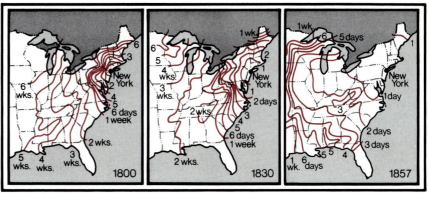

Figure 4.6 The impact of transport on travel time: 1800, 1830, 1857.

provincial governments built paved turnpikes to link the cities of the East Coast with the developing interior. The most ambitious of these was the National Road, a federal highway that ran from Cumberland, Maryland, westward to Vandalia, Illinois. These turnpikes reduced the cost of short hauls, but given the long distances involved, roads could not effectively connect the agricultural lands of the interior with population centers on the coast.

More important was the steamboat, which enabled goods to be transported thousands of miles along inland waterways. By 1820, 60 steamboats were plying the Mississippi river system; by 1860, there were more than 1000. Goods moved five times faster on steamboats than in wagons or on keelboats. Downstream moving costs were reduced by a factor of four; upstream costs, by ten or even twenty. The ability to transport goods to market was vastly extended by these steamboats. They opened the central part of the United States and, to a lesser extent, central Canada to commercial agriculture and industry.

Canals were also built to facilitate the movement of goods. The first of these was the Erie Canal, a 364-mile-long ditch finished in 1825 that linked the Hudson River with Lake Erie.

Thomas Jefferson had labeled the project "a little short of madness," but grain and other foodstuffs were soon flowing south and east in exchange for manufactures from New York City. People could now travel from New York to Detroit for less than $10. A water road to the west had been opened. The volume of traffic on the Erie Canal was so heavy that tolls paid the entire cost of construction in only nine years. Pennsylvania built a competing canal system linking Philadelphia with Pittsburgh. In the Middle West, canals joined the Ohio and Mississippi river systems with the Great Lakes.

The steam railroad, however, provided the most successful means of conquering the continental dimensions of the United States and Canada (Fig. 4.6). In the 1830s, a few minor railroad lines were built outward from coastal cities. Because of topography, however, they were unable to develop deep inland connections. By 1840, the United States had 3300 miles of rail in operation. But over the next two decades, the railroad network of the eastern part of the country grew to more than 30,000 miles in 1860.

All the major market cities of the North were linked by rail by 1860. Trunk lines spanned the Appalachians to connect the East and the

Middle West. Chicago became the railroad center of the continent. Over 20 million acres of public land were given to private companies building railroads.

The magnitude of this effort transformed the North American economy. Goods that had taken more than 50 days to move from Cincinnati to New York in 1817 could be hauled by rail in 6 days in 1860. Granted access to world markets by these gleaming lines of iron, farmers in the fertile prairies of the upper Mississippi Valley and adjacent regions in Canada as well as cotton planters in the interior South expanded production enormously. America became the world's single greatest source of food. Its railroad system brought American farmers closer to Europe. American wheat was baked in German bakeries, and American bacon was the breakfast of British clerks. Back home, America became a nation of movers endlessly and anxiously catching trains whose schedules were, their boosters claimed, "as inexorable as fate."

The Conquest of a Continent

At midcentury, the United States and, to a lesser extent, Canada, were growing and changing rapidly. A continental economy was integrating the regional diversity of North America's resource base. Improvements in transport bound previously relatively independent and isolated states together. This encouraged regional economic specializations that in turn fostered spectacular increases in commercial agricultural and industrial production. Frontier areas of settlement were drawn into this economic orbit on the basis of what they could contribute to the national economy.

A number of distinct economic regions began to emerge: the Industrial Northeast, the Agricultural South, the Middle West, Oregon and California, Mormon Utah, and the Great Plains.

In the Northeast, the Industrial Revolution had crossed the Atlantic, and a landscape of mills and factories was recreated in North America. In the South, cotton replaced tobacco as the principal agricultural commodity, and the slave population swelled to meet labor demands on a growing number of plantations.

East of the Mississippi, in what is today the Middle West, the agricultural frontier marched steadily westward, and the rich soil resources of the continental heartland were exploited. At the Great Plains, this steady advance faltered. In the 1840s, daunted by a treeless expanse of **prairie,** wagon trains of settlers set out for fertile, forested lands in the Far West, in Oregon, and in California. They were soon joined by thousands of fortune hunters lured westward by the discovery of gold in California. En route, many of these travelers passed through the Mormon colony established in Utah. Finally, the "last West," the Great Plains, was occupied by cattle ranchers and farmers. Remnants of the American Indian population were destroyed or interned, and the shape of the nation was complete.

The Industrial Northeast

The growing accessibility of southern and western markets for manufactured goods encouraged the development of industry in the northern United States. As early as 1850, 65 percent of all industrial goods in the United States were produced in the northeastern states.

There were three reasons for this rapid growth. First, Americans in the North were remarkably receptive to technological change. Yankee ingenuity was no idle boast. Visiting Europeans noticed the high level of education among working folks in the North, their liking for invention, and their desire to improve traditional procedures. Second, the opening of the western prairies made grain agriculture in New England unprofitable. The natural environment in New England was so poor for farming that only specialized dairy and market garden agriculture catering to the needs of local urban centers could prosper. New England farmers left the land. Some traveled west; others turned to factory work. Finally, because the cities of the eastern seaboard had been **entrepôts** of transatlantic trade for more than a century, New Englanders had considerable expertise in commerce. This initial commercial advantage accelerated as the natural resources of the West were harnessed and cotton production expanded in the South. Cities in the North, therefore, sprouted agricultural processing industries, such as flour mills, textile factories, leather works, and distilleries. Goods sold in domestic and world markets, although produced in the American interior, were processed in the cities of the Northeast.

The textile industry was the first to mechanize. Samuel Slater opened the first mill in 1790 in Pawtucket, Rhode Island. Soon cotton and woolen mills sprang up throughout southern New England. The first large-scale textile mills were constructed at Waltham and Lowell in Massachusetts, where young farm women provided a cheap and reliable labor force. These were among the first factories in the world to combine all textile operations under one roof.

Meanwhile, iron production was concentrating in Pennsylvania, a region endowed with rich resources of iron, coal, and wood. By 1860, Pennsylvania produced half the **pig iron** in the United States, and Pennsylvania coal fueled the expansion of New England factories. During the 1850s, New England manufactures grew 62 percent in value, compared with 7 percent in the Middle Atlantic region and 10 percent in the West. An industrial heartland was taking shape in the northeastern United States. In the opinion of the French traveler Alexis de Tocqueville, "the pursuit of industrial callings" was the psychic drive that motivated the American people.

The Agricultural South

In the South, large-scale agriculture was the economic base of the region. Early on, Southern agriculturalists concentrated on the production of cash crops for export. They had established plantations over large areas that extended from Maryland to Georgia. By 1800, however, this agricultural economy was in serious decline. More than half the population of Virginia, Maryland, and North Carolina depended on tobacco cultivation, and thousands of acres of once fertile land were being ruined by this soil-exhausting crop. Plantations were being abandoned. Gullied, brush-strewn, exhausted fields came to line the long-cultivated banks of the Atlantic tidewater. The price of slaves fell, and substantial numbers of black people were freed. Tobacco growing, which had sustained the early expansion of the southern economy, was failing.

What revived the faltering southern agricultural economy was the cotton gin, invented by the Yale graduate Eli Whitney. This machine solved the problem of separating the seeds of short-staple cotton from its precious fibers. Demand for cotton in the mills of New England and industrialized Europe was high, but removing the seeds from short-staple cotton by hand was so laborious that it took an able-bodied hand a full day

This cotton plantation on the Mississippi River produced America's most important export product in the nineteenth century. This lithograph vividly portrays the technology, transport, labor, and social structure of the plantation South.

to deseed a single pound. The cotton gin, a simple hand-driven machine, made it possible to clean cotton fifty times faster.

This problem solved, cotton could be grown profitably wherever rainfall was more than 24 inches a year and the **growing season** was longer than 200 days—in other words, throughout the entire South. Cotton cultivation spread inland throughout Georgia and the Carolinas, engulfed the rich black soils of central Alabama and northern Mississippi, and extended westward through Louisiana into Texas, where unreliable rainfall formed its natural limit. The forests of these regions, some of the densest in the nation, were systematically felled. Cotton production soared. By 1820, 400,000 bales (each weighing about 450 pounds) were produced each year. On the eve of the Civil War, this figure had risen to 4 million bales a year.

By the 1850s, cotton was king in the South. It was the most prosperous and dynamic element in the export economy of the United States. The agricultural South had blossomed into a 1000-mile-wide land-scape of cotton, 1 million square miles of raw wealth that produced three quarters of the world's cotton and two thirds of the exports of the United States. Vessels from Europe and New England landed at ports from Charleston to New Orleans to purchase bales of cotton for the mills of the industrial world, trading cheap cloth, diverse manufactured goods, and the luxury products of the age in exchange for this valuable raw material.

To the west, the steamboats that plied the Mississippi hauled cargoes of raw sugar from Louisiana northward to Saint Louis and Cincinnati to exchange for cheap corn, hogs, and vegetables because the cotton lands in the South were too valuable to be planted in food crops. Cheap food from the Central Plains made it possible for planters to keep their best land in continuous cotton cultivation. In less accessible and poorer areas in the upland South, land was still devoted to wheat, corn, and livestock production to feed local populations.

The pressure on the South was relentless: no matter how much cotton was produced, prices remained high, profits substantial, and the demand of northern mills insatiable. Something like the earlier triangular trade of the Atlantic developed, drawing the regional economies of the United States closer together: southern cotton flowed northward; northern manufactures traveled south and west; and western food went north and south. Basic to the structure of this triangular economic exchange were the legions of slaves who labored in the cotton fields down South.

The expansion of cotton cultivation led to a revival of slavery (Fig. 4.7). Earlier, slavery had become a declining, stagnant institution. But cotton changed all that. One field hand was needed for every 5 acres, so the demand for slaves soared. As the world looked on in fascination, a quarter of the United States became the world's premier commercial cotton farm. In a nation devoted to freedom and equality, the American South became the last stronghold of slavery, an institution already deemed barbaric in other technological societies.

The number of slaves in the South increased to 4 million in 1860, principally as a result of natural increase. Prices paid for slaves soared, reaching $1800 for a prime field hand (a figure equivalent in modern dollars to the price of a tractor). Slavery again became big business. Trainloads of blacks were illegally shipped from the worn-out tobacco-growing regions of Virginia and the Carolinas to the new cotton and rice fields of Alabama, Mississippi, Louisiana, and Texas. Free blacks from as far north as New York and New Jersey were trapped by slavers and transported to southern markets. It was a cruel and brutal business, frowned on by the best people and managed by the most depraved, but patronized by all who needed labor.

Conditions of life for southern slaves varied from one plantation to the next and from region to region. Conflicting accounts abound. Some describe whippings, brandings, and sadistic sexual abuse. More accurate is the picture of a wretched, insecure life of poverty described in Harriet Beecher Stowe's *Uncle Tom's Cabin*. The sheer monetary value of slaves, however, tempered mistreatment: maiming a slave lowered the price, imprisonment meant no work, and short rations impaired health.

There were revolts. In 1831, the visionary Nat Turner led a slave insurrection in Virginia. In 1845, 75 unarmed slaves from southeastern Maryland tried to fight their way to freedom in Pennsylvania but were rounded up and shot 20 miles north of Washington, D.C. Spurred by fear, southern states passed laws against blacks and, except in New England, black people could not vote, testify in court, intermarry with whites, get an education, or hold a meeting. With 40 percent of the South's 1860 population of 9 million enslaved, one disgusted Virginian proclaimed that "the land of Washington, Jefferson, and Madison had become the Guinea of the United States."

On the eve of the Civil War, the economy of the South was overwhelmingly agricultural. The im-

COTTON AND SLAVES, 1800–1860

Between 1800 and 1860, cotton production (Fig. 4.7a), and the number of slaves (Fig. 4.7b) in the American South increased dramatically. By 1860, the major areas of cotton production (Fig. 4.7c) correlated with the distribution of slaves (Fig. 4.7d). Concentrations of slaves were also found in coastal Texas, where sugar was the principal plantation crop; the Mississippi Delta, where sugar and rice were grown; and the coastal fringe of South Carolina and Georgia, also major rice-producing areas.

Adapted from: John A. Garraty, *The American Nation: A History of the United States to 1877.* New York: Harper & Row, 1971, p. 267 (Fig. 4.7a, 4.7b). Richard Hofstadter, William Miller, and Daniel Aaron, *The United States: The History of a Republic.* Englewood Cliffs, N.J.: Prentice-Hall, 1967, p. 349 (Fig. 4.7c, 4.7d).

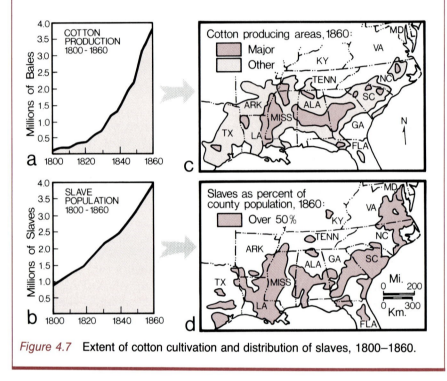

Figure 4.7 Extent of cotton cultivation and distribution of slaves, 1800–1860.

mediate profits from tobacco, rice, sugar, and cotton were higher than profits from industrial ventures, causing most southern capital to be invested in land and slaves. Levels of industrialization and urbanization, therefore, were low. Those few people with industrial interests, men like Cyrus McCormick, moved north because manufacturing was viewed as sordid and dirty in the South. The single town of Lowell, Massachusetts, had more textile mills than the entire South in 1860.

At least partly for these reasons, planter families who profited most

from the plantation system set the cultural tone for the entire region, although they formed less than 1 percent of the South's population. Fewer than 2000 of these masters owned as many as 100 slaves. At least three quarters of the white population had no slaves at all.

Most southerners were in fact poor, subsistence farmers who cultivated corn, cereal grains, sweet potatoes, and sorghum. They lived on small holdings tucked between cotton plantations in the lowlands and were concentrated in the Upland South. In the mountains, these small farmers, called hillbillies, formed a proud and distinctive group. Socially below them, the poor white trash or crackers, as they were variously known, were a class of illiterate victims of parasitic and nutritional diseases. These people became the most vigorous and embittered defenders of slavery—their color being their one source of pride and self-esteem.

Virtually all southerners aspired to the chivalrous code of the gentry and the romantic mystique of plantation life. Most obeyed the emotional, authoritarian preaching of diverse Protestant sects and shared a coherent, unified regional culture. It was this southern white culture—its moral attitudes, literature, language, and sense of tragedy—that was so disastrously and valiantly defended in the Civil War. Pitting a population of 9 million against the North's 22 million, southerners fought for four years with verve, courage, and brilliance in a war for southern independence. Short of soldiers, supplies, and resources, the South battled to certain destruction.

The Middle West

While industry flourished in the North and cotton in the South, manifest destiny was being converted into a reality in the American West. The impulse to settle open land and a prevailing optimism that the future offered great opportunities propelled people westward. They went by the thousands—farmers, miners, adventurers, entrepreneurs, religious groups, and ragged regiments of immigrants from Europe. The migration moved with speed and force, a headlong rush of Americans to little-known, diverse environments stretching from the Appalachian Mountains to the Pacific Ocean.

Between 1800 and 1830, settlers poured through gaps in the Appalachian Mountains into the Susquehanna Valley of Pennsylvania, the Mohawk and Genesee valleys of New York, and onto the rolling hill country of southern Ohio, Indiana, and

Illinois beyond the Appalachians—a region known as the Old Northwest.

Isolated clearings and wilderness farms soon gave way to organized commercial agriculture. The eastern forest was hacked away by an avalanche of new settlers. On turnpikes, steamboats, canals, and railroads, streams of wheat, flour, corn, pork, and beef flowed eastward and south from this fertile interior to seaboard cities, southern plantations, and European markets.

Towns sprang up to process the agricultural surplus of this lush land and to serve the needs of its growing rural population. Cincinnati, Saint Louis, and Chicago grew rapidly. Railroad companies and land speculators sold millions of acres to eastern farmers and immigrants with stories of cornstalks as large as tree trunks and cucumber vines that grew fast enough to strangle the unwary.

Soon agricultural settlements of English, Welsh, German, and Norwegian pioneers dotted the Upper Midwest. With land to spare and labor rare, each state attracted new settlers with claims of having the "greatest tract of fertile land on the surface of the globe." Other resources were also developed—lead mining in Missouri and southern Wisconsin, copper mining in Michigan, and iron mining near Pittsburgh and later along the far shores of Lake Superior.

As the agricultural frontier edged westward onto the prairie fringes of the unforested Great Plains, farmers faced a new set of environmental problems. The thick, tough, root-matted grassland soils of the prairie required a plow drawn by as many as fourteen oxen to cut and turn the turf. Professional land breakers with massive plows had to be hired at considerable expense. Poorer folk used sledgehammers and axes. Timber for building and for fuel was scarce. So were sources of water. There were no acorns and nuts to feed the hogs, and having carved their way through 1000 miles of forest, many settlers

viewed land without trees with considerable suspicion.

Yet the richness of the soils on the margins of the Great Plains was so great that even with the tools of the day, which limited the amount of land a farm family could cultivate to 40 acres, this region produced agricultural surpluses. Mastery of this environment, however, was accomplished not by manpower but by machines; between 1840 and 1860, the Middle West began to emerge as the breadbasket of America.

In the 1850s, John Deere, an Illinois blacksmith, produced 13,000 steel plows a year that were light enough to sling over the shoulder, yet could cut clean, deep furrows into the prairie soils. At the same time, Cyrus McCormick began to manufacture mechanical reapers in Chicago that cut the cost and labor of harvesting by a third. Secretary of State William H. Seward, who later stirred controversy by purchasing Alaska, credited reapers with pushing the farming frontier westward at a rate of 30 miles a year.

Binders, threshers, and other farm machines were rapidly developed and used; these inventions produced a golden torrent of grain. Even at the height of the Civil War, with large numbers of soldiers at war, the productivity of Midwestern agriculture was so great that the United States exported 140 million tons of grain.

Oregon and California

As grain farmers edged onto the eastern margins of the Great Plains, other Americans set their eyes on more distant horizons—the Pacific shores of Oregon and California. Trappers, fur traders, and mountaineers had come to know parts of this region. When the Lewis and Clark expedition opened up the Oregon Trail in 1804–1805, the Far West was still too remote for most Americans to think about.

But in the 1840s, Oregon fever struck. Pioneers from New England and the Middle West began to surge

Open land, opportunity, and optimism propelled thousands of pioneers across the Appalachian Mountains into the Middle West. The hard-scrabble, lonely battle they faced in establishing new homes is captured in these two photos of a pioneer family with covered wagons (above) and a sodbusting, corn-farming couple in Nebraska (below).

glers with broken wagons, limited supplies, or weak animals disappeared. The Oregon Trail soon was lined with discarded equipment, shallow graves, and advice to followers written on the skulls of fallen oxen. The worst part of the journey lay beyond the plains—the alkali flats of the arid Wyoming Basin and the 800-mile climb through the Rockies into the Oregon country.

Despite the dangers, more than 5000 farmer-settlers had made the 2000-mile trek by 1840. In 1848, competing British and American claims to territory in the Pacific Northwest were settled by a compromise agreement defining the Canadian-American border along the forty-ninth parallel, a pact that left both countries with outlets to the Pacific Ocean.

Although most transcontinental migrants veered northward to Oregon, a few thousand Americans and Mexicans filtered into California and established themselves as traders and ranchers in what was then Mexican territory. Some pioneers cut southward through the Rockies, others west from Santa Fe, and a few arrived on clipper ships from eastern ports. One of these, a Swiss pioneer named John Sutter, set up a California colony along the Sacramento River, which he received as a Mexican land grant.

Sutter tended cattle and grew wheat. He established a distillery, a tannery, and a blanket factory. On the American River in the foothills of the Sierra Nevada, he built a sawmill. In 1848, two years after the United States had wrested California from Mexico, a Scottish carpenter named James Marshall discovered gold nuggets in the millrace of this sawmill.

The news of gold soon spread to the East Coast and precipitated a rush to the goldfields. Some 25,000 forty-niners booked ship's passage for California via Cape Horn. An additional 55,000 simply walked and rode overland, following the Oregon and Santa Fe trails. In one year, San Francisco

across the Great Plains, attracted by tales of fertile land and virgin forests. The prairie schooner, or covered wagon, was hit on as the best means of transport. Wagon trains gathered at Independence, Missouri, and Council Bluffs, Iowa, to follow the course of the Platte River across the plains.

The hardships were severe: hostile Indians, cyclones, blizzards, disease, drowning, and exhaustion. Many people walked across the entire continent to save their animals. Strag-

mushroomed into a city of nearly 25,000, with its harbor jammed by clipper ships abandoned by crews who had left for the goldfields. In six years, gold production in the United States increased seventy-three times, and 50 percent of the entire world's gold came from California.

A restless, rootless society drawn from all over the world, many new Californians either returned to the East or spread through the Rockies as the flow of California gold dwindled in the 1860s. But others stayed on and sank roots in California, giving the state a distinctive regional tradition and culture.

Mormon Utah

Two years before the gold rush to California, a quite different regional culture was established in the valley of the Great Salt Lake in Utah. An astonishing body of fervently religious people, the Mormons, walked 1000 miles into the western wilderness to create an ideal society beyond the reach of civilization.

The Mormons were a quiet, prosperous, polygamous people who believed themselves chosen by God. Because of their prosperity and their belief in plural marriage, they were hounded westward through Ohio,

This discovery of gold in 1848 lured thousands of hopeful miners to California. Their essential equipment—hand tools, a pan, weapons, and whiskey.

Missouri, and Illinois. Their houses were burned, their banks looted, Mormon women were raped, and in 1844, their prophet Joseph Smith was shot to death in a jail cell in Carthage, Illinois.

Under the leadership of Brigham Young, the Mormons determined to build their holy city of Zion in the West where they could live without being harassed. After arriving in Utah, the disciplined Mormons laid out the streets of their holy city, built irrigation ditches, and converted the Salt Lake Basin into one of the most fertile agricultural regions in the American West.

In a single decade, ninety-five Mormon communities were founded. The Mormon population swelled to 200,000 as converts flocked to their well-ordered territory. Although the Mormons failed to establish an independent theocratic state in the American West, Brigham Young became the first governor of the state of Utah. A new culture hearth based on religious differences was implanted in the Great Basin country that has persisted to the present.

The Great Plains

The last West to be conquered and settled was the Great Plains, a semiarid grassland that encompasses nearly a quarter of the continental United States. The Great Plains slope eastward from the Rocky Mountains to the Mississippi Valley and extend northward from Texas into western Canada. Generally level, treeless, and dry, the Great Plains was incorrectly perceived to be unfit for cultivation, a "Great American Desert."

Prior to the California gold rush, many easterners considered the Great Plains a permanent barrier to westward migration. Indeed, in the 1850s, Congress allocated $30,000 to import two boatloads of camels from the Middle East in an effort to replicate Asian **pastoral nomadism** in the arid southern plains. Uncertain rainfall, scanty fuel, winter blizzards, and summer grass fires made the Great

Plains unattractive to trappers, miners, and pioneers. Thus, it remained the domain of mounted buffalo-hunting Indian tribes, except in the Southwest where New Mexico retained its Hispanic population and culture.

In 1860, some 250,000 Indians still inhabited the Great Plains. The strongest and most warlike tribes were the Sioux, Blackfoot, Crow, Cheyenne, and Arapaho in the north, and the Comanche, Apache, Ute, and Kiowa in the south. Trapped between cattlemen and farmers advancing from the east and miners rebounding eastward from California, the Plains Indians still lived as nomadic hunters, migrating northward in summer and southward in winter, feeding off enormous herds of buffalo.

Some herds included as many as 12 million animals, on which the tribes relied for food, shelter, and clothing. As the railroads penetrated the plains, buffalo hunters, farmers, and cattlemen began to eliminate the herds, encroaching on hunting grounds previously granted by treaty to the Indians. The very basis of Indian life was threatened. By 1873, only one large buffalo herd was still intact; by 1876, no more targets were left.

In desperation, the Indians fought back in hundreds of pitched battles with army troops. One by one, the tribes were subdued and herded onto reservations. Indian lands were taken by theft or purchase. The Indian population was drastically reduced by raids, disease, and hunger. Long before the pitiless massacre of the last of the Sioux at Wounded Knee in 1891, the extinction of the buffalo had sealed the fate of the Plains Indians (Fig. 4.8). The Great Plains was open to settlement.

In the ecological void left by the vanishing buffalo, several million semiwild longhorn cattle grazed on the Great Plains. When railroads from the East reached the margins of these plains, railhead towns became destinations to which longhorn cattle from the southern plains and northern prairies were driven for shipment to urban markets back East. Plains steak appeared in the restaurants of New York as the Indians of the Plains became an endangered species.

The first herd was driven from southern Texas up the Chisholm Trail to Abilene in 1867. The typical drive took three months as cowboys moved cattle at a rate of 15 miles a day along the 1200-to-1500-mile route. In the peak year of 1871, more than 600,000 cattle crossed the Red River heading north. Along the spreading rail lines, towns like Abilene and Dodge City sprang up—wild, disorderly boom towns with homicide rates ten to twenty times higher than that of modern New York City.

Battles over cattle ownership, grazing rights, and water generated lawlessness and violence quite unlike the romantic legend that has been preserved. But the cattle trails and the Wild West lasted briefly. In only twenty years, the wide open spaces

of the Great Plains were crisscrossed by rails and staked out by the barbed-wire fences of farmers and ranchers.

As the settlement of the Great Plains progressed, Congress passed the **Homestead** Act in 1862. This law entitled every adult American, on payment of $10, to ownership of 160 acres of land simply by agreeing to work it and produce a crop within five years. An area as great as Great Britain and France combined was thrown open to homesteaders. Most of it was located in the semiarid grasslands west of the 100th meridian. New settlers lured yet again by reports of fertile soil and almost free land cut farms into the prairie turf and lived in underground sod dugouts. They suffered drought, blizzard, locust plagues, windstorms, backbreaking work, and loneliness. It was a bleak, raw life that discouraged many.

But three inventions made farming possible on the open plains: the steel plow, which turned the sod and

opened the grassland soils to wheat farming; windmills, which pumped underground water to the surface; and barbed wire, which fenced off the plains and kept animals out of the grain fields. Although most western land ended up in the hands of land speculators and the railroads, the population of the Great Plains increased rapidly. Between 1870 and 1900, 430 million acres of new land were settled in the American Great Plains.

Centennial

In 1876, the Centennial Exposition opened in Philadelphia to celebrate the first century of American independence. The nation was in the midst of a business depression and was recovering from the political corruption that wracked the administration of President Ulysses S. Grant.

In the East, hordes of European immigrants were filling the cities. The South was beginning to recover from the ravages of the Civil War and the excesses of Reconstruction. In the West, where the first transcontinental railroad had joined East and West by rail in 1869, people were stunned by news that the Seventh Cavalry under the command of General George Custer had been annihilated by the Sioux on the Little Bighorn River in Montana. Farther west, the rapacious carnival atmosphere of the gold rush had given way to organized mining and agricultural development.

To the north, the new Dominion of Canada had a population of around 4 million, although 90 percent of its population still lived on the Atlantic Coast, in Québec, and southern Ontario. The government had put down a rebellion in the western province of Manitoba and the Canadian Pacific Railroad had been started under a cloud of scandal. Canadians had covered a continental space. An emergent sense of nationhood had developed—mostly in being politically separate from their very similar neighbors to the south. French Can-

Native Americans fought to maintain their ways of life against encroaching buffalo hunters, farmers, and cattlemen. They failed. Among the last to be conquered were the Chiricahua Apache led by Geronimo (front row, third from right). Here, Apache prisoners en route to Florida are photographed by their captors during a stop on the Southern Pacific Railroad near the Nueces River in Texas.

THE SEIZURE OF INDIAN LAND

Between 1784 and 1880, 370 treaties were signed and broken with Indian tribes. As the frontier moved west, vaulted over the Rockies, and then converged from both east and west on the Great Plains, millions of acres of land—two thirds of a continent—were wrenched from the Indians. The tragedy of their fate was poignantly summarized by Chief Joseph of the Nez Percé, who, after a 1500-mile fighting retreat over mountain and plain, surrendered just short of asy-lum in Canada on October 5, 1877, stating "I am tired of fighting . . . my heart is sick and sad. From where the sun now stands I will fight no more forever." Today, Indian reservations in the United States amount to 50 million acres, or 2.2 percent of the nation's total area.

Adapted from: Sam B. Hilliard, "Indian Land Cessions," *Annals of the Association of American Geographers,* Vol. 62 (1972). (Map Supplement No. 16)

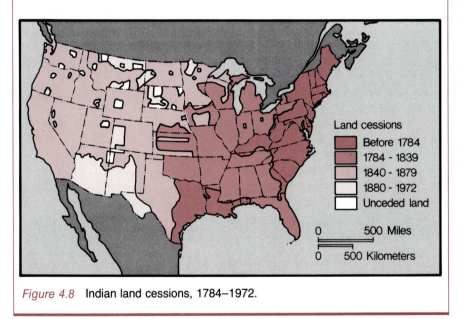

Land cessions
- Before 1784
- 1784 - 1839
- 1840 - 1879
- 1880 - 1972
- Unceded land

0   500 Miles
0   500 Kilometers

Figure 4.8 Indian land cessions, 1784–1972.

ada retained an isolated, self-defining culture in Québec, although French Canadians had migrated west to new lands in Manitoba like their English counterparts.

Overall, however, it had been a century of remarkable territorial expansion, population growth, and material progress in both the United States and Canada. North Americans' faith in growth, belief in progress, and relentless impatience with the mere achievements of the present, had won them a continent. A distinctive machine-run industrial economy was beginning to emerge. In a land rich in opportunity and re-sources and short of labor, North America would soon challenge Europe as the center of industrial power. The United States and Canada had already become the world's largest sources of cheap food, supplying the needs of their cities, providing purpose to the network of railroads that laced the continent together, and producing exports that profoundly changed their position in world affairs.

In short, North America was rapidly moving toward economic independence and, although the environmental losses in ravaged land, destroyed forests, and discarded re-sources were enormous, the United States and Canada accomplished in a matter of years what Europe had been working toward for centuries.

THE EMERGENCE OF INDUSTRIAL NORTH AMERICA

As the impact of the machine age and urbanization spread throughout the world, the beginnings of the twentieth century witnessed the full flowering of two **capitalist** societies on the North American landscape. The United States and Canada matured into dynamic technological societies with an increasing share of the world's wealth and a growing population. As they approached *The Drive to Industrial Maturity*, North Americans harnessed their diverse resource base to forge powerful national economies.

The process drew North Americans, native and immigrant alike, into new urban centers that exploded in size. Diverse peoples created unexpected social adaptations in *The Urban World* of North America as responses arose to problems reflecting the increasing intensity and complexity of Canadian and American life. Perhaps most urgent was the question of *The Distribution of Wealth*. Technology manufactured prosperity. But in nations that prized utility and productivity, wealth tended to concentrate among the strongest and most competitive. Ultimately, poverty among the less educated, the less mobile, racial minorities, farmers, and industrial workers resulted in the Great Depression, which raised fundamental questions and marked a turning point in the North American way of life.

The Drive to Industrial Maturity

Between 1850 and 1900, North Americans' efforts to develop their environments and resources gained momentum. The United States, an agricultural nation at the end of the Civil War, became an industrial giant. Comparable forces were at work in Canada in the southern margins of the country.

There were three reasons for this remarkable industrial growth. First, a storehouse of natural resources was discovered in these decades. Huge pools of oil were found. A substantial share of the world's coal was discovered. Large deposits of iron, lead, zinc, copper, and silver came under exploitation. One mining strike followed another, and a frenzied rush to exploit the richest resource concentrations began.

Second, a flood of new inventions altered life in the United States and Canada. Thomas Edison adapted scientific theory to practical needs, and single-handedly deluged the United States government with over 1000 requests for patents for new inventions. The telephone, telegraph, sewing machine, camera, typewriter, and automobile were invented. New industrial processes, machines, and motors were developed. These inventions increased the productivity of industrial workers. The system of mass production on which modern American society rests began to take shape.

Finally, the opportunity to become wealthy, to better one's lot, focused the energies of North Americans. Success became a moral obligation in the United States and Canada. The gospel of hard work made accomplishment mandatory. As a Massachusetts bishop put it, "wealth comes only to the man of morality." In the course of this saga of expansion, exploitation, and material progress, the United States became the world's foremost example of economic development.

Railroad Empires

Perhaps the single most important element in North America's economic development was its expand-

A celebration was held at Promontory Point, Utah, when the first transcontinental railroad was completed in 1869.

ing railroad network, which linked together the resources and people of the United States and southern Canada. In 1869, the first transcontinental railroad bridged the Rocky Mountains. The Central Pacific, built by Chinese coolies, and the Union Pacific, constructed by gangs of Irish laborers, met at Promontory Point, Utah. A golden spike was driven to complete the line. The first Canadian transcontinental railroad was completed in 1885.

By 1890, 166,700 miles of railroad track spanned North America. Five transcontinental lines connected the East Coast with the West. On the plains of the Middle West, dozens of feeder lines crisscrossed every state. These feeder lines had great economic significance for local communities. By 1900, state and federal governments had granted 180 million acres of land to the railroads. Railroad revenues were twice as high as those of the federal government.

This enormous system of rapid and cheap transportation that hauled a flood of goods and people to all settled parts of the United States was

owned by a few ambitious, powerful individuals. Cornelius Vanderbilt, once captain of a ferryboat, operated the New York Central Railroad, 4500 miles of track strategically located between New York City and the largest cities in the Middle West. Jay Gould, archetype of the robber barons of the period, rose from a position as grocery clerk in upstate New York to take control of the 9000-mile Southern Pacific Railroad system. Driven by fierce competition, these railroad monarchs forged a network of steel that interlaced the nation. Nothing like it existed anywhere in the world.

Monopolies in American Industry

Similar patterns of explosive growth and consolidation occurred in steel, oil, and electricity—the fastest growing segments of the American economy.

After the invention of the Bessemer process of purifying iron into steel, that once-rare commodity became widely available for bridges, buildings, and railroads. Steel production soared to 26 million tons in 1910. A substantial share of this production belonged to one man, Andrew Carnegie (1835–1919), the immigrant son of a Scottish weaver.

Recognizing that cheap steel was vital to the new industrial age, Carnegie began to buy up steel mills, iron and coal mines, limestone quarries, and the barges and railroads that connected ore fields to factories. The iron mines of Lake Superior were brought into production: the Menominee Range, the Vermilion Range, and—largest of all—the Mesabi Range. Here vast deposits of iron ore lay on the surface of the ground, and the ore was so soft that it could be **strip-mined** with steam shovels. Pittsburgh, in the heart of the Appalachian coalfields, burgeoned into the primary steel-producing center in America. In the 1880s, the Great Lakes canal at Sault Sainte Marie, which linked Lake Superior iron with Appalachian coal, was carrying three times the tonnage of the Suez Canal.

Carnegie built an integrated industrial empire which owned steel plants, coal mines, ore ships, and 1000 miles of railroad track. Having devoted his life to building this industrial empire, Carnegie sold the corporation to J. P. Morgan, retired to a castle in Scotland, and spent the rest of his life donating his fortune to charity.

John D. Rockefeller brought the same organization genius to the oil industry. For nearly a century, petroleum that seeped to the surface in the western Appalachians was used as a remedy for rheumatism, bronchitis, and a variety of other illnesses. In the 1850s, however, Edwin Drake drilled a well to tap this resource at Titusville, Pennsylvania. He struck oil at 70 feet, and the boom was on. More wells were drilled in the Appalachian field. By the 1880s, this region was producing over 30 million barrels of oil a year. The United States was, until Russian oil fields came into production in the 1890s, the world leader in oil, a role

it was to regain in the twentieth century.

Rockefeller brought order to the oil fields by buying up oil refineries. At one point, he owned 95 percent of the refining capacity of the United States through his corporation, the Standard Oil Company. Like Carnegie, Rockefeller aimed at controlling the entire industry. He purchased oil wells, barrel-making factories, and pipelines and oil cars for transport. He even owned the retail stores where kerosene was sold for lighting. Eliminating competitors, Rockefeller became one of the most powerful men in America. As more diverse uses for petroleum became known, Rockefeller dominated a business empire whose products included asphalt, the raw materials for fertilizer, lubricating greases and oils, gasoline, and heating oil. Rockefeller was the first billionaire in history.

Other large-scale monopolies developed in public utilities—Western Union, American Telephone & Telegraph, General Electric, and Westinghouse. Swift, Cudahy, and Armour controlled meat packing. Pillsbury consolidated the flour-milling industry. The scale of these operations made new economies and efficiencies possible, and from a purely quantitative viewpoint, the accomplishments of American industry were astonishing.

Total manufactures in the United States increased tenfold in the last half of the nineteenth century and doubled again before World War I. Living standards rose substantially. A combination of technological advances, the driving energy of competitive businessmen, and the work of willing immigrants from Europe were making the United States the most formidable industrial nation in the world.

Problems of Industrial Growth

Despite this high level of economic success, uncontrolled industrial monopolies in the United States created social problems. The elimina-

tion of small independent businesses was beginning to generate a new sense of helplessness among individual Americans. It was no longer certain that individuals could achieve success and prosperity through hard work and strong character. Workers' slums were not breeding grounds for millionaires, and in a nation of wage earners, the dream of economic independence was, for many, fading fast.

The rich viewed poverty as "the sternest of all schools" and unemployment as "an act of God." By 1893, the richest 10 percent of Americans owned three quarters of the national wealth. The rest of the population shared what was left. In desperation, factory workers formed unions to get a reduction in the sixty- to eighty-hour workweek, minimum safety standards, and some measure of job security. Corporations retaliated with private militias and federal troops. In the clash that followed, thousands of workers were killed in 38,000 strikes and lockouts involving 10 million workers.

Immigrants from Europe and southern blacks were hired as strikebreakers on the railroads, in the coal mines, and in urban sweatshops. Ultimately the unions won better working conditions and a more secure living. But a chasm of distrust separated corporate business and the nation's workers. Bitter ethnic and racial tensions, at least partially born in this conflict, seethed in America's industrial cities.

The Urban World

Urbanization and industrialization went hand in hand in the United States and Canada, with one process reinforcing the other. Although many Americans and Canadians continued to move west in search of land and fortune, many more were lured to a different frontier—the city. By 1900, 30 million of the 76 million Americans were urban residents, and one twelfth of the nation's population lived in three cities—New York, Philadelphia, and Chicago.

The population of New York City soared to over 3 million, and the city dominated the ocean traffic of the Atlantic. San Francisco and, to a lesser extent, Los Angeles and Seattle played similar roles in the Pacific. Philadelphia was the nation's third largest city with 1.3 million people. Pittsburgh, the nation's greatest forge, and Saint Louis, the prairie entrepôt, were sited at important river junctions. At either end of the Mississippi, New Orleans and Minneapolis–St. Paul were thriving cities. And Chicago, burned to the ground in 1871, had a population of 1.7 million by 1900.

The rate and intensity of urbanization differed from one part of the country to another. In 1910, the Industrial North included fourteen of the nineteen American cities with populations of more than 250,000, and all three of the nation's cities with over 1 million. Canadian cities with populations greater than 250,000 were Montréal and Toronto. Seven of every ten people in New England and the Middle Atlantic states lived in cities, as did half the Great Lakes population. On the West Coast, industrial growth based on exploitation of local resources, reliable railroad connections, and ocean commerce had spurred the growth of several large urban centers. By contrast, the interior West supported far fewer cities. The lowest rate of urbanization was in the South, where less than one of every five people lived in a city.

A Nation of Nations

Many of America's new urbanites were drawn from farming communities, but millions more were foreign immigrants who crossed the Atlantic Ocean in search of a better life. Between 1820 and 1880, 9 million foreigners entered the United States from the British Isles, Germany, Scandinavia, and even Canada.

For most immigrants, the decision to move was motivated by hard times in the old country. In the 1840s and 1850s, 1.7 million Irish sought refuge in the United States when life hit rock bottom in Ireland because of the potato blight. Clustered in the Northeast, the Irish gradually spread westward along the railroads they helped to build.

In the 1850s, political repression and crop failures in Central Europe pushed a million Germans across the Atlantic. In the 1860s and 1870s, Germans formed the largest share of the incoming immigrants. Although some were professional people and artisans, most were farmers driven off marginal agricultural land by cheap wheat flowing into Europe from the farmlands of North America and Russia. Along with Norwegians, Swedes, and a steady stream of English, Welsh, and Scottish immigrants, Germans settled on farms in the Middle West and the Canadian prairies, in the mining towns of Appalachia, and in the industrial towns of the Northeast.

Between 1880 and 1920, this immigrant stream swelled to a flood. Some 24 million people, the vast majority of them from southern and eastern Europe, arrived at East Coast ports. Anti-Semitic massacres in Russia in the 1880s launched a wave of Jewish migration to America. Cholera epidemics in the Italian south had the same effect. Population growth and the inefficiency of **peasant** agriculture in eastern Europe left many Hungarians, Czechs, Slavs, and Croatians with no way to earn a living in Europe. So they left for America by the hundreds of thousands. Emigrant trains starting deep in Russia picked up boxcars full of Austrians, Hungarians, and Lithuanians on the way to ports of embarkation.

With North America's rapidly expanding industrial economy in need of cheap labor, agents for American and Canadian land developers, factory owners, and mining companies encouraged potential immigrants to leave Europe. The agents made certain that these people had the three essentials for immigration—an exit paper, a $10 ticket, and $25 to spare.

Between 1900 and 1914, millions of Austro-Hungarians, Italians, Russians, and southeast Europeans made the two-to-eight-week passage across the Atlantic.

As many as 15,000 a day arrived at the immigration office on Ellis Island in New York Harbor, where they were sorted and given cursory medical checks. Speaking many languages and practicing different faiths, these immigrants shared a vision of America as a land of opportunity. They labored hard and long in this foreign culture to seize their chance.

Urban Immigrants

With the open lands of the West filling up, the bulk of the new immigrants poured into the factory towns of the Industrial North. In 1910, 79 percent of the new immigrants lived in urban centers. A full 60 percent of all industrial laborers were foreign born, two thirds of them from southern and eastern Europe.

Russian Jews and Italians entered the garment trades of New York City. Poles, Portuguese, Greeks, and Syrians joined the Irish in New England's textile mills. Slovak, Polish, and Italian miners worked the coalfields of Pennsylvania. Almost unnoticed in this European tide, southern blacks migrated northward, drawn by jobs in the expanding industrial belt. By 1910, 750,000 black Americans lived in the North and West, one third of them in New York, Philadelphia, Chicago, and Saint Louis. The urban collision of black and ethnic Americans was beginning.

The scale of this migration transformed the American urban landscape. Four of every ten New Yorkers were foreign-born. The city had twice as many Irish as Dublin, more Italians than Naples, and probably the largest Jewish community in the world. Only Berlin and Hamburg had more Germans than Chicago. In industrial cities, such as Milwaukee, Detroit, and Cleveland, more than a third of the inhabitants were immigrants. The same was true in the entry ports of Boston and San Francisco.

Poor, uneducated, and desperate for work, these people were rapidly shunted into the nation's factories and into airless tenement districts nearby. Large-scale immigration aggravated housing problems, sanitation conditions, street crime, and corruption in cities already strained by rapid growth. The newcomers clustered defensively in tightly knit urban neighborhoods, creating a new ethnic urban geography in most industrial cities. Each metropolis had its own "Little Italy" or "Little Ireland."

Threatened by this babel of new voices, Americans, themselves descendants of earlier northern European immigrants, railed against accepting any more new immigrants. They protested that the open immigration policy of the United States would lead to "racial suicide." As a result, the United States closed its door to large-scale immigration in the 1920s, but not before America had become not a melting pot but a nation of nations.

Urban Conditions

Most urban immigrants faced problems of health and housing whose solutions lay beyond the reach of any single individual. Sewage facilities were primitive in some cities, nonexistent in others. Cholera and typhoid epidemics were common, particularly in Philadelphia, whose provisions for clean water were so inadequate as late as 1883 that the death rate from typhoid fever was double that of New York City. In many American cities, street cleaning was left to pigs who survived on garbage thrown into public thoroughfares. In Cincinnati, which relied on these animals for garbage disposal, hogs were rounded up and sold at auction whenever their number reached 6000. A report of the day castigated the

Urban immigrants flooded into the Atlantic seaports of the United States in the 1800s. They were shunted into ghettos aggravating the problems of fire, crime, disease, and housing that afflicted most of America's rapidly growing cities.

pigs on Broadway in New York City because they were too "deficient in organization" to keep the city clean.

Public fire protection was a new idea in America's cities, and urban fire losses skyrocketed. The crime rate soared with population growth, making daily life risky and public safety a real concern. The national homicide rate tripled in the 1880s. The number of prison inmates increased by 50 percent. Everywhere urban growth outstripped road construction. Chicago had 1400 miles of dirt streets. The "engineer" that laid out Boston's streets must have been, according to Ralph Waldo Emerson, a "cow." Even before automobiles, urban traffic congestion was intense.

By the turn of the century, these urban problems began to ease. Police and fire departments were established. Garbage removal was systematized. Street were paved. Asphalt was thrown down on city streets to replace cobblestones and wooden blocks. Cable cars were introduced in San Francisco in 1873. By 1900, 10,000 miles of trolley track had been installed in American cities. These new transport systems considerably expanded the spatial reach of the city as circles of **suburbanization** widened ever outward. Trolleys did little, however, to relieve traffic congestion. First New York and then Boston went underground to construct subways for moving people to and from work.

Electric, gas, and telephone lines were installed in most American cities. Aqueducts reached deep into urban hinterlands to provide city dwellers with clean supplies of piped water. Epidemic disease dropped. With urban real estate values soaring, architects built upward in steel. Skyscrapers were introduced and the American city began to take on its modern form.

The most serious urban problem was housing. Tenement slums—crowded warrens in which more people were crammed into less living space than ever before—spread out around the avenues and skyscrapers of city centers. In lower Manhattan, population densities exceeded 900 people per acre, a staggering 575,000 people per square mile—and tenement buildings were rarely more than five stories high.

Living conditions in these housing blocks were barely endurable. Rates of infant mortality, turberculosis, crime, vice, and delinquency were extremely high. In 1900, only two of five infants survived their first year in one Chicago slum. A Boston report noted that the average lifespan of the urban Irish was only fourteen years. In New York, one of every twenty people lived in squalid cellars.

Some groups survived better than others. Russian Jews, who were experienced urbanites, had a very low rate of tuberculosis. Rural Italian immigrants usually had the highest death rates in the city. Unable and in some cases unwilling to leave crowded tenements for new **suburbs**, the urban poor were manipulated by slum landlords, land developers, and corrupt city administrators.

A century ago, Jacob Riis denounced the tenement in his classic study of New York City, *How The Other Half Lives* (1890). Tenement slums remain a persistent blight on the American urban landscape. A hundred years old or more, having housed generations of Irish, Italian, Polish, and German Americans, the same crumbling buildings now house newer refugees—black, Hispanic, and welfare Americans who bitterly resent their impoverishment in a land of obvious plenty.

The Distribution of Wealth

In the 1920s, Americans seemed to have discovered a way of maintaining permanent prosperity. The formula was scientific exploitation of resources and large-scale production and consumption of industrial goods. Unscathed by World War I, the agri-cultural and industrial resources of North America had been mobilized to such a degree that the United States was more powerful than any nation in human experience. It owned 40 percent of the world's wealth and was as rich as all of Europe.

President Calvin Coolidge remarked that "the business of America is business." Indeed, no people ever pursued wealth with such enthusiasm. Few societies had such faith in expansion and progress. Supported by a vast environment, the facts seemed to justify this faith. Industrial production in North America doubled in the 1920s, and the real incomes of workers increased. Americans consumed half the world's total available power.

On the farms, large-scale mechanization and new fertilizers raised yields. The United States was easily able to feed its 1920 population of 106 million and still be the foremost food exporter in the world. In agriculture, as in manufacturing, gains in productivity reflected new efficiencies, improved technology, and the electrification of manual work—all of which vastly increased the output of the individual laborer.

Under these circumstances, most Americans were uncritical admirers of their system of competitive enterprise and industrial growth. In 1928, Presidential candidate Herbert Hoover announced that the United States was "nearer to the final triumph over poverty than ever before in the history of any land." A year later, a director of General Motors noted that in America "anyone not only can be rich, but ought to be rich." Wealth was not only a social obligation; it was also a national goal.

Perhaps the automobile best symbolized the mastery that North Americans were gaining over material production. As early as 1908, advertising proclaimed the automobile to be an American necessity. That year, Henry Ford produced his first Model T. By 1927, Ford Motor Company had produced 15 million simple, sturdy cars. Always ready to move, America became a nation on wheels as registrations soared from 9 million vehicles in 1920 to 30 million in 1930. The automobile changed the focus of American life and landscape as surely as the railroads had done two generations earlier.

This rapid expansion was made possible by Ford's use of assembly-line techniques aimed at mass production and mass consumption. In 1913, it took twelve-and-a-half hours to build a Ford. A year later, Model Ts ran off the first electric conveyor belts at a rate of one every ninety-three minutes. By 1925, the production time was down to one car every ten seconds. Because of mass consumption, the price of a Model T had fallen by half.

Applied to other industries, these production methods led to store-bought shoes and clothing, department stores, and, eventually, to supermarkets, shopping centers, and drive-ins. The nation, woven together by a network of paved highways, became a society of self-satisfying producers and consumers.

Pockets of Poverty

Within America's prosperity, however, pockets of poverty, far broader and deeper than most people suspected, persisted. Some old industries, such as New England textile manufacturing, were in sharp decline. Among Appalachian coal miners hardship was acute.

Perhaps worst off were farmers who expanded their acreage and bought tractors to increase production to feed millions of Europeans during World War I. When this temporary demand for food evaporated, Canadian and American farmers found themselves producing too much. Grain prices plummeted, and small farmers were forced to abandon their land.

As new fertilizers, agricultural machines, and scientific cropping methods came into play, family-owned farms could not compete with large-scale farms—factories in the field. By

1930, the farm population had dwindled to 21 percent of America's people, one quarter that of a century earlier. Yet the output of the average farm increased by 41 percent between 1910 and 1931.

Racial minorities also fared badly in the twenties. The antiforeigner sentiment that led to restrictions on immigration reinforced repression of black Americans, Mexican Americans, and native Indians. Segregation held sway in the South. "Equal but separate accommodations for the white and colored races" had been approved by the Supreme Court in 1890. Fewer than 10,000 black students were attending high school in southern states in 1910—a purposeful barrier to participation in an increasingly complex society. An estimated 1100 black people were lynched in the South between 1910 and 1914. It seemed that America, a nation dedicated to democracy, was fast becoming a reactionary state.

When the 400,000 black Americans who enlisted in World War I returned to civilian life, many joined a growing northward migration rather than return to the South. The North's black population rose from 1.4 million in 1920 to 2.3 million in 1930. Race riots erupted in New York, Chicago, Detroit, and Cleveland. Blacks increasingly realized what American educator Booker T. Washington meant by "Negro two-ness—an American, a Negro; two souls, two thoughts, two unreconciled strivings."

Despite prosperity, signs of social unrest were widespread in the 1920s—strikes, race riots, rising crime rates, more divorces, and a taste for all kinds of luxury. The wilderness frontier had pitted pioneers against nature. Now competition among individuals, businesses, and ethnic and racial groups claimed new casualties in a new urban and industrial world. This world demanded cooperation and discipline for mutual economic advancement, but the American tradition of uninhibited individualism,

unplanned growth, and competitive enterprise remained unchallenged despite urban slums, poverty in the countryside, and neglected minorities.

North America's productive power had raced far ahead of its purchasing power. By 1929, 40 percent of all Americans earned less than $1500, and the 24,000 richest families earned three times as much money as the 5.8 million poor. For the first time in history, advertising stimulated the desire to buy, and easy credit provided the means. But neither increased the ability to pay the bills. With too much of the nation's money going into too few pockets, Henry Ford's system of mass production and mass consumption collapsed. This event—the Great Depression—caused a major restructuring of the human geography of North America.

The Great Depression

The Great Depression was one of the grimmest periods in the history of the United States. In October 1929, the bottom fell out of the New York stock market. Banks closed. Factories, business offices, and shops fell idle. Reduced purchasing power sped the downward economic spiral of the machine society.

Across the nation, 13 million people were unemployed. In the North, factory workers were laid off. In the Southwest, dust-bowl conditions buried farms in sand, blocked railroad lines, and drove thousands of migrants to California. In urban America, **shantytowns** grew up overnight filled with people who had lost their homes. In the Northwest, unemployed timber workers set forest fires to earn a living as fire fighters. In the midst of plenty, thousands of Americans actually faced starvation, while farmers burned crops they could not sell and threatened to cut off all food supplies unless prices were raised. Unemployed war veterans sold apples on street corners. Bread lines lengthened.

Under President Franklin D.

During the Great Depression, throngs of unemployed men and women stood in line to get a free Sunday dinner at the Municipal Lodging House in New York City.

Roosevelt, massive federal programs of construction were initiated to create jobs under the New Deal program. In New England, factory workers were put to work breaking rock. The Tennessee Valley Authority (TVA) was created to revive the eroded landscapes of the Southeast. In the West, huge dams were constructed. Labor unions were given the right to bargain, and federal jobs were created by the thousands. Despite these efforts, there were still 10 million unemployed in 1938. It was mobilization for World War II that ultimately brought economic recovery to both the United States and Canada.

But the Great Depression had forced a basic reexamination of American values and global **capitalism.** Under Roosevelt's New Deal, the federal government took responsibility for underwriting the costs of public welfare and for curbing the excesses of private enterprise. For the first time, Americans acknowledged that unemployment was not simply a product of laziness or irresponsibility. They recognized that even in the most affluent society, opportunities were not equal for all.

Government intervention, previously seen as destructive of individual freedom, was now viewed as the only way of restoring it. In Roosevelt's words, the nation must pursue "social values more noble than mere monetary profit." In this sense, Roosevelt was probably one of the most "conservative" presidents America ever had. These new attitudes impressed themselves on the American landscape and shaped the major issues of today.

THE HUMAN GEOGRAPHY OF NORTH AMERICA

North America, considered here as the United States (pop. 246.1 million) and Canada (pop. 26.1 million), is a striking example of a technological society impressed on an environmentally diverse but socially unified region (Fig. 4.9). To explain the extraordinary growth of the North American economy, most scholars cite the continent's rich natural resources, its diverse and technically

capable population of 272 million, its size, internal unity, political stability, and industrial capacity. All of these factors are indeed important, but the key to North America's human geography is that settlement of the continent and the Industrial Revolution were simultaneous events. After industrialization sparked European society to exploration and conquest, the environmental and economic transformations of North America took place in rapid succession.

Indian populations occupied North America for at least 40,000 years prior to the large-scale migration of Europeans, but they were few in number and technologically limited. Only in favored locations—along the coasts, on the shores of the Great Lakes, in the lower Mississippi Valley, the southern Appalachians, and in parts of the Southwest—were Indian population densities higher than two people per square mile. Nothing like the dense agrarian civilizations of India and China existed in North America to alter the direction and purpose of European settlement.

Weakened by newly introduced diseases and overwhelmed by European weapons, Indians melted away before the European advance. Despite, or perhaps because of, the close attachment of the American Indians to the world of nature, they were not effective in hindering and redirecting the European penetration of the continent. And because European settlement prior to the American Revolution was restricted to the Atlantic coastal plain, full exploration and conquest of the continent was deferred until the full effects of the Industrial Revolution came into play. Colonial America, with its French **seigneuries,** New England towns, and southern plantations, was dwarfed and transformed by the rapid geographic spread of a dynamic new type of economy and society. Indians dwindled and died in the face of this new society.

The human geography of North America, therefore, is of recent ori-

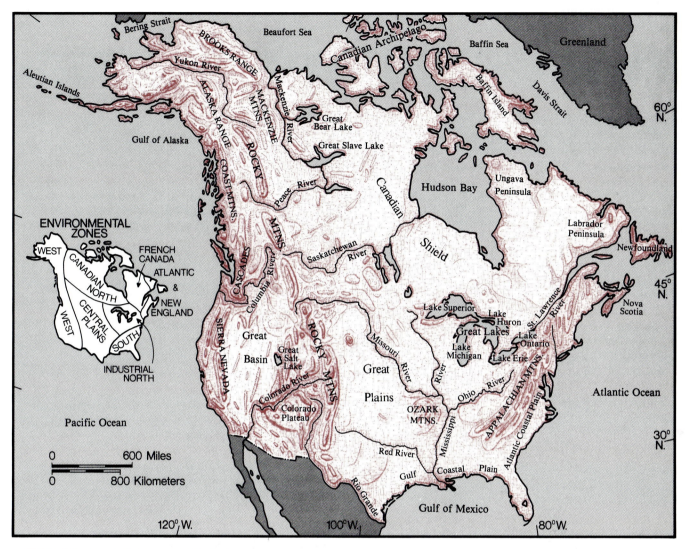

Figure 4.9 Physical features of North America.

gin and relatively homogeneous compared with other world regions. Large sections of the American West have even now been occupied within living memory, and settlement in parts of Alaska and the Canadian North is a contemporary event. For the most part, the political boundaries of North America—the provinces of Canada and the states of the United States—do not separate different peoples or beliefs. Instead, they represent expressions of the same culture set in different physical environments. There are exceptions—Mormon Utah, the Spanish Southwest, French-speaking Québec—but, by and large, the regionality of North America is based on large-scale en-

vironmental features and industrial processes rather than in different languages, customs, and moral attitudes. North American subregions, such as New England, the South, the Midwest, or the Canadian Prairies embody minor cultural variations compared with the differences between Spain and Germany, for example, or one region of Indian and another.

North America has no significant internal barriers to trade and communication, despite the Appalachian and Rocky Mountains. The United States and Canada form the largest platform of industrial economy, mobility, and communication in the world. Canada, with a national ter-

ritory of 3.8 million square miles and the United States with 3.6 million square miles, are the world's second and fourth largest nations.

Despite this apparent cultural homogeneity, Canadians and Americans have clung staunchly to regional identities, although most people are clearly integrated into the national society and economy. New Englanders draw their cultural inspiration from roots different from those of Southerners; French Canadians assert cultural independence in a nation built on English custom and law. At a more local level, Chinese immigrants, Germans, Italians, Greeks, and the Amish have typically formed small enclaves within specific cities and regions. Indians live on reservations implanted in a land they lost, and black and Puerto Rican Americans have become increasingly concentrated in the cores of metropolitan regions.

The difficulty in describing this cultural diversity within a unified framework of language, technology, and economy in North America is compounded by the variety of environments that slash across the continent and create vastly different settings for human activity. In an effort to compromise these differences, seven major regions are identified in this section: *The Canadian Northlands*, a vast, virtually uninhabited land of tundra and **taiga**; *French Canada*, testimony to the persistence of the French colonial experiment in the New World; *New England and the Atlantic Provinces of Canada*, one of colonial America's most influential culture hearths; *The Industrial North*, a belt of dense industrial and commercial activity stretching from the megalopolis on the Atlantic coast across the central Appalachian Mountains and the Great Lakes to the Upper Midwest; *The South*, an area set between the southern Appalachians and the plains of the Atlantic and the Gulf of Mexico, a regional culture with its own literature, lifestyle, and language; *The Central Plains*, the agricultural heartland of the continent; and *The West*, a vast sweep of mountains, **plateaus**, and deserts, densely urbanized on its Pacific periphery and thinly peopled elsewhere.

The Canadian Northlands

The virtually uninhabited northlands of the severely glaciated Canadian Shield is a landscape of taiga forests, shallow lakes, **muskeg** bogs, and **braided streams** (Fig. 4.9). The Shield covers about half the territory of Canada (1.8 million square miles), and projects southward into Minnesota, Wisconsin, Michigan, and the Adirondack Mountains of New York. The

Shield extends west to border the Canadian Rockies, and includes all of Canada's Northwest Territories as well as much of the area of Ontario and Québec. It is devoid of human presence except for occasional mines, air bases, and a small number of traders, trappers, schoolteachers, priests, and Indians. Taiga lands rich in mineral, timber, and hydroelectric resources form the basis of wealth in today's Canadian frontier.

In the farthest north, beyond the Shield, the Canadian **archipelago** is composed of a group of islands in the Arctic Ocean stretching over 60 degrees of longitude from Banks Island in the west to Ellesmere Island near Greenland and reaching southward some 1500 miles. The Canadian Arctic, a tundra landscape over one-half million square miles in extent, supports a population of less than 15,000 people. Most of these people are native Inuit (Eskimos) currently undergoing rapid change as modern communication systems, schools, and trading posts are constructed throughout the region. A distinctive physical province of North America, the Arctic islands and the Canadian Shield form the most difficult and least inhabited region in North America.

French Canada

French Canada is one of the most distinctive culture regions in North America. It is at the historical root of the existence of a separate Canadian identity in North America. French Canadians believe that Canada is their inspiration and that English Canada emerged only when British loyalists fled northward after the American Revolution in 1776. The debate on these issues of origin and identity still plays a major role in Canadian society.

Although communities of French Canadians are spread throughout Canada and northern New England, French Canada is basically synonymous with the province of Québec, the New France of colonial days (Fig.

4.1). With an area nearly three times as large as France, the province of Québec has only 6.7 million people, more than nine tenths of whom are direct descendants of the 65,000 French settlers who lived in the New World in 1763—a remarkable **demographic** persistence.

The French Canadians are concentrated in the lowlands of the St. Lawrence River Valley. Stretching 600 miles from the tip of the Gaspé Peninsula to the suburbs of Montréal, the St. Lawrence River Valley is framed on the north by the rugged terrain of the Canadian Shield and on the south by the Sutton Mountains, a northern extension of the Appalachians into Canada. The Sutton highlands of Québec, known as the Eastern townships, were settled by an English-speaking population of small farmers politically and culturally like the people of New England—indeed they were a northward extension of them in the 1700s. The French Canadian population, on the other hand, extends westward into eastern Ontario along the Ottawa River Valley between Montréal and Ottawa, the federal capital of Canada. Ottawa (pop. 718,000), is an enclave of English-speaking people surrounded by a French Canadian population.

The Changing Economy of French Canada

Well into this century, the St. Lawrence River Valley was a landscape of family farms and agricultural villages centered on parish churches. Agriculture still remains an important source of income for Québec. Production of apples, wrapping tobacco, hay, oats, dairy products, and maple syrup is substantial. Environmental conditions, however, limit the agricultural possibilities of French Canada. Even in the south, in Montréal, frosts occur late into May, and snow may fall in early October.

Increased exploitation of timber and mineral and energy resources in the province of Québec is altering this

French culture and society persists in the province of Québec, Canada. Ninety percent of the people of Québec are direct descendants of the original French settlers who migrated to the New World in the 1600s and 1700s.

traditional agricultural economy. The St. Lawrence River, tamed by the immense seaway project of the 1950s, provides access to the interior for seagoing vessels. This river now forms the outlet for the entire watershed of the Great Lakes.

This project, funded by state, provincial, and the national governments of Canada and the United States, has deeply affected the economy of Québec Province. Along the numerous rivers that pour southward off the Canadian Shield, the expansion of hydroelectric power resources has increased the production of the timber, paper, and pulp industries. Logging towns, such as Shawinigan and La Tuque on the St. Maurice River, have been revitalized by cheap hydroelectric power. With energy demand rising in Montréal, Québec City, Ottawa, and the northeastern United States, more remote reserves have been tapped by dams on the Manicouagan River—some 200 miles north and east of Québec City.

The province of Québec is now the principal producer of Canada's most important export—pulp and paper—and is endowed with a surplus of hydroelectric energy. Québec's immense engineering efforts to harness the wild rivers that pour off the Canadian Shield into Hudson's Bay are now bearing fruit. Hydro-Québec, the provincial power authority, supplied 14 percent of the power needs of New England and New York State in the late 1980s.

The mineral resources of the Canadian Shield have prompted a comparable growth in the mining sector. Iron ore, aluminum, titanium, copper, gold, and other minerals are mined on the Shield in isolated centers. Recently developed iron ore deposits in Labrador have benefited by supplying Great Lakes heavy industry with this vital metal at a time when high-grade Lake Superior ores are reaching exhaustion.

But the mineral resources of Labrador and Québec will not attract many people to this region. Efficient mining techniques require a minimum work force. Hydroelectric development in the north supports an economy of mineral treatment and metal production, but the more moderate environments of the St. Lawrence River Valley are far more attractive to settlers.

Population is still so thin on the Canadian Shield that fewer than 100,000 people inhabit the immense Saguenay region of Québec Province, which is 315,176 square miles in area. The economy of French Canada, redirected from agriculture to the exploitation of mineral resources, reflects a human geography common in the North American West. A dense core of intensive urbanization at Montréal serves a vast, thinly peopled hinterland.

Montréal, the premier port of the St. Lawrence River Valley, has a population of 2.8 million. It is Canada's second largest city and a major industrial, financial, transportation, and educational center. Montréal is

economically and culturally of overwhelming importance in French Canada. Compared with the city of Québec (pop. 576,000) or Trois-Rivières (83,000), the second and third cities of French Canada, Montréal is the residence of nearly half the French Canadian population. Marked by innovative urban planning, the city's **central business district (CBD)** is replete with an underground network of shops, offices, and restaurants— an articulated system of subterranean avenues shielded from the harsh weather of winter.

New England and the Atlantic Provinces of Canada

The six New England states (Maine, New Hampshire, Vermont, Massachusetts, Rhode Island and Connecticut), and the nearby Canadian provinces of New Brunswick, Nova Scotia, Prince Edward Island, and Newfoundland are located in the northern Appalachians, highlands that historically barred this subregion from easy access to the interior of the continent (Figs. 4.1, 4.9).

Generally below 3000 feet in altitude and forested by hardwoods and **conifers,** the low mountains of New England and the Atlantic provinces are composed of three separate ranges. First, a series of structurally related **folded mountains** including the Taconic Mountains, the Berkshire Hills, and the Green Mountains of Vermont extend northward into the Shickshock Mountains of the Gaspé Peninsula and the Long Range of northwestern Newfoundland. Second, a central mountain complex arches northeastward from the White Mountains of New Hampshire through Maine to the central highlands of New Brunswick and Newfoundland. Third, a band of uplands, noticeably lower in elevation, stretches from coastal Rhode Island and Massachusetts, dives under the Gulf of Maine and resurfaces in Nova Scotia and eastern Newfoundland. All three of these highland belts have

MAPSCAN

TOPOGRAPHIC MAPS

Topographic maps portray the physical features of a part of the earth's surface through the use of **contour lines,** which connect points of equal elevation above a reference point or **datum plane,** usually mean sea level. These lines are called contour lines because if they were actually drawn on the earth's surface, they would follow the contours of real-world landforms. By examining the pattern and spacing of contour lines, you can determine correct elevations at any point on the map. In addition, topographic maps illustrate drainage patterns, steepness of slope, and cultural features constructed on the physical landscape.

The logic behind topographic mapping of terrain is illustrated in the upper part of Figure 4.10, which shows a hilly island between 80 and 100 feet in elevation cut by horizontal planes spaced 20 feet apart. Each of these lines is a contour line. The spacing between lines, called the **contour interval** and selected by the cartographer, depends on the purpose of and area covered by the map. The smaller the contour interval, the more detailed the representation of terrain.

The lowest line, mean sea level, connects points along the shore. If you jogged along this line, you would maintain a constant elevation of zero (the datum plane). Going neither uphill nor down, you would ultimately return to the original point. The same is true for each of the horizontal planes at elevations above the datum plane. In the lower part of Figure 4.10, these paths of equal elevation are projected onto a flat plane as a series of contour lines. By viewing the pattern and spacing of these lines, you can easily envision the shape of the island with its twin peaks separated by a valley, and infer the elevation of any point on its surface. For these reasons, topographic maps are widely used to represent the third dimension, depth.

The upper illustration in Figure 4.11 shows an aerial view of a coast where a river flanked by hills flows into a bay partially enclosed by a hooked sandbar or **spit.** The river valley is relatively flat; the slopes of uplands on either side of the river have been cut by streams. The hills on the right have smooth, gentle slopes above a steep wave-cut cliff. The hills on the left rise steeply from the valley floor, then tilt

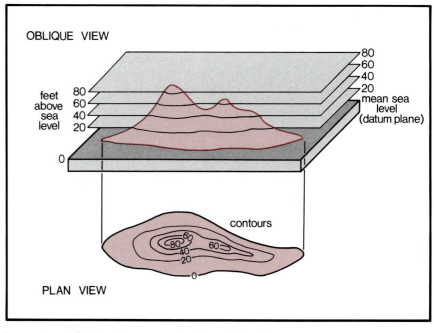

Figure 4.10 Contour lines on an imaginary island.

undergone severe glaciation, producing a beveled mountain landscape dotted by lakes, bogs, brooks, and streams. **Monadnocks,** the scoured peaks of the White Mountains, and elongated drumlins are distinctive landscape features of this area.

The Economy of New England and the Atlantic Provinces

Although largely depopulated today, the New England highlands were intensively farmed and logged over in the past. In the colonial period, these highlands supported subsistence farmers who grew hay, oats, rye, apples, and potatoes; raised poultry and dairy cows; cut timber and made maple syrup on the side. As commercial agriculture spread into more fertile environments in the Central Plains of North America, these eastern highlands lost much of their population, although local concentrations of activity remain.

Dairy farming is profitable in southern Vermont and New Hampshire, where ready access to metropolitan markets is an important advantage. The flat, sandy soils, adequate water, and long summer days of Prince Edward Island and the Aroostook Valley of Maine favor commercial potato production. Apples, pears, and cherries are grown in the Annapolis Valley of Nova Scotia. Along the northern coasts, fishing fleets are sheltered in small coves from Maine to Newfoundland. These fleets ply the North Atlantic Ocean catching shellfish along the coast and cod in offshore fishing grounds. The Grand Banks, where the cold waters of the Labrador Current collide with the

gently to an inclined **tableland** creased by small streams. An improved road follows the coast then curves inland up the river valley. An unimproved road and bridge cross the river to provide access to a church and several houses.

The lower illustration in Figure 4.11

shows the same coastal area in the form of a topographic map with elevations represented by contour lines. The contour interval is 20 feet. For ease of reading, every fifth contour (e.g., 100 feet, 200 feet) is accentuated as an **index contour.** The wide spacing of contour lines along the

river valley and where it empties into the sea indicates flat to gentle surfaces where you would travel a substantial distance before gaining 20 feet in elevation. By contrast, the closely packed contour lines along the wave-cut cliff and on the hill slopes to the left indicate steep slopes where rapid changes in elevation occur over short distances. Note that contour lines always point upstream because the bed of the stream is necessarily the lowest point along river valleys, tributary streams, and gullies.

The maps in the National Topographic Map Series of the U.S. Geological Survey (USGS) provide an invaluable source of information for geographers, regional planners, land-use analysts, and people engaged in outdoor recreational activities. Several map series are available for all or most of the United States at scales of 1:1,000,000 (1 inch equals 16 miles), 1:250,000 (1 inch equals 4 miles), 1:62,500 (1 inch equals approximately 1 mile), and 1:24,000 (1 inch equals 2000 feet). On these maps, contour lines and relief features are drawn in brown, water features in blue, vegetation of various types in green, and cultural features, such as roads, railroads, and buildings, in black. A complete listing of the extensive set of natural and man-made symbols used on these topographic map series is available from the USGS. Comparable topographic maps at various scales are available for Canada.

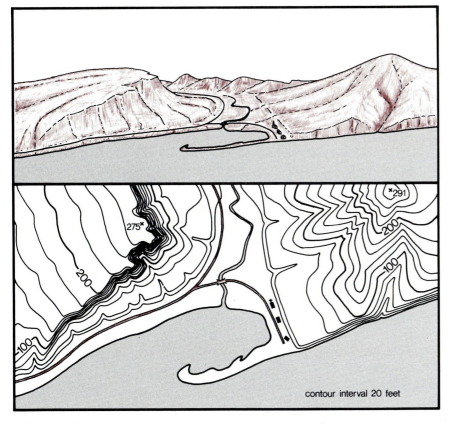

contour interval 20 feet

Figure 4.11 Aerial view and topographic map of coastal area.

warm waters of the **Gulf Stream,** are among the richest fishing grounds in the world. Increasingly, however, the economy of much of New England and the Atlantic Provinces depends on tourists from urban centers on the eastern seaboard, attracted to the rural vistas and rugged landscapes of this region.

In the Atlantic provinces, there are few cities of substantial size. The largest, Halifax in Nova Scotia (pop. 277,000) and Saint John's in Newfoundland (pop. 155,000), are oriented to the traditional economy of

fishing and logging. With incomes far below the average of the rest of Canada, the people of this area are poor. Government rejuvenation of the Atlantic provinces has played a role here since the 1950s. Efforts have centered on attracting skilled industries to the region's picturesque but languishing towns and cities and on developing more efficient techniques of exploiting local timber and mineral resources. With less than ten percent of Canada's population, the Atlantic provinces have stronger historical ties to Boston than to French-speaking

Montréal or the more distant Toronto. Their location north of the international border between Canada and the United States hinders natural economic and cultural connections with the south.

The New England Core

The heartland of this region is the narrow coastal plain of southern New England, where dense agricultural and urban populations are concentrated in a band of rolling glaciated land set between the mountains and the sea. As the regional capital of New

England's 12.7 million people, and as the northeastern outlier of the Industrial North, Boston has diminished in national importance as New York has grown. But with a population of 2.8 million, Boston is still the tenth largest city in the United States and the northern terminus of a near continuous belt of urbanization extending from Washington, D.C., through Baltimore, Philadelphia, and New York—a megalopolis of contiguous **metropolitan statistical areas.**

Boston's location on an excellent natural harbor, its seagoing commerce based on proximity to Europe, and its role as a service center for southern New England's dense network of small cities and towns account for its continuing importance. In the 1980s, the influx of high-technology industries has signaled the economic rejuvenation of both city and region.

South and west of Boston, the large industrial towns of Providence (pop. 919,000) and Hartford (pop. 726,000) dominate Rhode Island and Connecticut. The Connecticut River widens as it flows southward to form the most valuable stretch of agricultural land in New England. Dairy, grain, tobacco, and truck farms compete with suburban housing for space. Southern New England, a sprawling urban landscape, is a northern continuation of the intense concentration of population and industry characteristic of the Industrial North.

The Industrial North

The Industrial North is neither topographically nor culturally united. Its people live in environments ranging from the bedroom suburbs of cities lining the eastern seaboard to coal towns deep in the recesses of the Appalachian Mountains. Yet the westward expansion of the United States in the nineteenth century bound the three subregions of the Industrial North—Megalopolis, the Appalachian Highlands, and the Great Lakes Interior—into an interdependent industrial economy (Fig. 4.9). In the

process, one of the world's richest, most diverse, and most productive manufacturing complexes was created.

The initial east-west connection was made with the opening of the Erie Canal in 1825. It joined Buffalo on Lake Erie with Albany on the Hudson River, bringing the agricultural wealth of the awakening continent within the economic orbit of New York City. Railroads soon increased commerce and communication between interior plains and the coastal ports of New York, Philadelphia, and Baltimore, expanding the possibilities for industrial growth. Cities in the interior like Pittsburgh, Cleveland, Cincinnati, Chicago, and Milwaukee, exploited these possibilities and became industrial centers in their own right. With coal in Appalachia and iron in the Great Lakes, crop surpluses in the Middle West, and dense urban populations on the Atlantic coast, the Industrial North has the single greatest concentration of human activity in North America.

American Megalopolis

The cities of the Atlantic coastal plain from Boston to Washington contain half the industrial and commercial power of the United States in forty-two metropolitan statistical areas, ranging in size from New York (pop. 17.5 million) and four other cities of more than 2 million (Philadelphia, Boston, Washington, Baltimore) to a host of smaller urban centers. The cities of Megalopolis form a continuous urban belt with diminishing plots of farmland interspersed between them. This urban region—sometimes identified as "Boswash"—was the original focus for developing the concept of a megalopolis.

New Jersey and Rhode Island, entirely within this urbanized region, have the highest population densities in North America—over 900 persons per square mile, compared with California, the most highly urbanized state in the American West, with less than 200 people per square mile. Yet

Small towns, dairy farms, orchards, and vegetable gardens still dot the landscapes of New England, although the region now depends on tourism, high technology industry, and service employment to a large degree.

these statewide population figures convey neither the scope nor the intensity of the urban scene. New Jersey, despite its high population density, has relatively large open spaces in both the northwestern and southeastern parts of the state. Even today, the inhabitants of the pine barrens of southern New Jersey are principally trappers and blueberry pickers who retain a colonial accent and vocabulary much like isolated mountain folk in West Virginia and Kentucky. Areal statistics, therefore, do not reflect the true degree of urbanization. Where the people actually live in Megalopolis, densities are much higher.

With a metropolitan area population of nearly 17.5 million people located in three states, New York is one of the world's largest urban areas. Urbanization spreads from two towering groves of 500-foot skyscrapers in Manhattan outward in a 60-mile wide radius of suburban sprawl through Connecticut, the lower Hudson River Valley, Long Island, and New Jersey. As the nation's leading port situated at the mouth of the Hudson River, New York handles about half the nation's overseas air freight and passenger traffic. It is also the most important manufacturing and service center in the United States.

The scale of human energy compressed in New York City is difficult to grasp. The city employs 67,000 teachers, for 940,000 public school students. Some 3.6 million people are employed in the five **boroughs** of the city of New York. The borough of Brooklyn, an independent city until 1898, would be one of the largest cities in the United States were it independent today. Forty-eight states, all with more natural resources, have populations smaller than the New York metropolitan area. New York's black population is larger than the entire population of Atlanta. New York's Puerto Rican population dwarfs that of San Juan. The 7.3 million residents of the city of New York, many of them wealthy, as well as the 17.5

million annual visitors to the city, avoid the reality of those—1.8 million strong—who live in poverty. The cultural, social, and financial importance of New York to the nation as a whole cannot be overstated.

South of New York, the nation's fourth largest city, Philadelphia (pop. 4.8 million), is located at the head of the drowned estuary of the Delaware River. Straddling a narrow neck of land between the Schuylkill and Delaware rivers, Philadelphia's early industrial growth was based on waterpower. Today, Philadelphia has a broad manufacturing base including oil refining and chemicals.

Farther south, Baltimore (pop. 2.3 million), at the head of the Chesapeake Bay, is located in a transition zone between the Industrial North and the South. Although often perceived as a southern city, Baltimore is a center of heavy industry based on imported iron and coal transported overland from Appalachian fields. Baltimore is also, however, an important food-processing center for the agriculture of the Upper South.

Washington (pop. 3.5 million), the nation's capital, was originally situated along the Potomac River as a locational compromise between the North and the South. The French engineer Pierre L'Enfant planned a spacious city with a radial street pattern to display vistas of monuments and public buildings lining wide, tree-lined avenues. L'Enfant's image of the city of democracy, however, was quickly jeopardized by urban growth. As the site for disbursement of the federal budget, Washington is an administrative center that increasingly governs the growth and direction of the entire United States.

The Central Appalachian Highlands

From the top of a Manhattan skyscraper, it is possible to look well into the Appalachian Highlands, the western border of the urbanized Atlantic coastal plain. The **ridges and valleys** of the Appalachian Moun-

tains form a corrugated band of sparsely populated land running northeast to southwest—from the Catskill Mountains of New York south through the Alleghenies of Pennsylvania, western Maryland, and West Virginia, to the Blue Ridge Mountains of Maryland and Virginia. Still farther to the west, the coal-rich Allegheny Plateau, the largest **topographic** province in the Industrial North, is a highland zone extending west from New York into Ohio and Indiana and running southward through Kentucky and into central Tennessee.

At first glance, the thinly populated Appalachian Highlands appear to have little in common with the urban and industrial complexes in the interior and along the coast. Their intermediate location and strong resource base, however, have welded the economy of these highlands firmly to that of the Industrial North. Pittsburgh (pop. 2.1 million), the major metropolitan center of this subregion, is a classic example of the industrial geography of iron and steel. The city is located where the Allegheny and Monongahela rivers form the Ohio River. Coal lying close to the surface in the Appalachians was exploited early, fostering a wave of steel-based industrialization that brought labor and wealth to the area in the second half of the nineteenth century. Industrial towns set in the valleys grew up along the banks of the Allegheny, Susquehanna, and upper Ohio rivers. In their hinterlands, a population of small farmers and miners settled in isolated mountain valleys. As local iron deposits were exhausted, ore from the Upper Great Lakes was shipped by barge from Duluth at the western end of Lake Superior to ports on Lake Erie such as Cleveland and Erie, and then inland by rail.

Today, the metal-finishing factories of Pittsburgh utilize the coal resources of the Allegheny Plateau and import iron ore from Labrador and Venezuela. Saddled with high labor costs and aging industrial plants, this core of heavy industry today faces major problems in competing on world markets.

The Great Lakes Interior

Farther west, the band of industrialization continues along both the American and Canadian shores of the Great Lakes. Here, industrial centers are involved in the production of heavy metals, the transshipment of agricultural products to world markets, and the pursuit of integrated specialized industries, such as the manufacture of chemical, photographic, and pharmaceutical equipment as well as rubber and automobiles.

The ribbon of urbanization at the western end of Lake Ontario is dense. Rochester, New York, sprang up as a milling town processing grain from the rolling farmland of the Genesee Valley. Toronto and Buffalo are diversified centers of heavy industry. Toronto (pop. 3 million) serves a broad hinterland that encompasses much of Canada's effectively occupied territory.

Lake Erie's largest center of population is Cleveland (pop. 1.9 million), whose long list of manufactures reflects the industrial diversity typical of the Great Lakes region. Detroit (pop. 4.3 million) capital of the automotive industry, is situated at the narrowest point of the **strait** connecting Lake Erie with Lake Saint Clair and Lake Huron. Detroit has access to iron ore from Minnesota and Upper Michigan and coal from Pennsylvania, West Virginia, and Ohio. Despite these locational advantages, the selection of Detroit as a base of American industry was the result of decisions by a few early industrialists—David Buick, Ransom Eli Olds, and Henry Ford.

Farther west, Chicago (pop. 7.1 million) grew as a railroad hub whose lines of steel tapped the agricultural potential of the breadbasket of Amer-

This nighttime satellite photograph vividly displays the dense concentration of human activity in the Industrial North. This region extends from megalopolis on the Atlantic coast westward across the Appalachian Mountains to the Great Lakes interior.

ica. In 1852, Chicago was linked with New York by railroad, and a web of steel was drawn across the Middle West. Chicago evolved into a prairie metropolis, a heartland city of skyscrapers and stockyards. It has epitomized smalltown America grown up, a city of go-getters whose dreams of progress and prosperity financed the development of a large portion of North America. Third only to New York and Los Angeles in municipal population and the center of a substantial manufacturing belt, Chicago is the western focus of the Industrial North.

North of Chicago on Lake Michigan, Milwaukee (pop. 1.4 million) possesses a mixture of light and heavy industry characteristic of many Great Lakes cities. The twin cities on the Mississippi, Minneapolis and St. Paul

(pop. 2.2 million), are flour-milling centers for the northern plains as far west as Montana. Winnipeg (pop. 585,000), Chicago's alter ego to the north, is the center of the trans-Canadian transportation network. Marquette, Duluth, and Thunder Bay are port cities on Lake Superior that ship iron ore mined in the Mesabi, Vermilion, and other ranges on the southern fringe of the Canadian Shield.

The cities of the Great Lakes Interior from Syracuse to Milwaukee are surrounded by important agricultural landscapes. Along the shores of Lake Ontario and Lake Erie in both Canada and the United States, production of apples, pears, peaches, cherries, and grapes is substantial. Much of rural Michigan, under the warming influence of nearby Lake

Michigan, is devoted to fruit cultivation. Lake Michigan's southern shore is also well suited to the production of flowers and nursery stock—an important industry in a nation of suburban gardeners. Beyond the moderating climatic influence of the lakes, grain and hay farming is combined with dairying and poultry raising.

The South

The American South covers a variety of terrain in the south-central and southeastern United States (Fig. 4.9). It is an area distinguished by its warm climate and long growing season, and is occupied by a people bound to the fact and legend of the Civil War.

Much of the region remains intensely rural and relatively isolated, a landscape of small towns and specialized farming. Rural poverty is great, and outmigration to southern industrial centers and to the cities of the Industrial North has been strong in this century. Only recently have fast-growing centers, such as Houston, Atlanta, and Miami, attracted migrants from the rest of the United States and abroad.

Topographically the South embodies an extension of the Atlantic coastal plain, the Appalachians, and the Mississippi Valley—all areas that farther north form core elements of the American industrial belt. But the South has retained its cultural distance from the rest of the country. "The southern states are an aggregate of communities, not of individuals," said the South Carolinian John C. Calhoun in 1838. The region still preserves elements of its plantation economy and a coherent set of moral attitudes. Today, the full brunt of the American industrial economy is affecting selected parts of the South, modifying and integrating this distinctive culture region into the broader framework of American society.

The Coastal Lowlands

The lowland coast of the South is topographically similar from Virginia to Texas. Wide, open bays and inlets with **offshore bars** are set in a humid, swampy environment.

In contrast to the Industrial Northeast, urbanization is quite limited. On the Atlantic coast, Norfolk (pop. 1.3 million), Virginia, has grown because of important naval installations. Like Charleston, Savannah, and Jacksonville, Norfolk is an export center for products grown on the coastal plain: cotton, tobacco, peanuts, lumber, and naval stores.

Inland where the coastal plain abuts the piedmont in Virginia, the Carolinas, and Georgia, a string of cities grew up on the **fall line.** Richmond,

Raleigh, Columbia, and Montgomery utilized the waterpower generated at this topographical break as the basis for the textile industry, and today each city is an important manufacturing center.

Farther south, the lowland South projects nearly 400 miles into the Atlantic Ocean in the form of the Florida Peninsula and extends westward as a wide coastal plain bordering the Gulf of Mexico as far as the Rio Grande of Texas.

Until the early part of this century, the Florida Peninsula remained largely a wilderness, surrounded by warm water. A raised limestone platform, Florida's near year-round growing season proved ideal for citrus cultivation. Its warm climate at-

Atlanta, Georgia, is one of the fastest growing cities in the South. It reflects the powerful economic forces that are transforming this region.

tracted heavy migration from the North. Since World War II, much of Florida has become a suburban landscape of settlements designed for elderly citizens, refugees from megalopolis, and winter tourists. Tampa—St. Petersburg and Miami, both with populations of 1.8 million, are Florida's largest cities. Orlando has grown spectacularly to reach a population of 900,000. Florida's distinctive culture and society, however, are a purely twentieth-century phenomena. In 1900, Miami was a trading post and yacht harbor with only 1681 winter residents.

To the west, the **subtropical** Gulf Coastal Plain bordering the Gulf of Mexico is generally under 300 feet in elevation, while inland Gulf Coastal Plains reach up to 600 feet above sea level. The Mississippi River divides the Gulf Plain into eastern and western sections. With the longest growing season in eastern North America, hot summers, mild winters, and rain throughout the year, the Gulf Plain is an ideal environment for cotton cultivation. Cotton spread across this area in the first half of the nineteenth century. Much of the Gulf Plain, however, still remains in timber, and logging, especially in Louisiana and East Texas, is a large-scale industrial enterprise. Rice and sugarcane are important crops along the Louisiana and Upper Texas Gulf coast. The Texas cattle industry has bred animals uniquely suited to the hot, wet climate. In southern Texas, vegetable and citrus crops are grown in the Rio Grande Valley.

The major cities of the Gulf Coastal Plain are the ports of New Orleans (pop. 1.3 million) and Houston (pop. 3.2 million). New Orleans is the entrepôt of the Mississippi and the cotton capital of the southern coast. Built on a forested lowland **bayou**, Houston is now the fourth most populous city in the United States and one of the largest cities in the world in area, covering parts of six Texas counties. Houston's diversified industrial base

expanded when construction of a ship channel connected it to the Gulf of Mexico, diverting traffic away from the port of Galveston. The discovery of oil and natural gas in the region made Houston the petrochemical center of the United States. After the decision to locate NASA headquarters in Houston, the city became a leading center of high technology. North of Houston, a string of urban centers—the largest of which is Dallas–Fort Worth (pop. 3.5 million), serve both the lowland South and the Central Plains.

The Inland South

The inland South, composed of the southern Appalachians and related highlands to the west, is distinctly southern in culture, but differs substantially in economy from the lowland South. On the Appalachian piedmont, a tradition of small, family-worked dairy farms and orchards contrasts strongly with the large-scale peanut and cotton-plantation economy of the coastal plain. Still farther inland beyond the Blue Ridge Mountains, settlement followed the long valleys of major rivers like the Shenandoah, the Tennessee, and the Coosa.

Narrow Appalachian valleys widen southward, with Knoxville, Chattanooga, and Birmingham growing into industrial cities utilizing waterpower from the TVA and exploiting the coal and iron ore deposits of the Appalachians. Atlanta (pop. 2.5 million), the largest city in the southern Appalachians, influences much of the eastern part of the South. It diversified from a marketing and railroad center into metal refining, textiles, fertilizer, automobiles, and agricultural machinery. Now one of the fastest growing cities in the South and site of America's busiest single airport (Hartsfield), Atlanta is rapidly becoming the banking and commercial capital of the Southeast.

The valleys and plateaus that spread

north and west from the Blue Ridge Mountains form an isolated, poverty-stricken region with a history of hardship and human tragedy. Appalachia, as this region is generally called, remains a core area of unemployment. Because of technological advances, its rich coal and lumber resources are efficiently exploited by a dwindling labor force. Although federally sponsored programs have attempted to revitalize Appalachia's economy since the 1930s, the **mountain and valley** heartland of the southern Appalachians continues to be a zone of heavy out-migration and interior stagnation.

Farther west and north of Appalachia, settlement in the fertile bluegrass basins of Kentucky and Tennessee is more prosperous. Natural prairies in the hinterlands of Louisville and Lexington are rich farmlands noted for tobacco and finely manicured horse-breeding farms. Nashville (pop. 910,000), a center of country music and southern culture, is also an insurance and clothing center. The bountiful farmland of central Tennessee was sufficiently attractive to make Nashville the first city chartered west of the Appalachians in 1784.

Across the middle Mississippi River plain, dominated by the industrial transshipment port of Memphis (pop. 945,000), lie additional southern highlands—the Ozark Plateau in Arkansas and Missouri, the Boston Mountains in Arkansas, and the Ouachita Mountains of Oklahoma and Arkansas. Life here is similar to life in Appalachia, the original home of most of this region's settlers. Mining of coal, **bauxite** (aluminum ore), and iron ore is locally important, and lowland farms specialize in apple orchards and dairies. Upland farms are poor, and where the forest cover has been destroyed, erosion is severe. Little Rock (pop. 499,000), the largest city of the area, is on the western frontier of the South, and like Joplin and Springfield in Missouri, is a center for smelting aluminum, lead, and zinc ores mined in the uplands.

The Central Plains

The center of North America, a treeless prairie, was perceived as a vast dry land until the middle of the nineteenth century. After 1850, however, the thick sod of the Central Plains was turned over and the region became the most productive grain field in the world.

The extent of this natural prairie is defined by climate. To the north, the grasslands extend into central Alberta, beyond which the cold is too severe for abundant growth of grasses. Eastward, prairie stretches into Indiana and Illinois, where although rainfall is sufficient to support forests, the luxuriant growth of grasses (a single plant can put out 350 miles of roots in a year) choked off other vegetation. Fires, to which grasses are virtually immune, also repelled the eastern margins of the forests. To the south, the grasslands fade far into Mexico. The Central Plains are clearly defined on the west by the Rocky Mountains (Fig. 4.9).

In this agricultural environment, climate is of critical importance. Generally speaking, rainfall in the Central Plains declines from east to west because of the **rain shadow** effect of the Rocky Mountains. Average annual temperatures, as one would expect, rise from north to south. Two contrasting **air masses** dominate the Central Plains. In winter, polar air from the Arctic sweeps southward and temperatures below zero degrees Fahrenheit have been recorded as far south as Austin, Texas, on the edge of the Gulf Coastal Plain. Average winter temperatures in the north are severely cold. In summer, the land heats rapidly as Gulf air moves northward, pushing continental air back into the Arctic. Thunderstorms and tornadoes are

common in spring; high daily temperatures occur far north into the Canadian prairie. The frost-free season varies with latitude. The 100-day limit for wheat cultivation extends from Edmonton, Alberta, across central Saskatchewan to southern Manitoba. On the southern margins of the Central Plains, growing seasons of up to 240 days occur in Texas.

The Economy of the Central Plains

From the Canadian provinces of Saskatchewan and Alberta to the central United States, the Central Plains exhibit considerable topographical and agricultural diversity. Broad belts of specialized commercial farming cover the Central Plains in a series of agricultural regions graded according to climate and terrain.

In the far north, a zone of spring-planted wheat extends from the northern limit of profitability along a line from Edmonton to Winnipeg to the Dakotas and parts of Minnesota and Montana. Although called the spring wheat belt, more barley and rye grains are grown here than in any other section of America. Beef cattle, sold young for fattening in the corn belt farther south, are also important. Canada's cities in the spring wheat belt are much larger than those of the United States. The largest, Edmonton (pop. 554,000) grew with the development of the Alberta oil fields after World War II.

In Minnesota and Wisconsin, the dairy belt contrasts sharply with the wheatlands to the north and west. Rainfall is higher and winters less harsh. A wooded landscape of family dairy farms surrounded by hayfields predominates. Although not an environmental component of the grassland prairies, the dairy belt is a concentrated, contiguous market for grains from the Central Plains.

South of this area, in the heart of the Central Plains, the corn belt reaches from eastern Nebraska to the

Allegheny Plateau of Ohio. The economy of the corn belt, like other farming regions in the Central Plains, is directly related to local climate (Fig. 4.13). Ideal conditions for corn are average July temperatures in the mid-70s and summer rainfall totals near 11 inches. In the corn belt, where these conditions are met, a cultivated carpet of cornfields covers virtually all of Iowa, Illinois, and Indiana, and significant portions of Missouri, Ohio, Michigan, Minnesota, South Dakota, Nebraska, and Kansas. Corn land is rotated with soybeans, winter wheat, and pasture. Throughout the belt, cattle and hog feedlots fatten animals for market. The natural prairie sod of the corn belt has disappeared; the entire area is now a landscape of large-scale commercial agriculture.

Westward in the Central Plains, elevation rises from 2000 to 5000 feet and rainfall declines. This sparser grassland, often called the Great Plains, is a transitional zone between the humid East and the arid uplands of the West. The Great Plains are bounded by the Missouri River on the north, the Rocky Mountains on the west, and the Balcones **escarpment** of Texas on the south.

Water is the critical scarcity on the Great Plains, and periodic droughts have twice forced dramatic retreats of the agricultural frontier. After the Civil War, droughts struck homesteaders on the Great Plains in the 1880s leaving abandoned farms and human misery in their wake. But rising prices for wheat after World War I led to a renewal of speculative wheat farming on the Great Plains in the 1920s—a period of above-average rainfall. **Dust bowl** conditions resulted from below-average rainfall a decade later and again scarred the region with ecological disaster. Since that time, rural population has declined considerably, and modern farming methods—especially the no-till planting method of plowing and the utilization of former cropland for

GEOLAB

SPATIAL DIFFUSION

The culture regions of North America and elsewhere have been formed as people, material goods, and ideas spread, or diffused, across space and time. Culture regions are produced by population migration, by contact and communication between groups and individuals, and by the diffusion of innovations and ideas.

Some innovations originate in a single location, whereas others arise without communication or contact—in other words, through **independent invention.** Some elements spread widely, while others remain restricted in space. Every culture and culture region, however, is produced by innumerable innovations that have been adopted, rejected, or modified.

People have a justly deserved reputation for mobility in North America. **Spatial diffusion**—the spread of goods, people or ideas—has contributed directly to today's social and cultural patterns. The study of spatial diffusion, then, is central to understanding North America and is a major field of study in human geography.

Based on the research of Professor Hägerstrand at the University of Lund in Sweden, human geographers identify two major types of diffusion: (1) **relocation diffusion** and (2) **expansion diffusion.** In most cases of diffusion, innovations tend to weaken progressively farther from points of origin and are accepted less as time goes by. This characteristic of spatial diffusion is called **time-distance decay.** "Barriers" deflect, channel, or obstruct the spread of innovations. Barriers may be social or environmental. **Ab-**sorbing barriers block diffusions completely. For example, this occurs when governments effectively ban the introduction of a cultural element or group of people in their national territories, or alternatively, when a body of water halts the spread of an innovation beyond the coast. Most barriers, however, are **permeable barriers** that weaken, slow, or channel the diffusion of cultural elements and people. Obvious examples of permeable barriers are mountain ranges, deserts, and international boundaries.

Relocation diffusion takes place when people move from one area to another, carrying with them the ideas and institutions that make up their social fabric. Figure 4.12 shows the spread of ideas and folk culture in eastern North America inland from culture hearths on the eastern seaboard as an example of relocation diffusion. The spread of ideas was principally caused by migration of pioneers across the Appalachian Mountains into the American interior. In this case, the mountains acted as a permeable barrier. Gaps in the Appalachians and river valleys beyond provided natural routes of migration, channeling the diffusion of ideas and culture from coastal hearths in French Canada, New England, Pennsylvania, Virginia, and the South.

Expansion diffusion occurs when ideas spread outward from a point of origin throughout a population. The number of knowers (those who accept an innovation) increases and the spatial distribution enlarges. Expansion diffusion is called **contagious diffusion** when it spreads like a disease from individual to individual without regard to social status or power. Everyone accepts the innovation. It is called **hierarchical diffusion** when ideas spread from one important individual or group to another and then down hierarchical social chains. Examples of hierarchical diffusion include changes in fashion, taste in music, and expres-

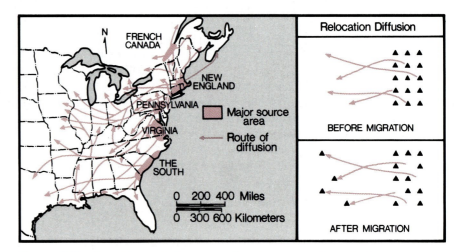

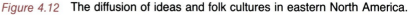

Figure 4.12 The diffusion of ideas and folk cultures in eastern North America.

permanent sheep and cattle grazing—have stabilized the economy of the Great Plains. In the Llano Estacado of the Texas Panhandle, irrigation has converted former wheatlands to cotton production, but underground water is limited, and exhaustion of the water supply looms as a definite possibility.

Chicago, defined earlier as an important city in the Industrial North, is also the dominant urban center of most of the Central Plains because of its transportation network. The city influences the distribution of local manufacturing, food processing, agricultural service industries, and commodity markets on the Central Plains. Smaller cities serve local hinterlands as processing and regional banking centers and as outposts of the U.S. Department of Agriculture, whose involvement in the organization of production and markets is considerable. Minneapolis–St. Paul is the center of the dairy belt; Des Moines, Omaha, Kansas City, and Topeka are the major service centers in the corn belt. Farther south, wheat farms and cattle ranches on the Great

sions of speech. **Stimulus diffusion** is a third type of expansion diffusion that occurs when a specific cultural element is rejected but the underlying concept is accepted.

Figure 4.13, showing the spread of hybrid corn in the United States, is an excellent example of expansion diffu-

sion. Varieties of hybrid corn were first accepted by farmers in a core area in Iowa and Illinois in 1936. In the next twelve years acceptance of hybrid corn spread rapidly across most corn-growing areas. Acceptance of hybrid corn was encouraged by the U.S. Department of Agriculture and local

country farm agents and was, in part, an example of hierarchical diffusion. Contagious diffusion undoubtedly also played an important role, however, as neighboring farmers exchanged information about the increased yields and disease resistance of hybrid strains.

Resistance to the diffusion of hybrid corn occurred in three areas. In the west, aridity is a barrier to the diffusion of hybrid—or any other—corn. In New England, more lucrative farming of dairy and market garden crops, and in Alabama and Georgia, important plantation crops prevented early acceptance. These barriers can be viewed as absorbing (corn requires too much water to grow in the arid West) and permeable (as economic circumstances changed, hybrid corn was accepted later in New England, Alabama, and Georgia).

The study of spatial diffusion by human geographers has barely begun; its processes are not yet fully understood. It is clear, however, that understanding culture regions and how they vary is directly linked to the acceptance, partial acceptance, or rejection of countless innovations over substantial periods of time. Today, the diffusion of women's rights as embodied in the Equal Rights Amendment, attitudes toward environmental quality expressed in local referenda, and views on quality of life as demonstrated by movement to the suburbs and the sunbelt are transforming the human geography of North America.

Adapted from: Henry Glassie, *Pattern in the Material Folk Culture of the Eastern United States.* Philadelphia: University of Pennsylvania Press, 1968, p. 38; Zvi Griliches, "Hybrid Corn and the Economics of Innovation," *Science,* Vol. 132 (July 1960).

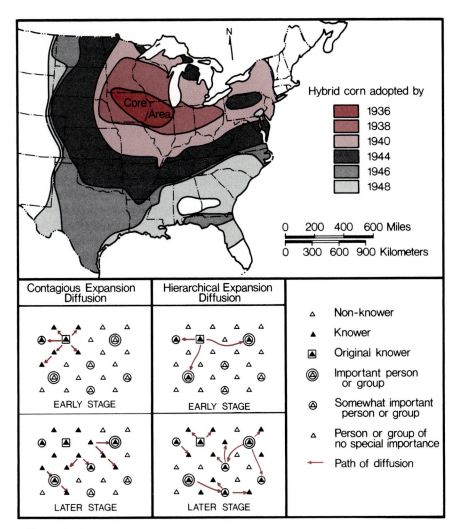
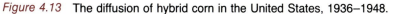

Figure 4.13 The diffusion of hybrid corn in the United States, 1936–1948.

Plains are served by Wichita in Kansas; Oklahoma City and Tulsa in Oklahoma; and Lubbock, Amarillo, and Forth Worth in Texas. Seemingly far to the east, but midwestern in industry and service is Indianapolis. St. Louis, at the junction of the Mississippi and Missouri rivers, controls the commodities and river traffic passing southward to the Gulf of

Mexico and northward into the corn belt and the spring wheat belt.

The West

The West is a region of huge internal distances, great topographical variety, and a diversified history of settlement. Thinly populated except on the Pacific coast, the West is gen-

erally perceived in terms of its physical geography–the Rocky Mountains, the **intermontane** basins and plateaus, and the Cascade, Sierra, and Coast ranges of the Pacific West (Fig. 4.9). Settled within living memory, it was for thousands of years the domain of agricultural and hunting Indian tribes. But wagon trains crossing the Great Plains and the Rockies brought farmers to Oregon, the Mormons to Utah, and gold miners to California, wave after wave of settlers seeking new lives and fortunes—a process that continues even today. Perhaps no other region has so captured the imagination of the North American people. Their restless movement has created a diversity of wests side by side from Los Angeles and Las Vegas to the forbidding recesses of the Rockies, the barren deserts of the Southwest, and the dense **rain forests** of Puget Sound.

The Rocky Mountains

The Rocky Mountains course southeast from the Brooks Range of Alaska through the Mackenzie Mountains of the Yukon and Northwest Territories to the Canadian Rockies, which trend southward between British Columbia and Alberta. In the United States, the American Rockies are characterized by long, rounded, domed ridges rising from wide valleys frequently paralleled by equally high volcanic ranges, such as the Absarokas of Montana and Wyoming. The easternmost ranges of the Rockies rise 10,000 feet above the Great Plains and are broken by only a few east-west passes. Farther north, the Canadian Rockies rise equally abruptly from a plain dotted by the lakes and wide rivers that course across the taiga of the Canadian Shield.

There are few large towns in the Rockies. Rural population is sparse, with most people engaged in sheep and cattle ranching, lumbering, and mining. Mining of copper, lead, gold, and silver is the basis of most cities in the Rockies, but the limited population in their vast hinterlands has inhibited urban growth. In both Canada and the United States, the largest cities serve both the Rockies and the Great Plains. Calgary (pop. 593,000) is the trading center for stockraisers and wheat farmers in the Canadian plains. The lumber mills of the city are based on nearby mountain forests. Denver–Boulder (pop. 1.8 million) has a diversified industrial base and provides service functions for both the central Rockies and the neighboring Great Plains.

The Intermontane Plateaus

Between the Rocky Mountains and the Sierra ranges of the Pacific, three high plateaus—the Columbia Plateau in the northwest, the Great Basin centered in Nevada, and the Colorado Plateau—form a dry, rugged swath extending from the Canadian border to northern Mexico.

In the north, the Columbia Plateau is a landscape of dry valleys and forested ridges. Dry-farming techniques make commercial grain agriculture feasible. In eastern Washington and British Columbia, irrigated valleys are major continental suppliers of apples and pears. In the more arid eastern and southern portions of the Columbia Plateau, thousands of unbroken acres of grain make this the wheat belt of the West. Water diverted from the Columbia River through the Columbia Basin Project has transformed the agriculture of the Columbia Plateau. Alfalfa and a wide variety of specialty crops, from mint to gladiolus, have been added to the agricultural economy of the region. Spokane (pop. 356,000), the largest city on the plateau, commands three passes through the northern Rockies and has a growing industrial base dependent on the abundant hydroelectric power of the Columbia River.

The Great Basin, centered on upraised, eroded highlands in Nevada, has one of the driest climates in the United States. In the Sonora, Mojave, and Colorado deserts in the south, rain may not fall for a year or more. Daytime temperature ranges are high, and life is restricted to irrigated **oases.** In general, the settled valleys of the Great Basin receive less than 10 inches of rain a year, with neighboring highland ranges receiving up to 20 inches. Agriculture is limited to cattle grazing, dry farming of grain, and cultivation in isolated irrigated zones.

The Salt Lake depression of Utah, the greatest population concentration in the Great Basin, is an oasis watered by streams coursing down from the surrounding Wasatch Mountains. Originally settled by Mormons, Salt Lake City (pop. 1 million) is the chief distribution center for the Great Basin. Other cities—Las Vegas, Carson City, and Reno—originally served gold, copper, lead, and zinc mining operations. But attractive scenery, gambling, and the hot, dry climate have drawn people to this area. The spectacular growth of Phoenix and Tucson, Arizona, can be attributed directly to the search for a winter-free climate. Phoenix expanded from a small vegetable and fruit-farming community of 5500 people in 1900 to become the ninth largest metropolitan area in the United States with a population of 1.9 million; Tucson's 1950 population of 45,000 grew to 586,000.

The Colorado Plateau consists of the largely uninhabited highlands of central Utah, northern Arizona, New Mexico, and western Colorado. The deeply **entrenched streams** of the area, best illustrated by the Colorado, are characterized by canyons incised into uplifted blocks of **sedimentary** rock. The area is rich in gold, silver, and copper, and its coal resources are attracting increasing attention. Albuquerque (pop. 464,000), founded as a regional capital of New Spain in 1706, serves a broad section of this thinly populated land.

The Western Ranges

West of the intermontane region, the land rises sharply in the Sierra Nevada of California and the Cascade Mountains farther north, falls abruptly in a succession of interior valleys, and rises again as the Coast Ranges along the Pacific. Over this varied terrain, many types of agriculture and settlement patterns prevail. Nowhere else in North America do such variations in climate occur over short distances.

The climate is dominated by polar Pacific air that reaches as far south as San Diego in winter. In summer, tropical air advances as far north as Vancouver Island. The seasonal shift of these Pacific air masses across rugged relief gives the Pacific West its special climates. The coasts from Alaska to San Francisco are characterized by humidity, high rainfall, and moderate temperatures. These climatic conditions contrast strongly with the winter **continentality** of the interior. Southern California, under dry air from spring until fall, exhibits characteristics of a Mediterranean climate, with little rainfall in summer and a maximum in winter because of the southward march of maritime **polar air** during that season. Throughout the region, the Coast Ranges, Cascades, and Sierra Nevada foster locally high rainfall totals.

The Sierra Nevada are young, folded mountains severely glaciated in their higher elevations and **faulted** on both eastern and western slopes. Rainfall totals of up to 70 inches on the western slopes of the Sierras provide a reservoir of water important for the expansion of agriculture in the valleys below and for urban populations along the coast. The entrapment and channelization of this runoff has been fundamental to the growth of modern California.

Two centers of irrigated agriculture—the Central Valley and the Los Angeles Basin—draw water from the Sierra Nevada through hydrological engineering complexes whose maximum expansion has apparently been reached. To the north, the Sierra Nevada and the Cascades sweep westward merging with the Coast Mountains in British Columbia to culminate in the Alaska Range. In Alaska, geologically recent uplifted mountains have created the highest peaks in North America. In the Alaska Range, Mount McKinley (also known by its Indian name, Denali) rises to 20,320 feet.

A series of topographical depressions—rich agricultural valleys—line the western face of the Sierra Nevada and the Cascades. The most important are Puget Sound in British Co-

lumbia and Washington, the Willamette Valley of Oregon, and the Central Valley of California. Filled with **alluvial** debris up to 200-feet thick, they form the agricultural heartland of the Far West. In the north, Vancouver (pop. 1.2 million), Seattle (pop. 1.7 million) and Tacoma (pop. 524,000) line Puget Sound. Portland (pop. 1.2 million) has grown to serve the specialized dairyland of the Willamette Valley. In California, a number of urban centers, most notably Sacramento (pop. 1.3 million), dot an agricultural landscape of fruit and nut orchards, vegetable gardens, and cotton fields in the Central Valley.

The Coast Ranges rise out of the Pacific Ocean to border California, Oregon, and Washington. Generally speaking, the Coast Ranges increase

in elevation northward, from rolling hills 2000 to 6000 feet high north of Los Angeles to the 8000-foot Olympic Mountains of Washington.

San Francisco–Oakland (pop. 3.5 million) is an immense urban area encircling San Franciso Bay, a drowned estuary that provides direct access to the Central Valley. On this natural harbor, San Francisco developed into the premier Pacific port of North America. Devastated by earthquake in 1906, San Francisco lost its lead as the largest city in the West to Los Angeles in the decade that followed. Now a center for a wide variety of manufactures—heavy industry, shipbuilding, electronics, and high technology—San Francisco is the home of two of the finest universities in North America, the University of California at Berkeley and

Tract housing, diversified industry, and a web of freeways blanket the landscape of the sixty-mile wide Los Angeles conurbation.

Stanford University. South of Stanford University, a series of communities known as "Silicon Valley" has developed as a center of innovation and diffusion of new technology in the computer industry.

The growth of Los Angeles is often perceived as a symbol of the structural changes of North American life during the twentieth century. The city has evolved from a trade center based on fruit and vegetable cultivation in the Los Angeles Basin into a multicored urban conurbation more than 75 miles broad linked by automobiles.

The work of Los Angeles is as varied as its population. Booming transport equipment industries—particularly aircraft—attracted thousands of Americans to southern California in the late 1940s and 1950s. Earlier, in the 1930s, refugees from the dust bowl migrated to California in search of employment. In 1900, southern California contained only a quarter of the state's population; by the early 1980s, the area from Santa Barbara to San Diego included two thirds of California's 26.4 million people. At the same time, the population of Los Angeles jumped from 102,000 in 1900 to 8.1 million now. Today, the unstructured nature of growth in the Los Angeles Basin endangers those very features that attracted people to the region.

South of Los Angeles, the California scene is dominated by San Diego (pop. 2.1 million), an important naval base, retirement center, and the United States' eighth largest city. San Diego was founded in 1769, the first of a number of Spanish colonial efforts to convert California's Indians to Catholicism and to redirect their hunting and gathering economy toward agriculture and herding. Inland, east of the Coastal Range, the arid Imperial Valley around the Salton Sea is now a center of intensive, irrigated agriculture conducted at elevations below sea level. Water diverted from the Colorado River by the All-American Canal allows the cultivation of cotton, alfalfa, date

palms, and a wide variety of vegetables for both California and national markets.

The Northwest and Alaska

From northern California along the Pacific coast to Alaska lies a wide expanse of land separated by great distances from the rest of urban North America. The coastal zones of the Pacific Northwest states (Oregon and Washington), British Columbia, and the twentieth-century frontier of Alaska are characterized by similar maritime environments. Sea and forest play important economic roles in the region. Farming is restricted to favored locations near the sea or carved out of forest. The port cities of the Northwest have grown in proportion to the wealth of their fishing, forestry, and farming, and each serves a large hinterland.

Although the salmon fisheries of the coast have steadily declined in output since the 1920s, the fishing industry has expanded to cover the entire northern Pacific. The amount of fish taken from the Pacific by competitive fleets from the United States, Canada, Japan, the Soviet Union, Britain, and Denmark is now forty times greater than the catch from the Atlantic.

Similarly, of all North American forests, those on the West Coast are by far the most valuable. The trees—dense stands of Douglas fir, western hemlock and cedar, ponderosa pine, Sitka spruce, and balsam fir—are used for construction, pulp, and furniture. The natural properties of these woods and the extent of the forests from Alaska to northern California have made lumbering the primary rural activity. Fully 70 percent of Washington and nearly 50 percent of Oregon is covered with a forest four fifths of which can be exploited. In British Columbia, 15 percent of the total value of production comes from wood. Logging is facilitated by the numerous rivers of the region, which along with truck and rail transport allow easy access to lumber mills.

Farming attracted the earliest pi-

oneers to the Northwest. They believed that thick forests were a sign of rich soils. But the wooded, mountainous landscape rendered farming profitable only in a few valleys. The Willamette River Valley of Oregon and the lowlands of the Puget Sound area became notable dairy, cattle, and fruit centers. Farther north, in British Columbia, farming is concentrated around the coastal cities of Victoria and Vancouver where vegetables and orchard crops can be produced owing to the 200-to-240-day growing season of the Fraser River delta and Vancouver Island. In Alaska, the Matanuska Valley, with good soils and shelter from harsh winds, was developed in the 1930s as a model for northern agriculture. Even though the growing season is barely over 100 days, the long, warm summer days make cultivation of vegetables, oats, hay, and potatoes possible.

The settlements of the Northwest are typically clustered on inlets where interior valleys meet the sea. Each is a trade center for the fishing, logging, and farming products of its hinterland. Specialized occupations have developed out of modern communications and the hydroelectric projects in the Columbia River Basin and along the fast-running streams of British Columbia. Industrial maturity and affluence have fostered diversification. Portland, at the juncture of the Willamette and Columbia rivers, boasts the busiest harbor of any American port, although the value and tonnage of cargo is not exceptionally high. Seattle is the dominant urban center of Puget Sound, a drowned valley set between the Cascade and Coast ranges. Its economic fortunes rest on the aeronautics industry, its strategic location as the closest American link with the Orient, and its position as the financial and transportation service center for Alaskan development.

At the head of Puget Sound, Vancouver Island lies between the Strait of Juan de Fuca facing the United States and the Strait of Georgia flanking Canada. At Vancouver Island, the island and fjord environment of mountains, glaciers, rivers, and forests begins and extends northward to Alaska, Victoria (pop. 234,000) the capital of British Columbia is an oddly English urban landscape and society. Vancouver, the metropolis of the Canadian West and third largest Canadian city, is located at the mouth of the Fraser River. The city began as a trading post of the Hudson's Bay Company in the early 1800s and was a lumber town early in this century. Today, Vancouver is an important industrial city and the export center for wheat from the prairie provinces.

Alaska, nearly 600,000 square miles large, 16 percent of the land area of the United States, is connected to the south by both the Alaska Highway and by the Inside Passage (Alaska Marine Highway), which threads through the coastal straits of the Pacific. Moderating maritime influences are strongly felt in the Alaskan Panhandle. Rainfall is heavy, reaching as high as 100 inches annually, and the climate is remarkably free from severe cold. Settlements in the south-central portion of the state and on the Aleutian Islands have capitalized on rich offshore fisheries and the dense forests of spruce, hemlock, and cedar. Anchorage (pop. 236,000) has functions similar to those of other cities in the Pacific Northwest.

High elevations are reached in the Alaska and Saint Elias ranges; peaks rising over 18,000 feet are common. Inland, beyond this great natural barrier, the Yukon Plateau is walled off from the far north by the Brooks Range. From the Yukon River Basin northward, rainfall declines to 15 inches or less in an Arctic desert. Extreme winter cold is interrupted by brief, yet surprisingly warm, summers. Beyond the Brooks Range, the vast tundra of the Arctic Coastal Plain stretches north to the Arctic Ocean. The Yukon Plateau, with little other natural wealth, attracted a population of miners in search of gold at the turn of the century and Alaska was organized into a territory in 1912.

With statehood in 1959 and a growing, if small, population, Alaska now is experiencing rapid industrial growth. With the discovery of substantial reserves of oil at Prudhoe Bay on the Arctic Ocean, the population of Alaska is now 521,000—more than a 25 percent increase in the last

The Trans-Alaska Pipeline carries oil 800 miles southward from Prudhoe Bay north of the Arctic Circle to the port of Valdez on the Gulf of Alaska. This is mile 562.

decade. The oil boom has launched Alaska toward a future fully integrated with that of the rest of the continent.

CONTEMPORARY NORTH AMERICA

After World War II, the United States became the leader of the free world. In 1961, President John F. Kennedy declared the United States was prepared to "pay any price, bear any burden, meet any hardship" to achieve its international role. It was a lofty goal: the price was high, the burden heavy, and success elusive. A costly postwar arms race with the Soviet Union drained U.S. national resources. Stung by the Soviet Union's space satellite Sputnik in 1957, the finest minds and most sophisticated technologies in the country were directed to hurtle an American into outer space. To maintain peace, international intervention seemed necessary. So American soldiers manned bases on every continent, fought skirmishes in Latin America, and endured bloody wars in Korea (1950–1953) and Vietnam (1965–1975).

International involvement was not confined only to the political arena. North American manufactures and foodstuffs dominated world markets, and _An Economy of Affluence_ beyond that of any other world region flowered in the United States and Canada. In the late 1980s, however, the rate of economic growth in the United States and Canada is slow. The war-torn economies of Europe, Japan, and to a lesser extent the USSR, recovered and produce competing products at lower cost in new factories. Successful competition has sprung up in the newly industrializing countries such as South Korea, Mexico, and Brazil. This competition, the rising price of energy in the 1970s, international debt, and shifts in the balance of trade, have forced North Americans to reevaluate their resource base as well as their patterns of living.

Moreover, as economic growth intensified during the three decades after World War II, Americans and Canadians in _Urban North America_ gradually began to desert aging central cities in favor of the suburbs, leaving behind blighted ghettos and pockets of poverty in the urban cores of the continent's most intensively settled regions. In the countryside, _Problems in Agriculture_, like those in other technological societies, have led to a mass exodus from America's farms, to increased concentration of production, and to a massive government-bought surplus of food and fiber. In addition to these pressures, North America's massive economy increasingly is forced to face trade-offs between _Environment and Economy_ as diverse problems of pollution are becoming more apparent.

An Economy of Affluence

In the postwar period, North Americans enjoyed a standard of living higher than any previously experienced. The gross national product (GNP) of the United States doubled in the 1950s, and redoubled again. By the late 1980s, North Americans were producing over $4 trillion worth of goods and services each year. Personal income rose steadily, and former luxuries became necessities without which people felt deprived. Median family income reached $28,000 in the United States. Furthermore, the lives of most people were protected by insurance, hospitalization, and retirement programs. Freedom in colonial America meant political liberty, but by the 1980s it had come to mean economic security and a diversified life.

Canada also embarked on a period of national prosperity. Its postwar resource-oriented economy diversified to complement the increasing raw material needs of the United States as well as its own strong industrial base. Canadian population grew as never before—from 12 million in 1945 to 26 million in 1988. In both coun-

tries, the resources of a continent were harnessed by industry to maintain the world's highest standard of living—what many refer to as the American way of life.

The Structure of the Economy

This American way of life was produced by the largest industrial machine in the world. Long unchallenged in world markets, the abundant resources of North America fueled an unprecedented rise in industrial production and consumption. Government and private industry became intimately involved in the structure of the national economy. Major corporations, most of them heavily reliant on federal contracts, came to control nearly half of the industrial assets of the United States. They deployed billions of dollars of equipment in dozens of locations, and employed hundreds of thousands of workers. These industrial giants applied complex technologies to the mass production and sale of material goods—a major reason why Americans were, compared with the rest of the world, well housed, well clad, and well fed.

Important technological breakthroughs were made in chemicals, computers, electronics, communications, and transportation—industries more mobile in location than those that process raw materials, such as iron and steel. Conversion from coal-based energy to petroleum and natural gas, and the increasing use of air travel for long-distance, short-term movement, enhanced this locational flexibility. By the late 1980s, four fifths of all corporate research and development efforts were concentrated in these industries. Virtually all new jobs being created in the American economy were for well-educated, white-collar workers in technical fields—the mark of a postindustrial society.

The innovations that sprang from such **multinational corporations** as IBM, DuPont, General Electric, General Motors, and Ford created products for which demand never before existed. The advertising industry usually managed to sell them. Indeed, the failure of Ford's Edsel automobile is remembered largely because failure was quite unusual.

With so many jobs and the welfare of so many at stake, the federal government increasingly attempted to both control and support large corporations. Monetary policies were manipulated to ease inflation, to regulate markets, and to consolidate and subsidize bankrupt enterprises—notably aerospace, automobile, and railroad companies. Now, government accounts for more than a quarter of all economic activity in the United States—a higher proportion than in some socialist countries. Free enterprise still exists in grocery stores, restaurants, and small shops, but im-

portant economic decisions in North America are made by a complex web of institutions—corporations, unions, universities, and government agencies—often not by individuals.

In the last two decades, the **gross domestic product (GDP)** of North America's economy tripled and energy consumption doubled. During this same period, the populations of the United States and Canada increased only 1.5 times so that there was proportionately more wealth and material goods to share. Now, however, rising costs of energy, increased international competition, and decreasing industrial productivity have slowed economic growth substantially. North Americans have gradually become aware of their vul-

nerability to world economic conditions and of the limits of their own resource base.

The Resource Base

The high levels of industrial production and consumption in the United States and Canada reflect the scale and vitality of the North American resource base. On this continent, productive potential, appetite for resources, and consumption of raw materials exceed those of all other countries in the Technological World. Indeed, energy consumption in the United States and Canada is equivalent to that of the rest of the entire Technological World minus the Soviet Union. The industrial complexes that mine, treat, and finish these re-

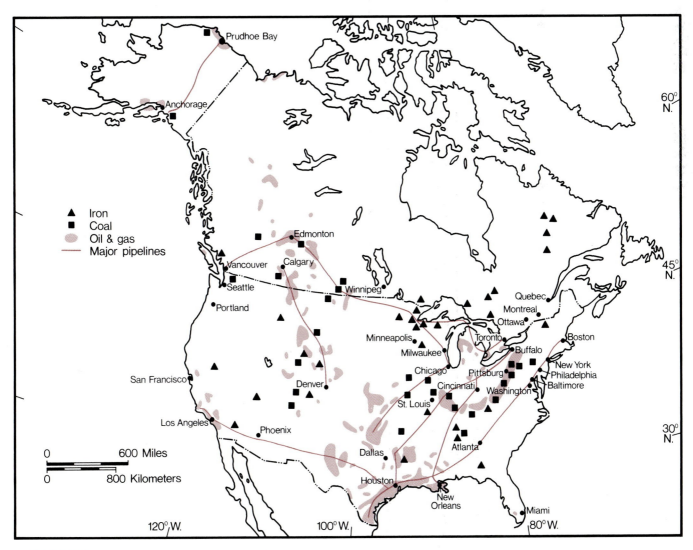

Figure 4.14 Economic patterns in North America.

sources are fired by large supplies of coal, oil, natural gas, and hydroelectric power. Taken as a whole, these basic energy reserves in North America are notable for their total output (26 percent of world production), their geographical dispersion, and their relative accessibility (Fig. 4.14).

The United States contains nearly half the world's proved reserves of coal. Coal accounts for 24 percent of the country's total energy production. Most underground mines are less than 1500 feet deep, and a large percentage of coal is mined by surface techniques. The Appalachian coalfield, stretching from western Pennsylvania and eastern Ohio southward through valleys in the Appalachians to northern Alabama, and the eastern interior coalfield, covering much of Illinois, produce three quarters of the nation's coal. Strip mining, carried out with gigantic earth-moving equipment, is practiced in both fields because it is in-expensive.

Today, increasing environmental awareness is forcing a recalculation of the long-term social and economic costs of strip-mined coal. In 1970, the Clean Air Act recognized that coal, the cheapest and most abundant American energy source, was also the dirtiest. By 1980, however, high prices and growing demand for petroleum and natural gas plus the political uncertainty of Middle Eastern oil provoked a reassessment of the importance of coal.

As pressure mounts for increased coal production, the ecological integrity of the eastern fields as well as remote areas of the West are in danger. Already, 2 million acres of land strip-mined in the eastern coalfields lie in ecological flux where the earth has been scarred by mechanical upheaval. In the Great Plains, Rocky Mountains, and Great Basin country, an estimated 86 billion tons of coal lie 50 to 100 feet beneath the surface. The coal reserves of the West—for use in eastern industries, regional electric power production, and the extraction of oil through a process of coal gasification—form a problematic new energy frontier.

In contrast to the United States, Canada has a scant 1.4 percent of the proved global coal reserves. Moreover, economically productive reserves in the western coalfields of Alberta are remote from industrial concentrations. Canadian industry has traditionally imported coal from closer sources in the eastern United States, but Canadian production has risen rapidly in recent years.

North America as a whole is self-sufficient in oil and natural gas, but strong differences exist between Canada and the United States (Fig. 4.14). Canada is a major world producer and exporter of oil. It has confirmed reserves of 9 billion barrels in central Alberta and a potential reserve equal to that of Saudi Arabia in the untapped oil-bearing **tar sands** of northern Alberta. Canada is one

The oil patch of Texas and Louisiana produces 60 percent of America's oil and 70 percent of America's natural gas.

CHANGING PATTERN OF ENERGY DEPENDENCE IN THE UNITED STATES

In the last twenty years, energy production leveled off in the United States, whereas consumption continued to increase in spite of conservation efforts spurred by the Arab oil embargo of 1973 and the OPEC price increase of 1979. Currently, nearly a quarter of the U.S. energy budget is imported. This shift in the U.S. energy economy is increasing America's sensitivity to international economic forces.

Adapted from: U.S. Bureau of the Census, *Statistical Abstract of the United States, 1982–1983.* Washington, D.C.: U.S. Department of Commerce, 1982, p. 570.

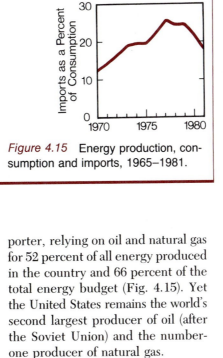

Figure 4.15 Energy production, consumption and imports, 1965–1981.

tion of production is in California, in and around Los Angeles, where large pools of oil are associated with folded rock structures.

The area of greatest undeveloped potential lies 200 miles north of the Arctic Circle, near Prudhoe Bay, Alaska. Here, on the North Slope of the Brooks Range, an estimated 10 billion barrels of oil—one of the largest fields in the world—lie 10,000 feet below the surface. In 1975, construction began on a 799-mile pipeline from Prudhoe Bay to Valdez, on Price William Sound. Although far removed from markets and consequently more expensive, Alaska currently produces 18 percent of domestic oil.

As new levels of energy demand are reached, new sources of oil and coal may be exploited for the first time. In the Arctic Ocean, the Gulf of Alaska, the Gulf of Mexico, and off the shores of southern California, New England, and New Jersey, oil and natural gas may exist in quantities far surpassing the potential of the North Slope. In the West, 16,500 square miles of public lands in Colorado, Utah, and Wyoming are believed to contain **oil-bearing shale** capable of supplying three times the known world reserves of oil. The extraction process is so difficult and environmental damage so likely that exploitation of oil-bearing shale may prove an ecological nightmare. The oil glut of the 1980s has depressed the price of oil sufficiently to deter any large-scale effort at development.

The rivers of North America are a valuable potential source of renewable energy—hydroelectricity. Per capita use of hydroelectric power is far more important in Canada, where a relatively small population is better situated near power sites than in the United States. The St. Lawrence Valley is served by dams located on fast-running streams dropping southward off the rim of the Canadian Shield and by the St. Lawrence Seaway project. Canada has become the world's largest producer of hydro-

of the few oil-exporting countries in the Technological World. Yet Canada's domestic oil situation is far from ideal. Canadian oil pipelines extend only as far east as Toronto. The industrial St. Lawrence Valley and Atlantic provinces must depend on imported foreign oil. However, exploration in the Hibernia field off the coast of Newfoundland has been promising. By 1974, Canada supplied one fifth of all U.S. oil imports; by 1986, Canada had become the United States' single largest source of imported oil. This relationship is likely to grow in importance as the 1987 trade pact between the two countries aims at eliminating all tariffs and other restrictions on the free flow of goods and services between them by 1999.

The United States was the world's largest producer of both oil and natural gas until 1975. Now, it is the world's largest consumer and im-

porter, relying on oil and natural gas for 52 percent of all energy produced in the country and 66 percent of the total energy budget (Fig. 4.15). Yet the United States remains the world's second largest producer of oil (after the Soviet Union) and the number-one producer of natural gas.

Today, 90 percent of all domestically produced oil and natural gas comes from three fields west of the Mississippi. Crude petroleum and natural gas production is concentrated in Texas and Louisiana, which together account for 60 percent of America's oil and 70 percent of America's natural gas. These oil and natural gas deposits are found in a wide, nearly continuous belt along the Gulf Coast from the Mississippi Delta to the Mexican border, both onshore and offshore. Inland, the midcontinental oil field encompasses much of Kansas, Oklahoma, and Texas. The third largest concentra-

electricity. Public power corporations in Québec, Manitoba, and British Columbia all deliver sizable hydroelectric exports to U.S. markets.

In the United States, hydroelectric power is important in three areas. New York State is a beneficiary of the harnessed energy of Niagara Falls, a natural dam at the entry to Lake Erie. In the southern Appalachians, the Tennessee River watershed has been extensively developed by the TVA. The authority maintains twenty-seven major dams, and sells hydroelectric power to 2 million customers in seven states. A third region of large-scale hydroelectric development is the Pacific Northwest. The Columbia River was harnessed by the construction of Grand Coulee Dam, which produces more electricity than any other dam in North America. Despite these massive hydroelectric power projects and others on the Colorado, the Missouri, and rivers in California, hydroelectric power in the United States accounts for a bare 2.7 percent of energy consumption.

Alternative energy sources play a minor role in the total energy budget of North America. In the late 1980s, there were 109 nuclear power reactors operating in the United States and Canada, fewer per population than in Western Europe. In the United States, nuclear generating capacity produces 16 percent of the total electrical supply. No new plants have been ordered since 1974; construction of new plants will cease after 1990. Public opposition to nuclear power has grown as incidents, like that at Three Mile Island in Pennsylvania (1979) have raised serious safety questions. Enormous construction costs of new plants have played a critical role in the end of the growth of nuclear power in the United States. In effect, U.S. nuclear capacity will peak in 1992; after that, production will slowly decline and the decommissioning of nuclear plants will become important. Both **geothermal** and solar energy are still in the experimental stage of development and

STRATEGIC MATERIALS IMPORTED BY THE UNITED STATES

Despite the extensive mineral base available in North America, the United States currently depends on imports for more than half of its supply of two dozen strategic raw materials. Sources of these minerals and metals range from neighboring Canada and Mexico to Australia, Zaire, South Africa, and the USSR. Efforts at stockpiling raw materials represent a short-term solution to the maintenance of America's highly complex military and domestic economy.

Adapted from: John D. Morgan, "Past Is Prologue: Strategic Materials and the Defense Industrial Base," *Defense Management Journal* (First Quarter), 1982, p. 17.

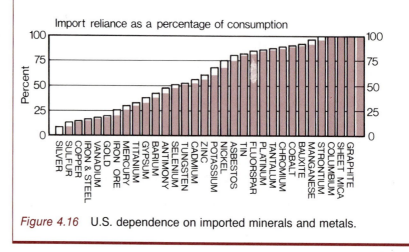

Figure 4.16   U.S. dependence on imported minerals and metals.

are very much tied to the cost of petroleum.

In terms of metal ores, North America is remarkably well endowed (Fig. 4.14). Both Canada and the United States are important producers of base metals, such as iron ore, copper, lead, and zinc—the resources of heavy industry. Two great metal and mineral bearing geologic structures exist in North America: the Canadian Shield and the **Cordillera,** the mountain system that arcs southward from Alaska through Canada to the Sierras and Rockies of the American West.

The concentration of production in the United States is remarkable. Arizona, Minnesota, and Utah produce half the American total of metal ores. As is true of energy sources, however, rising demand has outstripped supplies of metal ores, and the United States now depends on imports of base metals (Fig. 4.16). Domestic sup-

plies are decreasing in output and quality; foreign sources are less costly because of higher quality ores and lower labor costs.

Canada is an exporter of metals, and Canadian production can increase if the inaccessibility, rough terrain, and low population of the metal-bearing regions are overcome. Both Canada and the United States, it should be noted, are exporters or reexporters of virtually all minerals in the form of semifinished and finished manufactures.

Iron ore production is concentrated in the older mining districts at the western end of Lake Superior and in newer finds in the Canadian Shield along the Québec–Labrador border. Iron ore imports now constitute about half the United States' supply. Venezuela and Liberia are increasingly important exporters of iron to the United States, but Canada still supplies half of America's imports.

Expansion of Canadian production in the Shield has been remarkable. Even so, the greatest concentration of production in North America is still in the Lake Superior uplands. Some 80 percent of the iron ore mined in the United States comes from this region. Half the total U.S. production is strip-mined to a depth of 350 feet in the Mesabi field. Iron ore is shipped south and east through the Great Lakes to cities from Chicago to Toronto, where coal from the Appalachian field provides the energy base for the North American steel industry. The steady decline in quality ore from the Lake Superior upland has created a ready market for iron ore shipped from Labrador and Québec to the Great Lakes cities via the St. Lawrence Seaway.

Like iron ore, **nonferrous metal** ore deposits are distant from existing markets. Arizona produces half the nation's copper, and output is increasing. Utah and Montana are also significant copper producers. In Canada, copper deposits north of Lake Huron are the most important. The United States, first in copper production with 17 percent of the world total, is also an importer. Canada, the fourth largest copper-producing country, is the third largest copper exporter.

Large-scale production by both countries, but export by Canada and import by the United States, is true for other metals also. Lead and zinc are mined in widely scattered areas. Canada produces 23 percent of the world's nickel, largely from the Sudbury district. Cobalt, found in association with iron and nickel, is widely produced in North America. The continent's only significant source of bauxite in Arkansas produces but a fraction of demand so that the United States and Canada import 70 percent of the bauxite sold on world markets. Tin is absent in North America.

Overall, imports of both energy, minerals, and metals are playing an increasing role in the international economy of the United States (Fig. 4.16). Dependence on foreign sources is becoming an issue of national concern.

An awareness of the finite nature of domestic supplies, of wasteful patterns of energy consumption, and of the social and environmental costs of exploitation is growing. North Americans are now understanding with increasing clarity the systematic, global nature of their own industrial culture.

Changing Patterns of Industry

The unparalleled productivity and wealth of the United States in the 1950s and 1960s was based on cheap energy, an abundant resource base, a talented work force, and minimal competition on world markets from Europe, Japan, and the USSR, whose industrial structures had been badly damaged by war. As these conditions changed, the sources of America's affluence—churning smokestacks in the industrial heartland and armies of well-paid factory workers—began to come under severe pressure.

Decline in the "rust belt" and aging mills mark the nation's rapid shift from an industrial to a postindustrial society. Today, only 17 percent of all Americans work in manufacturing.

A 1400 percent increase in the price of energy in the 1970s forced a rehabilitation of America's aging industrial plants. Environmental concerns also required costly adjustments to new standards. Modern automated plant facilities staffed by lower paid work forces in Europe and Japan began to compete successfully on world markets and in the United States. By the late 1980s, the basic underpinnings of America's industrial economy—its steel, automobiles, and textiles—were no longer competitive on world markets, and a full quarter of the national economy was engaged in trade. The gradual deindustrialization of the American economy, punctuated by proposals to "revitalize" its manufacturing base, marks a pronounced shift in the American way of life as powerful and pervasive as those changes that accompanied the shift from horses to automobiles a half century ago.

This shift from an industrial to a postindustrial society strikes hardest in the factories and mines of the Northeast, the Middle West, Appalachia, and those parts of Canada where the closing of mills and mines in coal, iron, steel, automobiles, and textiles threatens the once-secure skills of millions of workers. In fact, employment in iron and steel has been eroding steadily for four decades as imports began to replace higher priced domestic products. Major U.S. steel makers have moved some factories overseas to reduce costs of production. No new steel plant has been constructed in the country in two decades. The automobile industry, which employed over a million workers has laid off a quarter of the work force. American automakers have seen their share of the U.S. market shift from 70 percent in 1986 to closer to 50 percent at the end of the 1980s. Foreign carmakers producing cars in the United States—"transplants"—have gained an increasing market share.

Needed improvements in productivity through increased use of computers and robots have revitalized production facilities and reduced costs of labor, but they are burying old factories, neighborhoods, and families in the aging industrial areas of cities like Detroit, Cleveland, Pittsburgh, and Toronto.

On the other hand, 68 percent of American workers labored in the tertiary, or services-producing, sector of the economy in 1988, compared with 17 percent in manufacturing. Much of the growth of the tertiary sector has sprung from high-technology industries associated with computers and telecommunications. The core areas of these new activities lie in the New York City area, in San Francisco's Silicon Valley, along Route 128 near Boston, in North Carolina's Research Triangle Park, in Austin, Texas, and in other areas with high-skilled workers, centers of education, and research institutions. Only a small fraction of new jobs were in industries that mine or process raw materials.

The U.S. industrial economy, which appeared to generations of Americans to be invincibly secure, is undergoing irreversible changes. Many experts believe that if America's industrial base continues to decline, the nation will be reduced as a world power, in international trade, and military strength.

The Changing Distribution of People

These changing economic conditions contributed to a spatial redistribution of wealth, power, and population in North America. A pro-

Assembly line production enabled the United States to become the world's leading industrial country. As this Nissan plant in Indiana shows, robots now perform many assembly line tasks and multinational corporations play an increasingly important role in manufacturing.

nounced geographic shift occurred in population from the North and East to the Southern Rim, a broad arc of southern and western states best known as the "Sunbelt," extending from Florida through the South and Southwest to southern California (Fig. 4.17). With America's mildest climates, most extensive coastline, well-developed inland waterways, and efficient rail and highway networks oriented to major ports, this region appealed to thousands of new and relocated industries. Nine of the thirteen fastest growing cities in the last decade were located in either California, Texas, Colorado, or Arizona.

Defense, aerospace, and high-technology industries settled in southern California, Texas, Georgia, and Florida. **Agribusiness** made California, Texas, and Florida the three largest farm states. In Canada, too, population moved westward to capitalize on the development of oil fields in Alberta, although many returned to Canada's centers of capital and industry—the already predominant metropolises of Montréal and Toronto. Resort and tourist businesses flourished and attracted hundreds of thousands of retired North Americans. Their numbers increased steadily as extended lifespans and earlier retirement resulted in a larger proportion of citizens living beyond their economically productive years.

The traditional economic core in the Industrial North suffered accordingly. This region accounted for 70 percent of North America's manufactures and industrial employees in 1940; by 1980, these figures had dropped considerably. Less than 15 percent of the 10 million new people added to the U.S. population settled in the North and Northeast. For a generation, the bulk of America's population growth has occurred in the Southern Rim. The new rhythms of American life seemed to demand a new living environment, more leisure, and a better quality of life. For many North Americans, these were found in the South and West. Yet, by the late 1980s, the high-paying, high-technology industries of south-

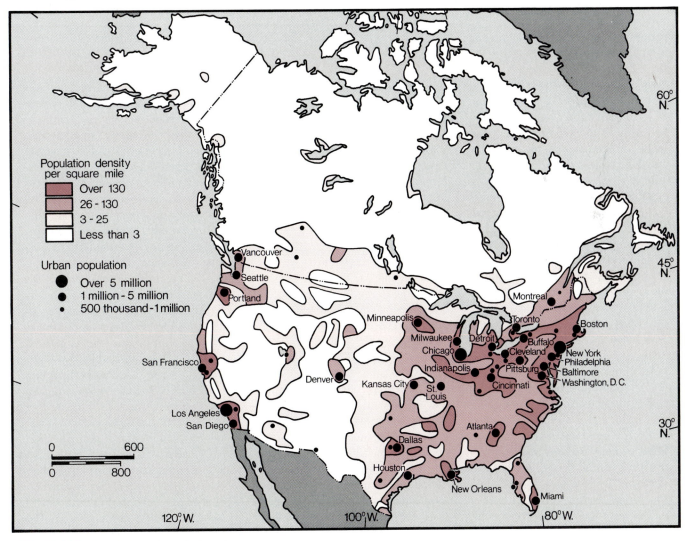

Figure 4.17 Population of North America.

ern New England and of dynamic centers throughout the Industrial North may have begun to reverse this exodus from north to south in America.

Urban North America

Far more North Americans, however, found their new opportunities not in the South or West, but in the suburbs. Beginning in 1950, suburban areas grew by 75 percent in population in two decades. Fully two thirds of the total population growth in the United States occurred on the developing peripheries of the largest cities (Fig. 4.18). In 1970, the population of America's central cities was about 68 million as compared with 87 million in the suburbs. By 1980, the central cities still had roughly the same total population because the huge losses in northern cities on the eastern seaboard and the Middle West were offset by growth and annexation in southern and western cities. Meanwhile, the suburbs had grown to 103 million, and population in the suburbs outnumbered that of the central cities by three to two.

Although metropolitan centers continued to exert a gravitational pull on the rural poor and minority groups, automobiles had extended what English historian H. G. Wells called "the magic radius" of the city. Lured by open environments and greater recreational opportunities and repelled by crime, neglected schools, and congestion in the cities, Americans became willing to travel long distances between home and job (Fig. 4.18). Suburbia spread in widening circles of decreasing density around each city, and the North American landscape was punctuated by **urban fields** or **daily urban systems** covering a substantial portion of the most desirable land of both Canada and the United States.

The term daily urban systems indicates the profound structural changes that occurred in North

THE URBAN FIELD OF CHICAGO

The urban field of Chicago is defined here by the distance commuters travel to work in the central city. The percentage of commuters decreases with distance from the city. The commuting range is broader today than in 1960 when this data was collected because of arterial improvements.

Adapted from: Brian J. L. Berry, "The Geography of the United States in the Year 2000," *Transactions of the Institute of British Geographers,* No. 51 (1970), fig. 10.

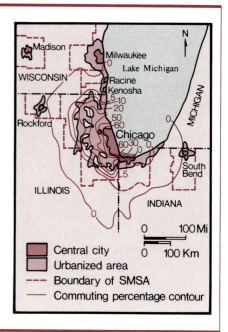

Figure 4.18   Commuting in Chicago.

American cities after World War II. Central business districts became barren landscapes of high-rise office buildings inhabited by workers only during the day. Once convenient and animated midcity neighborhoods became derelict districts rented to those least able to purchase suburban privacy and to those most dependent on the services of central cities. Incomes in the central cities are 26 percent lower than in the suburbs.

The middle and upper classes move over large urban fields to sleep, eat, school their children, and pursue their careers. These urban fields are the areas habitually traversed by the modern urbanite. Their geography is one of multiple suburbs focused on shopping malls, strip development, and schools, all of which are economic and social offspring of the central city. Los Angeles, the archetype of the automobile-oriented metropolis, is a metropolitan statistical area of 8.1 million people living in sixty-four separate municipalities spread over 455 square miles of territory. Between a quarter and a third of the land area of Los Angeles is devoted

to the needs of the automobile, and suburban growth stretches deep into its hinterland, making its urban field nearly four times larger than the area enclosed by Los Angeles' incorporated boundaries.

For the first time in over a generation, the largest cities of the United States are generally gaining population. Economic shifts toward the service industries—particularly real estate, insurance, finance, banking—as well as the search for a more dynamic lifestyle than that offered by the suburbs, have led to the regeneration of some cities, and the redevelopment of many areas in most cities. In a number of ways, the 1980s were a decade of urban revival. Old neighborhoods have been revitalized and younger Americans have settled in the cities after growing up in the suburbs. A process of **gentrification** has focused on rebuilding derelict housing and creating an urban lifestyle. Preservation reconstruction poured $11 billion into renovation of historic buildings across America between 1981 and 1988. Whole neighborhoods in Boston, Chicago, and virtually every large city have returned to new life. As this development proceeds, however, the urban poor—mainly black and Hispanic—often find themselves displaced by economic forces and with few geographic choices at hand.

Another trend shows that rural counties in proximity of metropolitan areas have increased in population. A preference for open spaces, and by implication, a better quality of life, is beginning to reverse the tide of migration that has brought Americans to town for over a century. Despite this trend, three quarters of the people of the United States and Can-

ada still live in cities. Most urban geographers foresee the coalescence of North American daily urban systems into gigantic multicored megalopolises that will continue to be society's most vital and densely populated centers.

Minority Groups in the Central City

With so many North Americans living in suburbia and connected to the city by private automobiles and high-speed freeways, and with youth preoccupied with new lifestyles, careers, and rising incomes, poverty in North American cities became less

visible and more concentrated. Although all Americans gained in absolute wealth, the poor were no longer temporarily disadvantaged immigrants or disorganized labor groups as in the past. They formed a lower class frozen by racial discrimination, poor education, or inadequate skills into continuing economic deprivation. The American poor remained outsiders to a technological society that yielded easy affluence to the well educated and the technically able. A permanent underclass, a **culture of poverty,** is developing.

Poverty remains closely identified with race. Nearly a third of all black, Mexican-American, Puerto Rican, and Indian families live below the poverty level. A geographical shift of poverty to the cities has occurred, so that 60 percent of the poor live in urban centers today (Figs. 4.19, 4.20). The ghetto poverty of large urban centers, where the twin issues of race and the physical structure of the city are closely entwined, is rapidly becoming one of America's most intractable problems.

The explosive demand for factory labor in northern and Middle Western cities during World War II accelerated the out-migration of black Americans from the South. Searching for jobs, better educational opportunities, and a less oppressive social existence, several million blacks moved to the North and West. In 1980, New York, California, and Texas led the nation in black residents, and only 53 percent of America's 26.5 million blacks still lived south of the **Mason-Dixon line** (Fig. 4.19). Similarly, Mexican-Americans began to disperse out of the rural southwest (Fig. 4.20).

This migration was more than a simple geographical shift. It was an economic move from field to factory, a social transition from small town to metropolis, a cultural leap from the segregated South to the city streets of black ghettos. Three of every four black Americans found themselves

Rapid transit systems exist in most large American cities to transport commuters back and forth between suburban homes and city jobs. Many Americans are willing to travel long distances each day rather than live in decaying inner cities.

living in metropolitan areas and nearly 60 percent in the central cities. The old black southern religious ideal of a black metropolis came to pass in a manner never before contemplated.

Clustered in metropolitan ghettos, the black population of America developed a philosophy of social action. The Supreme Court's separate but equal doctrine was successfully challenged when the promise of the Declaration of Independence that "all men are created equal" was taken literally. First, public schools were integrated and, later all public facilities. Voter registration procedures were simplified. As the civil rights movement gained momentum, disenfranchised blacks, Mexican-Americans, and Indians gained legal support. Although integration was expected to create problems in the South, the tenacious northern resistance to the integration of black and white was unexpected.

Efforts at residential integration in New York City, Boston, and Chicago were frustrated by discriminatory real estate practices, by the departure of whites from areas where blacks moved in, by intransigent city councils, and by newly formed resistance groups. The busing of black and white children to achieve racial balance in schools became an emotionally charged issue from New England to California. Treated by middle-class suburban whites as a moral issue, the clash of low-income minorities and whites in the central cities was a contest for housing, jobs, and education among the least advantaged people in the most technological society.

The Ghetto

The black and Puerto Rican populations of northern and western cities grew by natural increase and continued immigration. The boundaries of their ghettos expanded. Traditional Irish, Italian, Polish, and Jewish ethnic groups in the central city were displaced. Whites fled to the suburbs as the block-by-block spread of blacks into older urban areas induced panic

THE DISTRIBUTION OF BLACKS IN THE UNITED STATES

Black Americans numbered 26.5 million and formed 11.7 percent of the American population in 1980. Half of the blacks live in the South, with the remainder concentrated in the nation's largest cities. 1986 statistics showed that 12.2 percent of Americans are black.

Source: U.S. Bureau of the Census.

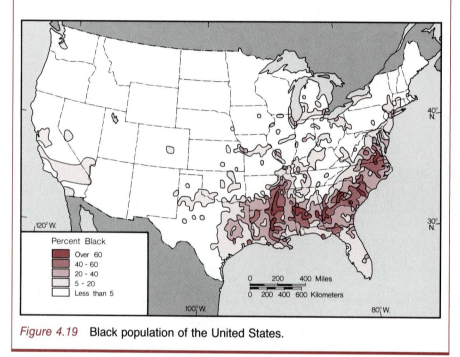

Figure 4.19 Black population of the United States.

selling. Only the old, the sick, and those too poor to move remained. Integration, as one black leader cynically remarked, was the time it took for the last white to leave a neighborhood after the first black arrived. Barred until the 1970s from suburbs, blacks could not escape the ghetto; they could only extend it another fraction of an inch on city maps. Spatial proximity did not produce harmony in urban America. Instead, America's deepest, most persistent division was exposed and exacerbated.

The ghettos became blighted zones of high crime, low income, inadequate housing, and high unemployment. These conditions culminated in bloody race riots in metropolitan

America in the 1960s, first in Los Angeles, then in Detroit, Newark, and most other large cities. The ghettos had become, as the English observer Kenneth Clark remarked, America's "social, political, educational—and above all economic, colonies." Although blacks represented only 11.7 percent of the total 1980 American population, they made up 28 percent of the metropolitan population. They formed 71 percent of the population in Washington, D.C.; 50 percent in Atlanta; more than 40 percent in Baltimore, Detroit, and Cleveland; 30 percent in Chicago; and 20 percent in New York City.

Minority groups did experience rising incomes and substantial educational gains within American soci-

THE DISTRIBUTION OF HISPANIC PEOPLE IN THE UNITED STATES

Some 14.6 million or 6.4 percent of the American population claimed to be of Spanish origin in 1980; 7.7 percent of the population was of Spanish origin in 1986. The vast majority are of Mexican, Cuba, or Puerto Rican descent. Still concentrated in the Southwest, Hispanics are now dispersing to California, Florida, New York, the Middle West, and the Pacific Northwest.

Source: U.S. Bureau of the Census.

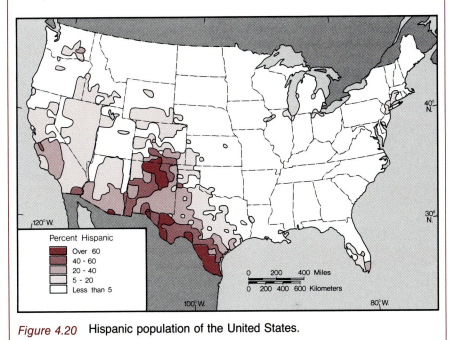

Percent Hispanic
- Over 60
- 40 - 60
- 20 - 40
- 5 - 20
- Less than 5

Figure 4.20 Hispanic population of the United States.

salary demands by teachers, fire fighters, police, and garbage collectors. High energy, rent, and land costs continue to drive up taxes. Traffic congestion, obsolete buildings, and a disproportionate share of society's disadvantaged mark the cores of virtually every large city in North America.

For the 29 percent of all Americans who live in the central cities of the United States in the late 1980s, housing, crime, economic security, and pollution are compelling social issues.

Problems in Agriculture

Now, American agriculture faces nearly as many difficulties as its largest cities. The costs of food production are rising, while the prices for farm products are going down. Huge price-depressing surpluses of wheat, cotton, and other farm products are piling up. Millions of bushels of grain and cotton purchased under government subsidy programs are being stored in silos, empty warehouses, and mothballed battleships.

Overproduction, declining world markets for food products, and the increasing role of large business in the farm sector are gradually pushing

ety as a whole, but the anger and frustration of ghetto communities remain strong. The discontent began, as Claude Brown noted in *Manchild in the Promised Land,* with an unfulfilled promise. The minorities migrated to the city for escape and salvation. Once there, deep-seated social prejudices in the form of spatial separation continue to blight their lives. Where, Brown asks, does one run to when you're already in the promised land?

The central cities of older American metropolitan areas could hardly be thought of as promised lands. Urban renewal efforts in New York, Boston, Chicago, and Detroit did not reverse the decay of the central city. The white middle class continued to move to the suburbs and was being replaced by the rural poor, racial minorities, and immigrants from countries new to the American experience, such as Korea, Vietnam, Haiti, Ecuador, and Trinidad. Continued suburban expansion, economic growth of the service sector in the CBD, and gentrification worked hardship on many of the urban poor.

Businesses that found it more profitable and pleasant to move to the suburbs left the urban unemployed geographically and socially removed from new job opportunities. Two thirds of all new manufacturing jobs located in suburban industrial parks and shopping centers.

With revenues declining, America's largest cities are saddled with

The ghettos of America's largest cities are landscapes of despair.

small farmers into other occupations. Farm indebtedness has risen to twelve times farm income, and the value of farmland is declining for the first time in three decades. In the 1980s, farm backruptcies reached levels comparable to the depression years of the 1930s. As the federal government instituted programs of farm price supports and paid farmers to leave a third of their wheat, corn, rice, and cotton land uncultivated, a basic restructuring of agricultural America took hold. North America's unique and productive farm system built on the broad-based ownership of agricultural land by millions of family farmers is, in the opinion of many agricultural geographers, on the verge of extinction.

Three trends mark this change in North America's rural landscape: (1) The total number of farms is declining, (2) the average size of farms is larger, and (3) the output of these larger farming units is increasing (Fig. 4.21). By 1988, only 5.4 million Americans lived on farms as compared with 23 million in 1950. The number of farms dropped from 5.4 million in the United States in 1950 to 2.3 million. Abandoned farms and farmland taken out of production blanket landscapes in the Northeast, the Middle West, and the South. Low crop prices, high interest rates, the high costs of agricultural machinery, fertilizers, and pesticides continue to spur the exodus. Many farmers, in an effort to hold their land, have taken to renting part of their acreage. Fully 40 percent of all farmland in the United States is now worked by someone other than the owner. Because nearly 70 percent of America's farmland is owned by people over 50 years old, this process may intensify. Part-time farmers have become a prominent category of farm operators.

The average size of American farms in 1988 reached 455 acres, double that of 1950. In part, this consolidation of agricultural land derives from economies of scale (Fig. 4.21). More

---

CHANGES IN FARMING

Between 1950 and 1980, a mass exodus of Americans out of farming coincided with a drop in the total number of farms and a dramatic increase in average farm size.

Source: U.S. Bureau of the Census. *Statistical Abstract of the United States, 1982–1983.* Washington, D.C.: U.S. Department of Commerce, 1982, p. 646.

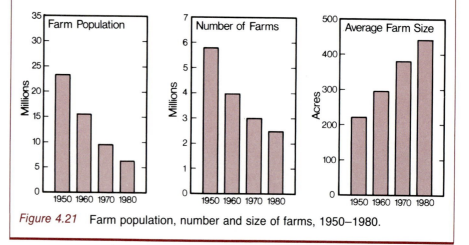

Figure 4.21 Farm population, number and size of farms, 1950–1980.

---

important, however, is the ability of larger operations to sustain the higher costs of agricultural production and lower farm prices over longer periods of time. Moreover, the entire range of federal farm programs tend to benefit the biggest producers, so that less than 5 percent of all farmers receive nearly half of all federal aid. Today, the largest 7 percent of all farms—those over 1000 acres in size—control 54 percent of the nation's farmland. The average productivity of these larger farm units is high. Approximately a tenth of the country's farm units produce two thirds of total food production.

Agricultural specialists speak of a "bimodal structure" in American agriculture as the 1990s unfold. As successful American farmers everywhere have substituted capital and technology for labor, a sorting out of farms and farmers has occurred. At the top end of the economic scale, consolidation of large farms continues. Large farms get larger. Ever more capital and technology is ap-

plied to production. Efficiency of production continues to improve, and Americans remain surrounded by a heightened choice of cheap—in global terms—food. It is likely that the large farm is still owned within a family, but the family has incorporated, is relatively affluent, and produces specialized products for the American food market. Some vertical production—where food processors and retailers, such as Purina or General Foods, actually produce the food on their company land—has occurred. Far more common, however, is for the conglomerate to contract out the production of crops to specific, independent growers, although in the production of fresh chickens, to take an example, vertical **agribusiness** has become dominant. Some chicken operations extend from chicken coop to supermarket shelf. Over 90 percent of fresh chickens in America, are grown, dressed, packaged, transported, and marketed in this fashion.

On the other hand, an important movement on the small farm is the development of part-time farming by former small full-time farmers and the acquisition of small farms by city folk. These new farm residents may actually work some of the land themselves or may rent it out to full- or part-time farmers. Thus the number of farms remains relatively stable, and the number of Americans actually living on farms has not changed significantly for over ten years. But in the center of the picture, the middle-sized farm has gotten squeezed out— the farmer with average acreage, modest capital, and modest outputs. So it seems to many that the family farm has disappeared from the American landscape and has been replaced by agribusiness.

The impact of these changes in American agriculture on the environment is a source of growing concern. Stewardship of the land becomes a social question. Corporations focusing on short-term profit and family farmers hard-pressed by debt are beginning to mine the soil. At issue is the question of whether or not soil erosion, overirrigation, and destruction of vegetation will lead to declining farm productivity and permanent damage to the environment.

The natural processes of soil erosion in America's most productive farming areas proceed at a rate in accord with the formation of new soil. A recent U.S. Department of Agriculture study, however, reports that 48 million acres, a tenth of America's farmland, is experiencing erosion rates as high as 100 tons per acre per year, twenty to twenty-five times higher than even deep soils can sustain without damage. More than 15 tons of topsoil flows out of the mouth of the Mississippi River each minute. The most affected areas are scattered across the country and include the corn belt in the Middle West, the rice lands of southern Mississippi, the dairy and fruit producing areas of the Willamette Valley in Oregon, and the potato fields of Maine. Overall, an estimated one third of the nation's topsoil has been lost since cultivation began in North America.

Farmers are increasingly using methods that intensify soil erosion and deteriorate soil productivity. **Contour plowing** and terracing, practices that preserve the soil, are not compatible with large eight-row machines that are designed to cultivate straight, square blocks of land. Rotation cycles between crops have been shortened or abandoned to maximize profits. Yields are maintained by increased use of fertilizer and pesticides. Continuous planting of corn and soybeans—crops that bring the highest returns—requires wide spacing between rows and leaves soil vulnerable to even normal rainfall. Further, shelterbelts of trees planted in the 1930s from the Texas Panhandle to North Dakota are being burned or bulldozed to increase agricultural acreage and utilize advanced tech-

Large-scale mechanized agriculture, as practiced on this farm near Blythe, California, is contributing to higher crop productivity, larger sized farm units, and abandonment of many small family farms across North America.

nology. Congressional action was taken in 1985 to reduce abuse of the land. The most effective anti-erosion measures, however, have been market forces, which determine that marginal cropland is removed from production. In the trade-off between environment and economy, the long-term effects of the restructuring of America's agriculture are now at issue.

Environment and Economy

Two conflicting views of environment and economy coexist in the United States today. America's farmers, unemployed factory workers, minorities, and poor people strive for secure jobs and higher incomes—goals not easily realized in an economy that is expanding at a slow rate. Many Americans, however, believe that lower rates of economic growth and lower levels of consumption promote more careful husbanding of resources essential to the long-term welfare of land and life in America.

Environmentalists view the ecological damage that the continent sustained during America's drive to affluence as unacceptable. They see North America as built on wasteful, rapid, and unplanned exploitation of resources that has severely degraded its human and natural environments.

In the South, soil exhaustion in the Appalachians gave farmers a powerful incentive for westward migration. The first soil conservation surveys of the 1930s revealed that 80,000 square miles of American soil—an area equal in size to England and Scotland combined—had been destroyed. In the North, timber was completely stripped from parts of southern Ontario and the Middle West. One geographer has demonstrated that early loggers and settlers in southwestern Wisconsin reduced the region's woodlands by 80 to 90 percent. In the Southwest and West, mineral resources were exploited with abandon to meet the material needs of America's expanding population and economy.

Some of the worst of these early environmental abuses were curbed by federal regulation in the first half of the twentieth century. Programs of soil conservation, the national park system established by President Theodore Roosevelt, the TVA, and the Prairie Farm Rehabilitation Act in Canada managed to preserve or renew substantial areas of North America. But today, new and more subtle environmental dangers have become apparent as scientists expose severe disruptions in natural ecosystems caused by what biologist Rachel Carson termed the "elixirs of death": the ecological side effects of the products and methods of a technological society.

Air Pollution

As in other technological societies, air pollution has become a serious problem in North America. Some 156 million registered vehicles in the United States pour hydrocarbons, sulfur dioxide, and nitrogen oxide into the atmosphere. The gasoline combustion engine accounts for 60 percent of all airborne pollutants. Metallurgical plants, iron and steel mills, petroleum refineries, fertilizer plants, and other industries contribute a further 25 percent. And with 90 percent of American electricity generated by burning coal and oil, power plants add their share.

Overall, some 260 million tons of refuse are spewed into the atmosphere each year. Despite the passage of a series of clean air acts, most importantly the Clean Air Act of 1970, this figure remains stubbornly high.

The haze of polluted air is the most widespread characteristic of atmospheric degradation. The natural distribution of smog is affected by local topography, the density of population, industrial concentrations, and weather conditions (Fig. 4.22). Areas with the highest potential for air pollution lie in the West, where the Rocky Mountains form a permeable barrier to air movement, and in the Appalachian Mountains in the East.

Locally, the intensity of smog is greatest near Los Angeles in southern California, where the automobile culture—an estimated 16 million vehicles—and the topography of the region concentrate pollutants. Similarly, the mountain folds of the Appalachians embrace the airborne pollutants of the Industrial North and Middle West. In both areas, pollutants are trapped in pockets of cool air and locked beneath stagnant warmer air that sits over populated

Skyscrapers in Los Angeles, California, rise above the dense surface layer of smog that covers the basin more than 200 days a year.

THE GEOGRAPHY OF AIR POLLUTION IN THE UNITED STATES

Figure 4.22 shows the number of days on which high air pollution potential, defined as smog covering 75,000 square miles or more for at least 36 hours, is forecast in the United States. Southern California and the Appalachian Mountains stand out as the most polluted areas, with 80 to 100 days of high air pollution occurring each year. This is largely because topography, population density, industrial concentration, and weather conditions play such an important role in determining this distribution.

Adapted from: Virginia Brodine, "Episode 104," in *Air Pollution.* New York: Harcourt Brace Jovanovich, 1973, p. 23.

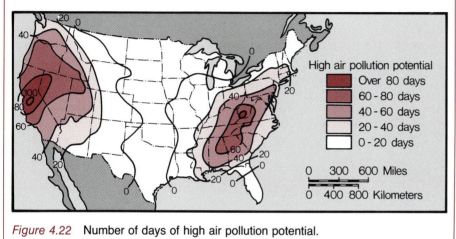

High air pollution potential

- Over 80 days
- 60 - 80 days
- 40 - 60 days
- 20 - 40 days
- 0 - 20 days

0   300   600 Miles

0   400   800 Kilometers

Figure 4.22   Number of days of high air pollution potential.

areas. When this occurs, regional death rates are measurably higher, illnesses soar to levels far above the norm, and people adjust their day-to-day activities accordingly.

Yet virtually every large city, whatever its topographical setting exhibits smog domes under certain weather conditions. In New York and Chicago, incoming sunlight during the smoggiest days is reduced by 25 to 40 percent. The capacity of urban industrial systems to concentrate the by-products of industrial energy and human activity in specific locations is producing a volume of waste that natural processes can no longer disperse.

In the last decade, air pollution has become a subject of serious environmental concern in the eastern United States and Canada. Here, acid rain forms when water vapor and other substances in the atmosphere combine with sulfur dioxide from coal-burning utility plants and nitrogen oxide from automobile emissions to form two very corrosive substances, sulfuric acid and nitric acid. According to the Environmental Protection Agency (EPA), about 26 million tons of sulfur dioxide and 22 million tons of nitrogen oxide are released into the atmosphere from sources in the United States each year. Comparable Canadian figures are 5 and 2 million tons. In the late 1980s, average rainfall in eastern North America was ten times more acidic than normal because of pollutants carried long distances by prevailing winds. Rains with acid levels 500 times the norm have been recorded in New Hampshire.

The impact of acid rain on plant and animal life in the Northeast is substantial. Fish life has been wiped out in thousands of high-acid Canadian lakes in Ontario and Québec. A four year study of the Adirondack Mountains identified 212 high-altitude lakes and ponds without fish and 256 other bodies of water near that point. Damage to crops and timber are more difficult to estimate, but experts suggest that timber yields may decrease 15 percent over the next two decades. Medical authorities doubt that acid rain has any direct effect on human health, but acidity increases the solubility of metals including toxic mercury.

The Northeastern states and eastern provinces blame acid rain on windborne pollution from the Middle West, particularly the highly industrialized Ohio River Valley. Paradoxically, the 1200-foot smokestacks on thousands of coal-fired boilers in Ohio, Indiana, and western Pennsylvania, which were intended to disperse pollution, simply throw it higher into the atmosphere and extend its range. Canada charges that two thirds of the sulfur dioxide that lands in its eastern provinces emanates from industrialized centers in the Middle West and eastern seaboard, blown north and east across the international border. In fact, largely because of the Clean Air Act of 1970, sulfur content in America's air was reduced 17 percent nationally between 1972 and 1982. In the mid-1980s however, levels of sulfur dioxide, nitrogen oxides, and particulates began to edge upward. Even more alarming is the realization that rising levels of carbon dioxide (CO_2) have had a globally cumulative effect such that a global warming trend is underway. As an unintended byproduct of industrialization, air pollution has initiated a long-term rise in atmospheric temperatures. Such large-scale changes raise doubts about the path taken toward economic progress. Some 84 coal-fired power plants were equipped with scrubbers to remove sulfur dioxide, and 34 more are being equipped with scrubbers.

Water Pollution

A similar concentration of pollutants is becoming a major problem in the

Public concern about waste disposal and other types of environmental pollution is intensifying in the United States. This acid dump in Riverside, California, was cleaned up after the water supply was contaminated. Similar incidents have occurred nationwide.

waterways of North America, although the danger is less acute than in Japan and parts of Europe where space is far more limited and population densities greater. Sources of water pollution are manifold: sewage disposal from cities located on rivers and lakes; industrial wastes; pesti-cides, herbicides, and fertilizers from America's scientifically based agri-culture; coastal oil refineries and off-shore drilling rigs—in short, the ele-ments that combine to produce the affluence of North American society.

Perhaps the most dramatic inci-dent of water pollution occurred on the Cuyahoga River in the late 1960s. Flowing through Cleveland into Lake Erie laden with industrial chemicals, the Cuyahoga burst into flames and damaged two railroad bridges. Far more serious, however, is the grad-ual and general deterioration of water quality in the great watersheds of the continent—the Hudson, the Missis-sippi, the rivers of the Central Valley of California, the Columbia, and the greatest reservoir of freshwater on earth, the 94,710-square-mile Great Lakes.

Nitrogen and phosphorus from ag-ricultural and suburban infiltration, industrial wastes from the heartlands of both the United States and Can-ada, and municipal sewage from shoreline urban centers threatened to convert large areas of the Great Lakes into a carpet of algae. In Lake Erie, particularly, these substances reduce the water's oxygen content, leading to luxuriant growth of algae that chokes off the normal self-re-newing biological processes of the water body. With less than 3.5 per-cent of the land area of the United States, the Great Lakes Basin is home to 37 million Americans and Cana-dians. Concerted action by both gov-ernments has now lowered the level of pollution in Lake Erie, but these 37 million people have a 20 percent higher exposure to toxic chemicals than do other North Americans.

The federal legislation enacted to regulate water pollution in North America utilizes different strategies from those in Japan, where polluters are forced to pay in proportion to the damage they cause. In the United States, costly suits based on environ-mental testing are required. For this reason, water quality has not signif-icantly improved. Industries and cit-ies have almost universally resisted the high costs of water restoration. Currently, some 10,000 communi-ties with 60 percent of the country's sewage plants have failed to meet deadlines established by the Water Pollution Control Act of 1972.

There are, however, exceptions.

Water in New York's Hudson River is gradually becoming cleaner largely owing to an upgrading of sewage plants along the river. Swimming and commercial fishing is still banned, but chemical and bacterial contamination is diminishing. Even more striking is the case of the Willamette River in Oregon. Here, a determined environmental action group forced the paper industry and its unions to clean up the river. Their success suggests that environmental issues are as much a matter of public concern and social commitment as of legislative enactment.

At the heart of the environmental debate is the extremely high per capita energy consumption of North Americans, which is double that of other technological nations and six times greater than world averages. This affluence has been achieved by the sophisticated utilization of the continent's natural abundance of energy sources—wood, water, coal, petroleum, natural gas—to continually increase the productivity of the industrial worker. Similarly, in agriculture, the lavish application of petroleum-derived pesticides and fertilizers enables farmers to increase their productivity. The synergistic relationship between economic growth and environmental degradation is now apparent.

Environmentalists argue for a reduction of wasteful consumption and a decrease in the various forms of pollution that inevitably derive from the use of coal, oil, or nuclear power to generate energy. Lawsuits are filed to preserve wildlife, to prevent industry from constructing pipelines, to eliminate offshore drilling for oil, to block the strip mining of western coal. But the proponents of cleaner air and water appear to be losing ground to those who champion still greater economic growth as an answer to immediate economic problems.

The National Cancer Institute has identified environmental pollution as a prominent cause of the rapid increase in this disease. In the 1980s, poisoning of the environment by toxic chemicals, nuclear wastes, and other dangerous substances is perceived as a serious national problem. The hazardous waste problem at Love Canal in Niagara Falls, New York, demonstrated that existing laws do not meet the issue, particularly because over 14,000 toxic waste sites are scattered across the American landscape. It is clear that the introduction of largely untested chemical agents into the American environment is of immediate concern for all North Americans.

Sobering questions face North Americans in the 1990s. Technology progresses, pushing the diverse, growing, and affluent population into new geographic situations. Most believe that plant shutdowns, economic dislocation, environmental disaster, and cultural discrimination "can't happen here." It does. Yet the economic strength and prosperity of the region as a whole increases. However, the disparities of wealth and poverty cannot forever, to paraphrase Lincoln, stand in a house divided against itself.

5

THE SOVIET UNION AND EASTERN EUROPE

*T*he Communist Revolution of 1917 ended centuries of Czarist rule in Russia and threw down a gauntlet to the industrialized West. The Communists rejected all forms of capitalism and predicted a future in which the societies of Western Europe and North America would experience a similar wave of Communist revolutions. Although Soviet rule was plagued for decades by social upheaval, purges, and wars, Communist ideology has guided the process of modernization and industrialization in the Soviet Union. Operating within its principles, the Soviet Union has restructured the human geography of a vast land and its people (Fig. 5.1).

The Soviet assertion that **communism** is the wave of the future still dominates global strategies of war and

peace. The Soviet example attracted attention in the Developing World with its clear-cut method of attaining rapid modernization. It has served as an alternative form of economic organization to capitalism, a system that most of the developing countries first experienced as subject colonial peoples.

The achievements of the Soviet Union, and particularly its quick transformation from a backward, agrarian society into a modern industrial state, allured some. Increasingly obvious, however, are the inefficiency of the Soviet economic order, the dictatorial suppression of the Soviet people, and the vast natural endowment of the Soviet earth—factors that contributed to the rapid economic progress of the Soviet Union. Although the

Figure 5.1   Political regions of the Soviet Union.

GEOSTATISTICS

	Capital	Area (square miles)	Population (millions)	Rate of Natural Increase (%)	Number of Years to Double Population	Population Projected for A.D. 2000	Infant Mortality Rate	Life Expectancy at Birth	Urban Population (%)	Per Capita GNP ($)	Energy Consumption (kg of oil equivalent per capita)
Albania	Tirane	11,100	3.1	2.1	33	3.8	43	71	34	840 (est.)	1,267
Bulgaria	Sofia	42,822	9.0	0.2	385	9.4	15	72	65	4,413 (1983)	4,332
Czechoslovakia	Prague	49,371	15.6	0.2	289	16.2	14	71	74	5,610 (1983)	4,853
East Germany	East Berlin	41,826	16.6	0.0	3,465	16.5	9	72	77	7,286 (1983)	5,680
Hungary	Budapest	35,919	10.6	−0.2	—	10.6	19	70	58	2,010	2,974
Poland	Warsaw	120,726	38.0	0.7	100	39.9	18	71	61	2,070	3,438
Romania	Bucharest	91,699	23.0	0.5	141	24.5	26	70	49	2,546 (1983)	3,453
USSR	Moscow	8,649,498	286.0	1.0	68	311.0	25	69	65	7,400	4,885
Yugoslavia	Belgrade	98,764	23.6	0.6	110	25.0	27	70	47	2,300	1,926

Sources: World Population Data Sheet, 1988; World Development Report, 1987.

struggle for hearts and minds in the Developing World goes on, attention has now shifted to the high cost of Soviet progress and to internal problems in the Soviet Union.

The most salient characteristic of the Soviet Union today is the near total dominance of the state in all phases of life. Because of this, modern Soviet leaders are faced with a dilemma. To create an efficient modern society, power and authority must be delegated to a widely based population. But once given power, the population could threaten the privileged position of the Communist leadership.

Thus far, the members of the Soviet Communist party have retained control. They wield the social and economic power to make crucial decisions that determine the human geography of the Soviet Union. Their current problem is to maintain economic growth, raise standards of living, and provide the economy of abun-

dance they frequently promise the Soviet people. Increasingly, Communist leaders are faced with tensions generated by the contradiction of running a totalitarian state whose avowed ideology demands no class distinctions.

To a certain degree, the forces that gave special character to Russian modernization have moderated. The anti-Western, nationalistic sentiments of the Soviet leadership are tempered by changes in technology, communications, and the attainment of modest levels of material comfort. Although the Soviet Union is still the most isolated of all technological societies, its defensiveness has been eased by control of an East European **buffer zone** and its military power. Unlike other industrial societies where countless individual decisions determine trends and policies, concentration of power in the hands of so few in the Soviet Union makes predictions of its future direction difficult.

THE MODERNIZATION OF RUSSIA

At the beginning of the twentieth century, Russia was a gigantic agrarian land stretching thousands of miles from Eastern Europe across Asia to the Pacific. It was neither European nor Asian. Ruled for three centuries by the Romanov czars, *Russia Under the Czars* lagged far behind the industrializing West. The central problem was the transformation of this agricultural society into an industrial power, but the huge investment required to build an industrial society was greater than Russia could pay. Through a combination of foreign aid and peasant repression, the last of the Romanov czars, Nicholas II, tried to sponsor industrial growth. To some extent he succeeded, but economic progress was aborted by ongoing social upheaval and Russia's disastrous defeat in World War I.

In 1917, a small group of revolutionaries picked up the reins of power determined to create a new socialist society. This marked *The Beginnings of Communist Rule in the Soviet Union.* A decade later, one of these men, Joseph Stalin assumed total power and brought about a veritable social revolution. This led to *The Creation of a Communist State.* No aspect of society was left untouched. The human geography of one sixth of the world's land area was transformed. **Collectivized** peasant farms and state industries became institutions in the Soviet Union at a fearful cost in human life. By the end of the 1930s, the Soviet Union had organized—through state planning—the outlines of a modern industrial economy.

Russia Under the Czars

In the spring of 1917, few suspected that Russia was on the brink of a social revolution that would topple three centuries of Romanov rule and set Russia on a course of cultural experimentation. True, protests and demonstrations occurred daily in Petrograd (today's Leningrad). But food shortages, bread riots, strikes, and peasant uprisings were common features of the social landscape of czarist Russia. The three central figures in the revolution—V. I. Lenin, Leon Trotsky, and Joseph Stalin— were all in exile. No one in power considered them important or dangerous. On March 6, the British ambassador cabled London from Petrograd: "Some disorders occurred today, but nothing serious." He was wrong. The Russian Revolution had begun; the rule of the czars was over.

Until this action, the power of the czars had been absolute. It had held the empire of the Russians together for centuries. Nicholas II, like his predecessors, was convinced that Russia could survive only through **autocracy**. His empire stretched through eleven time zones from the Baltic Sea on the west to the Pacific Ocean on the east, a vast 8.6-million-square-mile reservoir of illiterate peasants and untapped resources. Most of this land was barren of human exploitation, an endless expanse of tundra, forest, steppe, desert, and mountains.

For centuries, Russia's population had spread out from its forest heartland, centered on Moscow in western Russia, eastward across the Ural Mountains into Siberia and southward into Central Asia (Fig. 5.2). The most rapid period of expansion began in 1552 with Moscow's conquest under Ivan the Terrible of the Tatar stronghold of Kazan on the Volga River. Explorers, adventurers, and cossack troops moved across 5000 miles of Siberia in less than a century and reached the shores of the Pacific Ocean in 1640.

Russia under Peter the Great (1672–1725) gained a foothold on the Baltic Sea in the late seventeenth century. By the death of Catherine the Great in 1796, the Russians had pushed to the Black Sea. During the American Civil War, Central Asia was conquered and Russia became a Eurasian empire (Fig. 5.2).

For this reason, by 1900 less than half of Russia's 130 million people spoke Russian as their native tongue, although an additional quarter spoke related Slavic languages like Belorussian, Ukranian, and Polish. The remainder of the population was formed of non-Slavic linguistic and cultural groups—Jews, Germans, Lithuanians, Latvians, Estonians, Romanians, Georgians, Armenians, Buddhist Mongols, and a variety of Turkic-speaking Muslims in Central Asia. The Russian Census of 1897 identified some 200 nationalities who spoke 146 languages and belonged to dozens of religious groups.

The overwhelming majority of these people were simple peasants whose lives were mired in poverty caused by high taxes, medieval-like landlords, frequent droughts, early frosts, and famine. Relatively few Russians lived in cities or worked in factories despite the fact that Russia was experiencing rapid economic development at the end of the nineteenth century. To rule and control this vast and varied land was a monumental task. When Western Europeans criticized Nicholas II for his ruthless repression of the Russian people, his finance minister responded that the surprise was not that Russia had a repressive government but that Russia had any government at all.

The World of the Russian Peasant

Russia had always known great extremes of wealth and poverty. The social and economic gulf that separated Russia's nobility and landowners from the **peasantry** was enormous. It was a major obstacle to reform and progress. In the eyes of the West, Russia was a nation lost in its own vastness—a land of wretched roads and vermin-ridden villages spread from Europe into the arid

THE TERRITORIAL EXPANSION OF RUSSIA

From a core area centered on the principality of Moscovy, the Russian state expanded between A.D. 1300 and 1500 to include the Slavic peoples of the northwest. In the next two centuries, Russia extended its conquests eastward across Siberia. By the death of Peter the Great in 1725, the czarist empire extended from the Baltic and Caspian seas in the west to the shores of the Pacific Ocean. Expansion westward in the eighteenth century and southward in the nineteenth enveloped the peoples of European borderlands, the Ukraine, and Central Asia. Today, the Soviet Union is the only empire forged in the colonial period that is still territorially intact.

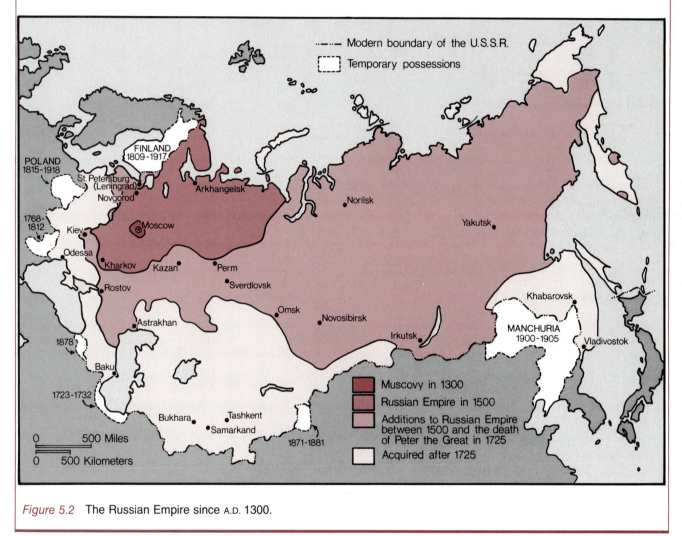

Figure 5.2 The Russian Empire since A.D. 1300.

plains of Asia. From the European viewpoint, this was true. A journey from London to Russia in 1900 was an expedition into the unknown.

At the turn of the twentieth century, Russia was still a nation of peasants. Four of every five Russians were villagers. Three out of four—100 million people—were farmers. The low productivity of Russian agriculture defined peasant life. Typical peasants ate 3 pounds of bread a day, with cabbages, beets, and cucumbers the other major elements in their diet. In most areas, land was still worked with premedieval wooden plows.

Grain was harvested by sickle and threshed by hand. One third of Russia's farms had one horse; another third had no horse at all. The soil was turned by men and women yoked to primitive agricultural implements. Some 90 percent of Russia's agricultural land was planted in grain, but

Russia was a nation of poverty-stricken peasants at the beginning of the twentieth century.

Early Russian Modernization

Despite the backward and isolated nature of the peasantry on the eve of the Revolution of 1917, Russia was not simply the dim, feudal world described by Western travelers. Broadscale social changes were at work. Starting in the 1880s, Russian industry began to expand, stimulated principally by foreign investment and state-sponsored expansion of the railroad system. This opened up new regions for colonization and new resources for exploitation. By 1917, Russia had 47,000 miles of track, including the longest single rail line in the world, the 5700-mile-long Trans-Siberian Railroad. Some of the new railroads were built for military reasons, but towns sprang up along the track, mines were established along the right-of-way, and previously isolated regions provided new markets for Russian manufactures.

New machinery was imported, paid for in grain wrested from the Russian peasants. Many factories and mines were financed by French, Belgian, and German capital. By 1900, half the total investment in Russian industry came from abroad. A new heavy industrial complex located in the Donets Basin in the Ukraine overtook the original industrial base built by Peter the Great in the southern Urals in the early 1700s. Moscow became an important textile center, and czarist Russia for a brief period produced more petroleum than the rest of the world combined. Russia, like Japan then and Germany earlier, was catching up after a late industrial start.

By 1914, Russia was a budding industrial power. But conditions in the factories and mines were scandalous. The work day averaged over twelve hours and was, more often than not, sixteen to eighteen hours long. Women and children made up nearly half the labor force. Low wages were paid because an endless flow of impoverished peasants—potential factory workers—coursed across the Russian landscape in search of work.

crop yields were one third those in Western Europe. The possibility of losing the entire crop to drought was three times greater in Russia than in Western Europe. The ethic of the Russian peasantry was brutally simple: "Another's tears are water."

As the new century unfolded, the situation grew worse. Russia's population of 60 million in 1850 doubled to 130 million by 1900 and in 1913 reached 160 million. Most of this population increase was absorbed in Russia's traditional communal villages, called **mirs**. After the emancipation of the serfs in the 1860s, village elders in these mirs collected taxes and communal dues, allocated justice, and periodically redistributed fields based on family needs. But farmland became increasingly limited as Russia's villages were forced to absorb more and more people.

As a result, by 1900 some 4 million villagers had fled to urban areas. In some cities, the population doubled within a generation. An additional 2.5 million landless farmers migrated eastward along the Trans-Siberian Railroad into the Siberian wilderness. But most Russian peasants remained bound to their home villages because movement required official permission. Faced with growing destitution in the villages, the Russian government provided no relief. Its policy was to export grain to Europe to pay for imported urban and industrial goods. In the face of growing hunger in the countryside, a czarist minister declared, "We shall undereat but we will export." It was the Russian peasants who underate.

This situation exploded in 1905 when riots broke out in numerous Russian cities. Triggered by disastrous defeat in a war with Japan, these riots actually reflected the social imbalance that accompanied the first phases of modernization in Russia. Peasants, kept home during the grip of winter, took up the banner when spring arrived: Crying "the land is God's," they burned farm buildings, occupied estates and raided towns throughout Russia. In retaliation, thousands were exiled to Siberia; others were summarily shot. The czar's authority was not to be questioned. In Saint Petersburg (modern Leningrad), troops slaughtered hundreds of peaceful demonstrators on Bloody Sunday, January 22, 1905. The reforms that followed these uprisings were too late to save Nicholas II and the Romanovs.

The 5700-mile-long Trans-Siberian Railroad is the world's longest single rail line. It links together the vast reaches of the USSR.

In western Russia, willing workers were always available. In Siberia, exiles and criminals formed the bulk of the work force. Armed cossacks, the czarist paramilitary, guarded the factories and mines. Between 1912 and 1914, strikes involved nearly 1 million workers. For these people, the Marxist appeal to revolt, "You have nothing to lose but your chains," made good sense.

Industry began to restructure the face of Russia. Cities grew so fast that by 1917 Russia was nearly 20 percent urban. The number of cities larger than 50,000 population grew from thirteen in 1850 to forty-four in 1900. Villagers flowed into cities poorly equipped to house, employ, and provide newcomers with municipal services. Discontent was widespread but unfocused.

A dual society, not unlike those of some modern nations in the Developing World, separated city from village and modern technology from traditional ways. Despite its urban and industrial advance, Russia remained a nation of peasants that lagged far behind the West in per capita wealth. Growing rural populations and declining availability of land were driving farmers to desperation. Despite the granting of a substantial part of the landed estates to freed serfs in 1861, the contest between landlord and peasant for land, a thread of blood running through centuries of Russian history, threatened the very roots of Romanov rule. Peasant deputies in the newly formed parliament, the Duma, clamored for the distribution of more land from the great estates. Landlords, having ridden out the revolution of 1905, would have none of it.

The government was hoping to develop a class of private landowning peasants by allowing communal village land to be divided into independent holdings. The intent was to form a conservative peasant bulwark against revolt without reducing the privileges of the landowning nobility. To some degree this happened. In the decade before the 1917 Revolution, one third of the 9 million peasant households in European Russia shifted to private ownership of their land. In Asiatic Russia, land-hungry peasants were settled on virgin territory.

But these reforms were largely ineffective in diverting the dramatic course of history. In Russia's cities, industrialization had created a dissatisfied working class of substantial size. Difficulties brought on by the huge debts of World War I led to demonstrations. Protestors carried placards with basic demands: "Bread," "Down with Autocracy." In the countryside, peasants—drained of their crops to pay for imported machinery and for the costs of World War I—were in ferment.

Trapped in the midst of an incomplete industrial revolution and an unwinnable war, the rule of Nicholas II crumbled under the impact of two different revolutions emanating from the two social worlds of Russia: urban workers and rural peasantry. Czar Nicholas II, last of the Romanovs, was forced to abdicate the throne. A provisional government under Alexander Kerensky took over. Shortly thereafter, peasants in the Russian countryside rose up, cast out the landlords, burned manor houses, and seized the land. In this vacuum of chaos, the three men who made a revolution—Lenin, Stalin, and Trotsky—returned from exile in the summer of 1917.

The Beginnings of Communist Rule in the Soviet Union

Stalin, traveling out of Siberia, arrived first on the Trans-Siberian Railroad. Trotsky, then lecturing in Canada, set sail from Montréal. Lenin was transported from Switzerland across Germany to Russia in a special sealed railroad car, courtesy of the enemy German government. After six months of political maneuvering, these men enabled the Bolsheviks—a small, extreme faction of the provisional coalition government—to overthrow the provisional government in a coup d'état and seize control of Russia in November 1917.

Their program for action was based on the precepts of the German social philosopher Karl Marx. According to Marx (1818–1883), the roots of industrial workers' problems were economic in origin. Misery was the result of the exploitation of one economic class by another. In his eyes, one class—the capitalists—had by luck and skill gained control over the means of production. According to Marxist theory, this economic power was used to enslave and impoverish workers. In Marx's view, the existing social system was designed to reinforce the power of the capitalist class and to protect its property. Shatter that social system, impose a revolution to overturn capitalist society, put the workers in power, and a better, more rational world—a world of social equality—would arise.

The first step in establishing this new society would be the abolition of privately owned property. This meant land and property—industries, mines, shops, as well as the land of the Russian Orthodox Church, which owned land throughout the realm—would be owned by the state in the name of the people. Class differences based on ownership would no longer exist. Although it puzzled Lenin, Stalin, and Trotsky that the long-awaited Communist revolution had taken root in their own backyard rather than in one of the older industrialized countries of Western Europe, they were determined to construct a new socialist order and to forge a classless society in Russia under the absolute control of the Bolshevik party.

The Bolsheviks in Power (1917–1921)

Between 1917 and 1921, the Bolshevik Revolution struggled with a number of issues crucial to all Russians: a humiliating peace treaty with Germany, a nationwide civil war, peasant revolt, and famine. Russia—renamed the Soviet Union in 1922—withdrew from World War I under the terms of the Treaty of Brest-Litovsk. Russia was forced to give up vast areas in eastern Europe—territory painstakingly acquired by the czars during the previous two centuries. Poland; Finland; the Baltic states of Estonia, Latvia, and Lithuania; the Ukraine; part of Belorussia; and Georgia were lost. The young Communist state was shorn of some of its most productive land. Some 62 million people and 1.27 million square miles of territory were lost. One third of the country's most fertile lands, one third of its factories, and three quarters of its coal and iron mines no longer belonged to the Soviet state.

In the territory remaining to the Bolsheviks, they had to contend with a civil war. The opponents of the revolution (Whites) gained control of Siberia, the Caucasus, and the Crimea. They received half-hearted support from British and American troops who occupied the northern port cities of Murmansk and Archangelsk and the Siberian port of Vladivostok. The Communists held Moscow, Saint Petersburg (renamed Petrograd during World War I and after the Revolution yet again renamed, this time Leningrad) and the Great Russian heartland. The bulk of both armies consisted of hungry peasants forcibly pressed into service.

In three years of savage warfare, famine and disease took the lives of an estimated 9 million people. By 1920, a third of the population in the cities and towns of northern and central Russia had fled to the countryside in search of food, reflecting the tenuous nature of urbanization at that time. Industrial manpower declined by half; grain production by a third.

Anarchy prevailed in many regions. The so-called "Green Revolutionaries," peasants concerned less with ideology than with agricultural land, took the Russian landscape by force.

Special detachments of Communist troops fanned out from the cities in search of the food that peasants cunningly hid. Villagers stood their ground and were slaughtered. The entire country was in the throes of a war for bread. Most people had little use for either the Communists or their opponents. A peasant folksong aptly described the politics of the peasant majority: "Oh you little apple, oh so bright; bash the Whites from the left and the Reds from the right." But by 1921, the Reds, although widely disliked, had defeated the still more hated Whites. Russia lay in ruins, its industry, transport system, and food production shattered by six years of war.

The New Economic Policy (1921–1928)

After the 1917 Revolution, Lenin dismantled Russia's market economy, so important in Western Europe's modernization. He nationalized every important sector of the Russian economy in line with orthodox Marxist thinking. Private property became state property. In the cities, factories, shops, and houses were taken over. In the countryside, land belonging to the crown, the Orthodox Church, and landlords was confiscated. Although 125 million acres of land were transferred from state to peasant control, the flight of 8 million city dwellers to the villages during the civil war negated the benefits of this transfer. In these early years, Lenin blindly persisted in viewing peasants in Marxist terms as "the class that represents barbarism within civilization." But lacking adequate control over territory, Lenin in effect legalized peasant control of the land.

Social upheaval swept both city and village. The Communists leveled the population into a primitive state of social equality. But this social transformation of Soviet Russia had awesome economic consequences. By 1921, the very survival of the Soviet Union as a country was at stake.

As the decline in Russian industrial and agricultural production became more acute, the need for a new economic policy became clear. By 1921, the bread ration in Moscow and Leningrad had to be cut by one third. The largest factories in these cities had been shut down because of fuel crises. Some provinces were in open revolt.

The Communist Revolution, only four years old, was trapped, as Leon Trotsky described it, in a pair of open scissors: the prices of manufactured goods rose as money declined in value, but the prices paid for farm products plunged. The widening gap between these prices—the two blades of the economic scissors—meant that peasants ate more of their produce and provided less to the cities. Unless the gap between the two blades was closed, to pursue Trotsky's analogy, the Communist Revolution was in danger of being beheaded.

In the face of these realities, Lenin retreated from socialism and made concessions to capitalism. He yielded to the demands of the peasantry and launched the New Economic Policy (NEP) in 1921, a profound change in direction. The objective was to encourage private and foreign investment to get Russia's crippled economy moving. During the first year of the NEP, drought in the Volga River Basin caused famine to stalk the Russian landscape. Some 5 million died, but the new policy soon took hold. Wealthier and more energetic peasants began to increase production and to trade freely in urban markets. This freer policy spread to industry. By 1927, Russian industrial production had returned to prewar levels. For the first time since before World War I, the Soviet Union experienced a return to normality. An economic revival ensued.

Individual farming was carried out on 25 million small holdings, and peasants made up 73 percent of the population. Restrictions on hiring labor, leasing land, and investing capital—all practices abhorrent to orthodox Marxists—were relaxed. Lenin's death in 1924 disturbed little. In the next four years, the gradual ascendancy of Joseph Stalin over the Communist party (as the Bolsheviks now called themselves) went largely unnoticed. Dismissed by most of his colleagues as a mediocrity, Stalin wielded absolute power over the Soviet Union for the next quarter century and became the architect of a new Russian empire after World War II.

The Creation of a Communist State

Alone among prominent Communists, Joseph Stalin had never lived in the West or learned any Western language. He believed that the Soviet Union should go it alone, that "socialism in one country," not world revolution, should be the Bolshevik objective. To Stalin, Russia was a country ringed by enemies who had consistently taken advantage of the country's backwardness. He profiled his attitude in a 1931 speech:

The history of Russia was that she was ceaselessly beaten for her backwardness. She was beaten by the Mongol Khans, she was beaten by the Turkish Beys, she was beaten by the Swedish feudal lords, she was beaten by the Polish-Lithuanian Pans, she was beaten by the Japanese barons, she was beaten by all for her backwardness. . . . We are fifty or a hundred years behind the advanced countries. We must make this lag good in ten years. Either we do it or they crush us.

Few in power disputed this view, and its appeal to the Russian people was considerable. For most Communist leaders, change was seen as a matter of timing and tactics. They were afraid that any drastic shift in economic policy would plunge the country into another civil war and destroy the regime. But Stalin was convinced that headlong **collectivization** of agriculture and rapid industrialization were essential to the survival of the Soviet Union. Somehow the peasants must be forced to feed the cities and to provide capital in the form of grain to pay for investment in heavy industry.

Stalin was determined to impose his will on the country whatever the

V. I. Lenin masterminded the Bolshevik Revolution of 1917. He made the USSR into the world's first communist society based on the teachings of Karl Marx.

cost. Stalin proposed that the Soviet economy be coordinated by the implementation of a **five-year plan,** set by the Communist Party, beginning in 1928. All aspects of national development were then orchestrated by a series of successive five-year plans. This was the beginning of the world's first **command economy.** Stalin's five-year plans transformed Russian agriculture and industry.

Collectivization

A new policy of collectivizing the millions of Russian peasants was inaugurated in 1929. Within a year more than half the farmland in the Soviet Union was organized into **kolkhozes,** collective farms in which the members of villages pooled their labor and land under government supervision and were paid in shares of the harvest. A smaller number of large state farms, or **sovkhozes,** on which peasants were paid cash wages, were also established on successful estates and in areas of climatic risk (Fig. 5.3).

The peasants responded with pre-dictable fury, their traditional craving for private land again thwarted by government edict. Faced with confiscation, peasants killed animals and burned crops rather than give them up to the collectives. Villages became battlefields where troops were sent to collect food, subdue riots, and protect the collectives. The countryside was once again on the verge of civil war, but Stalin prevailed. By 1937, 93 percent of the Russian peasants lived on collective farms (Fig. 5.3).

Despite the enormous human cost, which Stalin estimated at 10 million people, by 1938, at the end of the second five-year plan, the government had reorganized agriculture and solved the problem of feeding urban populations and subsidizing the growth of heavy industry. The 24 to 25 million individual peasant holdings had been amalgamated into 250,000 kolkhozes under direct Communist control and organization. The regime compromised by permitting each family a personally

worked garden plot. By the end of the 1930s, agricultural production was 50 percent higher than in 1928, although the number of livestock did not reach prerevolutionary levels until 1960. Nearly two thirds of the arable land was tractor-plowed and 90 percent of the grain mechanically threshed. The rural masses of the Soviet Union had been integrated into the **socialist** state, their opposition broken by the determination of Joseph Stalin.

Industrialization

Collectivization exacted a brutal price from the Russian people and disrupted society, but in Stalin's view, it was a sacrifice required for the young Soviet state to overtake and surpass the West in industrial and military power. To this end, the foundations of a new industrial society were laid. All industrial plants were brought under state control and assigned production quotas.

By 1940, the Soviet Union was producing 165 million tons of coal and

Agriculture was collectivized in the USSR despite peasant resistance. Here, farmers on a kolkhoz at Yaroslavl, northeast of Moscow, harvest potatoes.

THE COLLECTIVIZATION OF AGRICULTURE

The two graphs illustrate (1) the rapid collectivization of agriculture in villages in the 1930s under Joseph Stalin, (2) the gradual amalgamation of collective farms into larger units in the 1950s, and (3) the conversion of kolkhozes, where several villages pooled their labor and were paid in shares of the harvest, to sovkhozes, where the state paid cash wages to farm workers. From a geographical viewpoint, Stalin's collectivization of the peasantry marked the real socialization of the Soviet Union, a transformation of the relationship between land and life.

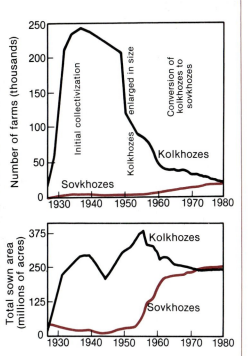

Figure 5.3 Collectivized agriculture in the Soviet Union, 1930–1980.

220 million barrels of petroleum from new fields that were developed between the Volga River and the Ural Mountains. The vast mineral resources of the country, previously barely tapped, were brought into production. Aluminum, copper, zinc, tin, nickel, and magnesium were mined. New railroad lines to Turkestan and the Arctic supplemented the old tsarist network. The Trans-Siberian Railroad and the railroad network connecting Leningrad, Moscow, the Donets Basin, and the Volga were double-tracked. A canal connecting Moscow with the Volga River was built by political prisoners, and the travel distance from the northern port of Archangelsk to Leningrad was cut by a factor of four by another new canal.

Some 20 million people migrated from the villages to the cities. The two largest cities—Moscow and Leningrad—doubled in size to 4 and 3.2 million people respectively by 1939. In these Communist metropolises, the working class was exhorted to increase production quotas. For the most part, these pleas fell on a dispirited population, sullen with hardship and deprivation. The skeleton of a modern industrial state was being forged in the Soviet Union, but the human dislocation caused by urbanization and industrialization—social tensions that were absorbed in Great Britain over the course of a century—were forced on Russians in a single decade.

The geographical distribution of new industry in the Soviet Union was influenced by both political and economic motivations. In conformity with Marxist philosophy, a more even allocation of industrial activity throughout the country was considered desirable, so that backward regions would not be exploited by powerful concentrations of economic activity in more favored regions. An attempt was made to locate industries as close as possible to sources of fuel and raw materials and to reduce dependence on interregional transport. And because of Stalin's obsessive fear of military conquest from the West, a major effort was made to reduce the concentration of industry in European Russia, the area most vulnerable to attack.

Economics prevailed however. The costs of expanding existing factories in Moscow, Leningrad, the Ukraine, and the Urals were much lower than creating new complexes, so that the traditional distribution of industry in the Soviet Union remained intact.

THE HUMAN GEOGRAPHY OF THE SOVIET UNION

The Soviet Union is the largest state in the world. Within its 38,000-mile borders, it embraces the eastern half of Europe and the entire northern half of the Asian landmass (Fig. 5.4). Two-and-one-half times the size of the United States and one sixth of the world's land area, Russia is a term used to refer to what is more correctly called the Soviet Union or Union of Soviet Socialist Republics (USSR). Properly, Russia refers to the homeland of the Russian people—one ethnic group in the Soviet Union. Russia is also one of fifteen union republics—the civil divisions of the Soviet Union. Given the special name, Russian Soviet Federated Socialist Republic (RSFSR), it is by far the largest Soviet republic, spanning the country from coast to coast. However, in common and historical usage, Russia refers to the landmass encompassed by the Soviet Union because the entire area operates on the basis of Russian traditions and customs.

Most of this sprawling country lies at latitudes north of the Canadian-U.S. border. The largest population centers of Russian society—Moscow and Leningrad—are located at latitudes comparable to those of southern Alaska. Monotonous stretches of treeless Arctic tundra and evergreen forests, the taiga, cover the northern half of the country. In the south, the forests give way to steppe grasslands and then to deserts. Outliers of the

Figure 5.4 Physical features of the Soviet Union.

Himalaya Mountains thrust into Soviet Central Asia and the Caucasus, ranges longer and higher than the Alps (Fig. 5.4). These harsh environmental conditions partly explain why Russia has an average population density of just over twenty-five people per square mile, half the world average.

Between these extremes of latitude and climate, a triangular wedge of fertile, well-populated land constitutes the effective territory of the modern Soviet state, the Fertile Triangle. The Fertile Triangle, broad in the relatively mild, well-watered European west, tapers eastward along an axis of Soviet industry and agriculture into an apex in south-central Siberia. Beyond that, nearly all people live within 20 miles of the Trans-Siberian Railroad. Within these generalized environments, virtually every climate short of tropical can be found. Sheer immensity ensures a national landscape of abundant variety and distinction.

In the czarist period, Russia was frequently characterized as a "prison of peoples," not simply to describe the absolute autocracy of the Russian state but to emphasize its cultural diversity. Over the course of centuries, Russians progressively expanded outward from their culture hearth in the forests between the Oka River and the headwaters of the Volga River (Fig. 5.2). They conquered Baltic and Slavic peoples on their western borders, the Muslims of Soviet Central Asia to the south, and numerous Asiatic peoples located in lands that extend 6800 miles between European Russia and the Pacific Ocean. The modern Soviet state, with a population of 286 million, includes over 100 different recognized racial, linguistic, and religious groups within its territory. Ethnic groups go by the special name of **nationality** in the Soviet Union. Large ethnic groups, such as the Russians themselves, or the Ukrainians, or Kazakhs, are the basis of the fifteen Soviet union republics. Cultural diversity complements environmental variation. Not surprisingly, patterns of human occupance are extremely complex.

Given vast distances, cultural differences, and environmental difficulties, human regions in the Soviet Union are defined by their environmental accessibility, effective settlement, and economic integration within the country as a whole. Four generalized regions basic to Soviet life can be identified: the Fertile Triangle, the Soviet North, the Southern Periphery, and the Far East.

In the west, *The Fertile Triangle* contains at least three quarters of the Soviet population, three quarters of all Soviet agriculture and industry, and a good deal of the country's developed energy, mineral, and metal resources. Thinly populated, *The Soviet North* encompasses more than half the land area of the country, a 1000- to 2000-mile-wide band of tundra and taiga that stretches across the entire breadth of the Soviet state. At lower latitudes, *The Southern Periphery* extends through the Caucasus and Soviet Central Asia to include a broken band of mountains, steppes, and deserts along the southern borders of the Soviet Union. At the Soviet Pacific, *The Far East* represents a frontier area whose development depends on the ability of Soviet planners to extend the relationship between east and west across vast distances.

The Fertile Triangle

The agricultural and industrial heartland of the Soviet Union, the Fertile Triangle, is a region of great social and environmental complexity. It lies wedged between Arctic Siberia to the northeast and the deserts and mountains ringing the Soviet Union's Southern Periphery.

The historic centers of Russian civilization—Moscow and Leningrad—anchor its northern quarter. Early established administrative and trading cities were supported by peasant farmers who cultivated the brown forest soils of the rolling plains of European Russia and benefited from the longer growing seasons and milder winters that prevail in this area. To the south, forests yield to the grasslands of the Ukraine, whose thick, fertile black soils called **chernozems**

support the highest rural population densities in the Soviet Union. The heavy industrial complex of the Donets Basin is located in the eastern Ukraine, north of the Black Sea.

Russian settlers have been attracted east of this European core by opportunities for centuries. The fertile fields and oil deposits of the Volga River plains, the mineral centers of the Ural Mountains, the grasslands of northern Kazakhstan, and the industrial core of the Kuznetsk Basin have drawn migrants in search of a better life, much like the American West drew pioneer settlers.

Overall, the Fertile Triangle supports 205 million of the Soviet Union's 286 million people, leaving much of the rest of the Soviet Union a thinly populated wilderness. It contains most of the nation's good agricultural land and all five of the major industrial concentrations—the light industries of Moscow and Leningrad and the heavy industries of the Donets Basin, the Urals, and Kuznetsk Basin.

By any measure, this is the heartland of the Soviet Union. It has six identifiable subregions—Moscow, the Baltic, and the Ukraine in what is the Soviet Union's European core; and the Volga, the Urals, and the Kuznetsk Basin farther to the east in what Soviet geographers identify as their Asian Frontier. Each of these parts of the Fertile Triangle differs considerably from each other by virtue of cultural and environmental distinctions. Together they stand apart from the rest of the country because of their high levels of social and economic development. For ideological and strategic reasons, Soviet planners have tried to divert development away from the Fertile Triangle into the Soviet North, Central Asia, and the Far East. But the Fertile Triangle has been and will remain the core of the Soviet state.

The European Core

The European core of the Fertile Triangle can be subdivided into three

areas—Moscow in the north, the Baltic in the northwest, and the Ukraine in the south. The Moscow subregion is a gently rolling, forested plain located in a transitional climatic zone on the southern margin of the taiga. Originally a rival princely state of the ancient capital of Vladimir to the east, Moscow benefited from its position at the hub of the extensive river systems of the East European Plain—the Volga, the Don, the Dnieper, and the Dvina—to become a trading center. Equally important, Moscow was a center of Mongol tax collection, and later it became the focal point of a rapidly enlarging state.

This locational advantage helped compensate for the meager resources of its hinterland—acidic, poorly drained forest soils that produce low grain yields; cold, damp winters with six months of snow; no energy resources except low-grade coal, wood, and peat; and few significant mineral deposits.

In the nineteenth century, Moscow's role as the social and political center of the Russian people was reinforced by the growth of the railroad network and by canals that linked the city with the Baltic, Black, and Caspian seas. Food, raw materials, and energy resources flowed along these routes into the administrative capital, promoting the emergence of the Moscow region as an industrial center. With a current population of over 9 million people, the city of Moscow—the center of the Communist world—is ringed by satellite industrial cities and suburbs. Moscow's economic landscape of textile mills and metal and machine plants has a combined product that is the largest in the country.

The Baltic region west of Moscow and north of the Ukraine is a glacial landscape of bogs, lakes, and forest. It is located so far north that the sun in midwinter barely rises above the horizon and in midsummer barely sets. Its importance in the national economy stems from Russia's historic

The Kremlin is the citadel of Moscow and the governing center of the USSR.

drive toward the Baltic Sea to gain access to Europe. This drive culminated in Czar Peter's establishment of the city of Saint Petersburg (now Leningrad) in 1703 on the poorly drained delta of the Neva River, the point on the Baltic shore closest to Moscow. In 1712, Peter made his city capital of Russia—a distinction it held until 1918.

Like Moscow, Saint Petersburg—Peter the Great's "window on the West"—was founded in an infertile region whose poorly drained glaciated soils, northern location, and paucity of energy and mineral resources had long retarded development. The creation of the city reflected centuries of conflict among Germans, Poles, Swedes, and Russians for political dominance in the Baltic. Strong water, and later rail, connections were created to link the city with the resources of the Ukraine, the Moscow region, and the Urals. Leningrad today has a population of 4.7 million. It is a major center of engineering, electronic, chemical, shipbuilding, and metalworking industries. Although clearly located outside the mainstream of contemporary Russian economic growth, Leningrad is a major center for ed-

ucation and the arts in the Soviet Union.

The third subregion in the European core of the Fertile Triangle is the Ukraine, offering the best-endowed and most productive farmland in the Soviet Union. Forested in the north and covered by grasslands in the south, almost the entire region is underlain by humus-laden chernozem. Its relatively southerly location provides the Ukraine with a far more moderate climate than either Moscow or Leningrad and allows for a longer growing season. These environmental factors make the Ukraine the breadbasket of the Soviet Union. It is a land of rolling plateaus and escarpments etched by a series of rivers—the Bug, the Dniester, the Dnieper, the Donets, and the Don—which flow from northwest to southeast.

In contrast to the more densely populated woodlands to the north, the Ukraine was a frontier area until the nineteenth century. Large wheat- and sheep-raising estates were established in pioneer fashion by nobles. With the discovery of the iron deposits of Krivoy Rog and the coal of the Donets Basin, the Ukraine was transformed into the agricultural and

industrial workshop of the Russian state. Currently, nearly 65 million people live in this region. They are spread across the old agricultural districts of the north and west, centered on the third largest city of the Soviet Union, Kiev (pop. 2.2 million), and concentrated in the industrial belt located between the Donets Basin and the Dnieper River bend. The entire region is populated by Slavic-language speakers, two thirds of whom are ethnic Ukrainians.

The Asian Frontier

East of the European core of the Fertile Triangle, there is a wedge of fertile agricultural land that narrows eastward from the Volga Plains to the low ranges of the southern Ural Mountains, past the Ob-Irtysh river system, and into south-central Siberia. This swath of cultivatable land with moderate climate is located between the taiga forests of the Soviet North and the southern mountains and deserts of Soviet Central Asia. An early industrial complex was established in the southern Urals during the 1700s, but for the most part, this area remained a Russian frontier for nearly two centuries. It served as a broad boundary zone between the civilized regions of European Russian and the Asian unknown.

In the last fifty years, the Asian Frontier has been opened to new settlement and exploitation. The discovery of energy resources and raw materials in the Asian Frontier has formed the basis for a new industrial axis where more than 70 million people live.

The Volga, the longest river in Europe and in many ways the eastern boundary of Europe, lies between the far-flung resources of the east and the dense populations of the west. Ivan the Terrible's armies conquered the Volga Plains in the middle of the sixteenth century. The middle and lower Volga regions were then occupied by Muslim Tatars and scattered peasant cultivators living in threat of flood and drought. During the reign of

Catherine the Great in the 1700s, German colonists were invited to settle in the middle Volga. Although endowed with navigable streams, the Volga Basin was not effectively industrialized until the Soviet period.

After World War II, the discovery of substantial oil reserves in the northeastern Volga Plains began to transform the economy and society of the region. New settlers and industries flooded into the Volga Basin, vast hydroelectric projects were initiated, and big petrochemical works were established. The Russian influx from the west began to diminish the importance of the non-Slavic nationalities who dominated the area until modern times—the Tatars, the Bashkir, and the Chuvash. The fastest growing industrial region in the Soviet Union today, producing one fifth of the country's petroleum, the Volga has vaulted into national prominence because of its oil resources, its development as a major trade waterway, and its intermediate location between Moscow and the Urals.

The Ural Mountains and the plains of western Siberia attracted some 7 million Russian migrants from the European core at the turn of this century. Grain farms were established on the more humid northern margins of these grassland steppes as peasants gambled on adequate rainfall, and new railroads provided access to markets for their crops. Regional development of the Asian Frontier lagged until the 1930s when the decision was taken to modernize older industries in the Urals through the establishment of the Urals-Kuznetsk combine. Implying the planned integration of diverse industrial resources across a vast geography, the Urals-Kuznetsk combine sent coal 1200 miles westward to the Urals from rich mines in the Kuznetsk Basin in Siberia. Iron ore was sent east to Kuznetsk. Steel complexes, furthering economic development, were built at both ends of the line. Greatly accelerated due to the Nazi threat in the western Soviet Union during World War II, industry in the Urals was facilitated by the development of a storehouse of metals and minerals, the most important of which are high-quality iron ore (now running out), copper, and a variety of **ferroalloys**.

Sverdlovsk (pop. 1.3 million) emerged as the principal center of a northern cluster of industrial cities in the Urals. To the south, the cities of Chelyabinsk (pop. 1 million), Magnitogorsk (pop. 400,000), and Orsk (pop. 250,000), have grown rapidly since the 1940s. Energy is provided by coal shipped from Karaganda (pop. 600,000), 500 miles east, and Kuznetsk. Today, the southern Urals house a strategic network of industrial cities on the Asian Frontier.

In addition, some 90 million acres of agricultural land in the steppes south of the southern Urals on the borders of Kazakhstan were put to the plow under the "Virgin Lands" program in the 1950s. Migration to this marginal farmland rapidly increased the population of the southern Urals and associated lowlands, but as in the American prairies, the threat of erosion, drought, and dust-bowl conditions make the future of these agricultural experiments uncertain.

In the headwaters of the Ob River, the Kuznetsk ("blacksmith") Basin begins to form the tapering eastern end of the Fertile Triangle (Fig. 5.8). To an even greater degree than the Urals to the west, the Kuznetsk Basin has experienced rapid industrial growth in the Soviet period. It is a cluster of cities set in rugged terrain. Cold northern climates and southern deserts converge at Kuznetsk to pinch off good land. Only the chernozem country of the Altai steppe at the headwaters of the Ob River has had adequate sources of water for large-scale agricultural development. State farm programs, then, have centered on irrigated cultivation. Despite the great distances from Russia's principal centers of population, coal- and steel-based cities have mushroomed in this distant frontier tip of the Fertile Triangle. Amidst immense coal deposits, an industrial zone focuses on new Soviet cities such as Novosibirsk (pop. 1.3 million), and Novokuznetsk (pop. 550,000).

Beyond the Kuznetsk Basin, the Fertile Triangle narrows to its apex at the cluster of new Soviet cities at Lake Baikal, the world's largest, deepest, and oldest freshwater body (Fig. 5.8). Rich in timber resources, the Baikal region is focused on Irkutsk (pop. 550,000), founded as a Russian trading post in 1652.

The Soviet North

The Soviet North, a 4-million-square-mile area, larger than either Canada or the United States, contains only 5 million people and is the least populated, least known, and least exploited region of the Soviet Union. Located along the deepest continental rim of the Arctic, the tundra environments of the Soviet Union prevail over a tenth of the country, and taiga occupies nearly half the country. Here winters are long and bitter. Despite continuous daylight in June and July, average monthly temperatures in the tundra remain below 50 degrees Fahrenheit. Trees in the tundra are but stunted birches. Vegetation is composed of mosses, lichens, and ferns, thinly rooted on the bare rock surfaces and frozen bogs of this glaciated region. Inhabitants of the Soviet North today range from traditional reindeer herders, to miners of scarce and valuable minerals, to the personnel of military bases and those prison camps so vividly described in Alexander Solzhenitsyn's documentary history *The Gulag Archipelago* (1974).

South of the treeless tundra, an enormous evergreen forest, the taiga, stretches 4000 miles across the country in a belt 1000 to 2000 miles wide. Most of the taiga is unpopulated, although it is a primary global source of timber. Summer temperatures are warmer than in the Arctic, but the

MAPSCAN

MAP PROJECTIONS

The only way that geographers can accurately replicate any large area of the surface of the earth is by using a globe. Globes, however, are too unwieldy to use in research, navigation, or planning. This poses a dilemma. It is impossible to map the curved surface of the earth on a flat sheet of paper without distortion. Any sizable curved surface when pressed flat will rip, wrinkle, or tear. To cope with this problem, geographers have developed a large number of **map projections.** The amount, type, and location of map distortion for each projection is known. This enables geographers to select the most appropriate map projection depending on the properties of the projection, the region under study, and the purpose of the map.

Every properly drawn map shows correct location on the surface of the earth, but the similarity ends there. Some maps show distance and direction from one point to another with accuracy. Other maps depict shape with precision. Some represent area accurately. But no map projection can embody all of these properties. Every map and the map projection has some distortion. Distance, direction, shape and area are never *all* accurate on a single map.

Every map projection, therefore, represents a compromise. In practice, geographers choose between **conformal projections,** on which the shapes of small areas are shown correctly, or **equal-area projections,** on which area is true to scale over the entire map. Generally, projections are classified into three families depending on their method of construction: **azimuthal, cylindrical,** and **conic.** Each

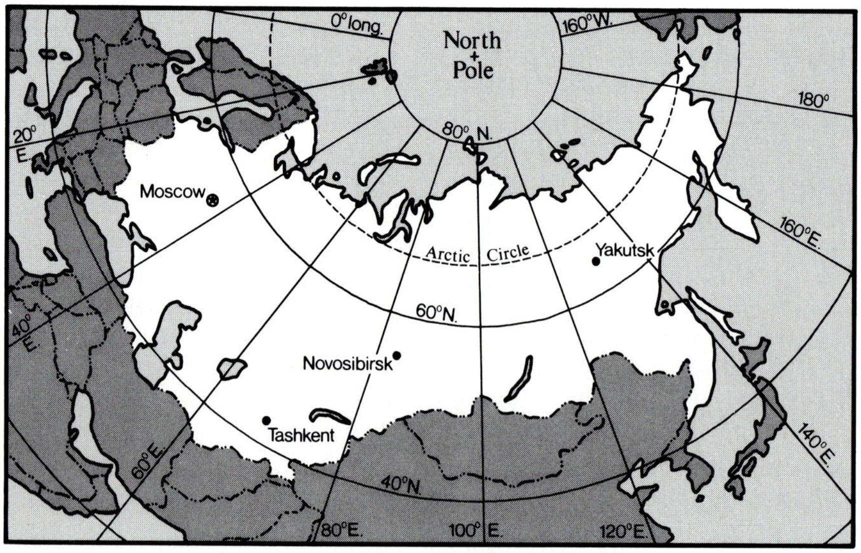

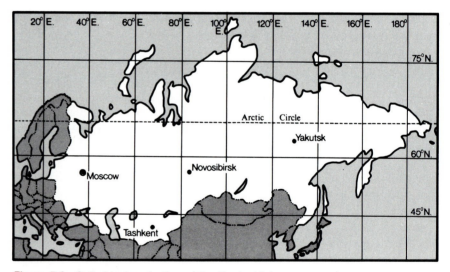

Figure 5.5 Azimuthal projection of the Soviet Union.

Figure 5.6 Cylindrical projection of the Soviet Union.

soils of the forest are extremely poor (Fig. 5.8). Taiga soils, called **podzols,** lack organic matter and have been leached of nutritive value. Cultivation requires heavy investment in soil reconstruction. Standing bogs cover much of the region. In many areas, the subsoil is permanently frozen, a condition called **permafrost.** In these areas, the alternate winter freezing and summer thawing of the topsoil provide an unstable foundation for rail lines, roads, and buildings. Across the northern half of the vast territory of the Soviet Union, therefore, human occupance is tentative and economic development is limited. But the Soviets are cold-country engineers without equal.

Distinct regional differences in levels of utilization can be identified

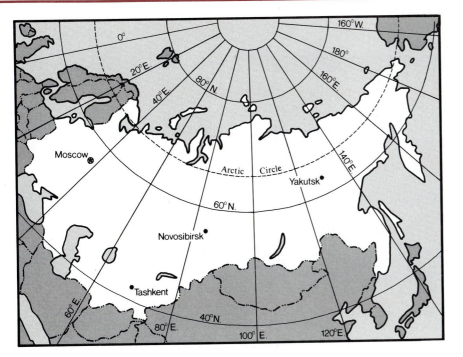

Figure 5.7 Conic projection of the Soviet Union.

family has its own set of properties, and when applied to a region as large as the Soviet Union, the differences between them are apparent. Within each family, projections can be conformal, equal area, or a compromise between the two, depending on the method of construction.

Azimuthal projections are projections of the globe onto a flat plane that touches (or is tangent to) the earth's surface at a single point. In Figure 5.5 the point of tangency is the North Pole. On this projection, meridians appear as straight lines radiating outward from the point of tangency; **parallels** are equally spaced circles drawn around this point. Scale is constant along the meridians because the circles of latitude are equally spaced. Direction is true from the central point

to any other point on the map. But distortion increases outward from the center, and although shapes are fairly well represented, areas near the edges of the projection are badly distorted. Azimuthal projections are generally used to show how the earth looks from outer space, on polar navigation charts, and on maps where relative distance from a given point is crucial. Note on this map that the Southern Periphery of the Soviet Union is vastly enlarged.

Cylindrical projections are constructed by fitting a cylinder around the globe that touches its surface along a given circle called the circle of tangency. The best known cylindrical projection is the standard Mercator (Figure 5.6), on which the equator is the circle of tangency. On the stan-

dard Mercator projection, parallels and meridians form a rectangular grid. This is a conformal projection, so that the shapes of small areas are well represented, but areal distortion increases rapidly poleward, enormously enlarging the Soviet North. Cylindrical projections are widely used for navigation charts.

Conic projections are constructed by fitting a cone over the globe. When the top of the cone sits above the pole, the circle or circles of tangency where the cone touches the globe coincide with one or two parallels. These are known as standard parallels. On conic maps, parallels are arcs of concentric circles focused on the apex of the cone and meridians are either straight or curved lines that converge toward that point. Shape and area are faithfully replicated close to the standard parallel or parallels; distortion increases with distance from these circles of tangency. On Figure 5.7, the Soviet Union is less distorted than on either the azimuthal or cylindrical projection because east-west distortion is minimized. Conic projections, therefore, are frequently used to map regions that stretch along parallels, like the United States or the Soviet Union. Conic projections are used as the basis for the topographic maps of the U.S. Geological Survey.

It is important that students of geography recognize that no single map or map projection accurately represents the surface of the earth and that different types of map projections distort distance, direction, shape, or area in specific ways. Although of little importance on maps of small regions, these three maps of the Soviet Union illustrate how dramatically the representation of space changes depending on which projection is selected.

in the Soviet North, however. In the European section, north of the Fertile Triangle and west of the Urals, where four fifths of the population of the Soviet North resides, the moderating maritime influence of Atlantic air masses eases the cold of win-

ter, limits permafrost conditions, and pushes vegetation boundaries farther north. Murmansk, an ice-free port on the White Sea, is connected by rail to Moscow. Fish and forest products are shipped south to the populated core of European Russia. Eastward,

a low, marshy glacial plain, mostly devoted to fishing and hunting, extends to the northern Urals. East of the Urals, the West Siberian Plain and the Central Siberian Plateau stretch monotonously to the rugged mountains of the Far East.

The Soviet North is covered by a 4000-mile swath of evergreen forest, the taiga.

Although two thirds of the Soviet Union's coal reserves, the vast natural gas fields of western Siberia, and a large proportion of the country's hydroelectric power potential are located in the frozen Soviet North, these resources are difficult and expensive to develop. Only a strong industrial power could develop these resources; the fact that the Soviet Union does is testimony to its economic strengths. The various reindeer-herding tribes who now number a million probably will continue to inhabit most of this northern environment, with Soviet energies concentrated in energy, mining, and lumbering centers.

The Southern Periphery

The Southern Periphery is composed of two far-flung regions: the Caucasus and Soviet Central Asia. Like the Russian North, it lies outside the primary axis of Soviet social and economic development. However, largely because of its location near the Middle East and the world of Islam, the Southern Periphery's distinctive traditional cultures and large

populations pose special questions in the Soviet Union today.

The Caucasus, located between the Black and Caspian seas, is a mountain refuge where non-Russians from 30 different nationalities, both Christian and Muslim, form the bulk of the population. The broken terrain of the Caucasus and its Middle Eastern historical connections have contributed to the region's environmental, cultural, and economic complexity. Grazing prevails in high mountain pastures, corn growing dominates in Transcaucasia (land to the south of the Caucasus), and the cultivation of tea, citrus, and vegetable crops is practiced on the shores of both seas, which have Mediterranean climates comparable to central California. These features give this region great diversity and provide a strong contrast with the Soviet heartland. The Caucasus' regions have ancient Georgian, Armenian, and Azeri cultures; Russian domination of these societies dates from the early 1800s.

The single most important national contribution of the Caucasus, beyond its role as a summer resort, is

the offshore oil production of the Caspian Sea. The oil industry is focused on the city of Baku (pop. 1.4 million), capital of the Azerbaijan union republic. Caspian production, however, has declined substantially with the development of the Volga and western Siberian oil fields. Two other cities of approximately one million population, which are also capitals of union republics, dominate the Caucasus. Tbilisi, in Georgia, is famed for its textiles, and supports a broad-based food processing industry reflective of its rich agricultural hinterland. So too, Yerevan, in Armenia, has grown as an administrative center but boasts a history as the focus of Armenian culture that goes back to the city's founding in 783 B.C.

Even more than the Caucasus, Soviet Central Asia—stretching from the Caspian to China—is a distinctly non-Russian part of the Soviet Union. It is non-European. The region is home to Muslim Asian peoples such as the Kirghiz, Kazakhs, Tadzhiks, Uzbeks, and Turkmen, each of which is the nucleus of a Central Asian union republic. Soviet Central Asia is separated from the Fertile Triangle by broad deserts and steppes surrounding the physical barriers of the Caspian and Aral Seas. Flat steppes and deserts are penetrated by lush river valleys in the southern sections of Soviet Central Asia; on the Soviet rim lie high mountains—the Hindu Kush and the Pamirs—forming the Soviet Union's boundaries with Afghanistan and China. This vast area—about 6 percent of the territory of the Soviet Union—is three times the size of California.

Conquered by Russians in the 1860s, the nomadic tribes of Soviet Central Asia were forcibly settled during the Stalinist collectivization period. Home to most Soviet Muslims, less than 10 percent of the people of Soviet Central Asia are Russian. Russians here are typically urban immigrants.

Settlement here has been tradi-

GEOLAB

FORMAL REGIONS: THE USE OF VENN DIAGRAMS

Geographers use regions to organize information about the world logically. Each region is a part of the earth's surface that has one or more cultural or environmental characteristics in common that distinguish it from other parts of the area under study. Some regions are defined by a single factor, such as population density, average annual temperature, political status, or type of vegetation. These are called single-feature regions. Often, single-feature regions are simply one of a number of categories on a single map separated from others by **class intervals.** This is the case on the maps of population density used in this book.

More commonly, several criteria are used to delineate regions. These multiple-feature regions are called formal regions if they are uniform throughout; they are called functional regions if they are designed to identify lines of circulation, patterns of organization, or connectivity around some focal point. **Formal regions** include many common terms used by geographers to identify areas with a set of interlocking conditions—for example, desert, rain forest, the Great Plains, the Fertile Triangle. **Functional regions** are often used to define city hinterlands, population movements, and land-use patterns.

One simple method of classifying regions is through the use of Venn diagrams. In these diagrams, single as well as interlocking sets of criteria are used to define formal regions. In Figure 5.8, four factors that unfavorably influence agricultural activity in the Soviet Union are classified in a Venn diagram. When each class is mapped, regions with cold temperature, low rainfall, poor soil, rugged terrain, and any combination of these conditions are defined. These single and multi-feature regions graphically illustrate the environmental limitations on agricultural development that exist in the Soviet Union.

The Venn diagram provides the car-

tographer with sixteen possible regions—four regions in which one factor is found, six regions with two factors, four regions with three factors, and finally two regions in which either all or alternatively none of the factors occur. The map reveals that cold temperatures and poor soils limit agricultural expansion in the Soviet North; rugged terrain, poor soils, and low precipitation are negative factors in the Southern Perimeter. The Ural Mountains stand out as a sliver of rugged terrain and poor soils cross-

cutting temperature belts in the Soviet Union. The best agricultural land is clearly found in the Fertile Triangle where none of the negative environmental conditions occur; the worst place to farm in the Soviet Union occurs in a small area of northern Siberia, which is cold, dry, rugged, and has poor soils.

Adapted from: John P. Cole and F. C. German, *A Geography of the USSR.* London: Butterworths, 1970, p. 116.

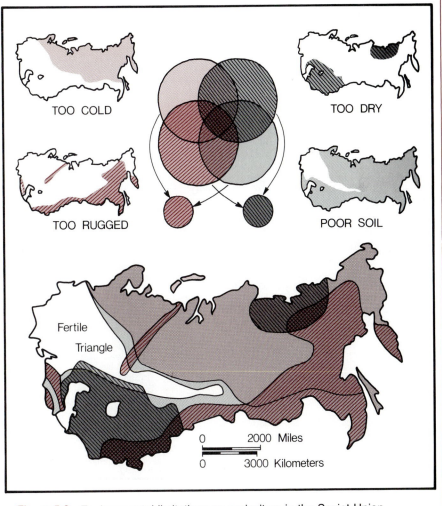

Figure 5.8 Environmental limitations on agriculture in the Soviet Union.

tionally concentrated in ancient oases such as Samarkand (pop. 500,000) and Bukhara (pop. 185,000) located at the foot of the southern mountains. But in recent history, some cities of Soviet Central Asia have undergone considerable expansion. For example, Tashkent (pop. 2 million), is the center of the region's railroad network and capital of Uzbekistan. Alma-Ata (pop. 910,000), the capital of Kazakhstan, was founded by the Russians as a fort in 1865. Although commercial cotton cultivation and the discovery of natural gas in the area have transformed the economy of Soviet Central Asia, its people have resisted and rejected **assimilation** into the mainstream of Soviet society. The countryside and peoples' lifestyles have changed little since the Revolution. Rates of natural increase in the Central Asian republics are the highest in the country—meaning that the composition of the Soviet population is changing and becoming less Slavic as Central Asian peoples become more numerous. Soviet Central Asia is one of the few remaining areas in the world conquered by col-

onizing nineteenth-century Europeans that has not secured its independence.

The Far East

By contrast, the Far East is almost completely inhabited by Russians and other European nationalities. European migration was not substantial until early in this century, when the Trans-Siberian Railroad provided a lifeline to the Russian heartland. The Soviet Far East showed faster population growth than any other region of the country for the period 1940–1970. Overall, the Far East remains a landscape of densely forested mountains whose soils are underlain by permafrost except in the basin of the Amur River, the dominant watershed of the Far East. Agricultural settlement is confined to patches of soil in the valleys, whereas fishing settlements are found on the Pacific coast, which is ice-free only during the summer months. Nakhodka and Vladivostok (pop. 600,000) to the south are two of Russia's few good harbors on the Pacific.

The Soviet Far East is chronically short of food supplies and has only begun to develop its natural resources. The difficult nature of the environment also poses distinct brakes to economic development and geographic integration with the rest of the country. Perhaps the greatest problem for the Soviet Far East is its sheer distance from other Soviet centers of population and industry. Distance has pushed the economy of the Far East into tighter trade relations with Japan. Japan has supplied equipment and technology for Far Eastern exports of its barely tapped resources of timber, petroleum, and coal.

As the 1990s unfold, both Siberia and the Far East will take on added significance in the Soviet economy. Indeed, exports from these regions are now vital to Soviet foreign policy as Siberian resources have been used to pay for Western technology, which in turn has been used to modernize the manufacturing base of the European core.

Muslims are an important minority group in the USSR. They are relatively free to practice their faith, as this scene of communal prayer at a mosque in Tashkent illustrates. The growth of minority populations in the Soviet Union is a threat to long-term Russian dominance.

THE SOVIET UNION: ECONOMY AND SOCIETY

The Soviet Union emerged from World War II as one of the two most powerful countries in the world. Over the course of twenty-five years, Joseph Stalin, the architect of Soviet modernization, radically altered the distribution of population in the Soviet Union, the structure of life in urban and rural areas, the distribution of industry and economic growth—indeed the entire human geography of a substantial portion of the earth's surface. His successors inherited a nation transformed by socialism and have maintained and accelerated the growth and development of a tightly controlled society and economy. Today, the Soviet Union reflects the impact of this ideology on its land, resources, and peoples.

In the twentieth century, *The Soviet Economic Order* initiated a planned economy in which high priority was given to investment in heavy industry. As a result, *The Growth of Soviet Industry* was rapid. The extensive resource base of the Soviet Union was explored and exploited. New centers of mining and manufacturing were implanted in the Southern Urals, Central Asia, and Siberia to complement and provide energy for older centers in European Russia. State controls yielded impressive growth in industry, but *Strategies for Socialized Agriculture* met peasant resistance. Collectivization of the land in communal farms failed to raise agricultural production; expansion of the arable land into the drier margins of Kazakhstan and Siberia also posed problems. Agriculture remains the weakest sector of the Soviet economy. Resistance to state planning is also evident in other areas of *Contemporary Soviet Society*. Rising death rates, problems of urbanization, and cultural resistance to assimilation into a Russian-dominated state are all indications that Lenin's goal of creating a "new Soviet man" is foundering.

The Soviet Economic Order

Lenin once defined communism as "Soviet power plus electrification." In modified terms, these two principles—the absolute power of the state over the economy and rigorous emphasis on heavy industry and energy—have remained central to the Soviet organization of Russian life.

Unlike the states of the industrial West, the Soviet Union has a command economy. All natural resources, sources of production, and financial institutions are owned by, or are at the command of, the state—water, land, minerals, property, transport, and communications. According to Marx, state ownership of property opens up limitless economic possibilities. But for these economic horizons to be realized, a new form of economic organization had to arise out of Communist doctrine. For this there was no plan.

In the Soviet Union, state planners and bureaucrats—not the marketplace—determine social and economic priorities. These planners project the kind, quantity, location, and price of all industrial and agricultural production as well as the wages and salaries of managers and employees. Collective bargaining and strikes do not occur in this system. In the Soviet Union, every decision dealing with resources and production derives from guidelines and directives set in Moscow. State ownership and control of all important sectors of the economy can be credited with both the past successes and current problems of the Soviet Union.

The Planned Economy

By the time of Stalin's death in 1953, the Soviet Union was a global superpower, second only to the United States and surpassing all others in environmental resources and industrial output. Critical investments in mining, manufacturing, and heavy industry backed by harsh discipline marshaled the vast natural resources of the Soviet Union. Although achieving breakthroughs in these sectors, the Soviet economy was still beset by problems.

The Supreme Economic Council was a sprawling collection of departments that reflected the efforts of a centralized and inflexible bureaucracy to deal with an increasingly complex Russian economy. The result was high levels of inefficiency and low productivity. The emphasis on achieving quantitative goals in terms of tons of steel, numbers of car loadings, and kilowatts of energy typically led to severe distortions in economic coordination. Ministries that competed for coal, iron, and timber hoarded resources so that their individual quotas were met. Local factories set production goals as low as possible to reduce the risk of failure. The Soviet planning system, unparalleled in size and completeness, slowed down as it became larger, less interconnected, and more rigid.

To cope with these problems, the post-Stalin leaders of the Soviet Union attempted to overhaul the nation's economic administration to provide more flexible and responsive regional bases for state economic planning. Beginning in the mid-1950s, Nikita Khrushchev attempted to make a series of fundamental changes in the Soviet system. The objectives of decentralization were to provide industrial plants and regional planners with the incentives to boost production and with the authority to rejuvenate and balance industrial growth on the regional level.

Although heavy industry and the development of military weaponry retained first priority, some concessions to consumer needs were made by the expansion of the production of consumer goods, the reduction of the average workweek, and the improvement of wages, benefits, and pensions. In agriculture, a program to cultivate vast areas of "virgin lands" was initiated in Kazakhstan with optimistic predictions that food shortages in the Soviet Union would become a thing of the past.

New industrial projects in the underpopulated regions of the eastern Soviet Union were restricted to capital-intensive, energy-oriented industries whose labor needs could be accommodated from local sources. New labor-intensive industries were scheduled for the well-populated towns of European Russia. It appeared to many observers that the Soviet decision-making process was becoming more responsive to economic forces and less arbitrary. Some even predicted a convergence between the Soviet command economy and Western capitalism.

These experiments at liberalization ended in 1964 with the dismissal of Chairman Khrushchev from his post as First Secretary of the Communist

This factory at Kharkov in the Ukraine produces turbines for atomic power stations. The high level of investment in heavy industry at the expense of consumer goods is a source of discontent in the USSR.

backward economy time to modernize by lessening international tensions, particularly with the West. Even the CIA called Gorbachev a "pragmatic visionary." But the problems involved in the economic overhaul of the Soviet Union are immense and long lasting, and they are as much social as anything else.

The Growth of Soviet Industry

Through the 1960s, Soviet industrial growth was, by any measure, impressive. Large-scale investment in heavy industry, energy resources, and military hardware led to the creation of a sizable industrial base, while other sectors of the Soviet economy languished. During the years 1975 to 1985, the rate of growth in the Soviet GNP slowed to two percent per year as bureaucratic inefficiency, poor planning, aging industrial facilities, and the gradual depletion of inexpensive, accessible raw materials took their toll. Productivity was low, the technological gap with the West was growing, and energy and other raw material costs were rising rapidly. By the late 1980s, the defense burden rose to 15 percent of the Soviet GNP—more than twice that of the United States.

The Resource Base

The Soviet Union claims more than half the coal reserves on earth, a third of all natural gas, and more petroleum reserves than any other country. Although methods of estimating energy reserves vary, it is clear that this country has an energy base larger than any other state in the world. The Soviet Union is also richly endowed with mineral and metal resources. It is virtually self-sufficient in the most important industrial ores—namely, nickel, copper, chromium, lead, manganese, and zinc—and has been the world's largest producer of iron ore for some time (Fig. 5.9).

Until 1950, coal provided two thirds

Party and Premier of the Soviet state. Central economic control was reimposed. In the long (1964–1982) Brezhnev era, Soviet leaders were faced with the old problems of central versus regional planning, capital versus consumer investment, and decisions about the allocation of Soviet resources. All crucial industrial commodities—coal, oil, iron, steel, chemicals—remained under direct central ministerial control. To some degree, the tendency to measure productivity in quantitative terms diminished. There was a marked shift toward the production of consumer goods. The Soviet economy appeared to be reaching maturation. Industrial output lagged during the 1970s, whereas consumer demands increased. Productivity fell and technological innovations came from Western imports. The work force was riddled with alcoholism and absenteeism.

After a period of faltering leadership following the death of Brezhnev, when a return to Stalinism actually seemed possible, the Soviet Union turned to younger, more dynamic leadership. The presence and ideas of Mikhail Gorbachev, former Secretary of Agriculture and named First Secretary of the Communist Party in 1985, captured the attention of the world. Policies of "glasnost"–openness in Soviet life—and "perestroika" restructuring of the Soviet economy, have begun to take hold. A new timetable for change has emerged in the Soviet Union, and part of the Russian agenda is to buy their technologically

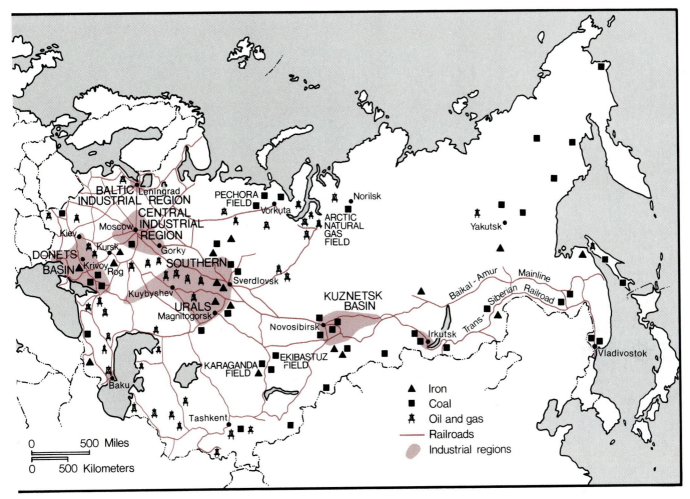

Figure 5.9 Economic patterns in the Soviet Union.

of the industrial energy in the Soviet Union. Today, four separate fields yield 60 percent of the country's total production and account for a large proportion of the country's higher grade coals.

The Donets Basin in the Ukraine produces 200 million tons per year. The coal seams of the Donets are thin, deep, and heavily worked, but the high quality of the coal and the proximity of Donets to factories and other coal-consuming facilities have maintained the primacy of this field. The Kuznetsk field in western Siberia, 2000 miles to the east, produces a fifth of Russia's coal. The Kuznetsk field is characterized by thick, easily worked seams, some as wide as 50 feet and located near the surface. These mines produce twice as much coal per worker as those in Donets,

which compensates for the locational disadvantage of Kuznetsk. The Karaganda and Ekibastuz fields, located between and south of the Ural Mountains and the Kuznetsk Basin, as well as the Pechora field in the Soviet Arctic at the northern tip of the Urals also produce significant but smaller quantities of high-grade coal (Fig. 5.9). Perhaps as much as 90 percent of the Soviet's coal reserves lie virtually untouched in two Siberian fields: the Tungskan Basin in the Central Siberian Upland, and the Lena River coal fields north of Yakutsk. Although coal currently accounts for only 25 percent of the total energy consumed in the Soviet Union, compared with 65 percent twenty-five years ago, it is still produced and used in greater quantities than in any other industrial nation.

In the 1960s, energy patterns in the Soviet economy were transformed by the development of the Volga-Urals oil fields, a series of geologic basins clustered east of the great bend in the Volga River. These huge deposits, which produce a third of the Soviet Union's current annual production of more than 4400 million barrels, have led to a lessening of transport of coal by railroad in favor of the easier transportation of petroleum and natural gas by pipeline. The development of these fields has also led to the Soviet Union's position as the world's leading petroleum producer since 1975. Oil and natural gas are piped west to the industrial centers of European Russia, an energy web connecting Moscow, Leningrad, Kiev, and the Donets Basin. Pipeline systems have been laid east-

This oil field near Baku in Azerbaijan was one of the first drilled in the Soviet Union and reduced Soviet reliance on coal for energy. Oil from the Volga-Urals fields is now much more important than the declining reserves at Baku.

ward from the Volga to Novosibirsk near the Kuznetsk Basin and to Irkutsk in eastern Siberia (see Fig. 3.16). Additional oil fields now exist on the eastern shore of the Caspian Sea and, most important, in the valley of the Ob River in western Siberia (Fig. 5.9). These new fields are growing rapidly. In the 1980's, western Siberia produced over half of the nation's petroleum.

The Soviet Union's diverse mineral and metal economy is also extremely strong; only the United States has a comparable resource base. The Soviet Union is number one in the world in a wide variety of metals ranging from cadmium through iron, lead, manganese, mercury, platinum, and gold; it holds first rank in such important nonmetals as asbestos, potash, and diamonds. Suffice it to say that the Soviet Union's ap-

pearance in the top ranks of world resources production is frequent.

Two thirds of the Soviet Union's iron production, the backbone of its steel industry, comes from three locations: Krivoy Rog, near the bend in the Dnieper River in the Ukraine; the Urals, particularly at Magnitogorsk (Iron Mountain); and the Kursk Magnetic Anomaly northeast of Kiev (Fig. 5.9). These three huge iron lodes form the resource base for the Donets Basin and the Urals industrial complexes. With existing technology, current levels of iron production can be maintained for a century, but as in the United States, higher quality ores are being depleted, so that over half the iron ore now being mined requires concentration. Indeed, scrap iron is now more important in steelmaking than iron ore.

Alloys used in the production of

steel are also in plentiful supply: manganese deposits in the Ukraine and in Georgia produce two thirds of the total world supply; nickel, from the Kola Peninsula and Norilsk in northern Siberia, and chromium deposits, found throughout the Urals, produce one third and one sixth of the world total respectively; and titanium, molybdenum, and tungsten are scattered from the Urals eastward through the mountains of Central Asia, Siberia, and the Far East (Fig. 5.9).

Industrial Location

During the 1930s, Soviet economists and planners executed ambitious schemes for industrial development in the eastern half of the Soviet Union. These decisions were made in accordance with principles of Soviet industrial location: (1) to build industries at existing mineral and energy sites and reduce transport costs, (2) to move Russian labor from the densely settled European core into minority areas in the east, (3) to reduce the disparity in development levels between different regions in the Soviet Union, and (4) to locate strategic industries in the inaccessible interior remote from the Soviet Union's borders with Europe.

Gradually, more industrial and population centers appeared in the east. Economic growth in the Urals, Central Asia, and Siberia was facilitated by the eastward migration of hundreds of thousands of Slavs. Some migrated as a patriotic response to national planning goals; others were hapless victims trapped in the web of Stalin's secret police. This heralded eastward movement did not, however, significantly shift the distribution of Russian industry before World War II. In 1940, two thirds of the Soviet Union's energy was still produced in European Russia. In fact, the building of new industrial centers in the east demanded the continued expansion of older centers of heavy industry in the west. It was the German onslaught in World War II that led to the relocation of hundreds of industrial plants to the Urals and Volga regions. At war's end, the industrial base of western Russia was rebuilt; centers of mining and manufacturing in the Urals and Siberia were intact.

The continuing disparity in the Soviet Union between the densely populated, resource-poor west and the thinly populated, resource-laden east remains a central problem for Soviet planners. They have come to realize that it is more efficient and less expensive to move raw materials from Siberia westward to industrial centers than to move people eastward into Siberia and create urban centers in the wilderness. A web of pipelines and railroads now carries oil from the Volga region and Western Siberia and coal from the Kuznetsk Basin and Lake Baikal to the rebuilt centers of heavy industry in the Ukraine and Moscow.

This spatial reorganization of mining and manufacturing was coupled with a tremendous post-war expansion of industrial production in the Soviet Union. By the late 1980s, annual coal production approached that of the United States, oil production was more than a fourth of the world's total, and annual steel production reached 152 million tons, 25 percent more than the combined output of the European Community and twice that of the United States. This explosive growth propelled Russia into its current position as the second leading industrial power in the world, despite sluggish growth in recent years. With vast territories only partly explored and huge proved energy reserves and mineral and metal resources, the Soviet Union has the raw materials to support extensive future industrial expansion.

Strategies for Socialized Agriculture

After a half-century of Communist control, Soviet agriculture is still plagued by wide-ranging problems—insufficient motivation to work, low productivity, and uncertain harvests on the farm. The Communist party has been unable to win the confidence of the peasants; Lenin's dictum that the material and social conditions of rural areas be equalized with those of the cities has never been successfully implemented. Peasants have resisted the socialist system of agriculture. Their disinterest, unwillingness to work, and lack of confidence have undermined every scheme designed by Communist planners to raise agricultural output.

The need for agricultural reform and more effective political control of the countryside demanded a reorganization of the collective farms after World War II. Collective farms were consolidated in the hope that this consolidation would make farm management more efficient and that mechanization would be furthered (Fig. 5.3). But these larger farms were

really administrative regions, and day-to-day work still revolved around the original 250,000 kolkhoz village centers. Khrushchev, the designer of this new policy, optimistically talked of the establishment of **agrogorods,** agricultural towns where farmers would enjoy urban amenities and where production would benefit from specialization of work and economies of scale.

The Virgin Lands Scheme

After consolidation of the collective farms, grain production was still far short of the needs of the Soviet Union's growing population. In 1954, a spectacular new measure was announced by Khrushchev to revitalize Soviet agriculture—the opening up of previously unplowed "virgin lands" in western Siberia, Kazakhstan, the Volga Plain, and the northern Caucasus to the cultivation of wheat and other grains. He believed that the level steppes and rich chernozem east of the Volga could be easily brought into permanent grain production.

In a single year, 32 million acres were put to the plow. By 1960, over 115 million acres of new land—an agrarian space somewhat smaller than that of West Germany and Great Britain combined—were in cultivation for the first time. Some 150,000 workers and technicians, mostly young people motivated by patriotic zeal, were exhorted to migrate and settle on new sovkhozes in the agricultural frontier.

This gigantic undertaking was an environmental gamble. The climate in Kazakhstan and western Siberia—long and severe winters, short growing seasons and frequent summer droughts—rendered large-scale grain farming a hazardous undertaking (Fig. 5.8). Traditional Marxist thought, however, suggested that a socialist society, suitably organized, could triumph over nature and that spirit and determination would overcome environmental risk.

Complementing cultivation of grain

Massive cultivation of wheat on the virgin steppes of Kazakhstan never solved the agricultural problem of the USSR, despite this propaganda photograph of a mechanized harvesting campaign.

MAKING RIVERS RUN BACKWARDS: CHANGE AND DEVELOPMENT IN SOVIET ENVIRONMENTALISM

Many of the mighty rivers of the Soviet Union empty their waters into the Arctic Ocean. On the face of it, these rivers, flowing northward into the wilderness, are underused and their waters are wasted. Meanwhile, in Central Asia, vast steppes remain uncultivated for lack of water. Many Soviets have looked at this situation and considered rectifying the geography of nature. For forty years, Soviet planners proposed reversing the flow of many of these rivers to solve the problems of Soviet agriculture by diverting water to arid southern regions. Soviet agricultural yields could thus rise by as much as 20 percent. In the process, by making the rivers flow backward, immense areas would be flooded, populations relocated, and, environmentalists claim, the climate of the entire Northern Hemisphere altered.

On the European side of the Urals, the Onega, Northern Dvina, and Pechora rivers have been candidates for restructuring. Great dikes would block their channels into the Arctic Ocean; 25 dams would raise water levels and reverse the flow of the rivers to the south (Fig. 5.10). Similar projects have been considered for the Ob and Yenisei rivers in Siberia. The Ob could be dammed and diverted into a 1500-mile canal to carry water to Central Asia (Fig. 5.10). All told, the river-reversal projects could take 50 years to build.

Soviet geographers and citizens expressed alarm at the unknown ecological consequences of such massive transformations of the environment. Changes in freshwater replenishment of the Arctic Ocean could reduce the size of the polar ice cap and thereby alter

in the vast virgin lands was the conversion of the more reliable agricultural lands of the Ukraine to corn production for feeding animals to supplement the Soviet Union's chronically poor meat supply. In five years, corn acreage expanded by a factor of seven, from 10 million acres to nearly 70 million. In one fell swoop, the Soviet government planned to solve the perennial food shortage of the Russian people: the virgin lands of the east would produce their bread; the Ukraine would serve as an immense factory for corn and meat production. Russia's total agricultural production increased quickly as crop and livestock production alone expanded by more than 40 percent. The extraordinary gamble to push back the frontiers of Soviet agriculture appeared to succeed through daring and

concerted effort. Cultivation in the Soviet Union seemed to be liberated from the environmental confines of the Fertile Triangle (Fig. 5.8).

The initial success of the virgin lands scheme led to great optimism. Personally worked household plots were denounced as a distraction to farm workers. In fact, the importance of garden plots revealed the deep-seated peasant rejection of collectivization and underlined the relatively low productivity of collective farms. In the 1980s, privately worked plots occupy 3 percent of the agricultural land, but produce a quarter of all field crops and most of the country's eggs, potatoes, and green vegetables—impressive testimony to the private enterprise of Soviet farmers.

Production gains on the collective farms, by contrast, were initially the

result of the expansion of the arable in the virgin lands in eastern regions. But disastrous droughts hit the Soviet Union in the 1960s, forcing the importation of millions of tons of wheat

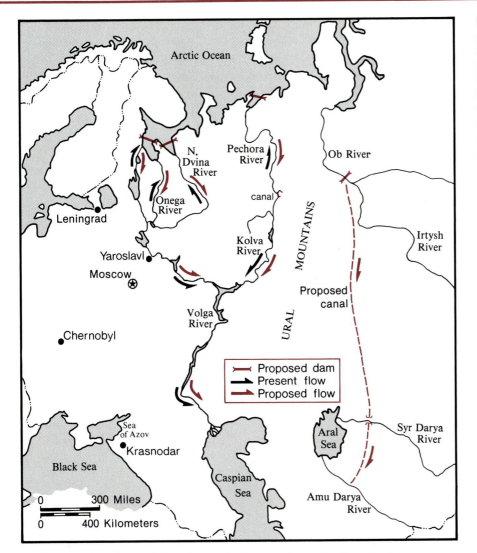

Figure 5.10 Proposed diversion of Arctic water to the Southern Periphery.

blew up, 31 people died, radioactive particles rained down on the Soviet Union's richest farmland, 100,000 people were evacuated, and contamination spewed around the world from Scotland to northern Italy. In a word that has come to define the environmental dangers of nuclear power to the world, Chernobyl changed the Soviet environmental agenda.

As in other industrialized countries, Soviet environmental consciousness has increased as technological developments have, perhaps, overarched their social bounds.

Events in the Soviet environmental movement have been rapid. In August 1986, the government announced that it was dropping plans to divert the Yenesei and Ob rivers. Concern for the health of Lake Baikal led to strict pollution controls in the lake. A two-year complete ban on fishing in the Sea of Azov (an arm of the Black Sea) was announced early in 1988, as authorities cited a dramatic drop in levels of the sturgeon catch and heightened pollution levels. At the same time, a massive chemical spill into the Volga at Yaroslavl testified to the quick response of Soviet authorities to environmental disaster. And construction of a nuclear power plant near the Black Sea at Krasnodar was abandoned in January 1988 in the face of public opposition. All 20 operating nuclear plants and most of those under construction were "bitterly opposed" by local citizens, reported one Moscow newspaper. Environmental opposition has also focused on battling a massive flood control project in the Leningrad delta lands.

In his first years as head of the Soviet Union, Mikhail Gorbachev routinely spoke on the theme of an interdependent world. He currently underlines the importance of acid rain and depletion of the ozone layer in public speeches. Transformations of the Soviet economy may come slowly, but it appears that the Soviet environmental movement has grown swiftly.

temperature regimes across the planet. Much of the world's oxygen is produced by the taiga forests of the Soviet North, and millions of acres of taiga would be flooded where the rivers make their turnabouts. Growing seasons could shorten due to vastly increased ice surfaces in the flooded areas. Arctic fisheries might well decline as the proportion of fresh to salt water is changed in the Arctic Ocean.

In the politics of the proposal, strong advocacy of the plan came from Central Asian leaders, with their growing rural populations and limited amounts of irrigated land. Opposition came from party officials and economists who recognized that investment costs would be high, huge losses of forest and developed farmland and infrastructure would be incurred, and that weighty ecological problems were at issue.

Then came Chernobyl. On April 25, 1986, a Ukrainian nuclear power plant

from the United States, Canada, Australia, and Argentina. The planned 70 percent increase in food production expected from the virgin lands amounted in the long term to only a

10 percent increase in national agricultural output. Wind erosion, depletion of soil fertility and inadequate rainfall all took their toll. This increase was not sufficient to fulfill the

needs of a growing population with rising consumer demands. Disappointments in agriculture added fuel to a general political crisis: Khrushchev was ousted from power.

Chronic Problems in Agriculture

The post-Brezhnev leaders of the Soviet Union have taken a more practical and less arbitrary approach to problems in Russia's agricultural sector. Environmental limitations are increasingly being viewed more scientifically and less ideologically (Fig. 5.10). The pressure to eliminate private plots has ceased, and restrictions on their use have been lifted. In hopes of raising crop yields, the state provides substantial funds for agricultural research into better plant varieties, greater use of fertilizer, better tillage practices, improved machinery, and better farm management.

For the first time since Stalin's drive to industrialize began with the first Five Year Plan in 1928, the agriculture sector is receiving high priority, more than a quarter of the national budget in the 1980s, which is higher than that for any state in the Technological World.

These relaxed Soviet economic measures in the 1970s and 1980s have resulted in a one-third increase in Russia's total crop production since 1970. Agriculture made gains well above the rise in population, mostly in grain consumed directly as bread. But bad harvests, waste, and planning problems continue to plague Soviet agriculture. The country's 27 million agricultural workers waste an estimated 20 to 40 percent of the crop through sheer mismanagement.

Chronic fodder-production problems have handicapped Soviet plans to expand livestock production. Most of the Soviet Union's imports from the West have been feed grains for animals. The country is now the world's leading producer of bread grains and potatoes, crops that do well in northern climatic conditions. The Soviet Union is able to feed its people, but the diet is low in animal protein.

Moreover, despite substantial investment, yields remain considerably lower than those in other technologically advanced societies. An estimated one fifth of the grain harvest is lost by late harvesting, poor distribution, and inadequate storage. It still requires 25 percent of the Soviet population to produce the country's food supply, compared with 2.3 percent in the United States.

In a broader context, the continuing migration of the young to urban centers has left an aging rural population to perform field work. As these people retire, the Soviet Union will experience a severe agricultural labor shortage. Soviet agriculture must modernize and adjust to social trends that take place outside the framework of the planned economy. In the early 1980s, an estimated 17 million people left villages and settled in urban areas. Overall, Soviet agriculture remains tenaciously resistant to collective patterns of organization and is the most inefficient, least productive sector of the national economy. The stagnation of that economy in recent years has deep roots in Soviet society. Changes in restructuring and intensifying the Soviet economy have been slow to come to the farm.

Contemporary Soviet Society

The Soviet Union is a centrally managed society, but forces of modernization, industrialization, and urbanization have generated trends similar to those in other nations of the Technological World, specifically patterns of population stabilization, a shift from rural to urban life, and problems associated with have-not minority groups. Despite these general structural similarities, however, differences in ideology, history, culture, and environment lend a special character to the human geography of the Soviet Union in the last decade of the twentieth century.

The Soviet Population

During the course of this century, the population of the Soviet Union has more than doubled from an estimated 130 million in 1900 to 286 million in 1988. In the process, the Soviet Union began to exhibit population patterns characteristic of the Technological World. Lowered birth and death rates led to a modest rate of natural increase and a conspicuous aging of the population. In the 1970s, the Soviet population grew by less than 1 percent or roughly 2 million people, with the greatest gains occurring among Muslim peoples living in Soviet Central Asia.

Population growth during the early decades of Communist rule was primarily caused by lowered death rates, which are now one-quarter those of prerevolutionary Russia. These resulted from advances in medicine, sanitation, and control of communicable diseases, much like the pattern followed in other rapidly industrializing societies. Whereas czarist Russia offered its people an average lifespan of roughly thirty years a hundred years ago, by the 1980s, life expectancy in the Soviet Union was sixty-five years for men and seventy-four for women. As the population became more urban, lower birth rates tempered the rate of population growth. In European Russia, birth rates also fell because of the millions of men and women killed in World War II as well as rising standards of education and increased urbanization. But birth rates among the predominantly rural non-Russian peoples of the Caucasus, Kazakhstan, and Soviet Central Asia remained high—double those of ethnic Russians, meaning that the Russians became a cultural minority within their own country during the mid-1980s.

The distribution of population in the Soviet Union, however, still retains its historic pattern (Fig. 5.11). More than 200 million people in the 1980s are concentrated in the more favorable environments of the Fertile Triangle in the long settled agricultural regions of European Russia. The remaining 60 million are scattered throughout the Caucasus, Central Asia, and along the Trans-

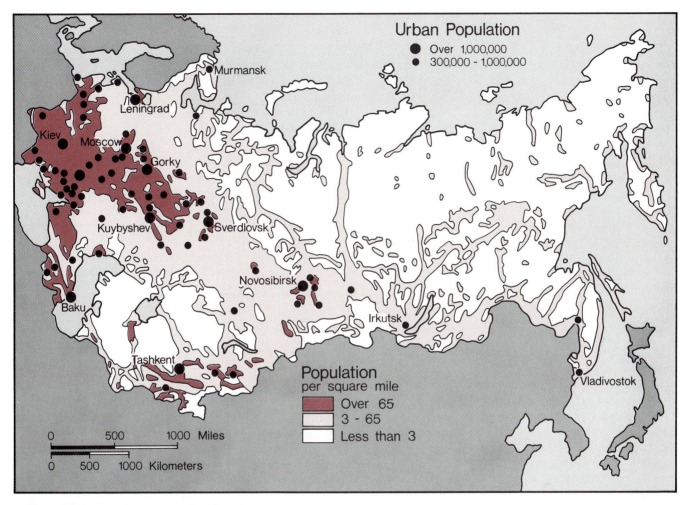

Figure 5.11 Population of the Soviet Union.

Siberian Railroad in eastern Siberia (Fig. 5.11). Dense populations are found along the east-west axis of the Fertile Triangle, along the Trans-Siberian Railroad, and in the irrigated oases of Central Asia. The eastward movement of the nation's industrial and energy economies means that nearly one fourth of the Soviet population now lives east of the Urals, mainly in Central Asian oasis settlements and in the new industrial complexes. Forbidding environmental regions, like the Soviet North, the Far East, and the unirrigated deserts of the Southern Periphery, are still essentially unpopulated.

Although population growth and distribution patterns in the Soviet Union have followed predictable trends, health conditions have not. In a startling reversal, health con-

ditions in the Soviet Union began to decline sharply in the 1970s. Infant mortality rose by more than a third, and death rates for every age group rose as well (Fig. 5.12). Life expectancy fell by more than four years for men and two years for women. Although Soviet food intake, educational levels, and number of available doctors are comparable to those in Western Europe, lifespans are six years lower; infant mortality rates are three times higher. The ostensible causes of this precipitous decline in health in the Soviet Union are rampant alcoholism (the average Russian spends as much on alcohol as Americans do on food), high levels of environmental pollution, industrial accidents, and inefficiency in health care delivery. Currently, no country in Europe has a lower life expectancy

than the Soviet Union. To the consternation of its own people, the Soviet Union appears to be exhibiting demographic characteristics that are comparable to the traits found in some countries of the Developing World.

Urbanization in the Soviet Union

In the 1980s, nearly two thirds of the people of the Soviet Union live in cities as compared with only 15 percent in the 1930s. Today, there are 271 cities with more than 100,000 people, 47 with more than 500,000, and 21 with more than 1 million residents in the Soviet Union. The metropolises of Moscow (9 million), Leningrad (4.7 million), and Kiev (2.2 million) are dominant political and economic centers in the Soviet heartland. Rural people have flocked to these centers and smaller cities, and rural population is steadily decreasing particularly in the agricultural lands of the European core. The rapid industrial modernization of the Soviet Union, therefore, is progressively converting Russia's sea of peasants into a country of urbanites.

The pattern of urbanization in the Soviet Union is a product of the regime's emphasis on industrial growth. The four older industrial zones—Moscow, Leningrad, the Donets Basin, and the Urals—stood as islands of modernization in an agrarian countryside before World War I. They were joined by the Kuznetsk Basin in the 1930s. After World War II, the urban population of Russia trebled in little more than a decade, but it remained concentrated in the long-standing industrial zones (Fig. 5.9). Regions of extreme environmental difficulty, such as the Russian North, remained relatively undeveloped, with only resource-extractive centers emplaced in the wilderness.

In the 1950s and 1960s, cities between the Volga Plain and Lake Baikal grew because of the discovery of large oil fields and the rapid Soviet energy shift from coal to petroleum. The regions of important urban growth today are the old geographic centers of Moscow and Leningrad as well as new cities strategically located in the Caucasus, Kazakhstan, and Soviet Central Asia, regions where new oil and gas fields have been exploited and where the rate of natural increase among the local population is high. Millions of people have left farming communities; two thirds of these migrants are young people seeking educations, jobs, and urban amenities. As this human tide continues to flow, it generates problems of urban congestion and rural decay in the Soviet Union similar to those in other industrial nations.

Soviet planners are attempting to direct the flow of urban migrants. Their goal has been to integrate urban growth with regional planning and to balance city size with regional

POPULATION AND HEALTH IN THE SOVIET UNION

In the twentieth century, the Soviet Union followed the demographic pattern common to most of the Technological World. Birth and death rates progressively declined; the rate of population growth was low. In the 1970s, however, death rates rose sharply in the Soviet Union for all age groups, suggesting a precipitous decline in health conditions. This represents a reversal of a trend that population geographers assumed to be a universal adjunct to modernization.

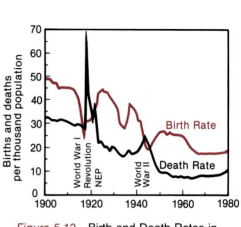
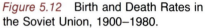

Figure 5.12 Birth and Death Rates in the Soviet Union, 1900–1980.

MOSCOW: THE SOCIALIST CITY

Moscow, a city of 9 million people, is encircled by a 700-square-mile greenbelt, which is under direct municipal control. Although this greenbelt has nearly a million residents, efforts have been made to restrict industrial activity. Encroachments along major transport lines suggest that Soviet planners have not been able to control urban growth, but they have been more successful than urban authorities in Western democracies. The suburban zone beyond the greenbelt houses nearly 3 million people, many of whom commute 45 miles each day to central Moscow. One million people own their own houses in the greenbelt, defying Communist principles, and, increasingly, the intent of the greenbelt itself.

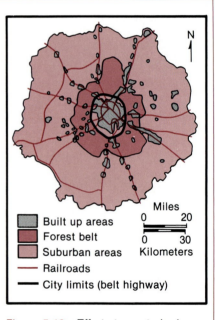
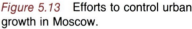

Figure 5.13 Efforts to control urban growth in Moscow.

environmental resources, population size, and other conditions in surrounding hinterlands.

Actions have been taken to try to limit the growth of the largest cities—Moscow, Leningrad, and Kiev (Fig. 5.13). Migrants are barred from large cities unless they have assigned jobs. Police permits are required for people to leave collective farms, and

new industries have been started in smaller towns. Efforts have been made to limit industrial and residential penetration in greenbelts that girdle the largest cities (Fig. 5.13). Despite these efforts to control urban growth, the Soviet Union today is a nation of cities and a society of urban problems.

The structure of Soviet cities is

strongly affected by Communist ideology and investment priorities. Housing is standardized according to Communist principles, which outline a classless city reflecting a uniformity of form. Low-cost, mass-designed, multistoried apartment buildings are found in every city in the Soviet Union. The amount of interior space per family, determined by the state according to family size, averages about one quarter that of American norms. Urban crowding and shortages of housing are found in virtually every city. The waiting period for an apartment ranges from two to five years.

Because all land is owned by the state, competition for space is eliminated, so that the internal patterning of urban space is more controlled than in Western cities, although the older urban cores remain virtually unchanged. Integration of all aspects of land use rather than separation into distinct residential, retail, and industrial areas is a guiding principle in new Soviet urban development.

To this end, strong efforts have been made to create self-sustaining residential units with services and sources of employment for local residents, particularly in Moscow. Ideally, these self-contained **communes** include residences, shops, schools, playgrounds, and a factory in which Soviet citizens live communal lives and share all tasks. These units create a distinctive urban structure in the Soviet Union—an administrative design of urban space more defined by social goals than is true in Western cities. The Soviet city is also more efficient in terms of transportation costs for residents.

A Multinational State

In the Soviet Union, Marxism presumed the gradual disappearance of cultural, linguistic, and religious differences among the more than 200 different nationalities that existed in the czarist empire and the subsequent emergence of a socialist society without class distinctions. But these expectations have not been re-

alized. Ethnic feelings are intense among the non-Russian peoples of the Baltic, the Ukraine, the Caucasus, and Central Asia. And these feelings are fueled by living in a multinational Soviet state where Russian language, Russian customs, and Russian institutions are foremost.

Since the early 1980s, Russians constitute less than a majority of the country's population. Russians number perhaps 140 million today (Table 5.1). Ukrainians (42 million in 1979), are the second largest minority culture, followed by Uzbeks and Belorussians with 12.5 and 9.5 million in 1979 respectively. In the Southern Periphery, Tatars, Kazakhs, Azerbaijanis, Armenians, and Georgians form separate national groups of 3 million to 6 million people each. On the European frontiers of Russia, the Estonians, Latvians, and Lithuanians of the Baltic region and the Poles and Moldavian Romanians farther south are significant non-Russian ethnic groups. With declining birth rates among Slavic nationalities and

This housing project in Strogino, a suburb of Moscow, embodies the classless society idealized in communist doctrine. Here, forty-two identical apartment houses have been built to alleviate the city's housing shortage.

TABLE 5.1 ETHNIC DIVERSITY OF THE SOVIET POPULATION

Nationality	1960		1980	
	Population (millions)	Percent of Total	Population (millions)	Percent of Total
All Nationalities	208.8	100.0%	272.0	100.0%
Russian	114.1	54.6	137.4	51.1
Ukrainian	37.3	17.8	42.4	15.8
Uzbek	6.0	2.9	12.5	4.7
Belorussian	7.9	3.8	9.5	3.5
Kazakh	3.6	1.7	6.5	2.4
Tatar	5.0	2.4	6.3	2.3
Azerbaijani	2.9	1.4	5.5	2.0
Armenian	2.8	1.3	4.1	1.5
Georgian	2.7	1.3	3.6	1.3
Moldavian	2.2	1.1	3.0	1.1
Lithuanian	2.3	1.1	2.9	1.1
Tadzhik	1.4	0.7	2.9	1.1
Turkmenian	1.0	0.5	2.0	0.7
Jewish	2.3	1.1	1.9	0.7
Kirghiz	1.0	0.5	1.9	0.7
German	1.6	0.8	1.8	0.6
Chuvash	1.5	0.7	1.8	0.6
Latvian	1.4	0.7	1.4	0.5
Bashkir	1.0	0.4	1.4	0.5
Mordvinian	1.3	0.6	1.2	0.4
Polish	1.4	0.7	1.2	0.4

Source: Soviet census data, January 1959 and January 1979. Small groups omitted.

higher birth rates among the peoples of the Caucasus and Central Asia, the slight Russian majority in the Soviet population has vanished, and the Slavic population as a whole—Russians, Ukrainians, Belorussians—is proportionately declining.

Viewing the old Russian Empire as an oppressor of all national groups, the early Communists established a federal system in which national groups were expected to assert their rights in preparation for the ultimate disappearance of both national and class differences. The union republics thus were designed on the basis of nationality. But from a practical viewpoint, the Soviet Union's place in the world depended on its Russian ability to retain control of the resources of its non-Russian areas—the fertile soil of the Ukraine, the oil of Baku, Central Asian cotton, and Polish coal. In the social turmoil of World War II, however, Stalin blatantly appealed to Russian nationalism for the preservation of Mother Russia from the crisis facing the nation. At the end of the war, several entire minority populations in the Caucasus and the Crimea as well as 1.5 million ethnic Germans long resident in the Volga region were forcibly transported to Central Asia as punishment for assumed group disloyalty. Since that period, the Soviet Union has consistently stressed the benefits of association with Russians to its non-Russian minorities, has attempted to undermine the strength of national customs and traditions, and tried to encourage the fusion of minorities into a common Russian-dominated culture in a process identified as **russification.**

Population migration has proved the most effective method of diffusing Russian language and culture in the Soviet Union. Russians are today a numerical majority in the large cities of the Ukraine and a growing number of Ukrainians identify Russian as their primary language. Heavy migration into the new economic regions of Kazakhstan has rendered this traditionally Asian region predominantly Russian today. Similarly, Russian migration into the Baltic has intensified—not, however, without increasing friction with local cultures.

Official policy under Khrushchev and Brezhnev was to encourage population movements in all directions to eliminate "national narrow-mindedness" and create a new "Soviet people." It is difficult, however, to estimate to what degree this ethnic objective has guided state decisions as compared with economic development, manpower needs, or other factors. Although official migration has effected a blending of peoples in the Soviet Union, the process has been slow. Not surprisingly, such cultural mixing is greatest in large cities and least in rural areas.

Language policy has been a second method for encouraging the russification of the Soviet population. After the Revolution, local languages were officially recognized in the Soviet Union to combat illiteracy. During the 1920s, elementary education was taught in sixty non-Russian languages, although the language of higher education remained exclusively Russian, except in the ancient cultures of Georgia and Armenia. In 1958, Russian was introduced as a second language in all Soviet schools with the choice of language studied by each child left to the parents. Despite the advantages to be gained through knowledge of Russian, surprisingly few have abandoned their native tongue. The official goal of making Russian a universal language in the Soviet Union is progressing slowly. As Central Asian rates of natural increase remain high, resulting in many non-Russian children, it becomes increasingly difficult to russify the central Asian population. It remains to be seen whether modern communication networks will accelerate the process.

The official goal of making Russian the universal language of the USSR is not working. This secondary school mathematics class at Ala-buka in Kirghiz is being conducted in Russian, a language few Muslims in Soviet Central Asia speak.

The multinational character of the Soviet population is posing increasing problems as the ethnic composition of the country changes. The lowest rates of population growth in the Soviet Union today are in the Slavic republics of Russia, the Ukraine, and Belorussia. In the last twenty years, these Slavic speakers declined from 76.2 to 70.4 percent of the total population (Table 5.1). Meanwhile, the highest rates of population growth are occurring in the Muslim republics of Soviet Central Asia. These shifts in the geographic distribution of the Soviet population work their way through Soviet life. Uzbeks are now the third largest ethnic group in the Soviet Union. As industrial labor shortages appear in the Slavic-speaking regions of European Russia, Uzbeks, Tatars, Azerbaijanis, Georgians, and other minorities are moving northward to man the factories; repressive measures

have been used to recruit labor. The increasing number of Muslims in the Soviet armed forces has led to interethnic conflict between Slavic-speaking officers and Asian-speaking soldiers. This factor altered Soviet military procedures during their occupation of Afghanistan. The Soviet state, despite seventy years of Communist ideology, remains geographically and socially segregated.

EASTERN EUROPE

Eastern Europe is an environmental and cultural transition zone between the Germanic and Latin societies of Western Europe and the Slavic-dominated Soviet Union. This region includes eight countries—East Germany (German Democratic Republic), Poland, Czechoslovakia, Hungary, Romania, Bulgaria, Yugoslavia, and Albania—with a combined pop-

ulation just under 140 million. Eastern Europe covers one-half million square miles of territory, stretching southward 1000 miles from the shores of the Baltic to the Mediterranean and Black seas, and it forms a latitudinal buffer zone 250 to 650 miles wide between Western Europe and the Soviet Union (Fig. 5.14).

Historically, Eastern Europe has suffered from its transitional location. Over the centuries, conflict and conquest have characterized the political geography of the region. With low-lying landscapes of the North European Plain through much of eastern Germany and Poland, and the Danube River Valley extending from the Black Sea to the Alps, much of Eastern Europe has been tossed between one political authority and another over time. The concept of *The Buffer Zone* identifies this geographic condition. Since World War II, Eastern Europe has served as a buffer zone for the Soviet Union. A zone of weakness, it has been controlled by a strong power, in this case the Soviet Union, to serve as a zone of separation between Russia and the West.

In the classic sense of the buffer zone, no local power in Eastern Europe is strong enough to dominate the region, and indeed, its people differ strongly from one another in language, culture, faith, and political traditions. It should be noted, however, that Austria and Poland have risen to political greatness at different points in history. The formulation of national states has proved difficult here, so that Eastern Europe's local boundaries come and go over time, its states frequently have competing interests, and they often have been, collectively, caught between conflicting interests of stronger powers. Thus, in the past, different powers—Germany, Austro-Hungary, Russia, the Ottoman Turks—have been able to dominate and control large portions of territory in Eastern Europe enclosing diverse populations and cultures. This has

Figure 5.14 Political regions of Eastern Europe.

been one of the Soviet Union's goals in political geography since the defeat of Nazi Germany.

Six countries are members of the Soviet-inspired Council of Mutual Economic Assistance known as CMEA or COMECON): East Germany, Poland, Czechoslovakia, Hungary, Romania, and Bulgaria. Only Yugoslavia and Albania, the two countries farthest from the Soviet domain, have had any real measure of political or economic independence during the last forty years. *Economic Development in Eastern Europe* is strongly influenced by the Soviet Union.

The Buffer Zone

The physical configuration of Eastern Europe has directly contributed to its political instability and cultural complexity. In the north, the North European Plain extends through East Germany and Poland along the coast of the Baltic Sea. Southward, this plain grades into a zone of rolling dissected hills, plateaus and basins of great topographic complexity. These uplands culminate in the Carpathian Mountains, an extension of the Alps, which arc from eastern Poland and Czechoslovakia and sweep through the heart of Romania where they are called the

Transylvanian Alps. These mountain ranges encircle the Pannonian Plains which extend from the borders of Austria to the Iron Gate, where the Danube River passes through a narrow gorge in the Balkan Mountains forming the border of Yugoslavia and Romania. In southeast Europe, mountain ranges, such as the Dinaric and Balkan Mountains fragment the territories of Yugoslavia, Albania, and Bulgaria to form what is usually called the Balkans as a whole. Although rugged topography has clearly influenced the distribution of peoples and economies in Eastern Europe, it has rarely functioned as a barrier to movement. Accessible passes and river valleys have enabled people, commerce, and communications to flow throughout Eastern Europe since ancient times.

During the last 1000 years, many different peoples swept into Eastern Europe, established settlements, and carved out territories that underlie the present political geography of the region. Slavic peoples moved in from the east, and Slavic cultures gradually differentiated themselves. The Western Slavs include Poles, Czechs, and Slovaks. In southeast Europe, the South Slavs include the Serbs, Macedonians, Croats, Slovenes, and Bulgars. The origins of the Romance-speaking Romanian people remain controversial. They see themselves as descendants of Roman legionnaires; their neighbors view them as refugee sheep herders from the Adriatic. Between the two major north-south Slavic groups, the Asiatic Magyars (or Hungarians) crossed the Carpathians and occupied the rich grasslands of the middle Danube Basin. Much later, Germans, Swedes, and Jews infiltrated Eastern Europe after the defeat of the Ottoman Turks.

The Christian faith emanated from two sources—Rome and Constantinople (modern Istanbul)—and accentuated ethnic divisions and influenced the orientation of various peoples toward Eastern or Western Christian culture. In the southeast,

The ancient ruins and Muslim architecture of Mostar on the Neretva River in Yugoslavia reflect the turbulent history of the Eastern European "shatter belt."

a third force, the Ottoman Empire of Turkey, held sway for several hundred years over the Balkans. The Ottoman Turks left behind as part of their legacy the Islamicized population in Albania as well as important Muslim minorities in Yugoslavia and Bulgaria.

At the beginning of the twentieth century, this welter of peoples was politically under the control of the German and Russian Empires in the north, the Austro-Hungarian Empire in the center, and a number of small, newly independent states formerly governed by the Ottoman Empire in the south—Romania, Bulgaria, Montenegro, Serbia, and Albania. (Greece had become independent from the Turks in the 1820s.)

After World War I, the map of Eastern Europe was completely redrawn with far-reaching effects when

American insistence on the application of the principle of self-determination was applied to the region. Small, weak, economically insecure states were established when the German, Russian, and Austro-Hungarian empires were dismembered. Poland, Czechoslovakia, and Yugoslavia (with the addition of Serbia and Montenegro) were carved out of the territory of these three former imperial powers. Hungary was separated from Austria, Romania emerged enlarged, and Bulgaria was somewhat diminished in size. Albania was created in 1921. Independent, each country attempted to build a viable self-sufficient state out of undeveloped economies, cultural fragmentation, and limited political experience.

Twenty years later, the map of Eastern Europe was again substantially changed by war. After German

domination during World War II, the independent states of Eastern Europe were brutally occupied by the Red Army and became a vast buffer zone between the USSR and Western Europe. Nearly 60,000 square miles of territory from Poland, Czechoslovakia, and Romania was incorporated directly into the Soviet Union. The Baltic republics of Lithuania, Latvia, and Estonia had already been taken early in the war. Poland gained substantial German territory in the west in partial compensation for its losses to the USSR in the east. East Germany was severed from West Germany, creating two German states, one oriented to the Soviet Union, the other to the West. More important, the Soviet Union dominated life throughout the entire region, except for Yugoslavia after 1948 and Albania after 1957.

As de facto Soviet satellites, the six

East European CMEA countries adopted a Soviet model of social and economic modernization under political pressure from Moscow. Command economies were implanted in each country with emphasis on the exploitation of raw materials, the development of an industrial base, and collectivization of agriculture, except in Poland (after 1956) and Yugoslavia. Central planners determined economic as well as social policy. Communist parties in East Europe attempted to resolve the difficulties of meeting local and Soviet aspirations and demands simultaneously. Unsuccessful revolts against Soviet domination occurred in East Germany in 1948, in Hungary in 1956, in Czechoslovakia in 1968, and in Poland in 1972, 1976, and 1980. In the late 1980s, these tensions remain unresolved in each state in Eastern Europe.

Economic Development in Eastern Europe

Under Soviet domination, Eastern Europe has experienced accelerated industrialization and urbanization in what was until recently a predominantly rural, agricultural region. Relatively poor in natural resources, imports of raw materials, such as petroleum, natural gas, and key minerals, from the Soviet Union supported the growth of East European industrial complexes. Equally important, Western governments and corporations made sophisticated technological knowledge available throughout the region.

Levels of development, however, vary sharply from country to country and region to region within Eastern Europe. In general, the progress of modernization has been greatest in the northern and western areas of East Europe that were part of developed Europe before World War II. Standards of living diminish toward the south and east. In every state, however, rapid change has transformed the human geography of the East European buffer zone.

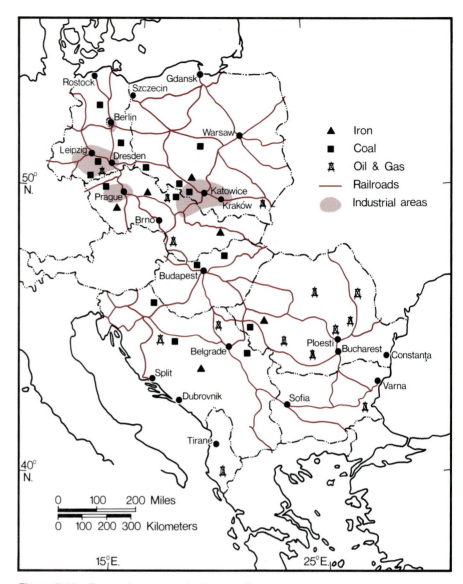

Figure 5.15 Economic patterns in Eastern Europe.

Industrial Growth

Historically, industrial growth in Eastern Europe has been slow to develop because of two factors. First, great power rivalries and shifting international boundaries tended to discourage long-term investment in industry, although Austrians and Germans both made substantial commitments. Second, Eastern Europe is relatively poorly endowed with the basic energy and mineral resources needed to sustain heavy industry (Fig. 5.15).

The oldest centers of industry are located in the more advanced states of the north. In East Germany, the industrial complex of Saxony is based on large deposits of lignite coal; it produces iron and steel, machine goods, and textiles. Indeed, throughout Eastern Europe, high rates of production of very low-grade **bituminous** coal and even lower grade lignite dominate the energy picture. In Poland, the bituminous coal mining district, Silesia, followed a similar course of development. Poland ranks as the world's fourth coal producer. In Czechoslovakia, iron deposits in the Erzgebirge or Ore Mountains were developed by German entrepreneurs. In Romania (pop. 23 million), the Ploesti oil fields were—prior to the discovery of North Sea oil—the largest source of petroleum in

Europe (Fig. 5.15). Today, Romania is a distant third in European oil production.

Elsewhere, industrial development occurred in the largest cities of Eastern Europe, mainly in the national capitals of Warsaw (pop. 1.6 million) in Poland, Prague (pop. 1.2 million) in Czechoslovakia, Budapest (pop. 2 million) in Hungary, and Bucharest (pop. 1.8 million) in Romania. Other important industrial concentrations are in Sofia, the capital of Bulgaria (pop. 1 million), and in Zagreb (pop. 562,000) and Belgrade (pop. 750,000) in Yugoslavia.

Today, industrial production in Eastern Europe is still concentrated in major cities and where important energy and mineral deposits are found, but the patterns of industrial location have greatly changed since the end of World War II. Each East European state has attempted to expand its industrial base under centrally planned socialist economies. Rapid industrial expansion is being pursued with emphasis on heavy industry, petrochemicals, and machinery. Consumer goods, as in the Soviet Union, receive less investment. Poland (pop. 38 million), East Germany (pop. 16.6 million), and Czechoslovakia (pop. 15.6 million) are still the leading industrial states in Eastern Europe, with per capita industrial outputs approaching those of Western Europe. Despite considerable industrial growth, the southern countries of Eastern Europe have less advanced industrial economies. Resource limitations have been overcome by imports of basic minerals and energy from the Soviet Union, and regional integration under CMEA has led to closer cooperation in industrial planning and production. Exceptions to this pattern are found in both Yugoslavia (pop. 23.6 million) and Albania (pop. 3.1 million). Yugoslavia retained its independence from the Soviet Union after World War II largely because of the charismatic leadership of Marshal Tito (died 1980) and support from the United States. Albania has pursued a path of independent Communist development in isolation from the other states of Eastern Europe.

With the exception of these two countries, interregional trade, focused on the Soviet Union, has increased in Eastern Europe since the formation of the CMEA, although with far less success than the European Community. Currently, East European dependence on raw materials from the Soviet Union, which have increased dramatically in price, and their need for expensive Western technology have contributed to economic deterioration. The Soviet Union maintains its interest in binding the industrial economies of Eastern Europe more tightly within its own sphere of influence, but demands for local autonomy are increasing. As a result, political unrest is growing throughout the region, most critically in Eastern Europe's largest country, Poland.

Agricultural Change

Agriculture plays a salient role in the economies of every country in Eastern Europe. In the past, this region served as a breadbasket for Europe, producing a quarter of its wheat, half of all its rye, and 70 percent of its corn. As population has grown, however, internal consumption has absorbed the surplus potatoes and rye cultivated in the cool, maritime climate of the northern regions of East Germany and Poland as well as the wheat and corn grown on the rich Hungarian Plain, on the Moldavian Plateau that borders Romania and the Soviet Union, and on the Wallachian Plains of the lower Danube River. Agriculture and livestock raising still are important activities in Eastern Europe, particularly in the south where better than half of the population lives in the countryside. Agriculture still forms a significant percentage of the gross national product (GNP) throughout Eastern Europe, although the region is no longer an important food exporter.

At the end of World War II, rural overpopulation was a major problem in Eastern Europe. In the best agricultural regions of the north and central sectors, large estates controlled the land, whereas in southeast Europe, subsistence farmers cultivating small plots of land were the norm. Soviet control of Eastern Europe led to a complete reorganization of agriculture, as the Soviets imposed socialism on the agricultural landscapes of the region.

As in the Soviet Union, it was expected that state control of agriculture would lead to larger land holdings, increased production, and greater specialization of labor. Collectivization was forced on most countries in Eastern Europe in the 1950s. By the 1960s, 95 percent of the cultivated land in Eastern Europe (except in Poland and Yugoslavia) was held in state or collective farms. Peasants were allowed to retain small private household plots and domestic animals. In Poland and Yugoslavia, where resistance was intense, a majority of the land remains in private holdings.

The impact of collectivization of agriculture in Eastern Europe varies, but overall agricultural productivity is much lower than in Western Europe despite more favorable agricultural environments. Investment in mechanization, higher yield grains, and fertilizer have not resulted in large gains in production. Indeed, in East Germany, Poland, and Romania, the food situation deteriorated so badly that meat and bread rationing was required in the 1970s and 1980s. In Poland, the diminution of food subsidies in 1980 contributed to the formation of the Solidarity movement, a direct workers' challenge to Soviet control of the Polish economy. The underlying forces are similar to those that plague Soviet agriculture—bureaucratic inefficiency, peasant discontent, and the policy of feeding urban industrial workers low-priced food at the expense of the total economy.

Overall, the countries of Eastern Europe have made considerable economic progress in the last forty years. They have moved from rural, agrar-

Catastrophic food shortages in Poland have increased tensions in Eastern Europe. This farm, located between Gdansk and Varsovie in northern Poland, is typical of East European agriculture.

ian states toward more industrialized economies with better developed transport systems, higher levels of urbanization, and slowly improving standards of living. But the costs of importing technology from the West and raw materials from the Soviet Union have driven the East European nations into debt and difficult economic positions. Consumer ex-

pectations for higher standards of living have not been met because of this deteriorating economic situation, and local resistance to Soviet pressures increased proportionately.

The future of this buffer region, closely tied to the Soviet Union, is difficult to calculate. Industrial growth is hampered by rising costs of production, aging technologies, and

worker discontent; the agricultural sector needs complete reorganization. In the face of these economic problems, it seems likely that citizens' resentments will grow. As new political directions in the Soviet Union take hold and bear social and economic change, Eastern Europe will follow.

6

JAPAN AND KOREA

Traditional Japan: Settlement and Society

The Tokugawa Shogunate

The Meiji Restoration

Japanese Expansion and Empire

The Human Geography of Japan

Hokkaido

Tohoku

Central and Southwestern Japan

Modern Japan: The Geography of Economic Growth and Social Change

The Rise of the Industrial State

Urban Japan

Agriculture in a Modern Economy

Problems of a Technological Society

Korea: The Bridge Between

The Korean Peninsula

The Two Koreas

In the last century, Japan changed from a country of rice-growing peasants into an industrial giant. The process was initiated in 1868 by a handful of militant **samurai** who were determined to build a powerful modern country. In less than fifty years, the samurai and those who followed transformed an isolated agricultural society into the first non-Western industrial state.

Peasant unrest and revolution were not important spurs toward modernization in Japan as was true in the Soviet Union and later in China. No middle class demanded liberal social and economic progress as they did in Western Europe and the United States. Instead, modernization in Japan was motivated by pride and a keen sense of national spirit. These values were combined with modern science and technology to accomplish an unparalleled leap to economic power. Japan now stands as the first cultural hybrid in the Technological World.

Japan's economic growth in the last two decades has been phenomenal. Militant pursuit of business has made it a truly affluent country. Yet Japan's wealth is fragile. The country is completely dependent on imports for virtually all energy, raw materials, and some food-stuffs. With a population of 122.7 million, Japan's well-being is founded on trade in a global arena well beyond Japanese regulation or control.

Further, Japan's industrial maturity has generated social and environmental problems in the narrow geographic confines of its habitable space. The Japanese have responded to these problems with intelligence and resolve. They have adjusted to wrenching changes in the world economic order, such as the emergence of the Organization of Petroleum Exporting Countries (OPEC), and they have formulated and enforced environmental policies as stringent as those anywhere in the world.

Social issues, however, have remained more intractable as decades of peace and affluence, following disastrous defeat in World War II, have substantially diluted the martial spirit of the samurai. For better or worse, the Japanese are committed to a technological society based on mastery of material processing, advanced electronics, and technology. But the country is now reaching its geographic limits of growth and must deal in an uncertain international arena. For these reasons, Japan's economic future is uncertain.

Like Japan's development, South Korea's economic growth has been rapid, although later. Within the Korean Peninsula, however, questions of division and political systems spanning a single culture between the two Koreas leave the future far more problematic than Japan. The region as a whole, however, seems bent on economic growth and a new world role.

TRADITIONAL JAPAN: SETTLEMENT AND SOCIETY

Japan is located off the extreme eastern shore of the Asian mainland, a group of four relatively small islands with few natural resources (Fig. 6.1). Historically, Japan was influenced by Chinese civilization, which spread to the island archipelago and which the Japanese superimposed on their native culture. For 1000 years, the Japanese learned and borrowed from Chinese thought, which was transmitted to the islands through Korea. Their people were exposed to Buddhist and Confucian doctrines; their leaders were influenced by Chinese systems of land utilization and taxation and by imperial models of government organization. But Japan's geographical distance from the Chinese core meant that despite this extensive borrowing, the Japanese retained their distinctive language, social organization, and identity. Racially a single people and geographically isolated, the Japanese still perceive themselves as unique and different, an island nation of lands and peoples sheltered from the tides of change during much of their history.

This section focuses on the union of land and people in Japan that, over the course of 400 years, led the Japanese from obscurity to empire, from an introverted agricultural society to the first non-Western industrial state.

For 250 years, well into the nineteenth century, Japan was under the rule of *The Tokugawa Shogunate*. This dynasty imposed isolation on Japan. It severed contacts between Japan and the outside world; it tried to maintain a static, stable agricultural society. Peace and prosperity under the Tokugawa, however, gradually led to economic and urban growth. These forces undermined the stability of the Japanese state and spawned social tensions. The intrusion of the

GEOSTATISTICS

	Capital	Area (square miles)	Population (millions)	Rate of Natural Increase (%)	Number of Years to Double Population	Population Projected for A.D. 2000	Infant Mortality Rate	Life Expectancy at Birth	Urban Population (%)	Per Capita GNP ($)	Energy Consumption per Capita (kg of oil equivalent)
Japan	Tokyo	143,749	122.7	0.5	133	130.0	5	78	77	12,850	3,116
North Korea	Pyongyang	46,541	21.9	2.5	28	28.2	33	68	64	—	2,118
South Korea	Seoul	38,023	42.6	1.3	52	48.8	30	68	65	2,370	1,241

Sources: *World Population Data Sheet*, 1988; *World Development Report*, 1987.

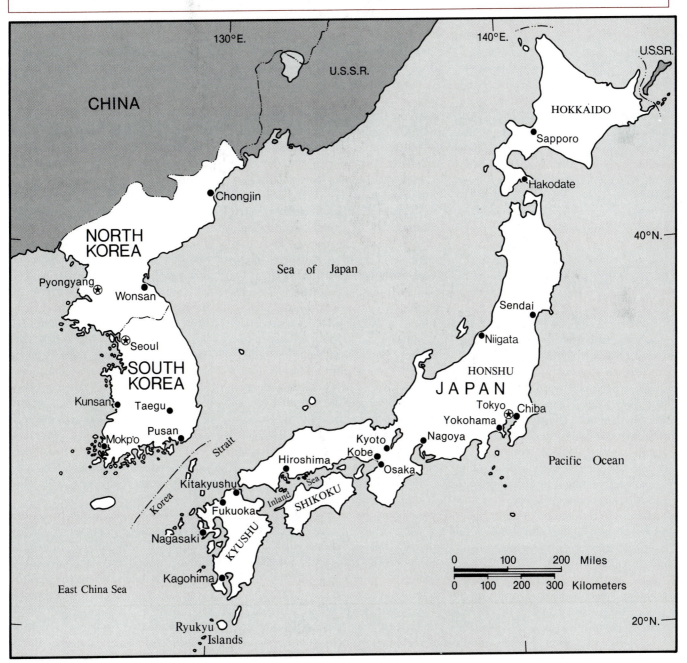

Figure 6.1 Political regions of Japan and Korea.

West in 1853 focused these tensions, broke Japan's self-imposed exile, and ended Tokugawa rule in 1867. The Tokugawa were replaced by a group of young samurai leaders who, in 1868, initiated *The Meiji Restoration.* This restoration involved a calculated policy of modernization aimed at achieving world stature through a marriage of traditional Japanese values with Western technology. Under the motto "wealthy nation, strong military," the Meiji leaders transformed the agricultural economy of Japan, built an industrial base on their islands, and propelled Japan into the modern world.

By the 1930s, this quest for world respect and power combined with the paralyzing impact of the depression on the Japanese economy led to *Japanese Expansion and Empire.* Japanese armies fanned out over Manchuria, China, and Southeast Asia in an effort to control a resource base independent of outside influence, capable of sustaining a world military and political power.

The Tokugawa Shogunate

For over 250 years (1603–1867), Japan was ruled by the Tokugawa clan under a series of feudal military leaders called **shoguns.** After initial contact with the West in the sixteenth century, the Tokugawa **shogunate** severed all but a few connections with the outside world and developed a static, inward-looking society.

In the seventeenth century, the government imposed economic and cultural isolation on Japan. Few foreigners were allowed to enter Japanese ports, although the Dutch were allowed a trading post on the human-built island of Deshima in Nagasaki Bay. Western books and foreign religions were banned. During their rule, the primary goal of the Tokugawa government was to insulate Japanese life from foreign influence—to remove Japan from the world of nations.

Stability and Change

These stringent measures of self-imposed isolation were part of a broader impulse to retard economic change in Japan and to preserve existing patterns of social organization. Japanese society was divided into five classes: (1) the **daimyo** or feudal barons; (2) their retainers, the **samurai** warriors; (3) the peasants; (4) merchants and townspeople; and (5) the outcasts of Japanese society. Government policies reinforced these class divisions and underlined the conservative, self-protective character of Tokugawa rule.

The daimyo, numbering less then 3000, comprised a landed elite who occupied some 250 feudal agricultural domains. This was the class from which the Tokugawa family rose to power and gained control of a quarter of the labor and agricultural produce of the country. On a spiritual level, the Tokugawa shogun and the daimyo paid homage to the symbolic figure of the emperor, but they, in fact, ran Japan. Holders of great wealth and power, the daimyo were forced to bear heavy expenses for the economic and political privileges they received under the Tokugawa.

Socially and economically bound to the daimyo were two million samurai, a stratified class trained in Confucian traditions of fidelity, obedience, and service. Samurai pride, loyalty to lord, and military preparedness were encouraged and applauded, despite the potential threat that the samurai posed to the stability of Tokugawa rule. They lived out the ideal and ethic that prevailed in medieval Japan.

Below the samurai were 28 million farmers, 80 percent of the Japanese population, on whom the economic burden of the country fell. These peasants were bound to the soil and to their lord. They could not change residence or occupation, and their lives were ordered in minute detail. Rigid obligations forced peasants to cultivate the agricultural land of the elite. Taxes paid in rice commonly amounted to 40 to 50 percent of a peasant's harvest and provided 80

percent of the revenues of the Tokugawa state. The general policy of the ruling class toward peasants was aptly summarized by a Tokugawa official, who wrote: "Sesame seed and peasants are much alike, the more they are squeezed, the more one extracts."

The fourth class, theoretically below but actually more wealthy than the peasants, were the artisans and merchants who were townspeople living in the castle towns and urban centers of Tokugawa Japan. Although merchants were considered inferior because of the Confucian belief that money corrupts, the ruling daimyo and samurai classes relied on them for loans to sustain their urban style of life. As a result, their influence was far greater than their status.

A fifth social class, the **burakamin** of Tokugawa Japan, were the outcastes of society. They swept the streets, buried the dead, and worked in other "untouchable" occupations.

At the beginning of the seventeenth century, Japan had four large cities with a combined population of 400,000. These were Kyoto, Fushimi (now a suburb of Kyoto), Osaka, and Sakai (Fig. 6.2). Grouped together at the eastern end of the Inland Sea, these cities were all located within a radius of 25 miles of one another. The Tokugawa shogun had just begun to establish a new capital at Edo (now Tokyo), purposely distant from this urban concentration at the eastern end of the Inland Sea. This curious urban concentration in a nation of isolated villages and subsistence farmers was complemented by occasional castle towns and ports of a much lower order.

The peace and prosperity generated under the Tokugawa shogunate inspired a gradual increase in urbanization throughout the country. Preindustrial Japanese cities, castle towns, became the focal points of local military and administrative activities. New castle towns were built in the economic centers of agricultural domains, not in outlying mountain passes where the old defensive for-

TOKUGAWA JAPAN: STABILITY IN CHANGE

The Tokugawa shogunate (1603–1867) ruled the major agricultural and urban areas of Japan, exercising their domain over the Japanese core area while powerful daimyo controlled the periphery. Edo (Tokyo), Osaka, and Kyoto were then among the largest cities in the world. After 250 years of rule, the Tokugawa were overthrown by two daimyo clans from Satsuma and Choshu in westernmost Japan. The samurai of these daimyo spearheaded the Meiji Restoration (1868) that opened Japan to Western science and technology and began the process of modernization.

Adapted from: Edwin O. Reischauer, *Japan: The Story of a Nation,* 3rd ed. New York: Alfred Knopf, 1981, pp. 80–81.

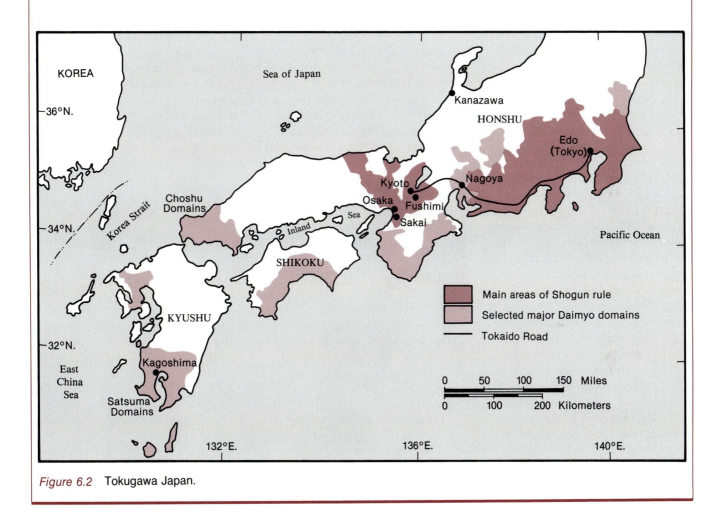

Figure 6.2 Tokugawa Japan.

tresses were located. As this network of small cities and towns came under the control of the shogunate, the spatial basis for a centralized state was formed.

Over several decades the feudal elite—lords and their retinues of samurai—moved from the countryside to castle towns. This created a dichotomy between peasants on the land and the newly urbanized feudal class in the towns. Feudal lords came to rely more and more on merchants to bridge the gap between city and countryside and to provide links between their agricultural domains, the castle towns and the national market system. The merchant class became a vital and aggressive element in a growing economy.

Urban and Economic Growth

By the beginning of the eighteenth century, Tokugawa urbanism had come of age, and Japan contained some of the world's largest cities. Edo (Tokyo) had nearly 500,000 people; Osaka and Kyoto had populations of 300,000; Kanazawa and Nagoya had grown to about 100,000 (Fig. 6.2). An estimated 10 percent of the Japanese lived in cities with populations larger than 10,000. Feeding the urban population and meeting its sophisticated needs began to emerge as the major business of Japan.

The burden of sustaining growing urban populations remained the task of the peasantry. Cultivated land in

Japan doubled between 1600 and 1730 as farming extended outward from the plains of the warm southwest to land located along the shallow bays and lagoons of the north. Cultivation of wet rice increased, commercial fertilizer came into use, **double cropping**—the cultivation of more than one crop in the same field in a given agricultural year—became more widespread, and yields increased. Waterwheels and treadmills were introduced, and the varieties of rice increased from 175 to over 2000.

Given this increase in agricultural production, the market economy of the castle towns spread to outlying rural areas. Industry-oriented crops, such as mulberry leaves for silk, cotton, sugarcane, indigo for blue dye, and tobacco were cultivated in suitable climates and soils. Handicraft industries grew in importance, and peasants, who began to receive cash payments for their produce, supplemented their incomes by spinning silk, brewing sake from fermented rice, making sandals, matting straw, and weaving cotton textiles. By the late Tokugawa period, regional agricultural specializations were developing—**sericulture** in the interior basins and on the Pacific coast of northern Honshu, sugar refining near Edo, and hemp weaving along the Sea of Japan in west-central Honshu.

Villages became product oriented. Enterprising and resourceful peasants bought land and rented it out to tenant farmers. Peasant landlords controlled village life and labored to maintain the proper peasant deference to those of higher social status. Through this commercialization of the Japanese landscape, villages were welded into a national spatial and economic system.

Commercial and urban growth in Tokugawa Japan created social tensions. The daimyo class could not generate enough income to sustain their urban way of life. Forced into debt, feudal lords lowered the stipends paid to their largely symbolic and idle samurai retainers. Large

numbers of masterless samurai roved from city to city, deprived of role, seeking jobs as government bureaucrats or in military academies that sprang up in large urban centers. The merchants, although benefiting from the growth in commerce and trade, were deprived of foreign opportunities. Peasant life remained unrewarding under the Tokugawas. Although some peasant landlords did benefit from the introduction of a money economy into rural Japan, money merely increased the costs of village life and heightened the level of silent misery for most.

The seeds of change and social discontent were deeply embedded in Tokugawa society long before the American naval Commodore Matthew C. Perry steamed into Edo Bay in 1853 and exploded Japan's self-imposed isolation.

The Intrusion of the West

All the internal problems confronting the Tokugawa shogunate in the middle of the nineteenth century—large numbers of unemployed samurai in the cities, the growing power of the merchant class, and peasant poverty and unrest—were intensified by the external threat posed by Perry's small naval squadron.

Japan, a country that had long ignored the outside world, could do so no longer. A growing awareness of the technical superiority of the West weakened confidence in Tokugawa rule. Enough European knowledge

Commodore Matthew C. Perry's arrival in Japan in 1853 broke the 250-year isolation of the country. It opened the island nation to the West.

had filtered into Japan from China, so that authorities respected the firepower of the American vessels. They were aware of the disastrous defeat of the Chinese of the Opium Wars with Britain a decade earlier. Perry demanded better treatment of shipwrecked sailors, aid for American vessels seeking shelter and supplies, and an opening of trade with the West. Nationalists led by some samurai demanded that the shogun expel these "barbarians." Perry left Japan to give them time to think it over.

Perry returned a year later with eight vessels. Rent with dissension and indecision, but terrified by this show of force, the leaders of the Tokugawa shogunate reluctantly agreed to open two ports to American vessels—Hakodate on remote Hokkaido and Shimoda on the isolated Izu Peninsula south of Edo. The technological significance of American gifts presented to the shogun—a miniature railroad, telegraph equipment, telescopes, and firearms—was not lost on the Japanese. Trade agreements were soon signed with England, Russia, France, and the Netherlands; Japan's long period of seclusion came to an end. Under this stimulus, trade increased rapidly. During the 1860s, Japanese silk, tea, and copperware were exchanged for imported cotton textiles, sugar, and ironware.

Opposition to Tokugawa rule, which had begun to form before 1853, then crystallized around a formidable core of young discontented samurai whose motto was, "Revere the emperor and expel the barbarians." It was not their intention that the emperor should have real power. Rather, they wished to use the emperor's symbolic status as a rallying point for opposition to the Tokugawa.

As antiforeign sentiment grew, some Japanese leaders decided that the only way to cope with the West was to adopt its military technology. The Choshu clan in extreme western Honshu began to form mixed battalions of samurai and commoner soldiers equipped with modern arms.

In an important incident, the British shelled the capital city of the Satsuma fiefdom at Kagoshima in southern Kyushu (Fig. 6.2). The Satsuma promptly hired British officers as naval advisers to train their men. In January 1868, the lords of Choshu and Satsuma marched toward Edo, overthrew the Tokugawa shogunate, and proclaimed the restoration of the emperor. The leaders of these two rural domains governed Japan under the symbolic guidance of the young Emperor Meiji, whose name is given to this important period in Japanese history.

The Meiji Restoration

The year 1868 was as important a date in the development of Japan as 1066 in England or 1776 in the United States. In that year, the Meiji government launched a program of reform and reorganization that responded directly to Western intrusion. Although Japan's economy had crystallized along feudal lines and was technologically backward because of the isolation of the Tokugawa period, other facets of Japanese society and environment were advanced.

Fully half the men and 15 percent of the women of Japan were receiving formal education in the 1860s. More than a million commoners were enrolled in religious schools. Many merchants and most samurai were well-educated.

The discipline of the traditional education system was soon translated into rapid understanding of new ideas and new technical methods. The market economy of pre-Meiji Japan was strong. People were used to dealing in accounts and money circulated throughout the realm. In addition, this literate population was influenced by the sophisticated urban culture of Edo, Osaka, and Kyoto.

Although the Tokugawa refusal to deal with outsiders had isolated Japan from the technological inventions of the West, its centrally governed society and well-organized hierarchy of urban centers left the Japanese well prepared to face the twentieth century.

Modernization and Industrialization

Modernization was a calculated policy of the young samurai leaders of Meiji Japan. Their aim was to upgrade Japan's position on the ladder of world power. They wanted to convert their small group of islands, scattered on the rim of the Pacific, into a respected military and commercial nation.

Their motivation was political rather than economic. Wealth was viewed as a source of power. The samurai ethic of discipline, loyalty, sacrifice, and selfless labor was harnessed to provide the momentum to propel Japan into a position of world leadership. Traditional values, the spirit of Old Japan, were preserved and reiterated in the culture of New Japan. Only those elements of Western science and technology that strengthened the nation were consciously acquired. Foreigners and things foreign were accepted for their usefulness, and delegations were sent to the United States and Europe to select the best models for the new society the Japanese were determined to create.

Modernization required a reorganization of space and society. The capital city of the new regime was established at Edo, renamed Tokyo. The feudal daimyo domains were abolished and consolidated into the forty-six prefectures that remain the basic civil divisions in modern Japan. In some new prefectures, feudal lords were installed as governors and paid generous stipends. The hereditary daimyo monopoly on national territory, however, was broken. Tolls and other economic barriers between domains were eliminated. Ports were thrown open to foreign trade.

Within four years, the first Japanese railroad was running the 18 miles between Tokyo and Yokohama. By

1914, Japan, a country of short distances, had constructed more than 7000 miles of track. As elsewhere, the railroad was a reliable measure of the progress of modernization.

A post office with telegraph and telephone service linking the islands of Japan by wire was inaugurated shortly after 1868. In less than a decade, the merchant marine doubled in size to serve the growing volume of foreign and internal trade. Innovations in mechanized transport and communications and less sophisticated improvements, such as the construction of dirt roads and the introduction of rickshaws (invented in 1870) and carts, exerted a powerful influence on the development of the Japanese economy.

The emergence of a unified national space was paralleled by social reforms aimed at creating a national society. The restrictive class barriers of the feudal period were eliminated. Universal conscription was introduced; a strong army and navy followed. This military role, previously reserved to samurai, brought rural and urban Japanese together and bridged the class distinctions of earlier times. Compulsory education was introduced in 1872, and by 1900, 95 percent of the Japanese population was literate.

The primary thrust of Meiji initiative was industrialization following the Western model of modernization. Heavy industry to support a modern military was especially favored. A variety of shipyards, machine works, and steel mills were built on northern Kyushu and in the cities of Osaka and Tokyo. Government-sponsored factories producing cotton and woolen textiles, silk, iron, paper, glass, and other manufacturers were set up as models to introduce Western technology to the Japanese. At the same time, the government subsidized private industry and sold model government factories to entrepreneurs. The Industrial Revolution was being deliberately copied on the eastern rim of Asia. The slogan

of the times, "Wealthy Nation, Strong Military," was becoming reality.

New factories, government administration of feudal domains, importation of Western technology and advisers, and development of a modern military were expensive. The costs of modernization were borne by the backbone of Japanese society—the peasants, who came into direct ownership of the land they worked early in the Meiji period and were forced to accept a new system of taxation based on land valuation.

Reform in Japanese agriculture was necessary to pay for the program of modernization. Agriculture generated 90 percent of state revenues. New seeds were introduced; intensive use of fertilizer, irrigation, double cropping, and better weeding practices became common. Rice yields

Farmers bore the costs of importing Western technology vital to Japan's rapid modernization during the Meiji period.

THE SAMURAI ETHIC

The samurai ethic (known as "bushido") played an important role in the modernization of Japan. Hard work, self-sacrifice, diligence, discipline, and loyalty provided the energy that enabled Japan to change from a feudal state to an industrial nation. Many early industrialists were samurai, and the largest corporations of modern Japan derive from these feudal roots. The house rules of the founder of Mitsubishi, a large international corporation, provide an example of old values carried into the modern period.

Mitsubishi: Founder's Rules

Article 1. Do not be preoccupied with small matters but aim at the management of large enterprises.

Article 2. Once you start an enterprise be sure to succeed.

Article 3. Do not engage in speculative enterprises.

Article 4. Operate all enterprises with the national interest in mind.

Article 5. Never forget the pure spirit of public service and *makoto* (sincerity, fidelity).

Article 6. Be hardworking, frugal, and thoughtful.

Article 7. Utilize proper personnel.

Article 8. Treat your employees well.

Article 9. Be bold in starting an enterprise but meticulous in its prosecution.

Source: Robert N. Bellah, "Tokugawa Religion," in Irwin Scheiner (ed.), *Modern Japan: An Interpretive Anthology.* New York: Macmillan, 1974, p. 86.

---

increased 80 percent between 1880 and 1920. Cultivated land expanded by a third. Competition from foreign imports forced a change in cropping patterns. Home-grown sugar and cotton, cultivated principally on the shores of the Inland Sea, were replaced by mulberry trees, tea, fruits, and vegetables.

During this period, tea and silk were the primary export products of Japan. Indeed, in the 1890s, raw silk accounted for nearly half of all Japanese exports. Experts disagree about the rate of agricultural progress, but it was the peasants who sustained Japan's plunge into technology by providing the labor supply for industrialization and by feeding the growing urban and industrial population.

The Social Impact of Modernization

The rapidity of modernization transformed the foundations of Japanese society. Peasant unrest became a serious problem as expectations outpaced structural changes in society. Rural disturbances over dissatisfaction with military conscription, compulsory education, and taxes were common. Major riots broke out in southern Honshu and in the mountains north of Tokyo. Steady taxation and falling food prices caused considerable misery. Some 100,000 farm families went bankrupt in 1885, and the number of tenant farmers rose sharply. Emigration to other islands in the Pacific and to North America was one release. Even the suicide rate rose.

Of greater concern to the government was the distress of the former samurai. Stripped of privilege and income, they were a dangerous and dissatisfied element in the urban population. Jobs were created for them in industry and the government issued them bonds. The new rulers of Japan were convinced that that the samurai class uniquely possessed the necessary qualities of morality, determination, and character to lead Japan in the national quest for power. Thus, many samurai were integrated into Japan's industrial leadership.

For factory workers, life in Japan was much like that in newly industrialized areas in nineteenth-century Europe. In the textile factories, women—half under the age of twenty—were used as cheap labor. Conditions in the mines were dreadful. Twelve-hour shifts kept industry producing day and night. Low wages preserved capital for factory expansion, and strikes were prohibited. Cheap housing and crowded workers' quarters sprang up in Japanese cities as industry reshaped the urban environment. An industrial capitalist system had penetrated to the heart of a non-Western society for the first time.

Despite these social tensions, the Japanese faced modernization with a sense of common national purpose, recognizing the importance of national power and accepting self-sacrifice to achieve this objective. Unlike other developing areas, industrialization in Japan did not alienate rulers from the governed. Instead, traditional loyalties to one's family and the emperor were intensified, and a new form of the stern ethic of the samurai became the prevailing ideal for all society.

Although change was predictably slower in rural areas than in cities, no important segment of the population questioned the goal of national power. To have done so would have been to cut themselves off from their cultural past and its rejuvenated values. In one generation, a medieval agricultural society was transformed into an industrial nation.

Colonial expansion for space and resources was an early lesson learned from the West. With newfound power, modern Japanese armed forces defeated China in war in 1895, were awarded Taiwan, and broke the dependence of Korea on China. Then, in 1905, the Japanese vanquished a Russian fleet and captured the Russian naval base of Port Arthur at the tip of the Liaodong Peninsula in Manchuria (northeast China).

The defeat of European Russia on

its Asian frontier by a non-Western nation sent a shock wave through the industrial West. The Japanese took the seat they so coveted among the powerful nations of the world. In 1910, Japan annexed Korea, creating its own empire of the "Rising Sun."

Japanese Expansion and Empire

When the Meiji emperor died in 1912, the industrial revolution planned and implemented by the young samurai during the previous fifty years was by any measure a success. Population had risen by two thirds to 50 million, reflecting the demographic impact of industrialization. Standards of living had risen with output, and the take-off stage of Japanese economic development was underway.

Recognized as a major military and political force in world affairs, Japan embarked upon a twenty-year period of territorial and economic expansion. After World War I, Japan was awarded a League of Nations mandate over the formerly German-held Caroline, Mariana, and Marshall islands in the western Pacific. Japanese merchants captured trade areas in East Asia that the old colonial powers were no longer able to supply. The industrial sector of the Japanese economy, however, developed much faster than the rural economy, and in the early depression years of the 1930s, this unequal growth in the economy played a major role in the rise of militarism in Japan.

With its growing population, Japan sought new sources of raw materials and new markets. An industrial economy was implanted in Manchuria following the Japanese invasion in 1931. Six years later, Japanese forces entered China itself, a key to the plan for a Japanese-ruled region to be called the Greater East Asia Co-Prosperity Sphere. In 1941, the Japanese attacked Southeast Asia and integrated the rim of Asia from Malaya to the Philippines to Manchuria into their new empire. With an immense field of commercial and industrial expansion in the offing, angered by American embargoes on oil and scrap iron and a British threat to cut them off from Southeast Asian oil, and encouraged by American commitments to fight in Europe, the militant Japanese attacked Pearl Harbor. The political ambitions that had accompanied the modernization of Japan reached their greatest territorial expression in 1943.

The Economic Base

In the first quarter of the twentieth century, Japanese industry and commerce expanded rapidly. The agricultural sector grew at a much slower rate. Cotton textiles and silk manufacturing tripled in production, and half of Japan's 2.5 million industrial workers were employed in these industries. A diversified industrial core, stretching from Tokyo to northern Kyushu, began to emerge. Heavy industrial plants—metallurgy, machinery, cement, and shipbuilding—were constructed in a string of cities along this 600-mile axis. Manufactured products formed an ever-increasing share of exports. Raw materials became vital imports.

Change in agriculture was much more limited, and a gap developed between this rural sector of the economy and the modern urban industrial sphere similar to the dual economy of countries in Africa, Latin America, and other parts of Asia. Rice continued to occupy half the cultivated land, but agricultural production barely kept pace with Japan's growing population. The best agricultural lands were already efficiently cultivated, and expansion of the cultivated area forced agriculturalists into marginal environments.

As a result, Japan came increasingly to rely on imports from its colonies in Korea and Taiwan to fill its food deficit. By 1930, these colonies produced a fifth of Japan's rice supply, even though half the Japanese labor force continued to work in agriculture. Pressure on cultivated land, the attractions of urban life, and the higher wages of factory workers drew a growing stream of rural poor to urban centers. By 1930, a third of the Japanese population lived in cities of 10,000 or more.

At the same time, the national income of Japan quadrupled in little more than a generation. Affluence, however, remained the privilege of a very few. Peasant and urban working families received only a small share of the country's wealth. Factory workers earned the equivalent of seventy-five cents a day. Industrial and commercial enterprises were concentrated in the hands of a few large family business combines, the **zaibatsu** (financial cliques). These business conglomerates, all family owned and run, had begun with the Meiji investment in the samurai class. The four largest—Mitsui, Mitsubishi, Sumitomo, and Yasuda—came to dominate all aspects of the Japanese economy.

The gap in income and material goods between the rich and the poor and between farmers and factory workers continued to grow. Resentment of the zaibatsu and their hand-picked politicians combined with the effects of the world depression strengthened the hand of Japanese militarists. Ultimately, the military, with assistance from the zaibatsu, was able to act independently of the government and to embark on a quest for empire.

The Rise of Militarism

The economic depression of the 1930s had a disastrous effect on the Japanese economy. Exports declined by 50 percent in two years. Silk prices dropped by two thirds and rice by one half. Rural indebtedness increased rapidly, as did suicide, infanticide, and crime. Young military officers, themselves sons of small landowners, and the peasants believed that cooperation with the international economic order had led to the depression that ruined their families and villages.

A Japanese empire extending over East Asia—independent of the rest of the world—became the military's answer and a new national goal. They would reassert the traditional virtues of selfless loyalty and honor—the true Japanese values—and eliminate the Westernized corruption that, in their view, had infiltrated Japan and brought about their present misery.

To achieve this ambition, Japanese forces—without direct orders from their government—fanned out over Manchuria in 1931. There, the army leaders gave priority to the development of strategic industries. The rich coal mine at the city of Fushuan was expanded; the iron and steel complex at Anshan increased production. Under military leadership, a flow of coal, iron, and steel poured down the South Manchurian Railroad toward Japan, with arrival and departure schedules printed in half minutes.

At home, the militarists increased arms expenditures and expanded heavy industry and shipbuilding. Textiles became less dominant because of the rapid growth of metal, engineering, and chemical industries. Now in league with both old and newly formed zaibatsu, the economic policies of the military pulled Japan out of the depression sooner than any other industrial country.

Japanese politicians who voiced dissatisfaction with these policies faced repression and often assassination. The militarists, having succeeded economically, were determined to establish a self-sufficient empire by gaining political control over sources of raw materials as well as the markets of China. In 1937, Japan invaded China and provoked a full-scale war, mobilizing the national economy and society on an emergency basis. Having earlier walked out of the League of Nations, which had censured their

aggression in Manchuria, the Japanese became increasingly isolated and resentful of what they perceived to be international encirclement. When the United States banned exports of strategic materials such as scrap iron, steel, and oil to Japan, the decision for war was taken. Japan would secure economic self-sufficiency by conquest of Southeast Asia and the Pacific. In December 1941, the military party under Premier Tojo gave the signal to carry out a plan for a surprise attack on the American fleet at Pearl Harbor in Hawaii. The attack—intended to immobilize the United States in the Pacific and give

Japan time to consolidate a hold on China and the European colonies in Southeast Asia—was a gamble that failed.

THE HUMAN GEOGRAPHY OF JAPAN

The Japanese archipelago consists of four main islands—Hokkaido, Honshu, Shikoku, and Kyushu—and 3400 lesser islands that arc 800 miles to the south and west along the eastern rim of Asia (Fig. 6.3). The Japanese

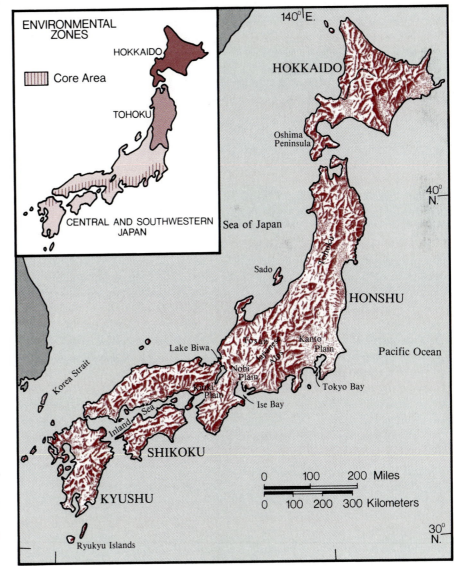

Figure 6.3 Physical features of Japan.

islands are the emerging volcanic peaks of young mountain chains, part of a discontinuous, fragmented string of rugged islands rimming the northwestern Pacific Ocean. **Volcanism** and earthquake activity are commonplace. With a land area smaller than that of California, these islands support 122.7 million people. Because the Japanese have occupied this island home for centuries, differences in race, religion, and culture are relatively minor from one region to another.

The principal distinctions are environmental—mountain versus plain, the cold north versus the subtropical south. Forested highlands dominate the landscape and constitute four fifths of the area of the four main islands. Sixty-five percent of Japan is wooded. Human activity is concentrated on small alluvial plains located along the coast where streams plunge to the sea, and in a few intermontane basins. In these areas, agriculture and industry compete for space. Because less than a quarter of the country is level enough for either activity, the human density per square mile of cultivated land in Japan is extremely high.

Climate is a second important factor in regional differences: if aligned along the eastern coast of the United States, the main Japanese islands would curve from the northern border of Maine southward to Florida. The subtropical south was the nucleus of Japanese civilization, a landscape of terraced rice fields and mulberry and tea plantations. The north, by contrast, has a short growing season and cold winters, and remains an area of frontier settlement even today. Japan extends over nearly 15° of latitude, from 30° N to almost 46° N.

On these bases, the Japanese recognize three generalized regional divisions of their country: *Hokkaido,* the northernmost island of Japan; *Tohoku,* the northern third of the island of Honshu, a transition zone between the southern core and the northern

frontier; and *Central and Southwestern Japan,* the subtropical heartland of Japanese industry, agriculture, and population.

Hokkaido

Hokkaido, the second largest island of the archipelago, differs from all other regions in Japan in its topography and climate, its isolation from the centers of Japanese civilization to the south, and its recent settlement. Hokkaido's volcanic mountains and plateaus contrast sharply with the dramatic peaks and plunging cliffs of Honshu. With a climate like northern New England's, much of the island is forested, and its snowbound winters and acid soils allow only one crop a year.

At the beginning of the Meiji period, when only 58,000 Japanese lived on Hokkaido, most of the island's inhabitants were fisherfolk clustered in small coastal villages on the southern Oshima Peninsula. Hokkaido was primarily occupied by scattered Ainu hunters and fishermen. The Ainu, a Caucasoid people of uncertain origin who probably never numbered more than 30,000, were Japan's original inhabitants.

Modern Japanese colonization was initiated in 1869, when military settlements were established to defend northern outposts from Russian incursions and to extract local fish, lumber, and mineral resources. Later, colonists received subsidies to settle the region, so that in the 1980s, 6 million Japanese live on Hokkaido, which, with an area of 78,000 square miles (a fifth of Japan), is the least densely settled region of the island archipelago. Only the city of Sapporo, with a population of 1.4 million, is a major urban center.

During the military and early colonial periods of settlement, a grid-pattern system of land ownership modeled on the American township and range system was imposed on the landscapes of Hokkaido. Nineteenth-century settlers adopted ag-

ricultural patterns similar to those in northern Europe by cultivating potatoes, oats, and hay on 12.5-acre rectangles. When cold-resistant and early-maturing strains of rice were developed at the turn of the century, this crop was introduced into Hokkaido. The original core of settlement, the relatively fertile, protected Ishikari Valley in western Hokkaido (focused on Sapporo), has been complemented by later settlement on less fertile eastern uplands and, more recently, on land reclaimed from the forested slopes and bamboo brushlands of the eastern coast (Fig. 6.3).

Although rice paddies cover a fifth of the agricultural landscape of Hokkaido today, beans, potatoes, oats, and sugar beets are much more important here than elsewhere in Japan. Animals, especially beef and dairy cattle, play a significant role in this area's agricultural economy. Until a century ago, the Japanese did not kill four-footed animals and had limited experience in animal husbandry or **mixed farming.** Japanese agriculture in this northern frontier region, therefore, reflects a practical cultural adaptation to environmental possibilities.

The nonagricultural and manufacturing economies of Hokkaido are still primarily extractive: fish, lumber, and coal and oil from the Ishikari Valley. Incomes are high and land holdings are four times larger than the national average.

Although Hokkaido drew a heavy stream of migrants after World War II, most Japanese now prefer the amenities of the urban-industrial core in the south to Hokkaido's harsh northern landscapes. With the completion of the 36-mile-long undersea rail tunnel connecting the island of Hokkaido with Honshu, however, travel time between Sapporo and Tokyo was cut by two thirds. The expected increase in demand for fresh vegetables and meat in urban Japan may again attract new farmer-settlers to Hokkaido.

Tohoku

Tohoku, the northern third of the island of Honshu, forms a transition zone between Hokkaido to the north and the subtropical south. A hilly and mountainous area in which level land is scarce, Tohoku is dominated by three highland zones that run north-south through the region (Fig. 6.3). Population is clustered in the intermontane basins between these volcanic and forested uplands. Although moderate by Hokkaido standards, winters in Tohoku are still cold and long. Except in protected inland basins, only one crop a year is grown, even along the east coast where the land is chilled when fog—from the clash of the warm, northward-moving Kuroshio ocean current and the cold, polar Kurile current—drifts inland.

Although settled between the seventh and ninth centuries, Tohoku is still viewed by the Japanese as a backward frontier region. It is less urbanized and more rural than any region in Japan except Hokkaido, and low incomes have led to considerable emigration. With 18 percent of Japan's area, Tohoku has a population of 9.5 million. Average population densities, although higher than on Hokkaido, are only half those of central and southwestern Japan. Mountainous topography, isolation from the coast, lack of raw materials, and absence of deepwater ports have all combined to retard industrial expansion. The region remains a bastion of rural life, with over half the labor force engaged in agriculture and other primary economic activities.

The broken relief of Tohoku is the primary factor influencing the distribution of rural population. The rugged eastern plateau, frequently called the Tibet of Japan because of its isolation, is a granite platform covered by infertile soils where farm yields are low and only the narrow valley floors are used for rice cultivation. The climate is too cold for winter rice, tea, or citrus cultivation, but mulberry trees and sweet potatoes, not found on Hokkaido, can be grown.

In the longitudinal basins that separate the eastern plateau from the more rugged central highlands, however, settlement is dense, and unirrigated terraced fields climb protected slopes. Although farms are small and fragmented, rice occupies two thirds of the cultivated area, and yields are high. Unlike other Japanese farm regions, in Tohoku, sup-

Mount Fuji (elev. 12,388 feet) is the highest peak in the mountain core that dominates Japan's main island of Honshu.

plemental industrial and craft activities play a smaller role in the family economy. The primary nonfarm occupations are the production of charcoal and lumbering in the coniferous forests of the highlands.

This same pattern of populated lowlands and sparsely occupied highlands extends through the western highlands to the west coast of Tohoku. There, the fertile soils of the narrow coastal plain are irrigated by spring meltwater from the snow cover that cloaks the western highlands in winter. Conditions are ideal for rice cultivation, and this area, sometimes called the rice basket of Japan, produces a quarter of the country's grain.

Central and Southwestern Japan

South and west of Tohoku, the traditional heartland of Japanese civilization stretches from central Honshu westward to include the southern islands of Shikoku and Kyushu—a variegated landscape of small farms, tidy villages, terraced rice fields, tea gardens, orange groves, growing cities, and industrial mills.

Over four fifths of Japan's population and most of its economic activity are set within this topographically diverse region. Forested highlands typically flank alluvial plans trapped between mountain and sea (Fig. 6.3). Here, intensive agricultural and industrial complexes vie for level land to support Japan's growing population.

From the volcanic peaks of Tosan in central Honshu, a mountain fist 2-miles-high known as the Japanese Alps, several ranges trend westward along the Inland Sea to form the tree-covered spines of southern Honshu, Shikoku, and Kyushu. The subtropical climate and ample rainfall of this area enable farmers to cultivate year round. Terraced fields climb hilly slopes to much higher elevations than in the colder frontier regions of Tohoku and Hokkaido.

Regional distinctions are more difficult to define in central and southwestern Japan than in the north. Each subregion is a mixture of hills and mountains that ring plains on which urban and industrial centers have developed. Typically, the cities of the plain are surrounded by **paddy** or fields of wet rice, which are, in turn, flanked by terraced fields on more elevated agricultural land. Highland coniferous and **deciduous** forests complete the regional framework.

This pattern is illustrated in the primary core areas of central and south Japan: Tokyo, Nagoya, Osaka, and northern Kyushu. The entire area has been settled by the Japanese for centuries and shares common traditions of land use and settlement. But recent economic growth in Japan has sharpened regional differences, provoking striking contrasts between the industrial, urban landscapes of the Core Area and the subregions of the northern and southern Periphery, which is composed of the less developed parts of Honshu, Shikoku, and Kyushu.

The Core Area

The Core Area of Japan is a latitudinal belt of disconnected lowland plains stretching 600 miles from the Kanto Plain in the east along the shores of the Inland Sea to northern Kyushu in the west. The Core Area is the setting for the Japanese megalopolis, a vast ribbon of cities, conurbations, and industrial complexes (Fig. 6.5). The Kanto Plain of Tokyo is Japan's largest patch of lowland, a 2500-square-mile plain blanketed by the country's fastest growing industrial complex, the Tokyo–Yokohama conurbation as well as a substantial agricultural expanse on which a tenth of this region's 36 million people cultivate rice, mulberry groves, and truck garden crops. Dairy farming is also important. The eastern side of the Kanto Plain is isolated from Tokyo by the marshes of the lower Tone River. Surrounding uplands are little used because of a scarcity of irriga-

tion water, and much land remains in its natural state of bamboo brush.

Tokyo, the world's second largest city (pop. 8.3 million), is also the heart of greater Tokyo and Japan's primate city. Yokohama (pop. 2.8 million), the second city in this vast conurbation, is Tokyo's traditional seaport. Tokyo has been destroyed twice in the twentieth century: once by earthquake and fire in 1923, again by U.S. bombing in 1944–1945. Reconstructed since 1945, one third of the Japanese population lives within 100 miles of the Emperor's Palace in central Tokyo. Density and overcrowding in Tokyo are unmatched anywhere else in the Technological World. Tokyo land prices, housing costs, and office space costs are a mirror to the packed nature of Tokyo's geography and the growth of the city's importance in global finance and trade. Eight of the world's top ten banks are today headquartered in Tokyo. The world's largest stocks and bonds firm is a Tokyo firm. The city has more than 150 institutions of higher learning. Clearly, in many strategic ways in the sphere of trade and investment, the world has come to Tokyo.

West of the Kanto Plain, the narrow Tokaido corridor connects a series of small, isolated deltas running along the Pacific coast to link Tokyo with Japan's second largest plain, the Nobi Plain of Nagoya. Along the Tokaido corridor, mild subtropical climate and plentiful rainfall have made the area a center for the production of tea and mandarin oranges, whose groves cover south-facing slopes.

On the Nobi Plain, the Chukyo industrial complex is centered around the city of Nagoya, which, with a population of more than 2 million, is surrounded by poldered rice fields with vegetables and other grains grown on nearby hillsides. Farther west, the Tokaido corridor reaches the Keihanshin industrial node, located in the ancient center of Japanese civilization at the head of the Inland Sea. Keihanshin includes the

farther east. Throughout the Core Area from the Kanto Plain to Kyushu, population is extremely dense. Mills, houses, and cultivated land are tightly packed; human occupance is intense. Blighted by smog and air pollution, this area is the vital heart of Japanese life today.

The Perihery

The Periphery of central and southwestern Japan flanks the Core Area to its north and south and includes the west coast and central highlands of the island of southern Honshu and the less industrialized southern halves of the islands of Shikoku and Kyushu (Fig. 6.3).

Westernmost Honshu, an area of low, forested ranges with poor soils on the coastal area facing the Sea of Japan, is thinly populated. Called "the shady side," its raw winter climate, dearth of level land, and isolation from urban centers have retarded industrial and agricultural development. Farther northeast along the coast of the Sea of Japan, farming is somewhat more intensive. Scattered lowlands are the focus of settlement, and a variety of fruit and vegetable crops are grown as well as rice. Some important industry has developed on this narrow coast where riverine plains provide level space for settlement in a largely mountainous region.

Inland, the rugged mountain complex of Tosan, the roof of Japan, forms the topographic core of Honshu and separates the rich, well-settled plains of the Pacific coast to the east from the cold, sparsely occupied western regions on the Sea of Japan. Here, in several separated basins, light industry, diversified agriculture, and tourism have become important in traditional silk-production centers.

The two remaining areas of the Periphery, southern Kyushu and southern Shikoku, have been isolated from the mainstrem of Japanese economic and industrial development. In southern Kyushu, folded block mountains and volcanoes limit communications with the Core Area. The

Craggy, indented coasts line the Japanese islands. Shinto shrines where fisherfolk pray for safety are marked by the traditional *torii*, or gateway.

cities of Osaka (pop. 2.6 million), Kyoto (pop. 1.5 million), and Kobe (pop. 1.4 million). It is the second largest industrial concentration in the nation. Lowland rice fields and terraced gardens ringed by largely deforested uplands complete the landscape (Fig. 6.5).

This industrial-urban complex continues in the form of a number of smaller urban centers scattered on both the Honshu and Shikoku shores of the Inland Sea. The Inland Sea unites this region. Communications between centers on southern Honshu and northern Shikoku have historically been easier by water than overland. The Core Area ends in the Kanmon node of northern Kyushu, at Kitakyushu, where coal mines supported the growth of heavy industry in the Meiji period. Kitakyushu, an amalgam of five older cities, is the largest urban center here (pop. 1 million).

This area has now been eclipsed by the trade-oriented port complexes of Tokyo, Nagoya, and Osaka–Kobe

region lacks level land or ports, and its forested highlands are occupied by subsistence farmers and people practicing shifting cultivation. Similarly, southern Shikoku is a backward, sparsely populated mountain region, although its warm climate makes double cropping possible wherever water is available and alluvial soils are found.

Altogether, Japan has great environmental diversity, set over 15 degrees of latitude and many degrees of development. Forest temples and Nissan-choked freeways coexist in modern Japan. So do the traditional land of the peasant and the urban landscape of the factory worker. The serene harmony of the being in nature, so aptly depicted in Japanese art and literature, stands in stark contrast with the increasing density of industry and urban populations in this technological nation.

Intensive cultivation and terraced slopes are hallmarks of Japanese agriculture.

MODERN JAPAN: THE GEOGRAPHY OF ECONOMIC GROWTH AND SOCIAL CHANGE

At the end of World War II, Japan lay in ruins, its population exhausted. Two thirds of Tokyo and Osaka had been burned to the ground. One of every four houses in Japan had been destroyed. Hiroshima and Nagasaki were atomic wastelands. Industry, shipping, transportation networks, and power plants were devastated, and the territorial empire had vanished. Hundreds of thousands of soldiers and administrators from previously Japanese-controlled territories were repatriated. The Japanese were again limited to the four islands of their homeland—the same area they held at the time of Commodore Perry's visit a century before.

Yet in four decades, Japan built a new and sophisticated economy and

became one of the wealthiest members of the Technological World. In large part, Japan's economic success was due to *The Rise of the Industrial State*. Lacking adequate sources of raw materials in their homeland, Japan's heavy industry was located on coastal lowlands and based on imports from abroad. As industry expanded in these areas, Japanese villagers migrated to *Urban Japan* for jobs, education, and social amenities. In the countryside, farm population fell but *Agriculture in a Modern Economy* remained relatively prosperous because of government rice subsidies and newly available part-time jobs in construction and industry.

The concentration of people and economic activity in Japan's Core Area, however, has led to *Problems of a Technological Society*. Economic change has spurred social change that is undermining the values that were vital to Japanese economic growth. Plagued by congestion and constrained by topography, economic well-being has spawned high levels of environmental pollution and basic questions concerning the quality of life. In Japan, these

problems are of deep concern and will influence the future human geography of these islands.

The Rise of the Industrial State

In the years after World War II, Japan experienced a phenomenal rate of economic growth. This transformed Japan's premodern manufacturing society into an industrial state of the first order. Overall, the Japanese economy expanded faster than that of any other country. It grew at a rate of 10 percent per year—double the average world rate. Manufacturing shifted from labor-intensive industries, such as textiles, to heavy industrial goods, and then to advanced technology. Japanese exports expanded twice as fast as average world rates, to the point where its merchant marine now ranks among the largest in the world. Under the postwar motto, "rich nation, strong enterprise," economic growth was pursued with single-minded skill and determination.

Japan's extraordinary postwar rate of economic growth was based on a rapid expansion of industry and manufacturing. Large-scale steel complexes were constructed at coastal locations to receive giant carriers of imported iron ore, coal, and oil. By the mid-1980s, Japan was producing 100 million tons of finished steel and 70 million tons of pig iron a year—second only to the Soviet Union. Metal, chemical, and engineering industries today employ over half of the Japanese work force. Japanese production of heavy industrial machinery, such as ships and automobiles, as well as specialized scientific apparatus, such as cameras, binoculars, and electronic goods, now forms a substantial percentage of the world's total. The unbroken drive to export led Japan's value of exports to reach $209 billion in the late 1980s, third in the world after West Germany and the United States.

The Resource Base

Unlike most industrial nations, Japan has a sharply limited natural resource base. Japan does not possess the domestic sources of energy and minerals needed to sustain industrial growth. As a result, Japan must compete in the world markets for basic raw materials.

To accomplish this Japan is striving to establish a network of economic and political relationships with resource-exporting countries. Today, Japan is more than 90 percent dependent on overseas suppliers for eleven key raw materials (Table 6.1). The Japanese economy is extremely vulnerable to disruptions in international trade.

Until 1955, coal filled half of Japan's energy needs. It was the primary source of power in the country. Japanese energy consumption, which rose 10 percent a year until the quadrupling of oil prices in 1973, quickly outpaced declining producing in the coal fields of northern Kyushu and Hokkaido (Fig. 6.4). Petroleum supplies two thirds of Japan's total energy today, and less than 1 percent of the country's oil and natural gas is

TABLE 6.1 COMPARATIVE DEPENDENCE ON RAW MATERIAL IMPORTS

Raw Material Imports	Japan	United States	Great Britain
Coal	79.2%	0%	1.6%
Oil	99.8	42.3	18.9
Natural gas	88.7	5.8	19.5
Iron ore	98.6	29.7	80.7
Wood	69.2	3.8	72.9
Cotton	100.0	0	100.0
Wheat	93.0	0	25.4

produced locally. Most is imported from Saudi Arabia and Indonesia, although minor oil fields are found along the west coast of Japan from central Honshu northward to Hokkaido. In an effort to reduce overseas dependence, Japan has engaged in joint development with the Soviet Union of gas fields off the coast of Sakhalin Island and coal fields in Siberia. Japan is also negotiating with China for potential oil reserves near the Senkaku Islands north of Taiwan.

Additional sources of energy in Japan include some 1500 hydroelectric plants scattered throughout the

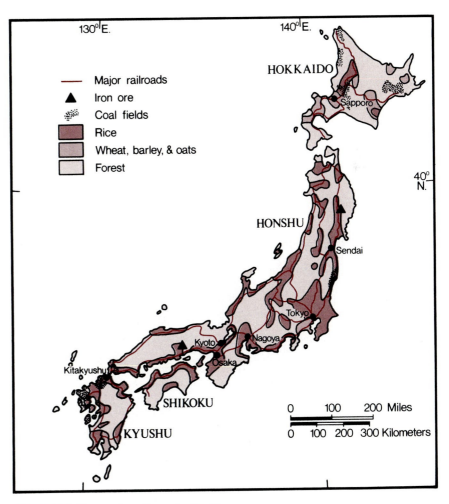

Figure 6.4 Economic patterns in Japan.

country, most of them of limited capacity; 400 thermal electric plants powered by coal or oil; and 44 nuclear power stations operating or planned by 1990. The latter, fueled by uranium imported from the United States, are seen as a major future source of energy in Japan. Japan's long-term dependence on foreign imports for 87 percent of the country's energy needs, however, seems likely to continue. National energy conservation policies—such as charging big electrical consumers higher rates—have had a positive effect in rendering Japanese industry more efficient and containing energy consumption.

Minerals and metals in Japan are equally limited. Japan imports 99 percent of the iron ore and 80 per-

cent of the coal used in heavy industry. Because mining the deep, thin coal seams of Japan is so dangerous, plans are to phase out all domestic production by the year 2000.

The backbone of Japan's economic growth—the iron and steel industry—relies on imports from Australia, the United States, India, Peru, and Chile. Virtually the entire supply of vital minerals, such as nickel, cobalt, copper, and aluminum, must be purchased abroad. Such mines as do exist in the archipelago are widely scattered, small, family operations. The Japanese are thus led to seek mineral concessions and purchasing agreements throughout the world. As with energy, Japan will pay high prices for the raw materials needed to sustain future economic growth. With

an annual trade surplus that averaged $90 billion in the late 1980s, however, Japan can pay the price.

Industrial Location

Partly because of the need to trade, but also for topographical and historical reasons, Japan's large-scale industry is densely concentrated along a narrow coastal band extending westward from Tokyo for some 600 miles to northern Kyushu (Fig. 6.5). More than three quarters of Japan's industrial production and four fifths of the total industrial labor force are located in the Core Area of Japan.

Four major industrial complexes can be identified: Kanto on Tokyo Bay, Chukyo on Ise Bay, Keihanshin on Osaka Bay at the head of the Inland Sea, and the Kanmon complex

This factory at the port of Nagoya smelts imported scrap iron to produce steel. The Buddhist shrine in the background reflects the intense competition for level land in this island nation, as well as its unique blend of tradition and modernity.

in northern Kyushu (Fig. 6.5). The first three of these industrial areas are located on bays rimmed by densely populated plains where large rivers enter sheltered harbors—excellent locations for concentrations of labor, water, and access to trade. The fourth center, northern Kyushu, developed as an early industrial region because of nearby coal mines.

These four industrial complexes produce 85 to 90 percent of Japan's iron and steel, two thirds of all engineering and textile products, and one half of all chemicals. With port facilities capable of handling fuel, ore, and raw fiber imports and with a readily available labor force, level land adjacent to protected harbors is at a premium in a country that is 80 percent mountainous. The industrial core of Japan continue to grow in size and complexity despite high levels of congestion. Land values are so high that coastal reclamation is profitable. Housing shortages, transport problems, and pollution are intense.

The Kanto complex consisting of the cities of Tokyo and Yokohama, forms a conurbation of 34 million people responsible for more than a third of Japan's industrial production. Chemicals, light industry, iron, steel, and electronics are most important. The Keihanshin node on the Inland Sea, the country's oldest commercial and industrial complex, includes the ancient inland imperial capital of Kyoto, the banking center of Osaka and Japan's largest port, Kobe. Keihanshin produces one fifth of Japan's manufactures. Heavy engineering and shipbuilding are the primary industries here. The Chukyo industrial complex, located between Kanto and the Inland Sea is centered on Nagoya. Somewhat less than a fifth of Japan's industry, primarily automobiles and textiles, is produced in Chukyo. Kanmon, focused on Kitakyushu in northern Kyushu, a center of older heavy industry, is now attracting high technology industries because of its mild

climate, relatively inexpensive land, and government efforts to decentralize industry.

Although the landscape, location, and structure of Japanese industry has assumed many of the general structural characteristics of other industrial countries in the Technological World, the social organization of manufacturing remains distinctively Japanese. Old samurai firms, such as Mitsui and Mitsubishi, manage two thirds of Japan's trade. Relative newcomers, such as Honda, Toyota, and Matsushita, have joined the national economic fabric. These modern conglomerates retain a traditional respect for loyalty, obedience, and mutual obligation, which results in industrial stability. Strikes are rare, job security is high (30 percent of the work force is hired for life), and increased industrial productivity is a consuming value. Alongside the large industrial conglomerates, a significant share of Japan's workforce is in hugely inefficient small family firms and retail sales, which use simple techniques and pay low wages. In industry, the Ministry of International Trade and Industry (MITI) masterminded Japan's emergence as a global producer of heavy industry in the postwar period. It is now propelling the country to a position of leadership in high technology.

The Shift to High Technology

A unique relationship between government and private enterprise in Japan has enabled the country to pursue coherent, long-term economic policies that anticipate the future rather than preserve the past. Traditionally, Japan's major industrial enterprises have centered on the import of raw materials and the export of high-value manufactured goods. As world economic conditions have changed and the cost of raw materials has risen, Japan has repeatedly scrapped older, less competitive industries and promoted investment in more technology-intensive products.

The degree of economic collaboration between government and private industry is not found elsewhere in the industrial world.

As early as the 1950s, Japan recognized that the textile industry in older industrial economies was no longer competitive with the lower labor costs of comparable textile products from the Developing World. Japanese firms producing cotton, rayon, and synthetic fibers were encouraged to switch to different products. In effect, Japan exported and financed this labor-intensive industry to the neighboring East Asian states of South Korea and Taiwan (Fig. 6.6).

Similarly in 1958, Japan decided to close its declining coal industry in Kyushu and to base future industrial expansion on imported petroleum. The MITI discouraged excessive energy consumption by letting domestic oil prices rise with world market prices. For this reason, the Japanese industrial base was able to survive the 1400 percent rise in oil prices better than other energy-importing industrial countries despite its total reliance on imported petroleum.

The oil crises of 1973 and 1979, however, provoked profound reorganizations in Japanese industry. Japan chose not to protect older, energy-intensive industries. They moved out of open-hearth steel production, aluminum smelting, and petrochemical-based manufacture of plastics, fertilizer, and fibers. Over 40 percent of the nation's shipbuilding capacity was abandoned. Instead, Japan invested in computers, electronics, and more productive and energy-efficient steel facilities (Fig. 6.6). Japan emerged from the energy crisis as the world's most efficient producer of steel and the leading manufacturer of automobiles, television sets, and consumer electronics. This policy of creative destruction of noncompetitive industries is a primary factor in the resilience and strength of the Japanese industrial economy.

GEOLAB

MEGALOPOLIS: A COALESCING OF CITIES

In the 1950s, the geographer Jean Gottmann developed the concept of megalopolis, a system of cities merging to form a nearly continuous urban and industrial belt. He used this concept to describe urban patterns on the northeastern seaboard of the United States between Boston and Washington.

In a megalopolis, large cities retain their character, but population growth and urban sprawl cause them to fuse, or coalesce. In the American northeast, population growth was favored in port cities, like Boston, New York, and Baltimore, which were landing points for millions of European immigrants in the nineteenth century. With new forms of transportation and advanced methods of communication, decentralization allowed for further growth in

the twentieth century. Instead of dense, compact, discrete urban centers, a vast polynucleated metropolitan area came to stretch hundreds of miles. Urban sprawl caused one city to blend with the next. Today, megalopolises are found in the United States, Europe, and Japan.

In Japan, a megalopolis stretches 600 miles from Tokyo along the Pacific coast to northern Kyushu (Fig. 6.5). This urban zone, called the To-

More than half the total population of Japan is clustered in the "Pacific Belt," or "Tokaido Megalopolis." The largest of these—Tokyo—spreads out over the Kanto Plain.

Japan today has shifted its industrial focus toward new industrial frontiers of high technology in such fields as advanced computers, robotics, semiconductors (the building blocks of computers), telecommunications, and genetic engineering (Fig. 6.7). Japanese industrialists, guided by MITI, have been encouraged to

create new products on which to build a technology-based economy within a decade. Miniaturization, automation, robotics, and the drive for higher productivity are moving the Japanese work force from assembly lines into service jobs.

Japan now is a primary exporter of semiconductors and memory chips.

The unquestioned lead in microprocessors once enjoyed by the United States is eroding. In biological engineering, Japan ranks as a world producer of antibiotics through fermentation and has moved into genetic engineering. Most Japanese gains have been achieved through new applications of existing research and

kaido Megalopolis, is connected by express rail and road connections and contains the bulk of Japan's people, industrial activity, and wealth. It is coincident with the Japanese Core Area. Like cities in the American northeast, the largest cities—Tokyo, Nagoya, Osaka, and Kobe—are important ports as well as cores of major industrial complexes.

Some geographers see the megalopolis as the principal human environment of the future despite problems of congestion, high land prices, air pollution, and energy and water supplies. Others believe that the megalopolis is an undesirable habitat that will decline as advanced technology enables still further geographic decentralization. Whichever proves to be the case, urban centers are still expanding and multiplying throughout the world despite the problems generated by such large-scale concentrations of people.

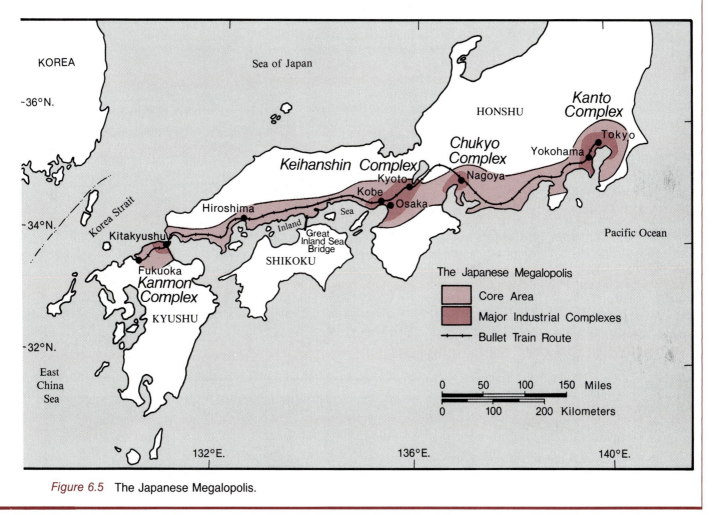

Figure 6.5 The Japanese Megalopolis.

developments borrowed or bought from other nations.

The movement of Japanese industry into high technology is resulting in the diffusion of Japanese manufacturing out of the densely settled, land-poor, congested plains into rural Japan. Encouraged by government investment in the regional economic development of depressed areas, high-technology industry has been attracted to rural Japan by pollution-free water, essential in the manufacture of computer elements; by less expensive land and labor; and by the more attractive quality of life outside the Japanese industrial core. Mountainous Tohoku produces a fifth of the nation's integrated electronic circuitry. The highland valleys of central Honshu, a major fruit-growing area, rank among the largest manufacturers of video cassette recorder components in Japan. To the south, the old steel center of Kyushu is now called "Silicon Island" because it produces 40 percent of Japan's semiconductors (silicon is the primary raw material used in their manufacture).

The government plans to build nineteen medium-size "science cities" throughout the country. Although 80 percent of Japan's engineers and researchers work in metropolitan centers, the Japanese countryside has a growing stake in the nation's high-technology export economy.

Urban Japan

The very rapid growth of the Japanese industrial economy has reordered the distribution of population in Japan (Fig. 6.8). Labor, drawn from farming communities in rural Japan, has moved to the sprawling cities of the flat, coastal plains. Long tied to their fields, Japanese farmers resisted urbanization for some time. Full-time farmers, 20 million strong, composed one fifth of the Japanese population as late as 1965—an extraordinarily high proportion for an industrial power. But by 1988, only 6 million Japanese were full-time farmers—less than 5 percent of the population (Fig. 6.9). Urban opportunities consistently attract Japanese youth to urban life; three of every four Japanese live in cities today. After a century during which the Japanese population quadrupled from 30 to over 120 million, all the added people are urbanities.

The factors that have infuenced the growth and distribution of cities in Japan are directly tied to patterns of economic development. But topography continues to control urban location and economic development today as it has in the past. Japanese cities are primarily confined to the coastal plains, particularly in the Core Area along the Pacific coast (Fig. 6.8). Few are found in mountain basins—city size and location are directly related to availability of level land. Four fifths of all cities are located on the one fifth of Japan that is relatively flat, and no city larger than 100,000 is located in the mountains.

JAPANESE INDUSTRIAL MATURITY: THE SHIFT TO HIGH TECHNOLOGY

The Japanese export economy has undergone three major shifts in the last three decades (Fig. 6.6). During the 1960s, Japan moved out of textiles because of lower labor costs in developing countries. In the 1970s, steel, television sets, and electronics became important industries. After modernizing their steel plants in the wake of the oil shortages of 1973 and 1979, Japan has become the world's leading exporter of automobiles.

Experts at miniaturization, assembly-line production, and refinements of existing technology, the Japanese are responsible for nearly a third of all new foreign patents filed in the United States (Fig. 6.7). A dramatic shift of the industrial base to high-technology products has occurred in an effort to build Japan into a technology-based nation. The key to their success is related to new scientific breakthroughs based on technological creativity and the ability to control and direct global financial markets.

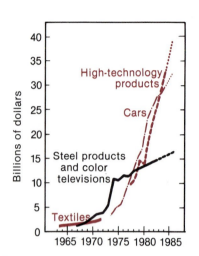

Figure 6.6 The Changing pattern of Japanese exports.

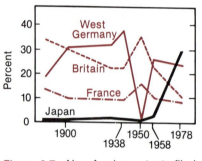

Figure 6.7 New foreign patents filed in the United States.

A Toshiba factory worker at Kawasaki near Tokyo specializes in mounting transistors into television units. Japan is now shifting its industrial frontier toward high technology.

The largest cities, the traditional "Big Six," all with populations of 1 million or more, are located on the fertile alluvial plains that line the core zone of south-central Japan (Fig. 6.8). Tokyo and Yokohama in the Kanto complex holds more than a quarter of the country's total population. Farther west, Nagoya in the Chukyo complex, is separated by high mountains from the cities of Osaka, Kobe, and Kyoto in the Keihanshan complex at the head of the Inland Sea. These three cities (about 1.5 million each) have spread inland toward the traditional heartland of Japanese civilization. To the Big Six one might add Hiroshima along the southern shores of Honshu and, at the far end of the Core Area, Kitakyushu and Fukuoka in the Kanmon complex on Kyushu.

With the exception of Kyoto, the cultural and religious center of Japan, all of these large urban centers extend to the sea, are equipped with port facilities, and have densely settled agricultural hinterlands. These and most other large cities in Japan, including thirty-four of the forty-six prefectural capitals, are former castle towns. This indicates the persistent attraction of fertile soil and mild climate in the Core Area of Japan to both the seventeenth-century daimyo and the modern corporation.

Japanese urban geographers today call the zone of urban and industrial activity between Tokyo and Kyoto the Tokaido Megalopolis, whose name is derived from an earlier post road, the "avenue along the eastern sea" (Fig. 6.5). Along this route, the palanquins of Tokugawa nobility, the rickshaws of Meiji, and now modern rail and highway systems link the premier industrial center of Tokyo with the imperial city of Kyoto and industrial ports on the Inland Sea.

More than 75 million people, well over half of the total population of Japan, are clustered in these ancient agricultural regions that together make up a small percentage of Japan's land area. This extraordinary

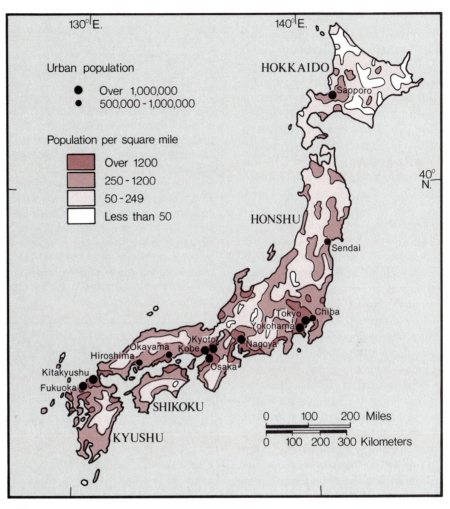

Figure 6.8 Population of Japan.

concentration of people, industry, commerce, and agriculture has generated fierce competition for space. Problems of congestion are considerably more intense than, for example, those of the eastern seaboard of the United States. Linked by highway and high-speed railroads, Japan's Core Area continues to grow despite government efforts at industrial dispersal and balanced regional development.

Agriculture in a Modern Economy

The dramatic modernization of the urban and industrial landscapes of the Core Area of modern Japan long had little resonance in rural areas of the island archipelago. Described as a country "where the stones show hu-

man fingerprints; where the pressure of men on the land has worn through to iron rock," the Japanese agricultural landscape remains a patchwork of intensively tended lowland rice fields and staggered upland terraces.

Rice, the primary crop, is grown on more than half the agricultural land. Other crops, such as wheat, barley, soybeans, and fruit, are planted as winter crops and wherever rice cultivation is not practical. Plots of land are tiny; eight of every ten Japanese farms are less than 2.5 acres (one hectare). Yields, however, are among the highest in the world and continue to rise because Japanese farmers lavish time, energy, and fertilizer on their small plots.

With two thirds of Japan in forested upland and only 16 percent in cultivation, intensive agriculture has overcome topographic limitations through sheer labor. Population density in the coastal plains and narrow upland valleys of agricultural Japan is greater than 4000 people per square mile, triple that of the Netherlands. Tokyo alone boasts 125,000 farmers, but like most Japanese farm families—75 percent—they are predominantly part-time farmers. The total agricultural acreage of Japan remains steady at 14 million acres, with newly reclaimed land on the coast and in marginal environments, like Hokkaido, counterbalanced by losses of agricultural land to urbanization.

Overall, then, the distribution and complexion of agriculture—crops grown, high yields, and patterns of intensive cultivation—have changed little when compared with the postwar flood of technology and capital that washed over urban Japan.

The social structure of agriculture, however, has undergone a fundamental reordering. Believing the poverty and misery of Japanese peasants a primary cause of World War II, American occupation forces implemented a land reform program after the war. This essentially eliminated landlords by confiscating agricultural land and redistributing it to **tenant farmers**. A total of 4.8 million acres of land was purchased by the government and sold to owner-cultivators at low rates of repayment. More than 27 million separate tracts—one third of Japan's agricultural land—changed hands. The number of tenant farmers fell from 46 to 8 percent of the agricultural work force. In a single stroke, rural Japan was converted into a nation of peasant landowners.

Considerable areas of paddy rice were reorganized into larger, more rectangular plots. Initially resented by peasants, deeply attached to the small bits of land they had acquired over the years, consolidation of fields made rice farming more susceptible to appropriate mechanization. By 1980, small garden tractors, tillers, planters, and harvesters were used

THE DECLINE OF JAPANESE AGRICULTURE

Over the last two decades, the number of farm households has steadily decreased in Japan (Fig. 6.9). Today, only 4.3 million families earn their living as agriculturalists. The decline has been greatest in peripheral areas along the coasts of Shikoku, Kyushu, and southern Honshu. The dramatic abandonment of farming in Hokkaido can be attributed to the rapid breakup of pioneer settlements initiated after the Meiji restoration in the late nineteenth century and the return of resettled World War II veterans and refugees to their rebuilt homes. The stability of farming in Tohoku in northern Honshu reflects the persistence of rural life in mountain villages that have retained their social cohesion. Areas within commuting distance of the industrial cores of Japan reflect the gradual penetration of urban and suburban populations into agricultural areas.

Adapted from: Motosuke Ishii, "Regional Trends in the Changing Agrarian Structure of Postwar Japan," in *Geography of Japan*, pp. 199–222. Tokyo: Association of Japanese Geographers, 1980. (Special Publication No. 4.); map, p. 219.

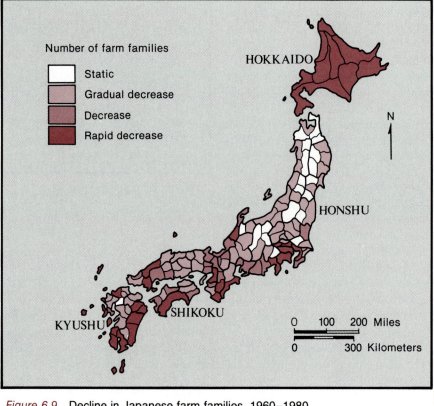

Figure 6.9 Decline in Japanese farm families, 1960–1980.

in nearly every Japanese rice field. This, combined with better drainage and irrigation, increased rice yields. Mechanization, fertilizers, better grade seeds, and hefty government subsidies have created a substantial rice surplus in Japan.

During this period, farm incomes rose. The standard of living gap that traditionally existed between the urban industrial populations and countryfolk was closed. Now, almost every Japanese farmer has a television set, refrigerator, and washing machine.

This standard of living is made possible by two factors. First, agricultural production is subsidized by the government, which guarantees farmers a minimum rice price six to eight times world market prices. Artificially high rice prices alone amount to an estimated 4 percent of Japanese personal consumption costs. The government also limits foreign imports of agricultural products, particularly rice, wheat, and sugar, although Japan still imports roughly half its food needs. Japan is the United States' biggest reliable farm export market. Political pressure is strong in international arenas to lower the rice price and open Japan to food imports from Korea, Taiwan, China, the EC, and North America.

The second factor that increases farm incomes is the commercial penetration of the countryside by industrial firms in search of cheap labor, land, and more amenable living environments. By 1988, 95 percent of all Japanese men living on farms worked part time in the manufacturing or tertiary sector of the economy. Better than half the income of Japanese farm families comes from non-agricultural activities. Fields tended primarily by women and on weekends by men signal a special transformation of the close-knit family and village structure, which conservative Japanese politicians consider essential to the preservation of Japanese culture and values.

Traditionally, the ideal Japanese family had three children: "one to sell (a daughter), one to follow (the first son), and one in reserve (a second son)." Families in each village were related by marriage and by the cooperative labor required to maintain complicated irrigation and drainage systems. Village harmony was a duty and a necessity. The hallmark of the entire system was order and continuity.

The commercialization of the countryside, population growth, and modern education have disrupted these traditions. During the 1950s, a stream of excess labor from rural Japan swept into industrial Japan, driven by population pressure on cultivated land and attracted by the amenities, jobs, and individuality of urban life. This migration continues. Each year agriculturalists form a declining percentage of the labor force; there are now only 4.3 million farm families left in Japan (Fig. 6.9). Family fields are tilled by women and old people, who constitute two thirds of the farm population. The over-65 age group is the only one in which the number of full-time farmers is increasing. The declining importance of village life in Japan and the weakening of those values of obedience, loyalty, and personal sacrifice that it embodied are now mourned by traditionalists.

Problems of a Technological Society

It was the resilience of strong traditional values that enabled Japan, defeated in war, to emerge as a world economic power in the last four decades. Economic growth became Japan's top national priority. The disciplined Japanese began to pursue increases in GNP as a matter of national honor. The condition of the country was perceived and measured in terms of manufacturing productivity. The goals of surpassing the West and achieving world respect remained the same, but the means to that end changed.

The benefits of economic growth penetrated all levels of Japanese society. Life expectancy is seventy-five years for men, eighty-one for women. Standards of living and Japanese incomes are among the highest in the world. The literacy rate approaches 100 percent. The material trappings of the technological world—television sets, VCR's, automobiles, home computers—have become ubiquitous.

These gains in comfort and convenience were achieved by the devotion of the Japanese to economic expansion. The sacrifices required to fulfill this single-minded Japanese drive for economic preeminence are now presenting the island nation with new challenges—problems of social change, environmental pollution, and quality of life.

Social Change

The Japanese industrial system succeeded by harnessing traditional values to high-volume production of manufactured goods. Discipline, self-sacrifice, obedience, respect for elders, and a sense of community powered industrial growth. These values were well suited to highly efficient assembly-line production. Dedication overcame shortages of raw materials; national commitment to economic growth linked duty and personal achievement to the creation of wealth. Productivity is still increasing in certain sectors of the Japanese economy, but changes generated by affluence are altering the values and social structure that enabled a resource-poor chain of islands to become a global economic power.

Social changes are beginning to alter three industrial practices that contributed significantly to Japan's success in manufacturing—lifetime employment, salaries based on seniority, and company unions. In declining industries, lifetime employment has created a "tribe by the window"—employees with little to do but gaze out of windows in a nation where high productivity is essential. In high-growth industries, automation is gradually decreasing the total number of manufacturing jobs in Japan at a time when women are aggressively moving into the workplace. Young middle-management Japanese executives, unwilling to abide by the seniority system of Japanese industry, have left their guaranteed jobs to create independent companies, an event unheard of in the past. Finally, company unions are beginning to demand more. Strikes, work slowdowns, and union activity are increasing annually.

Exacerbating these employment

POPULATION PYRAMIDS: THE GRAYING OF THE JAPANESE POPULATION

The three **population pyramids** shown here indicate the age and sex of the Japanese population in 1955, 1980, and 2015 (projected). The length of each bar represents the percent of the total Japanese population in each five-year age group. The vertical center line divides the percentage of males (left) and females (right).

During this sixty-year span, the shape of the population pyramid changes from a broad-based triangle in which a majority of the Japanese are young to a beehive-shaped block in which older people make up an increasing percentage of the total population (Fig. 6.10). Three factors account for this change: (1) the postwar baby boom, (2) a subsequent sudden drop in the birth rates in the early 1950s, and (3) the extension of average life expectancy with improved health care in Japan.

The implications of this graying of the Japanese population are substantial. Fewer workers will be supporting an expanding number of retired people, leading to higher taxes and welfare costs and a slower rate of economic growth. It is already forcing Japanese industry to reexamine employment policies, a key factor in Japan's rapid economic expansion. The relationship of demographic patterns to social and economic change is inescapable.

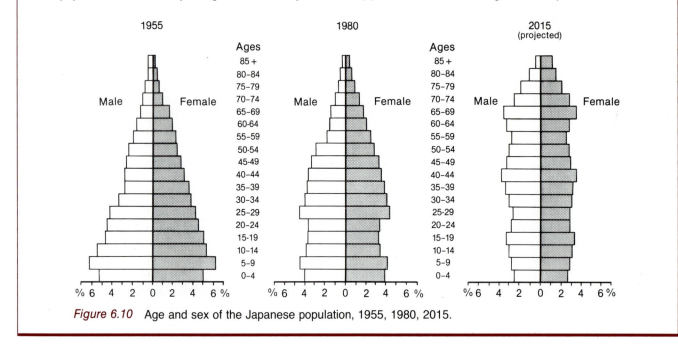

Figure 6.10 Age and sex of the Japanese population, 1955, 1980, 2015.

trends in Japanese industry are the predictable economic consequences of the rapid aging or graying, of the nation's population (Fig. 6.10). Currently, Japan has a relatively young population and welfare payments to retired people are minimal. In 1988, Japan had six employed workers for each retired person as compared with a ratio of three to one in the United States and Western Europe.

But since World War II, the lifespan of the average Japanese has increased by twenty years. In most large corporations, the retirement age is now fifty-five, with both men and women living well into their seventies. Social security is paid at age sixty.

In the next two decades, Japan's population will assume the characteristics of other industrial nations, and older people will account for a substantially higher percentage of the population (Fig. 6.10). This will increase the cost of social welfare and taxes, thereby reducing the investment capital available for industrial growth in Japan.

The shift to high technology to maintain Japan's level of economic growth implies still further social change. Japan's postwar economic success was achieved through importing technology developed in the industrial West. In the last thirty years, 30,000 licensing agreements gave Japan access to research developed principally in the United States. Currently, Japan exports more expensive and sophisticated products by making incremental innovations on known technology and transforming scientific knowledge into marketable products.

Now Japan faces a new challenge in high technology because it can no longer depend on other nations to provide scientific breakthroughs. Research and development expenses have risen sharply in Japan, and the number of engineers trained in the last decade have tripled each year. There is now widespread recognition that more basic research is needed

Air pollution is common in Japan's large cities. People wear masks for breathing.

in Japan, that creativity will be the key to future economic success (Fig. 6.7). Indeed, the government has created an entire "science city" at Tsukuba, 30 miles north of Tokyo. Japanese culture is build on community and consensus, not on individual initiative, so that research and development is often undertaken as a group effort.

Environmental Pollution

Environmental pollution is intense in Japan. With meager energy resources and little level land, Japanese industry is concentrated in large coastal towns, which earlier were the administrative and marketing centers of feudal agricultural regions.

Practical reasons dictated this concentration. On the coast, a skilled labor force was available. Here, new areas of flat land large enough for modern industrial complexes could be reclaimed from the sea. Moreover, coastal industrial complexes have access to ocean trade routes to import raw materials and export manufactured goods and are closely linked with one another by sea transport. Japan's industrial base is thus geographically sited on small, flat coastal plains. In these regions, the level of industrial concentration and economic activity per square mile is extremely high. So is the resultant level of environmental pollution.

The consequence of this concentration, in terms of noise, air, and water pollution, has been acute. Official complaints about pollution began to increase in the late 1960s, tripling from over 20,000 per year in the early 1970s to 70,000 per year now. In this same period, the number of prefectures defined as "free of environmental disruption" dropped considerably. Isolated environmental incidents in urban-industrial centers began to spread, forcing the government to recognize pollution as a national problem.

By 1970, air pollution had created smog domes in the atmosphere above every large city in Japan. Incidents of **photochemical smog** and heavy-metal poisoning increased; oxygen was sold from tanks on the streets of Tokyo. Dust and soot levels in the atmosphere diminished with the shift from coal to petroleum, but sulfur dioxide, carbon monoxide, and other petroleum-based residues rose steadily. In the 1970s, industrial production on the Kanto Plain doubled in value. Sulfur pollutants also doubled because of heavy reliance on Middle Eastern oil, which has a high sulfur content. The growing use of personal automobiles, which now number 33 million in Japan, also contributed to pollution.

Water pollution in the Inland Sea and coastal bays of Japan, where high densities of shipping and industry are found, has been equally intense. During the late 1960s, Tokyo Bay was branded the most polluted water body in Japan, and fishing and bathing were banned. At this same time, residents who ate fish caught in Minamata Bay in western Kyushu were struck by a disease of the central nervous system caused by mercury poisoning. At Nii-gata on the northwest coast of Honshu, a similar case of mercury poisoning from industrial pollutants led to a legal judgment against local industry.

These and other incidents have provoked public outrage. Decrees of compensation were awarded to victims of asthma from sulfuric acid mist and the *itai-itai* ("itch-itch") disease caused by cadmium discharges. By the 1980s, more than 80,000 people were officially diagnosed as suffering from environmental pollution and were receiving medical benefits and other compensation from the government.

Faced with these environmental by-products of the nation's commitment to unbridled economic growth, the Japanese government has enacted strict antipollution laws based on a policy of "polluters pay for pollution." Emission standards for air quality are established in law, and monitoring stations have been placed in major urban-industrial areas. Tokyo, which experienced over 300 days of photochemical smog in 1973, now exceeds health standards only 15 to 20 days a year. Sulfur dioxide and carbon monoxide levels are substantially lower in Japanese cities, although levels of nitrogen dioxide in the atmosphere have remained unchanged. Comparable efforts are being made to reduce the level of pollution in coastal waters, and Tokyo Bay again has a fishing industry. Noise pollution near new airports and highways is now the source of most environmental complaints received by the government.

Despite these efforts, Japan still has many pollution problems. Willingness to pay the high costs of environmental protection fluctuates with the state of the economy. The shift from heavy industry to high technology has, to some degree, eased the problem. But given the extraordinarily high geographical concentration of Japan's people and industry, the limited possibilities for industrial dispersion in the mountainous interior, and the costs of en-

MAPSCAN

URBAN MAPPING: TOKYO

Cartographers use a variety of mapping techniques to illustrate specific aspects of the contemporary urban scene. Among these are the rapid expansion of metropolitan centers in the twentieth century, the centrality of cities as employment centers for surrounding hinterlands, and the decentralization of urban cores. The three maps of the Tokyo Metropolitan Area (TMA) shown here present several cartographic methods used to map social and structural change in large urban centers: (1) a **time composite** map in Figure 6.11, (2) a **choropleth** map of employment and residence in Figure 6.12, and (3) a **flow map** of commuting in the TMA in Figure 6.13.

Figure 6.11 is a time composite map of the built-up area of Tokyo in 1888, 1914, 1946, and 1975. The time composite method is effective in showing the systematic areal expansion or contraction of a single phenomenon. Note that the time intervals selected coincide with crucial dates in Japanese history and that a different date selection would be used for metropolitan areas elsewhere. The map shows that in 1888, Tokyo was a compact city. By 1914, the city extended its built-up area along major roads, swelled into adjacent areas, and built-up outlying urban centers appear on the periphery at some distance from the center of Tokyo. After World War II, in 1946, Tokyo's expansion filled in the empty spaces between cities on the periphery and the metropolitan center. By 1975, Tokyo's built-up area extended 25 miles from the urban core, and a new urban periphery was beginning to appear.

Figure 6.12 is a choropleth map on which data on the ratio of employment to residence (E/R ratio) is mapped according to the areal units used for collecting information. The map illustrates the suburbanization of the population in the modern TMA. Within a range of 25 to 30 miles from the city center, most communities have less employment than residence, indicating that people are commuting to Tokyo's cen-

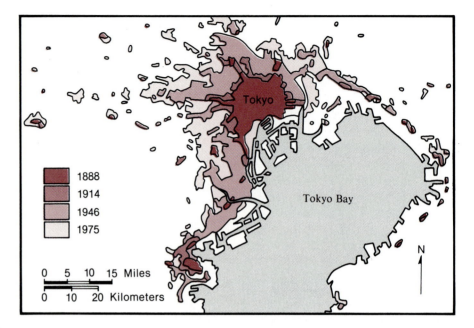

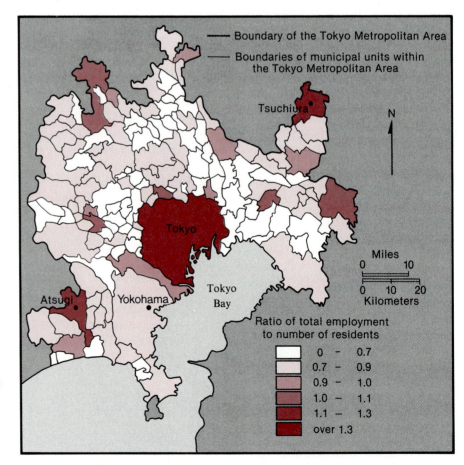

Figure 6.12   Commuting to central Tokyo: Ratio of employment to residence.

tral business district for work and living in outlying communities. Overall, in only 5 percent of the reporting regions in the TMA did employment exceed residence. Only two cities, Atsugi in the southwest and Tsuchiura in the northeast, drew a work force in excess of their residential populations.

Figure 6.13 is a flow map of current commuting within the TMA. On this map, each line illustrates a flow of more than 10,000 commuters between municipalities and central Tokyo. Given more accurate information, cartographers would use different thicknesses of line to differentiate higher and lower flows of commuters. This map pinpoints the commuting process more precisely than the E/R ratio, and it shows that Yokohama and Kawasaki have themselves become destination points for commuters.

These maps of urban expansion and suburbanization imply the problems of congestion, pollution, and progressive growth that large metropolises have undergone in the twentieth century. Cartographic techniques of this type, therefore, are widely used to demonstrate urban processes in many of the world's largest cities.

Adapted from: Teruo Ishimizu and Hiroshi Ishihara, "The Distribution and Movement of Population in Japan's Three Major Metropolitan Areas," in *Geography of Japan,* pp. 347–378. Tokyo: Association of Japanese Geographers, 1980. (Special Publication No. 4); maps, pp. 368, 371, 374.

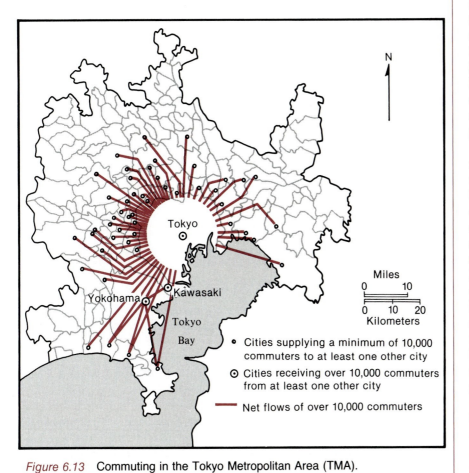

Figure 6.13 Commuting in the Tokyo Metropolitan Area (TMA).

Quality of Life

The determination to maximize its rate of economic growth has left postwar Japan deficient in public services except in the field of education. Despite its great prosperity, Japan still lags far behind other technological nations in roads, water and sewage supply systems, city parks, number of rooms per person, and other measures of social development—all except medicine. Japan has only one eighth as many roads as Great Britain, and only one third of them are paved. Traffic jams, called "traffic wars" by the Japanese, are legendary, particularly in Tokyo where only 11 percent of the land is given over to streets, compared with 25 percent in London and Paris and 35 percent in New York City. The rate of automobile movement in the Tokaido Megalopolis is less than 6 miles per hour during rush hours. Commuter lines in Tokyo run at 250 percent of capacity at peak hours despite substantial government investment in public transport.

These measures of congestion—most intense in Tokyo, but also typical of the Chukyo, Keihanshin, and Kanmon industrial complexes—are extremely high due to the shortage of level land in Japan. Housing is in short supply and spiraling land prices in urban centers prohibit many from living in traditional single-family dwellings. Under the slogan, "One house for one family," the government has constructed millions of new urban apartment buildings and houses, but the housing shortage has not noticeably changed. Water supply systems plagued by summer shortages, power brownouts due to limited generating sources, inadequate sewage systems, and park areas—which in Tokyo amount to only one half of those in Paris and one tenth of those in New York City—all

The level of congestion in Tokyo and other large Japanese cities is as high as anywhere in the world.

point to a serious deterioration of the Japanese urban environment.

The Japanese refer to these problems as the agonies: the evils of overconcentration caused by rapid economic growth, the confines of Japanese topography and resources, and the national policy of growth at any cost. With a declining birth rate and longer life expectancy, the proportion of Japanese over sixty-five is doubling in a society that spends less on social welfare than any other technological nation. The migration of the young to the larger cities is weakening family ties, leaving the old less able to rely on their traditional sources of support.

Furthermore, the modern generation is proving less willing to make sacrifices for national development and is critical of the government's lack of concern for the less fortunate. A growing number of public protests, strikes, and student riots mark this dissent. In the modern industrial state of Japan, then, discussion progresses on the question of whether economic progress alone is a sufficient national goal.

KOREA: THE BRIDGE BETWEEN

For centuries, the Korean Peninsula has been a bridge between Chinese civilization and the island world of the Japanese. Its location made it a battleground, a **marchland** set between great powers.

The Japanese periodically invaded Korea as a stepping-stone to China. Chinese sway over the peninsula ebbed and flowed with the power of the Chinese state. These incursions, however, were intermittent. The Korean peasantry suffered but endured. From the seventeenth century onward, they pursued the self-imposed isolation of the "Hermit Kingdom." This isolation was breached by Japanese diplomatic and commercial pressure in 1875. In 1895, Japanese forces occupied and colonized the entire region, integrating Korea's 10 million people into the new and expanding Japanese Empire.

Japan's colonial rule over _The Korean Peninsula_ ended in 1945 and was followed by the division of the peninsula into two states, one capitalist in the south, and the other communist in the North. This division

hardened in 1950 when North Korea invaded South Korea, triggering a devastating conflict between U.N. forces led by the United States on the one hand, and North Korean and Chinese forces on the other. The Korean War ended in a cease-fire in 1953. The land and people had been ravaged; 600,000 troops still patrol each side of the demilitarized zone (DMZ) along the thirty-eighth north parallel, and the economies of both North and South Korea remain on a war footing.

Today, the peninsula is occupied by 64.5 million Koreans united in language and culture but politically divided into two states. North Korea has developed under communist rule and is closely linked to the USSR. South Korea, by contrast, has a capitalistic society and is an ally of the United States, which has 42,000 American troops stationed there. As a whole, the peninsula is still a bridge between—encircled by China, the USSR, and Japan—divided by the demilitarized zone at the thirty-eighth parallel. Unification of _The Two Koreas_ does not appear likely in the near future.

The Korean Peninsula

The Korean Peninsula juts 500 miles southward from the Asian mainland into the Pacific Ocean between northern China and the Japanese archipelago (Fig. 6.14). Hills and low mountains dominate the Korean landscape, covering some 70 percent of the total land area of 84,715 square miles. Terrain is most rugged along the northern border. Here, a mountain mass and the gorges of the Yalu and Tumen rivers serve as absorbing barriers separating the peninsula from China, and are an important factor behind the evolution of a distinct Korean society. A mountain spine of broken low ranges runs from the Chinese border southward paralleling the east coast. Lowlands fan out to the west and south on the peninsula, but few are very large in area.

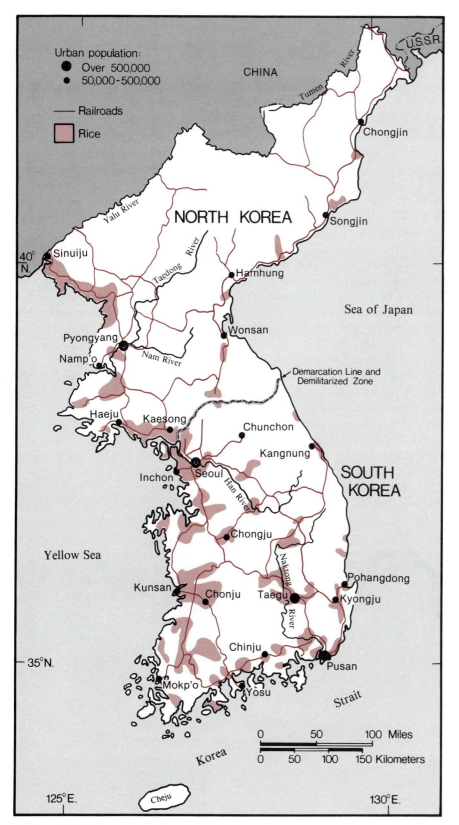

Figure 6.14 The Korean Peninsula.

Only 17 percent of the land is cultivated.

In the north, the hills and mountains are higher, more rugged, and covered with coniferous forests. The hills plunge steeply into the deep Sea of Japan along the east coast; to the west, swift-flowing streams course down narrow valleys and empty into tidal estuaries in the Yellow Sea. Climate is severe and more continental in character. Agriculture is limited by short growing seasons. Population and relief are closely related; hardy crops, like wheat, millet, and barley, are grown on hill slopes, rice on sheltered valley floors. The smaller total population of North Korea, despite its larger land base, reflects the difficulties topography and climate have presented to agriculturalists in this region over the centuries. The major level plain is located along the west coast and straddles the thirty-eighth parallel. This divided agricultural region supplies food to the capital cities of both North and South Korea, Pyongyang and Seoul.

In the south, local relief diminishes, valleys broaden out, and the climate is more moderate due to its more southerly location and maritime influences. Historically, the Korean south has been more densely populated than the north because the growing season is sufficiently long to allow for two crops a year. Irrigated rice is grown using the intensive garden-cropping Chinese system, so that level valley floors and adjacent terraces are covered with paddy. In the hills, wheat and barley are primary crops.

The most densely populated areas lie on plains adjacent to the western and southern coasts in the vicinity of the capital city of Seoul, the cities of Kunsan and Mokp'o, and the port of Pusan. High population density correlates with level land throughout the interior of the peninsula's south.

Korean agriculturalists lived in isolation for some 200 years until Japanese occupation in 1895 broke Korea's self-imposed solitude. At the time, Korea's population of 10 million was primarily engaged in agriculture, with villagers concentrated in the southwest and settlement relatively sparse in the uplands of the north and northeast. Forcibly driven to higher levels of production, regional economic differences between the industrial north and the agrarian south became more pronounced. Progress in material production was achieved under Japanese occupation, but it did little to improve the life of the Koreans. Lingering bitterness and resentment between Japanese and Koreans still exist.

The Japanese doubled the agricultural production of Korea during their fifty-year occupation by increasing irrigated rice land in the south. They extended water-control facilities, reclaimed tidal flats for cultivation, and introduced mechanization. In the hills, commercial crops, like cotton, tobacco, and commercial fruit orchards, were planted. The Korean fishing fleet, largely owned by Japanese, was modernized and catches increased substantially. Wood was harvested from the uplands, creating contemporary problems of soil erosion. Production was geared to supply Japan's expanding economy and empire.

Roads and railroads were constructed to connect producing areas with port cities and to enable the Japanese to exploit the mineral resources of the north. Anthracite coal and iron deposits were mined for Japanese factories. Local hydroelectric plants were constructed to facilitate manufacturing. As in Taiwan and Manchuria, the statistics of production reflected a remarkable rate of economic development under the Japanese. However, the conditions of production were distinctly colonial in nature. As Korea's population tripled to reach 28 million in 1945, most Koreans were living in increasingly exploited conditions. The quality of life for the average Korean was probably no better in 1945 when Japanese

occupation ended than it had been a half century earlier.

The Two Koreas

After the defeat of the Japanese, the Korean Peninsula was politically divided into two countries. North Korea, with a current population of 21.9 million became a communist state with strong links to the Soviet Union and China; South Korea, with a population of 42.6 million, became oriented to the West. Earlier, both halves of Korea under Japanese planning had developed a substantial degree of **geographic complementarity.** In North Korea, industry had been the principal area of Japanese investment; in South Korea, rice cultivation. After political division, each country attempted to redress the imbalance in its economy, and in the last three decades both have undergone substantial modernization.

North Korea, led by the hard line leader Kim Il Sung since 1948, embarked on a distinctive interpretation of communist doctrine following the Korean concept of "juche," roughly understood as national self-reliance.

North Korea pulled away from cooperation with foreign governments and foreigners, rendering the country one of the most isolated in the world. North Korea is also one of the most highly centralized, planned economies anywhere. It is also a police state of the first order.

Farmland was collectivized and farmers regrouped into large communes in the 1950s. The country is self-sufficient in food today. The emphasis of the centralized economy, however, has been on heavy industry. The capital, Pyongyang (pop. 1.5 million) has important industrial resources—coal and iron ore—in its immediate hinterland. A second industrial zone exploits a similar concentration of minerals in the far northwest near the Chinese border. Overall, North Korea yields four fifths of the mineral and metal production of the peninsula. Despite this advantage, North Korea has not experienced the rate of economic growth of the South, a fact most observers attribute to the inflexibility and inefficiency inherent in their uniquely Korean communist system. North Korea has thrown disproportionate public resources into the military

Some 42,000 American troops still patrol the DMZ, or "demilitarized zone," that separates the two countries of North and South Korea.

for a country of 21.9 million people. The country spends 25 percent of its GNP on the military, so that it has an army of 885,000 men—sixth largest in the world. No wonder, then, that North Korea has a GNP of $900 per capita, whereas the South Korean per capita GNP is two and a half times larger.

In sharp contrast to the North, South Korea has become a mighty industrial power—known as one of Asia's "Four Dragons" (South Korea, Hong Kong, Taiwan, and Singapore). Like the other "Dragons," South Korea has experienced extraordinary rates of economic growth since the 1960s. Personal income rose from $105 in 1965 to $2370 in 1988. Demographic indices showing a rising quality of life as well as South Korea's progression through the demographic transition portray a country that has gone beyond the take-off stage of economic development (see Geostatistics). In many ways, South Korea exhibits the most successful transition of a society from an agrarian-based to an industrial economy in recent decades: its development is a case study in the positive diffusion and reception of the Industrial Revolution in today's world.

South Korea has risen rapidly to become an urban country. Its population retains its rural roots, however, and the country exports rice and other agricultural products. Forestry is an expanding export industry. South Korea depends on local hydroelectric sources and imported oil for industrial energy, although current expansion of coal mines on the east coast is planned to increase domestic energy production. South Korea has five nuclear plants in operation and four under construction. Still, like Japan next door, South Ko-

South Korea is a rapidly growing industrial and technological society on the "East Asian Rim." This assembly plant in Seoul reflects the country's shift from agriculture to industry.

rea must trade to survive in the global arena.

South Korea's capitalist economic system combines strong government investments in large private enterprises run by an intimate circle of entrepreneurs. The economy has focused on steel, petrochemical products such as rubber and fertilizers, textiles and clothing, consumer electronics, automobiles, vast construction enterprises, and shipbuilding. South Korea exports not only machine and finished goods but workers as well. Private enterprises, particularly the merchant marine, construction, hospitals, hotels, and restaurants are run by South Koreans throughout the Developing World. Tourism is an important and growing local industry, witnessed most notably by the Seoul Olympics in 1988. Seoul, the national capital and one of the world's largest cities, has undergone rapid expansion. It reached a population of 1 million only in the 1940s. Seoul grew from a population

of 5.5 million in 1970 to 8.4 million in 1980 and was estimated to have exceeded 9 million in 1988. It is linked by rail and superhighway with Inchon (pop. 1.1 million), its port on the Yellow Sea. In the southeast, the port of Pusan (pop. 3.2 million) has grown as the major shipbuilding and textile center of South Korea (Fig. 6.14).

Today's questions in South Korea center on the liberalization of both the political and economic system. As students demonstrate and workers strike, they are testimony to the rapid development of the country and the need for South Korea's human aspirations to catch up with its material progress. On this, Korea's future holds. Movements toward the reunification of the "Two Koreas" seem far in the future and clouded by the divergent paths taken toward development. Their separate military alliances and economic systems militate against political unification of the Korean people.

7

AUSTRALIA, NEW ZEALAND, AND THE PACIFIC WORLD

239

Australia and New Zealand are European societies that were directly and successfully transplanted to the South Pacific. Peopled by British immigrants, both societies evolved from dependent colonies into independent states, although their ties to Europe still remain strong. Australia and New Zealand were remote from the cataclysmic changes that overtook the European continent in the twentieth century. So, as time passed, Australia and new Zealand developed policies and perspectives that increasingly reflected their own regional geographies, histories, and economies (Fig. 7.1).

World War II was a turning point in this process. It thrust the South Pacific—previously relatively isolated—into a world conflict, which ended with the decline of British influence throughout the world. Imperial Britain had previously shielded the people of Australia and New Zealand from direct encounters with Asia. The shield removed, both countries were faced with redefining their relationships to Britain, Europe, the United States, Japan, and their Asian neighbors.

Today, Australia and New Zealand bring to this task their own imperatives, a new sense of independence, and a new consciousness of their own distinctive character and location. This is apparent in changing patterns of trade, new international perspectives, and an emerging sense of responsibility for their own destiny. Yet their location relative to Asia and Europe poses a long-term problem. Australia and New Zealand are small, wealthy, white societies in an exposed position. Psychologically and geographically, they are confronted by Asian realities to a greater degree than other European-based societies in the Technological World.

In strong contrast, the new countries of the Pacific represent native peoples and entirely new societies emergent within the last few generations. Their roots go back in time to the successive peopling of the Pacific from west to east. Gripped by colonialism, Pacific peoples today struggle with futures that are as mixed as the geography of their islands.

In all, a new human experience has developed in Australia, New Zealand, and the Pacific World. This world region marks a significant blend of nonwestern and European cultures. Its prospects appear relatively bright.

THE COMING OF THE EUROPEANS

Early European Contacts

In 1606, the Spanish navigator Torres sailed through the strait between Australia and Papua New Guinea, which today bears his name. Shortly thereafter, Europeans charted the rough outlines of the northern and western coasts of the continent. The Dutch named Australia "New Holland," but little interest was aroused. Sailing out of the Dutch East Indies, Abel Tasman discovered New Zealand and Tasmania (which he named Van Diemen's Land) and circumnavigated Australia in 1642–1643. Yet well into the eighteenth century, European mapmakers still referred to Australia as "the southern continent not yet discovered." Indeed, it was not until 1769 that New Zealand's two islands were identified as separate from the Australian mainland (Fig. 7.1).

The vast size of the Pacific Ocean, negative reports by early explorers suggesting that these areas held little

When the Greek cartographer Ptolemy drew his world map in the second century A.D., he placed a huge unknown land (*Terra Incognita*) deep in the Indian Ocean far south of the shores of the Asian landmass. Some 1500 years later, European explorers discovered this Terra Incognita when Portuguese, Spanish, and Dutch mariners stumbled upon Australia and New Zealand in their quest for the riches of the Orient. *Early European Contacts* led to a peopling of these areas, and ultimately to a *Mastering of the Land*.

commercial value, and sheer remoteness from the pathways of European expansion caused Australia and New Zealand to be the last major world region to experience European exploration and settlement.

It was the voyage of Captain James Cook of the Royal British Navy in 1770 that first stirred European interest in Australia. Cook, who had been sent to Tahiti to record astronomical observations, sailed southward on his return voyage, circled New Zealand, and headed due west toward Australia.

On sighting land, Cook veered northward and charted the eastern shores of Australia. He landed first at Botany Bay (modern Sydney), then near Cooktown in modern Queensland, and finally on Possession Island off Cape York in the north. There he raised the British flag, formally de-

GEOSTATISTICS

	Capital	Area (square miles)	Population (millions)	Rate of Natural Increase (%)	Number of Years to Double Population	Population Projected for A.D. 2000	Infant Mortality Rate	Life Expectancy at Birth	Urban Population (%)	Per Capita GNP ($)	Energy Consumption per Capita (kg of oil equivalent)
Australia	Canberra	2,967,909	16.5	0.8	88	18.7	10	76	86	11,910	5,116
Fiji	Suva	7,065	0.7	2.3	31	0.8	21	67	37	1,810	—
French Polynesia	Papeete	1,544	0.2	2.4	29	0.3	23	71	57	—	—
New Caledonia	Nouméa	7,358	0.2	1.8	38	0.2	36	68	60	—	—
New Zealand	Wellington	103,736	3.3	0.8	87	3.6	11	74	84	7,110	3,823
Papua New Guinea	Port Moresby	178,259	3.7	2.4	29	4.8	100	54	13	690	235
Solomon Islands	Honiara	10,983	0.3	3.6	19	0.5	42	68	9	530	—
Vanuatu	Vila	5,700	0.2	3.3	21	0.2	38	69	18	—	—
Western Samoa	Apia	1,097	0.2	2.9	24	0.2	50	65	21	680	—

Sources: *World Population Data Sheet*, 1988; *World Development Report*, 1987.

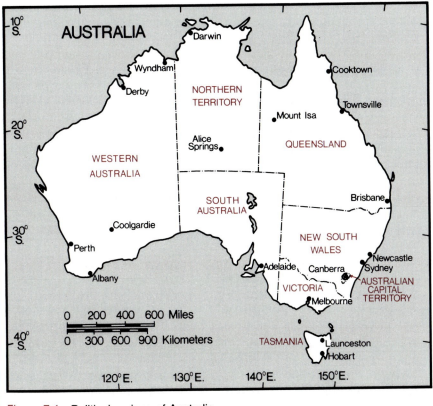

Figure 7.1   Political regions of Australia.

claring eastern Australia to be a possession of the British crown. He disproved the rumor of a great southern continent, instead identifying Australia as the large island-continent that it is.

Despite interest in Cook's discoveries, no effort was made to settle Australia until after Britain lost its American colonies in the Revolutionary War. No longer able to ship criminals to the colony of Georgia, Britain sought alternative places to send lawbreakers.

The very remoteness that had retarded European settlement in Australia now became a major asset. In 1787, a fleet of eleven ships carrying 1030 people, 736 of them convicts (188 of them women) landed at Botany Bay. They established their first colony in a protected harbor a few miles north of Botany Bay at Port Jackson. This settlement ultimately became Australia's largest city, Sydney.

For the first decade, the penal colony at Port Jackson was totally dependent on Britain for food. Gradually, however, land was brought into cultivation and exploration of the eastern rim of Australia progressed. A few free settlers left Australia to join seal hunters and whalers in outposts in northern New Zealand, 1000 miles to the southeast. The initial stage of European settlement was underway.

Exploration and Early Development

In the next several decades, exploration continued along the Australian coast. By 1813, the Great Dividing Range, which parallels the eastern coast, was penetrated. The Murray and Darling river systems, which flowed westward, were discovered. The difficult nature of the Australian interior long impeded full exploration. The first land traverse of the country was not made until 1862. Long into the nineteenth century, the idea that Australia would somewhere contain a great Mississippi or mountains like the Rockies held strong.

In 1987, Australia celebrated the bicentennial anniversary of the first landing of a fleet of British ships at Botany Bay near modern Sydney. The celebration was marred by protests by Australian aborigines.

Slowly, however, the realization that the interior of Australia was a barren and harsh land holding little promise for Europeans took hold. British settlements were slowly established in the more temperate, better watered peripheral regions of the Australian landmass. Settlement gradually reached outward from a southeastern core to extend northward along the Great Dividing Range but only 500 miles inland.

British financial support of Australia's penal colonies and military outposts continued for fifty years. Shipments of grain and manufactured goods from Europe subsidized the tentative development of the continent. Perth, Adelaide, Melbourne, Sydney, and Brisbane—all to become focal points of settlement—were founded. These cities later became the capitals of self-governing states under British control. British administrators were dispatched to Australia to maintain order, guide economic development, and protect the crown's investment in this remote corner of the British Empire.

In New Zealand, British interests and investments were more limited and came later. Public concern about

the scandalous treatment of the native Polynesian Maoris by traders and whalers led to the establishment of an Anglican mission at the Bay of Islands on North Island in 1814. Colonists made repeated appeals to the British to establish law and order. These appeals intensified as trade and settlement expanded. Finally, in 1840, the British abandoned their policy of minimal intervention because of the establishment of a competing French settlement at Akaroa on South Island, and also because of the formation of the British New Zealand Company, a corporate group dedicated to planned settlement and development of the islands. In 1842, New Zealand became a crown colony separate from Australia.

Mastering the Land

British support of the struggling colonies of Australia and New Zealand during the early stages of settlement was vital. Labor was in short supply. The native populations of Australian aborigines and New Zealand Maoris were too few in number to fill the labor needs of colonies under construction. Nor were aborigines and

THE EVOLUTION OF THE AUSTRALIAN ECONOMY

In the nineteenth century, strategic elements of the European agricultural economy were transplanted to Australia as part of the worldwide expansion of agriculture to meet the needs of growing urban markets of Britain and Western Europe.

As these elements penetrated Australia, land was sequentially devoted to four types of agricultural economy: (1) open-range pasturing of animals for wool and hides, (2) enclosed pasturing of animals for wool and meat, (3) extensive grain cultivation of wheat; and (4) intensive cultivation of wheat and dairying.

Gradually, less intensive types of land use were pushed farther from centers of population, each type successively replaced by a more intensive form of agricultural occupance following the sequence established above. The resulting distribution of types of human occupance accords well with Von Thünen's model of the distribution of agricultural activities presented in his classic work *The Isolated State* (See Geolab for Western Europe, Figs. 3.11 and 3.12).

The sequence of pastoral occupation in Australia after 1830 illustrated in Figure 7.2 shows how initial points of entry and routes into the interior channeled this pattern of economic development. In 1830, initial pastoral settlement existed at Sydney and Hobart; by 1845, it existed around each of the other settlements that later became state capitals—Perth, Adelaide, Melbourne, and Brisbane. The Great Dividing Range in the east had already been crossed. By 1860, a pastoral belt existed in the hinterland of every major city, extending

tentacles toward the arid core of Australia.

By 1880, pastoral land use had extended to the Great Artesian Basin in eastern Australia, and routes of penetration from the south and east had been supplemented by new northern centers of dispersion at Darwin, Wyndham, and Derby. By 1900, the contemporary extent of pastoral land use in Australia had been reached.

The pattern of modern agricultural land use in Australia reflects the European occupance of Australia. It also demonstrates the impact of distance from market on intensity of land use proposed by Von Thünen: the most intensive types of land use are located nearest major urban centers; the least intensive farthest away.

Adapted from: R. L. Heathcote, "Pastoral Australia," in D. N. Jeans (ed.), *Australia: A Geography.* New York: St. Martin's Press, 1978, p. 269.

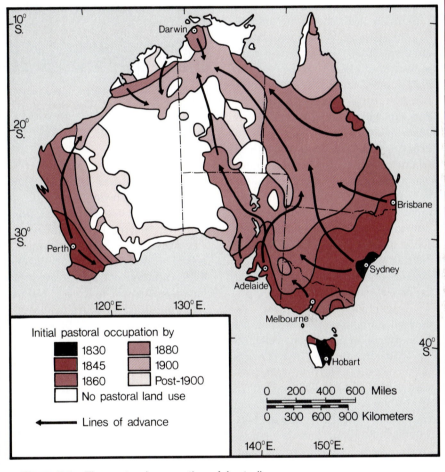

Figure 7.2 The pastoral occupation of Australia.

Maoris numerous enough to protect themselves from the onslaught of the Europeans. Australian aborigines reached a demographic maximum of 250,000–300,000 in 1800; the Maoris reached a similar number during the eighteenth century.

The British colonial economies in Australia and New Zealand were slow

to develop. Local agriculture barely met the food needs of the slowly expanding populations of the new colonies. Sealing and whaling were not lucrative enough to sustain them. Colonial governors granted free land to anyone who would employ convicts and assume responsibility for their feeding and clothing.

Australian Economic Growth

At the beginning of the nineteenth century, European plants and animals were imported into Australia to build the basis of an agricultural economy (Fig. 7.2).

Merino sheep were brought in from Cape Town, South Africa, and from the London suburb of Kew in England. Well adapted to the dry plains of central Spain, merino sheep found a natural habitat on the grassland fringes of the arid Australian interior. Pastoralists fanned inland from the coast of New South Wales onto the extensive pastures of Darling Downs on the inner slopes of the Great Dividing Range. Soon merino sheep were being kept wherever appropriate environments were found. By the 1930s, Australia was exporting to English markets 2 million tons of fine wool shorn from these animals.

Similarly, wheat growing diffused in southwestern Western Australia, at various points along the east coast of New South Wales, in the Queensland interior, and in the south in the hinterland of Adelaide, in what became known as South Australia. Early experiments at Swan River in Western Australia failed, as did others where rainfall was too variable to sustain permanent cultivation. But in the fertile lands of the Murray River Basin inland from Adelaide, on the semiarid grasslands between the Great Dividing Range and the deserts of central Australia, and in the hinterland of Perth in the southwest, wheat became the dominant export crop.

Geographic expansion and increased economic opportunities led to an Australian population of 400,000 by 1850. The original 736 convicts had become a country of 10,000 people by 1810 and 100,000 by 1830. In all, by the time forced migration of convicts to Australia ended in 1860, 150,000 prisoners had been sent "down under." Their rates of natural increase were responsible for most of the growth of Australia until the Gold Rush of the 1850s. Half a million settlers, largely from Britain, but even from America, poured into Australia in the 1850s to find riches in the new land. Public pressure forced Britain to end its use of Australia and Tasmania as overseas prisons. By 1859, the five Australian colonies of New South Wales, Tasmania, South Australia, Victoria, and Queensland had established their own constitutional

The Stuart Highway slices in a straight line across the flat, thinly peopled core of Australia. It runs from Alice Springs in the interior to Darwin on the northern coast.

governments as separate British colonies. The penal period was over; the colonial era had begun.

The push for colonial self-government was spurred by the discovery of gold at Bathurst, New South Wales, in 1851. Gold fever attracted a flood of adventurers, entrepreneurs, and miners to Australia much as it had in California. Rich finds in the alluvial gold fields at Ballarat and Bendigo in Victoria enlarged this immigrant surge. Vast tracts of land were opened to settlement in the 1860s, and railroads penetrated the Australian interior. Droughts, frontier-style conflicts, exploitation and abuse of Australian aborigines, and rivalry among colonies generated sectional bitterness. Eventually, intercolony tariffs to equalize differences in prosperity were levied; railroads of different gauges constructed.

By the end of the century, agriculture expanded in the eastern colonies of Australia because of the increased use of superphosphate fertilizers, which raised wheat yields; the introduction of drought-resistant varieties of wheat; and the opening of new lands to cultivation in the wake of railroad construction. Equally im-

portant, the invention of refrigerated ships enabled Australians to sell beef and mutton in the marketplaces of Europe. In Western Australia, gold discoveries at Coolgardie and Kalgoorlie spurred a second mining boom.

In 1901, by act of the British Parliament, the six independent Australian colonies of Queensland, New South Wales, Victoria, Tasmania, South Australia, and Western Australia became states in a federal government, the **Commonwealth** of Australia. Northern Territory joined in 1911. By 1914, the new country had a population of 4.9 million and the agricultural and mineral base of its economy was maturing.

The New Zealand Experience

The smaller size, more remote location, more humid climate, and mountain spine of New Zealand's two islands necessarily led to a different pattern of economic development. Colonization was encouraged by the New Zealand Company that transported farmers from England to initiate settlements at Wellington, Wanganui, and New Plymouth on the west coast of North Island and at Nelson on the northern tip of South Island. Inextricably tied to England, the main objective of these settlers was to exploit the resources of this small, remote colony and to develop export products capable of sustaining the local economy and trade with Britain.

Expansion of settlement led to a series of devastating clashes with the Maoris, even though they had contributed substantially to the early development of the timber industry and flax cultivation. On North Island, warfare went on for several decades until, in 1870, the Maoris exhausted their resources and manpower. On South Island, settlements, untroubled by war, progressed more rapidly.

Development in New Zealand's South Island was spurred by the discovery of gold in the 1860s at Otago near Dunedin on the east coast. These mineral finds attracted 100,000 migrants from Australia and elsewhere. They also brought in venture capital from Britain. This money was largely invested in the construction of roads and railroads on the Canterbury Plain in the hinterland of Christchurch, the best wheat-growing land in New Zea-

land. Deeper in the mountain interior, pioneer settlers pastured sheep.

By the early 1880s, the population of New Zealand had risen to 500,000. Falling export prices and economic depression, however, led thousands to leave New Zealand for opportunities in the more prosperous colony of Australia. As in Australia, the introduction of refrigerated ocean-going ships led to recovery in the 1880s. The rich pastures and reliable rainfall of New Zealand created an ideal environment for sheep raising, and direct access to European markets made the sale of meat and wool profitable. Mutton and wool accounted for 60 percent of all exports by 1900.

By the turn of the century, secondary industries had begun to supplement New Zealand's agricultural and pastoral economy. Better economic conditions, more enlightened social legislation, and growing self-confidence led New Zealand to decline an invitation to join the Commonwealth of Australia. New Zealand's growing population of 750,000 was about equally divided between its two islands. In North Island, Wellington (named capital in 1865), and Auckland were emerging

as the largest cities, Christchurch was developing rapidly on South Island (see Fig. 7.10). Britain formally terminated New Zealand's colonial status in 1907, whereupon the country achieved de facto independence. New Zealand did not, however, gain authority over its own foreign affairs until 1947.

AUSTRALIA: CONTEMPORARY HUMAN GEOGRAPHY

The Europeans came to Australia and discovered a continent that had escaped the attention of the colonizing societies of Asia. Thinly peopled by a population of 300,000 aborigines, the Europeans entered an empty land—virgin territory—to be developed and exploited much like the United States and Canada.

In the nineteenth century, these Europeans transferred a Western society and economy to Australia. Early settlement experience led to more permanent patterns of land use in *The Australian Environment*.

Today, Australia is a wealthy, literate, urban society with high standards of living, like those of other countries in the Technological World. Australia has often been called the "Lucky Country." Yet the total population of Australia is only 16.2 million, fewer people than live in the Mexico City, New York, or London metropolitan areas. The small size and concentrated distribution of Australia's people is strongly influenced by environmental opportunities and obstacles. For this reason, the country's densely settled, highly developed periphery and empty center has characterized the human geography of the region from the beginnings of European settlement to the present. The *Core and Periphery: The Distribution of People* is a distinctive feature of the continent. This has not been altered by *Australia's Changing Economy*.

The reliable rainfall and rich pastures of New Zealand provide an ideal environment for sheep raising. This scene of a sheep ranch backed by the snow-capped peaks of the Southern Alps is typical of New Zealand's South Island.

The Australian Environment

The Australian continent is a vast rectangle, 2000 miles long and 2500 miles wide, with an area four fifths the size of the United States (Fig. 7.3). Australia is twenty-five times larger than the British Isles and double the size of the Indian subcontinent. Its northern tip, Cape York, lies 10 degrees south of the equator; its southern margins dip well into the midlatitudes. Given Australia's wide latitudinal range and varied location, climate varies widely from one part of the continent to another. Topography, relatively little varied over the continent, has played a much smaller role in settlement and occupation in Australia than in the world's other large landmasses.

Topography

Topographically, Australia is the world's flattest continent. A huge central plateau, ranging in elevation from 600 to 1500 feet, extends over three quarters of its total area (Fig. 7.4). Highlands above 1800 feet cover only 5 percent of its total area. To the east, the Great Dividing Range, which parallels the coast inland, is a modest physical barrier with an average elevation of less than 3000 feet. Its highest mountain in the rugged southeast, Mount Kosciusko, only reaches 7313 feet above sea level. Smaller ranges exist in western Australia and in the tropical north. By and large, however, the major impact of topography on environment has been to reduce abrupt changes in regional climates. Gradual environmental transitions, largely governed by broad latitudinal differences over large distances, are characteristic of Australia.

Climate

The northern shores of Australia receive summer precipitation from rain-bearing tropical **easterlies** and asso-

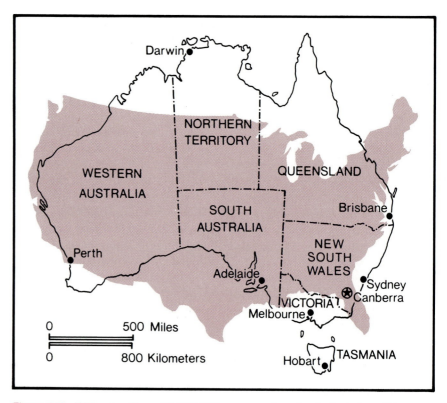

Figure 7.3 With a territory of 2,967,909 square miles, Australia is four fifths the size of the United States and sixth largest country in the world by size. Western Australia alone is as large as all the U.S. states in the Mountain and Pacific time zones.

ciated **monsoons** (Fig. 7.5). Parts of the Cape York Peninsula receive over 200 inches of rainfall a year, and a wide swath of northern Australia—extending as much as 500 miles inland—has 20 inches of precipitation or more. Tropical rain forests line the shores of Arnhem Land west of the Gulf of Carpentaria and extend intermittently southward along the Queensland coast. Inland from the coast, woodlands and tall grass **savannas** extend some distance into the interior, grading gradually into short-grass savannas and steppes as rainfall diminishes.

At the other end of the continent, the southern shores of Australia and the island of Tasmania receive rainfall from the midlatitude **westerlies** during the winter season, particularly in the southwest near Perth, in the southeast around Melbourne, and on the west coast of Tasmania (Fig.

7.5). Rainfall is highest on **windward** slopes, reaching 60 inches in the southeast and 40 inches in the southwest. Moisture decreases rapidly away from the coast. These areas and the eastern coast of Australia, which receives 20 to 40 inches of rainfall throughout the year, have the most dependable rainfall regimes in Australia. They are also the most densely populated regions of the continent, only 11 percent of which receives more than 40 inches of rain a year.

The heart of Australia is dominated by the Great Sandy, Gibson, Great Victoria, and Simpson deserts and their surrounding steppes (Fig. 7.4). Here, very low rainfall totals and high rainfall variability are the norm. An estimated 180,000 square miles of territory around Lake Eyre in South Australia averages between 4 and 6 inches of rainfall a year. One station, however, received 30 inches of rain-

Figure 7.4 Physical features of Australia.

fall in a single day, and no rainfall for an entire year. Such high variability makes permanent settlement quite difficult.

Between this arid core and zones of higher rainfall near the coasts, Australia's semiarid central plateau is covered with a thin vegetation of **xerophytic** acacia and dwarf eucalyptus shrubs that provide limited cattle pastures. This is also the principal sheep-raising environment in New South Wales and Western Australia. Vulnerability to drought is high and has caused major losses on seven occasions in the last century. In 1982, a devastating drought threatened Australia's rich eastern farmlands. Nearly two thirds of Australia has less than 20 inches of rainfall a year, mak-

ing it the world's driest as well as flattest continent. These factors have influenced the distribution of population in Australia.

Core and Periphery: The Distribution of People

The most salient characteristic of Australia's population is its small size as compared with other major world regions. Four factors have contributed to Australia having only 16.5 million people.

First, the dry interior and tropical north, which cover vast areas of the Australian landmass, discouraged European settlement. New migrants from England were attracted to the

midlatitude environments of the east coast and the south—those with which they were most familiar. Second, the remoteness of Australia from the main centers of world population undoubtedly limited the number of immigrants. Third, the narrow base of Australia's colonial economy and sheer distance from external markets limited local demand for labor. Livestock ranching and mining require relatively few workers. Fourth, and perhaps most important, European settlement in Australia is so recent that rates of natural increase have not had time to accumulate a larger population.

Environmental preference, location, economic history, and time have all contributed to the perception of Australia as an "Empty Continent." In fact, very little of the Australian landmass is suited to European technologically oriented settlement. Desert, steppe, mountain, and tropical rain forest environments cover large areas.

The Densely Settled Periphery

For these reasons, Australia's population is highly concentrated on the eastern and southern coasts and around major urban port centers in each of the country's states (Fig. 7.6). Some 85 percent of all Australians live within 50 miles of the sea, a degree of coastal concentration found only in maritime countries, such as Greece, Britain, and Japan. The vast interior core, which comprises 85 percent of the land area of Australia, contains the remaining 15 percent of the population.

Australia is the only continent with a completely coastal frontier. One result is that railroads typically extend directly from coastal cities to small agricultural and mining centers in the interior. The only large city located away from the coast is Canberra (pop. 219,000), in the Australian Capital Territory (A.C.T.), whose site was primarily determined in 1908 by early unresolved rivalry between Australia's largest metropolitan centers, Sydney and Melbourne.

Not only is Australia's population concentrated on the coastal fringes of the south and east, but an equivalent concentration of population is found within each state around the five mainland state capitals. Less than 1 million Australians live more than 300 miles away from these metropolitan centers. Only the well-watered island state of Tasmania varies significantly from this general pattern, with half of its population of 420,000 living in the south near the state capital of Hobart (pop. 170,000).

In Western Australia and South Australia, small dense clusters of population ring the state capitals of Perth (pop. 902,000) and Adelaide (pop. 934,000). In each state, 90 percent of the people are located on the tenth of the total area nearest each state capital. Small but economically important communities of people live in the interior of these states in mining and ranching areas like Pilbara Range and Kimberley Plateau in western and northwestern Western Australia. In New South Wales and Victoria, dense concentrations of people exist in the hinterlands of Australia's two largest cities, Sydney (pop. 3.2 million) and Melbourne (pop. 2.8 million). In Queensland, dispersion away from the state capital of Brisbane (pop. 1 million) is somewhat greater because settlements are located along its 1000-mile-long coast and in its extensive interior pastoral zone.

The Thinly Peopled Core

The reciprocal of Australia's remarkable concentration of population on the coast is its relatively small population in the interior (Fig. 7.6). Australia's dry core does not have the water or soil resources to nurture an agricultural economy comparable to that of the American Middle West. Isolated mineral deposits concentrated enough to sustain gigantic mining complexes are located at Bro-

MAPSCAN

MAPPING WATER NEED: WATER-BALANCE DIAGRAMS

The physical geographer, C. Warren Thornthwaite, developed a set of quantitative measures of water need **(potential evapotranspiration)** and classified world regions on the basis of whether or not they have a moisture surplus or a moisture deficit. Thornthwaite was concerned with the practical problems of crop irrigation. He developed his calculations of **water-balance budgets** to define water needs in given areas more precisely than by measures of rainfall.

In arid regions, the Thornthwaite calculations identify both the amount of the moisture deficit that must be made up to grow crops and the timing of moisture deficiency. This makes it possible to determine the period when irrigation is essential and the amount of water needed by any particular crop. This classification takes account of air temperature and season of rainfall, as moisture falling in the warm season evaporates more rapidly and in larger quantities than in the cool season. In Australia, where development has been closely related to available water, Thornthwaite's water-balance budgets are of crucial importance in measuring the land-use potential of each region.

The water-balance diagrams shown in Figure 7.5 for the five stations of Perth, Melbourne, Brisbane, Darwin, and Alice Springs are based on two curves: monthly mean precipitation in inches and monthly mean water need. Water need, or potential evapotranspiration, is the amount of water that will be lost to the atmosphere through evaporation and plant transpiration at any given temperature. During times of water need, water is withdrawn from the soil until it is used up and

then a condition of water deficiency exists. Potential evapotranspiration is higher when temperatures are higher and when days are longer. During times of water surplus, soils are recharged with moisture until a condition of water surplus exists.

When these two curves are plotted, four periods can be identified: (1) **Soil Moisture Utilization,** when water need exceeds precipitation and moisture is being withdrawn from the soil; (2) **Water Deficiency,** when water need exceeds precipitation and available moisture in the soil has been used up; (3) **Soil Moisture Recharge,** when precipitation exceeds water need and the soil is being recharged with moisture; and (4) **Water Surplus,** when precipitation exceeds water need and the soil has the equivalent of 4 inches of rainfall.

The water-balance diagrams for Perth, Melbourne, Brisbane, Darwin, and Alice Springs illustrate the variety of soil-moisture conditions found in Australia. The coastal city of Perth has a water-balance found in a Mediterranean-type climate with a subtropical wet winter, dry summer regime. A large water surplus exists during the southern hemisphere winter months of June, July and August. The deficit in summer (December, January and February) is equally large. The city of Darwin in northern Australia has an opposite seasonal pattern, with a distinctive wet and dry season in a tropical location.

By contrast, Melbourne and Brisbane on the eastern coast of Australia have more evenly distributed moisture regimes, with no marked seasonal surpluses or deficits. Alice Springs, a desert climate, has a year-round moisture deficit.

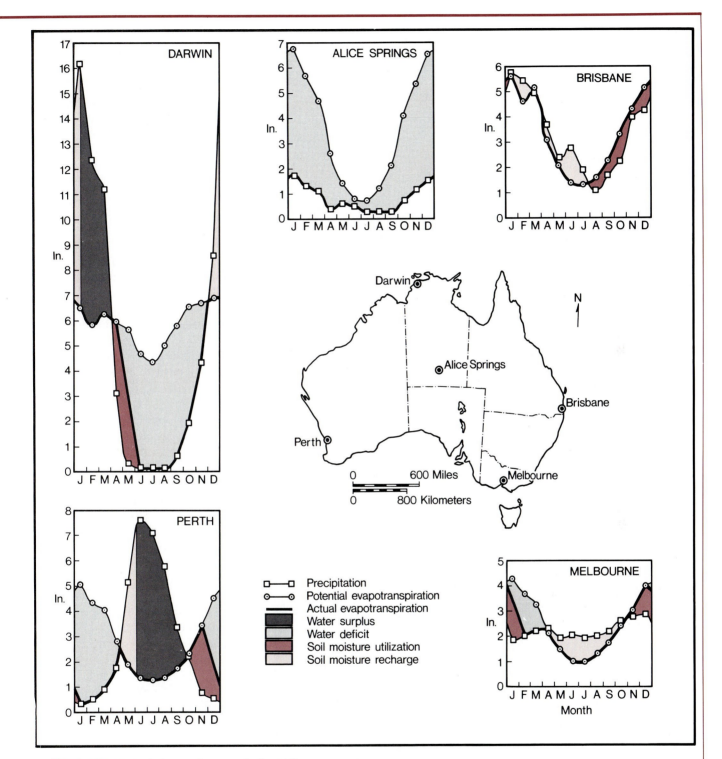

Figure 7.5 Water-balance diagrams in Australia.

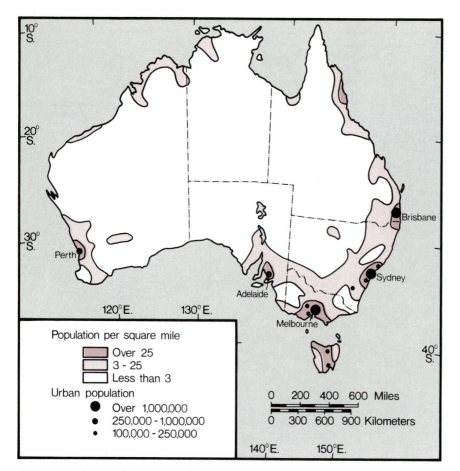

Figure 7.6   Population of Australia.

This view of Leigh Creek, a new town west of the Flinders Range in the interior of South Australia, suggests the sheer scale of the Australian landscape, a space almost as large as the United States.

ken Hill in northwestern New South Wales, at Mount Isa in western Queensland, and at emerging isolated points in Western Australia. There are no natural waterways, like the Mississippi or St. Lawrence rivers, connecting the interior to the coast. In short, the Australian core has vast mineral resources, but no surrounding agricultural environments to support urban industrial complexes of substantial size. Given the highly technical exploitation of the mineral and grazing resources in this vast region, relatively few people are engaged in producing the raw materials of the interior for shipment by rail to coastal cities. Extensive grazing results in high levels of sheep production in the Australian interior, "the Outback," but not many people are engaged in this modern, export-oriented industry. Several sheep ranches ("stations") in Northern Territory are the size of Connecticut, yet they employ fewer people than a Connecticut post office. Despite the image Australia cultivates, "Crocodile Dundees" are few and far between.

This distribution of population in Australia was undoubtedly influenced by the early establishment of a colonial, export-oriented economy. Only 3.5 million people were ever involved in the nineteenth-century economic development of Australia. Australians tended to concentrate their human and physical resources in compact coastal areas and to discount the huge expanse of land in the interior.

The burden of transportation on this small population was lessened by the development of semi-independent economies in each state. By concentrating people and industry in coastal metropolitan centers, the cost of transportation of raw materials from the interior and of goods and services among Australians living on the coast was lowered.

As a result, the myth of an internal frontier, which became solid reality in the United States, has remained a myth in Australia. Dispersion of population is limited. Despite Australia's substantial dependence on the production of raw materials, it is one of the most highly urbanized societies in the world. Some 86 percent of its people are city dwellers. Image, myth, and reality contrast strongly in modern Australia.

Australia's Changing Economy

Before World War II, Australia's economy was based on the production of agricultural and mineral resources for export to markets in Europe. After the war, manufacturing and processing industries grew rapidly. In the last two decades, service occupations have also expanded. Australia's reliance on primary production has diminished although it continues to play a major role in global trade. Today, agriculture and mining produce a tenth of Australia's wealth; manufacturing 20 percent. The service sector provides the balance. Australia, like other nations in the Technological World, has moved toward a postindustrial society.

Agriculture and Herding

Roughly 40 percent of the Australian landscape is used for farming and grazing, despite the arid climate of the continent. The most important activities are sheep and beef-cattle raising. These are pursued by using the latest advances in pasture and animal management, farm mechanization, and water technology. Fully 90 percent of the agricultural area is devoted to low-intensity grazing of these animals, whose products account for two fifths of the country's total export earnings.

About 15 percent of the world's sheep, an estimated 134 million animals, graze over wide areas of Australia (Fig. 7.7). East of the Great Dividing Range, sheep are grazed on land intermittently planted in wheat. West of these low mountains, sheep raising becomes more extensive. High

animal populations are found in the Great Artesian Basin in Queensland, where shallow wells reduce environmental risk. Lower animal densities occur in the savanna and steppe country of northern Australia. In favored locales, sheep raising extends well into the dry core of the continent. More than 90 percent of the wool produced on these ranches in exported to the European Community, Japan, and the Soviet Union.

Cattle raising is concentrated in more humid environments in Victoria and New South Wales on the western slopes of the Great Dividing Range around the basins of the Murray and Darling river systems (Fig. 7.8). Commercial wheat cultivation is also practiced in this same region (as well as inland from Perth), extending in a band from Adelaide in the south as far north as Brisbane. In these areas, more reliable sources of water support mixed farming and large cattle herds, a total of 25 million animals in the late 1980s. Wheat cultivation and cattle raising have recently extended into areas with higher rainfall variability through the application of contemporary scientific

techniques. Australia is thus the largest exporter of beef and veal in the world as well as a leading exporter of wheat.

Permanent cultivation is more limited in Australia. Largely for climatic reasons, only 1 percent of the continent is continuously cultivated. Dairying is a major agricultural pursuit in southeastern Australia and northern Tasmania, where rainfall is reliable, and in the hinterlands of Perth and Adelaide. Small enclaves of farming are found along the entire east coast and on the Darling Downs west of Brisbane. Other crops of significance in Australia include sugar, which is grown along the Queensland coast, and rice and citrus crops, grown under irrigation in New South Wales and Victoria.

Minerals and Energy

Australia is a world-level producer of minerals and metals—a prominent supplier of basic raw materials to other countries in the Technological World. In the last two decades, the value of mineral production has more than quadrupled, largely because of foreign investments. In the late 1980s,

Australia, the world's leading exporter of iron ore, taps the huge reserves of the Pilbara Range in Western Australia, using modern mining technology. Mineral wealth fuels the Australian economy.

SHEEP AND CATTLE IN AUSTRALIA

Sheep and cattle raising are vital elements in the Australian economy. The wide distribution of sheep raising in the semiarid zone is shown in Figure 7.7. Its penetration into the arid zone reflects the lower pasture and water demands of these animals as compared with cattle (Fig. 7.8). The impact of the Great Artesian Basin on the distribution of animal husbandry on the continent is apparent.

Adapted from: Dov Nir, *The Semi-arid World.* New York: Longman, 1974, pp. 136–139.

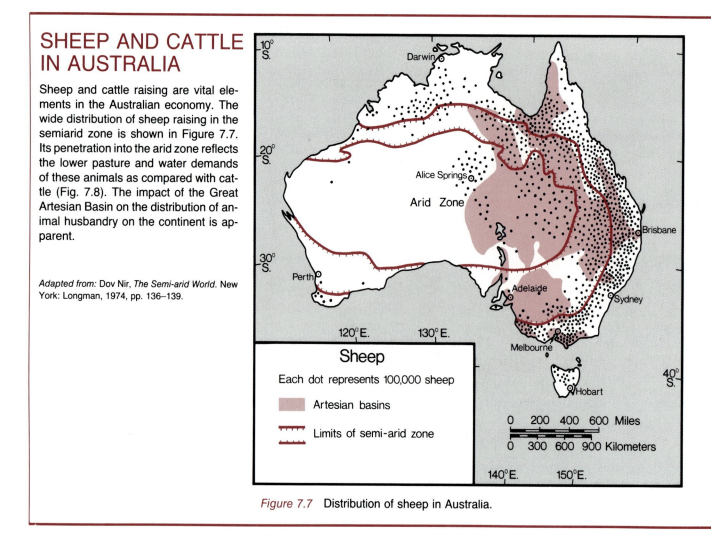

Figure 7.7   Distribution of sheep in Australia.

minerals and metals constitute a fifth of Australia's exports. If in earlier times Australia "rode on a sheep's back," today it is a major producer and exporter of iron ore, coal, bauxite, nickel, tin, manganese, lead, silver, zinc, and copper. New discoveries continue to be made, and Australia's capacity to produce minerals and metals is now greater than current world demand.

Australia is the third largest producer and the world's leading exporter of iron ore (Fig. 7.9). The four largest mines tap the huge reserves of the Pilbara range of Western Australia but operate at less than capacity because of the depressed world steel market. Smaller deposits of iron ore are widely scattered across the continent. Similarly, recoverable coal

reserves along the entire east coast from Victoria to the Cape York Peninsula, await more favorable market conditions for further development. The most important producing fields are located at Newcastle, Lithgow, and Bulli near Sydney in New South Wales. In terms of both iron and coal, Australia has huge reserves that far exceed the needs of domestic consumption. Indeed, most Australian iron ore and coal is sold to Japan, which uses these resources to make steel for automobile production and other manufactured export goods. Today, Australia's export value of coal and iron ore exceeds that of its agricultural production, indicating a profound change in its economic development.

Mining districts in which an as-

sociation of ores are found together are typical of Australia. The earliest and most famous of these mining complexes is Broken Hill, located west of the Darling River in New South Wales. Here, miners in search of gold found silver. Broken Hill is one of the world's largest producers of lead and zinc as well as an important source of copper and uranium. The Mount Isa mining district has developed a comparable diversity of mineral wealth since the early 1970s. It has the world's largest silver and lead mine, has the world's fifth largest zinc mine, and is ninth in production of copper. Manganese, silver, and uranium are also mined at Mount Isa (Fig. 7.9).

Additional major discoveries of nickel at Kalgoorlie and bauxite in

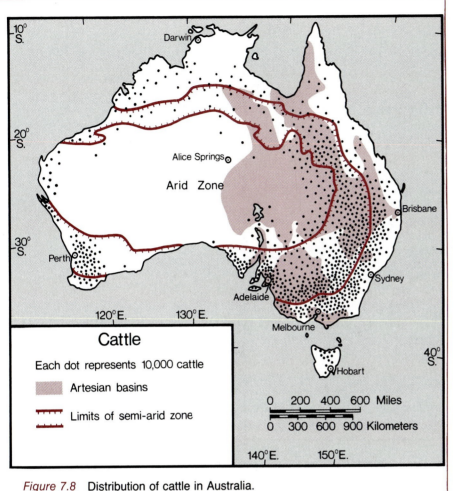

Figure 7.8 Distribution of cattle in Australia.

the Darling Range have been made in Western Australia. Bauxite has been found on the Cape York Peninsula, tungsten in Queensland, and copper in Tasmania. The array of metals and minerals found in Australia is awesome. The income they have produced has financed Australia's urban and industrial growth.

New discoveries are also changing the energy economy of Australia, which currently imports 30 percent of its crude oil. Australia's oil and natural gas comes from fields in the Bass Strait between Tasmania and Victoria and from Barrow Island off the west coast of Western Australia. Huge offshore natural gas discoveries have been made on the Northwest Shelf of Western Australia and in the Bass Strait. Exploration on the mar-

gins of the Great Artesian Basin in South and Western Australia has uncovered several promising new fields. These new discoveries, if developed, will make Australia self-sufficient in energy for the foreseeable future.

Manufacturing

Historically, Australia, like many colonial areas, played the role of supplying raw materials to the Technological World, particularly Britain. The country exported animal and mineral products and imported manufactured goods. World War I upset this relationship when trade between Europe and Australia was disrupted and the country was forced to produce its own manufactured goods. After World War II, the manufacturing sector expanded further. This growth

was financed by international investment and by revenues from newly developed mining ventures. Today, about one of every five Australians works in manufacturing, and this sector of the economy accounts for a fifth of the gross national product (GNP).

Australia now has a broad manufacturing base. Industries range from textiles, plastics, and food processing to precision instruments and electronics. Growth in heavy industries, such as automobiles, iron and steel, machinery, oil refining, and fertilizers, has been substantial. Most of these industries are located in Australia's largest cities, where the availability of skilled labor, sizable local markets, and port access to world markets are attractive locational incentives. Only the iron and steel industry, which draws on coal reserves in the hinterland of Sydney, is highly localized. Elsewhere diversified industry is found in each of the state capitals, with emphasis on industries that treat agricultural products and minerals from their respective hinterlands.

Today, Australia is moving rapidly toward a postindustrial society with a majority of its work force employed in service industries. A full 86 percent in its people are city dwellers, making Australia one of the most highly urbanized countries in the Technological World. Moreover, its agricultural and mineral wealth has enabled Australia to sustain a highly literate and skilled population at income levels of better than $10,000 a year in the 1980s. Tourism to Australia, particularly by Japanese and North Americans, has increased dramatically. Despite this, continued growth in manufacturing and advanced high technology is vital to maintenance of this standard of living. And here, Australia faces a number of obstacles.

Australia's internal market for manufactures is limited by its small population, despite a recent agreement to join New Zealand in a South Pacific "common market." This

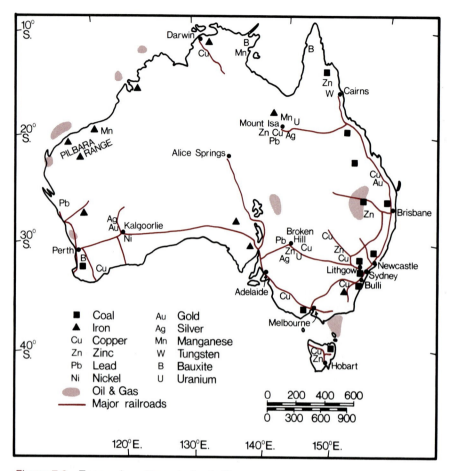

Figure 7.9 Economic patterns in Australia.

merger will increase trade across the Tasman Sea between two countries that are already each other's largest customers for manufactures. But the combined market of New Zealand and Australia is still under 20 million people. Moreover, Australia's domestic industries are protected by substantial tariffs on imports from abroad. High local production costs and long distances to potential markets make competition on world markets quite difficult. Australian exports of raw materials to Japan increased rapidly in the 1980s. In response, the Japanese requested lower tariffs on their manufactures, expecially automobiles. This places strong pressures on domestic automobile production. Australians are increasingly, concerned that their continent is becoming a quarry for Japanese industry.

Australia now exhibits many characteristics of a highly developed so-

ciety, but its position in world trade is comparable to that of many countries of the Developing World. Given Australia's extensive resource base and small population, however, the island continent is in a favored and flexible position in terms of future directions of growth. Australia remains the "Lucky Country."

MODERN NEW ZEALAND

Like Australia, New Zealand was settled by nineteenth-century Europeans who transferred a Western society and economy and replicated it in entirety in the Pacific. In the case of New Zealand, two Pacific islands previously occupied by a native Polynesian people, the Maoris, became

an integral part of the British Empire. Much smaller in size than Australia but equal in area to Great Britain, New Zealand's humid climate, mountainous terrain, and dearth of mineral resources encouraged a different pathway to economic development from Australia's. *The New Zealand Environment* posed different challenges.

New Zealanders capitalized early on the rich pasturelands of North Island and South Island to create an export economy based on animal husbandry (Fig. 7.10). Today they have a wealthy, skilled society of 3.3 million people. As they diversify into industrial and technological pursuits, the people of New Zealand are highly urbanized and have high standards of living (See Geostatistics). *Population and Economy* have grown apace.

The New Zealand Environment

New Zealand consists of two main islands and a number of smaller islands located more than 1000 miles southeast of Australia in the storm-prone westerlies between latitudes 34° and 47° S. This location is comparable to that of the American Pacific Northwest, so that New Zealand has a maritime west coast climate characterized by a moderate temperature regime and ample rainfall evenly distributed throughout the year. The islands are surrounded by a vast stretch of the Pacific Ocean. Abundant moisture is available. Variations in rainfall, therefore, are produced by prevailing winds and local topography.

New Zealand's North Island and South Island are dominated by mountain spines that slice cross country from northeast to southwest. Three quarters of the land lies at elevations over 650 feet. No place in New Zealand is farther than 80 miles from the sea. Of the two islands, North Island is somewhat smaller in area, has lower relief, and proportionately more level land. The corrugated terrain of its central highlands, however, reaches volcanic heights of more than 8000 feet at Mount Ruapehu and Mount Egmont. The terrain of South Island is considerably more rugged. The west side of this island is lined by the Southern Alps, a snowcapped mountain range whose highest peaks, Mounts Cook and Tasman, rise 2 miles above the sea. On both islands, the disposition of terrain is a strong factor in local climate as well as an important influence on patterns of settlement and economy.

Annual rainfall in most of New Zealand varies between 25 and 60 inches per year, but differences in total amount from one location to another are quite large. The western slopes of the Southern Alps receive upwards of 300 inches of precipitation, where warm, moist air masses from the west are forced to rise along the rugged mountain front. The eastern slopes of these mountains, however, receive as little as 13 inches a year as the rainshadow effect of terrain creates a sharp climatic divide. Because no part of New Zealand lies more than 80 miles from the sea, extremes of temperature are rare. Given this location, climate, and topography, forests and pastures cover much

Alpine pastures line the Kawarau River near the mountain resort town of Queenstown, South Island, New Zealand.

try, line the east coasts of both islands, cover the rolling hills of the western shore of North Island, and are found inland wherever vegetation, climate, and terrain permit. The most important lowland areas are the Auckland Peninsula of North Island and the Canterbury Plain inland from Christchurch on South Island. Here, fertile soils, ample rain, and a long growing season support lush pastures and cropland. In these areas and along the east coast, mixed farming, tree crops, and vegetable farms are interspersed with pastures. In the drier parts of South Island, wheat is cultivated.

Despite heavy reliance on pastoral products, only 145,000 New Zealanders are directly engaged in primary production and 84 percent of the population lives in cities. The highly mechanized, scientific nature of modern animal husbandry requires little labor. So, most people work in service jobs or processing industries in Auckland (pop. 825,000), Wellington (pop. 350,000), and Christchurch (pop. 330,000).

New Zealand, like Australia, is attempting to diversify its economic base. Unlike Australia, however, New Zealand has few natural resources (Fig. 7.10). Hydroelectric power is the only significant source of energy in New Zealand. Geothermal power is produced on North Island. New Zealand is one of the most hydroelectrified countries anywhere, with water-generated power meeting 87 percent of electrical needs. Coal, clay, and limestone are mined in small quantities. Iron sand deposits on the west coast of North Island support a small but growing steel industry at Auckland. Similarly, local bauxite is now refined near Invercargill on South Island. Natural gas is produced from the large Maui offshore gas field near New Plymouth on North Island. Paper and pulp plants at Nelson and Otago on South Island reflect growing commercial development of timber.

The entry of the United Kingdom into the EC in 1973 worked considerable hardship on New Zealand's economy. Suddenly, tariff-free entry of agricultural products like lamb, cheese, and butter into Britain, the mainstay of New Zealand's export economy, evaporated.

Economic diversification is proving difficult in New Zealand. Distance from markets for its animal products, the small size of local industries, the limited local market for domestic manufactures, and high labor costs are inhibiting factors. Forced to import machinery, energy, and food, New Zealand has been unable to develop textiles, consumer goods, or electronics industries that can compete on world markets. Virtually all local industry must be protected from outside competition by high tariffs, and many will suffer as Australia and New Zealand allow free trade between these two countries.

AUSTRALIA, NEW ZEALAND, AND THE PACIFIC

At the beginning of this century, Australia and New Zealand saw themselves as outposts of Britain, English cultural enclaves in a distant and alien world. Ties with the mother country were strong. England remained a reference point for the people down under long after British power dwindled in the Pacific.

Increasingly, however, Australia and New Zealand have evolved separate national identities. In the process, Australia and New Zealand have developed their own perspectives on international affairs, become more sophisticated and socially complex, and more aware of their distant location in an ocean fringed by large, densely populated Asian countries.

Both Australia and New Zealand were settled by immigrants who had to make a living, and have done so. Their standards of living are now as high as any of the world. To maintain these standards, Australia and New Zealand must find new ways of adapting to changing patterns of trade, social relations, and political affairs. Operating out of the conviction that a few million Europeans can sustain themselves in vast, underpopulated lands in a Pacific world rimmed by millions of Asians, Australia and New Zealand are now sensitive to two issues—treatment of *The Australian Aborigines and The Maoris* and their *Immigration Policies*.

The Australian Aborigines and the Maoris

Most European settlers in Australia and New Zealand came to occupy the land and were unswerving in their belief in the superiority of European culture. In Australia, aborigines were viewed as lesser peoples. They were despised, ignored, driven off the land, shot as sport, and finally housed on reservations. In New Zealand, the more sophisticated Maoris were treated with greater regard and respect, but pitched battles between these Polynesian people and Europeans led to the signing of the Treaty of Waitangi in 1840 that promised to respect the Maoris' rights to land. In the years that followed, however, the Maoris lost most of their land, were decimated by disease, and suffered social disintegration.

Today, the two countries are struggling with problems of race relations not unlike those found in the United States, Canada, and Britain itself. The movement of nonwhites into urban centers has led to racial incidents and a struggle for life space between them and poor whites. Simultaneously, resentment among aborigines, and to a lesser extent, Maoris to second-class status is growing. Their demands for compensation for past losses reflect a rising sense of cultural identity. In Australia and New Zealand, treatment of indigenous peoples echoes throughout the Pacific Basin. Here, race relations affect both domestic peace and international relations.

The Australian Aborigines

The Australian aborigines, a black Negrito-type people, lived as hunters and gatherers in Australia for thousands of years. When the Europeans arrived, the 300,000 aborigines who occupied the continent were divided into more than 500 separate tribes, each with their own language. These people had developed a complex and intimate association with the land, vegetation, and animal life within their tribal territories and were

widely distributed across Australia. Their way of life was destroyed by waves of European herders, miners, and settlers who occupied the best pastoral land and dispossessed hundreds of tribes. Of the original 4000 Tasmanians, the last died in 1876. By 1901, a scant 60,000 Australian aborigines had survived.

Today, there are 170,000 aborigines, many of mixed ancestry, in Australia. Scattered throughout the country, they live primarily in the Northern Territory, Queensland, and Western Australia (Fig. 7.11). Although they form only 1 percent of Australia's population, these aborigines are a difficult and pressing social problem in the country. As one recent prime minister notes, "Australia's treatment of her aboriginal people will be the thing upon which the rest of the world will judge Australia and the Australians," Until recently, that treatment has been one of indifference and neglect.

In the last two decades, the Australian government has attempted to redress the injustices of the past. Aborigines have been granted the right to vote and to collect welfare benefits. In the 1970s, new laws gave aborigines rights to own and occupy land on designated reserves, although the government retained mineral rights in these areas. Predictably, in clashes with mining corporations, the aborigines have been unsuccessful in resisting the erosion of land rights on their reserves.

About 65 percent of the aborigines now live on the fringes of urban areas in fenced squatter camps, subsisting on government allowances and assistance from missionaries. A full 50 percent are unemployed. The average life expectancy of aborigines is 50 years, 23 years less than Australians of European descent. Aborigines have higher infant mortality rates, a higher incidence of disease, and suffer rampant alcoholism. Clashes between aboriginal and white Australians are increasing.

GEOLAB

ENVIRONMENTAL PERCEPTION

Everyone has a mental image of the world surrounding his or her individual environment. In a general sense, the individual's images are shared by members of the same culture and society. Increasingly, geographers have discovered that these images, or **environmental perceptions,** influence spatial behavior, in some cases with surprising results. Few individuals command total knowledge of their local environment or of distant places, like Australia and New Zealand. As a result, people frequently make decisions on the basis of their environmental perceptions rather than on the actual character of environments. Briefly stated, they move in a world of mental maps.

Geographers have studied how people perceive their environments and how these perceptions influence behavior. American settlers moving onto the Great Plains in the nineteenth century perceived the region as having more rainfall that it actually did. They repeatedly viewed droughts as unusual events. In a different culture, they might well have perceived the same droughts as acts of God. Modern Americans continue to flow southward into the Sunbelt in search of employment despite factual information that jobs there are difficult to find. Similarly, decisions about where to live, where to retire, where to locate the headquarters of a business firm, and where to take a vacation have been shown to be strongly influenced by environmental perceptions.

Because environmental perceptions are shared within a group, societies often assess the desirability and potential of a given environment quite differently, drawing on their past experiences, social goals, technological levels, and observations. In Australia, aborigines and European immigrants differed sharply in their ways of life and in their perceptions of Australian environments. These differences are still reflected in the distribution of these two groups on the Australian continent.

Prior to the arrival of European settlers in Australia, aborigines were widely distributed across the continent. Although population density varied from one region to another, larger and more stable groups lived in the more humid north and south, along permanent streams, and on the coast. In the dry interior, population levels were much higher than comparable European population levels today—a marked difference in environmental perception.

Over 500 separate tribes of aborigines lived in Australia. They were hunters and gatherers intimately familiar with the animals and plants on which they lived. Men hunted kangaroos, emus (large fightless birds), and other large game. Women gathered staple commodities. All food was shared within the tribe.

Each tribe occupied a defined territory whose boundaries—creeks, hillocks, clumps of trees, and rock formations—were well known. A complete, indissoluble relationship existed among aborigines, animals, plants, and tribal territories. Aborigines now refer to the age before the coming of the Europeans as the "Dreamtime"—indicating an unending time of life in nature.

Aboriginal groups moved seasonally from one tribal territory to another and often engaged in raiding, but no aboriginal tribe attempted to occupy the land of another tribe because title to the land rested with the Dreamtime ancestors of each group as well as its living members. This system of spatial organization preserved free movement of aborigines in arid Australia. The ability to utilize different environments in different seasons was essential to maximal use of dry areas.

The European settlers who migrated to Australia perceived the environment in quite different terms. Wild animals were slaughtered to make room for sheep and cattle ranches as well as farms. British law did not recognize prior occupation as title to land, nor did it take cognizance of ancestral spirits. The European pattern of private ownership replaced communal occupance; individual enterprise not economic reciprocity was the basis of the European economy. Thus, environments which had amply supported nomadic groups of aborigines were wastelands to Europeans who were intent on establishing permanent settlements. As culture contact intensified, the southern aborigines closest to the European advance were de-

Ayers Rock, a huge monolith four miles in circumference, rises a thousand feet above the Great Western Plateau in the Australian outback. It is sacred to Australian aborigines and is also a major tourist attraction. It has become a symbol of aboriginal protests against discrimination and theft of their tribal lands.

stroyed, the best pasturelands were occupied by European animals and plants, and hundreds of aboriginal tribes were alienated from their land.

The different environmental perceptions of white and aboriginal Australians can be seen by comparing the distribution of the aboriginal population in Figure 7.11 with that of the total Australian population (Fig. 7.6). White Australians, who comprise 99 percent of the population, are heavily concentrated in the southeast and southwest portions of the continent in the hinterlands of Australia's largest cities—Perth, Adelaide, Melbourne, Sydney, and Brisbane. Population diminishes rapidly away from the coast. The interior is virtually uninhabited; the tropical north is sparsely inhabited.

By contrast, the distribution of aborigines outside major urban centers shows concentrations in the very

areas that Europeans consider to be less desirable. Rural aborigines live principally in the tropical north and in the steppes and deserts of Western Australia, Northern Territory, and Queensland.

Although the present distribution of Australia's aboriginal population has been strongly affected by two centuries of European dominance, it does provide some guide to past distribution. Moreover, it provides a clear example of how two very different cultures perceived Australia's varied environments within the contours of their different mental maps of the same geography.

Source: Fay Gale, "A Social Geography of Aboriginal Australia," in D. N. Jeans (ed.), *Australia: A Geography.* New York: St. Martin's Press, 1978, pp. 358–359.

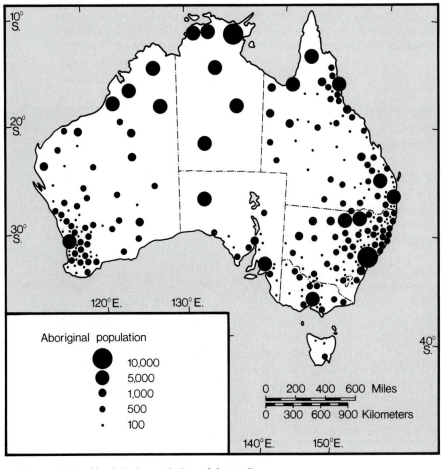

Aboriginal population

- 10,000
- 5,000
- 1,000
- 500
- 100

0 200 400 600 Miles

0 300 600 900 Kilometers

Figure 7.11 Aboriginal population of Australia.

A few communities still live the harsh, rigorous traditional life of the "bush," sleeping in makeshift shelters in dry riverbeds and practicing a mixture of hunting, gathering, and herding. But most aborigines are caught between two worlds. They live in government subsidized fringe settlements with nothing to do, few skills, and little confidence. On the other hand, some still live the life of the Dreamtime, and all know what they have lost in modern Australia. Like American Indians, they are victims of culture contact with Europeans.

The Maoris of New Zealand

The first colonists in New Zealand were the Maoris, whose voyages of discovery in the southern and eastern Pacific brought them to New Zealand somewhere around A.D. 750. In this new land, the Polynesian Maoris adjusted to new environments on islands far larger than others they settled. Primarily settling on North Island, they found climates temperate rather than tropical, and as they discovered New Zealand, they settled a diversity of environments open to human exploitation. Primarily hunters and gatherers, the Maoris also practiced **garden agriculture.** By the time James Cook discovered the islands in 1770, an estimated 250,000 Maoris lived in New Zealand, principally on North Island.

In contrast with the Australian aborigines, the Maoris had a highly developed, well-organized society led by astute leaders. In the early period of European colonization, Maoris played an important economic role in the development of New Zealand. As the European population grew, however, conflict over land led to war and ultimately to the Treaty of Waitangi in 1840 that guaranteed Maori rights to tribal land. But decimated by disease, dispossessed of land, and broken by social dislocation, the Maori population of New Zealand fell to 42,000 by the beginning of the twentieth century.

A small number of Australia's 170,000 aborigines still live the traditional life of hunters and gatherers in the Australian interior. Most live in government-sponsored squatter camps on the fringes of urban centers.

The twentieth century has witnessed a renaissance of Maori culture and society largely because of improved living conditions, increased resistance to European diseases, programs of government assistance, legal protection of Maori land, and vigorous tribal leadership. Today, the Maoris number more than 300,000, have had high rates of natural increase of more than 3 percent, and form 12 percent of New Zealand's population. Native Maoris intermarry freely with the **paheka,** or white New Zealanders, greatly facilitating the processes of adjustment and assimilation. Now Maori standards of living, life expectancy, and quality of life compare favorably with those of other New Zealanders—a tribute to the humanitarian idealism that generally governed European-Maori race relations despite early injustices.

The rapid growth and urbanization of the Maori population in recent decades has created some problems.

The renaissance of Maori culture in New Zealand is expressed in renewed interest in traditional crafts (the carved gateway) and dress.

The majority of Maoris are concentrated on the northern half of North Island, where, in some districts, they form a majority of the population. In the 1980s, three quarters of the Maoris live in urban centers, a fifth in the city of Auckland alone. The New Zealand government has acted swiftly to discourage acts of discrimination, improve housing conditions, and provide job training programs for Maori urban migrants.

Although Maoris clearly form an integral part of New Zealand society to a far greater degree than Australia's aborigines, Maori unrest is increasing because of their concentration in low-paying, blue-collar jobs. In addition, many Maoris believe that the paheka have failed to honor tribal land rights. Violent protests focused on a section of land called Bastion Point in Auckland have led to the establishment of a separate Maori political party. Despite these difficulties, New Zealand is attempting to accommodate the Maori minority. Efforts are being made to preserve Maori identity, while providing them with a place in the country's growth and development—a place that was nearly obliterated in the first century of European colonization.

Immigration Policies

Very early, Australia and New Zealand recognized that they were European outposts in the shadow of the Asian landmass. With small, white populations living on land areas less crowded than their much larger Asian neighbors, Australia and New Zealand carefully controlled immigration. Both countries provided active encouragement to European immigrants while barring the entry of any substantial number of Asians. Criticism of this racial discrimination is growing. Simultaneously, the economies of Australia and New Zealand are becoming more deeply entwined with those of nonwhite countries on the Asian perimeter, particularly Japan. Recently, Australia and New

Zealand have been forced to reassess their positions on immigration, which, like their treatment of indigenous peoples, is perceived as crucial to their future in the South Pacific.

Historically, Australia and New Zealand viewed their countries as racially white and culturally British. In both nations, restrictive immigration policies reinforced this reality. Immigrants of British origin were preferred to continental Europeans. Asians were excluded. In Australia, immigration became an issue when tens of thousands of Chinese and Indians entered the colony as cheap labor during the gold rushes of the 1850s. Popular resistance to Asian immigration, by the turn of the century, led to the enactment of a "White Australia" policy, supported by successive governments. A similar all-white immigration policy prevailed in New Zealand.

In the 1950s, Australia began to relax its "White Australia" policy, but a distinct preference for European immigrants continued in force. Since that time, several hundred thousand refugees and displaced persons— "New Australians"—have settled on the continent. Most of these people come from the British Isles, and 80 percent of all Australians are of English, Scotch, or Irish ancestry. But an increasing number of Dutch, German, Italian, Greek, Ukrainian, Lebanese, and Turkish immigrants live in Australia's largest cities, creating a cosmopolitan atmosphere in Australia that is less pronounced in more staunchly British New Zealand.

A trickle of Asian immigrants, roughly 10,000 a year, are also now admitted to Australia as well as thousands of Asian students. Moreover, a substantial number of refugee "boat people," driven to sea by desperation in Vietnam, Kampuchea (Cambodia), and other parts of Southeast Asia have sought haven in Australia and have been assisted by the government. Given the country's location, the problem of refugee "boat

people" is likely to recur in Australia as it has along the Caribbean perimeter of the United States. Although this will remain a contentious and difficult issue for Australia, greater liberalization of immigration policies seems likely as the country assumes more clearly defined regional perspectives and responsibilities.

New Zealand's immigration policies have been similarly liberalized. Upwards of 200,000 people from the Cook Islands, Tonga, and Fiji have become New Zealand citizens, as have a small number of "boat people" from Southeast Asia. Here, however, immigration policies are influenced by factors not found in Australia. People leaving New Zealand, mainly to take up residence in Australia, actually exceed new immigrants. More limited economic opportunities, a more restricted economic base, and the smaller population of New Zealand directly bear on immigration policies and on the future complexion of New Zealand's island society.

ACROSS THE WIDE PACIFIC

Australia and New Zealand are part of a large number of islands and peoples that make up the Pacific World. Set at the southwestern periphery of Oceania, Australia and New Zealand are, in some respects, at the economic and political heart of this vast oceanic stretch of the planet. Oceania is a collective place name for some 25,000 tropical Pacific islands lying generally in the southern and western quadrant of the world's largest ocean (Fig. 7.14). Oceania has emerged in the 1980s as a new place in the world. It is a new set of countries developed out of colonies, United Nations **trusteeships,** and islands tenuously connected to each other and to the outside world. In fact, most South Pacific islands are uninhabited and still unnamed.

Despite this, Oceania has rapidly

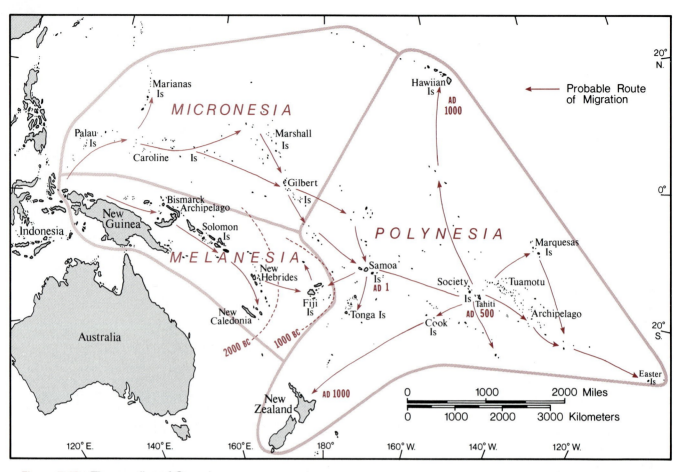

Figure 7.12 The peopling of Oceania.

become part of the political geography of our age. It has been claimed, demarcated, and divided into states very different from one another. The real coherence here is the dominance of the sea over the land, the distinctiveness of island life, the isolation of places, and the overwhelming distance between Oceania as a whole and anywhere else—even Australia and New Zealand.

Island Voyagers initially populated this region; later came explorers who initiated *The Europeanization of Oceania. The Human Geography of the Pacific World* was strongly influenced by local environments and resources that are only now, in *Contemporary Oceania*, being developed.

Island Voyagers

Three broad human regions exist in Oceania: Melanesia, Micronesia,

and Polynesia. Melanesia, the west and south of Oceania, and Polynesia, the east and northeast of Oceania, have been far more important in history than Micronesia, in the north and west of this region (Fig. 7.12).

Melanesia

Early in the last Ice Age, about 70,000 B.C., the Indonesian archipelago was inhabited by the ancestors of today's Melanesians. As the Ice Age proceeded, and more of the earth's water became locked up in ice, ocean levels throughout the world dropped by as much as 350 feet. In southeastern Asia and Oceania, the result was that it became much easier to voyage from island to island. The landmasses of Australia and New Guinea were slowly peopled by **paleolithic** migrants from Asia; these Melanesian peoples assumed their present distribution by

2000 B.C. (Fig. 7.12). When the Ice Age ended and sea levels rose, the geographic separation between Melanesia and Australia took hold. The land bridge between New Guinea and Australia gradually flooded, and the Torres Strait formed. Originally, then, Australian aborigines were Melanesians.

As a separate people, Melanesians came to occupy a variety of island chains extending toward the east, the general direction of settlement. Melanesia includes a broad band of islands across the southwest Pacific, north of Australia and south of the equator. Major island groups in Melanesia include the Bismarck archipelago, the Solomon Islands, the New Hebrides, New Caledonia, and Fiji. In all, Melanesia extends northwest to southeast for more than 2500 miles across the Pacific (Fig. 7.14).

New Guinea itself varies from the populations of Melanesia in race and in age of settlement (Fig. 7.12). In the interior mountains of New Guinea, the most isolated of the island's peoples are Pygmies who differ little from those in Africa. This suggests that the Negrito race was once continuous from Africa across the Indian Ocean. New Guinea's people, known as Papuans, are linguistically unrelated to Melanesians and may well be a far earlier—perhaps the first—people in the region.

Micronesia

North of Melanesia, the scattered atolls of Micronesia represent a northward push of Melanesian peoples into island groups stretching from the Marianas in the northwest; to Palau, wedged north of New Guinea and east of the Philippines; to the Carolines, running 1900 miles east-west between 5 and 10 degrees north; and the Marshall Islands, the eastern anchor of Micronesia (Fig. 7.12). Micronesians are physically similar to Melanesians, and have been in the region since the first millenium B.C. Like the Melanesians, Micronesians were exclusively hunters, fishers of the sea, and gatherers until very recent times.

Polynesia

Polynesians filled the Pacific from west to east (Fig. 7.12). People who had settled easternmost Melanesia, Tonga, began to become a separate culture after 1000 B.C. The Tongans colonized and settled Samoa after 300 B.C., and as they expanded into a new geography, they began to be identified as a separate people, the Polynesians.

Their navigational skills led these new people from Tonga and Samoa to the Marquesas by A.D. 300, and shortly thereafter to the Society Islands, Hawaii, and New Zealand (Fig. 7.12). Polynesians mounted voyages of exploration and discovery, deliberately colonizing the Pacific and peopling a far-reaching realm. No island worthy of settlement was overlooked by the Polynesians. Some attempts at colonization failed as Polynesians learned about the agricultural productivity of volcanic islands as compared with ecologically less promising coral reefs and atolls. Regular visits—social and ceremonial—kept the Polynesian sea lanes active paths of communication and commerce until the 1300s, when Polynesians became more island-bound. Why this geographic stabilization occurred remains a mystery. Demographic development was small; Hawaii and New Zealand each had populations of perhaps 250,000 at the time of European contact. The remaining Polynesians numbered around 100,000.

The Europeanization of Oceania

These distant lands were first traversed by Europeans during Magellan's epic voyage of global circumnavigation in the 1520s. Although Magellan was killed in the Philippines, his Spanish legacy lived on for several hundred years. The French and the British began to penetrate Oceania in the 1700s.

The three voyages of the British navigator, James Cook, marked the beginning of British influence in the region. Sent to the South Pacific to mark the transit of Venus, and thereby figure the earth's grid with greater precision, Cook discovered Tahiti, in the Polynesian islands. He voyaged west to circumnavigate New Zealand and identified the coast of eastern Australia. Out of interest, he returned in 1772–1775, whereupon he identified Australia as an island, visited the New Hebrides and New Caledonia in Melanesia, and skirted the waters of the even greater mystery at the bottom of the earth, Antarctica. Cook made a final voyage to the South Seas in 1776–1778, during which he rediscovered Hawaii, named the chain the Sandwich Islands, and was killed in a misunderstanding with native islanders. Cook's voyages laid the groundwork for the British presence in the Pacific, particularly in Australia and New Zealand, and established British claims to many islands in Melanesia and Polynesia.

Equally important was the voyage (1776–1779) of the Frenchman Bougainville. Bougainville, accompanied by naturalists and astronomers, circumnavigated the globe. As he passed through the Pacific, he visited Tahiti in the Society Islands, the New Hebrides, and rediscovered the Solomon Islands, the largest island of which was named after him (Fig. 7.14). His voyage gave France claim to the South Pacific much as Captain Cook's did for Britain. As a result of his voyage, the French held (as they still do) the Society Islands, focused on Tahiti. In western Polynesia, France later annexed a small set of volcanic islands known as Wallis and Futuna. And in Melanesia, France occupied the large island of New Caledonia in the 1850s and organized a prosperous agricultural colony and operated a penal colony there amid a population of native Papuans.

The Scramble for Colonies

By the end of the 1800s, the South Pacific was ruled by European colonial powers. Spain, losers in a war with America in 1898, ceded the Philippines to the United States. Far across the ocean, at the northeastern apex of Polynesia, American whalers, missionaries, sugarcane planters, and naval interests in concert with native Hawaiians maneuvered the overthrow of the Polynesian monarchy and U.S. annexation of the islands in 1898. In a stunning series of events, the United States had toeholds at both ends of the Pacific—Hawaii and the Philippines (Fig. 7.13).

The Spanish-American War had other Pacific side effects. The largest, most populous, and southernmost of the Mariana Island chain, the island of Guam, was ceded to the United States. Spain sold the rest of Micronesia to the Germans, already deeply

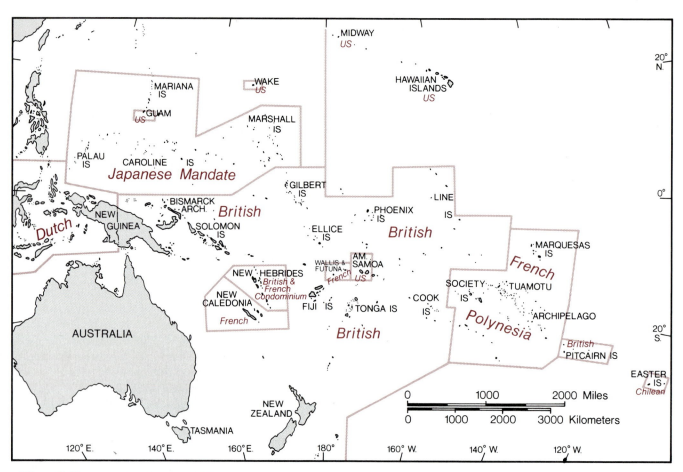

Figure 7.13 Oceania: The colonial Pacific.

involved in the Pacific. Spanish territories in Melanesia—New Britain and the Solomon Islands (Bougainville)—were added to the German Admiralty Islands and became known as German New Guinea (Fig. 7.13). And England had a Pacific empire too, made up of Australia, New Zealand, and many islands in Oceania.

Many British islands came to be governed by Australia and New Zealand. The southern half of eastern New Guinea became an Australian trusteeship in 1906 (the western half was Dutch, part of the Dutch East Indies). The Polynesian Cook Islands, 2000 miles northeast of Auckland, became a **dependency** of New Zealand in 1901. Tiny Niue and far-flung Tokelau (Union Islands) were bequeathed by Britain to New Zealand. In this fashion, colonies begot colonies. On the other hand, Tonga, the Gilbert and Ellice Islands, and Fiji,

perhaps the most important island group of all in the South Pacific, became full-fledged British crown colonies during the great age of European empire building in the Pacific from the 1870s to World War I (Fig. 7.13).

The scramble for Pacific colonies had, indeed, begun in the Polynesian heartland, the rich, fertile, and well-peopled volcanic islands of Samoa. The United States, Britain, and Germany all sent representatives to what was then an independent Samoan kingdom. The United States was the first to sign a treaty with Samoa, obtaining trading privileges and the right to establish a naval station at the capital, Apia. To placate the Germans and the British, similar privileges were accorded them in the following year, 1879. Ten years later, however, after a decade of island-grabbing throughout the Pacific, particularly

on the part of the Germans, and to a much lesser extent the British, the three powers were close to war over control of Samoa. Seven warships—three German, three American, one British—faced each other in a standoff in Apia harbor. Then a **typhoon** struck, Apia harbor was awash in rough seas, the German and American ships went down, and the British managed to survive by putting to sea in the eye of the storm and riding it out.

The three powers negotiated an agreement to rule the islands as a tripartate **condominium.** Eventually, Britain bowed out, leaving Samoa divided between Germany and the United States until World War I (Fig. 7.13). In a similar development, Britain and France forged an agreement to share responsibility over the New Hebrides in Melanesia, thereby establishing an Anglo-French condominium lasting until 1980 when the New Hebrides achieved independence and was renamed Vanuatu.

Britain, the United States, France, Germany, Australia, and New Zealand all held tropical Pacific territories in 1914. Chile annexed the most easterly of all Polynesian Islands, Easter Island, 2000 miles west of the Chilean coast (Fig. 7.13). The rush to gain colonies and imperial rivalry over bits of hitherto unknown territory closely resembled what occurred in Africa during the same period. And, as in the colonial map established in Africa, significant changes came from political influences far removed from the colonies themselves. With World War I, Germany lost its recently pieced together empire in the Pacific. German New Guinea became British and was then willed to the Australians; New Zealand grabbed German Samoa at the beginning of the war; German Micronesia was lost to a new Pacific power, Japan.

Japan energetically colonized Micronesia under a League of Nations **mandate** conferred after the war. So, on the eve of World War II, Japan was well positioned to expand in the Pacific. The Japanese pushed eastward into Polynesia attacking the American island of Oahu, in Hawaii, southward into Australian New Guinea, and westward into the American Philippines. As war was waged from island to island and Japan was eliminated from the colonial Pacific, the United States emerged as the owner of all of Micronesia, the last significant territorial conquest in the Pacific (Fig. 7.13).

In all, the Europeanization of the Pacific went largely unnoticed by the world at large. The American public's realization of its ownership-trusteeship of Micronesia was limited. Because of the enormous distances and the small, scattered populations involved, Oceania passed from one colonial power to another with the stroke of the cartographer's pen. Yet in Oceania itself, the changes wrought were profound and long lasting.

Demographic and Economic Change

Polynesians, for example, saw their population decimated by alien diseases—measles and smallpox—and their islands then repopulated by foreigners. In the most extreme case, Hawaii's native population declined from 200,000 in 1775 to 70,000 in 1850, and then to half that by 1900. Immigrants, largely from China, Japan, the Philippines, Portugal, and the United States, made up most of the total Hawaiian population of 150,000 in 1900 and 300,000 by 1925. Similar, but less dramatic, changes occurred in Tahiti, Tonga, Fiji, and New Caledonia.

Plantation agriculture was established on these islands. Hawaii was cleared of forest and planted to sugarcane and pineapple. Tonga grew coconuts. Fiji raised sugarcane and copra (fiber for rope) and Indian laborers were imported to work in the fields of Australian and British planters. New Caledonia was actively colonized by French farmers who established a French peasantry in Melanesia. On New Caledonia, however, the French founded a mining economy based on nickel, chrome, iron, gold, silver, cobalt, and copper. Samoa became dependent on the canning of tuna caught in Polynesian waters and marketed in world markets.

The Human Geography of the Pacific World

Looking at a globe, the Pacific Ocean is the single largest identifiable feature on our planet (Fig. 7.14). It covers some 70 million square miles and half the water surface of the globe. The Soviet Union could fit into the Pacific more than eight times, the United States more than seventeen times (Fig. 7.14). Land area in the Pacific is very unevenly distributed.

In Oceania, however, islands and island groups are far more numerous than elsewhere in the Pacific.

Australia accounts for 90 percent of the land area of Oceania; New Zealand and New Guinea, second in size to Greenland among world's islands, account for most of the remainder.

By size, smaller islands are generally in eastern Oceania, and larger islands are in the west. In western Oceania, large islands, such as New Guinea and New Caledonia, are related to continental land-building forces and were cut off from mainland Asia and Australia by rising sea levels.

Volcanic and Coral Island Formation

Volcanism is active in several of the Melanesian islands, and in the far east, in Hawaii. Islands shaped by volcanism and fringed by coral reefs stretch right across Oceania. On all of these islands, volcanic cones and their **ejecta** built plateaus. Subsequent erosion resulted in large islands etched by deep valleys with rich soils. On the largest of the volcanic islands, human occupance has been relatively dense and long-lasting. Volcanic islands provide favorable environments for a combination of fishing and agriculture. Fresh water is relatively abundant on volcanic islands and soils support cultivation of sugarcane, yams (sweet potato), cassava (manioc), and taro (another starchy root crop). Tree crops like banana, breadfruit, and coconut also flourish on volcanic islands. The forests provide forage for pigs, and wild fowl are plentiful.

The **coral reef** is another dominant feature of the natural environment of Oceania. The deep warm water surrounding islands is ideal for the growth of these living, lime-secreting organisms. Algae bind the coral together to form deposits of limestone rock. Coral creates a variety of physical environments: a **fringing reef** is a coral platform attached to the shore; a **barrier reef** lies outward from shore and is separated from the mainland by a

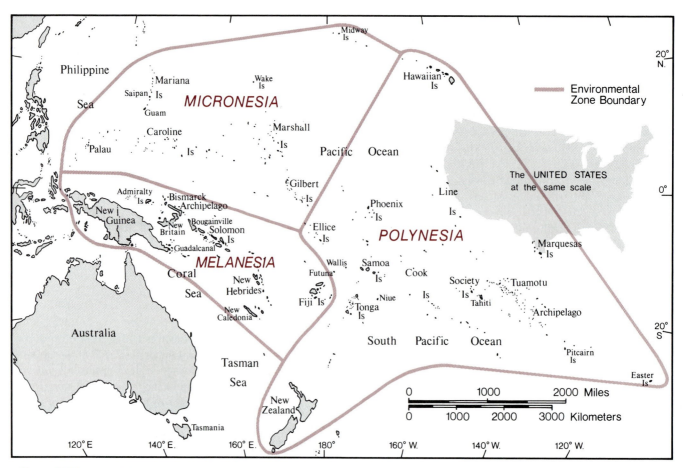

Figure 7.14 Oceania: Physical features.

Extinct volcanic islands ringed by coral reefs are found throughout the South Pacific.

lagoon; if the island is uplifted, as happened throughout the area at the end of the Ice Age, the reef dies and becomes a bench (or ridge) surrounding the island. Many Pacific islands are ringed by coral reefs. The world's single largest coral reef is Australia's Great Barrier Reef. It covers 400,000 square miles off Queensland and was declared a separate Australian territory in 1969.

A third type of land environment found throughout Oceania is the **atoll** (Fig. 7.15). An atoll is a series of coral islands ringing a shallow body of water, a lagoon. Atolls result from the growth of coral around sinking volcanic islands. It may be that the central island sank as Ice Age glaciers melted and ocean levels rose, or that the volcanic core was weathered away by wave action. A coral atoll is a ring of islands surrounding an empty lagoon. Atolls look like necklaces of is-

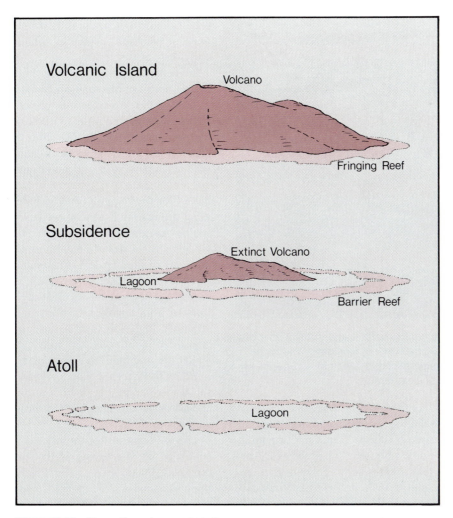

Figure 7.15 Formation of a coral atoll.

lets strewn across the Pacific. Atolls are built upon volcanic foundations.

The first to speculate on their formation was the English naturalist Charles Darwin in the 1830s. He proposed the subsidence theory, in which it is believed that an atoll originally was a volcano surrounded by a fringing reef (Fig. 7.15, top). As the extinct volcano became weathered by wave action, it began to subside, or sink. At the same time, the reef continued to grow upward, becoming a barrier reef (Fig. 7.15, center). Finally, the volcanic core sinks out of sight, and the reef islands ringing an empty lagoon are all that is left. The feature is now an atoll. Recently, geologists drilling into atolls have discovered that there has been as much

as 4000 feet of volcanic subsidence and 4000 feet of upward reef growth over the last 60 million years. It appears that Darwin was correct. As the central volcanic island sank, the reef continued to grow upward. Eventually, all that is left is the coral reef itself, shaped like a broken necklace surrounding the drowned former island (Fig. 7.15). The reef islands—islets—are wider on the lagoon-facing side of the atoll; the ocean-facing side of the islets have rough beaches of broken coral.

Atolls rise only a few feet above the open sea, and provide precarious habitats for human living. Soils are thin and infertile. Freshwater must be saved from rainfall. And atolls are under threat of devastation from

tropical cyclones, or typhoons. Atolls dominate in Micronesia. Interestingly, in Micronesia, which literally means "small islands," it is the few volcanic islands that are most important: Yap and Truk in the Caroline group and Guam, the largest Micronesian island, in the Marianas.

Human Ecology of the Pacific

Oceania was a laboratory of human ingenuity. On Micronesian atolls, for example, there is no clay, hence no pottery. Forage and pasture are virtually absent, so that domestic animals are few or absent altogether. Without rock other than sea-formed coral, all weapons, utensils, and tools were fashioned of wood, bone, or shells.

In Micronesia and Polynesia, the great distances between human places led to highly developed skills of seamanship, navigation, and boat making. In Polynesia, 100-foot-long outrigger vessels capable of carrying as many as sixty passengers and a crew besides, could sail through 2500 miles of open sea for a month at a time. Knowledge of the sea was precise. Polynesians knew that reflections in the clouds mirrored the location of island groups in the area.

The thatched houses of the entire region are environmentally sound, capable of withstanding the high winds and heavy rainfall of the typhoon. The coconut palm and pandanus (screw pine) were fully utilized. The coconut palm supplied drinking water (the green nuts); fruit, oil, and skin lotion (the ripe coconut); drink (the sap, fresh or fermented); rope and thread (the husk of the nut); lumber for boats and houses (the trunk); thatch for houses and fiber for mats (the fronds). Out of few resources, much was made.

Contemporary Oceania

With the end of World War II, Oceania stood at the doorway of a new era. Like Germany a generation before, Japan had disappeared from the roster of imperial powers. The

Nuclear testing in the Pacific has become a controversial issue. In 1985, this vessel belonging to Greenpeace (an ecological organization) was destroyed by an explosion in Auckland, New Zealand. It was preparing to sail to Mururoa Atoll in French Polynesia, a current site of French nuclear testing.

war in the Pacific had brought Americans to places barely heard of before: Guadalcanal, Solomon Islands, New Britain, Midway, Wake, Guam, and Saipan. Melanesia and Micronesia had seen the world's largest navies pass their way, wreak incredible destruction, and move on. But America stayed after the Japanese withdrew. Micronesia became American trust territory. Now under guidance from the United Nations, the old mandates and trusteeships of Australia and New Zealand, too, faced new futures. The winds of nationalism, strong in the postwar era among colonial peoples everywhere, began to blow gently across the Pacific.

Slowly, the path toward the reorganization of Oceania into new independent states was taken. In the 1980s a variety of formulas have been invented for the islands of Oceania in this new age.

The Changing American Presence

Micronesia, an area the size of the United States, administered as the U.S. "Trust Territory of the Pacific Islands," has less land area than the state of Rhode Island and a population of only 160,000 spread over more than 2000 islands. Following the results of a vote taken in 1986, Micronesia will emerge as three self-governing countries and one U.S. commonwealth by 2001. In the east, the Republic of the Marshall Islands is focused on the Kwajalein Atoll, where the United States built a major air force base (Fig. 7.16). "Kwaj" is the Pacific terminus of a U.S. missile range, over which rockets fired 4500 miles away in California are tested. The base at Kwaj has 3000 American civilians and a U.S. suburban environment. Between 1946 and 1958, the United States tested 66 nuclear weapons in the atmosphere over the Bikini and Eniwetok atolls, bringing a new dimension of change to Micronesian islanders. As with the other new states of Micronesia, the United States will continue to subsidize the economy of the Republic of the Marshall Islands during the transition period; their defense will also be guaranteed. In addition, the United States has established a $150 million trust fund to assist islanders harmed by the nuclear tests of the 1950s.

In central Micronesia, the Federated States of Micronesia (FSM) is a new country composed of four states—Kosrae, Pohnpei, Truk, and Yap—spanning the old Caroline Islands (Fig. 7.16). Volcanic Kosrae, with its fertile soils and good agricultural climate, is a potential breadbasket for the region. Tourism holds great promise in Kosrae as well as in the east-central state of Pohnpei, still steeped in the traditional Micronesian way of life. Truk, in the center of FSM, and Yap, the westernmost state of the Federation, are also largely isolated from major cultural change, although high rates of natural increase, dependence on imported foodstuffs, and modern education are building the forces of change. A strict social caste system is slowly eroding and Christian missionaries, too, bring changes to the islands.

The westernmost of the emerging countries of Micronesia is the Republic of Palau (Fig. 7.16). Palau's population of 15,000 people is divided into sixteen different states. Palau's fate, like that of many Pacific island countries, is jeopardized by its rapid rise in population, strong dependence on food imports, and limited resources. Continued reliance on American funds is likely.

In northern Micronesia, the Mariana Islands voted to retain association with the United States and even to strengthen their American links as they become the Commonwealth of the Northern Mariana Islands (Fig. 7.16). In the Marianas, on the large island of Saipan, the sugar industry has been augmented by the growth of tourism, particularly of Japanese revisiting World War II battlefields. The Marianas will gain U.S. citizenship and will be organized as a U.S. territory. Eventually they could elect to statehood, should their tiny population (15,000) grow large enough. Guam, pop. 105,000, owned by the United States since 1898, the south-

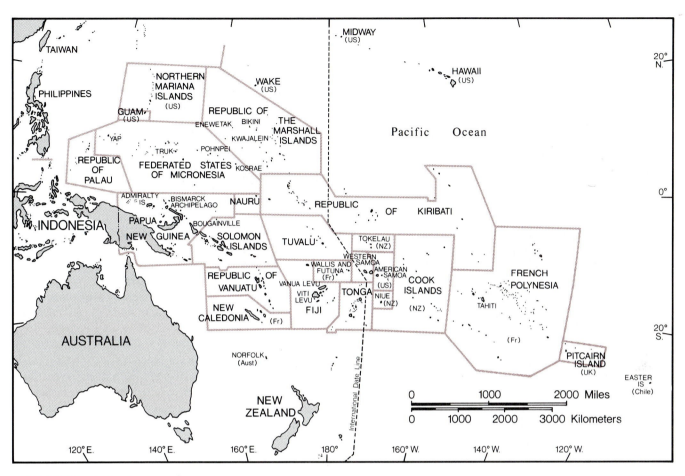

Figure 7.16 Political map of Oceania.

ern anchor of the Marianas, remains an unincorporated U.S. territory, and has extensive U.S. naval facilities.

Other American possessions in the Pacific have received different treatment. The Hawaiian Islands achieved statehood in 1959. Midway, two small islands at the far northern end of the Hawaiian chain, was not incorporated into the state of Hawaii and remains administered by the U.S. Navy. Wake Island, due north of the Marshall Islands, was acquired in 1898. It is too small (population less than 2000) to be anything other than unincorporated U.S. territory on an indefinite basis. In Polynesia, American Samoa (pop. 35,000; 76 square miles) consists of two main islands (Fig. 7.16). The backbone of the economy, tuna fishing and canning, provides livelihood for many people in the capital, Pago Pago (pop. 3075). Like Polynesians in general, most Sa-

The large American military installation on Guam is evidence of the growing strategic importance of the Pacific.

moans are smallholding farmers, growing the typical staples of the Polynesian diet—bananas, breadfruit, cassava, yams, taro, pineapples, and vegetables—for domestic consumption and small sales. Pago Pago is attracting more tourists, and U.S. government assistance brings in considerable cash to the islands.

The French in the Pacific

Alone of all imperial powers, the French have steadfastly maintained their Oceanian empire, such that New Caledonia, Wallis and Futuna, and French Polynesia have been granted "Overseas Territory" status, which means that their peoples have all the rights and privileges of French citizens elsewhere. The French have no intention of leaving their Pacific territories (Fig. 7.16).

New Caledonia (7358 square miles) contains one of Oceania's largest cities, its capital, Noumea (pop. 57,000). Native Papuans constitute slightly less than a majority of the island's population of 148,000; French colonists (**colons**) compose about 30 percent of the ethnic mix. Racial troubles have stirred in New Caledonia in the 1980s. The territory's main wealth lies in its minerals, particularly nickel, in which New Caledonia ranks third in world production. Unemployment, too, has generated unrest. France provides about one third of the revenues of the island.

Far to the east, French Polynesia (pop. 167,000; 1544 square miles) occupies five scattered island groups, of which the main island, Tahiti, is a major world tourist destination. Elsewhere in French Polynesia, however, low levels of employment and poverty have motivated many islanders to emigrate to Tahiti's capital, Papeete, or even to France. Some plantations—coconut, copra, sugar—have been established, but generally there has been a low level of development. Wallis and Futuna, two rainsoaked French islands 125 miles apart in western Polynesia, have a popu-

lation of 10,000 on 77 square miles; copra is the only export of note.

The British Retreat from the Pacific

The British have divested themselves of their empire in the Pacific, and only a few pieces of rock remain under the Union Jack. In far eastern Polynesia, the Pitcairn Group is still British (Fig. 7.16). Only Pitcairn Island itself is inhabited—fifty-five people on an island of 1.75 square miles. Pitcairn's history is one of the more curious in the Pacific. All fifty-five Pitcairn Islanders are descendants of the mutineers of the H.M.S. Bounty who took refuge on this uninhabited island in 1790 and burned their ship when they settled onshore.

In what was the British Empire in Polynesia and Melanesia, a set of new countries emerged in the 1970s, largely with British customs and methods of government. The first was Fiji, the largest in land area (7056 square miles) and population (700,000) (Fig. 7.16). Fiji's economy is largely based on its sugarcane and coconut plantations. The two main islands, Viti Levu and Vanua Levu, are surrounded by 300 other islands, many of which are uninhabited. Suva, the capital (pop. 64,000) on Viti Levu, has grown rapidly since independence. The establishment of the University of the South Pacific in Suva is testimony to the relatively high levels of achievement attained by Fijians. A racially mixed society, Fiji's population is composed of 47 percent native Melanesians and 49 percent Indians, originally imported to work in the sugarcane fields. Small Polynesian, Chinese, and European communities complete the ethnic mix. Racial animosity surfaced in Fiji in the late 1980s, resulting in a disputed election and military coup in 1987—the first modern military takeover in the South Pacific.

Elsewhere in the former British Empire, events have been as dramatic as in Fiji. Tonga, 1400 miles

northeast of New Zealand, received independence from Britain in 1970 and power was invested in the hereditary monarch (Fig. 7.16). The King of Tonga, through a Prime Minister and a partially elected Legislative Council, rules over his 107,000 subjects occupying 150 islands. The Tongalese have developed a unique form of landholding. All open land in Tonga is held by the Crown in reserve for the young men of the country. Upon reaching his majority, a young man receives a small farm from the king. Tonga has often been cited as one of the most successful modern agricultural economies in the Pacific, but high rates of natural increase will result in land shortages in the foreseeable future. Out-migration, too, has become an important factor in the island's economy.

In 1978 and 1979, the former Crown Colony of the Gilbert and Ellice Islands went their separate ways upon independence. The vast Gilbert, Phoenix, and Line Island groups became the Republic of Kiribati (pop. 68,000; 281 square miles) and joined the British Commonwealth of Nations (Fig. 7.16). To the west, the Ellice Islands (pop. 8400, 10 square miles divided among nine atolls), became the state of Tuvalu (Fig. 7.16). Both Tuvalu and Kiribati face difficult futures, with enormous geographic distances, tiny land areas, low populations, and very limited resources weighing against economic development. Grants-in-aid from Britain remain the main source of revenue for both new countries.

In Melanesia, the Solomon Islands, annexed by the British in the 1880s, were ruled as a British **protectorate** until 1978. Fully independent, the Solomons (pop. 271,000; 10,983 square miles), remain at levels of technology and agricultural subsistence not far removed from those of their ancestors. The capital, Honiara on Guadalcanal, is surrounded by copra, palm oil, and cocoa plantations. The timber and mineral resources of the twenty-one main and many smaller islands appear to be considerable (Fig. 7.16).

Finally, in 1980, the last of the British islands to gain statehood, the joint Anglo-French condominium of the New Hebrides, became the Republic of Vanuatu (pop. 138,000; 5700 square miles). These rugged Melanesian volcanic islands with densely forested mountains and intensively worked lowlands seem to have a promising future (Fig. 7.15). Communications and roads are good; manganese provides steady foreign currency. Farming, cattle raising, forestry, and fishing are all important economic activities. Tourism, especially by their Australian neighbors across the Coral Sea, is growing.

The Changing Roles of New Zealand and Australia

The territories governed by New Zealand and Australia, too, have taken different paths of political, economic, and social evolution in the postcolonial era of the Pacific. New Zealand has administered Tokelau (the Union Islands) as New Zealand territory since 1948 (Fig. 7.16). New Zealand has repeatedly encouraged emigration of the tiny population (today 1800) on the three widely scattered atolls to New Zealand, 2200 miles distant. The far different volcanic islands of Western Samoa, a former New Zealand mandate under the League of Nations and then the United Nations, obtained independence in 1962 (Fig. 7.16). Western Samoa (pop. 180,000; 1097 square miles) is made up of two main islands at the western end of the Samoan chain. Western Samoans are primarily subsistence farmers who grow the typical Oceanian plantation crops. Timber is being exploited, and tourism is in the early stages of development. Out-migration is a theme here; over 1000 Western Samoans emigrate each year to New Zealand.

In central Polynesia, the Cook Islands, athough granted self-government in 1965, are still linked to New Zealand through common citizenship in a "free association" (Fig. 7.16).

Cook Islanders live on broadly separated coral (northern Cook) and volcanic (southern Cook) islands stretching over 1000 miles of the Pacific from north to south. As in Western Samoa, migration to New Zealand is a prominent feature of contemporary economic life for the population of 21,500 Cook Islanders on their 91 square miles of land territory.

Finally, Polynesian Niue, due south of the Cook Islands, 1340 miles east of Auckland, became a self-governing New Zealand dependency in 1974 (Fig. 7.16). Niue, a single coral island (pop. 3000; 100 square miles) is entirely agricultural. Although it has its own elected assembly, Niue is likely to remain sheltered from the harsh realities of its limited resource base by continued assistance from New Zealand.

New Zealand, then, retains its power and influence over a broad stretch of the south-central Pacific. New Zealand looms as a continued center of importance for many of the peoples and economies of western Polynesia.

To the west, Australia, too, has given up its trusteeships in the Pacific as it readied native populations for independence following United Nations guidelines laid down in the 1960s and 1970s. Isolated between Micronesia and Melanesia, the oval-shaped coral island of Nauru gained its independence from Australian trusteeship in 1968 (Fig. 7.16). Nauru phosphate, widely used in New Zealand and Australian agriculture, is Nauru's sole source of income, but it has provided Nauruans with high incomes, and the profits from phosphates have been invested as a hedge against the day when the phosphates will run out on their tiny (8.1 square miles) island of 8000 people.

In 1975, Oceania's largest country gained its independence as Papua New Guinea (PNG) (Fig. 7.16), having been an Australian trust territory since 1906. With the German loss of the northern islands and northeast

coast in World War I, Australia annexed the German colonies and governed northern and southern New Guinea as separate League of Nations mandates. These combined in 1949 as the U.N. Trust Territory of Papua and New Guinea. The Australians recognized the importance of New Guinea—a vast land of paleolithic peoples rich in endemic flora and fauna—after World War II. An education system and the rudiments of the modern economy began to appear in the 1950s. Port Moresby, the capital, grew to a city of 150,000 by the mid 1980s. With a population of over 3 million and a land area of 178,765 square miles, Papua New Guinea has entered the modern world as a country with great potential in agriculture, fishing, forestry, and mining. The hydroelectric possibilities in this mountainous country are immense. Copper (mined on Bougainville Island) and coffee are the two most significant exports. As roads and the market economy reach into the interior, rapid transitions are being made. Like their fellow Pacific islanders, Papuans are witnesses to a century of profound change, development, and modernization.

Toward the Developing World

Oceania straddles the modern age. Like no other world region, the islands of the Pacific reflect the strategies of countries of the Technological World to forge colonial empires in distant places. Like African and native American societies, Pacific peoples had their own civilizations and histories—geographies unknown to the outside world. Magnificent kingdoms and cultures flourished in isolation. Touched by the West, brought into the orbit of the modern world, Pacific peoples now search for a new sense of identity in a global economy. Like people elsewhere in the Developing World, they live in a world of transition and new directions.

PART
THREE

THE DEVELOPING WORLD

8

LATIN AMERICA

*H*istorically, Latin America has been poorly understood. Latin America has remained on the periphery of the world stage, an economic dependency of Europe and North America. Vivid contrasts in culture and landscape disguise Latin America's geographic problems beneath a veneer of tourist resorts, colorful blends of people and culture, and a confusing and turbulent political history. Increasingly, however, the tide of events in Latin America is forcing North Americans to face the salient problems of the region—persistent poverty, social inequality, economic growth without social progress, deep political unrest, and a burgeoning population.

These ingredients have periodically exploded in revolution throughout Latin America, most recently in Central America and the Caribbean. North Americans are beginning to recognize the magnitude of Latin America's problems as well as the increasing interdependence of these two culture realms of the New World.

At the beginning of the nineteenth century, the economic and social future of Latin America could not have been predicted. Latin America had a large population, five times that of North America. It housed the greatest cities and finest universities in the New World. Its leaders were urbane and cultured world citizens, inheritors of a proud if rigid culture that gave them access to the scientific and technological progress of nineteenth-century Europe.

Despite this early lead, Latin America failed to develop its resource base, and never shared the immense wealth generated by the sale of its agricultural and mineral products among its people. It preserved a value system inherited from sixteenth-century Spain and Portugal, and to a lesser extent France, Britain, and the Netherlands.

After 170 years of independence, most of Latin America remains on the fringe of the industrial world as a producer of raw materials. The region has higher standards of living than those found in most of Asia and Africa, but lags far behind the Technological World in all indexes of social and economic development. The concentration of wealth in the hands of large landlords, the deprivation of the bulk of Latin America's population, the political fragmentation of the region, the failure to pursue social reform, growing populations, and rapidly expanding cities are generating discontent bordering on despair.

The contemporary human geography of Latin America cannot be understood in environmental or technological terms alone. In this region, lingering patterns of behavior and outmoded social structures retard balanced social and economic progress. Latin America reflects a value system etched on the landscape—a landscape of plantations and **haciendas,** of poverty-stricken peasants, of modern cities ringed by devastating slums, of extreme wealth and equally extreme poverty, of cultured societies led by military dictators backed by foreign and local elites that perpetuate a feudal system of social servitude.

In this light, Latin America is a relic society, belatedly pursuing economic development within the framework of an outdated set of perceptions and values. Alternatively, Latin America can be seen as a storehouse of resources capable of sustaining its people and providing all of its citizens with higher standards of living in the future. In fact, Latin America is both traditional and modern, developed and undeveloped. In this region, the future is present but never quite arrives. Complex as this may seem, Latin America is likely to be the most important region of the Developing World in influencing future development in North America.

TRADITIONAL LATIN AMERICA: SETTLEMENT AND SOCIETY

The interplay of settlement history and the physical environment is a central theme in the contemporary human geography of Latin America (Figs. 8.1, 8.2). For centuries, dense "islands of people" stood in stark relief against sparsely settled mountain, desert, and rain forest environments. The coastal rim of Central America and South America harbored the major centers of growth and development. The interior remained less developed, penetrated in most areas with indifferent success. Everywhere, the prism of Latin culture, focused during three centuries of colonial rule, generated modes of settlement and society that retain their vitality today. For this reason, much contemporary political, social, and economic activity can only be understood as an expression of preindustrial Iberian values impressed on the landscapes and societies of modern Latin America.

This section focuses on those traditional patterns of settlement and economy created by the collision of European, African, and American cultures. Before the Spanish and Portuguese settlement of the New World, civilizations with sophisticated political, economic, and social structures existed in the domains of *The Aztec, Maya, and Inca*. In Mexico and Peru, vast empires controlled the destinies of perhaps as many as 75 to 100 million people. But these high civilizations were literally beheaded during *The Spanish and Portuguese Conquest of the New World*. Their leaders were slain, their populations decimated by disease. Control of the region was assumed by new European conquerors who established institutions to meet the needs of their mother countries on

the Iberian Peninsula. For 300 years, *Colonial Development and Culture Change* in Latin America was directed from Europe. Patterns of landholding, economic growth, and cultural institutions were established that still survive. When *Independence in Latin America* was finally achieved early in the nineteenth century, surprisingly little changed. The traditional colonial patterns extend as a living legacy into the present. The sheer length of colonial rule had irrevocably transformed Latin America and its people.

The Aztec, Maya, and Inca

In the Valley of Mexico, in the dense forests of the Yucatán Peninsula, and in the Andes Mountains, civilizations flourished in the New World centuries before the Spanish arrived. Each of these societies had sophisticated religions and architecture, controlled substantial populations, and had productive agriculturally

based economies. Although very different from Old World civilizations and very different from each other, the Maya, Aztec, and Inca achieved levels of development equal to those of the Old World. Only recently have their accomplishments in art and science been appreciated, largely because the devastation wrought by the Spanish and Portuguese—the first European colonialists—was so intense and enduring. The old heritage lives on in the language and life of modern native Latin Americans, but the submergence of their culture under three centuries of Iberian rule has deeply changed the nature of most of the region.

The Aztec and Maya

The Aztec Federation that Cortés attacked in the sixteenth century was the last of many native American civilizations to occupy the fertile Valley of Mexico. Originally poor, landless, Nahuatl-speaking people from northwestern Mexico, the Aztec arrived in

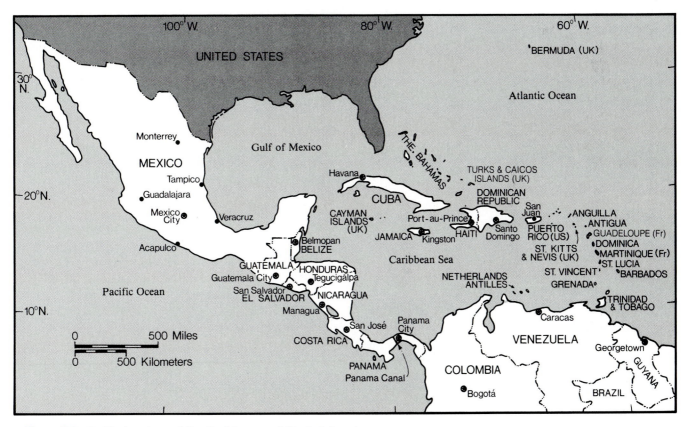

Figure 8.1 Political regions of the Caribbean and Central America.

Figure 8.2 Political regions of South America.

the Valley of Mexico in the 1300s. There, they built a village of reed huts, called Tenochtitlan, on some islands and sandflats in a lake. In the 1400s they rose to power, conquered neighboring peoples, and built an empire extending from the Pánuco River in the north to the border of Guatemala in the south.

The Aztec diet consisted of more than ninety different plants that had been domesticated in Mesoamerica (Central America). The most important of these—corn, squash, and beans—formed the basis of the Aztec economy. In the Valley of Mexico, a basin 30 to 40 miles wide, an agricultural population of between 1 and 2 million people supported the capital city of Tenochtitlan (Fig. 8.3).

In their capital city, the core of one of the most densely populated regions in **precolumbian** Middle America, the Aztec utilized an ingenious system of agriculture, the chinampa, a system in which artificial gardens were extended into freshwater lakes (Figs. 8.4, 8.5). Elsewhere, intensive cultivation, terraced farming, and irrigation were used in the fields of small, dispersed villages. Three to four crops in succession were produced during the year.

On the eve of the Spanish conquest, 12 to 15 million people lived in central Mexico, an additional 1 million lived in the highlands of Chiapas and Guatemala, and there were 500,000 people in the Yucatán. These populations were by no means homogeneous, culturally or politically. At the time of the Spanish conquest, eighty different languages belonging to fifteen language families were spoken throughout Middle America.

The best known of these groups, the Maya, had developed a civilization of artistic and agricultural sophistication in the tropical rain forests and surrounding dry highlands of Guatemala, Belize, and the Yucatán Peninsula. The Maya were led by a class of priests; their religion centered on the careful observance

The Spanish conquest of the New World began on October 12, 1492, when Christopher Columbus landed on the island of San Salvador (Watling) in the Bahamas.

of time and astronomical phenomena. Hereditary kings ruled independent city-states. Their religious and historical interests were inscribed on the pottery, monuments, and architecture of their cities in the most sophisticated hieroglyphic script of the New World. Their economy, based on the cultivation of corn, was sufficient to support a substantial population in the wet tropical lowlands. Recent geographic surveys using wide side-glancing radar have revealed that thousands of acres of ridged (raised) fields were under Mayan cultivation. Like the chinampas of central Mexico, these raised fields were the breadbasket of the Maya. The Maya abandoned their ceremonial centers around A.D. 900, perhaps because of ecological disaster. The Classic period was over. Some Maya groups thrived after the collapse of the Classic period particularly in the northern Yucatán and the Guatemalan Highlands.

By 1500, much of this region was still controlled by Maya fiefdoms, but the powerful Aztec Federation with whom the Maya traded was pressing southward. The Aztec and their western neighbors on the central plateau, the Tarascan, created powerful tribute states. The alien towns that the Aztec conquered paid annual gifts of grain, gold, textiles, cocoa, and human sacrifice to Aztec nobles in Tenochtitlan. The Aztec made no effort to integrate the varied people of the empire into their society. Political unrest was considerable, and the Aztec made repeated conquests to maintain order and ensure the payment of tribute. It was among these disaffected tribes that the Spanish found support in their bid for power, making it possible for Hernán Cortés, the gentleman from Estremadura, to conquer a New World realm of millions with a handful of men.

The Inca

Farther south at the time of Cortés's conquest, the Inca controlled an em-

GEOSTATISTICS

	Capital	Area (square miles)	Population (millions)	Rate of Natural Increase (%)	Number of Years to Double Population	Population Projected for A.D. 2000	Infant Mortality Rate	Life Expectancy at Birth	Urban Population (%)	Per Capita GNP ($)	Energy Consumption per Capita (kg of oil equivalent)
Antigua and Barbuda	St. John's	170	0.1	1.0	71	0.1	10	72	31	2,380	—
Argentina	Buenos Aires	1,068,297	32.0	1.5	45	37.2	35	70	85	2,350	1,468
Bahamas	Nassau	5,382	0.2	1.9	37	0.3	26	70	75	7,190	—
Barbados	Bridgetown	166	0.3	0.8	88	0.3	11	74	32	5,140	—
Belize	Belmopan	8,865	0.2	3.0	23	0.2	36	69	50	1,170	—
Bolivia	La Paz	424,162	6.9	2.6	27	9.2	110	53	49	540	263
Brazil	Brasília	3,286,475	144.4	2.0	34	179.5	63	65	71	1,810	781
Chile	Santiago	292,259	12.6	1.6	45	14.8	20	71	82	1,320	726
Colombia	Bogatá	439,734	30.6	2.1	34	38.0	48	64	65	1.230	755
Costa Rica	San José	19,575	2.9	2.9	24	3.7	19	74	45	1,420	534
Cuba	Havana	42,803	10.4	1.0	69	11.4	14	74	71	—	1,075
Dominica	Roseau	290	0.1	1.6	44	0.1	24	75	—	1,210	—
Dominican Republic	Santo Domingo	18,815	6.9	2.4	28	8.6	70	65	52	710	372
Ecuador	Quito	109,483	10.2	2.8	25	13.6	66	65	52	1,160	720
El Salvador	San Salvador	8,124	5.4	2.8	25	7.2	65	66	43	820	186
Grenada	St. George's	131	0.1	1.9	36	0.1	22	72	—	1,240	—
Guadeloupe	Basse-Terre	687	0.3	1.3	52	0.4	17	72	46	—	—
Guatemala	Guatemala City	42,042	8.7	3.2	21	12.2	65	61	33	930	176

	Capital	Area (square miles)	Population (millions)	Rate of Natural Increase (%)	Number of Years to Double Population	Population Projected for A.D. 2000	Infant Mortality Rate	Life Expectancy at Birth	Urban Population (%)	Per Capita GNP ($)	Energy Consumption per Capita (kg of oil equivalent)
Guyana	Georgetown	83,000	0.8	2.0	34	0.8	36	68	32	500	—
Haiti	Port-au-Prince	10,714	6.3	2.8	25	7.7	117	54	25	330	55
Honduras	Tegucigalpa	43,278	4.8	3.1	22	7.0	69	63	40	740	201
Jamaica	Kingston	4,243	2.5	1.7	41	2.9	20	73	54	880	954
Martinique	Fort-de-France	425	0.3	1.2	59	0.3	13	74	71	—	—
Mexico	Mexico City	761,602	83.5	2.4	29	104.5	50	66	70	1,850	1,290
Netherland Antilles	Willemstad	302	0.2	1.4	51	0.2	10	76	—	—	—
Nicaragua	Managua	50,193	3.6	3.5	20	5.1	69	62	57	790	259
Panama	Panama City	29,761	2.3	2.2	32	2.9	25	71	51	2,330	634
Paraguay	Asunción	157,046	4.4	2.9	24	6.0	45	66	43	880	281
Peru	Lima	496,224	21.3	2.5	28	28.0	88	61	69	1,130	543
Puerto Rico	San Juan	3,436	3.4	1.2	56	3.7	15	75	67	5,190	—
St. Kitts-Nevis	Basseterre	139	0.04	1.4	51	0.04	28	67	45	1,700	—
St. Lucia	Castries	239	0.1	2.2	31	0.2	22	69	40	1,320	—
St. Vincent and the Grenadines	Kingstown	150	0.1	2.0	35	0.1	27	69	—	960	—
Suriname	Paramaribo	63,039	0.4	2.1	33	0.5	33	69	66	2,510	—
Trinidad and Tobago	Port of Spain	1,981	1.3	2.2	31	1.6	13	70	34	5,120	3,641
Uruguay	Montevideo	68,039	3.0	0.8	83	3.2	30	71	84	1,860	745
Venezuela	Caracas	352,143	18.8	2.4	28	24.7	36	70	82	2,930	2,409

Sources: *World Population Data Sheet*, 1988; *World Development Report*, 1987.

TENOCHTITLAN: CAPITAL CITY OF THE AZTEC EMPIRE

In the 1300s, the Aztec were a small, poor Indian tribe who migrated into the Valley of Mexico and settled on two small, marshy islands in Lake Texcoco. The Valley of Mexico was a landlocked basin 3000 square miles in extent, perched a mile and a half above sea level, and surrounded by volcanic ranges. In the rainy summer season, the heart of the basin was covered by a sheet of water called by the Aztec the "Lake of the Moon." In winter, the lake evaporated into five shallow marshes, the largest of which was Lake Texcoco (Fig. 8.3).

Over time, the Aztecs extended their political control from the islands in this lake to the entire valley. In two centuries, they conquered surrounding regions and ultimately a vast empire.

By the Spanish conquest, their island village had become a shimmering, cosmopolitan metropolis, an administrative and political center that attracted traders and dignitaries from all over Mexico and Central America. In 1519, this island city—Tenochtitlan—covered an area of 4 square miles, was connected to the mainland by three causeways, and had a population of a quarter of a million. In the words of the invader Hernán Cortés, Tenochtitlan displayed such "excellence and grandeur . . . that in Spain there is nothing to compare."

The economic base that supported this ancient metropolis was a unique system of land reclamation and agriculture known as the **chinampa** system, which was practiced on the freshwater margins of the lake (Fig. 8.4). Each chinampa was a raised strip of land about 300-feet long and 15- to 30-feet wide and separated from other chinampas by canals. Fresh mud and weeds dredged from the canals were piled on the chinampa surface to ensure fertility. The edges of the chinampas were rimmed by trees and stakes to hold the structure in place. One end of each chinampa was used as a seed nursery. Crops, such as corn, beans, peppers, and tomatoes, were grown in small blocks of fresh mud, then transplanted as seedlings to the chinampa surface. Flowers, used as offerings to the Aztec gods, were also an

important crop. Fish were harvested from the canals. Overall, the chinampa system was one of the most productive and intensive systems of agriculture ever devised. It was this system that supported the large population of the Valley of Mexico and its Aztec capital, Tenochtitlan.

The center of Tenochtitlan was its Great Temple, the liturgical center of the Aztec Empire, a 200-foot-high step-pyramid topped with shrines. Surrounding the Great Temple were the palaces of

the emperor and his nobles, large public buildings, and the stone houses of prominent citizens. All raw materials—wood, stone, and lime—were shipped by boat from the mainland. Ingenious use of light volcanic rock and wooden pilings supported these huge structures on the unstable, spongy ground beneath. Out from the center of Tenochtitlan, the city was divided by a grid of canals (Fig. 8.5). These canals formed the edges of the chinampas and were crosscut by larger canals that formed

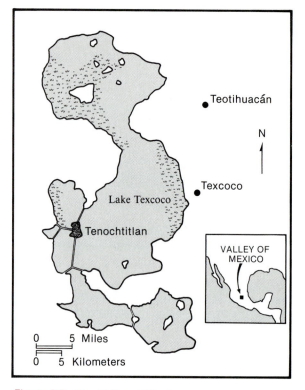

Figure 8.3 The Valley of Mexico.

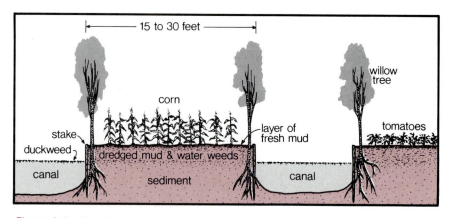

Figure 8.4 The chinampa system of agriculture.

the major arteries of the city. Roads and footpaths paralleled these larger canals.

The population of the city was composed of priests, administrators, merchants, craftsmen, and soldiers—the leaders of the Aztec Empire. Its wealth was based on tribute from afar, which—according to one list—amounted each year to 7000 tons of corn, 4000 tons of beans and other foods, 2 million cotton cloaks, as well as such precious goods as gold, amber, and quetzal feathers. Tenochtitlan, then, was a remarkable city of wealth, splendor, faith, and force until August 13, 1521 when it fell to the power of Hernán Cortés. Today, Tenochtitlan is buried beneath modern Mexico City.

Adapted from: Michael D. Coe, "The Chinampas of Mexico," *Scientific American* (July 1964), figs. pp. 91, 93, 94; pp. 90–98.

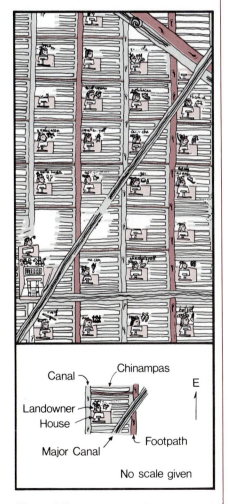

Figure 8.5 Aztec map of a section of Tenochtitlan.

pire of 380,000 square miles, 1500 miles long and 300 miles wide. It extended along the Andes from the southern border of Colombia through Ecuador and Peru to the fertile central valley of Chile. This territory, equivalent in size to the Atlantic states of the United States, had a large population. Most of these people had been conquered by the Quechua-speaking Inca and had been socially and economically integrated into the Inca state.

The center of the Inca empire, Cuzco, a town of 100,000 people, was located in the intermontane basin known as the **altiplano,** high in the Peruvian Andes at an elevation of more than 11,000 feet. From Cuzco, 5000 miles of roads extended outward in a network equivalent in size and quality to that of the Romans. These highways spanned the most difficult terrain in the New World. The orders of the Inca were relayed along them by runners. The entire system was implemented by a highly centralized bureaucracy. In this way, the smallest, most distant corners of the state were kept well under control and in constant touch with Cuzco. The empire was divided into four subregions within which households were arranged in social groups ranging in size from 10,000 to 40,000 families. A systematic distribution of people with respect to resources was constantly maintained by resettlement of families into new colonies.

The economic basis of the Inca state was the cultivation of potatoes, corn, manioc, peppers, tomatoes, beans, and squash. These were grown in irrigated valleys along the coast, in basins on the high plateau, and on terraced hillsides in the Andes. **Guano** (bird manure) was imported as a fertilizer from offshore islands to increase productivity. Fertile soil was carried from the lowlands to the highlands to enrich arable land. A well-planned system of canals, aqueducts, and reservoirs provided water and attested to the skill of Inca engineers. Communal pastures were grazed by herds of llamas and alpa-

cas. In this society, in which gold sheathed the temple walls, finely woven alpaca and cotton cloth was the most precious currency, serving as the medium of exchange.

In theory, all land belonged to the state, but in practice, one third of the harvest was allocated to the producing community, one third to the Inca priests, and one third to the ruler and his family. The royal family held a monopoly on precious metals and stones. Private property did not exist. Work on communal land was allocated according to family size within each agricultural community. Surplus food was placed in public storehouses for distribution in drought years. The cycles of poverty and hunger that characterize large parts of this region today did not exist under the Inca.

In short, Inca rulers established a benevolent dictatorship (or more properly, a **theocracy**) in the very difficult environment of the Andes. Personal freedom—from one's choice of residence to one's choice of spouse—was severely restricted, but lifetime social security was assured.

The Spanish and Portuguese Conquest of the New World

At the end of the fifteenth century, Spain and Portugal were among the strongest and most aggressive European nations. The fabled wealth of the East Indies had excited their interest in voyages of exploration, discovery, and conquest. The shipyards of Venice were busy building larger and swifter ships with enough space for provisions for longer voyages. Men like Christopher Columbus listened to Renaissance thinkers who claimed that the earth was round and that the East could be reached by sailing to the west.

After 700 years, the Spanish had driven the Muslim Moors out of the Iberian Peninsula. By 1492, Spain, a country of 10 million people, was spiritually and territorially united under the Catholic rule of Ferdinand

The fortress city of Machu Picchu in the high Andes is one of the best preserved ruins of the Inca Empire.

and Isabella. In this atmosphere, Queen Isabella of Spain dispatched a messenger to bring Columbus to her court. She pledged $30,000 to finance the first organized European venture westward, a decision that would ultimately bring the Old World into intimate contact with the New World. Later that same year, 1492, the Niña, the Pinta, and the Santa María sailed west. In October, Columbus landed on the tiny island of San Salvador in the Bahamas, and the Caribbean was claimed for Spain.

The Caribbean Experiment

Columbus returned from the New World to Spain with a small amount of gold, some Caribbean parrots, a few spices, six Bahamian Indians, and the electrifying news that land lay only thirty-three days' west of Europe. Spain immediately developed plans to transplant an Iberian society in miniature to the New World. A large fleet was outfitted with equipment, seed, and livestock. Some 1500 settlers were recruited to colonize the large island Columbus called Hispaniola (now shared by Haiti and the Dominican Republic). The three goals of the Spaniards were: (1) to find the wealth of the Indies, (2) to convert native peoples to Roman Catholicism, and (3) to establish permanent settlements as bases for further Spanish exploration.

In November 1493, the Spanish established the town of Isabella on the northern coast of Hispaniola. Within a few years, 12,000 Spanish colonists moved to the West Indies,

and thirteen chartered towns were established. Gold was mined in the interior. Cotton and sugarcane fields were planted in the lowlands. All the larger islands in the Antilles—the Caribbean islands—were explored. In these thirty years, the Spanish forged elements of a colonial policy that endured for over three centuries.

The guiding principle in establishing these policies was to create colonies that would be a credit to both Spain and the Catholic Church. The theory of mercantilism was to hold sway for several hundred years. Extensive power was given to colonial governors, the first of whom was Columbus. These men collected taxes, dispensed law, and distributed land grants. To establish permanent bases for further exploration, early governors directed the first colonists into agriculture. Columbus introduced horses, sheep, donkeys, cattle, and chickens as well as a variety of agricultural crops—wheat, barley, melons, and cucumbers—into the New World. Later governors introduced grapes, olives, citrus fruits, figs, bananas, and sugarcane. The agricultural economy of the Mediterranean world was gradually diffused and was replicated in the Caribbean. The environmental perception of the Spanish in the New World was that of a direct transfer of the Old World to the New. But they had much to learn.

To avoid manual labor, the Spanish created institutions to force native Indians (and later African slaves) to labor in the fields, tend the livestock, and mine the gold. The first of these labor systems was **repartimiento**. This was the temporary assignment of Indian labor to Spanish colonists for specific projects, such as building a church, clearing a field, or planting an orchard. By 1514, 20,000 Indians—peaceful Arawaks and hostile Caribs—labored to build and maintain Hispaniola's new economy.

Abuse, overwork, and epidemics created the need for a second labor system, the **encomienda** to protect Indians from annihilation. Under the encomienda, Indians were grouped into hamlets controlled by a Spanish protector who tutored them in religion and fed them in return for their labor. These encomiendas gave the Spanish permanent power over Indians and their land, subordinating their entire lives to the ambitions of Spanish colonists. Needless to say, the protectors failed to protect the Indians. By the 1530s, the native Caribbean labor force was virtually nonexistent—thousands were slain in abortive rebellions, shipped to Spain as slaves, killed by epidemics of Old World diseases like measles and smallpox (to which they had no resistance), or worked to death in gold mines on the rivers of the larger islands.

With native laborers in short supply, farms were abandoned and mines closed down. Adventurers disappointed by not finding precious minerals in the Caribbean Islands set off in search for the fabled golden city of El Dorado. Settlers, who never intended to become farmers in the New World anyway, quickly followed leaders like Hernán Cortés to Mexico and Francisco Pizarro to Peru. Despite severe punishments for those caught leaving the Caribbean, the economy of the islands lapsed into subsistence agriculture and cattle grazing. Attention instead shifted to the conquest of the mainland when rumors of populous and wealthy Indian civilizations in central Mexico lured Cortés to the land of the Aztec and the Maya.

The Conquest of Mexico

In 1518, Cortés, with 617 men, landed on the Mexican coast and established the city of Veracruz. With the support of dissident tribal groups, he mounted the eastern escarpment of the central plateau of Mexico and marched on the Aztec capital city of Tenochtitlan. On November 8, 1519, Cortés met the emperor of the Aztec Federation, Moctezuma. Less than two years later, after complicated maneuvering, the Spanish and smallpox killed Indians by the thousands, and the Aztec capital was burned to the ground. The most important center of high civilization in Central America was destroyed.

Spanish control quickly extended throughout the Aztec realm. Indian laborers were parceled out in encomiendas. The Pope sent priestly orders to preach Christianity to the natives and to establish missions on the settlement frontier. Mexico City was founded on the ashes of Tenochtitlan in the Valley of Mexico, Antequera (now Oaxaca de Juárez) was built in the valley of Oaxaca, and Colima was established in the rich gold, silver, and copper mining area on the Pacific slope of the western cordillera. Smaller towns were established at

strategic locations to maintain order.

There was little resistance to the extension of Spanish rule over central Mexico. Most Indians simply accepted the Spanish as new rulers who demanded the same tribute as their Aztec predecessors. Virulent epidemics of smallpox, measles, and typhus devastated them.

During the first century of Spanish rule, the Indian population of Central America declined from an estimated 12 to 15 million at the time of conquest to 1 million in 1580. For the Spanish, this meant less income from villages where Old World crops, such as wheat and sugarcane, were established and from the highland pastures and lowland savannas where livestock had been introduced.

The primary interest of the Spanish, however, was gold and silver. Despite strong Indian resistance, the highlands of southern Mexico and the escarpments of the central Valley were quickly brought under their dominion. In the silver belt of northern central Mexico, mining camps and missions became centers of Spanish influence. The more remote unproductive highlands of northwestern Mexico and the deserts of Baja California were not fully brought under control until nearly two centuries later.

The Conquest of Peru

Francisco Pizarro's conquest of Peru in the 1530s closely paralleled the conquest of the Aztec Federation in Mexico. A swineherd from Estremadura in western Spain, Pizarro left to seek his fortune in the New World. A man quite unlike the gentleman Cortés, Pizarro was an uneducated, illiterate man. He launched the conquest of the Inca Empire in 1531, sailing southward from Panama along the Pacific coast of South America to find the wealthy civilization reputed to exist in the Andes Mountains. A year later, Pizarro confronted the Inca ruler, Atahualpa, at Cajamarca, took him hostage to ensure the good behavior of the Inca army, and demanded a ransom of 20 tons of gold and silver from his followers. The ransom was paid, but, in August 1533, Atahualpa was strangled—a favor granted by the Spanish, who had agreed not to burn him if he converted to Christianity before his death.

Almost immediately, the Spanish marched southward on the Inca capital of Cuzco, destroyed its temples and took control of the Inca Empire. Within two years, this small band of Spaniards conquered the largest and best organized state in South America. Although Indian rebellions continued sporadically for the next forty years, Spanish dominance, once established, was never seriously challenged.

After the Inca ruler Atahualpa was killed and the capital city of Cuzco taken, the entire Inca domain with its thousands of acres of fertile land worked by hundreds of thousands of Indians fell under the control of Pizarro's invaders. The coastal city of Lima was founded in 1535 to connect Spanish Peru with the European world. The road system of the Inca was abandoned. As in Mexico, the Indians were parceled out to the conquerors in encomiendas.

Complex Inca irrigation networks gradually fell into disrepair, and traditional Inca techniques of maintaining high agricultural productivity were neglected. The impact of smallpox and measles on the Andean population was much the same as in Mexico: within fifty years, the number of people in the Inca realm was reduced by a third. At the same time, Spanish settlers flowed into Peru to manage farmlands, organize work in the mines, work as shopkeepers and artisans in new Spanish cities, and—as always—pursue the search for the mythical El Dorado.

Quito, the northern capital of the Inca, was taken and looted early in the conquest. A dissident group of Pizarro's soldiers also launched an expedition southward into Chile. But as the Spanish pushed outward from the well-ordered domain of the Inca,

they encountered Indians who resisted attempts at conquest and conversion. Despite this, the city of Santiago was founded in 1540, Valparaíso in 1544, and the southern towns of Concepción and Valdivia six years later. Other expeditions from Spain's colonies in Peru and Chile crossed the Andes into Argentina, ultimately reaching the Plata estuary. In the north, expeditions pushed over the high peaks of the Bolivian and Colombian Andes.

The Portuguese in Brazil

In 1494, two years after Columbus's first voyage, Pope Alexander VI divided the unexplored world into two spheres of influence—one Spanish, the other Portuguese—under the Treaty of Tordesillas to avoid competition. The **pope's line,** as it was called, was drawn 370 leagues west of the Cape Verde Islands along the fiftieth meridian, which cuts through the shoulder of modern Brazil from the mouth of the Amazon to south of São Paulo. All lands west of this line were granted to Spain; those east of it were ceded to Portugal. The Portuguese mariner, Pedro Cabral, claimed sovereignty for Portugal when he landed at Bahia (Salvador) on the northeastern coast in 1500. But this discovery stirred little interest in Portugal.

Brazil at that time was occupied by a thin scattering of Tupi-Guaraní Indians who lived as hunters, fishermen, and shifting cultivators along the coast and produced no gems, spices, or gold. Unlike the Spanish, the Portuguese were not interested in colonizing or converting the New World. Some thirty years later, however, French and Spanish expeditions to the Brazilian coast forced the Portuguese to press forward with settlement on the South American coast.

Portugal established firm possession of Brazil by dividing the entire coast from the Amazon to south of São Paulo into fifteen **capitanias.** These were large tracts of land extending inland. Each was granted to a wealthy Portuguese family. These

families held the right to found towns, levy taxes, and hold economic monopolies in their territories. In return, they were expected to bring in settlers, organize the countryside, and return a fifth of all profits to the Portuguese king.

Colonies were established at São Vincente near São Paulo, at Olinda near Recife, and at Bahia. Results were uneven—several of the noble families never came to South America, others lost fortunes financing new settlements, and a few made large profits. By 1550, Portuguese colonists were exporting dyewood, sugar, cotton, and tobacco, and cultivating European grains and raising cattle. In 1549, Brazil was brought under the direct control of a governor-general appointed by the Portuguese crown.

Gradually, the capitania families, themselves large landowners in Portugal, began to sense potential profits in establishing sugar plantations in Brazil. The first plantation was established in 1532 at São Vincente in the south. But the favorable location of the northern capitanias which were closer to European markets, soon led to expansion of sugar cultivation in the northeast. In 1576, Bahia had forty-seven sugar mills, and Recife and Olinda were wealthy towns. Native Indians died by the thousands on these plantations. The Portuguese then began to import slaves from Africa for the sugar plantations of Brazil as they had done earlier on farms on the island of Madeira off the coast of Africa. By 1600, an estimated 25,000 Portuguese colonists had settled along the coast of Brazil, the northeast had emerged as the world's chief source of sugar, and 14,000 African slaves and 18,000 Christianized Indians labored in the fields of the Portuguese New World.

Colonial Development and Culture Change

Spain transplanted Iberian patterns of administration, settlement, economy, and culture to the New World during the next two centuries. Following what have become known as mercantilist economic policies, relationships between the colonies and Spain were based on the premise that the Spanish Empire was the private property of the Spanish king. The duties of the colonists were to claim land for the Spanish flag, to fill the coffers of the Spanish monarch, and to convert native peoples to the Roman Catholic faith. A centralized system of political and economic administration was imposed on the colonies by the Council of the Indies, a small board composed of nobles, lawyers, and members of Spain's richest families. Rigid control of colonial trade and immigration was maintained by the House of Trade in Madrid. Missionaries pushed the frontier of Spanish settlement deep into the continent, often at their own peril. Spain governed this empire in the New World for three centuries, successfully repelling the territorial incursions of other European powers. Parallel to the vast Spanish dominion in Central and South America was the Portuguese colonial empire in Brazil.

The Colonial Economy

Despite the consuming Spanish thirst for gold and precious metals, the basis of their New World economy was agriculture. In most years, the value of agricultural exports to Spain exceeded that of the mines. Accountants of the Council of the Indies paid close attention to patterns of **land tenure** and land use in the colonies.

Wherever possible, Spanish commercial agriculture was introduced alongside the **subsistence** economy of the Indians. Wheat, barley, olives, and grapes were planted on vast tracts of land. On the Caribbean islands and in the tropical colonies of the mainland, Indians and African slaves worked on sugar, tobacco, cocoa, and indigo plantations. Olive trees were planted in the irrigated oases of coastal Peru, and Lima exported olive oil to the rest of the New World. Vineyards sprang up in central Mexico, the central valley of Chile, and the

Argentine piedmont. In recognition of the potential of this wealth, great tracts of land, called haciendas in Mexico and **latifundios** in South America, were bestowed on favorites of the king. Land was owned by the wealthy few, and the masses—in this case Indians, Africans, and a growing **mestizo** (mixed European and Indian) population—labored in servitude.

On the northern and southern margins of the Spanish Empire, a large-scale livestock industry arose. Herds of wild horses and cattle, descended from Iberian stock, flourished on rich grasslands, the New World prairies. A new culture of rancher-cowboys populated these regions—the **vaqueros** of the Rio Grande del Norte (Texas), the **gauchos** of the **pampas** of Argentina and Uruguay, and the **llaneros** of the Orinoco lowlands (**llanos**) of Venezuela.

Sheep were introduced to provide wool for a textile industry. Textile factories hired large numbers of skilled Indian weavers from one end of the continent to the other to produce cheap cotton and woolen cloth. Labor conditions in some of these mills were so notorious that reform-minded provincial officials imported African slaves and Chinese weavers to relieve the burden on Indian workers.

Despite the policies of the Council of the Indies, which limited the amount of land distributed to cattlemen to a maximum of 3 leagues each, great cattle ranches were established in northern Mexico, in the Plata lowlands, and on the plains, the llanos, of the Orinoco.

Supplementing this agricultural economy was the mineral wealth that had attracted the Spanish to the New World in the first place. The king of Spain held mineral rights on all occupied lands. A fifth of all precious metals went to the royal treasury. In Mexico, Colombia, Peru, and Bolivia, gold and silver miners worked feverishly to meet the voracious demand in Spain for raw gold and silver ore. Alexander von Humboldt, a nineteenth century German geog-

rapher, estimated that the New World exported more precious minerals to Spain in three centuries than all the world had previously produced. To do this, of course, required a virtually unlimited supply of labor.

In the Andes, where precious ores tended to be located close to the surface, forced-labor gangs of Indians dug small pits in the ground and carried baskets of ore up ladders to the surface. In the early colonial years, some 80,000 Indians were employed at the San Luis Potosí mines in Bolivia alone. Thousands died of mistreatment, underground flooding, and overwork. The replacement of exhausted workers with new laborers was a major colonial problem.

By contrast, the rich silver mines of northern Mexico were, by the end of the eighteenth century, worked by independent Indian labor. Here, mining was a more sophisticated venture, involving shafts, underground drainage, ventilation, and deep tunnels. Because of the special skills required in these mines, untutored labor gangs recruited from the fields were inefficient and costly. In the end, it was cheaper to pay wages to skilled laborers trained in the complexities of ore collection and processing.

Labor problems were an issue throughout the colonial period. The Spanish steadfastly refused to perform manual labor, so that the entire economic structure of the Spanish New World depended on native and African workers. Complicating the Spanish labor system was the paradox of saving Indian souls while placing harsh demands on their bodies. Some enlightened church leaders criticized and ultimately eliminated the worst abuses in the mines, on haciendas, and on lowland plantations. Missionaries even attempted to establish utopian religious communities to teach native Americans a new faith and a new way of life. Curiously, this clerical concern for Indians almost never extended to Africans. Indeed, it was religious concern that contributed to the beginning of large-scale slavery.

The Atlantic Slave Trade

In 1517, Bartolomé de Las Casas, a Spanish priest from Haiti, returned to Spain to plead for the lives of the Carib Indians. In the mines and plantations of the Caribbean, the Carib were rapidly dying off. As an act of mercy, Las Casas convinced the king of Spain to import black slaves into America—at a rate of twelve per colonist—to replace the Carib in the fields and mines of the New World.

In 1518, a cargo of slaves was shipped from Africa to Haiti. The Atlantic slave trade began.

Actually, slaves had been taken from Africa since time immemorial. The trade was largely directed toward the Mediterranean lands, the Middle East, and India. By 1500, an estimated 3500 slaves a year were imported from the West African coast to the slave markets of Portugal and Spain for use in domestic service, in

the fields, and on ships.

Even the practice of importing slaves for the economic development of new territories had precedent. In the Canary Islands and Cape Verde Islands, slaves were imported from the African mainland to tend vineyards, sugarcane fields, and orchards on Spanish and Portuguese plantations.

But it was the Atlantic trade that opened up an almost unlimited mar-

The Atlantic slave trade forced 10 million Africans to work on plantations in Spanish and Portuguese America. Descendents of slaves form a majority of the population in the Caribbean today, as this market scene from Saint Georges, Grenada, suggests.

THE ATLANTIC SLAVE TRADE

Some 10 million African slaves were imported to the New World during the four centuries of the Atlantic slave trade. The traffic reached its peak in the middle of the eighteenth century but did not decline appreciably until the middle of the nineteenth century. Half the slaves were delivered from the Slave Coast of Africa to Brazil and another third to the Caribbean, completely altering the cultural and racial composition of these Latin American societies (Fig. 8.6). Only 1 in 25 slaves (a recorded 399,000) arrived in the United States.

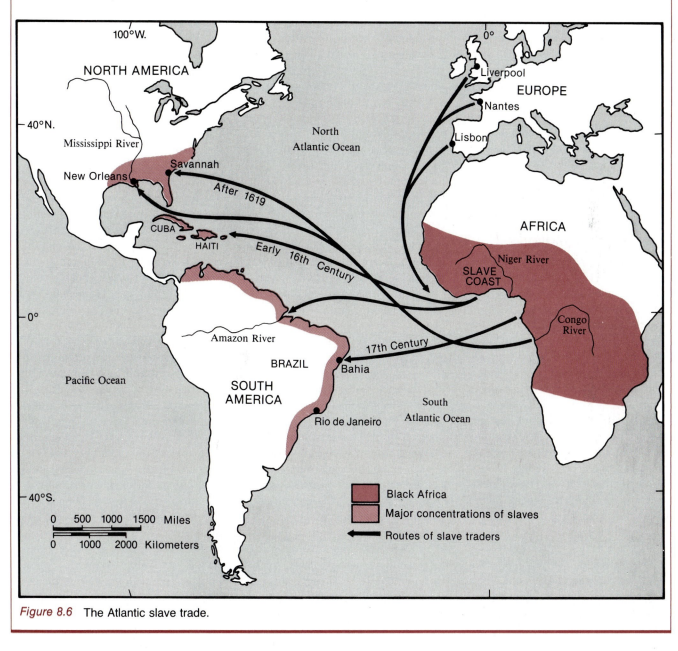

Figure 8.6 The Atlantic slave trade.

ket for human cargoes from Africa. It was a 400-year episode in human brutality that denied any standard except profit and that numbed the hearts of all who participated—trader, sailor, and slave alike.

Las Casas was correct: black slaves from Africa were better able to survive in the New World than American Indians, who lacked immunity to common Old World diseases. The death rate among blacks was only one third that among American natives. As a result, African slaves became an economic solution to labor shortages in the Americas.

As the need for a labor force to expand New World production intensified, so did the demand for African slaves. Between 1600 and 1650, Spanish and Portuguese colonies in the Americas imported an estimated 7300 slaves each year. Thereafter, competitive French and British economic interests in the New World doubled the rate of importation. All told, nearly 10 million Africans worked as slaves in the Americas. It was the largest enforced migration in history.

From 1650 on, Africans outnumbered Europeans in the New World. Approximately half the African slaves brought to the New World were sent to the Caribbean and another third were transported to Brazil (Fig. 8.6). In these areas, high death rates and high labor demands on sugar and coffee plantations continuously required new cargoes of slaves.

The New World Economy

From Spain's mercantilist viewpoint, the overseas empire existed to supply raw materials to the mother country in return for a supply of manufactured goods. For 250 years, the New World proved a storehouse of treasure worth $5 billion in an age that counted its wealth in pennies. The impact of this flow of metals on Spain was disastrous. Inflation drove prices beyond the reach of peasants and artisans, destroying the economy of Spain, although no one connected the flow of silver and gold to the economic plight of Iberia. The phenomenon of inflation was incomprehensible to Europeans of the time. How could gold be worth less one year than the year before? Ultimately, of course, inflation helped sink the Spanish seaborne empire, and Spain retreated to its own boundaries.

The objectives of the House of Trade were to maintain a total monopoly on all exchange and to prevent other European countries from engaging in trade with the Spanish colonial empire. By 1600, direct European control of virtually every aspect of life in the New World had resulted in a spatial distribution of economic activity that remained es-

sentially the same until the nineteenth century.

Distance from Western Europe played an important role. In tropical areas closest to Europe (3500 to 4000 miles), sugar, cocoa, indigo, and tobacco plantations were established in coastal Brazil, the Guianas, and the islands of the Caribbean. The high costs of land transport restricted the cultivation of these bulk commodities to the Atlantic coast. Near the mining centers of Mexico and Peru, adventurers, immigrants, and laborers were drawn to the silver and gold centers of Latin America. In the temperate grasslands more than 5000 miles from Europe, a livestock economy was established on the pampas of Argentina, the llanos of Venezuela, and in northern Mexico. In the Amazon region, southern South America, and the interior southwest in North America, vast stretches were populated by hostile Indians, runaway slaves, missionaries, pioneers, and occasional traders.

Independence in Latin America

The distances separating Spain from the New World possessions made it difficult for the mother country to maintain a tight rein on its colonies. In the course of three centuries, a new and complex society evolved in Latin America. The primary groups were a Spanish-born European elite (**gachupins**), a European commercial and landowning class born in the New World (**creoles**), mestizos, **mulattos**, native Indians, and Africans. In the early nineteenth century, an estimated 23 million people lived in Spanish America, nearly half of whom were Indians, a third mestizos, and the remainder whites, blacks, and mulattos.

Increasingly, these colonial societies felt constricted by Spanish control of their destinies. Large-scale smuggling was rampant. Local officials ignored unwelcome instructions from Spain. Spain came to distrust

anyone born in the colonies and appointed only Europeans to positions of power in the New World. Bitterly resentful of this discrimination, American-born creoles, who formed a wealthy, well-educated social class, brought independence to Latin America in the nineteenth century.

Measures were taken in the late 1700s to diminish resentment in the colonies. Trade restrictions were relaxed, so that all Spanish ports could trade with the colonies. The greater volume of commerce between Spain and the New World drove smugglers out of business, and a class of creole merchants grew wealthy during this period. Buenos Aires maintained bimonthly trading contacts with Spain. The number of hides exported in 1790 was ten times that in 1770. In Chile, freer trade strengthened the agricultural economy, and a growing urban population of 150,000 creoles and mestizos inhabited fifteen large colonial towns. Similarly, Cartagena, Havana, Veracruz, and Acapulco profited from the growth in trade among the colonies and with Spain.

But these concessions from Spain were too few and came too late. By the beginning of the nineteenth century, many citizens of Spanish America viewed their colonial homelands as separate from Spain. The stage was set for rebellion. Local revolts in Argentina, Mexico, and Central America ended in independent republics. The five new states of Venezuela, Colombia, Ecuador, Peru, and Bolivia were created under the extraordinary leadership of a young Venezuelan aristocrat named Simón Bolívar. Independence came peacefully to Brazil when the Portuguese dynasty fled Europe and came to the New World at the invitation of Brazilian leaders. In ten years, 1815–1824, the Portuguese and Spanish empires in the New World disintegrated, and eighteen independent nations emerged in the quarter-century of chaos that followed. The human geography of Latin America, however, changed little.

THE HUMAN GEOGRAPHY OF LATIN AMERICA

Latin America is a landmass consisting of the two triangles of South America and southern North America that join at the narrow Isthmus of Panama (Fig. 8.7). The region extends nearly 6000 miles from north to south. Its land area of 7.9 million square miles is more than twice the size of the United States. The northern triangle, composed of Central America and the Caribbean islands, is 1 million square miles in area. It forms the southern extension of North America. The southern and much larger triangle, South America, is set so far to the east that the distance between South America and Africa at one point is only half that separating North America and Europe. And almost all of South America is to the east of North America.

The equator slices across this region from the mouth of the Amazon to the Ecuadorian Andes. Most of Latin America lies between the Tropics of Cancer and Capricorn. Like Africa, the other tropical continent, the overall density of population in Latin America is quite low—less than fifty people per square mile. Clusters of dense population are found along the east coast of South America, in highland pockets in the Andes Mountains and Central America, and on the large islands of the Caribbean (see Fig. 8.14). These stand in juxtaposition to the empty stretches of the Amazon lowlands and the Andean cordillera.

This uneven distribution of Latin America's 429 million people is the result of two forces: (1) the nature of colonial settlement in the New World, which tailored the development of this huge area to the needs of Europe and (2) strong regional environmental variations.

This interplay of settlement history and physical environment is a central theme in the contemporary human geography of Latin America. The *Environments and Landscapes* of Latin America still reflect the early interpretations of the region by the Spanish and Portuguese despite the introduction of modern technologies. Within Latin America, one quarter of the land is mountainous, another quarter is covered with tropical swamps, and an additional tenth is barren desert. The traditional coastal and upland centers of colonial growth have become the dynamic cores of each country.

On the basis of settlement, environmental variation, and historical development, two major regions of Latin America can be identified. The northern triangle of *Central America and the Caribbean* includes the mainland of Mexico and upland Central America, a tropical and subtropical highland of haciendas worked by mestizo, and the Caribbean rimland, a tropical lowland environment of plantations occupied by mixed Indian and African people. The much larger and more diverse southern triangle of *South America* includes three major subregions: the Andean Cor-

Figure 8.7 Physical features of Latin America.

dillera, arching southward along the west coast of the continent and occupied by mixed Indian peoples; the Midlatitude South, the southern temperate extension of the landmass occupied principally by Europeans; and Brazil in the east with its densely populated coast and tropical interior. In all of these regions, *The Human Use of the Earth* has varied in patterns of land use, distinctions between native and European economies, and the length of occupance. Overall, environmental intrusion in Latin America has been less intense than in much of the Old World because of the comparatively recent efforts at large-scale development of its resource base.

Environments and Landscapes

Latin America stretches a full 80 degrees of latitude from the dry margins of Mexico and the tropical islands of the Caribbean in the north to the cold, windswept desert of Patagonia and clouded islands of Tierra del Fuego in the south. Two thirds of the region lies in the tropics, but rain forests in equatorial latitudes give way to **scrub forests,** grasslands, and drylands in the midlatitudes and to the mountain environments of the Andes and Central America in the west (Fig. 8.7). Within the borders of Latin America are found the greatest tropical forest on earth, the longest river, the most continuous mountain chain, and some of the world's most fertile grasslands.

The tropical rain forests (**selvas**) of Amazonia form the geographical core of Latin America, the largest and most continuous mass of vegetation on the planet. Located astride the equator, Amazonia is a rolling plain 2.3 million square miles in extent with high temperatures, high rainfall, and a continuous growing season. Moisture-laden **trade winds** from the Atlantic sweep over this lowland, dropping vast quantities of water (see Fig. 8.8). This water streams down the Amazon to the Atlantic with such volume and force that the ocean is stained with silt 200 miles offshore. Between November and June, the Amazon breaks over its banks, flooding sur-

rounding plains 50 to 60 miles away. Like the Congo Basin of Africa, Amazonia is occupied principally by people practicing shifting cultivation.

Near the equator, the tropical rain forest consists of tall, closely spaced broadleaf **evergreen** trees. These trees compete for light and form a complex mass of vegetation with more than 2500 separate species of large trees. Frequently, the tallest trees reach 150 feet above the surface, forming a continuous canopy of shade. Shade-tolerant trees form the second and third tiers of the tropical forest at heights of 100 and 50 feet respectively. This vertical stratification reaches its climax in the central Amazon where only 1 percent of the sunlight reaches the ground. Lack of light generally eliminates undergrowth (Fig. 8.8).

The nutrients for this mass of vegetation, in which 3000 or more plant species can be found in a single square mile, are drawn principally from leaves dropped from above. The soils beneath these leaves are leached by rain and, when cleared of vegetation, turn into iron-hard, sterile **laterites** (from the Spanish for brick). The atmosphere is one of pillared shade, a damp cathedral-like twilight. The impenetrable **jungles** known by travelers and made famous in the movies are only found along river banks, coasts, or in clearings where sunlight penetrates to the surface.

Moving away from the equator, the tropical evergreen forest of the equatorial zone gives way to more open deciduous forests. These trees drop their leaves during the cool season because of a more pronounced dry period and cooler temperatures. Here, the high canopy of dense vegetation is broken, forest stands are lower, undergrowth is thicker, and soils are more fertile. As the dry season increases in length with increasing latitude, a parklike scrub and savanna vegetation appears on the margins of the Amazon. The fertile

The tropical rain forests of Amazonia form the largest and most continuous mass of vegetation on the planet. The Iguacu Falls in southern Brazil are located on a tributary of the Paraná River.

THE VERTICAL LAYERING OF TROPICAL RAIN FORESTS

The tropical rain forests of Latin America frequenty exhibit a vertical layering with three separate tiers at the 150-, 100-, and 50-foot levels competing for sunlight (Fig. 8.8). The crowns of the topmost layer form a dense canopy above the continuous 100-foot layer.

Typically, these trees are broadleaf evergreens with smooth trunks. At the 50-foot level, different species of trees with slender trunks and narrow crowns reflect the hierarchy of trees competing for a place in the sun. Vines, some as thick as human torsos, drape the trunks and branches of all three tiers. Underbrush is generally absent because so little sunlight penetrates to ground level. Currently, rapid destruction of this complex and fragile ecosystem has become a global problem.

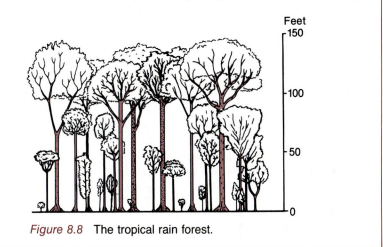

Feet
- 150
- 100
- 50
- 0

Figure 8.8 The tropical rain forest.

long grass savannas of the Argentine pampas and the llanos of Colombia and Venezuela are occupied by great cattle and sheep ranches. The Gran Chaco of Paraguay and the **campos cerrados** of Brazil are increasingly being used for stock raising despite their sterile, acid soils. In Mexico, a short-grass prairie supports a comparable but less intense livestock industry in the north.

Only in southern South America does this region extend deep into the midlatitudes, and colder temperatures combine with elevation to create the barren **heaths** of Patagonia, the glacial spillways of southern Chile, and the fog-bound islands of Cape Horn. It is in these transitional environments, on the more temperate coasts of Latin America and on upland plateaus, that the vast majority of Latin Americans live.

To the west, the towering ranges of Central America and the South

American Andes break the sequential progression of landscapes and environments from the tropics into the midlatitudes. Where the prevailing winds originate in the Atlantic, higher elevation and lower temperature transform the tropical rain forests into **montane forests** in Central and South America. With increasing elevation, these give way to **cloud forests** whose trees are covered with moss and finally to **elfin forests**—aptly named where trees have been dwarfed by wind and cold (Fig. 8.9). Above the forest line at about 12,000 feet, grassland, scrub, or desert is found, depending on the latitude and available precipitation.

On the west slopes of the Andes, quite a different pattern appears. Here, the moistureladen winds cannot surmount the barriers of the Andean and Central American highlands, so that the coasts of Peru and northern Chile are deserts immersed

in fog (Fig. 8.9). These **fog deserts** are created when Pacific winds are cooled as they cross the cold Humboldt ocean current parallel to the coast. Farther north in Ecuador, Colombia, and along the west coast of Central America, however, sufficient rainfall from the Pacific sustains tropical and temperate forests.

In Latin America, the sheer scale of the region combined with its latitudinal reach and topographic complexity has created a diversity of landscapes. The uneven distribution of population in Latin America mirrors the environmental problems generated by the mountains, rain forests, and deserts that constitute so much of its land area. In some uplands, people have been able to grow sufficient food to sustain dense populations. But the coasts, developed early, still retain the bulk of Latin America's population. The perceptions of the early Spanish and Portuguese governed this distribution of people, maintained a coastal orientation to society and economy, and left the Latin American interior relatively untouched. In each country, patterns of settlement are keyed to both environmental realities and historical process.

Central America and the Caribbean

Central America and the Caribbean together have a population of 144 million, one third of the total population of Latin America on only one eighth of its land area. Two generalized human habitats are recognized: the mainland and the rimland (Fig. 8.7).

Mainland Central America

Mainland Central America has a band of plateaus and mountains that sweep northwest to southeast through the eight countries that link North America with South America. In the north, steep escarpments 7000 to 13,000 feet in elevation flank either side of the central plateau of Mexico. This plateau is a mile above sea level, and even higher in its southern portions. Some 500 miles wide at its broadest, it tapers southward where the eastern and western cordilleras converge to form the mountain spine of Central America.

Mexico, with an area of 761,000 square miles and a population of 83.5 million, is the largest and most significant country in mainland Central America. The economic and social core of the country is located in the southern part of the central plateau. Here, at elevations of 6000 to 7000 feet, adequate rainfall, a temperate climate, and rich volcanic soils favored the early growth of dense agricultural settlement in precolumbian times. Currently, half of Mexico's people, primarily mestizo in ethnic background, are concentrated in this section of the central plateau.

As in the precolumbian era, intensive cultivation of corn, beans, squash, and wheat supports rural population densities of 200 to 300 people per square mile, some of the highest in Latin America. In especially favored locations, such as the Valley of Mexico, rural settlements blanket all but the steepest slopes with densities of 500 to 1000 people per square mile, figures rarely attained outside the rice-growing regions of Asia.

By any measure, Mexico City is today the world's largest city. When Cortés and his men first laid their eyes on the capital of the Aztec in November 1519, they were amazed at the splendor of Tenochtitlan, a city of 300,000 (Fig. 8.3). Today, the shining grandeur that was Tenochtitlan is Mexico City, a metropolis whose dimensions exceed those of the largest cities of Europe and North America. The setting for the city— elevation more than one mile; surrounding snow-capped mountains in a highland basin of shallow lakes at the focal point of the Valley of Mexico—made for a superb human environment. Superb it might be for a preindustrial metropolis or even for a city of several millions in the mod-

ern age, but it is a grim, spectral environment for the 18 million people who call Mexico City home today.

Authorities do not know the true population of Mexico City, but 18 million is an accepted estimate for 1988. About 1000 migrants stream into the urban area each day. The statistics of misery are abundant: Two million of the city's people have no running water; 3 million have no sewage facilities. Six thousand tons of garbage lies uncollected every day; 100,000 deaths per year can be attributed to pollution. It is pollution, in fact, that is the most startling phenomenon to the visitor. Polluted air rushes through the air vents of approaching airplanes, making passengers acutely aware of the landing they are about to make. On the ground, the air has a perpetual yellow or gray cast to it—a cloud of poisons resulting from the heavy density of factories and vehicles in this enclosed geography. Pollution controls are virtually nonexistent in Mexico's job-hungry atmosphere of laissez-faire capitalism. Mexico City is not simply a vast urban wasteland: it is a stylish and historic city with great cultural and economic power. Its social and environmental problems, however, threaten its future. And in Mexico City, with an anticipated population of 26 million by the year 2000, that future is today.

In northern Mexico, rainfall decreases to less than 20 inches per year. The densely settled fields of the central plateau give way to scattered oasis-like villages, ranches, and mining centers. Population densities fall to less than twenty people per square mile. In the states of San Luis Potosí and Zacatecas, discoveries of silver, lead, zinc, copper, and gold were the basis of Spanish settlement.

Landscape and culture also change south of the Valley of Mexico. Rainfall increases, cloaking the broken upland ranges of the escarpments with a mantle of trees that grade into the tropical rain forests of the Mexican south. Regional population densities

are low—the entire south has a total population of only 10 million.

In Morelos State, sugarcane and rice fields supplement the staple subsistence crops of Central America. Farther south, in Oaxaca, wheat, coffee, oranges, and tobacco are cultivated in the cooler piedmont uplands. In the Chiapas highlands, the agricultural economy is distinctly tropical. The major commercial crops here are cocoa and bananas. This pattern is repeated in the wetter part of the Yucatán, the lowland Caribbean peninsula of southern Mexico. Throughout southern Mexico, the people are Indians, 50 to 80 percent of whom speak indigenous languages such as Maya in the Yucatán. Major oil discoveries in the Mexican south are rapidly changing traditional patterns of life.

South of Mexico, the densely forested mountain core of Central America is formed by two volcanic ranges. One cuts eastwest across Guatemala, Honduras, and Nicaragua with peaks rising 11,000 to 13,000 feet above sea level. The second, less imposing, trends northwest to southeast through Costa Rica and Panama. Both are wet and densely settled. Roughly 80 percent of the 27.9 million people of the region live in highlands above 2000 feet. Most are of Indian, European, or mestizo descent in contrast to people of African heritage on the Caribbean coasts of Panama, Costa Rica, Nicaragua, Honduras, and Belize.

In Guatemala, roughly 60 percent of the population of 8.7 million are pure-blooded Indians—subsistence hoe cultivators who grow corn, squash, beans, and a variety of commercial crops on the mountain slopes and basins west of Guatemala City (pop. 750,000). By contrast, the rich coffee, cotton, and sugar haciendas of the Pacific piedmont and coastal plain, which produce 95 percent of Guatemala's exports, are run by a mestizo (or as they are called locally, **ladino**) aristocracy. In neighboring Honduras (pop. 4.8 million), popu-

Sugarcane plantations established by the British on Saint Kitts in the West Indies climb to the volcanic crest of this Caribbean island.

lation densities in the uplands are quite low, and the inhabitants—overwhelmingly mestizo—operate small gold and silver mines, raise cattle, and cultivate hillside plots.

By contrast, El Salvador (pop. 5.4 million), is the most densely populated country in Central America. With 27 percent of its land in cultivation—the highest percentage in Latin America—average densities approach 400 people per square mile. The best lands in the cool uplands are owned by a European elite who grow commercial coffee and cotton. Most Salvadorans are subsistence farmers whose diet is as meager as anywhere in Latin America.

In Nicaragua (pop. 3.6 million), the Honduran pattern is repeated, with coffee haciendas in the uplands, cotton and banana plantations in the lowlands. Population densities are low; and a preponderance of the people are mestizo subsistence cultivators.

Costa Rica, however, is a nation of small farmers, 83 percent of whom claim European descent. Historically, the country has had a stable government, a high literacy rate, a high standard of living, and a more equitable distribution of land. Over half of Costa Rica's 2.9 million people are clustered in the central highlands, cultivating coffee, sugarcane, and a variety of food products on small holdings. In Panama (pop. 2.3 million), the more general Central American pattern reappears: a predominantly mestizo population, low densities of population, and subsistence cultivation.

The Caribbean Islands

The Caribbean is a chain of tropical island environments, known as the Antilles, where the vast majority of the population of 33 million lives at elevations below 1000 feet (Fig. 8.7). Less isolated than the mainland, the Caribbean was a focus of competition among colonial powers. The Spanish maintained their early influence over three of the four major islands of the Greater Antilles: Cuba, the Dominican Republic on the eastern half of Hispaniola, and Puerto Rico. Northern European colonists held sway in Jamaica (British), Haiti (French), and some of the smaller islands of the Lesser Antilles (British, French, and Dutch). These Europeans developed profitable sugar plantations in the islands and along the Caribbean coast of Central America. For three centuries, African slaves were imported to labor in the fields, and eventually blacks became the dominant population virtually everywhere in the Caribbean.

Today, after the general decolonization of the region, many Caribbean islands have become heavily dependent upon tourism for their livelihood. Americans and Canadians, seeking winter sun, have created a hotel and service economy that dominates such islands as the Bahamas, Jamaica, and the Virgin Islands.

The Greater Antilles, composed of the four large islands of Cuba, Jamaica, Hispaniola, and Puerto Rico, includes nine tenths of the land area of the West Indies and an even larger percentage of the Caribbean population. The largest island, Cuba, is 800 miles long and has a population of 10.4 million. Most of its 44,000 square miles is flat or gently rolling terrain with three small mountainous areas rising to elevations of 3000 to 6000 feet above sea level. The climate of Cuba is subtropical and rainy, its topography rolling, its soils fertile—a natural endowment that has made the island the world's largest source of sugar.

On Hispaniola, the second largest island in the Caribbean, some 13.2 million people inhabit a land area far more mountainous and one-fourth smaller than Cuba. People are clustered along the coasts and in lowland ribbons located between parallel mountain ranges. Climate and vegetation vary with altitude and exposure, creating a complex of microenvironments. These are occupied by the Hispanic and European peoples of the Dominican Republic (pop. 6.9 million) and the black African population of Haiti (pop. 6.3 million).

Jamaica, the third largest island in the Greater Antilles, is one tenth the size of Cuba and has a population of 2.5 million. Most of the island is a heavily dissected limestone plateau occupied by peasant cultivators. Under three centuries of British rule, the windward coasts and lowlands were carved into sugar plantations. The American Commonwealth of Puerto Rico (pop. 3.4 million), the smallest and most easterly of the Greater Antilles, is, like Jamaica, spanned by a dissected plateau with a mountain core. Its wet, coastal lowlands are cultivated in sugarcane.

The four islands of the Greater Antilles, with their lowland plantations and African people, share two common problems: burgeoning populations and dependence on the export of tropical plantation products. In Cuba, Spanish occupation resulted in limited economic growth. At the turn of the century, the eradication of yellow fever led to an infusion of capital from the United States and preferential tariffs for Cuban sugar.

Some 3.5 million acres were planted to sugarcane. Large estates covered over half the arable land of the country and Cuba became completely dependent on a single crop. Fluctuations in sugar prices created periodic crises in the economy. The annual rhythm of sugarcane planting and harvesting threw a quarter of the island's people out of work for half the year. After Castro's revolution in 1959, the great estates were nationalized. Despite agricultural and industrial diversification, continued reliance on sugar is beginning to damage the best endowed environment in the Caribbean.

A surprisingly similar pattern occurred in Puerto Rico despite present-day contrasts in political orientation. Like Cuba, Puerto Rico was peripheral to Spanish colonial designs. In the nineteenth and twen-

tieth centuries, sugarcane cultivation expanded along the coast, tobacco estates were established in the humid east, and coffee was introduced into the western highlands. By World War II, large estates covered 85 percent of the cultivated land. After the war, land reform programs were instituted, diversified manufacturing introduced, and the lucrative tourist industry expanded.

But this economic growth in Puerto Rico was offset by a tripling of the population over the last seventy-five years to its current 3.4 million people. Population densities on arable land soared to 1695 people per square mile, and 67 percent of Puerto Rico's population today live in the capital city of San Juan (pop. 435,000) and in smaller cities like Mayagüez and Ponce. Although Puerto Rico's standard of living is one of the highest in Latin America, its limited land base poses problems.

On Hispaniola, quite different patterns of population and resource utilization evolved in Haiti and the Dominican Republic. Under French rule, Haiti became the richest plantation colony in the Caribbean until the slaves revolted, threw out the French, and destroyed the sugar mills and estates. Desperately poor, Haitian cultivators are squeezed into a country with 80 percent of its terrain in mountains. With an average density of more than 300 people per square mile, Haiti has the lowest standard of living in Latin America.

In the Dominican Republic, a former Spanish colony, a somewhat larger population occupies a territory twice as large as Haiti. Scarcity of land is not a problem. Large sugar and coffee plantations dominate the landscape, and the predominantly mulatto population has a substantially higher standard of living.

In Jamaica, a familiar pattern occurred. Sugar estates and banana plantations were established by British colonists on the humid coastal lowlands. Peasant farmers were pushed into the limestone uplands.

Only 15 percent of the land can be cultivated. Unlike the other Caribbean islands, however, Jamaica is endowed with a major mineral resource, bauxite, the ore from which aluminum is made. Producer of one eighth of the world's supply and with huge reserves, Jamaica is using revenues from mining to expand the island's economy.

Similar patterns of tropical agricultural development mark the economies of the Lesser Antilles, a 700-mile-long concave arc of islands that sweep across the Caribbean from Puerto Rico in the north to the coast of Venezuela. These islands are the peaks of a double line of submarine volcanoes: (1) an outer ring of low islands, old volcanoes, and limestone banks called the Leeward Islands; and (2) an inner ring of higher volcanic peaks called the Windward Islands. The volcanic peaks link near the coast of South America with Trinidad, Barbados, and the Netherlands Antilles—islands with a quite different geological history.

The largest of the low-lying or Leeward Islands are French Guadeloupe and independent Antigua. The mainstay of their economy is sugar grown on large estates. The usual problems of poverty and unemployment characteristic of the Caribbean plantation system prevail. Saint Kitts and Nevis (British) produce sugar; Montserrat (British) grows cotton.

On the higher Windward islands, agriculture is quite varied. Forested mountain spines rise to between 3000 and 4000 feet. Each island has rich volcanic soils, little level land, and abundant rainfall. Saint Vincent produces **arrowroot,** a starchy tuber; Dominica, limes; Grenada, cocoa and nutmeg; Martinique (French), sugar; Saint Lucia, bananas. On some islands, such as Grenada, small holdings dominate. On Martinique and Saint Lucia, however, so much land is devoted to commercial estates that most food must be imported. About 1.5 million people live in the Lesser Antilles, nearly half on the two French islands of Guadeloupe and Martinique.

Approaching the South American coast, the Lesser Antilles join with a string of continental islands. The most important of these are the former British territories of Trinidad and Tobago, Barbados, and the two largest islands of the Netherlands Antilles, Aruba and Curacao. Barbados (pop. 300,000) most closely emulates the Caribbean economic pattern: 95 percent of all exports are sugar, molasses, and rum. Population densities on Barbados reach levels of 1400 per square mile. In Trinidad and Tobago (pop. 1.3 million), settled much later, a mixture of black Africans (43 percent), Hindu Indians (37 percent), and Chinese (9 percent) were imported to work on sugar plantations in the nineteenth century. Although sugar and rum are still the major agricultural exports of Trinidad, petroleum has been discovered on the southern third of the island, and Trinidad now produces and refines more than 100 million barrels annually. This provides an economic balance rare in the Caribbean. In Aruba and Curacao,

petroleum refining is the dominant economic activity. Near-desert conditions limit agricultural development. Water is so scarce that distillation of seawater is required to maintain the population of 200,000.

South America

In South America, which includes two thirds of Latin America's 429 million people, three major subregions can be distinguished: (1) the Andean Cordillera, (2) the Midlatitude South, and (3) Brazil (Fig. 8.7).

The Andean Cordillera
The Andean Cordillera rises from the waters of the Caribbean in eastern Venezuela and extends southward for 4000 miles in a sinuous curve that forms the spine of South America. Much of the Andean highlands lies over 10,000 feet above sea level (Fig. 8.9). Individual ice-covered peaks in Ecuador, Peru, Bolivia, and Chile soar to 22,000 feet, a full 4 miles above sea level. In the Andean Cordillera, as in the mountains of Central America, the same altitudinal zonation of

land use is found. Three environments of human settlement and economy can be distinguished: **tierra caliente, tierra templada,** and **tierra fria**—lowlands, piedmont, and highlands (Fig. 8.10).

The Andean system broadens to a width of 400 miles in Bolivia. In Chile, it narrows to only 20 miles. Throughout most of their course, however, the Andes form a 200-mile-wide barrier of parallel mountain ranges, walls of ice and stone. These ranges are cut by fertile intermontane valleys and pocked with mountain-rimmed basins and plateaus. These are the primary centers of settlement for the Indian population.

The eastern slopes of the Andes are heavily watered, deeply dissected, and covered by tropical forests that extend eastward into the Amazon Basin. Virtually inaccessible, this transmontane region includes half of the national territories of Colombia, Ecuador, Bolivia, and Peru. It is inhabited by a thin scattering of hunters and gatherers, a few missionaries and pioneers, and oil-exploration teams.

This high plateau in the central Andes is a core of dense settlement surrounded by the snow-capped ranges of the Andean Cordillera.

GEOLAB

ELEVATION AND ENVIRONMENT

Most world maps of climate, vegetation, and soils are based on two factors: (1) the global distribution of sunlight (or latitude) and (2) location relative to atmospheric circulation (availability of moisture). By discounting local factors on these maps, geographers approximate the general patterns of environment found throughout the world. This provides students with insight into sets of complex environmental relationships.

In mountain regions, however, these general patterns break down because elevation in and of itself creates a complex series of microenvironments. Here, environments change with altitude above sea level, steepness of slope, and direction of slope. For this reason, highland environments are categorized separately from all other global environmental regions, such as rain forests, steppes, and deserts.

Atmospheric temperature, pressure, and humidity usually decrease with elevation, which directly affects plants, animals, and human beings. Atmospheric temperature decreases with distance above sea level at the **thermal lapse rate** of 3.3 degrees per 1000 feet. Atmospheric pressure also decreases with elevation, although less regularly. As temperature decreases, the ability of air to retain moisture (**absolute humidity**) decreases. Air masses pushed upward by mountain ranges drop this moisture in the form of **orographic precipitation** on windward slopes. On **leeward** slopes, the now drier, cooler air creates a rain shadow effect. These temperature and moisture conditions are responsible for well-known altitudinal zonation of plant and animal communities in major mountain ranges. They also affect patterns of human occupance.

In Latin America, the towering ranges of Central America and the Andes affect climate directly. In South America, warm, humid trade winds from the Atlantic cross the Amazon Basin and mount the eastern slopes of the Andes (Fig. 8.9). As this air cools, moisture condenses and falls as rain. Downpours are heaviest in the cloud forests, diminishing at higher elevations through the elfin forest, the tundra zone, and finally the snowbound Andean peaks.

The climate of the arid western slope of the Peruvian Andes, how-

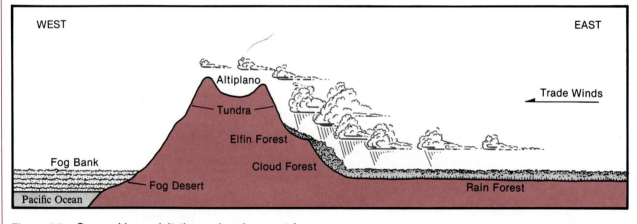

Figure 8.9 Orographic precipitation and environmental zones.

Tropical rain forests also cover the western slope of the Colombian and Ecuadorian Andes, where moisture-laden winds from the Pacific drop more than 100 inches of rainfall each year. South of the Gulf of Guayaquil, however, a stretch of desert runs along the coast of Ecuador, reaching its greatest intensity in the dune-covered Atacama Desert of northern Chile (Fig. 8.9). These drylands cut diagonally across the Andes to the south and reach into Patagonia. This coastal fog desert is produced by a cold northbound ocean current, the Humboldt. The ocean current cools on-shore subtropical air masses, reduces their moisture content, and lowers rainfall. Settlement here is limited to coastal oases dotted along streams that pour down from the Andes. Farther south, the Chilean Andes reach into the midlatitudes, producing a Mediterranean climate in the fertile central valley and cold, wet, temperate forests southward toward Tierra del Fuego.

In the northern Andes, the Andean Cordillera splits into several parallel ranges that slice through Ecuador, Colombia, and Venezuela and create three distinct environmental zones: (1) tropical coastlines thinly populated by a mixed mestizo and African population; (2) interior valleys and plateaus occupied by mestizo and Indian peoples; and (3) transmontane eastern rain forests drained by the Orinoco and Amazon rivers. These areas were the object of Simón Bolívar's early dream of a north Andean state to be called La

ever, is totally different. Here subsiding air becomes warmer and can hold its moisture, reducing chances of rainfall. Warm ocean winds from the Pacific cross the cold Humboldt current along the coast and turn to fog. Here, the Atacama Desert extends to the equator, its barren waste broken only by the unusual environment of the fog desert where a light vegetation is sustained by condensation in the form of dew.

Throughout the Andean Cordillera and in the mountains of Central America and the Caribbean, elevation is a principal factor in human settlement and economy. Away from the Humboldt current, both temperature and rainfall diminish with altitude. Typically, hot and humid coastal lowlands, the tierra caliente, are dominated by a plantation economy, where sugarcane, bananas, cacao, and other commercial crops are grown. On the warm piedmonts above 2500 to 3000 feet, the tierra templada, dense populations are engaged in commercial cultivation of coffee and subsistence cultivation. At elevations above 6000 feet, the cool uplands of the tierra fria are used for subsistence cultivation of grain and potatoes and, in places, for mining. Above 10,000 feet alpine pastures predominate in the high sierra. The elevations and temperatures in Figure 8.10, taken from the Cordillera de Merida of western Venezuela, reflect a widespread pattern of human occupance in the highlands of Latin America.

In addition to shaping the agricultural economy of the highlands, altitude has a direct physical impact on the human body. In Latin America, much of the population of Mexico and the countries of the northern Andes lives at elevations of 1 to 2 miles above sea level. In Peru and Bolivia, large numbers live in intermontane valleys and on the altiplano at elevations of between 10,000 to 13,000 feet. And one of the largest mining centers of the region, Cerro de Pasco in Peru, is located at an altitude of 13,800 feet.

At about 10,000 feet, lack of oxygen and low atmospheric pressure (roughly two thirds that of sea level) begin to have direct effects on animal and human physiology. During the Conquest, the movement of coastal people to mines at high elevations caused long-term infertility. Similarly, highlanders who were moved to the coast suffered respiratory diseases (as they still do). Ultimately, the Spanish were forced to abandon their plans to locate their capital at an elevation above 10,000 feet because European livestock became infertile, as did those Spaniards who ultimately settled in the region to manage the silver mines of the Incas.

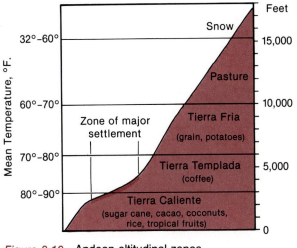

Figure 8.10 Andean altitudinal zones.

Adapted from: Gilbert J. Butland, *Latin America: A Regional Geography.* London: Longman, 1972, fig. 41, p. 195.

Gran Colombia. Although they share common cultural and environmental characteristics, Ecuador, Colombia, and Venezuela have had different patterns of development, as have the Guianas nearby—the three countries of Guyana, Suriname, and French Guiana—a coastal area that attracted neither Spanish nor Portuguese settlement.

Most of Venezuela's population of 18.8 million is located in the country's richest agricultural zone, the interior central highlands, where plantations of cocoa, sugarcane, cotton, and coffee support a large mestizo and European population.

Caracas, the capital (pop. 3 million), is located at an elevation of 3000 feet eight miles from the Caribbean. Birthplace of Bolívar, it is one of the continent's leading centers of education. Although agriculture remains the principal economic activity, Venezuela's energy wealth makes it one of the richest countries in Latin America. The 6500 oil wells in the 30,000-square-mile Maracaibo Basin yield 10 percent of the world's petroleum and half of Venezuela's export earnings. Venezuela was a founding member of **OPEC** in 1960.

Oil capital has made it possible for Venezuela to launch an ambitious program of industrial diversification in the llanos (grasslands) of the Orinoco Basin. In the llanos, large deposits of iron at El Pao and Cerro Bolívar north and east of Ciudad Bolívar in the Orinoco Basin are being developed, new oil fields are being brought into production, and a multipurpose dam is being constructed on the Guárico River. Today, less than 5 percent of Venezuela's labor force is engaged in industry and its population in the 1980s grew at the hefty rate of 2.7 percent per year. But Venezuela is endowed with a resource base capable of supporting a modern economy.

In eastern Venezuela, the Guiana Plateau grades into the three countries of Guyana, Suriname, and French Guiana, where sugar, rice, coffee, and bauxite production are the bases of more static economies.

In Colombia, the largest country in the northern Andes, the mountains divide into three separate cordilleras that finger northward toward Panama and Venezuela and are separated by the valleys of the Cauca and Magdalena rivers. Most of Colombia's 30.6 million people are scattered in fourteen separate valleys and basins dotting the highlands. Bogotá, the capital (pop. 4.2 million), is located at an elevation of 8500 feet in the Cordillera Orientale. Gold initially attracted the Spaniards to the area, but later cotton, sugarcane, cocoa, cattle, and coffee became important economic products.

Two major regions of Colombia have never attracted significant populations: the forested slopes of the Pacific coast and the grasslands east of the Andes (the **llanos orientales**), which constitute 60 percent of the total area of Colombia. On the Caribbean coast, a stockraising area, population is concentrated around port cities, like Barranquilla and Cartagena, which are export centers for agricultural products grown in the highlands. Coca, from which cocaine is derived, has emerged as a crop that tends to replace food-producing agriculture. Destined for the United States, the value of cocaine, far exceeds that anything else highland peasants can grow.

Ecuador is clearly divided into three separate environmental and cultural regions. The narrow Ecuadorian coast is populated by a small population of Indians, mestizos, and blacks who produce virtually all the agricultural and mineral wealth of the country. Cocoa, once the principal economic product of the coast, has given way to a large-scale expansion of rice and banana cultivation. All three products are exported through Guayaquil (pop. 825,000), Ecuador's largest city and most important port.

In the Andean highlands, where most of Ecuador's 10.2 million people live, the population is predominantly Indian. Here, population pressure is intense and subsistence cultivation of corn, barley, wheat, and potatoes is the basis of agriculture. On the eastern slopes of the mountains, the vast tropical forests of the Amazon **headwaters** are the homelands of the Jivaro Indian tribes whose previously undisturbed existence is now being disrupted by the discovery of oil in this, one of the most remote regions in Latin America.

The mountain spine of South America commonly reaches elevations above 20,000 feet in Peru and Bolivia. In Peru, two parallel ranges flank a broad, flat tableland, the altiplano, at 10,000 to 14,000 feet. The Peruvian altiplano is studded by jagged mountain blocks. In Bolivia, the altiplano forms a broad basin of interior drainage. These uplands were the core of Inca civilization in Peru and Bolivia. Subsistence cultivation sustained a relatively dense and prosperous precolumbian New World civilization. The dry, dune-covered coastal zone of Peru to the west was well developed by precolumbian peoples, whereas the Amazonian forests to the east were thinly settled.

The Spanish did not, however, establish their capital in the heavily populated uplands of Peru as they had in Mexico, Colombia, and Ecuador. Instead they founded Lima (pop. 4 million) as a commercial port to link the wealth of the Andes to Europe. Colonial landholdings and commercial mines were introduced

in the mountains. The social and economic gulf that developed between the mixed European population of the coast and the isolated Indian population of the highlands has been characteristic of Andean society ever since.

Modern Peruvian economic development has taken place along the 1500 miles of desert coast, a stark dune- and cliff-studded strip 20- to 80-miles wide. European-owned sugar and cotton plantations are located in the fertile valleys of streams that cascade down from the Andean highlands. Roughly one third of Peru's population, its richest agricultural land, and most of the country's manufacturing, fishing, and petroleum production, is found along the coast. Until recently, a small European elite owned 90 percent of the cultivated land and the factories in which mestizo and black populations labored. Indians have migrated toward coastal opportunities in large numbers in the last generation. Although land reform is now underway, the coast continues to be the economic heartland of Peru, and efforts at industrial diversification and agricultural expansion inevitably focus on the capital city of Lima.

By contrast, the Andean highlands, where most of Peru's 21.3 million people live, and the Amazon forests beyond are virtually undeveloped—even unknown. Quechua-speaking Indians, the descendants of the Inca, cultivate terraced fields of wheat, barley, and potatoes in intermontane valleys and on high plateaus, and they tend herds of sheep, llamas, and alpacas in mountain pastures.

Only three areas of dense settlement are found: (1) around Lake Titicaca, where the moderating climatic influence of the lake makes corn cultivation possible at high elevations; (2) near Cuzco, the old capital of the Inca Empire; and (3) at the mining complex of Cerro de Pasco, inland from Lima. Desperately poor and short of land (only 2 percent of Peru is under cultivation), the people of this region—and particularly the Indians—live outside the mainstream of Peruvian life.

In Bolivia, this social dichotomy is compounded by an extremely difficult natural environment. Trapped between the Atacama coastal desert and the Amazon rain forests, most of Bolivia's 6.9 million people live in small communities on the altiplano, in the gorges of streams flowing eastward to the Amazon, and in narrow intermontane valleys. Over one third of Bolivia is 1 mile or more high, and much of the rest is either rain forest or semiarid steppe. The people, two thirds of whom speak Indian languages, are divided by race, language, and local economy. The most significant concentration of population is found in the basin of Lake Titicaca, near the capital, La Paz (pop. 635,000).

Elsewhere, settlement is limited by climate and terrain, and primary settlement nodes are determined by the location of Bolivia's mining economy (tin and other metals), which provides 80 percent of the country's exports. Petroleum production and some commercial agriculture has begun on the eastern slopes of the Andes. A program of land reform has broken the grip of landlords on farmland. But the limited natural resource base of Bolivia makes it one of the poorest nations on the continent. As in Colombia and Peru, poor farmers have increasingly turned to cultivation of coca, to be transformed into coca paste (from the leaves of the shrub) and then into cocaine.

The Andean Cordilleras converge in the south to form a mountain spine that sweeps 2500 miles poleward, outlining the long, narrow Pacific republic of Chile. Despite the steep rise of the Andes from a narrow coastal plain, climate rather than terrain has been the primary determinant of human settlement in Chile.

In northern Chile, the Atacama Desert extends 600 miles along the coast, watered only with mists created by warm air blown landward across the cold Humboldt current. Some agriculture and herding are found in the southernmost part of this coastal desert. But inland, rich nitrate deposits located in an upland trough some 500 miles long and copper ores mined at Chuquicamata, El Salvador, and Potrerillos are vital contributions of the Chilean north to the national economy. The upland mines are connected by rail to Pacific ports, such as Arica, Antofagasta, and Iquique. Elsewhere, the barren landscapes of the north are virtually uninhabited.

The southern extreme of Chile, from the Bío-bío River to the tip of Tierra del Fuego, is also thinly populated. The cool, damp environment of forests and fjords in the Chilean south was a refuge for Araucanian Indians when they were driven from their homelands by the Spanish. Until the last century, the Chilean south was physically and culturally outside the society and economy of the nation. Today, forestry on the Pacific coast, sheep raising in high mountain valleys, and petroleum discoveries in Tierra del Fuego have integrated this region into the national economy.

The heartland of Chile lies between the northern deserts and the southern forests in the central valley, where some 65 percent of the nation's 12.6 million people live. Marked by Mediterranean climate and endowed with rich alluvial soils, the central valley is the most favored agricultural region of Chile. Focused on the capital, Santiago (pop. 3.6 million), land in the central valley is held in large haciendas (**fundos**), where wheat and beef cattle are raised. Extensive ranchland dominates the agricultural landscape.

The Chilean population, unable to expand in a countryside of fenced ranchland, has been forced to migrate to industrial centers, such as Santiago and Valparaíso on the coast (pop. 267,000). Four fifths of the Chilean population is urban. After considerable political turmoil, the great estates have been confiscated, but national development plans aimed at the redistribution of agricultural land stand in question. Agricultural exports of wine, fresh fruit, and cut flowers to North American markets have grown rapidly in recent years.

The Midlatitude South

The three temperate countries of Argentina, Uruguay, and Paraguay are part of a midlatitude prairie that stretches from the piedmont of the Andes to the South Atlantic (Fig. 8.7). Drained by the Paraná-Paraguay-Uruguay river system, this plain converges at the estuary of the Rio de la Plata, the region's outlet to the world. Throughout most of the colonial period, these grasslands were occupied by Indian hunting tribes, and the region was a backwater of the Spanish Empire. Thus separated from the rest of Spanish America, the Midlatitude South was peopled by immigrants from Europe during the nineteenth and twentieth centuries.

In Argentina, a distinctive Latin hybrid has been created by the early colonization of the Indians, strong European immigration, and the economic development of the fertile grasslands of the pampas. The settlement process was reminiscent of the American conquest of the Great Plains. Until just over 100 years ago, this region of temperate climate and rich **loess** soil supported a population of only 1.5 million. Buenos Aires, now the third largest city in the Southern Hemisphere, first reached the million mark in 1909. After the 1880s, 7 million Europeans—nearly half of them Italians and one third of them Spanish—immigrated to Argentina. Indians were driven from the pampas, and cattle ranches were founded to feed the expanding populations of industrial Europe. European grasses, windmills, barbed-wire fencing, and six-shooters were vital to the settlement of this South American prairie.

The Argentine *pampas* form one of the world's most fertile grasslands. Cattle ranches and wheat farms cover this South American prairie.

The range was parceled and fenced off, and wheat cultivation began, heralding the same struggle between rancher and farmer that occurred earlier in the North American Great Plains. A dense network of railroads—the best on the continent—connected the pampas with the bustling port of Buenos Aires.

The pampas are now the undisputed social and economic core of Argentina. Two thirds of Argentina's population of 32 million people, live on this grassland, which produces 80 percent of the nation's exports. Buenos Aires, with a population near 10 million, is a primate city—no other Argentine urban center approaches its size. The city has grown by a factor of fifty in a century; four fifths of Argentina's population is urban. The level of economic intensity diminishes with distance from Buenos Aires: market gardens are found nearest the city; intensive farming of wheat, fruit, corn, and flax farther out; and a purely

cattle-ranching economy on the periphery. Yet less than a fifth of Argentina's labor force is agricultural despite the importance of farming in the national economy.

The three backward regions of Argentina—the scrub forests of the Chaco in the north, the rugged Andean piedmont to the west, and the windswept, dry plateaus of Patagonia to the south—have gradually been welded into the national economy. Until recently, the hot, wet plains of the Chaco were marginal to anyone's interest, save Jesuit missionaries and their Indian converts. Largely due to modern-day immigration from Europe, the Chaco is now a pioneer region where lumbering and cattle raising are supplemented by cotton, sugar, and tobacco. Still largely populated by Indians, this frontier region has a tenth of the nation's population today.

A similar process of economic integration is occurring in the dry pla-

teaus and mountain valleys of the Argentine Andes, an area previously linked to the colonial economies of Peru and Bolivia. The northern province of Tucumán is the largest sugar producing area in Argentina; the irrigated western oases of San Juan (pop. 217,000) and Mendoza (pop. 471,000) are important regions for growing grapes and other fruits. Improved transportation links with the pampas have encouraged a rapid expansion of commercial agriculture and population.

On the barren tablelands of Patagonia, which stretch 1000 miles south from the pampas to the tip of the continent, population growth has been limited by political enmity between Chile and Argentina and by environmental constraints. Only a handful of Argentinians live in Patagonia. They are concentrated on sheep ranches in deep valleys that provide shelter from cold winter winds. Some 40 percent of Argentina's oil supply is produced near the city of Comodoro Rivadavia, a key base in the brief war with Britain over the Falkland (Malvinas) Islands. Iron resources have been discovered farther south, and Patagonia's role in the Argentine economy has increased in the last decade.

The two smaller La Plata countries, Uruguay and Paraguay, are studies in contrasts—in environment, population, and social and economic development. Uruguay with its mild climate, low-rolling terrain, and rich grasslands, became an independent state—a buffer zone between the two large and powerful nations of Brazil and Argentina. Spanish gauchos hunting wild cattle for hides settled the pastures of Uruguay and became large cattle ranchers. With the introduction of sheep and with immigration from Spain and Italy, Uruguay's stable population of 3 million is racially European and its economy is deeply anchored in animal husbandry. Sheep and cattle outnumber people by ten to one. Some 70 percent of the territory of the country is in pasture that produces the wool, hides, and meat that Uruguay exports.

Yet in Uruguay, the expectable social pattern of a wealthy landowning elite and a poverty-stricken working class did not evolve. The haciendas were complemented by large numbers of medium-sized and small farms on which wheat, flax, wine, and vegetable production has doubled in recent years. Enlightened government policies have provided social welfare to the poor. The Uruguayans, half of whom live in the primate city of Montevideo (pop. 1.3 million), have the highest literacy rate, the lowest rate of natural increase, the best diet, and one of the highest standards of living in any South American society.

In Paraguay, the evolution of society and economy followed a quite different course. Settled by the Spanish, the eastern third of Paraguay, with its rich soils, luxuriant grasslands, and gentle terrain, became a productive agricultural region. Under Jesuit missionaries, the western two thirds of the country, the wilderness scrub forest known as the Chaco, was brought into the Spanish domain. The expulsion of the Jesuits in the eighteenth century and a series of disastrous wars and revolutions in the nineteenth and twentieth centuries devastated Paraguay, literally erasing the economy of the country. After the worst of these, the five-year War of the Triple Alliance against Brazil, Argentina, and Uruguay in the 1860s, Paraguay's population was cut in half from 525,000 to 221,000. Only 28,000 adult males were still alive, and Paraguay lost 55,000 square miles of territory. The country has never recovered from this catastrophe.

Currently, the only productive agricultural zone in Paraguay lies in the immediate hinterland of Asunción (pop. 456,000), where half of the country's 4.4 million people live. Most Paraguayans are Guaraní-speaking mestizos; Guaraní is, in effect, the national language. Cotton, tobacco, cattle ranching, and market gardening are important here. Throughout the remainder of Paraguay, slash and burn agriculture of cotton, corn, manioc, and beans, and extensive cattle ranches are the rule. In the Chaco, the **quebracho** forests along the rivers provide tannin and lumber. Except on the 2100-square-mile colony granted by the government to Mennonites, modern agriculture and herding are rare. This isolated economy barely supports a Paraguayan population increasing at a rate of 2.9 percent a year—highest in South America.

Brazil

Discovered by accident in 1500 by the Portuguese explorer Pedro Cabral, Brazil is the fifth largest country in the world, largest in Latin America, and roughly ten percent smaller than the United States. Brazil reaches 2300 miles north-south and 2300 miles from the coast to its western boundaries. Largely through Spanish in-difference to the tropical forests in the inner core of South America, Brazil became a Portuguese empire in the New World. Brazil remains tiny Portugal's monument to its century of exploration and discovery. As the sole Portuguese-speaking country in the Western Hemisphere, Brazil is culturally isolated, and Brazilians are largely preoccupied with themselves, not with foreign affairs.

Throughout most of Brazil's history, its population has stubbornly clung to the east coast. Today, Brazil has a population of 144.4 million that increases by nearly 3 million a year. The pressure to expand into the vast territory of the interior has become a dominant theme in modern Brazilian life. A true twentieth century frontier extends through the geography of modern Brazil.

Brazil is unequaled for the diversity of its environments and resources in Latin America. In very broad terms, five basic regions can be detected in Brazil: the old Northeast; the East, focused on the throbbing industrial heartland of São Paulo and the traditional capital, Rio de Janeiro; the South; the Central West, brought into the modern age by the construction of a new capital in its wilderness; and Amazonia, the world's largest drainage basin and rain forest, a region poorly understood and threatened by human activity.

The old Northeast, surrounding the "shoulder" of Brazil, is the culture hearth of Portuguese America. As in the culture hearths of colonial North America, it was here that European colonists with the help of African slaves first established permanent settlements and developed institutions that influenced the later development of the entire country. The warm, rainy coasts of the Northeast are well suited to sugarcane cultivation, and despite unchanged cultivation techniques, the Northeast produces one third of Brazil's agriculture. In some places, the fertile red soils of the coastal lowlands have been producing cane and cocoa for

400 years. Cotton has been introduced in the drier coastal areas and in the fringes of the upland interior.

The bulk of the Northeast's population of 44 million lives east of a line drawn across the shoulder from the northerly city of Fortaleza (pop. 1.9 million) to the southerly city of Salvador (pop. 2.1 million). Recife, long the most important Brazilian settlement in the colonial period, has a population of 2.5 million today. The region grades off into hilly uplands and broad interior plains; rainfall diminishes sharply away from the coast and becomes erratic. Cycles of drought and flood characterize the land and shape the lives of its people. The culture of Brazil was largely formed in the backcountry of the Northeast, in what Brazilians call their **sertão.** The sertão is a barren, thinly peopled land covered by dryland grasses and thorny scrub.

The coast and the sertão are sharply different. Despite their contrasting densities of population, both are overpopulated. The cyclic nature of drought has been intensified by deforestation in the sertão. In the coastal lowlands, the persistence of rigid social barriers, patterns of absentee landlordism, and exhaustion of the soil have encouraged migration out of the Northeast to the more dynamic regions of contemporary Brazil, particularly the cities of the East and the new lands of the Amazon Basin. In all, more than 3.5 million have emigrated from the Northeast in the last generation—many to escape what remains one of the most poverty-stricken areas of the Hemisphere.

Eastern Brazil covers only one tenth of the land area of the country, but has nearly one half the population. Four of every ten Brazilians live in either the cities or densely settled countryside of Minas Gerais, Rio de Janeiro, and São Paulo states. The two largest cities, São Paulo (15.9 million) and Rio de Janeiro (10.2 million), form the most mature and diversified industrial region in Latin America. They also rank among the world's largest cities and have developed relatively recently in Brazilian history.

Early on, roving bands of pastoral adventurers crisscrossed the region in search of gold and precious stones. When diamonds and gold were discovered in the riverbeds in Minas Gerais state in the 1700s, thousands flocked to this new El Dorado (Fig. 8.11). The interior plateau, focused on Belo Horizonte (pop. 3.1 million) was opened to settlement and Rio de Janeiro was founded as an outlet for its mineral wealth.

By the 1800s, the minerals had been panned out. On patches of fertile red soil, coffee estates (**fazendas**) were established in the hinterlands of São Paulo and Rio de Janeiro (Fig. 8.11). A stream of 2 million European immigrants, principally Italians, Portuguese, Spanish, and later Japanese, flowed into this region after 1880 to labor on these coffee estates and on sugar, rice, and cotton farms along the coast and in the river valleys of the interior.

Two centuries after the gold rush, discovery of rich ore bodies in Minas Gerais state led to a panicky boom by international investors in the 1910s.

But Brazilians thought the resources should benefit Brazil directly, and development was delayed for a generation. Finally, to exploit the rich iron, manganese, and tungsten ores of the region, an integrated steel complex was constructed at Volta Redonda near Rio in the 1940s. Many others have been constructed since. The world's largest reserves of iron ore are found in Brazil; in Minas Gerais state, the famous "Iron Quadrilateral" has a hematite content of 66 percent. Brazil is both the top exporter and number one producer of iron ore in the world.

Despite extensive penetration of the upland interior and the creation of a new capital at Brasília in the 1960s, the coast remains the nexus of the Brazilian population. São Paulo produces 40 percent and Rio 20 percent of all Brazilian manufactuers. Very different cities from each other, São Paulo is a vast maze of skyscrapers, industrial plants, and residential suburbs spread over an ever-expanding urban field; Rio, cramped in between the Atlantic Ocean, Guanabara Bay, and the coastal mountains, grows uphill, with the city partitioned into a myriad of different

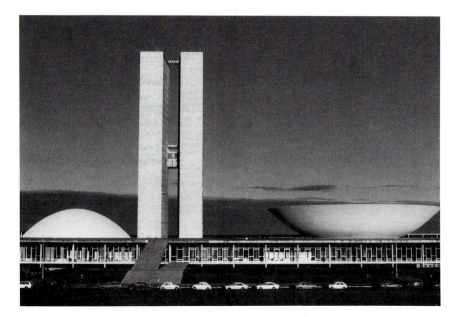

Brasília, the modern capital of Brazil, is located in the heart of the Amazon Basin. Modern in architecture, the city is a symbol of Brazil's determination to conquer and settle this region.

THE BOOM-BUST ECONOMY OF BRAZIL

Brazil has been historically adept at "harvesting the fruit without planting the trees," creating a cyclic boom-bust economy that has retarded balanced economic growth in Latin America's largest country. In the seventeenth cen- tury, a sugar boom led to the settlement of the Northeast; in the eighteenth cen- tury, the gold and mining boom in Minas Gerais state led to the establishment of Belo Horizonte. In the nineteenth cen- tury, rubber was harvested in the Am- azon and coffee cultivation created wealth in the Paraíba Valley. Today, the urban-industrial complex centered on São Paulo and Rio de Janeiro is the focus of Brazilian life. The capital cre- ated by these series of booms was never invested in economic growth in Brazil, a major reason the country has not fully developed its resource base.

Adapted from: John P. Cole, *Latin America: An Economic and Social Geography.* London: Butter- worths, 1975, p. 52.

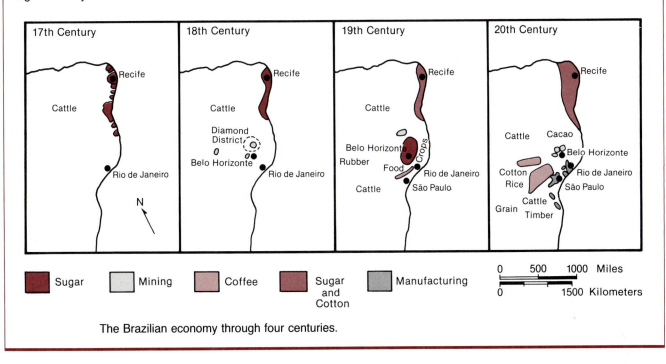

The Brazilian economy through four centuries.

urban areas. Stunningly beautiful from a distance, Rio's beauty becomes Third World reality up close. Trop- ical rains wash down the hillslopes and bring torrents of shacks and gar- bage in their wake. The casual "car- ioca" (Rio native) way of life is threat- ened by ecological pressures today.

A basic problem for Brazil has been energy resources. Until recently, no oil had been located anywhere in Brazil. To counter high petroleum costs in the 1970s, a massive program of dam-building was initiated. Gas- ohol—a response to costly imported gasoline—is made from a variety of agricultural crops grown specifically for this purpose. Gasohol now ac- counts for over 70 percent of the fuel used in Brazilian vehicles. In south-

eastern Brazil, the vast hydroelectric potential of the upper Rio Paraná has been harnessed for the rapid indus- trialization and urbanization of the region. Enormous hydro projects are underway along the Rio São Fran- cisco in Bahia state in the Northeast. The giant Itaipú Dam on the Paraná, costing $20 billion, a joint Brazilian- Paraguayan project, opened in 1982 as the world's largest hydroelectric project. Still, less than 15 percent of Brazil's hydro potential has been tapped. Today, with the discovery of oil off the Northeast coast, Brazil is expected to meet its own petroleum needs in 1990.

The Brazilian South, which sup- ports one sixth of the country's pop- ulation, experienced colonization in

waves that transformed the land- scape of this dissected upland pla- teau. But the **sequent occupance** and traditions of the settlers in the South were quite different from those else- where. The first European settlers filtered southward from São Paulo in the 1700s and 1800s and established a cattle- and sheep-raising economy like that in neighboring Uruguay. At the same time, gold seekers spread southward along the Atlantic coast and established fortified outposts at São Francisco do Sul, Florianopolis (pop. 187,000), and Pôrto Alegre (pop. 2.6 million). In the nineteenth and twen- tieth centuries, these coastal centers became destinations for a second ma- jor wave of immigrants from Ger- many, Italy, and Eastern Europe.

The first to penetrate the interior of the South were the Germans, who established a mixed farming economy of corn, rye, potato, and pig raising in the river valleys of Rio Grande do Sul state. Italian immigrants later extended the frontier, clearing the forests and planting vineyards deeper in the interior. The third major wave of change is the present development of the South's farmlands into extensive, high-technology agriculture based on cultivation of wheat and soybeans for export.

Brazil now earns as much from soybeans as from coffee. The diffusion of soybean production out of northeast China since the 1930s has proved to be one of history's great crop migrations, and today's Brazilian soybean crop—a key animal feed in the Technological World and human food in the Developing World—is exported round the world.

As high-tech farming now encloses the Brazilian South, small farmers are being closed out, and the South, too, bears the mark of a fundamental Brazilian problem—landlessness. At the same time, as food crops such as beans and corn have been replaced by sugarcane for gasohol and by soybeans for export, Brazil must face the fundamental problem of how to feed its people.

The Brazilian response—both official and among the people—has been to extend the frontier. The "first front" of the Brazilian frontier in the last generation has been the states of the Central West: Goiás and Mato Grosso do Sul (a new state, formed in 1979) as well as the Federal District focused on the capital, Brasília. Much of the surface geography of the region is composed of exposed shield materials. Here, soils are poor; in fact **lateritic** iron oxide often reaches a thickness of ten feet. Vegetation tends to be a mix of savanna and scrub woodland known as the **campo cerrado.**

Farming has expanded throughout the region, but the mainstay of the Central West is livestock raising. The most dramatic event in the Central

West has been the implantation of a new capital in the wilderness of the campo cerrado, Brasília. Symbol of the Brazilian desire (and need) to conquer the wilderness, Brasília was founded in 1959 as a planned, **forward capital**—an architectural design project intended to encourage settlement and to change the Brazilian environmental perception of the interior. Despite its problems, Brasília has grown to a population of 1.6 million in less than thirty years, and, particularly since the return of Brazil to democratic rule since 1985, has begun to work as a force to attract people to the Central West.

The vast Amazonian interior has been hailed as one of the world's last frontiers. The region's tropical environment stubbornly resisted all but the most determined efforts at permanent European settlement until recently. Settlement has traditionally been concentrated near the mouth of the Amazon River or far inland on patches of arable land directly along the Amazon and its many tributaries. Belém (pop. 934,000) gateway to the Amazon, is the focus for the development of the Eastern Amazon. Iron ore and hydropower are under development in the state of Pará. Inland, the 3900-mile-long river passes by Manaus (pop. 635,000), capital of Brazil's largest state, Amazonas. The Amazon continues another 2900 miles beyond Manaus, and is navigable as far inland as the frontier city of Iquitos, Peru (pop. 204,000).

The continuously hot, humid climate and infertile soils of the tropical rain forests that cover the Amazon basin kept it almost unoccupied by Europeans until modern times. Indians collected rubber and Brazil nuts and practiced slash and burn agriculture. A brief rubber boom at the turn of this century was frustrated by inaccessibility, plant diseases, and labor shortages (Fig. 8.11). The Ford (Fordlandia) and Goodyear rubber plantations are today in ruins, defeated in the end by the discovery of synthetic, petroleum-based rubber

in the 1940s. The government's determination, however, that the empty heart of Brazil should no longer remain empty has led to the construction of a Trans-Amazonian highway network linking the major regions of the Amazon.

It is in the far southwest, however, in Rondônia and Acre states, where the bulk of current human development on the Brazilian frontier is taking place. With the construction of a paved highway, BR 324, heavily financed by the World Bank and the Inter-American Development Bank, lumber companies, gold miners, peasant settlers, and cattle ranchers have stampeded into Rondônia state and are now protruding into the hitherto untouched Acre. In 1978, Rondônia welcomed 12,000 immigrants. Ten years later, 12,000 arrived each month from the East and South, given a sum of money by their mayors and sent west on a bus. Few arrive with a sense of the environmental qualities they are about to encounter in the diminishing wilderness. Indians beyond the advancing line of settlement are in immediate danger of extermination. Conservationists recognize that the Amazonian environment is fragile and cannot sustain dense agricultural populations over the long run (Fig. 8.8). Furthermore, clearing the rain forest may well affect climatic patterns in the East and South, thereby jeopardizing food production in Brazil's heartland. It is, however, in the Brazilian frontier where the needs and dreams of conservationists, frontier folk, Indians, and other Brazilians converge and conflict. The resolution of Brazil's problems is far from clear.

The Human Use of the Earth

Much of the environmental history of Latin America has involved the quest for forested land that could be cleared for planting or grazing. Before the 1500s, the population of this region was relatively small and pressure on the land was not intense except in areas of high civilization. In the realms of the Maya, Aztec, and Inca rather sophisticated systems of cultivation supported dense populations, but elsewhere settlement was light, people few, and vast tracts of land in Central and South America were relatively untouched.

For several thousand years, shifting cultivators cut and burned patches of forest land, abandoned the cleared fields when yields declined, and moved on to new settlement sites. Abandoned sites usually had time to recover before the human presence recurred. Soil erosion was limited by the small size and scattered distribution of the clearings. The modification of vegetation was gradual but cumulative. Small groups of people armed with primitive tools and their own physical energy did alter vegetation, but European eyewitness accounts of dense forests in locales like the Valley of Mexico and Peru during the conquest period suggest that their impact was limited. Close to the colonial cities, charcoal burners and cattle leveled vegetation, but elsewhere the natural environment prevailed. Deforestation and overgrazing were less intense in Latin America than in Africa, principally because animals played a limited role in native economies prior to the arrival of cattle and sheep from the Old World in the 1500s.

Environmental Transformation

Since the 1950s, growing Latin American populations, heightening demand for food, and the use of machine technology has led to a serious devastation of the forest environments of Latin America. This world region contains well over half of the planet's tropical forests, the bulk of them in the Amazon Basin, which stretches across the six countries of Brazil, Venezuela, Colombia, Ecuador, Peru, and Bolivia. Here, tropical forests cleared by chain saws and bulldozers are being converted to large-scale cattle ranches. The total size of the rain forest is estimated to

have shrunk some 15 percent since the arrival of the Europeans, but satellite pictures reveal that half the destruction has taken place in the last decade.

It is in the Amazon Basin that the greatest destruction of forest land has occurred. In the 1970s, the Brazilian government carved the Trans-Amazon Highway into the basin interior to develop the resources of the region and to relieve population pressure in the rapidly growing cities of the coast and in the drought-prone Brazilian Northeast. The Trans-Amazon Highway and linkage roads opened the rain forest to foreign investment in large cattle ranches. Impoverished workers from the Northeast were brought in to clear the land. When finished, they move deeper into the forest to clear plots for cultivation. Using tractors and heavy chains, teams are able to clear 125 to 150 acres a day as compared with the 2 to 3 acres a week that trained men had been able to clear with axes and sickles. Timber companies have built sawmills along river arteries to exploit the forest. Between 1975 and 1978, the cleared area grew an estimated 170 percent.

Elsewhere in Latin America, the same pattern of forest destruction for cattle raising, timber, and cultivation is in process. In Central America, Guatemala lost 65 percent of its forests between 1950 and 1980. In Costa Rica, forest land is disappearing at a rate of 150,000 acres a year, and if this rate continues, the country will be bereft of forest land by the year 2000. In El Salvador, with its dense population, a staggering 93 percent of the forested area of the country has been sheared, leaving a denuded, parched landscape, which observers have compared to the margins of the Sahara in Africa.

This rapid deforestation has led to rapid erosion, abandonment of cultivated land, and flooding in most Latin American countries. In Guatemala, some 40 percent of the agricultural land has been ravaged by

erosion, cleared areas have reverted to scrub, and flooding has become intense. In Panama, the water level in Lake Gatun, which supplies the Panama Canal, dropped dramatically because more than 35 percent of the land in the lake's watershed has been cleared for farming and, thus, the ability of remnant soils to retain moisture through the dry season has been reduced. Big ships have been diverted 10,000 miles around Cape Horn.

Paradoxically, much of the recently cleared forest land has already been abandoned. The rich green vistas of rain forests in the Amazon Basin and Central America deceived entrepreneurs and government planners alike. Most of the nutrients in the rain forest are tied up in the vegetation itself. Once cleared, the soils beneath are so sterile that the land cannot support continuous cultivation. As a result, farmers and cattle raisers are forced to leave their clearings when the topsoil washes away. At that point, regeneration of the forest is virtually impossible because of the complex structure of the rain forest ecosystem (Fig. 8.8).

With one fourth of the world's animal and plant species—a staggering half million species—the tropical rain forest has proven to be a nonrenewable resource. The unplanned, poorly executed destruction of this vast biotic realm marks a turning point in the human geography of Latin America.

MODERN SOCIETY, SETTLEMENT, AND REGIONAL DEVELOPMENT

Latin America's wars of independence did not bring prosperity, economic development, and social improvement as in the United States. After three centuries of European rule, the agricultural and mineral production of the region far exceeded that of North America. In both areas, vast reaches of valuable land awaited development in the interior. Yet today, after 170 years of independence, Latin America remains relatively underdeveloped. The combined domestic product of all of Latin America is one tenth that of North America. Latin America's standards of living are still many times lower than those found north of the Mexican-U.S. border.

Despite early occupation by Europeans and an excellent resource base, Latin America's delayed social and economic development can be traced to the persistence of the value systems and institutional structure inherited from sixteenth-century Spain and Portugal. In Latin America, *The Social Matrix* remained Iberian in inspiration well into the modern period. The feudal society with its defined classes and racial mixtures divide Latin Americans between wealthy and poor, the landed and the landless. This pattern was reinforced by *The Persistence of the Colonial Economy*. Although independent politically, the countries of Latin America continue to serve as producers of raw materials for industrial societies in the twentieth century. Only in the last twenty years have efforts been made to diversify and develop the national economies of the region, but entrenched landed elites have resisted social change and modernization. With *Population Growth and Urbanization,* social repression has led to political upheaval. The unequal geographical development of Latin America's resource base mirrors the unequal social development of its society.

The Social Matrix

The revolutions in the Spanish New World during the period 1810–1824 liberated the colonies from Spain. Many gachupins, the Spanish-born elite, returned to Europe. Latin America fell into the hands of native-born Americans. Simón Bolívar, a

brilliant orator and military leader, called for the first Pan-American Congress in 1826. He called for a federation of South and Central America whose proposed capital at the Isthmus of Panama would become the center of a dynamic new civilization. But only four new states sent delegates; Bolívar himself was unable to attend, and Bolívar died of tuberculosis in 1830, saying of his accomplishments, "We have plowed the sea."

Political Fragmentation

By 1850, the Spanish New World had crumbled into eighteen independent nations. By 1900 there were twenty; today, there are twenty-six independent countries and nineteen colonies or dependencies. Central America broke away from the Mexican Empire and within twenty years was subdivided into today's Guatemala, Belize, Honduras, El Salvador, Nicaragua, and Costa Rica. Bolívar's pan-Andean republic split into Colombia, Ecuador, and Venezuela. With the sole exception of Portuguese Brazil, local factions were triumphant. Political and economic fragmentation prevailed.

Regional differences, vast distances, and formidable physical barriers separated the centers of Latin America's population. The most striking difference between independent North and South America was that no single geographically unified nation emerged from the Latin revolutionary struggle. In most of the new republics, the long wars of revolution devastated agricultural land and disrupted local economies. Plantations lay in ruins; mines were flooded and abandoned. Insurgent bands led by local chieftains (**caudillos**) exploited the power vacuum by roaming the countryside in search of power, wealth, and prestige.

A pattern of government by generals, the so-called men on horseback, arose and was repeated again and again. Caudillos developed personal followings and launched revo-

lutions against incumbent strongmen. Personalities were more important than programs. Once in power, new leaders squandered their resources to prevent the emergence of yet another caudillo. Some of these leaders were cultured aristocrats. Others were local warlords, such as the one Charles Darwin met on his voyage up the Paraná River, whose hobby was hunting Indians.

Largely because of this kind of leadership, independence did not introduce social change in Latin America. Creoles replaced the exiled gachupins at the top of society. Mestizos moved up to fill the creoles' shoes. Blacks gained legal freedom but little else. Indians, who existed mostly outside the political process, gained nothing. Latin American economies were run by an **oligarchy** of landowners, mine operators, priests, merchants, intellectuals, and military officers whose interest in public welfare was minimal.

Race and Assimilation

In 1800, the Latin American population of 20 million consisted of 4 million Europeans, 8 million Indians, 2 million Africans, 5 million mestizos (people of European and American Indian parentage), and 1 million or so mulattos (people of European and African parentage) and **zambos** (people who are a cross between Africans and Indians).

With the passage of time, people of mixed blood outnumbered those of pure racial lineage in Latin America. Whites, however, retained the highest positions of social and economic power, forming a superior caste closed to people of color. Pure-blooded American Indians and Africans remained near the bottom of the social scale, and both groups became food producers and laborers in Latin America. Mestizos formed the middle class of officials, shopkeepers, and artisans, and became the binding core of Latin American society.

Social relationships between Europeans and their Indian and African

Racial mixing of native Indian, European, and African peoples is characteristic of many parts of Latin America.

subordinates were complicated by two factors that encouraged Europeanization of the population. First, plantation and large estate agriculture required large numbers of submissive laborers who, in Latin America, were organized into systems of peasantry and slavery. Second, the scarcity of white women in the New World forced Europeans to abandon questions of racial purity, and this rapidly resulted in a population of varied race.

Racial mixing and assimilation were extraordinarily rapid. Within two generations, substantial portions of land were divided between the mestizo sons, legitimate and illegitimate, of the Spanish ruling class. Mestizos today form the single largest Latin American racial component. Over half of the region's population—perhaps 220 million people—are mestizo. They predominate in Mexico, highland Central America, Colombia and Venezuela, the settled coastal zones of western South America, and eastern Brazil (Fig. 8.12). Pure Indians—approximately 70 million in

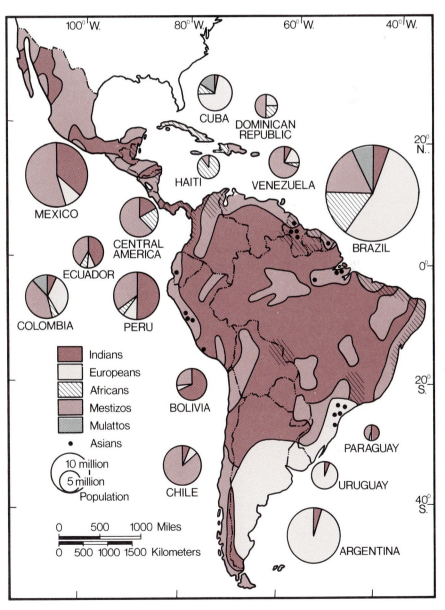

Figure 8.12 Distribution of races in Latin America.

number—remain strong elements of the population in the more remote regions of western and southern Mexico, the Yucatán, Central America, the Andean highlands, and the Amazon interior. African blacks number some 70 million in Latin America and are concentrated in northeastern Brazil, the West Indies (notably Haiti), and the coastlands of the Gulf of Mexico.

A somewhat smaller population of mulattos of varying degrees of racial mixture are found in the same area. The red-black zambos occur in small numbers in the Brazilian interior, the Guiana highlands, and the Colombia lowlands.

The extensive mixing of races in Latin America has made this region a laboratory of race relations in which prejudice and discrimination are comparatively subdued. Social values attached to race vary from region to region. In the traditional sugar center of northeastern Brazil, the slave heritage of the population has preserved a separation of race and class unusual in contemporary Brazilian society. In the interior, by contrast, the more democratic social norms of the cattle-raising frontier are dominant. The slums of São Paulo and Rio de Janeiro contain the dispossessed of all races.

In the Chiapas highlands of southern Mexico, the primary distinctions are between poor rural Indians and more commercialized mestizos. In Central America, race relations are complicated by the contrasting economic systems of highland Indian and European populations and the lowland plantations worked by Africans. In the West Indies, where blacks and mulattos make up a majority of the population, color and class prejudice are still visible, but primary allegiances are to island societies. Although the social pyramid throughout Latin America is consistently lighter in skin color at the top than at the bottom, there are no systematic racial barriers.

The Persistence of the Colonial Economy

The economic structure of Latin America, like its social matrix, changed little with independence, although the revolutions of 1810–1824 did free Latin America from the commercial restrictions of Spain. Trade with Britain, France, Belgium, and later Germany, Italy, and the United States increased substantially. Europeans exported manufactured goods to, and invested money in, Latin America. The European demand for raw materials was balanced by Latin America's need for manufactured goods. Britain emerged as the primary investor in Latin America.

Railroads were thrown across the pampas of Argentina and into the Andean Cordillera. The commercial wool industry of Uruguay and Argentina was established. Later, oil exploration was begun in Venezuela. In the 1920s, Americans developed the nitrate and copper deposits of Chile and oil wells along the Mexican coast. The banana empire of the United Fruit Company in the Caribbean became the symbol and reality of economic imperialism. Because almost all government revenues in Latin America came from trade tariffs, successive governments cooperated with foreign bankers to develop the resources of the region for export.

The Dual Economy

A dual economy evolved in Latin America in which a modern, technologically sophisticated economic sector drained raw materials from the region, whereas the bulk of the population labored in traditional economic endeavors. As in colonial Africa, the Middle East, and India, the most productive agricultural lands were given over to the growing of export crops. Brazil became world famous for rubber and then coffee production; Argentina grew wheat and beef for European markets. Sugar,

bananas, cacao, and cotton were grown on plantations in the Caribbean.

Improvements in transportation expanded the reach of commercial ventures in Latin America. Railroads opened hinterlands away from the coasts. Larger and faster refrigerator cargo ships made it possible to ship bulky perishable goods from Latin America to the ports of Europe in a matter of weeks instead of months. Mineral exports—tin from Bolivia, copper and nitrates from Peru and Chile, bauxite from the Guianas, and oil from Venezuela—were selectively exploited by modern mining ventures subsidized by foreign companies and governments. National economies and transportation networks in Latin America were geared solely to the maintenance of this flow of exports. Diversified economic development did not occur except in areas of commercialized agriculture and mining. As a result, whole regions foundered into unfocused economic backwardness.

Nowhere were the damaging effects of a dual economy forged by the ruling classes of Latin America and the bankers of Europe and the United States more pointed than in Argentina. At the turn of the century, large sums of British money were invested in Argentina. Railroads, port facilities, packing plants, and public utilities—the vital elements that opened up the pampas to commercial production of meats and grains—were constructed. A stream of European migrants—mostly German, Swiss, and Italian farmers—soon followed the flow of European money. By World War I, the Argentine economy and national politics were intimately linked to the British standard of living. From a purely statistical view, Argentina was indisputably the most developed country in Latin America.

In a typical exchange, British ships carried Argentine grain and meat to European markets. On the return voyage, the same ships carried British coal and manufactures back to Argentina. This trade significantly reduced local Argentine interest in the development of a balanced manufacturing and industrial economy. As a result, Argentina's economy was only partially modernized—and then only for the benefit of landlords and politicians. Technological change was not sufficient to create a nation capable of generating its own internal economic growth.

During the twentieth century, North American investments gradually replaced European capital in Latin America. The same encouragement of dual economies with **monocrop** export economies persisted. Almost half of all American investment abroad in the 1930s was in Latin America. A confusing array of Latin American military dictators drew heavily on American banks and arms, and security took precedence over national development.

When riots, rebellion, and rural unrest disturbed production on the plantations, haciendas, and in the mines, movements for social change were ruthlessly suppressed. In Mexico, the revolution of Emiliano Zapata (1910–1915) was particularly violent but also successful. Large Mexican haciendas were confiscated, land was redistributed to the peasants, the oil industry was nationalized, and Indians were granted some measure of social dignity. The Cuban revolution of the late 1950s brought the same objectives of economic balance and social equality to bear, but the pernicious dependence of the island on sugar exports still exists. In the 1980s, the Soviet bloc buys most of Cuba's sugar crop at several times the world price.

The growing role of the United States in Latin American affairs was prompted by its emergence as a world industrial power and by simple locational factors. The Caribbean is four times closer to the United States than to Europe. Only beyond the eastern bulge of Brazil is Latin America nearer to Europe than to North America. Nearly two thirds of Mexico's imports come from the United States; half the imports of the Caribbean nations and most countries of South America come from the United States. Only the economic powerhouses of Argentina and Brazil import less than 40 percent of their manufactures and food needs from North America. Thus, Latin American production of tropical agricultural products and raw materials for the needs of industrial North America has become the primary focus of their economies.

The economic development of Latin America has thus been characterized by conditions of dependency: Latin American states depend on exterior sources of capital for the development of their resources; the management and transport of these resources also depend on exterior markets for sale. Buyers, operating in global commodity markets, shift purchases from one producing world region to another to ensure lowest costs to the consumer. Market preferences and needs, too, can change overnight. The producer in the Developing World is thus a small—and replaceable—cog in a vast network of production and consumption and has little control over price. The economy of many agricultural products and minerals, then, is literally dependent on the Technological World for both capital and markets. Tourism is a more recent industry that functions in much the same manner. It is a difficult and dangerous position in which to be.

Economic Diversification

Latin American countries are today engaged in efforts to diversify their economies, to reduce their dependence on the export of raw materials, and to achieve higher standards of living. In the postwar period, major urban centers, such as Mexico City and Monterrey in Mexico, Medellín in Colombia, and Lima, Santiago, Buenos Aires, São Paulo, and Rio de Janeiro became centers of diversified light industry. But this late start together with rapid population growth, political instability, inadequate leadership, and environmental difficulties have sapped progress toward economic growth and diversification.

In the 1980s, manufacturing still

Emiliano Zapata's successful but bloody revolution in Mexico in 1910–1915 sent shock waves through Latin America. In 1915, his troops massed at the gates of Mexico City, which he threatened to put to fire and sword.

Many Latin American countries are dependent on the export of commercial agricultural products. Here, bananas are loaded on a freighter in the harbor of Guayaquil, Ecuador.

employs a fraction of the work force of Latin America, and three countries—Brazil, Mexico, and Argentina—produce three quarters of Latin America's manufactured goods. Consumption of steel is roughly equivalent to the level of pig iron consumption attained in the United States in 1900. Consumption of energy, considered a reliable index of economic development, is well below that of the industrial countries. The least developed Latin American countries—Bolivia, Guyana, El Salvador, Nicaragua, Honduras, and Haiti—are among the poorest of all the nations in the Developing World with per capita incomes of less than $1000 a year in the 1980s.

Those Latin American countries with petroleum resources have been able to afford programs of economic diversification better than most. As a whole, Latin America produces about one fifth of the world's petroleum and holds vast untapped potential of large-scale hydroelectric power. Except in Colombia, Latin America has virtually no coal (Fig. 8.13). Large areas in the interior of South America are only now being explored for petroleum and other sources of natural wealth. But mobilization of the resources necessary for the construction of expensive hydroelectric power sites is beyond the reach of many of the smaller countries. In general, the largest nations—Brazil, Mexico, Argentina, Colombia, Venezuela—are likely to play the dominant role in the development of new sources of energy. The

smaller, resource-poor countries of the Caribbean, Central America, and South America will remain energy dependencies.

The Caribbean is the focus of Latin America's developed petroleum resources. Of the five countries with an appreciable surplus of petroleum and natural gas—Venezuela, Mexico, Colombia, Trinidad, and Ecuador—four are located in this subregion (Fig. 8.13). Venezuela and Mexico are by far the most important, producing roughly four fifths of Latin America's petroleum. The primary Venezuelan oil field is located in the Maracaibo lowlands, where 6500 wells tap the richest single petroleum deposit in Latin America. Refining Venezuela's petroleum sustains the economy of the islands of

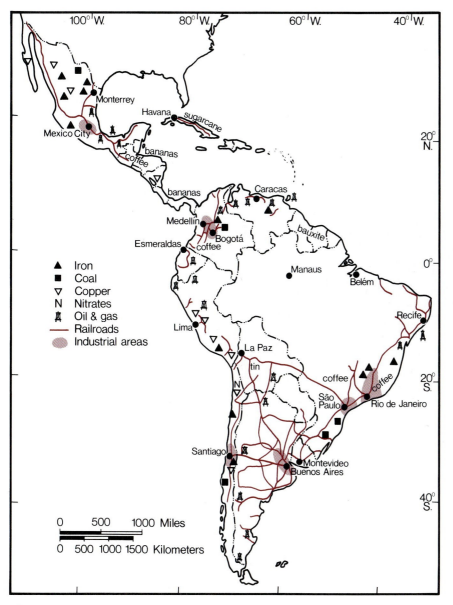

Figure 8.13 Economic patterns in Latin America.

trained manpower, these ventures have not yielded expected returns. Unchecked imports of capital and consumer goods have created trade deficits. Venezuela has failed to convert its nationalized oil riches into a better living standard for the average Venezuelan. They instead intensified the gap between rich and poor in the country. In Mexico, comparable problems have emerged with the flow of oil wealth into that country. Millions of Mexicans still live in poverty, the peasant agricultural sector is resistant to change, unemployment is high, inflation and debt are soaring. Whether Mexico can marshal its modern industrial potential to the benefit of its population is uncertain.

Elsewhere in Latin America, more modest petroleum production and reserves are crucial to the development of local economies. In Ecuador, like Venezuela a member of OPEC, oil deposits in the Amazon have been linked by pipeline across the Andes to reach the coastal port of Esmeraldas (Fig. 8.13). Oil is providing much-needed capital for internal development and can be credited with reducing Ecuador's historic dependence on bananas. Similarly, the discovery of oil in Trinidad has strengthened the economy of that island nation. The same is true in Colombia, whose oil field in the Magdalena River Valley, is vital to the Colombian economy. Argentina is now self-sufficient in energy and the oil fields of eastern Bolivia may provide some momentum to South America's poorest economy.

But if these countries have prospered by having developed energy resources, most Latin American nations have suffered. All of Central America and most Caribbean countries rely on high-priced oil imports to sustain economic growth. Yet revenues are usually heavily dependent on the export of lower priced mineral or agricultural products. Tin exports are crucial to Bolivia, as are copper in Peru and Chile and bauxite in Sur-

Aruba and Curaçao in the Netherlands Antilles, producing 2 million barrels of refined oil a day. Additional discoveries have been made in the Orinoco lowlands. Discoveries in Mexico, the world's largest petroleum producer in the 1930s, have returned that country to a prominent position in the world energy economy. The declining coastal deposits near Tampico and Veracruz are still locally important, but newly discovered fields offshore and in the southern state of Tabasco have filled domestic needs and fostered production

resulting in Mexico's fourth place in world production. Development of oil reserves in the northern states of Baja California, Chihuahua, and Coahuila will further strengthen Mexico's oil position in the future.

In both countries, however, petroleum created great wealth, but solid economic growth has been elusive. In Venezuela, capital has been invested in steel mills, aluminum smelters, and other manufacturing plants geared to the development of the enormous mineral resources of the Orinoco Basin. Lacking sufficient

The oil of the Maracaibo Basin is the mainstay of the Venezuelan economy. It is one of the few major energy deposits found in Latin America.

iname, Guyana, and Jamaica. Sugar is still the mainstay of Cuba and the Dominican Republic; bananas are pivotal in the Honduran and Panamanian economies, as they were in Ecuador until oil production. Fluctuations in the prices of these commodities on world markets periodically shatter the welfare of these societies.

Overall, agricultural products generate four fifths of the exports of fifteen nations of Latin America. Brazil and Mexico loom as the only large countries with a balanced export pattern. Brazil has diversified its production of food crops, soybeans, cotton, and sugar. Typical of Latin America, 80 percent of the Brazilian arable is owned by 5 percent of the population. Colombia has moved to boost production of sugar, flowers, and cotton. The Central American countries are interested in balancing bananas with cotton. In Venezuela and Chile, the iron industry is being promoted. Chile's winter fruits and vegetables have become standard fare in North American supermarkets. But in general, reliance on a single prod-

uct remains almost as strong today in Latin America as in the past. Paradoxically, by using the best lands to cultivate agricultural exports, Latin America in the 1980s must import one tenth of its food needs. Per capita food production actually dropped in Latin America in the 1980s. Underlying this complex state of underdevelopment in Latin America is a landholding system that dates back

to the conquest period.

External debt weighs heavily on the Latin American future today. Money from foreign sources, largely U.S., Canadian, and Japanese banks, and international lending agencies, such as the International Monetary Fund, the World Bank, and the Inter-American Development Bank, poured into Latin America in the boom times of the late 1970s and early 1980s. Bankers and investment analysts figured that the Latin American economy, fueled by rising petroleum, mineral, and agricultural exports, would continue to expand. $59 billion in loans were extended to Latin American countries in the single year, 1981. But as the world market for Latin America's export goods became stagnant and in some cases experienced a marked downturn, Latin Americans were faced with debts they could not repay (Table 8.1). Many private debts have become long-term public debts in the meantime.

Governments have been forced into difficult situations in renegotiating their countries' debts. Resentment of "Yanqui bankers" has become widespread. Some leaders, such as President Garcia of Peru, have ridden to power on their abilities to focus public dissatisfaction over the massive national debt. Many countries have

TABLE 8.1. TOP TEN LATIN AMERICAN DEBTORS

Country	1978	1982	1986	Debt Per Capita, 1986
	(In Billions of U.S. $)			(In Hundreds of U.S. $)
Brazil	53	91	111	781
Mexico	36	86	98	1200
Argentina	13	44	49	1562
Venezuela	17	32	34	1836
Chile	7	17	21	1667
Colombia	5	10	15	494
Peru	10	12	14	693
Ecuador	4	8	10	990
Nicaragua	1	3	6	171
Panama	2	4	5	214

Source: Inter-American Development Bank. *Economic and Social Progress in Latin America, 1987 Report.* Table 57, "Disbursed Total External Debt, by Country, 1978–86," p. 363.

barely kept up with the interest payments on their debt, not to speak of the principal. Compared with income or value of exports, repaying the debt seems almost impossible for many Latin American countries (Table 8.1).

Latifundismo: The Feudal Basis of Agriculture

The Spanish and the Portuguese had a passion for land acquisition, so they instituted a regime of feudal-like estates in Latin America. This landholding system, **latifundismo,** relied on cheap land, markets for produce, a submissive labor force, and an armed elite capable of controlling unrest. From these roots were born the haciendas of mainland Middle America, the **estancias** of Argentina and the La Plata states, the fundos of Chile and Peru, the coffee fazendas of Brazil, and the sugar plantations of the Caribbean. Rural society in Latin America is still divided into two classes. A wealthy, landed elite owns great estates, the latifundios; the mass of the peasantry live on tiny plots, **minifundios,** unable to sustain their families and forced to work as **sharecroppers.** Currently, half the agricultural land of Latin America is held in large estates.

In Argentina, the pampas were subdivided into huge estancias on which beef and dairy cattle, sheep, and horses were raised. Until recently, the 100 wealthiest cattle baron families owned more than 10 million acres. The 2000 largest farms represented one fifth of the total area of Argentina. Millions of European-born farmers migrated to Argentina to work the great ranches as tenant farmers, sharecroppers, and day laborers. These peasants and ranch hands earn subsistence incomes by cultivating the wheat fields and tending the herds belonging to **absentee landowners.** Now technology has begun to push the peasantry off the land and into the cities.

Although market pressures and the inheritance system have broken up some estancias, 60 percent of Argentina's arable land remains in holdings larger than 5000 acres. In Uruguay, sheep ranches are operated in similar fashion. The Uruguayan government has made an effort to increase small agricultural holdings, but only a small amount of land has been transferred to small farmers. Large estates are also dominant in Paraguay. Although half the country's labor force is engaged in agriculture, only 3 percent own their own land.

In Peru, 400 families own half of the agricultural land in the fertile central valley. One estate alone is as large as the original state of Israel. In the late 1980s, half of Chile's farm families are landless, and three quarters of the rest own only 5 percent of the land. The same pattern is repeated on the coffee haciendas of highland Colombia, where large landowners control half the agricultural land in units of 250 acres or more. The ownership of Brazil's agricultural land is equally imbalanced, although on the coffee fazendas in the hinterland of São Paulo and the grain fields of the South, the living conditions of European-born sharecroppers are better than in most of Latin America. These farmers live in fazenda colonies, tend up to 100,000 coffee trees each, cultivate private garden plots, and tend livestock nearby. This plantation model of agriculture, with its emphasis on the cultivation of a single crop for export, is repeated in the sugar- and banana-producing regions of the Caribbean. Despite a long history of slavery and the vagaries of price fluctuations, these plantations and state-owned

Most good land in Latin America is held in large estates (latifundismo) devoted to commercial agriculture like this coffee plantation in Colombia.

farms are the only modern, efficient agricultural systems in Latin America.

These restrictive forms of land ownership are a basic source of rural poverty, agricultural stagnation, and social inequality in Latin America. Landowners maintain their haciendas for status and income. There is little impetus for investment in more intensive land utilization or in modernization of cropping and marketing methods. In contrast the sharecroppers's minifundio (small subsistence farm) is too small, inefficiently run, and located on marginal land. It produces barely enough food to sustain a peasant family. As a result, diets are poor; incomes are low. Unemployment is high in rural areas, and dissatisfied tenants can easily be replaced.

In some areas, out of a desperation born of extreme poverty, peasants have squatted on—occupied illegally—cropland. In Peru, some 200,000 Andean peasants occupied private estates in the 1950s until the military intervened. Similar peasant takeovers have occurred in Mexico, Colombia, and Venezuela during the last thirty years. The current political turmoil in Central America finds its roots in peasant discontent. Sheer landlessness is at work. In Guatemala, 2 percent of the population own nearly 80 percent of the farmlands; in neighboring Honduras, 44 percent of the rural poor own no land at all.

More frequently, the dispossessed move to the cities or become migrant agricultural laborers traveling from one rural scene to another. In Guatemala, nearly one third of the rural labor force move about the highlands for the coffee harvest each year. Four million Colombians travel to Venezuela each year in search of work. Perhaps one of every two minifundio peasants regularly migrates in search of seasonal employment. The flight of illegal aliens from Mexico, Central America and the Caribbean to the United States is part of this general

Virtually all Latin Americans are members of the Roman Catholic Church, whose staunch opposition to birth control contributes to high birth rates in this region. The power of the Church in Latin America is symbolized by this view of the city of Antigua Guatemala, in Guatemala.

state of affairs in rural Latin America.

With over half of all Latin Americans engaged in agriculture, rural poverty is the most compelling problem facing national governments. Agricultural productivity per worker declined by 3 percent in the 1960s. In the 1970s, arable land increased at a rate of only 1 percent per year. In the 1980s, food production failed to keep up with population growth. Latin American grain production reached a peak in 1981 and has since declined. Population pressure on agricultural land has become more intense, and the size of the already tiny minifundios has steadily decreased.

Governments have responded to these conditions by initiating half-hearted land distribution and reform programs. Even these limited efforts at reform, which are made as a matter of political expedience, meet with continuing resistance from the entrenched elite. As external debt has risen, many countries have curtailed the importation of fertilizers to conserve foreign exchange for interest payments on their debts (Table 8.1).

Social upheavals in Latin America resulting in the destruction of the landlord class have struck fear of revolution into this elite. After the revolt of the illiterate tenant farmer Emiliano Zapata in Mexico in 1910–1915, which left the states of Morelos and Guerrero in ashes, the great estates were broken up and peasant cooperatives were established. "Land, bread, and justice," the objectives of the peasants, were achieved. But agricultural productivity on Mexico's **ejidos** (or cooperative farms) remains low even today, and 40 percent of all rural workers are unemployed.

In Cuba, Castro's agrarian reforms of 1959 banned large landholdings and sharecropping. Huge American-owned sugar estates were nationalized and redistributed to Cuban farmers in lots of 67 acres each. Later these were recombined, and cane cutters now work on large government farms organized under a state monopoly—a huge national sugar factory in the field.

Sweeping social reforms in 1952 in

Bolivia were similarly dependent on the transformation of the traditional social order. More than 2 million new small landholders were given parcels of land secured by the nationalization of great estates, but environmental problems and limited financial resources have retarded Bolivian agriculture. The 1979 overthrow of the Samoza dictatorship in Nicaragua and current turmoil in El Salvador are products of social inequality in agriculture.

Elsewhere, agrarian reform has been tentative. Small numbers of families in each country received land from expropriated private estates through land reform programs during the 1970s. In Venezuela significantly larger numbers of people were given land. In the 1980s, Brazil's new democratic government, too, promised sweeping land reform. But pressures to export and maintain social order delayed action on promises. As in Mexico, the Brazilian landless occasionally sweep in and take over large farms as squatters. But with population growing at increasing rates and land reform and industrial production providing limited relief, rural poverty and social inequity are vivid evidence of a continuing failure of leadership in Latin America.

Population Growth and Urbanization

The population of Latin America is currently estimated at 429 million and is increasing by 9.26 million a year, at an annual rate of 2.2 percent per year, meaning that the Latin American population is growing three times faster than that of North America. Although the balance between population and resources is more favorable in Latin America than in either India or China, its population has doubled since 1950. This factor alone defeats efforts to raise standards of living and improve the quality of life. People have fled from rural poverty to the cities. There, the poor of Latin America have taken refuge.

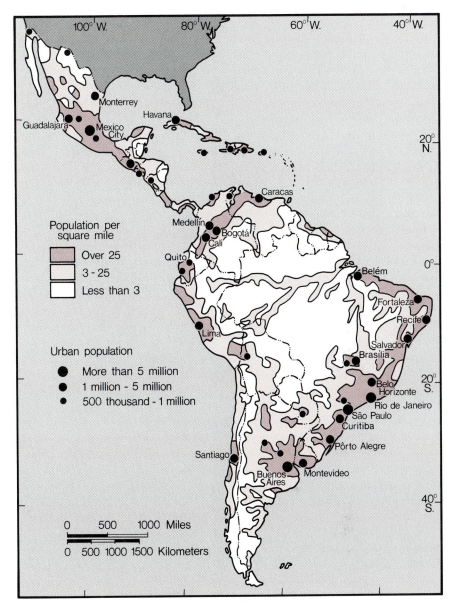

Figure 8.14 Population of Latin America.

Some Latin American countries are approaching the limits of their natural resources. Others lack the money and organization needed to provide education, jobs, and social services to their growing societies. Some of the more developed countries, notably Argentina and Uruguay, have minimal population growth problems.

It is increasingly clear to Latin Americans generally that population growth in Latin America acts as a brake to economic development. Planners in every country are scram-

bling to provide a reasonable life for populations that may reach 537 million by the year 2000.

Population Growth

Between 1930 and 1960, an unprecedented rapid decline in the death rate served to extend the average life expectancy of Latin Americans from thirty-five years to fifty-five years. In 1988, average life expectancy in Latin America had reached 66 years—about that in Europe and North America in 1950. Previously, high birth rates were offset by high death rates, and population growth was limited. In the 1940s, a child in Latin America had only a 50 percent chance of living to age thirty-five. By the 1960s, the three major killers in Latin America—malaria, yellow fever, and typhoid fever—were brought under control. The **Organization of American States (OAS)** paid for hospitals, medical training, water supply, and sewage systems. Communicable and infectious diseases, which had traditionally decimated the population, were replaced by the chronic diseases of old age. As a result, in the 1980s, Latin America's population is six times larger than in 1900.

The population explosion in Latin America does not stem simply from advances in medicine, sanitation, and personal hygiene. From Mexico to Argentina, Latin America is a Catholic society. The Church, although under social pressure to change its views, adamantly opposes artificial methods of contraception. As a result, few Latin American governments have sponsored public birth-control programs. Mexico, one of the few, dropped its opposition to family planning in the 1970s. In ten years, the population growth rate fell one third, although until 1972, Mexico was the fastest growing large country in the world.

Still, as population has burgeoned, the human situation is not entirely bleak. Levels of **scholarization** have increased in all age groups in all Latin American countries since 1960. School enrollment rates for all levels—primary, secondary and university—have steadily risen, such that 65 percent of children, ages 12–17 were in school in 1985, versus 40 percent in 1960.

The distribution of population growth in Latin America has been concentrated in areas already densely settled (Fig. 8.14). Pioneer settlement is hindered by environmental difficulties, the grip of latifundismo in rural areas, and the heavy concentration of economic and social development programs in and around existing urban centers. As a result, in the 1980s, a third of all Latin Americans are crowded onto 3 percent of the land area, whereas half of the region—nearly 4 million square miles—is occupied by only 5 percent of the population.

Today, the regions of highest population density are the islands of the Caribbean, central Mexico, the Andean agricultural highlands from Venezuela through Colombia and Ecuador to Peru, and the Brazilian coast from the eastern shoulder to the Plata estuary (Fig. 8.14). Small clusters of settlement are found in the central valley of Chile, the Bolivian highlands, and parts of Central America. Elsewhere, people are few: the vast rain forests of the Amazon, the scrub forests of the Chaco, and the bleak wastes of Patagonia have less than ten people per square mile. For all intents and purposes, South America has remained an empty continent surrounded by islands of people. But this map is changing for the first time in 300 years as Latin Americans strike out for the wilderness and forever change the nature of their environment.

Urbanization

The largest cities in Latin America are located at the cores of these islands of settlement (Fig. 8.14). They have been growing three to four times as fast as the population at large. Between 1970 and 1980, the urban population of Latin America increased from 125 million to 230 million, resulting in a considerably more urbanized population than in either Asia or Africa. Some 68 percent of all Latin Americans are urban dwellers in 1988. Currently, twenty-three cities in Latin America, nine of them national capitals, have populations of more than 1 million. The metropolises of Mexico City and Buenos Aires have populations of 18 and 10 million respectively. São Paulo and Rio de Janiero, Brazil's largest cities, have respective populations of 15.9 million and 10.2 million. Bogotá now has passed the four million mark. Caracas, Lima, and Santiago have 3 million or more; Guadalajara, Monterrey, Medellín,

Cali, Barranquilla, Havana, Recife, Salvador, Fortaleza, Curitiba, Belém, Brasília, Belo Horizonte, Pôrto Alegre, and Montevideo have more than 1 million inhabitants.

Industrialization has not kept pace with urbanization in Latin America.

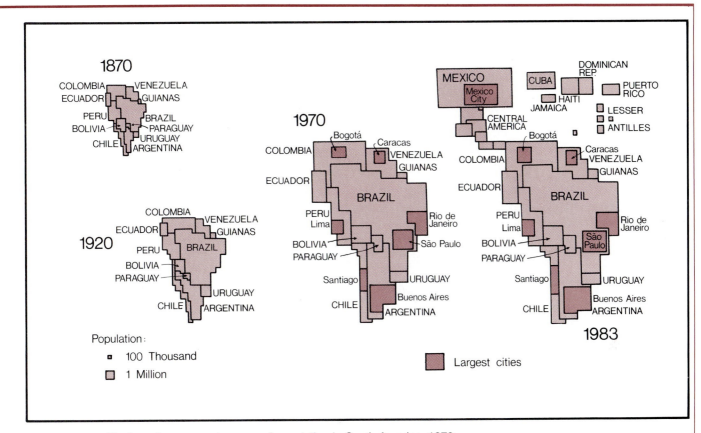

Figure 8.15 Rectangular area cartograms of population in South America, 1870, 1920, 1970, and 1983.

to the magnitude being illustrated, producing a **rectangular area cartogram.** Rectangular area cartograms maintain a considerable degree of continuity but sacrifice accuracy in shape and proximity. If studied closely the regions do not have shapes corresponding to geographical reality, nor do they fit together as they would in the real world. Rectangular area cartograms are widely used because they convey a sense of relative magnitude with clarity, and they are easy to construct using graph paper. Such techniques are easily computerized.

In the four rectangular area cartograms of South America and Latin

America shown here (Fig. 8.15), the area of each country is proportional to the size of its population, not to the size of its territory. These rectangular area cartograms portray the historical growth of South America's population from 26 million in 1870 to 389.4 million in 1983. The shapes of each country are geometrically distorted, but their relative location (but not exact position) are well maintained.

The general growth of the continent's population, the dominance of Brazil, Argentina, and Colombia as the three most populous countries in the region, the importance of primate cities in 1970 and 1983, and the dispar-

ity in populations between the largest and smallest countries of South America are clearly shown. But distinctions of a lesser scale, such as the lower rates of population growth in Bolivia (for economic reasons), Paraguay (disastrous wars), and Uruguay (lower birth rates) are less easy to identify. The ability of an area cartogram to convey general impressions correctly makes it an attractive method of portraying relative magnitudes in graphic form.

Adapted from: John P. Cole, *Latin America: An Economic and Social Geography.* London: Butterworths, 1975, pp. 5, 426.

Numbers and jobs do not match. Manufacturing employs 26 percent of the work force in the 1980s, somewhat more than the 19 percent in 1950. On the other hand, the percentage in agriculture dropped from 54 to 32 percent over the same pe-

riod, and those in the service sector grew from 27 percent in 1950 to 42 percent in 1980. In the midst of increased numbers and stagnating urban economies, the poverty and unemployment of the countryside has been transferred to the cities. Nearly

2 million people, one fifth of the population of Rio de Janeiro, live in the nearly 300 slum communities (**favelas**) that blanket the hillsides of the city. In Lima, a quarter of the population resides in **squatter settlements** inside the city and on its mar-

Primary cities have exploded in size in Latin America. Slums like these draping the hillsides near Rio de Janeiro are found in and around every large urban center.

gins. A similar percentage is found in Buenos Aires and Mexico City. Overall, as many as 25 to 30 million people may live on the fringes and in the marginal economies of Latin America's largest cities. They are a miserably poor and depressed class whose flight to the city in search of alternatives to poverty has overwhelmed the capacity of urban planners to provide them with adequate housing, education, and health services.

Primacy and Regional Development

The irreversible flow of immigrants from rural areas into the largest cities of this region has reinforced and intensified the concentration of population in Latin America (Fig. 8.14). Primate cities are poles of economic and social growth, centers of influence, and theaters of change. During the last century, the growth rates of the capital cities of the twenty largest nations of Latin America have outpaced the national population growth

rate. A third of all Argentines and Uruguayans live in either Buenos Aires or Montevideo. Lima, Santiago, Havana, Caracas, Asunción, Panama City, and San José account for one fifth of their national populations. In seven other countries, 10 percent or more of the population lives in one major urban center. Dominating in numbers and influence, urban primacy is more obvious in Latin America than in any other world region.

Although the political and economic dominance of modern Latin America's primate cities was established in the colonial times, the cities were not population magnets until the modern period. Caracas, for example, was designated as the capital of a new captaincy-general in 1777, but its cultural and political leadership did not make it a center of commerce. Only under the impact of the petroleum industry has Caracas become a diversified commercial and industrial center so attractive to rural immigrants that it now houses 17

percent of Venezuela's population.

Santiago is another example of an early center of Spanish rule whose long role as a political and cultural capital was not accompanied by growth. Now housing one third of Chile's total population, Santiago has expanded over the last thirty years by changing raw materials into processed and manufactured goods for the Chilean market.

Similarly, Buenos Aires experienced a loss of population immediately after independence, but with a distant locational advantage, a rich hinterland, and large-scale foreign immigration and investment, it has become a Latin American primate metropolis containing one third of the population of Argentina.

The exaggerated importance of primate cities in the development of modern Latin American economies and societies has led to a growing disparity between the core regions of urban development and the rural periphery (Fig. 8.16). Lima, for example, with one fifth of Peru's population, handles virtually all the country's financial affairs, supports half its commerce, employs two thirds of its industrial workers, and produces between 80 and 90 percent of its manufactured goods every year. In Mexico, 60 percent of the new factories constructed in the last thirty years were built in Mexico City. With a total population of more than 18 million and an incredible 131,000 factories, Mexico City is the commercial, financial, and industrial core of the country. Similar urban concentrations surrounded by intensive agriculture characterize the heartlands of Venezuela, the Caribbean, eastern and southern Brazil, the central valley of Chile, and highland Colombia. These islands of dense human settlement are the geographical foci of opportunity that have attracted the rural poor.

Modern Latin American governments, concerned with patterns of unequal regional growth within their countries, are now moving to develop the periphery and integrate frontier regions into their national economies (Fig. 8.16). In a dramatic move to counter its pattern of restricted development, Brazil decided to shift its capital city 600 miles into the undeveloped wilderness of the Amazon interior. Within a decade, the new city of Brasília had a population of 300,000. It has since grown five times in size, and a network of roads to divert migration away from São Paulo and Rio de Janeiro has been built. In the Andean countries of Colombia, Bolivia, and Peru, roads have pushed eastward over the Andes into the Amazon forests in search of petroleum. In Venezuela, the Orinoco lowlands are projected as a secondary center of population. Mexico is opening up new agricultural land in the Yucatán and the northeast, and the construction of new factories in Mexico City is under constant discussion. Settlers in Argentina are moving south and west of the pampas. Only the densely populated islands of the Caribbean have no frontiers to be conquered.

It is now difficult to predict whether this new colonization will substantially transform the geography of human activity in Latin America. Migrants continue to prefer the established core areas to life on the periphery. Furthermore, the redistribution of economic activity is taking place within more than thirty self-contained states whose integration with one another is poorly developed. If, as predicted, the population of Latin America doubles in the next thirty years and the proportion of urbanites remains above 65 percent, it seems likely that the existing urban cores will become even more dominant. By the year 2000, Mexico City may well have a population of 26 million, São Paulo 25.8 million, and Rio de Janeiro 19 million. At that time, the 300 to 500 million city dwellers of Latin America concentrated in these clusters of settlement will pose social problems of a magnitude barely suggested by present conditions.

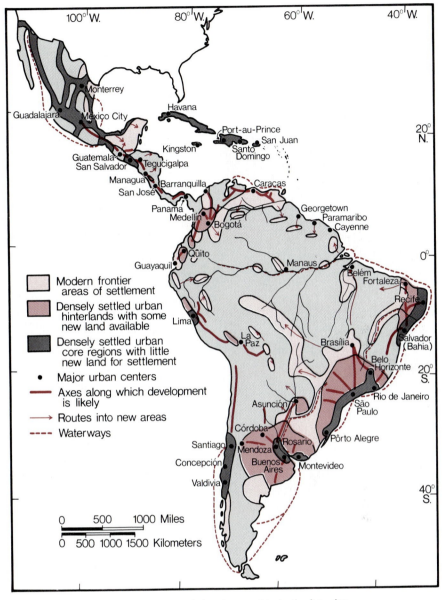

Figure 8.16 Primacy and regional development in Latin America.

9

CHINA

PROLOGUE

The leaders of modern China are grappling with crucial decisions on how to confront the problems of modernization. After four decades of Communist rule, living standards have risen only marginally. Considerable doubt exists as to whether the Chinese can ever achieve the prosperity enjoyed by the Chinese in Hong Kong and Taiwan. For decades the Chinese people have been oppressively instructed in what to do and think. No society on earth has been so stringently regulated. Yet progress has been grudgingly slow. Promises—confidently made—have been difficult to keep.

At its root, the question is addressed to the Communist system itself. Can it propel China into the ranks of those nations that have succeeded in integrating the benefits of the scientific transformation into their societies? This nation's success is of concern to the entire world because China, the "colossus of Asia," has within its realm one fifth of the human race. No government past or present has ever faced the problem of ruling 1 billion people.

Until recently, China was the dominant civilization in eastern Asia. With a history spanning 4000 years, China, as late as 1800, was the most stable, prosperous, and successful nation on earth. One dynasty after another managed to deal with natural disasters, foreign invasions, political succession, and internal reform. A sense of timelessness pervaded Chinese life which bred in its leaders a "serene contempt" for the outside world, a confidence in their own superiority. This confidence was badly shaken when the industrial powers of the West invaded the Asian perimeter in the nineteenth century. At least partly for this reason, the Chinese have been slow to view themselves as a developing society in today's international world.

Today, China debates questions involving how to de-velop the resource base to meet the needs of its people. What level of emphasis should be placed on heavy industry versus light industry? To what degree should military considerations take precedence over consumer demands? How best can China feed its 1 billion people on a land base whose agricultural area is comparable in size to that of the United States? How wide should the door be opened to foreign technology, investment, and trade? What combination of Communist and capitalist principles should govern the organization of Chinese society and economy? The future is uncertain.

In many ways, however, Communist China can be viewed as a modest success. In 1949, the Communists inherited a nation rent by a half century of civil war and foreign invasion. They instituted programs of revolution and reform. A nuclear power by the early 1960s, the country is now viewed as a potential world power. In the international arena, mainland China replaced Taiwan in the United Nations in 1971. The world now vies for closer cultural and economic relationships with the Chinese. Closed to the world until the late 1970s, thousands of Americans and others visit China every year.

On the domestic scene, the Communists have managed to feed their people despite the fact that the Chinese population has nearly doubled from 583 million in 1953 to an estimated 1,087 million in 1988. Notwithstanding rigorous programs of birth control, China's population continues to increase at a rate of 15 million a year. This reality, more than any other single factor, underlies the doubts concerning China's future. On a limited land base, China has the largest population of any nation in the world. If China fails to solve the very real social and economic problems of modernization, its failure will shake the world.

TRADITIONAL CHINA: SETTLEMENT AND SOCIETY

The trademark of Chinese geography and history is its continuity. China's human geography played an important role in shaping the lives of gen-erations of the Chinese. Successive dynasties were measured by their ability to cope with **population pressure,** floods, droughts, and repeated invasions from Central Asia. Disruption of the agricultural base—whether caused by environmental or social stress—created changes in leadership. But the **human ecology,** polit-ical culture, and organization of space in China retained their basic character for 2000 years (Fig. 9.1).

The central question geographers now debate is whether or not the leaders in Beijing (Peking) are more Chinese or more Communist. In other words, after a century of struggle with forces generated by the European in-

GEOSTATISTICS

	Capital	Area (square miles)	Population (millions)	Rate of Natural Increase (%)	Number of Years to Double Population	Population Projected for A.D. 2000	Infant Mortality Rate	Life Expectancy at Birth	Urban Population (%)	Per Capita GNP ($)	Energy Consumption per Capita (kg of oil equivalent)
China	Beijing	3,705,390	1,087.0	1.4	49	1,212.0	44	66	41	300	515
Hong Kong	Hong Kong	402	5.7	0.8	83	6.3	8	76	93	6,720	1,264
Macao	Macao	8	0.4	1.7	41	0.5	12	68	97	—	—
Mongolia	Ulaanbaatar	604,247	2.0	2.6	26	2.8	53	62	52	—	1,313
Taiwan	Taipei	12,456	19.8	1.1	63	22.4	7	73	67	—	—

Sources: World Population Data Sheet, 1988; World Development Report, 1987.

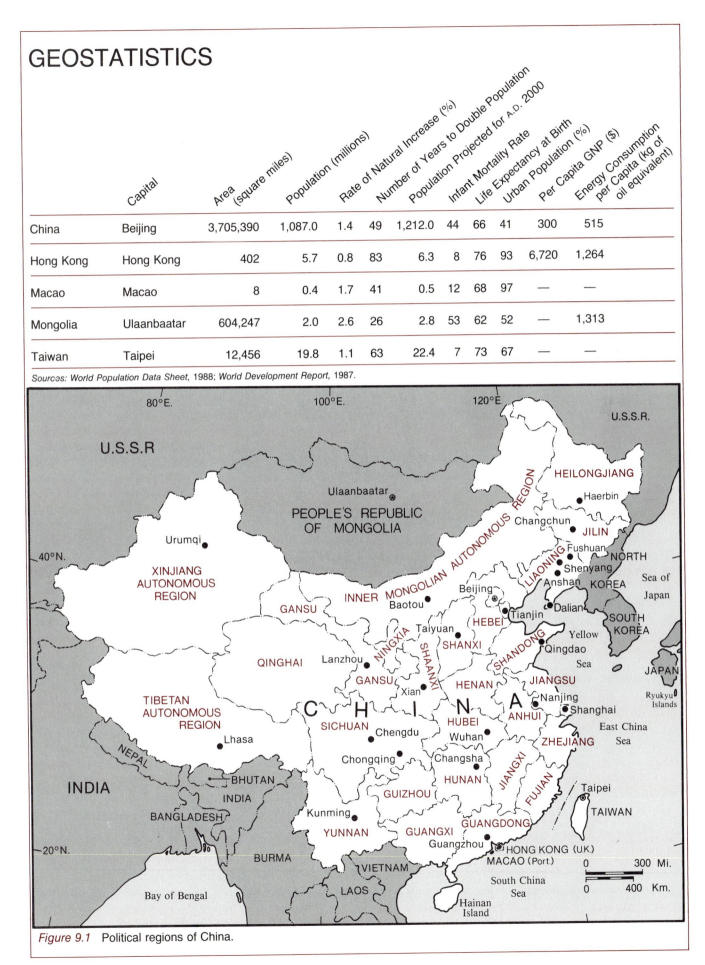

Figure 9.1 Political regions of China.

325

dustrial revolution, will China interpret its environment and resources primarily in terms of traditional Chinese values or, alternatively, in terms of Communist values? The answer to this question will have a profound effect on the human geography of China.

This section focuses on the historical geography of China, providing a background for understanding the forces that are transforming modern China. In *The North China Culture Hearth,* the origins of Chinese civilization on the North China Plain are described. A garden style of irrigation agriculture formed the economic basis of the state, and this agricultural economy diffused to the various environments that today comprise most of Agricultural China. *The Political Culture of Traditional China* was based on the teachings of Confucius. These teachings formed the core of Chinese culture and behavior and provided the basis for administration of the Chinese Empire. The Confucian system of social and political institutions had a direct impact on *The Organization of Space in Traditional China,* a landscape shaped and molded by continuous human effort. In the nineteenth century, however, population pressure on cultivated land and Western intervention led to *The Fall of the Qing (Manchu) Dynasty* that had ruled China for 250 years. The stage was set for *The Struggle for a New China* between the Nationalists led by Chiang Kai-shek and the Communists under Mao Zedong (Mao Tse-tung). In 1949, the Communists won control of the Chinese mainland, shaping the pathways toward modernization that China has pursued for the last three decades.

The North China Culture Hearth

Chinese civilization originated on the loess plateau and alluvial plain of the Huang He (Yellow River) in North China. This plain is covered with wind-driven loess and alluvial soil, and has a **subhumid climate** and open vegetation. Water for irrigation, wood and rock for building material, and excellent soils were abundant in the landscape. Even in paleolithic times, this region's 300,000 square miles were probably more densely settled than adjacent areas.

Because the fertile soils of this region were easily worked with a hoe or spade, the local environment favored a garden style of agriculture different from those practiced in other Asian centers of civilization. Irrigated garden cultivation of wheat and millet involved intense human effort applied to small plots of land. This became the hallmark of the Chinese agricultural system. Average peasant holdings were less than half those of plow-using Europeans in medieval times because virtually all work in China was done by hand. Food production per acre was high—even today Chinese production per acre is higher than in the United States. But productivity per farmer was low. Drought, the most dangerous natural hazard, was mitigated by simple irrigation and drainage canal systems.

The formative period of the North China culture hearth began 3000 years ago when a group of semipastoral people, the Chou, conquered the region in 1111 B.C. The Chou settled as permanent farmers on the loess soil of Shaanxi (Shensi) Province. In time, these people consolidated their power and established walled cities throughout the middle reaches of the Huang He Valley. Their city-states served as nuclei of relatively autonomous economic regions. From these urban bases, the Chou expanded their dominion eastward to the Shandong (Shantung) Peninsula and southward as far as the Chang Jiang (Yangtze River). Over the next 1000 years, carpets of fields spread over the North China Plain. Terracing and irrigation systems were constructed. Key innovations and techniques—wet field rice, the ox-drawn plow, a formal style of writing, and a unifying language—emerged in North China.

Finally, in 221 B.C., a young Chin prince (whence Chinese), Qin Shi Huang Di, consolidated all of North China into a single state. The 1500-mile-long Great Wall, the only man-made structure visible from the moon, was begun in this period. The wall was intended to provide a barrier between the nomads of Central Asia and the agriculturalists of North China. It was Qin Shi Huang Di who laid the foundations on which his successors, the Han, built a vast empire that endured for 2000 years.

Expansion and Empire

During the four centuries of Han rule (207 B.C.–A.D. 220), the agriculturalists of North China extended their sway over virtually all of modern China (Fig. 9.1). In the west, the Chinese overran the Central Asian oases at the foot of the Nan Shan Mountains and spread Chinese rule through the Tarim Basin as far west as the Syr Darya River in the modern Soviet Union. In the north, Chinese armies maintained frontier control over the Northeast (known to Westerners as Manchuria) and political influence in Korea, reducing nomadic pressure on the core area of the Chinese state (Fig. 9.2).

The most important geographical expansion of the Han political and cultural system, however, lay to the south. At that time, southern China was inhabited by a variety of non-Chinese Tai peoples native to Southeast Asia. Chinese peasants spread southward beyond the alluvial plains of the Chang Jiang into the hill country of South China and onto the tropical delta of the Xi Jiang (West River).

The Chinese conquered the Tai peoples of the south by assimilation, driving conservative, less responsive groups out of lowland environments into the hills. Level land suitable for hoe cultivation was their goal. They settled so extensively on alluvial lowlands and plains that even today nine tenths of China's population is clustered on this one sixth of the country.

The gradual drift of Chinese peas-

PLACE NAMES IN CHINA: THE PINYIN SYSTEM

The problem of **transliterating** (putting a language into another alphabet) Chinese from its original characters into Western languages has plagued students of China for a long time. Over the years, a somewhat standardized system for spelling Chinese in English became widely accepted. Transliteration became more standard during World War II, when the need for maps, air charts, and gazetteers was high, and translation of Chinese into English became part of the war effort. The U.S. Board on Geographic Names, for example, published a gazetteer of China with over 100,000 place names. Virtually complete map coverage of China in English was published. Geography textbooks, atlases, library reference works, periodicals, and newspapers all came to use standard spelling.

However, many Chinese words rendered into English had little relationship to the actual pronunciation in Chinese or to the form of the word in standard Chinese dialect (North Mandarin Chinese). Westerners may have come to know the place name through the dialect of Guangzhou, for example, or simply misheard the word in this tonal language. And there were variations of the same word in English, and more importantly, there were variations between different Western languages. The capital was Peking in English but Pekin in French. Neither bore much relation to the actual Chinese word.

The Chinese government adopted a new, simplified system of transliteration in 1958: Pinyin. The Chinese established Pinyin as the standard spelling of Chinese characters. In 1979, Pinyin was adopted for transliteration of all texts into Western languages.

Based on the pronunciation of Chinese characters in the Northern Mandarin dialect, the letters, with some exceptions, sound exactly as they do in English.

These exceptions are: q equals ch; c and z equals ts; zh equals j; and x equals hs. In this text, the new Pinyin system of transliteration is generally used, and Pinyin is followed on first reference by the old form in parentheses. The exceptions to this arrangement are those instances where a historical discussion involving use of the traditional form of the word seems useful, as in the case of Guangzhou (Canton), and those few instances of places and people long known in the West by a significantly different name from that given them in modern standard Chinese. These are Tibet, Hong Kong, Macau, and Manchuria, and the political figures Sun Yat-sen and Chiang Kai-shek.

All this is to say that there are still enormous problems in this field, and they typically arise when students attempt to compare data over time, or even to recognize the same word in both systems. This list of place names and persons under both systems shows names used in this chapter.

Pinyin	Old System	Pinyin	Old System	Pinyin	Old System
Provinces		**Cities**		**Rivers**	
Anhui	Anwei	Anqing	An-ch'ing	Chang Jiang	Yangtze
Fujian	Fukien	Baoshan	Paoshan	Huang He	Hwang Ho
Guangxi	Kwangsi	Baotou	Pao-tou	Songhua	Sungari
Guizhou	Kweichow	Beijing	Peking	Xi Jiang	Hsi
Hebei	Hopeh	Benqi	Penchi		
Heilongjiang	Heilungkiang	Chengdu	Chengtu	**Basins, Peninsulas, Islands**	
Henan	Honan	Chongqing	Chungking	Jungarr	Dzungarian
Hubei	Hupeh	Daqing	T'a-ch'ing	Liaodong	Liaotung
Jiangsu	Kiangsu	Fushuan	Fushun	Penghu	Pescadores
Jiangxi	Kiangsi	Guangzhou	Canton	Qaidam	Tsaidam
Jilin	Kirin	Haerbin	Harbin		
Ningxia	Ninghsia	Lanzhou	Lanchou	**Persons, Dynasties**	
Shaanxi	Shensi	Luta	Darien	Deng Xiaoping	Teng Hsiao-ping
Shandong	Shantung	Nanjing	Nanking	Mao Zedong	Mao Tse-tung
Sichuan	Szechwan	Qingdao	Tsingtao	Qing	Manchu
Zhejiang	Chekiang	Shenyang	Mukden		
Xinjiang	Sinkiang	Taiyuan	T'ai-yuan		
		Tianjin	Tientsin		
		Urumqi	Urumchi		
		Yichang	Ichang		

ants into the tropics was apparently motivated by disasters in the north and by the lure of new land in the south. According to some observers, nomadic pressures from the north and west on the Huang He and Chang Jiang valleys produced a ripple effect that pushed colonists farther and farther south. Floods and droughts also played an important role. Records exist of some 48 floods and 17 droughts in North China during the Han period. Each of these natural disasters undoubtledly dislodged farmers from their land. The south, known and perceived as a land of plenty by peasants in North China, attracted families in search of a better life. This view was fully justified; the south provides over 60 percent of the total food supply of modern China.

The southward advance of Chinese colonization spread a network of walled cities—called **hsien** (county capitals)—throughout the valleys and intermontane basins of southern China. The hsien functioned as administrative and economic centers for surrounding regions. By the end of the Han period, this network of central places covered most of the territory of modern China (Fig. 9.2). The Chinese Empire was comparable in size, population, and cultural complexity to its counterpart in Europe, the Roman Empire.

Over the centuries, the garden agriculture of the Han Chinese and their successors was productive. China's population grew from 100 million in the year 1100 to 150 million in 1600, 220 million in 1750, and 430 million in 1850. Population pressure gradually pushed farmers into less attractive environments.

In South China, a new rapid-maturing rice introduced in the twelfth century made it possible to grow two rice crops in one year on the same piece of land. This new variety, called Champa rice, doubled the productivity of the land and required less water. It could be planted in hitherto marginal environments—on sloping land, in regions of poorer soil, and on more rugged terrain. Dry land crops, like wheat, barley, and sorghum—which filtered southward from North China—further extended the environmental range of the Chinese agricultural economy.

In the sixteenth century, American crops, such as corn, sweet potatoes, and peanuts, were introduced. This pushed peasant cultivation still deeper into the dry hills and mountains of the south. The forested uplands of central and southern China were cleared for cultivation. As many as 12 million acres of forested land were cut down by colonists in search of land. This ultimately led to erosion and abandonment of fields in upland China and silting and flooding in the lowlands.

The Great Wall of China slices 1500 miles across North China. It was built to separate the agricultural peoples of China from the barbarian nomads of Inner Asia.

The Political Culture of Traditional China

Population pressure on the environment continued throughout the course of Chinese history. Dynasties fell twenty-five times in 2000 years, leaving the administrations of new rulers to cope with environmental and social catastrophes caused by drought on the North China Plain or floods in the tropical south. Yet China maintained its cultural and territorial continuity. This was largely because the principles and ideals of the teacher-scholar Confucius (about 551–479 B.C.) were adopted, practiced, and retained as a state cult from the Han period to the present. China is thus the world's oldest continuous civilization.

Confucian teachings embody three basic concepts that were of supreme importance in the organization of life and landscape in China. First, the Chinese ruler was considered accountable for human conditions. Second, imperial administrators were selected on the basis of competence. Third, the Chinese people were encouraged to value order, continuity, and social cohesion above the pursuit of personal gain. Although imperfectly practiced, these teachings defined the appropriate behavior of the three most important social groups in China: the royal court, the imperial administrators, and the peasantry. All were expected to live by Confucian ethical and moral codes of conduct—and these became an indelible mark of Chinese culture.

At the apex of society was the emperor, ruler of the dynasty, on whom a mandate was conferred by Heaven, making him universal monarch, the Son of Heaven. Inherently superior to all other rulers, his task was to achieve harmony through the practice of good government and moral conduct. Evidence of this harmony was to be found in human conditions in China. Drought, flood, famine, and disorder were signs that the emperor was not fulfilling his duty. This personal obligation set limits on the emperor's power and justified his replacement by a new dynasty when chaos prevailed.

The ideal administrators in traditional China were not military leaders, but men of wisdom and learning. These "scholar-officials" were representatives of the imperial government. They were bureaucrats who levied taxes, supervised public works, ran police forces, and administered law courts throughout China. Even the lowest ranks of this class commanded great influence, often being solely responsible for the public affairs of districts populated by as many as a quarter of a million people. They were the product of an elaborate recruitment scheme, the imperial examination system.

The Confucian principle that excellence was a matter of education and conduct rather than inheritance was applied to the task of establishing a reliable bureaucracy to govern China. An exhausting series of examinations attracted hundreds of thousands of student-scholars from the lower reaches of society. Success quotas on some examinations were less than 3 percent. But the rewards of the system were so great that all over China young men spent as many as twenty years honing their knowledge of Confucian teachings.

Since agriculture was always the leading source of wealth in China, peasants were encouraged to value submissiveness to authority, respect for tradition, reverence for the past, prudence, caution, and moderation—Confucian virtues that contributed to conservatism, order, and harmony in society. Harmony existed when, as the proverb went, "Superior men diligently attend to the rules of propriety, and men in an inferior position do their best." The Chinese peasantry, embedded in this Confucian political culture for centuries, supplied city dwellers with food and were the principal organizers of the Chinese landscape.

The Organization of Space in Traditional China

The social and economic world of the Chinese peasant was rooted in a basic **market town** located within walking distance of the farming villages of China. In densely settled eastern China, market towns served hinter-

For 2000 years, the Chinese spread out from the North China Plain. They colonized South China and converted lowlands into rice fields. This typical landscape scene is from Guizhou Province in South China.

GEOLAB

CULTURE REGIONS: CORE, DOMAIN, AND SPHERE

Although a distinctive Chinese culture dominates a large area of East Asia, mapping the exact dimensions of the Chinese culture region—or any culture region—is not an easy task. The difficulty lies in identifying the elements that make Chinese society and economy unique. Is the Chinese culture region simply the area where ethnic Chinese make up a majority of the population? Is it the territory politically controlled by China? Or is it those locales where the Chinese garden style of agriculture and centuries of Confucian administration have systematically transformed the landscape? In an effort to resolve the difficulties of mapping culture regions, the geographer Donald W. Meinig has made use of general concepts to express significant gradations in the content and situation of the culture under study. The culture region is then expressed in areal dimensions in terms of these concepts: **core, domain,** and **sphere.**

The core area of a culture, according to Meinig, is a "centralized zone of concentration displaying the greatest density of occupance, intensity of organization, strength and homogeneity of the particular features characteristic of the culture under study." In China, the culture core was established during the Han period (207 B.C.–A.D. 220) when the Chinese empire expanded into the Northeast, westward into the oases of Central Asia, and across the hill lands of South China (Fig. 9.2). The eighteen provinces conquered and administered by the Han form a cohesive spatial entity in which life and landscape are indelibly Chinese, molded by their specialized agricultural economy and guided by the Con-

fucian code. The Chinese refer to this core region as "China Proper or Chung Kuo, the Middle Kingdom." Note that in defining the culture core, a qualitative judgment based on intimate knowledge of the region and its processes is being mapped. No single criterion is used.

The domain refers to those areas in which "the particular culture under study is dominant" but with less intensity and complexity of development than in the core. Here, regional variations are evident; bonds of connection within the domain are less developed. In China, the domain extends over large areas peripheral to the core re-

gion of eastern China. Among these areas are Tibet, Xinjiang (Sinkiang), Inner Mongolia, Mongolia, the Northeast (Manchuria), Taiwan, and parts of Vietnam (Fig. 9.2). Certain areas in the domain have recently—in Chinese terms—become intensely Chinese, among them the three provinces of the Northeast and parts of Inner Mongolia and Ningxia (Ninghsia). Historically, the Chinese domain, although frequently under Chinese political control, has retained its distinctive environmental and cultural features. The Chinese imprint is less complete in the domain than in the core.

The sphere of a culture is defined

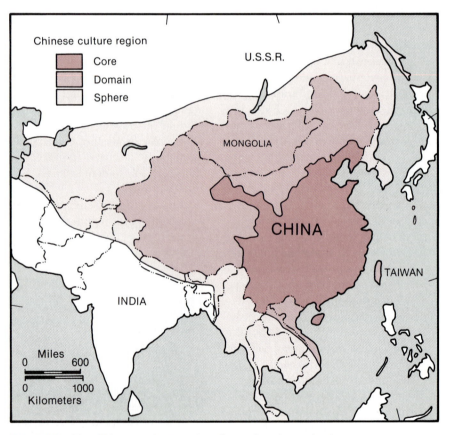

Figure 9.2 The Chinese culture region: Core, domain, and sphere.

lands about 20 square miles in area. In lowland eastern China, the basic market towns usually served fifteen to eighteen farm villages and a total population of some 7000 people. In less intensely settled mountain dis-

tricts and in the deserts of Outer China, basic market towns served larger areas with smaller populations. In any case, the basic market town was the focus of peasant life throughout China. This pattern of

settlement in traditional China is a prime example of the regularity and rhythm in human geography apparent in many preindustrial societies (Fig. 9.3–9.5).

In nineteenth-century China, some

as its "zone of outer influence and, often, peripheral acculturation." Here, the culture under study is represented only by certain of its elements and its people often reside as a minority among those of a different culture. The sphere is difficult to define precisely because its boundaries lie in a transition zone where culture changes rapidly. In China, the sphere extends over southern Vietnam, Central Asia, Afghanistan, Korea, parts of the Soviet Union adjacent to the Northeast, and the Ryukyu Islands in the East China Sea (Fig. 9.2). In these areas, Chinese political and cultural influence has had a strong effect on resident peoples, but the Chinese are a minority population residing in a transitional culture region.

It should be noted that the core, domain, and sphere concept developed by Meinig to map culture regions is based on two assumptions. First, it assumes that the culture under study is expressed most intensely at its point of origin or culture hearth and in the core and that it diminishes outward. Diffusion of culture by migration of people, ideas, and technology is presumed. Second, the concept assumes that this culture will affect land and life less intensely as the friction of distance diminishes its influence. In short, it is both a diffusion and a distance decay model.

Adapted from: Donald W. Meinig, "The Mormon Culture Region: Strategies and Patterns in the Geography of the American West, 1847–1964," *Annals of the Association of American Geographers,* Vol. 55 (1965), pp. 191–220.

MAP BASE: Variations on maps in Don R. Hoy, *Geography and Development: A World Regional Approach.* New York: Macmillan, 1978, pp. 616–617.

45,000 basic market towns were distributed across the landscape so evenly that virtually all peasants in the country's 900,000 villages had access to the goods and services they offered. Basic market towns and their

Villages like this one outside the city of Nanjing formed the social world of the Chinese peasantry for centuries.

surrounding hinterlands stretched across China in a regular, almost mathematical pattern. These basic market towns were the foundation in a **hierarchy** of towns and cities, or **central places,** that provided the countryside with urban services.

The hierarchy of urban central places extended from the basic level of the market town up through progressively larger towns and cities and their collective **marketing areas.** All over China, the agricultural products and crafts of the peasants were brought to basic market towns for sale; manufactured and specialized goods filtering down through the hierarchy of central places were exchanged for the peasants' products.

The basic market town, the cell in this pattern of economic exchange, was the Chinese hometown. It was a meeting point between the worlds of the scholar officials, merchants, and peasants. Virtually every good or service needed by a peasant—soap, matches, oil, incense, a barber, a tailor, a scribe—could be found in the basic market town. The marketing area surrounding the town was the social terrain that peasants knew intimately. By the time peasants

reached age fifty, they had visited their basic market town more than 3000 times, dealt with merchants with whom they had become closely acquainted, and recognized on sight peasants from their own and nearby marketing areas. Because the population of these districts tended to remain stable, local social cohesion was reinforced.

In turn, each of these basic market towns was part of a network of larger settlements with an increasingly large range of goods and services. These higher level market towns were important in traditional Chinese society because they were the major transfer points between the villages, the basic market towns, and the metropolises of China. The relationship between populations and markets was repeated through each successive stage in this hierarchy of settlement. It culminated in the largest central place of all, the imperial capital.

At each higher level in the system, economic activities became more specialized, administrative functions broader, and occupations more diversified. In traditional China, then, the theoretical precision of central place theory was closely approxi-

GEOLAB

CENTRAL PLACE THEORY

Theoretical geographers have studied regularities in the patterns of settlement in rural societies to develop logical, deductive models of the organization of human activity. One of these models is called **central place theory.** The assumption underlying this theory is reasonable: it assumes that human activities are regularly, not randomly, distributed in space. The ultimate goal of theoretical geographers is to understand the order and logic that underlie this regularity in complex human societies throughout the world. In essence, they are searching for mathematical laws that underlie human spatial distributions.

The problems that theoretical geographers face are substantial. A mountain range, a political boundary, a river, or an accident of history will change local patterns of human activity. This makes every location on earth unique. To resolve this complexity, theoretical geographers assume an idealized, flat, undifferentiated landscape; they remove topographic, political, and cultural variations from the region under study to identify principles of spatial distribution. Although the geometric regularity of the idealized central place model is never perfectly realized in the landscape, a more universal appreciation of the ways in which people organize and use space becomes apparent.

The three figures of a rural area near the city of Chengdu (Chengtu) in Sichuan (Szechwan) Province shown here demonstrate how a real landscape can be understood as a logical organization of settlement and economic activity through the use of cen-

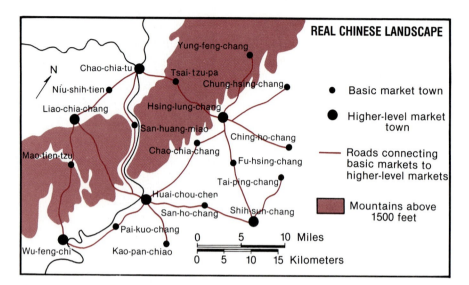

Figure 9.3 Real Chinese landscape.

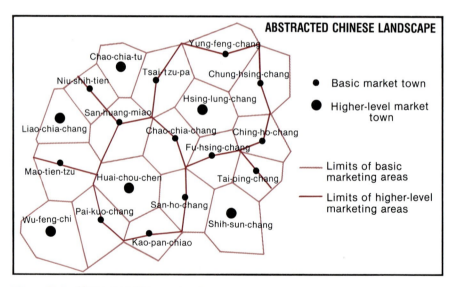

Figure 9.4 Abstracted Chinese landscape.

mated by the geographical distributions, the economic functions, and the administrative systems of the real world (Figs. 9.3–9.5).

The Fall of the Qing (Manchu) Dynasty

During the 1500s and 1600s, China under the Qing dynasty was the rich-est, most prosperous society in the world. The empire was well administered by its Confucian bureaucracy. A stream of new ideas, crops, and goods had filtered into China without disrupting its political culture. Space was efficiently and effectively organized to meet the needs of the Chinese people and their leaders. Population rose from 100 million in 1500 (same as it had been in 1100) to 160 million in 1700. The Qing dynasty, which had ruled China since 1644, was secure.

At the beginning of the 1700s, the Chinese state was still secure. But the two forces that were eventually to dislodge the Qing—peasant anguish and Western intervention—were just over the horizon.

tral place theory. In Figure 9.3, nineteen basic market towns are shown as they actually exist in the Chinese landscape. Roads connecting basic market towns with **higher level market towns** are influenced by rugged terrain crosscutting the region from north to south and by a river that flows through these mountains. It is along these roads, the veins and arteries of this spatial system, that villagers and their products move back and forth between the smaller and larger centers.

Figure 9.4 is an abstraction of this area, dividing it into theoretical hinterlands, or marketing areas, served by the basic market towns (bounded by the lighter lines) and by the higher level market towns (bounded by the darker lines). Note that the hinterlands served by each of the basic market towns is absorbed within the larger marketing areas of the higher level market towns. These larger settlements provide more specialized goods and services for the Chinese populace.

Figure 9.5 is a theoretical model of this region in which all environmental and cultural differences have been filtered out. Seen in mathematical relief, all basic market towns and their hinterlands revolve around the higher level market towns of this district in geometric fashion.

This simplified, theoretical vision of reality suggests that there is a spatial order underlying the organization of human activity. By applying central place theory to rural China and other parts of the world, theoretical geographers have been able to use deductive theory to reveal the almost geometrical precision of human activity.

Adapted from: G. William Skinner, "Marketing and Social Structure in Rural China, Part I," *Journal of Asian Studies*, Vol. 24 (November 1964), figs. 2.1, 2.2., 2.3, pp. 22–23.

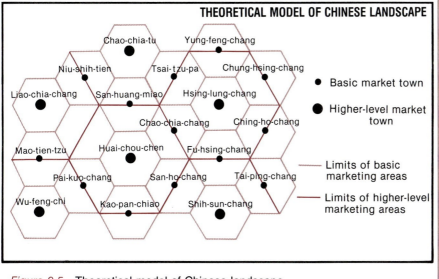

Figure 9.5 Theoretical model of Chinese landscape.

In the countryside, population pressure was causing fragmentation of fields into tiny plots too small to support a family. Population doubled during the 1700s, growing past the 300 million mark by 1800. Forced into debt, peasants lost their land to moneylenders, and over 30 percent of Chinese farmers became landless tenants. This condition was aggravated by corrupt tax collectors determined to squeeze more income from the peasantry. The decline of the agricultural economy of China, which produced 80 percent of the empire's wealth, was not perceived until late in the 1700s. A general uprising, coinciding with the American Revolution, signaled the decline of the Qing Dynasty.

The Qing had also not perceived the growing economic and military power of the West. The physical isolation of China and long-standing sense of cultural superiority had engendered contempt in China for peoples living beyond the borders of their empire. In 1793, for example, Lord Macartney sought trading facilities in China for Great Britain. He was told that China had no need of Western manufactures and that Britain should prepare to "swear perpetual obedience" to the emperor of China.

China Confronts the West

Confucian China and the industrial West came into direct confrontation in the 1840s over the issue of the lucrative opium trade. Opium had been known in China for centuries and was used medicinally for diarrhea and dysentery. In the eighteenth century, imperial edicts banned opium because of its increased use as an addictive drug. Europeans, however, continued to import opium into China. During the 1830s, some 30,000 chests of the drug were shipped annually to China from the opium fields of British India. Finally, the emperor appointed an administrator, Lin Tse-hsu, to eliminate this opium smuggling.

This seemingly minor appointment triggered the first direct confrontation between China and the West. In 1839, Lin Tse-hsu arrived in Guangzhou (Canton), the only city open to Western traders. He ringed the foreign enclave on the Xi Jiang with troops, cut off all food supplies, and demanded that Western traders surrender their opium. Approximately $11 million worth of opium was confiscated and publicly burned. Although the Chinese were acting within their sovereign rights, their actions offended British pride and threatened British trading interests. In 1839, the British Parliament declared war on China.

During this First Opium War, the British inflicted one defeat after another on the imperial Qing armies who were completely overpowered

HONG KONG: ONE OF THE LAST TREATY PORTS

Until the eighteenth century, Asia was ruled by land-based empires whose great cities were located in the interior. Their primary functions were to administer territory, organize agricultural surpluses, and govern large agricultural populations. When the Europeans arrived, they constructed trade bases on the coast. These ports were beachheads of an alien culture that became focal points of confrontation between the land-oriented societies of the East and the sea-oriented intruders from the West. It was from these tiny centers of commercial development that ripples spread inland in the nineteenth century, setting in motion many of the changes that appear on contemporary landscapes. Many of these early port cities—places like Bombay, Calcutta, Singapore, and Shanghai—have become the modern urban nuclei of Asia.

In eighteenth-century China, foreign trade was restricted to the port of Guangzhou (Canton) and was under strict government control. European traders sold silver to the Chinese in return for silk and tea. When silver became more difficult to obtain, Europeans, notably the British, illegally smuggled opium from India into Guangzhou. The Qing attempted to halt this illegal traffic in the 1830s, which led to direct confrontation between Britain and China in the First Opium War of 1839–1842. In the aftermath of China's defeat, Hong Kong was ceded to Great Britain and a number of port cities, the

so-called **treaty ports,** were opened to Western influence. Still more coastal cities were opened to European trade after the Second Opium War of 1856–1858, some twenty-five commercial centers in all (Fig. 9.6).

As Qing power declined, the British, French, Portuguese, Americans, Germans, and Japanese all established colonial footholds on the Chinese coast and built colonial suburbs in these cities where their citizens held extraterritorial rights and were immune from Chinese law. The Chinese gradually ceded mineral rights, land for railroads into urban hinterlands, and tax concessions to foreigners. Outsiders gained almost complete control over China's commerce. Bitter Chinese resentment at this intrusion exploded in the Boxer Uprising of 1900, during which hundreds of Christian missionaries were slaughtered and

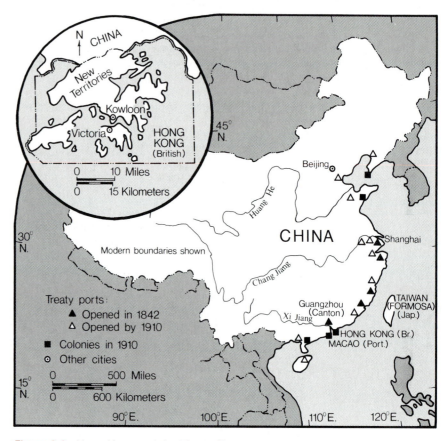

Figure 9.6 Hong Kong and the Treaty Ports.

by British gunboats and marine landings. The myth of Chinese invincibility abruptly vanished. In the Treaty of Nanjing of 1842, Chinese sovereignty was completely abrogated. The island of Hong Kong was ceded to Britain in perpetuity; five other ports were opened to Western trade (Fig. 9.6). Lin Tse-hsu, the administrator who had enforced the imperial ban on opium, was exiled.

Within a few years, China was open to the West. The opium trade flourished. Chinese control of its land and economy was eroding. High-quality, inexpensive textiles from factories in the industrial West were outselling the more expensive handloomed products of Chinese villagers. In the countryside, the growing number of Chinese farmers was reaching its environmental limit. Forced to leave

their fields, thousands of country folk became beggars in the growing ports of Guangzhou and Shanghai.

In these deteriorating circumstances, bandits and rebels sprang up across the face of China. This culminated in the bloodiest civil war in history, the Taiping Rebellion (1848–1865). Twenty million people, twice the number slaughtered in World War I, were killed as Taiping

Beijing (Peking) was held under siege for fifty-five days. Europeans, however, never established firm control over the Chinese interior. Until the end, Chinese treaty ports remained "isolated Western islands in an alien and resistant Chinese sea," as the geographer Rhoads Murphey has noted. Only Hong Kong and nearby Macao (Portuguese) still remain under European control.

Today, Hong Kong, one of the last of the treaty ports, is a bustling center of capitalist trade and commerce on China's doorstep. Situated on one of the finest natural harbors in Asia, Hong Kong is located east of the mouth of the Xi Jiang, 80 miles southeast of Guangzhou. The Crown Colony includes Hong Kong Island, the neighboring Kowloon Peninsula, and adjacent areas of the mainland called the New Territories (Fig. 9.6). The New Territories, leased from China for 99 years in 1898, compose 89 percent of the colony's territory. Hong Kong currently has a population of 5.7 million people and one of the highest standards of living in Asia.

Since the end of the Cultural Revolution in 1976, trade has boomed with the People's Republic. Some 35 to 40 percent of China's foreign exchange ($7 billion in 1984) is earned through the trading and banking facilities of the colony. Hong Kong's role in global business has expanded many times over.

Yet Hong Kong's future, despite its economic prosperity and importance to China, is now cast in doubt. A key date is 1997, when the 99-year lease on the New Territories expires. The New Territories, covered with large industrial parks and new towns, form the bulk of the colony. Hong Kong would hardly be viable without them.

In the early 1980s, the Chinese indicated that they wanted to recover the entire colony. British Prime Minister Thatcher's visit to Beijing did not lead to agreement. Hong Kong was plunged into uncertainty, and Asia's premier banking center suffered commensurately. Two years later, however, negotiations led to an Anglo-Sino agreement that Hong Kong—the entire colony—would become part of China in 1997. The Chinese insistence on recouping the leased territories forced the British hand.

The agreement allows Hong Kong to continue as a capitalist enclave within Chinese territory. China has agreed to permit capitalism to persist until 2047 in the "Special Economic Zone" that Hong Kong will become. Whether China's rulers will in fact permit Hong Kong to continue its pursuit of free enterprise remains open to doubt, as does the status of its two million residents who are British subjects.

More recently, Beijing has also signed an agreement with the Portuguese government for the return of Macao by the turn of the century. Macao, just 40 miles west of Hong Kong, has been held by the Portuguese since 1557. The end of the last vestiges of the treaty ports is nigh.

This is a view of the Hong Kong skyline at night. Hong Kong is one of the busiest and most prosperous trade centers in Asia. In 1997, it will become part of mainland China when Britain's 99-year lease expires.

Adapted from: Rhoads Murphey, "Colonialism in Asia and the Role of Port Cities," *East Lakes Geographer,* Vol. 5 (December 1969), pp. 24–49.

and Qing forces crisscrossed the Chang Jiang Plain. Finally, Western troops joined the Qing in destroying the Taiping rebels.

For the next fifty years, external intervention and internal disorder intensified in China. In 1856, the Second Opium War broke out. The Chinese lost. They were forced to sign the Treaty of Tianjin (Tientsin), opening eleven ports and the interior of China to Western merchants and missionaries. In the sparsely populated northwest, Muslim rebellions flared. On the North China Plain, drought and famine killed 13 million people in 1877. In the Northeast (Manchuria), China was humiliatingly defeated by a reenergized Japan in 1894. The Treaty of Shimonoseki forced China to recognize Korea's independence and cede the Liaodong Peninsula, the Penghu (Pescadores) Islands, and Taiwan to imperial Japan.

Stung by these defeats, antagonized by missionary activities, and resentful of new European **concessions** for railroads and mineral rights, anti-Western and anti-Qing sentiment grew. Finally, in 1911, an unplanned uprising overthrew the Qing. Its leader, Sun Yat-sen, curiously

China's defeat by Britain in the opium wars in the middle of the nineteenth century undermined Qing rule, destroyed the myth of Chinese invincibility, and opened China to Western intrusion. Here, a clash between British and Chinese forces in 1856 is dramatized in the *Illustrated London News*.

enough raising money in the United States at the time, proclaimed the birth of the Republic of China. The stage was set for a new China: the question was whether the commercial, Western-oriented vision of Chiang Kai-shek or the peasant-based revolution of Mao Zedong would prevail.

The Struggle for a New China

China never became a colony of Western powers as did India and most of Africa. European territorial control was confined to the port cities. Widespread disorder in the countryside and Chinese hostility to foreigners prevented Western traders and merchants from penetrating Chinese society. Few railroads were built to the interior. As a result, the industrial West was unable to control agricultural production or to restructure the economy of China.

The Rise of the Nationalists

Nevertheless, in the Northeast and in the port cities of China, Western industry and commerce created a new class of merchants, bankers, and industrialists. These people facilitated the flow of raw materials, like tobacco, tea, and fiber crops, from the interior to the ports. They constructed and ran processing plants in cities like Guangzhou, Shanghai, and Tianjin. It was they who acted as intermediaries between China and the West. Two leaders derived their support from this emerging middle class: Sun Yat-sen, the well-educated, Western-trained son of a Cantonese farmer, and his disciple and follower, Chiang Kai-shek, son of a middle-class merchant.

But the leaders of the Republic of China and the class they represented did not control the interior of China. Local rulers prevailed in the provinces as warlords or puppets. Poverty worsened with frequent breakdowns in public order and armed struggles among rival warlords. Finally, in 1926, Chiang Kai-shek, with financial aid from the Soviet Union, brought the Chang Jiang Valley and the northern capital of Beijing under Nationalist control. When Sun Yat-sen died in 1925, Chiang Kai-shek emerged as the most powerful figure in China. He purged the only viable competitors to his vision of a new China, the Communists, destroying thousands in pitched battles and leaving a tattered 10,000 survivors. It seemed that the question of dynastic succession had been resolved. A stable, unified China led by the middle class and oriented to Western capitalism would begin the process of modernization.

The Communists

In the villages of Hunan Province, however, one Communist leader—Mao Zedong—was inspecting Communist peasant associations and thereby escaped the anti-Communist purges. What he saw in Hunan convinced Mao that "in a very short time, in China's central, southern and northern provinces, several hundred million peasants will rise like a tornado . . . and rush forward along the road to liberation."

Mao was the only revolutionary—Communist or otherwise—who envisioned a new China built on the peasantry rather than on the urban working class. For the next decade, however, Chiang Kai-shek pursued the Communists deep into the recesses of rural China. Between 1934 and 1936, on the epic Long March, Communists under Mao crossed 18 mountain ranges and 24 rivers while fighting a running battle to escape Nationalist forces. By 1936, Mao and the Communists had retreated to the dry mountain interior of Shaanxi Province.

The contest for dominion over China between the Communists in the interior and Nationalists on the coast was obscured by the Japanese invasion of the Northeast in 1931. While Chiang concentrated on the destruction of the Communists (and in a sense retained his focus on the main issue), Japan invaded China Proper in 1937. Within a year, Japan conquered all of the lowland north. Nationalist armies lost 800,000 men, and Chiang Kai-shek retreated to Chongqing (Chungking) in the mountain fastness of Sichuan. The early accomplishments of the Nationalists—2000 miles of rail lines, 50,000 miles of road, and the growing industries of the port cities—fell into Japanese hands.

When the Japanese withdrew from China at the end of World War II in 1945, the Communists and the Nationalists renewed the conflict that would determine the future of modern China. Conditions were bad. Death and starvation in the countryside seeped into the cities. In Shanghai alone, 20,000 bodies were cleared from the streets each year. On the plains of eastern China, vast areas had been damaged by warring armies. Some 5 million armed men had been preying on Chinese villagers for two decades. The peasantry, driven to desperation during the Taiping Rebellion a century earlier, was again ripe for revolt. It was this force the Chinese Communists hoped to harness.

The Communists were outnumbered five to one in both manpower and materials. The Nationalists had heavy equipment and transport and an unopposed air force. But in the countryside, the Communists attracted popular support by opposing and destroying landowners and redistributing the land to peasants. This, and their appeal to national pride, caused Communist party rolls to swell to 1.2 million members by 1945. On this basis, they opposed the U.S.-equipped 3-million-strong army of the Nationalists.

In 1946, the illusion of Nationalist military superiority evaporated when entire Nationalist regiments surrendered to the Communists. In 1948, Nationalist forces in the Northeast were surrounded and forced to submit. In a battle of annihilation that raged for two months, central China changed hands on January 1, 1949. A half-million Nationalist troops were killed or captured. By the end of the year, Chiang Kai-shek fled from mainland China to Taiwan. His military forces were destroyed, his opportunity to lead the largest nation in the world gone. China had opted for the peasant from Hunan—Mao Zedong.

THE HUMAN GEOGRAPHY OF CHINA

The human geography of China is marked by an intimate relationship

Limestone towers and domes form a backdrop for irrigated rice fields ringing a farm village near Guilin in the Xi River Basin in South China.

between man and nature. In the words of the geographer Yi-Fu Tuan, no other landscape has been more "pervasively humanized" than China's. In history, the fortunes of China's leaders have been directly influenced by their effectiveness in managing the nation's environmental base. Economically, land was the source of all wealth and small plots were handed down from generation to generation: "Man dies; the land remains." An almost mystical bond has tied Chinese peasants to the land, providing an order and pattern to life.

In brief, China divides into an Outer China in the west and an Agricultural China in the east. In turn, Outer China consists of Tibet, Xijiang, and Inner Mongolia. Agricultural China can be broken down into the North China Plain, centered on the Huang He lowlands; Central China, which is defined by the course of the Chang Jiang; and South China, focused on the Xi Jiang lowlands. The Northeast, what has been traditionally known as Manchuria, rounds out the map of Agricultural China.

This section deals with the contemporary human geography of China. A land of diverse *Environments and Landscapes*, China's topographic and climatic contrasts play critical roles in the geography of its people and economy. The environmental difference between the arid western highlands and the more humid eastern lowlands of China is the most salient geographic feature of the country. *Outer China* is a vast, remote, thinly populated region as barren as any on earth. Its three major cultural and topographic regions include half of all Chinese territory but only a small fraction of the population. In contrast, the eastern lowlands of *Agricultural China* form the heartland of the country's society and economy. From the subtropical coasts of the south to the more recently settled valleys of the Northeast, this is where most of the Chinese population lives. It is here that the drama of *Man and Nature in China* has been

written in the landscapes and lives of its people.

Environments and Landscapes

China is a vast country slightly larger in area than the United States. Its boundaries enclose some 3.7 million square miles of territory (Fig. 9.7). Outer China includes over one half the land area of the country but is sparsely inhabited (Fig. 9.8). Agricultural China is one of the most densely settled environments in the world. In China, the alternation between mountains and plains dominates the landscape. Climate also varies in the extreme. Human occupance of the landscapes of China is strongly influenced by the physical environment.

The western frontier of Outer China embraces the mountain core of the Asian continent. The center of this mountain domain is the three-mile high plateau of Tibet, surrounded by the Himalaya, Karakorum, and Kunlun mountains. To the north of Tibet lie the two mountain-ringed basins of Xinjiang Province—the Tarim and the Jungarr (Dzungarian). To the east, the Gobi Desert occupies 500,000 square miles in Chinese Inner Mongolia and the independent country of Mongolia. Cold, windswept plains in Inner Mongolia provide the only easy access to Agricultural China from the north. It was along this Mongolian frontier that the Chinese built the Great Wall, forming a perimeter of stone stretching from 600 miles northeast to 900 miles west of Beijing. Not a single wall, but an amalgam of walls built beginning in the 200s B.C., the Great Wall proved, over time, to have little military utility in keeping barbarians from Central Asia out of China.

The climates of Outer China are severely **continental**. Winter air masses from Siberia sweep the entire region with cold, dry winds. Moisture-bearing air from the Pacific penetrates deep into China in the sum-

mer, providing limited rainfall. In all, Outer China is an inhospitable land. Unknown to all but the most determined explorers until modern times, Outer China is a vast, isolated wilderness equal in size to India.

Stretching eastward from Tibet, a series of mountain ranges reach like rigid fingers into the lowlands of eastern, or Agricultural, China. These form and bound the three major river systems of China—the Huang He, the Chang Jiang, and the Xi Jiang—that flow from the interior highlands eastward to the sea (Fig. 9.7). Only in the Northeast, home of the Qing dynasty, do mountains separate small basins from interior continental influences.

Climate correlates with latitude in Agricultural China. As in Eastern North America, rainfall and temperature tend to increase from north to south. But Chinese latitudes have average annual temperatures some 20 degrees cooler than those on the U.S. East Coast. Ice regularly forms in Po Hai Bay east of Beijing, at the same latitude as Washington, D.C. At the same latitude and position on the coast, winter temperatures in Charleston, South Carolina, are usually 20 degrees warmer than in Shanghai. Only southernmost China is free of frost year round. Thus, although Agricultural China is structurally similar in climate to the Eastern United States, the more severe temperature regimes of eastern Asia have important consequences for life and livelihood in the world's most populous country.

Agricultural China is the China that matters. Ninety-five percent of all the Chinese are crowded into the industrial core of the Northeast and the lowland agricultural regions associated with its three major river systems (Fig. 9.7). In the lowland river districts of the Huang He, the Chang Jiang, and Xi Jiang, population densities reach upward of 2500 people per square mile in rural areas (Fig. 9.9). As one writer put it, without birth control, the Chinese would have

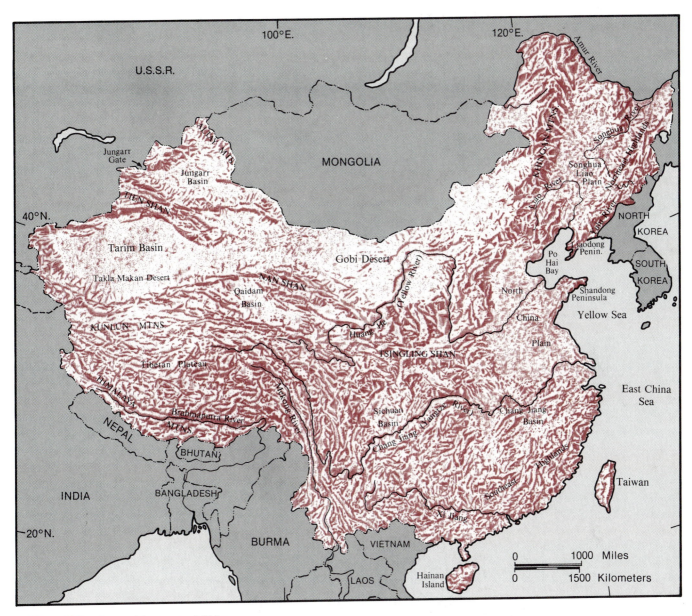

Figure 9.7 Physical features of China.

Figure 9.8 Environmental zones of China.

no place to stand in these lowlands.

Agricultural patterns in eastern China reflect broad north–south climatic patterns. In the north, it is too cool and dry to grow rice, so wheat, millet, sorghum, and soybeans are cultivated. Rice begins to be grown just south of a major environmental boundary that cuts across the North China Plain north of the Chang Jiang (Fig. 9.10). As the climate becomes warmer and more humid toward the south, rice fields come to dominate the landscape. The south's rugged, dissected hills contrast sharply with the flat plains of the north (Fig. 9.7).

These hills, once forested, have been molded into terraces through the efforts of Chinese peasants to bring every square foot of available land into rice cultivation. In the deep south, near Guangzhou, the climate is warm and humid enough to enable farmers to cultivate two rice crops on the same land in one year, a practice called **double cropping**.

Among the regions of China, then, the most basic geographic division is between sparsely settled Outer China and the densely occupied human landscapes of Agricultural China. The boundary separating these two re-

MAPSCAN
MAPPING WITH ISOLINES

Isolines are lines that connect points of equal value on a map. These lines are frequently used to construct maps of continuous distributions, such as population density, elevation (called **contour lines**), temperature (called **isotherms**), or rainfall (called isohyets). All points on an isoline have the same value. For example, 20 inches of rainfall or 1000 feet of elevation, are lines of equal value. Points between isolines can be determined through the use of a cartographic procedure called **interpolation,** which is described in every basic text on mapmaking.

On an isoline map, the distribution of the phenomenon under study is clearly shown when a series of isolines are shown together. To create an isoline map, cartographers decide how many isolines to draw and how close together to space them. In other words, they determine the class interval between isolines that is most appropriate. Further, a decision is made whether to use a **constant class interval,** where the values between all isolines are equal, or a **variable class interval,** where they are not equal. These decisions will determine overall isoline distribution. Along with the intensity of shading patterns between isolines, class intervals affect the visualization of the distribution by the map reader.

Figure 9.9 shows the distribution of population throughout China on a shaded isoline map. The isolines are not spaced numerically; the class in-

terval varies. The class intervals have been selected by the cartographer to emphasize the contrast between the dense population of lowland eastern China and the sparse population of the upland interior. On this map, the isolines connect points of equal population density and are more correctly called **isopleths** because they connect points of an abstract concept—population per square mile. It is un-

likely that any single area in China actually exists where 25 or 250 people per square mile reside. Comparing this map with the map of terrain, Figure 9.7, the student can easily visualize the close association in China between dense populations and lowlands, sparse populations and uplands. Understanding and reading shaded isoline maps is a vital skill for students of geography.

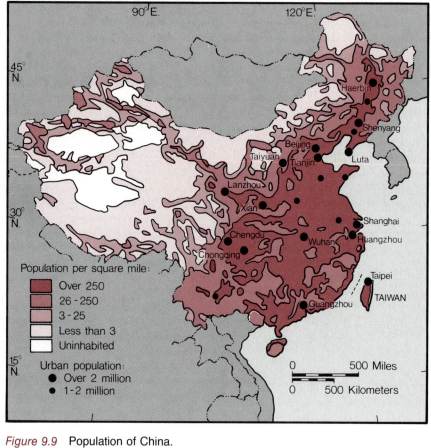

Figure 9.9 Population of China.

gions parallels the 20-inch rainfall **isohyet** and cuts from northeast to southwest from the Khingan Mountains to the city of Lhasa in Tibet (Fig. 9.8).

Outer China

Outer China is a land fractured by high plateaus, towering mountains, and forbidding deserts (Fig. 9.7). It is a land relatively empty of people. Taken together, the four major physiographic regions of Outer China— Xizang, Xinjiang, Inner Mongolia, and Mongolia itself—make up more than half the territory of China. But they produce only a tiny amount of China's food and contain less than 4 percent of China's total population. Vast areas, such as the northern half of the Xizang Plateau, the deserts of the

Tarim Basin, the eastern Jungarr Basin, and the windswept mountain deserts of Inner Mongolia, are virtually uninhabited.

In Outer China, people live in scattered mountain valleys sheltered from wind and cold, in nomadic encampments located near pastures, and in scattered oases where water is available. Extensive mineral discoveries suggest large-scale industrial potential. The relentless hostility of the people of Outer China to the Chinese and the difficulties of development in these extreme environments have thus far thwarted efforts at modernization. Mao Zedong believed that of the three great assets of China, the minority peoples of Outer China possessed territory and resources, whereas Agricultural China possessed people. After 40 years of Communist Chinese rule, Mao's statement still rings true.

Tibet

The plateau of Tibet lies at an elevation of roughly 10,000 to 15,000 feet. It is a cold, treeless area covering some 750,000 square miles. Surrounded by jagged, snow-covered peaks, this plateau is one of the most inaccessible regions on earth. Some have referred to it as the world's "third polar region."

Here, 2 million Tibetans lived in isolation until the Communist takeover of mainland China in 1949. Tibetans were traditionally subsistence barley farmers and herders of the yak, a large, long-haired domesticated ox. The Tibetans were organized into a theocracy, a religious state governed by Buddhist monks headed by the Dalai Lama. In 1950, Chinese troops invaded this region and attempted to replace this **feudal,** religious society with Communist political and agricultural cooperatives. This intrusion was deeply resented by the Tibetans, who revolted in 1958. Their revolt spread to the capital city of Lhasa (pop. 120,000) and Chinese troops moved into the region in force, subjugated and disarmed the Tibetans, and forced the Dalai Lama to flee his country.

The Chinese consolidated their control of Tibet, driving monks out of their fortress monasteries, destroying shrines, nationalizing agricultural land, and instituting programs of forced land reform. New roads and some 260 small mines and factories were constructed, particu-

For centuries, Tibet was governed by Buddhist monks headed by the Dalai Lama, who ruled the country from this palace-monastery in Lhasa. Chinese intrusion into Tibet is deeply resented by Tibetans.

larly in the mineral rich Qaidam (Tsaidam) Basin. Intense pressure was exerted on the Tibetans to assimilate themselves to Chinese culture. These efforts have failed.

After the death of Mao Zedong in 1976, the Chinese changed their policy toward the Tibetans, although 200,000 Chinese troops still occupy the region. In the 1980s, Beijing admitted that the basic needs of the Tibetan people—such items as saddles, milk bowls, churns, and barley—had been ignored in favor of Chinese-inspired crops and industries. The current Chinese policy, although less oppressive, has continued to subjugate Tibetan culture to a point where widespread anti-Chinese demonstrations and acts of resistance against Chinese occupation broke out in 1987–1988 and continue to thwart Chinese political and cultural advances.

Xinjiang

Xinjiang is a vast, sparsely settled expanse covering some 650,000 square miles (Fig. 9.1). It is occupied by about 12 million people. Located to the north of Tibet, Xinjiang is com-

posed of two enormous mountain-ringed basins: the Tarim Basin in the south and the Jungarr Basin to the north (Fig. 9.7). These basins are separated one from the other by the towering peaks of the Tien Shan Range. The center of the Tarim Basin is a rainless, dune-covered desert, the Takla Makan. In this environment, settlement is confined to oases on the **alluvial fans** that spread out from the base of the Tien Shan. Here, traditional Muslim farmers use canals and **qanats** (subterranean horizontal wells) to irrigate grain. Herding is virtually absent in the Tarim because the land is too barren for grazing. In the colder Jungarr Basin to the north, however, higher rainfall supports a lowgrass steppe on which upward of 1 million Muslim nomads herd their animals.

When the Communists assumed power in China in 1949, almost all of the people in Xinjiang were Turkish-speaking Muslims who were similar in life and culture to their neighbors across the border in the Soviet Union. The largest single tribal group, the Uighurs, number 5 million people and dominate the productive oases on the fringes of the Tarim Basin. Other important Muslim groups include the Kazakhs of northeastern Xinjiang and the nomadic Kirghiz who occupy the high mountain pastures of the southwest. In 1953, only 300,000 Chinese lived in Xinjiang.

For political and economic reasons, the Chinese government forcefully encouraged migration from China proper to the frontiers of Xinjiang. Culturally, they wanted to consolidate their control over the western provinces through the process of **acculturation** called **sinification**, or "becoming Chinese." Politically, they wanted to secure this border region. They hoped to create a buffer zone of Chinese people in Xinjiang and discourage potential nationalist movements among native peoples.

As a result of these policies, Chinese immigrants now comprise nearly half the population of Xinjiang. They live in the rapidly growing cities of the Jungarr Basin, where agricultural production has quadrupled since the Revolution, and near the large petroleum center of Karamai, the third largest oil field in China. New roads have been built along the historic caravan routes of Central Asia connecting the regional capital of Urumqi (Urumchi) (pop. 400,000) with Karamai and other urban centers near the Soviet border. A railroad and pipeline now link Urumqi with Lanzhou (Lanchou) 1100 miles to the east, midway between the western deserts and the great cities of the east. The effect of these policies has been to establish a strong Chinese presence on the country's western frontier—an intentional display of Chinese power to discourage Soviet ambitions in Xinjiang.

Inner Mongolia

Migration from the east has also increased in Inner Mongolia, the third region of Outer China, although Chinese have lived in this region far longer than in either Tibet or Xinjiang (Fig. 9.1). Physically, Inner Mongolia is a huge rolling plain arch-

ing from the Gobi Desert in the west along the Great Wall of China in the south and east (Fig. 9.7). Inner Mongolia experiences severe climate: searing heat in summer, bitter cold and punishing winds in winter. In the north and west, sand and gravel deserts and low-grass steppes prevail. These gradually give way to grass-covered rolling hills as rainfall increases eastward. In this transition zone, rivalry between nomadic Mongol horsemen and Chinese cultivators has gone on for centuries.

Today, more than 90 percent of the estimated 18 million people of Inner Mongolia are Chinese. On the rolling plains beyond the Great Wall, many Chinese are descendants of peasant pioneers who carved agricultural land out of the grasslands. In the great loop of the Huang He, large numbers of Chinese cultivate land irrigated by new dams and canals. New industrial centers, the largest of which is the iron-rich steel town of Baotou (Pao-tou) (pop. 950,000), have been built and the road and railroad network extended. The 1 million or so Mongols in this region have been pushed westward to the windswept, dry borders of the Soviet satellite state of Mongolia. The Chinese tried to

force these nomads to settle as farmers farther to the south. But many Mongols still live in the traditional yurt, or felt tent, herding goats and sheep. The Chinese recently announced that steel frames are replacing the 180 wooden branches used to construct each yurt. In many ways this modest technological change symbolizes the Chinese determination to absorb minority peoples within the framework of the Chinese state.

Mongolia

Mongolia is populated by Mongolian Turkic-speaking peoples and is given definition by the Gobi Desert in the south and central parts of this 900,000-square-mile region. The high Altai Mountains frame the southwest of Mongolia and separate it from Xinjiang. In the north, forest lands in Siberia mark the limits of Mongolia; to the east, the Gobi Desert grades into steppe and more corrugated topography before the great North China Plain is reached. It is from Mongolia that skilled horsemen have swept into China to establish short-lived empires, impart something of their culture, and then retreat back

Many Mongols still live as nomadic herders on the dry, windswept plains of Inner Mongolia. Here, a Mongol horseman ropes a horse with an *urga*, a long pole with a leather loop. Two yurts are located in the background.

to the Mongolian heartland. Mongolians are pastoral nomads who follow their flocks of goats and sheep in summer, covering great distances, and live in yurt communities during the rest of the year. They are skilled in riding, wrestling, shooting, and archery, and their strength and fierceness are legendary. Perhaps the greatest Mongol was Jenghiz Khan, who united the Mongol tribes and then sent out armies to capture much of Asia within an arc spanning from Korea to Persia to the Ukraine in the 1200s.

China subjugated the Mongols in the 1700s. In the chaos following the end of the Qing Dynasty in 1911, Mongolia broke away, only to become a communist state allied with the Soviet Union in 1921. The landlocked Mongolian People's Republic spans environments from the cool, forested, and lake-strewn lands of the north to the harsh confines of the Gobi Desert in the south. With a population of just under 2 million in its 604,000 square miles, it is one of the least densely populated countries in the world. It is also perhaps the world's only country past or present of communalized nomads. One out of every four Mongolians lives in the capital, Ulaanbaatar ("Red Hero" in Mongolian). The country is still largely pastoralist, with nomads organized into state cooperatives much as in other communist countries. The Mongolian People's Republic abounds in timber and mineral resources in the northern third of its territory. Most industry today is centered on conversion of the pastoral resources of the country—hides, wool, dairy products, and meat. A railway built in the 1950s to connect the Soviet Union and China slices through 1000 miles of Mongolia, connecting the country to the outside world.

Agricultural China

Agricultural China includes less than half of China's territory but is occupied by 95 percent of the total population (Fig. 9.9). Three quarters of these people, an estimated 750 to 800 million, are clustered in three lowland areas. These are the North China Plain of the Huang He; the Lower, Middle, and Sichuan basins of the Chang Jiang in Central China; and the Xi Jiang Delta of South China (Fig. 9.7). An additional 100 million people live and work in the industrial Northeast.

In the best agricultural areas, average rural population densities reach 2500 people per square mile. Elsewhere in Asia, this intensity of human occupance occurs only along parts of the Indus and Ganges rivers of South Asia, the Mekong and Red rivers of Southeast Asia, and on the island of Java. Because Agricultural China produces virtually all of the food for this country of over 1 billion people, because farmers comprise 80 percent of the total Chinese work force, and because China's largest cities and most important industrial centers are located here, this is the China of human consequence (Fig. 9.9).

North China Plain

The North China Plain includes the provinces of Hebei (Hopeh), Henan (Honan), and Shandong (Fig. 9.1). It covers only 5 percent of the Chinese earth, but it has a population of 210 million people, a fifth of the people in China. It includes 35 percent of China's cultivated land. This region, the flat delta plain of the Huang He, is covered with a dense carpet of cultivated fields (Fig. 9.7). The fertile wind-blown loess soils of the plain are planted in winter wheat, barley, millet, and kaoliang (sorghum). The area is too cold for rice. Rainfall is unreliable, averaging only 17 to 21 inches a year. This makes agriculture hazardous, particularly on the western perimeter where Mongolian winds scour the soil.

Erosion has deposited vast quantities of **silt** in the bed of the Huang He, so that flooding is a constant threat to farmers. Over the years, the Chinese have widened the bed of the river to accommodate summer floods and reduce the risk of flooding. This has increased deposition of silt and raised the river bed so that it flows through channels as high as 20 feet above the surrounding landscape. Any breach in these **levees** containing the river spells human disaster. The government has recently constructed a series of steplike dams to try to reduce siltation, alleviate flooding, and control the course of the Huang He.

Despite these **natural hazards**, the North China Plain remains a crucially important agricultural area in China. Its wealth supports Beijing, the national capital, which has a municipal area of 6900 square miles and a population of 9 million people. Together with its port city of Tianjin (Tientsin) with 7 million people, Beijing is one of China's three largest industrial regions based on the rich iron ores of Shandong and the coal deposits of Hebei provinces directly to the south.

Central China

Central China is the land dominated by the Chang Jiang. The river's course divides the landscape into three distinct regions: the Lower, Middle, and Upper basins of the Chang Jiang.

The Lower and Middle basins of the Chang Jiang include the five provinces of Hubei (Hupeh), Hunan, Jiangxi (Kiangsu), Anhui (Anwei), and Jiangsu (Kiangsu) (Figs. 9.1 and 9.7). These provinces encompass only a tenth of China's territory, but 237 million Chinese, a quarter of the country's population, live here. This is the granary of China.

The Lower Chang Jiang Basin is a vast, gently sloping lowland that stretches from the Chang Jiang delta 700 miles northward to connect with the lowlands of the Huang He. The entire region of lowland East China is connected by the Grand Canal, which runs from Beijing in the north to Hangzhou (pop. 1.5 million) south of Shanghai, 1000 miles in all. Built in stages over several hundred years, the Grand Canal has connected the

The Chang Jiang River is a major artery of commerce in Central China. This country boatman is navigating strong rapids where the river flows through a series of gorges between Sichuan and Hubei provinces.

major cities of the North China Plain since A.D. 610. The main route of trade through eastern China, the Grand Canal was safe from pirates in the East China Sea and assured the flow of foodstuffs northward to food-poor Beijing. As the age of the steamship brought commerce to China's east coast in the 1800s, the Grand Canal declined proportionately in importance.

Inland, the Lower Chang Jiang Basin extends 400 miles along the river. The density of population here is as high as anywhere in China. A carpet of rice fields covers the Lower Chang Jiang Basin, over 50 percent of which is cultivated. Agricultural production is immense.

It is north of the Lower Chang Jiang Basin that the important transition between the northern wheat and southern rice belts of eastern China occurs (Fig. 9.10). This is a significant cultural as well as agricultural boundary; one third of China's cultivated area lies north of the line, two thirds to the south. In the south, irrigated rice fields spread out over the lowland landscape, with tea and fruit crops more important in the hills. Southern China also contains two thirds of the country's principal food animal—the pig. Taken as a whole,

the rice-tea agriculture of Central and South China produces 60 percent of the country's food supply on less than half the cultivated area of all China.

Near the Chang Jiang's mouth, the

huge port city of Shanghai has a population of 12 million. Shanghai is probably the largest city on the Asian mainland, rivaled only by Calcutta in India. Shanghai grew rapidly in the 1800s as a treaty port where foreigners with special rights and privileges traded over the wealth of the interior. Today, Shanghai handles fully half of China's external trade and is an expanding center of diversified industry (Fig. 9.6).

The Chang Jiang, unlike the Huang He, can be navigated far inland, rendering the Chang Jiang one of China's major transport arteries. Both Wuhan (700 miles from the East China Sea) and Yichang (Ichang), at the geographic center of the country, can be reached by ocean-going vessels. Smaller vessels can reach still further to the city of Chongqing, 1000 linear miles from the coast.

The Middle Basin of the Chang Jiang begins at Anqing (pop. 250,000) 400 miles upriver. The Middle Basin,

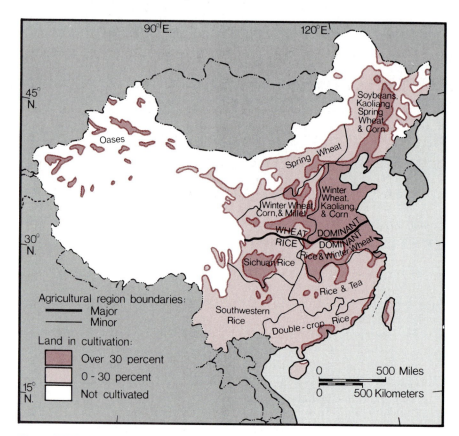

Figure 9.10 Agricultural patterns in China.

SHANGHAI: CHINA'S METROPOLIS

Shanghai is China's largest city, biggest industrial center, and most important port. It is to China what New York is to the United States. Shanghai's population of 12 million makes it the largest city in Asia after Tokyo. Its rise to prominence dates back only a century when it was opened to foreign trade as a treaty port in 1842.

An insignificant town earlier, Shanghai rapidly became China's principal center of foreign trade largely due to its location on an estuary of the Chang Jiang, China's most important waterway. Prior to the Communist victory in 1949, almost half of China's trade passed through Shanghai. Silk, tea, tung oil (used in paints and varnishes), and ores were the primary exports. Food, manufactured goods, oil, steel, and chemicals were important imports.

Shanghai was a city dominated by foreign interests—thus it began to look foreign. Still today, Shanghai has a distinctly European flavor in its buildings and avenues. Paralleling this commercial preeminence, Shanghai was the birthplace of the Communist party in China in 1921. More recently, Shanghai was a turbulent locale of Red Guard activity during the Cultural Revolution (1966–1976). Politically and economically, Shanghai was and is China's most important city.

Today, Shanghai shares many characteristics with other burgeoning Third World metropolises. With 12 million people and an incorporated area of 2250 square miles, Shanghai is China's most crowded space—a place where visitors appreciate that they are in a country of 1 billion people. Shanghai has a population density that is seven times higher than that of New York, five times that of London, and three times that of Tokyo. Average living space is about 45 square feet, or one 9-by-5-foot room per family. Approximately 1 million families in Shanghai have living quarters of 11 square feet or less. Recreational space in the city is about the size of one newspaper page per person.

Shanghai records more traffic accidents than any city in China. Its public transport system handles 12 to 13 million commuters on a busy day. The city has China's highest incidence of cancer, perhaps because of severe industrial pollution. Unemployed young people have contributed to a growing crime problem.

Shanghai accounts for one eighth of China's industrial output, one sixth of all revenue turned over to the government, and one quarter of the country's exports. The city supplies almost half of China's manufactured products; per capita income and productivity are well above the national average. Now a major center of heavy industry as well as a producer of refined copper, lead and zinc, it is also China's dominant center of culture. It has many universities, research institutes, publishing houses, museums, and theaters.

A distributary of the Chang Jiang weaves through the urban core of Shanghai, China's largest city, most important port, and most productive center of industry.

which connects a series of large lakes, has often been called the "rice bowl" of China. The urban focus of the Middle Basin is the tri-city hub of Wuhan (pop. 3.5 million), site of one of China's largest steel complexes. At Yichang (pop. 200,000), 1000 miles inland, the river enters a series of spectacular steep-walled gorges rendering navigation impossible at times.

The Sichuan (Szechwan) Basin is the Upper Basin of the Chang Jiang (Fig. 9.10). Deep in the interior, elevated and remote, Sichuan Province has a population of 100 million, two thirds of whom live in the Sichuan Basin itself. Except round the western city of Chengdu (pop. 2.5 million), the landscape is actually hilly—it is a basin only in respect to the much higher topography directly to the west (Fig. 9.7).

The protected location of Sichuan gives it a milder climate than Shanghai's; because of rugged terrain, however, only a fifth of the land is cultivated. This complex topography has generated a diversity of local microclimates. Cropping patterns are sophisticated and strongly related to local climate and relief. Terraced slopes are planted to rice in summer and wheat in winter. Tea and mulberry groves are planted on steeper slopes; corn and potatoes are planted at higher elevations.

Chongqing, largest city in the Upper Basin, has a population of 6 million. Political capital of China during World War II, Chongqing continues to grow in industrial importance, based on extensive local coal, iron, petroleum, and natural gas resources.

South China

The third lowland agricultural core of eastern China is the Xi Jiang Delta of South China. Separated from the basins of the Chang Jiang by the rugged hills of Central China, this small plain—only 3100 square miles in area—has a population of 15 million people. Pressure on irrigated land is intense. Entire hills have been transformed into terraces; canals and distributaries have been diked to divert water to level land. Rice is the dominant crop, but because of its subtropical climate, sugarcane, silk, and fruit are also cultivated here.

At the river's mouth on the South China Sea lie the British colony of Hong Kong and the Portuguese enclave of Macao. The population of the plain and its great port city of Guangzhou is Chinese. The city itself has a population of 5 million. But in the rugged interior, some 15 million non-Chinese people still speak a variety of Tai languages and still resist acculturation. The largest of these groups are the rice-growing Chuang, who with 8 million people form the most sizable minority group in China. Other groups, such as the Mia-Yao (3 million) and the Tai, are subsistence cultivators who practice slash and burn agriculture in the remote interior. Discouraged from this way of life by the Communist government, these people are enduring the same pressures of sinification as the minorities of Outer China.

The Northeast

The Chinese Northeast, known traditionally as Manchuria, the fourth and final region of Agricultural China, is composed of the three provinces of Heilongjiang (Heilungkiang), Jilin (Kirin), and Liaoning (Fig. 9.1). With about 9 percent of China's land area, the Northeast has a population of roughly 100 million people concentrated in the southern lowland of the Liao River in Liaoning Province which abuts directly on the North China Plain (Fig. 9.7). The Northeast was the original home of the Qing, a nomadic people who conquered China in 1644 and ruled the country until 1911. For centuries, Chinese infiltrated northward into this region whenever disaster struck the North China Plain, but the Qing maintained their racial and political independence. In the early twentieth century, however, revolution, civil war, famine, and floods ravaged the basin of the Huang He. A tidal wave of Chinese immigrants swept into the Northeast. The Qing were absorbed and dispersed. Only a million or so remain in the upper Songhua Basin in Heilongjiang. The Northeast now is fully Chinese in blood, culture, and economy.

Flanked on the north and east by the Soviet Union and North Korea, conquered by Japan in World War II, the Northeast is China's most important and sensitive border region. Soviet and Chinese armies are poised near each other's territory along the Amur and Ussuri rivers bordering the Northeast.

Climatically, the region has a short growing season and severe winters due to its northern location. Droughts are an additional **natural hazard.** Over one third of the southern province of Liaoning is cultivated, and irrigation and drainage networks are being extended to every potentially arable part of the region. The primary crops in the Northeast are spring wheat, barley, corn, kaoliang, and soybeans, which grow well on the fertile soils of the Liao Basin. North of Liaoning Province, the watersheds of the Northeast flow north into the Songhua River and enter the Amur River at the Soviet border. In the west, the Khingan Mountains of Heilongjiang

This billboard in Guangzhou reflects China's new open-door policy toward the West. Modern science, technology, and consumer goods are flowing into the country's large cities.

produce one fifth of China's timber, a precious commodity in a country that has been largely deforested (Fig. 9.11).

Of far greater importance are the Northeast's extensive deposits of coal, iron, and an abundance of other natural resources in the central Liao Basin and in the far north (Fig. 9.13). These make the Northeast China's most important industrial region. The major industrial centers of the Northeast are Shenyang (Mukden), Fushuan (Fushun), Benqi (Penchi), and Anshan. Each of these centers has coal and iron ores within local transport range to support heavy industry. Shenyang with a population of 6 million is the primary steel-producing city. It draws its coal from Fushuan (pop. 1.7 million) and its iron ore from Anshan (pop. 1.5 million), both of which are located nearby. In addition, important deposits of manganese, molybdenum, magnesite, lead, and limestone lie within reach by rail. On this basis, Shenyang has become the major diversified manufacturing and agricultural-processing city in the Northeast. It is one of the key centers in China's drive toward industrial self-sufficiency.

In the early 1980s, Chinese leaders devoted special attention to the implementation of programs of industrial growth and technological efficiency. In this region, the industrial landscape marched northward. From the port city of Luta (Darien) (pop. 4 million) at the tip of the Liaodong Peninsula to the important railroad junction and steel town of Haerbin (Harbin) (pop. 3.5 million) in the Songhua Valley, an industrial-agricultural complex similar to that stretching from Chicago to Pittsburgh is emerging. Skilled workers are attracted to the Northeast by specialized jobs, higher wages, and better facilities. It is here that the aspirations of the new leaders of China to open their nation to modernization are being played out. Success or failure in this endeavor will determine China's economic future.

Man and Nature in China

The diversity of topography and climate in Agricultural China have posed many difficulties to human occupance. The flood-prone plains of North China, the rugged hills of the south, and the mountain basins of the interior, however, were infiltrated and ultimately dominated by Chinese agriculturalists (Fig. 9.10). Hillsides were terraced for dry farming in the north and for rice cultivation in the south—probably the most substantial feat of agricultural engineering in the world. Massive flood control and water conservation schemes involving hundreds of miles of **dikes** and canals were constructed. These were needed to organize an environment capable of supporting dense rural and urban populations in eastern China.

The problems of maintaining these environmental systems are compounded by natural hazards. Droughts and floods are frequent in the north, as are typhoons in the tropical south. The maintenance of this resource base has exacted a price. Soil destruction, devastation of forests, and erosion became widespread. In the end, however, Chinese civilization was achieved by 2000 years of backbreaking toil, by what the French philosopher Teilhard de Chardin called "an enormous mass of concentrated peasant."

Environmental Transformation

Chinese garden agriculture originated on the loess plateau inside the great loop of the Huang He and spread across the North China Plain, south-

These terraced hillsides and lowland rice fields in South China illustrate the humanization of the Chinese landscape by what philosopher Teilhard de Chardin called "an enormous mass of concentrated peasants."

ward across the Chang Jiang, and into the hill lands of southern China. The system required level land, fertile soils, and intense human effort. Century after century, the Chinese sculpted and molded their landscapes. They produced ever-increasing yields of grain to feed the densest human concentration of any preindustrial agricultural-based society.

The principal characteristics of this unique agricultural system relied on the channeling of water and nutrients onto a relatively small agricultural area. Only 11 percent of China is under cultivation. Irrigation is practiced to provide water to lowland rice fields and to cope with the wide variations in rainfall found in Agricultural China. Fertility is maintained by deposition of eroded soils from the upper reaches of major rivers onto the plains and by the application of human and animal manure to the cultivated land. Because virtually no land has been left uncultivated or fallow, few draft animals are used except where pasture exists in nearby hills. Virtually all work, then, is done by people with simple tools. The sheer intensity of human energy invested in the land has led to almost a complete humanization of the landscapes of eastern China. Over thousands of years, China's plains became a human mat of grain crops, soybeans, and vegetables, interspersed by small market towns (see Central Place Theory Geolab and Fig. 9.11).

The impact of the Chinese on hillsides in the hinterlands of Agricultural China is nearly as great as in the lowlands. Forests were destroyed over extensive areas. Even the grass and shrub vegetation that replaced the woodlands of the uplands is used for fuel or fodder. About half the Chinese domain was forested at one time. By 1980, only 13 percent of China was wooded, although China was number three in the world in felled timber production (roundwood). Recognizing the environmental problem at hand, large-scale programs of reforestation have been

HUMAN IMPACT ON VEGETATION IN CHINA

Centuries of human use have transformed the patterns of natural vegetation in China. Humanized landscapes, where natural vegetation is virtually absent, cover all of Agricultural China. Forests are found in the Northeast, in the hills of South China, in Sichuan, on Hainan Island, and in the Central Mountains of Taiwan. Elsewhere, they have been removed (Fig. 9.11). The grasslands and deserts of western or Outer China are produced by low rainfall; the tundra and the **alpine vegetation** of Tibet reflect altitude.

Adapted from: Joseph Whitney, "East Asia," in Gary A. Klee (ed.), *World Systems of Traditional Resource Management.* London: Edward Arnold, 1980, fig. 18, p. 104.

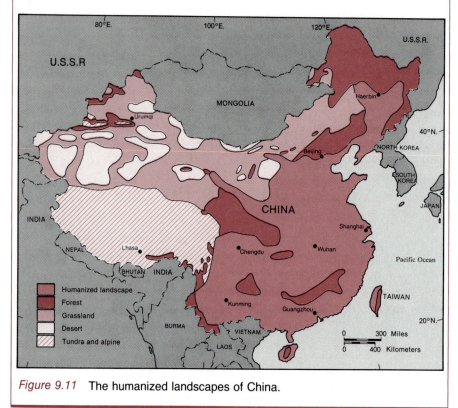

Figure 9.11 The humanized landscapes of China.

instituted by Communist leaders under the slogan "Make China Green." Remaining forests are located in the remote Khingan Mountains of the Northeast and in the deep recesses of rugged South China in the provinces of Sichuan, Yunnan, and southeastern Tibet (Fig. 9.11). A new program of reforestation is now underway whereby every able-bodied Chinese, eleven years of age and older, is asked to plant three to five trees each year. China's goal is to cover more than 20 percent of its nearly 3.7 million square

miles with trees.

Paradoxically, the denuding of the Chinese landscape that led to soil erosion, the raising of riverbeds to levees 20 or more feet above surrounding agricultural areas, and the subsequent danger of flooding has been vital to maintaining the ongoing productivity of China's major agricultural areas. The blanket of soil stripped from China's hills renews soil fertility on the plains each year. This has made it possible to support large numbers of people in the same locations for centuries.

By any reckoning, total agricultural production in China is prodigious. Well it should be in the country of one billion people. China is the world's number-one producer in an astonishing range of foodstuffs—from chicken and eggs to goats, hogs, melons, pears, cucumbers, pumpkins, onions, and millet. China is the world's biggest tobacco producer, harvesting about 10 percent more than the United States. China produces an amazing amount of sweet potatoes, in fact, most of the world's output. China has seven sheep for Australia's every ten, and produces twice as many peanuts as the United States. More to the point, China produces 36 percent of the world's rice—twice as much as any other country and 22 times that of the United States, although the United States is the world's largest exporter of rice. Chinese annual rice consumption is 264 pounds per person.

The ability of this agricultural system to maintain large urban centers through profound modifications of the natural environment is three to five times higher than less intensive farming systems. China's present program of restoring its forests, then, assumes that fertilization by factory-produced chemical fertilizers will replace natural fertilization by silt-laden river water. The purpose is to eliminate flooding along the densely populated lower reaches of the Huang He and Chang Jiang.

Natural Hazards

The two primary natural hazards in eastern China are drought and floods. Although these disasters have been intensified by human abuse of the land, the root causes of these catastrophes lie in the environment. Most Chinese live in climates in which conditions fluctuate drastically from year to year (Fig. 9.12). In four provinces on the North China Plain, records kept between 1600 and 1900 document some 317 floods and 168 droughts that plagued farmers living

in that region. Along the coast of South China, typhoons sweep in from the sea in late summer and deluge the countryside. In the subhumid north and northwest, drought is the principal hazard, the greatest killer.

For centuries, hundreds of millions of Chinese have lived in this zone of climatic uncertainty. In 1981, China was battered by both drought and flood. Conditions were so bad that the Chinese appealed to the United Nations for aid. In the provinces of Hebei near Beijing and in Hubei farther south, drought caused widespread malnutrition. The crisis was compounded by floods along the middle Chang Jiang.

Severe flooding along the Chang Jiang and the Huang He is a historic problem in China. Early Chinese paintings illustrate the bizarre scene of walled cities surrounded by flood waters with peasants fishing from the walls, their fields inundated and their crops destroyed. For centuries, the Chinese have attempted to manipulate and control these rivers, particularly the Huang He, aptly called "China's Sorrow."

The Huang He rises in the lake country of eastern Tibet and flows through the fine-grained, easily eroded loess lands around the Great Loop, picking up a large volume of silt. Rainfall here is concentrated in July and August—the more rain, the more silt, and the greater the risk of damaging floods. Stream flow in the Huang He is among the most unpredictable in the world for a river of this importance. Recorded volumes of water in high rainfall years are 250 times those in years of severe drought.

The Chinese responded to these hazards by building dikes and levees along the lower course of the river in an effort to contain its flow. But with its bed high above the surrounding landscape, the Huang He has often broken through the levees and flooded the North China Plain. Fifteen times in recorded history, the river has changed course and entered Po Hai Bay through different chan-

nels, sometimes hundreds of miles south of its current outlet north of the Shandong Peninsula. The causes of these shifts are not known, except for the last three, which occurred in 1855, 1937, and 1947.

In 1855, the Huang He swung north when its dikes broke because of poor maintenance in the preceding decades. The river channel became unstable. In succeeding years, some 2 million people drowned or died from starvation. In 1938, the banks of the Huang He were deliberately breached by the Nationalist Chinese in a vain effort to stop the advance of invading Japanese armies with floodwater. The river swung southward again until 1947, when it was redirected northward to its present position. The human cost of the 1938 military decision cannot be measured, but some 2 million acres of China's finest farmland was taken out of production.

The recurrence of natural disaster in China has had a profound impact on the Chinese conception of human relationships with the physical environment. In traditional Confucian thought, man and nature were integral parts of a cosmos dominated by nature. Contentment and harmony could only come through acceptance of the natural world to which people belonged. Despite the close and intensive occupation of the Chinese earth over the centuries and its transformation from a natural to a cultural landscape, the traditional Chinese attitude was one of respectful stewardship of the natural world. Although abuses abounded, the historic Chinese system of land management did not philosophically pit man against nature. Harmony was seen as the key to continuity.

The Communist Revolution has reversed the roles of man and nature. The confident, pioneering Communist human being was viewed as the **ecological dominant.** Nature was to be conquered; it was an enemy to be defeated to increase agricultural production and meet the needs of the Chinese people. Mountains were to

NATURAL HAZARDS AND ENVIRONMENTAL PRODUCTIVITY

This map presents information on the natural productivity of China's environments and the risk of drought or flooding in various parts of the country. On Figure 9.12, the heavy-shaded line—which coincides with the transition line between the northern (wheat) and southern (rice) agricultural patterns in eastern China—separates those areas on the North China Plain where plants experience **moisture stress,** which makes irrigation essential, from those areas farther south that have a moisture surplus. The lighter lines are a complex measure of environmental productivity expressed in tons of vegetation per acre per year. Note that environmental productivity decreases northward and toward the interior because of colder temperatures and less rainfall. By this measure, South China is seven to eight times more productive than the dry fringes of northern and western China. The close spacing of these lines on the North China Plain shows rapid changes in productivity over short distances, indirectly suggesting a substantial level of environmental variability.

Natural hazards are a frequent occurrence in China, and moisture stress is only one problem Chinese farmers must face. Circled values on Figure 9.12 indicate the probability (measured in number of years in 100) of crop failure through drought; boxes indicate the probability of flooding. In the eastern part of North China, drought occurs 20 percent of the time; farther west in the Huang He Basin and on the loess plateau, 60 percent of the time. Flooding also occurs in this area and in South China

where typhoons strike. Taken together, drought and flood make agriculture a risky venture in North China. The chances of a good farming year are less than 50 percent.

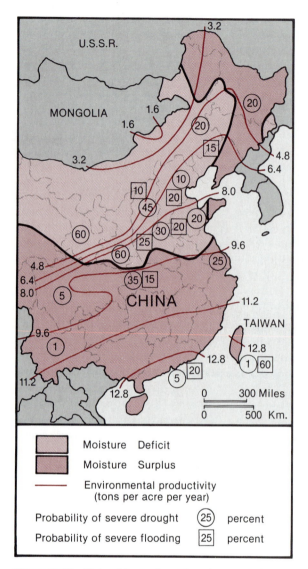

Figure 9.12 Natural hazards and environmental productivity in China.

Adapted from: Joseph Whitney, "East Asia," in Gary A. Klee, ed., *World Systems of Traditional Resource Management.* London: Edward Arnold, 1980, fig. 19, p. 105.

be leveled by mass labor; large-scale planning would wrest wealth from the Chinese earth. Today, Confucian and Communist thought coexist in uneasy juxtaposition in China—on environmental and many other issues.

THE NEW CHINA

The Communist triumph in 1949 did not mark an end to turmoil in China. Mao Zedong was determined to

transform the organization of Chinese society, to break completely with the past—no small task. Programs in agriculture, industry, and social organization were implemented to create a model Communist society.

The major goals of *The Communist Agenda for Change* involved the collective reorganization of agriculture, expansion of heavy industry, and elimination of traditional patterns of thought and behavior. When population growth and peasant resistance threatened this program of modernization, China's villages were organized into large communes, and China's leaders attempted to achieve instant economic development by redoubling their efforts in one "Great Leap Forward" into the future. By the 1960s, however, China's people were living at a standard only slightly higher than two decades earlier.

New *Pathways to Modernization* were sought. In the 1960s, Mao's determination to rekindle the revolutionary spirit of the Chinese people initiated the Cultural Revolution in 1966, which threw the country into chaos for a decade. Society was divided between radical revolutionaries and more moderate pragmatists. Since Mao's death in 1976, leaders in Beijing have been busy easing the ideological constraints of Communist doctrine in an attempt to graft market capitalism onto a centrally planned socialist economy under a program called the Four Modernizations. Successful control of population growth is vital to the achievement of their goals.

In contrast, the economic success of the Republic of China, *Taiwan*, is both a reproach and a model for China today.

The Communist Agenda for Change

In 1949, the Communists set forth on a program to transform Chinese society. They wanted to reestablish the integrity of the Chinese state. They had promised security to the peasants of China. Mao's followers brought to this task a new social philosophy based on the teachings of Marx and Lenin. Communist goals were three: (1) to restructure the relationship between the Chinese peo-

One of the goals of the Communist Party under the leadership of Mao Zedong was to eliminate class differences in Chinese society, to create a homogeneous society.

ple and the Chinese earth, (2) to build the industrial basis of a modern nation, and (3) to destroy the hold of the Confucian order on the Chinese mind. The intent was to create a new society based on Communist principles as interpreted by Chinese leaders, specifically Mao Zedong.

Agricultural Reorganization

The central problem, the paradox facing every aspiring nation of the Developing World, was that farmers, the largest segment of society, had to provide the money needed for investment in modern industrialization and technology. The price of progress in China fell where it had always fallen—on the backs of the peasants.

Chinese agriculture had to be reorganized if economic development was to be achieved. An absolute increase in the production of rice and other foodstuffs was needed. More land had to be brought into cultivation, more efficient techniques of cultivation employed, better protection afforded against floods and droughts, and new transportation networks created. In addition, a fairer distribution of the harvest among the

peasants of China was necessary—landlord control of rural production would have to be broken.

This goal of breaking the power of the landlords was accomplished during the initial period of land reform between 1949 and 1952. The Communists paid off a longstanding promise to the Chinese peasants by redistributing agricultural land. Landlords and rich peasants (anyone with 5 acres or more of land) who had collected taxes, lent money at high interest rates, or supported the Nationalists were destroyed. A million members of this class were killed by firing squads, lynch mobs, and in "reform through labor" camps. The Confucian gentry who had controlled the landscapes of rural China for 2000 years disappeared. Some 120 million acres of land were thus redistributed among 350 million peasants.

The elimination of landlords and rich peasants led to problems. Giving the "land to the tiller" was not enough to change conditions in rural China. Redistribution of land left some peasants with agricultural land, others with draft animals, still more with tools but no land to farm.

Partly to solve these problems and also to ensure political control over the countryside, the Communists started a program of collectivization throughout village China. By 1954, 10 million groups of six to fifteen village households were organized into mutual-aid teams. These groups pooled their land, animals, and tools; they shared the harvest while retaining individual ownership of the means of production. But the inconsistency of individual ownership and collective sharing soon became apparent.

Mutual-aid teams were merged into larger agricultural producer cooperatives in which individuals were paid on the basis of the amount of land and labor they contributed to the harvest. Finally, following the Soviet example of the sovkhoz, these cooperatives were reorganized into still larger collective farms, so that by 1957 some 740,000 of these units, averaging 168 households in size, accounted for 90 percent of China's rural population. All land was commonly owned, all boundaries removed, and all workers paid on the basis of work points and quota fulfillment.

Results of this social reorganization of Chinese agriculture were disappointing. Because of limited government investment in agriculture in the 1950s, the average annual increase in Chinese agricultural productivity was only 2.6 percent—barely enough to feed the annual 2 percent growth in the Chinese population. It was not enough to subsidize any large-scale industrial expansion. Chinese peasants were becoming increasingly restive. Given collectivized harvests, the peasants simply ate more. Rigorous checks on food consumption were instituted. At the same time, the government was devoting all available resources to the growth of heavy industry. As a result, economic exchanges between city and village became increasingly one-sided; harvests went to the city, little returned.

Further, the Communists believed that human misery sprang primarily from exploitation of the poor

by the wealthy. They tended to underestimate the importance of environmental conditions. So, many of the forestry projects and irrigation schemes designed to increase agricultural production were ill conceived. In the province of Hubei, for example, four out of five of the newly constructed water reservoirs and ponds dried up in the drought of 1959. Similarly, half the 500,000 new reservoirs in Jiangsu Province were useless. Deep wells sunk on the western margins of the North China Plain failed when climatic variations made the wells vulnerable to both drought and flood. By 1957, the face of Agricultural China had been transformed—spatially and socially—but this had not solved the centuries-old problem of food shortage. The Communist leaders of the People's Republic of China became keenly aware of what starvation in the countryside had meant to earlier dynasties.

The life of plenty, that Communist party cadres had been promising agricultural cooperatives for years, was steadily retreating into the future. The policy of draining agriculture to support industry was reaping a harvest of peasant restlessness and resistance. Rural food consumption continued to go up; productivity was declining. Agricultural surpluses were desperately needed by Communist planners to support industrial growth, to maintain the external trade funneled through Hong Kong, and to pay the debts incurred by importing technology in the early phases of industrialization. Through the 1970s, the planners mobilized these surpluses by buying grain from the villagers at a low price and then selling it in the cities and abroad at higher prices. China doubled its output of food grains during three decades of Communist rule, but by the 1980s, more than 100 million peasants were still living in a state of hunger.

A New Industrial Map

In the industrial sector, the results of Communist planning were much more encouraging. During the first

five-year plan in the 1950s, China's industrial output (not counting handicrafts) rose by 240 percent as compared with a 25 percent expansion of agricultural production. This expansion of industry was largely the result of direct imitation of the development plans used earlier in the Soviet Union. A full 40 percent of the national budget was invested in industrial products, such as coal, steel, electric power, and oil. The agricultural sector received only 3 percent. Overall, industrial growth in 1980 was still increasing at a rate of 8.5 percent. Aided by Soviet technicians and modest Soviet financial and technological investment until 1959, the Chinese Communists were intent on building a modern industrial nation.

As in the West during the initial period of industrialization, coal, which represented 93 percent of all energy sources in China, was important in the achievement of these aspirations. Within three years, the Communists reached the Japanese level of production (60 to 70 million tons) in the primary coal-producing region of the Northeast. By 1958, the government reported a total annual coal production of 270 million tons, third highest in the world, behind the United States and the Soviet Union. By 1980, coal accounted for only 70 percent of China's energy, reflecting the development of alternative sources, principally petroleum. In 1984, China became the number-one coal producer in the world, outproducing the United States to reach 759 million metric tons per year.

With high-quality coal reserves located at or near existing industrial sites, two thirds of China's coal production is concentrated in the north and northeast (Fig. 9.13). In this region, large strip mines are worked at Fushuan in Liaoning Province, coke mines are found in the Northeast near the Soviet border, and a broad arc of coal deposits sweep across to the North China Plain from the vicinity of Beijing southward to the banks of the Huang He. Other coal-producing areas, from centrally located Hebei

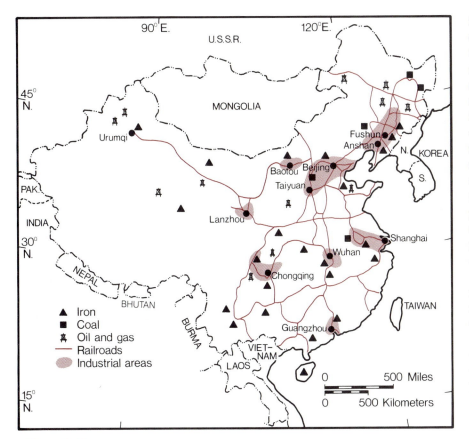

Figure 9.13 Economic patterns in China.

Province and the Sichuan Basin northward to the borders of Inner Mongolia, enabled the Chinese to diversify and decentralize their industrial base—a politically desirable goal.

Chinese leaders determined not only to intensify the growth of the coastal industrial complexes that produced three quarters of China's industrial output but also to introduce industry into the interior. The primary emphasis was on heavy industry, especially machine building. The great steelworks at Anshan and Benqi in the Northeast remained the leading producers of steel. But centers of heavy industry were also developed in Taiyuan (Tai-yuan) (pop. 3 million) based on the local Shaanxi coal deposits; in Chongqing to the south; in the tri-city hub of Wuhan; at Lanzhou to the northwest; and at Baotou north of the great bend of the Huang He in Inner Mongolia (Fig. 9.13). Shanghai retained its leadership in industrial production, largely due to cheap electricity produced by

inexpensive waterborne coal, but a new industrial map was emerging in China. Fully two thirds of the major industrial projects launched during the first five-year plan (1953–1957) were located away from the coast.

As the first five-year plan progressed, it became clear that China had the resource base needed to build a modern industrial state. Indeed from 1952 to 1978, China's industrial output reportedly increased at an average annual rate of 11.2 percent, an extraordinary figure by U.S. standards.

Iron ore, although not available in either the quantity or quality of coal, was discovered and mined in Sichuan, Xinjiang, Inner Mongolia, and on Hainan Island, supplementing production from the mining centers of the Northeast (Fig. 9.13). Ferrous and ferroalloy minerals exist in sufficient quantities to support a major iron and steel industry.

Important new discoveries of petroleum in Xinjiang, in Sichuan, and

in the Qaidam Basin led to the production of 3 million tons of oil from these western fields by 1980. More recently, a new field Daqing (T'ach'ing), in the Northeast, has become the major petroleum-producing region in China, accounting for 40 percent of China's total production in 1980 (Fig. 9.13). Although not developed, the Chang Jiang has enormous waterpower potential—more than the total developed capacity in the United States—which could supplement and ultimately replace nonrenewable sources of energy.

To integrate these new factories and mines into the state economy, the network of roads and railroads in China has been expanded. Between 1949 and 1958, 8000 miles of new track were added to the 16,200 miles the Communists inherited. An unknown number of roads were constructed, repaired, and resurfaced. Most of the new construction was in the less developed provinces of the west and the northwest.

The objectives of the new lines were both political and economic. Shanghai was connected to Guangzhou, the Chang Jiang was bridged, and new lines were extended to the Taiwan Strait and the borders of Vietnam. The Communists took no chances on a Nationalist counterrevolution. The Lunghai rail line was built from Beijing to the steel plants of Baotou in Inner Mongolia and the oil fields of Urumqi in Xinjiang. A similar, although less dramatic, rail track was built northward through Ulaanbaatar, the capital of Mongolia, to the Irkutsk Basin in Siberia, linking by rail the world's two largest Communist nations. As in agriculture and industry, the transportation network of Communist China was viewed through the prism of politics.

The Great Leap Forward

Despite the impressive industrial gains during the first decade of Communist rule, by 1957 a number of disturbing social and economic problems had appeared. In the cities, the growing estrangement of intellectuals had led Mao to encourage free discussion and criticism. A period known as "Let a Hundred Flowers Bloom" ensued. But when open discussion became highly critical of the Communist party, numerous intellectuals were silenced and a return to "right thinking" was implemented. At the same time, the minority peoples of Outer China, particularly in Xinjiang, began to demand autonomy. The peasants, as noted earlier, had resisted collectivization, and agricultural production was too low to sustain China's program of rapid industrialization.

When the level of China's food exports fell in 1957, it became clear that the gap between agricultural production and industrial aspirations would have to be resolved. Attempts were made to attract financial and technical aid from the Soviet Union, but the Soviets were increasingly concerned over the threat of a strong China, particularly one with nuclear potential. The Soviet Union would no longer assist China. Mao made a decision. China would not settle for a period of retrenchment. China would advance by the coordinated, disciplined labor of peasants and urbanites. In one "Great Leap Forward," China would overcome the central problem facing all developing nations: sheer labor would be converted into working capital. People would work twice as hard: they would "Walk on Two Legs"—one agricultural and one industrial.

The Great Leap Forward of 1958 demanded extraordinary feats of human labor from the Chinese people so that the industrial growth of China might continue unchecked. The Chinese were asked to produce both bread and steel. Millions of peasants labored by day tilling the fields and were forced to work in factories at night. The average working day was extended. Small steel furnaces and forges were built in the villages of China. Within a matter of months, approximately 600,000 of these backyard furnaces dotted the landscape. Production goals were revised upward almost monthly. Grain production, 185 million tons in 1957, was reported to have reached 375 million tons in 1958; steel production appeared to have more than doubled from 5.3 to 11 million tons. On paper, the Great Leap Forward was a success.

Simultaneously, one of the most revolutionary social changes of the century was implemented in China. The spatial basis of rural Chinese society and economy was completely reorganized. The 740,000 agricultural producer cooperatives were amalgamated into some 24,000 peoples' communes. The communes roughly approximated the ancient Chinese counties and averaged 20,000 people on about 10,000 acres of land. People were housed in communal dormitories and mess halls. Communal nurseries freed women for work in the fields, which continued around the clock. In some villages, the walls of private dwellings were done away with to create communal living quarters. Kitchen utensils, door hinges, and other bits of metal from these destroyed walls fed village furnaces to increase the steel production of China. Of particular importance, food consumption in the communal dining halls was carefully supervised. A single ounce of grain per person per day in China, if saved, could amount to 7 million tons a year. This was of vital importance because per capita production of grain, the staple of the Chinese diet, was declining in village China.

Beijing planners ordered great labor battalions to embark on large-scale irrigation and construction projects. Nothing like this scale of human effort had ever been seen before. Crops were planted closer together on the theory that more rows of grain in a given space would produce more grain. Deep plowing was fostered by using winches and cables to pull plows across rice fields. A campaign to kill sparrows and weaverbirds was launched because these birds ate newly sown seed. In the field, hundreds of Chinese men, women, and children would dance and yell to keep the birds in the air

The communalization of agriculture in China was intended to create a new social and moral order as well as to increase food production. Here, members of a commune in Wuhan weed a soybean field.

until they fell to the ground exhausted. In the final statistical reckoning, a sparrow kill of 1 billion birds was claimed—probably accurate, given the insect infestation that later overtook China.

On a larger scale, labor battalions affecting tens of thousands of workers constructed dams and irrigation projects; new deep wells brought marginal land under irrigation. A nationwide drive to plant trees under the slogan "Make China Green" led to nearly 100 million acres of new forest land, but the vast majority of capital investment—almost 65 percent—still went into heavy industry. The peasants were increasing agricultural production with their bare hands, their traditional tools, and with what had once been their time to drink tea and sleep.

The results of the Great Leap Forward in grain and steel production were less than expected. The inflated announcement of 375 million tons of food grains in 1958 was eventually revised downward to 250 million tons. Some experts believe the actual harvest was 190 million tons, only 5 million tons greater than the 1957 harvest. In steel, the figure of 11 million tons was adjusted to 8 million tons. It was finally admitted that the 3 million tons produced in backyard furnaces was so poor in quality as to be useless. Whatever the truth, at the end of the effort, the work force of China was exhausted. Illness and absenteeism were spreading.

Certain aspects of this incredible social experiment clearly failed. Deep plowing where topsoil was thin turned up layers of infertile soil. Faulty irrigation practices caused waterlogging and increased salinization in some soils. The digging of deep wells in dry regions lowered water tables. The massacre of the sparrows encouraged local insect population explosions. Above all, peasant resistance to the commune, which Mao had called "the most appropriate organizational form in China for accelerating the transition to Communism," was intense.

At this critical juncture, environmental disaster hit China. Between 1959 and 1962, the specter of famine shadowed the Chinese landscape. Fear of hunger was the primary preoccupation of planner and peasant alike. Drought settled over the North China Plain, and insect damage to crops was extremely high. In the tropical south, heavy floods and typhoons destroyed thousands of acres of cropland. In 1960, a rare drought also occurred in this normally humid region.

The impact of these calamities on grain production was devastating. In 1959, the total grain crop was substantially below the previous year's harvest. The figures for 1960 were so low that no official announcements were made. Experts believe the total grain crop amounted to only 160 million tons, a harvest that would have been considered exceptional in 1952 but that was totally inadequate eight years later. The Chinese population had increased by 50 million people between 1952 and 1960, the equivalent of an entire France. To avert mass starvation, the Chinese were forced to buy large quantities of grain from Canada, Australia, and Burma.

The Great Leap Forward also led to changes in the organization of space of rural China. Although the Communist commitment to the commune as the basic form of spatial and social organization remained firm, centralization in the communes was reduced. The old, much smaller agricultural producer cooperatives were remade the basic accounting unit of agricultural production. These brigades were further subdivided into still smaller production teams, which corresponded reasonably well with the single Chinese village. The millions of peasants of China were now allowed to maintain privately owned garden plots that covered 5 to 7 percent of the total cultivated area, and they were even allowed to sell produce in free markets and to hold village fairs. Despite these efforts at reorganization, China was forced to import 5 million metric tons of grain each year from 1961 to 1976.

A New Communist People

The social organization of Chinese life was changing as rapidly as China's physical landscape. A primary Communist goal was to eliminate the centuries-old Confucian code of ethics and behavior and to replace it with the principles of communism. Mao's vision was to break the long cyclical wave of Chinese history. The goal of communalization in agriculture and industry was not, then, simply economic development but rather the creation of a new social and moral order. To accomplish this, Communist China: (1) initiated major programs of education and health care; (2) attempted to prevent the rise of an urban elite, separated from the peasantry; and (3) tried to integrate the minority peoples of the Chinese domain into the mainstream of Chinese life and culture. Although less measurable than acres of cropland or tons of grain, the most fundamental change in the human geography of China is being forged in the minds of its people. Hence the debate: Is China more Chinese or more Communist?

Education was the principal instrument available to create this new society. Learning was considered one of the four collectivizations of Communist China; the other three were dining, living quarters, and labor. Adult education centers were established in the communes, in factories, and in the streets of the cities and villages of China. By 1958, 40 million people were attending classes, and another 31 million were studying part-time. The process was facilitated by the introduction of simplified Chinese characters and a phonetic romanized script, the Pinyin system of standard Chinese. Primary school enrollments increased from 24 million in 1949 to 90 million a decade later. Secondary schools increased proportionately, and some 810,000 students were enrolled in institutes of higher education. By 1960, over 90 percent of the school-age children of China were receiving education in one form or another.

The costs of this educational expansion were paid by an application of the Walking on Two Legs policy. Students at universities and technical schools set up small factories. Secondary and elementary school pupils built small dikes, cleared irrigation channels, and worked in the fields. Educational units became production units that were supposed to be self-supporting. This integration of study and work was designed to avoid the ancient Confucian separation between mental and manual labor. Emphasis was placed on technical and administrative training to fill the manpower needs of expanding industries. The curriculum, however, was political as well as technical. The goal was not simply to produce engineers and chemists but to create new Communist people.

Paralleling the drive for education, the Communists attempted to raise health levels in rural China by eliminating the "five plagues and the four pests." As late as the 1930s, two thirds of the people of South China were afflicted with malaria. A little-known disease called kala-azar, which affects the functions of the liver and spleen, was endemic to the North China Plain. In addition, typhus and plague, the diseases of poverty, were widespread throughout China. Some 10 million people had schistosomiasis and from 50 million to 100 million suffered from hookworm, two parasitic infestations.

To cope with the five plagues—malaria, schistosomiasis, kala-azar, filariasis (another parasitic disease), and hookworm—Communist planners instituted campaigns of mass inoculation, improved sanitation, and established rural infirmaries. The four pests—flies, mosquitos, rats, and sparrows—were likewise the targets of extermination campaigns.

Most of these accomplishments were the products of an experiment in delivering health care to China's millions of peasants—by means of "barefoot doctors." On completion of a year's training in the rudiments of both Western and traditional Chinese medicine, each barefoot doctor was sent out to an agricultural commune to labor with its members and provide health care as needed. Periodically, they returned to a training center for refresher courses.

Both in education and in health, the Communist government tried to reduce the gap between conditions of life in the city and in the village. Their goal—to prevent the emergence of a Confucian-style urban elite ruling in comfort over a starving peasantry. To a greater degree than most developing countries, China has succeeded. These policies in education and health along with economic diversification have slowed the rate of urbanization in China.

In 1953, 18.5 percent of China's population, or about 108 million people, were urban dwellers. Only nine cities had populations of more than 1 million. Although the number of million cities rose to seventeen by 1960, the greatest increase in urban dwellers occurred in small towns of 50,000 or less. By 1980, 183 million people lived in China's largest cities. In 1988, 41 percent of the Chinese were urban residents.

Communist theory advocates self-determination for oppressed national minorities, but traditional Chinese insistence on the superiority of their own culture caused ambivalence on this issue. Although ethnic Han Chinese form the vast majority of the country's population, there are 55 non-Chinese ethnic groups numbering 56 million people (6 percent of the population) in the 1980s. Minorities populate more than half the country's territory, much of it the deserts, mountains, and dry lands of Outer China.

These include such diverse peoples as Tibetans, Mongols, Koreans, Thais, Vietnamese, Russians, and Turkic-speaking Muslims. The largest of these groups are found in the five autonomous regions (provinces) located in the humid south and arid western portions of China: Guangxi (Kwangsi), Tibet, Xinjiang, Ningxia (Ninghsia), and Inner Mongolia (Fig. 9.1). Government policy has wavered between praise of the racial,

Under the policy of "Walking on Two Legs," students labored on communes while pursuing their studies. Members of this commune, in Sichuan, are widening a road.

cultural, and linguistic diversity of China and rigorous enforcement of the assimilation of minorities into the cultural patterns and national goals of the People's Republic.

Modernization has meant sending trained, political cadres of Chinese to direct programs of medical, educational, economic, and political integration in the autonomous regions. Conflict has developed because minority values are often at variance with those of the Chinese. The most dramatic example of physical resistance is in Tibet. Minority groups find themselves subject to the traditional Chinese pride and scorn for other peoples. In many cases, this has proved stronger than the ideal of universal brotherhood proposed in Communist thought. The Cultural Revolution of the late 1960s and 1970s set out to eradicate the four olds—religious beliefs, traditional culture, customs, and habits—all of which are the basis of differences between minority peoples and the Chinese. Ethnic policies illuminate the ongoing struggle between Communist and Confucian thought in China.

Pathways to Modernization

The struggle between Communist and Confucian thought has had profound effects on the direction of China's pursuit of modernization for the last three decades. Pure Communist policies are based on the Marxist principle of "to each according to his needs," whereas Confucian principles are based on "to each according to his labor." A struggle ensued between Communist ideologues and more moderate pragmatists. This battle of ideas was fought in every city and village in China bearing directly on the human geography of the country.

The Cultural Revolution led to the purging of the pragmatists as well as the rising class of technocrats guiding China's development. This purge threw the country into chaos. After Mao's death in 1976, the pragmatists regained power, instituting a more

moderate, less ideological course. The central problem they now face is one of population and resources: supporting 1 billion people on China's land base. By opening the country to the West, they are attempting to achieve a level of development comparable to that of the "other China," Taiwan.

The Cultural Revolution

The Confucian ethic and the Communist ideology of Mao Zedong were inherently contradictory. Confucianism, one of the most durable codes of human behavior ever devised, proposed that "superior" men should lead the nation by example and excellence. Embedded within its social fabric is the assumption of a static, unchanging set of social classes. Although appropriate to the agricultural-based dynasties of China's past, it was poorly suited to a society aspiring to development. Confucianism was already moribund when European traders, technology, and military power intruded on the Qing dynasty in the nineteenth century.

Chinese communism, by contrast, asserted that there should be three equal classes in society—the army, the workers, and the peasants. And China's economic policies, although based on the early development plans of the Soviet Union, reflected this social commitment. Until his death, Mao Zedong envisioned a new Communist society in which all shared a perfect equality.

By the 1960s and 1970s, Mao's utopian goal seemed threatened by the rise of a counterrolutionary educated elite and trained bureaucracy who viewed themselves as apart from the people, superior to the peasantry. The old Confucian division between mental and manual labor seemed to be erasing the revolutionary gains of communism. As tensions increased, Mao launched a decade-long Cultural Revolution in 1966 to revive the revolutionary spirit of the Chinese people and to initiate once more the drive toward a Communist future.

The universities were closed and

college examinations abolished. Revolutionary Red Guards, most of them students, were encouraged to deride and harass public officials. These radical, young visionaries were exhorted to purge "bad elements" in Chinese society. Millions were exiled to the countryside. Until the army took over in 1968, the resultant turmoil paralyzed China. Its political and social institutions were relentlessly attacked; revolutionary committees of Red Guards took control and violence broke out. Millions of orthodox Maoists supported the Cultural Revolution; millions more opposed its excesses. China stood divided.

The impact on the Chinese economy was substantial, although production figures for this period are not reliable. Dissent rent the fabric of the urban and rural communes of China. Industrial growth apparently continued, but the peasants were no better off in the 1970s than in the 1950s. This was largely due to the erosive effects of population growth and to the heavy drain of funds from rural areas to support industrialization. A recent study discovered that grain consumption in China's cities increased 10 to 15 percent between 1957 and 1978, but declined 6 percent in the countryside. Average incomes in the metropolitan centers of Beijing and Shanghai are now triple those in the villages.

Provision of new fertilizers, modern farm machinery, and high-yielding rice and wheat seed virtually stopped. Many of the 17 million student Red Guards sent "up to the mountains and down to the villages" to participate in peasant life were urbanites with little knowledge of life on a rural commune. In the cities, the purging of intellectuals, technocrats, and administrators eroded the efficiency of an economy already too heavily dependent on manual labor. The result is a ten-year gap in technical training with a prolonged effect on China's development.

The Four Modernizations

In the early 1980s, the new leadership in Beijing shattered many of Mao's most cherished dreams by charting a new course toward modernization. In 1980, they recognized that China was still a developing nation with 80 percent of its population engaged in agriculture and that its only surplus was human energy. Under Deng Xiaoping (Teng Hsiao-ping), a program called the Four Modernizations—in agriculture, industry, defense, and science and technology—was initiated. This dramatic shift in strategy was more practical and less doctrinaire. The planners of modern China set their sights on achieving: (1) improvements in agriculture to feed China's 1 billion people and release manpower for industry; (2) renovation of the army, which had been badly mauled in the 1970s in skirmishes with the Soviet-equipped Vietnamese; (3) modernization and diversification of the industrial base with a new emphasis on light industry and consumer goods; and (4) importation of foreign science and technology to make China a first-rate world power by the year 2000.

In agriculture, the pragmatists changed the nation's approach to China's food problem. The 52,000 agricultural communes were subdivided into production fields over which local groups were given direct responsibility. By 1980, more planting and harvesting decisions were allowed at the village level, and traditional one-family farms were revived in some regions. The government now allows peasants to carry on a certain amount of private production and trade. Each peasant family can farm a small plot of land outside its home or in the vicinity of its village. Produce from these fields can be sold in newly opened free markets where the peasants are allowed to set their own prices. Privately owned land now makes up 5 to 7 percent of the cultivated area of the country. Perhaps most important, the state raised the purchase price of grain 20 percent in 1980 and lowered the quota peasants were forced to sell to the state.

Politics now is the politics of pro-

In the late 1980s, student protests for more democracy are expressed on wall posters like these in Beijing.

duction. Emphasis has been placed on higher rewards to those who work harder. Beijing also modified Mao's almost mystical view that grain is the "key link" in the Chinese economy and has encouraged the planting of more profitable commercial crops, such as cotton, jute, tea, sugar, and vegetables. Priority is being given to the production and distribution of farm machinery and fertilizer.

In short, the agricultural reforms of the pragmatists directly challenged Mao's concept of a Chinese countryside occupied by vast homogeneous communities. Decentralization and private incentives are now seen as keys to China's ability to feed its growing population without importing grain. Deng Xiaoping's practical maxim, "It does not matter whether the cat is black or white, as long as it catches mice," is being tested among China's 800 million farmers.

Results in agriculture are vital to the Chinese economy. Thus far, under the new program, these are promising. The gap between rural and urban living standards, although still large, has been narrowed. The peas-

ants are better off, and total food production has increased. In 1979, China produced a record harvest of 332 million tons of grain; in 1981, the figure was 318 million tons in spite of floods and drought. By the mid-1980s, China was producing 400 million tons of grain.

Comparable reforms have been introduced into the industrial sector which produced nearly half of the country's gross national product in 1981. The command economy in which all economic decisions were made by the state has been modified to take account of market demands. Decision-making powers have been shifted to individual enterprises, and the profit motive has been introduced into factory management. Under this new system, each business is assigned a production quota, but after fulfilling this quota, surplus production may be sold directly to consumers. Similarly, workers are paid bonuses each month if they work longer hours or are more productive. Factory managers are encouraged to compete with one another, and they have more discretion in the purchase of raw materials and the sale of their manufactured goods. All factories, except those producing armaments, are expected to make a profit. A market-oriented economy is rapidly replacing the highly centralized system of the recent past.

In addition, more attention is being paid to previously neglected areas of industry in China, such as transportation, housing, and consumer goods. The demands of the state are giving way to the demands of the marketplace. By 1981, the Chinese government had increased investment in agriculture and light industry at the expense of heavy industry. To fund new enterprises, foreign countries are being encouraged to invest in joint ventures in mining, manufacturing, and energy exploration. Britain has built a coal mine at Tatung (pop. 300,000), west of Beijing, and the Dutch have constructed a new coal-exporting port on the lower Chang Jiang. The Japanese are involved in a steel project at Baoshan (Paoshan) on the Chang Jiang Delta. Beijing has signed agreements with U.S. corporations for offshore oil exploration in the South China Sea. Newly drilled wells here and in the East China Sea have yielded promising test samples. The uranium sector is also being opened up to foreign corporations. China's trade with the West is expected to increase rapidly.

This new pathway to modernization involves recognition that China's slow pace of modernization over the last forty years must be accelerated through technology if the country is to compete as a major world power. The decision to open China's doors to the West is not unlike that made by Japan in the late nineteenth century. Previously cautious about all foreign involvements, China's new leadership has allowed a large number of foreign firms to establish branch offices in Beijing. Joint ventures with the United States expanded trade between the two countries to the $5 billion level by the mid-1980s. Currently, China's major trading partners are Japan and Hong Kong, with exchanges of goods estimated at $3 billion each. Just as important for China, this expansion of trade will involve the training of thousands of scientists and engineers in foreign technologies, a step that was unheard of under Mao Zedong. The attraction for industrialized nations in these new ventures are inexpensive Chinese land, labor, and raw materials. The old question of "Who will light the lamps of China"—the lure of a market of 1 billion people—has drawn world economic attention to the previously impervious colossus of Asia.

Whether the new pragmatic pathway to modernization initiated by Deng Xiaoping and his colleagues will succeed in propelling China into a more secure future is uncertain. The sheer scale of China's population and economy is daunting. In the late 1980s, the per capita gross national product of China is barely over $300, less than 2 percent that of the United States. The total investment in health, education, and science amounts to only $10 per person per year. Millions of new jobs will have to be created each year to employ the 300 million Chinese under the age of sixteen and the 650 million under the age of thirty. Further, Maoist resistance to recent changes remains strong, if muted. But the ultimate test of the reforms of the post-Mao period will come in China's 2 million villages where 800 million peasants, one third of all the farmers in the world, still live. Today, as in the past, the fate of the Chinese state lies in the relationship between its land and people.

1 Billion People

One fifth of humanity, slightly more than 1 billion people, live in the People's Republic of China. The Chinese population has great momentum, growing by 15 million people each year—and this in spite of the institution of rigorous programs of birth control. Unfortunately, China's agricultural base is finite and stable.

In China, 7 percent of the world's arable land feeds 1 billion people. Of the 11 percent of China that is under cultivation, only about 40 percent, mostly in the southeast, is double cropped. This means that the sown area of China is roughly equal to that of the United States. Due to the large Chinese population, less than one-half acre of cultivated land is available per person. As China increases at a rate of 15 million people a year, China adds the equivalent of an entire U.S. population to its nation every seventeen years. It is unlikely that this growth can be stemmed because 300 million of China's 1 billion people are under sixteen years of age.

The initial response to the problem of numbers was to increase the productivity of agriculture. During the Great Leap Forward, enormous amounts of energy were devoted to expanding the agricultural acreage in China. Millions of acres of marginal land were brought under cultivation in the Northeast, Xinjiang, and the subhumid fringes of Agricultural China. Later this policy was abandoned in favor of intensified cultivation in the traditional croplands of eastern China. Mechanization, new varieties of seed, more efficient irrigation practices, and a disciplined, totalitarian reorganization of rural Chinese society effected a small increase in individual productivity. But per capita grain output is not much better than in the 1930s, and food shortages are widespread.

Chinese farms have yielded somewhat higher harvests, but the environmental and technological parameters of Chinese agriculture have remained remarkably stable. Population is distributed across the landscapes of China now as in the past; rising density levels have been repeatedly sustained (Fig. 9.9). Today, this stable agrarian living space looms as an environmental confine that may thwart the goals of the Chinese state.

Producing a son in traditional Chinese society was an act of moral responsibility, a duty to the memory of one's ancestors and security for the future. Because the infant mortality rate in rural China was always high, a peasant family strove to have at least three sons to ensure the survival of one. Given the laws of probability, families of six or more children were the rule.

The effects of this high birth rate on population growth were mitigated by malnutrition and disease, which caused high death rates. Female infanticide was widely practiced. As late as 1943, the Nationalist government of Chiang Kai-shek found it necessary to prohibit the drowning of girl infants. But large families remained a blessing in rural China, as in most agricultural societies. As a result, the birth rate was high; the best estimates suggest a prerevolutionary rate of 40 to 45 births per 1000 population—much like that of preindustrial societies everywhere.

In the 600 years for which estimates are available, the population of China grew ten times, the amount of cultivated land increased four times, and grain yields doubled (Fig. 9.14). In spite of the clear implications of these reasonably well-known statistics, the Communist government of Mao Zedong was ambivalent on the population issue.

When they assumed power in 1949, Communist propagandists asserted that China could support ten times her current population. Birth control was denounced, and people were considered to be "the most precious of all categories of capital." From the Communist viewpoint, human misery was not produced by overcrowding but by a social order ruled by capitalists. The results of the 1953 census changed planners' minds: 100 million extra Chinese turned up in the 583 million figure. Thereafter, abortion and contraception were viewed with greater leniency. Birth control was justified as desirable for the health and well-being of mothers and children. But efforts to reduce the birth rate in the 1950s probably had no effect in rural China and only limited success in the cities.

The optimism of the Great Leap Forward of 1958 led to a reversal of government support of birth control. The implausible argument that there was a labor shortage in China; that "a man's hands can produce more than his mouth can eat," was again disseminated. Disastrous food shortages and nationwide hunger during the next two years, however, led to a sustained program of birth control in the 1960s aimed at lowering the birth rate.

The approach was initially indirect. Although marriage laws in Communist China allowed a man to wed at twenty and a woman at eighteen, it was argued that early marriage was bad for one's work, study, and even health (through excessive sexual activity). The most appropriate age of marriage, according to Chinese leaders in 1970, was twenty-three to twenty-seven for a woman and twenty-five to twenty-nine for a man. Premarital sex was considered totally reprehensible. These values took hold with the young, who make up a fertile two thirds of the population of China.

To be effective, however, a variety of birth control devices had to be introduced into the countryside. Abortion clinics were established; sterilization operations were made more readily available. More to the point, thousands of barefoot doctors were also made bearers of China's birth control devices. Although it is difficult to determine which of these forces was most effective in lowering the birth rate in Communist China, by the end of the second decade of Communist rule the birth rate had dropped to about 32 per 1000 population. In 1987, China's birth rate was a reported 21 per 1000 population.

This dramatic drop in births has occurred because China's leaders realize that unless population growth is halted, the country's economic progress, political stability, and ability to feed itself will be threatened. In the early 1980s, a "one couple, one-child" policy was adopted to restrict the families of the 160 million young people who reached marriageable age by the mid-1980s. Exceptions are made only when the first child is abnormal or adopted, or if the parents remarry. Farmers whose only child is a girl may also have a second child. For the first time, China's national minorities, previously exempt, are subject to population control.

Statistics vividly demonstrate the magnitude of the problem. If a "one couple, one-child" policy is followed by the Chinese people, the nation's population will stabilize at about 1.2 billion and then fall to about 700 mil-

China's population problem is especially intense because the country has more than 320 million youngsters under 15 years of age.

POPULATION GROWTH IN CHINA

For more than 1500 years, the Chinese population remained stable. Then, in the Qing period (1644–1911), population increased dramatically. The 1953 census estimated a population of 583 million, which doubled to 1087 million in 1988. In 1982, some 5 million census takers, 100,000 coders, and twenty-one IBM computers engaged in the largest census of record in history. Population growth has forced China to launch the most severe, restrictive birth-control program in the world. If this program fails, economic modernization will be extremely difficult.

Adapted from: Keith M. Buchanan et al., *China: The Land and the People.* New York: Crown, 1980, p. 133.

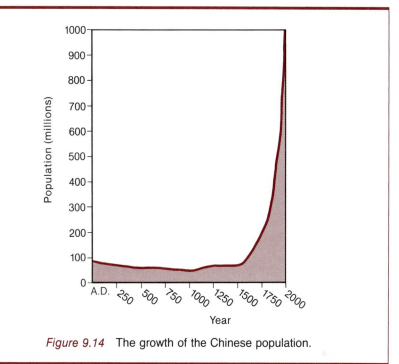

Figure 9.14 The growth of the Chinese population.

lion over the next 100 years. If, however, each couple in China has three children, China's masses will number an untenable 4.26 billion a century from now—a population nearly equal to that of the entire world today.

To encourage compliance with the "one couple, one-child" policy, a system of rewards and punishments has been instituted in China. Couples who sign a contract to have one child receive larger living quarters, extra food coupons, free education and health care for the child, and larger pensions. Penalties begin when a couple has a second child. The family not only loses, but must pay back, all benefits gained under the one-child plan. If a third child is born, the family's rations are cut, wages are reduced, and the woman comes under severe criticism from local Communist cadres. Contraceptives and abortions are encouraged; enforced sterilization has been reported.

Currently, some 10 million families are forced to comply with the "one couple, one-child" program, but most of these people live in China's largest cities—Shanghai, Beijing, Chongqing, and Guangzhou. The success of China's population policy, however, will be determined in rural China, where political control is less restrictive, the desire for sons is stronger, population density is less

This "one child" billboard in Beijing exhorts the Chinese to "practice birth control to benefit the next generation." This policy has been revised to allow a second child, if the first is a girl, because of substantial peasant resistance.

acute than in China's cities, and extra labor for individually owned garden plots is welcome. China's leaders are aware of strong rural opposition to compulsory birth control, and this issue is becoming a painful source of conflict between the Chinese peasantry and the Communist state. But if China is unable to control population growth, the communes of the new society will communalize only hunger, and even harsher measures will be required to maintain order and social commitment in the world's largest society.

Taiwan

Modern Taiwan, the Republic of China, was born in defeat under threat of invasion from mainland China. Replaced in the United Nations by the People's Republic, Taiwan is now given official recognition by very few foreign powers. When, in 1949, Chiang Kai-shek and 2 million of his followers retreated to the island, 125 miles off the southern coast of the mainland, most observers expected the Nationalists to be overrun by the Communist armies of Mao Zedong. But protected in the 1950s and 1960s by U.S. naval power and assisted by

U.S. aid, Taiwan has emerged as a model of East Asian economic development. The island's high per capita income represents a standard of living surpassed only by Singapore, Hong Kong, and Japan in all of Asia.

The Settling of Taiwan

Taiwan was known to the Chinese for well over 1000 years. Beginning in the 1950s, ethnic Chinese, mostly farmers and fisherfolk from the mainland, infiltrated the island via the Penghu Islands off its western shore. Through weight of numbers, the Chinese gradually drove the original inhabitants of Taiwan, believed to be of Malay stock, deep into the recesses of its mountain spine. Today, an estimated quarter-million of these Southeast Asian people still live in some 240 mountain villages. They are divided into nine tribes, each with its own language.

When the Portuguese discovered the island in the 1500s, they named it "Formosa"—the beautiful island. For many years, Westerners referred to the island as Formosa, although the Chinese have always known it as Taiwan. In the 1600s, the Dutch established small provisioning stations for their ships on the southwest coast near Tainan and at Tanshui in the north. But some 2 million Chinese, fleeing the mainland before the invading Qing armies, sought refuge on Taiwan in the 1660s and erased the imprints of this early European occupation. The Qing conquered Taiwan in 1683, ruling the island for 200 years. Chinese culture and economy were firmly implanted on Taiwan. In 1895, after Qing armies were defeated in the Sino-Japanese War, Taiwan was ceded to the Japanese. The Japanese initiated a large-scale program of economic development on the island, creating a skeleton of modernization that the Nationalists would flesh out one-half century later.

Located astride the Tropic of Cancer and smaller than Denmark or the Netherlands, Taiwan has a climate similar to that of South China, sub-

tropical in the north and tropical in the south. Rainfall is heavy, in places in excess of 200 inches per year. But rainfall varies considerably because Taiwan is situated in the typhoon belt. These vast tropical storms lash the island in summer at a rate of three every year; more than 200 have been recorded in the first half of this century.

Local climate is primarily determined by elevation because the island is quite mountainous (Fig. 9.15). The ranges of the Central Mountains rise out of the sea on its eastern shores to elevations approaching 13,000 feet. Some sixty-two peaks in Taiwan are higher than 10,000 feet. Level land is concentrated along the west coast; smaller patches are found in the Ilan River Basin in the northeast and the Taitung Valley parallel to the east coast. Except in these lowland areas, the island was originally covered with tropical and subtropical forests. Patterns of land utilization

reflect these environmental realities.

In the lowlands of the west, Chinese immigrants cleared away tropical woodland and reclaimed swampland to implant their garden-style, intensive agriculture (Fig. 9.15). Irrigated rice fields spread along the west coast of the island, with sugarcane, tea, and bananas planted in more hilly areas. Double cropping was widely practiced. The Ilan Plain was also brought into rice cultivation. The Taitung valley was less densely settled; its primary crop is sugarcane. In the mountains, forests were heavily cut for the valuable comphor tree. The Japanese expanded this agricultural base by extending the irrigated area, initiating schemes of water conservation, increasing production of rice and sugar, and slowing the destruction of forests. During their occupation, Taiwan became an important source of food and raw materials for Japan.

Having first concentrated on increasing agriculture, the Japanese

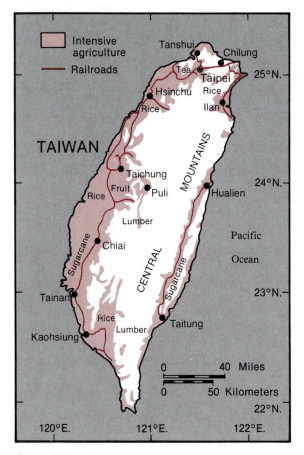

Figure 9.15 Taiwan.

soon harnessed the rivers plunging off the flanks of the Central Mountains by building hydroelectric plants, which provided cheap power for the initial stages of industrialization. Road and rail communications linked the entire west coast. Chemical and metallurgical industries were begun early. Japanese development was geared to permanent occupation of Taiwan. Their language was taught in the schools and became the language of the marketplace. This ended with their defeat in 1945, when Taiwan was returned to China, and after a brief four years, became a refuge for the defeated Nationalist armies of Chiang Kai-shek.

Modern Taiwan

The Nationalist flight to Taiwan provided Chiang Kai-shek with a second chance to implement the program of modernization conceived by his mentor Sun Yat-sen, although the arrival of the 2 million "mainlanders" was not greeted with enthusiasm by the Taiwanese. Two key policy decisions were made early: (1) the institution of a land reform program that distributed cultivated land to Taiwanese peasants and (2) the development of factories to produce textiles and fertilizers, goods that had previously been imported. Large landlords were appeased by payments of stock in the new industries. Peasant incomes and productivity rose dramatically once they owned land that they had previously leased. Both policies were successful. Taiwan, with a population of 19.8 million, now produces 85 percent of its food supply and is the twentieth largest industrial producer in the world.

Taiwan's economic progress is apparent in Taipei, the capital of the country. Taipei is a modern city of 2.25 million people with 5 million automobiles, traffic jams, pollution problems, and one of Asia's highest standards of living. Taiwan's second largest city and leading port, Kaohsiung (pop. 1.2 million) in the southwest, is a thriving industrial center. The industries in these cities produce

Taipei, the capital of Taiwan, is a modern Westernized city and the major center of one of the fastest growing economies in Asia.

light machinery, bicycles, electronic components, textiles, and shoes for export to the United States, Europe, the Middle East, and even mainland China—quietly through the intermediary port of Hong Kong. The country is gradually moving from labor-intensive manufacturing into high technology—the production of steel, oil tankers, and satellite communications. New industrial cities like Taichung and old urban centers like Tainan reflect this shift in emphasis. Although only one fourth of the island is cultivated, rural incomes have kept pace, electricity is available everywhere, and literacy rates exceed 90 percent. With the completion of the South Link Railway in the mid-1980s, the east coast of the island is experiencing greater levels of development.

Economically prosperous and socially stable, Taiwan's political future is uncertain. It is no longer recognized by most countries in the world; the United States severed diplomatic relations with Taiwan in 1979 and gave formal recognition to the People's Republic of China. Although still linked to the United States through defense treaties, Taiwan is increasingly isolated in the international arena.

The policy of the United States is to maintain the status quo between the two Chinas, but the opposing views of each will make this difficult. Mainland China is unalterably committed to the "liberation" of Taiwan. Taiwan's former president, Chiang Kai-shek's son, declared that he will never, under any circumstances, deal with the Communists.

In the early 1980s, mainland China issued its "Message to Compatriots on Taiwan," suggesting that the island become part of a reunified China. Under this plan, the Taiwanese would be allowed to maintain separate armed forces (400,000 strong and modern) and be guaranteed positions of "leadership" in a unified government. The Taiwanese are understandably suspicious of mainland motives and reluctant to cede their de facto autonomy. They view their country as a "spiritual fortress of the free world." But rejection of this and subsequent offers will further isolate the Taiwanese in world opinion. Acknowledgment, on the other hand, will commit them to negotiations. With the People's Republic now pursuing a more open policy toward the outside world, political pressure on Taiwan seems certain to increase in the future.

10

SOUTH ASIA

PROLOGUE

The six states of South Asia—India, Pakistan, Bangladesh, Sri Lanka (Ceylon) Nepal, and Bhutan—have a combined population of 1.07 billion people, a fifth of humanity (Fig. 10.1). Since independence, these countries have struggled to raise the standards of living of their people, to build stable political states, and to modernize their economies. The scale of this struggle is monumental. Within this region of diverse environments and equally diverse peoples, each country is engaged in a battle with poverty at the most basic level.

Some human geographers view South Asia as a human treadmill with little prospect of improvement; others see the region poised for rapid modernization. Nowhere are these conflicting views more apparent than in India, the dominant power in South Asia. A nuclear power, India still obtains most of its energy from cattle—indeed a bullock cart hauled an Indian space rocket to its launching pad in 1981. Although India successfully fed its growing population when many predicted large-scale starvation, its 817 million people still live in one of the world's poorest countries and have an average income of less than $300 a year. Plagued by industrial inefficiency and growing unemployment, India is currently engaged in a massive program of resource development and industrial revitalization. Frequently compared unfavorably with China, India—the world's largest democracy—has achieved remarkable gains

without resorting to the pervasive oppression of the human spirit found in its huge Asian-neighbor.

In each of the South Asian states, the processes of economic development and modernization are underway, but how successful their programs of change will be remains in question. If the region's population soars to 1.3 billion by the year 2000, as most believe it will, can the land base of South Asia support the stress of more intensive cultivation? With the bulk of the region's people still engaged in agriculture, how will South Asia cope with growing urban populations and provide jobs in industry for people moving off the land? Will South Asia be forced to accept solutions that simply make rural life more tolerable?

Each country in South Asia brings to this struggle for modernization a distinctive political system, different cultural legacies, varied resource opportunities and limitations, and different strategies of economic development. The region is a laboratory in which the future roles of developing countries in the world's political economy are evolving. But many predictions on South Asia made by regional experts during the last four decades have proved wrong, lending a note of caution to most current projections. The sheer complexity of South Asia remains a distinctive feature of the region. For some, this complexity breeds frustration, for others fascination.

TRADITIONAL SOUTH ASIA: SETTLEMENT AND SOCIETY

Life and landscape on the Indian Subcontinent is the product of two forces: first, the geographical isolation of this region from many currents of change that swept Asia throughout the course of history; second, the gradual evolution in relative isolation of a distinctively South Asian society and economy. South Asia's human geography was strongly influenced by the virtually impenetrable barrier of the Himalaya Mountains to the north and by its ocean borders on the west and east. Only the mountain passages of the northwest afforded invading Arabs, Persians, and Afghans entry into the subcontinent, and although these people influenced the region, they never disrupted the pervasive "Indianness" of South Asia.

On the Subcontinent, the internal dynamics of life and livelihood evolved slowly over the centuries. South Asia nourished an underlying unity of culture while sustaining regional diversity across its varied landscapes of hill and plain, valley and desert, jungle and rain forest. For these reasons, traditional modes of settlement and society are living realities in this region. Its people are deeply influenced by traditional sources of wisdom—India by Hinduism, Pakistan and Bangladesh by Islam, and Sri Lanka by Buddhism. As the geographer David Sopher explains, the distinctiveness of South Asia today is a product of the "slow churning of the ocean of Indian life."

GEOSTATISTICS

	Capital	Area (square miles)	Population (millions)	Rate of Natural Increase (%)	Number of Years to Double Population	Population Projected for A.D. 2000	Infant Mortality Rate	Life Expectancy at Birth	Urban Population (%)	Per Capita GNP ($)	Energy Consumption per Capita (kg of oil equivalent)
Bangladesh	Dacca	55,598	109.5	2.7	26	145.8	135	50	16	160	43
Bhutan	Thimbu	18,147	1.5	2.0	34	1.9	139	46	5	160	—
India	New Delhi	1,269,340	816.8	2.0	35	1,013.3	104	54	25	270	201
Nepal	Kathmandu	54,363	18.3	2.5	28	23.8	112	52	7	160	17
Pakistan	Islamabad	310,402	107.5	2.9	24	145.3	121	54	28	350	218
Sri Lanka	Colombo	25,332	16.6	1.8	38	19.4	31	70	22	400	139

Sources: World Population Data Sheet, 1988; World Development Report, 1987.

This section examines the persistent cultural unity and regional diversity that have characterized South Asia and strongly influence its patterns of development today. In *Culture and Society in South Asia,* Hinduism as a faith and caste as a social system are discussed as foundations that defined the organization of life in South Asia. These cultural realities framed the destinies of a majority of people on the subcontinent who for centuries lived in villages that were, for the most part, connected to the outer world by footpaths. These villages formed *The Economic Basis of Traditional South Asian Society,* providing work for the region's peasant population, wealth to support the dynasties that ruled South Asia, and a social and natural environment within which people lived out their lives. But oceanic exploration opened India to influences from the West, and for nearly two centuries, the region's landscapes and economies were shaped by *The British in South Asia.*

First under company rule and later as a colony, South Asia was converted into a region producing raw materials and food for foreign mills and mouths. The problems of population growth, urbanization, and

Hindu pilgrims from throughout South Asia bathe in the sacred waters of the Ganges River at Varanasi (Benares).

Figure 10.1 Political regions of South Asia.

environmental decay that South Asia faced once independence was achieved in 1947 were in large part a British legacy.

Culture and Society in South Asia

Before Muslim invasions from the west converted a fifth of the people of the Subcontinent to Islam, before the British built a colonial empire in India in the eighteenth and nineteenth centuries, and before Mahatma Gandhi and his colleagues began attacking the problems of creating an independent Indian nation, the people of South Asia were overwhelmingly Hindu by faith and caste members by birth. These two insti-

tutions, Hinduism and the **caste system,** molded the human geography of the Subcontinent for centuries. Now four fifths of the Indian population is Hindu. Adherents of other faiths—Muslims, Buddhists, Sikhs, Parsis, Jains, and Christians—are important religious minorities in India. Pakistan is an Islamic state, Bangladesh is overwhelmingly Mus-

THE DECLINE AND FALL OF INDUS VALLEY CIVILIZATION

Around 2000 B.C., when the Egyptians of the Nile Valley and the Sumerians of Mesopotamia were thriving, a third great civilization existed in the Indus River Valley of modern Pakistan. Known through excavations at two major centers—Harappa and Mohenjo-Daro—this civilization held sway over a triangular domain 1000 miles to a side that extended from the Iran-Pakistan border in Baluchistan northward to Harappa near modern Lahore and southward to the Gulf of Cambay near modern Bombay. Until recently, scholars believed that this civilization was sacked by Indo-European invaders. Now it appears more likely that natural disasters and environmental exhaustion played major roles in the decline and fall of civilization in the Indus Valley, as shown in Figure 10.2.

At its peak around 2000 B.C., Mohenjo-Daro, the largest city in the Indus Valley, had an estimated 40,000 people supported by cultivation on the fertile soils of the river plain (1). Like Harappa, Mohenjo-Daro was a well-planned city with flat-roofed, multistoried dwellings of fired brick. Massive fortifications, ceremonial centers, grain storage buildings, and household architecture testify to the sophistication of Indus Valley artisans. A thriving international trade apparently was carried on through seaports along the Arabian Sea Coast, and this undoubtedly added to the wealth of the Harappans and the citizens of Mohenjo-Daro. Irrigated cultivation of barley, wheat, vegetable crops, and cotton in the valley was the mainstay of their economy.

Apparently, rapid geological faulting 90 miles downstream from Mohenjo-Daro gradually undermined the wealth of the people in the Indus Valley. This faulting is believed to have raised natural dams that turned the upstream section of the Indus into a natural lake, inundating the city of Mohenjo-Daro and surrounding agricultural settlements (2). The people of Mohenjo-Daro re-

sponded with dogged determination. They built massive fired-brick dikes to hold back the encroaching waters, and they rebuilt the town itself no less than seven times (3). But periodic flooding must have badly damaged the agricultural economy of the central Indus.

Regional uplift also cut off coastal communications and severed the commercial life of the Indus Valley (4). At some point, reconstruction was abandoned at Mohenjo-Daro and the capital moved northward to Harappa. Re-

source exhaustion progressively left the inhabitants open to incursions by hill tribes in adjacent regions. The fine pottery, jewelry, art, and architecture disappear in the archeological record, as do the people of the Indus Valley whose civilization once matched those of the Egyptians and the Sumerians.

Adapted from: George F. Dales, "The Decline of the Harappans," in Gregory L. Possehl (ed.), *Ancient Cities of the Indus.* Durham, N.C.: Carolina Academic Press, 1979, p. 310.

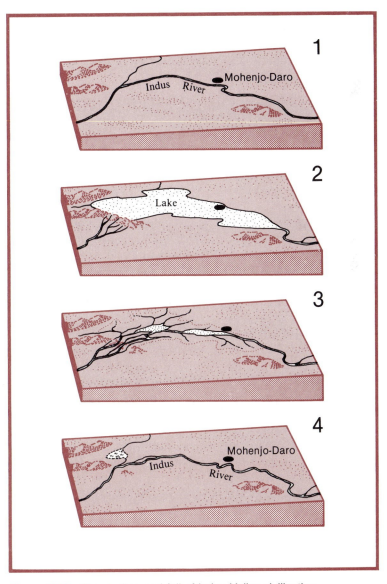

Figure 10.2 The decline and fall of Indus Valley civilization.

lim in population, and Sri Lanka is primarily a nation of Buddhists. All three countries, however, have been deeply influenced by the Indian cultural experience.

Hinduism: The Pursuit of Sanctity

Hinduism began in South Asia when Aryan tribes from the northwest repeatedly invaded India in the second and first millennia B.C. Prior to their arrival, a great civilization had flourished in the Indus Valley, but geologic changes in the earth's surface eventually destroyed the established resource base (Fig. 10.2). Successive waves of invasion led to the assimilation of the native **Dravidian**-speaking peoples of the northern Subcontinent and bequeathed the ancient language of Sanskrit to them. This contributed to the region's heterogeneity and tolerance of differences.

Hinduism and its growth have often been likened to the growth of a tree. It has no single founder, no single location or date of origin, and no single tenet of belief that unites all Hindus. Yet it has an observable structure that is both obvious in practice and visible in the landscape. Hinduism started to take form as early as 100 B.C., when a set of writings known as the Vedas ("Knowledge") appeared. These deal with the many gods and the nature of the universe and creation. The Upanishads, commentaries on these works, followed. Brahmans, those who became the priest class of Hinduism, spread their knowledge throughout India. These new beliefs generally developed in response to the growth of Buddhism on the Subcontinent, although much of Buddhism was incorporated into Hinduism as the religion developed. Many common customs, modes of social organization, and settlement practices spread throughout the region. But these common features did not weld India into a single country or provoke a single code of belief within Hinduism.

The outlines of Hinduism began to become clear, however. By A.D. 200, the principal works of Hindu scripture had been written. Perhaps the most notable of all is the Mahabharata, compiled between 200 B.C. and A.D. 200. This series of epic tales about the gods and humankind contains the **Bhagavad-Gita,** which outlines many of the rules concerning social caste and begins by praising the system of discipline, or ways to knowledge, known as yoga.

As is true of any great religion, individuals of different classes, different temperaments, and different intellects can find a satisfying faith within the broad range of Hindu practice and belief. The world's 650 million Hindus range from **monotheists** who pursue the worship of a single god to **pantheistic** believers who venerate many gods. All Hindus agree, however, on the belief in an omnipresent spirit that provides continuity in an endlessly changing physical world. Every creature's soul and the innumerable deities in the Hindu pantheon are integral parts of this spirit. Despite the lack of organized structure in this intensely personal religion, three basic concepts are generally shared by all: (1) dharma, or duty within society; (2), reincarnation—the cycle of life, death and rebirth; and (3) karma, an accounting of good and evil behavior.

Foundations of Hindu Belief

In Hinduism, each individual is born with a personal duty, or dharma, which sets forth a preordained role in life. In the Bhagavad-Gita, performing one's own role poorly is deemed better than performing another role well. The social position of the individual is determined by one's group, or caste. Each caste has a dharma within society and when every group performs its duty, society functions in harmony. Hindus, then, have a personal destiny conferred at birth. Because this destiny cannot be altered by education, by the accumulation of wealth, or by the attainment of power, social mobility and self-improvement have different meanings in the Hindu system than in Western society.

Reincarnation—the cycle of life, death, and rebirth—is the second fundamental tenet shared by most Hindus. Life is viewed as open-ended, with birth, growth, and death occurring repeatedly. The Western belief that time moves in a straight line from the past through the present into the future plays no role in Hinduism. The body is thought of as a suit of clothes, donned at the beginning of each life and discarded for another at death. Because souls can occupy any life form from ape to insect, all creatures have sacred qualities in Hinduism. Western belief (ecologists excepted) that people and nature are separate finds no place in Hinduism.

People strive for release from this cycle of reincarnation by searching for **moksha** (or in Buddhism **nirvana**)—unity with the universal spirit and freedom from the painful mortal cycle of birth and death. Different paths can be taken to achieve moksha, reflecting the variety of travelers making the effort. Each path is a variety of **yoga** (discipline), and four are widely recognized.

The Way of Knowledge is for those people who approach the search for cosmic unity through reason and thought; the Way of Love is for emotional people and is pursued by prayers to one of the gods in the Hindu pantheon; the Way of Work is for socially active people, like Mahatma Gandhi; and the Way of Mystical Experience is for people who engage in rigorous self-discipline to achieve mastery over mind and body. In providing valid paths to moksha for people of different temperaments, Hinduism has retained the flexibility to unite diverse peoples under one general body of belief.

The third and final central tenet of Hinduism, the law of **karma,** can be thought of in terms of a ledger in which an accounting, as inexorable as the law of gravity, holds everyone responsible for his deeds and thoughts

This holy man on pilgrimage at Palni in South India personifies the importance of faith in South Asian life.

in all past existences. Good deeds produce good results, such as birth into a wealthy, powerful, or priestly Brahman family; evil acts produce the reverse, namely, rebirth as a lower creature—as an insect, an animal, or as a member of those considered outcastes, the Untouchables. Linked to the social order by the cycle of rebirth, karmic law justifies and explains the relative position of each individual and group within the hierarchy of Hindu society. Chance is eliminated, environment irrelevant; one's birth is no accident. Poverty, suffering, disease, and human degradation are preordained social states earned through past misbehavior and are appropriate to each individual and group.

Caste: In Search of Purity

Hindu society is separated into four broad groups, or castes, each with its own **dharma.** These four groups are: (1) Brahmans, who traditionally study, teach, and perform religious rituals and sacrifices; (2) Kshatriyas, the warriors, political leaders, and kings; (3) Vaisyas, the farmers, tradesmen, and merchants; and (4) Sudras, the

servant class. Untouchables stand outside all four groups; they are seen as not quite human.

According to this idealized social plan, important religious distinctions separate the three upper groups from the lowborn Sudras. The upper groups are initiated into their communities through sacred ceremonies; they experience a second birth that makes them doubly holy or twice-born. The once-born Sudras, who form the bulk of Hindu society, hold lower status. Beyond them, "in outer darkness," stand the Untouchables, or as renamed by Mahatma Gandhi, Harijans ("children of God"). Until recently, these caste distinctions pervaded Indian law. Group discrimination is now illegal, but 2000 years of tradition are not discarded easily.

In practice, these four broad caste orders of Hindu society (Brahman, Kshatriya, Vaisya, and Sudra) are fragmented into a host of smaller subgroupings called **jati:** ("birth"). Each jati, revolving around its caste, forms an exclusive social group whose members eat together, often practice the same occupation, intermarry, and share the same dharma within society. Each group holds a unique position in the social hierarchy. Members of different groups typically live in segregated sections of a village, town, or city, although they often work together. Their social interactions are marked by complex codes of deferential behavior. By the 1800s, more than 2000 jati existed in India. Most villages had a number of jati from a handful to 20 or more, and a given linguistic region might well have over 100 different jati.

At the root of this hierarchical social system was the fear that pollution through contact with ritually "unclean" groups might lead, however accidentally, to defilement. Each caste held a hierarchical ranking in degree of "purity" within the Indian caste pyramid.

Brahman castes have traditionally enjoyed the highest rank, although frequently they were neither the

wealthiest nor the most powerful group within a given community. Orthodox Brahmans went to great lengths to preserve their high status, taking food only from the hands of other Brahmans and keeping to a vegetarian diet. Some Brahman as well as other higher caste groups would not eat eggs, which they considered to be nascent life. They avoided intimate contact with lower castes, leading lives of social isolation in groups as small as fifteen families. The strong emphasis on food habits was based on the belief that the nature of human beings was affected by the food that they ate. As a result, many cooks in modern India are Brahmans. Restaurants reflect adjustments to different castes.

At the other end of this graded scale were the Untouchables. Untouchables today make up more than a sixth of the population of India. In the past, Untouchables were forbidden to use some roads because they might contaminate members of higher castes by their proximity. If the shadow of an Untouchable were to pass over food, higher groups, however hungry, would not touch it. Yet even among the Untouchables, the Hindu principle of hierarchy took root, and each caste within the Untouchables was scaled against the others.

Despite efforts to legislate against discrimination toward Untouchables and guarantee better places for them in Indian life by quota hiring in government service (one eighth of all jobs, one seventh of the seats in national and state legislatures), most villages retain a segregated Untouchable quarter. Upper class Hindus still clash with Untouchables, killing hundreds each year. Untouchables continue to perform the "contaminating" tasks of Hindu society and are generally despised and avoided. Between these two extremes are many hundreds of castes and subcastes whose members know with some certainty their relative place in this traditional hierarchy.

Fear of pollution was a critical force

in maintaining these caste compartments in Hinduism, but it was not the only force. The caste system also provided benefits on a day-to-day basis. Castes offered security to their members, both in the broad sense of a cultural group with shared customs and values and in the more narrow sense of financial aid for members struck by disaster or misfortune. In addition, each caste had its own internal system of justice, a caste council that punished members who broke caste rules and that defended caste honor against outsiders. Finally, specialized caste occupations led to reciprocal exchanges of goods and services among castes in each community and region, a fact of vital importance to the functioning of Indian society and economy.

In Indian villages, there were usually a number of hereditary castes, for example, priests, traders, farmers, carpenters, potters, smiths, oil pressers, washerfolk, and landless laborers. Each caste performed an exclusive function that others needed. Even if their task were viewed as unclean, they were, after all, fulfilling their dharma. They were also contributing to the functioning of the total community, and in the final analysis, there were groups beneath them with fewer rights and privileges.

The reciprocal exchange of services among landlords, dependent artisans, and field workers was formalized into what was called in North India the **jajmani** system. This system provided a share of the annual harvest to each contributing member of village society, however lowborn, and a place for each person within the social fabric. Stable, resistant to change, and until recently relatively isolated from outside influences, village Indians based their social life on Hinduism and caste.

The Economic Basis of Traditional South Asian Society

The traditional setting of life in South Asia has always been the village, where nearly four of every five people still live. In these small settlements, South Asians were bound together by ties of religion, caste, and obligations to other villagers. Disputes in villages were settled by councils of elders and caste organi-

Indian villagers huddle under sheets of plastic during a torrential downpour associated with the onset of the summer monsoon. Monsoon rains are crucial to agriculture in South Asia.

zations. Any sizable village had its own priests, traders, moneylenders, blacksmiths, barbers, and shopkeepers. To some degree, caste groupings functioned on a regional basis, but poor roads and inadequate communication systems tended to reinforce the self-sufficient nature of local village society.

Over time, the technology and techniques of farming changed little. Cultivated land in northern India was generally planted to cereals. Rice became dominant on the well-watered plains of the northeast, especially in Bengal at the mouths of the Ganges and Brahmaputra rivers as well as on the coastal plains of the south. On the Deccan Plateau, cotton, sorghum, and millet were planted. Throughout the peninsula, peasant life fluctuated with the weather. A good crop depended on the **summer monsoon** (see Figs. 10.5–10.8). The monsoon produces 80 to 90 percent of the annual rainfall over large areas of the Subcontinent.

Agriculture was a gamble on the monsoon rains. The Indian farmer coped with this by spreading seed thinly over the land and by cultivating only food grains—agricultural practices that reduced yields and produced little profit but that were relatively safe. Most years the summer monsoon failed in one or another part of the subcontinent, forcing peasants to migrate, abandon their land, become tenant farmers or wage laborers, or simply fall deeper into debt. Even when rains were plentiful, most soils in South Asia were so overused that crop yields were minimal.

Of the various sources of poverty and misery that afflicted South Asian villagers, none was more basic than low productivity. Even today rice and wheat yields per acre in India are one third those of Japan and one half those of China. These extremely poor yields for India's two largest food grains meant that over two thirds of the population was engaged in a subsistence occupation. Peasants sometimes tried to hedge their bets by

planting several crops in the same field.

In the eighteenth century, some commercial crops, such as tobacco, opium, and Gujarat indigo (from which a blue dye is obtained) were planted. But limited transportation networks hindered the development of large-scale commercial cropping. In Madras, for example, the cost of hauling grain was so expensive that the value of the grain doubled every 24 miles. River tolls were also quite high, and roads were so poor that it took three months to go 800 miles by cart from Delhi to Calcutta.

Despite these conditions in the villages, it was agriculture that supported the Mogul dynasty (1526–1857), which ruled the Subcontinent until the middle of the eighteenth century and held title to power well into the nineteenth century. The Moguls established a well-conceived system of land taxation or tax farming, which, at its best, was very good indeed. Instead of paying military leaders and ministers who performed public services directly from the royal treasury, Mogul emperors assigned the royal share of taxation for a given area, whether a single village or a large district, to

individuals as rewards. Land taxes usually amounted to one third the value of the crop and were assessed on the village as a whole and paid in kind. Taxes on many villages were collected by local authorities called **zamindars.**

The zamindari system worked effectively for the Moguls because the Subcontinent was then underpopulated and had large areas of uncultivated fertile land. The scarce resource was not land but labor. So, zamindars were careful not to tax villagers too harshly, fearing they would flee to empty lands outside Mogul jurisdiction. Peasants were exhorted to cultivate their land. In the past, then, the availability of uncultivated land acted as a check on oppressive taxation.

As population increased generation by generation in the nineteenth century, this land was filled and village conditions worsened in South Asia. More people attempted to live off the land, and village fields became more and more fragmented. This meant that little land could be left uncultivated or fallow; fields had to be cultivated every year. Population pressure also led to large-scale destruction of forests in the nine-

The scratch plow that symbolizes the traditional technology of Indian agriculture is still in wide use across the Subcontinent.

teenth century, which increased erosion. Lacking wood, peasants were increasingly forced to burn cattle dung as fuel, eliminating an important source of fertilizer that could have increased yields.

As if cultivating infertile and unfertilized tiny patches of land were not difficult enough, other factors contributed to the poverty of South Asian farmers. The **scratch plow** commonly used in this region cut the soil so shallowly that birds frequently ate large percentages of newly sown seed. The poorest farmers could not afford even a scratch plow, so that even now nearly a tenth of India's seeded fields are unplowed, reducing yields to a minimum. Not unexpectedly, peasants were frequently in debt to moneylenders at extremely high rates of interest. Landlords drained the Indian peasantry still further, leaving a standard of living so low that one observer referred to the traditional South Asian village as "the one phenomenon that lasted where nothing else survived."

The British in South Asia

British rule introduced Western values and techniques of public administration, education, and manufacturing into South Asia, creating the spatial basis for the establishment of the modern countries of the Subcontinent. The British transformed society and economy throughout much of the region.

British rule over the Subcontinent began modestly on December 31, 1600, when Queen Elizabeth I chartered an association of 125 business leaders and merchants as the British East India Company to ply the rich trade of the Orient. India, then under the Islamic rule of Mogul Emperor Akbar (1542–1605), was economically self-sufficient, exporting both raw materials and finished goods to the world. The quality and variety of Indian products were incomparably better than those of Europe. By contrast, Britain was an underdevel-

oped country. The royal treasury of Queen Elizabeth was only one eightieth the size of that of the Mogul emperor.

For the first fifty years, the British clung to India in a small number of trading posts, such as Surat, a small town north of Bombay; Madras, in the south; and a fort on the Hooghly River in the Ganges Delta, which later grew into the city of Calcutta. So too did the Portuguese and French have their trading footholds in India. From such entrepôts on the western, southern, and eastern flanks of South Asia, the British ultimately gained control of the Indian Subcontinent.

Mogul Rule (1526–1857)

When the British arrived in India, the Subcontinent was ruled by a Muslim dynasty that had established its center of power on the Gangetic Plain and extended its hold over much of India. Fusing elements of both Hindu and Muslim culture, the Moguls created one of the most brilliant and dynamic empires in world history.

When the first three vessels of the British East India Company set sail from London in 1601, the Moguls were near their peak of military power and cultural efflorescence. Mogul rulers fostered new and distinctive Indo-Islamic styles of painting, music, and architecture in their cities. In the countryside, they conducted extensive land use surveys and fostered systems of taxation and land ownership on which society and economy are still partially based.

The spatial jurisdiction of Mogul power expanded in the last half of the seventeenth century, and the population of India increased to perhaps 150 million. This period marked both the zenith of Mogul rule and the beginnings of its decline. For fifty years, beginning in 1658, Emperor Aurangzeb (1618–1707) fought a series of military campaigns to conquer both Hindus and Shi'ah Muslims.

The resources and treasury of the empire were poured into an unceas-

ing series of military campaigns. The population was decimated. Villagers were taxed unmercifully, milked by government armies and marauding bands alike. South Asia was visited by famines and plagues spawned by the breakdown of the Mogul system of law and justice. By 1700, the largest empire ever created on the Subcontinent was drained by the ulcers of war. In the 1750s and 1760s, British merchants—coastal spectators in India's wars—assumed direct territorial control over Bengal, Bihar, and portions of the eastern coast of South Asia.

As Mogul rule deteriorated, the British East India Company, lodged in its three coastal bases, began to assume increasing authority over local law and order and the organization of agricultural production. Everywhere, Marathas, Rajputs, Afghans, Moguls, and Sikhs were engaged in bitter, self-destructive warfare. Under these circumstances, Sir Robert Clive with 3000 troops put to flight the Mogul army in a mango grove at Plassey (north of Calcutta) in 1757. In one stroke, the rich province of Bengal in the Ganges Delta fell into the hands of the British East India Company. In the next century, three fifths of India was incorporated under company rule, and the political map of the subcontinent took roughly the form it would hold until independence in 1947 (Fig. 10.3).

The British East India Company (1757–1858)

The British soon made changes in the system of land taxation, although technically the Moguls still ruled. The zamindars who previously collected taxes under the Moguls were issued deeds to agricultural land and assumed the full rights of landlords after 1793. They charged peasants exorbitant rentals, threw villagers off the land if they refused or were unable to pay, forced agriculturalists to take out high interest loans, and then foreclosed when anyone failed to pay. About 40 percent of the agricultural

THE SPATIAL REORGANIZATION OF SOUTH ASIA UNDER THE BRITISH

Under the British, the center of gravity on the Indian Subcontinent shifted from an agrarian society based on inland centers of power on the Indo-Gangetic Plains and in the Dravidian south to a coastal society engaged in trade with Europe. Cities, like Karachi, Bombay, Madras, and Calcutta, grew from small towns to metropolises, whereas traditional inland urban centers withered. This reversal of the spatial organization of the Subcontinent is an enduring reality fostered by British rule. It still affects the distribution of people, goods, and services in Pakistan, India, Bangladesh, and Sri Lanka.

Adapted from: David E. Sopher, "The Geographical Patterning of Culture in India," in Sopher (ed.), *An Exploration of India: Geographical Perspectives on Society and Culture.* Ithaca, N.Y.: Cornell University Press, 1980, p. 318.

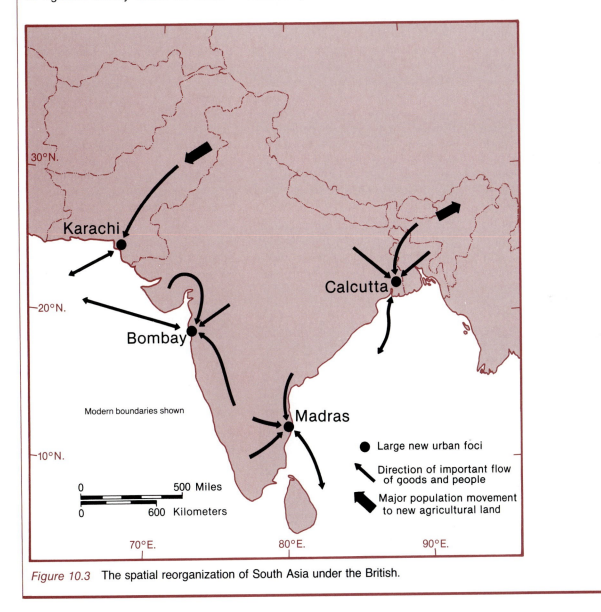

Figure 10.3 The spatial reorganization of South Asia under the British.

land in South Asia ended up in the hands of largely urban moneylenders, accelerating a trend toward parasitic landlordism.

Further, the British required that taxes be paid in cash rather than kind. This forced peasants and landowners to grow cash crops. As a result, the area cultivated in cotton, indigo, opium poppies, and jute—all **commodity crops** destined for export—increased significantly. And in the nineteenth century, tea and coffee, two products in great demand in Europe, were introduced. South Asia rapidly became an agricultural hinterland of Great Britain, an entire Subcontinent assigned the task of producing consumer goods and raw materials to feed the mouths, machines, and mills of industrial England.

In the cities of India, the impact of Britain's industrial revolution was also keenly felt. Cheap manufactured cotton cloth from the textile mills of Manchester and Birmingham flooded urban markets. By 1850, 45 percent of India's imports were textiles. Native spinners and weavers, unable to compete with these inexpensive machine-woven goods, were driven out of business. These handicraft workers and artisans had to abandon their craft activities and seek work as agricultural laborers on already overcrowded lands. Perhaps most important, the spatial organization of the subcontinent was completely transformed (Fig. 10.3). Expanding trading cities on the coast—Calcutta, Bombay, Madras, and Karachi—became enduring centers of power and wealth. Most inland cities declined in population, power, and prestige.

British reformers next began to suppress certain traditional Hindu practices they found offensive. Caste courts were subordinated to civil courts, a change in law that was deeply resented by upper caste Hindus. Such practices as **suttee** (in which widows were immolated on the funeral pyres of their dead husbands), child sacrifice, and female infanticide were made illegal. Finally, permission was granted Hindu widows to remarry, a major violation of traditional belief. What the British viewed as social reform spurred Indian unrest and provided causes to sustain a rebellion that led to a transfer of power from the British East India Company to the British Parliament.

From Company to Colony (1858–1947)

The change from company to colony came with the Sepoy Rebellion of 1857, when Indian sepoys (soldiers) were punished for not biting cartridges supplied with the new Enfield rifles, believing them to be greased with pig or beef lard and, therefore, unclean to both Hindus and Muslims. A full-scale war erupted between native Indian and British forces largely composed of loyal Indian troops, with the military superiority of the latter soon evident. When it was over, India became a British colony. Sixty thousand British troops were garrisoned on Indian soil, costing India one third to one half the country's total revenues annually. To reinforce security, the British established a system of railroads across the Subcontinent. The peasants, taxed more heavily than ever to pay the costs of military garrisons and railroads, were pushed deeper into debt. Bit by bit three factors overwhelmed the peasant farmers of South Asia: (1) rising taxes, (2) the commercialization of agriculture, and (3) a rapidly growing population.

New and heavier taxes pushed an already oppressed peasantry deeper into debt. Land prices rose steadily during the last half of the nineteenth century. In many areas, as prices rose, the traditional structure of South Asian villages was destroyed when cultivators lost their land.

By the 1920s, the rate of indebtedness of India was twenty-five times higher than property taxes, and one fourth of all taxpayers were landowning moneylenders. In these circumstances, few technical innovations were introduced into the wheat and rice fields of India, and the yields on crops remained substantially below those of Japan and China for example. What emerged was a society with a small, wealthy elite that drained produce from the poor and discouraged technical innovations to protect their own status. Even after independence, when the zamindari system was abolished, one fifth of the villagers in India and Bangladesh (then East Pakistan) owned no land, and a large number of cultivators owned less than an acre. In Pakistan, circumstances were much the same.

Paradoxically, agricultural acreage

The British ruled India for 200 years, co-opting local leaders and draining the peasantry through heavy taxes. This 1907 photograph honors His Highness, the Raj Sahib of Kutch, a region northwest of Bombay.

increased somewhat during this period, reflecting the continuing commercialization of agriculture in South Asia and an expansion of irrigation. In part, this happened because of the revolution in transportation. By 1880, there were 20,000 miles of surfaced roads in South Asia. Many of these roads fed into the rail system, carrying commercial crops from the agricultural hinterlands of the interior to the coastal ports of Karachi, Bombay, Madras, and Calcutta. The production of commodity crops, such as cotton, jute, coffee, tea, and indigo (until synthetic dyes were invented), increased proportionately.

The third factor underlying the impoverishment of the peasantry was population growth, which first became noticeable in rural South Asia in the late nineteenth century. Between 1872 and 1921, population increased from less than 250 million to 319 million despite several devastating famines. The immediate cause of famine was the failure of the monsoon rains, but commercialization of agriculture, which took land out of food production, aggravated the situation. Local famines were exacerbated by overall food shortages, high prices, and unemployment. But as rudimentary Western medicine and sanitation practices took hold, India's population began to grow steadily.

Remarkably, at the end of the nineteenth century, India was no more urbanized than a century earlier—scarcely more than one South Asian in ten was an urban resident. A principal reason for this was that British policies deliberately inhibited the development of Indian industry. South Asia retained its status as a producer of agricultural products for Britain. In the villages, population growth led to fragmentation of the land. Agricultural employment was parceled out among larger numbers of people without increasing production. Hunger became widespread.

Commercial and factory growth in the large seaports of Bombay, Mad-ras, and Calcutta converted these cities into metropolitan centers, but this growth was counterbalanced by cities in the interior that declined except for those located at railroad junctions or the capitals of princely states closely related to the British crown. At the outbreak of World War II, less than 2 million people in India were employed in factories. South Asia was poorly prepared to face the tasks of modernization that came with independence. Two centuries of British policies had left their mark on the culture and economy of both city and village in South Asia.

THE HUMAN GEOGRAPHY OF SOUTH ASIA

Within South Asia, one of the world's great civilizations has persisted for millennia, creating a distinctive human geography marked by a unity of culture and custom despite its welter of faiths, languages, and ethnic groups. Separated from the rest of the Asian landmass by mountains and oceans, South Asia has long been recognized as a discernible world culture region with a complex mosaic of subregions.

The political fortunes of the countries of South Asia—India, Pakistan, Bangladesh, Sri Lanka, Nepal, and Bhutan—largely rest on these relationships. Effective plans of resource utilization must be executed quickly if South Asia's immense population, nearly four times that of the United States, is to be fed. The success of modernization programs in every country rests on building a more productive agriculture. A primary goal is to improve the lives of farmers, who comprise over 70 percent of the region's population. The well-being of one fifth of humanity depends on accomplishing a productive and stable balance between the populations and environments of South Asia.

This section focuses on the contemporary human geography of the South Asian Subcontinent. Varied in topography, its *Environments and Landscapes* are principally differentiated on the basis of climate and particularly on the availability of water from the summer monsoon. Only recently exploited intensively, the agricultural land of South Asia is subject to higher population pressure now than at any time in the past. This pressure, however, varies considerably among the three major geographical divisions of South Asia. Along *The Himalayan Frontier* in the north, rainfall is plentiful and rugged terrain is the most important environmental constraint on dense settlement. By contrast, the fertile lowlands of *The Indo-Gangetic Plains* form the economic and social heartlands of Pakistan, India, and Bangladesh. South and east of these lowlands, the **dissected hills,** plateaus, and coastal plains of *Peninsular India* are marked by a bewildering diversity of climates, landscapes, and cultures. But the overriding theme of *Man and Nature in South Asia* is based on longstanding Hindu and Buddhist beliefs in harmony between people and their environments. The environmental rhythm of rural life in South Asia, however, is dominated by the summer monsoon, which governs landscape and behavior throughout most of this region.

Environments and Landscapes

South Asia is a huge world region roughly half the size of the United States (Fig. 10.4). Its frontiers span thousands of miles of harsh and rugged terrain. Deserts surround South Asia on the west, the forbidding heights of the Himalayas define it on the north, and the tropical mountains of Burma delimit South Asia on the east. The southern flanks of South Asia are bounded by oceans; 4000 miles of coastline runs along the Arabian Sea and the Bay of Bengal, arms

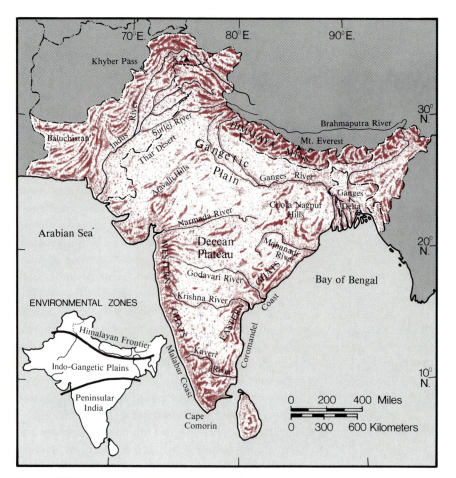

Figure 10.4 Physical features of South Asia.

of the Indian Ocean.

South Asia, often referred to as the Subcontinent by geographers, stretches 2000 miles east-west and 2000 miles north-south, culminating at Cape Comorin at the tip of India. Largely protected from the continental climatic extremes of Central Asia by mountain walls, most of South Asia is dry to humid-tropical in climate. However, more than half of the region's 1.07 billion people live north of the Tropic of Cancer, which is relatively far north for tropical environments to occur. The tropics extend north here by virtue of India's projected geography and the occurrence of the monsoon (Figs. 10.5–10.8). The seasonal nature of the monsoon is critical to the people's lives in these rural, peasant, and village-dominated countries.

Rainfall and Environmental Change

Rainfall varies from year to year in amount and intensity across the Subcontinent. In general, however, rainfall declines from east to west. This reflects the direction and declining strength of the summer monsoon as it pushes inland. Precipitation is reliable along the coasts of South India where air masses climbing the Eastern and Western Ghats spawn rainfall along the Coromandel and Malabar coasts. Similarly, the Bay of Bengal funnels air north and eastward across the delta of the Ganges and Brahmaputra rivers into Bengal. To the north, along the upper reaches of both the Ganges and the Indus rivers, streams cascade down from the mountains to provide plentiful water for irrigation. But in the in-

terior heartland of the Subcontinent, known as the Deccan Plateau, water is far less available. Savanna grasslands prevail over the dissected Chota Nagpur Hills in the northeast fringes of the Deccan Plateau, but these give way to more arid steppe climates in the interior. Far to the west, past the Aravalli Range, steppe gives way to the Thar Desert, which straddles the border between India and central Pakistan. Many soils of the Deccan are rich but lack adequate sources of irrigation water.

As South Asia came under British rule during the last two centuries, the natural environments and human landscapes of the region were transformed. In earlier times, much of South Asia was forested. Tribal farmers, fishers, and herders prevailed throughout the Himalayan arc and occupied a wide swath across eastern India, the northern Deccan Plateau, and the Western Ghats farther to the south. Rice was grown in Bengal, wheat in the Upper Ganges, and millet and sorghum on the Deccan Plateau. Pastoral herders exploited the dryland environments of what is now Pakistan. Hunting and herding usually supplemented the agricultural economy, with fishing important along major streams and in coastal waters.

After the onset of British rule, the area in forest was greatly reduced, double cropping of land increased, and village fields expanded to meet the environmental limits of peasant farming in the Subcontinent. The population was integrated into a national economy forged upon vaguely designed colonial needs. Held together under British rule until 1947, the diverse peoples of South Asia have rapidly intensified pressure on the resource base as their numbers have tripled in this century. The vast majority of this increase was absorbed in the more than 500,000 villages that dot the landscapes of the region.

Unlike China, the environmental problems of India were principally generated by the recent past. The colonial legacy of environmental change is a central theme of South Asia's human geography and a primary factor in the question of whether the 1.07 billion people of South Asia can lead adequate lives.

The Himalayan Frontier

The convex arc of the Himalaya Mountains forms a physical barrier on the northern frontier of India and Pakistan some 150 miles wide, 2000 miles long, and 4 miles high (Fig. 10.4). In the west, the Himalayas branch into the Karakoram and Hindu Kush ranges, an elevated country beyond the Indus River watershed. To the east, the Himalayas grade into the rain-forested hills of the Burmese borderlands. The Himalaya barrier, impressive as it is, is not impermeable. Narrow valleys in the northwest, such as the Khyber Pass set between Afghanistan and Pakistan, serve as gateways to the Subcontinent. These passes have historically channeled migrants and invaders down through the hills of the Punjab onto the plains of the Indus and Ganges. They still do.

Kashmir and Jammu: the Northwest

One of the few widely and densely settled areas of the Himalayan Frontier is Kashmir in the northwest. Kashmir, a former princely state in dispute between India and Pakistan since 1947, is mostly administered by India. The political situation is similar in the adjoining disputed territory of Jammu. Fertile lowlands at the foot of the Himalayas provide the setting for landscapes of startling beauty in Jammu and Kashmir, today focused on the Kashmiri capital city of Srinagar (pop. 500,000).

Central Himalayan Frontier

The central portion of the Himalayan Frontier is occupied by the countries of Nepal and Bhutan and the Indian state of Sikkim—landlocked, mountainous places that have served as refuge and buffer zone between the major powers, India and China, on either side of the Himalayas.

Nepal, with an area of 54,363 square miles and a population of 18.3 million, is a completely Himalayan country. Sheltered behind a curtain of wet and malarial forests on the Himalaya's lower slopes, Nepal never came under Muslim domination or the influence of Christian missionaries. Nepal remains a rich cultural mix of minority Buddhist hillfolk and majority Hindus originating from the crowded Gangetic plains. In the fertile Kathmandu Valley, southwest of Mount Everest, most likely the highest mountain in the world, population densities reach more than 2000 people per square mile. Harsh questions concerning the relationships among population, resources, and environment are posed in Nepal today. Rapid population growth has led to severe ecological pressures in many narrow Nepalese valleys. Strong population increases, deforestation, and even the pressures arising from mass tourism to the mountains have created an intertwined set of problems that threaten the health of the Nepalese environment.

Bhutan (pop. 1.5 million) and Sikkim (pop. 650,000) also occupy the Indian side of the roof of the world. Bhutan became a British colony late (1910) and gradually emerged as an independent state in 1971. Like their neighbors in Sikkim, the Buddhist Bhutanese are highland herders and farmers of rice, corn, wheat, and barley in neatly terraced mountain lowlands. Tiny (2744 square miles) Sikkim, however, voted to abolish its monarchy and ended its independent existence by merging with India in 1975.

Northeast Himalayan Frontier

The eastern reaches of the Himalayan frontier include the hills of the Indian territory (not yet a state) of Arunachal Pradesh, the Burma border ranges in the east, and the valley of the Brahmaputra River, the focus of Assam state. This region forms an eastern economic and political frontier of India today as it did throughout the colonial period. The entire territory of Arunachal Pradesh, mostly claimed by China, is occupied by less than 500,000 tribal peoples. Its difficult, elevated terrain, extremely wet climate, and thick forests have deterred most efforts at colonization. This remote area is the least developed in India.

Assam, lowlands wedged between the Himalayas to the north and the Burmese border ranges to the south, is rich in timber resources; the lower mountain slopes are planted in well-developed tea plantations. Rice and jute are grown in the lowlands by native Assamese, who feel a sense of jeopardy as they see the fringes of their lands settled by the far more numerous, land-poor Bengalis, primarily from Bangladesh to the south.

Finally, in the Burmese border ranges, three Indian states—Nagaland, Manipur, and Tripura—and the Indian territory of Mizoram complete the mountainous frontiers of the Subcontinent. Scores of Mongoloid tribal peoples, each with their own dialect, practice slash and burn agriculture in the rugged hills of these districts. The people of the Burmese border ranges have been strongly Christianized and represent the beginnings of distinctly different human regions to the north and south.

The Indo-Gangetic Plains

The plains of the Indus River of Pakistan and the Ganges river of India and Bangladesh form the heartland of the Subcontinent (Fig. 10.4). Both the Indus and Ganges river systems carry torrents of water down from the heights of the Himalayas. In the west, drainage from the Himalayas trends through the Punjab ("the five rivers"). From the Punjab, water flows southward nearly 2000 miles down the Indus River to the Arabian Sea. The Ganges flows eastward 1550 miles to the Bay of Bengal. Near the mouth of the Ganges, the Brahmaputra River joins its course to form the world's largest river delta in the watery lowlands of Bengal, today mostly within the country of Bangladesh.

Both river systems break down into a series of human regions. The Indus contains the Punjab and the Sind; the Ganges divides into the Upper, Middle, and Lower Ganges River plains, with the Lower Ganges given the name of its indigenous population, Bengal. These alluvial plains are each country's core of social, political, and economic development.

The Indus

The Indus River Valley was the easternmost of the three ancient arid zone riverine centers of civilization stretching to the Tigris-Euphrates and the Nile. Today, the Indus is the heartland of the Islamic Republic of Pakistan, to use the country's official name.

In its upper reaches, the river's tributaries flow across the plains of the Punjab at the foot of the Himalayas in both India and Pakistan. The Punjab, split between India and Pakistan upon independence from Britain in 1947, is a densely populated and fertile region. The Punjab is also home to the Sikhs, one of the Subcontinent's major religious minorities—also split between India and Pakistan.

The Punjabi environment is richly endowed for **perennially irrigated** grain agriculture in the flat, alluvial plains of the region. Canals here lace the fields and rivers of the Upper Indus. Wheat, cotton, and rice dominate the farms of this grain-exporting region. On both sides of the border, the Punjab's Sikhs have reached a degree of wealth as farmers and traders rarely attained elsewhere in the Subcontinent. Lahore (pop. 3

These yak herders of Nepal live high in the Himalayas, a mountain barrier that separates South Asia from the Eurasian landmass.

million), in Pakistan hard by the Indian border, is the major city of the Punjab. The new forward capital of Pakistan, named Islamabad ("city of Islam") (pop. 110,000), is strategically located in the Pakistani Punjab so as to make a political and geographic statement about the disposition of the disputed territories of Jammu and Kashmir to the north (Fig. 10.1). They have been claimed by both countries since independence but are administered by India. It is over these territories that India and Pakistan have twice gone to war since 1947.

The Punjab is clearly defined to the south, where dry environments deprived of the benefits of the monsoon grade into the Thar Desert. Efforts have been made, particularly in India, to extend the water resources of the Punjab southward into the drylands. The Rajasthan canal projects several hundred miles south and west into the heart of the Thar Desert. A line of cities from Delhi, India's capital (pop. 5.7 million) southward through Udaipur (pop. 230,000), to Ahmadabad (pop. 2 million) frames the edge of the drylands.

Southward in the Indus River watershed, the many tributaries of the Indus join to form the Indus proper in Central Pakistan. The climate becomes progressively drier and hotter downriver. In the south, the Indus widens and forms a second major agricultural region known as the Sind— the Indus delta lands. Traditionally focused on the Mogul fort-city of Hyderabad (pop. 800,000) at the head of the delta, the Sind's urban center of gravity shifted in the colonial period toward the port city of Karachi (pop. 5.1 million) on the Arabian Sea. The first capital of independent Pakistan, among the fastest growing large cities in the world, Karachi has become a major manufacturing center and the import-export focal point of Pakistan. The Sind, meanwhile, has seen its arable increase through large dams; the wheat, rice, cotton, and oilseed production of the region is vital to Pakistan's growing food and manufacturing economy.

In both the Sind and Punjab, however, problems of environmental deterioration and sheer human pressure on the land are becoming acute. In the piedmont of the Himalayas and the Karakoram Mountains, deforestation has accelerated erosion; erosion has accelerated problems of siltation downstream. As more intense populations attempt to heighten yields, problems of **waterlogging** and salinization grow in the Punjab and the Sind.

Pakistani Borderlands

Westward of the Indus River system, much of Pakistan is occupied by nomadic tribes who do not respect national frontiers. They herd sheep and goats over vast dry and upland ranges in Baluchistan, southwest Pakistan, and Iran. Along the Afghan border, the outliers of the Hindu Kush Mountains trend southward to form steep ramparts that gradually lower toward the south and west. Just west of Peshawar (pop. 2 million), the only city of note in Pakistan's northwest, the Khyber Pass is a strategic ravine leading into Afghanistan. The city of Quetta, at the northeast frontier of Baluchistan, now holding perhaps a million Afghan refugees, is similarly placed at the foot of mountain passes. Since the beginning of the Soviet occupation of Afghanistan in 1979, several million Afghans have sought safety by following the Khyber Pass into this country—Pakistan—whose resources are already stretched to the limit.

The Ganges

From the edge of the dry plains of the Punjab in the west to humid Bengal in the east, the 200-mile-wide Ganges Plain is densely settled, continuously cultivated, and highly productive. The principal divisions of the Ganges Plain—Upper, Middle, and Lower (Bengal)—reflect differences in rainfall and the resultant differences in human patterns on the land.

The Upper Ganges Plain extends over some 65,000 square miles eastward from the dry Delhi-Agra region. The terrain is flat and rainfall gradually increases to the east. Population densities are high; pressure on resources is intense. Farming methods are rudimentary; levels of poverty and debt are extreme. Cat-

tle, seen as wealth in Hindu India, are numerous. Irrigation is widely practiced as a hedge against the uncertain summer monsoon. Wheat is the primary food crop, and sugarcane is the principal commercial crop. No clear-cut boundary separates the wheat fields of the Upper Ganges from the rice lands of the Middle Ganges (Fig. 10.13).

Although the region is overwhelmingly rural, there are a number of important urban centers in the Upper Ganges Plain. On its western margins, the city of Delhi (pop. 5.7 million) is the third largest in India and the biggest inland city of the Subcontinent. Farther east on the Upper Ganges Plain, the traditional Hindu cities of Varanasi, or Benares (pop. 800,000) and Allahabad (pop. 650,000), the Mogul city of Agra (pop. 785,000), Kanpur (pop. 1.7 million), and Lucknow (pop. 1 million) are all important administrative and commercial centers.

The Middle Ganges Plain is comparable in area and terrain to the Upper Ganges. It is, however, more affected by the monsoon, and considerably wetter. Rainfall, 90 percent of it associated with the monsoon, rises from 40 inches per year on the western border of the region to more than 70 inches per year toward Bengal. Rice is grown on half of the estimated 20 million cultivated acres, followed by wheat, barley, sugarcane, and jute in the east (Fig. 10.13). The transition is gradual. As one moves down the Ganges, irrigation becomes less important, wheat fields are increasingly rare, and rice fields come to cover the landscape. Population densities are extremely high, averaging 1800 people per square mile in some districts. Food production has not kept pace with population growth in the Middle Ganges, creating strong deficits in grain production. The Middle Ganges is an area of bitter poverty, hunger, and malnutrition—it is among the least industrialized, least urbanized, and most densely populated regions of India.

The easternmost stretch of the Ganges Plain is its broad delta formed by the confluence of the Brahmaputra River. It is a flat, hot, and humid land. This is Bengal, a region home to several ancient Indian kingdoms, mostly Muslim in belief, and divided today between India and Bangladesh. Rainfall is heavy—ranging from 50 inches per year in western Bengal in India to over 200 inches a year in parts of Bangladesh, where the summer monsoon hits the coast early in June. Although monsoon rains cause frequent large-scale flooding, these rains are essential for the cultivation of rice and jute. Over 60 percent of the rich, alluvial land is cultivated. Of that total, four fifths is planted to rice, most of which is double cropped; a tenth is planted to jute. As in other parts of the Subcontinent, land is highly fragmented. The familiar Gangetic pattern of poverty and hunger caused by overpopulation is repeated in its clearest form in Bengal. Calcutta (pop. 9.2 million), India's largest city, serves this vast agricultural hinterland.

The new country of Bangladesh, centered on the delta of the Ganges and Brahmaputra, was established in 1971 as it, the former East Pakistan, broke away from the former Union of Pakistan. Bangladesh may well prove the least viable, most overpopulated country in the world. Most of the country's 109.5 million people are farmers working small holdings in an area equal in size to Illinois. Subject to strong typhoons and heavily dependent on international agencies for economic support, the future of Bangladesh is precarious.

Peninsular India

The Deccan Plateau, a broad triangle of forests, fields, scrub, and mountains, is separated from the Ganges Plain by the low, forested Vindhya Range on the north and west and the rough, dissected Chota Nagpur Plateau on the east (Fig. 10.4). On either side of the Deccan Plateau, two escarpments, the Western and Eastern Ghats (steps), rim the peninsula, separating the grassy scrub of much of the interior from the lush, tropical, heavily populated coasts of India.

The northern margin of the Deccan Plateau is a complex region of **scarped plateaus,** river valleys, and erosional plains. In the dry western state of Rajasthan, the majority of people are cultivators who fall back on herding when the monsoon fails. Where irrigation is possible, **jowar** (an Indian sorghum) and **bajra** (a local millet) are grown. In the eastern Vindhya Range, rainfall increases to 20 to 25 inches per year. Here, cultivation is more permanent, but bajra is still the predominant crop. On the eastern side of the Deccan frontier in Chota Nagpur, development of iron and coal fields, mica mines in Bihar state, and deposits of bauxite and gypsum have brought a moderate level of industrialization. But generally the north of the Deccan is among the poorest regions in India.

On the Deccan Plateau proper, a subhumid climate prevails, with rainfall exceeding 60 inches per year in parts of the northeast and falling to 20 to 30 inches per year in the drier south and west. Only the mountain rims of the plateau, the Western Ghats and Eastern Ghats, receive higher amounts of rainfall. The plateau is relatively sparsely populated and is a drought-prone land in which agriculture is dependent on the monsoon.

The heartland of the Deccan Plateau is a broad tableland formed by the Maharashtra Plateau, a heavily eroded, deforested zone of rich **volcanic soils.** In spite of low rainfall, it is relatively prosperous owing to concentration on commercial crops, especially cotton (Fig. 10.13). The principal food crop is jowar. Mechanized farming has been introduced on expanses of fertile volcanic soil, making the Deccan one of the better developed regions of India. Until the nineteenth century, the wet, forested highlands of the peninsula's tip

A variety of grains are cultivated on the Deccan Plateau where agriculture depends on the monsoon. Here, a village woman in Mysore is cleaning wheat by hand.

were the domain of tribal cultivators, herders, elephants, and rain forest, but the region now supports tea and coffee plantations. Offshore, the island nation of Sri Lanka (Ceylon) forms part of the Indian periphery, discussed at the end of this chapter.

The Deccan coastal littorals of India—the Malabar Coast on the west and the Coromandel Coast on the east—are well-watered, tropical environments, whose fertile soils make them productive agricultural regions. These southern coastal plains

are carpeted with rice fields. Rubber, tea, pepper, and coconut plantations dot the Western Ghats along the Malabar Coast. The largest city on either coast is Madras (pop. 4.3 million) on the eastern Coromandel Coast. Farther north along the Coromandel Coast, the climate becomes less tropical; rice remains the dominant crop. The east coast narrows in Orissa state and ultimately opens onto the delta lands of Bengal.

In the west, the Malabar Coast broadens northward into the plains of Gujarat state. Cotton is produced in large quantities. The long, straight western coast is dominated by the city of Bombay (pop. 8.3 million). Bombay, capital of Maharashtra state, is India's premier financial center, a focal point in the world's diamond trade, and India's major gateway for cotton and cotton textiles as well as the many products from Bombay's enlarging industrial base.

Man and Nature in South Asia

The landscapes of South Asia have been profoundly affected by Hindu and Buddhist religious beliefs concerning harmony with nature, beliefs that have subtly transformed the human topography of this region. Among Hindus and Buddhists, the doctrine of **ahimsa** dictates that people refrain from harming sentient creatures. This ethic takes concrete form in celebrations and rituals, in the preservation of wild creatures, in respect for the value of animal life, and until recently contributed to the perpetuation of forest and jungle environments.

Now villages and fields dominate the South Asian scene. The rapid increase in South Asia's population during the past 150 years has obliterated many natural landscapes of the past. Forests are being leveled for timber. In the Himalayas, there is little remaining forest below 9000 feet and the **tree line** ends at around 12,000 feet. Forests still exist in the northern Deccan, but observers believe that less than 100 million acres of timber exist in India, half the official estimate. People now take much longer to collect wood than they did a decade ago, and most villages must rely on cow dung for their energy needs. Partly for this reason, the tigers of Bengal and the elephants of Sri Lanka are reduced in number, and dense occupance by an agrarian society prevails across the region. Yet deep currents of religion and culture still bind South Asians to nature, a

fact that some Western observers often find disconcerting.

People, Land, and Cattle

In modern India, cow worship is one explicit expression of the Hindu concept of the oneness of human beings with other living creatures. According to Mahatma Gandhi, "the central

fact of Hinduism is cow protection," and this central fact has permeated the ecological relationships between people, land, and animals across the Subcontinent. The Hindu taboo against slaughtering and eating its 180 million cattle and 60 million water buffalo does deprive many Indians of much needed protein in their diets,

Cows wandering through the streets of Jaisaimer in northwestern India reflect the unique relationship between people and cattle in Hindu India.

GEOLAB

THE MONSOON

The dominant climatic force affecting South Asia is the monsoon, a word derived from the Arabic, meaning "season." Geographers define a monsoon as any air current blowing steadily from one direction for weeks or months. South Asia is affected by two monsoons: the wet summer monsoon, moving inland from the sea (Fig. 10.8); and the dry winter monsoon, flowing from land to sea (Fig. 10.6). The summer monsoon pushes warm, moist ocean air over the Subcontinent from June through September (Fig. 10.5). By contrast, the winter monsoon is a current of dry air moving across the continent producing little rain (Fig. 10.6).

Monsoons are most simply explained in terms of the more rapid heating of land surfaces as compared with water surfaces. When **solar radiation** increases in spring, this differential heating leads to the development of a **low pressure** area with warm buoyant air over the Indian subcontinent in summer and **higher pressure** areas of cool moist air over the Arabian Sea and the Bay of Bengal. The relatively cool air over the ocean collects moisture rapidly through evaporation and is drawn down the **pressure gradient** into the low pressure area over the Subcontinent (Fig. 10.7). Once over land, this monsoon air is warmed and rises, causing water vapor to condense and fall as rain. As this air rises, it intensifies the low pressure area, which, in turn, intensifies the monsoonal flow from sea to land. The area of maximum surface heating gradually moves inland because rainfall has cooled the land surfaces closer to the coast. Thus, on average, the monsoon rains lash the coasts of southern India and Bangladesh about the beginning of June, progress to the middle Ganges Valley by mid-June, and reach Pakistan by the beginning of July (Fig. 10.8).

During the winter season, a reverse flow of air is generated by high pressure over cooler land surfaces as compared with the warmer oceans nearby. Extremely cold, dry air flows out of Central Asia across this region, resulting in little rainfall in South Asia during the winter months.

This explanation of the monsoon circulation of South Asia based on thermal differences and pressure gradients is incomplete. As a result, space satellites and complex mathematical analogues have not been able to predict the precise timing, intensity,

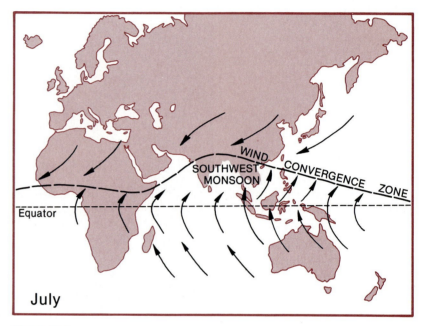

Figure 10.5

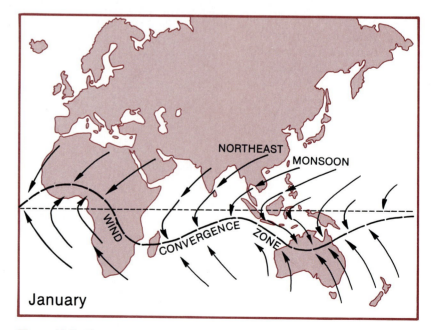

Figure 10.6 The winter monsoon in South Asia.

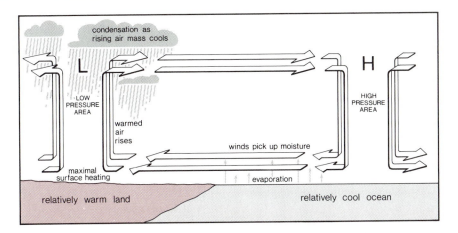

Figure 10.7

or duration of the monsoon. Currently, climatologists and physical geographers are examining the behavior of **jet streams,** great rivers of air in the upper atmosphere that guide storm tracks, as well as the overall **global heat balance** and detailed mechanisms of heat transfer between air masses to understand more fully the causal mechanisms that power the monsoon.

Adapted from: Peter J. Webster, "Monsoons," *Scientific American* (August 1981), pp. 109–118.

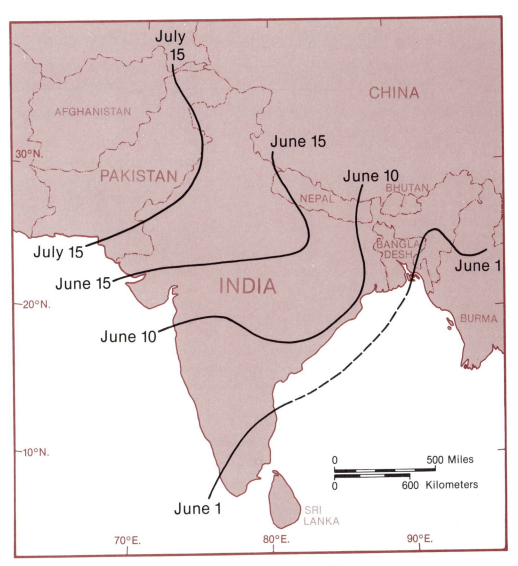

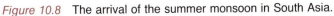
Figure 10.8   The arrival of the summer monsoon in South Asia.

although most cattle are eaten by Untouchables if the animals have died of natural causes. Many others are not particularly religious in this regard today. But thousands of cattle, many owned by urbanites, graze along highways and scavenge through the streets of India's largest cities. These cattle are, at the very least, a major traffic hazard. But some scholars have argued that the relationship between people and cattle in India is mutually beneficial; that the success of India's agriculture is intimately tied to the Hindu concept of cow protection.

Cattle are vital to food production in South Asia as plow animals. When the monsoon arrives, all farmers need plow animals at precisely the same time. Sowing must be done quickly during the first monsoon showers; harvesting, likewise, must be done by animal power when the grain matures. This leaves two thirds of India's rural households without a minimum plow team at critical points in the agricultural year.

To cope with this problem, rural India supports a dense population of cows to ensure the birth of vital draft animals. But farmers can provide little or no fodder for them because natural landscapes have been denuded by overgrazing. The resulting malnutrition of India's cows means that they breed irregularly. Large numbers of cows must be maintained to ensure an ongoing population of transport and plow animals.

A second contribution of cattle to the village economy is dung. Cattle scavenge for food, converting grain by-products and scrub vegetation into 800 million tons of dung annually. This is the principal source of cooking fuel and manure in India. Cows and buffalo are also India's primary milk producers. In addition, they produce hides to make leather products and bone for bonemeal fertilizer. The Indian use of the cow, therefore, seems well adapted to agriculture; removing the taboo against slaughtering and eating cattle, would significantly alter the ecology of Indian agriculture.

This rich and diversified cultural complex involving cattle and people in India cannot be adequately explained in practical terms alone. It has been generated by deeply held Hindu beliefs and practices, which take concrete form in the hundreds of cattle hospitals and rest homes for cows throughout India. This heritage complicates the task of development planners who are currently attempting to modify traditional cultures in South Asia to provide food to growing populations.

The Monsoon

The single most important environmental factor affecting food production in South Asia is the monsoon, a seasonal climatic factor that determines the availability of rainfall, the success of harvests, and the rhythm of the agricultural year (Figs. 10.5–10.8). In the summer, air masses from the southwest sweep over the Indian ocean and push inland across India carrying warm, moist air to the parched plains of the subcontinent (Fig. 10.5). This summer monsoon produces between 80 and 90 percent of India's total annual rainfall, which falls between June and September. In the winter, a reverse current of cool, dry air flows seaward off the Indian subcontinent inhibiting rainfall (Fig. 10.6).

Except where agricultural land is irrigated, summer monsoon rains are the lifeblood of agriculture. Good monsoons substantially increase harvests in Pakistan, India, Bangladesh, and Sri Lanka; poor monsoons lead to food shortages and purchases of expensive grain on world markets—not famine, as in earlier times. The climatic mechanisms that control these monsoon circulations are still poorly understood and accurately forecasting the arrival of the summer monsoon is not yet possible (Fig. 10.7). About once every three years, floods or droughts destroy crops in South Asia, making agriculture on the subcontinent a "gamble in the rains."

The timing of the summer monsoon and the amount of rainfall it produces is crucial to agriculturalists throughout South Asia (Fig. 10.8). Plowing and sowing of the principal wet season crop begins with the rains. If planting occurs too early, seeds wither in the fields. If too late, seedlings rot in waterlogged soils. If the monsoon is delayed or too little rain falls, the crops die before maturation. With too much rain, flooding can wipe out the entire year's crop and may destroy whole villages as well. The monsoon orchestrates the lives of Indian farmers.

Despite recent advances in irrigation, the use of fertilizers, and the introduction of high-yield grains, failure of the monsoon can leave parts of South Asia perilously close to famine. The good monsoon of 1981 meant that India's production of food grains was 20 percent higher than in 1980 when drought hit the subcontinent. In 1987, a bad monsoon severely affected production.

The arrival of the summer monsoon generates a spurt of frenetic activity in villages in South Asia. It is the single most important event affecting the agricultural year, the well-being of villagers, and the national economies of the states of South Asia. The seasonal linkage between climate and life is so intimate that much personal behavior is influenced by the monsoon in one way or another. The pace and purpose of village life is sharpened and focused by the meteorological calendar. Plans for economic growth and agricultural modernization—plans on which the future of the entire region rest—are successes or failures depending on the monsoon.

DIVERSITY, DEMOGRAPHY, AND DEVELOPMENT IN INDIA

In 1947, the new leaders of India inherited a legacy of British colonial rule and the sobering realities of the

Subcontinent's human geography. Their task was to transform the world's second most populous nation—361 million Indians in 1951 and 817 million in 1988—into a modernized state, to achieve Gandhi's poetic ambition of "wiping every tear from every eye." For the last 40 years, they have attacked this task, but four major problems have persistently thwarted their drive for human and economic development.

First, divisive religious, language, and caste loyalties create tension between national unity and regional cultures. Although South Asia was subdivided into two countries, Muslim Pakistan and primarily Hindu though secular India, *The Struggle for National Unity* is still central to the South Asian scene. The transition from the "eternal India" of caste and community to a modern state has been slow and halting, and cultural diversity remains a problem to national unity in India and the other states of the region. Second, growing population and low agricultural productivity mean that India faces the continuing issue of *Population and Food.* After decades of food imports to ward off famine, the institution of birth control programs, and some agricultural modernization, India has achieved self-sufficiency in food grains. But rural poverty still prevails in many regions. Raising agricultural productivity and reducing the rate of population growth is basic to India's future. Third, poverty in the countryside combined with better living conditions in the cities is now swelling the population of *Urban India.* Unless *The Industrial Economy* of India can expand to provide productive jobs for new urbanites, the goals Indians have set for their country may be impossible to achieve.

The Struggle for National Unity

India achieved independence from Britain in 1947. Overnight, India became the most culturally complex, diverse, and varied independent country in the world. The loyalties of most Indians are still defined by religion, language, caste, and tribe. This extraordinary mix of peoples, languages, and faiths created the richness of India's social fabric and generated its cultural energy. But it also threatened to split the Subcontinent asunder.

The most dramatic territorial division in South Asia came with the separation of Muslim Pakistan from predominantly Hindu India. But even after this division, the Indian government faced separatist movements based on language, faith, and tribe in many parts of their new country. Not that the new Union of Pakistan didn't face them too. These cultural differences persist today. Riots between Hindus and the 85 million Muslims resident in India are not uncommon. The Sikhs of Punjab have struggled for a realignment of Indian political geography. Dravidian-speakers in South India have yet to accept Hindi as a national language. Separatist movements draw wide support round the Subcontinent. The struggle for national unity is a primary task and ongoing process in modern India and on the Subcontinent in general.

South Asia Divided: India and Pakistan

In 1947, the British gave India its independence. Mahatma Gandhi and his fellow Indians had achieved their primary political goal: self-government. Independence celebrations were marred by riots between Hindus and Muslims in northern India. Lacking the order imposed by British rule, the Subcontinent divided along traditional religious lines, and this division created mass migrations and severe economic dislocations.

The Muslim-majority regions of the northwest (now Pakistan) and northeast (now Bangladesh) of British India became the geographically separated Union of Pakistan; the remainder, India. But the new borders left millions of Hindus and Muslims on the wrong side of their respective boundaries. Some 17 million people migrated—Hindus and Sikhs to India, Muslims to Pakistan. Hundreds of thousands died. Territorial conflict between India and Pakistan spurred two wars (1948 and 1965) over the disputed northwest. Another war in 1971 led to the independence of Bangladesh, formerly East Pakistan. Moreover, 85 million Muslims are still left in India.

The economic disruptions caused by the partition of British India were many. West Pakistan, a principal food-producing region of the Subcontinent, was separated from the iron and coal resources of India. The cotton fields of Sind and the jute-producing areas of Bengal belonged to Pakistan, yet the cotton mills and the jute factories were in India. Everything was divided between the two new states: criminals, mental patients, government supplies, and railroad cars. The underlying cultural and economic problems of the subcontinent were also shared: a rapidly expanding population, a slowly expanding and poorly exploited resource base, widespread poverty, and problems of local and regional separatism and isolation.

Unity and Diversity in India

Hinduism was a major common cultural denominator on the subcontinent, providing a unity of the spirit that transcended local distinctions. Within this unity, however, a variety of races, religions, and languages flourished, so that at independence, India embraced within its borders a greater array of cultures than ever existed in Europe.

India included approximately 600 princely states, some of them large enough to have their own postal systems and currencies. Almost all of these were quickly absorbed by the central government—New Delhi. Fourteen major languages and 1652 separate dialects were spoken on the subcontinent (Fig. 10.9). The largest language group (Hindi, Hindustani, and Urdu) accounted for 40 percent of the population. But these Indo-European languages were confined

LANGUAGES AND PEOPLES OF SOUTH ASIA

Language, a mirror of history, reflects past battles and conquests, migrations, and assimilation. Modern Indian languages express the historical experience of the subcontinent.

India was wholly inhabited by Dravidian-speaking peoples until about 1500 B.C. when Aryan nomads from Central Asia, speaking a variety of **Indo-European** languages, moved through the northern passes of the Himalayas onto the plains of India. Over the next 1000 years, the Dravidians were pushed southward onto the Deccan Plateau and down the coasts of peninsular India (Fig. 10.9). Four Dravidian languages are included among the fifteen recognized in the Indian constitution, and each is the principal language of a state: Telegu (Andhra Pradesh state), Tamil (Tamil Nadu state), Kannada (Karnataka state), and Malayalam (Kerala state).

North of the Dravidian speakers of

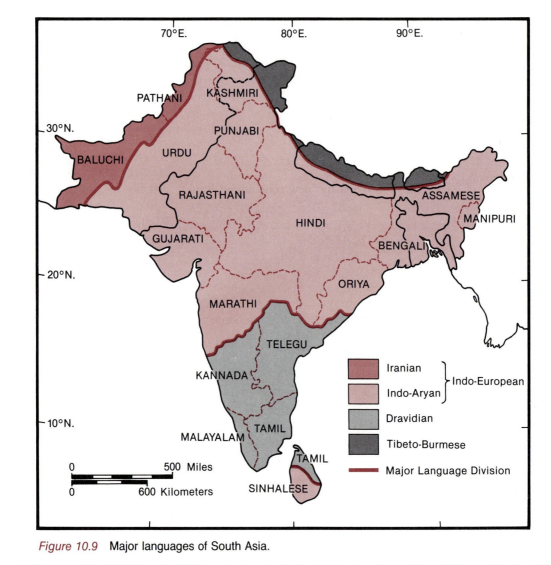

Figure 10.9 Major languages of South Asia.

mainly to north India. English remained important everywhere. Thus, the normal bases for communication and nationhood were weak. Welding a single nation out of these diverse peoples became a central goal of the new leaders of Indian society.

Indian leaders correctly perceived that strong linguistic and religious loyalties were one of the most dangerous legacies of the Indian past. What they feared was a **balkanization** of the country into a series of small religious and linguistic states whose ties to the national government at New Delhi would wither. Religious differences and linguistic rivalries could destroy the hope of a strong and unified twentieth-century India. India still experiences religious and linguistic riots each year. The state map

South India, languages belonging to the Indo-European family are spoken. Sanskrit, the oldest written Indo-European language, dates back to 500 B.C. in the Indo-Gangetic Plains. It has died out today, kept alive by scholars in the same fashion as Ancient Greek or Latin, and has often been cited as the progenitor of all Indo-European languages—from Hindi to English. All we really know is that it has survived longer than any other member of this vast language family. In the North, Hindi, Urdu, Bengali, Marathi, Gujarati, Bihari, and Rajasthani are the most widespread languages—but no language is truly national in scope. Hindi is spoken most widely, accounting for some 30 percent of the Indian population. It has played something of a national role, but is still largely restricted to north-central India. Languages on the Subcontinent are regional in nature.

Muslim Persians and Turks invaded northern India between the eighth and twelfth centuries. These conquerors developed a mixed language, Urdu, to communicate with the Indians. Although Urdu is an Indo-European language, Urdu borrows much vocabulary from non-Indo-European Arabic and Turkish, and is written in modified Persian script, which is itself modified Arabic script. Today, Urdu is the language of educated Muslims throughout North India and is the official language of Pakistan.

Brought to India by the British in the 1600s, English is spoken by a small percentage of India's population, but it is spoken widely by India's educated elite. English is spoken by the groups that run the country's government and economy. Considered an **introduced language,** English, the by-product of colonialism, is the lingua franca of the Subcontinent today.

of India continues to adjust to these differences and their articulation in the national scene.

Lacking a single national language, local languages have been a serious threat to national cohesion in India. During their long struggle against

British rule, Indians had used English as their means of communication, their **lingua franca.**

At Independence it was thought that India needed a national language because continued use of English would widen the gap between the country's well-educated politicians and its people. Mahatma Gandhi, himself a native speaker of Gujarati, sponsored the North Indian language of Hindustani, understood by both Hindi and Urdu speakers. With its related languages, Hindustani was spoken by about 40 percent of the Indian population. The constitutional selection of Hindi was very unpopular among the Dravidian-speaking peoples of the South and also among speakers of Bengali and Marathi whose languages had richer literatures.

When the new constitution went into effect in 1950, the North Indian language of Hindi was designated as the "official language of the Union." In addition to Hindi, the constitution recognized thirteen other "languages of India"—Urdu, Punjabi, Telegu, Bengali, Marathi, Tamil, Gujarati, Kannada, Malayalam, Oriya, Assamese, Kashmiri, and Sanskrit (Fig. 10.9). English, spoken by about 1 percent of the population, would continue to be used until 1965 for "official purposes."

But the issue was highly charged with emotion. The Telegu-speaking population of Madras state, resentful of the dominance of Tamil-speaking bureaucrats in the province, demanded the establishment of a separate language-based state to be called Andhra Pradesh. After hunger strikes, the central government acquiesced to local demands, and the new Telegu-speaking state was created in 1953.

Three years later, the language commission recommended a spatial reorganization of India into fourteen states and six territories, recognizing "linguistic homogeneity as an important factor conducive to administrative convenience and efficiency." In

Mahatma Gandhi led India to independence from British rule. He is shown here attending an independence meeting; note the pocket watch hanging from his waist.

1960, Bombay state was subdivided into two new linguistic states, Gujarat and Maharashtra. That same year, the fiercely individualistic and militant Sikh community began to press the government for a Punjabi-speaking state. In 1966, the old state of Punjab was subdivided, ostensibly on linguistic grounds, into a new Sikh-dominated Punjab and Hindu-majority, Hindi-speaking state of Haryana.

The Sikhs of the Punjab belong to a casteless religion that combines elements of Hinduism and Islam. Sikh religion emerged in the Punjab at the end of the 1400s from monotheistic teachings that stress religious tolerance and a code of behavior that, among other things, prohibits men from cutting their hair. Male Sikhs, all given the name Singh ("lion"), are thus readily recognizable by their turbans and closely rolled beards and hair. They have migrated widely throughout the Western world in search of education and commercial opportunities. In the Subcontinent, they are industrious people who form a merchant class virtually everywhere, and at home in the Punjab,

Sikh demands for an independent state in the Punjab have sparked bloody confrontations between Sikhs and Hindus. This religious gathering of Sikhs inside the Golden Temple of Amritsar took place shortly after government troops stormed this holy shrine and killed Sikh extremists.

they are responsible for making India and Pakistan self-sufficient in wheat. Sikhs account for about 15 percent of the Indian Army and a comparable number of the country's civil servants. Many are doctors, lawyers, engineers, and scientists. The Sikh population of India numbers only 15 million, however—less than two percent of India's population. They are a bare majority in their native Punjab. When the Punjab was split between India and Pakistan upon independence, many of the Sikhs of India suddenly found themselves landless. The creation of a separate Indian state of Punjab has not been enough to quell Sikh unrest in recent years. Sikh demands for autonomy or even independence as a new state ("Khalistan") led to repression of Sikh extremists and the assassination of Prime Minister Indira Gandhi by her trusted Sikh bodyguards in 1984.

In Assam, protesters, fearful of cultural submergence by incoming immigrants, demanded the expulsion of all outsiders and stopped the flow of oil (30 percent of India's total) from the region in 1981, damaging the national economy for a few months.

Similar demands for regional autonomy in India came from certain of the tribal communities, who numbered some 30 million people concentrated in remote hill and forest areas on the Deccan Plateau and the Northeast. Leaders of the Congress Party (the dominant political party) granted tribes in the Chota Nagpur Hills a series of important concessions and temporarily averted the formation of a tribal state. In Nagaland, the demand for a separate state in the hills along the Assam-Burma border was met in 1963 when the state of Nagaland was created after years of rebellion by Naga tribesmen against Indian rule. Movements for tribal states are still strong in some tribal areas, and several have resulted in the creation of new states and centrally overseen union territories.

The formation of linguistic and tribal states in India, despite initial government opposition, has provided the geographical foundation for a fragmentation of the Indian union into subnational groupings, but the strength of these forces is difficult to ascertain. In part because of these pressures, English has been retained

Villagers in the Assam Valley armed with spears and bows have fought to halt immigration into their region from other parts of India and neighboring Bangladesh.

as an "associate language" in India. This has delayed making Hindi mandatory in the South, where it is considered an alien language.

This compromise solution is an awkward attempt to resolve regional differences. In the end, the most significant factor in this conflict between local and federal power may be economic—the allocation of government development funds, particularly in depressed agricultural regions where linguistic and tribal dissent is strongest.

Population and Food

In the late 1950s, India's leaders claimed that Indians were born with "two hands capable of work and only one mouth to feed." They saw their principal task as one of economic development, and they underestimated the serious drain on resources that a burgeoning number of new births would require of their newly independent nation. By 1961, India's population had increased to 439 million. By 1983, it had grown an additional 60 percent to 730 million. There is little doubt that India's population will reach 850 million in the early 1990s. Indian planners have long recognized that population growth defeats their efforts to improve the lives of India's people. Planners stand alone.

Most of India's new people have been villagers who draw their sustenance from the land. Their agricultural tools are simple, their techniques traditional. In many parts of India, land remains in the hands of landlords, and crops depend heavily on the summer monsoon. Yields of wheat and rice—India's staple foods— are low. Food production has barely kept pace with population growth. Until the 1970s, India fought off famine through food imports and grants from international agencies. Gradually, however, modern agricultural elements have been introduced through the **Green Revolution**. Dams have been built to increase the area under irrigation and reduce the im-

Rural poverty, traditional agricultural techniques, and uncertain monsoons are at the root of India's crisis in agriculture. Here, women transplant rice seedlings by hand in a village in the Mahanadi River Basin in Orissa.

pact of bad monsoons on India's food supply.

In the 1980s, India has achieved self-sufficiency in basic grains, and population growth has steadied at a rate of 2.1 percent per year. But three quarters of India's people are still engaged in farming, average incomes hover around $250 per year, yields are still extremely low, diets are inadequate, and hunger prevails across wide regions of the Subcontinent.

A Growing Number of People

Death control was accepted quickly in India; birth control was not. Consequently, more babies survive and Indians have longer life expectancies—by 1988 an average age of 54. The population of India has grown from 278 million in 1933 to 817 million in 1988. Today, death rates have dropped dramatically, and the infant mortality rate, in particular, is in the process of rapid decline in India. The birth rate is in slower decline.

Before 1921, high death rates were caused by malaria, plague, influenza,

and famine; thereafter, these large-scale disasters were held in check by death control. Until the 1950s, India's population grew at the relatively modest rate of 1.0 to 1.25 percent each year, and in some decades it actually fell. But improved public health services have allowed the rate of growth to increase to 2.1 percent. Each month India's population increases by more than 1 million, each year by 14 million. At current rates, India's population will double in thirty years. **Demographers** project an Indian population of over 1 billion by the year A.D. 2000.

At independence in 1947, Gandhi believed that if "all labored for their bread and no more," the resources of India would provide "enough food and leisure for all." Few Indian leaders then recognized that population growth had to be checked if significant economic development were to occur on the Subcontinent. By the mid-1950s, the population issue had been recognized as an urgent problem. During the 1960s, birth control

---

MAPSCAN

MAPPING POPULATION

Several methods are utilized by cartographers to map the areal distribution and density of population. Among them, shaded isoline maps (used throughout this book), choropleth maps, and dot maps are the most common.

Shaded isoline maps (Fig. 10.10) are constructed with lines connecting points of equal value. In this case, these lines represent population density expressed in numbers of people per square mile. Note that unlike contour lines, these isolines connect points of symbolic (e.g., density) rather than actual (e.g., elevation) value: It is unlikely that any single square mile on the map has precisely the density of population indicated by the isoline symbol. But when used together isolines have the effect of demarcating areas of relatively similar levels of population density. The areal differences in relative population density are visually enhanced by shading the areas between lines with tones of different value or intensity. The selection of isolines and the class intervals between them is at the discretion of the cartographer and determines the

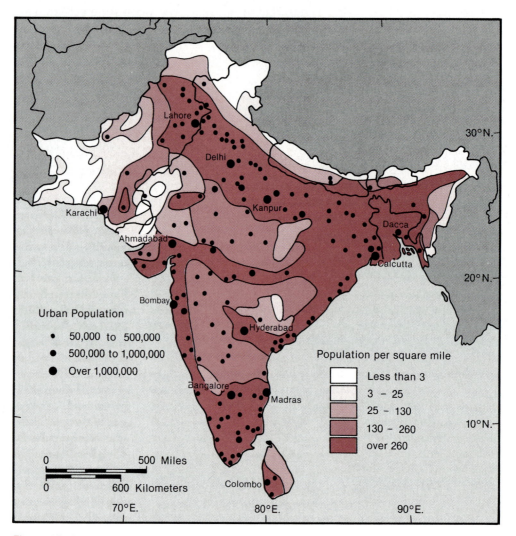

Figure 10.10   Shaded isoline map of the population of South Asia.

clinics were established in both urban and rural areas. But in the Indian context of more than a half-million villages, these efforts amounted to little more than pilot projects. When both the 1971 and 1981 censuses indicated that population had grown by 25 percent in each of the preceding decades, the cautious approach of Indian planners to birth control was abandoned. India, preceding China, was the first large Asian country to inaugurate serious efforts to reduce the number of births.

A national birth control program

spatial form of the distribution, the perception of population regions, and the appearance of the map. The major drawback of shaded isoline maps is that they may give the map reader the impression of a steplike rather than continuous distribution.

Choropleth maps (Fig. 10.11) are a second method used to portray density of population. Unlike shaded isoline maps, which delineate areas of

similar densities, choropleth maps use data-collection regions (here the states of India) and classify these regions according to their average population density. Once again, the class interval is chosen by the cartographer, and each region is assigned a value or intensity, depending on the system of classification. The boundaries of population regions on choropleth maps, however, are usually those of

political units; this intensifies the impression of a disjointed distribution because of sharp breaks in the overall pattern. One additional problem is that the choropleth technique assumes even population distribution within each collection region, and although this can be partially corrected, it further distorts the impression and appearance of the map.

Dot maps (Fig. 10.12), a third

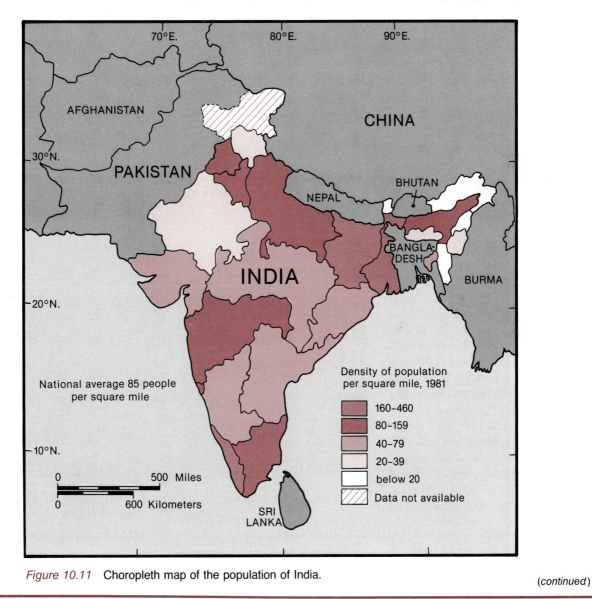

Figure 10.11 Choropleth map of the population of India.

(continued)

was mounted. Throughout India, posters with inverted red triangles flanked by a family of four carried the message, "Two children are respectable, three a menace." Billboards in-

structed Indians that "a small family is a happy family." In the 1970s, millions of men underwent voluntary sterilization at sites as varied as railroad stations and community devel-

opment offices. Enforced mass sterilization efforts in 1976 met with armed resistance by villagers. Now women are paid the equivalent of $22 for accepting sterilization, men $15.

MAPSCAN (*continued*)

method of presenting areal-population data, are constructed by assigning a specific value to each dot (in this case 100,000 people), dividing the total population by this value to determine the number of dots needed and, then, distributing the dots across the map. More dots are placed in areas of high population and fewer dots in areas of low population. In many ways, dot maps illustrate the spatial distribution of population more accurately than either shaded isoline or choropleth maps, but they have several drawbacks. First, the distribution of dots reflects the units of population data collection—in South Asia either districts or states—and can create sudden breaks across political boundaries. Second, dense concentrations of population in river valleys, such as the Brahmaputra of Assam, or in large cities, such as Calcutta, Madras, and Bombay, are distributed within the collection units, diluting their visual impact. Finally, the human eye tends to underestimate the level of concentration of the dots, distorting the map reader's perception of regional density. Finally, dot maps are difficult to construct, although in the hands of a skillful cartographer they can be quite effective.

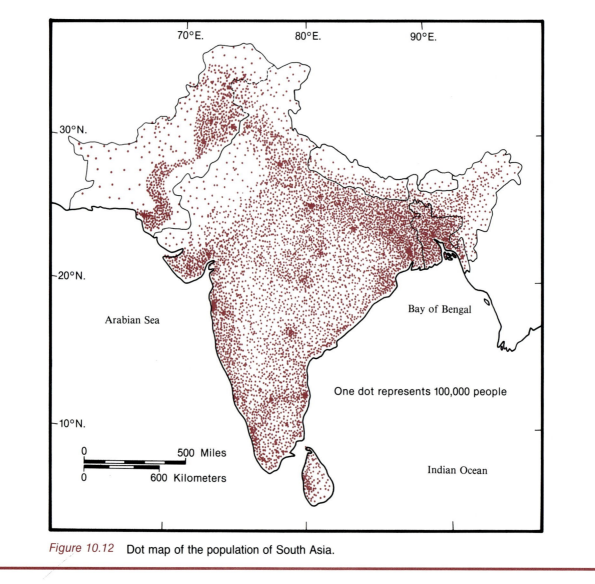

Figure 10.12 Dot map of the population of South Asia.

An estimated 20 to 30 million people have participated in India's birth control program.

These figures pale, however, in the face of the total population of India and a growth rate of more than 1 million a month (Fig. 10.10). Demographers now project a population over 1 billion for India by the year 2000. The rate of growth in the 1970s, 24.6 percent, was more than anticipated. It was the result of a continually lowered death rate rather than any significant increase in the birth rate. In fact, birth rates have gone down, but not as rapidly as have death rates.

On this scale, the Indian population requires an additional 1.5 million tons of food grain each year, 2.5 million new houses, and 4 million new jobs. Despite agricultural progress and a broad industrial base, the Indian economy has never operated at a level capable of sustaining such a rapidly growing population. In rural India, poor grain yields, rising production costs, and low grain prices have left villages with too little food, too many mouths to feed, rising food prices, and unemployment—in short, with a crisis in agriculture.

A Crisis in Agriculture

Few countries at their birth had such idealistic leadership as India. Its leaders were democratic socialists, whose goal was an "equitable distribution of the national wealth." Publicly they condemned caste and communal, linguistic, and provincial divisions—forces that fragmented national life. Privately, many vied for the votes of caste lobbies and language groupings. Throughout India, the elite developed a taste for pomp, ceremony and personal luxury. Nowhere was the discrepancy between oratory and reality more striking than in the half-million villages of India, where millions of small farmers and landless laborers existed on the fringes of starvation, many with per capita incomes of less than $60 per year.

To cope with rural poverty and insufficient food, the Indian government of Prime Minister Nehru proposed two policies: (1) the distribution of land to the peasants, raising agricultural productivity by giving the cultivator actual title to the land and thereby reducing high rents and peasant indebtedness; and (2) the growth of peasant productivity through technical assistance under community development programs. But the passage of laws to distribute land was left to the state assemblies, where landlord interests were strongly represented. India did not sufficiently change patterns of land ownership in its villages, and this failure

had an inhibiting effect on the community development program.

Under this program, which was begun to "improve all aspects of village life," the village was naively viewed in the new India as a vital repository of traditional Indian values. These villages, however, were less coherent social units than in the past; their unity had been broken by population growth and modern social values. Nonetheless, new schools, medical centers, and marketing facilities sprang up in villages across the Subcontinent. The program ignored the caste system, property rights, and village unemployment—three important realities in village India. A host of elements sponsoring rural change—land reform, tractors, new types of seed, and cooperative markets—found their way into villages in every region of India. But the basic reform needed, a change in land-ownership patterns, was halfhearted. The market surplus of India's villages continued to be drained off by well-to-do farmers and landlords. Per capita agricultural productivity did not substantially increase, although per acre yields did increase.

This failure, however, was not immediately apparent to economic planners. Huge irrigation projects, like those constructed in the Damodar Valley west of Calcutta and on the Mahanadi River, brought 3.4 million acres of land into cultivation. Beneficial monsoons raised agricultural production and disguised deteriorating conditions in rural areas. Government planners believed that India's goal of self-sufficiency in food grains was within reach.

By the 1960s, however, rural India was hungry and food riots broke out in Calcutta. Low standards of living dipped to the point of starvation, and looting of grain stores occurred nationwide. Food shortages were officially attributed to hoarding by landlords and grain dealers. The real problems were population growth and rural stagnation. Indian planners tried to increase investment in agricul-

ture. Once again the goal was self-sufficiency in food grains; once again there was poor performance in the agricultural sector.

In 1965, the summer monsoon failed. The next year the country was 17 million tons short of grain. Indian politicians called on the elite to observe "supperless Mondays" to conserve food. Rationing was imposed. The United States sent 6 million tons of food. But rice yields continued to hover at the same levels recorded in the 1920s when India had half as many people to feed. In the villages, moneylenders still handled peasant loans and landlords still charged rents. Clearly, a new agricultural strategy was needed.

The Green Revolution

The strategy that the Indian government adopted was called the **Green Revolution.** Its goal was to make India self-sufficient in food grains by raising the total production of food in India. The attack was three pronged: (1) introduction of new seeds and modern agricultural techniques, (2) concentration of these improved inputs in irrigated areas, and (3) price incentives to encourage participation in the program. The new strategy focused on those regions best suited to modern agriculture, like the states of Punjab and Haryana in North India.

The key element in this increase in food production was the introduction of high-yielding strains of wheat and rice, seeds that were highly responsive to chemical fertilizers in areas with reliable water supplies. By 1970, the new "miracle wheats" contributed to a 52 percent increase in grain production and a 28 percent increase in productivity per acre. Although only one fifth of India's wheat fields was planted to these new varieties, the Green Revolution accounted for one third of India's wheat production.

The core area of this revolution was the Punjab, India's traditional breadbasket, where 80 percent of the land was devoted to "miracle wheats" (Fig. 10.13). A large number of deep wells

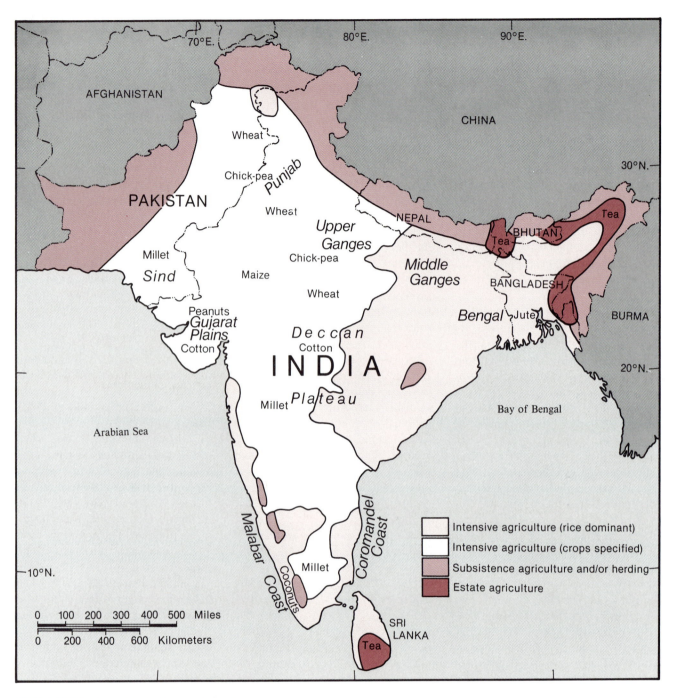

Figure 10.13 Agricultural regions of South Asia.

were drilled to provide water to these new wheat fields. The use of chemical fertilizers tripled. Pesticides were introduced. Wheat yields doubled overall and in some newly irrigated areas rose tenfold.

Progress was less striking in rice-producing areas despite significant yield increases in local districts along the Malabar and Coromandel coasts and in West Bengal (Fig. 10.13). The new varieties of rice were susceptible to damage by pests and diseases. Most rice farmers were unable to afford the chemical fertilizers or pesticides required by the new seeds and, unlike the Punjabi farmers, did not have sufficiently reliable irrigation and drainage facilities. High-yielding rices have been accepted principally in South India where plant diseases are less prevalent, fertilizers and pesticides are in greater use, water is available, and popular rice dishes are prepared with ground rice rather than whole grains—an important factor because the new rice varieties lump when cooked.

The breakthrough in food production made possible by the Green

Revolution averted widespread famine in India, but it is far from a full-fledged agrarian revolution. Only a minority of India's millions of peasant families have benefited from the introduction of the new wheat and rice crops. Because three quarters of India's agricultural land is not irrigated, this may remain true for the foreseeable future. The Green Revolution has created islands of agricultural prosperity in the bleak agrarian landscape of India's rural poverty. And these islands are now experiencing rising production costs due to increasing prices for pesticides, chemical fertilizers, and petroleum.

Indian Agriculture Today

The Green Revolution and gradual expansion in irrigated land have, however, enabled India to achieve its goal of self-sufficiency in food grains. For the last twenty years, food production has grown slightly faster than population. In the 1980s, therefore, famine no longer casts its shadow over the Indian countryside. But agricultural India still harbors a reservoir of poor, hungry farmers. In the villages, 120 million peasants are landless and an additional 240 million farmers work on patches of agricultural land of two acres or less. These two rural groups make up half the Indian population and form the bulk of the Indian poor.

In India, nearly three quarters of the population earn their living directly from the land, but agricultural products make up only 40 percent of the national wealth—a common structural condition in the Developing World. India's agricultural productivity (Green Revolution islands excepted) is exceedingly low. The country ranks thirty-fifth in the world in wheat yields per acre, thirty-eighth in rice, and forty-second in cotton. Although India has the largest acreage of sugarcane in the world, sugar yields are half those found elsewhere. Despite having an agricultural area one-third larger than that of China and a population one-fifth

INDIA'S PRODUCTION OF FOOD GRAINS

In the last twenty years, India's production of food grains has increased from 70 million to over 130 million tons of wheat and rice. During that same period, India's population grew by 291 million. Nonetheless, production has kept pace with population growth, so that levels of imported grain have steadily decreased and stockpiles against famine are available. The jagged curve of food production is graphic evidence of the impact of the monsoon on Indian agriculture.

Source: Government of India.

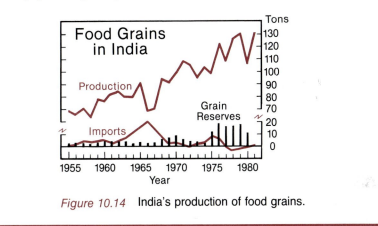

Figure 10.14   India's production of food grains.

smaller, most Indians still live with hunger, and government policies with respect to food supplies are highly controversial.

The highly efficient farmers of North India, who fully implemented the elements of the Green Revolution, have seen production costs rise three times faster than government agricultural subsidies. They demand higher prices for grain sold in the cities. Large landholders on the Deccan Plateau who have not introduced modern techniques have experienced a comparative gain because the wages for landless laborers have remained low. Still other Indian villages are awaiting their turn for agricultural assistance. With grain reserves estimated at anywhere from 10 million to 14 million tons, the Indian government has become a food exporter (Fig. 10.14).

The future of Indian agriculture is uncertain. India is the fourth largest producer of grain in the world. It has the largest potential for increases in agriculture of any major power. In-

dia, nevertheless, suffers an extremely low standard of living in its more than half-million villages. Grain self-sufficiency has left 300 million Indians without sufficient protein to lead healthy lives. State patronage affects almost every aspect of farming. Land reform has not been adequately implemented, and the level of investment in agriculture has never risen above a quarter of the Indian budget. Much agricultural land remains under the sway of large landowners. A few Indians have highly productive farms, but most villagers live marginal lives. The poorest of them all are little more than rural scavengers.

By most estimates, about half of India's population lives below the austerely defined poverty line—a mass of people larger than the population of Western Europe. With farmers demanding higher prices and urbanites resisting any increase in the cost of food, regional and social tensions are mounting. Despite impressive gains in food production, stockpiles of grain to prevent famine, and additional land available for irrigation, India remains one of the world's most inefficient farming nations and for that reason hunger is common.

Urban India

India has historically harbored two worlds: urban India, where political and economic power is concentrated, and rural India, where millions of peasants produce enough to feed themselves and city dwellers as well. As the gap in standards of living between urban and rural India has widened, villagers have moved to the country's large cities. The trickle of migrants in the 1950s and 1960s is now becoming a human flood. Expanding urbanization is swamping India's abilities to provide adequate employment, housing, and services to the growing populations of its largest cities.

The growth of urban centers in India has been slow compared with that in other regions of the Developing World (Table 10.1). Although poverty was widespread in rural India, ties to village, clan, caste, and family delayed migration to the city. The recent, sharp growth in the numbers of people moving to cities reflects the loosened hold of rural cultures on India's villagers.

In 1971, 20 percent of India's population lived in cities (Table 10.1). This figure increased to only 23 percent in 1983. But because the total population of India had risen to 730 million in 1983, 168 million people were classified as urban. In 1988, 25 percent of all Indians, more than 200 million people, live in cities.

Although contemporary Indian urban percentages are as low as those of the United States in 1850 and England in 1800, the total number of urbanites is growing twice as fast as India's population—an additional 55 million people in the last decade. India's difficulty in providing jobs for city dwellers is generating an urban crisis of major proportions in one of the world's most rural countries.

Urban growth in India has taken place in old settings. Calcutta (pop. 9.2 million) and Bombay (pop. 8.3 million) grew from trading ports of the British East India Company into major centers of Asian banking and trade. Calcutta served as a port for the agricultural produce of the Indo-Gangetic Plain, the jute production of Bengal and modern Bangladesh, the tea of Assam, and most recently the industrial production of Chota Nagpur. Bombay, the second leading manufacturing city in India, tapped the cotton production of the Deccan Plateau, the hydroelectric reserves of the Western Ghats, and capitalized on its western location (closer to Europe) to become a major center of

East-West commerce and banking. Delhi (pop. 5.7 million) and Madras (pop. 4.3 million) have maintained their roles as administrative and service centers. Cities grew despite government efforts to regulate growth by prohibiting unplanned accretion. This growth, in turn, has created massive contemporary problems of housing, transportation, and sanitation.

Cities with more than a million people—which include Calcutta, Bombay, Delhi, Madras, and seven other cities—have grown dramatically since the 1960s. The decade of the 1970s saw the population of Calcutta grow by 2.2 million, Bombay 3.3 million, Delhi 2.1 million, and Madras 1.8 million. With nearly a quarter of a million new people each year, urban conditions have deteriorated.

Rapid growth has generated slums, serious crowding, and almost unmanageable problems of public health and transport. The density of population in Calcutta averages 36,000 people per square mile and that of Madras 28,000, Bombay 24,000, and New Delhi 22,000 per square mile. In poorer sections of these cities, densities approach 500,000 per square mile. (By contrast, the far more vertical cities of New York and Chicago have average population densities of 24,000 and 16,000 per square mile, respectively). Within these Indian cities, dwellings are being added at a rate of 200,000 per year, but population increase demands a construction rate eight times higher. Immigrants from rural India pile up on the outskirts of these cities and in scattered open areas in shantytowns (**bustees**)—urban zones that lack rudimentary water, medical, or sewage facilities.

India's urban centers are unable to provide employment for this rising tide of citizens; even menial jobs are difficult to find. The invisible poverty of the countryside is now evident in every large Indian city. Unless Indian industry can generate jobs for

TABLE 10.1 URBAN INDIA, 1901–1983

Year	Total Population (millions)	Urban Population (millions)	Percentage Urban of Total Population
1901	236.3	25.7	10.9
1911	252.1	26.6	10.6
1921	251.4	28.6	11.4
1931	279.0	33.8	12.1
1941	318.7	44.3	13.9
1951	361.1	62.6	17.3
1961	439.2	78.8	18.0
1971	545.5	108.8	19.9
1981	688.6	163.2	23.7
1983	730.0	167.9	23.0

Source: Government of India.

CALCUTTA: THE CITY OF THE DREADFUL NIGHT

Nowhere are India's urban problems more pressing than in its largest city, Calcutta, where 9.2 million people are crowded into 490 square miles. Located on the wet, flat delta of the Ganges and Brahmaputra rivers, Calcutta is India's largest seaport and most productive manufacturing center. Its cosmopolitan population is drawn from virtually every region, religion, and language grouping on the subcontinent. Four Nobel prizes have been won by people living and working among the poor of Calcutta.

The central business district along the Hooghly River is so crowded that an estimated half-million pedestrians, an array of cows, and 40,000 vehicles cross the Howrah Bridge each day. Traffic jams choke movement; power blackouts are constant. Residential apartment complexes and slums surround the central city, and higher class suburbs lie to the south. Three quarters of the population live in overcrowded tenement districts. Many live in unbaked brick houses.

More than half the families in the city have only a single room to live in, with an average of 30 square feet of living space for every family member. A quarter of Calcutta's population live in shantytowns, locally known as bustees; thousands more live and sleep in railroad stations, temple grounds, and on sidewalks. An estimated 100,000 beggars live off refuse. In the slums, each water tap serves twenty-five to thirty people; each latrine serves some twenty people. Garbage is simply not collected.

In the bustee quarters of Calcutta, cholera and other waterborne diseases are endemic. The city has between 35,000 and 40,000 lepers in eight colonies around the city. Epidemics are frequent, disease is commonplace. Everywhere a formidable array of beggars, day laborers, and pieceworkers scour the streets. In the words of one writer, "Calcutta is like a stone astride my chest."

The problem in Calcutta is that industrialization is not proceeding rapidly enough to employ, house, and feed its growing population. Further, Calcutta's physical development has not been sufficient to cope with this rapid growth.

Before 1970, no new water supply had been provided in a century. The last major road was laid in 1930, the last major sewer line in 1896. One Indian poet describes the human despair: "Blind herds in the bazaar; Tin-roofed hovels, wormy lanes; Meshes of bones, pits of eyes; People rotting, unable to die."

One of every four people in Calcutta, India's largest city, live in slums (bustees). Thousands more live in the streets.

these people, the tensions of unemployment, appalling living conditions, and brutal poverty may ignite the misery that is compacted in India's largest cities.

The Industrial Economy

During the colonial period, the Indian Subcontinent produced goods for domestic consumption and for the markets of the British Empire. Principal exports were agricultural commodities, craft goods, and a few minerals. Imports were limited to small amounts of machine and manufactured goods, which left India with low rates of internal industrial growth. This colonial economic pattern ended with independence. Since then, India's leaders have attempted to create a diversified modern industrial state. India is no longer content merely to produce raw materials for the industrial West.

To accelerate industrial growth, sophisticated machinery and scarce raw materials for manufacturing were imported. Petroleum was purchased to sustain industrial growth, and fertilizers were bought to increase commercial agricultural production. In absolute terms, this policy had the desired effect. By the 1980s, the Indian industrial product had expanded six times since independence. In the context of India's economy, however, this rate of growth was too slow. No significant percentage of the population was able to shift from agriculture to industry.

Periodically, agricultural deficits forced India to import grain to avert famine. The high costs of petroleum shocked India into moving ahead with oil exploration, something delayed for years by bureaucratic red tape and distrust of foreign multinationals. Modern India does possess an integrated, if aging, national transportation system and the energy and mineral resources necessary to build a powerful industrial state. But low agricultural productivity slows industrial growth, and rising popula-

tion has retarded the modernization process. After thirty-five years of government economic planning, most Indians still rely directly on the land. Economically, India has been gaining ground too slowly.

The Resource Base

India has the potential energy sources to sustain rapid industrial growth but, with the exception of coal, these resources have remained largely undeveloped. Coal is the principal source of industrial energy in India. Annual coal production is over 100 million tons, making India the sixth leading producers in the world. Roughly one quarter of this output is used up by the railroads, a fifth by heavy industry, and the remainder for thermal electric generation and domestic consumption. Although coal reserves are scattered over many areas of the peninsula, mining is concentrated in the Chota Nagpur Hills where the Damodar fields yield 50 percent of the national output (Fig. 10.15). Most of India's coal reserves, however, are bituminous or lower grade coal. High-grade coking coal for steel production is in short supply.

Alternative sources of energy have great potential in India. Older petroleum production in Assam and Gujarat states traditionally amounted to one third of India's needs. In reaction to the rise in oil prices in 1973–1974, the Indian government opened large areas of exploration to multinational corporations. Major oil and gas discoveries were made off the coast of Bombay such that 70 percent of petroleum needs were met by domestic sources in 1985 (Fig. 10.15). Similarly, the hydroelectric potential of India is sizable, although this potential has been developed mainly along the Western and Eastern Ghats and in the Damodar Valley of Bihar and West Bengal states. India also has an abundance of resources that can be transformed into the raw materials of atomic energy. India has exploded a nuclear device, and six atomic power stations now produce 3 percent of the nation's energy.

India also has the resources to support a world-scale heavy industry. The largest reserves of high-grade iron ore in the world and substantial reserves of important alloy minerals are found on the subcontinent. The major iron-

The living conditions for the poor in Calcutta, like other fast-growing cities in the Developing World, are appalling. Slums ring the city.

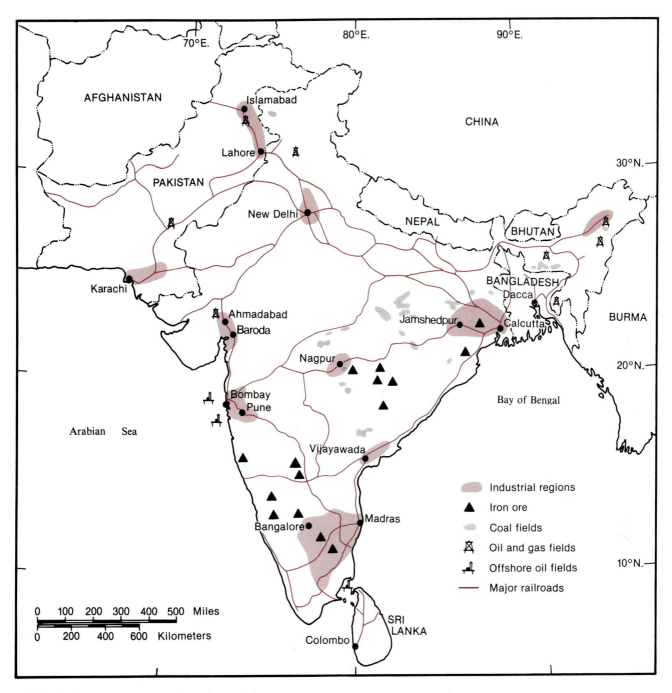

Figure 10.15 Economic patterns in South Asia.

producing area is in Bihar state where a range of iron some 40 miles in length is estimated to hold some 3 billion tons of exploitable ore. New iron fields in a number of regions are being developed for export purposes. Similarly, India is a world producer of manganese, and the fields in Orissa, Madhya Pradesh, Goa, and Karnataka produce over a million tons a year, 80 percent of which is exported.

Industrial Regions

Major industrial complexes in India are located near these energy and mineral resources as well as in the urban centers that expanded during the colonial period (Fig. 10.15). Around the nucleus of the steel city of Jamshedpur in the Chota Nagpur Hills of southern Bihar, India's largest heavy industry complex developed 150 miles west of the industrial port of Calcutta. Based on the rich coal and iron resources of West Bengal, Bihar, and Orissa states, Indian planners conceived of this region as an "Indian Ruhr." But production has been disappointing. India's steel production in 1983 was 10.1 million tons, a fourth that of China. Power failures, labor strikes, and costly transport has forced India, once self-sufficient in steel, to import substantial amounts.

Calcutta is the core of the largest manufacturing region of India. In earlier times, Calcutta was a jute-manufacturing center (rope, carpet backing, and burlap bags). Partition, however, separated the jute-producing areas of what was then East Pakistan (now Bangladesh) from the Calcutta factories. The city is now a diversified manufacturing center engaged in light industry, chemicals, engineering, agricultural processing, and cotton textiles. In this, Calcutta is similar to centers of Indian, manufacturing in the south and west, all of which are diversifying their industrial base and moving away from mercantile activity and textiles.

In the south, Bangalore (pop. 2 million) grew up as a cotton textile center in the hinterland of Madras (pop. 4.3 million), a port used by the British to export the products of the region. Cement plants, light industry, machine tool plants, and food-processing industries are changing the nature of Bangalore's economy. The two western manufacturing regions, Bombay and Ahmadabad-Vadodara (pop. 2 million) have had similar experiences. Both began as cotton textile centers; both diversified into other industries. With the offshore oil discoveries in the Arabian Sea, considerable expansion of the petrochemical industry is beginning.

The Slow Pace of Industrial Growth

It is clear that India possesses the manufacturing skills and the energy and mineral resources necessary for industrialization. The rate of industrial growth, however, has been far too slow to relieve endemic rural poverty. Through the Green Revolution and expanded irrigation agriculture, India is releasing workers from villages for urban jobs, but in-

dustrial jobs have not been forthcoming. In the 1980s, only 15 percent of all Indians are employed in handicraft industries and manufacturing, a figure that has remained relatively static since independence in 1947.

Slow industrial growth has meant few jobs for the rural poor who are now carrying their poverty to India's largest cities. The problems in industry are complex and interrelated. The coal industry needs more power to produce more coal; thermal electric plants need more coal to produce more power. Both industries need more efficient railroads, themselves badly in need of repair. The vast distances on the Subcontinent require efficient coordination on a national scale, but India's bureaucracy has failed to provide that coordination. Thus, strikes, power shortages, heavy investment in military hardware, deteriorating industrial plants and railroads, and endless debates among politicians and planners about the merits of public versus private enterprise have all contributed to industry's failure to keep pace with India's needs. Now launching a new program of industrial expansion and revitalization, the coming decade will clarify whether India's economic base can be organized sufficiently well to complete the process of economic modernization.

THE INDIAN SPHERE

Pakistan, Bangladesh, Sri Lanka, and the mountain kingdoms of Nepal and Bhutan ring the heartland of South Asia. Two of these countries—Pakistan and Bangladesh—are among the ten most populous nations in the world. Together, the people of the Indian sphere number 253 million, a population equivalent to that of the United States.

Each of these countries has a distinct and unique culture and society:

Pakistan and Bangladesh, formerly a single nation, share the Islamic faith; Sri Lanka is a country dominated by Buddhists, but with a substantial Hindu minority; Nepal and Bhutan have retained their separate societies in the fastness of the Himalaya Mountains. Yet each of these countries has felt the sheer mass and cultural weight of India and have participated in the heritage of South Asia. Moreover, all share with India the difficulties and frustrations of forging modern countries out of traditional societies influenced by two centuries of British rule.

The problems facing each of the countries in the Indian sphere differ in kind and intensity. In _Pakistan: Islamic Republic,_ the hostilities that ensued after partition from India, traditional agricultural utilization of the Indus Valley, and a limited industrial base have retarded modernization. In _Bangladesh: Population Pressure on the Land,_ the sheer number of agriculturalists attempting to survive on the fertile but disaster-prone delta of the Ganges is the central struggle. In _Sri Lanka: An Island Divided,_ efforts to diversify a colonial plantation economy are complicated by ethnic and religious differences that have rent the nation. All seek similar futures. All lie in the shadow of India, peripheral states on the flanks of their powerful South Asia neighbor.

Pakistan: Islamic Republic

In 1947, South Asia was partitioned on the basis of religion into two separate nations: Muslim Pakistan and primarily Hindu, but secular India. Muslim Pakistan was composed of two quite different core areas on either flank of India, separated by 1000 miles of Indian territory. West Pakistan is centered on the arid Indus Valley, which had been converted to Islam by invading Muslims in the 700s A.D. East Pakistan, occupying the heartland of Bengal, became independent Bangladesh in 1971. Bengal had become Muslim in the 1200s A.D., well before the Moguls spread their domain across the face of North India to the wet delta plains of Bengal.

At the time of independence in 1947, Muhammad Ali Jinnah, the principal Muslim spokesman for partition, envisioned two independent countries, different in faith but united in the purpose of building a progressive and prosperous South Asia. In his view, partition would reduce religious strife between Muslims and Hindus and eventually bring the two countries closer together. In fact, partition was bitter and bloody; Muslims and Hindus were driven farther apart. In its wake, two wars were fought between India and Pakistan over the disputed territories of Jammu and Kashmir on the northwestern edge of the Himalayan arc. After much bloody agitation for independence in East Pakistan, Indian troops invaded East Pakistan in 1971, precipitating the independence of Bangladesh. Today, large-scale arms buildups in South Asia underscore the persistent hostility between India and Pakistan.

Historically, what is now Pakistan was a zone of transition between the arid Muslim Middle East and Hindu-dominated South Asia. Culturally, religion is the principal unifying factor in Pakistan. Over 98 percent of the country's population are Muslims. An Islamic Republic, Pakistan's legal code is based on the Koran. Linguistically and ethnically, however, the country is diverse. The Baluchi and Pathan peoples in the rugged mountain regions on its western and northern frontiers speak languages related to Persian (Farsi). The official national language of Pakistan, Urdu, is spoken by less than a tenth of the population. Panjabi, the native tongue of more than half of all Pakistanis, is the most widely spoken language in the densely settled north; Sindhi predominates on the plains of the south. In part because of this cultural diversity born of location and history, orthodox Sunni Islam is basic to Pakistan's national identity.

A splendid synthesis of Muslim and Hindu culture was achieved during the Mogul period (1526–1857). It is apparent in the architecture of the buildings that line this street in Peshawar in northwest Pakistan.

The economic base of Pakistan is irrigated agriculture practiced on the fertile alluvial plains of the Indus River (Fig. 10.13). The Punjab and the Sind dominate the Pakistani regional scene. Over half the population are farmers.

Pakistani agriculture, however, has failed to keep pace with population growth, so that the country must now import food. Low productivity and yields, environmental abuse, and the use of traditional technologies has produced rural poverty in Pakistan, just as it has in India. Meanwhile, Pakistan's population has soared from 33 million in 1950 to 107.5 million people in 1988. At current growth rates, population will double in the next twenty-four years (see Geostatistics). Efforts at land distribution and reclamation in the 1970s were aborted by a military coup that erased a trend toward a more equitable distribution of income. Average GNP is below $400 per year, a fact that retards programs of economic development.

To absorb and support its rapidly growing population, Pakistan has launched programs of industrial development. The fifth five-year plan,

(1978–1983) which called for economic growth of over 7 percent per year, was fulfilled. Industrial and agricultural development has promise in Pakistan despite dire conditions at present.

Pakistan has no major deposit of iron or coal. Oil production in the northern fields near Rawalpindi is in decline, although promising new oil and gas finds are reported in Baluchistan and Sind. These may reduce the country's heavy dependence on imported oil (Fig. 10.15). The massive earth-filled Tarbela Dam on the Indus River north of Islamabad is Pakistan's primary source of hydroelectric power.

Despite this limited resource base, Pakistan has constructed at Karachi (pop. 5.1 million) a huge integrated steel mill based on imported coal and iron, a project that may in the long run prove costly, although it will reduce Pakistan's total reliance on imported steel. Meanwhile, the vital textile industry based on home-grown Indus Valley cotton has suffered from the continuing threat of government **nationalization** of the industry. Mills are now producing less efficiently because programs of modernization have been deferred. Overall, the economic future of Pakistan is uncertain. Many Pakistanis—particularly the educated—have sought employment abroad. Pakistani emigrants are numerous in Britain and North America. Many others have served overseas as migrant laborers in the oil-rich states of the Arabian Peninsula.

Despite a growing population, slow progress in agriculture, a limited resource base, and uncertainty in the industrial sector, gains in the standard of living have been made since independence. International aid from a wide variety of sources plays an important role in Pakistan. The political system, stifled by dictatorship since 1977, will face increasing pressure to admit more democratic forces. Afghan refugees and the war in Afghanistan generally have placed harsh burdens upon Pakistan. Whether these explosive forces can be contained will determine the future of the people of the Indus River Valley.

Bangladesh: Population Pressure on the Land

Bangladesh is the world's eighth most populous country, with some 109.5 million people living in an area no larger than the state of Illinois. Located on the fertile plain of the Ganges-Brahmaputra Delta, population densities on agricultural land in Bangladesh are double those in India. Only in the Chittagong Hills on its eastern border and along the flood-prone coast do population densities fall below 1000 people per square mile. In this densely crowded country, 80 percent of the population relies directly on agriculture. Agriculture provides half the country's budget and all its export earnings. Food production, however, has failed to keep pace with population growth. Excepting natural gas, Bangladesh has no important resource other than land. The search for offshore oil is in process. Muslim, Bengali-speaking

Bangladesh, a country less than 20 years old, is, except for Ethiopia, the poorest country on earth.

The land of Bangladesh, however, is fertile and well watered. Two thirds of Bangladesh is under cultivation (Fig. 10.13). Three crops of rice— the basic grain—are grown each year, and there is substantial room for increases in food production. These natural advantages, however, are counterbalanced by the country's vulnerability to the vagaries of the monsoon and to large-scale flooding associated with typhoons along the coast. Despite the advent of improved strains of rice, agricultural yields are extremely low. Grain production has increased at less than 2 percent a year since independence, while the rate of natural increase has hovered close to 3 percent per year. Malnutrition afflicts 60 percent of the population, and the average person has less to eat than twenty years ago. A country of farmers, Bangladesh is the world's largest importer of rice and biggest beneficiary of food aid. The United States has donated much food aid to Bangladesh in an effort to

avert famine. But Bangladesh has failed sufficiently to increase its own food production. The food it has received from overseas has been poorly managed.

Inexpensive food for city dwellers, particularly in the capital city of Dacca (pop. 2 million), has encouraged urbanization at the expense of the rural economy. City dwellers make up only 16 percent of the population, although urbanization is occurring so rapidly that Dacca is projected to grow to 11 million people in the next 15 years. Inexpensive food exacerbates the desperate living conditions in the country's villages. In these villages, half the people of Bangladesh are landless laborers. A quarter of the land is worked by sharecroppers. Plots of land are tiny, technology is limited, and per capita production is low. Yet land reform—an obvious remedy for rural poverty—has been blocked by the power of landowners, just as the provision of low-cost food to the cities has been maintained by middle-class urbanites.

These social inequities, common in many countries in the Developing

Large-scale floods often wash over the low-lying coastal plains and villages of Bangladesh, killing thousands of people.

World, are especially pressing in Bangladesh. It is a country on the edge of disaster. A drought or a flood-producing typhoon could create a famine comparable to that of 1974, when people died in the streets of Dacca for lack of food. Without any significant industry except jute processing, the fate of Bangladesh lies in its use of the land, and patterns of land use have resisted change. Given these conditions, its seems unlikely that the future of Bangladesh holds any more promise than its past.

Sri Lanka: An Island Divided

Sri Lanka (formerly Ceylon) is the third large country in the Indian sphere, a teardrop-shaped island some 20 miles off the coast of South India across the Palk Straight (Fig. 10.16). The island republic currently has a population of 16.6 million people crowded in an area slightly larger than West Virginia. Densities of population on agricultural land are 1500 people per square mile, lower than in Bangladesh, but higher than in either Pakistan or India. Economically, it shares with the other South Asian states the difficulties of feeding a growing agricultural population on a limited resource base while attempting to build a diversified economy. Culturally, Sri Lanka's distinctive Buddhist society faces severe problems of national integration due to migrations of Tamil-speaking Hindus from the Indian mainland.

Sometime in the distant past, an Indo-European people, the Sinhalese, migrated from northern India and took up residence in Sri Lanka. By the first millennium B.C., the Sinhalese established an advanced civilization based on irrigation of the subhumid northern half of the island. Maintaining close contacts with South India, the Buddhist culture and language of Sri Lanka were strongly influenced by periodic infusions of Dravidian-speaking Hindu Tamils. Political and economic competition kept the Sinhalese and Tamils apart.

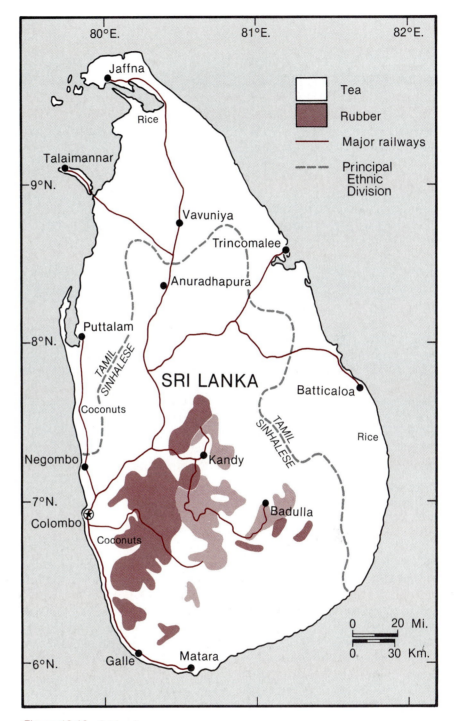

Figure 10.16 Sri Lanka.

Gradually the Hindu Tamils became dominant in Jaffna in the lowland north; the Sinhalese controlled the mountainous central and southern sections of Sri Lanka (Fig. 10.16). In the nineteenth century, the British imported more Tamils from South India to work on Sri Lankan tea and rubber plantations.

Today, sectarian violence between these two ethnic groups is a major social problem. The Sinhalese, who comprise 70 percent of the population, have resisted the demands of

In the 1800s, the British imported Tamil laborers from India to work on tea plantations like this one at Tandy in Sri Lanka. Conflict between Tamils and the majority Sinhalese erupted in the 1980s.

Tamils in the lowland north, some 1.5 million people, for a separate state. In addition, the government is systematically repatriating a large proportion of the "plantation" Tamils, more than a million strong, back to India. Civil war has broken out. The resulting social chaos is retarding the efforts of the Sinhalese to modernize the agricultural economy of the island.

This economy is closely tied to Sri Lanka's environment. The southwestern quadrant of the island, with its densely forested mountain core rising to peaks in excess of 8000 feet, is well watered and densely settled. In the nineteenth century, the British built roads into this wet forested zone and established a plantation economy in an area previously occupied by subsistence cultivators and cinnamon collectors. Gradually, tea and later rubber plantations were carved out of the forested slopes of this hilly region (Fig. 10.16). These two commercial crops became the mainstay of the economy of the country. After independence from Britain in 1948, these crops retained their importance in Sri Lanka's export economy, generating today some half of the national wealth. The capital city of Colombo (pop. 800,000) is the primary port and industrial city, serving this rich and productive hinterland.

Uncertain rainfall affects the lowland north and southeastern coast. In most years, rainfall is everywhere sufficient to support rice cultivation, but these regions are susceptible to periodic dry spells caused by the failure of the monsoon. Forced to import substantial quantities of food, the government of Sri Lanka has embarked on construction of large-scale irrigation facilities, focused particularly on a river diversion scheme on the Mahawali River, which flows to the east coast, to increase food production. The process of lowland agricultural settlement gained momentum after the near eradication of malaria, but the economy of Sri Lanka is still in difficulty.

The country has few mineral resources other than gemstones and is forced to import high-cost petroleum and food. Sri Lanka is now attempting to diversify its economy by establishing a light industry in the vicinity of Colombo and a free-trade zone in the city to attract commerce and achieve the higher standards of living found on island nations farther east, such as Hong Kong, Singapore, and Taiwan. Its standard of living has risen risen to become one of the highest on the Subcontinent. Yet the country has borrowed heavily in international money markets and is engaged in a civil war. With half its people in primary production, a population growing at a rate of a million every four years, and ethnic conflict splitting its society, Sri Lanka faces many difficulties. Sri Lanka may become, however, the first South Asian country to escape the classification of "poorest" in the roster of developing countries.

11

SOUTHEAST ASIA

Southeast Asia is a region of incredible cultural and environmental diversity. Perhaps no other world region contains such distinctive environments and peoples as does Southeast Asia.

The land area of Southeast Asia is roughly half that of the United States, a mere 3 percent of the land area of the globe. This area, however, stretches over vast seas. The distance from Burma on the west to the eastern rim of Indonesia is as great as that from Boston to Seattle. Southeast Asia's southernmost islands are as far from the mountain crests of the northern mainland as the Gulf of Mexico is from the Arctic Circle.

Geographic fragmentation in Southeast Asia is less a matter of scale and distance than of nature's design. Narrow river valleys on the mainland are set apart from one another by rugged highlands. The island archipelagos of Indonesia and the Philippines include upwards of 23,000 mountainous islands, only 3000 of which have names. A pivotal position astride world trade routes, Southeast Asia has historically been a zone of population movement, cultural convergence, and international conflict. But parts of this region remain as unaffected by historic and modern forces as any in the world.

Today, the ten states of Southeast Asia face problems similar to those in other parts of the Developing World. Centuries of colonial rule left much of the region politically and culturally divided. Most countries in the region have dual economies, with a modern sector providing minerals and agricultural raw materials to the Technological World, while an overwhelming majority of their people earn subsistence livings directly from the land. Although population pressure is less acute in Southeast Asia than in India and China, rural migration to the cities is beginning to swell these places.

In most of Southeast Asia's capitals, industrial jobs for growing populations are not available. Strategies for economic development vary from one country to another. But most states are handicapped by limited physical and human resources. There is strong reason to believe that some countries of Southeast Asia, racked by war, culturally divided, and politically unstable, will face difficulties in raising the standards of living of their people. Vietnam, Laos, and Kampuchea (Cambodia), are certainly in this category. Burma remains a virtual hermit in the world. Malaysia and Thailand, on the other hand, have made rapid strides in industrializing and improving the lot of their people. The city-state of Singapore is a rich mercantile enclave of global capitalism in Southeast Asia. By GNP, Brunei is the richest country in the world. Oil-rich Indonesia is a rural country with a rich cultural heritage and is a Third World demographic giant. The Philippines are closely tied to the United States by history and military commitments. Their people live between hope and the harsh realities of underdevelopment.

The picture, then, in Southeast Asia is very mixed. The future of the region is clearly tied to global politics and to the future of Asia more specifically. Taken as a whole, the region looms as a partner in development with Japan, China, Australia, and the United States. It is also a region focused on a great variety of traditional cultures. Bringing these cultures and their 433 million people into the present is Southeast Asia's great challenge.

SOUTHEAST ASIA: CROSSROADS OF CULTURE

Southeast Asia is accurately known as a crossroads of **culture**. Over the centuries, the mainland geography of Southeast Asia from Burma to Vietnam and the maritime realms of Malaysia, Indonesia, and the Phillippines became human watersheds (Fig. 11.1). Regions of different peoples who perhaps most differed in being either upland or lowland folk were repeated across the map of this highland-lowland, mainland-island region of the world. Each country contains a broad variety of people within its borders. They practice different religions, speak different languages, originate from different racial stocks, and are engaged in different ways of life. The native peoples of this region have been affected by each of the great civilizations to the north and west: first India, then China, and then Islam. In more recent eras, the impact of Europe, and even America, has been substantial.

This array of peoples and cultures

GEOSTATISTICS

	Capital	Area (square miles)	Population (millions)	Rate of Natural Increase (%)	Number of Years to Double Population	Population Projected for A.D. 2000	Infant Mortality Rate	Life Expectancy at Birth	Urban Population (%)	Per Capita GNP ($)	Energy Consumption per Capita (kg of oil equivalent)
Brunei	Bandar Seri Begawan	2,228	0.3	2.7	25	0.4	11	71	64	15,400	—
Burma	Rangoon	261,216	41.1	2.1	33	51.6	103	53	24	200	74
Indonesia	Jakarta	735,355	177.4	1.7	40	213.7	88	58	22	500	219
Kampuchea (Cambodia)	Phnom Penh	69,900	6.7	2.3	31	8.5	134	48	11	—	58
Laos	Vientiane	91,429	3.8	2.5	28	5.0	122	50	16	—	58
Malaysia	Kuala Lampur	127,317	17.0	2.4	28	20.9	30	67	35	1,850	826
Philippines	Manila	115,830	63.2	2.8	25	85.5	51	66	41	570	255
Singapore	Singapore	224	2.6	1.0	71	2.9	9	73	100	7,410	2,165
Thailand	Bangkok	198,456	54.7	2.1	33	66.4	52	64	17	810	343
Vietnam	Hanoi	127,243	65.2	2.6	27	86.0	53	63	19	—	76

Sources: World Population Data Sheet, 1988; World Development Report, 1987.

in Southeast Asia was fostered by four basic but crucial geographic factors. First, Southeast Asia is located in a transition zone between the civilizations of India and China. Thus, *Indian and Chinese Influence in Southeast Asia* has played an important role across most of the region. Second, Southeast Asia is positioned astride the maritime trade routes connecting the Indian and Pacific oceans. *Traders from the West: Muslims and Europeans* forged new spiritual and economic relations in Southeast Asia. Finally, *The Impact of European Colonialism* on Southeast Asia set in train movements that contributed to the present political complexion of

states in the region after *Independence in Southeast Asia.*

Indian and Chinese Influence in Southeast Asia

Southeast Asia entered world history as its people developed systems of agricultural village life early in the **Neolithic** era. Lowland cultivation of water chestnuts and beans dates back to 10,000 B.C. in Burma; indications are that the Southeast Asian bronze industry had begun by 3000 B.C. These developments are certainly as early as what was happening in the ancient Middle East.

By 3000 B.C., village-based agri-

cultural societies were on the march in mainland Southeast Asia, expanding in all directions. The inhabitants of Southeast Asia gradually developed preindustrial village societies based on the cultivation of tropical vegetables and fruit crops, such as yams, taro, breadfruit, bananas, and coconuts. They also kept domesticated pigs and chickens. By migration and diffusion, elements of this mainland Southeast Asian culture hearth, focused on the Mekong and other lowlands, spread eastward into the Pacific, north into China, and even west across India to southwest Asia and Africa. The wide dispersal, early occurrence, and economic signifi-

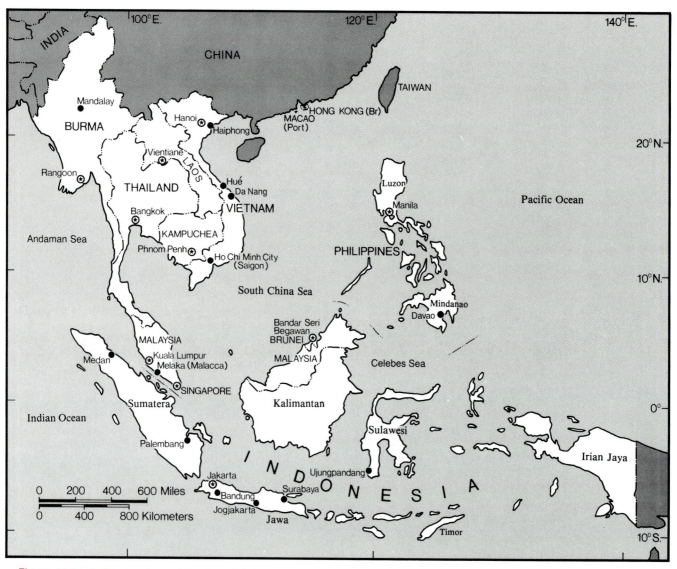

Figure 11.1 Political regions of Southeast Asia.

cance of these food sources prompted the American geographer Carl Sauer to speculate that Southeast Asia—not the Fertile Crescent—was the original hearth of plant and animal domestication.

The discovery of food production was achieved in Southeast Asia by complex stratified societies populated by people receptive to many innovations that diffused across Southeast Asia. By the first millenium B.C., dry and wet rice technologies existed throughout the region, although the development of agriculture in many of the outlying islands of the Philippines and Indo-

nesia occurred much later. Dry (nonirrigated) rice was grown on terraces throughout the upland river valleys. Irrigated rice augmented an ample subsistence economy based on orchards, gardens, fish raised in ponds, chickens, pigs, and dogs. In contrast, scattered groups of hunters and gatherers populated isolated regions, as they do even today.

What did not indigenously occur in Southeast Asia was the local development of primary urban centers and dependent peasantries—large city-states—as happened in other early centers of civilization. The food surplus for more intense human de-

velopment was available, however, when influences from India and China penetrated Southeast Asia and led to the establishment of organized states, beginning about 2000 years ago.

The Indian Influence

The most decisive cultural influence on Southeast Asia came from India. In the early centuries of the Christian era, a floodtide of Indian adventurers, teachers, and traders, bringing their Hindu and Buddhist values with them, moved eastward along the coast exploring the seaways between India and China. Indian trading outposts were established along the coast

Rice is the staple crop that historically has sustained the population of Southeast Asia.

of Burma, the length of the Malay Peninsula, at the Chao Phraya Delta in the Gulf of Thailand, near the mouth of the Mekong River, and on the east coast of Vietnam (Figs. 11.2 and 11.6). The diffusion of Indian culture in Southeast Asia was accomplished without substantial migration. Only small numbers of Indian Brahmans, Buddhist monks, merchants, and traders actually settled in the region.

Because the impact of India came by sea, the earliest Indianized kingdoms in Southeast Asia grew out of trading stations located on the sea routes to China—the goal of the Indian traders. Later, these coastal kingdoms were to shift to inland bases of power.

The states of Funan on the lower Mekong River and Champa on the Annam coast of central Vietnam were the earliest and largest Indian coastal centers on the mainland. Other early mainland states included the coastal kingdoms of the Mon people of Burma and Thailand, and the early interior

Khmer kingdom of Kampuchea. The Khmer built the world's largest religious structure, the temple complex known as the "Wat," at their capital, Angkor (Fig. 11.2).

In maritime Southeast Asia, Palembang on the island of Sumatera (Sumatra) was an early precursor to the great Indian-influenced trading empire of Srivijaya. Later, the Portuguese trading entrepôt of Melaka (Malacca) on the Malay Peninsula took over Srivijaya's role. All these states— maritime and mainland—had direct access to the sea and were located on river deltas with good harbors.

Through strong Indian influence in literature, art, architecture, and religion—Buddhism and Hinduism—these Southeast Asian kingdoms came to be ruled by kings who claimed to be divine within local interpretations of Hinduism. Their impressive palaces and cities were appropriate residences for divine royalty. They were tangible signs of the presence of the gods on earth. These mainland kingdoms and Sriv-

ijaya were supported by the cultivation of wet rice in low-lying delta plains, whereas other, still smaller maritime states relied more on trade for their livelihood.

On the mainland, in Thailand and Burma, the coastal kingdoms were conquered by larger, more highly organized states located in upland river valleys. This shift in gravity in medieval mainland Southeast Asia was caused by the infusion of new migrants from the north and supported by the more extensive land base from which inland states could draw their wealth.

The Mongol invasions of China in the 1200s and 1300s A.D. triggered a southward movement of tribal peoples. The Thai, among others, descended the valleys that crease the Southeast Asian mainland from north to south. They established inland kingdoms in rich agricultural river valleys and eventually subdued the coastal states (Fig. 11.2).

Dense populations were more easily supported in inland river valleys.

HISTORIC CULTURE CORES AND EXTERNAL INFLUENCES IN SOUTHEAST ASIA

Historically, three major cultures influenced Southeast Asia. Indian Hindu-Buddhist traditions penetrated much of mainland Southeast Asia as well as the early, influential centers of culture in Jawa and Sumatera. Chinese Confucian influence was confined to Vietnam. Later, Islam swept through the Indonesian archipelago, reaching its farthest extent in the southern Philippines where it abuts the Spanish Catholic area of those islands.

During this extended period, culture core religions developed in the river valleys and coastal plains of mainland Southeast Asia, on Jawa, and at strategic maritime locations on major sea routes. These core areas are the antecedents of modern Southeast Asian states.

Adapted from: Joseph E. Spencer and William L. Thomas, *Asia, East By South: A Cultural Geography,* 2nd ed. New York: Wiley, 1971, p. 347.

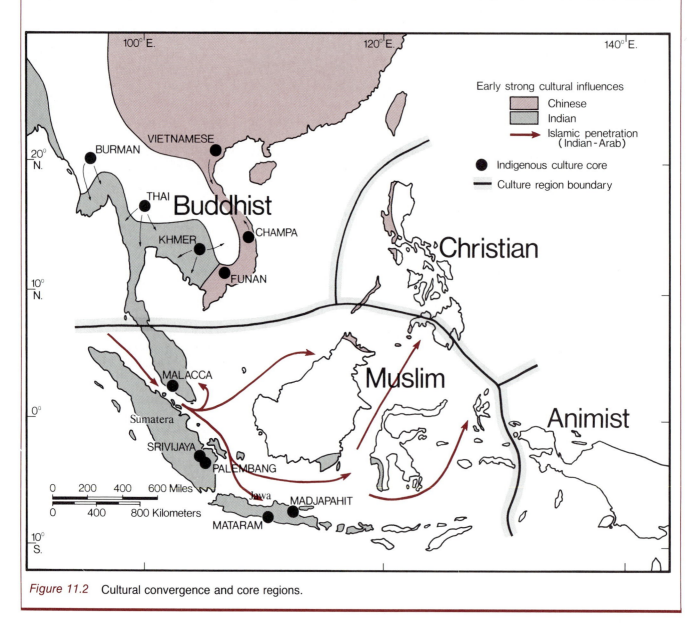

Figure 11.2 Cultural convergence and core regions.

Problems of water control were less difficult, vegetation was more easily cleared for irrigated cultivation, and natural hazards—drought, floods, and typhoons—were less severe inland than on the coast. By contrast, the low-lying, heavily forested, seasonally flooded mouths of the Irrawaddy, Chao Phraya, and Mekong rivers were much more difficult to bring under environmental control. Important kingdoms developed around the cores of these inland agricultural river states. Irrigated rice provided the staple food for dense populations and rivers provided the transport network to maintain territorial control. Except on Jawa, where the same spatial shift to an inland state (in this case, Madjapahit) occurred, maritime Southeast Asia did not give rise to large agrarian-based Indianized kingdoms. The supply of agricultural land was too limited.

Given the corrugated nature of Southeast Asia's topography, riverine compartments separated by uplands become the territorial basis of modern states. Historic Burma corresponds well with the Irrawaddy Valley, Thailand with the Chao Phraya River watershed. The narrow trough of the Salween River in eastern Burma, however, has a more rugged watershed, with limited interior lowlands. The Salween itself is not navigable. Occupied by Shan and Karen hill peoples, the Salween never emerged as a Southeast Asian culture core. The compartmentalized nature of the Mekong contributed to the establishment of two separate states along the river—Laos in the upper Mekong and Khmer in the Tonle Sap region downstream in the heartland of modern Kampuchea. These interior riverine kingdoms governed substantial populations from elaborate capital cities that were highly Indianized in culture, faith, and form.

The Chinese Periphery

Chinese influence in Southeast Asia was more limited than the Indian penetration of the region. The Chinese maintained maritime trade links with the Indian Ocean, and overland migration down the longitudinal valleys occurred sporadically. But Indian culture prevailed as the primary exterior force over most of Southeast Asia.

This, however, was not the case in Vietnam. The Annamese Cordillera, extending along the western border of Vietnam as far south as latitude 18° North, is as important a physical boundary as the Arakan Yoma, which

The main temple at Angkor Wat, built in the 12th century A.D., reflects the strong influence Indian traders and missionaries had on religion and culture in Southeast Asia.

separates Burma from Bengal. East of the Annamese Cordillera, Chinese influence was predominate.

On the plains of the Red River in the Tonkin region of northern Vietnam, the early independent kingdom of Nan Yüeh was absorbed into Imperial China for over a thousand years following conquest in 111 B.C. Chinese ideographic writing, Confucian thought, Chinese systems of political administration, and advanced methods of water control were adopted thoughout today's northern Vietnam, focused on the Red River Valley. Local languages remained important. The Red River Delta became the first coastal plain in Southeast Asia to be brought under effective irrigation control. Tonkin, as the region became known, was soon the most densely settled part of mainland Southeast Asia (Fig. 11.2).

When the Vietnamese regained their independence from the Chinese in A.D. 939, they thrust southward to conquer the coastal kingdom of Champa in Annam and later seized the mouth of the Mekong River from the inheritors of the Khmer. As they conquered territory, they spread their

blend of cultures over this large area. Chinese influence never erased Vietnamese identity; rather, it added more dimensions. Indeed, Vietnamese independence of Chinese rule is a persistent theme in the history of Vietnam. Elsewhere in the region, Chinese culture generally had little permanent impact, although Chinese merchants and seafarers moved throughout the area. Many of the coastal cities of Southeast Asia, however, came to harbor large Chinese mercantile populations—as they still do.

Traders from the West: Muslims and Europeans

Like the Indians and the Chinese, Muslims and Christians were drawn to maritime Southeast Asia by trade. The region lies athwart the major sea passages between the Indian Ocean and the Mediterranean Sea to the west, and China and Japan to the east. For some time, merchant ships had carried Venetian glass, Levantine wool, Damascus cloth and brasswork, and Indian textiles to Southeast Asia in exchange for gold, tin, ebony, teak, and ivory. With the collapse of overland trade routes through Central Asia as a result of Mongol expansion, this maritime trade increased substantially during the 1300s and 1400s. Southeast Asia itself was the principal source for spices sold in market in the Middle East and Europe. Pepper, cloves, nutmeg, and camphor were in great demand and of great value.

The Coming of Islam

In the fourteenth century, Muslim armies, which six centuries earlier had swept across the Middle East into northern India, conquered Gujarat, an important trading center on the west coast of India. Gujarati merchants, who acted as brokers in Southeast Asia's international trade and had long-established trading links throughout maritime Southeast Asia, converted to Islam. The trade routes between India and Southeast Asia became channels of the new religion as Gujarati merchants spread Islam throughout the Indonesian and Philippine archipelagos (Fig. 11.2). Early on, these Indian traders were responsible for the conversion to Islam of port cities on the Malay Peninsula, northern Sumatera, and northern Jawa.

Of these commercial centers, Melaka (Malacca)—founded in 1403 on the southwest coast of the Malay Peninsula—was by far the most important (Fig. 11.3). Sited on the Strait of Malacca at a **choke point** in the trade triangle linking China, Southeast Asia, and India, the city of Melaka rapidly became the most important entrepôt in the region. Chinese junks sailed southward on the winter monsoon to Melaka, found anchorage in the river mouth below the city, and exchanged goods there with Arabs and Indian traders arriving on the summer monsoon. The magnificent bazaar of Melaka, its warehouses filled with gold, tin, precious woods, and spices, became the commercial center of the richest seaport in Southeast Asia.

The Iberian Vanguard

Islamic control of the rich trade emporium of Melaka lasted only a century. In 1511, a heavily armed Portuguese fleet attacked and captured the city. For some time, Europeans had sought a direct sea route to Asia. Indeed, this search was a primary factor in Europe's "Age of Discovery." Centuries earlier, Marco Polo (1254–1324) had passed through the Strait of Malacca on his return from Cathay. He described Sri Lanka (Ceylon) as an island whose "treasure is beyond computation," where "all the spices in the world can be found." Somewhat later, Columbus led four voyages across the Atlantic to find a direct spice route; he died believing he had reached Asia.

Until the Portuguese took Melaka, spices reached the Mediterranean after a long sea voyage from Southeast Asia and a dangerous overland trek across Asia Minor. By the time they arrived in Venice, the cost of spices was so high that they were well beyond the means of all but the wealthy. Because Europeans ate no fresh meat during the winter months and salt-cured meat was more palatable when spices were added, whoever captured the Indies would garner great wealth.

This was the motive that propelled the Portuguese eastward and brought the Portuguese fleet with its vastly superior firepower to Melaka. As a Portuguese explorer noted, "whoever is lord of Malacca has his hand on the throat of Venice." Control of trade and markets, not political conquest, was the goal of the first Europeans involved in Southeast Asia (Fig. 11.3).

Once established at Melaka, the Portuguese attempted to gain control of the Maluku (Moluccas) Islands, then known as the Spice Islands (Fig. 11.6). The goal of Portuguese expansion was direct control over the primary source areas of pepper, nutmeg, cloves, and mace. A number of small islands at the eastern end of the Indonesian archipelago fell within Portuguese orbit during the sixteenth century, some

by capture, others by commercial treaties with local Muslim rulers. Later, they acquired Macao, a peninsula near Guangzhou (Canton). The Portuguese never did achieve their goal of a monopoly over the spice trade, but their profits nonetheless were enormous. The Portuguese retained control of the eastern end of the island of Timor (in modern Indonesia) until their colony was forcibly annexed in the 1970s. The Portuguese also retain the title of "Last European Imperial Power in Asia," as they will withdraw from Macao after the British relinquish control over Hong Kong in 1997.

The Portuguese soon had European competitors for this wealth. In 1521, the sole surviving ship of Magellan's voyage around Cape Horn landed in the Maluku Islands. The Spanish had opened up a new trans-Pacific route from Europe to Southeast Asia, thus challenging Portuguese domination over the spice trade. The Spanish were unsuccessful in dislodging the Portuguese from the Malukus, however, and moved northward into the Philippines, conquering the island of Cebu and establishing a fortress settlement at Manila in 1571. Manila soon became a large city, the Asian center of the Spanish trans-Pacific trade where the silver of Mexico and the silks and porcelains of China met.

The Philippines became the only area in Southeast Asia to have its culture profoundly altered by Europeans before the region fell under colonial rule in the nineteenth century (Fig. 11.2). The Philippines had been less influenced by India and China than other parts of Southeast Asia, so that no precolonial religious establishment blocked conversion to Christianity. Very quickly, the lowland and coastal people of the northern island of Luzon and neighboring islands adopted Spanish systems of administration, landholding, and religion. For the next three centuries, the Filipinos embroidered upon their Spanish colonial system, creating an

MELAKA (MALACCA): TRADE EMPORIUM OF THE EAST IN 1500

Trade in Southeast Asia remained much the same during the centuries preceding European colonization. The basic pattern was the exchange of cloth from India for the cloves, mace, nutmeg, pepper, precious woods, and gold of maritime Southeast Asia. China and Japan contributed silk, fabrics, pottery, and salt. Spices were the most important attraction to Indian, Arab, and European traders.

This trade flow, which revolved around the populous, rich and colorful trading port of Melaka in the year 1500, included a wide variety of imports and exports. From Arabia and India came rosewater, carpets, tapestries, incense, and seeds offered to Southeast Asian traders in return for camphor, tin, bird plumage, and batik as well as spices, precious woods, and gold. Indians, Arabs, Portuguese, and Dutch all attempted at one time or another to establish a trade monopoly in this region.

Adapted from: G. J. Missen. *Viewpoint on Indonesia: A Geographical Study.* Melbourne, Australia: Nelson, 1972, p. 112.

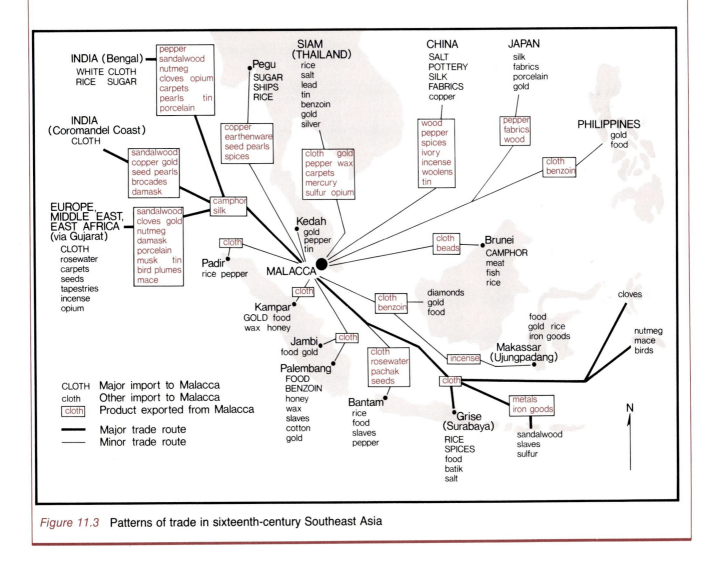

Figure 11.3 Patterns of trade in sixteenth-century Southeast Asia

outpost of Iberia in Southeast Asia that was ruled by New Spain in the Americas. Independence for the Philippines did not come with the independence of the New World. The United States conquered and paid for the Philippines after the Spanish-American War of 1898. The Philippines represent, then, a blending of Asian cultures, have a strong cultural overlay of Spanish and Roman Catholic influences, and show profound effects of their American stewardship earlier in this century.

The Dutch East India Company

Portuguese and Spanish interests in maritime Southeast Asia were soon challenged by the Dutch East India Company, a merchant company of private investors who sought wealth through trade with this world region. Dutch forces captured Melaka from the Portuguese in 1641, established their own trade center at Batavia (now Jakarta) on the north coast of Jawa, and were able to secure control over maritime trade in Southeast Asia for nearly two centuries. The Dutch called maritime Southeast Asia the "East Indies."

Like the Portuguese before them, the Dutch attempted to create a trade monopoly in maritime Southeast Asia and to control the region's most valuable export crops—spices. Initially, the Dutch were content to reap profits by transporting these goods in Dutch ships. Increasingly, however, they became involved in control over source areas of production as well as systems of marketing. This involved the Dutch in the economic life of maritime Southeast Asia to a far greater degree than in earlier periods, and set the Dutch in contrast to their mercantile predecessors.

The Dutch introduced new export crops, like coffee, into western Jawa and expanded the production of crops like sugar, indigo, tapioca, tobacco, the oil palm, and pepper. Cultivation of spices in the Maluku Islands was ruthlessly limited in order to control supply and maintain high prices. Small, semi-independent East Indian states were forced to pay tribute in coffee, which took good agricultural land out of food production. A dual economy, with a modern export sector and a traditional local food economy, was in the making. As Dutch territorial control increased, forced deliveries of cloves, nutmeg, coffee, pepper, and mace were imposed on local rulers.

Although the Dutch were hampered in implementing these policies by the rugged topography of the Indonesian archipelago and its far-flung dispersal of resources, this early colonial economy became more and more entrenched as time passed. Despite considerable regional variations, the Dutch began to develop Southeast Asia's commercial potential in the modern world—but not its people. The Colonial powers that followed the Dutch elsewhere in Southeast Asia pursued similar policies in the second half of the nineteenth century (Fig. 11.4).

The Impact of European Colonialism

As late as 1850, the European colonial presence in Southeast Asia was peripheral. True, the archipelagos of maritime Southeast Asia were under the direct rule of the Spanish in the Philippines and the Dutch in Indonesia. On the mainland, the British had made tentative inroads in Burma and secured their control over the three settlements of Penang, Melaka and, most important, Singapore on the Strait of Malacca during the 1830s. Here they established their colony known as the Straits Settlements, forerunner of modern Malaysia. But the remainder of mainland Southeast Asia was ruled by local kings and sultans. Even in the archipelagos, most villagers remained removed from external forces, labored at subsistence pursuits as they had for centuries, and seldom interacted directly with Europeans.

In the last half of the nineteenth century, however, the entire region, except modern Thailand, was subjugated by Europeans (Fig. 11.4). In this brief period, intensive colonial exploitation led to changes in the distribution of population, to the creation of colonial political compartments that emerged in the twentieth century as independent states, and to the restructuring of the economies of many areas in Southeast Asia.

Colonial Dominance

The final surge of European colonialism in Southeast Asia began in Burma in the 1850s. Here, the British, attracted by commercial opportunities and propelled by an exaggerated sense of national prestige, annexed coastal Burma and its hinterland. Three decades later, upper Burma was included in the British colony. On the Malay Peninsula, local Chinese aspirations for commercial expansion encouraged British political consolidation of the peninsula to exploit its tin resources. To these Malay territories were added Sarawak, the private kingdom of the British adventurer Sir James Brooke, and Sabah, the site of a British commercial venture—both located on the northern shores of the island of Kalimantan (Borneo). The sultanate of Brunei on the north Kalimantan coast was reduced to two separated slivers of land.

British expansion on the western mainland of Southeast Asia was paralleled by French domination in Vietnam, Laos, and Kampuchea (Cambodia), although the French conquest of this region, known as Indochina, met stiff resistance. French demands for commercial opportunities and diplomatic representation at the Vietnamese imperial capital of Hué led to a successful French attack on the port of Da Nang. Somewhat later, the French occupied the Mekong delta, the rice bowl of Vietnam, and the provincial town of Saigon (now Ho Chi Minh City).

Moving up the Mekong River in search of direct access to China, the French expanded their territorial control over Kampuchea. The discovery that the Mekong was not navigable in its upper reaches soon led to a French assault on the Red River Delta of northern Vietnam and the city of Hanoi. Ultimately, the Vietnamese imperial court at Hué was reduced to impotence. French officials conducted Vietnamese foreign affairs from Paris, disbanded all Vietnamese armed forces, and placed local leaders under strict French control.

Laos was added to the French do-

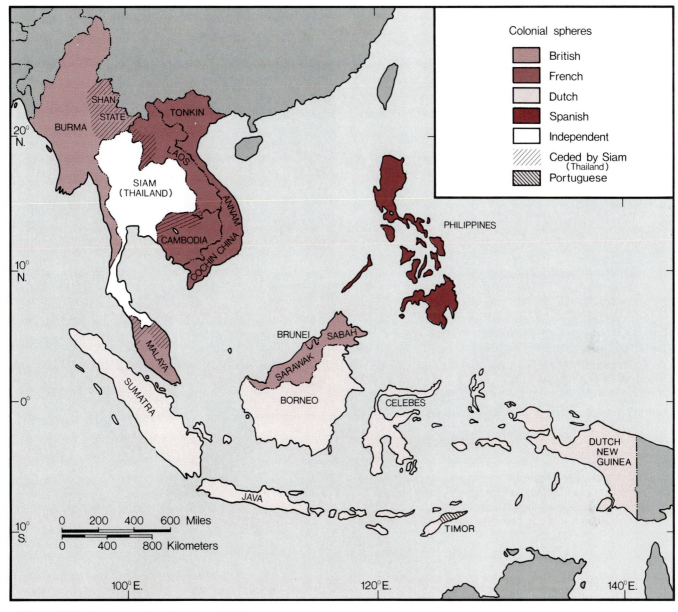

Figure 11.4 Colonial rule in Southeast Asia.

main as one of the territorial concessions forced on Thailand in return for its tenacious maintenance of independence. Thailand remained a buffer zone between the empires of the British and the French thoughout the colonial period, but it lost a land area on its borders roughly equal in size to the United Kingdom.

Economic Transformation

Colonial rule in Southeast Asia led to far-reaching changes in the economy and distribution of people throughout the region. Before 1850, European influence in Southeast Asia was primarily concentrated in scattered coastal areas and rarely extended very far into the interior. But the introduction of steam-powered ships and the opening of the Suez Canal in 1869 changed all that. The faster sea route opened up new economic frontiers. Rapid telegraph communications allowed greater inland control over colonial territories. These factors stimulated an expanding investment in the production of Southeast Asian raw materials for international markets. So, the European powers staked out claims to every square mile of the region, except for the residual buffer state of Thailand. For the first time, the lives of a large segment of the region's population were directly affected by European incentives and ambitions.

In a brief half century, European regimes shifted the center of gravity of power and population in Southeast Asia from the interior to the coast (Fig. 11.4). Invariably, the Europeans selected major ports as their capitals and principal economic centers. The city of Saigon expanded into a

Port cities grew rapidly in Southeast Asia during the Colonial period to facilitate trade between this country and Europe. Singapore, now an independent city-state at the tip of the Malay peninsula, is one of the busiest commercial centers in Southeast Asia.

Millions of acres of farmland is devoted to commercial crops in Southeast Asia. Here, terraced groves of clove trees form a backdrop for a vegetable field in Jawa, Indonesia.

major metropolis on the site of a small provincial town. Phnom Penh in Kampuchea and Rangoon in Burma grew out of villages. Kuala Lumpur in Malaysia started as a crude tin mining camp. Even in Thailand, which had eluded colonial rule, the port city of Bangkok grew into the country's largest urban center. In maritime Southeast Asia, Singapore, Batavia (Jakarta), and Manila became great cities where no earlier settlements had existed. Meanwhile, the inland culture cores of traditional kingdoms withered and their capitals—places like Hué, Mandalay, and Jogjakarta—faded into obscurity.

Railroads and roads radiated out from rapidly growing port capitals into the interior. Except for a few important mining areas, the principal scene of European economic development was along the coastal fringe. With new irrigation technology available, the huge deltas of the Irrawaddy, the Chao Phraya, and the Mekong rivers became irrigated granaries—vast mosaics of canalized rice fields that stretched from one horizon to another.

Elsewhere, cash crops were cultivated on a large scale and new mines were established. Under the Dutch, large acreages of raw land in Sumatera were planted to tobacco. In Jawa, coffee, tea and sugar predominated. Tin mines were opened on the islands of Bangka and Billiton off southeast Sumatera. Spice and tea cultivation expanded along the eastern rim of the island archipelago.

In the British-controlled Malay States, much of the virgin jungle on the west side of the peninsula was planted in rubber, a plant transported from Brazil to Kew Gardens (near London) by a young botanist and subsequently introduced into Southeast Asia. Giant dredges were also imported into the Malay States to mine tin more efficiently. In British Burma, rice fields covered the delta, and the petroleum and timber resources of the interior were tapped. In French Indochina, European-managed coffee, tea, and rubber estates produced crops for world markets and the coal resources of the north were mined. In the Philippines, export of sugar, tobacco, copra, and hemp continued to form the basis of the economy, as the islands passed from Spanish to American dominion in 1902.

Population Change

The rapid economic development of Southeast Asia as a world producer of rice, plantation crops, and minerals triggered internal population movements, population growth, and immigration throughout the region. People in the interior were rapidly drawn to the labor-poor plantations and rice lands on the coast, which had previously been covered by natural forests. Increasingly, they abandoned the self-sufficient subsistence economies that filled their needs in the past, and they became enmeshed in commercial economies producing goods for export to Europe.

As great tonnages of rubber, sugar, rice, tin, and oil began to flow westward through the Suez Canal, Southeast Asians were pushed into the world economy in new and powerful ways. By the 1930s, the region was producing better than 90 percent of the world's rubber, export rice, and quinine-rich cinchona; and more than 50 percent of all tin, palm oil, and copra exports.

Such large-scale production required political stability. The introduction of improved medical and sanitation practices into Southeast Asia plus stable colonial political systems and booming plantation economies, generated a regionwide population explosion. In little more than a century, Southeast Asia's population increased by a factor of six. Only the deep recesses of upper Burma, Laos, and the interior of Kalimantan were unaffected.

Despite strong demographic increase, large numbers of Chinese and Indian immigrants migrated to the region, attracted by jobs in new economic ventures. As their numbers swelled in the 1900s, these industrious outsiders became miners, merchants, artisans, craftspeople, and moneylenders—middle-class operatives interposed between the European colonialists and the local population. The continued presence of large numbers of Chinese and Indians in Southeast Asia remains an explosive problem in many countries today.

Independence in Southeast Asia

By the beginning of the twentieth century, nationalistic fervor was gaining momentum in Southeast Asia as discontent with European rule became widespread. The gap between the rich and the poor, between developed regions and backward regions, increased. Education contributed to higher levels of expectations. Attention focused on the growing disparity of life and livelihood in each European colony, as Southeast Asians began to aspire to greater control over their own destinies.

Conditions varied from one country to another, but World War II swept away the last obstacles to full independence in most of Southeast Asia. The Philippines gained independence in 1946, Burma in 1947, and Indonesia in 1949. The Federation of Malaya (including Singapore) gained independence in 1957. In 1965, Chinese-dominated Singapore withdrew from the Federation, which was expanded to include Sabah and Sarawak on northern Kalimantan and was renamed Malaysia.

In French Indochina, Laos and Kampuchea became independent states in 1949; after the defeat of French forces at the key outpost of Dien Bien Phu in 1954, Vietnam was divided into two countries, North Vietnam and South Vietnam. These were ultimately united by force in 1975 after three decades of guerrilla and civil war which ultimately involved the United States. The American Vietnam War, fought to maintain the non-communist government of South Vietnam, was the United States' longest war, escalating into a major conflict after 1964. In an effort to shore up a disorganized and corrupt series of regimes in Saigon against the determined North Vietnamese, 8.7 million Americans served in Vietnam, and 58,000 American lives were lost. In turn, the war left much of Vietnam—North and South—derelict and outside the world economy.

As in much of the Developing World, the achievement of political independence in Southeast Asia has not erased the legacy of colonial rule. Except in Malaysia and Vietnam, political boundaries remain those of the colonial period. New political regimes locked within these territorial compartments must assimilate divergent peoples into unified polities. Moreover, for the first time in centuries, no stabilizing Western colonial or military presence is present in Southeast Asia today.

In addition, the countries of contemporary Southeast Asia must deal with growing populations, rapid urbanization, and continued dependency on economies designed by former colonial rulers.

Raising standards of living is a primary goal in every country in Southeast Asia. Efforts are being made to diversify economies, increase literacy rates, improve health conditions, and achieve social and economic well-being. To accomplish these objectives in a region of great cultural diversity, rent by war, and in states designed in earlier times is a daunting task. It is the primary thrust behind modern Southeast Asia's changing human geography.

SOUTHEAST ASIA: CONTEMPORARY HUMAN GEOGRAPHY

At first glance, Southeast Asia's total population of 433 million people appears modest given the land resources of the region. Only one tenth of the total area in this region is cultivated. By comparison with China and India, Southeast Asia has large tracts of thinly peopled land that is potentially productive.

This apparent land surplus is deceptive, however, because the population of Southeast Asia is growing far more rapidly than cultivated land. In 1950, only 173 million people lived in all *Southeast Asian Environments*. At current rates of growth, Southeast Asia's present population of 433 million will nearly double to 720 million in 30 years. Already, migration from the countryside reflects mounting population pressure on the land base of Southeast Asia. As population continues to increase, the region's largest cities will have to accommodate a growing number of people (Fig. 11.5).

This process of population growth is occurring in a region where four of the five largest countries—Indonesia (pop. 177 million), Vietnam (pop. 65 million), Thailand (pop. 55 million), and Burma (pop. 41 million)—have over 75 percent of their people engaged in agriculture. The Philippines (pop. 63 million), the only other sizable country in the region, is 40 percent agricultural.

Regionwide, agriculture is the basis of life in Southeast Asia. Any substantial improvement in standards of living will require far-reaching changes in the *Land Use Patterns in Southeast Asia*. It is likely that *Urban Southeast Asia* will grow to mas-

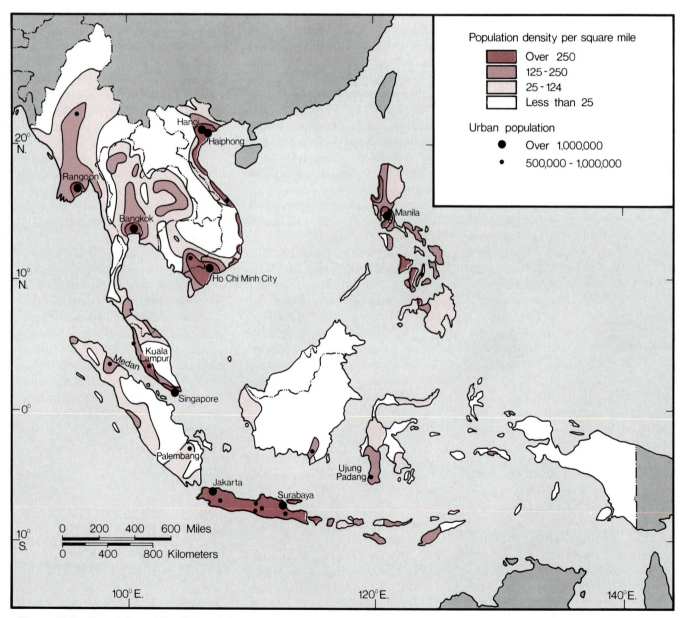

Figure 11.5 Population of Southeast Asia.

sive proportions in the near future in this struggling developing region.

Southeast Asian Environments

Most people in Southeast Asia are involved in either subsistence or commercial agriculture. The distribution of population, therefore, is directly related to land use (Fig. 11.5). High densities coincide with intensive subsistence cultivation of wet rice in alluvial valleys, on coastal plains, and in places like Jawa where available water and soil fertility sustain dense permanent cultivation. In a few locations, commercial agriculture and mining ventures provide the economic basis for local population clusters. But large areas of mainland Southeast Asia (Burma, Thailand, Laos, Kampuchea, and Vietnam) and maritime Southeast Asia (Malaysia, Indonesia, the Philippines, and the ministates of Singapore and Brunei) are little used. Environmental factors are crucial to understanding land and life in both mainland and maritime Southeast Asia.

Mainland Southeast Asia

Mainland Southeast Asia is a corrugated region of broken mountains, high plateaus, and narrow, deeply entrenched streams (Fig. 11.6). Uplands cover most of the region's 800,000 square miles. Just to the north, the eastern end of the Himalaya Mountains makes a sharp right-angle bend to the south and penetrates deep into mainland Southeast

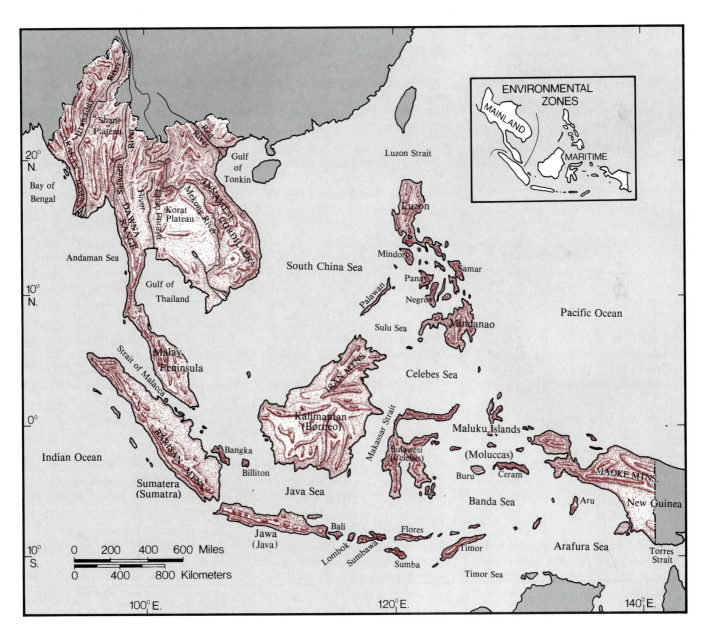

Figure 11.6 Physical features of Southeast Asia.

Asia. Outliers of this mountain **massif** crease the region, compartmentalizing its narrow valleys and encircling its upland plateaus.

The most formidable of the Southeast Asian ranges lie on its western and eastern flanks. The Arakan Yoma in western Burma forms a mountain wall separating Southeast Asia from the Indian realm; the Annamese Cordillera to the east curves southward through Laos and parallels the Vietnamese coast for hundreds of miles, its steep face fronting the sea. Between these two mountain chains, which bound mainland Southeast Asia, broken but formidable hill ranges line the political boundary between Burma and Thailand and extend down the length of the Malay Peninsula. Somewhat lower ranges in Thailand separate the drainage basin of the Chao Phraya River to the west from the Korat Plateau and the lake region of Kampuchea to the east, both of which are part of the drainage basin of the Mekong River (Fig. 11.6).

In the valleys framed by this upland architecture, lie the great rivers of the Southeast Asian mainland—the Irrawaddy and Salween of Burma, each more than 1400 miles long, the Chao Phraya of Thailand, the 2600-mile-long Mekong of Laos, Kampuchea and Vietnam, and the Red River of Vietnam. Despite their lengths, these rivers are extremely narrow in their upper courses, broadening gradually as they flow toward the sea. Yet, in these lowland compartments, separated from one another by difficult highlands, and on the region's deltas and coastal plains, there live 170 million people, roughly 45 percent of the total population of Southeast Asia.

The climate of Southeast Asia, like that of India, is largely a product of seasonal fluctuations in air flow, that is, the summer and winter monsoons. In summer, the southwestern monsoon blankets the region with dense clouds and yields heavy precipitation. In winter, the drier, cooler northeastern monsoon produces less rainfall except on windward facing slopes. Generally, temperatures are uniformly high and have little effect on human activity in Southeast Asia, except in northern Vietnam, the only part of the entire region that experiences a distinct cool season. But on mainland Southeast Asia, seasonal variations in rainfall alter vegetation and soil conditions, thereby influencing the distribution of agricultural activities.

The summer and winter monsoons have a telling effect on the seasonal distribution of precipitation on the mainland. Largely because of a location more distant from the equator, much of mainland Southeast Asia has a pronounced and protracted dry season, with four to five months each year having rainfall totals of less than 2 inches. Local variations abound, however, because the north-south grain of the mainland's topography crosscuts the flow of monsoonal air. The west coast of Burma, which receives the brunt of the summer monsoon, for example, is drenched with more than 100 inches, in some places 200 inches, of rainfall in the summer season. By contrast, central Vietnam receives most of its precipitation from the winter monsoon.

Topography exerts a strong influence on rainfall patterns over much of the region. In lowland valleys and interior basins, the rain shadow effect of surrounding mountains lengthens the dry season and reduces total precipitation. This occurs most notably in the dry zone of Burma near Mandalay and on the Korat Plateau in central Thailand (Fig. 11.6).

Generally, vegetation and soils change with rainfall regimes, except in the alluvial valleys, coastal lowlands, and deltas of mainland Southeast Asia, where human activity has profoundly transformed natural landscapes. Throughout much of the region, **monsoon forests** composed of stands of individual species of deciduous trees, unlike the diverse tropical rain forests, are widespread. Here, timber extraction is less difficult than in other forests. Moreover, monsoon forests have broken canopies open to sunlight and dense ground covers that provide the soils beneath them with a greater store of nutrients. Where dry seasons are pronounced, soil **leaching,** promoted by continuous rainfall, is slowed down, so that soil fertility is higher. With most people in this region engaged in agriculture, these environmental variations are of great significance.

Maritime Southeast Asia

Maritime Southeast Asia contains an estimated 23,000 islands scattered in chains and clusters that extend 2500 miles into the Pacific Ocean (Fig. 11.6). The Malay Peninsula defines the western border of maritime Southeast Asia; Papua New Guinea marks the eastern frontier. Most of the islands in this region rise as densely forested mountain cores from shallow seas. Generally, dense tropical rain forests blanket deeply incised hills and mountains in the island interiors. Mangrove swamps and tidal marshes line the shores of the region's elongated peninsulas and islands. Short rivers run from the island interiors to the sea. Dense settlement is usually confined to narrow coastal plains and delta fans at the mouths of these streams, except where fertile soils support intensive agriculture.

Some 900,000 square miles of land area exists in maritime Southeast Asia, but surrounding seas cover an area four times larger. Maritime pursuits, location on trade routes, and coastal environments play an important role in the distribution of people. The largest land areas are the Malay Peninsula; the islands of Sumatera, Kalimantan, Sulawesi (Celebes), and Jawa in Indonesia; and Luzon and Mindanao in the Philippines. Some 260 million people, 55 percent of all Southeast Asians, live in this island world.

Most of maritime Southeast Asia lies in the equatorial zone. Continuous heat, dense cloud cover, high

tility. A string of active volcanic islands stretch from the islands of Sumatera and Jawa eastward through the Sulawesi and Maluku (Moluccas) Islands of Indonesia and sweep northward to the Philippines. Volcanic materials spewed forth from these mountains produce young fertile soils capable of supporting populations as dense as those in the alluvial valleys, **floodplains,** and deltas of Southeast Asia. The uneven distribution of these volcanic and alluvial soils is a principal factor in the striking variations in land use and population density in this region where upwards of 100 million people live on the small Indonesian island of Jawa, yet, large areas of eastern Sumatera, Kalimantan, and Irian Jaya (western New Guinea) are virtually unoccupied.

Land Use Patterns in Southeast Asia

Three very different agricultural systems exist in Southeast Asia (Fig. 11.7). **Shifting cultivation** is practiced by tribal groups in the highlands of the Southeast Asian mainland and its island archipelagos. **Sawah,** the cultivation of wet rice, sustains people in the region's most densely settled alluvial valleys, deltas, coastal plains, and terraced hillsides. Commercial or plantation cultivation of **commodity crops**—rubber, coffee, sugar, and coconuts—was established by colonists throughout the region. Each of these agricultural systems engages people in intimate association with their environments. Once established, each has been resistant to change.

Shifting Cultivation in Southeast Asia

Shifting cultivation is the principal agricultural economy of tribal peoples in the forested uplands of Southeast Asia. Climate, terrain, vegetation, and soil conditions inhibit permanent agricultural settlement (Fig. 11.7). Shifting cultivators cut

The rugged terrain dominating much of mainland and maritime Southeast Asia is only now being penetrated by forces of modernization.

humidity, and rainfall totals of 60 to 100 inches a year are the rule. Tropical rain forests underlain by lateritic soils are common. Only the northern and southern fringes of maritime Southeast Asia have extended dry seasons and more open, monsoon vegetation. These conditions exist in parts of the northern Philippines,

southern Sulawesi, and eastern Jawa, which have four- to five-month dry seasons. Some locations situated in the rain shadow of mountain barriers also have pronounced dry seasons.

Perhaps more important than climate and vegetation in understanding patterns of human activity in maritime Southeast Asia is soil fer-

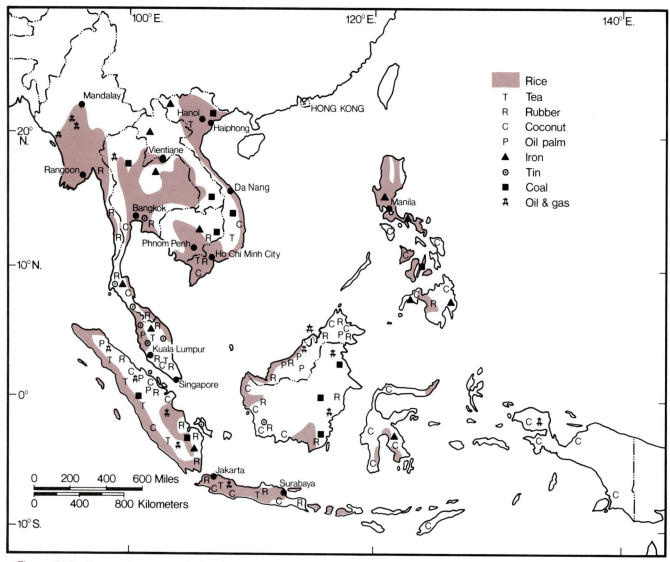

Figure 11.7   Economic patterns in Southeast Asia.

clearings in the forest, burn the felled trees to ashes to increase soil fertility in the clearings, plant a variety of crops on these temporary fields, and abandon them when soil fertility diminishes and food production declines. The agricultural cycle consists of relatively short three- to four-year periods of cultivation punctuated by lengthy periods of fallow that commonly last for eight to twelve years.

The technology of shifting cultivation is simple, involving only hoes, digging sticks, and machetes. Crop combinations, however, reflect a sophisticated ecological knowledge of tropical forest environments. Some

400 cultivated plants are grown in forest clearings in Southeast Asia, often as many as 100 in a single field. Tubers—cassava, yams, sweet potatoes, taro—and the produce of tree crops form the basic diet of shifting cultivators. Cereals are of less importance.

Shifting cultivation requires extensive areas of forest land to support small groups of people. Most of the highlands in the Annamese Cordillera of Vietnam and Laos, the uplands of eastern Thailand, and the mountains of Burma are occupied by shifting cultivators. In maritime Southeast Asia, it is the predominant

economy in Kalimantan, Irian Jaya, much of Sumatera, and the eastern side of the Malay Peninsula. However large the area given over to shifting cultivation, less than 30 million people, the vast majority of them members of minority tribes, are supported by this way of life. But their impact on the environment is substantial.

The area occupied by shifting cultivators has shrunk over the last century as lowland rice farmers and commercial plantations have pushed into the foothills. Contact between these people and tribal groups like the Lao, Thai, and Montagnard of mainland

Southeast Asia introduced rudimentary medical care into the highlands, causing tribal populations to increase. Because of larger numbers and more restricted environments, destruction of forest land has increased.

As a result of this demographic growth, many shifting cultivators have been forced to return to their abandoned clearings prematurely, accelerating impoverishment of the soil, and leading to the spread of tough, fibrous grasses into large areas of once cultivated land in the Philippines, Thailand, and Vietnam. Overall, an estimated 115 million acres of forest land in Southeast Asia has been affected by shifting cultivators, and an estimated 10 million new acres is cleared annually. Viewed by most governments in the region as a destructive system of agriculture, shifting cultivation is being actively discouraged in some countries.

Sawah: The Rice Economy of Southeast Asia

Within Southeast Asia, a remarkable percentage of the region's intensively cultivated land is planted in wet rice, or paddy (Fig. 11.7). This is known as sawah in the region. Rice occupies more than half the agricultural area of every country in Southeast Asia, except in Malaysia where commercial agriculture prevails. Moreover, the amount of cultivated land devoted to rice in Southeast Asia has doubled in the last half century, total production has tripled, and rice has maintained its place as the preferred food of a vast majority of the people in this region. The economies of Burma, Thailand, Kampuchea, and Vietnam rely heavily on rice exports; Indonesia is the world's leading rice importer. Few world regions are as dependent on a single crop as is Southeast Asia.

The key to rice cultivation in tropical Southeast Asia is the sawah, an embanked field in which water is impounded during the life cycle of the plant. Flooded sawahs located on soils of varying quality consistently produce

Cultivation of rice on coastal lowlands in *sawahs,* embanked fields, provides a livelihood for most people in Southeast Asia.

one or more rice crops on the same field year after year with no decline in yields. Once constructed, embanked fields are permanent and productive components of the Southeast Asian agricultural landscape, whether they are located on delta plains, in river valleys, or on terraced hill slopes. Over 3000 different varieties of rice, with growing periods ranging from 60 to 300 days, are cultivated in Southeast Asia.

The basic requirement for wet rice cultivation is a reliable, controlled source of water. This condition is met in much of the Philippines and on the Irrawaddy Delta of Burma through adequate rainfall; on the plain of the Chao Phraya River of Thailand, on the lower reaches of the Mekong River in Kampuchea and Vietnam, and in the Palembang region of Sumatera, through natural river flooding; and on the islands of Jawa, Bali, Luzon, and on the Tonkin Plain in northern Vietnam, through intricate artificial irrigation systems.

A majority of the agricultural population of Southeast Asia is engaged in rice production, although sawahs cover only a tiny fraction of the land area in each country. Villages rise as tree-ringed islands above carpets of flooded fields in these densely settled rice-producing regions (Fig. 11.8). Further extension of rice cultivation is physically difficult and prohibitively expensive. Large scale expansion of rice cultivation in the future is not likely. Instead, most countries in Southeast Asia are attempting to increase rice production by raising yields rather than by expanding the amount of land under irrigation.

With rice yields one third to one half of those in Japan and Taiwan, there is ample room for large increases in rice production in Southeast Asia through the use of new seed varieties, fertilizers, and other elements of the Green Revolution.

The Green Revolution was introduced into the region in the early 1970s. Confident predictions were made that Southeast Asia would have substantial rice surpluses. These assessments were based on rapid increases in rice production, particularly in Indonesia and the Philippines, where good weather, the planting of "miracle rices" in the best irrigated areas, inexpensive repairs to neglected irrigation systems, and cheap fertilizers and pesticides contributed to substantial gains.

It soon became apparent, however, that successful cultivation of high-yielding varieties of rice was limited to those regions where precise water control in irrigation and drainage of fields was possible. But in much of Southeast Asia, wet rice cultivation depends on rainfall or seasonal flooding. In these areas, the technology of water management is not sufficient to meet the demands of the "miracle rices." Moreover, the rising cost of fertilizer and pesticides

in the 1970s placed these expensive imports well beyond the reach of many local producers. Although Southeast Asia now produces twice as much rice as it did thirty years ago, the number of people in the region has doubled. In Southeast Asia, then, the Green Revolution postponed large scale food shortages, but the problem of feeding rapidly growing populations remains of central concern.

Commercial Agriculture

Commercial, or plantation, agriculture is the third system of cultivation of importance in the agricultural economies of virtually every country in Southeast Asia (Fig. 11.7). Native spices, pepper, cloves, and nutmeg, have been grown in Southeast Asia for sale on world markets for centuries. Today, however, the most important commercial crops in Southeast Asia are rubber, coconuts, the oil palm, coffee, tea, and tobacco. Some of these crops were introduced into the region by Europeans in the 1700s. Throughout the region, the most important factor in determining the location and scale of commercial cultivation—whether on large scale plantations or by small holders—is market conditions in Europe, the United States, and Japan. Southeast Asia thus finds itself in a condition of economic dependency much like Latin America.

An estimated 20 million acres of land are cultivated in commercial crops in Southeast Asia. Natural rubber is by far the most important crop. More than half the area under commercial cultivation in Southeast Asia is planted in rubber. This region is the source of 85 percent of world rubber production. Except in the Philippines, where coconuts—the region's second most important commercial crop—is dominant, rubber accounts for better than 30 percent of commercial agricultural exports in every country. In peninsular Malaysia and southern Vietnam, an overwhelming 80 percent of total export income from agriculture is gen-

GEOLAB
RURAL SETTLEMENT PATTERNS

In rural areas, the cultural landscape is composed of fields and farm buildings. These are arranged in different patterns and with differing degrees of clustering. The distribution of dwellings in each region varies with the type of agriculture, local culture, and environmental conditions.

Geographers generally distinguish two types of rural settlement depending on the arrangement of dwellings on the land. **Agglomerated settlements** are clusters of dwellings variously called hamlets or villages, depending on size. All are characterized by a concentration of buildings surrounded by the gardens, fields, and pastures of the settlement. Different patterns of concentration in agglomerated settlements take different shapes on the landscape. The two most common are nuclear villages and linear villages. **Dispersed settlements,** by contrast, are composed of isolated farmsteads often far removed from neighbors.

In Southeast Asia, agglomerated settlements are the most common form of farm settlement (Fig. 11.8). Some of these are nuclear villages, like the walled settlements of central Burma and the less concentrated but still nuclear villages of central Thailand. Two smaller types of nuclear settlements are the clumped hamlets of Jawa and Sumatera in Indonesia and the hamlets of shifting cultivators in the highlands of mainland Southeast Asia and Kalimantan. Linear nuclear settlements occur throughout the region along rivers, canals, roads, and on the plantation estates of Malaysia and Sumatera. Dispersed settlements composed of widespread individual farmsteads occur occasionally on rented rice fields in the river lowlands of Southeast Asia. Only in Timor, however, is dispersed rural settlement common.

Adapted from: Colin S. Freestone, The Southeast Asian Village: A Geographic, Social and Economic Study. London: George Philip and Son, 1974, pp. 6–7.

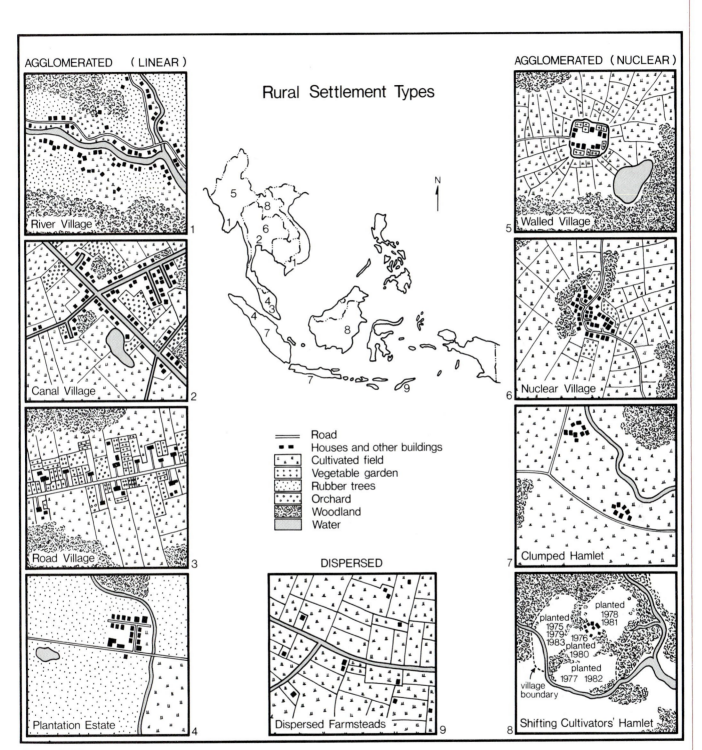

Figure 11.8 Rural settlement in Southeast Asia.

erated by the sale of rubber. Other commercial crops, palm oil, coffee, tea tobacco, and sugar, are more localized in cultivation and less important to national economies.

The concentration on commercial production of rubber in Southeast Asia is largely the result of the advantages that the rubber plant, *Hevea brasiliensis*, holds for both small farmers and large estates in the region's tropical environments. Rubber trees can be grown under a wide variety of environmental and social conditions. It can withstand an extended dry season, makes limited demands on soils, can be grown on sloping as well as flat land, requires little labor, and can be harvested year round.

For these reasons, rubber is grown under a wide variety of conditions in Southeast Asia. Large scale, capital intensive rubber plantations are found in peninsular Malaysia and Sabah, on the island of Sumatera, and on the tropical fringes of southern Vietnam. Yet, rubber is also widely cultivated by small farmers throughout Southeast Asia.

Villagers plant rubber trees in abandoned sawahs in river valleys, on sloping land adjacent to rice fields, in forests within range of small settlements, and even on the vacated clearings of shifting cultivators. Because rubber is a native of the tropical forest environment, it requires little attention. Farmers can supplement their earnings with a minimum of added capital or labor.

Elsewhere in Southeast Asia, the oil palm is grown on the coastal fringes of Malaysia and on the shores of a number of islands in the Indonesian archipelago, coffee and tea are grown in the Indonesian highlands, sugar in the Philippines, and spices in the Maluku Islands. The importance of coconuts instead of rubber in the agricultural economy of the Philippines was prompted by political considerations not by environmental or economic factors. Although these products contribute to the export economies of the region, they are vulnerable to shifts in market demand, changing prices on world markets, and the development of synthetic substitutes.

Despite their economic impor-tance, then, commercial agricultural commodities leave most Southeast Asian states dependent on factors well beyond regional control. Most countries are initiating programs of crop diversification to reduce the dangers inherent in this situation. But overall, the contemporary states of Southeast Asia cannot significantly improve living conditions in the countryside by crop substitution or agricultural expansion. With increasing numbers of villagers migrating to Southeast Asia's rapidly growing cities, new urban-based economic opportunities will have to be created to accommodate the region's growing population.

Urban Southeast Asia

As in India, most Southeast Asians live in the countryside, are engaged in farming, and are poor. Now that populations are expanding rapidly because of falling death rates, the ability of villages to sustain large numbers of people is declining. Many have left their villages and moved to cities in the last thirty years (Fig. 11.5).

Throughout Southeast Asia, urban population is growing twice as fast as total population. In Malaysia, the Phillippines, and Indonesia, cities may be expanding three times as fast. Large metropolitan centers exist in every Southeast Asian country, except Kampuchea and Laos. But industrialization is not keeping pace with urbanization, jobs are few, and urban services lag far behind urban growth. Southeast Asia—rural and agricultural in population and economy—is facing an urban crisis of increasing magnitude.

The Growth of Urban Centers

The growth of modern Southeast Asian cities began in the colonial period when Europeans established commercial centers to facilitate the export of raw materials from the region. The earlier royal capitals of indigenous Southeast Asian states were

Millions of acres of land in Southeast Asia is devoted to the cultivation of commercial crops like rubber for export to the industrial world.

primarily inland administrative and religious centers. In contrast, the cities built by the Europeans were coastal in location, international in orientation, heterogeneous in population, and often located where no previous settlement existed. Although Europeans in Southeast Asia were always few in number, the commerce and trade stimulated by their activities attracted some 32 million Chinese to the region who acted as merchants and service workers in European commercial centers.

Port cities became the focal points of economic growth in Southeast Asia. Only a few towns grew up in the tin-mining areas of Malaya, along railroads, and where Europeans established administrative centers to control or protect areas of primary production. Trade, the principal source of wealth, profited indigenous Southeast Asians only when it expanded the production of exportable raw materials.

Manufacturing, which spurred and supported urban growth in the Technological World, was virtually nonexistent in Southeast Asia. Europeans had little interest in incorporating the natives of colonial possessions into the fabric of their own industrialized world. Nor did Southeast Asia possess deposits of coal and iron, then the two most important industrial resources.

The largest Southeast Asian cities were run by European and nonindigenous Chinese elites whose concerns focused on services oriented toward international enterprise. The central business districts were European in aspect; the residential quarters that housed the Europeans and their clients were strictly segregated from the indigenous population. They occupied the urban periphery, living in squatter settlements.

Urban Primacy in Southeast Asia

In the 1980s, the cities established by Europeans in Southeast Asia swelled in size. Migration from the countryside and natural increase led to complete domination of social and economic life in most countries in the region by a single metropolitan center.

On the mainland, Rangoon, Burma has a population of 2.3 million; Greater Bangkok in neighboring Thailand holds a population of 5.4 million. In Vietnam, Ho Chi Minh City in the south is the country's largest city with 3.4 million people, despite the ravages of war and the expulsion of the Chinese. Hanoi, the northern capital, and its port city of Haiphong, have populations of 2.6 and 1.3 million respectively. In maritime Southeast Asia, Manila is an urban metropolis of 4.5 million, Jakarta has a population of 6.5 million, and Surabaya is over a million. The city-state of Singapore holds 2.6 million people. Regionwide, only landlocked Laos, rural Kampuchea, Malaysia after separation from Singapore, and the tiny sultanate of Brunei do not have cities of 1 million or more inhabitants (Fig. 11.5).

In most Southeast Asian countries, these great urban metropolises are primate cities that dwarf other urban centers in size, economy, and influence. Indonesia is the sole exception to this rule because of its large total population and geographical fragmentation. Here, secondary urban centers like Medan and Palembang on Sumatera and Ujung Pandang in Sulawesi have populations of between 500,000 and 1 million people.

These colonial capitals, now primate cities, have been transformed by the construction of agricultural processing industries, mineral and energy refineries, textile factories, and service activities. But the process of job creation and urban development is too slow to accommodate human needs. And the regional imbalance caused by the location of most jobs in a single urban center creates serious problems of regional development. Nowhere is this more apparent than in Bangkok, the capital city of Thailand, which has a population

ten times larger than the combined population of the three next largest cities in the country.

The Primate City of Bangkok

The city of Bangkok was never a colonial city, but in many ways, it illustrates the problems of large urban centers created throughout the Developing World during the colonial period. Bangkok is located near the coast on a bend in the Chao Phraya River in the most populous and economically important region of Thailand (Fig. 11.9). In recent years, the city has fallen victim to its own rapid growth—growth stimulated by falling death rates, migration from the countryside, and the concentration of political and economic power in this single primate city.

In the early 1970s, Bangkok had a population of 2.3 million. By 1988, the number of people in the city swelled to an official 5.4 million, although the actual population may have been closer to 7 million. This represents a substantial share of Thailand's total population of 55 million. It also marks Bangkok as the premier primate city in Southeast Asia. Thailand's second largest city, Chiang Mai, in the north, is fifty times smaller. In addition, current growth patterns suggest that Bangkok's 597 square miles of flat, swampy land will accommodate a total of 14 million people in the next fifteen years.

Over the last three decades, canals that branched off the Chao Phraya River were paved over to provide streets for automobiles. This blocked the natural drainage channels that in earlier times protected the city from flooding. As the population of Bangkok expanded through mass migration from the Thai countryside, some 11,000 wells were sunk to provide drinking water to the city's people. With drainage blocked by the flat terrain, and the land subsiding because of the withdrawal of underground water, Bangkok—once hailed as the Venice of the East—now lies under several feet of water during

MAPSCAN

REMOTE SENSING OF THE ENVIRONMENT

Mapping the surface of the earth through direct field work is difficult, time consuming, and expensive. In recent years, new capabilities of **remote sensing** of the environment have been created through space satellites. Satellites with special sensing devices record the reflections of electromagnetic energy from the surface of the earth. This data is transmitted from satellites to recording stations, which translate this information into images. The process is analogous to the transmission of impulses from television studios to television receivers.

Applications of remote sensing techniques to the study of the earth have revolutionized the accuracy of weather forecasts, mapping of surface features, identification of zones of potential mineral exploitation, agricultural development, crop disease, and patterns of resource utilization. They are one of the most powerful new tools available to modern geographers.

Among the most widely used of these satellite images are the **Landsat** series generated from an altitude of 570 miles above the earth's surface. Four scanners and three television cameras on the satellite sense the same scene on different wavelengths. Images based on these wavelengths can be artificially combined to produce false color images, each 115-miles square. Because the satellite orbits the earth rephotographing the same area every eighteen days, it is possible to monitor the progress of crops, patterns of urban growth, and other short-term changes in the physical and human environment.

The Landsat image and accompanying map of Bangkok, Thailand, illustrated in Figure 11.9 provides an example of the uses and limitations of the Landsat series. Each dot in the matrix of the image (as on a television set) is 1.1 acres in size. Small-scale features, therefore, are difficult to identify. The Landsat series does,

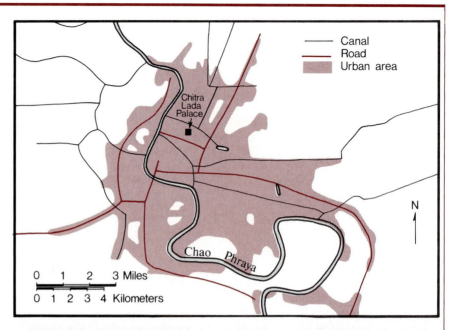

Figure 11.9 Landsat image and map of Bangkok, Thailand.

however, provide broad regional views of large areas in which point and line symbols are clearly visible. On the image of Bangkok, for example, the urban area of the city, the Chao Phraya River, and linear features, like canals and highways, stand out. The precise grading of the rice fields surrounding the city into tree crops and forests is less easily discerned.

As remote-sensing techniques become more sophisticated, the resolution of surface features is increasingly detailed. The future use of satellite photography in identifying patterns on the landscape for a variety of purposes will find many applications.

Source: Landsat image courtesy of Technology Application Center, University of New Mexico.

the rainy season. Engineers have issued warnings that unless action is taken, the entire city of Bangkok may sink below sea level by the end of the century.

Services in Bangkok have failed to keep pace with urban development. Sewers are nonexistent, so that waste products flow directly into the Chao Phraya River. Piped water is delivered to only half of Bangkok's urban population. With 600,000 automobiles competing for space on inadequate roads, pollution and traffic problems are acute.

Bangkok summarizes the confusing mixture of urban land use characteristic of Southeast Asia's primate cities. Western-style skyscrapers, office buildings, and condominium complexes coexist with small, family-run, bazaar-style shops in the central business district (CBD). Beyond the inner residential quarters, an estimated 1 million people live in Bangkok's 400 slums. Demand for new housing requires the construction of 40,000 new units each year, but less than a fifth of this need can be met. As the focal point of Thailand's national economy, the city of Bangkok reflects the problems of development facing most Southeast Asian countries. By comparison, Bangkok and Thailand in general are much better off than most of their Southeast Asian neighbors.

Traffic jams and smog are common in Bangkok and other cities in Southeast Asia that have experienced rapid, unplanned growth.

Land and sea meet at this floating market in Bangkok, Thailand.

DIVERSITY AND DEVELOPMENT IN SOUTHEAST ASIA

Since independence, most countries in Southeast Asia have faced problems of economic development similar to other states in the Developing World. Throughout the region, population growth has outpaced economic expansion. Primary production of raw materials initiated in the colonial period persists to the present. Standards of living are low, agricultural productivity is limited, industrialization has been slow to develop, unemployment is increasing, and government economic programs are not meeting the rising expectations of the people of the region.

Two additional factors complicate efforts to improve the quality of life in Southeast Asia. First, questions of *Cultural Diversity and National Identity* are central issues in many countries where significant minorities undermine national unity. Second, despite Southeast Asia's miniscule role in world trade, the strategic position of this resource-rich region has made Southeast Asia a focal point of international conflict. Within this geographic context, *Strategies of Development* vary sharply between the closed and open national economies of the region.

Cultural Diversity and National Identity

Within Southeast Asia, every country has a variety of ethnic and regional groups within its borders. The native peoples of Southeast Asia speak some 25 languages and over 250 dialects, practice three major religions, and differ in race, culture, and economy. The intensity of problems arising from this diversity of peoples varies from one country to another. Ethnic and cultural divisiveness is a political reality that undermines national unity throughout Southeast

Asia. As these countries strive to establish coherent, integrated national economies, minority groups pose social and political problems that must be addressed.

Cultural Diversity

In mainland Southeast Asia, the principal axis of cultural division is between the dominant lowland cultures and the subordinate upland peoples. In Burma, Thailand, Kampuchea, Laos, and Vietnam, hostilities between these societies—different in race, language, culture, and economy—has existed for centuries. With the achievement of independence, differential treatment of minority upland populations threatens national unity and retards economic development.

In Burma, the lowland Burmese of the Irrawaddy Valley are able to exert only intermittent control over the Shan, Karen, and Kachin tribes in the uplands. These minority hill people are largely excluded from the economic and political life of the country. Attempts by the Thai government to assert political control over the northern highlands have been met with resistance from resident hill tribes. In Laos, too, the historic hostility between the valley-dwelling Lao and upland tribal groups has taken political form. The highland minorities support the political left, the Pathet Lao, in the ongoing struggle to control the country. In Vietnam and Kampuchea, the Montagnard people of the uplands became pawns in the warfare that raged throughout the region in the 1960s and 1970s.

Malaysia eased the conflict between its indigenous Malays and immigrant Chinese when Singapore became a separate political state in 1975. But elsewhere in maritime Southeast Asia, regional loyalties in the far-flung national territories of Indonesia and the Philippines have provided the basis for separatist movements. In Indonesia, the Javanese dominate national policy, a fact resented by separatist cultural groups on Suma-

tera, Kalimantan, Sulawesi, and most other islands in the archipelago. In the Philippines, one separatist movement involves the Muslim Moros of the south, who oppose the Catholic Filipino elite of the north. Land-hungry Filipinos have also found a voice in the communist insurgency led by the New People's Liberation Army (NPLA). Conflict between different

Filipino factions threatens the future development of the country.

The Chinese in Southeast Asia

A second contentious problem of cultural diversity in Southeast Asia involves the millions of overseas Chinese who entered the region in the latter half of the nineteenth century to work in the tin mines of Ma-

Hill tribes who practice slash-and-burn agriculture are excluded from modern social and economic development in mainland Southeast Asia.

laysia, the agricultural estates of Kalimantan, the plantations of Vietnam, and the European-built port cities in general. Although they represent only 4 percent of the population of the region, the estimated 15 million overseas Chinese in Southeast Asia are concentrated in large cities. In Malaysia, they comprise 35 percent of the total population; in Indonesia, the Philippines, Thailand, and Vietnam only 3 percent. Yet, throughout Southeast Asia, the Chinese are viewed with suspicion and distrust and are envied for their commercial success.

The distrust by native Southeast Asians of the overseas Chinese has intensified since independence. The Chinese maintain their own culture, language, and tradition. They live in separate residential quarters in the largest cities in the region. They control crucial sectors of national industries, ranging from commercial agricultural land in Malaysia to rice processing in Vietnam. Their prominence in banking, moneylending, and trade has long engendered hostility among Southeast Asians. With the rise of mainland China as a force in the Pacific, their loyalty is now questioned, which adds a political dimension to what was already a serious problem in many Southeast Asian states.

These cultural differences have frequently erupted in violence. The expulsion of the Chinese from rural Jawa in 1959 was one of a series of attacks on Chinese communities in Indonesia and the Philippines over the centuries. In the wake of a purported Communist coup in 1965, there were further assaults on the Indonesian Chinese. In northern Sumatera, Chinese were rounded up and deported. Many Chinese were killed in riots on Kalimantan. More recently, Chinese in southern Vietnam were driven to the sea following the military conquest of the south by the north. Millions of the "boat people" seeking refuge throughout the Pacific Basin were from the Chinese

suburb of Saigon, or what is now Ho Chi Minh City.

It seems clear that if the overseas Chinese are to retain positions within the social orders of the independent states of Southeast Asia, they will have to abandon elements of their cultural identity and give undivided loyalty to their adopted homelands. Southeast Asian countries are increasingly unwilling to tolerate their presence or prominence as alien minorities in states actively engaged in the **nation-building process.**

Strategies of Development

The larger countries of Southeast Asia share similar problems in transforming their subsistence agricultural economies into more balanced, productive societies through developmental planning. The need for sustained economic growth is acute, particularly as growing populations

Political instability is a threat to economic growth throughout the Developing World. Here, Corazón Aquino attends a graduation ceremony at the Philippine Military Academy after her successful overthrow of the Marcos regime.

demand more jobs, social services, and access to higher levels of income.

Two development strategies have evolved in Southeast Asia since independence in the 1940s and 1950s. One group of countries has been outward looking and has pursued policies that emphasize greater participation in the world economy. Thailand, Malaysia, the Philippines, and the ministates of Singapore and Brunei are in this group. All have recorded high rates of economic growth over the last two decades. The second more inward-looking group of countries—Burma, Laos, Kampuchea, and Vietnam—is more concerned with internal conflict, ideological concerns, and the maintenance of existing social orders than accommodation to the economy of the modern world. The economies of these latter countries have registered lower rates of economic growth. Indonesia fits neither category well, with tendencies that have been both inward and outward looking.

The Outward-looking Economies of Southeast Asia

The outward-looking economies of Southeast Asia—those of Thailand, Malaysia, the Philippines, Singapore, and Brunei—have pursued development policies that involve realistic appraisals of their human and natural resources, greater participation in international economic cooperation, and capitalist incentives to economic growth. They are the relatively wealthy and fast-growing economies in Southeast Asia.

It is difficult to account for the higher levels of economic performance of these countries, as compared with their Southeast Asian neighbors, except in terms of the social and economic policies pursued by their respective governments. Thailand, Malaysia, and the Philippines do not have richer environmental bases for agriculture than their neighbors in Southeast Asia, nor do they possess (with the exception of the oil-rich sultanate of Brunei) mineral and energy resources of significantly greater potential value. Environmentally, Thailand has more in common with Burma and the Mekong River states on the mainland than with either Malaysia or the Philippines. The city-state of Singapore is an economic enclave that, like Hong Kong, has translated locational advantages and mercantile skills into an island of economic prosperity. Singapore withdrew from the Federation of Malaysia in 1965 to become an independent state whose population is 76 percent ethnic Chinese. Today, with a population of 2.6 million, Singapore is the third most active port in the world and, although it has no oil of its own, is the world's third largest refiner of petroleum products.

The economy of Thailand is firmly rooted in the land. Agriculture, forestry, and mining provide employment for the bulk of the Thai population. Rice, rubber, tin, and teak are the most important export products of Thailand; petroleum, machinery, and manufactured goods are its leading imports. Most local manufacturing involves the processing of agricultural, fish, and forest products; tin mining is also important.

The major threats to Thailand's continued economic growth— which has averaged nearly 7 percent per year over the last fifteen years—are the high costs of imported energy, rapid exploitation of the forest (which has declined from 56 to 30 percent of the Thai national territory in two decades), and the growth of rural population, which is increasingly pressing against the ecological limits of the country. Little new arable land is available for expansion. Through a series of five-year plans for economic development, the Thai government has promoted the establishment of industrial parks in the Bangkok area, expanded the handicrafts industry, and increased investment in the profitable agricultural export sector. Thailand's economic growth has been fostered by the country's ample agricultural surpluses, plentiful fish resources, and an abundance of tropical hardwoods. But as the economy of the country matures, more manufacturing and service jobs will have to be created to absorb expanding urban populations and sustain economic growth. The political system, too, awaits development because Thailand's constitutional monarchy has been set aside by military leaders.

The Philippines' economy is also rooted in the primary sector of the economy. Leading Filipino exports are coconut oil, sugar, bananas, timber, nickel, and copper. Energy and machinery are the leading imports. Mining and manufacturing are growing rapidly, however, providing a more diversified economic base than in Thailand. Textiles and clothing, shoes, electrical equipment, and electronic components have benefited from low labor costs and have attracted substantial Japanese and American investment. A sixth of the labor force is in manufacturing. Moreover, the opening of new copper, nickel, and chromite mines on various Filipino islands promises new jobs in dispersed locations. Paralleling industrial expansion are strong investments in the technology of the Green Revolution, which is more widespread in the Philippines than anywhere else in Southeast Asia.

Social and political unrest have plagued the Philippines in recent years. The transition from authoritarian rule to more democratic government occurred dramatically after President Marcos left the scene in 1986. Unrest today centers on a growing rural communist movement to which many landless Filipinos are drawn in hopes of a more equitable distribution of farmland.

Malaysia is the richest of the large Southeast Asian countries. The economy is still highly dependent on the export of rubber, tin, palm oil, lumber products, and, to an increasing degree, petroleum from offshore fields. Malaysia has experienced very different levels of development in its far-flung territory. Sarawak and Sabah form an economic periphery of Malaysia with special problems of regional development. But more than in other countries of the region, Chinese entrepreneurship and policies encouraging foreign investment have led to rapid growth in manufacturing in Malaysia.

Malaysia has moved from an industrial policy of import substitution—producing everything domestically, often at high costs, to avoid imports—to production of specific goods geared for export. Malaysia successfully pinned its hopes on the production of textiles, electronic goods, and products made from local raw materials. Rapid industrial expansion has occurred in chemicals, electrical machinery and appliances, construction materials, and transport equipment. Malaysia began to export cars to North America in 1988. Malaysia is thus able to afford imports on the basis of a successful policy of export orientation.

Overall, the Malaysian economy is distinctive in its balance, ability to create new jobs, and the degree to which urbanization and higher incomes have been sustained. Ethnic tensions between the Chinese and Muslim Malay communities have abated as economic development has been the common national quest. Political stability, focused on a system of parliamentary democracy, has been the rule in Malaysia. These factors have created an attractive investment environment in Malaysia. The country is now clearly embarked on the path taken earlier by Taiwan and South Korea toward higher levels of social and economic development.

The Inward-looking Economies of Southeast Asia

In Burma, Laos, Kampuchea, Vietnam, and Indonesia—the inward-looking economies of Southeast Asia—economic growth is more limited and problematic. On the mainland, Burma is pursuing a course of self-imposed economic isolation. Since the early

Warfare has ravaged the economies and peoples of Vietnam, Laos, and Kampuchea. This "killing field" is the city of Phnom Penh, capital of Kampuchea, after its conquest by the Khmer Rouge. Its fall marked the beginning of a six year reign of terror followed by Vietnamese occupation.

1960s, the government has closed the country to foreign influence, expelled the mercantile class of Burmese Indians, and socialized the economy. This policy is based on the simplistic notion that the natural endowment of the country will produce wealth once all external exploitation is removed. So agriculture, fishing, forestry, and mining continue to be the major economic activities in Burma. Now faced with a growing population, the economy of Burma is stagnating and per capita incomes are falling. New government plans call for increased investment in the development of petroleum fields in central Burma, but industrial and economic growth in the future will have to overcome two decades of neglect.

In Vietnam, Laos, and Kampu-

chea, the aftermath of war has seriously disrupted all plans for economic development. In Vietnam, warfare destroyed the coal-based industrial complex of the north and badly disrupted the rice-based economy of the south. Now unified politically, large military expenditures, the ineffectiveness of socialized agriculture, and limited foreign investment is delaying any substantial restructuring of the economy. The geographic complementarity of the agricultural Vietnamese South and the industrial Vietnamese North would seem to provide the basis for future economic expansion, but even Vietnamese officials expect that it will not be before the mid-1990s that they regain prewar standards of living in Vietnam. Harsh social conditions continue. Vietnam is making slow

movements toward reopening its closed Southeast Asian economy to the world.

Neighboring Laos and Kampuchea are perhaps more permanent victims of the political and military turmoil that engulfed the region between the 1940s and 1970s. Under the Khmer Rouge communist faction, which took control of Cambodia (and renamed it Kampuchea) in 1975, the economy of the country was shattered. The short-lived but devastating policy of driving city people into the countryside to create a classless agricultural society had the immediate effect of killing at least 500,000 people (some estimates range between 2 and 3 million), and created long-range social and economic dislocations that continue to have profound negative effects on the country. Until 1988 under the de facto control of Vietnamese armed forces, the future of Kampuchea will be difficult at best.

Similarly, in communist Laos, political turmoil has prevented the development of the country's abundant agricultural, forest, and mineral resources. Widely viewed as potentially the richest of the three Indochinese states, Laos may well have the lowest standards of living in Southeast Asia. Partially as a result of the isolation of Laos, partly in response to the country's severe levels of poverty, Laos has become a major producer of opium for sale in world markets. It is transformed into the legal drug morphine or is sold as illicit opium or heroin, which is derived from opium. In this regard, Laos has taken its cue from isolated Burma, the world's largest producer of opium and the heart of the so-called Golden Triangle of opium production.

Indonesia includes 40 percent of the population of Southeast Asia and is the world's largest Muslim country. Indonesia is the world's fifth largest country by population and Southeast Asia's largest in area by far. Indonesia's failure to achieve a reasonable level of economic develop-

ment after independence from the Dutch in 1949 is more difficult to explain than that of the inward-looking economies of the region.

During the 1950s and 1960s, neglect and mismanagement of the economy, concentration on political problems, and social tensions all but paralyzed the once-rich Indonesian economy. The demographic transition also began to affect Indonesia's already substantial population as birth rates remained high and death rates began to plummet. Since that period, economic expansion, fueled by capital from offshore petroleum and natural gas fields and foreign investment, has been rapid. Yet growth has not kept pace with the country's needs. Indonesia is in the curious position of being a key member of OPEC and, as an essentially agricultural country, a net importer of its basic foodstuff, rice. In 1980, the government estimated that nearly 60 percent of the population lived in absolute poverty. One third of the labor force is without work. Despite its extensive plantation economy and its diverse geography of small freehold farms, imports of food are as important as those of machinery, iron and

steel, and chemicals. Virtually all export income derives from petroleum, although reserves of nickel and tin have been developed in recent years. Indonesia has large untapped reserves of bauxite, copper, and manganese; coal is mined in Sumatera. The future is not without promise. Indonesia's strong rates of natural increase and its inability to conserve its forest resources, however, jeopardize economic gains. One of the most resource-rich states in the Developing World, Indonesia ranks among the poorest.

Southeast Asia's present is built upon its complex geographic past. Influences originating from strong civilizations elsewhere in Asia have molded the region into its present tapestry of cultures and human regions. In the modern world, Southeast Asia's cultural experience is reflected in its political struggle—a dynamic region, recipient of impulses from both the capitalist and communist worlds. The real struggle, however, is the integration of the region into larger economic systems and the reinterpretation of the local environment by local cultures in a new human world.

Historically, the Middle East has been a crossroads located at the juncture of three continents. International trade sustained the region's largest cities, as this nineteenth-century market scene in Cairo, Egypt, suggests.

nomic pressures were brought to bear. Finally in 622, Muhammad and about 70 Muslim converts fled northward from Mecca to the oasis city of Medina. This emigration, called the **hegira** (or "exodus"), marked the emergence of Muhammad as a recognized social and political leader.

During the ten years before his death in 632, Muhammad unified the tribes of Arabia under the Muslim banner. The power of the sword was added to the power of the word. Within a generation after the death of the Prophet, Arab armies spread north, bearing the message of Islam. They broke through the southern frontiers of Mediterranean Byzantine civilization, through the western boundaries of the Persian Empire, and conquered Egypt, the eastern Mediterranean, Mesopotamia, and Persia. A century later, Islam held sway from the Atlantic coasts of Morocco and Iberia to the Indus River of the Subcontinent. Muslim armies established a new civilization with its own faith, language (Arabic), laws, and institutions over the landscapes of conquest. The speed and success

of Islam's victory were extraordinary.

The diffusion of Islam remains one of the great spiritual events of history. The expansion and wide acceptance of Islam outward from its culture hearth in Western Arabia has never been satisfactorily explained. Demographers estimate that the economy of Arabia during the period of conquest could not have supported a population of more than 100,000 men from which to form an army. This population is tiny compared with the empires the Arabs challenged and defeated. The cultural synthesis of peoples and regions that emerged completely overshadowed Europe of the day. A Golden Age of Islam was made possible by a single fundamental force: the belief of the people of the Middle East and North Africa in the divine inspiration of Muhammad's message and the common practice of a code of behavior and religious ritual based on his teachings.

The Five Pillars

Islam today provides 840 million Muslims around the world with a

straightforward guide to daily living (Fig. 12.2). Islamic prescriptions for life are rooted in the geographic context of the religion's origins—Arabia. The model to be followed by each believer is the word of God as found in the holy book of Islam, the **Koran.** The life of Muhammad and the oral traditions concerning early Islam and Muhammad's successors—the caliphs—are equally important. Together, these sources define the appropriate courses of action open to people in their everyday lives. Interpretation and application of religious doctrine are provided by respected and learned men, the **ulama.** By and large, however, Islam has no formal religious hierarchy. Each human community holds the democratic potential for spiritual understanding and righteous guidance.

For the vast majority of believers, the righteous way of life is clear-cut, almost technical. Five basic acts, or "pillars," upon which people build their lives are universally accepted by Muslims. The Five Pillars of Islam are: (1) bearing witness to God and his Messenger, Muhammad—the expression of faith; (2) practicing daily prayer at designated times and places; (3) giving alms to the needy; (4) fasting during the month known as Ramadan; and (5) making a pilgrimage to Mecca, the spiritual center of Islam, once in a lifetime. These patterns of behavior lend unity to the *dar al Islam* (the House of Islam, meaning the Muslim community) and bind Muslims together throughout the world.

The first pillar of Islam is the verbal expression of faith, as stated in the formula, "There is no god but God, and Muhammad is His Messenger." By making this statement, an individual becomes a member of the community of Islam. The simplicity of the act makes it relatively easy to gather converts. At least partly for this reason and because Christianity is identified with European colonialism, Islam is the most successful religion in attracting new converts in Asia and Africa today.

THE WORLD OF ISLAM

The World of Islam extends far beyond the confines of its culture hearth in the Middle East. The second largest world religion, with a variety of believers spread throughout the world but clearly focused on point of origin, Mecca, Islam has 840 million believers, as compared with 1.6 billion Christians. Its adherents stretch across the Eastern Hemisphere. Indonesia, with 138 million Muslims, India with 88 million, and Pakistan and Bangladesh, each with nearly 80 million Muslims, have the highest Muslim populations. The Soviet Union, with 51 million Muslims, has the world's fifth largest Muslim population. But the Islamic heartland is in the Middle East, astride the crossroads of three continents. It is here that Islam finds its fullest expression.

Islam is today undergoing a major revival in the Middle East and the world. Religious values have been injected into modern systems of law and government. In Iran, the Islamic Revolution of 1979 derailed one of the most rapidly modernizing countries in the region. Law codes in Kuwait have been revised to incorporate the **sharia,** the religion-derived Islamic law code. Pakistan revitalized the sharia and instituted Islamic law as the basis of justice following the emergence of General Zia as head of state in the late 1970s. Bangladesh announced a new Islamic legal code in 1988. Governments everywhere in the Middle East and North Africa have seen a resurgence of Islamic political activity.

Paradoxically, Islamic politics has held a distinct attraction to the youth of the Middle East and North Africa. Many see a revitalized Islam as the answer to the welter of problems facing the Middle East, which some have reduced to a struggle between the *dar al Islam* and the West. Islamic resurgence in an age of social, economic, and technological change represents more than a disdain of Western values, however. It represents a reassertion of self-esteem by one of the world's great civilizations. Like other world regions transformed by contact and domination by the West, Islam has reacted in a search for stability and roots.

Data from: Richard V. Weekes, ed., *Muslim Peoples: A World Ethnographic Survey.* London: Greenwood Press, 1978, pp. 499–527.

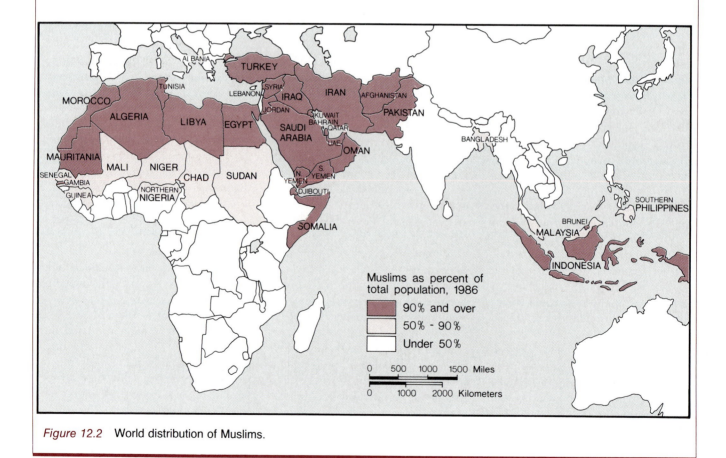

Figure 12.2 World distribution of Muslims.

The second pillar of Islam, prayer, is required of all Muslims five times a day: at dawn, at noon, in mid-afternoon, after sunset, and on retiring. The form and content of the prayer do not vary from one country to the next. In the towns and cities of the Middle East, the call to prayer is now broadcast over loudspeakers, fixing the rhythm of daily life. Mosques, Muslim houses of worship, with their tall towers, or minarets, are dominating structures in Middle Eastern cities and villages alike. Although all five prayer sessions are not observed by everyone, every family owns a prayer rug or prayer stone to aid in the proper discharge of this religious responsibility.

Although private prayer is common, congregational prayer inside a mosque is encouraged by religious leaders. The most important prayer meeting occurs on Friday, the Muslim holy day, when the entire community gathers at noon to pray. Inside the mosque, the faithful arrange themselves in rows, men at the front, women at the rear. They are led in prayers by an **imam,** a man of learned authority in religious matters, and members of the local ulama. This ritualized communal prayer is a binding tie among Muslims and provides a disciplined rhythm to daily life.

The third pillar of Islam, almsgiving, obliges Muslims to give part of their wealth to the poor as a sign of piety, as a means to salvation, and as an expression of the common concern of one human being for another. In Islam, the wealthy have a defined social responsibility to care for the broader community.

In early Islam, alms taxes were levied on most private property. Alms were distributed to slaves, widows, orphans, new converts, debtors, and travelers. Today, the principle of almsgiving is still respected. It eases the lives of the poor and the sick in countries where hospitals, orphanages, and asylums are few and extremes of wealth and poverty are common. In smaller towns, the

The collision of modern technology and traditional values in countries like Saudi Arabia has been intensified by the resurgence of Islam throughout the region.

wealthy personally distribute alms to the poor, particularly during the month of fasting, Ramadan.

Fasting during the ninth month of the Islamic calendar, Ramadan, is the fourth pillar of Islam. The fast is the most rigidly observed obligation in Islam. Observation of the fast lasts twenty-nine consecutive days and requires abstinence from all food, drink, tobacco, and sexual relations from dawn to dusk. Although the aged, sick, pregnant and nursing women, and travelers are exempt from strict observance of the fast, many often make up missed fast days at some later point in the year. This extended exercise in discipline binds Muslims in a community of abstinence that creates feelings of spiritual solidarity among most Middle Easterners.

Daily life takes strikingly different form during Ramadan. In many countries, breaking the fast—at least in public—is illegal. Cafés and restaurants are closed by day. On the other hand, come sundown, people break their fast in public or in private. Social gatherings lasting into the night relive Islamic days of yore.

Public life lasts till just before dawn, when the last food is served, prayers are said, and many go to bed. Day and night become reversed.

The twelve-month Islamic calendar is based on the phases of the moon, so that the calendar rotates through the seasons. When Ramadan falls during the Middle Eastern summer, when days are hot and long, the fast is truly arduous. Weariness increases and tempers flare. Economic productivity declines markedly. In the 1960s, President Bourguiba of Tunisia tried to end this situation and declared Ramadan fast unnecessary as the country struggled against underdevelopment. He failed. Ramadan holds strong. The month of fasting, feasting, and devotion forms a powerful focus in Islam. Many view the fast as symbolic of the vitality of Islam as well as a sign of resistance to Westernization.

The fifth and final pillar of Islam, the pilgrimage to Mecca, is the duty of every adult Muslim at least once. At Mecca, the pilgrim recreates many of the key holy acts in the lives of Muhammad and earlier prophets, particularly Abraham. Like Ramadan, the pilgrimage is an act that unites the community of Islam across national boundaries. But the pilgrimage represents a direct geographic convergence of believers into a single time and place the likes of which is found nowhere else.

In the past, the pilgrimage was the voyage of a few; for some, from far away places like Morocco, it was literally the trip of a lifetime. Today, jumbo jets bring some two million pilgrims from more than 70 countries to Mecca each pilgrimage season, which is specified as the first ten days of the last month of the Islamic year. Again, if the pilgrimage season falls during the intense Meccan summer, the pilgrimage represents a significantly difficult journey. Providing for the needs of two million pilgrims for two weeks is a considerable undertaking for the Meccan authorities, and the degree of organization is remarkable. Saudi authorities have recently announced a limit of 1000 pilgrims for every 1 million Muslim population for any given country.

The traditional function of the pilgrimage as a point of encounter for Muslims from throughout the world continues. Mecca's cosmopolitan population is testimony to the global nature of Islam. In recent years, with the development of a more politicized Islam, the pilgrimage itself has become a focus of Islamic differences and disturbances—a development abhorrent to most Muslims.

A Cultural Mosaic

A mosaic of religious, linguistic, and ethnic minorities populates the Muslim world. Religious diversity in the Middle East and North Africa is the legacy of the universal religions of Judaism, Christianity, and Islam which were born in the region. The Middle East, particularly Palestine, is truly a "Holy Land," sacred to all three. Peoples of many languages and ethnic ties continued to inhabit and

Pilgrimage to Mecca, the holy city of Islam, is the duty of all adult Muslims once during their lifetime. Pilgrimage is one of the "five pillars" of Islam. In the 1980s, over 2 million Muslims from throughout the Islamic World converge on Mecca each year during the month of the pilgrimage. Here, pilgrims rest and recite verses from the Koran in the Great Mosque.

come to the Middle East after the establishment of Islam as the dominant faith, indicating the vitality of the region as a world crossroads.

In a different setting, these minorities might well have disappeared either by assimilation or extermination. But two factors—one spiritual, the other geographic—militated against this happening in the Islamic Middle East. First, Islam recognized the spiritual validity of the "Peoples of the Book"—those who believe in a single God, the Prophets, and the Day of Judgment—as communities to be tolerated and protected within Islam. Thus Jewish and Christian communities, despite intermittent persecution, were able to retain and practice their own laws and customs. Their people are seen as belonging to the same tradition, which the Muslims incorporate with their own interpretation of Old Testament prophets and Jesus.

Second, Islamic rulers were rarely able to control the vast desert and mountain regions of the Middle East. Generally, the power of centralized Islamic governments was limited to

the well-watered coasts and fertile lowlands of the region. This left large areas where heretical sects and tribes could find sacred refuge and live in a geographic isolation that preserved language and tradition. If they paid their taxes and did not pose a threat to government, these communities were left to pursue their own beliefs and customs. In the early 1800s, the Turkish Ottoman Empire, then ruling over most of this world region, harbored a variety of religious communities, known as **millets,** whose leaders, under the watchful eye of the imperial government in Constantinople (now Istanbul), regulated the personal affairs of group members.

Deeply ingrained allegiances to religious and tribal traditions have proved an obstacle to the national unity now sought by modern Middle Eastern leaders. Most important in this world region was the growing sense of being Arab—a category beyond religion. Arab identity has been most strongly rooted in language. Persian and Turkish nationalism, too, has been forged on the basis of linguistic, not religious, identity. Although most Middle Eastern countries have a tradition of pluralistic harmony, new territorial boundaries, new aspirations, and new identities have created a massive change in the cultural makeup of countries throughout the Muslim world.

Religious Diversity

Some 80 percent of all Muslims in the world belong to the orthodox or Sunni branch of Islam, the dominant faith of North Africa, Arabia (except Oman and Yemen), Jordan, Syria, northern Iraq, Turkey, and Afghanistan. After Muhammad's death, a struggle for succession developed between the followers of his son-in-law Ali and several powerful Meccan families. Those Muslims who sided with the Meccans became known as the Sunnis, accepting the first four elected caliphs, or successors to Muhammad as head of the faith, as rightful heirs to Muhammad, and authoritative heads of the Muslim community. Today, Sunni Muslims base their religious beliefs and practices on the Koran and the **Hadith,** a compendium of sayings of the Prophet written after his death. The strictest and most orthodox Sunni group is the Wahabis, an eighteenth-century revivalist movement that conquered Saudi Arabia early in this century.

Shi'ism, the other major denomination of Islam, is based on the belief that the caliphate should have been bestowed on Ali, the son-in-law of Muhammad, and his descendants. When Ali was assassinated in 661 and his two sons Hasan and Husayn were, respectively, poisoned and beheaded, a bitter schism erupted in Islam. These events engendered a division in Islam into Sunni and Shi'ah sects.

Shi'ah Muslims accept the Koran and the Hadith as the fundamental sources of faith but assign exceptional importance to Ali. They do not accept the legitimacy of the first three caliphs and, because they differ among themselves about the proper line of succession, there are numerous Shi'ah sects. Shi'ahs are found in Iran, southern Iraq, Lebanon, Pakistan, Syria, and Yemen. Offshoots of Shi'-ism include the Alawi of northern Syria, the Druze in the highlands of Syria, Lebanon, and Israel, and the Kharijites of Oman and the Algerian Sahara. Finally, mystical Sufi orders, in which individuals strive for enlightenment through ascetic and ecstatic discipline are common in both Sunni and Shi'ah Islam. Sufism has provided the basis of powerful political movements throughout much of Islamic history.

Religious differences between separate communities with different languages, customs, and lifestyles also exist among the 5 million Christians of the Middle East. When Christianity became the official state religion of the Roman Empire in 313, four religious provinces were established with centers at Rome, Constantinople (Turkey), Antioch (Syria), and Alexandria (Egypt). Each gave rise to a separate Christian church. In a series of disputes over the nature of Christ, Egyptian Copts and Syrian Jacobites were declared heretics by Rome. The Copts, an important group in Egypt, number over 1 million today and claim direct racial and linguistic descent from the ancient Egyptians. The Greek Orthodox and the Armenian Orthodox (or Gregorian) churches, which also broke with Rome, each have 600,000 members scattered throughout the Middle East. Subsequently, additional Christian sects were created when some Eastern Christians reestablished connections with Rome but retained their local rites and customs. Only one group, the Maronites, completely reunited with Rome. A large minority in modern Lebanon, the Maronites can trace their religious history back to the Crusades of European popes and kings as they attempted to remove Islam from the Holy Land in the Medieval Age. Economic and religious differences between these Lebanese Christians and the Muslim majority lie at the heart of Lebanon's long civil war (Fig. 12.3).

Middle Eastern Jewry is considerably less fragmented than either Christianity or Islam. A majority of Israel's 2.6 million Jews are Orthodox Rabbinites who accept the **Talmud,** the authoritative body of Jewish tradition, as it is interpreted by Orthodox rabbis or teachers. But the age-old Middle Eastern Jewish communities that migrated to Israel after 1948—a total of 600,000 people from throughout the Middle East and North Africa—brought to the new Israel their own traditions, beliefs, and language. Outside Israel, Jews continue to live in Turkey, Morocco, Yemen, and, until the Revolution of 1979, in Iran—those parts of the Middle East least directly affected by the Arab-Israeli conflict.

In addition to three world monotheisms, adherents of a number of other faiths are found in the Middle East. In Iran, Zoroastrians still practice the faith of ancient Iran and maintain their sacred firetemples in Tehran, Yazd, and Kirman. The Bahai, followers of a nineteenth-century Persian reformer, live in Israel, Lebanon, and Iran. In northern Iraq, two Kurdish religious groups are found who mix elements of both Sunni and Shi'ah Islam. In southern Iraq, the Mandeans practice a fertility cult that combines aspects of Christianity and Manichaeism, a religion of the early Roman Empire.

Linguistic Diversity

The distribution of languages in the Middle East is less complicated than regional religious patterns. A major language divide follows the southern slopes of the Taurus and the western slopes of the Zagros mountains. Arabic predominates south of this boundary. The language of Arabia spread throughout the region during the Islamic conquest, is the official language of countries from Mauritania to Iraq to Somalia, and forms the essential basis of Arab identity. The development of Hebrew as a

LEBANON: CULTURAL DIVERSITY, CIVIL WAR

Many students of modernization have underestimated the power of religious affiliation as a motivating force in contemporary life. Lebanon and Northern Ireland loom as prime examples, however, of the strength of religion to define and develop ethnic tensions. Nowhere has the destruction potential of religious differences been more apparent than in Lebanon.

Before 1975, Lebanon was a prosperous, wealthy country. Beirut became a fulcrum of the world economy in the 1950s and 1960s and was often called the "Paris of the Middle East." Lebanon was, however, a fragile creation carved out of Syria by the French as a Christian-dominated state on the Mediterranean. In 1975, civil war between Muslim and Christian groups broke out, ultimately reducing the country to ruins. Today, over thirty private armies hold sway in Lebanon, and sporadic fighting between Catholic and non-Catholic Christians, Sunni and Shi'ah Muslims, Druze, Palestinian refugees, occupying Syrian forces, and Israelis has devastated Lebanon.

The four major religious communities in Lebanon (17 are recognized in the national constitution) are the Christians (Catholic and non-Catholic), the Sunni and Shi'ah Muslims, and the Druze. No group today holds a demographic majority, as did the Christians when the

first—and last—census of Lebanon was taken by the French in the 1930s. That census, however, was used as the statistical basis to apportion political power on the basis of religious communities in the new state of Lebanon. This is termed Lebanon's "confessional" style of government. But Lebanon's population has changed considerably since the 1930s. It is agreed that Christians are no longer in the majority and that the Shi'ah population, in particular, has grown rapidly. Palestinian refugees, only in Lebanon since 1948, hold no political status at all in Lebanon. Lebanon's Jewish community in Beirut has dwindled in number to only a few hundred.

Great differences separate the different Lebanese religious communities. Generally Christians are at the top of the economic ladder; the Druze are in the middle, and the Sunni and Shi'ah

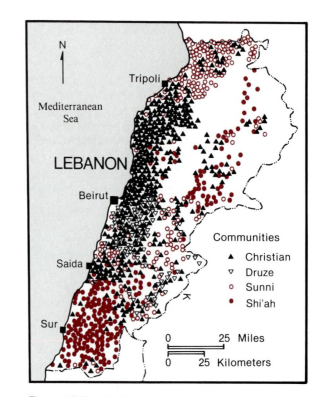

Figure 12.3 Distribution of "communities" in Lebanon.

modern language in Israel is the major exception to the use of Arabic throughout the Central Middle East and North Africa. North of the Taurus, Turkish, modernized to be written in Latin script, is the national language of Turkey; Persian (Farsi) is spoken in Iran, and Pashto is the predominant language of multilingual Afghanistan. In most Middle Eastern countries, however, tiny social minorities—Armenians, Greeks, Jews, Europeans—have retained islands of

linguistic presence, and French and English are widely spoken as second languages.

Some locally important language minorities have persisted. In the Maghrib, Berber dialects are widely spoken in the Moroccan and Algerian interior. Berber, the language of North Africa's original inhabitants, has not served as a vehicle for political consciousness largely because of the use of Arabic as the language of devotion for Berbers and Arabs alike.

But in the highlands of eastern Turkey, northern Iraq, and northwestern Iran, two million Kurds have demanded a separate political state for a long time. Kurdish identity is more complex than the use of Kurdish language alone. Although they are Sunni Muslims, the Kurds see themselves as a separate nation of people, a people long fixed in place, maintaining their separate outlook on the world. They have struggled against all the national governments that surround

are at the bottom. These economic differences exacerbate tensions between Christians and Muslims. Geographic segregation of the communities has also been a hallmark of the Lebanese state. As Figure 12.3 shows, each community has traditionally dominated a separate region of the country. Christians are sprinkled throughout the Lebanon Mountains but are concentrated in the northern mountains and coast between Beirut and Tripoli. Druze communities dominate the mountains just south of Beirut, where they are interlaced with Christian communities. Sunni Muslims are almost completely absent from the interior highlands, but they predominate on the coast south of Beirut and in the far north of Lebanon. Shi'ah Muslims are concentrated in the Lebanese South. The strategic Beqaa Valley between the Lebanon and Anti-Lebanon mountains has a mixed population.

For forty years after the creation of Lebanon, these communities lived uneasily with their confessional-style government. During the 1970s, however, this system began to disintegrate. Age-old social identities came to the surface as the unequal apportionment of political power became increasingly divisive. The surge of Palestinian refugees into Lebanon in the early 1970s helped upset the delicate balance established in Lebanon and helped militarize conditions as well. Differences in wealth between the different communities became even more apparent. Regional and ethnic factionalism overshadowed the central government.

During the 1970s and 1980s, Lebanon has been shredded by Palestinian raids into Israel and Israeli retaliations into Lebanon, Syrian and Israeli invasions, and communal strife. Beirut itself has been the focus of war between the different groups and was the object of the Israeli army's invasion in 1982. Attempts to resolve differences have led nowhere, and for the United States, caused the death of hundreds of its Marines in 1983. The use of Westerners as hostages in Lebanon—weapons for motivations of uncertain purpose—became the calling card of Lebanese factions in the 1980s.

The image of luxury hotels as fortresses for snipers, the use of hostages as policy, and urban armies composed of teenagers contradicts the assumption that material progress in the Developing World produces stability. In Lebanon, the cultural mosaic of the Middle East stands in explosive, tragic, relief.

Fifteen years of civil war have reduced Beirut, Lebanon, once a thriving commercial and banking city, to rubble.

Adapted from: E. de Vaumas, "La répartition confessionnale au Liban et l'équilibre de l'état libanais, *Revue de Géographie Alpine*, Vol. 43 (1955), pp. 511–604.

and enclose them; they were unwilling victims of the Iran-Iraq War.

Like the Kurds, Armenians, who are Christian Middle Easterners with a homeland spanning Turkey, Iran, and the Soviet Union, are a country that never happened. There is, of course, an Armenian S.S.R. in the Soviet Union, but the Armenian goal of an independent Armenian state— largely forged on the identity of Armenians defined by language—has been thwarted by more powerful political movements. Although dominant in northeast Turkey, the Turks do not recognize Armenians' separate identity. Armenians are thus scattered throughout the cities of the Middle East, and emigration to the United States has been strong.

One final Middle Eastern ethnic conflict, that between Greeks and Turks on the island of Cyprus, is rooted in the age-old animosity between these two cultures. Cyprus is viewed by Greeks as part of their national territory, despite its location only 40 miles off the coast of Turkey. In 1974, nearly 80 percent of the island's population of 700,000 were Greek; the Turkish minority was scattered throughout the north of the island. Greek political moves to encourage Greek Cypriot union with Greece led to a Turkish invasion. The island was partitioned between a Turkish north and a Greek south. Economically and culturally, the two parts of the island remain completely sealed off from each other, stark testimony to the rugged sense of ethnicity in today's Middle East.

Although these ethnic distinctions often strike Westerners as arcane, Middle Easterners have built their lives and communities around them for centuries. When the Ottoman Empire began to crumble in the 1800s, these differences provided the basis for conflicting loyalties in the emerging modern Middle East. The mosaic of people, a distinctive feature of the Middle East, is basic social terrain in the new states of the region. Modernization has not eroded these differences. The Middle East is a meeting ground, not a melting pot, of peoples.

The Ecological Trilogy

The human geography of the Middle East was characterized until very recently by a cellularlike system of settlement. A kind of ecological trilogy involved interactions between three different types of community: the city, the village, and tribal nomads. Each of these components formed a distinctive society, evolved over centuries of experimentation with the local environment, resonating to the culture and institutions of Islam. Nomads, villagers, and urbanites produced their distinctive products in their different geographies to create a variety of Middle Eastern human regions within the world of Islam.

City, Village, and Tribe

Middle Eastern cities have shared a number of common features. These are, in a broad sense, characteristics of preindustrial cities. The mosque, a central feature of the Muslim community, was the realm of the ulama. Commerce was pursued in nearby **bazaars** (central business districts) whose social and economic structures reflected the interplay of religious and economic life. Residential quarters spread outward from the central mosques and bazaars. Adaptation to heat and emphasis on pri-

vacy characterized urban structures. Overall, Middle Eastern cities from Marrakech to Mashhad were strikingly uniform in appearance and organization. Many remain so.

Villages were more closely tied to local environments, and their organization was thus more diverse. This is still largely the case. Villages also reflected the need to minimize risks in a variety of agricultural and pastoral environments—riverine, oasis, desert, and highland. Common patterns in Middle Eastern village economy and society can be readily detected: economic relations generally confined to the hinterland of a regionally dominant Islamic city, cooperative fieldwork, localized kinship systems, simple technology, and the seasonal rhythm of the agricultural cycle.

Similarly, tribal nomads in the Middle East and North Africa are defined in terms of their migratory cycles, adjustments to limited resources, harsh environments, herd composition, and the degree to which agriculture played a role in their economy. Categories of nomadic life have developed on that basis. Nomadism ranges in degree of intensity. "Pure" nomads are best illustrated by the Arabic-speaking desert Bedouins who migrate from point to point within their tribally defined territories according to the seasons. Transhumants often combine herding with agriculture but are defined by their movement of herds up and down slope during the course of the year so as to capitalize on the seasonal differences in climate found in mountainous areas. **Seminomadism** is a catchall term that reflects the fact that many nomads practice some combination of farming with their herding.

Interactions among cities, villages, and nomads delineate functional human regions. Caravan routes linked cities together, but relations between individual cities and the people in their hinterlands were complex and varied. In Anatolia (central

Turkey), villages traded grain with their cities in return for urban goods and services. In Iran, villages were commonly owned by urbanites, creating a veritable patchwork of city-states held together largely by mercantile relations. In southern Mesopotamia, in Arabia, and in the fringes of the Sahara, it was common for villages to pay tribute to controlling nomadic tribes. Distinctions between peasant and nomad blurred in these areas. People of all walks of life minimized risk by combining a variety of pursuits—trade, farming, herding.

As the nineteenth century wore on, the breakdown of order and trade in the Ottoman Empire resulted in lower population levels in some areas. Large areas of once-cultivated land were abandoned as nomads became more aggressive. At the same time, Ottoman tax collectors bled peasants dry in those areas still under government control. In the cities, death rates were high. The economy of the Middle East was stagnant; intellectual life was barren. Political power fell into the hands of corrupt and ineffective rulers. Much thought, but little action, was given to rejuvenating the military strength of the Ottoman Empire. The Empire began to disintegrate as the Balkans and Greece fought for their independence and European powers began forging economic links and then controlling territory in the Middle East. The ecological trilogy, too, began to fall apart.

The Traditional Middle Eastern City

Muslim cities were the cornerstones of Islamic civilization. The preeminence of Middle Eastern cities in society was especially strong because Muslim political, religious, and economic leaders were normally urban based. Urban social and economic institutions dominated the countryside.

In the early Islamic period, Arab geographers defined their cities as any place with a mosque and a permanent marketplace, or bazaar. Many of the cities of early Islam had long been important centers, founded in Phoenician, Greek, and Roman times. But under Islam, Middle Eastern cities came to share a set of new, distinctive, internal spatial patterns. Several characteristics consistently appeared in the cities of the region: (1) an emphasis on enclosure and security in urban structure and domestic architecture, (2) the allocation of central space to a mosque/bazaar complex, and (3) the organization of living space into neighborhood residential quarters, each with some degree of ethnic, religious or occupational unity and self-regulation.

Every important Middle Eastern city was surrounded by high walls and fortifications. The contrast between city and country was thus complete. An enclosing wall 40 to 50

feet high was pierced by gates leading to major avenues inside. These often extended directly to the centrally located mosque/bazaar complex. In many cities, a citadel with still stronger fortifications occupied a prominent position inside the city.

The emphasis on enclosure and security also influenced the structure of residential quarters and the houses within. The internal patterns of the quarters were irregular: streets and lanes formed a maze of dark, twisting passageways, alleys, and culs-de-sac. Most streets were less than 12 feet wide and were framed by the high outer walls of household compounds. Street signs and house numbers were unknown. Privacy, protection, and security were paramount in their construction. Today, contemporary architects are attempting to replicate

the vernacular architecture of the Middle East, recognizing that it embodies a thoughtful response to the harsh social and environmental realities of the region.

Central space in these walled cities was allocated to the most prestigious institutions, the mosques and bazaars. The central mosque was often the most beautiful and impressive building in the city. Some, like the Al Azhar mosque in Cairo, Hagia Sophia in Istanbul, and the Masjidi Shah in Isfahan, were also major centers of education and administration. As cities evolved, new mosques became focal points of new bazaars. Most larger cities came to have several centers of urban life. Each mosque was a hub of activity for the ulama, the religious elite who applied Islamic law to family life, regulated

High walls surround cities, houses, and gardens throughout the Middle East and North Africa. This defensive architecture reflects the turbulent history of the region.

markets and water supply, and managed the city's religious, educational, and legal institutions. The pervasive influence of Islamic values on the structure of Middle Eastern cities probably derived from the paramount importance of these men in urban administration.

The second central institution in Middle Eastern cities, the bazaar, was a welter of crowded lanes, covered stalls and associated caravan warehouses (caravansaris). These were noisy, bustling, aromatic places at the heart of Middle Eastern and North African trade routes. The bazaar was the locus of virtually all wholesale and retail trade within the city. In the bazaar, a concentric spatial hierarchy of trades and crafts existed. The shops of prestigious craftsmen and merchants—booksellers, carpet merchants, jewelers, and silversmiths— were located at the center of the bazaar; lesser crafts progressively inhabited the bazaar's margins.

Most of the space in these cities was subdivided into residential quarters that were social and geographical entities. During the Ottoman period, the millet (or "community system") recognized the legal existence of these separate social communities. In Antioch, Syria, for example, forty-five quarters existed. Jews, Armenians, Greeks, Europeans, and Muslim sects each lived in specific sectors of the city. Every quarter formed an independent community walled off from the others, a city within a city, with its own temple, customs, laws, and milieu. In smaller cities, walled quarters were usually absent, although residential differentiation remained fundamental to Muslim urban social organization.

In the nineteenth century, Cairo, Baghdad, Constantinople, and Fez were the only cities in the region with populations larger than 250,000. Cities as famous as Aleppo and Damascus were slightly larger than 100,000; Jerusalem and the future capital of Iran, Tehran, had populations of only

10,000. Modern cities such as Abu Dhabi and Casablanca were tiny fishing villages.

Both natural and social factors limited the size of traditional Middle Eastern cities. Although Constantinople, Damascus, Baghdad, and Isfahan were known in the West as international trading centers, less than one tenth of their populations were employed in commerce. Most were engaged in producing, collecting, and processing raw materials from the countryside—wool for carpets and shawls, grain and vegetables to feed the urban population, and nuts, dried fruits, hides, and spices for export. Many urban residents were, in fact, urban peasants who tended fields outside city walls by day. Because regional transportation networks were poor, the size of the rural hinterland from which cities could draw agricultural surpluses was limited.

Even when large territories were organized by the governments of the Ottoman and Persian empires, natural factors inside preindustrial Muslim cities limited their size. When urban populations grew by migration from the countryside, problems of water distribution, poor sewage disposal, and inadequate food supplies caused high urban death rates. Fires and earthquakes also took their toll.

The Middle Eastern Village

Villages were the economic foundation of society in the Middle East and North Africa. Some 70 to 80 percent of the people lived in small, rural agricultural communities. Occupied with cultivating wheat, barley, the date palm, and a host of lesser crops, villagers formed a majority in every major Middle Eastern region, except Arabia and the Sahara, where nomads held sway. Their role within the ecological trilogy was to supply grain and other foodstuffs to urban centers in return for goods and services and to nomadic tribes in return for meat, milk, and wool.

In general, villages were located

wherever a reliable supply of water was available or could be made available through wells, subterranean horizontal tunnels (**qanats**), waterwheels, or other lifting devices. Dense rural populations were located on the coasts of the Mediterranean, Black, and Caspian seas; in the uplands of the Fertile Crescent where winter rains provided water; and in the river valleys of the region. Only the highest mountain regions and the cores of the great deserts of the Middle East—the Sahara, the Empty Quarter (Rub al Khali) of Arabia, the Syrian desert, and the barren regions of the Iranian Plateau—had no settled village populations.

Most Middle Eastern villages were small, compact clusters of dwellings with few facilities besides a mosque, a mosque school, a shrine, a few shops, and sometimes a public bath. The adobe houses, constructed of mud bricks or tamped earth, blended in with surrounding landscapes. Houses were walled and faced inward to courtyards, creating an urbanlike network of alleys even in small villages.

Housing patterns varied with differing building materials, local environments, and architectural traditions. In the marshes of southern Iraq, elaborate reed houses formed floating villages. Along the western coast of Saudi Arabia, houses took a beehive form that is also found near Aleppo, Syria. In Saharan oases and in southern Arabia, palm fronds were a principal building material. In Libya, sandstone was used; along rivers, adobe. In the highlands of Anatolia and Iran, wood and stone villages were interspersed with settlements where villagers solved the problems of construction and heating by living underground.

These clustered settlements were well adapted to local environmentnts and to daily patterns of village life. Where water was plentiful, houses, mosques, and shops were frequently surrounded by walled orchards. Grain

on the success of the harvest. The villagers' few cash transactions took place in the nearest town or city, which they visited infrequently.

The primary economic relationship between cities and villages in the Middle East was rooted in food surpluses produced at the village level. The lot of the peasant in the Middle East and North Africa was one of hardship, toil, and poverty. Moneylenders, absentee landlords, nomadic tribes, and urban governments exacted tolls from the only important source of revenue—village producers. To be sure, the diminished population of the region throughout the nineteenth century meant that sufficient land was available, but peasants were rarely able to cultivate enough land to better their conditions. Armed only with family strength and a simple technology, they endured famine and plague, insecurity and drought. The observations of Western travelers about the "fatalism" of the Middle Eastern peasantry was, in fact, a sophisticated assessment of local realities.

Middle Eastern Nomads

Until this century, the trade routes that passed through the deserts and mountain ranges separating major population centers in the Middle East were controlled by some 5 million nomads. The domain of these nomads included the habitable fringes of the Sahara Desert, the Arabian Peninsula, the Levant, and the mountain and plateau regions of the Maghrib and the Northern Highlands. The largest tribal federations were powerful autonomous semimilitary groups. This has changed with the formation of modern states in the region.

Nomadic pastoralism as practiced in the Middle East and North Africa has been traditionally organized into three general types: (1) **horizontal nomadism,** the periodic movement of herds over long distances in search of pasture; (2) **vertical nomadism,** or

Bazaars like this one in Tabriz, Iran, were the major business districts in traditional cities in the Middle East. Today, commercial activities are moving to modern avenues in the region's rapidly growing urban centers.

fields radiated outward beyond the enclosed area. Cultivation was limited primarily by the energy and determination of village families.

Frequently, the village was strung out along a watercourse. Houses and walled gardens were located upstream; grain fields fanned out downslope. In these villages, the location of each household compound determined the quality and quantity of its water supply. The homes of the prosperous lay in the upper sections of the village where water was clean and plentiful. The poorer households were located downstream where water was polluted and reduced in volume.

Water administration was a critical social task and resolution of water conflicts a vital necessity.

Village life, then, was intimately tied to local environments. Most villagers were farmers whose lands provided the staple grain of their diet, whose few sheep and goats provided protein and wool products for clothing, and whose entire lives were regulated by the rhythm of the agricultural cycle. Villagers were essentially self-sufficient. Their most important dealings were in kind rather than cash. The local barber, potter, and carpenter were paid in grain at harvest time. The amount depended largely

transhumance, the seasonal shifting of herds of sheep and goats between lowland and highland environments; and (3) **seminomadism,** a combination of herding and cultivation on the fringes of settled agricultural communities. All three of these nomadic economies are adaptations to marginal environments.

Horizontal nomadism is still practiced in the Sahara Desert, on the margins of agricultural North Africa, and in the desert cores of the Arabian Peninsula, the Rub al Khali in the south and the Nafud in the north. These regions have extremely thin vegetation, stemming partly from climate and partly from overgrazing. Fewer plant species are found in the Sahara than in any world region except the polar zones. Most Saharan plants are succulents or thorny bushes low in nutritive value. Rainfall is so rare in some areas that houses in desert oases can be built with blocks of salt without danger of dissolving. By necessity, pastoral migrations take the form of broad movement in search of pastures for the camel herds.

Camel nomads tend to stay out of the desert as much as possible. Instead, they set up camps on the steppe margins or in oases during the summer. In search of pasture, they range out from these bases into the desert on long seasonal migrations covering as much as 1000 miles and lasting as long as nine months.

Camel nomads rely principally on their herds, but every sizable tribe has access to agricultural products. In the past, nomadic tribes often controlled the harvests of desert oases and steppe villages by threat of force or by direct ownership. Commonly, nomads owned a quarter to a third of the date palm groves in desert oases. In the central Sahara, these palm groves were tended by an African slave caste, the Haratin, who for all practical purposes were owned by the nomads. In areas where nomads did not own cultivated land, they often exacted tribute from villagers in return for protection from

other nomads. Similarly, in Arabia, where nomads effectively controlled the entire landscape—desert pasturage, wells, oases, small and large—oasis cultivators were the slaves, clients, or tenants of nomads. Until the introduction of Western technology in the Middle East, the desert ecosystem was largely controlled by camel nomads.

In the mountain and plateau areas of Iran, Afghanistan, Turkey, and the Maghrib, vertical nomadism, or transhumance, is still practiced on seasonal pastures not suitable for year-round grazing or permanent cultivation. Transhumant nomads use cool upland pastures in summer and milder lowland pastures in winter. If herds of sheep and goats were kept in either zone year round, approximately 70 to 80 percent of the animals would die. The logic of this system is to exploit each environment during its period of maximum productivity.

In Iran, transhumant tribes living in the Zagros and Elburz mountains own a large proportion of the country's livestock. But patterns of nomadic herding have led to overgrazing and destruction of plant resources. Each transhumant family requires a flock of forty sheep or goats to survive. The primary environmental

Nomadic encampments, like this one in eastern Syria, are rare sights in the modern Middle East. Nomads are abandoning their traditional way of life and settling in cities and villages, often under government supervision.

threat to herds is not drought, but cold spells during spring lambing time. An untimely frost can kill 50 percent of a herd overnight. Maintenance of large herds, therefore, makes sense. In the long run, however, this logic has degraded grazing resources.

The third type of nomadism found in the Middle East, seminomadism, encompasses a wide variety of agricultural and herding combinations designed to fit local environmental conditions. Patterns vary from year to year depending on rainfall, social and political conditions, and, in some cases, market factors. Along the Euphrates, short-distance sheep and goat nomadism is practiced to take advantage of nearby upland pastures. In North Africa, nomadic tribes frequently cultivate the steppe margins. Even among the mountain nomads of Iran and Afghanistan, some villages are occupied by nomads who farm when necessary and revert to herding when conditions allow. Many of these patterns have changed in recent years, but nomadism, in one form or another, generally lives on in the Middle East and North Africa.

The European Impact on the Middle East and North Africa

The traditional patterns of human geography—the ecological trilogy—remained intact well into the nineteenth century. Until then, the Middle East was insulated from the growing power of Europe by a cultural frontier across the Mediterranean Sea, separating Christian Europe from the Islamic Middle East. Closer to Europe in distance than any other non-Western people, nineteenth-century Middle Easterners knew little about Europe's scientific and technological discoveries. And Europeans knew as little about such places as Morocco and Yemen in 1800 as they did about Tibet.

The Ottoman Empire was still territorially intact, but some local regions had achieved quasi-independent status, and Bedouin incursions into settled areas were increasing. When an Ottoman sultan attempted to introduce Western military techniques and weapons into his armed forces in the 1850s, the elite troops of the Empire threatened revolt rather than adopt these "Christian devices." Plagued with ineffective rulers, the Ottoman Middle East was poorly prepared to face the impact of the first waves of the Industrial Revolution that washed over this region in the latter half of the nineteenth century.

Poor leadership in the Ottoman Empire was accompanied by the progressive breakdown in law and order. Tax revenues began to decline. In an effort to modernize the army and civil service, Ottoman sultans began to take loans from European powers. Belated efforts at reform yielded little increase in military power. One by one the Balkan provinces of the empire attained independence. In Anatolia itself, leaders of powerful local families refused to pay taxes to the seat of Ottoman administration in Constantinople. In North Africa, Barbary pirates ruled the cities of Algiers, Tunis, and Tripoli (Libya).

Successive sultans signed commercial treaties with European powers to get additional revenue. In the 1840s, the British were granted trading rights anywhere in the Ottoman Empire. Within a few years, Britain began to import substantial quantities of grain, carpets, wool, and opium from Anatolia in return for textiles and other manufactured goods. Under pressure from European powers, Ottoman sultans granted a series of concessions, called **capitulations,** to foreigners in return for loans. Under the capitulations, Europeans were exempt from local taxes, could not be tried in their home countries for crimes committed in Ottoman territory, and paid low export tariffs.

With these incentives, European banks were established in Mediterranean port cities. European investors bartered for railroad concessions, mineral rights, public utilities, and agricultural land throughout the Ottoman Middle East and North Africa. Additional revenue was raised when sultans sold land in Palestine to Zionists, a financial measure that had enormous repercussions on the future of the entire region. As the debt grew, so did European control of the Ottoman economy. Finally, in 1875, the once-powerful Ottoman Empire was declared bankrupt. The Middle East and North Africa became an economic colony of Western Europe.

Commercial Penetration

The initial effects of European commercial activity in the Middle East were felt in Mediterranean port cities, such as Constantinople, Smyrna (Izmir), Beirut, and Alexandria, and spread inland along trade routes. The introduction of machine-made European textiles had a devastating effect on traditional handicraft industries in many cities. Thousands of cotton spinners were forced out of business when cotton cloth was imported in volume from the mills of industrializing Europe. Indigenous textile products such as damask, muslin, and gauze, disappeared from marketplaces. Craftsmen were driven out of urban occupations and into the villages in search of work. This factor undoubtedly retarded the emergence of an industrial class in the Middle East and North Africa.

As European economic penetration intensified, many important sectors of the Middle Eastern economy passed into the hands of foreigners. Except in Egypt, all railroads and ports were foreign owned and foreign operated. In the large cities, water, electricity, and public transport, were owned by foreign firms. In the North African countries of Morocco, Algeria, Libya, and Tunisia, finance, commerce, real estate, and manufacturing came under European control. The local merchants used as in-

MAPSCAN

THE BEGINNINGS OF CARTOGRAPHY

We do not know when the first map was drawn by a cartographer. Sketches of direction and distance undoubtedly preceded those that have survived. The oldest map now extant is a clay tablet, small enough to fit in the palm of one's hand, which dates back to 2500 B.C. (Fig. 12.4). This tablet, excavated from the ruins of the city of Ga Sur located about 200 miles north of Babylon, shows a river valley (possibly the Euphrates) flowing between two mountain ranges and then subdividing into three deltaic streams that empty into a swamp, lake, or sea. Directions are indicated in inscribed circles; the map is aligned in conformity with cardinal directions. The probable purpose of this tablet was to identify land holdings in a local region of Mesopotamia. Comparable land surveys undoubtedly existed in Egypt at the time.

Modern cartography began with the Greeks. They developed mapmaking into a science that was unsurpassed until Europe emerged from the Middle Ages. It was the Greeks who first recognized the spherical shape of the earth, calculated its approximate size, developed the initial system of longitude and latitude, and designed the first map projections. The most famous of these geographers was Ptolemy (Claudius Ptolemaeus) who lived in the Egyptian city of Alexandria—the intellectual center of the Western world—in the second century A.D. His work had an enormous influence on geography and cartography, the principles of which he delineated in an eight-volume work, *Geographia*.

One of his most famous maps shows the known earth, which then extended from the shores of the Atlantic to the Ganges Valley, projected on a cone (Fig. 12.5). On this map, the Indian Ocean is shown as a landlocked sea, India is truncated, and the island of Sri Lanka (Taprobana) is as large as the Iberian Peninsula. The Middle East lies at the center of the map; the breadth of Europe and Asia

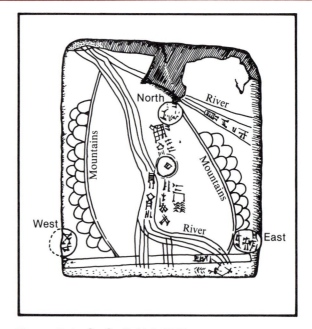

Figure 12.4 Ga-SurTablet, 2500 B.C.

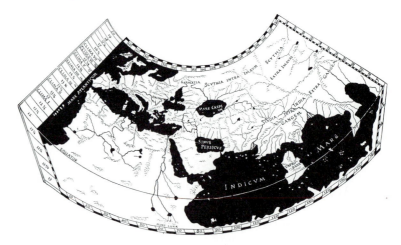

Figure 12.5 Map by Ptolemy.

Figure 12.6 The map of Saint Beatus.

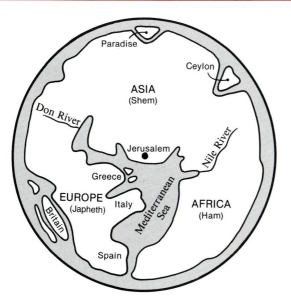

Figure 12.7 "T-in-O" map.

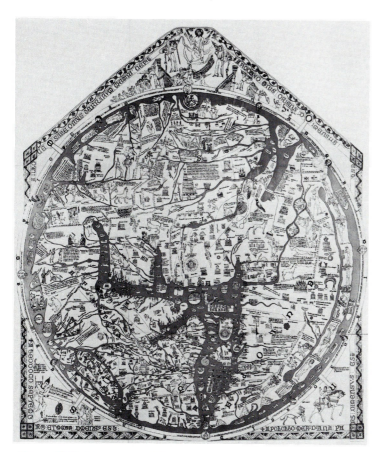

Figure 12.8 Hereford world map.

are exaggerated. Degrees of latitude line the right side of the map; climatic zones based on the length of the longest day (12 hours at the equator, 20 hours in Scandinavia) line the left side of the map. Despite some distortion, which derived primarily from Ptolemy's underestimation of the size of the earth, his maps formed the basis of geographic studies in the Arab World for centuries.

The work of Ptolemy was lost to Western civilization until the fifteenth century. Subsequent Roman maps were deeply imbued with Christian faith. The map of St. Beatus in 776, for example, delineated the world to fit Christian theology (Fig. 12.6). Jerusalem is at the center of the map; the Holy Land is enormous in size. Paradise (Oriens) with its four rivers lies at the top of the map. The outlines of land areas are smoothed to present a more decorative product.

This tendency to mix theology and cartography continued well into the Middle Ages in the form of the circular world map, the **Orbis Terrarum** of the Romans. Such maps are known as "T-in-O" maps in which the three continents of Asia (at the top), Europe, and Africa are pierced by water bodies in the form of a *T* (Fig. 12.7). The Mediterranean Sea formed the leg of the *T*, the Nile and Don rivers the crossbar. Jerusalem was located at the center of the map, following the biblical injunction, "This is Jerusalem: I have set her in the midst of the Nations and countries are round about her" (Ezek. 5:5). One of the most elaborate of these maps is the Hereford world map drawn in the Hereford Cathedral in England in the 1200s (Fig. 12.8). It was not until the Age of Discovery that the early Greek and Arab advances in cartography were rediscovered and mapmaking entered its modern period.

Adapted from: Figure 12.4 (clay tablet), Figure 12.5 (map by Ptolemy), Figure 12.6 (St. Beatus)—Erwin Raisz, *General Cartography,* New York: McGraw-Hill, 1948, p. 5, p. 12, p. 14 respectively. Figure 12.7 ("T-in-O" map), from Arthur H. Robinson and Randall D. Sale, *Elements of Cartography.* New York: John Wiley, 1969, p. 6. Figure 12.8 (the Hereford map) from The Library of Congress.

termediaries by the Europeans were usually non-Muslims: Jews, Greeks, Armenians, and other Christian minorities.

In the countryside, the Western impact was no less dramatic. Progress was equated with increases in the production of raw materials for export to Europe. In Anatolia, mineral resources were mined. But in the Arab countries of the Middle East, the only available exploitable resource was often agricultural land. Europeans expanded cultivation in Anatolia and Syria. In southern Iraq and in Egypt, irrigation projects enlarged the arable. In North Africa, substantial portions of the cultivated land along the Mediterranean coast were settled by French colonists, in Libya by Italian colonists.

The major agricultural change Europeans effected in the Middle East was the replacement of subsistence crops by commercial crops grown for export. Cotton became the principal crop of Egypt and parts of Anatolia. Tobacco was introduced into Syria and Turkey. The export of dates from Iraq and oranges from Palestine became the bases of their economies. The impact was greatest in the most accessible regions—coastal districts and areas penetrated by the spreading net of railroads. Even in these areas, however, little progress was made in the technology of cultivation, so that improvements in productivity were minimal. Economic development was geared to benefit European-dominated trade. It did little to change the social and economic backwardness of the region.

Egypt: Growth Without Development

Nowhere was the lopsided pattern of growth described above more pronounced than in Egypt. After the death of the brilliant and energetic Ottoman ruler Muhammad Ali in 1849, Egypt fell into debt, was declared bankrupt in 1880, and was occupied by British troops. Egyptian resources were rapidly developed in

line with British interests. Egypt's soil, climate, and water supply were ideal for the cultivation of cotton. When the Civil War in the United States eliminated the American South as a major exporting area, agricultural acreage was expanded and cotton was introduced as an export crop. By 1865, Egyptian cotton production had quadrupled; by the turn of the century, cotton and cottonseed accounted for 90 percent of Egypt's exports.

But the cultivation of cotton in Egypt did not mean industrial growth. The thirty-odd mills established by Muhammad Ali fell into disrepair. The British made certain that the local textile industry did not revive. As Lord Cromer, the British consul general of Egypt, noted, "It would be detrimental to both English and Egyptian interests to afford any encouragement to the growth of a protected cotton industry in Egypt." As late as World War I, therefore, the total number of Egyptians engaged in manufacturing enterprises amounted to only 30,000.

On the basis of a number of economic indexes, however, Egypt appeared to be a relatively well-developed society. With a 1913 population of 12 million, Egypt had a per capita income higher than that of Japan and twice that of India. In terms of foreign trade, few industrialized countries surpassed Egypt in value of foreign exports. With more than 2500 miles of railway and the navigable Nile, Egypt was as well provided with transport facilities as most countries in the world.

Despite these indexes, the level of social development in Egypt was low. The illiteracy rate, 93 percent, was higher than that in many less commercial societies. During thirty-five years of British rule, less than 1 percent of the government budget was spent on education. Few Egyptians were sent abroad for education, and of these, only one of every four studied any field directly related to social and economic development.

The effects of this lopsided pattern of growth in Egypt became apparent in the twentieth century. Reliance on one commercial crop led to severe economic fluctuations reflecting world cotton prices. Internal transport networks, geared as they were to international marketing, had no multiplier effects in terms of Egypt's internal economic development. Most businesses and public services were, after all, in the hands of foreigners or non-Muslim minority groups. Finally, population growth spurred by advances in health care exceeded agricultural expansion, and landless peasants piled up in the growing cities of Egypt. For Egypt, colonialism meant commercial growth without social development.

Colonial Patterns of Change

Colonial patterns of change—commercialization of the economy, low levels of social development, foreign control of important sectors of the economy, and orientation toward the production of raw materials for export—affected many areas in the Middle East. In the Gulf, the primary interest came to be petroleum; in the Levant, agricultural production. In North Africa, nearly 2 million European settlers took over the agricultural economy of the Maghrib. Only the more remote parts of the region—the interior of Arabia, the Sahara, Afghanistan, and parts of Iran—were not substantially affected.

Nationalism and Independence

On the eve of World War I, Ottoman Turkey still retained territorial control over its Arab provinces in the Levant, Mesopotamia, western Arabia, and Yemen. Great power rivalries had preserved a delicate balance of distrust that enabled Ottoman sultans to maintain physical and economic rule.

But in 1914 the Sultan, spurred by Turkish nationalists, rashly declared

In the 1800s, fertile land in Egypt was planted in cotton under British colonial rule. Today, cotton remains Egypt's most important commercial crop.

a "holy war" on the Allies (the British, French, and Russians) and joined forces with Germany. The Allies agreed by secret treaty to partition the Ottoman Empire. The Russians would take control of the straits between the Black and Mediterranean seas. Greece was to regain parts of western Anatolia. The Italians were to keep their holdings in the Adana region in the southeast and the Zonguldak coal basin in the northwest of Turkey proper. The British would remain in Palestine and Mesopotamia. The French would receive Syria. The Ottoman Empire faced political extinction.

Turkey and Iran

The plans of the allied powers were abandoned when Turkish national-ists, under the leadership of the army officer Mustafa Kemal (later called Ataturk), drove occupying French, British, and Greek armies from Anatolia. He focused the national spirit of the Turkish people on the establishment of an independent republic. The Ottoman caliphate was abolished and religious courts were replaced by a Western code of civil law in Turkey. The special privileges of the minorities were withdrawn, and a secular state was created. Efforts were made to develop the economic resources of Anatolia and to industrialize without foreign interference. The first independent Middle Eastern state, Turkey, sought parity in the world through intensive Westernization.

Similarly, Iran (then called Persia) was on the verge of becoming a dependency of the British Empire. For years, Britain and Russia had gained internal railroad, bank, tobacco, and loan concessions from local rulers. But in 1921, Reza Khan, an officer in the Iranian cossacks, led a *coup d'etat* in Tehran and took over the Iranian state. Like Ataturk, Reza Khan was an ardent nationalist. After subduing rebellious tribal groups in the Zagros, he embarked on an extensive program of modernization. Religious officials were stripped of authority and religious property was confiscated. Western legal codes were introduced and concession agreements with foreigners were nullified.

Over the next twenty years, the road system was extended from 2000 to 17,000 miles and the lengthy Trans-

Iranian railroad was built to connect the Gulf in the south with the fertile provinces of the north. Light industry was introduced, and some progress was made in agriculture, although the power of absentee landlords prevented any fundamental land reform. As in Turkey, the pattern of developmental change was Western.

The Arab Lands

In the Arab Middle East and North Africa, no single charismatic leader emerged to unite national aspirations. Divided for centuries into provinces of the Ottoman Empire, islands of dense population were separated from one another by deserts and mountains. Independence was achieved in different ways in each region. In Cairo, Damascus, Baghdad, Beirut, and the port cities of North Africa, nationalists concentrated on ending European colonialism in their respective countries. In the interior, Arab governors, tribal leaders, and local rulers fought to gain independent power bases.

Rivalries, geographical isolation, and the disruptive tactics of colonial authorities frustrated any concerted action among Arab leaders. Vague British promises of Arab independence in exchange for their support against the Turks in World War I were quickly converted into partition of the Arab Ottoman domains after the war. Only the Arabian Peninsula attained independence. In the desert interior, the conservative Wahabis led by Ibn Saud conquered the Hijaz and unified most of the peninsula in 1933. Yemen, too, became independent, although Aden had become an important British port on the route to India. The Gulf states and Oman remained under British domination.

In Egypt, a monarchy was established and granted nominal independence in 1924, but British influence remained strong in the Nile Valley throughout the interwar period, thwarting the aims of nationalists. British commercial and military interests remained paramount until the regime of King Farouk was finally dislodged in 1952 by an army revolt led by Gamal Abdel Nasser.

In Iraq, a similar pattern evolved. The British mandate was relinquished in 1932, but it was not until 1958 that the pro-Western Hashimite dynasty was overthrown by a military revolt.

In the British mandate of Palestine, Jewish immigration and colonization led to a complicated international conflict between Jews and Arabs. A Hashimite monarchy was established in part of Palestine east of the Jordan River, which became the state of Transjordan (modern Jordan). The British withdrew from the rest of Palestine in 1948, turning the territorial conflict between Zionist settlers from Europe and Palestinians over to the United Nations. Modern Israel emerged in the outcome.

In Syria, the French were more determined than the British to retain their mandate. Severe fighting between Syrians and the French preceded final French withdrawal after World War II. Two new republics—Syria and Lebanon—were created.

In North Africa, the struggle for independence was complicated by the presence of 2 million French nationals who were determined to stay. Libya gained independence from Italy in 1952; Morocco and Tunisia from France in 1956. The most severe conflict occurred in French Algeria, where eight years of bloody guerrilla warfare were required to dislodge the French in 1962.

THE HUMAN GEOGRAPHY OF THE MIDDLE EAST AND NORTH AFRICA

The Middle East and North Africa form a vast swath of deserts, steppes, and mountain plateaus located at the juncture of the three continents of Europe, Africa, and Asia (Fig. 12.9). Nearly twice the size of the United

Gamal Abdel Nasser, who became the leader of Egypt after an army revolt in 1952, was an articulate proponent of Arab nationalism.

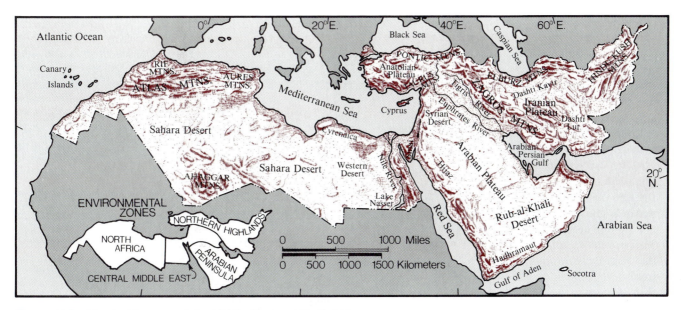

Figure 12.9 Physical features of the Middle East and North Africa.

States, this region stretches 6000 miles eastward from the dry Atlantic shores of the Sahara to the high mountain core of Afghanistan. It includes twenty-two separate political states, the boundaries of which were drawn by colonial cartographers in the nineteenth and twentieth centuries. By world standards, the population of the Middle East is small: roughly 325 million people. But over half of the Middle East is too dry or rugged to sustain dense populations, and only 5 to 10 percent of the entire region is cultivated. Stark contrasts prevail between core areas of human settlement where water is plentiful and the empty wastes of surrounding deserts and mountains.

These environmental contrasts play an important role in the developmental plans of both the oil-rich countries of the Gulf and the poorer countries in this region. The *Environments and Landscapes* of the Middle East and North Africa still govern the distribution of population in this region. Well-watered areas on the Mediterranean coasts, in the river valleys, and in the mountains and plateaus of Turkey and Iran have been occupied for millennia. These cores of population are still surrounded by

sparsely settled deserts, steppes, and high mountains. On the basis of climate and terrain, four regions can be identified: *The Northern Highlands*, a 3000-mile-long zone of plateaus and mountains in Turkey, Iran, and Afghanistan, stretching from the Mediterranean Sea to Central Asia; *The Arabian Peninsula*, a 1-million-square-mile desert jutting southward into the Indian Ocean and flanked by the Gulf and the Red Sea; *The Central Middle East*, the rich valleys of the Nile in Egypt, the Tigris and Euphrates in Iraq, and the intervening Fertile Crescent countries of Israel, Jordan, Lebanon, and Syria; and *North Africa*, a band of watered mountains and plains set between the Sahara Desert and the Mediterranean Sea that includes Libya, Tunisia, Algeria, and Morocco. In all of these regions, *The Human Use of the Earth* has been long, intense, and hazardous.

Environments and Landscapes

The landscapes and environments of the Middle East evoke stock images in the West: the oasis of palm trees set in sand, a green slice of riverine land framed by barren plains, camel

caravans crossing desert wastes, snowcapped mountains stripped of vegetation, nomads grazing flocks on thin pastures, and the shores of the Mediterranean—blue sea against verdant land. Everywhere the environmental key is water (Fig. 12.10).

The climate of the Middle East is distinctly seasonal. In the winter, storm tracks shift southward from Europe, course across the Mediterranean, and collide with its eastern and southern shores—the Levant and the Maghrib. These storms pass inland dropping rainfall on the southern slopes of the Taurus Mountains in Turkey and the western flanks of the Zagros Mountains. In summer, by contrast, the dry Saharan climate pushes northward, providing the Mediterranean Basin with cloudless skies. Rainfall, therefore, is concentrated in the winter season; summers are dry. As in Mediterranean climates generally, this pattern defines the agricultural seasons and sets the seasonal rhythm of rural life throughout the Middle East.

Topography plays an important role in the distribution of rainfall. The Atlas Mountains of North Africa trap westerly air masses, enabling Mediterranean-style agriculture to be practiced on the northern coast of Africa. Inland from these coastal mountains, vegetation grades from Mediterranean scrub, or **maquis,** to grass-covered steppes, and the deserts of the Sahara (Fig. 12.10). In the Levant, low ranges in Syria, Lebanon, and Israel intercept rain-bearing air masses that provide sufficient moisture for cultivation without irrigation. The melting snows of the Taurus and Zagros mountains provide water to the Tigris-Euphrates river system, the culture hearth of ancient Mesopotamian civilization. In Egypt, the Nile flows as an **exotic stream** from the highlands of East Africa through desert to the Mediterranean. Only the northern fringe of the Middle East receives a surplus of rain. Regionwide, however, subhumid or arid conditions prevail.

The importance of these environmental factors can be seen in the distribution of population. Dense concentrations exist only where water can support agriculture either through rainfall or by irrigation. The margins of the Anatolian and Iranian plateaus sustained important civilizations on the basis of agricultural surpluses generated by more favorable agricultural environments. The river-based civilizations of Mesopotamia and the Nile date back millennia. The coasts of North Africa and the Levant formed the breadbaskets of the Roman Empire. Elsewhere in the Middle East, people are few, settlements scattered. In the deserts of North Africa, Arabia, Turkey, and Iran, the land until recently was used principally by nomads.

Traditional technologies, like subterranean tunnels (qanats) and waterwheels, along with sophisticated methods of trapping and channeling water for irrigation remain widespread in the Middle East. These systems of water extraction were in balance with natural supplies but supported limited populations. The introduction of modern technology into the region—the dams of Mo-

POPULATION AND RAINFALL IN NORTH AFRICA

The direct correlation between rainfall and density of population in the Middle East is clearly illustrated in Fig. 12.10. Where settlement extends beyond the 10-inch rainfall line into drier areas, Moroccan farmers have dug wells or constructed small dams, or live along riverine oases. Beyond the Atlas Mountains, irrigated agriculture supports small, dense populations of date and grain farmers in oasis settlements, many of which are along rivers from the Atlas that drain into the Sahara. Because irrigated agriculture is more restricted in space than rain-fed agriculture, population diminishes where average precipitation falls below 10 inches a year.

Adapted from: Marvin W. Mikesell, *Patterns and Imprints of Mankind.* Chicago: Rand McNally, 1969, p. xxvi.

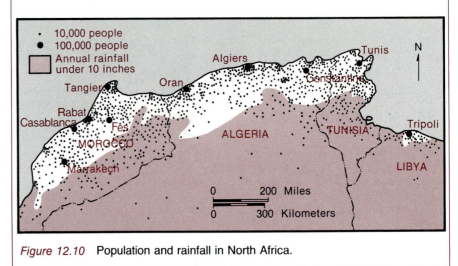

Figure 12.10 Population and rainfall in North Africa.

rocco, Algeria, Egypt, and Iraq; deep wells in the subhumid fringes; and water canals and pipeline facilities for urban centers—tap nonrenewable **fossil water tables** of limited capacity. The long-term future of settlement in the Middle East is contingent on intelligent and restrained use of available water.

The human geography of the Middle East and North Africa today reflects the traditional environmental constraints that bound past generations in this region. Modern environmental change has taken the form of intensification of land use in old Middle Eastern core areas. Extension of economic activity beyond these cores into the uplands or drylands of the Middle East has been directly related to the search for oil and the expansion of irrigated surfaces through

the construction of dams. The process of economic intensification, spurred by population growth, has altered the environments of this region in major ways. In each of its subregions—in the Northern Highlands, the Arabian Peninsula, the Central Middle East, and North Africa—regional landscapes reflect the impact of modern technology. Current programs of economic and social modernization in the Middle East will hinge on the effectiveness of water use in this arid environment.

The Northern Highlands

The Taurus and Zagros mountains of southern Turkey and western Iran, a physical and cultural barrier, divide the Arabic-speaking peoples of the south from the plateau-dwelling peo-

Palm trees are grown in pits in the Souf Oasis in Algeria. This is one of the few permanent settlements located in the deserts of the Middle East and North Africa.

sides by water—the Black Sea to the north, the Aegean Sea to the west, and the Mediterranean Sea on the south. In the north and the west, the Turkish coast is rainy, densely settled, and intensively cultivated.

About 40 percent of the population is clustered in four areas: (1) on the narrow, wet Black Sea coast; (2) on the lowlands around the Sea of Marmara—in both European and Asiatic Turkey; (3) along the shores of the Aegean; and (4) on the fertile Adana Plain in the southeast.

By contrast, the center of Turkey—the dry, flat Anatolian Plateau—is sparsely settled. Cut off by the Pontic Mountains to the north and the Taurus Mountains to the south, the core of the plateau is too dry to sustain dense agricultural settlement. In the east, the rugged terrain of the Armenian highlands limits agricultural development.

Turkey's population of 52.9 million has doubled over the last forty years and continues to grow at a rate of 1 million people each year. Turkey's rate of natural increase has begun to decline, however. The country is still an agrarian society; half of the population still works the land. Cultivated land has increased two-and-one-half times in the last twenty-five years. Wheat harvests have doubled, and cultivation of cotton, tea, and citrus fruit has greatly expanded. But only 7 percent of the land is in agriculture.

Many rural Turks in search of economic security have migrated to cities such as Istanbul (pop. 3 million), to the capital Ankara (pop. 3.2 million), or to smaller provincial centers. Their success in finding jobs depends on continued industrial and agricultural growth. With about 3 percent of its national territory in continental Europe, Turkey's industrial success in the 1980s and its close labor migration relations with Western Europe have led Turkey to apply for membership in the EC.

Although the environmental base of Iranian society is similar to Tur-

ples of Turkey, Iran, and Afghanistan (Fig. 12.9). About 40 percent—some 119 million—of the people of the Middle East and North Africa live in the Northern Highlands, on the An-atolian and Iranian plateaus, and on the flanks of the Hindu Kush Range of Afghanistan.

Turkey is a large, rectangular peninsula plateau bounded on three

GEOLAB

CLIMOGRAPHS OF HUMAN COMFORT

Comfort **climographs** are graphic representations of climatic data, relatively simple methods for graphically illustrating the felt weather conditions for human beings in different climates.

The bottom axis on the climograph is **relative humidity,** which is expressed as a percentage. Relative humidity is the amount of water vapor present in the air at a given temperature relative to the maximum amount of water vapor the air could hold at that temperature. The higher the relative humidity, the muggier or damper the air. The vertical axis is temperature expressed in degrees Fahrenheit. Wet bulb temperatures (temperatures taken from a thermometer covered with a damp cloth) are used to take account of the cooling effect of evaporation.

Data for monthly relative humidity are plotted against monthly wet bulb temperatures for each city, and these points are connected by lines. Comfort zones are listed on the right side of the climograph. Note that points with high temperatures and low relative humidity are defined as scorching, high temperatures and high relative humidity as muggy, low temperatures and low relative humidity as brisk, and low temperatures and high relative humidity as raw.

In the top climograph (Fig. 12.11), the comfort conditions for two cities in

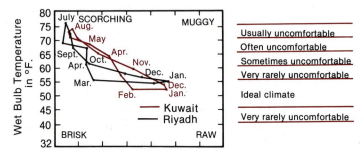

Figure 2.11   Climograph of the Northern Highlands.

Figure 12.12   Climograph of the Arabian Peninsula.

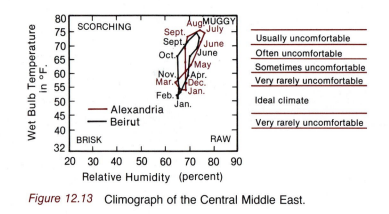

Figure 12.13   Climograph of the Central Middle East.

key's, the topography is more dramatic, and contrasts between cultivated land and barren wilderness are more sharply drawn. High mountains ring the dry Iranian Plateau on all sides, except the east. In the west and south, the folded ranges of the Zagros Mountains curve south-eastward for a distance of 1400 miles, from the Turkish frontier in the northwest to the deserts of Sistan province in the southeast. In the

north, the steep volcano-studded El-burz Range sharply divides the wet coast of the Caspian Sea from the dry Iranian interior. The encircled plateau covers over half the area of Iran. Here, large stretches of salt waste in the Dashti Kavir to the north and of sand desert in the Dashti Lut to the south are uninhabited. In contrast to Turkey, only one third of the people of Iran are agricultural villagers. Because population has quintupled from

10 million to 51.9 million in this century, settlement has intensified in regions favorable to agriculture.

Along the Caspian littoral, which receives up to 60 inches of rainfall per year, intensive cultivation of rice, tea, tobacco, and citrus fruits supports a dense rural population. Similarly, in Azerbaijan in the northwest and in the fertile valleys of the northern Zagros Mountains, rainfall is sufficient to support grain cultivation

the Northern Highlands, Tehran and Ankara, are plotted. The high temperature and low relative humidities of summer produce scorching conditions; the winter rains and low temperatures, raw conditions. The extremes of temperature reflect the continental locations of both cities. In the middle climograph, (Fig. 12.12), the desert climates of the Arabian Peninsula are seen in the temperature and moisture regimes of Riyadh and Kuwait. Hot, dry, scorching conditions prevail except in winter. The bottom climograph (Fig. 12.13), presenting data for Beirut and Alexandria in the Central Middle East, shows high relative humidities year round and a limited range of temperature because of the maritime locations of these cities on the Mediterranean.

Throughout the Middle East, people are acutely aware of daily and seasonal variations in climate. Offices and shops close in the afternoon; government officials are rarely available in the summer season. Trips are planned or deferred to take advantage of "good weather" to a far greater degree than in American society. Climate is a crucial concern and is expressed on the landscape in narrow streets, courtyard houses, wind towers, thick adobe walls, and other indigenous architectural features.

Adapted from: Peter Beaumont et al., The Middle East: A Geographical Study. London: John Wiley, 1977, p. 77.

The Tigris and Euphrates rivers join in southern Iraq. This region of fertile alluvial soils, irrigated grainfields, and date palm groves is the birthplace of Mesopotamian civilization.

without irrigation. The high pastures of this region support an estimated 3 million transhumant nomads of Turkish origin.

But in the rest of Iran, rainfall is low and irrigation is essential. Oasis settlements are common. In Khuzistan, on the Mesopotamian plain, new dams on the Dez and Karun rivers are aimed at creating major industrial-agricultural complexes. Growing urban populations in the mushrooming city of Tehran (pop. 6 million); in Mashhad, Isfahan, Tabriz, and Shiraz (each with more than a half million people); and in smaller cities in the north mean that Iranian agriculture cannot feed the country's people. How Iran's revolutionary government will deal with these problems after the war with Iraq is not clear.

In the remote country of Afghanistan, the easternmost of the Northern Highlands, the processes of population growth, agricultural expansion, and urbanization have barely begun. The country's center is oc-

This fortified village in the Salang Valley of the Hindu Kush, north of Kabul, is on a highway built by Soviet engineers. The road through the Salang Pass, one of the few passageways through the Hindu Kush, has been the scene of bitter battles between Russian troops and Afghan insurgents.

cupied by the Hindu Kush Mountains, a rugged snowbound highland that is one of the most impenetrable regions in the world. Deserts to the east and south are cut by two major rivers, the Hari Rud and the Helmand, both of which originate in the mountains of central Afghanistan and disappear into the deserts of eastern Iran. In the north, the Amu Darya (Oxus) flows into Soviet Central Asia. Settlements are scattered in alluvial pockets on the perimeter of the Hindu Kush Mountains, wherever there is level land and reliable water.

Over 70 percent of Afghanistan's estimated 14.5 million people live in these villages, cultivating wheat and barley and herding small flocks of sheep and goats. An additional 15 percent are nomadic tribesmen, whose political power is still felt in this traditional society. In central and eastern Afghanistan, Pathans are dominant; in the north, Turkish-speaking Uzbeks and Persian-speaking Tadzhiks predominate. This cul-

tural diversity reflects a tradition of isolation in a countryside that has been largely unconnected with the modern world. At least two thirds of Afghanistan's rural produce never enters the market economy; urbanization is slight (Kabul has only 600,000 people), and modern agricultural expansion has just begun with irrigation projects in the Hari Rud and Helmand valleys. Despite this, population growth has forced the country, formerly self-sufficient in foodstuffs, to begin imports of basic grains. The Soviet invasion and occupation of Afghanistan (1979–1988) disrupted the life of this once-isolated land. Afghan out-migration has been strong; as many as three million Afghans have left the country in the wake of warfare in this preindustrial land. Afghan political groups continue to struggle for a unified country.

The Arabian Peninsula

The Arabian Peninsula is a huge desert platform bounded on three sides

by water and on the fourth by the deserts of Jordan and Iraq (Fig. 12.1 and 12.9). In the west, the slopes of the Hijaz and the rugged highlands of Yemen form the topographical backbone of this platform. The remainder tilts eastward to the shore of the Gulf, rising only in the extreme southeast to higher elevations in the Jabal al Akhdar (Green Mountains) of Oman.

Although the peninsula is the largest in the world and nearly four times the size of the state of Texas, it supports a population of only 29 million people. The majority of these people live in two countries. Saudi Arabia (pop. 14.2 million), which governs nine tenths of this region, and North Yemen (pop. 6.7 million), whose highlands trap sufficient moisture to support cultivation without irrigation. South Yemen (pop. 2.4 million) and Oman (pop. 1.4 million), both large states in area, occupy the southern and eastern periphery of Arabia. Small states along the Gulf—none with populations over two million—include Kuwait, Bahrain, Qatar, and the United Arab Emirates.

As elsewhere in the Middle East, the principal determinant of human settlement in Arabia is availability of water. The region receives less than 3 inches of rainfall each year, with slightly more in the north. Only the highlands of Yemen and Oman at the southern corners of the peninsula receives over 10 inches of rainfall. Parts of Yemen receive over 30 inches of rain per year, in high mountains rising to over 10,000 feet—making for a remarkably different human environment in southwestern Arabia. Daily temperatures commonly rise above 100 degrees Fahrenheit. Given this harsh environment, the Arabian landscape has no permanent lakes or streams. Vegetation is sparse. Settlement is confined to oases; only 1 percent of the region is under cultivation. Vast stretches of the peninsula are completely uninhabited, devoid of human presence except for the passage of Bedouin camel herders.

In this difficult physical setting, two thirds of the people of the Arabian Peninsula are rural agriculturalists, seminomads, and nomads. Oases based on wells and springs provide water for the cultivation of barley and dates—the staple food of the desert—and the maintenance of herds of camels, sheep, and goats. The distribution of these oases is determined by a network of wadis, dry river valleys, carved into the surface of the plateau in earlier and wetter geological periods. These wadis are the most favored locations for commercial and agricultural settlement, and the most convenient routes for caravan traffic.

In the western highlands, where population density is above average, the largest urban centers are Mecca, Medina, and Taif. In central Arabia, underground water percolates down from these uplands and surfaces as artesian wells, which support a string of agricultural oases both north and south of the Saudi Arabian capital of Riyadh. Farther east, on the shores of the Gulf, this same water emerges as freshwater springs in Kuwait, eastern Saudi Arabia, and the United Arab Emirates. Similarly, in South Yemen, springs in the Wadi Hadhramaut, a gash several hundred miles long parallel to the coast of the Gulf of Aden, provide the basis for oasis settlement. Only in North Yemen and Oman is this dry-land-oasis pattern broken. In North Yemen, the highland rainfall allows terraced cultivation of coffee, cotton, and the highly profitable shrub qat, a stimulant chewed by Yemenis young and old. In Oman, grains, dates, pomegranates, and limes are cultivated, and cattle breeding is an important economic activity.

The prevailing harshness of the Arabian environment, however, has always required that any sizable settlement on the peninsula exist partially on resources brought in from outside—on revenues from the pilgrimage traffic, coastal trade in the Gulf, or commerce in the Indian Ocean. Today, oil resources in Saudi Arabia, Kuwait, the island state of Bahrain, the United Arab Emirates, and (to a lesser extent) Qatar and Oman are providing the capital for rapid economic growth. North and South Yemen have been left in isolation and poverty, although the discovery of oil in the North Yemeni desert bodes rapid change for that country.

In the Gulf, glittering modern cities like Dhahran, Dammam, Jubail (in Saudi Arabia), Kuwait City, Manamah (Bahrain), and Emirate centers, like Abu Dhabi, Dubai, and Sharjah, are creations of the oil industry. Less directly but equally dramatically, the traditional centers of Riyadh (pop. 700,000), Jidda (pop. 600,000), and Mecca (pop. 400,000) are growing rapidly as farmers, Bedouins, and migrant laborers from abroad seek salaried employment in expanding urban industries and services.

With apparently limitless capital, the governments of the oil-producing states of the Arabian Peninsula are now drilling thousands of new water wells, establishing desalinization plants along the coast, and investing heavily in agricultural expansion and forestation—all to the purpose of establishing a viable post-oil economic base. But whether the arid environment of the peninsula can sustain these larger populations on a permanent basis is a matter of conjecture.

The Central Middle East

The Central Middle East is flanked on the west and east by two great river valleys, the Nile of Egypt and the Tigris-Euphrates of Iraq. Between these riverine states, the small nations of Israel, Lebanon, and Syria line the shores of the eastern Mediterranean; Jordan is landlocked (Fig. 12.9).

The total population of this region is 94 million, which reflects a more reliable water supply. In the north, rain is delivered by winter storms coursing eastward through the Mediterranean Basin. In the drier south, the dependable fertility of the river valleys is maintained by runoff from the Northern Highlands into Iraq and from the East African Highlands into Egypt.

The environments of these six nations are as complex as their histories. Four thousand years of human civilization have left an essentially denuded landscape—barren hills, steppes overgrazed by sheep and goats, and rivers choked by the erosional silt of human activity. Faced with rapidly expanding populations, each state has developed strategies to cope with increasing pressure on environmental resources.

In Egypt, population pressure on agricultural land is more serious than anywhere else in the Middle East. An estimated 96 percent of Egypt's 53.3 million people are crowded into the Nile Valley, a narrow trough 2 to 10 miles wide that cuts northward across the arid plateau of north-eastern Africa to the Mediterranean Sea. The sources of the Nile River lie 2000 miles south of the Mediterranean in the highlands of Ethiopia and East Africa. Summer rainfall in the Ethiopian Highlands pours into the Blue Nile, joins the White Nile at Khartoum, and causes the river to flood regularly from August to December, raising its level some 21 feet.

For centuries, the Nile flood formed the basis of Egyptian agriculture. Specially prepared earthen basins were constructed along the banks of the Nile to trap and hold the floodwaters. This provided Egyptian farmers with enough water to irrigate one and, in some areas, two crops of wheat and barley each year. Silt deposited by the swollen waters refertilized Egyptian fields every year and ensured continuing soil fertility and high yields.

Early in the twentieth century, British and Egyptian engineers constructed a series of low dams on the Nile to hold and store the floodwater year round. Their goal was to change traditional **basin irrigation** into **perennial irrigation,** thus enabling the Egyptian peasant to plant three or four crops each year on land previously left uncultivated when the level of the Nile was too low. Corn and cotton replaced wheat and barley as the primary crops. Rice and vegetables were grown for export. By 1960, the area under cultivation had increased from 4 million to 6 million acres, and crop yields of wheat and corn were up by one third.

This transformation of Nile agriculture was completed in 1971 with the construction of the Aswan High Dam, a massive earthen barrier more than 2 miles across, one-half mile wide at the base, and 365 feet high. Behind it, Lake Nasser, the dammed Nile River, stretches 300 miles southward into Sudan. Although the

dam has added to the cultivated area of Egypt by about one third, this is not enough to sustain Egypt's rapidly growing population. Politically expedient, the environmental impact of the High Dam on the Nile Valley may be severely negative in the long run.

As agricultural engineers labored to increase the scope and productivity of Egyptian agriculture, Egypt's population quintupled from an estimated 10 million at the turn of the century to its current 53.3 million. During this same period, urban population expanded eight times, and Greater Cairo (pop. 11 million) and Alexandria (pop. 2.8 million) emerged as the two largest cities on the African continent. Peasants from Upper Egypt (the south) migrated from less productive areas of basin irrigation to richer agricultural areas downstream

in Lower Egypt. In the Delta, rural densities have reached over 6000 people per square mile in some areas. Overall, the average size of agricultural holdings in Egypt diminished from 5.7 acres in 1900 to less than 2 acres today. The amount of crop area per person has been halved.

Contained within a narrow ribbon of fertile land in the valley and delta of the Nile, Egypt's population continues to grow at a rate of more than a million people each year. Intense overcrowding and mounting population pressure can only be relieved by substantial emigration or, alternatively, through rapid economic development at home. Attempts to reduce the birth rate have met with little success. Ultimately, Egypt's fate may depend on all three of these developments.

In contrast to Egypt, the basic

Oil wealth has created a string of modern cities on the western shore of the Gulf.

problem in the other great river valley of the Middle East, the Tigris-Euphrates of Iraq, or what has been known traditionally as Mesopotamia, is not overpopulation but environmental management. Both of these rivers rise in the mountains of eastern Turkey and course southward for more than 1000 miles before merging in the marshes of the Shatt al Arab at the head of the Gulf. North of Baghdad, both rivers run swiftly in clearly defined channels. To the south, they meander across flat alluvial plains.

Only in the northeast of the country, in the Kurdish highlands, is rain-fed agriculture possible. Elsewhere in Iraq, human existence depends on the waters of the Tigris and Euphrates. But unlike Egypt, where every available acre of farmland is intensively utilized, Iraq's agricultural resources are not used effectively. Only one sixth of the potentially arable land is under cultivation. Iraq clearly has the resources to support a substantially larger population than its current 17.6 million.

Yet the Tigris and Euphrates rivers have always proved less manageable than the Nile. Fed by melting snows in the Taurus Mountains, springtime floods pour down the Euphrates toward Baghdad, where the river begins to spread out over the vast plains of Mesopotamia. Here the Euphrates and Tigris become laced together, the land is flat, and elevation changes only 4 to 5 feet over distances of 50 miles. As some 70 percent of Iraqis are farmers, floods are a direct threat to the economy of the country.

Modern dikes and dams on the rivers have brought widespread flooding under control, but drainage and irrigation are difficult downstream from Baghdad. The accumulation of salts in the soil, salinization, is a constant problem. Improved control of the environment, however, has encouraged nomads in Mesopotamia to settle as wheat and barley farmers in good agricultural years and to revert to herding in bad agricultural years. Although cultivation is widespread, large areas still lie fallow, and yields are low. In the far south, the rivers join to form the swampy marshes of the Shatt al Arab. Three quarters of the world's dates are produced here, where the environment is less hazardous, and dense populations of peasants produce an agricultural surplus.

Iraq's growing population and the attractions of urban life have caused a flight of villagers from rural areas to the cities, in particular to the capital city of Baghdad (pop. 3.2 million). In spite of available agricultural land and relative underpopulation, many of the same problems that plague Egypt are affecting Iraq. The available resources and potential oil revenues of Iraq would seem to make future progress much more likely. In the 1980s, however, prolonged war with Iran drained Iraq of needed development funds and proved disastrous to Iraq's southernmost environments.

The Fertile Crescent countries of Syria, Lebanon, Jordan, and Israel are located on the east coast of the Mediterranean, in what has been known traditionally as the Levant. Environmental patterns are extremely complex. Aridity increases eastward. The coastal plain, narrow in the north but widening southward, is backed by dissected, rugged highlands that reach elevations of more than 10,000 feet in Lebanon. These are the Lebanon Mountains. Throughout their length, these uplands have been stripped of forests—notably the famous cedars of Lebanon—by centuries of overgrazing, cutting, and warfare.

In Syria, the coastal highlands capture ample rainfall to support life in the oasis cities of Aleppo, Homs, Hama, and Damascus. As in Lebanon and northern Israel, runoff from the highlands sustains important commercial and agricultural areas along the coast. Farther south, the highlands flatten out into the Negev Desert of Israel.

Inland, a narrow belt of intermontane valleys separates the coastal highlands from secondary, more arid, mountains to the east. Between Israel and Jordan, south of the Sea of Galilee, the Jordan River flows 150 miles along one of these valleys to the Dead Sea, 1300 feet below sea level. Farther north, a similar trough in Lebanon, the Beqaa Valley, is drained by the Litani and Orontes rivers. East of these lowlands, the rugged Anti-Lebanon Mountains grade inland to the grass-covered steppes of Syria in the north and the dry stone pavement of the Jordanian desert in the south. The elevated Syrian Desert, much of it strewn with volcanic debris, dips eastward toward Mesopotamia.

In this varied terrain, the distribution of population is extremely uneven. In Israel, with a population of 4.4 million (excluding the 1.5 people in the Occupied Territories), some 80 percent of the population is clustered on the northern coastal plain between Haifa and Tel Aviv. In the south, the Negev, which makes up 70 percent of the country's area, is virtually empty, although political considerations and ideological commitments have led to the establishment of some communal agricultural settlements (**kibbutzim**) in this desert.

Similarly in Lebanon (pop. 3.3 million), population is dense along the coast and thinner in the interior highlands, with a secondary concentration in the Beqaa Valley between the Lebanon and Anti-Lebanon mountains. Olives, grapes, citrus fruit, and other Mediterranean crops are grown commercially along the Lebanese coast, as they are to the south in Israel. Neither state, however, is primarily agricultural. Unlike most Middle Eastern countries, Israel and Lebanon (before it became a battleground) are urban nations with sophisticated, literate populations and diversified economies. More than 50 percent of all Lebanese live in either Beirut (pop. 1.5 million) or Tripoli; in Israel, a like percentage resides in Tel Aviv (pop. 350,000), Jerusalem (pop. 400,000), Haifa (pop. 370,000), and other towns.

In Syria and Jordan, the primary economic activity is village farming. Some 90 percent of Syria's 11.3 million people live in the more humid western part of the country. On the narrow coastal plain and in the foothills of the Jabal Ansariah, a prolongation of the Lebanon Mountains, wheat, olives, and the famous latakia tobacco are cultivated. On the eastern slopes of these mountains, wheat fields and tree crops cover a vast plain stretching from Homs to Aleppo. In the south around Damascus (pop. 1.1 million), olives, fruit, and wheat are primary products. Southeast of Damascus, the volcanic Jabal Druze rises above the plain to shelter the homeland of one of the Levant's most significant ethnic groups—the Druze. Druze people, numbering somewhat less than one million, are spread throughout the Levant today. Their distinct Muslim beliefs have given rise to their separate identity, particularly apparent in the politics of modern Lebanon. In the Syrian interior, only the far northeast, the Jezira, has sufficient rainfall to support nonirrigated grain agriculture. Important irrigation projects have been established along the Syrian Euphrates, providing opportunities for Syria's population, which is growing faster than that of any other Middle Eastern country.

In Jordan (pop. 3.8 million), five-sixths of the land is a desert plateau suitable only for a nomadic existence. On either side of the Jordan River, subsistence wheat cultivation is supplemented by small, intensive farms oriented toward exports to the Gulf and Saudi Arabia. This economy has been severely disrupted by politics and war. Approximately half of Jordan's population is now composed of refugees from Israeli territory.

North Africa

North Africa is the largest subregion of the modern Middle East, but it is settled by only 85 million people. North Africans are clustered on the southern shore of the Mediterranean Sea and the Atlantic plains of Morocco—between the sea and the Sahara (Fig. 12.9). Much as Egypt is the gift of the Nile, occupied North Africa is the realm of the Atlas Mountains, which divide into a variety of ranges between the Sahara and the Mediterranean. Collectively, Morocco, Algeria, and Tunisia are known as the Maghrib. Libya stands apart.

Most of the territory of the modern states of the Maghrib consists of Sahara Desert. The Sahara stretches 3000 miles across Africa from the Atlantic Ocean to the Egyptian border. And the Western and Eastern deserts of Egypt are an extension of the Sahara. One seventh of this area is sand dunes or **erg;** the remainder is rockstrewn desert plains and plateaus or **hammada.** Aridity in the Sahara is not interrupted even by the jutting peaks of the Ahaggar and Tibesti massifs at 11,000 feet, which receive as much as 5 inches of rainfall per year. In scattered Saharan oasis environments, an estimated 3 million people wrest a living from one of the earth's most difficult environments. Only in the north, along the mountain-backed coasts of the Mediterranean and Atlantic, is rainfall sufficient to sustain substantial concentrations of people. The Atlas Mountains form a diagonal barrier that isolates the nomads of the deserts and steppes to the south and east from the sedentary agriculturalists in the Mediterranean north.

The former Spanish Sahara, incorporated into Morocco since 1975, is totally desert. Before the discovery of extensive phosphate deposits and the promise of rich iron ore lodes, this territory was of little interest to anyone but the 70,000 indigenous pastoralists and the Spanish troops occupying the area. Although the

territory has been absorbed by Morocco, resistance from the local population has been strong. Many Saharans have fled to refugee camps in Algeria, where they have regrouped as the Polisario Liberation Front.

In Morocco, the Atlas Mountains form a succession of mountain ranges dominating the landscape. In the north, the Rif, geologically separate from the Atlas system, is a concave arc of mountains that rise steeply along the Mediterranean, reaching elevations of 7000 feet. In the center of Morocco, the limestone plateaus and volcanic craters of the Middle Atlas reach elevations of 10,000 feet. Farther south, the snow-capped peaks of the High Atlas attain elevations of 13,400 feet and separate the watered north from the Sahara. Finally, the Anti-Atlas, the lowest and southernmost of the Moroccan ranges, forms a topographic barrier to the western Sahara.

Historically, the Atlas Mountains provided a refuge for the original Berber-speaking inhabitants of Morocco, whose descendants make up a substantial portion of that country's population. Today, most of Morocco's 25 million people are Arabic-speaking farmers who till the fertile lowland plains and plateaus that stretch from the Atlantic Ocean to the foothills of the Atlas Mountains. Two types of agricultural economy—modern and traditional—are intertwined and juxtaposed in Morocco as well as in Algeria and Tunisia. All agricultural regions, however, have felt the impact of Morocco's rising population, which has more than tripled in this century. In the countryside, extensive government efforts to increase the cultivated area have not stemmed the flow of migrants to the rapidly growing coastal cities of Casablanca (pop. 2.8 million) and Rabat (pop. 900,000). Inland centers such as Fez and Marrakech, both with populations of approximately 500,000, have grown much more slowly.

Farther east, along the west-east axis of the Atlas Mountains in Al-

DESTRUCTION OF VEGETATION IN THE MIDDLE EAST

The two maps in Figure 12.14 are of past and present distributions of vegetation in the Middle East. They vividly document the degree of human interference in the landscapes of this ancient region. The original natural vegetation, as reconstructed by biogeographers, included forests in the Elburz and Zagros ranges of Iran as well as in the uplands that encircle the dry core of Anatolia and extend southward along the Levant coast. Forests also were dominant in Yemen and Oman in Arabia and in Cyrenaica and Tripolitania in Libya. These forests gave way to evergreen shrub, continuous grasslands, semiarid steppes, and deserts in Iran, Arabia, and the Sahara. Regionwide, a lush cover of natural vegetation existed before the origins of agriculture and animal domestication in the Middle East about 10,000 years ago.

Today, the forests of the Middle East are confined to the rim of the Anatolian Plateau and the Elburz Mountains of Iran. Evergreen scrub has been stripped from the mantle of Iraq, Saudi Arabia, and much of western Iran. Semiarid steppes and deserts exist in regions formerly covered by evergreen scrub or continuous grasslands. Human abuse of the earth has been intense. This legacy of resource exploitation is a major hindrance to development in most Middle Eastern countries.

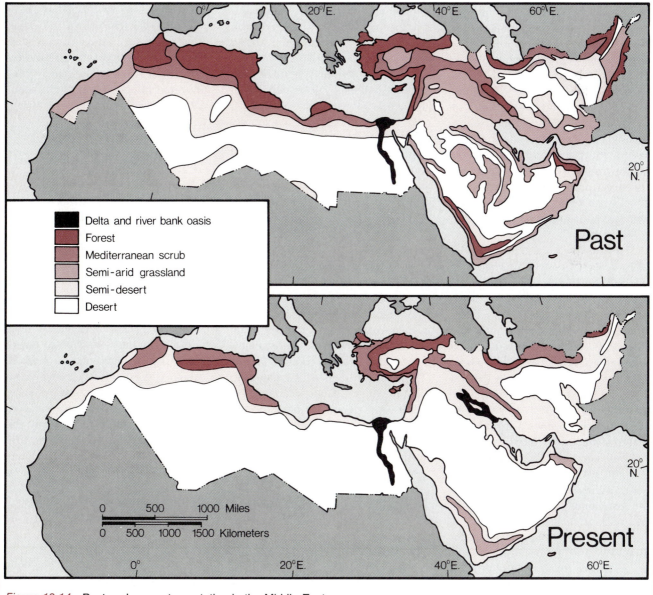

Legend:
- Delta and river bank oasis
- Forest
- Mediterranean scrub
- Semi-arid grassland
- Semi-desert
- Desert

Figure 12.14 Past and present vegetation in the Middle East.

geria, the primary environmental contrast is the typical Maghribi distinction between fertile, well-watered, and densely settled valleys set between Atlas ranges in the north and the dry reaches of the Saharan interior. The Algerian coast is backed by the Tell Atlas, reaching little more than 7000 feet, but forming an important reservoir of Berber peoples. Defining the edge of the desert, the Saharan Atlas rise to comparable elevations but are much drier. Between these two ranges, highly differentiated topography is given some definition by a series of high plateaus pockmarked by salt lakes that fill with water in rainy years. These **shatts**, interior drainage lakes, form the focus of important nomadic migrations. The Tell and Saharan Atlas ranges merge in eastern Algeria to form the rugged Aures Mountains. South of the Aures, and into Tunisia, enormous shotts cover the landscapes of the northeastern Sahara—dangerous, salt-encrusted shallow lake pans that pose problems for any kind of development. Algeria reaches far into the Sahara, running 1200 miles due south of Algiers.

Settlement and economy across the environmental zones of Algeria closely mirror those of Morocco. The humid coast and mountain ranges of the north are fairly densely settled; the desert interior is virtually empty. Some one million French settlers established small farms and vast plantations of Mediterranean agriculture on the best farmland between their arrival in the 1830s and their abrupt departure in the 1960s. Europeans organized the export economy of Algeria until independence was achieved in 1962. Algeria may well be one of the best world examples of the effects of both **settler colonialism** and the creation of a colonial dual economy.

At the end of their struggle for freedom from France, one million Algerians had died and all but a few tens of thousands of the French settlers returned to France in one dramatic year, 1962. The near-cata-

strophic effects of independence were eased by Algeria's use of oil wealth for industrial development, steady emigration to France, and stable, if at times harsh, leadership throughout the period. Algeria's path toward "Islamic socialism" has been marked by the creation of large, state-owned, industries and programs of land reform eliminating large estates in the countryside.

Algeria (pop. 24.2 million) has the highest population growth rate in the Maghrib, however, and this has been evident in its strong levels of urbanization and emigration. Algiers has a population of 2 million; Oran, Constantine, and Annaba have also grown rapidly. Algeria's continued strong human relationship with France has led to an Algerian population in France of about 1 million today—an ironic turn of events.

In Tunisia and Libya, topography is less dramatic than in Morocco and Algeria, but the same environmental sequence from northern Mediterranean coast to southern desert prevails. Two thirds of Tunisia's 7.7 million people live in the northern third of the country's territory. The country's central highlands and interior steppes, marginally important in the past, have become sites of innovative development projects. Today, Tunisia is an example of self-motivated, serious, and successful state planning. Tunisia has also become a model for family-planning projects in the Third World, contradicting the oft-held notion that family planning and Islam contravene each other.

In Libya, the population of 4 million is concentrated on the coast and in the hilly back country of Tripolitania and Cyrenaica, the western and eastern islands of vegetation that bracket the Gulf of Sidra. The Mediterranean landscapes of Libya's Jabal al Akhdar in Cyrenaica decline rapidly into full desert. Cultivation of Mediterranean crops prevails on the coast; to the south, except in oases and oil towns, the desert—the vast Fezzan district—is vacant.

Population has grown rapidly in both Libya and Tunisia from very small premodern bases. Tunisia, the most urbanized of the states of the Maghrib, has one third of its urban residents in the capital, Tunis (pop. 1.1 million). Libya, the most urban (76 percent) of all large states in the Middle East and North Africa, has seen its capital, Tripoli, triple in size in twenty years to reach a population of 900,000. Benghazi has a population of 400,000. The remarkably different domestic and foreign policies conducted by these two North African neighbors have led to uneasy relations between them, as indeed, have prevailed between Libya and much of the world over the last two decades. Libya's oil wealth has been used for a variety of public programs, from the rapid militarization of the country to extensive programs of irrigation in the Fezzan.

The Human Use of the Earth

Since the end of the last Ice Age some 12,000 years ago, the climate of the Middle East has changed little. The temperature and rainfall regimes of the past were apparently much as they are today. The natural vegetation of the Middle East and North Africa, however, was quite different. The Taurus, Elburz, Zagros, Lebanon, and Atlas mountains were cloaked in thick forests. Conifers interspersed with alpine pastures dominated at high elevations; these gave way to deciduous woodlands of oak and pistachio mixed with grasslands downslope. Along the coast of the Levant and southern Turkey, a cedar forest prevailed. Reed swamps filled the lower Tigris-Euphrates, Nile, and other river valleys. Steppe and desert vegetation were characteristic of the Sahara, Arabia, central Iran, and Anatolia (Fig. 12.14).

Environmental Transformation

About 10,000 years ago, plants and animals were domesticated in the foothills of the Taurus and Zagros mountains. Here, barley and wheat were brought into cultivation in small villages, and sheep and goats were kept in these settlements or grazed in nearby pastures. By 9000 years ago, village farming sites extended over a wide arc, spanning the western flanks of the Zagros Mountains, southern Anatolia, and northern Palestine. After 1000 years of experimentation in this nuclear zone, village settlement began to diffuse throughout the uplands of the Middle East, down into the river valleys, and along the shores of the Mediterranean. Population densities increased in those locales most suitable for farming. The broad outlines of today's population distribution in the Middle East began to become fixed; the transformation of the environment was underway.

Farming and herding initiated slow but irreversible changes in the natural environments of the Middle East. In the uplands, forests were cleared for cultivation of wheat and barley (Fig. 12.14). Herds of sheep and goats grazing on stubbled fields made clearings permanent landscape features. As these clearings expanded to meet the food needs of growing populations, forests disappeared from accessible areas. Wood was used as timber, for domestic cooking and heating, and for the firing of kilns. Early on, the mountain rim at the head of the Euphrates Valley was totally deforested when timber was sent downriver on rafts to meet the needs of cities in southern Iraq. The cedars of Lebanon, prized for their aroma and color, embellished the households of the elite. The forests of the Middle East were gradually cut down, reduced in their extent today to small remnants of their original, and potential, range (Fig. 12.14). The decline of these fragile woodlands set in motion environmental changes that extend to the present.

Mediterranean hillsides denuded of woodlands erode quickly. The sudden downbursts of winter rain in Mediterranean climate only add to

Vital irrigation water is distributed to reclaimed fields in eastern Turkey. Throughout the Middle East, drought is a major environmental hazard.

the process. In turn, soil and silt increase in volume in the densely settled river valleys of the region. Middle Eastern technologies have long been developed to exploit this "free" endowment of natural fertilizer and to cope with the heightened floods that result from the increased **runoff.** Predicting the floods of the Nile and coping with their waters was crucial to Egyptian society and gave birth to many scientific concepts. But generally over time, the degradation of the Middle East's environment has led to increased human pressures on delicate and limited arable landscapes. Current efforts in many countries to reverse these forces and to create new land for agriculture are a measure of the degree to which degraded landscapes have impeded development in the region.

Natural Hazards

The most fundamental natural hazard for farmers in the Middle East is drought. Every important center of population in the region lies either on its more humid northern fringe or relies on irrigation. Precipitation is sharply seasonal, occurring in winter

and spring. Agriculture is geared to the long summer drought that follows.

In the past, villagers coped with environmental risk by planting as much as 90 percent of their land in wheat and barley—low value but dependable crops. The introduction of Western technology, however, transformed traditional Middle Eastern farming. More complex and productive systems of commercial cultivation requiring greater levels of environmental control have become widespread.

The most dramatic examples of change are in river valleys, where entire ecosystems have been transformed. Agricultural expansion and intensification have occurred virtually everywhere in the region to some degree. Over the long historical view, it is clear that intense use of the resource base has led to periodic disaster in the Middle East. There is no reason to believe that modern development will be able to sustain current levels of population growth indefinitely.

In addition to drought and floods, erosion, and salinization, Middle

Easterners endure periodic hazards from earthquakes, desert locusts, and unexpected frosts, all of which can devastate local regions. The primary environmental risk, however, appears to be the decision of most governments to exploit their natural resources to feed their people with little regard for the long-run environmental consequences. Deep wells are drilled to obtain water for agricultural and urban expansion, using finite supplies of **geologic water** for the first and last time. The wealth of Saudi Arabia has enabled that country to become a net exporter of wheat—grown with deep-well irrigation—in a world swimming in surplus wheat. In poorer countries, efforts to shift to higher levels of industrial growth are hampered by a basic lack of water or the inability to pay for expensive water schemes. More profoundly, no society, rich or poor, technologically advanced or not, has solved the long-term problems of sustaining dense human populations in arid environments.

THE MODERN MIDDLE EAST AND NORTH AFRICA

The achievement of political independence was the predominant goal of the nationalist leaders of the Middle East and North Africa during the first half of this century. The central issues facing Middle Easterners today are the development of national resources, the achievement of economic stability, and the quest for higher standards of living.

These goals, shared by every government in the region, are being pursued within new social and spatial frameworks. The traditional ethnic mosaic has broken down. Community allegiances are now submerged in most societies. Loyalty to country is now primary, but the revival of Islam in the region argues for the tenacity, or a yet undefined transla-

tion, of older patterns of living in a new age. Petro-dollars have flowed into the coffers of a few countries; most remain poor and undeveloped. New patterns of unity and diversity have emerged around issues of Westernization, oil wealth, Israel, and relations with the superpowers.

In the modern Middle East and North Africa, the human setting now accommodates twice as many people as have ever lived in the region. Still confined to core areas of dense population, Middle Easterners have absorbed the initial impact of changes wrought by the introduction of Western science and technology.

The ecological trilogy has been supplanted by the development of modern states and economic forces in the Middle East. The old urban centers of the region have been restructured by new economic and political patterns, so that *The Modern Middle Eastern City* differs in size, structure, and function from the Islamic cities of the past. In their hinterlands, *Change in the Village* has been fostered by programs of land reform and agricultural expansion, although agricultural growth has not matched population growth in most countries. *The Settling of the No-mads* in the Middle East and North Africa has been intentionally fostered by the governments of virtually every state in the region. In this welter of change, *The Economics of Oil* has propelled this region onto center stage in the international arena, where the conflict between *The Arabs and the Israelis* dominates discussion. Perhaps no region of the Developing World so concerns the United States and other nations of the Technological World today. Its contemporary unity and diversity, expressed in new patterns of human geography, are of global importance.

The Modern Middle Eastern City

The integration of the Middle East and North Africa into large-scale modern economies has led to the growth and redistribution of its urban centers. Historically, Middle Eastern cities were international trading centers, connecting points on continental trade routes crisscrossing the Old World. The largest cities were often located in the interior. Many—Damascus, Mashhad, Marrakech—were entrepôts on the desert margins. Others, such as Cairo and

Modern urban and suburban growth encircles the old city of Tangier, Morocco. Like most coastal cities in the Middle East, Tangiers has exploded in size.

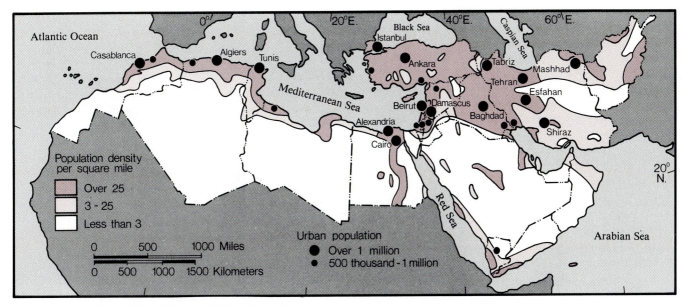

Figure 12.15 Population of the Middle East and North Africa.

Baghdad, primarily fulfilled religious and administrative functions. Smaller cities were strung out like beads along the caravan routes between major centers. These cities prospered or perished depending on local conditions of security, trade, food supplies, and water.

In the nineteeth century, Western merchants and capital penetrated the region and integrated it into wider, Western-oriented trade networks. The distribution of urban centers changed as seaports, such as Istanbul, Beirut, Tripoli, Alexandria, and Casablanca, swelled in population and commercial importance. The great cities of the interior began to lose their demographic superiority.

Urban Growth

Urban growth in the Middle East has been so dramatic in this century that fifteen cities now have populations of more than 1 million and roughly 100 are larger than 100,000 (Fig. 12.15). In North Africa, Casablanca (pop. 2.8 million), Tunis (pop. 1.1 million), and Algiers (pop. 1.2 million) have grown from coastal backwaters to modern world metropolises. The urban area of Cairo (pop. 11 million) has expanded from 5 to 150 square miles, making the old city a small district

in the new. With Alexandria (pop. 2.8 million), these two cities house one fourth of the Egyptian population. Tehran, the capital of Iran, has grown from 100,000 in 1940 to more than 6 million today; Mashhad, Isfahan, Tabriz, and Shiraz have more than a million people each. Baghdad has 3.2 million people, Beirut an estimated 1.5 million, and Damascus 1.1 million. In Turkey, the port city of Istanbul retains cultural supremacy with a population of 3 million, and the interior capital of Ankara has a population of 3.2 million.

In most Middle Eastern countries, more than a third of the population lives in urban centers, a much higher percentage than in other regions of the Developing World. As these primate cities continue to grow at a rate of 6 to 10 percent a year, economic and political decisions are increasingly concentrated within their bounds. Although growth rates vary in tempo and magnitude from city to city, two factors underlie urban growth in the Middle East: (1) the doubling of population regionwide caused by sharply declining death rates and (2) immigration of peasants and tribesmen from the countryside.

Roughly two thirds of current urban population growth is a result of

natural increase among urban residents. Better medical and health facilities have made the **mortality rate** lowest in the cities. Rising aspirations and limited educational levels have combined to maintain high birth rates of 35 to 45 per 1000. The status of women in the Middle East is improving slowly, but early marriage and abundant procreation are still highly valued cultural factors. Only in countries where non-Muslims form a substantial part of the population— Israel, Cyprus, and Lebanon—is the birth rate relatively low. In the oil-rich countries, continued high birth rates and much lowered death rates have combined to result in explosive population growth. Overall population growth in the region is close to 3 percent per year.

The remaining third of the population growth in Middle Eastern cities is generated by expanding rural populations who flow out of the countryside away from the villages and nomadic camps of another era into the new urban social and economic centers.

Urban Environments

The modern cities of the Middle East differ physically and socially from those of the past. Often the same city has distinct old and modern sections. Broad avenues suitable for motor transport cut wide swaths between older residential quarters and more modern parts of the cities. Commercial activity has abandoned the old bazaars, and modern buildings have sprung up on the new streets. Skyscrapers house government offices, banks, hotels, and department stores. Slum shantytowns filled with new urban immigrants frequently occupy empty spaces in these unplanned, incoherent centers.

Urban sprawl has accompanied the enormous growth of city populations. Motorized suburbs have spread far beyond the confines of ancient city walls. The cemeteries and shrines that once acted as collars on urban expansion have been leveled. The exodus of the urban elite to modern suburbs, where houses are less crowded and street patterns less torturous, has increasingly relegated the central sections to the lower classes.

These cities reflect the social premises that leaders of Middle Eastern societies have advocated for their people. Traditional emphasis on family ties, religious affiliation, and occupational groupings is weakening. Ethnic division of labor, the hallmark of the old cultural mosaic, will be less significant in the future. In the larger cities of the Middle East, a residential mixing of races and religions, previously unthinkable, is now quite common. A social analysis of Cairo detected a general movement toward the economic, class-based configuration of Western metropolitan society. A new urban milieu is evolving rapidly in the Middle East, although the revival of Islam may redirect its character.

The most important new social group in the urban Middle East is the emerging middle class. These city dwellers, still numerically small, account for perhaps 10 percent of the populations of Turkey, Iran, Egypt, Lebanon, and the Maghrib; in Saudi Arabia, Yemen, Afghanistan, and other traditional societies, the mid-

The processes of change are vividly demonstrated in the generational differences in attitude and orientation in this Moroccan family. The middle class is now a primary force for modernization throughout the Middle East and North Africa.

dle class is far smaller. Yet the aspirations of this handful of men and women have had a dramatic impact on life and landscape in the Middle East and North Africa.

Armed with the knowledge and skills of modern education, the middle class has broken the traditional power of guilds, extended families, and in many countries religious associations. Today, they play important roles in the development and transmission of ideas, in the formulations of plans to modernize society, and in implementing programs of reform. This group runs the petroleum industry and state and private corporations. They work in government ministries, staff the schools and hospitals, and participate in the growing service economy of the region. Small in size but large in influence, the emergent middle class is now being challenged by the resurgence of Islam.

Change in the Village

The early twentieth century found the mass of peasants and tribesmen

in the Middle East and North Africa poverty stricken and chronically in debt to an elite resistant to change. Given these conditions, national programs of economic and social development in the countries of the Middle East and North Africa have taken similar directions, despite important cultural and ecological variations. Among their common objectives were (1) the institution of land reform and land distribution, (2) an expansion of the cultivated area, and (3) the settling of the nomads.

Land Refrom

The widespread poverty and low standards of living of most peasants in the villages of the Middle East and North Africa derived from three factors. First, in many countries, absentee landowners held a monopoly over both the cultivated land and the capital to develop it. Second, during the course of colonial rule, few new agricultural techniques were introduced into the villages, except in Egypt, parts of Lebanon, the Zionist settlements in Palestine, and European farms in North Africa. As a result, per capita productivity and income remained extremely low. Finally, because of low rainfall and rugged terrain, the agricultural base of the Middle East and North Africa was and is extremely limited. Only five countries—Turkey, Syria, Israel, Lebanon, and Cyprus—cultivate more than a fifth of their total land surface. An equal number of countries cultivate less than 1 percent. The cumulative effect of these factors meant that hopes for progress in the villages of the Middle East focused on three areas: (1) elimination of the landlords, (2) introduction of modern agricultural techniques, and (3) expansion of the arable.

Land redistribution was effected in one country after another by a series of social and political revolutions. When Gamal Abdel Nasser came to power in Egypt in 1952, 72 percent of all Egyptian farmers owned less than half an acre of land, although 2 acres was considered minimum subsistence level. An additional 1.5 million peasant families were totally landless. The bulk of Egypt's highly productive commercial agriculture was in the hands of urban landlords. The revolution eliminated the landlords, confiscated royal properties, and limited individual holdings to 200 acres and subsequently to 50. In the next fifteen years, a fifth of Egypt's agricultural land was redistributed to tenant cultivators.

In Syria, a land distribution law was passed in 1958 as the government attempted to break up large holdings and provide land for the peasants. In Iraq, the overthrow of the monarchy in 1958 led to the expropriation of large estates, limits on the size of private holdings, and redistribution of the land to tenant farmers. In Algeria, an estimated 2.5 million acres vacated by French colonists in 1962 was expropriated by the government. In Iran, where an estimated 70 percent of the fertile land was owned by a small number

of large landlords, the former Shah's White Revolution (optimistically signifying bloodless change) limited land ownership to one village per landlord. Despite these reforms, great disparity still exists between the wealth of landlords and the poverty of peasants in the Middle East and North Africa.

The introduction of modern agricultural techniques into the region has accelerated. A web of new roads, communications media, and government hierarchies is spreading out from the cities, introducing new crops and field methods, marketing cooperatives, agricultural credit, and educational programs to the rural hinterlands. In one remarkable Syrian case, urban merchants invested in mechanized agriculture in the rain-fed north; grain production increased by 60 percent, and cotton yields increased by a factor of eight. Similarly, in Egypt, agricultural techniques are now sophisticated enough to produce wheat, corn, and cotton at higher yields per acre than in the United States and Europe. And in Israel, great pride is taken in "making the desert bloom"—transforming desert into gardens, fields, orchards, and new forests.

Overall, the productivity of Middle Eastern peasants is estimated to be only one eighth to one quarter of the productivity of their European counterparts. This stems from many environmental and social factors. Most soils in the region have low organic content because of dry climate, high soil temperatures, and the deforestation of much of the region. Irrigated fields, the most productive agricultural land in the Middle East, are subject to salinization. In addition, illiteracy is common, diets marginal, poor health endemic, and debt chronic in many areas. Programs of primary education, health services, and agricultural reform now exist in all but the most remote countries of the region. These may ultimately transform both the peasantry and land use patterns in the Middle East and have done so in the small, oil-rich nations of the Gulf. But elsewhere, today's growing populations and attendant food shortages must be met by an increase in productivity and production.

Expansion of cultivated land is a limited option in the dry lands of the Middle East and North Africa (Fig. 12.9). In Turkey, the cultivated area has tripled in twenty-five years. Sig-

Programs of primary education exist in virtually every country in the Middle East and North Africa, including revolutionary Iran.

nificantly, wheat harvests in the same period only doubled, reflecting the extension of agriculture into increasingly marginal environments. In Morocco, Algeria, Syria, and Iran, similar extensions of cultivation have been initiated by the construction of dams, the drilling of new wells, and the cultivation of semiarid steppes. Region-wide, however, agricultural production has failed to keep pace with population growth, and the Middle East is now a net importer of food. After forty years of economic development and planning, rural incomes in the Middle East and North Africa remain low, except in Kuwait, Lebanon, Israel, Cyprus, and the oil-exporting countries of Iran, Iraq, Libya, and the Gulf.

Expansion of the Arable: The River Valleys

Nowhere have the frustrations of this failure to raise standards of living been more acute than in the large river valleys of Egypt and Iraq, where the environmental basis of agriculture has been transformed in an effort to increase production. In Iraq, destruction of forests and subsequent erosion, silting of the rivers, and flooding badly damaged the environmental basis of irrigated agriculture. The primary effort, therefore, has been to control annual variations in the flow of the Tigris-Euphrates river system. A series of dams has been constructed to reduce flooding (Baghdad was ravaged by flood in 1968) and to open up new areas for cultivation. Four major irrigation works have been built. These and others currently planned are expected to double the agricultural area of Iraq, provide adequate protection against floods, and supply electricity for industrial development. Still massive irrigation projects and programs of land reform, begun in 1958, have failed to raise standards of living in rural Iraq. Population growth is a factor, but the underlying cause is environmental. These problems have plagued Mesopotamia since the earliest days of civilization.

The Aswan Dam transformed agriculture in Egypt. It succeeded in expanding the amount of farmland, but these gains have been largely absorbed by population growth.

In southern Mesopotamia, flat terrain and impermeable soils cause water to stand on the surface. As surface water evaporates, salts are deposited on the land, accumulate, and eventually render the soil infertile. In the past, Iraqi farmers coped with these environmental limitations by cultivating the land only once every two years. Small groups settled on the land, constructed canals, and irrigated soil. When salt levels began to rise and harvests fell, farmers moved to new areas. This pattern of agriculture was able to support the small population of Iraq in the past, but with 17.6 million people today and an annual population growth rate of 3.5 percent, new agricultural projects involve a more intensive form of agriculture, which has led to higher levels of salinization. Self-sufficient in foodstuffs prior to 1958, Iraq now must import grains and vegetables.

In Egypt, as in Iraq, the Aswan High Dam converted Egypt's agriculture from the traditional one-crop system of basin irrigation into two- and three-crop perennial irrigation. Although the agricultural area increased by one third and crop production rose even more, these gains

were completely absorbed by Egypt's population growth.

In addition, it now appears that serious environmental problems associated with the damming of the Nile have emerged. The rate of evaporation over Lake Nasser behind the dam was seriously underestimated. The dam now holds less water than the two smaller dams and natural flow it replaced. Engineers are studying the feasibility of spreading acetyl alcohol over the surface of Lake Nasser to reduce evaporation or, alternatively, of cutting a canal through the Sudd swamps south of the lake to increase flow. Water is also seeping in beneath the dam, undermining its structure. Some engineers estimate that the life span of the structure may not extend far beyond the year 2000. The trapping of sediment behind the dam has also had serious effects farther downstream. The coastline of the delta is eroding for lack of natural siltation. Fishing in the Mediterranean has been seriously damaged as the nutrient content of Nile River water pouring into it has decreased. Egyptian farmers must use large quantities of expensive factory-produced chemical fertilizers to replace natural silt. Increased use of pesticides pollutes a wide swath of the eastern Mediterranean.

With water now standing year round in the lake and in irrigation canals, the incidence of waterborne disease is more common than ever. Malaria and schistosomiasis, parasitic diseases transmitted by mosquitoes and snails that breed in quiet water, afflict more Egyptians. Faced with a doubling of population to 106 million in 24 years, Egypt's leaders have little choice but to try to resolve the new ecological problems the Aswan High Dam has created.

The Settling of the Nomads

The introduction of modern transport and military technology gave governments in many Middle Eastern countries the capacity to control their deserts, steppes, and mountains. Nomadic tribes, which had for centuries ignored government rule in these marginal environments, were quickly brought to heel. National boundaries, which cut across the historical grazing areas of their forefathers, are patrolled by well-equipped government troops. Tribal raids to redress the balance have been met with machine guns, tanks, and airplanes.

In North Africa, this process was accomplished during the French and Italian "pacification" periods. Army posts manned by the Foreign Legion were constructed throughout the Sahara. In the new security imposed by Western forces, peasant cultivation was extended into the grasslands of the Maghrib formerly grazed by tribesmen. In the oases, the Haratin slave caste was freed from tribal control. Nomads had to pay taxes—a great disgrace—to the central governments. The nomads suffered a loss in revenue when transport services for camel caravans lost out to trucks. Constricted in space, reduced in prestige, economically pressed, and administered by government officials, many tribes of the Sahara have

settled down in villages on the steppes, at wells in the deserts, or in the rapidly growing cities on the Mediterranean coast.

In the mountains and plateaus of Iran and Turkey, the transhumant tribes of the Zagros and Caucasus mountains were also stripped of their economic and political independence. In Iran, Reza Shah led army campaigns against tribesmen and disarmed and disbanded the tribes by breaking their patterns of migration. The tribesmen were relocated on marginal land in northeastern Iran.

In Anatolia, the process of tribal pacification was less violent and less complete, and many groups in eastern Turkey retain their traditional pastures while accepting taxation by the central government. In Israel, Syria, Jordan, and parts of Egypt, nomadic groups have been disrupted by warfare between Arabs and Israelis. Only in Iraq, where the Kurds successfully defied the central government in Baghdad well into the 1970s, has tribal autonomy been maintained. In the 1980s, Kurdish territory became a battleground in the war between Iran and Iraq.

In Saudi Arabia, where Bedouin nomads make up as much as half the population, a similar process of sedentarization is being pursued but for quite different reasons. Here, the government, itself of nomadic origins, drilled wells in the desert to create a series of watering points for the nomads.

The goal of this expensive program was to consolidate tribal alliances on a national level. But religious considerations also played a role. The government's aim was not simply to settle the Bedouins for purposes of security and control, but also to enable the nomads to lead truly religious lives in fixed locations where mosques could be built. These new oasis settlements, called al-Hijra in memory of the exodus of Muhammad to Medina, now number more than 200. Plans exist for settling an additional 10,000 nomads in the vicinity of Riyadh, a project requiring the

planting of some 600,000 tamarisk trees to fix the soil and prevent encroachment by sand dunes.

The effect of these varied government policies on the economic and social life of nomads has been severe. Nomadism is in serious decline, leaving a void in resource utilization in those regions unsuitable for cultivation but productive under a grazing economy. Despite the cost in lost meat, milk, and wool products, the governments of the Middle East have been determined to destroy the independence and mobility of the tribes, preferring peace and order to protein. Less than 3 percent of the people of the Middle East and North Africa continue to live a predominantly nomadic way of life: 2 million to 3 million in the Sahara, an estimated 1 million to 2 million in Arabia and Turkey, less than 1 million in Iran, and 300,000 to 400,000 in Syria and in Iraq.

The Economics of Oil

Despite the relatively modest progress most states of the Middle East and North Africa have made in the improvement of life in their societies, recent changes in the economics of oil have made parts of this region rich (Fig. 12.16). Unlike some developing countries that must limit industrialization and agricultural growth because of limited capital, some Middle East oil exporters have abundant cash reserves and foreign credits with which to finance programs of economic and social development.

In the five largest producing countries—Saudi Arabia, Iran, Kuwait, Libya, and Iraq—over 60 percent of the total revenues of each government and 70 percent of their foreign exchange earnings accrue directly from oil. Similar figures apply to the lesser producers, and in an indirect fashion to the transit countries of Jordan, Syria, and Lebanon through which oil is piped to Mediterranean ports. These revenues have risen 1400 percent since the oil-producing na-

OIL: THE MIDDLE EAST AND THE WORLD

The oil reserves of the Middle East comprise more than 60 percent of the world's total and three quarters of the reserves of the non-Communist world. The proved oil reserves of the Middle East have increased eight times since 1950. Each year more new oil is discovered than is produced. Of the 33,000 oil fields discovered throughout the world, half of all production is from only 33 giant fields, each of which originally had at least 5 billion barrels. Of these 33 giant fields, 28 are located in the Middle East; 9 of the 10 largest are also located here. The crucial role the Middle East plays in the economies of the Technological World is apparent from the destinations of oil exports—the largest consumers are Western Europe, Japan, and the United States.

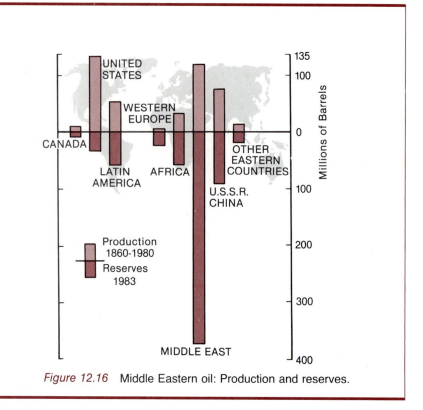

Figure 12.16   Middle Eastern oil: Production and reserves.

tions joined together in the Organization of Petroleum Exporting Countries (OPEC) in 1960 and renegotiated oil concessions and contracts with European and American oil companies. The rate of economic growth in the Middle East is double that of any other region in the Developing World, although falling oil prices have forced retrenchments.

Patterns of Industrial Growth

Until recently, industrial growth in the Middle East and North Africa was limited, employing less than 15 percent of the population. Since independence, the countries of the Middle East have tried to stimulate industrialization, but growing populations, increasing urbanization, and intensifying pressure on farmland have forced them to invest in social welfare programs and land reform, rather than industrialization. Few states have had the money or human resources to establish substantial industrial complexes. In addition, mineral resources in the Middle East, except for oil, are widely scattered, of variable quality, and distant from labor pools that are concentrated in cities (Fig. 12.17).

The paucity of coal in the region has meant that most other ores cannot be processed or concentrated locally. Instead, these ores have been carried in raw form to distant ports or foreign countries for refining. Rising oil prices in the early 1970s and

The economics of oil have brought immense wealth to the countries of the Gulf. In Saudi Arabia, new discoveries of oil continue to exceed production every year.

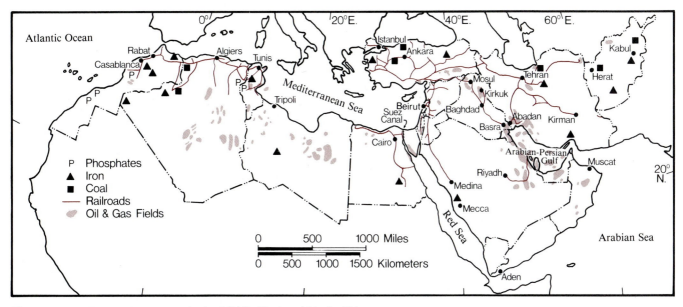

Figure 12.17 Economic patterns in the Middle East and North Africa.

increased local control of the oil industry have suddenly provided oil-producing nations, such as Iran, Iraq, Saudi Arabia, Libya, and Kuwait, with the capital necessary for the development of broader, more diversified industrial economies. Although light industries, particularly textiles and food processing, still predominate in the large cities of the region, the political and economic aspirations of these states are leading to a more intensive search for raw materials and minerals that will change the industrial map of the Middle East and North Africa. Nonetheless, the 21 states of the Council of Arab Economic Unity produce less than 1 percent of the world's industrial goods.

The Evolution of the Oil Industry

The Middle East and North Africa make up the largest oil-producing and oil-exporting region in the world (Fig. 12.16). In the early 1970s, this region produced over 40 percent of the world's crude oil. New discoveries continue to be made. Petroleum is by far the most significant resource here. All told, Middle East oil reserves in the 1980s are greater than those of the rest of the free world combined.

The costs of producing oil in this region are low. In the Gulf, the production costs of a barrel of oil range form six cents in Kuwait to thirty-five cents off the shores of the Emirates, compared with $3 per barrel in Texas. One reason for this cost differential is that Middle Eastern oil is close to the surface and free flowing. An average well produces 4500 barrels of oil per day as compared with 15 barrels in the United States. The Middle East is the world's leading supplier of crude oil. The people of the Middle East utilize only a small proportion of the region's vast production. Even with higher prices, new discoveries, and greater fuel conservation, the Middle East and North Africa, with over 60 percent of the world's proved petroleum reserves, will remain the world's primary exporter of oil.

In the Technological World, imported oil is an economic fact of life. Japan, for example, depends on oil for more than three quarters of its energy needs. Western Europe depended on oil for 30 percent of its energy needs in 1960; by 1970, this figure had risen to 53 percent, by 1980, 58 percent. Through conservation and alternative fuels, the United States reduced oil imports to

20 percent in the early 1980s. This has now risen to 40 percent. Despite market surpluses of oil and programs of fuel conservation in most industrial societies, however, competition for Middle Eastern Oil will remain a fundamental feature of the world economy.

The Middle East oil industry began early in the twentieth century when demand for oil to power the expanding machine technology of the Industrial Revolution led to European penetration and exploration of the region's oil fields. Currently, a variety of national and international oil companies operate in joint ventures with Middle East governments to exploit the oil and natural gas resources of the region.

The most important oil-producing field in the Middle East is located in a vast sedimentary basin known geologically as the Gulf geosyncline (Fig. 12.17). Lining the Gulf shores, the largest oil-producing countries are Iran, Saudi Arabia, Kuwait, and Iraq. The largest oil fields in Iran, the Khuzistan fields, lie on the western flanks of the Zagros Mountains just north of the Gulf. Here, oil trapped in a subsurface limestone reservoir is brought to the surface and piped to the huge port and refinery complex at Abadan and to a ten-berth, deep-water tanker terminal at Khark Island (Fig. 12.18).

In Iraq, the largest oil field is located in the north and is directly connected by pipeline to Mediterranean ports in Lebanon and Syria. Other important fields are located still farther to the north near Mosul and, in the deep south, near the port city of Basra.

The oil industries of the other Gulf states were not developed until after 1945. The postwar expansion of oil production in Kuwait transformed that country into the largest Middle Eastern producer of crude oil, a position only recently relinquished to Saudi Arabia and Iran. During the 1960s, some 2 million barrels of crude oil flowed each day from eight Kuwaiti fields. Produced at exceptionally low cost because the oil is near the surface and pushed up from below by water pressure, Kuwaiti oil is transported less than 15 miles from the oil fields to refining and port facilities.

In Saudi Arabia, Aramco, the largest oil company in the world, has been bought outright by the Saudi government. Near the Gulf coast, the enormous Ghawar oil pool—150 miles long and up to 22 miles wide and with reserves equivalent to those of the entire United States—was discovered in the late 1940s. This field, and others farther to the north and offshore, pipe oil to local refining terminals at Ras Tannurah and Bahrain and nearly 2000 miles westward to the Mediterranean. These fields have propelled Saudi Arabia into a primary place in Middle Eastern oil production (Fig. 12.17). Similar patterns in the production and export of Gulf oil are found in Bahrain, Qatar, Dubai, Abu Dhabi, Sharjah, and Oman.

Similar, less spectacular, discoveries of oil on the North African shield have converted this region into a major exporter of crude oil and natural gas. In Libya, a dozen major fields clustered in Cyrenaica now have ap-

GEOPOLITICS OF THE GULF

International rivalry in the Middle East focuses primarily on the Gulf, the vital energy lifeline on which the United States, Europe, and Japan rely. Approximately 40 percent of the free world's oil flows through the narrow bottleneck at the mouth of the Gulf, the Strait of Hormuz. The religious revolution in Iran followed by the outbreak of war between Iran and Iraq seriously disrupted this flow of oil. This political situation created deep concern in the United States, which declared the Gulf to be an area in our vital interest in 1980. Locally, the Arab Gulf states formed a joint security pact, the Gulf Cooperation Council (GCC). Together however, the six GCC countries—Saudi Arabia, Kuwait, Bahrain, Oman, Qatar, and the United Arab Emirates—have a total population of only 20 million people and about 140,000 armed troops. Defense of the region will ultimately lie in the broader realm of international geopolitics.

The Strait of Hormuz at its narrowest point is 21 miles wide, and the depth of the main tanker channel that passes near the Omani shore varies from 250 to 700 feet. The estimated 40 to 50 tankers carrying 10 million barrels of oil that pass through this point each day are vulnerable to attack. Pipelines in the area are also vulnerable to sabotage. Today, the Strait of Hormuz is patrolled by the navies of Oman, the USA, Britain and France. As a choke point in the world's flow of petroleum, it remains one of the most sensitive geographical areas in the world.

The Straits of Hormuz at the mouth of the Gulf is patrolled by the navy of Oman which guides 40 to 50 tankers carrying 10 million barrels of oil through the 21 mile wide bottleneck each day. In 1987, the U.S. Navy began patrolling the Gulf.

proximately 1000 producing wells (Fig. 12.17). Libyan fields have the advantage of being located relatively close to the Mediterranean, and pipeline terminals now exist at five locations on the coast.

Farther to the west, in Algeria, the

third largest natural gas field in the world has been discovered at Hassi R'Mel, some 200 miles south of Algiers near Ghardaïa. A series of major oil strikes have also been made in the interior of southern Algeria, and four pipelines now connect these

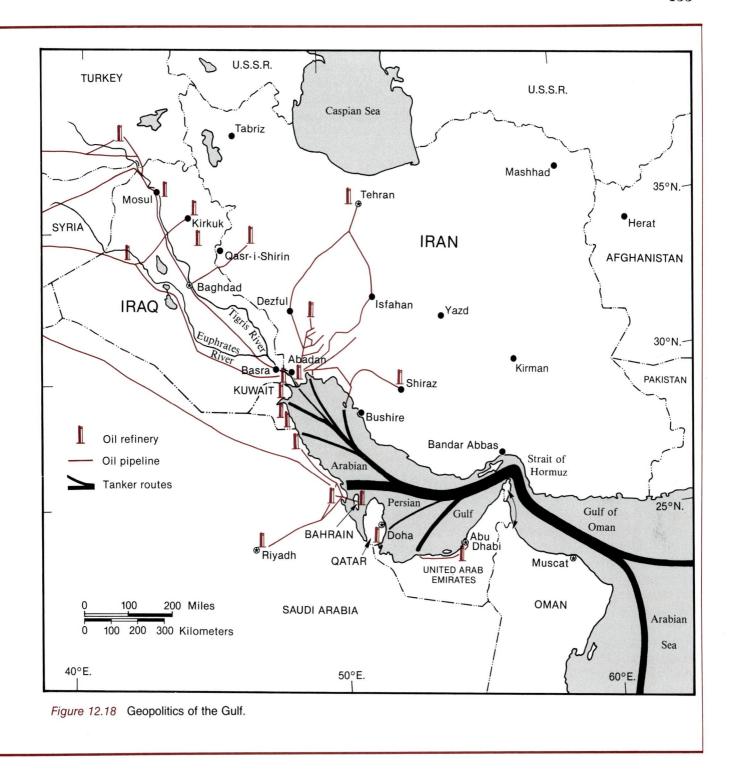

Figure 12.18 Geopolitics of the Gulf.

fields with the Mediterranean. In Tunisia, offshore oil near Kerkennah Island is in production. Moroco has had little success in discovering oil. Egypt has recently begun to export oil from offshore finds in the Gulf of Suez, from older wells at El Alamein,

and in the Sinai.

The petroleum industry of the Middle East and North Africa in all its phases—from exploration and discovery to pipelining and distribution—is one of the most complex and strategic of all world industries (Fig.

12.18). The international tensions that bear on every aspect of the industry lend it an air of immediacy and global strategy. Middle Eastern domestic priorities, Arab politics, multinational capitalism, and global energy needs all play a part in rendering the

Middle Eastern oil industry critical in a world of growing aspirations and limited resources.

The world's advanced industrial nations are now intimately entwined economically and strategically with distant, small, and relatively underdeveloped Middle Eastern countries. Further complicating this new economic reality is one of the most explosive and difficult political struggles of this century, the continuing conflict between the Arabs and the Israelis.

The Arabs and the Israelis

In the late nineteenth century, the brutal persecution of the large Jewish communities of Russia and Eastern Europe led to the formation of Zionism, a worldwide Jewish philosophical movement devoted to securing a political refuge for the Jews. Nearly 2000 years of Christian intolerance had convinced Zionists that lasting safety for Jews could be guaranteed only by the establishment of an independent Jewish state. They explored alternative sites in Africa and Latin America, but no place held the powerful religious and emotional appeal of Palestine.

It was in Palestine that the last sovereign Jewish community existed until Roman legions ravaged Jerusalem in A.D. 70, destroyed the temple of Herod, and dislodged the Jews from their Holy Land. Thereafter, during the long **diaspora**, or exile, Jews lived as alien minorities—they could call no country their own. Orthodox Jews believed that the land of Palestine had been promised to them by God, sanctioned in scripture. Others felt that in Palestine, Jews would experience a cultural rebirth and a spiritual redemption by which they would reestablish self-identity. For these reasons, the First Zionist Congress, held at Basel in 1897, defined its primary goal as the creation of a "home in Palestine secured by public law" for the Jewish people. Palestine was then part of the Ottoman Empire and

populated by a mosaic of peoples. Twenty years later, as the Ottoman Empire was disintegrating during World War I, the opportunity arose. Influential Zionists secured a commitment from the British government in the Balfour Declaration to support the "establishment in Palestine of a national home for the Jewish people." Subsequently, in 1920, Palestine became a British mandate under the League of Nations and was controlled by the British until the independent State of Israel was established in 1948.

In 1920, 700,000 Arabs, the majority of them farmers, lived in villages dotting the fertile coastal plain and lowland valleys of Palestine. Some 80,000 Jews, largely new emigrants from Eastern Europe, comprised an urban minority of 11 percent of the Palestinian population. For the Zionists, physical possession of the land was a political imperative, and they began to buy land—a practice previously forbidden to foreigners by the now-defunct Ottoman government.

Tensions between the Arab and Jewish communities began to mount, foreshadowing the hostilities that dominate the eastern Mediterranean today. By 1936, a tide of Jewish immigration from Nazi Germany increased the Jewish population significantly. Jewish land purchases doubled and redoubled. Taxes on land transactions quadrupled in three years, and the price of land soared well beyond the means of most Arab farmers. The increase in Jewish immigration and widespread fear of the establishment of a Jewish national home caused social and economic unrest among Palestinian Arabs. The situation deteriorated into a guerrilla rebellion that lasted until the beginning of World War II, which placed a temporary closure on the local situation.

In 1947, the British, occupied by problems closer to home, turned the issue over to the United Nations, which devised a scheme for partitioning Palestine into two countries:

(1) a Jewish state, to include 56 percent of Palestine—the Mediterranean lowlands from Haifa to south of Tel Aviv, the fertile northern coast, and the Negev; and (2) an Arab state, 43 percent of Palestine—Acre and Nazareth in the north, the central hill lands, and the Jordan Valley, Gaza, and part of Beersheba. Jerusalem, sacred to all three Middle Eastern religions, was to remain under permanent U.N. administration (Fig. 12.19).

The Jews agreed to the partition plan, the Arabs did not; both communities prepared to fight. On the eve of civil war, the 590,000 Jews in Palestine—still heavily concentrated in the urban districts of Jerusalem, Tel Aviv, and Haifa—made up 31 percent of the population and owned 450,000 acres of land, or roughly 7 percent of the entire area. Arabs formed 69 percent of the population

Figure 12.19   The changing map of Israel.

of 1.9 million and owned 93 percent of the land.

The Emergence of Israel

On May 14, 1948, the British withdrew from Palestine, the State of Israel was declared, and war between the Arabs and the Jews began. In fourteen months of fighting, Israel achieved what decades of immigration had not accomplished. Palestine was transformed into a Jewish homeland.

Under the armistice of 1949, Israel occupied nearly four fifths of the territory of the former mandate and virtually all its good agricultural land. Roughly 750,000 Arabs fled or were driven from Israeli-controlled areas and became refugees in the Gaza Strip, Jordan, Syria, and Lebanon. In their place, Jewish survivors of European concentration camps and Jews from the Arab countries of North Africa and the Middle East flocked to Israel. Some 250,000 arrived in 1949 alone. The Jewish population of Israel increased a staggering 108 percent in the four following years to compose more than 80 percent of the population.

In the next quarter century, the ingathering of Jews from various world regions proceeded under the Law of Return, which provided that "every Jew shall be entitled to come to Israel as an immigrant." Social and political upheavals in Iraq, Yemen, the Soviet Union, Hungary, Poland, and North Africa brought thousands on thousands of Jews to the new nation-state. By 1962, 2 million Jews lived in Israel. An additional 500,000 non-Jews, most of them Arabs, still lived in Israel.

Israel attempted to absorb the tide of new immigrants by expanding agricultural settlement into the less densely populated parts of the country. The motivations were several. First, self-sufficiency in food seemed a desirable goal, given the continuing hostility of the Arab world; the considerable lands abandoned by Arab refugees provided an attractive economic resource. Second, the Zionist commitment to cultural redemption by return to the soil appealed to a strong minority. Finally, the heavy concentration of Jews in Haifa, Tel Aviv, and Jerusalem posed security problems.

A master plan based on central place theory was designed to achieve an optimum distribution of the Israeli population and to create a close-knit hierarchy of settlements. At the lowest level were primary villages: the **kibbutz,** a unique Israeli collective farm, and the **moshav,** a cooperative composed of independent small farmers. Although these settlers were never a significant percentage of the population, the tough survival philosophy forged in these pioneer settlements has had a strong influence on Israeli national policy. At higher levels in the hierarchy, rural service centers, small towns, and urban centers are linked in a network composed of twenty-four planning regions, including the three large cities of Jerusalem, Tel Aviv, and Haifa (Fig. 12.19).

By the 1970s, the number of rural settlements in Israel doubled, and virtually all agricultural land in the country was occupied. Thousands of acres had been reclaimed from deserts and marshes, and 480,000 acres of land—nearly half the total in cultivation—were under irrigation. Traditional extensive dry farming methods of former Arab farmers were replaced by modern intensive horticulture. Cultivation of citrus crops became an important agricultural sector, with oranges the largest export product of Israel. Dairying, cattle raising, market gardening, and cereal cultivation also expanded.

This transformation of agriculture in Israel attracted international acclaim. Making the desert bloom became both a spiritual goal and a political slogan in Israel. Thousands of evergreens were planted on the barren limestone uplands of Galilee, Samaria, and Judea from which topsoil had been scoured by centuries of erosion. The malarial swamps of the Jezreel Valley were converted to agriculture. In the south, Beersheba, once occupied by nomads and dry farmers, became an important center of irrigated farming. Experiments in drip irrigation, hydroponics, and the

Communal farms, like this *kibbutz,* were established throughout Israel in order to "make the desert bloom."

use of brackish underground water extended agricultural settlements into the Negev.

Despite these well-publicized efforts, however, Israel remains a predominantly urban society and the concentration of population in the urban centers of the well-watered north has gradually been accepted by Israeli planners. Severely limited by the lack of water, 85 percent of which is already used for agricultural purposes, farming occupies only 8 percent of the labor force and accounts for 6 percent of the national product. By contrast, fully a quarter of Israel's national income derives from manufacturing, the highest such figure for any Middle Eastern country.

Palestinian uprisings in the Occupied Territories are a continuation of forty years of bitterness and bloodshed between Israelis and Palestinians. Both groups claim the land as their own.

The Palestinians, the Arabs, and the Jews

If Westerners applauded Israel's success in establishing a modern industrial and agricultural economy in an ancient and ravaged land, this view was not shared by the displaced Palestinians or other Arabs. For the Arabs, Israel was a colonial state created by Europeans during a time when Westerners were able to impose their will on others and dispose of territory as they chose. To them, Israelis were imperialists who, like the Crusaders before them, had occupied the homeland of the Arabs and had succeeded, at least temporarily, in dislodging the legitimate population of Palestine. The Palestinians—stateless, rejected, living as burdens in other Arab countries or as wards of the United Nations—view the Israelis as a foreign army occupying the land where they, the Palestinians, lived for 1400 years.

For forty years, this impasse has persisted and escalated into the current Arab-Israeli conflict. After the 1948 war, the Arab countries—humiliated in defeat—refused to absorb the 750,000 homeless Palestinian refugees because to do so would be to acknowledge the permanence of Israel. Most Palestinians ended up in

the two areas of Palestine unoccupied by Israel—the West Bank of the Jordan River and the thin sliver of land surrounding the city of Gaza on the Mediterranean. Or, alternatively, they found themselves in U.N. refugee camps where they have lived for the last generation. Intermittently, Palestinian frustrations were vented by border raids into Israel. These were met by massive Israeli retaliation.

In 1956, threatened by Egyptian President Nasser's nationalization of the Suez Canal, Israel joined France and Britain in an invasion intended to return the canal to European control. Israeli armies swept across the Sinai and into Gaza, but under heavy pressure from the United States, all three armies were forced to abandon this adventure and return the invaded territories to Egypt. Finally, in 1967, when Nasser imposed a blockade on Israeli shipping through the Straits of Tiran at the southern tip of the Sinai Peninsula, Israel launched a preemptive strike on Egypt, Syria, and Jordan that resulted in a catastrophic defeat for Arab forces and the transformation of the

political map of the eastern Mediterranean (Fig. 12.19).

In the June 1967 war, Israel occupied the Sinai Peninsula, the Gaza Strip, the Golan Heights in Syria, and the entire West Bank of the Jordan River. Some 1.5 million Palestinians were registered as refugees with the United Nations, half of them in Jordan, a third in Gaza, and a quarter on the West Bank. In the occupied territories, 1 million Arabs were under Israeli administration and the area of the Jewish state had quadrupled in size. The Israelis, having secured safe borders, initiated an extensive building program in the occupied territories. In October 1973, Syrian and Egyptian armies attacked Israel in the Sinai and Golan Heights. After bitter fighting, a cease-fire was signed, with Israel still in control of the occupied territories. But the Arabs had fought credibly for the first time.

The October War in 1973 and the oil embargo that followed revealed the growing political and military power of the Arab states. To cope with these new realities, the world's industrial powers embarked on efforts to reconcile the conflict between the Arabs, the Palestinians, and the Jews. The Arabs demand return of all territories occupied in the 1967 war. For the Israelis, the creation of a Palestinian state on the West Bank poses a direct threat to national security; for the 1.8 million Palestinians in refugee camps, it is a minimal demand. The city of Jerusalem remains a difficult emotional and symbolic issue. The Israelis annexed the Old City in 1967, thus returning the Wailing Wall, Judaism's most sacred place of worship, to Jewish control for the first time in 2000 years. As a religious center of Islam, the Arabs view Jerusalem as nonnegotiable. The Camp David accords of 1978 led to a phased withdrawal of Israelis from the Sinai Peninsula that was completed in 1981, but in the same year, Israelis unilaterally annexed the Golan Heights. In 1982, Israel invaded Lebanon. Forty years of bitterness and bloodshed complicate peace efforts. Palestinians and Israelis seek national identity on the same land.

13

AFRICA

*T*he forty-eight countries of Africa south of the Sahara Desert have a combined population of 508 million (Fig. 13.1). For three decades, these states have struggled to throw off the residual effects of colonialism, to build strong national economies, to achieve parity in the marketplaces of the world, and to raise the standard of living of their people. With few exceptions, they have failed. Of the twenty-nine poorest countries in the world, twenty-one are found here. By any measure, the people of Africa are the poorest in the world. Their lives are spent in a battle for survival.

Ignored by the Western World until the nineteenth century, Africa is still the least studied of all major world regions. Valued for a few vital minerals, as pawns in world politics, and as the original home of a substantial segment of the New World's population, the countries of Africa receive minimal aid and little attention in their battle for equity in the modern world.

Poverty is now a permanent reality in sub-Saharan Africa. Poverty is rooted in small, poorly located countries carved into colonies by Europeans. Poverty is expressed in underdeveloped economies, and in nations with few natural or human resources on which to draw.

Barring the emergence of a system of regional economic cooperation, like the European Community, or the input of intensive technological and financial assistance from the Technological World, the extreme levels of poverty in Africa will intensify. Many observers predict political upheaval and social chaos in the near future.

The notion of progress comes naturally to the Western mind and until recently was an unchallenged assumption. But Africa denies the inevitability of progress. Independence has brought neither personal freedom nor material well-being. Literacy rates, health care, and incomes are not improving in most parts of the region—in the poorest sections of the continent, hunger and famine are contemporary realities. In the late 1980s, Africa is an economic backwater unobtrusively sinking into deeper levels of human misery. When queried about the future of Africa, the novelist V. S. Naipaul, one of the most perceptive observers of the contemporary Developing World, replied, "Africa has no future." A harsh judgment, but one that cannot be ignored by modern geographers.

AFRICANS AND EUROPEANS: THE TRANSFORMATION OF A CONTINENT

To a greater degree than most culture regions, Africa was geographically isolated from other civilizations. The Sahara Desert to the north, narrow coastal littorals, and falls at the mouths of rivers prevented Africans from experiencing large-scale contact with Asia and Europe until well into the nineteenth century. Long-distance commerce was practiced by the medieval West African kingdoms, but most African communities were small kin-oriented groups who practiced subsistence agriculture and herding. African isolation is sharply silhouetted by technological backwardness when compared to the history of Europeans and Asians: fundamental innovations, such as the plow, the wheel, irrigation devices, and iron smelting, came late and spread slowly across the African domain.

When sustained interaction with these civilizations began in the 1500s after developments in shipbuilding and navigation, *Early European Contacts* began with coastal trade at the mouths of the great rivers of West Africa. This trade supplanted the old caravan trade routes across the Sahara. Although limited in scale and incidental to European voyages to India and the Orient, these early contacts strengthened the economic ties between Africa and Europe. The influx of European manufactured goods gradually swelled. African raw materials were exchanged for European finished goods. This trade mushroomed in scale when demand for slaves on plantations led to the massive forced migration of upwards of 10 million Africans to the New World.

The European presence, although pervasive, was limited to coastal trading stations. By the 1800s, however, European explorers and missionaries penetrated the African interior. Finally, at the end of the nineteenth century, *The Colonialization of Africa* began. European colonial powers took control of the continent, reshaped its economies,

Figure 13.1 Political regions of Africa.

subjugated its people, and destroyed the integrity of local cultures.

Early European Contacts

Despite the proximity of Africa to Europe, the heart of this continent remained unknown to Europeans well into the nineteenth century. Environmental and economic circumstances produced Europe's ignorance of Africa. In the north, the Islamic world bridged but separated the peoples of North Africa and those of sub-Saharan Africa. Although the products of Africa—gold, ivory, and slaves—were prized in the Mediterranean world, the routes of commerce across the Sahara Desert were controlled by the Muslims of North Africa. Islam thus served as a perme-

GEOSTATISTICS

	Capital	Area (square miles)	Population (millions)	Rate of Natural Increase (%)	Number of Years to Double Population	Population Projected for A.D. 2000	Infant Mortality Rate	Life Expectancy at Birth	Urban Population (%)	Per Capita GNP ($)	Energy Consumption per Capita (kg of oil equivalent)
Angola	Luanda	481,351	8.2	2.6	27	11.5	143	43	25	—	207
Benin	Porto-Novo	43,483	4.5	3.0	23	7.1	115	45	39	270	35
Botswana	Gaborone	231,803	1.3	3.4	20	1.8	67	58	22	840	300
Burkina Faso	Ouagadougou	105,869	8.5	2.8	24	11.8	145	46	8	150	20
Burundi	Bujumbura	10,745	5.2	2.9	24	7.3	119	48	5	240	26
Cameroon	Yaoundé	183,568	10.5	2.6	26	14.5	126	50	42	910	145
Cape Verde	Praia	1,556	0.3	2.6	26	0.5	77	60	27	460	—
Central African Republic	Bangui	240,533	2.8	2.5	28	3.8	148	45	35	290	33
Chad	N'Djamena	495,753	4.8	2.0	35	6.3	143	39	27	—	—
Comoros	Moroni	694	0.4	3.4	21	0.7	96	55	23	280	—
Congo	Brazzaville	132,046	2.2	3.4	21	3.2	112	55	48	1,040	232
Djibouti	Djibouti	8,494	0.3	2.5	28	0.4	132	47	74	—	—
Equatorial Guinea	Malabo	10,830	0.3	1.9	37	0.4	130	45	60	—	—
Ethiopia	Addis Ababa	471,776	48.3	3.0	23	71.1	118	50	10	120	17
Gabon	Libreville	103,347	1.3	1.6	44	1.6	112	49	41	3,020	—
Gambia	Banjul	4,363	0.8	2.1	34	1.1	169	36	21	230	—
Ghana	Accra	92,100	14.4	3.1	22	20.5	72	58	31	390	131
Guinea	Conakry	94,927	6.9	2.4	29	9.2	153	41	22	—	53
Guinea-Bissau	Bissau	13,946	0.9	2.4	29	1.2	132	45	27	170	—
Ivory Coast	Abidjan	124,502	11.2	3.1	22	17.3	105	52	43	740	166
Kenya	Nairobi	224,961	23.3	4.1	17	38.3	76	54	19	300	103
Lesotho	Maseru	11,718	1.6	2.6	27	2.3	106	50	17	410	—
Liberia	Monrovia	43,000	2.5	3.1	22	3.6	127	50	42	450	345
Malagasy Republic (Madagascar)	Antananarivo	226,656	10.9	2.8	25	15.6	63	51	22	230	33

GEOSTATISTICS (continued)

	Capital	Area (square miles)	Population (millions)	Rate of Natural Increase (%)	Number of Years to Double Population	Population Projected for A.D. 2000	Infant Mortality Rate	Life Expectancy at Birth	Urban Population (%)	Per Capita GNP ($)	Energy Consumption per Capita (kg of oil equivalent)
Malawi	Lilongwe	45,745	7.7	3.2	21	11.4	157	46	12	160	39
Mali	Bamako	478,764	8.7	2.9	24	12.3	175	43	18	170	25
Mauritania	Nouakchott	397,954	2.1	3.0	23	3.0	132	45	35	440	127
Mauritius	Port Louis	718	1.1	1.2	58	1.3	27	68	42	1,200	—
Mozambique	Maputo	309,494	15.1	2.6	27	21.1	147	46	19	210	86
Namibia	Windhoek	318,259	1.7	2.8	24	2.4	111	49	51	1,020	—
Niger	Niamey	489,189	7.2	2.9	24	10.6	141	44	16	260	48
Nigeria	Lagos	356,668	111.9	2.9	24	160.9	122	47	28	640	165
Réunion	Saint Denis	969	0.6	1.8	38	0.7	12	70	60	3,940	—
Rwanda	Kigali	10,170	7.1	3.7	19	11.2	122	49	6	290	43
São Tomé and Príncipe	São Tomé	371	0.1	2.7	25	0.2	62	65	35	340	—
Senegal	Dakar	75,749	7.0	2.6	26	9.8	137	44	36	420	110
Seychelles	Victoria	108	0.1	1.9	37	0.1	17	70	37	—	—
Sierra Leone	Freetown	27,699	4.0	1.8	38	5.4	175	35	28	310	82
Somalia	Mogadishu	246,201	8.0	3.1	23	10.4	147	41	34	280	82
South Africa	Pretoria	471,444	35.1	2.3	31	45.3	66	60	56	1,800	2,184
Sudan	Khartoum	967,494	24.0	2.8	24	33.4	112	49	20	320	61
Swaziland	Mbubane	6,703	0.7	3.1	23	1.0	124	50	26	600	—
Tanzania	Dar es Salaam	364,900	24.3	3.6	19	36.6	111	52	18	240	39
Togo	Lomé	21,927	3.3	3.3	21	4.9	117	54	22	250	47
Uganda	Kampala	91,135	16.4	3.4	20	24.7	108	50	10	—	24
Zaire	Kinshasa	905,564	33.3	3.0	23	47.9	103	51	34	160	73
Zambia	Lusaka	290,583	7.5	3.7	19	11.6	87	55	43	300	412
Zimbabwe	Harare	150,803	9.7	3.5	20	15.1	76	57	24	620	427

Sources: World Population Data Sheet, 1988; World Development Report, 1987.

495

able barrier between Africa and Europe.

For Africans, the stimulus for trade was salt, a commodity needed in West Africa, plentiful in the Sahara. Trade was brought about by Muslims who carried salt southward to the city of Timbuktu on the Niger River and traded for gold, kola nuts, ostrich feathers, ivory, ebony, and slaves. Barred by Muslims from direct contact with tropical Africa, Europeans remained distant and envious consumers of Africa's exotic wealth.

It was not until the fifteenth century that direct sea contact between Europe and tropical Africa became technically possible. The struggle to divert lucrative African commodities, especially gold, from the trans-Saharan trade routes was on. A member of the Portuguese royal family, Prince Henry the Navigator, established a school of navigation and sent ships to sail down the west coast of Africa and then eastward to the Indies. Previously, no European vessel had dared voyage beyond Cape Bojador, due south of the Canary Islands. These ships were equipped with triangular lateen sails that could carry the Portuguese beyond the African bulge and tack into the winds to bring them back again.

In 1446, the Senegal River was reached; the Gold Coast (today's Ghana) was visited by 1475. Contact with the Kingdom of the Kongo (the modern Congo region) was established in 1483; five years later Bartholomeu Dias rounded the Cape of Good Hope. But Portuguese mariners discovered few natural ports or harbors on the west coast of Africa, and most trade was carried on in ships anchored at the mouths of rivers.

During the next four centuries, from the time of these early Portuguese contacts to the late nineteenth century, European traders conducted business on the coastal fringes of Africa. The early traders—Portuguese, Dutch, British, and French—constructed forts and trading posts at key points along the west coast of

In the 1400s, Portuguese advances in shipbuilding brought Europeans to Africa as coastal traders. This engraving (dated 1470) depicts a ship of the type that opened the African world to European merchants.

Africa from Mauritania to southern Angola. Inland from these trading posts, a web of trading partnerships with African kingdoms developed. European trade goods were introduced from Senegal to Angola. In return, the Europeans received gold, ivory, and slaves.

Over time, cloth goods, metals, firearms, and New World crops like corn and manioc, diffused throughout a wide area of sub-Saharan Africa. In the interior, African kingdoms vied for control of the trade routes along which gold and slaves flowed to the coast. Cooperation between native Africans and European traders only required a European coastal presence.

But even if economic motives had attracted Europeans to the African interior, environmental obstacles to such penetration were formidable. The interior of most of Africa is a plateau flanked by narrow coastal lowlands. Only a limited amount of Africa can be explored by river ca-

noes, the simplest means of transport, because waterfalls occur along sharp breaks in elevation near the coast. Bypassing these river barriers and using pack animals was difficult. A dense tangle of jungle lined the waterways, beyond which the tropical forests of the African lowland were infested with **tsetse flies,** which carry diseases fatal to pack animals. Moreover, any trading expedition entering the African interior risked hostile kingdoms jealous of their trading rights and had to be large enough to carry all provisions and trade goods by hand.

Beyond these physical obstacles, perhaps the single most important factor that discouraged European entry into Africa was disease, specifically malaria, dengue fever, and yellow fever. Africa developed a well-deserved reputation as the "white man's grave" because of the high death rate among Europeans. Some 40 to 60 percent of newcomers from Europe died during their first year of residence in Africa. For all these reasons, Europeans stayed out of Africa and knew little about its land, people, and resources. Cartographers labeled the interior of Africa as "uninhabited," meaning that only Africans lived there. African people formed an unknown mass, objects of trade until slavery was abolished, invisible thereafter.

The Slave Trade in Africa

Europeans did not start the slave trade. Centuries before the Portuguese ever sailed southward, Africans had exported slaves to the Mediterranean world and to Asia. Nor did European slaving expeditions comb the African interior in search of laborers for the plantation economy that burgeoned in the Americas in the 1600s and 1700s. Topography, disease, and African trading policies restricted Europeans to the coastal margins of the continent. Only 1 or 2 of every 100 slaves shipped to the New World were actually captured by Europeans. The rest—an esti-

AFRICAN STATES AND EMPIRES BEFORE THE EUROPEANS

Recent geographical research has established that large-scale, well-organized central states and empires existed in Africa for centuries before the continent was conquered by Europeans. These states played a major role in the organization of society and economy, and some participated actively in the slave trade.

Adapted from: Jeffrey Holden, "Empires and State Formation," in John N. Paden and Edward W. Soja (eds.), *The African Experience,* Vol. 1. Evanston, Ill.: Northwestern University Press, 1970, p. 178.

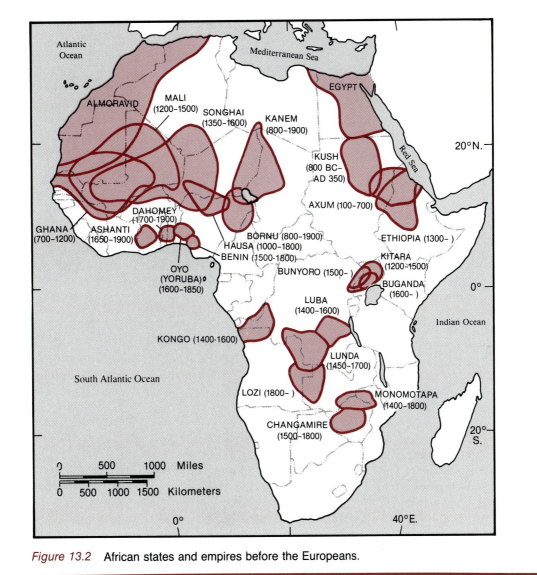

Figure 13.2 African states and empires before the Europeans.

mated 10 million human beings—were caught, transported, and sold into slavery by fellow Africans.

The Africans who profited from the growth of the Atlantic slave trade were for the most part members of thriving agricultural societies ruled by kings in centrally organized states (Fig. 13.2). The West African kingdoms were part of a trading network that linked tropical West Africa with the grasslands of the Sudan, the Sahara Desert, and the shores of North Africa beyond. It was to these states that European ships came filled with trade goods to exchange for slaves.

African kings entered into partnership with slave traders, lured by the products of an industrializing Europe. This introduction of the commercial and industrial revolutions to

African kingdoms organized the slave trade in the interior of the continent, marching their captives to European trading stations on the coast for shipment to the New World. Slaves were often traded for guns (note print), precipitating a gun–slave cycle.

Africa is comparable to what happened in other parts of the Developing World. But the legalized, international trade in human souls that evolved was viciously different. In Africa, as elsewhere, Europeans opened up new commercial horizons, reorganized internal political and commercial networks, and introduced new goods, techniques, and ideas.

The arrival of European traders in West Africa meant that the old trans-Saharan trade links were bypassed. The Sahara diminished in importance as north-south trade declined. West and Central African products could be directly transported to European markets in European ships. Previously, the centers of economic activity in West Africa lay in the interior. Here powerful groups, like the Kanem-Bornu of Lake Chad and the Songhai and Hausa states of the Niger River, controlled crossroads locations where the products and people of tropical Africa converged for transshipment northward to market centers in North Africa (Fig. 13.2). States near the west coast like Ashanti, Dahomey, and Benin were peripheral to this Sudan trading network by reason of distance. With the emergence of Atlantic commerce, however, the coastal regions became centers of a new, important commercial system.

Most major Atlantic trade centers were located at the mouths of rivers, which provided easy access to the interior. On the northern Atlantic coast, goods flowed down the Senegal River from the interior of modern Mauritania and Mali. Several hundred miles to the south, a similar trade center existed in the islands off the mouth of the Gambia River. For the next 1000 miles, trading stations were few. But near the mouth of the Volta River on the Gold Coast (modern Ghana), 27 European outposts were established to tap the gold resources of the Ashanti kingdom in the interior.

Trade was heavy along the entire Guinea coast (Fig. 13.4). The Gold Coast was a natural outlet for goods from the Volta River Basin in the interior. From here westward to the delta of the Niger River, slaves were marched along trails and small streams to the coast. Finally, along the Bight of Biafra, the easternmost trade center of West Africa was located at the mouth of the Calabar River. European-oriented trade was limited on the next 700 miles of the African coast, along the shores of Cameroon, Equatorial Guinea, and Gabon. Far-

ther south, coastal trade complexes were located at the mouth of the Congo River and at Luanda in Angola. Here, Europeans carried on a rich trade with the organized states of central Africa. South of Luanda, the coastal plain narrowed. The Namib Desert in the interior, a poor, thinly populated region, held little interest for European traders.

The products of Europe flowed through these coastal trading regions into the most densely populated sections of Africa. Manufactured cloth, metal goods, knives, brass kettles, copper and iron bars, rum, brandy, tobacco, firearms, and gunpowder diffused from the hands of one African leader to another. The most significant innovations, however, were New World crops: corn entered the Congo Basin in the sixteenth century and by 1900 was cultivated on savanna grasslands and cleared forests throughout tropical Africa; manioc was introduced into Angola around 1600 and by the 1850s was cultivated as far east as modern Zimbabwe.

Over a long period of time, African societies became dependent on these imports. Native metalworking declined because of the availability of inexpensive European axes, hoes, and knives. Machine-made textiles had the same effect on cloth weaving. More disruptive, however, were African rulers, who came to rely on this merchandise to attract loyal retainers. These rulers participated willingly in the European trade as sellers of slaves.

As the demand for slaves in the Americas increased, economic life in West Africa became dependent on a steady outflow of human cargo. The area between Senegal and Angola produced roughly 85 percent of all the slaves exported to the New World. But economic and social conditions varied from one local region to another. In Benin, the slave trade was a tightly controlled royal monopoly on which the state was almost completely dependent. In the Senegal Valley, the Futa Toro tribe were never slavers, but they taxed shipments of slaves passing through their territory. In the Niger delta, city-states sent armed war canoes into the interior to collect slaves for export. In Nigeria, the Aro people used religious ritual as a method of collecting slaves for export. In East Africa, Arabs controlled the slave trade.

The vast majority of slaves, however, were captured in intertribal wars. Native warfare increased dramatically with the introduction of firearms. This precipitated a gun-slave cycle. Africans were provided with arms, arms were used to enslave enemy tribes for profit, and the profit was used to buy more guns.

The Impact of Slaving on Africa

The long-term impact of the slave trade on Africa is difficult to discern. Only in two areas, Angola on the west coast and Mozambique on the east, did this massive export of human beings cause extensive depopulation. In West Africa, the slave trade may simply have drawn off a population increase that could not have been supported by the existing economy and technology, although some agricultural land was abandoned and reverted to forest. Paradoxically, then, although 10 million of the healthiest people of Africa were removed from their societies, there is little evidence that this had any long-term effect on the demography of the continent.

The effects of the slave trade on African politics and economics were more direct. Some states were literally eliminated by the slave trade, but others, like the Ashanti and the Yoruba, gained prominence. Poorly organized societies, like the Ibo, suffered the greatest losses; highly structured societies, like Benin, the least. One effect was universal. When the tentacles of the slave trade reached deep into the continent, distrust, fear, and warfare increased among the peoples of Africa. Already culturally fragmented into more than 500 different language groups, Africans were further alienated from one another by the terror created by the trade in lives.

The most enduring effect of the slave trade on Africa and its people may have been psychological. It strongly influences the concepts Africans hold of each other as well as European perceptions of Africans. White prejudice was generated by a basic ignorance of the societies and environments of Africa. Deep-rooted notions of African inferiority supported the Western vision of Africans as ignorant and uncivilized. When the slave trade finally became unprofitable in nineteenth-century Europe and America, it was a curious distortion of these biases that laid the foundation for European conquest. Explorers penetrated the interior in search of the unknown. Missionaries came to enlighten the "savages" by diffusing Christianity and the "benefits" of Western civilization.

Explorers and Missionaries

The exploration of Africa by Europeans began with the journey of the Scottish explorer James Bruce to the highlands of Ethiopia in 1769 and ended a century later with the death of the missionary David Livingstone. Bruce was an explorer and geographer drawn to Africa by curiosity. His goal was to discover the source of the Nile. Although he failed, his writings fired the imagination of Europe. Others like Bruce were obsessed with the drama and glory of conquering the "Dark Continent" and played a significant part in opening up Africa to the Western world.

Twelve wealthy English gentlemen, intrigued by the unknown, joined together in 1788 to solve the riddle of the Niger River—to identify its source and direction of flow. The club's first four expeditions were disasters, but the fifth, led by Mungo Park, succeeded in establishing that the Niger flowed eastward. More explorers were lost before cartographers could delineate with confi-

dence the major features of the West African interior.

As questions concerning the topography of West Africa were answered, impetus for continued exploration of the African interior came from a new motivation: the movement to abolish slavery. Penetration of the African interior was deemed essential to eliminate the slave trade at its source. In 1833, after the British made slavery illegal throughout the British Empire, a British expedition fitted out with two steamships sailed up the Niger River for this purpose. The expedition ended in disaster when thirty-eight Europeans died of disease.

By the 1850s, the discovery of quinine, an antimalarial drug, enabled Europeans to penetrate Africa more safely. Thereafter, consulates and commercial stations were established throughout West Africa. Trading depots dealing in palm oil, ivory, and rubber were scattered along the three great rivers of the region—the Senegal, Gambia, and Niger.

The same complex of events and motives also opened up East Africa to Europe in the nineteenth century. Richard Burton, accompanied by John H. Speke, traveled inland to Lake Tanganyika, igniting the celebrated controversy over the source of the Nile River. Speke returned to Africa (1861–1862) to prove that Lake Victoria was the ultimate source of the Nile. This dispute riveted the attention of contemporary Europe on East Africa, which until then had been little known.

But a more serious motive than geographical curiosity brought the greatest of the African explorers, David Livingstone, to Africa in 1841—the conversion of Africa to Christianity. For more than thirty years, Livingstone tramped across Africa from Luanda on the west coast to the mouth of the Zambezi River on the east. He was the only explorer to reject what he called "the stupid prejudice against color" and the first missionary to bring the suffering of the

A Royal Geographical Society expedition on the Zambezi River sets out in search of David Livingstone, the most famous European missionary in Africa.

African people to the attention of Europeans. Livingstone embodied the three great motives that brought Europeans to Africa: curiosity, Christianity, and commerce.

The population of East Africa was ravaged by slave raids organized by Arab and Indian traders from the off-shore island of Zanzibar. This eastern slave trade, although smaller in volume (total exports, 2 million Africans) than the defunct Atlantic trade, was similarly organized. Native leaders bought cloth, metal goods, and guns from slavers in return for captives, who were marched in chains to Arab sailing vessels on the coast. The abolitionists, who had eliminated the Atlantic traffic in human beings, were inspired by Livingstone to demand a cessation of slavery in the east. Expeditions similar to those on the Niger opened up East Africa to Christianity and commerce.

As late as the 1880s, Africa remained politically independent, but the economic and moral foundations for European conquest had been laid. In West Africa, the British and French were established along the Atlantic coast between Senegal and the Niger delta. Farther south, the American

adventurer Henry Stanley was exploring the basin of the Congo River for the king of Belgium. In South Africa, British and Dutch (Boer) colonists broke over the question of slavery. The Calvinist Dutch moved into the interior, which brought them into direct conflict with the powerful Zulu nation. Meanwhile, the British diamond magnate Cecil Rhodes was advocating a British colony extending from the Cape of Good Hope to Cairo.

Thus, information on the geography, peoples, and economic conditions of Africa flowed into Europe through the journals of explorers and missionaries. Yet there were few Europeans in Africa. The swift partitioning of Africa, which began after the Berlin Conference of 1884–1885, must have come as a total surprise to most Africans. After four centuries of European contact, Africa fell under direct European political control in a brief thirty years.

The Colonialization of Africa

Europeans had common political and economic goals when they colonialized Africa. The methods used to

achieve these aims were adapted to fit local environmental and economic conditions. They reflected each European nation's political philosophy and approach to colonial rule.

Between 1884 and 1914, Europeans fought to control Africa and to partition its society and territory. Successful commerce and settlement demanded security. The European need for order took precedence over European concern for justice. Boundaries were forged in bitter commercial competition and were arbitrarily drawn on new European maps. These boundaries reduced clashes between rival European powers, but native societies and economies were disrupted by the new political barriers.

With the establishment of colonial law and order, the African continent was opened to trade. Africans were forced to produce and transport goods for export to Europe. Farmers and herders across the continent left their traditional livelihoods to work in cash economies oriented to European needs. Transportation systems, plantations, and mines were paid for by taxes on Africans. Africa was not only conquered, it was conquered cheaply.

Although the colonial era spanned only seventy years, fundamental changes were set in motion that laid the foundations of Africa's modern human geography. Territory was subdivided by Europeans into what became the states of modern Africa (Fig. 13.3). Traditional societies were subordinated or destroyed, and even the poorest peasant farmers understood that political power was in the hands of colonial administrators.

Similarly, the economy of Africa was transformed. Transportation systems were built to maintain order and exploit Africa's resources. Africans planted new crops and labored in the mines, railroads, and ports built by, and for, Europeans. The process of change reached into the countryside of Africa in the form of new economies, continuous taxation, forced labor, and Western administrative

THE "SCRAMBLE FOR AFRICA": 1884–1914

The "Scramble for Africa" between 1884 and 1914 brought the entire African continent except Liberia and Ethiopia under direct European colonial control.

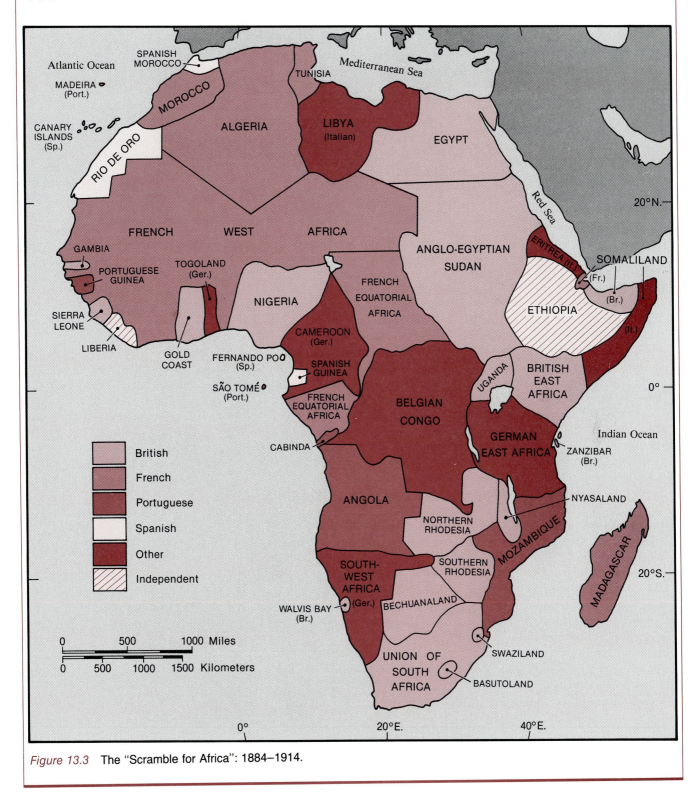

Figure 13.3 The "Scramble for Africa": 1884–1914.

organization. For Africans, colonialism was an invasion of European political and economic interests that shattered their societies and cultures.

West Africa: Colonial Administrators, Peasant Producers

The European presence in West Africa was modest in the middle of the nineteenth century. British and French trading posts existed from Senegal to the Niger River, and commercial agents were involved in shipping gum, palm oil, and rubber to Europe. All told, there could not have been more than 1000 Europeans in West Africa in 1850. But from these unimposing outposts, the Europeans partitioned one third of Africa's sub-Saharan population into seventeen different colonies.

By the turn of the century, the French had carved out an empire in West Africa nine times the size of metropolitan France. French colonial policy, based on their experience in Senegal, was applied to the Sudan (modern Mali), Mauritania, Burkina Faso, Niger, Guinea, Ivory Coast, and Benin (Fig. 13.3). These seven territories were amalgamated into French West Africa shortly after 1900 and were centrally administered by a governor-general in Dakar, Senegal. Civilian administrators were sent to control local populations. In theory, every West African subject could become a citizen of France, but education in French, military service, and ten years of French employment were required. Of the 17 million people under French rule in West Africa, only 2500 met these conditions and became French citizens.

Economic policy in French West Africa was influenced by France's successful cultivation of peanuts on the grassy plains of the Senegal Valley. Because the majority of territory under French control was covered by savanna grasslands, the principal goal was to convert the African population

This photo, commemorating the British annexation of Ado, Nigeria, reflects the clash of cultures that accompanied the colonization of Africa in the late 1880s.

into commercial cultivators of export crops. Except on the coast, however, the population of the region was thinly scattered and trade routes were poorly developed. To cope with transport difficulties, railroads were constructed. Head taxes were levied on the population to finance the railroads. Taxes had to be paid in cash, which forced Africans to cultivate commercial crops, in effect reducing them to servitude.

Inland cultivation of peanuts and cotton never proved profitable in French West Africa, so French attention turned to coastal environments. Here cocoa, timber, coffee, and bananas from the Ivory Coast, palm products from Benin, and bananas from Guinea became important export commodities. Railroads were built inland from major port cities, creating narrow corridors of considerable wealth. But the vast majority of French West Africa's estimated 17 million people were scattered over 4.8 million square miles of countryside, most of which remained isolated and undeveloped during the colonial period. These differences in regional development

stimulated large-scale labor migrations to the coast in times of economic stress.

By contrast, the four British colonies in West Africa were small in area, more densely populated, and possessed important mineral as well as agricultural resources. The Gold Coast (modern Ghana) rapidly became the richest territory in West Africa after railroads were constructed inland from the coast. Gold, manganese, and bauxite became important export products, although these were later overshadowed by the large-scale commercial development of cocoa plantations. In Nigeria, development came later because most of the colony's 24 million people lived in the interior. Eventually, however, two railroads opened up peanut cultivation in the interior to supplement Nigeria's export of palm oil and cocoa from coastal districts. In Sierra Leone, a similar pattern evolved. The tiny colony of Gambia, although an important source of peanuts, was the poorest of Britain's West African colonies (Fig. 13.3).

Unlike the French, the British never developed a single method of administering their possessions in West Africa. Instead, they allowed local conditions to dictate techniques of government. As in the French territories, revenues from peasant producers on the coast were used to finance the development of the interior. The higher productivity of the British colonies, however, enabled them to rely on export duties instead of head taxes. Ultimately, the coastal districts were governed by direct British rule, whereas the interior was administered indirectly. The increase in trade that came with the extension of British rule and railroads in West Africa created a sizable middle class of well-educated Africans who spoke out for developments in medical services, education, and social services to a far greater degree than in French West Africa.

In the German colonies of Togo and Cameroon, rigid discipline was imposed; in Portuguese Guinea, colonialism took a less clearly defined form. In Liberia, the only noncolonial territory in West Africa, none of this happened—neither the establishment of European rule nor economic development. Former slaves from America who returned to Africa in the 1820s clung to the coast, lacking the wealth, the trade, and the cultural power to control the interior. Finally in 1925, the Firestone Rubber Company leased 1 million acres of Liberian forests and developed rubber as the one-crop economy of this state.

Central Africa: The Concession Companies

In the Congo River Basin of Central Africa, colonial development was influenced by different environmental and economic conditions. The tropical rain forests of the region were thinly populated by isolated groups of hunters, fisherfolk, and subsistence farmers. There were denser populations on the northern and eastern rims of the Congo Basin, but the potential for large-scale exchange of European trade goods was quite

limited. Central Africa, then, had neither the precolonial economies nor the trading systems on which King Leopold of Belgium's Congo Free State (modern Zaire), the French colonies of Equatorial Africa (Chad, Central African Republic, Congo, and Gabon), and the British colonies of Nyasaland (Malawi) and the Rhodesias (Zimbabwe and Zambia) could graft a system of colonial development and exploitation (Fig. 13.3).

Central Africa had few peasant producers to convert to commercial farming, no substantial trading networks to tax for revenues, and no dense, settled populations from which head taxes could be collected. The formidable task of developing the Congo Basin had to be financed by money invested by private entrepreneurs seeking large long-term profits. Mineral and agricultural rights (concessions) were granted to any private company that guaranteed to finance the construction of highways, railroads, and navigational routes to stimulate commercial production. Central Africa thus became the realm of the concession company.

Leopold II of Belgium managed to achieve international recognition of his personal domain over the Congo Free State (modern Zaire). Beginning in 1886, concession companies were granted rights to territory in return for constructing railroads. Early in this process, policies were introduced to accelerate commercial exploitation. All lands not under cultivation, "waste lands" as they were called, were declared government property. Because most farmers in the Congo Basin were shifting cultivators, moving from one area to another every few years, the effect on native African agriculture was disastrous. Forced labor and payment of taxes were demanded of all Africans. An armed police force ensured that these obligations were met. In a reign of terror that lasted nineteen years, from 1889 to 1908, roughly half the population of the Congo was killed by arms, forced labor, and starvation.

In 1908, Leopold II was forced to cede the Congo to the Belgian government.

The first products brought out of the Congo were ivory and rubber, but concession companies established cotton plantations, palm groves, sisal farms, and mines in many dispersed areas throughout the region. The invention of the pneumatic tire in Europe, however, led to a rubber boom. Africans were forced to leave their patches of cultivated land to tap rubber trees in the forests. As the demand for wild rubber declined with the establishment of rubber plantations in Southeast Asia, similar tactics were employed to provide labor for other commercial enterprises. The resulting destruction of the food economy of the Congo was the principal reason for the depopulation of the basin. Although the Belgian government ameliorated the worst of Leopold's excesses, it never questioned the ethics of forcing Africans to work for European profit.

In the French territories in Central Africa, a similar pattern of economic development through concession companies was pursued. These companies were granted monopolies over large territories in the four colonies of Gabon, Middle Congo (Congo), Ubangi-Shari (Central African Republic), and Chad, which were amalgamated into French Equatorial Africa in 1910 (Fig. 13.3). Africans were forced to work on palm plantations in Gabon, to harvest wild rubber in the forests of the Middle Congo, and to tend coffee and cotton plantations in Ubangi-Shari. The effects of reorganizing African labor from subsistence to commercial production were much the same as in the Congo Basin, although colonial policies were less brutal.

South Africa: The Boers and the British

In South Africa, the imposition of colonial rule followed a quite different course from that of West or Central Africa. The Europeans came to

South Africa seeking trading posts to guard their interests in the East Indies. In 1652, the Dutch established a trading station at Cape Town on the southwestern tip of the continent. During the next century the European population slowly grew and spread out from Cape Town. They established large farms on which Malay, West African, and local slave labor worked in wheat fields and vineyards. As settlement moved inland, the Dutch exterminated native Africans in their path. A class of mixed-race people, white and black, known as the Coloureds, emerged in this early period. They are still predominantly located in the cities and towns of the Cape.

By the middle 1700s, after a century in residence, the Dutch, called Boers (farmers), had developed a distinctive culture whose language, Afrikaans, was simpler than standard Dutch. Their rigid orthodox Calvinist faith justified the master-slave relationship. And this became an issue when Britain, in the wake of Napoleon's defeat in Europe, seized Cape Town in 1806 to protect its naval interests in the Indian Ocean.

By 1820, 5000 British immigrants had settled in the Cape Colony as town dwellers. Friction arose between British colonial authorities and the pastoral Boers. Each Boer considered it his birthright to possess 6000 acres when married. The Boers, therefore, insisted on an aggressive policy of territorial expansion. The British, however, were appalled by Boer cruelty to Africans. The British extended legal protection to remnant groups in the Cape Colony; in 1834, London forbade the Boers to keep slaves. These acts deeply offended the Boers and set in motion a new phase of colonial settlement in South Africa.

One by one, in ox-drawn wagons, the Boers began to leave the Cape Colony, trekking northward across the Orange River to escape the confines of British rule. This Great Trek of the Boers into the interior brought them into conflict with Bantu-speaking peoples who were simultaneously moving into the rich pastures of the high **veld.** On the high veld, the trek Boers and Bantu groups vied for control of the fertile lands of the interior of southern Africa. By 1850, the issue was resolved in favor of the better armed Boers. The Bantu peoples of the high veld were subjugated. Two Boer republics, the Orange Free State and the Transvaal, were established north of the Orange River beyond the reach of British influence in the Cape Colony and Natal.

By now, the combined European population of the British colony and the interior Boer republics amounted to about 300,000. In these territories, the African population numbered between 1 and 2 million. As European rule spread, land was alienated from the Africans. So Africans left their land and migrated to the Cape in search of work and food. The pattern of African migration to white-dominated urban centers intensified as the British and Boers settled on the best farmland, leaving poorer, less fertile environments for native peoples. Urban jobs were created by the discovery of diamonds at Kimberley in 1867 and of gold at Witwatersrand near Johannesburg in 1884. Nonetheless, sporadic warfare continued as it had for three centuries between Europeans and Africans. Finally, the Africans were disarmed and forced to submit.

The great mineral finds of South Africa intensified problems between the British and the Boers. Thousands of foreign miners, entrepreneurs, and adventurers, mostly British, immigrated to the Boer republic of Transvaal. Led by Cecil Rhodes, the British sought an alliance with the Boers to develop the wealth of South Africa. The Boers, already outnumbered, feared their distinctive way of life would be destroyed by British intrusions. The resulting tensions ultimately triggered the fierce Anglo-Boer War at the turn of the century that ended in British victory. The Union of South Africa was formed in 1910, composed of the British Cape and Natal colonies and the Boer Orange Free State and Transvaal.

During the next half century, this union of British and Boer interests transformed South Africa from an agricultural to an industrial economy. Economic change occurred faster and on a larger scale here than anywhere else in Africa. The Witwatersrand became a major industrial and mining complex, with Johannesburg, the largest city in southern Africa, as its focus. A web of railroads was flung across the country connecting the inland industrial districts with port cities. Africans were assigned reserves located in the least desirable areas of South Africa, foreshadowing the policy of **apartheid** (apartness), rigidly enforced after 1948.

Africans participated in the economic development of South Africa as cheap labor in the mines and factories of the industrial centers and on the cotton, rice, and sugar plantations of Natal. Asian plantation laborers, immigrants recruited after slavery ended, emigrated to the towns to become shopkeepers. Although Africans made up three quarters of the population, native reserves included only 13 percent of the land area. Although South Africa's economy depended on gold mined by Africans, the native population earned one eighth the income of whites in similar jobs. They lived in slums in restricted areas near the larger cities, on white farms, and in native reserves. Thus, when the tides of nationalism swept Africa after World War II, South Africa differed substantially from other areas of Africa. Here the largest European population on the continent had built a modern economy on the backs of a subjugated majority, and unlike other colonial regimes in Africa, the Europeans were determined to stay in Africa and stay in power.

European Settlers in East and South-Central Africa

In the highlands of East Africa, from Kenya southward to the Cape of Good

NÉGRITUDE AND COLONIALISM

The colonialization of Africa has caused many Africans to reject Western values, such as objectivity, progress, and productivity. In the view of Aimé Césaire, Africans, who "never invented anything, explored anything, conquered anything," have unique and precious attributes—emotion, sensibility, and comprehension—that taken together make up négritude, the quality of being African and the sense of African blackness. This became the basis of Césaire's passionate condemnation of colonialism as a force of alien destruction. Here, he voices the protest for the end of colonialism:

It is my turn to formulate an equation: colonization equals thingafication.

I hear a storm of protest. They speak to me of progress and "accomplishments," sickness conquered, higher standards of living.

I speak of societies emptied of themselves, of trampled cultures, undermined institutions, confiscated lands, of assassinated religions, annihilated artistic masterpieces, of extraordinary possibilities suppressed.

They throw up to me facts, statistics, the number of kilometers of roads, canals, and railways.

I speak of thousands of men sacrificed in the Congo ocean. I speak of

Aimé Césaire speaks of millions of men "knowingly brought to their knees." This 1896 print of the submission of the Ashanti king, Prempeh, to British rule, is aptly entitled *The Final Act of Humiliation.*

those who at the time I am writing are in the process of digging out the port of Abidjan by hand. I speak of millions of men torn away from their gods, their land, their customs, their way of life, their livelihood, their dance, and their wisdom.

I speak of millions of men in whom

fear, trembling, feelings of inferiority, despair, toadyism were knowingly inculcated and who were brought to their knees.

Source: Aimé Césaire, "On the Nature of Colonialism," in I. L. Markovitz (ed.), *African Politics and Society*, pp. 41–42. New York: Free Press, 1970.

Hope, land sparsely populated by Africans and climatically attractive to European settlement was available. The British, the Germans, and the Portuguese all encouraged settler immigration (Fig. 13.3).

British policies in East Africa varied from colony to colony, but the establishment of a cash economy to pay the costs of administration and to generate trade occurred everywhere. In Kenya, 17,000 square miles of good land in the highlands were reserved for Europeans, although no official government policy of immigration was declared. In Nyasaland (Malawi), dense African populations on the best farmland limited European settlement. In Uganda, the

powerful Buganda people received grants of land in return for helping the British, and they converted large areas into highly profitable commercial cotton production.

In the Rhodesias (Zambia and Zimbabwe), Cecil Rhodes promoted European settlement to further his dream of a Cape-to-Cairo colony. Large grants to land were set aside for settlers; other immigrants were attracted by jobs in the copper mines of Northern Rhodesia (modern Zambia). The native inhabitants of the Rhodesian plateau lost large tracts of land to incoming whites. By 1914, there were nearly 20,000 British settlers in these colonies in East and South-Central Africa.

In contrast to Britain, Germany followed a rigorous state-sponsored form of colonization. German settlers were exhorted to emigrate to overseas African colonies, particularly Tanganyika (Tanzania) on the east coast and South-West Africa (Namibia) on the west coast. In both colonies, the goals were to impose German discipline and techniques of production on the native labor force, to create a new German homeland in Africa for the growing peasant population of Germany, and to produce revenue and raw materials as efficiently as possible. German administrators ruthlessly suppressed opposition to colonial rule, levied heavy taxes on native peoples, and forced African subsistence farmers into commercial agriculture. In both Tanganyika and South-West Africa, the German impact on native peoples was disastrous.

In South-West Africa, German policy called for the concentration of the African population in the dry environment near Windhoek, an interior capital. But most natives were seminomadic cultivators and herders who lived in small settlements well adapted to the arid climate. Enforced settlement met with armed resistance and then reprisals. All territory was declared part of the German colony, so that Africans no longer owned any land. By 1906, after two years of warfare, two thirds of the native population was killed. The remainder entered employment on German farms and ranches.

In Tanganyika, African resistance began almost immediately after the Germans bought the coastline from the sultan of Zanzibar in 1884. Better armed, the Germans were able to suppress Swahili resistance on the coast. But in the interior, much larger groups fiercely resisted the implantation of German garrisons. The Germans responded with a scorched-earth policy. In four bloody and chaotic years, 125,000 Africans died and the settlement system of Tanganyika was laid waste. The stain of German colonial rule on Tanganyika was so pervasive that development in this territory was retarded for two generations.

In their colonies of Angola and Mozambique, the Portuguese practiced one of the least coherent, most radical colonial policies on the African continent. Professing a desire to assimilate the Africans into Portuguese culture and society, a policy of intermarriage was encouraged with the ultimate aim of producing a population of mixed blood that was loyal to Portugal. The practice, however, was quite different from the theory. Some 3 million blacks were shipped as slaves to Brazil from Angola. Other Africans worked on coffee plantations. In Mozambique, palm and co-

coa plantations were hacked out of the coastal jungles. When local sources of labor failed, Indians were imported from South Asia to work on the estates of the Portuguese colonists. The Portuguese policy of assimilation was never fully implemented and less than 1 percent of the African population achieved Portuguese citizenship. The lowest levels of literacy and health care in Africa existed in the two Portuguese "provinces" of Angola and Mozambique.

THE HUMAN GEOGRAPHY OF AFRICA

Africa south of the Sahara, often perceived as a lush and verdant land, is composed of a series of difficult natural environments. Throughout much of the region, rainfall is low and uncertain, soils are of poor quality, and agricultural potential is limited. Where rainfall is plentiful and rain forests prevail, soils are leached and acidic. Here, winter, the great natural destroyer of insects and disease, never comes. For uncounted centuries, however, Africa supported small communities of subsistence farmers and herders and even a number of well-organized agricultural kingdoms. High birth rates were balanced by high death rates, leaving a stable population to manipulate the arid, subtropical, and tropical environmental systems of the region. With the coming of the Europeans, this stable pattern of land use and living was changed. Today, conditions of life in Africa are as bad as anywhere on the globe.

In the late nineteenth and early twentieth centuries, European powers subdivided Africa into colonies, introduced commercial cropping, destroyed native African systems of communal land ownership and land use, and perhaps most important, initiated measures of health care and disease control that substantially

lowered death rates. The balance between population, resources, and environment was upset. African economic systems required large land areas to support small populations. Hunting and gathering societies required an estimated 65 square miles per person, pastoral herding supported only 8 people per square mile, and subsistence grain cultivation anywhere from 65 to 400 people per square mile, depending on local environmental conditions. With African women bearing an average of six children and infant mortality rates in decline, population growth became an underlying cause of environmental deterioration.

Today, the same environments that supported small, cohesive populations in the past are being pressured by populations doubling in size every twenty-five years. Agricultural production has increased at a slower rate than population. Hunger is widespread; famine is on the horizon. The limitations of Africa's *Environments and Landscapes* have now become apparent and pose problems to development schemes throughout the region. In *The Rain Forests of Central and West Africa*, deforestation has wiped out one third of the natural vegetation and population pressure is intense. In *The Sahel*, a latitudinal swath of grasslands stretching across the midsection of the continent, the southward migration of the Sahara Desert during the last twenty-five years has created a belt of famine that extends into the highlands of *The African Horn*. In *East Africa*, environmental use varies with elevation and precipitation. Population is clustered in favorable agricultural environments. In *Southern Africa*, racial prejudice has strongly influenced the distribution of people on the landscape.

Environments and Landscapes

Sub-Saharan Africa is a massive, compact block of land extending 3200 miles southward from the Sahara De-

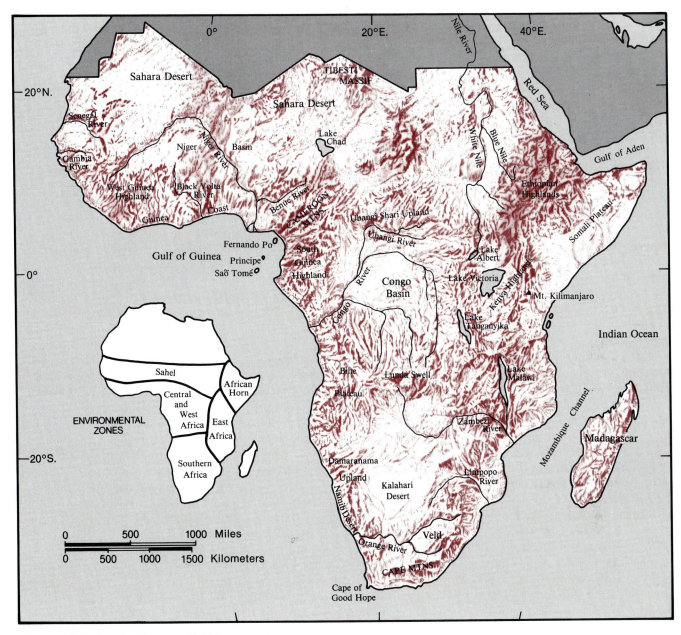

Figure 13.4 Physical features of Africa.

sert to the Cape of Good Hope (Fig. 13.4). Approximately three times the size of the United States and 4600 miles at its widest, Africa lies astride the equator. Climates from its southern tip to the southern shore of the Saharan Desert, the Sahel, are either tropical or subtropical. Despite this relatively uniform climate, Africa is thinly peopled. With a total population of 508 million, this region has an average density of 40 people per square mile, a figure lower than that of any other continent save Australia.

The principal reasons for this are environmental. Africa has a greater proportion of valueless land than most other world regions. The lowlands of western and central Africa are infested by tsetse flies and have poor, heavily leached, laterite soils. Rainfall in the highlands of eastern and southern Africa, in the Kalahari Desert, and on the plains of the Sahel is either too little or too unreliable. Thus, in Africa, whose population is increasing faster than that of any world region except Latin America, the

pressure of people on the resource base—despite relatively low densities—is a serious problem.

As one might expect, population pressure on resources in Africa varies in cause and intensity from one environmental zone to another. Natural regions, however, are less clearly defined here than on other continents where major divides, like the Alps, the Andes, and the Himalayas, compartmentalize human activity. In Africa, broad transition zones are more common than compartments. From the hot, wet, **equatorial forests** of West and Central Africa, the environment gradually changes to savanna grasslands in the Sahel to steppes and deserts in the Sahara. A comparable southward environmental gradation occurs between the rain forests of the Congo Basin and the Kalahari Desert. East-west transitions occur from the lowlands of West and Central Africa to the highlands of eastern and southern Africa. On the basis of these two variables, rainfall and elevation, the following subregions can be identified.

A northeast to southwest line cuts across the African continent from the highlands of Ethiopia to the coast of Angola. West of this line, the vast lowlands of western and central Africa—an area below 3000 feet in elevation—are drained by the great river systems of the Niger, the Congo, and the Nile. In these lowlands, rainfall diminishes both northward and southward from the equatorial core of Zaire in the Congo Basin. Here, and along the coast of West Africa, tropical rain forests flourish because of year-round high temperature and high humidity. The forests gradually change in complexion from dense evergreen woodlands in the basin to deciduous forests on its subtropical margins. Northward, rainfall diminishes and a pronounced dry season predominates in the Sahel, a belt of savanna grasslands and steppes stretching from the plains of Senegal and Mauritania on the Atlantic coast eastward through Mali, Burkina Faso, Niger, Chad, and southern Sudan to the rugged western slopes of the Ethiopian highlands.

East of this line and above 3000 feet, highland Africa includes the African Horn, composed of the Ethiopian Highlands and the deserts of the Somali Plateau; East Africa, composed of the uplands of Kenya, Uganda, and Tanzania; and Southern Africa, composed of the eastern highlands of Zambia, Zimbabwe, and South Africa as well as the dry Kalahari Desert and the steppes of Na-

mibia, Botswana, and western South Africa.

The Rain Forests of Central and West Africa

Tropical rain forests cover much of the Congo Basin—a vast, shallow saucer ringed by low hills. The lowland coasts of West Africa along the Gulf of Guinea are also cloaked in tropical rain forest (Fig. 13.4). Bisected by the equator, all parts of this region are constantly wet. Rainfall exceeds 60 inches a year; there is no dry season. Rainfall totals exceed 400 inches a year in coastal Cameroon. This climatic region supports the most imposing and luxuriant plant association known. A three-tiered canopy of evergreen trees at 50, 100, and 150 feet arches over the land, blocking out sunshine from the surface. Along river channels, where sunshine can penetrate to the ground, a dense **gallery forest** stretches unbroken along the banks. Here, an impenetrable tangle of mangrove shrubs, palms, and lianas (vines) lines the riverbanks.

An estimated two thirds of the Congo forest remains intact, although deforestation is proceeding rapidly. A full third of the rain forest has been cleared by lumber companies and shifting cultivators. Along the Guinea coast, rain forests line the shore from Sierra Leone eastward to western Nigeria, where a wide tongue of savanna grassland planted in palm trees breaks its continuity. On the outer fringes of the Congo Basin, in the hills of Cameroon, Congo, Gabon, and the Central African Republic and inland from the West African coast, evergreen rain forests give way to deciduous woodlands and savannas.

Despite the luxuriant vegetation in rain forest areas, this ecological system is sensitive to change, delicately balanced, and vulnerable to human activity. The myth of the encroaching jungle suggests rapid growth, but, in truth, tropical forests

grow 20 to 100 times slower than forests in the midlatitudes. Areas cleared for cultivation or lumbering take generations to recover. The astonishing complexity of the plant association, with as many as 100 different species found in 1 square mile, makes reforestation virtually impossible. Further, these rain forests are underlain by thin, acid lateritic soils that are leached of plant nutrients by heavy rainfall and are susceptible to rapid erosion when forest cover is removed.

Damage to the rain forest environment has already become a problem in the densely populated coastal belt of West Africa, where a year-round growing season, the fertile soils of river deltas, and trading opportunities have encouraged intensive commercial cultivation of cocoa, palm products, and rubber as well as subsistence food crops. In Ghana (pop. 14.4 million), Togo (pop. 3.3 million), and Benin (pop. 4.5 million), over half the population lives on the coast. Similar clusters of population are found near major port cities in the Ivory Coast (pop. 11.2 million), Liberia (pop. 2.5 million), and Guinea (pop. 6.9 million). In western Nigeria (pop. 111.9 million), the higher quality soils of the forest-savanna borderland support a comparable agricultural population with densities of 400 to 500 people per square mile.

Generally, in West and Central Africa, concentrations of population have set in motion forces of environmental deterioration. In Sierra Leone (pop. 4 million), rising population has pressured farmers practicing slash and burn agriculture into shortening the fallow period in the rain forest from a traditional seven to ten years to less than three years. Soil destruction and severe erosion have ensued. A similar process of erosion is afflicting densely settled parts of eastern Nigeria and the uplands of Cameroon (pop. 10.5 million) where growing numbers of agriculturalists have pressured the land base, leading to deforestation, gully erosion, frag-

Tropical rain forests cover much of West and Central Africa. Despite their luxuriant appearance, rain forests are delicate, easily disrupted ecosystems.

mentation of holdings, declining soil fertility, and frequent land disputes. In the vast rain forests of Zaire (pop. 33.3 million), Congo (pop. 2.2 million), Gabon (pop. 1.3 million), and the Central African Republic (pop. 2.8 million), however, population pressure is not yet an obvious problem. Here, poor soils, dense vegetation, and swarms of tsetse flies have kept population densities low for as long as anyone knows. In this area, roughly the size of Europe, the total population is less than 55 million.

On the northern fringes of the rain forests of West Africa and the Congo Basin, the forest grades into savanna grasslands and open woodlands. In West Africa, the "middle belt" (as it is called) is thinly populated compared with the dense populations of the coast and the inland commercial farming areas on the savanna-steppe boundary of northern Nigeria. In the middle belt, tsetse flies are more common than on the coast, soils are poorer in quality than those of the interior, and rainfall is too low to sup-

port tree crops. None of these environmental factors, however, sufficiently explains the relative underdevelopment of this region.

Farther inland, in the northern belt of West Africa, although the dry season lengthens, it is not underpopulation but overpopulation that is the problem. In the densely settled nodes of the old African kingdoms, the high natural fertility of the grassland soils has been maintained by heavy applications of fertilizer.

But in outlying areas, overgrazing has reduced herds. And continued cultivation without fertilization is destroying the natural basis of the agricultural economy. In places, this has led to land abandonment and **migration** to urban centers. Recently, migration has turned into a human flood as the interior of West Africa, a transition zone between the tropical environments of the equatorial zone and the desert to the north, has been afflicted by a southward movement of the Sahara Desert, a twenty-five-year invasion that has spread drought across sub-Saharan Africa.

The Sahel

On the northern margins of the savannas of West and Central Africa, annual rainfall diminishes to 20 inches or less. The long grasses of the humid south are replaced by the short-grass steppes of the Sahel (Fig. 13.4). Here the six states of Senegal, Mauritania, Mali, Burkina Faso, Niger, and Chad—with a combined population of 38.3 million—face an environmental crisis of major proportions. With the exceptions of the peanut-growing regions along the Senegal River, the cotton farms of the Upper Niger, and central Burkina Faso, this 4000-mile-long region is thinly populated, with cultivation restricted to the humid south. Cattle and camel herding predominate in the dry, tsetse-free north.

The population of the northern regions of the Sahel doubled in the early 1960s among the herding peoples of

GEOLAB

NATURAL HAZARDS: DESERTIFICATON IN THE SAHEL

Between 1968 and 1974, a catastrophic famine occurred in the Sahel, stretching from the Atlantic shores of Senegal to the highlands of Ethiopia. Drought led to death, malnutrition, destruction of herds and crops, displacement of people, and disruption of the ecological basis of human life in the region. In 1977 and 1980, 1987, and 1988, drought hit again. Climatologists suggest that a worldwide shift in climatic belts, leading to a southward expansion of the Sahara in Africa and of other drylands in comparable latitudes elsewhere, caused the drought. Demographers have emphasized the increase in population and herds, which occurred after the introduction of deep wells into the region, as forces of environmental deterioration. Historians note that the colonial expansion of commercial cultivation deep into the dry margins of the Sahel forced farmers and herdsmen into zones of higher environmental risk. Social scientists have stressed failures of local leadership, inequitable distribution of resources, and government inefficiency as primary factors in exacerbating the distress of the people of the Sahel.

At its roots, the Sahelian drought has been generated by human and natural events that disrupted the delicate ecological balance that sustained the people of this region for centuries. Geographers have attempted to unravel the causes and consequences of desertification in the Sahel and to formulate policies to deal with natural hazards worldwide. Some of the factors under consideration: theories of dust accumulation in the atmosphere, leading to a decline in rainfall; population pressure on the resource base; destruction of vegetation; climatic change; government strategies of predicting natural hazards; and appropriate resettlement policies for drought victims.

Thousands of people are fleeing the famine-stricken regions of northern Ethiopia, streaming southward in search of food.

Chad (pop. 4.8 million), Niger (pop. 7.2 million), Mali (pop. 8.7 million), Mauritania (pop. 2.1 million), and the Sudan (pop. 24 million) when vaccination programs and the drilling of deep wells temporarily improved the chances for people and animals to survive (Fig. 13.5). In the south, population growth led to soil exhaustion. The peanut growers of Senegal (pop. 7 million) were forced to abandon existing fields in favor of new land. Large-scale erosion occurred in Burkina Faso (pop. 8.5 million). Population pressure was already high when drought invaded this region in 1966 and the Sahara Desert began to

extend southward, in some places by as much as 100 miles. In the late 1980s, **desertification** continues to reach southward at a rate of 4 to 5 miles a year.

The impact of this long-term cycle of drought, the most recent of many recorded in times past, has been disastrous. In a wide band from the Atlantic Ocean to the Red Sea as many as one third of the 111 million people of the Sahel (Ethiopia and Sudan included) have faced resettlement or starvation (Fig. 13.5). The major rivers of the region, the Senegal and the Niger, recorded their lowest water levels in a century in the late 1960s

and again in the early 1980s. Lake Chad evaporated to one third its former size, leaving fishing villages that once lined its shores stranded miles away from the new waterline. The cycle of drought, famine, and death has been intensified by overpopulation.

In Mauritania, three quarters of the cattle died in the 1960s drought; epidemics of cholera and diphtheria broke out. In Mali, Burkina Faso, and Chad, an estimated one half of the cattle died. In Niger, most camels and cattle perished, leaving herders and farmers with no stock with which to rebuild their herds when

The importance of this geographic research is obvious. If the Sahara is moving southward as a result of a global shift in climatic belts, the Sahel will have to be abandoned as a farming and herding region. If reforestation, controlled utilization of pastures and fields, and effective government action can reverse the trend, the Sahel will be able to sustain human populations for the foreseeable future. It is clear that research into people-environment interactions, a core of geographic research, is of crucial significance in dealing with natural hazards.

Detailed studies of the drought in the Sahel include: Richard W. Franke and Barbara H. Chasin, *Seeds of Famine: Ecological Destruction and the Development Dilemma in the West African Sahel*. New York: Universe Books, 1980; Noel V. Lateef, *Crisis in the Sahel: A Case Study in Development Cooperation.* Boulder: Westview Press, 1980; Michael H. Glantz (ed.), *The Politics of Natural Disaster: The Case of the Sahel Drought.* New York: Praeger, 1976.

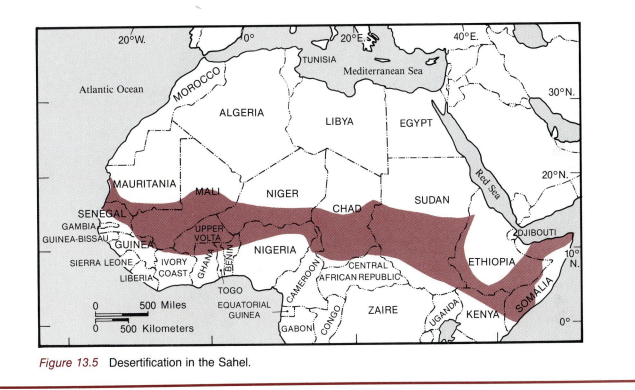

Figure 13.5 Desertification in the Sahel.

more humid conditions returned in the mid-1970s. Herdsmen fled to more densely settled, better watered regions to the south and west. In Senegal, shantytowns sprang up on the outskirts of cities, like Dakar (pop. 1 million), to house emigrants from Mauritania. Along the Niger River, refugees from Mali and Niger occupy resettlement camps set up by international agencies.

The drought has had a ripple effect southward through the vegetation zones of West Africa. Nigeria's peanut harvest has been cut by two thirds. Coffee and cocoa crops on the forests of the Ivory Coast, Ghana, Togo, and Benin have dropped off sharply. If this drought is caused by a permanent shift in weather patterns, the six nations of the Sahel may well deteriorate into chaos. Even if rainfall increases, the reestablishment of vegetation, herds, and former livelihoods may prove impossibly difficult.

The African Horn

The African Horn, the northernmost region of highland Africa, is composed of the three states of Ethiopia, Somalia, and Djibouti which are believed to have populations of 48.3 million, 8 million, and 0.3 million respectively, although no country has taken a census. Rugged escarpments separate the Ethiopian Highlands from the plains of the Sahel to the west (Fig. 13.4). Southward, the dry plains of northern Kenya isolate the African Horn from East Africa. The highland itself is partitioned by the Great Rift Valley, which cuts southward through the middle of Ethiopia, separating the densely settled western highlands from the dry hills of the eastern upland.

The entire region is broken into a jumble of hills, mountains, scarps, canyons, and valleys. The topogra-

The human impact of the disastrous drought in the Sahel is apparent in this photograph of people near the border of Mali and Burkina Faso scouring the sands for the remains of bundles of bran sticks dropped from airplanes for cattle. People eat them to survive, but bran sticks do not relieve thirst and they cause intense pain.

phy of this dissected mass has reinforced the cultural isolation of its people. Upwards of 90 percent of Ethiopians are agriculturalists, generally clustered on the 10 percent of the country that is neither too dry nor too rugged to be cultivated—the western highlands between the capital city of Addis Ababa (pop. 1.4 million) and Lake Tana. By contrast, the eastern lowlands of Ethiopia and Somalia are hot and dry. Covered with bush scrub, these areas are mainly used for grazing. Three quarters of the people eke out livings as cattle, camel, goat, and sheepherders, still collecting and selling frankincense gum as they have for centuries to supplement a bleak existence.

Overgrazing by cattle and camels has depleted the scant resources of the dry lowlands of Somalia and northern Ethiopia, and cereal cultivation on the eastern plateau has in-

duced some soil erosion. But the well-watered western highlands of Ethiopia have long been viewed as underpopulated. In the past, development specialists have speculated that this highland could become the breadbasket of the region. In the 1980s, few see this as a viable possibility.

Since 1966, when the southward migration of the Sahara mounted the western escarpments of the highlands, Ethiopia has been in the grip of drought, much the same as the nations of the Sahel (Fig. 13.5). In the dry provinces of the north, famine and cholera have been taking lives for a decade. In the barren deserts of Harar Province, the Danakil tribesmen are in danger of extinction. In the 1980s, over 20 million people here and in East Africa are affected. An estimated 1 million people died of famine in Ethiopia in 1984.

Drought restruck with a vengeance in 1987–1988. Relief efforts have been stymied by the compound problem of strong political liberation movements in the northern Ethiopian provinces of Tigré and Eritrea. Because between one third to one half of the Ethiopians live more than 20 miles from any transportation link, there is little likelihood of effective food distribution. Whereas in the Sahel, overpopulation existed before the drought, in Ethiopia and neighboring East Africa, the drought has just begun to change the environment and to damage badly the productive potential of the land.

East Africa

The highland countries of East Africa, Kenya (pop. 23.3 million), Uganda (pop. 16.4 million), Tanzania (pop. 24.3 million), Rwanda (pop. 7.1

million), and Burundi (pop. 5.2 million) form the roof of the continent, a high plateau studded with volcanoes, the highest of which is Mount Kilimanjaro at 19,340 feet (Fig. 13.4). On the west, the East African highland is bordered by a branch of the Rift Valleys, a system of geologic troughs running 6000 miles from the Red Sea to South Africa. A second branch of the Rift, 30 to 80 miles wide, cuts through the center of the plateau. Lake Victoria lies in a shallow depression between the two branches and is the core area of one of the most densely populated, productive agricultural zones of East Africa. In the northern and southern highlands, the plateau slopes gently to a broad coastal plain fringing the Indian Ocean; in the central section, the coastal zone is quite narrow.

Vegetation in East Africa varies with elevation and precipitation. In the north, the steppes of Kenya grade imperceptibly into the dry lands of Somalia and southern Ethiopia. An arbitrary political boundary has been drawn between the two regions, which divides and isolates related groups of Somali cattle herders. But the vast majority of the plateau is covered by open parkland. These rich, tree-dotted grasslands form the premier big game hunting region of Africa. Forests make up only one seventieth of the region and are primarily found on the slopes of the higher volcanoes. Coastward, the upland savannas give way to mangrove swamps in the deltas of rivers that course down the eastern slope of the plateau to the sea.

The distribution of reliable rain-

fall, soil fertility, and the tsetse fly in East Africa have strongly influenced population patterns. About 30 inches of rainfall are required for settled intensive cultivation in this region. Nearly all densely populated parts of East Africa—whether on the coast, the highland plateau, or the elevated peaks—are in areas where this amount of rainfall is attained four out of every five years. In Kenya, only one sixth of the land receives this much rainfall on a regular basis. As a result, 90 percent of Kenya's 23.3 million people are clustered in well-watered zones on the shores of Lake Victoria that extend eastward into the former "White Highlands," the land taken over by European colonists around the capital city of Nairobi (pop. 1 million). Except for a few nodes of population around coastal ports, espe-

The open tree-studded grasslands of East Africa once housed vast herds of wild and domesticated native animals. Today, wildebeest herds like this one in the Serengeti National Park survive because of government protection.

cially Mombasa (pop. 400,000), the rest of Kenya is thinly settled. Three quarters of the country has less than 10 people per square mile.

In Tanzania, similar stretches of low rainfall and low population are found on the central plateau, the Serengeti Plain, and large areas of the low eastern plateau. Over 60 percent of this region is infested with tsetse flies. This factor, combined with unreliable rainfall, substantially explains the distribution of people. Tanzanian population clusters occur near Lake Victoria and on the eastern shores of Lake Malawi. Along the coast, the port city of Dar es Salaam (pop. 1 million) forms the urban core of a rich agricultural hinterland. Elsewhere in East Africa, population is dense in the fertile, well-watered crescent of southern and eastern Uganda around the capital city of Kampala (pop. 460,000) and in the highlands of Rwanda and Burundi, which have some of the highest population densities of any countries in Africa.

In East Africa, Europeans were attracted to the temperate, tsetse-free regions of the highlands. This attraction strongly influenced the development of the agricultural economy of the region. Commercial and subsistence crops were planted on rich volcanic soils in the highlands. European plantations of tea, coffee, and pyrethrum (a chrysanthemum used in the manufacture of insecticide) were established in areas of reliable rainfall. Cattle ranches were developed in the drier zones. In Kenya and, to a lesser extent, in Tanzania, this had the effect of pushing Africans into less productive environments. This, combined with population growth, has generated pressure on the resource base of selected parts of East Africa.

In the herding country of the Masai in southern Kenya and northern Tanzania, for example, a minimum of six cattle per person is required to maintain the nomadic way of life. Because 10 acres of the dry plains are required to support one animal, areas where densities exceed ten people

per square mile are likely to be overgrazed. Similarly, in central Kenya, the land of the agricultural Kikuyu tribe, one third of the tribesmen are landless. Half the agricultural holdings here are smaller than 3 acres, the size generally assumed to be necessary for subsistence cultivation. Even the fertile lands in the basin of Lake Victoria are experiencing population pressure, where densities reach two to three times the critical point in areas of cotton cultivation. Here, as elsewhere in Africa, population pressure on the land is marked by a decline in food supply, a lower quality of diet, deforestation and attendant erosion, soil exhaustion, fragmentation of land holdings, migration to urban islands of development, and social conflict.

Southern Africa

South of the highlands of East Africa and the lowland Congo Basin, a vast upland plain stretches in an arc from eastern Zambia through Zimbabwe to the Atlantic coast of Angola and the dry Kalahari Basin of Botswana, South Africa, and Namibia (Figs. 13.1 and 13.4). This upland plain is generally covered by thin, deciduous woodland. Heavier vegetation is found on its northern tropical margins; to the south, it grades into grassland steppes. The region is generally unfavorable for both agriculture and pastoralism except at higher elevations in Zimbabwe, Angola, and South Africa. Economic development in southern Africa is based on mining, which has created isolated centers of population at mining sites with poorly developed economic hinterlands.

To the south and east, the Rift Valley plunges between Malawi and Mozambique, and reappears in the form of the rugged Drakensberg Mountains of eastern South Africa. The escarpments of the Drakensberg Mountains separate the high veld of the interior from the densely populated, subtropical coast of Natal. Al-

though environmental factors have played an important role in this part of Africa, racial policies (discussed later) have influenced human occupance of the land to a degree found nowhere else.

Except for the urban, industrial centers of the Copperbelt, the factors that influence the distribution of population in Zambia (pop. 7.5 million) are dry season water supplies (because half the year has less than 1 inch of rain), the presence or absence of tsetse flies, and fishing opportunities along the important rivers of the region. Only the plains of Barotseland in the southwest, the riverine country of the upper Zambezi, and fishing grounds in the swamps of Lake Bangweulu are densely settled. The rest of Zambia is either sparsely populated or virtually empty. This is also true of western Zimbabwe (pop. 9.7 million), Botswana (pop. 1.3 million), the lowland Karoo region of South Africa (pop. 35.1 million) and of Namibia (pop. 1.7 million) where the dry desert and steppe country of the Kalahari and fog deserts along the coast have discouraged dense populations except in favored local environments.

In Malawi (pop. 7.7 million), the better watered lands of eastern Zimbabwe, the uplands of Mozambique (pop. 15.1 million), and the high veld of South Africa, rainfall was an important influence on the type of rural economy. Most European settlement in these temperate uplands is mixed farming, although plantations are also well developed. In Zimbabwe and South Africa particularly, native Africans have been preempted from settling the better watered, more fertile lands. These cultural majorities have been shunted into unfavorable environments in the Zambezi and Limpopo lowlands and on the dry margins of the good earth.

Along the coasts of Mozambique and South Africa, population densities increase southward, reflecting the more temperate, less tropical climate

The Rift Valley, whose floor is here adorned by a large baobab tree, slices southward along the entire length of East Africa.

of the region as well as the intensity of European development. In Mozambique, subsistence cultivation is the rule, except where sugarcane and cotton are cultivated near ports, like the capital city of Maputo (pop. 755,000). In South Africa, the well-watered coast of the eastern province of Natal is densely populated. Sugarcane, cotton, citrus fruits, and bananas are grown.

Two factors have caused population pressure on the resource base of Southern Africa. First, the dry climate of the Kalahari Desert extends inland from the southwestern quadrant of the continent to the western parts of Zambia and Zimbabwe. Second, the racial policies of European colonists who usurped African lands contributed to an imbalance between human activity and environment. In Zimbabwe, both factors came into play until recently. Here the African reserves were overstocked and overpopulated. These reserves constituted one fifth of the land area of the country but supported two fifths of the population. In Zambia, population pressure is less severe, although

population growth in favored areas (described earlier) foreshadows future problems.

By contrast, the entire country of Botswana, the domain of the Hottentots and the Bushmen (Basarwa), suffers from severe overgrazing and overpopulation. This country appears destined to remain a perennial recipient of relief supplies from private and international agencies. In South Africa, population pressure is a matter of race, not resources. In general, population increases eastward with rainfall, but the enforced settlement of Africans on restricted reserves has generated serious problems.

CONTEMPORARY AFRICA: THE WINDS OF CHANGE

Independence spread swiftly across Africa after World War II. In 1955, only two states, Liberia and Ethiopia, were independent. A decade

later, however, thirty-one independent states existed in sub-Saharan Africa, seventeen born in 1960 alone. The process began in West Africa when the Gold Coast, under the charismatic leadership of Kwame Nkrumah, became the independent state of Ghana in 1957. By 1960, virtually all of the former European colonies of West and Central Africa had achieved independence, and East Africa soon followed suit. In the south, the Portuguese reluctantly withdrew from Angola and Mozambique in 1975. In 1980, the black majority in Rhodesia gained independence after years of white-minority rule and oppression, and they renamed their state after the ancient ruins at Zimbabwe. Now only South Africa and the aspiring state of Namibia are still controlled by white settlers.

Political independence in Africa did not, however, bring prosperity, political stability, or an end to poverty. The reasons were several. First, in *Independent Africa: Space and Economy*, the legacy of the colonial period frustrated development plans for economic growth. The boundaries of old colonies remained the boundaries of new independent states. Their relations with neighboring states were constricted, reinforcing economic dependence on former colonial rulers. Second, the colonial dual economy remained intact, making the independent states of Africa as dependent on the export of raw materials and as vulnerable to world markets as they have been in the past. In fact, Africa's society and economy function at two different levels, in two different worlds. In *Islands of Modern Economic Development*, production of minerals and commercial agricultural products for export continue to be the major source of government revenue in most countries. Meanwhile, *African Subsistence Economies*, such as shifting cultivation, grain cultivation, mixed farming, and pastoralism have received little attention. The failure to invest in rural development has meant a continuation of poverty, underdevelopment, and inequity. These forces are intensifying because of population growth, and *Population, Poverty, and Development* are central issues in many African countries with limited facilities and poorly developed human resources. As a result, Africa is the poorest, least developed region in the world.

Independent Africa: Space and Economy

By the 1960s, colonial powers turned over governance in Africa to native political leaders. But fifty years of European rule had created the political and economic framework within which newly independent African states functioned. Colonial boundaries became the boundaries of new countries. These form the spatial perimeters within which each country seeks social and economic prosperity. The economic system created by colonial administrators engendered wealth without well-being, leaving Africa the most underdeveloped of continents. More than in other world regions, the two factors of European-designed boundaries and European-oriented economies influenced patterns of political and economic development in Africa.

The Organization of Space

In the late nineteenth century, European powers divided Africa into colonies inside which African ethnic groups were amalgamated. The boundaries of these colonies were drawn arbitrarily (Fig. 13.6). Little attention was paid to the African environment and even less to the African population. When independence came to Africa, nearly half of all boundaries were parallels or meridians, another third were straight lines or arcs of circles, and the remainder followed the courses of rivers, mountain ranges, watersheds, or valleys.

Fourteen states—Mali, Burkina Faso, Niger, Chad, the Central African Republic, Uganda, Rwanda, Burundi, Malawi, Zambia, Zimbabwe, Botswana, Lesotho, and Swaziland—were entirely landlocked, having no access to the sea. Others, like Gambia, Sierra Leone, Togo, Benin, Equatorial Guinea, and Guinea-Bissau, were absurdly small. About 200 important ethnic, or tribal, territories were split apart by national political boundaries, although it is difficult to define ethnic groups, or tribes, with any precision. In any case, like people were separated and unlike people were joined by the colonial spatial system that was superimposed on the African continent (Fig. 13.6).

Political leaders in the new states of Africa inherited truly new countries with great ethnic and cultural diversity. The problem they faced was a complete reversal of the European national experience. In Europe, people sharing a common language, faith, or ethnic background aspired to form their own independent states. In Africa, independent states whose people had little in common aspired to national unity.

Immediately, secessionist movements became a major problem for the central governments of the new African countries. In Zaire, secessionist movements in the provinces of Shaba (Katanga), Kasai, and Kivu threatened to fracture the country into several smaller states. After five years of confused fighting, these movements, rooted in cultural diversity, were suppressed. In nearby Burundi, civil war broke out between two major tribal groups, the Tutsi and the Hutu, culminating in a massacre of the Hutu in 1972.

The tendency toward fragmentation led to war in Nigeria. The most populous country in Africa, with 111.9 million people, Nigeria has more than 250 ethnic groups. In 1967, one group, the Ibo of eastern Nigeria, seceded and declared the independence of the state of Biafra. Bloody fighting between federal Nigeria and secessionist Biafra ended with a starvation blockade of the Ibos in 1970 and the reestablishment of federal control.

Many new nations in Africa have experienced similar violent attempts at boundary revision. Currently, ethnic loyalties are playing major roles in fighting in Ethiopia, Chad, Uganda, Angola, Namibia, and Zimbabwe. The local interests of ethnic and linguistic groups are threats to the security and stability in new states throughout the continent. Observers note that this return to tribal politics is a major factor retarding development in sub-Saharan Africa.

Despite these problems, no major colonial boundary has changed in Africa since independence, partly because the Organization of African Unity (OAU) agreed to preserve inherited boundaries to stem chaos, but mainly because these frontiers circumscribe the transportation systems along which people, goods, and knowledge move. Colonial entrepreneurs constructed 50,000 miles of railroad track in Africa. Their purpose was to bring the mineral and agricultural resources of the African interior into the orbit of the world economy. Most of these communication lines connect interior trading cities with coastal ports. They acted as channels of economic activity as well as extensions of colonial power. When the railroad system matured, feeder lines were added to open up inaccessible regions. Still later, a road network intensified interconnections between channels of penetration and centers of economic activity.

But all this took place inside each colony's boundaries. Few roads or railroads crossed colonial frontiers, except to gain access to the sea. In West Africa, different track widths were deliberately adopted to forestall movement across boundaries. As a result, most colonies had better connections with Europe than with their immediate African neighbors. This transportation network confines the process of modernization within what one geographer has identified as communication "bubbles."

THE COLONIAL REORGANIZATION OF AFRICAN SPACE

The colonial boundaries of Africa were drawn without regard to African cultural and economic realities. The independent countries of modern Africa are struggling to weld nation-states out of these spatial compartments, which are occupied by people of different ethnic, linguistic, and cultural backgrounds.

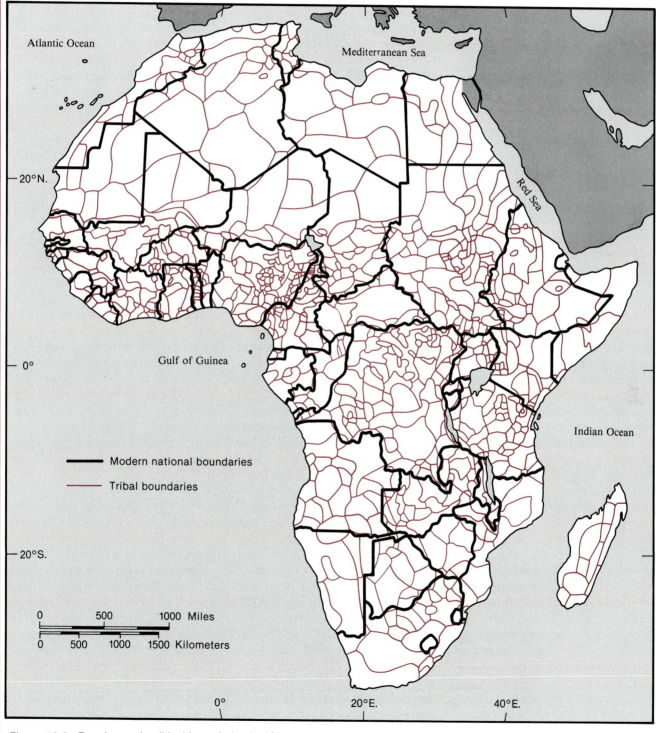

Figure 13.6 Peoples and political boundaries in Africa.

Although African leaders have verbally supported the concept of pan-Africanism and the notion of an amalgamation of former colonies into large political units, these circulation systems tend to isolate partners and defeat unification. Each country pursues its plans for social and economic development within compartments defined by the frontiers of colonial Africa. These development plans, like the spatial domain in which they are implemented, are influenced by the legacy of colonialism.

The Dual Economy

Perhaps the greatest paradox of this colonial legacy, from an economic viewpoint, is that few profited. After a half century of colonial development and investment, the standard of living of the average African peasant had not improved. In many places it had declined. In a majority of countries, less than one tenth of the adult population was literate, few lived in towns, and only a small percentage worked for wages. Most lived as pastoralists and subsistence peasants. They were aware of, but not connected to, the currents of economic change that were sweeping Africa.

Nor did the European powers substantially benefit from the possession of this continent. Their colonies were liabilities rather than assets. They produced a few scarce minerals and some luxury tropical foods, but Africa proved an insignificantly small market for industrial goods. The costs of administration and development outweighed the profits from exploitation. In the end, Africa accounted for only 5 percent of world trade. In short, colonialism impoverished the Africans without enriching the conquerors. It was an all-round failure, mainly because colonialism introduced a dual economy that initiated growth without development, and wealth without well-being.

The dual economy in Africa, as elsewhere in the Developing World, involved heavy investment in modern, export-oriented activities but little investment in regional economies or human resources. Two economies paralleled each other in most African countries: (1) a modern industrial or commercial agricultural sector run for and by Europeans, and (2) a vastly larger traditional subsistence economy in which most Africans participated. Economic growth in the modern sector produced export products desired in the Technological World. The lack of development in the traditional sector meant low living standards for the bulk of the African population.

This growth without development was most intense in resource-rich regions like South Africa, Zimbabwe, Nigeria, Ghana, Gabon, and Zaire. In poorer countries like Niger, Chad, and Mali, there was neither growth nor development. Growth meant more miles of railroad track, larger cities, and better roads. In the countryside, there was a shift to commercial agriculture, intense pressure on the resource base, and a deceptive rise in per capita income. In fact, the native population in wealthy regions remained impoverished. They lived poorly in the native reserves of South Africa, the mining compounds of Witwatersrand and Katanga, and the shantytowns of cities across the continent. Three exceptions to this pattern were Ghana, the Ivory Coast, and, before the reign of Idi Amin, Uganda. In these countries, small farmers engaged in the commercial cultivation of cotton, coffee, and cocoa, and were able measurably to improve their standard of living.

Generally, the shift to commercial agriculture, in which plants were grown for export rather than for food, did not increase the social well-being of Africans. Peanut, cotton, palm oil, cocoa, and coffee plantations hired Africans as wage earners. Colonial powers invested in commercial plantations, but not in the subsistence agriculture of the African people.

What African leaders inherited at independence, then, was a dual economy: (1) a relatively small, modern commercial sector devoted to the production and international sale of selected minerals and agricultural products coexisting with (2) a much larger subsistence agricultural economy whose methods of cultivation, crops, land-tenure systems, and patterns of social organization were generally ignored by the colonial powers.

The effect of the dual economy was to create islands of economic growth in Africa, whose expanding cities, mines, and commercial farms attracted migrant wage laborers from undeveloped hinterlands. Because most of these areas depended on a single crop or mineral, the economies of independent Africa were generally unstable. A rise or fall in the price of one commodity on the world market could alter the economy of an entire country in a matter of days. In addition, industrial countries soon developed synthetic substitutes for such crops as rubber, cotton, and sisal. In short, the colonial dual economy, like the colonial spatial matrix, placed a heavy burden on independent states. It created economic dilemmas that appear virtually insoluble for many countries in Africa.

Islands of Modern Economic Development

European exploitation of agricultural and mineral resources created islands of modern economic activity in Africa. These islands include the largest cities in sub-Saharan Africa, every important industrial complex, and the most productive zones of commercial agriculture and mineral production. The producing areas for these raw materials are nuclei of urbanization and industry, zones of dense population, and destinations for migrants from vast and thinly populated hinterlands.

These islands of modern development are based on two types of economic activity in Africa. First, coastal zones of commercial and ur-

Cape Town, the first Dutch settlement in South Africa, is now a highly diversified city that attracts migrant laborers to its industries and port.

ban development exist along the Gulf of Guinea in West Africa from Senegal to Cameroon, along the coast of South Africa, and to a lesser degree near the entrepôts of East Africa. Second, heavy investment has been made in the major zones of mineral production: the Witwatersrand in South Africa, the highlands of Zimbabwe, the Copperbelt of Zambia, and the Shaba (Katanga) region of southern Zaire. These mineral-rich regions and their nearby urban centers have attracted hundreds of thousands of labor migrants.

Coastal Economic Development

By far the largest and most diverse region of coastal commercial development is located in West Africa from Senegal at the African bulge to Cameroon in the Bight of Biafra. This coastal zone is the most densely populated, highly urbanized, and economically diverse region in Africa (Fig. 13.7). Only white-dominated South Africa is more highly developed.

The economy of the coast of West Africa gained momentum at the end of the nineteenth century when commercial cultivation of palm oil began in earnest. Used for soap, candles, lubricants, margarine, cooking oil, animal feed, and in a wide variety of other products, palm oil was an important addition to world commodity crops. Palm cultivation was confined by climate to the wetter portions of the coast, particularly in the delta of the Niger River. Palm oil was gradually supplemented by cultivation of other commercial crops for export. On the dry plains of the Senegal Val-

ley, peanut cultivation was introduced and diffused throughout the savanna interior of West Africa. In Guinea and the Ivory Coast, coffee and bananas became important products. Cocoa was the major crop in Cameroon and Ghana, rubber in Liberia. The interior of northern Nigeria was planted in cotton and peanuts. Only in Togo, under German rule, was any effort made to generate a diversified economy.

These patterns of resource utilization and trade still influence the economic growth of the countries of West Africa today. Exports of commercial agricultural products and selected minerals, such as diamonds from Sierra Leone, aluminum from Guinea and Ghana, iron ore from Liberia, manganese from Ghana, petroleum from Nigeria, and phos-

LABOR MIGRATION AND ISLANDS OF ECONOMIC DEVELOPMENT

Labor migrations to islands of modern economic development in Africa have been going on for some time. Usually, single men move to mining centers or commercial plantations to work, maintaining contact with their home villages through frequent visits. As unemployment has risen, the urban centers in these highly developed areas are being swamped by a tide of migrants for whom there are no jobs nor basic facilities. Failure to invest in rural development and the growing gap in standard of living between urbanites and villagers is accelerating this process of urbanization through migration.

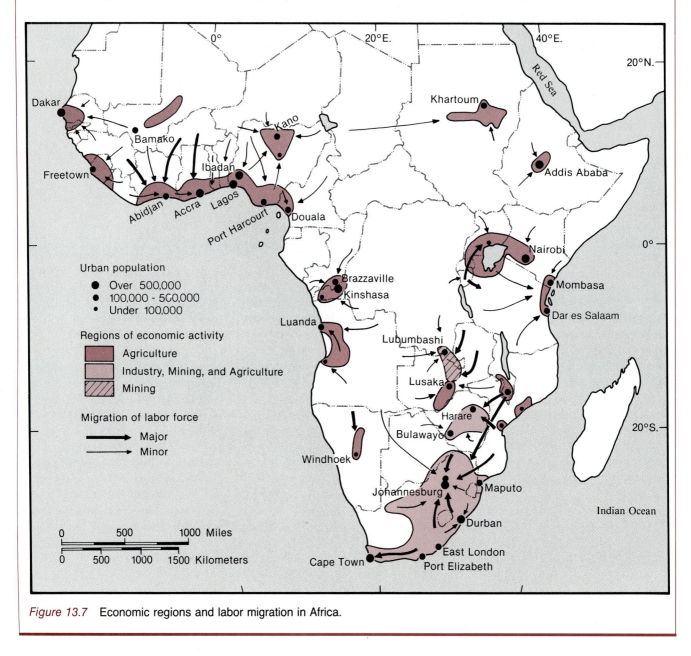

Figure 13.7 Economic regions and labor migration in Africa.

phates from Togo, are the significant generators of wealth in this region. Peanuts make up four fifths of Gambis's exports; iron ore, 70 percent of Liberia's; diamonds and iron ore, 75 percent of Sierra Leone's; and cocoa and aluminum, 70 percent of Ghana's.

Railroads connect producing areas with the coast. As a result, Nigeria's trade with other nations of West Africa is negligible. Intra-African trade figures for Ghana and Sierra Leone are under 10 percent and falling. Some new crops have been introduced since independence—ginger in Sierra Leone, manioc in Togo. And major oil finds have fueled development in eastern Nigeria, Cameroon, and Gabon. But the pattern of West Africa's economy remains basically what it was under colonial rule.

The major urban centers of West Africa are coastal ports, end points of interior railroads that tap densely populated environments. Most countries depend on a single major port city—Dakar in Senegal, Banjul in Gambia, Bissau in Guinea-Bissau, Conakry in Guinea, Freetown in Sierra Leone, Monrovia in Liberia, Abidjan in the Ivory Coast, Accra in Ghana, Lomé in Togo, Porto-Novo in Benin, and Douala in Cameroon. Dakar has a population of 1 million, as do Conakry, Abidjan, and Accra. Douala has more than a half-million people. The rest are small towns. Only Nigeria is large enough to sustain two major port cities, Lagos (pop. 2 million) and Port Harcourt (pop. 300,000).

Most of these cities include half of the urban population of each country, but with the exception of Liberia, Benin, and the Ivory Coast, urban populations in West Africa make up less than one third of the total population. Except for Dakar and Lagos, the cities of West Africa are relatively small. Nevertheless, these cities and the areas of intense commercial cultivation around them are now centers of fast-paced and often incoherent industrial economic development.

The patterns of labor migration to these cities and their surrounding areas are complex (Fig. 13.7). In some ways, however, they reflect general characteristics of population movements in Africa. Men, usually not accompanied by wives and children, travel long distances to work for a few months or years in the mines, factories, and fields located in economically advanced areas. Because many agricultural and mineral centers in Africa are remote from rural agricultural populations, the lure of cash wages draws people from villages to

urban recruiting agencies that seek workers to fill the labor needs of emerging industries. Both employers and employees are reluctant to form permanent relationships. Indeed, in 1983, Nigeria expelled migrant workers from hard-pressed Ghana in the wake of a slowdown in Nigerian economic growth.

Few rural Africans have been attracted to cities on a permanent basis, which is the reason why Africa, with less than a third of its population living in cities, is the least urbanized continent. For their part, employers do not want to provide the housing and facilities needed by a permanent labor force. For these reasons, hundreds of thousands of Africans live their lives in two very different worlds. They are driven from the countryside by lack of opportunity, and they are attracted to (but uncomfortable in) the cities, mines, and factories of developing Africa.

In Senegal and Gambia, farmers migrate seasonally to Dakar and to peanut plantations in Mali, Guinea, and Senegal. Cultivating the landlord's fields, these workers receive the right to farm a plot for themselves, a variation of traditional sharecropping arrangements. In Liberia, four fifths of the labor force that tends the 12 million rubber trees on the Firestone plantations are migrant laborers. The same is true in the diamond fields of Sierra Leone. In the most advanced economic regions in West Africa, men outnumber women two to one, reflecting the prevailing pattern of male migration.

In the Ivory Coast and Ghana, two important migrant destinations in West Africa, the cocoa and coffee plantations, mining areas, and coastal urban centers draw many workers from the Saharan fringe. Similar movements although on a smaller scale, occur on the coasts of Togo, Benin, and western Nigeria. All told, 3 million people are migrant laborers in West Africa, half of whom migrate to Nigeria, the Ivory Coast, and to a lesser extent Ghana. And this figure is rising rapidly because of drought

in the Sahel. These migrations intensify regional disparities between the coastal islands of development and subsistence hinterlands of West Africa.

The industry and commerce of coastal ports in South Africa, such as Durban, Cape Town, Port Elizabeth, East London, and Richards Bay, are more highly developed than in the cities of West Africa. This reflects the fact that South Africa is by far the richest, most powerful, and most industrially advanced country in Africa. In Cape Town, despite apartheid, only 40 percent of the population is now white. The majority are black African migrant laborers and local "Cape Coloureds" attracted by factory employment to this city—which, with its suburbs, has a population of 1.8 million (Fig. 13.7). Cape Town is the most diversified city in Africa. It processes the agricultural products of the southwestern cape.

Durban, a metropolitan center of 1.2 million people, plays a comparable role in eastern South Africa. It is the leading port of the country because of its rail connections with the Witwatersrand mines near Johannesburg. In addition, Durban has sugar refineries, textile factories, oil refineries, and other industries sufficient to rival Cape Town in commercial output. As in Cape Town, African laborers, many of them migrants living in conditions of poverty and humiliation, provide the muscle for industrial growth.

The East African entrepôts from Maputo in Mozambique to Mombasa in Kenya form a third area of coastal commercial activity in Africa. Dar es Salaam is the leading port of Tanzania and handles the export of such commercial crops as cotton, coffee, sisal, cloves, and cashew nuts. The largest industrial city on the East African coast, it attracts migrant laborers from the interior to work in industry and, since the completion of a Chinese-built railroad in 1975, is the port of exit for Zambian copper as well. Mombasa plays a similar role in Kenya. Linked by rail to the coffee- and cotton-growing regions of Lake Victoria, Mombasa is a regionally important industry center. Recent mining discoveries north of the city have attracted new migrants to the coast in addition to those working on landlord-owned plantations in the immediate hinterland.

Zones of Mineral Exploitation

Modern mining has created European-run islands of development in the rich mining belt that sweeps northward from the Witwatersrand district of South Africa through Zimbabwe to the Copperbelt of Zambia and Shaba (Katanga) Province of southern Zaire (Fig. 13.8). Mining development in Africa began in 1867 when diamonds were found on the banks of the Orange River in South Africa. Within three years, 50,000 miners were combing the South African interior for precious gems, and the Kimberley diamond mines were established. Twenty years later, gold was found in the Witwatersrand some 300 miles to the northwest. A year later, Johhnnesburg, destined to become one of the largest cities of Africa, was founded nearby. Wealth from the Kimberley diamond mines provided money for the development of the Witwatersrand gold mines. Wealth from gold plays a vital role in the sustained growth of the South African economy.

A complex combination of geological events created this rich mineral-bearing region in the Witwatersrand. In an area of a few thousand square miles, coal, precious minerals, and underground water are found adjacent to one another. This resource base now supports a 50-mile-long, 20-mile-wide industrial and commercial complex centered on Johannesburg, which has a metropolitan population of more than 3 million. Gold is still the most important single mineral resource in the region, accounting for one half of South Africa's mineral output and employing 600,000 workers. But the production of uranium, platinum, nickel, coal, iron ore, and

MAPSCAN

MAP SYMBOLS

Cartographers use three general types of map symbols to present locational, directional, and quantitative information. These are **point symbols, line symbols,** and **area symbols.**

Point symbols by their very nature emphasize location. They refer directly to the place where a given commodity or condition is found. A wide variety of point symbols are used by cartographers.

On Figure 13.8, geometric shapes are used to show the location of iron (solid triangle), copper (inverted hollow triangle), coal (solid square), and important cities (black circles). The symbol used for oil and gas fields is called a **pictographic point symbol,** because the miniature oil derrick suggests the phenomena being located. Additional minerals and crops are indicated directly by name. In some cases, point symbols may be used to indicate quantitative amount as well as location. This is the case on Figure 13.9 where cities with different size populations are shown by progressively larger circles.

The most common devices used to present point symbol data are changes in shape (Fig. 13.8), size (Fig. 13.9), texture (density of pattern), differences in color, and differences in color intensity.

Line symbols are used to suggest connectivity, direction, and differences between areas on one side as compared with the other. On Figure 13.8, railroad lines (solid) are linear phenomena that express continuity and connectivity along their course. By contrast, political boundaries (dashed lines) illustrate differences in political status as one crosses the line.

Lines with arrows attached, such as those showing labor migration on Figure 13.7, indicate direction. The use of two widths of lines with arrows on this figure suggests the number of migrants as well as their destination. Among the most common geographic phenomena illustrated by line symbols are rivers, roads, railroads, and boundaries. As with point symbols, line symbols can be presented using changes in size, texture, color, or color intensity.

Area symbols are used to present geographic information that extends over regions. On Figure 13.8, different shading and color patterns are used to identify those areas in which pastoralism, shifting cultivation, and grain agriculture and mixed farming are found in Africa.

When cartographers want to convey changes in magnitude as well as distribution, **quantitative area symbols** are used such as the terrain shading employed on Figure 13.4. To show changes in magnitude, variations in size, texture, color, and color intensity are used. As on the physical features map, these often give a three-dimensional impression to the map reader.

Map symbols are one of the primary vehicles cartographers use to present real-world information in a coherent and understandable way. A large array of point, line, and area symbols are available for use. Considerable thought, therefore, is given to which symbol will create the precise information the cartographer wishes to convey. For this reason, it is essential that students learn to read map legends carefully. By doing so, maps can become simple and direct tools that summarize complex patterns of information.

manganese has increased substantially. Because extracting 1 ounce of gold from the mines requires crushing 3 to 4 tons of rock, other economic minerals, particularly uranium, are processed from the vast **tailing hills** found in the mining regions.

The major problem in the Witwatersrand is procuring labor to work in the mines, steel mills, and factories of this urban belt. At the turn of the century, 50,000 indentured Chinese were imported for this pur-

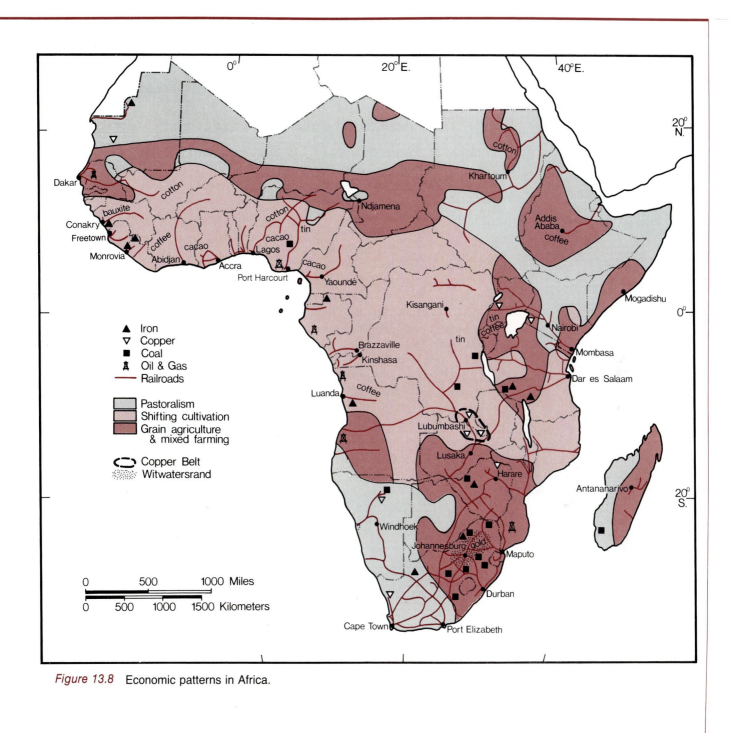

Figure 13.8 Economic patterns in Africa.

pose, but they were later repatriated. Since then, labor has been recruited from the neighboring countries of Mozambique, Botswana, Lesotho, and Swaziland. Only men without families are allowed into South Africa. They cannot remain in

the country after their labor contract is fulfilled. In small Lesotho, whose men have been specialists in sinking mining shafts for three generations, three fifths of the adult male labor force is absent at any one time. These labor policies have discouraged the

growth of a resident black work force that might demand fair treatment. Currently, migrant blacks receive one fifth the wages of whites in comparable jobs.

In Zimbabwe, similar but less extensive mining opportunities were an

Gold mining is the backbone of the South African economy. Here, a worker in a Johannesburg refinery carefully stamps gold bars worth thousands of dollars each.

incentive for European settlement. Gold had been mined in Zimbabwe by native Africans for nearly 1000 years, from the founding of the ancient urban center after which the country is named, to the beginnings of European penetration. When the Matabele Zulu were defeated by British troops in 1893, white settlers and miners moved northward from South Africa in search of another Witwatersrand. They found one, although on a much more limited scale, in a belt extending from the capital city of Harare (formerly Salisbury; pop. 700,000) southward 300 miles to Bulawayo (pop. 400,000). Initially,

gold was the most important mineral produced. In the 1980s, exports of asbestos, copper, nickel, and chrome, especially, are more significant. Although Zimbabwe produces only one sixth as much chrome as South Africa, it is, after South Africa, the noncommunist world's second producer of this mineral. Zimbabwe is a less important magnet for migrant laborers than the Witwatersrand, but the same pattern of male migration without families prevails.

The two remaining mineral and mining regions of Africa, the Copperbelt of Zambia and Shaba (Katanga) Province of southern Zaire, join at a border originally drawn to separate Cecil Rhodes's South Africa from King Leopold II's Congo (Fig. 13.8). In Zambia, the huge ore resources of the Copperbelt were developed in the 1930s to meet growing world demand. Currently, this region covers a zone 80 by 20 miles. Here, seven towns account for nine tenths of Zambia's urban population and an equivalent share of its industrial and mining activity.

The copper from this region is produced in sufficient quantity to rank Zambia as the fifth leading producer of this metal. More important, it provides half the government's revenue and is Zambia's only important export. Worker strikes and subsequent labor laws have bettered the living conditions and wage scales of miners and factory employees. Migrant laborers have brought their families to the Copperbelt, creating a relatively stable working population. Zambia's problematic landlocked location, however, weighs increasingly against the country's development. Zambia fell from the world's third largest copper producer to fifth between 1975 and 1985.

In Zaire's Shaba Province, mining activities were developed by concession companies under the Belgians. As in neighboring Zambia, copper was the most important mineral export from the region. But now Shaba (Katanga) produces tin and zinc, 40 per-

cent of the world's cobalt (a steel alloy), and almost all the world's radium. Zaire is number two in diamond production (after the Soviet Union). However, unlike South Africa (number three), Zaire's diamonds are largely of industrial quality. The labor force in the mining and smelting centers of Lubumbashi (pop. 500,000) and Likasi (pop. 200,000) is relatively stable. The need for workers in the mines, however, still attracts migrants from throughout Central Africa.

African Subsistence Economies

Away from the port cities and the mining centers, the vast majority of Africans depend on their fields and herds for survival. Only one of every three modern Africans is an urbanite. Many were never touched by expanding transportation networks, market economies, and the diffusing waves of commercialization during the colonial period. Society and economy are still pursued in small, semiisolated ethnic groups throughout the continent. They are closely tied to local environments, separated from other groups by language and belief, and are threatened by warfare, famine, drought, and disease. A majority of Africans today, perhaps as much as 70 percent of the population occupying the 4 million square miles of sub-Saharan Africa, live as subsistence cultivators and herdsmen in the traditional sector of the African dual economy.

The small scale of these traditional economies differs sharply from the industrialized Westernized societies in the cities and mining zones. The cultural diversity of Africa, where more than 500 different languages separate ethnic groups, militates against larger scale settlements and marketing systems. Critical environmental limitations in Africa also play a role. In West and Central Africa, soils are of poor quality, with less than one tenth of the organic content of midlatitude cultivated soils. Over much of East Africa, rainfall is low and erratic. The level of environmental risk is frequently directly proportional to the density of population. Animal diseases, tsetse flies and ticks, malaria and schistosomiasis discourage dense agricultural populations except in highly favored environments. Finally, the rudimentary technology of African agriculture restricts the area of cultivation to the limits of a tribe's physical endurance. Given these cultural, environmental, and technological realities, small-scale economies are the rule in Africa, although they are neither simple nor crude.

The three major traditional African economies are: (1) shifting cultivation in the wet, tropical core of West and Central Africa; (2) grain agriculture and mixed farming in the subhumid savanna and mixed forest belt that stretches eastward from the interior of West Africa, bending south through the highlands of East Africa to the South African veld; and (3) pastoralism in the sub-Saharan fringe, the semiarid zones of East Africa, and the margins of the Kalahari Desert (Fig. 13.8). All are sophisticated African adjustments to local environments.

African cultivators adapt their agricultural methods and cropping patterns to the limitations of these environments. They fallow to increase soil fertility, move when a minimum threshold of agricultural productivity threatens the well-being of the group, and employ patterns of land use that minimize soil deterioration. Similarly, pastoralists adjust their migrations to take account of annual and seasonal grazing resources and to maintain the size and quality of their flocks. In this way, the rural economies of Africa achieve some degree of equilibrium with complex environments.

All these African economic systems, however, were predicated on precolonial concepts of space, prop-

erty, and resources. These concepts are now threatened by changes stemming from the modern sector of the economy. In most African populations, private property and individual ownership of land and resources do not exist. Instead, regions and their raw materials are cultural domains that any member of the group has the right to utilize. Unlike most of the Developing World, where a small landowning elite controls production and peasants labor for shares, space and resources are viewed in communal, egalitarian terms in Africa.

But the colonial intrusion disturbed this equilibrium between Africans and their land. The introduction of medicine and health care spurred population growth that is now occurring at a rate of nearly 3 percent per year—exceeded only in parts of Latin America. Traditional economies, well adapted to small populations and extensive resource areas, feel the impact of rising population in terms of disturbance of the ecological systems of cultivated areas and in overgrazing of communal pastures.

In Central Africa, the colonial sale of "unoccupied" land to concession companies took away those areas to which shifting cultivators could move when soil fertility declined. In East Africa, national boundaries block pastoral migrations. In the hinterlands of Zambia, Zimbabwe, and parts of South Africa, the flight of the men from villages to factories has made the pursuit of subsistence agriculture impracticable. And in the settler areas of South and East Africa, Europeans took land for themselves. These forces have created new pressures on traditional agricultural and pastoral economies, pressures most experts, Africans and others, believe are forcing their integration into the commercialized national economies of independent Africa.

Shifting Cultivation

Shifting cultivation—or as it is sometimes called, slash and burn agriculture—is widely practiced in the trop-

ical forests of Central Africa and along the Guinea coast as well as in the savanna reaches of the interior of West Africa and highland East Africa (Fig. 13.8). In these regions, land is cultivated in patches as long as it retains sufficient productivity to support the group, usually four or five years. Then, the group moves to a new location and establishes new fields. Former fields, if possible, are allowed to lie fallow long enough to regain their fertility.

The key variable in shifting cultivation is the character of the soil. On the rich volcanic soils of Mount Kilimanjaro and in Buganda, near continuous cultivation of bananas and plantains is achieved. On weak, highly leached soils in the rain forest, it takes from twenty to twenty-five years for the soil to recover sufficiently to be recultivated.

Given the nature of shifting cultivation, a vast amount of land is required to support a low density of population, rarely more than fifteen people per square mile. For this reason and because it was considered destructive of vegetation, most Western experts, until recently, considered shifting cultivation to be a primitive form of agriculture. In fact, this system is a sophisticated form of economic improvisation designed to cope with changing soil and weather conditions, levels of health, and other circumstances beyond the control of most Africans.

In forested regions, the settlements of shifting cultivators usually amount to a dozen or so huts surrounded by vegetable gardens, banana trees, and palm and fruit trees. Paths radiate out from the village to patches of land where maize, yams, and manioc are planted. The clearings, usually located on slopes, are opened to sunlight by chopping down small trees and girdling and burning large ones. Most families can clear, weed, and cultivate only 2 to 3 acres a year. Each crop is planted in its most favored microenvironment. Bananas are grown in the most fertile

These huts and cornfields of shifting cultivators in the Kisii region of Kenya east of Lake Victoria are more permanent than most. They will, however, be abandoned when soil fertility and crop yields decline.

soil, pumpkins and sweet potatoes in areas with high ash content, yams in moist depressions, and grains where nothing else will grow.

In the first year, fertility is high. Then, the forest begins to close in, soils stripped of vegetation erode, the crops drain nutrients from the soil, and the productivity of each patch declines. As long as enough food is produced, the settlement remains fixed. When fertility declines and the distance between clearings and the settlement becomes overlong, the group moves to a new location, abandoning the fields to the natural processes of forest growth. They or others will reclaim the land in twenty years or so, although population growth is causing shorter cycles of renewal with correspondingly less improvement in soil fertility.

In the savanna, shifting cultivation varies considerably with local environment and tribal traditions. On the northern plateau of Zambia and in southern Zaire, a simple form of ash burning is practiced. Trees are cut over a large area, stacked on the fields, and burned. The potash residue fertilizes the soil. Heat from the fire breaks the soil down, and this makes cultivation easier. Sorghum, millet, manioc, and other crops are grown for at least two years before soil exhaustion forces abandonment. In other savanna areas, more advanced systems of cultivation have evolved. Among the Hausa of northern Nigeria, for example, the application of animal fertilizers to burned areas prolongs soil fertility and postpones the necessity of relocation. Similarly, groups located near towns and large villages utilize human and animal manure to make their agricultural locations more permanent.

The standard of living of these groups is usually quite low. The growth of settled communities is negated by the periodic necessity to shift locations. Seasonal droughts, pests, and epidemic diseases afflict many shifting cultivators. As in most marginal environments, the risk is high and so is the death rate. Food intake is generally sufficient, but protein deficiency is acute. Kwashiorkor, a protein-deficiency disease common among children under five, is widespread. To some degree, farming is supplemented by hunting, fishing, and gathering, depending on local environmental opportunities, but few

animals are kept because most of Central Africa is infested by the disease-carrying tsetse fly.

Grain Cultivation and Mixed Farming

A belt of grain cultivation and mixed farming encircles the equatorial core of tropical Africa, occupying the subhumid transition zone between the hot, wet environment of the rain forests and the deserts to the north and south (Fig. 13.8). Grain is a staple food in the middle belt from Senegal on the Atlantic Ocean to the Ethiopian highlands as well as in a north-south strip from the highlands of East Africa to the high veld of South Africa. Among Africans, mixed farming, in the European sense of combined animal and crop raising, is rare. Where found, it usually represents collaboration between two ethnic groups, a pastoral group on the dry steppe margins of the savanna and an agricultural group in its more humid core. In the temperate highlands of East and South Africa, however, mixed farming is extensively practiced by white planters who transferred this agricultural economy from Europe to Africa.

Upland rice is cultivated by villagers in Senegal, Sierra Leone, Liberia, and the Ivory Coast. Eastward in the interior of West Africa, sorghum, millet, and corn become the principal crops. Conditions of cultivation vary with elevation, rainfall, local soil conditions, and the technological skill of the cultivators. In more remote sections of this grain belt, the digging stick is still the principal agricultural implement. More commonly a short-handled hoe is used to till the soil. In northern Nigeria, villagers hire the pastoral Fulani to herd their flocks. Similar exchanges occur between the cattle herders of East Africa and nearby settled farming communities. As noted, Africans rarely engage in mixed farming. Among the exceptions are settlers near Lake Victoria, whose intensive mixed-farming economy supports a population of 600 people per square mile, and the hill dwellers of northern Togo, who crop irrigated fields and keep cattle in corrals.

In areas of colonial settlement—the "White Highlands" of Kenya, the plantations of Mozambique, the ranches of Angola, and in the mixed-farming belt of South Africa—combined crop and cattle raising is quite common. Western technology, knowledge of fertilization and crop rotation practices, and seizure of the most suitable agricultural environments from the Africans enabled the colonialists and their descendants to establish permanent farms on the African continent.

These regions of permanent settlement and sedentary life have already felt the impress of modernization. They have begun to change from subsistence to market agriculture. In northern Nigeria, Ghana, and Uganda, full commercial agriculture exists. In less well located regions of West Africa, a system of **periodic markets** provides the basis for agricultural exchange. In East Africa, the growth of circulation networks and settlement hierarchies are integrating rural Africans into national systems. The transformation of African agriculture is the single most important economic change now taking place on the continent. If it progresses, regional inequities generated by the colonial dual economy may be eased.

Pastorialism

The majority of African pastoralists are cattle keepers who live in environmental transitional zones between desert and forest. They are located on the dry land margins of the grain belt from Senegal to the Horn, from highland East Africa to South Africa, and between the forests of the Congo Basin and the Kalahari Desert (Fig. 13.8). Camel herders are found on the Saharan fringe and in the eastern part of the African Horn. Goats are widespread in the drier regions of Africa and are herded in large

numbers on the Serengeti Plain of Tanzania and in other areas of East Africa. The greatest concentrations of cattle are found on the dry plateaus east of Lake Victoria, along the eastern coast of South Africa, and in the valleys of the Senegal and Niger rivers.

But vast areas with low precipitation, particularly in East Africa, are inhabited by a thin scattering of pastoralists. In Kenya, for example, three quarters of the country has a population density below ten people per square mile. These lands are occupied by the cattle-keeping Masai, Jie, and Turkana tribes. Similarly in Tanzania, the Serengeti Plain, Masai Plain, and the dry central plateau are occupied by pastoralists. The distribution of these people is directly related to climatic conditions, to the nature and quality of grazing resources, and to the absence of tsetse flies.

African cattle keepers live much as pastoralists do in other world regions. Grazing land for the herds is secured by moving animals from one pasture to another throughout the year. Most pastoralists occupy dry lands not suited for agriculture. Complex patterns of cooperation, conflict, tension, and trade are common near the boundaries between settled farmers and nomadic herders. Migration routes and patterns of social organization vary widely. Among cattle herders between the White Nile and Lake Chad, a strategy of constant movement—as many as sixty moves per year—is typical. In the wetter highlands of the eastern Cape, herders migrate only with the changing of the seasons.

The Turkana of northern Kenya herd more than 1 million cattle between dry lowland plains with as little as 2 inches of rainfall per year and massive granite hills that seasonally receive 20 inches of rainfall. Split up into tiny groups to maximize use of thin pasturelands, these people lack political cohesion as compared with the Jie, a tribe living in better watered

country in northeastern Uganda. In Nigeria, groups of nomadic Fulani cattle herders have settled as town dwellers and farmers in the wetter south. Exchanges of animal and crop products between Fulani groups in two distinct environments are handled within the larger tribe. Each pastoral system is keyed to local ecology, but in many areas, environmental circumstances have already been altered by the impact of modernization.

The primary impact of modernization on pastoral groups in Africa has been to encourage sedentarization. Early in this century, the great rinderpest epidemics that destroyed cattle herds in West and East Africa forced the Fulani, Kikuyu, and Masai tribes temporarily to settle down in villages. When Europeans entered East Africa, land vacated by these nomads was occupied by white colonists. When Europeans controlled the rinderpest epidemics and cleared environments of tsetse flies, the most favorable areas were kept by them and taken from cattle herders. The realm of the nomadic herders was reduced; environmental risk increased. Paradoxically, however, the introduction of pest control led to a dangerous expansion of the herds. Pastoralists continued to view their herds as bank balances—the larger, the better—and higher survival rates among cattle are causing overgrazing and deterioration of pastures.

Indirectly, the growth of population has also played a role in the sedentarization of pastoralists. Agriculture pushing deeper toward the dry margins of cultivation denies the herders their most reliable pastures. In addition, the new states of Africa are eager to count and control pastoral populations and their herds. Taxes on cattle are high, reducing the herders' margin of profit. Raiding, a dignified and honored method of increasing herds in the past, is not tolerated. The future of pastoralism in Africa, therefore, is uncertain. Mixed farming and cattle ranches in-

Pastoralism is a declining way of life in Africa because of overgrazing, drought, encroachment by agriculturalists, population pressure on the land, and government interference.

creasingly supply the protein needs of settled populations. Pastoralists are being pushed deeper into unattractive environments.

Population, Poverty, and Development

Poverty is Africa's central problem. In the United States, the poverty level for an American family is fifteen to thirty times higher than the annual income of an *average* African family. The total gross national product (GNP) of the African continent is one twentieth of the GNP of the United States. Its role in international trade is less than any other world region. Per capita energy consumption is one fifth of the world average, and Africa consumes only 2 percent of the world's energy.

These statistics rank Africa as the poorest continent in the world. But

they mask the great regional variation in scale and level of development that exists among the forty-eight countries of sub-Saharan Africa. Most of these countries are small as well as poor. Currently only seven states have populations of more than 20 million—Ethiopia, Kenya, Nigeria, South Africa, Sudan, Tanzania, and Zaire. An additional six countries have between 10 million and 20 million people; the remaining thirty-five countries, less. South Africa stands out with a per capita GNP of $1800, as the only large, developed economy in Africa. Two other small countries (tiny islands excepted) have per capita GNPs of more than $1000— Gabon through the production of oil and Congo because of oil and minerals. Thirty states in Africa have per capita GNPs of less than $500 a year. More than 100 million Africans live in absolute poverty with annual incomes of $100 or less.

Even these low income levels are not secure. National incomes are generated by exporting unprocessed mining products—like diamonds, gold, copper, cobalt, manganese, uranium, petroleum, and platinum—and tropical agricultural products—like coffee, cocoa, peanuts, and palm oil. Although serious attention has been paid to building industrial complexes in the region in the thirty years since independence, most African countries have continued to export raw materials to generate capital.

In addition, production in the crucial agricultural sector is increasing at a slower rate than population growth. In the 1980s, less than 2 million Africans south of the Sahara are employed in mining and manufacturing. If the independent states of Africa remain agriculturally based, and many of the smaller countries have little choice, Africa will undoubtedly remain the poorest region in the Developing World for the foreseeable future.

Population and Poverty

Africa south of the Sahara has about 508 million people, roughly one tenth of the world's total population (Fig. 13.9). Although population densities are low, the region's population has doubled since independence and in most countries will double again in twenty to thirty years. In the 1980s, Africa has both the highest birth rates and the highest death rates in the world. Women have an average of six children as compared with four elsewhere in the world. One of every seven children die in their first year.

In the last decade, the African population grew 15 percent faster than the rest of the Developing World. But today, only eight countries have a population planning policy aimed at lowering the rate of population growth. Eight others are encouraging population growth. Abortion is illegal throughout the region; birth control measures are limited. For these reasons, a population explosion is fully underway in Africa. The total population will reach 732 million in the year 2000. Already caught up in social and political upheavals with eleven wars, more than fifty coups,

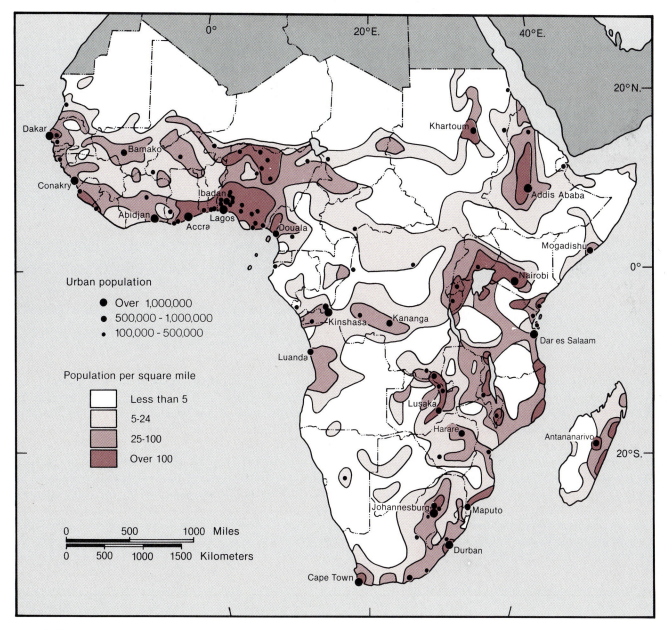

Figure 13.9 Population of Africa.

and fourteen presidential assassinations in the last two decades, Africa is rapidly moving toward what British writer Joseph Conrad called the "heart of darkness."

Compared with other continental areas, population density is low in Africa (Fig. 13.9). But most people are concentrated in islands of economic development with their adjacent urban centers or in those parts of rural Africa where soil fertility, available water, or favorable location sustains a dense population. Perhaps 80 percent of all Africans are still engaged directly or indirectly in agriculture and pastoralism. With population growth increasing at double the rate of food production, population pressure on available resources is intense. This pressure is manifest in various forms of rural poverty and deprivation.

Most obviously, the burden of disease still weighs heavy in Africa. Malaria, eradicated throughout much of Asia and the New World, remains a scourge that contributes to high levels of infant mortality. Snails carrying the parasite that causes schistosomiasis have spread into most lakes, rivers, and streams. Of the 12 million people with leprosy in the world, 5 million live in Africa. Sleeping sickness has undergone a resurgence in the last two decades, and 20 million people are afflicted by river blindness contracted from worms spread by black flies that breed in rapidly flowing rivers. One of every five Africans suffers from malnutrition or protein deficiency. Life expectancy—fifty years—in this region is the lowest in the world; infant mortality is the highest.

These bleak indicators of the human condition mirror broader development problems in Africa. Although economies in the rest of the Developing World grew in the late 1970s and early 1980s, those in Africa—with few exceptions—declined. The tenfold increase in the price of imported oil, a decline in the

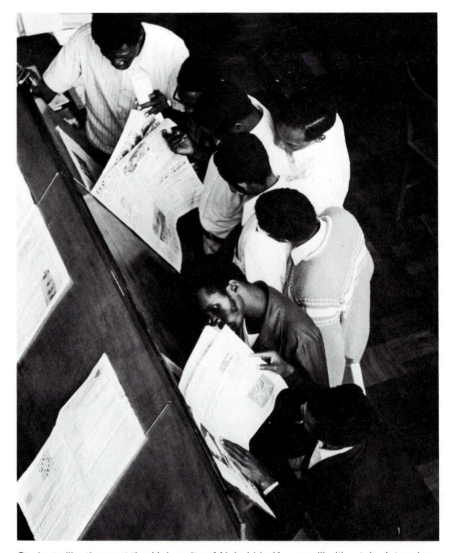

Students like these at the University of Nairobi in Kenya will ultimately determine the future of the world's poorest continent.

value of exports of minerals and tropical agricultural products, and the failure to industrialize has contributed to staggering levels of international debt. Africa's share in world trade and industry has fallen. Perhaps most important, agricultural production has failed to increase, leaving Africa, in the words of the president of the World Bank, "the poorest part of the world's economy." Resources for food, health programs, education, and housing are not available in most countries. And as the gap between levels of living in city and countryside widens, Africans are moving in larger numbers

to overcrowded islands of urban population where rudimentary facilities are available.

Urbanization and Modernization

Throughout Africa, wars of secession, insecurity and corruption, inadequate health services, and high rates of population growth have plagued most countries. The integration of modern mining and agricultural centers into more diversified industrial urban regions is proving to be a difficult process. Patterns of national and regional integration are slow to develop. And governments have consistently neglected the develop-

CIRCULATION SYSTEMS, THE ORGANIZATON OF SPACE, AND ECONOMIC DEVELOPMENT

The organizaton of space is a critical dimension of modernization and economic development. This simplified model illustrates the imprint of spatial systems originally developed in the colonial period on the organization of life and economy that still exist in modern Africa. In the precolonial period (1), local centers dotted the African coast, taking advantage of the abundant food supplies found where land meets sea. In the colonial period (2), selected local centers became trading posts for the export of gold, ivory, and slaves. In many colonies, railroads or roads were built into the interior to connect areas of agricultural and mineral production with port cities, which were emerging as major centers of economic activity. In the late colonial period (3), transportation networks were extended deeper into the interior, and connections with other major centers along the coast were strengthened. After independence (4), the modern states of Africa made substantial efforts to develop articulated national economies with fully developed circulation systems. The persistence of the colonial patterns of transportation and communication, however, has been virtually indelible.

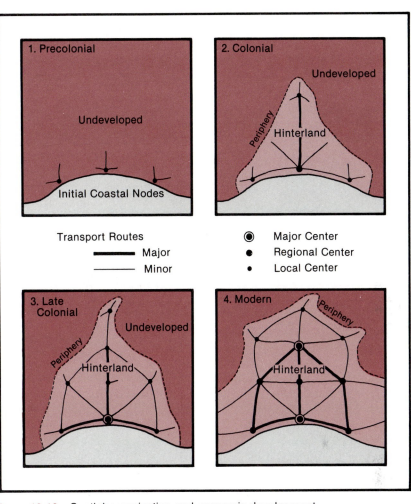

Figure 13.10   Spatial organization and economic development.

Adapted from: H. C. Weinand, "A Spatio-Temporal Model of Economic Development," *Australian Geographical Studies,* Vol. 10 (1972), pp. 95–100.

ment of peasant agricultural and pastoral economies in favor of high-image urban industries that drain funds and produce few jobs. This concentration of spending in urban centers—most often the capital city or leading port—has widened the income gap between city and village. Subsequent migration has led to high rates of urbanization and to the emergence of primate cities as the premier nodes of modernization in Africa (Fig. 13.9).

Africa, with only one of every four of its people living in cities, is the least urbanized region in the Developing World. It is also, however, experiencing a rapid rate of urban growth. Large cities are expanding at rates between 10 and 20 percent per year in many countries, swelling these centers four to five times faster than population is growing. The principal force behind this accelerating process of urbanization is migration from the countryside. It leaves most large cities in Africa besieged by unskilled, unemployed immigrants who exceed the number of jobs available.

Urban employment is forcing migrants into long-term migration because the job search often takes months. Women are still left behind in the villages to continue agricultural production. Family separation is frequent in Africa. In urban settings, migrant living conditions are dreadful. Few cities have a basic water supply, sewage, medical facilities, or housing to serve rapidly expanding populations. Unemployment and other social security benefits are unknown. Slum working quarters—shantytowns or **bidonvilles**—encircle every major city in West Africa, on the coast of East Africa, and in the south. Severe urban poverty is endemic. Despite this, new migrants from overcrowded hinterlands set out for the new African frontier, the city, buoyed by hopes of jobs and opportunities when few are available.

Migrants are continuing to flood primate cities in Africa because the town, as one geographer notes, "is the window through which Africa is entering the modern world." It is in these cities that wealth and power are largely concentrated. In small countries, like Gabon, Gambia, and Liberia, fully 100 percent of all manufacturing is found in the capital city. In most other countries, investment is largely confined to the one or two largest cities. Many of these urban centers are ports or mining centers built during the colonial period (Fig. 13.10). Their explosive growth reflects the prevailing patterns of production and trade where fourteen of the forty-eight countries of Africa depend on one or two export products for 70 percent of the national wealth. Urban growth also mirrors the centralized nature of governments in the region, the concentration of administrative and economic control in the hands of a small urban elite, and the disposition of many African leaders toward the construction of symbolic edifices of modernity. The less glamorous articulation of local and regional economics required for economic growth and material progress has received little attention.

Geographers have studied the close relationship between urban centers, transportation networks, and the diffusion of modernization in Tanzania and in Sierra Leone with comparable results (Fig. 13.10). In both cases,

the spread of modernization from the primate city was intimately related to transport networks. Cities are centers of social and economic development, growth poles of modernization, and pivots of rising aspirations. The prospect of increasing urbanization will strengthen these processes while compounding the real inability of African governments to cope with swelling urban populations. Only in South Africa are active measures being taken to deal with urban populations, but these measures are less influenced by aspirations for economic growth than by racial discrimination.

SOUTH AFRICA: THE GEOGRAPHY OF RACE

Three centuries ago, three ships of the Dutch East India Company anchored at Cape Town at the southwestern tip of the continent. The year was 1652. On landing, the Dutch were met by a party of about fifty cattle-herding Hottentots. Within six weeks, the Dutch, needing labor to establish a refitting station for ships trading in the Orient, captured the Hottentots, seized their cattle, and sold the able-bodied men into slavery. Because the Hottentots were non-Christian, "pagans beyond redemption" according to Dutch Calvinism, they could be enslaved. Discrimination in these early days was based on religion rather than race. Racial prejudice began eight years later in South Africa. In 1660, a hedge was planted on a hill overlooking Cape Town beyond which no Hottentot could venture. The color bar had been established.

For the Dutch, the welfare of their colony demanded that blacks be subjugated, dispossessed of their lands, divested of their herds, and forced to labor in the colonists' fields. When sufficient slaves could not be found locally, others were imported from Jawa, Madagascar, and India. Until

the nineteenth century, slaves outnumbered their white masters by a substantial margin.

As European control spread across the African continent, the Dutch stereotype of Africans as inferior, lazy, and ignorant people lacking in history and culture became the justification for the establishment of stratified color-based societies. The colonial economic system depended on the maintenance of master-servant relations between whites and blacks. It was fundamental to the political existence of European regimes.

When the winds of change swept over Africa after World War II, European governments reassessed the costs of maintaining white rule. Faced with a rising tide of African resistance, the colonial powers found the price in money and lives too dear. By contrast, South Africa initiated *Apartheid: A Spatial Plan of Racial Segregation* which created *Economic Integration, Spatial Segregation* within that country. The British, French, Belgians, and Spanish abandoned their colonial empires. In the Portuguese colonies of Angola, Mozambique, and Portuguese Guinea, which provided a quarter of the total budget of the home country, the Portuguese stayed until 1975. In areas of dense white settlement, independence came slowly and grudgingly. Southern Rhodesia did not become the Republic of Zimbabwe until 1980. The United Nations is still debating the fate of Namibia (South-West Africa) today. But in South Africa, the white minority is determined to stay. Their history is different.

Apartheid: A Spatial Plan of Racial Segregation

In 1948, the National Party, dominated by Afrikaners, was elected to power on a platform of apartheid, economic prosperity, and withdrawal from the British Commonwealth. Apartheid promised to segregate spatially the African majority from the European minority. The ultimate goal was to create a series of color-based, semiindependent territories in South Africa. In these territories, or **homelands,** each racial group—whites, blacks, Asians, and Cape Coloured (people of mixed blood)—ideally would develop its own society and traditions. Racial pollution and antagonism would be averted. White dominance over the greater part of South Africa would be maintained.

Some 250 fragmented areas in South Africa were set aside as reserves from which ten African states called **Bantustans,** or tribal homelands, would emerge. Similar plans or urban-based residential segregation were developed for the Cape Coloured and the Asians. Specific locations apart from the white population were designated for each group. By the late 1950s, the blueprint for implementation was drawn up in South Africa. All nonwhites were denied the right to vote. A spate of apartheid legislation was passed, giving segregation the force of law. South Africa was thrown out of the Commonwealth and became the R.S.A. (Republic of South Africa).

For the last three decades, society and economy in South Africa have been guided by the determination of the white minority to retain control of the country. The conscious development of apartheid as a government policy stemmed from white fears that in any integrated society, the Europeans would be swamped by the overwhelming black African majority. In the 1980s, South Africa's total population of 35.1 million was composed of 25.9 million (74 percent) Bantu-speaking Africans, 5.2 million (15 percent) whites of predominately Afrikaans and English descent, 3.2 million (9 percent) Cape Coloured, and 700,000 (2 percent) Asians of Indian extraction. By the year 2000—which is not so far away—there will be 5.4 million whites accounting for 12 percent of the total population. Black Africans will number 39.9 mil-

lion or 78 percent of South Africa's total population.

The African majority are almost all Bantu speakers from two major groups, the Nguni (including the Zulu, Xhosa, Ndebele, and Swazi) and the Sotho. Originally, they were herders and farmers who lived in small villages. By the 1980s, rural black Africans lived on assigned homelands or as laborers on white-owned Afrikaner or English farms. Urban blacks were crowded in racially segregated ghettos like Soweto (pop. 1.5 million), a black ghetto near Johannesburg, in the four major industrial regions of South Africa near the cities of Johannesburg, Durban, and Cape Town, each with populations of more than 1 million, and Port Elizabeth (pop. 500,000).

Two thirds of the 5.2 million whites in South Africa are native speakers of Afrikaans, and one third are English speakers. The descendants of the Boers outnumber the British, particularly in the old Boer republics of the Orange Free State and the Transvaal. Afrikaaners have guided the economic development of South Africa, dominating much of the economic life of the country. It is they who hold positions of power in South African society and rule its mines, industrial establishments, and plantations. Originally, rural dwellers, the Afrikaaners now live in urban centers. Directly and indirectly, however, they control the most fertile, productive land in the South African countryside.

The 3.2 million people known as Cape Coloured in South Africa are ethnic products of two and a half centuries of mixed breeding among Asians, Europeans, and Africans. Most of them live in racially segregated townships adjoining Cape Town and in the rural areas of Cape Province. Except for a small English-speaking group in Natal, the majority speak Afrikaans. Originally the Cape Coloured had an advantage over Bantu-speaking Africans because of their close affiliation with Europe-

ans. But racial discrimination has condemned them to low-skilled jobs as farm laborers, servants, and factory workers. Now the Cape Coloured have the highest mortality rate of any group in the country.

The smallest racial group, the Asians, are Indians and Mauritians who were imported to the sugar plantations of Natal in the 1860s as indentured laborers. Hindu and Muslim traders, service workers, and market gardeners, have a standard of living approaching that of the Europeans.

Faced with the demographic reality of being a white minority and with the successes of African nationalists farther north, the Afrikaaners decided on apartheid as the only policy that would keep them in power in South Africa (Fig. 13.11). In 1964, the first homeland was established in the Transkei. In theory, 250 other Bantustans or homelands were to be consolidated into ten political units. Most of these Bantustans are scattered throughout northern and eastern South Africa on broken, isolated, or desolate land. Cities, industries, railroads, and the most fertile agricultural lands are located in the white homeland. Only 13 percent of South Africa is devoted to the homelands. Outside these reserves, Africans are not permitted to own land or occupy property. They cannot vote and are forbidden to join any political group or association, and they are spatially restricted to residence in some 150 "black spots" located in the vicinity of the larger cities and industrial areas.

Currently, the homelands are called nation-states by the South African government. There are now four of these "independent" states within the traditional boundaries of South Africa (Fig. 13.11). Transkei was granted "independence" in 1976, Bophuthatswana in 1977, Venda in 1979, and Ciskei in 1981. They are recognized by no other government, except that of South Africa; they do not even recognize each other. Nonetheless, the policy proceeds and six

THE GEOGRAPHY OF APARTHEID IN SOUTH AFRICA

Apartheid, or separate development, has been implemented in South Africa by the formation of a series of ten racial homelands or Bantustans in which the 25.9 million black Africans will have de jure residence and legal rights. As Figure 13.11 shows, these homelands are scattered throughout the east and northeast quadrants of South Africa. They comprise only 13 percent of the total land area of the country, enclose no major urban or industrial center, and occupy some of the least desirable land in South Africa. Indeed, 55 percent of all black Africans live outside these de jure homelands. No other country has recognized these homelands as countries, nor are they economically viable. The policy of separate development, a geographical solution to segregating the races in South Africa, has been denounced worldwide.

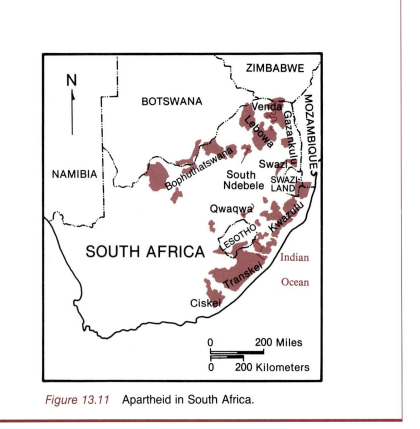

Figure 13.11   Apartheid in South Africa.

other former homelands are being readied for "independent" status against the wishes of their inhabitants. In pursuing this policy of apartheid, a well-established pattern of economic growth based on African labor and European management has been distorted, disrupting the entire functioning of South Africa as a geographical complex.

Economic Integration, Spatial Segregation

The political and social engineering of South Africa's population into this program of separate and unequal development denies the reality of an integrated modern economy. In the nineteenth century, black Africans migrated to the emerging industrial and mining centers of South Africa— to Johannesburg, Cape Town, Durban, Pretoria, and Port Elizabeth. Currently, over half the population of the Witwatersrand industrial com-

The Reverend Desmond Tutu, awarded the Nobel Peace Prize in 1984, leads a peaceful demonstration against racial discrimination in South Africa.

plex near Johannesburg is composed of native Africans. Although the African population is still predominantly rural, no major city in South Africa has a white majority.

After a century of life and work in these urban centers, few Africans have acquired either the skills or the education necessary for the management of a modern economy. But their contribution to industrial production is vital to the economy of South Africa. When separate homelands were established in the hinterlands of the industrial centers, these urban black Africans were stranded in white areas. With no rights in the white-controlled urban centers, they are faced with the alternative of returning to the rural bush where there are no cities and few jobs outside of agriculture and government service.

This problem is compounded by a flow of migrant laborers from the assigned homelands to white areas, an exodus that at any one time probably amounts to 40 percent of the able-bodied work force. On the Bantustans, every male is forced to pay both a poll tax and a hut tax in cash. Paradoxically, a majority of black Africans leave the reserves and become permanent residents in white homelands. Approximately 55 percent of the black population now lives outside their homeland, half working as laborers on white farms, the other half in urban industry. This migration leaves the native homelands without adequate manpower. The migrants are residents of two worlds—one without jobs, the other without rights.

Whatever the theoretical attractions of separate cultural development for black Africans, the cynicism of the South African government in implementing apartheid has disenfranchised the African majority. They have been alienated from the land and resources of the nation and reduced to poverty, humiliation, and pain. On the Bantustans, the economic crisis is so intense that an official government commission reports that fully half of the population would have to be removed for the remainder to achieve minimum living conditions. Plans exist for programs of agricultural stabilization and industrial transformation in the homelands. But these goals cannot be achieved in regions devoid of resources, lacking in transportation, facilities, with no large cities, and among people who have never participated in urban, industrial life.

The policy of apartheid is a decisive political effort by a white minority to retain supremacy over an impoverished African majority. In the short run, at least, it has been successful. The British, Portuguese, French, Belgians, and Spanish have all been forced out of Africa; the Afrikaaners remain. The price is heavy, both economically and politically. Each year violence and suppression increase in South Africa. Incidents on the frontier between white-dominated South Africa and black-controlled Southern Africa are becoming more frequent. The future is uncertain for this rich, strategic land.

GLOSSARY

Absentee landlordism system of land tenure where owner does not work agricultural land; see *land tenure, sharecropping, tenancy.*

Absolute humidity the actual quantity of moisture present in the air, defined as the weight of water vapor contained in a given volume of air.

Absorbing barrier barriers that block the spread of ideas, goods, and people; see *diffusion.*

Acculturation the process of cultural adjustment on either an individual or social level; see *assimilation.*

Acid rain rain, snow, fog, or mist with an acidic pH value caused by the conversion of industrial pollutants (sulphur and nitrogen) to acid oxides in the atmosphere. Acid rain damages plant and animal life; on already acidic soils, it results in pollution of rivers and lakes through leaching of minerals from the soil, rendering the water lifeless. Global circulation of winds determines the occurrence of acid precipitation often far from the source area.

Adobe sun-dried bricks made of mud; may be mixed with straw or chalk; used in building construction; associated with arid regions but found in a variety of climates; if tamped directly into a building frame, known as rammed earth. Strong, insulating, and durable if well protected, adobe building techniques are among the world's oldest and most widely *diffused.*

Agglomerated settlement a form of rural settlement, usually a village, in which buildings are grouped together, as compared with *dispersed settlement* where people live in scattered farmsteads.

Agrarian agricultural; used with reference to land or people.

Agribusiness a huge farm under corporate management, dependent on reserves of capital and sale to a large geographic market.

Agrogorod a large agricultural town in the USSR where, in theory, farmers have access to urban amenities and production is increased by economies of scale and specialization of work.

Ahimsa the doctrine in Hinduism and Buddhism dictating that people refrain from harming sentient creatures.

Air mass a mass of relatively homogeneous air covering a considerable area of the surface of the earth. Usually classified by *region* of origin as *tropical* or *polar, maritime* or *continental.*

Alluvial fan cone- or fan-shaped deposits of *alluvium* laid down in a plain or open valley.

Alluvial plain a level stretch of land along a stream on which *alluvium* has been deposited through periodic floods.

Alluvium rock fragments, soil, and *silt* deposited by water in low-lying areas such as stream beds, *deltas*, and *estuaries.*

Alpine meadow grasslands found at high altitudes in the Alps and other mountain systems located above *coniferous* forests and below permanent snow.

Alpine vegetation the typical altitudinal zonation of vegetation in the Alps and other *midlatitude* mountain systems from lowland grassland and *deciduous* forest, to *coniferous* forest, *alpine meadow*, and *tundra* vegetation.

Altiplano a mountain-ringed high *plateau* in Bolivia and Peru; the largest interior drainage *basin* in South America.

Animate energy energy derived from human or animal sources: people or work animals.

Anthracite hard, natural coal, generally containing little volatile matter as compared with soft or *bituminous* coal.

Apartheid a spatial solution to the problems posed by the multiracial nature of society in the Republic of South Africa. In theory, apartheid envisions the creation of a loose federation of independent, racially based *homelands*, or *bantustans*. In practice, it is a political device to preserve the power of the white population in a society where they form a minority of the total population.

Arable the agricultural space of a society; land suitable for cultivation.

Archipelago a group of islands located in close proximity to one another. Originally restricted to the islands of the Aegean Sea, the term now embodies the idea of a chain of islands.

Area symbols like *line* and *point symbols*, used to present information on a map. Area symbols are typically utilized for phenomena that extend over regions. Graphic variations in color, pattern, and intensity are used to identify different phenomena.

Arrowroot a family of *tropical* American plants cultivated for the starch in their tuberous roots.

Assimilation the process by which a minority group gives up its distinctive cultural traits and adopts those of the larger or more powerful society; see *acculturation.*

Atoll a circular or partly circular *coral reef*, formed by a series of low, coral reef islands enclosing a central lagoon. No central island exists; passages to the open sea divide the component islands. Common in west and central Oceania, especially Micronesia.

Autocracy government by an absolute ruler, or autocrat; a dictator is an autocrat usually viewed as oppressive. Autocracy also refers to the community governed by an autocrat.

Azimuthal projection a type of *map projection* created when a flat plane touches (or is tangent to) the earth's surface, usually at the North or South Pole.

Balkanization the breaking of a previously united *region* into many small and often mutually hostile units. The term comes from the political evolution of the Balkan *peninsula* of southeastern Europe; see *buffer zone.*

Bantustan a separate, self-governing *homeland* for the black population of South Africa; see *apartheid, homeland.*

Barrier reef type of *coral reef* separated from a body of land—a central island, a mainland—by a *lagoon*. Common in Oceania, Australia's Great Barrier Reef is the world's largest, 1250 miles long and 10–90 miles wide.

Barrio the term for *shantytown* used in Mexico.

Bar scale known also as graphic scale, a line on the map to show the lengths of units of earth (real) distance. The left end of the bar is often subdivided into smaller units to allow for more precise estimation of distance.

Basin a hollow or trough in the surface of the earth often filled with water.

Basin irrigation a system of *irrigation* in which the floodwaters of a river are trapped in a series of *basins;* seasonal in nature, it supplements inadequate rainfall; see *perennial irrigation*.

Bauxite the ore from which aluminum is made.

Bayou a local term for the slow-moving marshy creeks, *tributaries*, and minor rivers of the Gulf coastal plain of the southern United States.

Bazaar a traditional Asian or Middle Eastern market consisting of rows of shops or stalls selling a variety of merchandise.

Bergslag the traditional communal agricultural organization in central Sweden, conceived as a self-sufficient pioneer economic unit.

Bidonville the term for *shantytown* used in French-speaking Africa.

Birth rate the number of births per thousand population per year.

Bituminous soft coal, generally containing less than a third volatile matter; refined into *coke*, it provides the energy for most iron and steel production; see *anthracite*.

Bodhisattva one whose essence is enlightenment and who is worshipped as a diety in Buddhism.

Bog a low-lying area of waterlogged ground composed of decaying plant life, especially moss; characteristic of the *taiga* and of the shallow standing water of *glacial* lakes and ponds known as *muskeg* in Canada.

Borough a political subdivision; New York City is divided into five boroughs—Brooklyn, Queens, the Bronx, Staten Island, and Manhattan.

Brahman the omnipresent spirit in Hinduism that provides continuity in a changing world.

Braided streams a complex pattern of interweaving shallow channels of a river system, each stream with insufficient volume or velocity to carry its load of *alluvium*.

Buffer zone a country or *region* situated between two or more powerful states.

Burakamin the underclass of Japan. Traditionally workers in leather or metals, the burakamin also dealt with human and animal wastes in the cities (nightsoil). Still part of the social fabric of Japan, forming a socially and spatially segregated urban class.

Bustee the term for *shantytown* used in India.

Campos cerrados a *savanna* grassland with many trees located in central Brazil south of the Amazonian *rain forests*.

Capitalism, capitalist modern economic system signaled by private ownership of property, means of production, and large financial institutions encouraging growth of industry, trade, and consumption. Although capitalism has existed in part since early civilizations, capitalism is generally seen as replacing mercantilism with the rise of the Industrial Revolution and as antithetical to *communism* in the modern world.

Capitanias large feudal estates stretching inland from the coast of Brazil awarded by Portugal to noble families to encourage settlement and development in the colonial period.

Capitulations a series of *concessions* granted by Ottoman sultans, under pressure from European powers, to foreigners in return for loans.

Caravan a merchant group, or train, of pack animals transporting goods through *deserts*, or in *preindustrial* times, any kind of land *environment*. Caravan routes are marked by strategic stops at caravansaris, warehouse-hotels that may be in city or in country.

Cartogram a device used by *cartographers* to convey in map form an overall impression of different magnitudes of data by distorting the geographical area of a map.

Cartography the science of map making; the representation of three common measures of geography—distance, area, and *scale*—in map form.

Caste the traditional social system of Hindu society in which the members of each social group or caste eat together, often practice the same occupation, and share the same *dharma* or duty.

Caudillo the "man on horseback," or military leader in Latin America.

Central business district (**CBD**) the "downtown" or main commercial district of a city, characterized by a high concentration of business, usually lodged in a core of vertical office buildings, in a small area.

Central place a location that functions as a service center for a surrounding area or *hinterland*, by providing various goods, employment, and services. Central places, usually towns, may be ranked in a *hierarchy* of importance by population, the number and range of goods and services provided, and the area over which their influence is felt; see *central place theory*.

Central place hierarchy network of settlements or *central places* of greater size and complexity increasingly more widely spaced than small, less complex *central places*; see *central place theory, urban hierarchy*.

Central place theory a *model* of the *hierarchy* of settlements or *central places* of different size and complexity.

Chernozem a Ukrainian word for the fertile black soils that cover much of the Ukraine in the Soviet Union and in *prairie* environments around the world.

Chinampa a system of land reclamation in the form of raised strips of land in the freshwater lakes of Aztec Mexico.

Choke point a strategic pass, typically a *strait* at sea or narrow crossing on land, along trade routes. Due to location between or near hostile entities and its geographic composition, a choke point has the distinct possibility of being cut off by military action.

Choropleth map a map on which data is plotted by the areal units used for collecting information.

City-state an autonomous state consisting of a city and its surrounding territory.

Civil division the creation of different levels of government within an established political body, so as to form a *hierarchy* of smaller administrative units; in the United States, for example, (1) federal, (2) state, (3) county, and (4) municipal levels of government.

Class interval the interval between two categories of data (classes) on an *isoline* map where the lines between classes connect points of equal value. The selection of class intervals is decided by the *cartographer* and determines the spatial form of the distribution shown on the map.

Climate the average weather conditions that exist in a given place or *region* throughout the year.

Climax vegetation a stable community of plants established over time.

Climograph a graph on which two or more *climatic* characteristics such as monthly mean temperature and precipitation are plotted.

Cloud forest forests located on cloud-shrouded slopes like the eastern Andes, characterized by dense trees covered with mosses, ferns, and other epiphytes.

Coastal plain a generally flat or rolling land surface (plain) of varying width lying at low elevations adjacent to a sea or ocean. Coastal plains are covered with sediment washed down from higher elevations and form rich *environments* for human settlement.

Coke *bituminous* coal that has been burned at high temperatures in a closed oven (retort) and transformed into a residue that burns at higher temperatures than coal; see *anthracite*.

Collectivization an administrative restructuring of rural society in which all land holdings are grouped together into a single unit and operated under the cooperative control of those who live and work on the land; generally associated with *communist* land reform programs.

Colonialism control by one power over a dependent area or people.

Colonialization the process by which one power exerts control over a dependent area or people. Also called *colonization*.

Colons French *settler colonists* who owned and worked the land and directed the colonial economy in the French colonies.

Colony settlement in a territory by people from the outside, usually another country. A colony thus often becomes subject to the laws of and becomes a *dependency* of the parent state. A colony is often established in a newly conquered or hostile territory in which settlement is already substantial. A colony established for trade (as opposed to a *settler colony*) is termed a *mercantile colony*.

Command economy an economy in which the allocation of resources depends on a central planning council as in the Soviet Union and supply and demand play a limited role in production decisions. All resources are at the command of the state.

Commodity crops an agricultural product produced under economic conditions allowing it to be bought and sold in international markets. Commodity crops are often produced as *monocrops* with advanced technology.

Commonwealth a self-governing territory organized into association with a federation, the government of which takes responsibility for common concerns, such as defense. The link between the territory and the federal government varies in strength according to the arrangement made.

Commune a settlement based on collective ownership and use of property, goods, and the means of production; strongly associated with *communist* societies.

Communism modern economic system, derived from the ideas of Karl Marx (German, mid-1800s), that advocates the creation of a classless society based on common ownership of property and means of production and distribution. In theory, the state becomes less important and self-management more important over time. Common ownership of property has been found in a variety of societies, but communism as a political philosophy was first implemented in Russia following the Revolution of 1917.

Concession the rights to land and resources granted to private companies that invested in central Africa in the *colonial* period.

Condominium in political geography, an area jointly administered by two states, neither of which has exclusive authority or sovereignty over the area.

Conformal projection any map projection on which the shapes of small areas are shown correctly.

Conic projection a *map projection* constructed by fitting a cone over a globe. On conic projections, *parallels* are concentric circles focused on the top of the cone and *meridians* are lines that converge on that point.

Conifer a conically shaped tree with straight trunk, short branches, and needlelike leaves. Most conifers, such

as the spruce, fir, and pine, are *evergreen;* a coniferous forest is characterized by little undergrowth and poor, acidic soils.

Constant class interval maps on which the spacing of intervals between *isolines* is constant; see *class interval*.

Contagious diffusion a type of *diffusion* that spreads like a disease from individual to individual without regard to social status or power; see *diffusion*.

Continental climate a *climate* characterized by extremes of temperature, low rainfall, and low humidity generally found in the interiors of large land masses.

Continentality measure of indexes of a *continental climate*, which is characterized by seasonal extremes of temperature and marked seasonal differences in precipitation, due mainly to great distance from the sea.

Contour interval the interval or difference in elevation between two *contour lines* on a map; see *class interval*.

Contour line a line on a map connecting points of equal elevation above a *datum plane*, usually mean sea level; see *isoline*.

Contour plowing plowing parallel to the contours of the land to reduce *runoff*, retain moisture, and lessen *erosion*.

Conurbation an extensive urban area formed of two or more cities, originally separate, which have coalesced to form a single continuous *metropolitan* region with multiple nodes; see *megalopolis*.

Coral reef a type of coast created by coral and algae, organisms that grow together as colonies to produce rock-like deposits of limestone as they die. New colonies are built on top of old to create a growing, living phenomenon near the surface of warm, *tropical* waters. Coral reefs grow in conditions of clean sea water exposed to vigorous wave action. Coral fragments torn free by wave action accumulate as sand beaches on shore. Coral reefs are of three types: *fringing, barrier,* and *atoll*.

Cordillera a *continental* mountain system consisting of numerous ranges set in parallel ridges.

Core, Core Area the centralized zone of a *culture region* displaying the greatest density of occupance, intensity of organization, and homogeneity; see *culture region*.

Core and periphery a geographical reference to the gap between the *core*, or *heartland* of a *culture*, economy, or society, and its *periphery*, or *spatial fringes*, where the intensity of the phenomenon under study is much less and may begin to merge with the culture of yet another core.

Creole an American-born member of the landowning class of Europeans in *colonial* Latin America.

Crevasse a deep crack in a *glacier*, not unlike a fault line. Crevasses frequently occur either at the top of a valley glacier where the ice is brittle and fractures easily, or downslope where a glacier moves more rapidly over a steeper grade or is bent around a curve.

Crop rotation a farming technique designed to protect and even increase soil fertility and yields. In its simplest form, as in *shifting cultivation*, crop rotation involves the successive use of different planting sites. More generally today, the same field is used to produce different crops during each growing season.

Cross plowing tilling a field with a wooden plow first in one direction and then across the furrows, reworking the entire field to break up the soil. With the appearance of the heavier iron plow in Europe in the early medieval period, cross plowing was no longer necessary.

Cultural landscape the impress of a society on its physical *environment*. In early twentieth-century geography, the study of the cultural landscape was seen as a fundamental area of inquiry.

Culture learned behavior; elements of culture include technology, language, historical experience, religion, politics, economics, and values. Culture is generally divided into material aspects (arts, sciences) and less tangible aspects; culture operates among and between groups.

Culture hearth a region in which a distinctive cultural complex either originated or exists. In North America, for example, modern American civilization can be traced to four culture hearths in French Canada, New England, the Middle Colonies, and the South—each with different economic foci, social organization, and patterns of intellectual development.

Culture of poverty according to the anthropologist Oscar Lewis, a set of behavior, a culture, derived from relative deprivation.

Culture region a defined area in which a distinctive cultural complex exists. Modern examples include China, India, Latin America, and other *culture regions* used as the basis for organization and analysis in this book.

Cumulative causation a theory of developmental change based on the idea that the play of market forces tends to increase rather than decrease inequalities among countries.

Cylindrical projection a *map projection* constructed by fitting a cylinder around the globe that touches its surface on any given circle. The best known cylindrical projection is the standard Mercator.

Daily urban systems the *urban field* within which the *suburban* American upper and middle classes sleep, eat, live, and pursue their careers.

Daimyo feudal baron in medieval Japan.

Datum plane the reference point, usually mean sea level, above which *contour lines* connect points of equal elevation.

Death control application of basic medical technology, such as sanitation and vaccination, to populations previously without them typically producing a rapidly lowered *death rate* with no corresponding downward shift in the *birth rate*. Such relatively easy changes in the single demographic factor of the death rate constitute death control.

Deciduous descriptive of plants that shed leaves seasonally—at the onset of winter or a dry season—and renew them in spring or with the arrival of wet season rains.

Decolonization (1) the process of achieving independence in a colonial territory, or (2) the process of removing the effects of *colonization* following the independence of a former colonial state. Decolonization may involve transformation of the state's culture, economy, or political organization, and was most prominent in the postcolonial Africa of the 1960s and 1970s.

Deforestation the clearing or destruction of forests.

Delta a flat, fertile lowland plain formed by a river as it deposits its burden of *alluvium* near its mouth.

Demographer a specialist in *demography*, the study of populations.

Demographic transition a four-stage *model* of the impact of the Industrial Revolution on population growth. In the early phases of industrialization, a population is characterized by high *birth rates* and, before the general introduction of modern health practices, high *death rates*. Population remains static. In the second stage, fertility remains high but death rates decrease as sanitary conditions dramatically improve; a sharp increase in population ensues. In the third stage, the birth rate declines to a level comparable with the death rate, slowing population growth. In the final stage, the total population is much larger than at the beginning of the cycle of growth, but is again stabilized with both birth and death rates at low levels.

Demography the study and description of population by nationality, race, age, sex, religion, health, education, and other vital characteristics.

Dependency a territory that depends on, or is subject to, the control of another country from which it is separated by some considerable distance.

Desert tract of land in which precipitation is so scanty and undependable that vegetation is noticeably absent. *Sedentary* human activity is restricted to the extraction of specific minerals and metals or to irrigated *oasis* agriculture.

Desertification changes in climate, often induced by environmental mismanagement, that expand *deserts* into once productive land on its *subhumid* fringes.

Dharma the Hindu concept of duty within society.

Diaspora the settlement of scattered colonies of Jews outside Palestine beginning with the Babylonian exile of the Jews in 586 B.C.

Diffusion geographic spread of cultural elements from a given point over a progressively wider area. Geographers identify the study of cultural diffusion—its causes and effects, propagation, amplitude, and direction—as an important means of understanding the relationships between different societies and the course of culture through time and space.

Digging stick a primitive agricultural implement used to plant, weed, and clear stones.

Dike an earthen bank constructed

alongside low-lying ground to prevent it from being flooded by the sea, a lake, or a river.

Dispersed settlement settlement by individual families on widely scattered single farmsteads, as compared with centralized or *agglomerated settlement*.

Dissected hills an upland or series of hills where a number of valleys have been etched into the surface by *erosion*.

Distributary an individual channel formed by the splitting of a river that does not rejoin the main stream but reaches the sea independently.

Domain the area of a *culture region* in which the particular culture is dominant but with less intensity than in the *core*; see *culture region*.

Dot map map showing spatial distributions (often population) by an array of dots, each assigned a specific value. Dot maps can provide a quick and visually realistic representation of spatial distribution.

Double cropping the practice of planting two crops in succession in the same field in the same year.

Dravidian a member of an ancient Australoid race in southern India; also a family of languages spoken in that region including Tamil, Telegu, and Malayam.

Drumlin an elongated, oval-shaped hill found in *glaciated* regions.

Dry farming techniques used in arid and dry-season environments to retain as much moisture as possible in the soil.

Dual economy an economy split into a small, intensive modern sector geared to export and a large traditional sector; characteristic of many countries in the Developing World.

Dual society a society in the Developing World in which an urban elite owns and operates the main lines of the economy, whereas the remainder of society, primarily rural, lives at low standards of living and has little political, economic, or social power. In reference to a *dual economy*, it is the same elite that owns the small modern sector of the economy; the traditional economic sector belongs to the social underclasses.

Dust bowl a semi-arid area from which exposed topsoil is being or has been removed by the wind after a period of low rainfall. Dust bowl conditions can be accelerated by poor soil management techniques.

Easterlies the continuously flowing east to west wind system of the low *latitudes* at low elevations. Also called the *trade winds*.

Ecological dominant an organism, species, or life form whose influence over a given area or life complex is substantial.

Ecology the study of the mutual relationships of organisms and their *environment*.

Ecosystem an organic community of plants and animals within its *environment*—for example, a *bog*, an *oasis*, or a *lagoon*.

Ejecta the variety of volcanic materials—dust, ash, rock, lava—ejected by volcanoes.

Ejido a cooperative farm in Mexico.

Elfin forest a forest located at high elevation (often above 10,000 feet) characterized by twisted trees and shrubs.

Encomienda a labor system in colonial Latin America under which Indians were grouped in *hamlets* under control of Spanish colonists.

Energy slave primary energy source or sources of a society, ranging the technological gamut from man and beast to nuclear, petroleum, or natural gas.

Entrenched stream a deeply incised stream flowing at a markedly lower elevation than that of the surrounding terrain.

Entrepôt a center to which goods in transit are brought for temporary storage and transshipment; often a port city.

Environment the sum of the surrounding conditions within which organisms or communities exist.

Environmental niche a small, specialized *environment* that an organism or an activity is especially well suited to occupy.

Environmental perception the mental image of the physical *environment* held by an individual or a group.

Equal area projection any *map projection* on which area is true to *scale* over the entire map; see *map projection*.

Erg a *desert* whose surface is covered with sand dunes.

Erosion the wearing away of the earth's surface by the action of water or wind.

Escarpment a sharply defined inland cliff produced by *faulting* or *erosion*, rimming a *plateau*.

Esker a long narrow ridge of sand, gravel, and rocks that was once the bed of a stream flowing under or in a *glacier*.

Estancia a large estate in the Argentine *pampas* on which beef and dairy cattle, sheep, and horses are raised.

Estuary the tidal mouth of a river where fresh water mixes with sea water; a delicately balanced aquatic *ecosystem* noted for shellfish production and a rich variety of marine life.

Ethos characteristic spirit of a society, community, or people, often implying a distinctive set of moral values. An ethos takes geographic form in the principles underlying the order of landscapes.

Evergreen a descriptive term for plants that remain green throughout the year; plants with such persistent leaves or needles include *conifers*, many grasses, and succulents.

Exotic stream a stream originating in a well-watered *environment* that subsequently flows through dry areas as, for example, the Nile River of Egypt.

Expansion diffusion the spread of goods, people, and ideas outward from a point of origin to one area after another; see *diffusion*.

External debt money owed by a country to exterior, foreign sources—banks, international monetary lending agencies (*World Bank*), or governments. Weighed against assets and the total value of trade, the amount of external debt is an indicator of the strength or weakness of a national economy.

Fall line a line joining points where parallel-flowing rivers drop suddenly from a *piedmont* to a coastal plain in falls or rapids; the upstream limit of river navigation.

Faulting the fracturing of the earth's crust into blocks of land along lines of pressure. Along with *folding*, it is one of the principal mountain-building processes.

Favela slum ringing Rio de Janeiro, São Paulo, and other fast-growing cities of Brazil; see *shantytown*.

Fazenda a large coffee *plantation* in Brazil.

Fen low-lying land often covered by a thin sheet of water, and characterized by plants and animals adapted to a water *environment*.

Ferroalloy any of the many minerals such as tungsten, vanadium, or *molybdenum* that are alloyed with *pig iron* to yield steel of a desired quality.

Fertile Crescent a well-watered, semi-circular band of land arcing northward from the southeastern coast of the Mediterranean, through the Lebanon Mountains, east to the *alluvial plains* of Mesopotamia, and south again along the foothills of the Taurus and Zagros mountains.

Feudalism the most prevalent system of political organization in Europe during the Middle Ages, based on bonds of loyalty between *peasant* and lord. Feudal systems were also characteristic at various periods in China, Japan, India, and the Middle East.

Fiefdom in medieval Europe, a territory controlled by a feudal lord and worked by his serfs, workers bound in servitude to the lord by personal or hereditary ties.

Five-year plan an economic document established by planners to set the direction and goals for national economic progress over a five-year period. Closely associated with the development of the Soviet economy since Stalin's first five-year plan in 1929, many developing countries have established central economic planning that operates under the direction of five-year (or other set period of years) plans.

Fjord long, narrow *inlet* of the ocean; characteristic of Norway; known as sounds in New Zealand. Scoured and deepened as valley *glaciers* made their way to the sea, fjords were filled with seawater after the retreat of the glaciers.

Floodplain level, low-lying valley floor bordering a river, subject to flooding when the river rises and overflows its banks.

Flow map a map on which lines, often of different thicknesses to illustrate higher or lower quantities, are used to show movement and volume of movement.

Fog desert *desert* on the west coast of a continent between 15° and 30° latitude. When cool air overlying cold ocean currents paralleling the shore moves inland, these deserts are blanketed by fog.

Folded mountains mountains constructed by the compression of the earth's crust into alternating *ridges and valleys*, much like a washboard.

Food surplus food production greater than that consumed by the producers; a necessary precondition for the existence of cities.

Formal region among other types of *regions*, a formal region is a given area in which a likeness of forms and features—a uniformity of characteristics—is present. Geographers have traditionally conceived the formal region as homogeneous in nature.

Forward capital a capital city so located within the territory of the country that it makes a statement concerning the territorial extent of that country. The position of the capital promotes the desire of the country to occupy territory in adjacent, still-unoccupied or contested areas.

Fossil water table underground water accumulated over a long period of time that when utilized loses water at a rate faster than it can be naturally recharged.

Fragmentation successive subdivision of inherited land into ever-smaller and less economic parcels.

Francophone French-speaking; may be applied to societies and countries as well as individuals.

Fringing reef a type of *coral reef* that is continuous with the shore, forming a platform attached to the shore with no intervening *lagoon* separating reef from shore. Fringing reefs grow outward as a result of corals that become established on rocks near shore.

Functional region a *region* delineated by patterns of circulation, organization, or connectivity around a single, focal location.

Fundo a large estate in Chile and Peru.

Gachupin a Spanish-born member of the landowning class of Europeans in colonial Latin America.

Gallery forest a corridor of tropical *rain forest* along a stream. Also called *jungle*.

Garden agriculture the Chinese and Polynesian system of intensive, horticulture-style agriculture in which intense human effort is invested in small plots of land.

Gaucho a rancher/cowboy in Argentina and Uruguay.

Gentrification beginning in the 1970s, the movement to restore and rebuild decaying, potentially desirable habitats in urban areas of North American cities that has resulted in social change in many cities; implies replacement of low-income communities by young, often single, higher income residents—a kind of urban "gentry."

Gentry a rural social class of high standing, characterized by ownership of large properties, economic privilege, and conspicuous wealth.

Geographic complementarity that condition when two or more geographical areas produce different goods and engage in mutual exchanges beneficial to each other.

Geologic water water laid down in an aquifer (a water-bearing rock formation) in an earlier, rainier period. Little or no water has been added to the aquifer since then. Geologic water is characteristic of desert aquifers, is finite, and once used, will not be replaced. See *fossil water table*.

Geothermal of or relating to the heat of the earth's interior. Geothermal electricity is produced by capturing this heat in locations where instability in the earth's crust has brought it near the surface in the form of *geysers*, whose hot water is capped or drawn off to generate power.

Geyser a deep hot spring that at intervals shoots a jet of steam and hot water as high as 200 feet.

Glacial drift the debris of rock, sand, and gravel left behind on the *landscape* after a *glacier* has melted.

Glacial landscape a *landscape* modified by being covered by a large mass of ice; characterized by rock-strewn soils, lakes, *bogs*, and disrupted drainage patterns.

Glaciation general term for the entire process of glacial growth and *landscape* modification.

Glacier a river of ice, of one of two types: valley (or alpine), found where thick accumulations of ice in highland zones begin to move downslope; and continental (or sheet), which occur when cold climates cause a higher proportion of the earth's water to be stored in ice, as in the *polar latitudes*.

Global heat balance the global transfer of heat from low to high latitudes by ocean currents and air movement.

Global village associated with Canadian media observer Marshall McLuhan (d. 1980), the result of being plugged into modern telecommunications networks; a globally connected, instantaneous, interactive society.

Graying of society the steady increase in average age of population in the industrial economies, resulting in similar growth in the percentage of retired workers. The percentage of the population in the work force declines proportionately. This tendency is heightened by the steady decline in the *birth rate* in such societies. Sustaining old-age pensioners' programs such as Social Security in the United States becomes increasingly difficult. Taken together, these processes are identified as the graying of society.

Greenbelt encircling swath of forest and farmland on the periphery of a built-up urban area.

Green Revolution term for a complex of agricultural advances including new high-yielding varieties of seed, fertilization, and cultivation techniques. These have increased agricultural production, principally in *monsoon* Asia.

Gross domestic product (GDP) like *gross national product (GNP)*, the total market value of goods and services produced in a country in a year; unlike GNP, GDP does not include income derived from overseas investments but does include production within the country produced by foreigners. The distinction between GDP and GNP is slim, and variations in definition are found from country to country and among economists.

Gross National Product (GNP) the total value of all goods and services produced within a country (or smaller administrative unit) in any given year.

Ground water subsurface water that saturates pores and crevices in the soil at a given depth below the surface and moves by gravity.

Growing season generally the number of frost-free days at any given location on the earth.

Guano hardened deposit of bird or bat excrement, rich in nitrates and used in the manufacture of fertilizers and explosives.

Gulf Stream a warm-water ocean current that flows out of the Gulf of Mexico, passes through the Florida Straits, parallels the east coast of the United States, and turns eastward across the North Atlantic toward northwestern Europe, where it is known as the North Atlantic Drift. The Gulf Stream is responsible for higher than average temperatures in adjacent coastal zones.

Hacienda a large estate in Central America.

Hadith in Islam, a compendium of sayings of the Prophet Muhammad written after his death.

Hamlet a tiny, usually *agglomerated*, village, often related to a nearby larger settlement.

Hammada rock-strewn desert plains and *plateaus* in the Sahara.

Headwaters the source of a stream or river.

Heartland the center of action, a vital and strategic place.

Heath a tract of wasteland where heather, a shrubby *evergreen*, berry plants, mosses, and sorrel have replaced woodlands as the dominant vegetation.

Hegira the flight of Muhammad, Prophet of Islam, from Mecca to Medina in A.D. 622; the date on which the lunar-based Muslim calendar begins.

Hierarchical diffusion the spread of ideas or goods from one important individual or group to another down hierarchical social chains; see *diffusion*.

Hierarchy generally a graded series; in geography a ranked series of settlements or type of *diffusion*.

Higher level market town one level in a *hierarchy* of settlements or *central places*; see *central place theory*.

High pressure a reference to level of atmospheric pressure as registered in millibars. High pressure as compared with adjacent areas is associated with outflowing air and clear, settled weather conditions.

High stationary the first phase of the *demographic transition*; see *demographic transition*.

Hinterland the surrounding area over which a city or any *central place* exerts influence, and on which it draws to sustain services, industry, and population.

Homeland alternative term for *bantustan*, a racially segregated self-governing reserve for the black African population of South Africa; see *apartheid*.

Homesteading a movement in North America rooted in the belief that the public domain belonged to the people and that every family was entitled to a debt-free home or farm. It culminated in the Homestead Act of 1862 under which all heads of family in the United States were entitled to 160 acres of land in the public domain after occupancy and cultivation for five years. Similar legislation was passed in Canada.

Horizontal nomadism the periodic movement of herds over long distances in search of pasture.

Hsien term used for walled city, a county capital, or the county itself in traditional China.

Human ecology the science of the mutual relationship between human beings and their *environment*.

Hunting and gathering subsistence way of life based on food collection instead of food production.

Iberia a 230,000-square-mile peninsula in Europe composed of Spain and Portugal.

Imam a man of learned authority in religious matters in Islam; prayer leader.

Inanimate energy energy derived from nonliving sources: mineral (coal, petroleum, natural gas), solar, geothermal, nuclear.

Independent invention inventions or innovations that arise independently without communication or contact; see *diffusion*.

Index contour a *contour line* accentuated by darkening to facilitate ease of reading a topographic map.

Indigo a plant whose leaves yield a dark blue dye.

Indo-European descriptive of a world family of languages, encompassing most European languages, and having more speakers than any other language family (over 2 billion people). So named because speakers of Indo-European languages are spread from India to Europe, although some languages spoken in this area are not Indo-European. Shared characteristics have led linguists to speculate that there may be a common ancestor to languages from English to Italian to Greek to Persian to the languages of North India.

Industrial Revolution the transformation of life in eighteenth-century Britain that involved advances in the use of inanimate energy and resources, the development of the factory system, industrialization, and *urbanization*.

Infant mortality rate the annual number of deaths of children under age one per 1000 live births in a given year.

Infrastructure those elements of financial, transportation, communication, and industrial systems that make economic development possible. The infrastructure supports and generates further economic development and capital investments.

Inlet a small opening in the shoreline of an ocean, lake, or river.

Intermontane, intermontane basin, in-

termontane valley descriptive of land lying between mountain ranges.

Interpolation a *cartographic* procedure used to determine the values of points located between two *isolines*.

Introduced language a foreign language, introduced through *colonial*, *mercantile*, or military policy, that plays a distinctive role in the society into which it has been implanted. An introduced language may come to hold equal rank with the native language(s) and even replace preexisting languages.

Irrigation artificial distribution of water by the construction of channels from the water source or storage place to a point of need.

Isohyet a line on a map that connects points of equal precipitation in a given period of time; see *isoline*.

Isoline a line that connects points of equal value on a map.

Isopleth a line on a map that connects points having the same value of an abstract concept such as population density; see *isoline*.

Isotherm a line on a map connecting points of equal temperature over a given period of time; see *isoline*.

Isthmus a narrow strip of land, bounded on two sides by water, that connects two larger land masses.

Jajmani system of reciprocal exchange of services among landlords, dependent artisans, and field workers in North India.

Jati the Indian word for "birth" or sub-caste; see *caste*.

Jet stream fast-moving rivers of air in the upper atmosphere in the *midlatitudes*.

Jowar a sorghum cultivated in India.

Jungle a dense, impenetrable tangle of low trees, climbing vines, and thick undergrowth that occurs where streams and highways in the *tropics* open *rain forests* to sunlight. Also called *gallery forest*.

Karma in Hinduism, the concept of an accounting of good and evil.

Kettle lake water-filled depression in *glaciated* landscape formed after a large ice block embedded in *glacial drift* melts.

Kibbutz a *collective* farm or settlement in Israel.

Kibbutzim people who live on *collective* farms or settlements in Israel.

Kolkhoz a *collective* farm in the Soviet Union in which the members of a village or villages pool their labor and land under government supervision and are paid in shares of the harvest; see *collectivization*.

Koran the book composed of writings accepted by Muslims as revelations made to Muhammad by Allah through the Angel Gabriel.

Ladino a member of the *mestizo* aristocracy in Guatemala.

Lagoon a stretch of coastal water separated from the open sea by a narrow strip of land—a *coral reef*, *atoll*, island, *offshore bar*, or *spit*.

Landlocked descriptive of a country or region with no seacoast and thus without direct access to the sea.

Land reform the giving of farmland to landless *peasants* to achieve a more equitable distribution of agricultural land among the rural population and to end *absentee landlordism* and *tenancy*.

Landsat name of two *remote sensing* satellites and the images derived from them that are orbiting the earth at an elevation of 570 miles.

Landscape the visible scene including both man-made and natural elements and patterns; see *cultural landscape*.

Land tenure a variety of forms of land ownership and control including *absentee landlordism*, *sharecropping*, and *tenancy*.

Large-scale map a map that covers a small area in detail, usually at a *scale* of 1:1,000,000 or 1 inch equals 16 miles or more; see *scale*.

Laterite a soil commonly found in the humid *tropics*, rich in iron and aluminum but poor in humus, and *leached* of other soil nutrients.

Latifundio great estates owned by the landed elite in Latin America.

Latifundismo the landholding system in Latin America in which a small wealthy elite owns large amounts of land.

Latitude arc of a *meridian* or line of *longitude* between the equator and a given point on the globe; see *parallel*.

Leaching a process by which minerals and organic matter percolate downward through successive layers of soil, or are entirely removed from the soil structure by intense and prolonged rainfall.

Leeward a coast or mountain range that faces away from the direction of prevailing winds; see *rain shadow*.

Legumes fruits or seeds from leguminous plants used for food. Leguminosae is a large plant family that includes clovers, beans, peas, and lentils. Most legumes have root nodules with nitrogen-fixing bacteria and are thereby useful in enhancing nitrogen in the soil.

Levee a natural or artificial embankment (*dike*) along a low-lying river that protects the surrounding area from flooding.

Linear scale a form of map *scale* that uses a small ruler on the map to measure units of distance on the map in terms of real-world distance in whole numbers of miles or kilometers; see *scale*.

Line symbol the most widely used map symbol. It is utilized to suggest connectivity from one point to another, similar characteristics along the length of the line, or differences on either side of the line. Like *point symbols*, line symbols can suggest differences in intensity on a map through changes in size, texture, color, or color intensity.

Lingua franca a common language. Originally, lingua franca was a distinct language derived from a number of others and served as a common language in the mercantile society of the Mediterranean. Today, any language that allows communication between peoples with different languages is considered a lingua franca.

Littoral a seacoast that is directly affected by its neighboring water body; a seashore.

Llanero a rancher-cowboy of the Orinoco lowlands of Venezuela.

Llanos a tropical *savanna* grassland located in the Orinoco Basin of Venezuela and the Guiana Highlands on the northern margins of the Amazon Basin; see *pampas*, *savanna*.

Llanos orientales tropical *savanna* grasslands on the eastern slopes of the Andes.

Loess airborne dust that is carried on prevailing air currents and falls to create a deposit of fine soil that in some places may cover large areas with a thick mantle. Loess soil is highly porous and generally very fertile.

Longitude arc of a *parallel* between the prime *meridian* (longitude 0°) and a given point on the surface of the globe; see *meridian*.

Long lot long, narrow parcel of land stretching back from a river, road, or canal in French Canada and elsewhere.

Low Countries the European countries of the Netherlands, Belgium, and Luxembourg. Northern Belgium and the Netherlands (Holland) form a low plain, much of which is below sea level; southern Belgium and all of Luxembourg are in the upland Ardennes Plateau. However, they are collectively known as the Low Countries, a term not so topographic as political and historic.

Low pressure a reference to level of atmospheric pressure as registered in millibars. Low pressure as compared with adjacent areas is associated with inflowing air and cloudy, unsettled weather conditions.

Lut salt-encrusted *desert* in Iran.

Mandate system of *trusteeships* established by the League of Nations following World War I to administer former Turkish territories and German colonies. Obligations to the League and to the populations of the mandates were intended to avoid the pitfalls of *colonialism*. Mandates remaining after World War II became United Nations Trust Territories.

Map projection a number of systems by which the curved surface of the earth is projected onto a flat plane in the form of a map. Map projections may be *conformal* or *equal-area*. Three families of map projections classified by method of construct are *azimuthal*, *conic*, and *cylindrical*.

Maquis thick, *scrub* underbrush found along the shores of the Mediterranean Sea.

Marchland a frontier or border *region* whose boundaries are vaguely defined and subject to conflicting national claims, invasion, and repeated transfers of power.

Maritime climate a climate characterized by moderate temperature, medium to high rainfall, and high humidity generally found along coasts.

Market area, market center, market town trading center where the produce of the surrounding countryside (the *hinterland* or *market area*) is sold, exchanged, or bartered for a limited number of urban services and non-agricultural goods. Basic-level market towns are small, lower-order settlements woven into a network throughout the countryside; *higher level market towns* offer a greater range of services, have larger populations and draw on this network; see *central place theory*.

Mason-Dixon line the cultural boundary between the North and the South in the United States.

Massif a mountainous block of land whose peaks do not form lines as in a mountain range.

Mediterranean climate transition *climate* between the *subtropical deserts* nearer the equator and the cool, moist climates farther poleward. Best displayed in the Mediterranean Basin, this climate is characterized by summer drought and a winter rainfall maximum.

Megalopolis a great urban *region* including many cities that have expanded and coalesced to form an extensive continuous zone of urbanization.

Mercantile colonialism colonies established for trade with the mother country; colonies in which the primary interest was trade, not *settler colonialism*.

Mercantile enclave usually on a coast, a small colony established for trading purposes.

Mercantilism European economic system, generally preceding and supplanted by *capitalism*, that held that the economic and political strength of a country could be measured in the amount of silver and gold it acquired, that imports were bad, and that colonies should be established to serve the resource needs of the mother country. In turn, manufacturing was discouraged or prohibited in the colonies.

Meridian a line of *longitude* stretching 180° from pole to pole and serving as a measurement of distance east or west of the standard meridian (0°), which passes through Greenwich, England. One degree of *longitude* (one *meridian*) progressively decreases in distance poleward.

Mestizo a person of mixed American Indian and European ancestry in Latin America.

Metes and bounds the system of land division used in settling the American South based on landmarks and property lines.

Metropolitan Statistical Area (MSA) United States Bureau of the Census measure of urbanization; a county that contains a central city of 50,000 population or more, or a group of contiguous counties, each with a central city of 50,000 or more.

Metropolis a very large and important urban center.

Microclimate *climate* of a shallow layer of air near the ground or of a small area.

Midlatitude the zone between 35° and 55° north and south *latitude* on either side of the equator. Here, contrasts between seasons are strong, but neither winter nor summer is harsh enough to seriously limit human activity.

Migration the movement of people, *migrants*, from one country, place, or locale to another.

Millet an officially recognized ethnic, linguistic, or religious community in the Middle East during the Ottoman period.

Minifundio tiny plots of land owned by *peasants* in Latin America; in contrast with the great estates or *latifundios*.

Mir traditional communal village in Russia.

Mixed farming agricultural system based on combination of crop cultivation and animal husbandry.

Model in the social sciences, a representation of reality, or some aspects of reality, selected to explain relationships or assertions about reality. A model may attempt to represent reality in totality; a model may be an analog of reality or a mere symbol of reality. A model presented in this text is the Demographic Transition.

Moisture stress condition under which plants are affected by insufficient moisture.

Moksha the Hindu term for unity with the universal spirit or *atman* in Hinduism, called *nirvana* in Buddhism.

Monadnock an isolated hill of resistant rock which rises above the surrounding countryside.

Monocrop a crop produced as the sole product in a given agricultural operation. A monocrop is usually a *commodity crop* produced under high technology conditions.

Monotheism a religion focused on a single god.

Monsoon any air current that blows steadily from one direction for weeks or months.

Monsoon forest the forest of *monsoon* regions, in which the marked dry season is interrupted by the annual monsoon, bringing 40 to 80 inches of rain. The resultant monsoon forest is composed of *deciduous* broadleafed trees, most of which are hardwoods. Teak is an important commercial tree in the monsoon forest.

Montane forest forest vegetation characteristic of cool upland *environments* in the *tropics*.

Moraine masses of boulders, rocks, and soil carried and ultimately deposited by a *glacier* and the resulting landform. *Moraines* left behind during a period of glacial retreat often appear on the *landscape* as parallel ranges of low hills, their surfaces pockmarked by depressions, holding ponds, or small lakes, with an irregular drainage pattern.

Mortality rate the number of deaths in a given time or place or the proportion of deaths to population; see *death rate*.

Moshav a cooperative agricultural settlement composed of small farmers in Israel.

Mountain and valley a corrugated topography of parallel ridges and valleys, notably found in the central Appalachians. Also called *ridge and valley*.

M·latto a person of mixed white and black descent.

Multinational corporation a business enterprise that operates in several countries but with headquarters in only one.

Muskeg a *bog* in the *coniferous* forests or *tundra* zone in Canada.

Nationalism movement of people sharing a common language, faith, or ethnic background to form their own independent state.

Nationality in the Soviet Union, ethnicity. One of the more than 100 officially recognized ethnic groups—a people with a separate historical heritage, language, religion, race, traditional homeland, or other aspect of ethnicity.

Nationalization the act of the state in taking control over a private enterprise or private property more generally, with or without compensation.

Nation-building process in former colonial societies, or in new countries with few common traditions, the progress toward development of national consciousness.

Natural hazard an extreme natural event that threatens or affects human activity.

Natural increase the surplus of births over deaths in a given place and population.

Neocolonial descriptive of (1) structures in a former colonial state that maintain colonial economic, political, or social relationships; (2) a situation in which a powerful foreign power intervenes in the affairs of a former colonial state. The two countries may not necessarily have been joined as colonial power and colony in the past.

Neolithic referring to people or culture of the New Stone Age (in Britain 2500–1900 B.C.). Varies in time from place to place, usually followed by Iron Age.

New town an urban center constructed in a nonurban landscape, designed and financed by a central government to plan and regulate urban growth.

Nirvana the concept of unity with the universal spirit in Buddhism.

Nomad member of a migratory group of *pastoralists*.

Nonferrous metal any metal not containing iron. Nonferrous metals fall into two general categories: those used alone or in combination with other nonferrous metals to yield materials known for specific properties, such as copper, aluminum, or brass; and those alloyed with iron to yield special irons and steels—the *ferroalloys*.

Oasis: a fertile, watered area in the midst of a *desert*.

Offshore bar ridge of sand deposited a short distance offshore by the action of the waves, winds, and currents.

Oil-bearing shale a kind of rock containing oil in dispersed form.

Oligarchy government by a few people, usually a self-selected and self-limiting group, often a group of the rich.

OPEC cartel of oil-producing and exporting nations, the Organization of Petroleum Exporting Countries, formed in 1960.

Orbis Terrarum circular world map combining theology and *cartography* common in the Roman and medieval periods in Europe.

Organization of American States (OAS) a pan-American international organization, founded in 1948 and with permanent headquarters in Washington, D.C., to promote cooperation, raise living standards, and defend the territorial integrity and independence of the Western Hemisphere states. A significant nonmember is Canada.

Orographic precipitation precipitation caused by the forced rise of moist air over a mountain barrier.

Outwash plains flat or gently sloping plain built up by water flowing out of melting *glacier*; see *glaciation*.

Paddy, Padi fields of wet rice.

Paheka Maori term for whites in New Zealand.

Paleolithic of the Old Stone Age, the longest period of human development, generally coinciding with the Pleistocene, or Glacial, geologic epoch; began about 1.5 million years ago, and ended variously between 40,000 and 8,000 B.C. It identifies a period of evolution of humankind from apelike creatures to true human beings, all of whom were *Homo sapiens* at the end of the Paleolithic period. Paleolithic human culture was marked by hunting and gathering and achievement of stone and bone tools, weapons, and ornaments.

Pampas the *midlatitude prairie* grasslands of Argentina.

Pantheism religion that tolerates or encompasses all gods of different creeds.

Parallel a line drawn parallel to the equator (0°) in ever smaller concentric circles to the north or south. One degree of *latitude* (one *parallel*) is equal to approximately 69 miles everywhere on the earth's surface; see *latitude*.

Pastoral descriptive of cultures, economies, and societies dependent upon herding of grazing animals.

Pastoralism; pastoral nomadism way of life based on animal herding practiced by shepherds and *nomads*.

Pays a small, distinctive *culture region* in France.

Peasantry an agricultural class of low status in a society of rigid class structure; often landless agricultural laborers.

Peat a black or brown fibrous low-grade fuel of decomposed organic matter that accumulates in a *bog*.

Peninsula a stretch of land projecting into a sea or lake.

Perennial irrigation man-made system of water storage and distribution that makes water for *irrigation* available year round; see *irrigation*.

Periodic market nonpermanent markets that are held in the countryside or urban centers, usually at regular intervals.

Periphery the spatial fringes, see *core and periphery*.

Permafrost permanently frozen subsoil found in subarctic or arctic *regions*.

Permeable barrier a cultural or physical obstacle that weakens, slows, or channels *diffusion*; see *diffusion*.

action of sunlight on pollutant gases produces new toxic gases and compounds; see *pollution, smog.*

Pictographic point symbol   point symbol whose shape indicates the phenomena being located, e.g., an oil derrick; see *point, line,* and *area symbols.*

Piedmont   hilly, rolling land, lying at the foot of a mountain range and forming a transition between mountain and plain.

Pig iron   iron ore that has been partially refined by burning with *coke.* Cast into molds called "pigs," this crude iron may be further refined into cast iron, wrought iron, or steel.

Plantation   large agricultural estate, usually devoted to the cultivation of a single export crop such as rubber, bananas, cotton, sugarcane, sisal, or coffee; see *monocrop, commodity crop.*

Plateau   an extensive level stretch of land raised above the surrounding *landscape,* often exhibiting sharply defined edges in the form of *escarpments.*

Podzol   acid, infertile soil that underlies *evergreen* forests (*taiga*) in cool, moist climates and covers large areas of Canada and Russia.

Point symbols   a wide variety of marks on a map that refer to the specific, point-location of a phenomenon through graphic representation. A dot on a *dot map* is a point symbol. Distinguished from *area symbols* and *line symbols* by reference more to place than to line or area.

Polar air   cold air mass originating in *polar latitudes.*

Polar latitudes   those *latitudes* located between 66½° and 90° N and S.

Polder   land reclaimed from the sea or an inland lake by the construction of protective *dikes;* the enclosed area is pumped dry and the resulting polderland is brought under cultivation.

Pollution   contamination of land, water, and air by chemicals, and/or gases that are often by-products of human activity; see *photochemical smog, smog.*

Polytheism   religion that encompasses several gods, for example Hinduism.

Pope's line   line drawn 370 leagues west of the Cape Verde Islands by Pope Alexander VI to divide the unexplored New World into a Spanish (western) and a Portuguese (eastern) sphere of influence. Located on the fiftieth *meridian,* the Pope's line cuts through the shoulder of modern Brazil.

Population pressure   not a specific den-

try's capacity to sustain its population given its level of economic development and natural and human resources.

Population pyramid   a type of bar graph illustrating the percentage of a given population by age group and sex.

Postindustrial   descriptive of a form of society and economy believed by some observers to be replacing industrialized societies and economies of the Technological World; most characterized by pronounced shift of labor force into *service* or *tertiary* sectors of the economy; implies structural changes in population and spatial order characteristic of high technology societies.

Potential evapotranspiration   water need; the rate of evaporation and transpiration estimated to occur from a continuous cover of growing plants supplied with all the soil water they need.

Prairie grasslands   grass-covered land found in *subhumid climates* in the *midlatitudes.*

Precolumbian   descriptive of societies and environments of the Western Hemisphere before the voyages of Columbus (1492–1504), which marked the end of isolation for the Americas and the beginnings of European conquest and transformation.

Preindustrial   before the Industrial Revolution, and following the Agricultural and Urban Revolutions of ancient times. Such societies were characterized by lack of industry based on fossil fuels; little specialization of labor; predominantly rural populations that supported minority urban populations in which power and civilization resided; and rigid kinship systems, ensuring little social mobility.

Pressure gradient   the slope in atmospheric pressure between areas of *high pressure* and adjacent areas of *low pressure.*

Primacy, primate city   a measure of the relative dominance of a given city over the total urban system of an area, usually a country, as expressed in terms of population size vis à vis other national cities.

Primary sector   *sector of the economy* that encompasses activities dealing with materials drawn directly from the earth: agriculture, mining, quarrying, forestry, fishing, hunting. Also referred to as primary industry and primary activity.

Protectorate   a form of colonization in which a country and its existing government are placed under the overseership ("protection") of a colonial power. In some cases, a colonial power was asked to provide authority over a society in order to keep it from being taken by another colonial power; in other cases, the establishment of a protectorate was merely a cover for full-blown colonial intentions.

Qanat   a gravity-fed subterranean *irrigation* tunnel in the Middle East and North Africa.

Quantitative area symbol   map symbol used to convey changes in magnitude by variations in texture, color, or color intensity. Used for phenomena that extend over regions; see *area, line,* and *point symbols.*

Quebracho   forest and *scrub* composed of semideciduous trees and shrubs in South America.

Rain forest   forest located in a belt straddling the equator where rainfall is heavy and there is no dry season. Because of high temperatures and sustained precipitation, forest growth is luxuriant, and a leafy canopy of *evergreen* trees forms a roof over the forest floor. The number of different species of flora and fauna in the tropical rain forest is greater than in any other natural *environment.*

Rain shadow   an area with relatively lower precipitation on the lee side of a mountain range. When moisture-laden air crosses a mountain range, it is forced to rise and drop its moisture on the *windward* slopes as the *air mass* cools; when it descends, this air is warmed and dried, so that the lee area receives less rain than surrounding areas.

Rectangular area cartogram   a *cartogram* in which each *region* is transformed into a rectangle proportionate to the magnitude of the data being presented; see *cartogram.*

Reef   see *coral reef.*

Region   in geography, the name for a distinctive set of physical or cultural features that lend special character to a place and set it off from other places. An elastic term, region may refer to large-scale areas such as the world regions discussed in this book or to smaller scale, more local areas.

Relative humidity   amount of water va-

perature relative to the maximum amount of water vapor the air could hold at that temperature. The higher the *relative humidity,* the muggier or damper the air.

Relocation diffusion   *diffusion* effected by the movement of people from one area to another; see *diffusion.*

Remote sensing   rapidly growing area of geographical information gathered from airborne surveillance of the earth by sensing devices mounted on aircraft and satellites.

Repartimiento   a labor system in *colonial* Latin America under which Indian laborers were temporarily assigned to Spanish colonists for specific projects.

Representative fraction   a method of expressing map scale stated as the ratio of map distance to earth distance; see *scale.*

Ridge and valley   a corrugated band of alternating uplands and lowlands in the Appalachian Mountains.

Runoff   rain and other precipitation that run off the land through stream flow; a major agent of *erosion.* The amount of precipitation that becomes runoff is largely determined by the intensity of rainfall and the permeability of the soil.

Russification   process of inculcating Russian culture into non-Russian ethnic groups in the Soviet Union; language is a primary agent; part of the Soviet *nation-building process.*

Salinization   the accumulation and concentration of salts in the upper levels of the soil. Salinization is a problem wherever *irrigation* is practiced if salts carried by irrigation water accumulate in fields.

Samurai   the warrior class of medieval Japan; also their rigid code of behavior called *bushido.*

Savanna   a grassland with scattered trees and bushes usually found on the margins of equatorial *rain forests.*

Sawah   Indonesian term for *paddy* or wet rice cultivation.

Scale   the factor or ratio used to reduce distance measured on the surface of the earth in miles or kilometers to distance on a map measured in inches or centimeters.

Scarped plateau   *plateau* set sharply above adjoining lowlands by a cliff or steep slope.

Scholarization   percentage of school-age children actually in school.

Scratch plow   light, primitive wooden or metal-tipped plow often made of a tree branch.

Scrub   area covered with vegetation consisting of low trees, bushes, and drought-resistant plants, often found on the margins of forests where rainfall is insufficient or soils too poor for the growth of denser plant life.

Section   a 640-acre subdivision equal to one thirty-sixth of a *township* in the United States *township and range* system of land surveying; see *township and range.*

Sectors of the economy   division of the economy into three sectors, separated by the type of activity conducted: *primary, secondary,* and *tertiary* (or *service*).

Sedentary, sedentarization   permanently settled, fixed to fields and towns; the process of anchoring *nomads* and *shifting cultivators* to a permanently settled existence.

Sedimentary   descriptive of rocks formed by the deposition of *alluvial* materials in distinct layers called strata.

Seigneur   a feudal lord in French Canada who held land (a *seigneurie*) by feudal tenure until 1854; see *feudalism.*

Seigneurie   large tracts of land in French Canada awarded to French noblemen (*seigneurs*) and the church by the French kings. These land grants were later subdivided into smaller tracts for individual settlers, who organized them into landscapes of *long lots* along the St. Lawrence River.

Selva   term for *rain forest* used in Latin America; see *rain forest.*

Seminomadism   a combination of herding and cultivation practiced on the fringes of settled agricultural communities.

Sequent occupance   a sequence of settlements or *cultural landscapes* suggesting distinctive stages of occupance.

Sericulture   the raising of mulberry trees and silkworms to produce commercial silk cloth. The silkworm (a moth larva) thrives on the leaves of the white mulberry tree; it weaves a web of raw silk that is subsequently harvested and spun into cloth.

Sertão   thinly occupied, pioneer land in Brazil.

Service sector   *sector of the economy,* also identified as *tertiary,* that deals in selling of goods and services—wholesaling, retailing, education, health, government administration, construction, design, and information industries.

Settler colonialism   *colonialism* with an aim to settle significant numbers of people from the mother country in the colony. The colony may be previously unpopulated, lightly populated, or relatively densely populated—all cases exist.

Shantytown   unplanned residential zone constructed of cast-off materials on vacant land in or near the city; generated by population growth and urban migration and usually inhabited by people new to urban life and unable to find housing and jobs. The shantytown is known by different names in different societies; *favela* in Brazil, *bidonville* in French-speaking Africa, *barrio* in Mexico, *bustee* in India.

Sharecropping   a system of farming in which the cultivator raises crops and pays for the use of the land by giving a fixed share of the harvest to the landlord as rent; see *absentee landlordism, land tenure, tenancy.*

Sharia   the religious principles of Islamic law.

Shatt   in Arabic, a beach or strand. The word has taken on a more specific meaning as a shallow, brackish, interior-drainage saltwater lake in North Africa. In Iraq, at the mouth of the Tigris-Euphrates, the mixed salt and freshwater Shatt al Arab is a similar phenomenon.

Shield   continental platform of extremely ancient rocks exposed above sea level; soils are poor and human population densities low; mineral deposits may be exposed and readily extracted.

Shifting cultivation   cultivation by the periodic, piecemeal removal of forest or *scrub* cover by burning or slashing; also known as *slash and burn* agriculture.

Shogun   feudal military leader or generalissimo in medieval Japan.

Shogunate   the feudal government of Japan, under which a *shogun* (generalissimo) and his clan ruled in the name of the emperor, who was kept cloistered and powerless.

Silt   a deposit of fine particles deposited in rivers, streams, lakes, and seas.

Sinification   process of inculcating Chinese culture into non-Chinese ethnic groups in the People's Republic of China; major agent is Chinese language. Part of the Chinese *nation-building process.*

Slash and burn agriculture alternative term for *shifting cultivation;* see *shifting cultivation.*

Slum a densely populated urban area characterized by crowding, run-down housing, poor services, poverty, and social disorganization.

Small scale map a map that covers a large area, usually not showing much detail; see *scale.*

Smog mixture of particles and chemical pollutants in the lower atmosphere, usually found over urban areas; see *pollution.*

Socialism; socialist economy a variety of political and economic theories and systems of social organization based on *collective* or governmental ownership and administration of the means of production and the distribution of goods.

Soil moisture recharge restoration of depleted soil water by infiltration of precipitation; see *water-balance budget.*

Soil moisture utilization depletion of soil water by natural process and human utilization; see *water-balance budget.*

Solar radiation solar energy received by an exposed surface.

Sovkhoz a government-owned *collective* farm in the Soviet Union in which the members of a village or villages work for wages; see *collectivization.*

Spatial diffusion the spread of goods, people, and ideas through space; see *diffusion.*

Sphere the zone of outer influence of a *culture region* with lower levels of concentration, intensity of occupance, and homogeneity than either the *core* or the *domain;* see *culture region.*

Spit a narrow, fingerlike extension of sand into the open water of a bay.

Squatter settlement see *shantytown.*

Standard parallel the circle (or circles) of tangency where the cone touches the surface of the earth on a *conic projection;* see *map projection.*

Steppe *midlatitude* grassland, generally treeless and level plain, that covers a vast area in the interior of the Eurasian landmass.

Stimulus diffusion a type of *expansion diffusion* where a specific culture element is rejected but the underlying concept is accepted; see *diffusion.*

Strait a narrow stretch of sea connecting two extensive areas of sea or ocean.

Strip farming a pattern of cropping in medieval Europe whereby fields were laid out in long, narrow strips.

Strip mining the removal of the earth's soil mantle to expose a vein or lode of minerals near the surface.

Subhumid climate the climate of the drier margins of moist *regions.*

Subsistence agriculture an agricultural system in which most of the produce is consumed directly by the farm family rather than being traded or marketed.

Subtropics *latitudes* from the *tropics* to approximately 35° both north and south of the equator characterized by distinct seasonal changes in *climate.*

Suburb smaller community or communities adjacent to or within commuting distance of a city or large town.

Suburbanization the extension of residential areas outward from the *central business district (CBD)* of a city.

Summer monsoon an air current that flows from sea to land in summer in South Asia associated with heavy precipitation; see *monsoon.*

Suttee the now-outlawed custom of a Hindu widow to willingly be cremated on the funeral pyre of her husband.

Tableland a broad, level elevated mass set off from the sea or adjoining lowlands by steep, clifflike edges; see *plateau.*

Taiga the *coniferous* forests that cover much of subarctic Russia, Scandinavia, and North America.

Tailing hills mounds of crushed rock debris from which ore has been extracted located near mines and ore processing plants.

Take-off that stage in the development of an industrial society when the conditions for an internal industrial revolution are met and sudden change—"the great watershed in the life of modern societies"—begins to take hold. Thereafter, increasing production, consumption, wealth, and the notion of continual progress become the normal and expected course of events.

Talmud the written authoritative body of Jewish tradition.

Tar sand sand holding vast quantities of petroleum in a suspended, dispersed state; see *oil-bearing shale.*

Temperate latitudes alternative term for the *midlatitudes;* see *midlatitude.*

Temperature inversion an increase of warm air with altitude so that warm air overlies colder, contrary to the normal state. Temperature inversions can be induced by concentrations of *pollutants* and heat production with a stable *air mass.*

Tenancy a system of farming whereby a farmer pays the landowner cash rental for the right to farm the land; see *sharecropping.*

Terrace in agriculture, a raised and embanked plot of hillside land made level and planted to crops.

Tertiary sector see *service sector.*

Theocracy a government directed by religious officials or a single leader regarded as divinely guided.

Thermal lapse rate the rate of 3.3 degrees per thousand feet that atmospheric temperature decreases with elevation.

Tideland; tidewater the coastal plain of eastern Virginia, a lowland cut by rivers and indented by *estuaries.*

Tierra caliente the hot, coastal lowlands and *piedmont* (usually below 2,500 feet in elevation) in the Andes Mountains of Latin America.

Tierra fria the cool upland elevations (usually above 6,000 feet) in the Andes Mountains of Latin America.

Tierra templada the *temperate* middle elevations (usually between 2,500 and 6,000 feet) in the Andes Mountains of Latin America.

Time composite map a map showing the areal expansion or contraction of a single phenomenon at different time intervals.

Time-distance decay the progressive weakening of a *diffusion* farther from the point of origin and with a decreasing level of acceptance through time; see *diffusion.*

Topography the configuration of a land surface including its elevations and the position of its natural and man-made features.

Township an area of 6 square miles; the basic unit of land division in the United States *township and range* system of land surveying; see *township and range.*

Township and range system by which most of the United States west of the Appalachians was laid out and mapped. The basic unit of land division was the *township*, 6 miles square in area, laid out along an east-west base line—a line of *latitude* also called the township line. Every 6 miles along it, a line of *longitude* called a range line divided the townships into equal units. In this way, a geometrical grid of latitude and longitude (here called *township and range*) was imposed on the landscape in advance of settlement.

Trade wind the continuously flowing *easterly* wind system of the low *latitudes* at low elevations also called the *easterlies*.

Transhumance the seasonal movement of people and animals from lowland to highland *environments* in search of pasture. Also called *vertical nomadism*.

Transliteration the reproduction of the sounds of words in one language or alphabet with those of another language or alphabet. Although internationally accepted systems exist for transliteration, and despite the fact that general agreement exists that the place-names used in the language of the country in which they are found should be used internationally, this is not likely to occur. Entrenched usage of such a common place-name as "Cairo" in English is not likely to be replaced by "Al Qahira" (as it should be according to the Arabic).

Treaty port in China, port cities that were opened to foreign trade under treaty.

Tree line the upper limit of tree growth in mountains or high latitudes.

Triangular trade a three-part trading pattern between *colonial* America and England, Africa, and the Caribbean; the slave trade was the cornerstone of this exchange.

Tributary a stream or river that joins a larger one.

Tropical; tropics the area between the Tropic of Cancer (23½° north *latitude*) and the Tropic of Capricorn (23½° south latitude), characterized by the relative absence of a cold season, high daily temperatures, and strong sun.

Trusteeship a territory administered by authority of the United Nations, as was Papua New Guinea by Australia before independence. Inheritor to the League of Nations' *mandate* program.

Tsetse fly fly of the African *rain forest* that infects people and animals with parasitic diseases such as sleeping sickness.

Tundra a zone between the northern limit of trees and the *polar* region in North America, Europe, and Asia. Tundra areas have only one summer month with an average temperature above freezing; their vegetation is composed of grasses, sedges, lichens, and shrubs.

Typhoon an intense moving cyclone of *tropical* and *subtropical latitudes* in the Pacific and Indian Oceans with heavy rain and high winds.

Ulama the learned and respected religious leaders in Islam entrusted with the responsibility of interpreting and applying religious doctrine.

Urban field the *daily urban system* within which the American upper and middle classes sleep, eat, live, and pursue their careers. Also called *daily urban system*.

Urban hierarchy a group of *central places*, usually towns and cities, ranked in importance by population, the number and range of goods and services provided, and the area or *hinterland*, being served; see *central place, central place hierarchy, central place theory*.

Urbanization the *migration* of people to urban centers; the percentage of a given population living in urban areas.

Vaquero the Spanish term for a rancher-cowboy in Rio Grande del Norte (modern Texas).

Variable class interval maps on which the spacing or interval between *isolines* changes; see *class interval*.

Veld the open grassland that covers the *tableland* of South Africa.

Vertical nomadism the seasonal shifting of herds between lowland and highland *environments* in search of pasture. Also called *transhumance*.

Volcanic soils soils formed of volcanic dust, ash, rock fragments, and weathered lava; if well watered, they are very fertile.

Volcanism the entire range of processes associated with the movement of molten rock and other volcanic materials from the interior of the earth into the earth's crust or onto the earth's surface. The element within volcanism, called the *volcano* is best known but only a part of the entire process.

Volcano conical hill or mountain composed of lava flows, rock fragments, and ash spewn from a vent in the earth's crust.

Voyageurs the fur traders and trappers of French Canada.

Wadi term for the dry gully, valley, or bed of an intermittent stream in the Middle East and North Africa.

Water-balance budget budget of precipitation, evapotranspiration, and changes in soil water storage for a given place over a given period of time.

Water deficiency when water need exceeds precipitation and available moisture in the soil has been used up; see *water-balance budget*.

Waterlogging a rise in the *water table* that brings ground water into the root zone of plants.

Watershed the drainage *basin* of a given stream. As streams join, their watersheds merge into a single system.

Water surplus when precipitation exceeds water need and the soil has the equivalent of four inches of rainfall; see *water-balance budget*.

Water table upper surface of the subterranean zone saturated by *ground water*.

Westerlies prevailing surface winds in the *midlatitudes* that generally blow from the southwest.

Windward coast a coast that faces the direction from which the wind is blowing.

World Bank an arm of the United Nations, the International Bank for Reconstruction and Development (IBRD), or World Bank, is headquartered in Washington, D.C. It functions, with the closely associated International Monetary Fund (IMF), to make loans to governments, furnish technical economic advice, expand international trade, and promote stability in currency exchange.

Xerophyte a plant adapted to an arid *environment*.

Yoga one of a number of paths individuals take to achieve union with the universal spirit in Hinduism.

Zaibatsu financial clique in Japan.

Zambo a person of mixed American Indian and black African ancestry in Latin America.

Zamindar an individual holding tax rights over cultivated land; tax collector in Mogul India.

Zero population growth (ZPG) a contemporary term indicating a population in equilibrium (births and deaths per 1,000 population approximately equal).

Ziggurat a step pyramid in ancient Mesopotamia.

BIBLIOGRAPHY

Chapter 1

Adams, R. M. *Land Behind Baghdad: A History of Settlement on the Diyala Plains.* Chicago: University of Chicago Press, 1965.

——. "Strategies of Maximization, Stability, and Resilience in Mesopotamian Society, Settlement, and Agriculture," *Proceedings of the American Philosophical Society*, Vol. 122 (1978), pp. 229–235.

——. *Heartland of Cities: Surveys of Ancient Settlement and Land Use on the Central Floodplain of the Euphrates.* Chicago: University of Chicago Press, 1981.

Adams, R. M. and Nissen, H. J. *The Uruk Countryside; The Natural Setting of Urban Societies.* Chicago: University of Chicago Press, 1972.

Ashton, T. S. *The Industrial Revolution: 1760–1830.* London: Oxford University Press, 1948.

Bloch, M. *Feudal Society.* Chicago: University of Chicago Press, 1961.

Bobek, H., "The Main Stages in Socioeconomic Evolution from a Geographic Point of View," in P. L. Wagner and M. W. Mikesell (eds.). *Readings in Cultural Geography.* Chicago: University of Chicago Press, 1962.

Braudel, F. (trans. S. Reynolds). *Civilization and Capitalism, 15th–18th Century,* Vol. I, *The Structures of Everyday Life.* New York: Harper & Row, 1981.

——. *Civilization and Capitalism, 15th–18th Century,* Vol. II, *The Wheels of Commerce.* New York: Harper & Row, 1982.

Bronowski, J. *The Ascent of Man.* Boston: Little, Brown, 1973.

Butzer, K. W. *Early Hydraulic Civilization in Egypt.* Chicago: University of Chicago Press, 1976.

——. *Archaeology as Human Ecology.* Cambridge: Cambridge University Press, 1982.

Butzer, K. W. et al. "Irrigation Agrosystems in Eastern Spain: Roman or Islamic Origins?" *Annals of the Association of American Geographers,* Vol. 75 (1985), pp. 479–509.

Clout, H. *The Land of France, 1815–1914.* Winchester, Mass.: Allen & Unwin, 1983.

Darby, H. C. (ed.). *A New Historical Geography of England.* Cambridge: Cambridge University Press, 1973.

Denevan, W. M. *The Native Population of the Americas in 1492.* Madison: University of Wisconsin Press, 1976.

Duby, G. *Rural Economy and Country Life in Medieval Europe.* Columbia: University of South Carolina Press, 1968.

Gregory, D. *Regional Transformation and Industrial Revolution.* Berkeley: University of California Press, 1982.

Grigg, D. B. *The Agricultural Systems of the World: An Evolutionary Approach.* New York: Cambridge University Press, 1974.

Harris, D. R. "Alternative Pathways Towards Agriculture," in C. A. Reed (ed.), *Origins of Agriculture.* The Hague: Mouton, 1977.

——(ed.). *Human Ecology in Savanna Environments.* New York: Academic Press, 1980.

Isaac, E. *Geography of Domestication.* Englewood Cliffs, N.J.: Prentice-Hall, 1970.

Kramer, S. N. *The Sumerians.* Chicago: University of Chicago Press, 1963.

Langer, W. L. "The Black Death," *Scientific American,* Vol. 231 (1964), pp. 114–121.

May, T. *An Economic and Social History of Britain, 1760–1970.* Harlow, Eng.: Longman, 1987.

Pounds, N. J. G. "The Urbanization of the Classical World," *Annals of the Association of American Geographers,* Vol. 59 (1969), pp. 135–150.

——. *An Historical Geography of Europe, 1500 to 1840.* Cambridge: Cambridge University Press, 1979.

Pred, A. *The External Relations of Cities During the Industrial Revolution.* Chicago: University of Chicago, Department of Geography, 1962.

——. *Urban Growth and City Systems in the United States.* Cambridge: Harvard University Press, 1980.

Rorig, F. *The Medieval Town.* Berkeley: University of California Press, 1971.

Sauer, C. O. *Agricultural Origins and Dispersals.* New York: American Geographical Society, 1952.

Siemens, A. H. "Wetland Agriculture in Pre-Hispanic Mesoamerica," *Geographical Review,* Vol. 73 (1983), pp. 166–181.

Simmons, I. G. and Tooley, M. J. (eds.). *The Environment in British Prehistory.* Ithaca, N.Y.: Cornell University Press, 1981.

Turner, B. L., Hanham, R. Q., and Portarero, A. V. "Population Pressure and Agricultural Intensity," *Annals of the Association of American Geographers,* Vol. 67 (1977), pp. 384–396.

Ucko, P. U. and Dimbleby, G. W. (eds.). *The Domestication and Exploitation of Plants and Animals.* Chicago: Aldine, 1969.

Ucko, P. U., Tringham, R., and Dimbleby, G. W. (eds.). *Man, Settlement, and Urbanism.* London: Duckworth, 1972.

Vance, J. E., Jr. *This Scene of Man: The Role and Structure of the City in the Geography of Western Civilization.* New York: Harper & Row, 1977.

Vigier, F. *Change and Apathy: Liverpool and Manchester During the Industrial Revolution.* Cambridge: MIT Press, 1970.

Wheatley, P. *The Pivot of the Four Quarters.* Chicago: Aldine, 1971.

White, L. T., Jr. *Medieval Technology and Social Change.* Oxford, Eng.: Clarendon Press, 1962.

Chapter 2

Barke, M. and O'Hare, G. *The Third World: Diversity, Change, and Interdependence.* Edinburgh: Oliver and Boyd, 1984.

Beckford, G. L. *Persistent Poverty: Underdevelopment in Plantation Economies of the Third World.* New York: Oxford University Press, 1972.

Berry, B. J. L. "Hierarchical Diffusion: The Basis of Development Filtering and Spread in a System of Cities," in N. M. Hansen (ed.), *Growth Centers in Regional Economic Development.* New York: Free Press, 1972.

Berry, B. J. L., Conkling, E. C., and Ray, D. M. *The Geography of Economic Systems.* Englewood Cliffs, N.J.: Prentice-Hall, 1982.

Black, C. E. *The Dynamics of Modernization: A Study in Comparative History.* New York: Harper & Row, 1966.

Boserup, E. *The Conditions of Agricultural Growth: The Economics of Agrarian Change Under Population Pressure.* Chicago: Aldine, 1965.

Brookfield, H. C. *Interdependent Development.* London: Methuen, 1975.

Brown L. R. *The Global Economic Prospect: New Sources of Economic Stress* (Worldwatch Paper No. 20). Washington, D.C.: Worldwatch Institute, 1978.

Chisholm, M. "The Wealth of Nations," *Transactions of the Institute of British Geographers,* Vol. 5 (1980), pp. 255–276.

———. *Modern World Development: A Geographical Perspective.* Totowa, N. J.: Barnes & Noble, 1982.

Clarke, J. I. *Population Geography.* New York: Pergamon Press, 1975.

Cole, J. P. *The Development Gap: A Spatial Analysis of World Poverty and Inequality.* New York: John Wiley, 1981.

de Souza, A. R. and Porter, P. *The Underdevelopment and Modernization of the Third World.* Washington, D.C.: Association of American Geographers, 1974.

Dickenson, J. P. et al. *A Geography of the Third World.* London: Methuen, 1983.

Drakakis-Smith, D. (ed.). *Urbanisation in the Developing World.* London: Croom Helm, 1986.

El-Shakhs, S. "Development, Primacy, and Systems of Cities," *Journal of Developing Areas,* Vol. 7 (1972), pp. 11–36.

Foust, J. B. and de Souza, A. R. *The Economic Landscape: A Theoretical Introduction.* Columbus, Ohio: Charles E. Merrill, 1978.

Friedmann, J. and Weaver, C. *Territory and Function: The Evolution of Regional Planning.* London: Edward Arnold, 1979.

Gilbert, A. (ed.). *Development Planning and Spatial Structure.* New York: John Wiley, 1976.

Ginsburg, N. (ed.). *Essays on Geography and Economic Development.* Chicago: University of Chicago Press, 1960.

Ginsburg, N. "From Colonialism to National Development: Geographical Perspectives on Patterns and Policies," *Annals of the Association of American Geographers,* Vol. 63 (1973), pp. 1–21.

Grossman, L. "The Cultural Ecology of Economic Development," *Annals of the Association of American Geographers,* Vol. 71 (1981), pp. 220–236.

Hoyle, S. B. (ed.). *Spatial Aspects of Development.* New York: John Wiley, 1974.

Johnson, E. A. J. *The Organization of Space in Developing Countries.* Cambridge: Harvard University Press, 1970.

Lösch, A. (trans. W. H. Woglorn and W. F. Stolper). *The Economics of Location.* New Haven, Conn.: Yale University Press, 1954.

Myrdal, G. *Economic Theory and Underdeveloped Regions.* London: Methuen, 1957.

———. *Rich Lands and Poor.* New York: Harper & Row, 1957.

Peters, G. L. and Larkin, R. P. *Population Geography: Problems, Concepts, and Prospects.* Dubuque, Iowa: Kendall/Hunt, 1979.

Pred, A. *City-Systems in Advanced Economies.* London: Hutchinson, 1977.

Reynolds, L. G. *Economic Growth in the Third World: An Introduction.* New Haven: Yale University Press, 1986.

Rodgers, A. *Economic Development in Retrospect: The Italian Model and Its Significance for Regional Planning in Market-Oriented Economies.* New York: Winston, 1979.

Rostow, W. W. *The Stages of Economic Growth: A Non-Communist Manifesto,* 2nd ed. Cambridge: Cambridge University Press, 1971.

———. *The World Economy: History and Prospect.* New York: Macmillan, 1978.

Smil, V. and Knowland, W. E. (eds.). *Energy in the Developing World: The* *Real Energy Crisis.* Oxford, Eng.: Oxford University Press, 1980.

Stöhr, W. B. and Taylor, D. R. F. (eds.). *Development from Above or Below? The Dialectics of Regional Planning in Developing Countries.* New York: John Wiley, 1981.

Taaffe, E. J., Morrill, R. L., and Gould, P. R. "Transport Expansion in Underdeveloped Countries: A Comparative Analysis," *Geographical Review,* Vol. 53 (1963), pp. 503–529.

Teitelbaum, M. S. "Relevance of Demographic Transition Theory for Developing Countries," *Science,* Vol. 188 (1975), pp. 420–425.

Warntz, W. *Macrogeography and Income Fronts.* Philadelphia: Regional Science Research Institute, 1965.

Wilkinson, R. G. *Poverty and Progress: An Ecological Model of Economic Development.* London: Methuen, 1973.

Zelinsky, W., Kosinski, L. A., and Prothero, R. M. (eds.). *Geography and a Crowding World.* New York: Oxford University Press, 1970.

Chapter 3

Bamford, C. G. and Robinson, H. *Geography of the EEC: A Systematic Economic Approach.* Plymouth, Eng.: MacDonald and Evans, 1983.

Beaujeu-Garnier, J. "Toward a New Equilibrium in France," *Annals of the Association of American Geographers,* Vol. 64 (1974), pp. 113–125.

Berentsen, W. H. "Regional Policy and Industrial Overspecialization in Lagging Regions," *Growth and Change,* Vol. 9 (1978), pp. 9–13.

Berg, V., den L. et al. *Urban Europe: A Study of Growth and Decline.* Oxford, Eng.: Pergamon Press, 1982.

Boal, F. W., Douglas, J., and Neville, H. (eds.). *Integration and Division: Geographical Perspectives on the Northern Ireland Problem.* London: Academic Press, 1982.

Browne, G. S. (ed.). *Atlas of Europe: A Profile of Western Europe.* New York: Scribner's, 1974.

Burtenshaw, D. et al. *The City in West Europe.* New York: John Wiley, 1981.

Claval, P. "Contemporary Human Geography of France," *Geoforum,* Vol. 7 (1976), pp. 253–292.

Clout, H. D. (ed.). *Regional Development in Western Europe.* New York: John Wiley, 1981.

Clout, H. D. et al. *Western Europe: Geographical Perspectives.* New York: Longman, 1985.

Demko, G. (ed.). *Regional Development: Problems and Policies in Eastern and Western Europe.* London: Croom Helm, 1984.

Diem, A. *Western Europe: A Geographical Analysis.* New York: John Wiley, 1979.

Dutt, A. K. and Heal, S. "Delta Project Planning and Implementation in the Netherlands," *Journal of Geography,* Vol. 78 (1979), pp. 131–141.

Foster, C. R. (ed.). *Nations Without a State: Ethnic Minorities in Western Europe.* New York: Praeger, 1980.

Gottmann, J. "The Dynamics of Large Cities," *Geographical Journal,* Vol. 140 (1974), pp. 254–261.

Goudie, A. *The Human Impact: Man's Role in Environmental Change.* Cambridge: MIT Press, 1982.

Hall, P. (ed.). *Europe 2000.* London: Duckworth, 1977.

Hall, P. and Hay, D. *Growth Centres in the European Urban System,* Berkeley: University of California Press, 1980.

Hoare, A. G. *The Location of Industry in Britain.* Cambridge: Cambridge University Press, 1983.

Hoffman, G. W. *The European Energy Challenge: East and West.* Durham, N.C.: Duke University Press, 1985.

Hoffman, G. W. (ed.). *Federalism and Regional Development: Case Studies on the Experience in the United States and the Federal Republic of Germany.* Austin: University of Texas Press, 1981.

———(ed.). *A Geography of Europe: Problems and Prospects,* 5th ed. New York: John Wiley, 1983.

House, J. W. (ed.). *U.K. Space.* London: Weidenfeld and Nicolson, 1979.

Jones, E. L. *The European Miracle: Environments, Economies, and Geopolitics in the History of Europe and East Asia.* Cambridge: Cambridge University Press, 1981.

Jordan, T. G. *The European Culture Area,* 2nd ed. New York: Harper & Row, 1988.

Langston, J. *Geographical Change and Industrial Revolution.* Cambridge: Cambridge University Press, 1982.

Maclennan, D. and Parr, J. B. (eds.). *Regional Policy: Past Experience and New Directions.* Oxford, Eng.: Martin Robertson, 1979.

Manners, I. R. *North Sea Oil and Environmental Planning.* Austin: University of Texas Press, 1982.

Minshull, G. N. *The New Europe: An Economic Geography of the EEC,* 2nd ed. London: Hodder & Stoughton, 1980.

Nystrom, J. W. and Hoffman, G. W. *The Common Market,* 2nd ed. (New Searchlight Series). New York: Van Nostrand, 1976.

O'Brien, P. *Railways and the Economic Development of Western Europe, 1830–1914.* New York: St. Martin's Press, 1983.

Odell, P. R. "The Energy Economy of Western Europe: A Return to the Use of Indigenous Resources," *Geography,* Vol. 66 (1981), pp. 1–14.

Organization for Economic Cooperation and Development. *The State of the Environment in OECD Member Countries.* Paris: OECD, 1979.

Parker, G. *The Logic of Unity: A Geography of the European Economic Community,* 2nd ed. New York: Longman, 1981.

Rostow, W. W. *How It All Began: Origins of the Modern Economy.* New York: McGraw-Hill, 1975.

Seers, D. et al. (eds.). *Underdeveloped Europe: Studies in Core-Periphery Relations.* Atlantic Highlands, N.J.: Humanities Press, 1979.

Short, J. R. and Kirby, A. (eds.) *The Human Geography of Contemporary Britain.* London: Macmillan, 1984.

Stone, K. H. "Geographical Effects of Urbanizing on Ruralizing in Europe, 1920–2000," *European Demographic Information Bulletin,* Vol. 6 (1975), pp. 2–24.

Tames, R. *Economy and Society in Nineteenth-Century Britain.* London: Allen & Unwin, 1972.

Tuchman, B. W. *The Proud Tower.* New York: Macmillan, 1966.

Wagret, P. *Polderlands,* New York: Barnes & Noble, 1972.

White, P. *The Western European City: A Social Geography.* London: Longman, 1984.

Chapter 4

Abler, R. and Adams, J. S. *A Comparative Atlas of America's Great Cities.* Washington, D.C.: Association of American Geographers: Minneapolis University of Minnesota Press, 1976.

Adams, J. S. (ed.). *Contemporary Metropolitan America,* Vol. 1, *Cities of the Nation's Historic Metropolitan Core.* Cambridge, Mass.: Ballinger, 1976.

Bailyn, B. *The Peopling of British North America: An Introduction.* New York: Knopf, 1986.

Baumann, D. and Dworkin, D. *Water Resources for Our Cities.* Washington, D.C.: Association of American Geographers, 1978.

Bennett, C. F., Jr. *Conservation and Management of Natural Resources in the United States.* New York: John Wiley, 1983.

Berry, B. J. L. "The Geography of the United States in the Year 2000." *Transactions of the Institute of British Geographers,* Vol. 51 (1970), pp. 21–53.

———. "Inner City Futures: An American Dilemma Revisited," *Transactions of the Institute of British Geographers, New Series,* Vol. 5 (1980), pp. 1–28.

Beyers, W. B. "Contemporary Trends in the Regional Economic Development of the United States," *Professional Geographer,* Vol. 31 (1979), pp. 34–44.

Birdsall, S. S. and Florin, J. W. *Regional Landscapes of the United States and Canada,* 2nd ed. New York: John Wiley, 1981.

Blackbourn, A. and Putnam, R. G. *The Industrial Geography of Canada.* London: Croom Helm, 1984.

Davies, C. S. "Life at the Edge: Urban and Industrial Evolution of Texas, Frontier Wilderness—Frontier Space, 1836–1986," *Southwestern Historical Quarterly,* Vol. LXXXIX (1986), pp. 443–554.

Dicken, P. and Lloyd, P. E. *Modern Western Society: A Geographical Perspective on Work, Home, and Well-Being.* New York: Harper & Row, 1981.

Doughty, R. W. *At Home in Texas: Early Views of the Land.* College Station: Texas A&M University Press, 1987.

Estall, R. A. *Modern Geography of the United States.* Harmondsworth, Eng.: Penguin, 1976.

Getis, A. "The Economic Health of Municipalities Within a Metropolitan Region: The Case of Chicago," *Economic Geography,* Vol. 62 (1986), pp. 52–73.

Harris, R. C. *The Seigneural System in Early Canada.* Madison: University of Wisconsin Press, 1966.

Hart, J. F. "Cropland Concentrations in the South," *Annals of the Association of American Geographers,* Vol. 68 (1978), pp. 505–517.

Jackson, J. B. *American Space: The Centennial Years, 1865–1876.* New York: W. W. Norton, 1972.

Jakle, J. A. *The American Small Town: Twentieth-Century Place Images.* Hamden, Conn.: Shoe String Press, 1982. (Archon Books)

Jakubs, J. F. "Recent Racial Segregation in U.S. SMSAs," *Urban Geography,* Vol. 7 (1986), pp. 146–163.

Johnston, R. J. *The American Urban System: A Geographical Perspective.* London: Longman, 1982.

Jordan, T. G. *Texas Log Buildings: A Folk Architecture.* Austin: University of Texas Press, 1978.

————. "Evolution of American Backwoods Pioneer Culture: The Role of the Delaware Finns," in N. Polk (ed.), *Mississippi's Piney Woods: A Human Perspective.* Jackson: University Press of Mississippi, 1986, pp. 25–39.

Lewis, P. F., Tuan, Yi-Fu, and Lowenthal, D. *Visual Blight in America.* Washington, D.C.: Association of American Geographers, 1973.

Lithwick, N. H. *Urban Canada: Problems and Prospects.* Ottawa: Government of Canada, 1970.

Louder, D. R., Morissoneau, C., and Waddell, E. "Picking Up the Pieces of a Shattered Dream: Québec and French America," *Journal of Cultural Geography,* Vol. 4 (1983), pp. 44–56.

Meinig, D. W. "The Mormon Culture Region: Strategies and Patterns in the Geography of the American West, 1847–1964." *Annals of the Association of American Geographers,* Vol. 55 (1965), pp. 191–200.

————. *The Shaping of America: A Geographical Perspective on 500 Years of History.* Vol. 1., *Atlantic America, 1492–1800.* New Haven: Yale University Press, 1986.

Morrill, R. L. and Wohlenberg, E. H. *The Geography of Poverty in the United States.* New York: McGraw-Hill, 1971.

Muller, P. O. "Transportation and Urban Growth: The Shaping of the American Metropolis," *Focus,* Vol. 36 (1986), pp. 8–17.

Muschett, F. D. "Spatial Distributions of Urban Atmospheric Particulate Concentrations," *Annals of the Association of American Geographers,* Vol. 71 (1981), pp. 552–567.

Palm, R. *The Geography of American Cities.* New York: Oxford University Press, 1981.

Patterson, J. H. *North America,* 6th ed. New York: Oxford University Press, 1979.

Pred, A. *Urban Growth and City Systems in the United States 1840–1860.* Cambridge: Harvard University Press, 1980.

Rees, J. "Technological Change and Regional Shifts in American Manufacturing," *Professional Geographer,* Vol. 31 (1979), pp. 45–54.

Rooney, J., Zelinsky, W. and Louder, D. (eds.). *This Remarkable Continent. An Atlas of United States and Canadian Society and Culture.* College Station: Texas A&M University Press, 1982.

Rose, H. M. *Black Suburbanization.* Cambridge, Mass.: Ballinger, 1976.

Sawers, L. and Tabb, W. K. (eds.). *Sunbelt/Snowbelt: Urban Development and Regional Restructuring.* New York: Oxford University Press, 1986.

Shortridge, J. R. "Changing Usage of Four American Regional Labels," *Annals of the Association of American Geographers,* Vol. 77 (1987), pp. 325–356.

Smith, David M. *The Geography of Social Well-Being in the United States.* New York: McGraw-Hill, 1973.

Sommers, L. M. *Michigan.* Boulder: Westview Press, 1984.

Vale, T. R. *Plants and People: Vegetation Change in North America.* Washington, D.C.: Association of American Geographers, 1982.

Walker, D. F. *Canada's Industrial Space-Economy.* Toronto: John Wiley, 1980.

Ward, D. *Cities and Immigrants: A Geography of Change in Nineteenth Century America.* New York: Oxford University Press, 1971.

————(ed.). *Geographical Perspectives on America's Past: Readings on the Historical Geography of the United States.* New York: Oxford University Press, 1979.

Watson, J. W. *Social Geography of the United States.* London and New York: Longman, 1979.

Yeates, M. H. *Main Street: Windsor to Québec City.* Toronto: Macmillan, 1975.

Yeates, M. H. and Garner, B. *The North American City,* 3rd ed. San Francisco: Harper & Row, 1980.

Zelinsky, W. *The Cultural Geography of the United States.* Englewood Cliffs, N.J.: Prentice-Hall, 1973.

————. "North America's Vernacular Regions." *Annals of the Association of American Geographers,* Vol. 70 (1980), pp. 1–16.

Chapter 5

Bandera, V. N. and Melnyk, Z. L. (eds.). *The Soviet Economy in Regional Perspective.* New York: Praeger, 1973.

Berentsen, W. H. "Regional Change in the German Democratic Republic," *Annals of the Association of American Geographers,* Vol. 71 (1981), pp. 56–66.

Black, C. E. (ed.). *The Transformation of Russian Society.* Cambridge: Harvard University Press, 1960.

Bond, R. B. and Lydolph, P. "Soviet Population Change and City Growth, 1970–79: A Preliminary Report," *Soviet Geography: Review and Translation,* Vol. 20 (1979), pp. 567–586.

Brown, A. (ed.). *The Cambridge Encyclopedia of Russia and the Soviet Union.* Cambridge: Cambridge University Press, 1982.

Campbell, R. W. *Trends in the Soviet Oil and Gas Industry.* Baltimore, Md.: Johns Hopkins University Press, 1976.

Cole, J. P. *Geography of the Soviet Union.* London: Butterworths, 1984.

Conn, S. H. *Economic Development in the Soviet Union.* Lexington, Mass.: D. C. Heath, 1970.

Demko, G. J. and Fuchs, R. J. (eds. and trans.). *Geographical Perspectives in the Soviet Union.* Columbus, Ohio: Ohio State University Press, 1974.

————. "Mobility and Settlement Systems and Integration in the USSR," *Soviet Geography: Review and Translation,* Vol. 24 (1983), pp. 547–559.

Dewdney, J. C. *The USSR.* Boulder, Colo: Westview Press, 1976.

Dienes, L. "Soviet Energy Resources and Prospects," *Current History,* Vol. 71 (1976), pp. 114–118, 129–132.

———. "Modernization and Energy Development in the Soviet Union," *Soviet Geography: Review and Translation*, Vol. 21 (1980), pp. 121–158.

Dienes, L. and Shabad, T. *The Soviet Energy System*. New York: V. H. Winston, 1979.

Dostál, P. and Knippenberg, H. "The 'Russification' of Ethnic Minorities in the USSR," *Soviet Geography: Review and Translation*, Vol. 20 (1979), pp. 197–219.

Fischer-Galati, S. (ed.). *Man, State and Society in East European History*. New York: Praeger, 1974.

French, R. A. and Hamilton, F. E. I. (eds.). *The Socialist City. Spatial Structure and Urban Policy*. Chichester, Eng.: John Wiley, 1979.

Gianaris, N. V. *The Economics of the Balkan Countries: Albania, Bulgaria, Greece, Romania, Turkey and Yugoslavia*. New York: Praeger, 1982.

Harris, C. D. *Cities of the Soviet Union*. Chicago: Rand McNally, 1970.

———. "Urbanization and Population Growth in the Soviet Union, 1959–1970," *Geographical Review*, Vol. 61 (1971), pp. 102–124.

Hoffman, G. W. "Rural Transformation in Eastern Europe Since World War II," in I. Volgyes et al. (eds.), *The Process of Rural Transformation*. New York: Pergamon Press, 1980.

———. "Variations in Centre-Periphery Relations in Southeast Europe," in J. Gottmann (ed.), *Centre and Periphery*. Beverly Hills, Calif.: Sage Publications, 1980.

Hooson, D. J. M. *The Soviet Union: People and Regions*. Belmont, Calif.: Wadsworth, 1966.

Jackson, W. A. D. (ed.). *Soviet Resource Management and the Environment*. Columbus, Ohio: American Association for the Advancement of Slavic Studies, 1978.

Jensen, R., Shabad, T., and Wright, A. (eds.). *Soviet Natural Resources in the World Economy*. Chicago: University of Chicago Press, 1983.

Kosinski, L. A. (ed.). *Demographic Developments in Eastern Europe*. New York: Praeger, 1977.

Kostanick, H. L. (ed.). *Population and Migration Trends in Eastern Europe*. Boulder, Colo.: Westview Press, 1977.

L'vovich, M. I. "Research Coordination on Proposed Soviet Water-Diversion Projects," *Soviet Geography: Review and Translation*, Vol. 19 (1978), pp. 698–738.

Lydolph, P. E. *Geography of the USSR: Topical Analysis*. Elkhart Lake, Wis.: Misty Valley Publishers, 1979.

Micklin, P. "Soviet Plans to Reverse the Flow of Rivers: The Kama-Pechora Project," *Canadian Geographer*, Vol. 13 (1969), pp. 199–215.

———. "The Status of the Soviet Union's North-South Water Transfer Projects Before Their Abandonment in 1985–86," *Soviet Geography: Review and Translation*, Vol. 27 (1986), pp. 287–329.

North, R. N. "Soviet Northern Development: The Case of NW Siberia," *Soviet Studies*, Vol. 24 (1972), pp. 171–199.

Nove, A. *An Economic History of the U.S.S.R.* Harmondsworth, Eng.: Penguin Books, 1982.

Pipes, R. *Russia Under the Old Regime*. London: Weidenfeld and Nicolson, 1974.

Rugg, D. S. *The Geography of Eastern Europe*. Lincoln, Neb.: Cliffs Notes, 1978.

Salisbury, H. E. (ed.). *Anatomy of the Soviet Union*. Camden, N.J.: Thomas Nelson, 1967.

Singleton, F. (ed.). *Environmental Misuse in the Soviet Union*. New York: Praeger, 1975.

Turnock, D. *Eastern Europe. Studies in Industrial Geography*. Boulder, Colo.: Westview Press, 1978.

Wixman, R. "Demographic Trends Among Soviet Moslems (1959–1979)," *Soviet Geography: Review and Translation*, Vol. 25 (1984), pp. 46–60.

———. *The Peoples of the USSR: An Ethnographic Handbook*. New York: M. E. Sharpe, 1984.

Chapter 6

Alden, J. D. "Metropolitan Planning in Japan," *Town Planning Review*, Vol. 55 (1984), pp. 55–74.

Allen, G. C. *A Short Economic History of Modern Japan*. New York: St. Martin's Press, 1981.

Association of Japanese Geographers. *Geography of Japan* (Special Publication No. 4). Tokyo: Association of Japanese Geographers, 1980.

Bartz, P. *South Korea*. Oxford, Eng.: Clarendon Press, 1972.

Burks, A. W. *Japan: Profile of a Postindustrial Power*. Boulder, Colo.: Westview Press, 1981.

Cumings, B. *The Two Koreas*. New York: Foreign Policy Association, 1984. (Headline Series No. 269.)

Fisher, C. A. and Sargent, J. "Japan's Ecological Crisis," *Geographical Journal*, Vol. 141 (1975), pp. 165–176.

Fukutake, T. *Japanese Rural Society*. London: Oxford University Press, 1967.

Gibney, F. *Japan: The Fragile Superpower*. New York: W. W. Norton, 1975.

Glickman, N. J. *The Growth and Management of the Japanese Urban System*. New York: Academic Press, 1979.

Hall, R. B., Jr. *Japan: Industrial Power of Asia*, 2nd ed. New York: Van Nostrand, 1976. (New Searchlight Series)

Harris, C. D. and Edmonds, R. L. "Urban Geography in Japan: A Survey of Recent Literature," *Urban Geography*, Vol. 3 (1982), pp. 1–21.

Hayami, Y. *Agricultural Growth in Japan, Taiwan, Korea, and Philippines*. Honolulu: University Press of Hawaii, 1979.

Hofheinz, R., Jr., and Calder, K. E. *The Eastasia Edge*. New York: Basic Books, 1982.

Johnson, C. *MITI and the Japanese Miracle: The Growth of Industrial Policy, 1925–1975*. Palo Alto, Calif.: Stanford University Press, 1982.

Joo, K-S. "Urbanization and the Urban System of Korea," *Geographical Review of Japan*, Vol. 55 (1982), pp. 1–20.

Jun, U. "Japan as an Advanced Polluting Nation—Its Responsibility," *Japan Quarterly*, Vol. 27 (1980), pp. 321–332.

Kirby, S. *Japan's Role in the 1980's*. London: Economist Intelligence Unit, 1980.

Korean Overseas Information Service. *A Handbook of Korea*. Seoul: Ministry of Culture and Information, 1978.

Kornhauser, D. H. *Urban Japan: Its Foundations and Growth*. London and New York: Longman, 1976.

Maki, F. "The City and Inner Space," *Japan Echo*, Vol. 6 (1979), pp. 91–103.

Masazumi, H. "Minamata Disease as a Social and Medical Problem," *Japan Quarterly*, Vol. 25 (1978), pp. 20–34.

McCune, S. *Korea: Land of Broken Calm.* Princeton, N.J.: Van Nostrand, 1967.

Moulder, F. V. *Japan, China, and the Modern World Economy.* Cambridge: Cambridge University Press, 1977.

Nakano, H. "Japan's Internationalization: Becoming a Global Citizen," *International Journal of Comparative Sociology*, Vol. 25 (1984), pp. 114–122.

Park, S. "Rural Development in Korea: The Role of Periodic Markets," *Economic Geography*, Vol. 57 (1981), pp. 113–126.

Patrick, H. and Rosovsky, H. (eds.). *Asia's New Giant.* Washington, D.C.: Brookings Institute, 1976.

Pitts, F. *Japan.* Grand Rapids, Mich.: Fideler, 1974.

Reischauer, E. O. *Japan: The Story of a Nation*, 3rd ed. New York: Knopf, 1981.

Rondinelli, D. A. "Land-Development Policy in South Korea," *Geographical Review*, Vol. 74, (1984), pp. 425–440.

Sakamoto, H. "The Regional Distribution of Comparatively Large Farms in Japan." *Geographical Review of Japan*, Vol. 55 (1982), pp. 37–50.

Seidenstricker, E. *Low City, High City: Tokyo From Edo to the Earthquake.* New York: Knopf, 1983.

Shimpo, M. *Three Decades in Shiwa: Economic Development and Social Change in a Japanese Farming Community.* Vancouver: University of British Columbia Press, 1978.

Shishido, H. "Economic Growth and Urbanization: A Study of Japan," *International Regional Science Review*, Vol. 7 (1982), pp. 175–191.

Simmons, I. G. "The Balance of Environmental Protection and Development in Hokkaido, Japan," *Environmental Conservation*, Vol. 8 (1981), pp. 191–198.

Smith, R. J. *The Price of Progress in a Japanese Village: 1951–1975.* Palo Alto, Calif.: Stanford University Press, 1978.

Sternheimer, S. "From Dependency to Interdependency: Japan's Experience with Technology Trade with the West and the Soviet Union," *Annals of the American Academy of Political and Social Science*, Vol. 458 (1981), pp. 175–186.

Totman, C. "Forestry in Early Modern Japan, 1650–1850: A Preliminary Survey," *Agricultural History*, Vol. 56 (1982), pp. 415–425.

Trewartha, G. T. *Japan: A Geography.* Madison: University of Wisconsin Press, 1965.

Chapter 7

Berry, B. J. L. "The Economics of Land-Use Intensities in Melbourne, Australia," *Geographical Review*, Vol. 64 (1974), pp. 479–497.

Bolton, G. *Spoils and Spoilers: Australians Make Their Environment, 1788–1980.* Boston: Allen & Unwin, 1981.

Brookfield, H. (ed.). *The Pacific in Transition: Geographical Perspectives on Adaptation and Change.* New York: St. Martin's Press, 1973.

Burnley, I. H. (ed.). *Urbanization in Australia: The Post-War Experience.* Cambridge: Cambridge University Press, 1974.

Clark, A. H. *The Invasion of New Zealand by People, Plants and Animals: The South Island.* New Brunswick, N.J.: Rutgers University Press, 1949.

Cochrane, P. *Industralization and Dependence: Australia's Road to Economic Development, 1870–1939.* St. Lucia, Austral.: Queensland University Press, 1980.

Cox, D. "Refugee Settlement in Australia: Review of an Era," *International Migration*, Vol. 21, (1983). pp. 332–344.

Crabb, P. "A New Australian Railroad—Then North to Darwin," *Geographical Review*, Vol. 72 (1982), pp. 90–93.

Cumberland, K. B. *Southwest Pacific: A Geography of Australia, New Zealand and Their Pacific Neighbors.* New York: Praeger, 1968.

Cumberland, K. B. and Whitelaw, J. S. *New Zealand.* Chicago: Aldine, 1970.

Daly, M. *Sydney Boom, Sydney Bust.* Sydney: Allen & Unwin, 1982.

Donaldson, I. and Donaldson T. *Seeing the First Australians.* Sydney: Allen & Unwin, 1985.

Gentilli, J. *World Survey of Climatology, Climates of Australia and New Zealand.* Amsterdam, The Netherlands: Elsevier, 1971.

Gibson, K. D. and Horvath, R. J. "Global Capital and the Restructuring in Australian Manufacturing," *Economic Geography*, Vol. 59 (1983), pp. 178–194.

Gilpin, A. *Environmental Policy in Aus-*

tralia. Brisbane: University of Queensland Press, 1980.

———. "Problems, Progress, and Policy: An Overview of the Australian Environment," *Environment*, Vol. 25 (1983), pp. 7–38.

Heathcote, R. L. "The Evolution of Australian Pastoral Land Tenures: An Example of Challenge and Response in Resource Development," in R. G. Ironside et al. (eds.), *Frontier Settlement.* Edmonton: University of Alberta Press, 1974.

———. *Australia.* New York: Longman, 1976.

Howe, A. and O'Connor, K. "Travel to Work and Labor Force Participation in an Australian Metropolitan Area," *Professional Geographer*, Vol. 34 (1982), pp. 50–64.

Howe, K. R. *Where the Waves Fall: A New South Sea Islands History from First Settlement to Colonial Rule.* Honolulu: University of Hawaii Press, 1984.

Jeans, D. N. *Australian Historical Landscapes.* Sydney: Allen & Unwin, 1984.

Jeans, D. N. (ed.). *Australia: A Geography.* New York: St. Martin's Press, 1978.

Linge, G. J. R., "Australian Manufacturing in Recession: A Review of the Spatial Implications," *Environment and Planning*, Vol. 11 (1979), pp. 1405–1430.

Linge, G. J. R. and McKay, J. (eds.). *Structural Change in Australia: Some Spatial and Organizational Responses.* Canberra: Australian National University, 1981.

Livingston, W. S. and Louis, W. R. (eds.). *Australia, New Zealand, and the Pacific Islands Since the First World War.* Austin: University of Texas Press, 1979.

Lonsdale, R. E. and Holmes, J. H. (eds.). *Settlement Systems in Sparsely Settled Regions: The United States and Australia.* New York: Pergamon Press, 1981.

McKnight, T. L. *Australia's Corner of the World.* Englewood Cliffs, N.J.: Prentice-Hall, 1970.

———. *Friendly Vermin: A Survey of Feral Livestock in Australia.* Berkeley: University of California Press, 1976.

Meinig, D. *On the Margins of the Good Earth: The South Australian Wheat*

Frontier, 1869–1884. Chicago: Rand McNally, 1963.

Nicholls, J. L. "The Past and Present Extent of New Zealand's Indigenous Forests," *Environmental Conservation*, Vol. 7 (1980), pp. 309–310.

Oliver, W. H. with Williams, B. R. (eds.). *The Oxford History of New Zealand.* Oxford, Eng.: Clarendon Press, 1981.

Robinson, K. W. *Australia, New Zealand and the Southwest Pacific.* London: University of London Press, 1974.

Saddler, H. *Energy in Australia: Politics and Economics.* Sydney: Allen & Unwin, 1981.

Sahlins, M. D. *Islands of History.* Chicago: University of Chicago Press, 1985.

Veblen, T. T. and Stewart, G. H. "The Effects of Introduced Wild Animals on New Zealand's Forests," *Annals of the Association of American Geographers*, Vol. 72 (1982), pp. 372–397.

White, R. *Inventing Australia: Images and Identity, 1688–1980.* London: Allen & Unwin, 1981.

Wilde, P. D. "From Insulation Toward Integration: The Australian Industrial System in the Throes of Change," *Pacific Viewpoint*, Vol. 22 (1981), pp. 1–24.

Williams, M. *The Making of the South Australian Landscape: A Study in the Historical Geography of Australia.* London: Academic Press, 1974.

Chapter 8

Balan, J. "Regional Urbanization Under Primary-Sector Expansion in Neo-Colonial Societies," in A. Portes and H. L. Browning, *Current Perspectives in Latin American Urban Research.* Austin: University of Texas Press, 1976.

Bethell, L. (ed.). *The Cambridge History of Latin America.* Cambridge: Cambridge University Press, 1984.

Blouet, B. W. and Blouet, O. *Latin America: An Introductory Survey.* New York: John Wiley, 1981.

Bromley, R. D. F. and Bromley, R. *South American Development: A Geographical Introduction.* New York: Cambridge University Press, 1982.

Browning, D. "Agrarian Reform in El Salvador," *Journal of Latin American Studies*, Vol. 15 (1983), pp. 399–426.

Cardona, R. and Simmons, A. "Toward a Model of Migration in Latin America," in B. Du Toit and H. I. Safa, *Migration and Urbanization: Models and Adaptive Strategies.* The Hague: Mouton, 1975.

Cardoso, F. H. and Faletto, E. *Dependency and Development in Latin America.* Berkeley: University of California Press, 1979.

Clark C. G. *Kingston, Jamaica: Urban Development and Social Change, 1692–1962.* Berkeley: University of California Press, 1975.

Cole, J. P. *Economic and Social Geography*, 2nd ed. Washington, D.C.: Butterworths, 1975.

Denevan, W. M. *The Native Population of the Americas in 1492.* Madison: University of Wisconsin Press, 1976.

Dickenson, J. P. *Brazil: Studies in Industrial Geography.* London: Dawson, 1978.

Doolittle, W. E. "Aboriginal Agricultural Development in the Valley of Sonora, Mexico," *Geographical Review*, Vol. 70, (1980), pp. 327–342.

————. "Agricultural Change as an Incremental Process," *Annals of the Association of American Geographers*, Vol. 74 (1984), pp. 124–137.

Freyre, G. *The Masters and the Slaves.* New York: Knopf, 1956.

Friedmann, J. *Regional Development Policy: A Case Study of Venezuela.* Cambridge: MIT Press, 1966.

Ghosh, P. K. (ed.) *Developing Latin America: A Modernization Perspective.* Westport, CT.: Greenwood Press, 1984.

Gilbert, A. *Latin American Development: A Geographical Perspective.* Baltimore: Penguin, 1974.

————. "The State and Regional Income Disparity in Latin America," *Bulletin of the Society for Latin American Studies*, Vol. 29 (1978), pp. 5–30.

Gilbert, A. with Hardoy, J. E. and Ramirez, R. (eds.). *Urbanization in Contemporary Latin America.* New York: John Wiley, 1982.

Hardoy, J. H. *Urbanization in Latin America: Approaches and Issues.* New York: Doubleday, 1975. (Anchor Books)

Hoberman, L. S. and Socolow, S. M. (eds.). *Cities and Society in Colonial Latin America.* Albuquerque: University of New Mexico Press, 1986.

Hoy, D. R. and Belisle, F. J. "Environ-mental Protection and Economic Development in Guatemala's Western Highlands," *The Journal of Developing Areas*, Vol. 18 (1984), pp. 161–176.

Hunter, J. M. and Foley, J. W. *Economic Problems of Latin America.* Boston: Houghton Mifflin, 1975.

Jones, D. M. "The Green Revolution in Latin America: Success or Failure," *Proceedings of the Conference of Latin American Geographers* (Muncie, Ind.), Vol. 6 (1977), pp. 55–64.

Katzman, M. T. *Cities and Frontiers in Brazil: Regional Dimensions of Economic Development.* Cambridge: Harvard University Press, 1977.

Lowenthal, D. *West Indian Societies.* New York: Oxford University Press, 1972.

Moran, E. *Developing the Amazon.* Bloomington: Indiana University Press, 1981.

Moran, E. (ed.), *The Dilemma of Amazonian Development.* Boulder: Westview Press, 1983.

Morris, A. S. *Regional Disparities and Policy in Modern Argentina.* Glasgow: Institute of Latin American Studies, 1975.

————. *South America.* London: Hodder & Stoughton, 1979.

————. *Latin America: Economic Development and Regional Differentiation.* Totowa, N.J.: Barnes & Noble, 1981.

Morse, R. M. *The Urban Development of Latin America, 1750–1920.* Stanford, Calif.: Center for Latin American Studies, 1971.

————. *From Community to Metropolis: A Biography of São Paulo.* New York: Farrar, Strauss & Giroux, 1974. (Octagon Books)

Odell, P. R. and Preston, D. A. *Economies and Societies in Latin America: A Geographical Appraisal*, 2nd ed. London: John Wiley, 1978.

Pedersen, P. O. *Urban-Regional Development in South America: A Process of Diffusion and Integration.* The Hague: Mouton, 1975.

Preston, D. A. "Contemporary Issues in Rural Latin America," *Progress in Human Geography*, Vol. 7 (1983), pp. 276–282.

Richardson, C. B. *Caribbean Migrants: Environment and Survival on St. Kitts and Nevis.* Knoxville: University of Tennessee Press, 1983.

Sauer, C. O. *The Early Spanish Main.*

Berkeley: University of California Press, 1966.

Smith, N. J. H. *Rainforest Corridors: The Transamazon Colonization Scheme.* Berkeley: University of California Press, 1982.

Stöhr, W. *Regional Development Experiences and Prospects in Latin America.* The Hague: Mouton, 1975.

Turner, B. L., II, "Population Density in the Classic Maya Lowlands: New Evidence for Old Approaches," *Geographical Review*, Vol. 66 (1976), pp. 73–82.

Veblen, T. T. "Forest Preservation in the Western Highlands of Guatemala," *Geographical Review*, Vol. 68 (1978), pp. 417–434.

Wagley, C. (ed.). *Man in the Amazon.* Gainesville: University of Florida Press, 1974.

Webb, K. *Geography of Latin America: A Regional Analysis.* Englewood Cliffs, N.J.: Prentice-Hall, 1972.

West, R. and Augelli, J. P. *Middle America: Its Lands and Peoples*, 2nd ed. Englewood Cliffs, N.J.: Prentice-Hall, 1976.

Chapter 9

Baum, R. (ed.). *China's Four Modernizations, the New Technological Revolution.* Boulder, Colo.: Westview Press, 1980.

Buchanan, K. *The Transformation of the Chinese Earth.* London: G. Bell and Sons, 1970.

Chang, S-D. "Modernization and China's Urban Development," *Annals of the Association of American Geographers*, Vol. 71 (1981), pp. 202–219.

Chu, D. K. Y. "Some Analyses of Recent Chinese Provincial Data," *Professional Geographer*, Vol. 34 (1982), pp. 431–437.

Ding, C. "The Economic Development of China," *Scientific American*, Vol. 243 (1980), pp. 152–165.

Dwyer, D. J. "Chengdu, Sichuan: The Modernization of a Chinese City," *Geography*, Vol. 71 (1986), pp. 215–227.

Ginsburg, N. "China's Development Strategies," *Economic Development and Cultural Change*, Vol. 25 (1977), pp. 344–362.

Greer, C. *Water Management in the Yellow River Basin of China.* Austin: University of Texas Press, 1979.

Ho, S. P. S. *Economic Development of Taiwan.* New Haven, Conn.: Yale University Press, 1978.

Hsu, R. C. *Food For One Billion: China's Agriculture Since 1949.* Boulder: Westview Press, 1982.

Huang, P. C. C. *The Development of Underdevelopment in China.* White Plains, N.Y.: M. E. Sharpe, 1980.

Knapp, R. (ed.). *China's Island Frontier.* Honolulu: University Press of Hawaii, 1980.

Lardy, N. R. *Agriculture in China's Modern Economic Development.* Cambridge: Cambridge University Press, 1983.

Lo, C. P. "Spatial Form and Land Use Patterns of Modern Chinese Cities: An Exploratory Model," in L. Ngok and L. Chi-Keung, eds., *China: Development and Challenge*, (Vol. 2). Hong Kong: University of Hong Kong, 1979.

Ma, L. J. C. and Gui, G. "Administrative Changes and Urban Population in China," *Annals of the Association of American Geographers*, Vol. 77 (1987), pp. 373–395.

Ma, L. J. C. and Hanten, E. (eds.). *Urban Development in Modern China.* Boulder, Colo.: Westview Press, 1981.

Ma, L. J. C. and Noble, A. (eds.). *The Environment: Chinese and American Views.* New York and London: Metheun, 1981.

Moise, E. E. *Modern China: A History.* London: Longman, 1986.

Murphey, R. "The Treaty Ports and China's Modernization," in M. Elvin and G. W. Skinner, eds., *The Chinese City Between Two Worlds.* Stanford, Calif.: Stanford University Press, 1974.

——. *The Fading of the Maoist Vision, City and Country in China's Development.* New York: Metheun, 1980.

Pannell, C. W. and Ma, L. J. C. *China: The Geography of Development and Modernization.* New York: John Wiley, 1983.

Pannell, C. W. and Welch, R. "Recent Growth and Structural Change in Chinese Cities," *Urban Geography*, Vol. 1 (1980), pp. 68–80.

Salter, C. L., "Chinese Experiments in Urban Space: The Quest for an Agrapolitan China," *Habitat*, Vol. 1 (1976), pp. 19–35.

Salter, K. "Windows on a Changing China," *Focus*, Vol. 35 (1985), pp. 12–21.

Shabad, T. *China's Changing Map: National and Regional Development, 1949–71*, rev. ed. New York: Praeger, 1972.

Skinner, G. W. "Marketing and Social Structure in Rural China," *Journal of Asian Studies*, Vol. 24 (1964–1965), pp. 3–44, 195–228, 363–400.

—— (ed.). *The City in Late Imperial China.* Stanford, Calif.: Stanford University Press, 1977.

Spencer, J. E. *Oriental Asia: Themes Toward a Geography.* Englewood Cliffs, N.J.: Prentice-Hall, 1973.

——. "A China Geographer's Bookshelf," *China Geographer*, Vol. 10 (1978), pp. 63–71.

Tregear, T. R. *China, a Geographical Survey.* New York: John Wiley, 1980.

Tuan, Y-F. "Discrepancies Between Environmental Attitudes and Behaviour: Examples from Europe and China," *Canadian Geographer*, Vol. 12 (1968), pp. 176–191.

——. *China.* Chicago: Aldine, 1969.

Wheatley, P. *The Pivot of the Four Quarters: A Preliminary Enquiry into the Origins and Character of the Ancient Chinese City.* Chicago: Aldine, 1971.

Whitney, J. B. R., "Temporal and Spatial Change in the Productivity of Chinese Farming Ecosystems," in L. Ngok and L. Chi-Keung, *China's Development and Challenge* (Vol. 2). Hong Kong: University of Hong Kong, 1979.

——. "East Asia," in G. A. Klee, ed., *World Systems of Traditional Resource Management.* New York: John Wiley, 1980.

Chapter 10

Brush, J. E. "Some Dimensions of Urban Population Pressure in India," in W. Zelinsky et al. (eds.). *Geography and a Crowding World.* New York: Oxford University Press, 1970.

Chakravati, A. K. "Green Revolution in India," *Annals of the Association of American Geographers*, Vol. 63 (1973), pp. 319–330.

——. "The Impact of the High-Yielding Varieties Program on Foodgrain Production in India," *Canadian Geographer*, Vol. 20 (1976), pp. 199–223.

———. "Population Growth Types in India, 1961–1971," *Journal of Geography*, Vol. 75 (1976), pp. 343–350.

Dikshit, R. D. *The Political Geography of Federalism: An Inquiry into Origins and Stability.* New York: John Wiley, 1975.

Dutt, A. K. et al. *India: Resources, Potentialities, and Planning.* Dubuque, Iowa: Kendall/Hunt, 1973.

Dutt, A. K. and Nawajesh, A. "Population Pressure in Bangladesh," *Focus*, Vol. 15 (1974), pp. 1–10.

Faaland, J. and Parkinson, J. R. *Bangladesh: Test Case for Development.* Boulder: Westview Press, 1975.

Fox, R. G. (ed.). *Urban India: Society, Space and Image.* Durham, N.C.: Duke University Press, 1970.

Frankel, F. R. *India's Political Economy, 1947–1977.* Princeton, N.J.: Princeton University Press, 1978.

Geddes, A. (ed.). *Man and Land in South Asia.* New Delhi: Concept Publishing, 1982.

Hardgrave, R. L., Jr. *India: Government and Politics in a Developing Nation*, 3rd ed. New York: Harcourt Brace Jovanovich, 1980.

Islam, N. "Islam and National Identity: The Case of Pakistan and Bangladesh," *International Journal of Middle East Studies*, Vol. 12 (1981), pp. 55–72.

Johnson, B. L. C. *South Asia.* London: Heinemann, 1969.

———. *Bangladesh.* London: Heinemann, 1975.

———. *Pakistan.* London: Heinemann, 1979.

Kayastha, S. L. "An Appraisal of Water Resources of India and Need for National Water Policy," *GeoJournal*, Vol. 5 (1981), pp. 563–572.

Khan, A. M. "Rural-Urban Migration and Urbanization in Bangladesh," *Geographical Review*, Vol. 72 (1982), pp. 379–394.

Lodrick, D. O. *Sacred Cows, Sacred Places.* Berkeley and Los Angeles: University of California Press, 1981.

Murton, B. J. "South Asia," in G. A. Klee (ed.), *World Systems of Traditional Resource Management.* London: Edward Arnold, 1980.

Noble, A. G. and Dutt, A. K. (eds.). *India: Cultural Patterns and Processes.* Boulder: Westview Press, 1982.

Oza, G. M. "An Indian View of Man and Nature," *Environmental Conservation*, Vol. 10 (1983), pp. 331–335.

Pollard, H. J. "Development from an Agricultural Base in the Punjab," *Geography*, Vol. 68 (1983), pp. 16–24.

Possehl, G. L. *Ancient Cities of the Indus.* Durham, N.C.: Carolina Academic Press, 1979.

Raju, S. "Regional Patterns in the Labor Force of Urban India," *Professional Geographer*, Vol. 34 (1982), pp. 42–49.

Rawling, E. "Improving the Quality of Life in Indian Cities," *Geography*, Vol. 67 (1982), pp. 145–148.

Roy, B. K. "Population Regionals: A Perspective in Geographic Space of India," *GeoJournal*, Vol. 6 (1982), pp. 173–182.

Saha, K. R. et al. "The Indian Monsoon and Its Economic Impact," *GeoJournal*, Vol. 3 (1979), pp. 171–178.

Schwartzberg, J. E. "The Distribution of Selected Castes in the North Indian Plain," *Geographical Review*, Vol. 55 (1965), pp. 477–495.

———. *A Historical Atlas of South Asia.* Chicago: University of Chicago Press, 1978.

Sharma, U. *Women, Work, and Property in Northwest India.* New York: Tavistock, 1980.

Simoons, F. "Contemporary Research Themes in the Cultural Geography of Domesticated Animals," *Geographical Review*, Vol. 64 (1974), pp. 557–576.

Singhal, D. P. *Pakistan.* Englewood Cliffs, N.J.: Prentice-Hall, 1972.

Sopher, D. E. "Pilgrim Circulation in Gujarat," *Geographical Review*, Vol. 58 (1968), pp. 392–425.

———. "Temporal Disparity as a Measure of Change," *Professional Geographer*, Vol. 31 (1979), pp. 377–381.

Sopher, D. E. (ed.). *An Exploration of India: Geographical Perspectives on Society and Culture.* Ithaca, N.Y.: Cornell University Press, 1980.

Sukhwal, B. L. *India: Economic Resource Base and Contemporary Political Patterns.* New York: Envoy Press, 1987.

Veit, L. A. *India's Second Revolution: The Dimensions of Development.* New York: McGraw-Hill, 1976.

Visaria, P. "Poverty and Unemployment in India: An Analysis of Recent Evidence," *World Development*, Vol. 9 (1981), pp. 277–300.

Chapter 11

Abdul Rahim Mokhzani, D. B. *Rural Development in Southeast Asia.* New Delhi: Vikas, 1979.

Aiken, R. S. "Squatters and Squatter Settlements in Kuala Lumpur," *Geographical Review*, Vol. 71 (1981), pp. 158–175.

Burling, R. *Hill Farms and Padi Fields: Life in Mainland Southeast Asia.* Englewood Cliffs, N.J.: Prentice-Hall, 1965.

Doeppers, D. F. "Ethnic Urbanism and Philippine Cities," *Annals of the Association of American Geographers*, Vol. 64 (1974), pp. 549–559.

———. "The Philippine Revolution and the Geography of Schism," *Geographical Review*, Vol. 66 (1976), pp. 158–177.

Drake, C. "The Spatial Pattern of National Integration in Indonesia," *Transactions of the Institute of British Geographers, New Series*, Vol. 6 (1981), pp. 471–490.

Dutt, A. K. (ed.). *Southeast Asia: Realm of Contrasts.* Dubuque, Iowa: Kendall/Hunt, 1974.

Dwyer, D. J. *The City as a Centre of Change in Asia.* Hong Kong: Hong Kong University Press, 1972.

Eden, J. F. *Who Shall Succeed? Agricultural Development and Social Inequality on a Philippine Frontier.* Cambridge: Cambridge University Press, 1982.

Fisher, C. A. *Southeast Asia: A Social, Economic and Political Geography.* New York: E. P. Dutton, 1966.

Freestone, C. S. *The South-east Asian Village: A Geographic, Social and Economic Study.* London: George Philip and Son, 1974.

Fryer, D. W. *Southeast Asia: Problems of Development.* New York: Halstead, 1978.

———. *Emerging Southeast Asia: A Study in Growth and Stagnation*, 2nd ed. London: George Philip and Son, 1979.

Hill, R. D. "Integration in Agricultural Geography with some Southeast Asian Examples," *Philippine Geographical Journal*, Vol. 25 (1981), pp. 98–107.

——— (ed.). *South-East Asia: A Systematic Geography.* New York: Oxford University Press, 1979.

Jones, G. W. "Population Trends and Policies in Vietnam," *Population and*

Development Review, Vol. 8 (1982), pp. 783–810.

Lee, D. *The Sinking Ark: Environmental Problems in Malaysia and Southeast Asia.* Kuala Lumpur, Malaysia: Heinemann, 1980.

Lee, Y. L. "Race, Language, and National Cohesion in Southeast Asia," *Journal of Southeast Asian Studies,* Vol. 11 (1980), pp. 122–138.

McGee, T. G. *The Southeast Asian City: A Social Geography.* New York: Praeger, 1967.

Parker, G. J. et al. *Diversity and Development in Southeast Asia.* New York: McGraw-Hill, 1977.

Rambo, A. T. "Human Ecology Research on Tropical Agroecosystems in Southeast Asia," *Singapore Journal of Tropical Geography,* Vol. 3 (1982), pp. 86–99.

Salita, D. C. and Rosell, D. Z. *Economic Geography of the Philippines.* Bicutan: National Research Council of the Philippines, 1980.

Seavoy, R. E. "The Shading Cycle in Shifting Cultivation," *Annals of the Association of American Geographers,* Vol. 63 (1973), pp. 522–528.

Spencer, J. E. *Shifting Cultivation in Southeast Asia.* Berkeley: University of California Press, 1966.

———. "Southeast Asia," *Progress in Human Geography,* Vol. 6 (1982), pp. 265–269.

Sternstein, L. "Migration and Development in Thailand," *Geographical Review,* Vol. 66 (1976), pp. 401–419.

Tap, D. V. "On the Transformation and New Distribution of Population Centers in the Socialist Republic of Vietnam," *International Journal of Urban and Regional Research,* Vol. 4 (1980), pp. 503–515.

Taylor, A. (ed.). *Focus on Southeast Asia.* New York: Praeger, 1972.

Wheatley, P. "India Beyond the Ganges—Desultory Reflections on the Origins of Civilization in Southeast Asia," *Journal of Asian Studies,* Vol. 42 (1982), pp. 13–28.

Chapter 12

Abu-Lughod, J. *Rabat: Urban Apartheid in Morocco.* Princeton, N.J.: Princeton University Press, 1980.

Allan, J. A. *Libya: The Experience of Oil.* London: Croom-Helm, 1981.

———. "Some Phases in Extending the Cultivated Area in the Nineteenth and Twentieth Centuries in Egypt," *Middle Eastern Studies,* Vol. 19 (1983), pp. 470–481.

Barth, H. K. and Quiel, F. "Riyadh and Its Development," *GeoJournal,* Vol. 15. (1987), pp. 39–46.

Beaumont, P., Blake, G. H., and Wagstaff, J. M. *The Middle East: A Geographical Study.* London: John Wiley, 1976.

Beeley, B. W. "The Turkish Village Coffeehouse as a Social Institution," *Geographical Review,* Vol. 60 (1970), pp. 475–493.

Blake, G. H. and Lawless, R. I. (eds.). *The Changing Middle Eastern City.* London: Croom-Helm, 1980.

Bonine, M. E. "The Morphogenesis of Iranian Cities," *Annals of the Association of American Geographers,* Vol. 69 (1979), pp. 208–224.

Butzer, K. W. *Early Hydraulic Civilization in Egypt: A Study in Cultural Ecology.* Chicago: University of Chicago Press, 1976.

Clarke, J. I. and Bowen-Jones, H. (eds.). *Change and Development in the Middle East: Essays in Honour of W. B. Fisher.* London: Methuen, 1981.

Clarke, J. I. and Fisher, W. B. (eds.). *Populations of the Middle East and North Africa.* London and New York: Africana, 1972.

Clawson, M., Landsberg, H. H., and Alexander, L. T. *The Agricultural Potential of the Middle East.* New York: Elsevier, 1971.

Cole, D. *Nomads of the Nomads: The Al Murrah Bedouin of the Empty Quarter.* Chicago: Aldine, 1975.

Costello, V. F. *Urbanisation in the Middle East.* Cambridge: Cambridge University Press, 1971.

El Mallakh, R. *The Economic Development of the United Arab Emirates.* New York: St. Martin's Press, 1981.

English, P. W. *City and Village in Iran: Settlement and Economy in the Kirman Basin.* Madison: University of Wisconsin Press, 1966.

———. "Geographical Perspectives on the Middle East: The Passing of the Ecological Trilogy," in M. W. Mikesell (ed.), *Geographers Abroad.* Chicago: Department of Geography, University of Chicago, 1973.

Entelis, J. P. *Algeria: The Revolution Institutionalized.* Boulder: Westview Press, 1986.

Efrat, E. *Urbanization in Israel.* London: Croom Helm, 1984.

Fisher, W. B. *The Middle East: A Physical, Social and Regional Geography,* 7th ed. New York: Methuen, 1981.

———. "Middle East," *Progress in Human Geography,* Vol. 7 (1983), pp. 429–435.

Fowler, G. L. "Decolonization of Rural Libya," *Annals of the Association of American Geographers,* Vol. 63 (1973), pp. 490–506.

Gischler, C. *Water Resources in the Arab Middle East and North Africa.* Cambridge: Menas, 1979.

Gradus, Y. "The Role of Politics in Regional Inequality: The Israeli Case," *Annals of the Association of American Geographers,* Vol. 73 (1983), pp. 388–403.

Haynes, K. E. and Whittington, D. "International Management of the Nile—Stage Three?," *Geographical Review,* Vol. 71 (1981), pp. 17–32.

Hidore, J. J. and Albokhair, Y. "Sand Encroachment in Al-Hasa Oasis, Saudi Arabia," *Geographical Review,* Vol. 72 (1982), pp. 350–356.

Johnson, D. L. *The Nature of Nomadism: A Comparative Study of Pastoral Migrations in Southwest Asia and Northern Africa.* Chicago: Department of Geography, University of Chicago, 1969.

———. "The Human Dimensions of Desertification," *Economic Geography,* Vol. 53 (1977), pp. 317–321.

Kolars, J. "Earthquake-Vulnerable Populations in Modern Turkey," *Geographical Review,* Vol. 72 (1982), pp. 20–35.

Lesch, A. M. and Tessler, M. A. "The West Bank and Gaza: Political and Ideological Responses To Occupation," *The Muslim World,* Vol. 77 (1987), pp. 229–249.

Manners, I. R., "The Middle East," in G. A. Klee (ed.), *World Systems of Traditional Resource Management.* London: Edward Arnold, 1980.

Mikesell, M. "The Deforestation of Mount Lebanon," *Geographical Review,* Vol. 59 (1969), pp. 1–28.

Miller, J. A. *Imlil: A Moroccan Mountain Community in Change.* Boulder: Westview Press, 1984.

Niv, D. *The Semi-Arid World.* London: Longman, 1974.

Perkins, K. J. *Tunisia: Crossroads of the Islamic and European Worlds.* Boulder: Westview Press, 1986.

Roberts, H. *An Urban Profile of the Middle East.* New York: St. Martin's Press, 1979.

Shwadran, B. *Middle East Oil: Issues and Problems.* Cambridge, Mass.: Schenkman, 1977.

Smith, C. G. "Water Resources and Irrigation Development in the Middle East." *Geography,* Vol. 55 (1970), pp. 407–425.

Swearingen, W. D. "Sources of Conflict Over Oil in the Persian/Arabian Gulf," *The Middle East Journal,"* Vol. 35 (1981), pp. 315–330.

Tibi, B. "The Renewed Role of Islam in the Political and Social Development of the Middle East," *The Middle East Journal,* Vol. 37 (1983), pp. 3–13.

Walton, S. "Egypt After the Aswan Dam," *Environment,* Vol. 23 (1981), pp. 31–36.

Weinbaum, M. G. *Food, Development, and Politics in the Middle East.* Boulder, Colo.: Westview Press, 1982.

Wheatley, P. "Levels of Space Awareness in the Traditional Islamic City," *Ekistics,* Vol. 253 (1976); pp. 354–366.

Yinon, O. "The Significance of Egypt's Population Problem" *Middle Eastern Studies,* Vol. 18 (1982), pp. 378–386.

Chapter 13

Adalenro, I. A. *Marketplaces in a Developing Country: The Case of Western Nigeria.* Ann Arbor: University of Michigan Press, 1981.

Akenbode, A. "Population Explosion in Africa and Its Implications for Economic Development," *Journal of Geography,* Vol. 76 (1977), pp. 28–36.

Altschul, D. R. "Transportation in African Development," *Journal of Geography,* Vol. 79 (1980), pp. 44–56.

Berg, R. J. and Whitaker, S. J. (eds.) *Strategies for African Development.* Berkeley: University of California Press, 1986.

Bernard, F. E. and Walter, B. J. *Africa: A Thematic Geography.* Washington, D.C.: U.S. Department of Health, Education, and Welfare, 1971.

Best, A. C. G. "Angola: Geographic Background on an Insurgent State," *Focus,* Vol. 26 (1976), pp. 1–8.

Best, A. C. G. and de Blij, H. J. *African Survey.* New York: John Wiley, 1977.

Beyer, J. L. "Africa," in G. A. Klee (ed.), *World Systems of Traditional Resource Management.* London: Edward Arnold, 1980.

Bohannon, P. and Curtin, P. *Africa and Africans.* Garden City, N.Y.: Natural History Press, 1971.

Christopher, A. J. "Partition and Population in South Africa," *Geographical Review,* Vol. 72 (1982), pp. 127–138.

Church R. J. H. et al. *Africa and the Islands,* 4th ed. New York: John Wiley, 1977.

Clarke, J. I. and Kosiński, L. A. *Redistribution of Population in Africa.* London: Heinemann, 1982.

Datoo, B. A. "Peasant Agricultural Production in East Africa, The Nature and Causes of Dependence," *Antipode,* Vol. 9 (1977), pp. 70–78.

de Blij, H. and Martin, E. (eds.). *African Perspectives: An Exchange of Essays on the Economic Geography of Nine African States.* New York: Methuen, 1981.

Gould, P. R. "Tanzania, 1920–63: The Spatial Impress of the Modernization Process," *World Politics,* Vol. 22 (1970), pp. 149–170.

Hance, W. A. *The Geography of Modern Africa,* 2nd ed. New York: Columbia University Press, 1975.

Hidore, J. J. "Population Explosion in Africa: Some Further Implications," *Journal of Geography,* Vol. 77 (1978), pp. 214–220.

Holz, R. K. with Helfert, M. "Multisource Verification of the Dessication of Lake Chad, Africa," in G. Ohring and H. J. Bolle (eds.), *Advances in Space Research: Space Observation for Climate Studies,* Vol. 5, pp. 379–384. New York: Pergammon, 1985.

Howell, P. "The Impact of the Jonglei Canal in the Sudan," *The Geographical Journal,* Vol. 149 (1983), pp. 289–300.

Kesby, J. D. *The Cultural Regions of East Africa.* London: Academic Press, 1977.

Kilson, M. L. and Rotberg, R. I. (eds.). *The African Diaspora: Interpretive Essays.* Cambridge: Harvard University Press, 1976.

Knight, C. G. and Newman, J. L. *Contemporary Africa: Geography and Change.* Englewood Cliffs, N.J.: Prentice-Hall, 1976.

Lamb, D. *The Africans.* New York: Random House, 1982.

Lockwood, J. G. "The Causes of Drought with Particular Reference to the Sahel," *Progress in Physical Geography,* Vol. 10 (1986), pp. 111–119.

Mabogunje, A. L. *The Development Process: A Spatial Perspective.* New York: Holmes & Meier, 1981.

Martin, P. M. and O'Meara, P. (eds.). *Africa.* Bloomington: Indiana University Press, 1977.

Oliver, R. and Crowder, M. (eds.). *The Cambridge Encyclopedia of Africa.* Cambridge: Cambridge University Press, 1981.

Osei-Kwame, P. *A New Conceptual Model of Political Integration in Africa.* Lanham, Md.: University Press of America, 1980.

Paden, J. N. and Soja, E. W. *The African Experience,* Vol. I. Evanston, Ill.: Northwestern University Press, 1970.

Prothero, R. M. *People and Land in Africa South of the Sahara.* New York: Oxford University Press, 1972.

Richards, P. "Spatial Organization as a Theme in African Studies," *Progress in Human Geography,* Vol. 8 (1984), pp. 551–561.

Rogge, J. R. "Population Trends and the Status of Population Policy in Africa," *Journal of Geography,* Vol. 81 (1982), pp. 164–173.

Sabbagh, M. E. "Some Geographical Characteristics of a Plural Society: Apartheid in South Africa," *Geographical Review,* Vol. 58 (1968), pp. 1–28.

Smith, D. M. (ed.). *Living Under Apartheid.* Winchester, Mass.: Allen & Unwin, 1982.

Stamp, L. D. and Morgan, W. T. M. *Africa: A Study in Tropical Development.* New York: John Wiley, 1972.

Taylor, A. (ed.). *Focus on Africa South of the Sahara.* New York: Praeger, 1973.

Thompson, B. W. *Africa: The Climatic Background.* Ibadan, Nigeria: Oxford University Press, 1975.

Thompson, L. and Butler, J. (eds.). *Change in Contemporary South Africa.* Berkeley: University of California Press, 1975.

Timberlake, L. *Africa in Crisis: The Causes, The Cures of Environmental Bankruptcy.* Philadelphia: New Society Publishers, 1986.

Turnbull, C. M. *Man in Africa.* Garden City, N.Y.: Doubleday, 1976. (Anchor Books)

Udo, R. K. *The Human Geography of Tropical Africa.* Exeter, N.H.: Heinemann, 1982.

Watts, M. *Silent Violence: Food, Famine, and Peasantry in Northern Nigeria.* Berkeley: University of California Press, 1983.

Western, J. "Outcast Cape Town" *Focus,* Vol. 32 (1982), pp. 1–12.

Willmer, J. E. (ed.). *Africa: Teaching Perspectives and Approaches.* Tualatin, Ore.: Geographic and Area Study Publications, 1975.

Winters, C. "Urban Morphogenesis in Francophone Black Africa," *Geographical Review,* Vol. 72 (1982), pp. 139–154.

PHOTO CREDITS

Chapter 1

Opener: Culver Pictures. Page 6: George Holton/Photo Researchers. Page 9: Paolo Koch/Rapho-Photo Researchers. Page 10: The Bettmann Archive. Page 12: Carl Frank/Photo Researchers. Page 17: Courtesy The Pierpont Morgan Library. Page 19: (top) The Bettmann Archive, (bottom) Culver Pictures. Pages 20 and 21: The Bettmann Archive. Page 23: BBC Hulton/The Bettmann Archive. Page 26: Culver Pictures.

Chapter 2

Opener: Pablo Bartholomew/Gamma-Liaison. Page 34: (top) R. Neven/Gamma-Liaison, (bottom) Mirella Ricciardi/Sygma. Page 36: Ellan Young/Photo Researchers. Page 38: Bradley Smith/Photo Researchers. Page 41: (top) Bernard Pierre Wolfe/Photo Researchers, (bottom) Rick Smolan/Stock, Boston. Page 46: Noel Habgood/Photo Researchers. Page 47: Rick Smolan/Contact Press Images, Inc. Page 48: Stuart Franklin/Sygma.

Chapter 3

Opener: B. Annebicque/Sygma. Page 56: John Constable. *The White Horse.* © 1944, Courtesy The Frick Collection. Page 58: BBC Hulton/The Bettmann Archive. Pages 59, 61, 62, and 63: The Bettmann Archive. Page 67: Ellis Herwig/Stock, Boston. Page 69: Don Morgan/Photo Researchers. Page 72: MOPY-Maurice Charbonnieres/B.D. Picture Service. Page 74: Dirk Reinartz/VISUM 1981/Woodfin Camp. Page 76: Courtesy Swiss National Tourist Office. Page 77: J. Allan Cash/Rapho-Photo Researchers. Page 82: Photo News/Gamma-Liaison. Page 86: Jean Louis Atlan/Sygma. Page 88: Brucelle/Sygma. Page 89: G. Rancinan/Sygma. Page 91: Pavlovstzy/Sygma. Page 95: Regis Bossu/Sygma.

Chapter 4

Opener: J. Barry O'Rourke/The Stock Market. Page 107: Courtesy New York Historical Society, New York City. Page 110: (top) Culver Pictures, (bottom) The Bettmann Archives. Page 115: Courtesy The Harry T. Peters Collection, Museum of the City of New York. Page 118: (top) Courtesy Denver Public Library, (bottom) Tom McHugh/Photo Researchers. Page 119: Courtesy The Collection of the Minnesota Historical Society. Page 120: Courtesy The Smithsonian Institution. Page 122: The Bettmann Archive. Page 125: Courtesy The Library of Congress. Page 128: UPI/Bettmann Newsphotos. Page 131: Ken Straiton/The Stock Market. Page 134: Grant Heilman. Page 136: NOAA/NESDIS/NCDC. Page 137: J. Messerschmidt/The Stock Market. Page 143: George Hall/Woodfin Camp. Pages 145 and 148: Owen Franken/Stock, Boston. Page 151: Grant Heilman. Page 152: Courtesy Nissan. Page 155: UPI/Bettmann Newsphotos. Page 159: Courtesy USDA. Page 160: Geoff Tuckes/The Stock Market. Page 162: Bill Ross/Woodfin Camp.

Chapter 5

Opener: Alain Nogdes/Sygma. Page 170: L'Illustration/Sygma. Page 171: Henri Cartier-Bresson/Magnum. Page 173: Culver Pictures. Page 174: Henri Cartier-Bresson/Magnum. Page 182: Inge Morath/Magnum. Page 184: Paolo Koch/Rapho-Photo Researchers. Page 186: Tass from Sovfoto. Page 178: Peter Menzel/Stock, Boston. Page 188: Henri Cartier-Bresson/Magnum. Pages 190, 195, and 197: Tass from Sovfoto. Page 199: Schuster/Leo de Wys. Page 202: Jean-Pierre Laffont.

Chapter 6

Opener: Jean Pierre Laffont/Sygma. Page 210: Courtesy U.S. Naval Academy. Page 212: Culver Pictures. Page 217: Georg Gerster/Photo Researchers. Page 219: Robert Alexander/Photo Researchers. Page 220: Burt Glinn/Magnum. Page 222: Jean Pierre Laffont/Sygma. Page 224: Georg Gerster/Photo Researchers. Page 226: Paolo Koch/Photo Researchers. Page 231: Norman Myers/Bruce Coleman. Page 234: Peter Menzel/Stock, Boston. Page 236: Jean Pierre Laffont/Sygma. Page 237: T. Matsumoto/Sygma.

Chapter 7

Opener: G.R. Roberts. Page 242: P. Durand/Sygma. Page 244: Courtesy Australian News and Information Bureau. Page 245: Bill Bachman/Photo Researchers. Page 250: Jean Guichard/Sygma. Page 251: Robert Frerck/Odyssey Productions. Page 256: Bill Bachman/Photo Researchers. Page 258: Jean Guichard/Sygma. Page 260: Courtesy Australian News and Information Bureau. Page 266: Claudia Parks/The Stock Market. Page 268: Gil Hanly/Sygma. Page 269: Jean Pierre Laffont/Sygma.

Chapter 8

Opener: Pascal Maitre/Gamma-Liaison. Page 279: Mary Evans Picture Library/Photo Researchers. Page 284: Carl Frank/Photo Researchers. Page 288: J. Allen Cash/Rapho-Photo Researchers. Page 292: Nat Norman/Rapho-Photo Researchers. Page 295: Fritz Henle/Photo Researchers. Page 297: Hans Silvester/Rapho-Photo Researchers. Page 302: Alain Keler/Art Resource. Page 304: Alain Keler/Sygma. Page 309: (top) Laimute Druskis/Taurus Photos, (center) Nicholas Sapicha/Stock, Boston, (bottom) Jerry Frank/Design Photographers International. Page 311: The Bettmann Archive. Page 312: FPG. Page 314: Diego Goldberg/Sygma. Page 315: Jerry Frank/DPI. Page 316: Reininger/Leo de Wys. Page 320: Carl Frank/Photo Researchers.

Chapter 9

Opener: Henri Bureau/Sygma. Page 328: Paolo Koch/Photo Researchers. Page 329: Ira Kirschenbaum/Stock, Boston. Page 331: Paolo Koch/Photo Researchers. Page 335: Judith Canty/Stock, Boston. Page 336: Courtesy Library of Congress. Page 337: Bruno Barbey/Magnum. Page 341: Wang

Zhiping/Sygma. Page 342: Paolo Koch/ Rapho-Photo Researchers. Page 344: Charles Marden Fitch/FPG. Page 345: Audrey Topper/Photo Researchers. Page 346: Francie Manning/The Picture Cube. Page 347: Georg Gerster/Photo Researchers. Page 351: Ira Kirschenbaum/ Stock, Boston. Page 354: Photos Bureau/ Sygma. Page 356: J. P. Laffont/Sygma. Page 358: Gérard Taxis/Sygma. Page 360: Daniel Simon/Gamma-Liaison. Page 361: Owen Franken/Sygma.

Chapter 10

Opener: Jean-Claude Lejeune/Stock, Boston. Page 367: George Bellrose/Stock, Boston. Page 371: Henri Cartier-Bresson/Magnum. Page 372: Donald Mc-Cullin/Magnum. Page 373: Bernard Pierre Wolfe/Photo Researchers. Page 376: The Bettmann Archive. Page 380: Stuart Cohen/Stock, Boston. Page 382: Baldev/ Sygma. Page 383: Bernard Pierre Wolfe/ Photo Researchers. Page 389: Culver Pictures. Page 390: (top) Habans/Sygma, (bottom) Bhawan Singh/Magnum. Page 391: Courtesy Information Service of India. Page 399: Hubert le Campion/Sygma. Page 400: Baldev/Sygma. Page 403: Ed Grazda/Magnum. Page 404: Alain Nogues/Sygma. Page 406: Bernard Pierre Wolfe/Photo Researchers.

Chapter 11

Opener: Nancy Lockspeiser/Stock, Boston. Page 413: Bernard Pierre Wolfe/Photo Researchers. Page 415: George Holton/ Photo Researchers. Page 420: (top) Dale Boyer/Photo Researchers (bottom), Steven R. King/Peter Arnold. Page 425: Rick Smolan/Leo de Wys. Page 427: Georg Gerster/Photo Researchers. Page 430: Bernard Pierre Wolfe/Photo Researchers. Page 432: Courtesy Technology Application Center, University of New Mexico. Page 433: (top) Robert Nicklesberg/Gamma-Liaison, (bottom) Hella Hammid/Photo Researchers. Page 434: Leo de Wys. Page 435: Baguio/Sygma. Page 437: Christine Spengler/Sygma.

Chapter 12

Opener: Elkoussy/Sygma. Page 445: Culver Pictures. Page 447: Alain Nogues/ Sygma. Page 448: Elkoussy/Sygma. Page 451: Chauvd/Sygma. Page 453: Owen Franken/Stock, Boston. Page 455: Georg Gerster/Photo Researchers. Page 456: Paul Almasy. Page 458: (center) Courtesy The New York Public Library-Picture Collection, (bottom) Raisz, *General Cartography*, © 1948, McGraw-Hill, reprinted by permission. Page 459: (bottom) Courtesy Library of Congress. Page 461: Georg Gerster/Rapho-Photo Researchers. Page 462: UPI/Bettmann Newsphotos. Pages 465 and 467: Georg Gerster/Rapho-Photo Researchers. Page 468: Paolo Koch/Rapho-Photo Researchers. Page 470: Georg Gerster/Rapho-Photo Researchers. Page 475: Owen Franken/Stock, Boston. Page 476: Georg Gerster/Photo Researchers. Page 478: Owen Franken/Stock, Boston. Page 479: Christine Spengler/Sygma. Page 480: Jacques Pavlovsky/Sygma. Page 482: Robert Azzi/Woodfin Camp. Page 484: Sygma. Page 487: Carl Rubin/Photo Researchers. Page 488: Moshe Milner/ Sygma.

Chapter 13

Opener: John Flannery/Bruce Coleman. Page 496: Anonymous Northeast Italian artist, Courtesy National Gallery of Art, Washington. Pages 498 and 500: Culver Pictures. Page 502: Mary Evans Picture Library/Photo Researchers. Page 505: BBC Hulton/The Bettmann Archive. page 509: Carl Frank/Photo Researchers. Page 510: A. Keler/Sygma. Page 512: Alain Nogues/Sygma. Page 513: Coleman and Hayward/Photo Researchers. Page 515: Lynn McLaren/Rapho-Photo Researchers. Page 519: Georg Gerster/Photo Researchers. Page 524: William Campbell/ Sygma. Page 526: Marc & Evelyne Bernheim/Woodfin Camp. Page 528 Georg Gerster/Rapho-Photo Researchers. Page 530: Owen Franken/Stock, Boston. Page 534: Chambeau/Gamma-Liaison.

INDEX

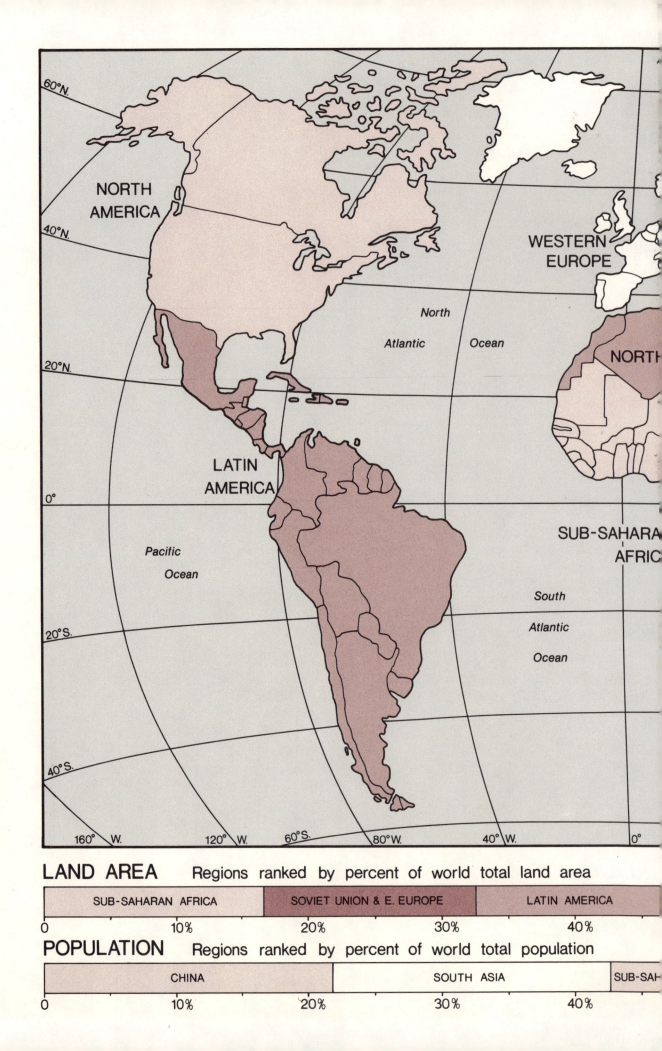

60°N.

NORTH
AMERICA

40°N.

WESTERN
EUROPE

20°N.

North

Atlantic   Ocean

NORTH

LATIN
AMERICA

0°

SUB-SAHARA

AFRIC

Pacific

Ocean

South

20°S.

Atlantic

Ocean

40°S.

160° W.   120° W.   60°S.   80°W.   40° W.   0°

LAND AREA   Regions ranked by percent of world total land area

SUB-SAHARAN AFRICA	SOVIET UNION & E. EUROPE	LATIN AMERICA

0   10%   20%   30%   40%

POPULATION   Regions ranked by percent of world total population

CHINA	SOUTH ASIA	SUB-SAH

0   10%   20%   30%   40%